Jewish Law and Decision-Making

A Study through Time

Aaron M. Schreiber

Professor of Law, Temple University School of Law

Jewish Law and Decision-Making
A Study through Time

Temple University Press
Philadelphia

Temple University Press, Philadelphia 19122
© 1979 by Temple University. All rights reserved
Published 1979
Printed in the United States of America

Publication of this book has been assisted by a grant from the
Publication Program of the National Endowment for the
Humanities, School of Law, and the Temple University
Law Foundation.

Library of Congress Cataloging in Publication Data

Schreiber, Aaron M
  Jewish law and decision-making.

  Bibliography: p.
  Includes index.
  1. Criminal law (Jewish law)—History.
I. Title.
Law   345′.002′403924   79-18872
ISBN 0-87722-120-0

To my wife, Rivka,
without whose selfless sacrifices, encouragement, and endless patience,
this book could never have been completed

Contents

Part Two
Talmudic Law in the Eras of the
Second Jewish Commonwealth,
Ancient Greece, the Hellenist States,
Rome, and the Early Middle Ages,
350 B.C.E.–630 C.E.   181

Thanks and Acknowledgments

My deepest gratitude is due to many persons who aided in the preparation of this book. Professor W. Michael Reisman, of Yale Law School, provided the stimulus, encouragement, and overall guidance for the structure of the book and for resolving the many problems that arose during its preparation. Much of whatever merit there is in the book is due to his profound insights, judgment, and dazzling range of knowledge. Professor Myres M. McDougal's pioneering jurisprudential approach first inspired me to begin research in this area while I was still a student of his at Yale Law School and he has continued to encourage me since. It was due to the foresightful urging of Dean Peter J. Liacouras, of Temple Law School, that I began to offer a regular course in comparative Judaic law at Temple Law School (possibly the first such regular course offering at an American law school), out of which this book developed. Dean Liacouras has devotedly supported my work and made yeomen efforts to provide the financial and academic support necessary for the preparation and publication of this work. His aid made its completion possible. I have benefited greatly from the enormous erudition of Rabbi Issac Sender of the Hebrew Theological College of Chicago, who reviewed the manuscript and made numerous and extremely helpful suggestions and comments. Professor Sol Cohen, of Dropsie University, placed at my disposal his great expertise in ancient Near Eastern languages, culture, and literature, the Bible, and Rabbinic texts. Finally, the book was greatly enhanced by the encyclopedic knowledge of the Talmud, its commentaries, and the wide range of Responsa literature by my son, Baruch D. Schreiber, whose indefatigable resources I gratefully acknowledge. Ms. Ann Newman, a student research assistant, performed outstanding services in preparing the index and in proofreading. Ms. Cassie Stankunis was a model of patience in typing numerous drafts.

I should also like to acknowledge the permission kindly granted by the following authors, editors, translators, publishers, journals, and organizations to reprint excerpts from the works indicated below.

Birnbaum, P. "Talmudic Exposition of the Scriptures." In *Daily Prayer Book* (Hebrew Publishing Co., 1969).

Chajes, Z. H. "The Oral Law and Its Relation to the Written Law." In J. Schacter, *Students' Guide through the Talmud* (P. Feldheim, Inc., 1960).

Diamond, A. S. "An Eye for An Eye," 19 *Iraq* (1957). With the kind permission of the British School of Archaeology in Iraq.

Elon, M. "Takkanot" and "Takkanot ha'Kahal." In *The Principles of Jewish Law* (Keter Publishing House Jerusalem Ltd., 1975).

Finkelstein, J. J. " 'Babel-Bible': A Mesopotamian View." With the kind permission of Dr. Philip Finkelstein.

Finkelstein, J. J. "Bible and Babel: A Comparative Study of the Hebrew and Babylonian Religious Spirit." Reprinted from *Commentary*, by permission; copyright © 1958 by The American Jewish Committee. With the kind permission of Dr. Philip Finkelstein.

Finkelstein, J. J. "Sex Offenses in Sumerian Laws." *Journal of the American Oriental Society* 86 (1966). With the kind permission of Dr. Philip Finkelstein.

Finkelstein, L. "Synod of Castilian Jews of 1432" and "Takkanot of R. Tam." In *Jewish Self-Government in the Middle Ages* (The Jewish Theological Seminary of America, 1924).

Freehoff, S. "Origins and Development of the Responsa." *The Responsa Literature* (Jewish Publication Society of America, 1955).

Friedlander, M., ed. *Moses Maimonides: The Guide For the Perplexed* (Dover Publications, 1956).

Greenberg, Moshe. "The Biblical Conception of Asylum." *Journal of Biblical Literature*, vol. 78 (Scholars Press, 1959).

Greenberg, Moshe. "Some Postulates of Biblical Criminal Law." *Yehezkel Kaufmann Jubilee Volume* (Magnes Press, 1960).

Greenberg, Moshe. "Avenger of Blood," "Banishment," "Blood Guilt," and "City of Refuge." From the *Interpreters Dictionary of the Bible*, vol. 1, copyright © 1962 by Abingdon Press. Used by permission.

Greengus, Samuel. "A Textbook Case of Adultery in Ancient Mesopotamia." XL–XLI *Hebrew Union College Annual* (1969–1970).

Jackson, B. S. "Reflections on Biblical Criminal Law." In *Essays in Jewish and Comparative Legal History* (Leiden: E. J. Brill, 1975) and in *Journal of Jewish Studies* 24 (1973), published by the Oxford Centre for Post Graduate Hebrew Studies.

Jacobsen, Thorkild. "Primitive Democracy in Ancient Mesopotamia" and "An Ancient Mesopotamian Trial for Homicide." Reprinted by permission of the publishers from TOWARD THE IMAGE OF TAMMUZ AND OTHER ESSAYS ON MESOPOTAMIAN HISTORY AND CULTURE by Thorkild Jacobsen, William L. Moran, editor, Cambridge, Mass.: Copyright © by the President and Fellows of Harvard College.

Jewish Publication Society of America. Selections from *The Torah* (1967).

Leemans, W. F. "King Hammurapi as Judge." In *Symbolae Iuridicae et Historicae Martino David Dedicatae* (Leiden: E. J. Brill, 1968).

Maimonides, M. "Laws Concerning a Murderer and the Preservation of Life." From *Book of Torts*, trans. H. Klein, and "Laws of the Sanhedrin," from *Book of Judges*, trans., A. D. Hershman (New Haven, Conn.: Yale University Press, 1954).

Paul, S. M. "The Problem of the Prologue and Epilogue to the Book of the Covenant," from *Studies in the Book of the Covenant in the Light of Cuneiform and Biblical Law* (Leiden: E. J. Brill, 1970).

Pritchard, James B., editor. *Ancient Near Eastern Texts Relating to the Old Testament* (edited by James B. Pritchard; copyright © 1969, reprinted by permission of Princeton University Press):

    The Code of Hammurabi, translated by Theophile J Meek.

    Lipit-Ishtar Law Code, translated by S. N. Kramer.

    The Laws of Eshnunna, translated by Albrecht Goetze.

    The Middle Assyrian Laws, translated by Theophile J. Meek.

    The Hittite Laws, translated by Albrecht Goetze.

    The Laws of Ur-Nammu, translated by J. J. Finkelstein.

    Results of a Trial for Conspiracy, translated by John A. Wilson.

    The Edict of Ammisaduqa, translated by J. J. Finkelstein.

Rosenzweig, Bernard. "The Hermeneutic Principles and Their Application." *Tradition*, 13 (Summer, 1972).

Soncino Press, Ltd. English translation of *The Talmud* (selections from the volumes entitled *Baba Mezia, Gittin, Makkot, Menahot, Sanhedrin, Shabbat, Yebamot*).

Speiser, E. A. "Cuneiform Law and the History of Civilization." *Proceedings of the American Philosophical Society*, vol. 107 (Nov. 6, 1963).

Speiser, E. A. "Early Law and Civilization. In J. J. Finkelstein and M. Greenberg, eds., *Oriental and Biblical Studies* (Philadelphia: University of Pennsylvania Press, 1967).

Speiser, E. A. "The Manner of the King." In B. Mazar, ed., *World History of the Jewish People*, vol. 3 (New Brunswick, N.J.: Rutgers University Press, 1970), with the kind permission of Massada Press, Ltd.

Soloveitchik, J. B. "Thoughts and Visions: The Man of Law" (Hebrew). I *Tadpiot* (*Yeshiva University*, 1944).

Soloveitchik, J. B. "The First Rebellion Against Torah Authority." In *Shiurei Harav: A Conspectus of the Public Lectures of Rabbi Joseph B. Soloveitchik* (New York, 1974).

Twersky, Isadore. "The Shulhan Aruk: Enduring Code of Jewish Law." *Judaism* (American Jewish Congress and World Jewish Congress, Spring, 1967).

Wilson, John A. "Authority and Law in Ancient Egypt." *Journal of the American Oriental Society* (April 1, 1959).

Jewish Law and
Decision-Making
A Study through Time

Introduction

Jewish law is the oldest applied legal system in the world, spanning more than three thousand years. It has been operative in most civilized countries and continents, throughout the full spectrum of recorded human history and in all stages of societal development, ranging from rural to urban, and from agricultural to commercial and industrial. It has experienced the greatest variety and change in social conditions, including shifts in economic contexts, cultural and political milieus, dramatic crises, and drastic fluxes in both power and powerlessness.

The term "Jewish law" is used in this book to refer to the law of the Jewish people throughout the Biblical Era, the first and second Jewish commonwealths in the land of Israel, the Middle Ages, and up to the present time in numerous lands in which Jewish communities existed all over the world. Although significant differences may be found between the various epochs, it would not be useful in a book of the general character of this one to distinguish between "biblical law," "Israelite law," "talmudic law," "Jewish law," and like terms since there are dominant unifying themes running through all of these periods. As Henri Frankfort succinctly stated:

> What constitutes the individuality of a civilization, its recognizable character, its identity which is maintained throughout the successive stages of its existence? . . . We are not, of course, looking for a formula; the character of a civilization is far too elusive to be reduced to a catchword. We recognize it in a certain coherence among its various manifestations, a certain consistency in its orientation, a certain cultural "style" which shapes its political and its judicial institutions, its art as well as its literature, its religion as well as its morals. I propose to call this elusive identity of a civilization its "form." It is this "form" which is never destroyed although it changes in the course of time. And it changes partly as a result of inherent factors—development—partly as a result of external forces—historical incidents. . . . These changes [are] the "dynamics" of a civilization. . . . [This] cultural style . . . amounts to a point of view from where seemingly unrelated facts acquire coherence and meaning. . . . It imparts to their achievements—to their arts and institutions, their literature, their theology—something distinct and final, something which has its own peculiar perfection.[1]

In addition to its many other values, Jewish law permits the comparative study of the law and social dynamics of society at different stages of development and allows the examination of various hypotheses regarding decision-making, by enabling scholars to isolate different variables in the multitude of observed societies.[2] In this sense, Jewish law may come closer than any other legal system in affording the opportunity for legal studies as an empirical science.

Approaches to Jewish Law

Traditionally, however, the study of Jewish law and the Talmud has often proceeded on the assumption that law is a body of rules, operating as a closed system, completely divorced from human events and societal conditions and detached from developments resulting from the interactions of people competing for societal values in a variety of activities and institutional patterns. So, too, little regard has been paid to the effects on decisions of the perspectives, personalities, and backgrounds of decision-makers. Similarly, students of Jewish law have often paid slight attention to the underlying, sometimes unspoken, assumptions of Jewish law regarding values, ethics, and tradition, along with the social contexts, historical antecedents, and converging social forces.

This prevailing approach to Jewish law implies that a legal decision, especially by a court, would be reached on any "issue" of law simply and solely by first determining the "applicable" legal doctrines and principles and then by logically analyzing and following deduced conclusions through a winding rational maze, until one eventually emerged with a "legal" decision, dictated solely by application of deductive logic to these *a priori* principles of law. When carried to extremes, as is all too often the case, this process deteriorates into derivational exercises in which there is little conception of either the role of policy in the decision processes or the effects on decisions of conditions in the social contexts. Scholarly work in the area of Jewish law, including contemporary scholarship, has in this vein tended to concentrate on the examination of various doctrines and rules of law that are allegedly to be applied by courts, has largely ignored policy, social conditions, and contexts, and has frequently disregarded decisions made by nonjudicial decision-makers.

1. H. Frankfort, *The Birth of Civilization in the Near East* (New York, 1955), pp. 2–3, 25.

2. See E. A. Hoebel, *Law of Primitive Man* (Cambridge, Mass., 1954), pp. vii–viii.

The proponents of the foregoing approach have often seemed completely unaware of its fatal defects. It has long since been pointed out that, even in the area of judicial decision-making, one can often find conflicting lines of case precedent and legal doctrines, all of which can be applied with equal logic to the case at hand.[3] The issue then becomes, which line shall be selected by the decision-maker and why? Similarly, any line of legal precedents that one may choose to follow can legitimately be given a narrow or a wide interpretation, resulting in greatly differing applications to the case at hand. In the same way precedent cases can be "classified" and interpreted, both as to the facts and law, in many different ways, leading to divergent results. Which facts of any given case are emphasized and which are relegated to a position of minor importance can also play a vital role in judicial decisions. The above factors alone should indicate the difficulty, if not the impossibility, of relying solely on the application of deductive logic to given "principles" of law in order to reach decisions in judicial cases.

In addition, of course, there are other substantial difficulties in maintaining such a view of law. It has been observed that a judge often reaches a decision on one ground but then proceeds to justify and rationalize it by writing a legal opinion in which he cites legal principles and precedent cases that are not the real reasons for the decision. Often the real grounds for his ruling are affected by unconscious motivations, unknown even to the judge himself.[4] The American legal realists, in leveling their devastating criticism of traditional approaches to law, have greatly emphasized and elaborated upon such "hidden" factors in judicial decision-making and the sometimes "instinctive" reaction of judges to fact patterns. It is also by now widely recognized that the social, economic, and cultural class and background of the judge as well as his personality, can have a substantial effect on his decisions. Similar complex factors affect the many vital nonjudicial areas of legal decision-making.

Clearly, too, a "mechanical" approach to law without regard to social developments assumes a very stable legal system and presupposes the certainty of the law.

This is regarded as shaped exclusively by rules and principles that themselves are unchangeable. What this view ignores is that for law to be effective and "just" it must reach and further accepted basic goals. As society and its underlying conditions change, as they invariably do, so the law also must change if it is to avoid undesired and even ludicrous decisions. Vital to the law are "the creation of techniques that efficiently and effectively solve the problems posed . . . so that the basic values of the society are realized through the law, and not frustrated by it."[5] Exclusive concentration on how a particular norm fits syntactically into a rule structure can be of little use in developing a well-ordered society, although it may have mystical connotations and satisfy an aesthetic feeling for logical symmetry.

Furthermore, the manner in which norms are applied is vital. It has been aptly remarked:[6]

> Even when . . . rules are known and clear in words, one does still not know the legal system, save as he studies case after case in which rules have come into question, or have been challenged or broken. Thus only as one makes cross-check in action on how far the known "rules" are rules which are followed and on how they are "followed," and on what else happens in addition to their being followed, can he be certain what his data are. A fortiori must one go to the cases of hitch or trouble when procedural and remedial matters lack ritual or verbal form.
>
> For, to repeat, the idea of "legality" carries with it the idea not only of right, but of remedy. It includes not only the idea of prescribed right conduct, but that of prescribed penalty (or type of penalty) for wrong, . . . [the] recognizably proper persons to deal with offenders, or of recognizably proper ways of dealing with offenders and of recognizable limits on proper dealing with them. . . .
>
> The techniques of *use* of any legal form or rule, are, if anything, more important than the form and rule themselves. The techniques of operation of the legal personnel, and the latter's manner of handling the techniques, these commonly cut further into the nature of a society's legal system than does the "law" itself. But they must be dug out of the cases in which actual troubles have been dealt with.

In order for law not to strait-jacket society, authoritative decisions must take account of changed conditions and new developments in many diverse areas, ranging from social customs, to religious, philosophical, and ethical perspectives, to new instruments of production, forms of credit, ownership devices, and modes of travel. Law, then, must stress its overriding goals and assess existing and projected societal conditions, deter-

3. See R. Von Jhering, *Law as a Means to an End*, trans. Husik (Boston, 1913), and *The Struggle for Law* (Chicago, 1879), p. 12; B. N. Cardozo, *Paradoxes of Legal Science* (New York, 1927); M. McDougal, "The Ethics of Applying Systems of Authority: Balanced Opposites of a Legal System," in H. Lasswell and H. Cleveland, eds., *The Ethics of Power* (New York, 1962), p. 221.

4. K. N. Llewellyn, "Some Realism about Realism—Responding to Dean Pound," 44 *Harvard Law Review* (1931): 1222; J. Frank, *Law and the Modern Mind* (New York, 1931), p. 130; see also his *Are Judges Human?* 80 *University of Pennsylvania Law Review* (1931): 17, and his *Courts on Trial* (New York, 1949).

5. Hoebel, *Law of Primitive Man*, p. 281.

6. Llewellyn and Hoebel, *The Cheyenne Way* (Norman, Okla., 1941), pp. 26, 27.

mining which decisions will best attain such goals. This makes it necessary for decision-makers, as well as scholars, to determine precisely what the goals are (along with the relative weights of each, if they clash in a given case), to isolate the basic social postulates and criteria of choice on which the legal system rests, and to discover the key concepts, without which the prescribed and applied law of a culture cannot be understood.[7] As Whitehead expressed it:[8]

> In each age of the world distinguished by high activity, there will be found at its culmination, and among the agencies leading to its culmination, some profound cosmological outlook, implicitly accepted, impressing its own type upon the current spring of action. This ultimate cosmology is only partly expressed, and the details of such expression issue into derivative specialized questions . . . which conceal a general agreement upon first principles almost too obvious to need expression, and almost too general to be capable of expression. In each period there is a general form of the forms of thought, and, like the air we breathe, such a form is so translucent, and so pervading, and so seemingly necessary, that only by extreme effort can we become aware of it.

This book attempts to apply to the study of Jewish law the methodology and approach that is called for in the study of any legal system. It focuses on law in contextual perspective, as one aspect of social interactions relating to all societal values in which the force of organized society is employed to allocate values, to regulate individual and group behavior, and to apply sanctions and indulgences to repress, punish, and prevent deviance from prescribed mores and encourage compliance. Law is viewed herein as a process of authoritative decisions, not as a body of abstract rules and legal doctrines. This book seeks a realistic view of Judaic law and is concerned with all decisions and choices made in Jewish society. It is not limited to choices and decisions by judges and governmental units but focuses as well on decisions by groups and individuals, both formal and informal. Contrary to the prevailing approach in Jewish legal studies, it emphasizes those decisions that were in fact made, and it does not simply deal with the doctrinal formulations offered as a guide or justification for decisions.

Accordingly, this work attempts to be empirical in approach, observing decision-making behavior and the attempted ordering of human society as well as the fac-

tors that have affected decisions through time. The dangers of concentrating on formalized decisions or prescriptions, rather than examining the decisions actually made and the choices in fact selected, are obvious. One need only look at some of the authoritarian, inhumane, and unfree countries of the world to realize that to embody noble principles, such as freedom of religion or speech, in a constitution or in other laws, does not necessarily reflect the reality of social life there.

The approach taken here follows that pioneered by Professors Myres M. McDougal, Harold D. Lasswell, and W. Michael Reisman. An examination is accordingly made of many of the intellectual tasks that they recommend, including examination of the goals established and clarified in Jewish law and such issues as what the goals were and to what extent decision-makers were aware of these goals. What clarification of goals occurred through time, and to what extent did decision-makers rely on these goals to override technical legal doctrine?

Similarly, the book will examine certain trends of decision-making throughout history, and the various societal conditions that played a role in these trends. Among the crucial factors to be examined are the religious and ethical perspectives of the participants. Perceptive scholars have noted that religious attitudes and conduct influence human behavior in many areas of activity. It has been claimed, for example, that the capitalist system developed in the west in part because of the Protestant belief in predestination and election by God, which was held to be evidenced by success in business. This notion, together with an ascetic perspective against self-indulgence in wealth, allegedly resulted in a work ethic and the reinvestment of profits back into business.[9]

Other factors to be examined in this book are the backgrounds and assumptions of decision-makers and whether, for example, the particular epochs and locales of decisions were characterized by distinctive modes of thought that assumed certain facts and types of decisions as basic and unchallengeable, or considered certain methodologies as inherently acceptable approaches

7. See Hoebel, *Law of Primitive Man*, pp. 13, 16; F. S. C. Northrop, "Jurisprudence in the Law School Curriculum," 1 *Journal of Legal Education* (1949): 489; Frankfort, *Birth of Civilization*, p. 2.

8. A. N. Whitehead, *Adventures of Ideas* (New York, 1933), pp. 13, 14; S. P. Simpson and R. Field, "Law and the Social Sciences," 32 *Virginia Law Review* (1946): 58.

9. See M. Weber, *The Protestant Ethic and the Rise of Capitalism*, trans. Talcott Parsons (London, 1930, 1948). For other examples of the influence of religion on conduct, see Weber, "Religious Rejections of the World," in *Essays in Sociology*, ed. by H. H. Gerth and C. W. Mills (New York, 1946); and J. Freund, *The Sociology of Max Weber* (New York, 1968), pp. 179–80, 209. Weber's analyses of Jewish law were, however, heavily influenced by his reliance on J. Wellhausen and other German Bible scholars of the nineteenth century (see his *Ancient Judaism*, trans. Gerth and Martindale [New York, 1952], pp. 425–29, n. 1). The theories of these scholars have been substantially eclipsed and superseded by the archeological finds and biblical scholarship of the past fifty years, thus destroying the underpinnings of Weber's analysis in this field.

to problem-solving, and defined only certain questions, and not others, as important and worthy of solution. It has been noted that even in the natural sciences, the data that people observe and their perceptions concerning them are dependent on their paradigmatic conceptions, which determine *what* they see and *how* they see it.[10] Hopefully, the McDougal-Lasswell-Reisman paradigm followed here, which views law as a process of authoritative decision, will lead to the observance of new data and the perception of existing data in ways that will help to form a much more realistic picture of Jewish law.

This work thus attempts to examine many aspects of the broad social contexts of decision-making, including economic and social forces, interactions with non-Jews, and changes in the power and authority systems in Jewish communities. It will attempt to focus, in each area, on the participants involved in decisions, their strategies, objectives, resources, locales, and contexts of the decisions, and their short- and long-term results. A relatively brief study of the Biblical Era has been included as a necessary introductory backdrop for the studies about law in the subsequent eras; the latter are the focus of this book, since much more data is available for those epochs. Moreover, sketches of the salient social, religious, and economic factors have been included in this volume for each era studied.

This volume will emphasize the decisions actually made and not limit itself to the stated perspectives or goals. It will examine those individuals or groups that had effective control over decisions as well as the factors of authority and the expectations of the community regarding the persons who should make decisions, the methods by which they should be made, and the substance of those decisions.

Since the study of the operation of law over a long span of time can throw much light upon the role of law in shaping society under assorted conditions, it follows that the broader and more contextual the study, the greater can be its relevance and benefits. It is also highly desirable, indeed vital, to study law on a comparative basis in order to see how other contemporaneous societies dealt with similar problems and with what results. Furthermore, only by comparative examination can we determine in what ways the stance of Jewish law is unique and assess its consequences. Hence this book also attempts to make a number of comparative, albeit brief, studies of Jewish law with other contemporaneous systems of law. Here, too, a proper methodology and approach are vital. Comparative legal studies are often "marked frequently by the barren dissection of verbal

texts"[11] that compare only similarities in legislation and judicial decisions. Often an inadequate method is used to realistically describe and appraise the flow of authoritative decisions through time, resulting in the failure to make beneficial comparisons.[12]

> The greatest confusion continues to prevail about what is being compared, about the purposes of comparison, and about appropriate techniques. The law that is being studied is still, too often, regarded as a body of doctrine or rules divorced from power and social processes. . . . The conception of law as a decision-making process and a process in which the decision-makers are influenced by many variables, has had, as yet, but few effects.[13]

It is hoped that the emphasis here on a continual examination of trends and conditions will help to avoid the aforementioned pitfalls and the telling criticism leveled at contemporary legal studies.

> First, it must be clear that a comparison restricted to *one* legal phenomenon in two countries is unscientific and misleading. A legal system is a unity, the whole of which expresses itself in each part; the same blood runs in the whole organism. Hence, each part must necessarily be seen in its relation to the whole. An identical provision of the law of two countries may have wholly different moral background, may have been brought about by the interplay of wholly different forces, and hence the similarity may be due to the purest coincidence—no more significant than the double meaning of a pun.[14]

11. J. Wigmore, "More Jottings on Comparative Legal Ideas and Institutions," 6 *Tulane Law Review* (1932): 244, 263.

12. See McDougal, *Studies in World Public Order* (New Haven, 1960), p. 952.

13. Ibid., p. 953.

14. P. LePaulle, "The Function of Comparative Law," 35 *Harvard Law Review* (1922): 838, 853. A similar point of view, but with important distinctions, is that "to make some rule or accepted formula covering a definite point of doctrine in one system of law, find a similar expression in one or more other systems . . . neither involves important mental processes by the writer nor excites contributory stimulation in the reader. A numerically selective robot could produce as fruitful results from a good shelf of statutory compilations. . . . To understand the history of the rule, to trace its principal sources, its developing vicissitudes and its final formation and acceptance, to appreciate its relation to other parts of the instant system and, most important of all, to learn its actual operation, to see what it does as distinct from what it says, by consultation of the commentators and more importantly, by examination of the actual decisions of the courts, to carry through this analysis for each of the great systems of law . . . to discover and set forth the similarities and differences in the existing solutions and, then to make a summation of the whole resultant with a view to an at least partial and temporarily valid prediction as to the tendency of current doctrines and lines of decision, more correctly constitutes the real purpose of comparative law. . . ." W. Hug and G. Ireland, "The Progress of Comparative Law," 6 *Tulane Law Review* (1931): 68, 73.

10. T. Kuhn, *The Structure of Scientific Revolutions* (Chicago, 1962).

Nevertheless, since this book concentrates essentially on Jewish law (and even here aims mainly at criminal law), it does not purport to be a comprehensive, comparative study of Jewish law in all areas. That vast task is beyond the more modest scope of this work.

Since it is impossible for a scholar's values not to affect his study or orient his mind, including the selection of matters to be studied and those to be ignored,[15] it is important for any scholar to state his values and observational standpoint. It therefore should be made clear that the author has been steeped from childhood in love and respect for the personalities and teachings of Jewish law and that these have undoubtedly affected his appraisal of the subject.

The Value of Comparative Judaic Law Studies

The oldest system of continuously applied law in the world, Jewish law has been in constant operation for the past three millennia at every stage of human society and under a myriad of conditions: in agricultural milieus as well as commercial and industrial ones, in rural jurisdictions as well as heavily urbanized areas. It has been exposed to varied religious and cultural environments and to radical changes in social and political institutions. It therefore is possible to isolate desired variables and to test the operations and responses of this legal system as in a "laboratory" situation. One can observe the responses and gauge their effectiveness with regard to all of the major problems that have faced mankind during most of recorded history. Jewish law thus permits the comparative study of law and social dynamics of society at different levels of development. It allows the examination of various hypotheses regarding decision-making, by enabling scholars to isolate discrete variables. In this sense, Jewish law may come closer than any other legal system in affording the opportunity for legal studies utilizing an empirical approach. It is important to realize that, after all,

> the technical law of the modern state requires only to be viewed as a world of working tools measured against a body of stated objectives and problems not posed by it but given to it for solution. . . .
> When seen thus, each legal concept becomes a candle to illumine the working of society. It became a concept because some type of problem has recurred often enough, has required to be wrestled with often enough to be not only felt, but seen as a type of problem.[16]

This book focuses on responses in the criminal law area, including decisions as to which behavior should be regarded as sufficiently deviant to require a sharp societal response and on the disposition and treatment accorded in practice to deviants in Jewish law.

Additionally, although Jewish law dealt in its initial stages with a society much simpler than today's, its study can be most helpful for a better understanding of legal decision-making in our more complex contemporary society, for it directs attention to fundamental societal problems and similarities of human behavior in decision-making. The study of Jewish law through time also helps us to see the effect of specific conditions on the course of law and legal decision-making. Since many of these conditions exist in essentially similar form today, we can learn from the past how to meet current problems and which approaches to avoid.

More importantly, studies in Jewish law furthermore permit us to examine the methods by which high ethical and moral standards were sought to be implemented in law and to determine the measure of success achieved. This too is crucial for modern society.

The study of Jewish law over this long time span also permits one to see its responses to the sudden crises and changes in circumstances that have arisen repeatedly during its long and turbulent history. Crisis-ridden contemporary society has much to gain from observing how Jewish law has reacted to crises, what decisions were taken, why, by whom, and what the effects of the decisions were.

Jewish law often dealt with Jews who dwelled in different countries with radically divergent cultural and social environments. Its long history of ordering the lives of these Jews, who lived alongside and interacted with many diverse peoples, cultures, and religions, can provide many valuable lessons and insights in decision-making for our own pluralistic society, which exists in an interdependent and ever-shrinking world.

Clearly, the foregoing problems are formidable in today's world too. The successes, failures, and insights of Jewish law in dealing with these areas can be highly instructive for contemporary society. Its relevance is enhanced by the fact that a greater portion of our American legal system than is realized is rooted in Jewish law. Consequently, a deeper understanding of its development and the insight it affords can help us to comprehend and utilize our own legal system to greater advantage.[17]

---

15. See R. Dahrendorf, "Values and Social Science," in *Essays in the Theory of Society* (Stanford, 1966), pp. 1–18.
16. Llewellyn and Hoebel, *The Cheyenne Way*, p. 42.

17. The examination of a legal system and of the underlying culture that it reflects over a long period of time can be beneficial in still another vein, that of conflict resolution. Obviously, conflicts cannot be removed unless the conflicting groups understand each other. Not infrequently, this process may be aided by the comprehension of the symbols used in a particular culture to denote political objectives and achievements. Failure to grasp and comprehend these symbols can often lead to unnecessary friction. For example, in Western societies the written

Furthermore, the detailed study of an ancient legal system necessarily entails the examination of political crises that have ensued throughout history from close encounters between different civilizations and the role of an informed elite[18] in dispelling conflict, establishing trust and terms of reference for the conduct of domestic and foreign relations, and determining areas and principles of agreement, which may be more meaningful than the ones presently in use. This also may have relevance for ultimate accommodation of conflicting groups in the contemporary world.

Problems and Methodology in the Study of Ancient Law

The study of Jewish law, with its origins in ancient history, entails many problems. Prime sources for the study of law and civilization in the ancient Near East are the written records remaining from that era. Hundreds of thousands of texts have been uncovered, completely overshadowing in number any other type of records from ancient civilizations, even from the classical world. The study of those records is far more reliable than secondhand information, although it requires an intimate understanding of the languages used. Much of these written records, however, remains unpublished, and a large part is still undigested; but enough has been deciphered to form a valuable basis of study.

Unfortunately, the plethora of written documents from Mesopotamia, Syria, and other portions of the ancient Near East, is counterbalanced by the scarcity of documents, other than the Bible, from ancient Jewish society. This phenomenon is due to a number of factors.[19] Clay was not readily available to the Jews for writing, as it was in Mesopotamia. Instead, highly perishable materials, such as skins and papyrus, were utilized. Those documents were prey to the ravages of time because the climate of ancient Israel—unlike that of Egypt—was generally inhospitable to these materials. The dearth of surviving written records of the Jewish people was exacerbated by the strategic location of Israel as a land bridge between two continents. This made it a prime target for conquest, with resulting frequent plunderings and destruction.[20] Furthermore, until Alexander the Great's conquest of the Near East, and its subsequent Hellenist cultural unification, few outside of Israel were interested in Jewish culture or society, except for the relatively few periods when it was a fairly important military or mercantile power. All of the foregoing factors coalesced to result in very few literary finds in Israel. In fact, it is startling that, despite all of these conditions, the Bible itself survived and managed to capture the hearts and minds of so many diverse peoples throughout the world.

Another major obstacle to the study of ancient legal systems is the incompleteness and accidental character of the data available. For example, archaeological discoveries in Ebla, Syria, in 1976 seem likely to result in major revisions in our understanding of the civilization and history of the ancient Near East. All that one can study are the data that have been uncovered but perhaps may not be typical of the society as a whole and, consequently, may be misleading. A number of approaches have been utilized by scholars to overcome this deficiency. For example, detailed philological examinations have been made, based on intensive study of a particular site and the period to which its records relate. Prosopography, the study of the career of a particular person derived from a thorough examination of all of the records from a particular site, has also been found to be helpful.

---

word (e.g., as reflected in a treaty) is a trusted frame of reference. This is not true in the case of certain Eastern societies. Consequently, a Western society in conflict with an Eastern one may strive to end the conflict by the symbolically significant Western act of signing a treaty, which may be meaningless to an Eastern society. In the same way, constitutions, which may be very helpful in regulating certain societies, may not be congenial to the other groups of people.

So, too, by studying the law and underlying culture of a society one can ascertain the values that it recognizes as major principles and the meanings that a nation traditionally attributes to significant terms such as "peace," "war," "freedom," "truth," and "authority." These terms have radically different meanings for different societies. Mutual understanding between societies can only come about with the correct comprehension of the meanings of the significant terms utilized in formulating agreements.

The study of significant patterns of decision-making—the hub of legal activities in a society and of political thoughts and behavior there, can help to uncover the real affinities between different cultural and political systems and can uncover common sources of cultural strengths. This can aid conflicting societies in reaching accords.

Additionally, the study of comparative law over a long time span can help to analyze the political and cultural relations between different societies and how these are affected by miranda that are prevalent in those societies. Myths that are accepted as truth in a society acquire a reality of their own. Thus, the myth that the Muslim world was once politically unified helps to shape the policies of Arab countries today. So, too, China has a myth that it was once the solitary, universal power. Although this was not in fact true, this myth shaped the patterns of China's political organization and had a profound effect upon it and its legal system.

18. See, in general, A. Bozeman, *Politics and Culture in the Ancient World* (Princeton, 1960); P. Koschaker, "Scope and Methods of History of Assyrio-Babylonian Law," 35 *Proceedings of the Society of Biblical Archaeology* (1913): 230.

19. See N. Sarna, *Understanding Genesis* (New York, 1972), p. xviii.

20. See, e.g., 2 Maccabees, which tells of Judah's efforts, after his victory over the Seleucids, to gather books that had been lost during the wars. See also 4 Esdras regarding the burning of scrolls during the wars that led to the destruction of the Second Jewish Commonwealth and Temple in 70 c.e.

Fundamentally, however, one cannot analyze one aspect of a society without placing it within the total framework of that society and era. This requires a comprehensive understanding of that society. For example, records unearthed at Lagash disclosed extensive land holdings by the local temple. Other studies of the ancient Near East, however, indicate that during that period not all land throughout the Near East was owned by temples and that individuals also owned land. Similarly, the existence of records dealing with slave labor does not mean that all, or even most, of the work of a society was done by slaves. Study is required of the role of the semifree workers. Unfortunately, a number of monographs have been written concerning slavery in Mesopotamia without sufficient consideration of the relative roles of and the differences between these working classes. At the same time, records of widespread temple activities should not be taken as an indication that all countries of the area had a purely temple economy. In fact, there were non-temple economies too.

Additionally, in analyzing data from ancient societies it is important not to try to force the scant evidence into a Proscrustean bed, according to preconceived notions. Thus social stratification is often classed as "horizontal" (based upon differences in language, ethnic grouping, religion, etc.) or "vertical" (based on differentiations in power, such as master-slave, or on wealth); it is clear, however, that what may be "vertical" in one stratification is "horizontal" in another. The rich may not necessarily have a higher status in the church than the poor. Slaves can sometimes be powerful and even rich. Again, although ancient Greece has often been labeled "democratic," women could not vote.

A similar snare lies in the fact that incomplete information can be interpreted in quite different ways, depending upon the ideological viewpoint of the interpreter.[21] Thus, the data concerning land tenure in ancient Sumer can be interpreted either from a Marxist point of view, as representing the emergence of a class society, or simply as the transformation of a tribal society into a more complex one. While one clearly should avoid trying to squeeze the materials into a preconceived mold, the normal mode of human comprehension is to fit perceived data into a particular mental framework.

Another pitfall is to apply blindly to the study of ancient law the methodology of social anthropologists. There are substantial differences between the study of ancient civilizations, including their legal systems, and the examination of primitive societies that continue to exist today. For one, the social anthropologist studies societies that are still primitive, while ancient civilizations may have had quite sophisticated cultures, even then. Furthermore, the social anthropologist is concerned with society at only one point in time—when he observes it. In ancient society, however, evidence regarding a particular institution, such as marriage, often spans millennia, during which there may have been substantial changes in social institutions and interactions within, and among, different ethnic and social groups. There is, of course, a further difficulty in applying the methods of social anthropology to the study of ancient legal systems. There are widely divergent approaches used by social anthropologists themselves, such as the structuralist school of Claude Lévi-Strauss, the functionalistic methodology of the Anglo-Saxon school, the approach of P. W. Schmidt and his "Vienna School," or the cross-cultural school of P. Murdock. Accordingly, this book approaches Jewish law with the same methodology required of research in any legal system.

Another difficulty with the study of ancient law is that we are out of touch with its contextual background and the cultural setting in which it existed, despite the records that have come down to us. Even in those records, as has been indicated above, words can have different meanings in their distinct contexts and may have evoked different thoughts at the earlier time than they do in our own society. This makes it more difficult to evaluate their testimony accurately. We must be careful not to project the norms and thought habits of the present day into the past. Conversely, it is often insuperably difficult to formulate an alien mode of thought in terms of current notions and terms of expression.[22]

Nevertheless, there remains much of value in the study of ancient law, particularly in the study of Jewish law, with its continuous flow of authoritative decisions since the dawn of recorded human history.[23]

21. See J. Renger, "Who Are All Those People?" in 42 *Orientalia* (1973): 263–64.

22. Frankfort, *Before Philosophy: The Intellectual Adventure of Ancient Man* (Baltimore, 1972), p. 7, and *The Birth of Civilization*, p. 9.

23. See, in general, T. J. Colb, "Approaches to the Study of Ancient Society," in 81 *Journal of the American Oriental Society* (1967): 188; Renger, "Who Are All Those People?" p. 263.

Part One

Law in the Ancient Near East, 2200 B.C.E.–350 B.C.E.

I. The Social Contexts of the Ancient Near East

A. *Regional Contexts*

1. INTRODUCTION

Law reflects the values and practices of a society and also serves as an instrument for change. In order to comprehend the law and legal systems of the ancient Near East, it is necessary to grasp the broad contexts in which that society operated, including the fundamentals regarding the power structures and processes, the religious and cultural perspectives, and the social and economic factors that molded societies in the ancient Near East and are reflected in their law. Teaching experience with the materials incorporated in this book has demonstrated the great advantage and time saving for students in having readily available a concise summary of the historical and social contexts of the law. In order to save the student the considerable time and effort that would otherwise be required to gather the relevant data, sketches of the salient background of the law have been included in this book for each era studied.

2. THE DEVELOPMENT OF MESOPOTAMIAN AND EGYPTIAN CIVILIZATIONS

Civilization as we know it seems to have begun about four thousand years ago in the ancient Near East, in Mesopotamia, spreading soon afterwards to Egypt.[1] We do not have adequate records to establish whether similar civilizations also existed at the same time in the Indus Valley and in China on the banks of the Yellow River. Civilization seems to have developed earliest in Mesopotamia and Egypt, apparently encouraged by the good soil and climate, which provided sufficient food without absorbing all of the people's time and energy, thus permitting them to engage in civilized pursuits. It is possible that other areas with climates that supplied food with little effort may have been too hot, thereby stultifying initiative, or too cold, thereby immobilizing men for too long within their artificial shelters. In both Mesopotamia and Egypt, however, the appropriate natural conditions existed for the development of civilized life. Both regions had moderate climates and fertile

valleys, fed by rivers that supplied water and constantly brought new soil to replenish the exhausted earth.

Another reason contributing to the rise of mankind's earliest civilizations in the ancient Near East was the fact that this area had been a strategic center of gravity since the dawn of mankind. This was largely due, no doubt, to the region's central location, its possession of vital communications and trade routes, and its natural resources and climate. Since the dawn of history it had therefore attracted settlers who contributed their talents to making it the cradle where advanced cultures developed. This in turn attracted more settlers and may have led to further advances until the Near East became the cultural center of the world. At the same time, the region continued as a key to world power and prestige, and therefore the target of all rulers who would aspire to world power.

The epicenter of this region is Palestine. For millennia it served as a land bridge for trade and communications between Mesopotamia and Egypt, and in general between Africa and Asia. It also served as a cultural thoroughfare and as a landing area for traders from around the entire Mediterranean basin.

Mesopotamia and Egypt had some remarkable similarities; both possessed writing, monumental architecture, representational art, and political coherence. Yet there were striking differences between these two lands in the functions and structures of these features of civilization.[2]

Topographically, each of these two civilizations was centered about a great river valley: the Nile in Egypt and the Euphrates in Mesopotamia. Both river valleys have remarkably rich and fertile soils, permitting abundant harvests of a variety of agricultural crops. Although both areas have scant rainfall and require irrigation to make farming possible, they are blessed with mighty rivers that each year bring fresh supplies of water and rich soil in the form of silt. (The Tigris River was of far less importance than the Euphrates or Nile for irrigation because its deep bed carried waters too low beneath the levels of the surrounding countryside to permit the stream to be tapped by a simple system of canals.)[3]

---

1. See J. Hawkes and L. Wooley, *Prehistory and the Beginnings of Civilization* (History of Mankind, vol. 1; New York, 1963), pp. 345–51, 359–61; H. Frankfort, *The Birth of Civilization in the Near East* (New York, 1955), pp. 28–29.

2. Frankfort, *Birth of Civilization*, p. 50.
3. C. H. King, *A History of Civilization* (New York, 1964), pp. 27–28; Hawkes and Wolley, *Prehistory*, p. 417.

Both Mesopotamia and Egypt developed cultures that were quite advanced. Egyptian architecture served as models for the Greeks and other peoples; the pyramids, remarkable monuments to many skills and built with incredible accuracy, constituted some of the largest structures ever erected, structures that other civilizations found it difficult to emulate. Mathematics, and particularly astronomy, reached a high degree of evolution. Egyptians became proficient in medicine and pharmacology, as well as in a host of other technical specialties. In Mesopotamia, too, both the arts and sciences were advanced. Accurate charts were made of the stars, and prodigious feats of engineering were performed.[4] Many beautiful examples of the fine arts and poetry have been discovered in both countries, and techniques of government and administration reached new heights. Both civilizations were the building blocks on which much of modern society has been based.

3. ETHNIC MOVEMENTS AND POWER ALIGNMENTS AMONG THE NATION-STATES OF THE ANCIENT NEAR EAST

Massive ethnic migrations significantly shaped both the power processes in the ancient Near East and the development of empires by the nation-states of that region. They also made the area a melting pot for a wide variety of ethnic groups.[5]

At the dawn of history separate city-states developed in Sumer, in the south of Mesopotamia, and in Akkad in the north. Some time later, under Sargon I of Akkad (*circa* 2300 B.C.E.) and his son Naram-Sin, Sumer and Akkad were united into one state, thereby ending their traditional rivalry. This represented the emergence of a Semitic element of Akkad as a leading ethnic factor in the entire area.[6] The unification of Sumer and Akkad gave them greater strength and led to a blending of the cultures and spirit of its peoples. The new state increased in size until it became a large empire, extending from Iran to Asia Minor. This, however, exposed it to counterattacks from regions that were formerly remote from the capital cities of Sumer and Akkad.

As was to be the case in that region for millennia thereafter, the empire was short-lived. After only one century of rule, it was utterly destroyed by immense hordes of barbarians, the Umman-Manda, who were recalled with horror in legend and myth for almost two thousand years thereafter. Some time later (exact dates

before the first millennium are not easy to establish and are the subject of heated scholarly debates), in about 2000 B.C.E., a Sumerian revival took place, centered around the city of Ur. While this rule nominally included both Akkad and Sumer, many areas of that region in fact retained considerable autonomy. This regime, while it lasted for only one century, reached great heights, including the first known compilation of laws, called the Laws of Ur-Nammu after the founder of the dynasty. Many ethnic groups participated in this dynasty, and a number of its rulers had Akkadian, Subarian, and Hurrian names. Eventually the dynasty, under King Ibbi-Sin, came to an end with its conquest by Elamites.

At this point in time there is evidence of a new ethnic group in the area, the Amurru, often referred to by scholars as Amorites, as they were called in the Bible. They are described in Mesopotamian literature of that time as barbarians who had no houses and no agriculture and ate raw meat. Much information about them has been elicited from the discoveries at the city of Mari, an important urban area located between the Mediterranean and Mesopotamia. Their entry into the area is typical of the constant influx of new ethnic groups, mostly from the mountainous areas of Anatolia and Asia Minor in the northwest (see Map 1).

In about 1800 B.C.E. a trio of rulers became prominent in the region: Hammurabi, Shamshi-Adou, and Rim-Sin. The records of that era disclose that Rim-Sin of Larsa reigned during a long era of peace and prosperity and magnanimously spared the capital city of Isin when he conquered it. Shamshi-Adou of Assyria was an Amorite king who had business colonies in Cappadocia. His state had its own calendar and considerable prosperity. Hammurabi (more accurately Hammurapi), today the most famous of the trio because of his authorship of the Laws of Hammurabi (see Chapter II, Section E 4 *a*), was king of Babylon (Sumer). Some of his letters, which have been preserved, show him to have been methodical, shrewd, and skillful as well as determined to become the overlord of all Mesopotamia. He made alliances with his neighbors, whom he had already secretly decided to destroy one by one. Eventually he was successful. At the start, however, he clearly was not the most powerful ruler in the area.

There is no king who is all powerful on his own; ten or fifteen kings may march behind Hammurabi, the Babylonian; just so, after Rim-Sin of Larsa; similarly after Ibalpiel of Eshunna; similarly, too, after Amutpiel of Qatanum. Perhaps, twenty kings march behind Yarim-Lim of Yamhad.[7]

---

4. See E. A. Speiser, in *World History of the Jewish People*, vol. 1, ed. E. A. Speiser (London, 1964), p. 231.

5. M. Noth, *The Old Testament World* (Philadelphia, 1966), pp. 243–44.

6. Speiser, in *World History of the Jewish People*, vol. 1, p. 199.

7. Letter found in Mari, written to its king, Zimri-Lin; see ibid., p. 211.

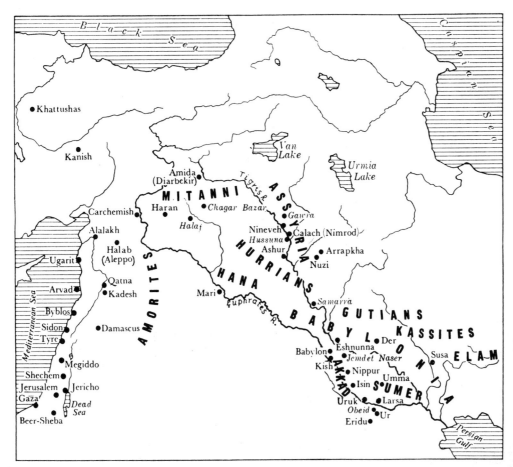

Map 1. States and Peoples of Ancient Mesopotamia. From E. A. Speiser, ed., *World History of the Jewish People* (London, 1964), I, 245.

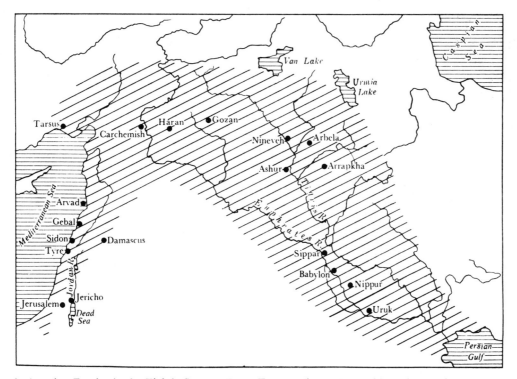

Map 2. Assyrian Empire in the Eighth Century. From E. A. Speiser, ed., *World History of the Jewish People* (London, 1964), I, 245.

The law code of Hammurabi is probably the most famous single document preserved from that era, and it will be examined by us later.

About one hundred and fifty years after the reign of King Hammurabi, Mursillis, king of the Hittites of Asia Minor, sacked Babylon and left it desolate. Some time after the invaders left, another people, the Kassites, entered the area in substantial numbers.

It is worthy of notice that the sacking of Babylon reflected the same chain of events that had taken place some centuries earlier and was to be constantly repeated in the history of the region: the invasion by a new ethnic group from the direction of Anatolia, causing widespread devastation and the collapse of a celebrated Mesopotamian dynasty, with ensuing rule by an obscure people from the nearby northeast mountains who enter the area after the Anatolian invaders leave. The fall of Babylon replicated the fall of Akkad some centuries earlier. There were, however, two important differences: the conquering Hittites were clearly a civilized state, unlike the Umman-Manda hordes which had toppled the Akkadian empire; also, the Hittite invasion constituted only one portion of a series of dramatic events in the Near East at that time that profoundly changed the political and ethnic structure of the area for many centuries thereafter.

For reasons still unclear, a migration of immense magnitude brought to all portions of the Near East large groups of peoples who had superior methods of warfare and communication. This caused long-lasting upheavals in the area, leading to a period referred to in the literature of the time as "the dark age." This large-scale migration apparently was started by Indo-Aryans, who also ushered in the Vedic Era in India at that time. The Indo-Aryan movement seems to have originated in Transcaspia, or Transcaucasia, and swept many groups ahead of them: Kassites, Hurrians, and other Semitic elements. While great numbers of Indo-Aryans did not enter the Near East because they were so far away, they nevertheless disrupted and uprooted other peoples, who then entered the area and caused havoc and a "dark age" in the territories of the Hittites, Syria, Assyria and Babylonia, and Egypt, lasting from about 1600 to 1500 B.C.E.

During this period of upheaval, and as part of the same drive, a people best known as the Hyksos invaded and conquered Egypt, and dominated it thereafter for a substantial period of time. At the same time the Mittani kingdom emerged. The success of these peoples in conquering the area was apparently due to their use of horse-drawn chariots on a large scale. This was a technological revolution with which the several peoples of the area were unable to cope.

A result of this turmoil was the emergence of the Hurrians, who originated in Armenia. They ruled Assyria and dominated the Mittani area and portions of Syria as well. The Kassites, who had entered Babylonia after the Hittite sacking, ruled there.

Subsequently the Egyptians, after expelling the Hyksos, attempted to expand into Syria, and encountered the Hittites, who were pressing down from the north. They fought a notable battle at Kadesh in about 1285 B.C.E. This resulted in a treaty between Pharaoh Ramses II and the Hittite king, Hattusilis III, which divided Syria into two spheres of influence, dominated by these two powers.

Gradually, the Mittani kingdom declined and Assyria reemerged. In about 1250 B.C.E., Assyria, under King Tu Kulti-Ninurta, defeated Babylonia and dragged off an idol of its chief god, Marduk. This king, who is celebrated in one of the most illustrious poetic epics in Mesopotamian literature (and who has been identified by some scholars as the biblical Nimrod), was eventually killed by his son.

At this juncture (about 1200 B.C.E.), there occurred another of those periodic massive incursions, which threw the entire Near East into a turmoil again. Vast migrations began, originating in the area around the Black Sea. Some people came by sea, others over land. They were a diverse ethnic group of Danaans, Philistines, Lycians, and others, who had lived in an area abounding with iron and had learned to use it with deadly efficiency for war. With it they were able to sweep all before them. They sacked Hattusas, ending Hittite rule in Anatolia, and conquered Carchemish, Aleppo, Alalakh, and the Amorite kingdom of southern Syria. One group conquered Cyprus. Others, the Etruscans, went to Italy and Sicily. The epic of Troy, described by Homer, appears to have been one of the episodes in this ethnic movement.[8] Many invaded Egypt, where they were known as the "sea peoples." At the same time, the eastern Mediterranean was subjected to incursions by Philistines.

Some have surmised that it was at this time that the Israelites left Egypt and conquered the land of Canaan. During this same period Elam conquered Babylonia and removed the stone stele on which King Hammurabi had engraved his code of laws. The stele was carried to Susa, where it was ultimately uncovered by archeologists at the beginning of this century. Soon, however, Babylonia drove out the Elamese Kassites, and Nebuchadnezzar I became king. Assyria too became independent and, under Tiglath-Pileser I, began another slow ascendancy to power, which was to last for a very long while. Eventually the expanding Assyrian empire

8. Hawkes and Wooley, *Prehistory*, pp. 394–95.

came into direct contact with Israel. King Shalmaneser III (859–824 B.C.E) attacked Damascus, which was allied with King Ahab of Israel. The latter allegedly furnished ten thousand foot soldiers and two thousand chariots to his allies.[9]

Some time later King Tiglath-Pileser III (746–727 B.C.E.) instituted a new policy of forcible ethnic migrations, which was to have a profound effect upon the peoples of the area. In order to weaken opposition by conquered peoples, he began to interchange populations systematically and deliberately transferred them from one end of his vast domains to the other. As a result of this policy, the Aramaeans were dispersed and nullified as a military power. This, however, helped to spread their language throughout the Near East.

The ten tribes of Israel were similarly uprooted and brought to the furthermost reaches of the Assyrian empire. Sennacherib (705–681 B.C.E.) wished to expand his Assyrian empire even further by challenging Egypt. As part of this drive, he invaded Judah (*circa* 701 B.C.E.), but his armies were allegedly devastated by an act of God and Jerusalem was saved on Passover Eve.[10] In 689 B.C.E., however, he captured Babylon and razed it to the ground, desecrating its religious shrines. Like his predecessor Tukulti-Ninurta, some six hundred years earlier, he too was killed by his own son while worshipping in his elaborate new capital at Nineveh.

The Assyrian empire continued, however, to grow. His son, Esarhadon, who became king with the help of his mother, Naqiya, finally succeeded in conquering Egypt in 671 B.C.E., the first time in history that Egypt and Mesopotamia were brought under a single rule. At his death Naqiya, who still ruled the family with an iron hand, selected her grandson Ashurbanipal to rule instead of his older brother. Ashurbanipal's name has come down in history, particularly, because he gathered a huge library, some twenty thousand tablets, dealing with all phases of ancient Mesopotamian culture. These have been uncovered and have provided one of the richest sources of information about the ancient Near East, including detailed lexicons and grammatical works of languages that had long been extinct.[11]

This Assyrian empire also was short-lived and came to a sudden, violent end. After Ashurbanipal's death the Medes conquered Nineveh in 612 B.C.E. and completely destroyed it, despite the help that Assyria received from its new ally, Egypt. Pharaoh Necho had now come to the aid of his old-time enemy, Assyria, because he feared the Medes and Neo-Babylonians even

more. Syria and Israel, which opposed Assyria, both resisted this Pharaoh, leading to a battle at Megiddo at which the Judaean king, Josiah, was killed.[12] The Neo-Babylonians later defeated the Egyptians at Karkhemish in 605 B.C.E.

The destruction of Assyria by the Medes was so complete that less than two hundred years later Xenophon and his Greeks passed within eyesight of Nineveh and did not even know they were treading so close to the former mighty world capital. Thus, Assyria was destroyed less than sixty years after it had reached the pinnacle of its power, ruling over a vast empire stretching from the Persian Gulf to Asia Minor and including both Mesopotamia and Egypt (see Map 2). This is typical of the constant upheavals that took place throughout the ancient Near East.

Soon Media controlled the northern tier of Near Eastern territories, from Iran to Anatolia. The southern section of the Near East fell under the sway of Nebuchadnezzar II, whose rule (605–562 B.C.E.) extended from Chaldaean Babylonia to the Mediterranean. During this period (586 B.C.E.) Nebuchadnezzar sacked Jerusalem, destroyed the Jewish Temple there, and deported masses of its inhabitants to Babylonia, beginning the "seventy years of Babylonian captivity." These events had profound effects on the Jewish nation and its law.

Even these two mighty empires, Media and Babylonia, did not long endure. By 539 B.C.E., Cyrus II of Persia had conquered both the Medes and the Babylonians, opening a new chapter in world history.

4. POWER PROCESSES AND ALIGNMENTS AMONG THE ANCIENT NATION-STATES

As we have seen from our thumbnail sketch of ancient Near Eastern history, the center of power in Mesopotamia gradually shifted in a northwesterly direction, up the Euphrates River Valley. Sumer merged with Akkad. Both gave way to Babylonia. Other centers of power emerged slowly further north. Assyria eventually superseded and absorbed the southern areas. Finally, the Medes and then the Persians, who succeeded them to power, expanded the sphere of power further in all directions.

The geographic boundaries of empires constantly expanded and eventually included many different ethnic groups: Sumerians, Akkadians, Amorites, Assyrians, Hittites, Elamites, Gutians, Hurrians, Aramaeans, Medes, and Persians. There were epochs during which there seemed to be two distinct tiers of states, one in the north (Israel, Assyria, Media) and one in the south

9. 1 Kings 20; Speiser, in *World History of the Jewish People*, vol. 1, p. 221.

10. 2 Kings 19:35; Isa. 37:36.

11. Speiser, in *World History of the Jewish People*, vol. 1, p. 226.

12. 2 Kings 23:29; 2 Chron. 35:20.

(Judah, Babylonia, and Persia), with the western states being gradually overwhelmed by those further east. Thus Israel and Judah were conquered, respectively, by Assyria and Babylonia. These in turn were then overwhelmed by Media and Persia. These northern and southern centers of power were eventually amalgamated to form the huge Persian empire. (See Map 1 for the locations of the various ethnic groups and states in Mesopotamian history.)

Egypt, as mentioned, was the second major power in the ancient Near East. At first it expanded its power and ruled over Libya and Nubia, and was the focus of power in Northeast Africa, at the juncture of the Asian and African continents. Unlike Mesopotamia, Egypt remained largely isolated from outside invasion due to her barriers of desert and sea. Subsequently the Egyptian empire expanded to dominate the eastern Mediterranean shores and Syria. Eventually it was overwhelmed by Assyria. Prior to this time Egypt had remained independent throughout most of her history, with the exception of isolated invasions, such as those by the Hyksos and the "sea peoples."

The major powers in the Near East who existed the longest were the Egyptians and the Hittites (one may add the Cretan Federation, since it too was in the eastern Mediterranean region). Other important powers of substantial duration were Babylonia, Elam, Mittani, Assyria, and Persia. These states were all mostly agricultural and self-sufficient (except Crete, which was largely commercial). In addition to the major powers, there were satellite states of varying strengths that moved in different power orbits, occasionally shifting their allegiances.[13]

The power processes, both external and internal, that took place in the Near East cannot be clearly understood, however, without a grasp of the relationship between power, law, religion, and culture in the ancient world.

5. THE COMMON LAW, CULTURE, AND LANGUAGES OF WESTERN ASIA

It is an interesting and crucial fact that Mesopotamia was the main source of cultural influence throughout the Near East, from Elam (in present-day Iran) to the Mediterranean and beyond, for a period of nearly two thousand years (from about 2500 B.C.E. to about 500 B.C.E.). This was true even in those parts of the Near East that were not dominated politically by Mesopotamia, such as the lands near the Mediterranean from 2000 to 1000 B.C.E. In this large area nearly all of the

countries had a common culture, which included shared concepts regarding law, government, and religion, the use of the cuneiform script, cylindrical seals, and the use of Akkadian as the international language of diplomacy and business.

The widespread use of a language is not simply limited to a form of expression. Language is a part of, and a reflection of, the culture.[14] Language, religion, myths, arts, and science are interdependent functions and products of the collective workings of the human mind.[15] Language has significant symbolic value, and it is even claimed that man cannot be understood without comprehending the symbolism inherent in his language.[16] Adoption of a foreign language results in a deep cultural influence that is expressed in part by the forms used in the language. The common language employed throughout the ancient Near East reflected its common cultural heritage.

The Akkadian language was used in the ancient Near East during the middle of the third millennium B.C.E. The popularity of Akkadian and of the cuneiform script apparently was due to the culture that it reflected:

> The spread of Cuneiform and of Akkadian coincides, by and large, with a marked attention to the law in many of the adoptive lands. What we are confronted with is a package deal, so to speak, embracing script, language and law, all imported from, or influenced by, Mesopotamia. The law is not necessarily, or prevailingly, Mesopotamian in content, but is markedly Mesopotamian in form, and, above all, in its status within a given society.[17]

Thus, in Elam there was widespread use of legal documents that were written in the Akkadian language and utilized provisions that originated in Akkad. Even the Hurrians, who after 1500 B.C.E. had a feudal system that differed sharply from the Mesopotamian concept of a state, still used legal documents that closely followed the Babylonian practice. Many such documents were uncovered at Nuzi in Arrapkha. So, too, the law codes of Anatolia and the Hittite codes bore similarities to the codes of lower Mesopotamia.

Although the history of Mesopotamia was marked by constant change—usually caused by vast ethnic movements and displacements—its overall culture nev-

13. A. Bozeman, *Politics and Culture in the Ancient World* (Princeton, 1960), p. 28; see also M. A. Levi, *Political Power in the Ancient World* (New York, 1965).

14. D. Hydes, "Directions in Ethnic Linguistic Theory," in 66 *American Anthropologist*, no. 3, pt. 2 (1964): 6 (section on "Transcultural Studies in Cognition").

15. Ibid. See also J. Gomperz and A. Hymes, "The Ethnography of Communication," in 66 *American Anthropologist*, no. 6, pt. 2 (1964); E. Cassirer, *Philosophy of Symbolic Forms*, vol. 1 (New Haven, 1953); B. Malinowski, *Coral Gardens and Their Magic*, vol. 2 (London, 1925).

16. See E. Cassirer, *An Essay on Man* (New Haven, 1944).

17. Speiser, in *World History of the Jewish People*, vol. 1, p. 252.

ertheless remained uniform. There was thus ultimate harmony despite the underlying diversity of ethnic and racial groups and the constant change. This success at peaceful coexistence may be of interest to our own age.

This Mesopotamian cultural unity is perhaps best exemplified by the Assyrian Prince Ashurbanipal, who in the seventh century B.C.E. (when there was bitter strife between Assyria in the north and Babylonia in the south) took pride in saying: "I read the involved texts in Sumerian and in the obscure Akkadian, so difficult to understand. And I took up the . . . stone records before the Flood."[18] His study of ancient texts in discarded languages apparently reflected his belief that they shared the same culture.

Besides its momentous contributions in government, law, and writing, this ancient Mesopotamian culture also developed the twenty-four-hour day, the solar calendar with its reckoning of years by the sun and weeks by the moon, the naming of days of the week after planets, the use of a sexagesimal system of measuring time (computing time by the hours, minutes, and seconds according to a 360-degree circle), systems of weights and measures, and many of the industrial and agricultural arts that are still vital to civilization today. Even under Elam, Mesopotamian cultural unity was maintained. The kings took Akkadian names, and the Laws of Eshnunna were written in Akkadian.

In contrast, Egypt had its own distinct language and culture. Civilized life revolved around the divine king. The Pharaoh was the living fount of law, and his decrees were regarded as inspired decisions. There is no mention of a legal code in ancient Egyptian history. This is probably due primarily to the perceived lack of need, since the king was the sole source of law, and secondarily to the perishable nature of Egyptian writing materials of papyrus and leather.[19] Eventually the Pharaohs appointed an official who acted as chief justice and as head of all government departments.[20]

B. *National Contexts: The Internal Power Structure of the Ancient Nation-States*

1. THE INTERRELATIONSHIP OF RELIGION, POWER, AND LAW IN THE ANCIENT WORLD

a. POLYTHEISTIC RELIGIONS IN THE ANCIENT NEAR EAST

Because our data regarding ancient religions is so incomplete, it is well to remember that the perils of Scylla and Charybdis lie before one who would speculate about religion in the ancient Near East. One may imagine too much of the emotions and ideas involved in the beliefs or blind oneself to the theological perspectives that actually did exist.[21]

It seems clear, however, that the uncertainty and instability of Mesopotamian life was reflected in its religious perspectives. The people believed in a hierarchy of deities who, although usually motivated by what was just, sometimes acted unpredictably and even out of whim or malevolence.[22] The cosmos of Mesopotamia therefore was not guided by constant ethical and moral principles. Consequently, mortals had always to be prepared for the worst, even though they hoped for the best. This constant fear that one or another of the gods would wreak havoc upon humans forced the Mesopotamians to develop extensive rituals to appease the gods for the myriad of acts for which they could take offense. These complex forms contributed toward the formation of a specialized priestly class. In any event, this accent on external forms, accompanied by the lack of constant ethical and moral principles, contributed to the spiritual decay against which the Israelites were, so tellingly, to revolt.

b. THE EARTHLY STATE AS PART OF THE POLYTHEISTIC COSMIC POWER STRUCTURE

An underlying assumption throughout Mesopotamia was that power was the supreme arbiter of destiny.[23] The standing of each participant in the ordering of the cosmos depended upon the extent of his power, the entire cosmos being considered as one state with its own ordered system of relationships.[24] An assembly of deities was held to rule the entire cosmos.

Each city was conceived as being ruled by a god. This phenomenon appears to have been caused by the constant anxiety of Mesopotamian man. He was all too aware of the constant threats to his existence from the recurrent and disastrous floods that could result from the frequent gales, abnormal rainfall or snowfall, landslides, and other phenomena that could cause the rushing Tigris River to burst its banks. Accordingly, he felt dependent upon a superhuman power for eternal protection. This, apparently, led to the perception that there

18. Ibid., p. 232, citing *Vorderasiatische Bibliothek*, vol. 7, 254.15.

19. Frankfort, *Birth of Civilization*, p. 99.

20. Ibid., p. 100; Levi, *Political Power in the Ancient World*, p. 2.

21. Hawkes and Wooley, *Prehistory*, p. 334.

22. Speiser, in *World History of the Jewish People*, vol. 1, p. 236; see also "Bible and Babel: A Comparative Study" (Chapter II, Section F 1, below).

23. Bozeman, *Politics and Culture in the Ancient World*, p. 21.

24. T. Jacobsen, "The Cosmos as a State," in H. Frankfort, *Before Philosophy: The Intellectual Adventure of Ancient Man* (Baltimore, 1972), pp. 142, 152.

existed a particular deity who was concerned with the city, watched over it, and ruled it.[25]

The earthly state was regarded only as an extension of the political domains of one of the deities. The local deity of a geographic unit served as a deputy of Enlil, the chief god, to administer its affairs. He in turn appointed a human steward, the king, who similarly would delegate powers to other lesser rulers. Accordingly, the entire cosmos, the empire, the city-states, and the local village were all organically linked into one cosmic government.[26] Some claim that the city-state was viewed as a secondary power structure within the universal state. It constituted the estate of one of the gods in his capacity as a private citizen of the cosmic state. The national state, on the other hand, was run by a god in his capacity as an official of the cosmic state and it constituted an extension of that state.[27]

As a result, the king derived his power from heaven but was not a deity. He was at most a mediator between man and the gods. This was different from the Egyptian concept of the king-deity on the one extreme and, on the other hand, the ancient Israelite concept of a king who was the delegate of the people. The Mesopotamian king's functions, then, included a priestly one, representing god to man and beseeching the deities to intervene on behalf of his subjects. As such, his relations with the priestly caste were very different from those in Egypt, where he himself was the deity.

Thus the entire structure of the government in Mesopotamia, and obedience to its orders, was based upon religious perspective concerning the operation of earthly states as units of the cosmos, ruled by local deities through their agents, the kings. Nevertheless, the city served as the political and sometimes economic unit, while the religious-economic unit was the temple. Each citizen belonged to one temple community.[28]

c. The Sharing of Power by King and Assembly

In the Mesopotamian religious perspective, as discussed above, the state was an integral part of the cosmic order and followed the same rules. This meant that the earthly state, like the heavenly exemplar, could not be ruled by one individual. Just as heaven was ruled by a heavenly assembly of deities, and even the chief god could not have his way without the consent of the others, so too no ruler on earth could have absolute authority. The consent of a popular assembly was required. Although the perspectives concerning a heavenly pantheon may have only reflected the practices of human decision-making on earth, this theological belief served to reinforce a nonauthoritarian order in the earthly state. The result was to circumscribe and limit the powers of the monarch and to require the consent of the governed. Religious beliefs thus played a crucial role in the development of power structures in the Mesopotamian state, in which religion, government, and law were firmly intertwined (see Chapter III, Section A 2 a below).

Accordingly, leading scholars of the ancient Near East believe that the king in Mesopotamia was rarely deified. Neither Hammurabi nor Sargon of Akkad, both mightly rulers, claimed to be a deity. In fact, during the New Year celebration in Babylonia the kings would customarily allow priests to slap them on the cheeks, box their ears, and divest them of the insignia of rule to emphasize their unworthiness.[29] Assyrian kings would be called *issakku*, or governors, since only gods were sovereign. The power of the earthly king was therefore sometimes severely limited by the will of the people, as expressed in popular assembly. Furthermore, the Mesopotamians believed that the king was responsible to the gods and received his mandate from them. This was another factor that helped to circumscribe the king's power and gave rise to a consultive government by an active assembly (called *ukkin* in Sumerian and *puhrum* in Akkadian). In the epic tales of floods the heros Utanapishtim and Gilgamesh both had to obtain the consent of a council for journeys and wars. In the epic of *Etana* mankind was in a state of barbarism until "consultation" was sent to earth by heaven.[30]

The Mesopotamian king's functions on behalf of the ruling deity in administering the government and in military affairs were, accordingly, religious in nature. He merely acted as the deity's messenger, carrying out his will. When Hammurabi conquered all of southern Mesopotamia, he and his subjects attributed this to the fact that his local deity had been chosen by the divine assembly to administer for Enlil. This local deity, in turn, appointed Hammurabi as ruler. When Hammurabi conquered and administered, it was for the gods. Not only were victories handed to the king by the gods, but he administered their lands as their agent. In administering the law he also acted in the gods' name. Men

25. Frankfort, *Birth of Civilization*, p. 54.
26. Bozeman, *Politics and Culture in the Ancient World*, p. 21.
27. Jacobsen, "The Function of the State," in Frankfort, *Before Philosophy*, pp. 200–201, 207.
28. Frankfort, *Birth of Civilization*, p. 64.

29. F. Thureau-Dangin, *Rituels Akkadiens* (Paris, 1921), p. 144, cited by Speiser, in *World History of the Jewish People*, vol. 1, pp. 238–39; see also S. A. Hooke, ed., *Myth, Ritual and Kingship: Essays on the Theory and Practice of Kingship in the Ancient Near East, and in Israel* (New York, 1958).
30. Speiser, in *World History of the Jewish People*, vol. 1, p. 238.

were therefore bound by religious faith to obey the laws and respect the authority of the king, who was a source of law and responsible to the gods for their enforcement.[31]

d. THE CITY-STATES

Since Mesopotamia did not have a geographic unity, there developed early in its history divisions into local urban groupings, each one of which formed a socio-economic unit of its own.[32] Each unit had its separate sovereign, priests, and gods. Yet there was a unity of thought among all of the various urban areas. All were dependent upon the same rivers, all shared the same civilization, and all had priestly castes that acted as mediators between man and his gods and administered the temple estates. All developed essentially the same form of government.

The city-states of ancient Mesopotamia resembled those of early Greece, the Hanseatic League, and Renaissance Italy in a number of respects. In all of these there was local autonomy and the notion that habitat, as distinct from kinship, determined the affinities of their citizens. The sovereignty of the cities rested with an assembly of citizens who were guided by an oligarchy of influential individuals.[33]

This was the way in which Mesopotamian man related to his gods and formed the basis of his moral and ethical beliefs. His perception of the alignment of society and nature, no less than economic and social factors, inevitably shaped the relationships between individuals, between man and the state, and the nature of society in general.

e. THE ROLE AND STATUS OF LAW IN MESOPOTAMIAN SOCIETY

Just as the heavens, in the Mesopotamian view, were governed according to immutable cosmic truths, so too the earthly state had to follow the same cosmic order. The king was chosen by the gods as their delegate and one of his prime functions was to conform life on earth to the cosmic power and apply those immutable truths in his rule. This not only included rule by assembly, rather than by the king as a dictator, but also implied that it was the king's duty to implement justice, which was an integral part of the cosmic order, and to provide proper care for the needs of his subjects. Functionally, this amounted to a concept of individual "rights." Any king who did not carry out justice would be punished

by the gods. Indeed, as we shall see, the kings strove valiantly to convince the gods that they were carrying out justice.[34] Some of these "rights" were later incorporated in written law codes.

Furthermore, obedience to the authority of the law was a religious duty, since law was simply an extension of cosmic truths. Law, accordingly, had a sacred and elevated status in Mesopotamia.

The Mesopotamian legal systems and form of government therefore reflected the underlying cultural concept of a state that was influenced by (and was partly a product of) religious perspectives. Thus religion had a crucial effect upon law and the sharing of power, and it determined the individual's relations with society and with other individuals. This illustrates the truism that law does not develop in a vacuum but is intimately related to social contexts.

The Mesopotamian ruler was not, then, the original source of law, only its agent. He was not the master of law but only its servant and was bound by law, like his humblest subject. One of the king's principal duties was to institute *mesarum* (justice), and he was accountable to the gods for any lapses or any errors in commission.

The existence of a well-established system of law and the expectation of legal decisions in accordance with accepted tradition is evidenced by the tens of thousands of juridical documents of all types that have been preserved from Mesopotamian civilization. These legal documents were in wide use even by the Hurrians after 1500 B.C.E., although they had a feudal system that was very different than the Mesopotamian concept of state. Nevertheless, they profusely utilized legal documents that closely follow Babylonian practice, as evidenced by the many tablets uncovered at Nuzi and Arrapkha. Even far away Anatolia, in Asia Minor, had its Hittite Code, which was similar in many respects to the codes of lower Mesopotamia.

The widespread appeal of Mesopotamian law, which was part of the cultural unity of the area for many thousands of years, was perhaps responsible for the widespread use of Akkadian (the primary language of that law), rather than the reverse. Unlike a script, a foreign language would normally not be adopted in preference to one's native tongue, unless it served as an indispensable vehicle for the cultural features desired to be adopted. In a similar way Latin was utilized as a vehicle for the application of Roman law, and gained adoption

---

31. Levi, *Political Power in the Ancient World*, pp. 8, 11.
32. Ibid., p. 13.
33. Frankfort, *Birth of Civilization*, p. 77.

34. It should be noted that in Egypt, too, justice was regarded as the social aspect of the cosmic order and pervaded the Egyptian commonwealth. The pharaohs came to be regarded as trustees who were to ensure the well-being of the community (Frankfort, *Birth of Civilization*, p. 24). See also J. A. Wilson, "Authority and Law in Ancient Egypt," Chapter II, Section E 2, below.

for other purposes as well. It is possible that Akkadian, too, may have been accepted in part because of the legal system and concept of state that it embodied. Thereafter, that language may have become utilized for international diplomacy as well. The Mesopotamian legal forms, if not always their content, thus became established elements of importance in the cultures that adopted them. One of the results was that these cultures also subscribed to similar concepts of government, meaning that the power of the ruler was strictly circumscribed since he too was bound by the law, which was a product of the gods, not of a person. This was one of the chief differences between the legal system of the Mesopotamians (including Elamites, Hurrians, Syrians, and Hittites, although each of these Mesopotamian cultures differed in many ways from one another), and that of Egypt. As a result, the assembly was a significant feature of power and decision-making in the Mesopotamian states, but not in Egypt.

These religious concepts concerning law may have led to (or at least were reflected in) the written law codes, although these were designed, in part, to testify that the king had carried out the will of the gods in instituting justice throughout the land. According to some scholars, these law codes were acts of piety, carrying forward the gods' acts of creation[35] by instituting justice in the land. The written law codes testified to what we might today call the "rights" of the king's subjects and, in effect, limited the king's powers. The masses were not, therefore, dependent upon the king's mercy, which he could arbitrarily exercise.

One scholar has speculated that "the abiding appeal of the law in Mesopotamia was due, in the final analysis, to its proved ability to protect the basic rights of the individual and to serve as a buffer against absolutism."[36] In fact, the codes could be looked at as a form of contract, which indicated that the subjects were expected to obey the king and his laws, but only when he acted according to the codes. These codifications were, therefore, looked upon by some scholars as a crucial point in the history of political ideas.[37] Other scholars, however, have claimed that the codes were not regarded as binding law (see Chapter II, Section E 4 *g*). Nevertheless, they appear to have reflected highly accepted perspectives prevalent in Mesopotamian culture.

It is also possible that the codes helped to restrict the power of the priestly class and of the local aristo-crats, thus gaining for the king the support of the masses, although perhaps antagonizing these privileged groups. The idea that the codes were made by man, rather than by gods, seems to have been further developed by the Hittites. Since the details of the laws were not made by the gods, it followed that they could be broken without committing a religious sin. It is possible that for this reason the Hittite Code provides punishments that are much more lenient than some of the other codes.

f. THE ROLE AND STATUS OF LAW IN THE EGYPTIAN STATE

The pattern of internal power in the Egyptian state was radically different from that in the Mesopotamian states, since the king was the state, the god, and the law. Without him there was nothing. In the Egyptian perspective, Horus, the son of the supreme deity Ra, was reincarnated in every pharaoh. Through this process of autogeneration, no matter which pharaoh sat on the throne he was always the same god. The death of a pharaoh and the coronation of a new ruler was analagous to the setting of the sun and the rising of the same sun the next morning. In the Egyptian perception, everything came about solely because the king so willed it. The deified pharaoh was therefore infallible. Accordingly, all political questions were treated solely in theological terms. As a result, there are no records of written codes or of a legal tradition in ancient Egypt. There was no need for a written law code since the pharaoh himself was the living law. It is possible that the limited amounts of arable land surrounded by desert also helped to give Egypt its rigid regimentation under a deified ruler, for strict control and proper management of the arable land was absolutely necessary if Egypt was to survive and prosper. This dominant theme of the divine ruler continued for some three thousand years. Even during the later Persian and Greek conquests, and as late as the Roman Era, a local pharaoh was needed to govern Egypt.

A deified pharaoh meant that there were no distinctions between his religious, military, and civil functions. In all of these he acted as a god. Still, there was a moderating influence on the authoritarian rule of the pharaoh. The Egyptians came to believe that the king had a duty to bring peace, security, and happiness to his peoples and to destroy his enemies who did not believe in his divinity. Egyptian theology later provided that a pharaoh had to account for his actions to the other gods after his death. If he did not act according to *ma'at* (the divine and cosmic order), even the pharaoh was to be cast into the flames of the nether world. The inevitable result was a diminution of reverence for

---

35. Compare the saying in Judaic law that any judge who rules justly becomes a partner with God in the creation of the world (Talmud, *Shabbat* 10a), and that the creation of the world was conditioned upon the subsequent acceptance of God's law (Talmud, *Shabbat* 88b).

36. Speiser, in *World History of the Jewish People*, vol. 1, p. 240.

37. Levi, *Political Power in the Ancient World*, p. 11.

the pharaoh. This belief received greater emphasis after the introduction of the cult of Osiris, which preached that all men would be reborn after death.[38]

Respect for the authority of the king and obedience to his rules were based upon religious faith in the king's divinity. The divine nature of his powers extended as well to his representatives and to all who wielded political power in his name. Obedience to their commands, and participation in all the activities of society, was, therefore, an act of faith. As a result, religion served as an all-important power base for the Egyptian monarch and his delegates in much the same way as in the Mesopotamian states.

g. THE PERSIAN STATE

The Persian kingship appeared to be an amalgam of the notions of two civilizations: the Egyptian, with the king as god, and the Indo-European Hittite, with the king as head of a cavalry-warrior class. The Persian king was a military leader, dependent upon his warriors, yet also a sovereign majesty and tyrant to those over whom he had power. This blend of notions meant that the powerful aristocracy had to be kept satisfied by being made *satraps*, or local governors. They in turn contributed militarily and financially to the king's support. A powerful bureaucracy also developed, which dealt with the king through their leader.

The Persians and the Medes lived as privileged races among the countries conquered by Persia. The subject classes, whose existence and acts were not regarded as important, were usually given the freedom that they needed for practice of their religious, commercial, and private lives. The elitism of the ruling classes eventually led to their decline. They ultimately became unwilling to bear the sole burden of the country's defenses. Consequently, the king was forced to conscript soldiers from the conquered masses. This gave the masses power and made them dissatisfied with the special favors accorded to the Persians and Medes, leading eventually to the Ionian revolt.

In short, the Persian empire was weakened by the existence of the elite class of Medes and Persians, with their unjustifiable privileges. The need to delegate power to aristocrats who ruled over local provinces, and the dissatisfaction of the conquered masses with their privileged overlords, helped to intensify governmental weaknesses. Additionally, the lack of adequate internal communications and the lack of adequate navies to control the coast and trade lines contributed to the later Persian downfall at the hands of the Greeks.[39]

In summary, two systems of political control emerged in the ancient Near East. First was the Egyptian system, in which the sovereign leader was a god, to whom obedience was required by religious dogma. This meant an absolute standard of justice administered by the king and a centralized administration whose personnel acted as agents of the deified ruler. Thus all men were equal in theory before this king-god. In practice, however, the king had to rely for administration of the country on bureaucrats, soldiers, and priests who gradually acquired privileges that in fact destroyed the equality of all people before the king. This, eventually, led to injustices and internal strife.

The second system of political control existed in Mesopotamia and was personified by the Hittite and Persian empires. This phenomenon of a state with a military aristocracy settling among a conquered race and governing it by right of conquest resulted in a decentralized administrative system with conflict between the aristocracy and monarch, on the one hand, and between the privileged aristocrats and the conquered masses, on the other hand. The results were political conflicts, injustices, and disharmony that made compromise essential.

2. OTHER SOCIAL CONTEXTS OF LAW

a. CLASS STRUCTURE AND THE ECONOMY

(1) *Mesopotamia*

Mesopotamian society was divided along economic lines into three classes: the free, the semifree, and the slaves. The free class (*awlium* or *amelu*) were apparently free citizens of various social grades, who filled the higher ranks of the army and were officials of the king. They had large kinship units, such as tribes and clans, as well as nuclear families consisting of husband, wife, and children. In the course of time the family became largely confined to unmarried children, the married ones forming their own households. There were also *mushkenu*, who were a class above slaves but below the *awlium* or *amelu*. This lower, and perhaps semifree, class constituted the main working force for the households and received rations of food and necessities, but could not be sold. They were punished less severely than the upper classes for their torts or violence and were compensated less for torts inflicted upon them. Some scholars feel that they probably could only be tenants but were not permitted to own land outright and were rarely allowed to carry arms, although they were liable to conscription.[40] It has also been argued that the main distinction between the *amelu* and the *mushkenu*

---

38. Ibid., p. 5.
39. Ibid., pp. 18–26.

40. Cf. Frankfort, *Birth of Civilization*, p. 64.

was not so much between rich and poor but between the full citizen and the half-free.

Much of Hammurabi's code was framed for the protection of this citizen class. Furthermore, while the temple communities operated as planned societies, there was considerable private enterprise in Mesopotamia.[41]

Among the Hittites, however, there appears to have been a sharp distinction between free men and slaves (who had a very low status),[42] but, apparently, there was no middle class of semifree men. In addition, there were the kings, noblemen, priests, and scribes who had special status in society.

(2) *Egypt*

The Egyptian economy, though basically agricultural, nevertheless had highly developed crafts and a vast bureaucracy. In terms of power, the pharaoh, a god, was superior to any mortal. As a ruler, however, he required officials to carry out the varied functions of government. He therefore had representatives in all the provinces who ruled practically as independent governors, with their own assistants and armed retainers. Until the end of the Middle Kingdom, even the priesthood was still only an incidental office held by a layman.[43] This resulted in a situation where the people could be classified into two main groups according to power: the officials who administered the pharaoh's orders and the subjects who obeyed them.

After the Hyksos were driven out (*circa* 1500 B.C.E.), Pharaoh Ahmose swept all these local overlords out of power. All of Egypt became the personal property of the pharaohs. As a result of the subsequent, continuous wars, which required powerful military forces, the army soon became dominant in the state. The priesthood,

too, came to occupy an important power and wealth position, with a large staff to administer the temples and temple revenues. The high priest of Amon, at Thebes, stood at the head of the priesthood, which gained increasing political power.

A census official of the eighteenth dynasty divided the Egyptian population into "soldiers, priests, royal serfs, and all the craftsmen."[44] (This classification, however, omits the royal family and the nobility at the top of the social and power ladder, as well as the slaves at the bottom.) From the eighteenth dynasty on, this middle class increased greatly in wealth and in the comforts of living. Many fairly elaborate tombs of this class have been uncovered. Even houses of petty clerks and artisans sometimes contained from four to seven rooms. The royal palace and the mansions of "nobility" were, of course, on a magnificent scale.

The artisans and lesser craftsmen of Egypt were forbidden by law to change their occupations. They were also not allowed to participate in civic affairs. Some farmers were independent. Others worked on royal estates and temple lands but owned their own homes and could not be sold. The slaves, however, were tied to the land and passed on to the new master if the lands were sold.

b. Miscellaneous Social Contexts

Even a superficial glance at the Mesopotamian legal codes and legal documents discloses that they, like the biblical code, deal with social institutions that had developed from earlier times. The Mesopotamian laws did not attempt to change most of these legal institutions, such as the family, marriage, or commercial contracts. Rather, the law sought to mediate disputes and to protect the rights of the parties in accordance with the established institutions and expectations of the society. In these cases, too, the law reflected, and was inexorably tied to, underlying social institutions and practices.

In addition to the effects of the social contexts examined herein and the consequences of growing urbanization[45] and commerce, there are still other, though less significant, ways in which the law of the ancient Near East was affected by political, religious, social, and other factors of the underlying culture.

It has been contended, for example, that in practice the stronger the degree of central authority within a state, the less self-help is tolerated by the law and the more the oppressed individual is compelled to resort to the courts for aid. This is principally because self-help

41. *Ibid.*, p. 73.

42. Thus, one of the Hittite records states, "And if ever a servant vexes his master, either they kill him, or they injure his nose, his eyes or his ears; or he [the master] calls him to account and also his wife, his sons, his brother, his sister, his relatives by marriage, and his family, whether it be a male servant or a female servant. . . . If then anyone vexes the feelings of a god, does the god punish him alone for it? Does he not punish his wife, his children, his descendants, his family, his slaves, male and female, his cattle, his sheep and his harvest for it, and remove him utterly?" (*ibid.*). These indicate, if taken literally, that the Hittite slave could be put to death for his offenses, and could probably be sold. Nevertheless, a Hittite slave could own property, and could marry a free woman. If he were assaulted, the assaulter could be sued and be forced to pay a fine. It is not, however, clear whether the fine was paid directly to the slave or the master. Apparently, the slave was, therefore, not a mere chattel but received some protection from the law (Hawkes and Wooley, *Prehistory*, p. 473). See also I. J. Gelb, "Approaches to the Study of Ancient Society," 81 *Journal of the American Oriental Society* (1957): 1, 7; I. Mendelsohn, *Slavery in the Ancient Near East* (New York, 1949).

43. Hawkes and Wooley, *Prehistory*, p. 468.

44. *Ibid.*, 469.

45. See Sections 1 and 2, above.

mitigates against the power of the central authority, which desires to be the sole source of power within the state.[46] If so, it is understandable that in Mesopotamia the central authorities' desire for order sometimes found expression in the extreme legal provisions that local authorities were to be held responsible for offenses of murder and robbery if the offenders themselves were not caught.[47] Similarly, brigandage, which constituted a threat to central authority, has always been treated harshly under the law;[48] the law also was said to be highly suspicious of herdsmen, who were often the associates of brigands.[49] Similarly, while the growth of the talio provisions of Mesopotamian law may have been due to religious and cultural perspectives, it has been claimed that this draconian legal norm came into effect following the growth of central authority, which desired to curb individual acts of violence since it saw these as threats toward authority. The same applies to the intense hostility to sorcery (which usually flourishes when central governmental and religious authorities decline). This may reflect the concerns of the central governmental authority to preserve its power, and the efforts of

the central religion to conserve its role as the sole contact with the supernatural.[50] In these cases, the law reflected the underlying cultural beliefs and institutions.

Another important economic fact, inflation, has often resulted in revision of fixed fines.[51] We shall study the effects of economic conditions upon Jewish law and the responses of the law to changed economic conditions in the institution of the *prusbul* (the assignment of debts to the court, in order to avoid their cancellation by passage of the Sabbatical year) (see Part Two, Chapter V, Section C 4), and in the devices developed to circumvent restrictions on usury in law.[52]

All practices and applications of law are, of course, shaped by societal conditions. Thus, scholars have argued that even the tradition of following legal precedent and the utilization of hermeneutics and settled methods of legal reasoning develop when the underlying social conditions provide overall stability and limit the role of the jury. Some scholars have seen in this the reasons why sophisticated methods of legal reasoning did not develop in Greek law but did develop in Jewish, Roman, and Islamic law.[53]

---

46. B. Jackson, "Evolution and Foreign Influence in Ancient Law," in 16 *American Journal of Comparative Law* (1968): 372, 385.

47. See e.g., Code of Hammurabi, sec. 24. See Jackson, "Evolution and Foreign Influence," n. 79, for citations to other legal systems.

48. See, e.g., Talmud, *Sanhedrin* 25; Theodosian Code 9.31.1, Constitution of 409 C.E.

49. Jackson, "Evolution and Foreign Influence," p. 386.

50. Ibid., pp. 386–87.

51. See E. Balogh, "Adaption of Law to the Economic Conditions in Ancient Greece," in *Studi in Onore Vincenzio Arangio-Ruiz* (Rome, 1962), pp. 181–98; Balogh, *Adaptation of Law to Economic Conditions According to Roman Law* (New York, 1957).

52. See also H. Schacht, *Introduction to Islamic Law* (Oxford 1964), p. 79, for similar phenomena in Islamic cultures.

53. See Jackson, "Evolution and Foreign Influence," pp. 389, 390.

II.   Biblical Law in Contextual Perspective

A. *An Overview of Jewish History in the Biblical Era*

Jewish history is unique. There is no other history quite like it. It is more than just a history of a people, a nation, or a religion. The Jews have actively participated, as Jews, in every phase of the development of Western civilization. Their history is, accordingly, intimately interlocked with the larger surrounding cultures and societies, each phase of Jewish history being deeply affected by those interactions with the surrounding world.

The history of the Jews cannot, therefore, be studied in isolation, separated from the realities of the world at large. One must pay close attention to the developments and patterns of non-Jewish peoples in all eras—in the ancient Near East, the Greco-Roman eras, the Middle Ages, and thereafter. At the same time, one must pay close attention to distinctively Jewish developments during those epochs, although often these could not help but be shaped by non-Jewish institutions and developments regarding modes of governing and maintaining public order, language and forms of literary and legal expression, the spread of Hellenistic culture and practice, the evolution of feudalism, capitalism, commerce, imperialism, and religious developments in Christianity and Islam.[1]

1. SOURCES OF JEWISH BIBLICAL HISTORY

The Bible is far and away the best and most informative source for the history of the Jews in the Biblical Era. Doubts of scholars have been substantially dissipated as a result of excavations in the ancient Near East that have corroborated the reliability of the Bible in sketching the background of events recounted therein, as well as the practices and customs of those times. Even the truthfulness of minute, accompanying details have been verified. These could not have been invented by human imagination, for the significance of many of their details had been lost and forgotten for many thousands of years by the time the Bible was re-

corded.[2] The Bible, accordingly, appears to reflect an accurate tradition faithfully recorded.

There are, however, other subsidiary sources of information for this era:[3]

1. Data unearthed by archaeological investigations, including Egyptian execration texts from about 1800 B.C.E., listing the enemies of Egypt by name, including both individuals and states.

2. The texts unearthed in Mari, a Mesopotamian city, from the time of Hammurabi and Abraham (*circa* eighteenth century B.C.E.). These include archives of the king, economic and legal texts, and political correspondence.

3. The Amarna Tablets, found in Egypt, which date from the fourteenth century B.C.E. These contain what is probably the first documentary mention of the Jewish people in Palestine.

4. The Ras-Shamra (*Ugarit*) Tablets, an extensive cache of documents from royal archives (*circa* 2000 B.C.E.) in Syria.

5. Egyptian reports on the campaigns of the pharaohs, beginning with the fifteenth century B.C.E. These include references to Palestine.

6. The documents unearthed at Nuzi in Syria from about 1500 B.C.E. These probably constitute the most important findings regarding the social backgrounds of the biblical patriarchs. These documents shed much light on many biblical motifs that would otherwise have remained obscure, such as the wife-sister tradition mentioned in connection with Abraham and Isaac (Gen. 12:13, 26:7), the tradition that a childless wife could have her husband marry a concubine (Gen. 16:20, 30:3, 9), the selling of the birthright by Esau to Jacob (Gen. 25:31–4), and the stealing of the *teraphim* (household gods) by Rachel (Gen. 31:19).

Discoveries in Ebla, Syria, by Italian archaeologists in 1976 may overshadow the foregoing in their importance for biblical studies.

1. See E. Rivkin, *The Shaping of Jewish History* (New York, 1971).

2. E. A. Speiser, *World History of the Jewish People*, vol. 2 (London, 1964), pp. 160, 168.

3. See Speiser, "The Patriarchs and Their Social Background," ibid., vol. 2, p. 163; M. Noth, *History of Israel* (New York, 1958); M. Burows, *What Mean Those Stones?* (New York, 1958); A. Malamat, "Prophecy" in the Mari Documents (Heb.; Israel, 1956); E. A. Speiser, *The Idea of History in the Ancient Near East*, ed. R. C. Denton (New Haven, 1955), p. 82; E. L. Ehrlich, *A Concise History of Israel* (New York, 1962), pp. 1–2; B. Mazar, "Historical Development," in *World History of the Jewish People*, vol. 2, p. 19.

2. THE EARLY HEBREWS

The Bible, the most authoritative and extensive source of information about the history of the Jews in the Biblical Era, reflects the perceptions concerning history that were to affect Jewish law. Accordingly, the following summary of Jewish history during that time is based upon the biblical account, as amplified by some of the extrabiblical sources mentioned above.

The first Jews were Hebrews who came from Ur in southern Babylonia. It is not clear if there was any connection between these Hebrews and the *Habiru* or *Apiru* mentioned in Mesopotamian, Egyptian, and Syro-Palestinian sources from the nineteenth to the twelfth centuries B.C.E.[4]

Nevertheless, it is interesting to note one of the earliest nonbiblical references to the Jews, found in a hymn of the pharaoh, *Mer-Ne-Ptah*, of the thirteenth century B.C.E.:

> Plundered is Canaan with every evil;
> Carried off is Ashkelon, seized upon is Gezer;
> Yanoam is made as that which does not exist;
> Israel is laid waste, his seed is not;
> Hurru is become a widow for Egypt.[5]

This report of Israel's destruction was a harbinger of its many later tribulations. Despite the premature report of its complete annihilation, Israel managed to survive and outlive this threat, as well as all of its later enemies.

It should be noted here that while the Hebrews were called Semites, the word "Semitic" is not a racial concept, and many different races utilize the Semitic language, including the Akkadians (in North Babylonia since 2000 B.C.E.), the Amorites, (who founded Babylon and penetrated Syria about 2000 B.C.E.), and the Aramaens as well as the Arabs in the seventh century B.C.E.[6]

3. THE PATRIARCHS

The Bible portrays Abraham, Isaac, and Jacob, the three patriarchs, as the recipients of divine promises and prophecies who communicated directly with God. The first divine command to the patriarchs, recorded in the Bible, was the command to Abraham to leave Mesopotamia. Although the Bible does not state the reason for this difficult divine imperative to forsake family and homeland, it seems clear that key factors were the polytheistic religions and the immoral practices of the Mesopotamians. Abraham and his family

then moved to Haran, on the Balikh River in the middle Euphrates Valley in northwestern Babylon.[7] This was probably between the seventeenth and twentieth centuries B.C.E., although exact dating for this era is the subject of much scholarly debate. Shortly thereafter Abraham and his family moved on to the eastern coast of the Mediterranean Sea. His moves were favored by the hegemony of the Amorites, who ruled from what is today western Iran to the Mediterranean Sea until their chief city, Mari, was conquered by King Hammurabi.[8]

The Bible records that Abraham actively propagated the belief in monotheism, gained many converts, and entered into a solemn covenant with God. This included the promise that henceforth he and his descendants would have a special relationship with God and that the land in which he dwelled would be given to his descendants. Abraham's move from Mesopotamia to that land and, especially, the perception of his covenant with God were to be of overriding importance for Jewish history.

In terms of the development of civilization, the patriarchal era corresponds roughly with the Middle Bronze Age. While Mesopotamia and the northeastern Mediterranean coast were then controlled by the Amorites, many of the cities along the eastern Mediterranean were dominated by Egypt. Nevertheless, the behavior of Abraham and his family, who originated in Mesopotamia, was shaped by many of the customs of Mesopotamia and particularly of the Hurians, whose center was near Haran. This is attested to by many of the texts unearthed at Nuzi, which throw light on a number of the biblical narratives, including concubinage (Gen. 16, 30), laws of adoption and inheritance, (Gen. 15:1), Jacob's work for Laban and his marriage to Laban's daughters (Gen. 31:50), and others. At that time Syria-Palestine apparently did not yet play a role as a vital land bridge between Egypt and Mesopotamia. It served in this capacity only after the arrival of the Hyksos there in the seventeenth or eighteenth century B.C.E.[9]

4. THE BONDAGE IN EGYPT

The Hebrews entered Egypt, driven by hunger from the land of Canaan, apparently during the sixteenth or seventeenth century B.C.E. (the precise dating continues to be the subject of scholarly dispute). There is evidence from Egyptian papyrus texts of a number of

4. M. Greenberg, *The Hab/Piru* (New Haven, 1955); Ehrlich, *A Concise History of Israel*, pp. 7–8.

5. J. A. Wilson, in J. B. Pritchard, *Ancient Near Eastern Texts Relating to the Old Testament* (Princeton, 1955), p. 376.

6. Ehrlich, *A Concise History of Israel*, p. 7.

7. Cf. Commentary of Moshe ben Nakhman (Ramban), to Gen. 11:31 (Jerusalem, 1962).

8. Noth, *History of Israel*, p. 127; Ehrlich, *A Concise History of Israel*, p. 4.

9. Noth, *History of Israel*, p. 27.

groups from Asia that were admitted into Egypt and permitted to settle there during times of adversity.[10] Scholars have speculated that the move to Egypt took place during the reign there of the Hyksos, who had conquered Egypt largely as a result of a new deadly weapon, the horse-driven chariot.

Some scholars have theorized that there is a connection between the Hyksos' invasion and rule of Egypt and the status of the Hebrews there. According to this theory, all went well with the Hebrews in Egypt until the Hyksos were driven out (in about the sixteenth century B.C.E.). Then the eighteenth Egyptian dynasty returned to power and enslaved the Jews. This would explain the biblical reference (Exod. 1:8) to the reign of a "new king" who did not "know" Joseph (son of the patriarch Jacob, who had saved Egypt from a severe and sustained famine). It would also explain the biblical account that the Egyptians feared that the Hebrews would join their enemies (presumably the Hyksos) in war, since both were alien peoples and not ethnic Egyptians.[11] In any case, the Bible records that the Hebrews multiplied rapidly and, as slaves, built the cities of Pithom and Ramses in the Delta. Ramses was the capital of Egypt in the nineteenth dynasty (the thirteenth century B.C.E.), which may help to date the period of the Hebrew enslavement in Egypt. It has been speculated that the pharaoh Ramses II (approximately 1290–1223 B.C.E.), who utilized the city of Ramses as his residence, was king at the time of the Jewish exodus from Egypt and that the pharaoh Seti I (approximately 1313–1301 B.C.E.) was the pharaoh of the oppression.

5. THE EXODUS FROM EGYPT AND THE SINAI COVENANT

The Bible records that after a sojourn of a few hundred years in Egypt, the Hebrews prayed to God, who then sent them a redeemer, Moses. He was a Hebrew who had been adopted as a baby by Pharaoh's daughter and had been raised as an Egyptian prince. After many plagues were miraculously visited upon the Egyptians, the Hebrews were permitted to leave, and they were joined by a multitude of people of diverse ethnic origins. The biblical account of the exodus from Egypt has not been found mentioned in Egyptian sources.[12] This is not surprising, however, since it was customary for Egyptians, like many other peoples of the ancient Near East, to record their victories and not their defeats; for example, the conquest and rule of Egypt by

the Hyksos was mentioned only *after* they were expelled from Egypt.

Following the exodus of the Hebrews from Egypt into the desert, the Bible records that they made a covenant with God at Mount Sinai, where they were then given the Divine Law which was recorded in the Bible. The Bible views this religious experience as the central event and focal point in the history of Israel, the event that made Israel unique among the nations. There has, of course, been much scholarly controversy regarding this event. Some contemporary scholars of ancient Near Eastern studies have been extremely skeptical. Others have held and accepted the truth of this event, stating, for example, "It cannot be doubted that this Sinai tradition, the content of which is unique in its essential matter, and cannot be derived from other stages in general religious history, has its origin in an actual train of events."[13] What cannot, however, be doubted is the perception of the Jewish people in subsequent generations that they had in fact entered into a covenant with God and received the law from Him. This is the crucial factor that has made that people unique in its outlook and, moreover, has profoundly influenced the course of human history.

6. THE CONQUEST OF THE LAND OF CANAAN

After a forty-five year stay in the desert, Moses died (*circa* 1200 B.C.E.) and the Israelite tribes invaded the land of Canaan. At that time the influence there of both Egypt and the Mesopotamian states was minimal because of their own internal difficulties. The land was inhabited by extremely diverse ethnic groups, including Hittites, Amorites, Canaanites, Perizzites, Hivites, and Jebusites. The Canaanites and Jebusites appear to have been Semitic peoples indigenous to the land. The Amorites are thought to have been the remnant of peoples who came out of the Arabian Desert at the beginning of the second millennium B.C.E. and had been the dominant power in the eastern Mediterranean lands for some time. The Hittites were a non-Semitic group who originated in Asia Minor, while the Hivites were probably synonymous with, or related to, the Hurrians, a group of unknown origin, who entered northern Mesopotamia at the end of the third millennium and constituted a majority of the population of northern Syria in the fourteenth and fifteenth centuries B.C.E. Over a period of years the Israelites conquered the land and settled it. Yet a number of fortified cities (for example, Gezer and Jerusalem [see Josh. 9:13]) were bypassed and remained in non-Israelite hands. A number of Canaanite cities, together with their inhabitants, appear

---

10. Ehrlich, *A Concise History of Israel*, p. 12.

11. See, ibid., pp. 10–11.

12. See, however, the claims of E. Velikovsky in *Worlds in Collision* (New York, 1949) and in many of his subsequent works.

13. Noth, *History of Israel*, p. 128.

to have been "incorporated" in the new Israelite territory and were permitted to remain. These included the cities of Gibeon, Shechem, Hepher, and Tirzah (see Josh. 9:15–18; 13:13; 16:18; 17:11). As a result of the social interaction between the Israelites, the remaining Canaanite elements, and the peoples of neighboring states, the Hebrew religion and culture had to compete with Canaanian and other cultures that had very different religious perspectives.

The Hebrew religion was based upon a strict monotheism, with no visual representation, or secret ceremonies, and a minimum of dramatic rituals. Its primary emphasis was on compliance with very demanding moral and ethical standards. The Canaanite cultures, on the other hand, were based upon polytheism, visually ubiquitous and closely connected with the earth and its vegetation. The Canaanite civilization, however, appears to have been technologically more advanced and richer materially than that of the Israelites. As was to be expected, the Canaanite religion and culture influenced many Israelites and resulted in the waging of a perpetual *kulturkampf* between the two differing perspectives. Furthermore, since the Israelites were a loose confederation of tribes, without any central authority, neighboring peoples (i.e., Edom, Mohab, Ammon, etc.) were often tempted to attack the disunited Israelites.[14]

7. THE ERA OF THE JUDGES

After the conquest of the land of Canaan, Israelite society was structured in a loose tribal confederation (somewhat like the Greek *amphictyony*), grouped around a common central sanctuary (e.g., Gilgal and Shiloh). The individual tribes were expected to cooperate to maintain peace and for mutual defense. In practice, however, despite the religious and political ties between the tribes, they would often refuse to come to each other's aid in time of war (see Judges 5:16). In addition to the looseness of the tribal political confederation, there were also geographic barriers to unity. The Plain of Esdraelon, ruled by undefeated Canaanites, divided Galilee from the area ruled by the tribes of Menasseh and Ephraim. The fortress city of Jerusalem also acted as a barrier between the Israelites living in the Judean hills and those living on the hills of Ephraim. The leaders of the loose Israelite tribal confederation were called judges and, as was common in the ancient Near East, often acted as the supreme judges of their region and decided disputes and other legal issues.[15]

This era of the judges coincided with the beginning of the Iron Age in the eastern Mediterranean.[16] Prior to the introduction of iron, copper and bronze (made from a mixture of tin and copper) had been used for tools. It has been speculated that it was the Hyksos who introduced bronze into the ancient Near East in about 1700 B.C.E. Subsequently the Hittites of Asia Minor, using a complicated smelting process, perfected the use of iron. Its tensile strength and other valuable features made it a much more effective tool for war, agriculture, and building. The process seems to have been kept secret until the fall of the Hittite empire about 1200 B.C.E. At about that time the use of iron was introduced into the eastern Mediterranean, apparently by the Philistines.

The Philistines came to the eastern Mediterranean as part of the massive invasion of "sea peoples" and settled there in great numbers, particularly after Ramses III successfully kept them out of Egypt.[17] They are thought to have originated in Crete, and perhaps Illyria.[18] Their five major cities in the southeastern Mediterranean, adjacent to the area occupied by the Israelite tribes, were Gaza, Ashkelon, Ashdod, Ekron, and Gath. Some scholars believe that the Philistines constituted a warrior upper class, superimposed upon an indigenous Canaanite population.[19] Although the Israelites had repelled many invasions by neighboring people, their most serious danger came from the invasions of the Philistines. For a long time the Philistines were successful and ruled over substantial portions of Israelite territory, even capturing Sampson, one of the most famous Israelite judges,[20] and later capturing the Holy Ark of the Israelites.[21]

To maintain their military dominance, the Philistines forbade the Israelites to manufacture iron instruments, thus maintaining their technological superiority for war. This Philistine domination was the final factor that impelled the Israelites to unite politically and choose a king.[22]

8. THE MONARCHY IN ISRAEL

a. THE FIRST KING

Monarchy was an established institution in the ancient Near East, as discussed above (Chapter I, Section B 1). The Mesopotamian king, unlike the Egyptian

14. Ehrlich, *A Concise History of Israel*; see also the biblical Book of Judges.
15. S. Loewenstam, *World History of the Jewish People*, vol. 2, pp. 231–32; see Chapter II, Section B, below.

16. Ehrlich, *A Concise History of Israel*, p. 25.
17. See Chapter I, Section A 3, above.
18. See Amos 9:7; Jer. 47:4; Ehrlich, *A Concise History of Israel*, p. 27; Noth, *A History of Israel*, p. 35.
19. Ehrlich, ibid., p. 27.
20. Judg. 16:21.
21. 1 Sam. 4:11.
22. See 1 Sam. 8:5.

model, was not usually deified, although he would act as a representative and appointee of a deity. There were a number of factors that tended to limit the authority of the Mesopotamian king. For one, there was often a popular assembly whose deliberations were thought to be essential to civilized existence. More importantly, the king was believed to have a mandate from the gods and was obligated to account to them. He had to obtain divine approval, by use of omens, for all major undertakings. These tended to emphasize his complete dependence upon the gods. So, too, in the religious perspective of the ancient Mesopotamians, even a deity lacked complete power, and was subject to the rules of an assembly of gods. In the Mesopotamian view, the political structure on earth had to follow the model in heaven, where the chief deity had only limited powers. It is quite likely, however, that the Mesopotamian perspective of heavenly rule by an assembly of gods merely reflected the already existing political situation on earth.[23]

In a similar fashion, when the Israelites chose a king, his powers also were severely limited. Of even greater importance than the Mesopotamian tradition of a king with limited powers was the Israelites' firm belief in monotheism, which clearly prevented any king from claiming to be a deity. Upon the demand of the Israelites for a king to lead them in war, the prophet Samuel, who had heretofore acted as leader and judge, chose Saul, of the tribe of Benjamin, to be king.

In addition to Saul's personal qualities, the fact that he was from the tribe of Benjamin may have had substantial political advantages. First of all, his tribe was one of the smallest. His choice could eliminate fears by the other tribes that his clan would attempt to dominate them. Furthermore, the area of the tribe of Benjamin had a central geographic location, enabling easy communication with the other tribes.

Besides its vital political ramifications for governing and decision-making, the rise of the monarchy eventually led to the undermining of the social importance of the individual tribes. It furthermore led to increasing friction and later open hostility between the kings, who attempted to increase their authority, and the prophets, who spoke up, attempting to check injustice and to protect the weak and lower social and economic classes. The prophets emphasized that even the king had to submit to biblical law and morality.

Saul, the first Israelite king, was killed when his army suffered a major defeat at the hands of the Philistines

(circa 1000 B.C.E.). Yet his death gave rise to one of the most decisive turns in Israelite history, due to the personal qualities of his successor, David.

b. THE DAVIDIC DYNASTY

David, who had his origins as a shepherd, became a well-known warrior, married Saul's daughter, and succeeded in arousing Saul's intense jealousy, due to his growing popularity. He was a man of great poetical and musical abilities and of deep religious feelings, which are reflected in the immortal poems that he composed and that are enshrined in the Book of Psalms.

Following Saul's death, David proclaimed himself king in Hebron, the chief city of the tribe of Judah, of which he was a member. At first Saul's only surviving son, controlled by Abner, his commander-in-chief, ruled over substantial portions of Samaria, Galilee, and Trans-Jordan. Eventually, however, Abner went over to David's side and Saul's son, Ishbosheth, was murdered by two soldiers without David's approval.[24] David then became king over all of the Israelite tribes and subsequently defeated the Philistines so decisively in a number of battles that he ended forever their domination over Israel and their threat as a major power in the area. He embarked on a long series of successful wars, until his kingdom eventually stretched from the Gulf of Aquaba to Homs in the north and from the Euphrates River to the Mediterranean coast.[25] The Jewish state then became a major power in the Near East and for size and influence was without any precedent on the soil of Syria-Palestine (a name later applied to the area, partly derived from the former Philistine presence). It should be remembered that at this time both Egypt and Assyria were at the low point of their international influence because of their internal difficulties. They were, however, to reemerge as the supreme powers in the area a short time later.

David institutionalized his monarchy by establishing Jerusalem as the capital city for all the Israelites. This was the first time that all Israel had one capital city, now called the "City of David." The choice of Jerusalem as a capital city had many advantages. It was immediately adjacent to the site selected for the Temple, which was to serve as the religious center for all Israel and the site of mass pilgrimages. It had not been allotted to any one tribe and had remained a non-Israelite enclave until that time. It was geographically in the center of the country and was situated on a hill encircled by deep valleys, which made it easy to defend as a fortress city. Its location there also tended to max-

---

23. See Speiser, "Historiography and Historical Sources in Ancient Mesopotamia," in *World History of the Jewish People,* vol. 2, pp. 3 ff.; see also Speiser, "The Idea of History in Ancient Mesopotamia," pp. 37–76, 361–62, in Denton, ed., *The Idea of History in the Ancient Near East.*

24. 2 Sam. 4:7.
25. 1 Kings 5:1.

imize tribal support of David since the city was located between the territory of the tribe of Judah (David's tribe) and the territory of the tribe of Benjamin (the tribe of Saul, who formerly had the allegiance of the other Israelite tribes).

c. THE INTERNAL POWER STRUCTURE OF THE DAVIDIC MONARCHY

David established an extensive bureaucracy (not unlike that of other states in the area, particularly Egypt) to administer the affairs of the new Hebrew state. With time, this bureaucracy acquired a significant measure of power. Of greater importance, however, was the military organization of mercenaries, who were bound to David personally. This military force was supplemented by the militia, raised from the tribes. Both forces were apparently headed by Joab, who acted as overall supreme military commander. The most important power element, however, was David himself, because of his personality and charisma, his support by the prophets (augmented by his being anointed as king by the Prophet Samuel in the name of God) and by the subsequent pronouncement of the Prophet Nathan that his royal reign was to pass to his children in perpetuity.

David, however, failed to designate his successor to the throne, which gave rise to palace intrigues. The latter part of his life was also marred by a series of personal family tribulations, including fratricide and attempted patricide. His oldest son, Ammon, raped his stepsister Tamar and was in turn killed by David's younger son, Absalom. The latter eventually rebelled against his father, attempting to kill him and set himself up as king. He was subsequently slain in battle with David's army. The Bible records David's well-known lament for Absalom upon hearing of his death: "My son, Absalom, my son, my son, Absalom. Would that I had died instead of you, Absalom, my son, my son."[26] There was also a revolt by Sheva ben Bikhri against David and against the establishment of a Davidic line of kings.[27] Later another son, Adoniyah, with the support of Joab the general and Aviathar the priest, tried to set himself up as the successor to David, while the latter still lived. David's son Solomon won out, however, with the support of his mother, Bethsheba (David's favorite wife), and with the help of the Prophet Nathan and Beniah, the commander of David's mercenaries, as well as Zadok the priest. Solomon was then designated as David's successor.[28] David, the poet-war-

rior, became a legend in his own lifetime and was later held up as a model of piety, humbleness, and selflessness for subsequent kings to emulate.

During the reign of Solomon, commerce and trade flourished. Large Jewish merchant fleets sailed into the Indian Ocean, the Mediterranean Sea, and possibly beyond. There was also much construction activity, and a magnificent Temple was erected in Jerusalem.

9. THE DIVISION OF THE JEWISH STATE: JUDAH AND ISRAEL

The heavy burdens of taxation and forced labor imposed upon the people to support these activities engendered much resentment among the masses. This culminated in a revolt led by Jeroboam (circa 933 B.C.E.), who appears to have been aided by Egypt and by the tactlessness of Solomon's successor and son, Rehoboam.[29] Only the king's own tribe of Judah and the neighboring tribe of Benjamin remained faithful to him. The revolt was successful and the ten tribes in the north set up a separate kingdom called Israel (circa 920 B.C.E.). From that time on Judah and Israel went their own separate ways. They were sometimes in alliance and sometimes hostile. Occasionally they even fought with each other.

Jeroboam, however, perceived a threat to his reign from the customary festival pilgrimages to the Temple at Jerusalem. This sanctuary was an enclave within the territory of Judah and was regarded as closely linked with the Davidic dynasty.[30] Accordingly, Jeroboam feared that the pilgrimages would result in reuniting the two kingdoms under the reign of the Davidic king at Jerusalem. To meet this threat, he established idolatrous shrines to compete with the Temple in attracting pilgrims. To ensure the success of his shrines, he took steps to prevent the people of his kingdom from going on pilgrimages to Jerusalem. This posed a deep and dangerous threat to the continued existence of monotheism in Israel.

This political and religious split among the Israelites greatly weakened them and heralded the downfall of both kingdoms. At this time Shoshenk I (the "Shishak" of the Bible) became the pharaoh, founded the twenty-second (or Lybian) dynasty, and restored Egypt to its former power. Shortly after the secession of the ten tribes, he attacked Judah and plundered the Temple, demonstrating forcefully the renewed might of the Egyptian state.

---

26. 2 Sam. 19:1.
27. 2 Sam. 20:1.
28. 1 Kings 1:38–39.

29. 1 Kings 11:40, 12.
30. See Talmud, Yoma 25a, which records a tradition that only a king of Davidic lineage could sit in the Temple courtyard, while all other monarchs had to stand.

10. ROYAL RULE IN JUDAH AND ISRAEL

In the kingdom of Judah the Davidic dynasty was generally well-liked and remained firmly established. No serious challenges arose to its reign as such. All the quarrels that did occur were between members of the dynasty, and concerned only the choice of which individual should rule. The Davidic dynasty in Judah received further support from the fact that Jerusalem, the royal seat, continued to serve as the secure political and religious center for the tribe of Judah, which was by far the more populous and powerful of the two tribes, Judah and Benjamin, that dwelled in the kingdom. This helps to account for the fact that many of the Judean kings had long reigns. For example, Asa ruled for forty-one years and Jehoshaphat for twenty-five years. By contrast, in the kingdom of Israel there was considerable and constant political unrest. During this same period, Israel had seven different kings, many of whom were assassinated and replaced by the successful rebels. One of these, however, Omri, succeeded in establishing a powerful state and subdued many of his neighbors. His power was so respected by neighboring states that the Assyrians later designated the kingdom of Israel as *Bit-Humri* ("House of Omri"). This designation was retained by the Assyrians for more than one hundred and fifty years and is last mentioned, some nine years after the fall of the Israelite kingdom,[31] in an inscription of Sargon II, who conquered Samaria in 713 B.C.E.

For the next one hundred and fifty years the fortunes of the kingdoms of Judah and Israel rose and fell sporadically. In Israel, Ahab (869–850 B.C.E.), who succeeded his father, Omri, spread the idolatrous cult of Baal, aided by his wife Jezebel, daughter of the king of Phoenicia. He was bitterly opposed by the prophets, notably Elijah.

During Ahab's reign, Assyria, on its road to renewed ascendancy in the ancient Near East under the rule of Shalmanesser III (859–824 B.C.E.), became very aggressive. It attacked the states of Hamath and Damascus. Assyrian records indicate that Ahab came to the help of Damascus in the Battle of Qarqar with two thousand Israelite war chariots and ten thousand foot soldiers.[32] Due to the constantly shifting alignment of states in the ancient Near East, however, Ahab later fought against Damascus and was killed in battle.

A short time later the entire dynasty of Omri, along with the priests of Baal, was exterminated in a revolt led by Jehu, who had the active encouragement of the Prophet Elisha and of the Rekhabites, an ascetic group that appears to have protested against urban civilization and idealized a nomadic existence.[33] The king of Judah, Ahazia, was also killed by Jehu. In the ensuing strife all of David's descendants, except for one child, Joash, were exterminated.

Because of the ascendancy of the neo-Assyrian empire, which threw its shadow over all of the smaller states of the ancient Near East, Jehu and his kingdom became tributaries of Assyria. The Assyrian king recorded: "As a tribute of Jehu of Bit-Humri [sic], I received the following: silver, gold, a golden bowl, . . ."[34]

Despite this Assyrian dominance, power rivalries continued among the smaller states, which had their individual ups and downs. At times the Aramaens in Syria overpowered the kingdom of Israel, reducing it to a tiny army of fifty horsemen and a few thousand infantry.[35] Yet a short time thereafter, when Amaziah, king of Judah, challenged Joash, king of Israel, to battle, Israel won. It captured Amaziah, razed some of the fortification of Jerusalem, and even plundered the temple there.[36]

Under Jeroboam II (786–746 B.C.E.) the kingdom of Israel again became the most powerful state in Syria-Palestine. It was able to attain this position as a result of quarrels among the Syrian states and noninterference from mighty Assyria. Its elevated status brought great economic improvement to Israel and accumulation of wealth, particularly by a few individuals. This was accompanied by exploitation of the poor and lower moral standards, arousing bitter protests by the prophets, notably Amos and Hosea, who warned against the greed of the rich, their oppression of the poor, the cultivation of Baal, and the breaches of the ancient Hebrew covenant with God.[37] Later the kingdom of Judah, too, again increased its power, under the kingship of Uzziah.

11. THE RISE OF ASSYRIA AND BABYLONIA AND THE DEMISE OF THE NORTHERN JEWISH STATE

At this time, aided by the internecine warfare of the smaller states in the area, Assyria became more and more dominant. Tiglath-Pileser III (745–727 B.C.E.), the king Pul of the Bible,[38] forced the kingdom of Israel to pay him a tribute of one thousand talents of silver. This was an enormous sum, equal to approxi-

---

31. See Mesha inscription of 835 B.C.E. in Pritchard, *Ancient Near Eastern Texts*, pp. 284, 320; Ehrlich, *A Concise History of Israel*, p. 47.
32. Pritchard, *Ancient Near Eastern Texts*, pp. 278, 761; A. Parrot, *Nineveh and the Old Testament* (1955), p. 32; Rivkin, *The Shaping of Jewish History*, p. 48.

33. See 2 Kings 10:15; Jer. 35:1 ff.
34. Pritchard, *Ancient Near Eastern Texts*, p. 281.
35. 2 Kings 13:7.
36. 2 Kings 14:14.
37. See Amos 2:7, 3:10, 4:1; Hos. 1.
38. 2 Kings 15:19.

mately three million silver shekels.[39] Subsequently, when the kingdoms of Damascus and Israel joined forces to attack Judah, its king appealed for help to Tiglath-Pileser, who responded by attacking Damascus. He captured it in 732 B.C.E. and incorporated the entire kingdom of Aram into Assyria. He likewise incorporated parts of the kingdom of Israel into Assyria, deported parts of the population,[40] and confirmed Hoshea as king of Israel, after the latter had revolted and murdered King Pekah. One of Tiglath-Pileser's inscriptions reads: "I set Hoshea as king over them . . . ."[41]

The growing power of the Assyrian empire clashed with Egypt, which was then also reemerging as a major force in the ancient Near East. The states of Judah and Israel attempted to choose sides with the power that they thought would most protect their interest and sovereignty. In the process King Shalmanesser, the successor to Tiglath-Pileser III, captured Israel's capital, Shomron, terminating the kingdom of Israel (*circa* 722 B.C.E.). Shalmanesser's successor, Sargon II (722–705 B.C.E.), deported the population of the kingdom to distant portions of Assyria and resettled people from other states in the area.[42] This wholesale shifting of populations from one end of the vast Assyrian empire to the other was part of the new Assyrian policy designed to ensure the continued dominance of Assyria over the peoples of the entire Near East.

The power and boasting of the conquering Assyrians has been captured in the immortal words of the Prophet Isaiah:

Are not all my officers, kings?
Is not Kalno like Karkemish?
Is not Hamath like Arpad?
Is not Samaria like Damascus? . . .
And I pushed back the frontiers of the nations.
And plundered their treasuries.
I cast down into the dust those who sat on thrones.
My hand grasps for the riches of the peoples
    as a hand grasps for a nest,
and as one gathers the abandoned eggs,
so, have I collected the entire world.
There was not a wing moved against me;
not one opened his beak or twittered.[43]

The fall of the kingdom of Israel helped to spark a religious reformation in the remaining Jewish state of Judah. King Hezekiah rid the country of idolatrous cult

symbols, including Assyrian ones, and enforced monotheistic worship. This helped to arouse the wrath of Assyria, since political domination in the ancient Near East commonly brought in its wake acceptance of the religious cult and symbols of the dominating power. Judah's abolition of Assyrian cult symbols therefore had political overtones of revolt. Egypt, under Shabaka (who founded the twenty-first, or Ethiopian-Egyptian, dynasty), supported Hezekiah in his show of independence against Assyria.

To fortify the city of Jerusalem, Hezekiah constructed aqueducts, which included long tunnels bored through solid rock, in order to supply water to Jerusalem during any siege. The inscription in one tunnel, made at the place where the diggers from both ends met, has been found and preserved.[44] Later Hezekiah revolted openly against Assyria. Its king, Sennacherib, thereupon marched on Judah. On the way he defeated a small Egyptian army, conquered the Philistine cities of Ashkelon and Ekron, and then laid siege to Judah. Sennacherib recorded: "I beseiged and conquered forty-six of his strong cities with walls, and the small towns in their vicinity, without number. I shut him, himself [Hezekiah] up like a bird in a cage in the city of Jerusalem, the seat of his kingdom."[45] Hezekiah was forced to submit and to turn over all of the silver in the royal treasuries and presumably to submit hostages for transport to Nineveh.[46]

Hezekiah, nevertheless, revolted again, and Jerusalem was once more beseiged by Assyria. This time Hezekiah was successful and Sennacherib was forced to leave empty-handed. On Passover Eve, according to the Bible, "An angel of God went out and smote one hundred and eighty five thousand in the camp of Assyria. They arose in the morning and, behold, they were all dead corpses."[47] Some time thereafter, Sennacherib was killed by his own sons, in Nineveh, while prostrating himself in prayer in his shrine.[48]

Despite this setback, Assyria continued to grow in power under King Esarhaddon and then under King Ashurbanipal. (The latter, incidentally, amassed a huge library of ancient tablets that have been preserved and have proved to be a veritable treasure trove of information on the ancient Near East.) In the seventh century B.C.E., Assyria even conquered portions of Egypt and reigned supreme in the entire Near East, being the first nation to rule simultaneously over both ancient seats of power, Egypt and Mesopotamia. Its empire now stretched from present-day Iran to Asia Minor and

39. See Pritchard, *Ancient Near Eastern Texts*, p. 283.
40. 2 Kings 15:29, 16:9.
41. Pritchard, *Ancient Near Eastern Texts*, p. 284.
42. 2 Kings 17:6, 24; see the record left by Sargon II, in Pritchard, *Ancient Near Eastern Texts*, p. 284.
43. Isa. 10:8, 9, 13, 14.

44. Pritchard, *Ancient Near Eastern Texts*, p. 321.
45. Ibid., 287.
46. 2 Kings 18:13, 15; Noth, *History of Israel*, p. 267.
47. 2 Kings 19:35; Isa. 37:36; cf. 2 Kings 19:7; Isa. 37:6.
48. Isa. 37:38; 2 Kings 19:37.

from Anatolia in the north to Egypt and the Persian Gulf in the south.

Toward the end of the seventh century B.C.E. decisive changes suddenly took place again in the power alignments of the Near East. In 626 B.C.E. the Chaldeans revolted and set up an independent state in Babylonia, under Nabopolassar. In 614 B.C.E. the city of Ashur was captured by the Medes, and in 612 B.C.E. an army of Babylonians, Medes, and Scythians conquered and completely razed Nineveh, the capital city of the Assyrian empire. This resulted in the sudden collapse and end of this once mighty world empire, only a few years after it had reached an unprecedented pinnacle of power.[49]

While Assyria was being conquered by its rivals, King Josiah of Judah attempted to eradicate all foreign cultic elements and idolatry, and to reemphasize the study of the Bible.[50] Egypt was trying to profit from Assyria's downfall and seize some of its former territories in Syria. Egypt was then also interested in preserving a remnant of the Assyrian empire (its former archenemy) in Haran, in order to minimize the threat from the rising powers of the Medes and Babylonians, whom it regarded as even greater dangers. Pharaoh Necho marched his armies through Judah, which by then formed part of a thriving and vital land bridge between Egypt, Syria, and Mesopotamia. Josiah, trying to avoid a new Egyptian overlord, attempted to block the pharaoh's passage and was killed. Judah then became a vassal state of Egypt.[51]

The new Egyptian ascendancy was short-lived, however. The Medes and Babylonians made an agreement that recognized the rule of the Medes over the northwestern portion of the former Assyrian empire and over what is today the Iranian and Armenian hill country. In return, the Babylonians were to rule over the remaining portions of Mesopotamia, as well as over Syria and Palestine. The rival claims of Babylonia and Egypt to this latter area resulted in the Battle of Karkhemish (*circa* 605 B.C.E.), which ended with a crushing defeat for Egypt.[52] Babylon, under the victorious King Nebuchadnezzar, became the new overlord of Judea.

12. THE DESTRUCTION OF JUDAH AND OF THE TEMPLE

Egypt, however, still hoping to regain its former power, inspired repeated Judean insurrections against Babylonia. In 598 B.C.E., Nebuchadnezzar took the Judean King Jehoyakhin and major portions of the population as captives to Babylon, thus beginning the "Babylonian captivity." When the new king, Zedekiah, continued to conspire against Babylonia, Nebuchadnezzar again attacked Jerusalem (*circa* 586 B.C.E.), sacked the city, and destroyed the Temple, which had served as the national shrine and center of religious life for many hundreds of years. King Zedekiah, forced to look on while his sons were killed, was blinded and led into Babylonian captivity, along with the bulk of the population of Judea.

Thus, at one stroke, was ended the Jewish state with its Davidic dynasty, which had tied the remnants of Jewish people together politically, and its temple worship, which had helped to unite the people religiously. All the Jews were now forced to exist in an alien environment as a powerless minority, subject to the whims and dictates of the non-Jewish majority. The profound anguish and shock of this event was eloquently recorded by an eyewitness, the Prophet Jeremiah, in the Book of Lamentations.[53]

13. THE BABYLONIAN EXILE AND THE RETURN TO JUDEA

In faraway Babylonia, the Jews were gradually given considerable freedom. They became active in agriculture, commerce, metalsmithing, and government administration. They lacked the religious center of Jerusalem and had no political independence, but they did have internal political organizations, headed by "elders."[54]

True to the perennial upheavals in the ancient Near East, the power of the Medes and Babylonians was also short-lived. In 553 B.C.E. the Persians, under Cyrus, overthrew the Medes, and in 539 they conquered Babylonia. Under Kambyses they went on to conquer Egypt in 525 B.C.E. The vast Persian empire now stretched from Iran to Greece and remained intact until its conquest by Alexander the Great two hundred years later, in 331 B.C.E.

The Persians' national policy was to permit their subject peoples to lead their own religious and cultural lives. King Cyrus, accordingly, granted the request of the Jews to rebuild their Temple at Jerusalem and to return there to settle.[55] Zerubabel, a Jew, was appointed

---

49. Ehrlich, *A Concise History of Israel*, p. 63; Parrot, *Nineveh*, p. 76.
50. 2 Kings 22:23.
51. 2 Kings 22:33.
52. See Jer. 46:2; Ehrlich, *A Concise History of Israel*, p. 66.

53. For archeological evidence of the enormous destruction in Judah at that time, see Wright, *Biblical Archaeology* 18 (1955): 14.
54. See Ezek. 8:1, 14:1, 20:1; Ehrlich, *A Concise History of Israel*, p. 72.
55. Cyrus' proclamation is preserved in the Book of Ezra, 1:2–6.

governor of Judah. Despite the freedom given to return from the exile, fewer than fifty thousand Jews elected to migrate to Judah. The rebuilding work at Jerusalem dragged on for many years, but finally, in about 515 B.C.E. (this date has been the subject of much dispute), the Temple at Jerusalem was rebuilt and consecrated. When Darius became emperor, he divided his empire into twenty sections (called *satrapies*) and placed Jerusalem in the fifth *satrapy*.

The Judaic resettlement was opposed by its neighbors, who thwarted the rebuilding. The Persians then appointed Nehemiah, a Jew, as governor. Under his vigorous leadership the walls of Jerusalem were rebuilt, making the city safe from attack. From a traditional Jewish religious point of view, however, the Jewish community there left much to be desired. Many of the Jews had married non-Jewish women, the Sabbath was widely disregarded, and their mother tongue was not Hebrew but Aramaic, which had also become the official language of the Persian empire. Eventually Ezra, under a mandate from the Persian king, succeeded in accomplishing a spiritual rejuvenation. He forbade intermarriages with non-Jews and forced the wholesale termination of such existing marriages. Jewish judges were installed to rule in accordance with the norms of the Torah, and Ezra undertook extensive activities to educate the people in the Torah. Assemblies were established where portions of the Torah were read a few times per week. This, incidentally, may have laid the foundation for the existence of Jewish lay communities.[56] Ezra's activities were successful in helping to make knowledge of the Torah widespread among all of the people, rather than limited to an educated elite.[57]

It should be noted that at this time most of the Jewish population was still situated outside of Judah. The largest concentration was in Babylonia, with a very sizable number in Egypt and also scattered about the Mediterranean Basin. There were even colonies of Jewish mercenaries in a number of lands. The one best remembered today is that at Elephantine, an island on the Nile River near the present site of the Aswan Dam. That Jewish military colony is believed to have existed even before the Persian conquest of Egypt in 525 B.C.E. The soldiers there then became mercenaries for Persia, thereby arousing the hostility of the indigenous inhabitants. The mercenaries were paid by the Persian government, apparently had Babylonian or Persian commanders, and lived partly as civilians, engaging in commercial activities. Some of the papyrus documents

they left, recording their activities, have shed light on the development of Jewish law.

B. *The Social and Cultural Contexts of Biblical Law: The Pre-Pentateuchal Basis of Post-Pentateuchal Practices*

1. THE CULTURAL CONTEXTS

Biblical law did not arise in a vacuum. It emerged in a geographic area that was dynamic, sophisticated, and had an old cultural heritage, social institutions, and established traditions. These institutions and traditions were part of the common cultural and social heritage that the Jewish people shared with the other peoples of the ancient Near East. Many institutional patterns were regarded as natural and as the "proper" way of arranging human affairs.

Numerous traditional institutions and cultural practices are reflected in the Bible and its law, a fact that has been acknowledged by the most fundamentalist Jewish legal scholars (see, e.g., Maimonides,[58] who explains many of the laws of the Bible as based upon existing cultural and religious practices). For example, the institutions of marriage and divorce, and the forms they took (e.g., with the man as the active, dominant partner), are nowhere specifically defined in detail in the Bible, which presumes knowledge of the existence of these practices[59] and refers to them only in passing in its legal provisions. Accordingly, the sole reference to divorce in the Pentateuch[60] merely prescribes that if a man marries a woman (pursuant to a form or ceremony presumed to be known by all) and writes and gives her a bill of divorce (which again is nowhere detailed as to form and content) and she remarries another man, then the first husband may not remarry her. Nowhere does the Bible provide detailed procedure and norms for either marriage or divorce, such as that "if a man desires to marry, he must go through the following ceremony . . . ," or that if he decides to divorce his wife, he must go through another ceremony, and then describe this in detail. Only a "Book [document] of Divorce" is mentioned, without details as to its contents and requirements.[61] In the same vein, biblical law[62] makes only a passing reference to primogeniture, by

56. S. Baron, *Social and Religious History of the Jews*, vol. 1 (Philadelphia, 1952), p. 140.

57. See Ezra 7:10, 10:1–44; Ehrlich, *A Concise History of Israel*, pp. 77–82.

58. Maimonides, *Guide for the Perplexed*, trans. M. Friedlander (reprinted New York, 1956), bk. 3, chs. 29–32.

59. See Exod. 21:9–10, 22:15–16; Deut. 24:1–4; M. Ha'-Meiri, *Beth Habkhira, Yebamot* 4a.

60. Deut. 24:1–4.

61. See B. Epstein, *Tosefot Berakha* (reprinted Jerusalem, 1965), Deut. 21:17.

62. Deut. 21:16–17; see also Gen. 25:31–34, 48:17–19, 49:3.

providing that if a man has two wives, one "beloved" and the other "hated," he cannot circumvent the rule of primogeniture by designating the child of his beloved wife as the "first born." This also presumes prevalent knowledge regarding the institution of primogeniture and the cultural perspective that the greater inheritance portion falls to the first-born male issue. So too, with regard to the laws requiring a man to marry the widow of his deceased brother, if there were no issue of the marriage,[63] the Bible itself describes a similar practice as having been followed by the family of Judah before the giving of the law to Moses.[64] Mention is made in the Bible of Joab's attempt to take advantage of the traditional sanctuary granted by seizing the corners of the altar[65] and of the customary practices employed to grant validity to contracts.[66] The same acceptance of common underlying cultural practices applies to many other legal and nonlegal features of the Bible.

There are also many laws recorded later in the Talmud (*circa* 200 C.E.) that, while not recorded in the Bible, may be remnants of ancient customs that prevailed in Mesopotamia, such as: the three years of occupation by which the occupier of a field acquires good title, the treatment of a wife who refuses to cohabit with her husband, the details of the marriage contract with the wife, and perhaps the modes of acquiring good title to real property and chattels.[67]

Although it is impossible to establish whether any of the above views is correct, in whole or part, it seems clear that in order to understand biblical law we must understand the older traditions, social institutions, and practices that existed in the Near East in general at that time. "It is only by starting with that common background, that we can discover, evaluate, and understand the difference between the message embodied in Scriptures and the joint testimony of other contemporary records; the basic difference between the enduring, and so much that was to prove ephemeral."[68] There are many views regarding the relation between custom (including the prepentateuchal traditions) and so-called "legal" provisions. For example, Henry Maine has theorized that societies move through an epoch of "customary law" in which only a small class has a monopoly on the knowledge and preservation of the customs of society.[69] This is debatable, particularly in view of

our knowledge today concerning the very widespread use of many legal documents in ancient Mesopotamia (see above, Chapter I, Section B 1 *e*).

It has also been suggested that the Bible was not intended to constitute a legal codex, nor to establish a completely new and self-contained system of law. Instead, while asserting some revolutionary changes in certain areas of existing law and customary practices (completely negating some and changing the thrust of others), it accepted much of the institutional practices and norms of preexisting Mesopotamian legal systems.[70] It has been contended that this would clarify why entire, vital areas of the law were wholly or largely ignored (e.g., marriage, divorce, commercial documents, and rental of real property, all of which were extensively utilized and were well established in the ancient Near East) and why the Bible's phraseology, style, and even choice of subject matter to be covered by norms is so similar to that of the Mesopotamian codes. Some of the biblical phraseology clearly seems to reflect long-established literary-judicial expressions of the ancient Near East. As the Talmud later put it, the Torah speaks in the common language of the people.[71]

On the other hand, as mentioned, there were extra-biblical, postpentateuchal state laws prescribed by the king, and there was probably substantial reliance and expectancy by the people that, in addition to preexisting biblical norms, new state laws would be promulgated from time to time to deal with new situations.[72] It has even been suggested that the biblical norms were never meant to be, and were not in fact, enforced as the law of the land, but were only meant to appeal to conscience.[73] This, however, appears untenable, since the Bible itself details a number of instances in different epochs where kings applied the "Law of Moses."[74]

2. THE ECONOMIC FRAMEWORK

Although we will examine biblical law in greater detail later on, it should be noted here that, on its face, it reflects a very simple society in terms of economic development and social structure. Unlike contemporary

---

63. The so-called Levirate marriage, see Gen. 38:8, 14, 18.
64. See Commentary of Moshe ben Nakhman (Ramban), to Gen. 11:31.
65. 1 Kings 2:28; See Exod. 21:14.
66. Ruth 4:7.
67. See C. Chernowitz, *History of Hebrew Law*, vol. 3 (Hebrew; New York, 1953), p. 162 ff.
68. Speiser, in *World History of the Jewish People*, vol. 2, p. 343.
69. H. Maine, *Ancient Law*, ch. 15; see also Maine, *Early History of Institutions* (London, 1847).

70. Y. Antoli, *Melamed La'talmidim*, sec. *Mishpatim* (Berlin, 1866); Nissim Gaon, *Commentary to Talmud, Berakhot*, intro; M. Sofer, Responsa, *Y.D*, no. 319; A. Shapiro, Responsa, *Dvar Avraham*, vol. 1, no. 1; U. Cassuto, *A Commentary on the Book of Exodus* (reprinted Jerusalem, 1974), p. 181. See also Chapter II, Section C, below, for other examples.
71. Talmud, *Berakhot* 31b; Torat Kohanim to Lev. 20:2.
72. See, e.g., I Sam. 30:24–28; Isa. 10:1.
73. Cassuto, *Commentary on the Book of Exodus*.
74. See, e.g., 2 Kings 14:5–6, where the king himself followed the law of Moses and refused to kill the sons of his enemy for the sins of their father. See also, 2 Chron. 17:9 and 19:5–11, where the king directed his judicial appointees to apply the biblical laws, and his agents, to teach it.

Mesopotamian law, the Bible has no provision for tariffs on services and merchandise and no laws regarding rentals or tenancy of land. This contrasts with the situation in Mesopotamia, where rich land owners often lived in the city, with their land worked by peasants who leased the land. There are very few norms in the Bible concerning commerce, and even the sale of land is viewed as occuring only when the land owner is in dire need of raising money.[75] There is no mention of sales for purely commercial and profit motives. Unlike Mesopotamia, there are no norms regarding architects or professional soldiers, and only one passing mention of physicians. All of these may reflect a lack of substantial economic and technical development of society,[76] as well as the adoption in biblical law of many preexisting societal norms and institutions.

3. THE SOCIAL STRUCTURE

Throughout the Biblical Era the social structure of the Israelites apparently revolved around three units:

• *The father's house.* This included the father's unmarried offspring, his married sons, their wives and children. This unit reflected great patriarchal influence and prominence.

• *The family.* This term was often used to represent a larger unit, comprising a number of "father's houses."

• *The tribe.* This large group comprised the descendants of one of the sons of the Patriarch Jacob and included many "families" and "father's houses." The tribe was therefore a unit related by blood, not a class or territorial unit. It provided protection and security for its members, particularly when there was no central authority to maintain order. This was reflected in the institution of the "Redeemer of Blood" (see Chapter III, Section B 3) and the required redemption of poor relatives who had been sold into slavery or forced to part with their patrimonial lands.[77]

In the aforementioned model of the social structure, the family units were also economic units, and the heads of the father's houses and families, called "elders," were the communal leaders. They participated in important societal decisions and had vital societal functions, including communal responsibility for widows and orphans and for law and order. When the Israelites settled in the land of Canaan, the resultant urbanization and the agriculturalization of their tribal society eventually undermined some of the important economic and social foundations of the tribal structure. This ultimately led to its weakening.

The importance of blood relationships in Israelite society might explain the complete lack of adoption laws in the Bible, in sharp contrast with the situation in other parts of the ancient Near East. Blood kinship was apparently the sole determinant of status, and no individual could change the resulting social arrangement at will.[78]

For a period of a few hundred years following the conquest of the land of Canaan by the Israelites, many of the tribal leaders were called "judges." Some of these appeared to have had charismatic and military qualities and were active in repelling invasions by enemies. Others, if not all, served as judges in the traditional sense, settling disputes and participating in the prescription of norms.[79] The institution of the judges continued as long as there was no strong central Jewish government. With the later growth of the monarchy, the various judges were replaced by the king. Additionally, the tribes then had to relinquish their individual freedoms and became subject to taxes, corvee, and military service imposed by the king (see Chapter III, Section B 1, regarding courts in the Biblical Era).

C. The Effect of Mesopotamian and Egyptian Cultures on Biblical Law

Although the Jewish people lived in much closer geographical proximity to the Egyptians than to the Mesopotamians, the cultural and legal influence of Mesopotamia was greater for many reasons. Abraham, the patriarch and first Jew, came from Ur and Harran, in Mesopotamia, and carried with him its cultural traditions. Furthermore, the dynamic culture of Mesopotamia extended beyond Sumer, Babylonia, and Assyria. Its influence reached far and wide, to Anatolia and the Black Sea on the northwest and to the lands of the Mediterranean, including the land of Canaan, on the west. It is also possible that the forced stay of the Israelites as slaves in Egypt produced a revulsion against

75. Lev. 25:25.

76. Loewenstam, "Law" in *World History of the Jewish People*, vol. 2, p. 232 ff.

77. W. Robertson-Smith, *Kinship and Marriage in Early Arabia* (reprinted Boston, 1973); J. Liver, "The Israelite Tribe," in *World History of the Jewish People*, vol. 2, pp. 183, 184, 187–88.

78. Liver, "The Israelite Tribe," pp. 189, 191–92. The role of "elders" is mentioned in many of the biblical books, e.g., Num. 7:2, 36:1; Josh. 22:14; 1 Kings 8:1; Judg. 8:14, 5:15, 10:18; tribal pilgrimages are referred to in 1 Sam. 20:29; see H. Orlinsky, "The Tribal System of Israel and Related Groups in the Period of Judges," in *Oriens Antiquus* 1 (1962): 11–20, and in *Studies and Essays in Honor of Abraham A. Neumann* (Philadelphia, 1962), pp. 375–87.

79. Liver, "The Israelite Tribe," p. 193; see F. Fensham, "The Judges and Ancient Israelite Jurisprudence," in *Die Ou Testamentriese Werkgemeenskap in Juid-Afrika*, papers read at the second meeting (Pretoria, 1959), p. 15; Y. Kaufman, *The Book of Judges* (Hebrew; Jerusalem, 1962).

Egyptian culture and practices that persisted among the Israelites:

> The exodus from Egypt was, above all, an act of liberation from intolerable spiritual bondage, imposed by the Egyptian way of life . . . . Remembrance of the Egyptian horror was to become a dominant note in all biblical history. Only an indelible spiritual experience could have left so deep an imprint on the whole national consciousness.[80]

Abraham and the Israelites sharply rejected the polytheistic religions of Mesopotamia, with their immoral way of life. God's covenant with Abraham, therefore, is another dominant theme in the Bible. Yet many of the Mesopotamian cultural influences and institutions continued to exert a profound influence. It is only through an understanding of this common Mesopotamian heritage that one can comprehend many of the motifs in the Bible, in both its narrative and legal portions. These include the narratives regarding the interactions between Abraham, Sarah, and their maid Hagar;[81] the claims by both Abraham and Isaac that their wives were their sisters;[82] the transfer of the birthright by Esau to Jacob;[83] Jacob's position in Laban's household and his marriage to Laban's daughters Leah and Rachel;[84] and the removal of the house gods of Laban by Rachel.[85] Some scholars have even called attention to an institution in the city of Mari which, in its outspokenness, resembled prophecy. There, individuals who were not priests or officials spoke up to ruling authorities regarding civil or religious matters and were accorded great weight. It has been claimed that the prior existence of such institutions provided the framework for the acceptance among the Israelites of the institution of prophecy with its constant rebukes to mighty kings.[86]

With regard to the legal portions of the Bible, one should be wary of the many allegations of "borrowing" of laws by the Bible from the Code of Hammurabi (prompted by the finding of the Hammurabi stela in 1902). Many of these claims were wildly superficial and without proof. One must, however, be aware of the pervasive influence of prebiblical cultural traditions and institutions. It has been speculated that the Hurrians, among whom Abraham, and later Jacob, dwelled, acted

as cultural intermediaries between the Mesopotamians and the Bible.[87]

Nevertheless, the Bible is a document of overwhelming originality that stresses numerous revolutionary fundamental perspectives. In addition to absolute monotheism, these include the absolute transcendance of God as *sui generis* and who was above and not a part of nature, and who controlled nature. This negated the view that each of the natural phenomena was brought about by independent actors. The perspective that man is unique, sacred, and in the image of God, and is to bring about the realization of the will of God through obedience to a detailed divine law was staggeringly novel. So too was the radical perspective that God supervises human activity in minute detail and intervenes to reward and punish in accordance with consistent principles of justice and ethics.[88] The notion that disobedience to God is sinful, and not simply a pragmatic possible cause of divine retribution, was an innovation, as were many other notions, some of which will be examined hereafter.

While the Code of Hammurabi and other Mesopotamian codes do have similarities to the laws of the Bible, they also have many sharp differences. It is only by studying the common cultural heritage and examining these differences that one can understand the ways in which biblical law departed from Mesopotamian law and can comprehend the direction of the biblical thrust.

The documents regarding legal practice unearthed at Nuzi, Alalakh, and Ugarit indicate the widespread influence of Mesopotamian culture and law upon the practices among other civilizations. Some of these same institutional patterns are reflected in the Bible. These include institutional practices such as marriage and divorce, inheritance, polygamy, slavery, primogeniture, and monarchy. In addition, the Bible refers to such Mesopotamian practices as the use of the cylindrical seal;[89] the recording, witnessing, and sealing of the documents for sale of land;[90] the existence of "elders" who wield considerable influence;[91] and the acts of "the people," the "men of Judah" and the "assembly" in selecting a king.[92] The Bible uses forms of expression similar to those found in Mesopotamian literature; these range from use of the term *sefer* for document,[93]

---

80. Speiser, *World History of the Jewish People*, vol. 2, p. 346.

81. See Gen. 16, 30.

82. Gen. 12:13, 26:7.

83. Gen. 25:29–34.

84. Gen. 29:18–29.

85. Gen. 31:19.

86. Speiser, *World History of the Jewish People*, vol. 2, pp. 257–58.

87. Ibid., p. 158.

88. See, e.g., H. Frankfort, "The Emancipation of Thought from Myth," in *Before Philosophy*, pp. 241–48.

89. Gen. 38:18.

90. Jer. 32.

91. Exod. 3:16, 4:29, 24:1, 9, 14; 17:5, etc.

92. 1 Sam. 11:15; 2 Sam. 2:4, 5:3; 1 Sam. 19–20.

93. Deut. 24:1.

as in Akkadian, to "you shall cut off her hand,"[94] references to injuries to an eye or tooth (in that order),[95] and numerous other expressions and literary forms utilized in the Mesopotamian codes. All of these resemble cultural institutions and literary traditions of Mesopotamia.

Yet in spite of these similarities, the Bible has sharply different changes in cultural perspectives and legal concepts that are profound, fundamental, and revolutionary. Their significance can only be grasped if the Mesopotamian milieu is understood.

D. *Studies in Biblical Legal Documents*

1. INTRODUCTION TO SELECTIONS FROM THE TORAH (THE PENTATEUCH)

One can only sense the scope, grandeur, spirit, and religious fervor of the Bible by study of its entire text. Unfortunately, much of its beauty and power is lost in translation from the original Hebrew. The selections that follow contain some of the more prominent, but by no means all, of the legal provisions in the Bible, specifically in the Pentateuch, which form the basis of Jewish criminal law. They constitute some of mankind's very oldest legal writings and have been preserved from the dawn of history. Discussions of the scholarly conflicts regarding editing, dating, and interpolations have been avoided here, since these have only subsidiary relevance to the Jewish perspectives or practices that are reflected in the Jewish legal tradition with which we are concerned.

It should be noted that while our examination of biblical norms is empirically oriented, it commences by accepting the fact that the Jewish people and its decision-makers operated on the premise that God was the source and prime mover of the biblical laws. No attempt is made herein to go beyond this and to examine whether or not divine nature of biblical law is an empirical reality. That subject is properly beyond the scope of this work.[96]

The following selections of legal provisions from the Torah, from the portion known as the Pentateuch, since it consists of the first five books of the Bible, should be read with an eye to grasping the main thrust of these provisions, the spirit behind them, and the perspectives on which they are predicated. They form the basis of Judaic law. The student should attempt to fathom how its underlying concepts, as well as its detailed provi-

sions, differ from the other systems of law in the ancient Near East. Note that the Pentateuch dates from approximately the thirteenth century B.C.E. and the Code of Hammurabi from approximately the nineteenth century B.C.E.

In examining the following selections, particular attention should be paid to the biblical norms dealing with homicide found in the following places: Genesis 4:8–16, 9:5, 6; Exodus 20:13, 21:12–14, 20, 21, 23, 28–32; 22:1, 2; Leviticus 24:17, 18, 21, 22; Numbers 35:15–27, 30–33; Deuteronomy 19:2–5, 9, 11, 12; 21:1–9, 24:16. The biblical provisions regarding "an eye for an eye" are found in Exodus 21:24–25, Leviticus 24:19–20, and Deuteronomy 19:21. It also should be borne in mind that there are very few case materials regarding the actual practice and application of biblical law, only the prescriptions themselves.

The long tradition of Jewish law has generated its own questions concerning the meaning and implications of the biblical verses dealing with legal principles and norms. Some of these queries are incorporated in the notes herein, together with comments that have a more modern context. It is hoped that exposure of the student to these two facets of biblical prescriptions will lead to a deeper understanding of the Jewish legal tradition and its relevance to modern issues.

The reader should be aware that in the Bible, as in other documents in the ancient Near East, prescriptions are not formulated in broad abstract terms that may apply to a number of different situations. Instead, the legal tradition was to describe a concrete situation, or case, and the rule to be applied thereto. Analogies were expected to be made to similar cases, to which the norm would also apply.

2. SELECTIONS FROM THE TORAH (PENTATEUCH)

The translations of biblical verses appearing hereafter are based upon the Jewish Publication Society translation of the Torah (1960) with a number of changes made to reflect the Jewish legal tradition more faithfully for our purposes.

a. GENESIS

The first three chapters of the Book of Genesis introduce a number of revolutionary and profoundly significant concepts regarding man, God, and nature that differ fundamentally from the perceptions prevalent in all of the cultures of the ancient Near East. The very first biblical verse stresses that there is only one God, who created the entire cosmos and is above, not part

---

94. Deut. 25:12.
95. Exod. 21:22–27.
96. See E. A. Hoebel, *Law of Primitive Man*, p. 6.

of, nature. This was a radical departure from the then universally accepted view regarding the theogony of many deities, with their epic battles. In the Bible, God himself has no history and is above nature. The elevated concept of God goes far beyond the Mesopotamian concept of whimsical deities who themselves are part of nature and who constantly battle with each other. It is also profoundly different from the view of Pharaoh Amenothop that the sun-god, who was also part of nature, was the chief deity who created the world.

The biblical view of man, too, is totally different. In the prevailing cultures of the time the creation of man and the earth is incidental to the theogony and strife of the gods and is an afterthought. Man is only another of many creations. In the Bible, however, the creation of man and the world is a deliberate and planned act. Furthermore, man is unique and is the very pinnacle of creation. He is the only one created "in the image of God" (Gen. 1:27) and who is animated directly from God with a "breath of life" (Gen. 2:7). Furthermore, he is not helpless before the blind forces of nature, but is designated to rule over the earth and all of its creatures (Gen. 1:28). This also emphasizes that he is distinct from beasts. His unique possession of intellect, free will, conscience, and self-control is further exemplified in the story of the testing of Adam in the Garden of Eden (Gen. 2:15–25, 3:1–21).[97]

(1) *Homicide, Repentance, and Punishment (Genesis 4:8–16)*

8. And Cain said to his brother Abel . . . and when they were in the field, Cain set upon his brother Abel and killed him.

9. The Lord said to Cain, "Where is your brother Abel?" And he said, "I do not know. Am I my brother's keeper?"

10. Then he said, "What have you done? Hark, your brother's blood cries out to Me from the earth!

11. Therefore, you shall be cursed from the soil, which opened its mouth wide to receive your brother's blood from your hand.

12. If you till the soil, it shall no longer yield its strength to you. You shall become a ceaseless wanderer on earth."

13. Cain said to the Lord, "My sin is too great to bear!

14. Since You have banished me this day from the soil, and I must hide from Your presence and become a restless wanderer on earth—all who find me will kill me!"

15. The Lord said to him "Therefore, whoever kills Cain, shall be avenged sevenfold." And the Lord put a mark on Cain lest anyone who meet him should kill him.

16. And Cain left the presence of the Lord and settled in the land of Nod, east of Eden.

Notes to Genesis 4:8–16

1. The Cain-Abel incident clearly emphasizes the notions that homicide is a fundamental crime and that God is aware of and concerned with all human deeds. Even secret acts committed out "in the field" (Gen. 4:8) are known to God; thus, "Your brother's blood cries out to me from earth" (Gen. 4:10). Moreover, God will punish injustice.[98]

2. *"Am I my brother's keeper?"* (Gen. 4:9). God's refusal to accept Cain's defense implies the concept, later expanded in Judaic law, that an individual *is* responsible for his brother's welfare (see Lev. 19:16, "Do not stand by the blood of your neighbor," and Part Two, Chapter VI, Section C 1, below).

3. *"You have banished me . . ."* (Gen. 4:13). Note the early use of the penalty of banishment and exile, where the slayer was not subject to capital punishment (see Exod. 21:13). Compare the practice in ancient Greece.

"I must hide from your presence" (Gen. 4:14). Cain's exile may also reflect the notion that the slaying was both an offense against society and against God. Hence, his banishment from the presence of both man and God. Notice that punishment was restricted to Cain and not directed at his children, reflecting the notion of individual responsibility and negating collective guilt (see Part Two, Chapter VI, Section C 1, below).

4. Why wasn't Cain killed for murdering his brother, Abel, according to the formula in chapter 9: "Whoever sheds the blood of man, by man shall his blood be shed"? The relatively mild punishment meted out to Cain is one of the sources for the notions (which we shall examine later) in Judaic law that justice is to be tempered with mercy, and is affected by a transgressor's repentance. (Note Cain's acknowledgment that he acted wrongfully: "My sin is too great to bear.")[99] It also

97. See U. Cassuto, *From Adam to Noah* (Jerusalem, 1944), pp. 1–11; N. Sarna, *Understanding Genesis* (New York, 1972), pp. 14–15.

98. Cassuto, *From Adam to Noah*, p. 124; Sarna, *Understanding Genesis*, p. 31. For the view of some scholars that Abel represented a nomadic ideal, see Pritchard, *Ancient Near Eastern Texts*, p. 40; S. Kramer, *Sumerian Mythology* (New York, 1961), pp. 49, 53; R. DeVaux, *Ancient Israel*, vol. 1 (New York, 1965), p. 13; Cassuto, *From Adam to Noah*, p. 115; H. L. Ginsberg, "Hosea's Ephraim, More Fool Than Knave," *Journal of Bible and Religion*, 16 (1961): 346; Kaufman, *Toldot Ha' Emunah Ha' Yisraelit*, vol. 2 (Tel-Aviv, 1942–1956), pp. 65, 625; Sarna, *Understanding Genesis*, p. 28.

99. *Midrash Rabbah* (New York, reprinted 1953), Genesis 22:25; see Moshe ben Nakhman, Commentary to Genesis 22:25 (Jerusalem, 1962).

reflects the important perspective that punishment may not be inflicted unless the offender was warned beforehand of the punishment that would be imposed for his act. Cain had received no such warning. Furthermore, Cain's death would have severely penalized Adam and Eve, leaving them without any sons. His demise would have little deterrent effect, since there were few others to learn from his punishment, whereas his lifelong exile and wandering would be a constant reminder to those who would be born later. It is also not clear that Cain knew that his blows would irrevocably end Abel's life, or that his murder was coldly premeditated.

5. *"And Cain said, 'All who find me, will kill me.' The Lord said to him, 'Therefore, whoever kills Cain . . . shall be avenged.' And the Lord put a mark on Cain, lest anyone who met him should kill him"* (Gen. 4:14–15). Cain's fear that all who met him would kill him appears to presage the ancient institution in which members of a victim's clan would avenge his death. All persons would be descendants of Adam and Eve, and therefore related to Abel and bound to avenge him (except, perhaps, for Cain's own descendants). God's pronouncement against killing Cain may indicate the biblical perspective against this practice (see Chapter III, Section B 2, for later biblical attempts to limit this practice).

(2) *A Reckoning for Life (Genesis 9:1–6)*

1. "God blessed Noah and his sons and said to them, "Be fertile and increase, and fill the earth.

2. The fear and the dread of you shall be upon all the beasts of the earth and upon the birds of the sky—everything with which the earth is astir—and upon all the fish of the sea; they are given into your hand.

3. Every creature that lives shall be yours to eat; as with the green grasses, I give you all these.

4. You must not, however, eat flesh with its life-blood in it.

5. [For] your life-blood I will demand [a reckoning]; of every beast will I demand it; and from man, from every man for his brother, will I demand [a reckoning for] human life.

6. Whoever spills the blood of man,
By man shall his blood be spilled;
For in the image of God
Was man created.

Notes to Genesis 9:1–6

1. *"Every creature that lives shall be yours to eat, as with the green grasses, I give you all these"* (Gen. 9:3). This indicates the conception that, except for other humans, all living things are subservient to the needs of man, who may consume them when necessary for his benefit. The analogy, "as with green grasses," is to the prior permission given to Adam to eat vegetation (Gen. 1:30) but not to consume living creatures. With regard to slaying human beings, however, verses five and six spell out the death penalty for murder.

2. *"For your life-blood I will demand [a reckoning]; of every beast will I demand it; and from man, from every man for his brother, will I demand [a reckoning for] human life. Whoever spills the blood of man, by man shall his blood be spilled; for in the image of God, was man created"* (Gen. 9:5–6). The phrase "I will demand [a reckoning]" indicates a demand for an accounting and punishment of those who are guilty of the murder of humans. Why, then, does the passage repeat this concept by saying, "from man," and repeat this still a third time by saying, further, "from every man for his brother," and state this still once again in verse 6: "Whoever spills the blood of man, by man shall his blood be spilled"?

Is there any significance in the wording of verse 5 that "I" will demand a reckoning and the phraseology of verse 6, which provides that a murderer shall have his blood shed "by man"? Is there any significance in the specific description of the criminal act in verse 6, "Whoever *spills* the blood of man," compared with the rather generalized and vague description of the offense, "for your life-blood, too" in verse 5? (See below, Part Two, Chapter VI, Section C 1, for the detailed talmudic exposition of these verses, attributing a different norm to each passage, with important consequences for criminal defendants. Talmudic jurists were, as we shall see, sensitive to delicate shadings of meanings, repetitions, and nuances of phraseology in scriptures.)

3. *"For your life-blood, I will demand [a reckoning]; of every beast will I demand it; and from man, from every man for his brother will I demand [a reckoning] for human life"* (Gen. 9:5). This may reflect the perspective that both animals and man were equally entitled to formal court proceedings before punishment (see below, Part Two, Chapter VI, Section C 2).[100]

4. *"From every man for his brother . . ."* (Gen. 9:5). The implication is that all men are brothers and that all homicide is like Cain's slaying of his brother Abel.

5. *"Whoever spills the blood of man, by man shall his blood be spilled"* (Gen. 9:5). In the original Hebrew text, in which the Bible was written, the Hebrew letter *"beth"* in the word, *"be 'Adam,"* (translated here as "by man") may also be understood as meaning "as payment for" or "instead of." This is the way it is used in Deuteronomy 19:21, *"Nefesh Be'Nefesh"* ("a soul for a soul"). The sense of the verse would then be that whoever sheds the blood of man shall have his own

---

100. See J. J. Finkelstein, "The Goring Ox," 46 *Temple Law Quarterly* (Winter, 1973): 169.

blood shed. Furthermore, the penalty clause ("By *man* shall his *blood* be *spilled*") in the original Hebrew version utilizes the identical key expressions as those used in describing the crime ("He who *spills* the *blood* of *man*"), but in reverse order. This verse would then be the first mention in the Bible of the principle of *jus talionis*, "measure for measure."

This norm also implies that, as was the case with Cain, only a murderer, not his family, shall be punished for his crime. This was an important advance in the humane application of criminal sanctions, and a radical departure from prevailing practices.

6. *"Shall his blood be spilled . . ."* (Gen. 9:6). Does this indicate anything about the manner of executing the murderer, i.e., that the murderer's blood must literally be made to "spill," as by execution with the sword? This would exclude execution by drowning, which was found in other contemporary cultures in the ancient Near East. (A number of widely divergent interpretations of this phrase have been made by talmudic scholars, some applying the verse to feticide.)

7. *"For in the image of God was man created"* (Gen. 9:6). Regardless of how the term "image" may be understood, does it have any significance for the treatment of criminal offenders? Does it imply that man is exalted and even sacred like God? Does this supply the reason for the extremely severe punishment provided for murder? Could it, on the other hand, be utilized to protect the accused, who was also created in God's image?

Note that the reason given in these verses for killing a murderer is not revenge but to punish the affront to God. The offense appears to be akin to blasphemy, since it entails destroying one who is in God's image, and who is the prime handiwork of God. The Jews later expressed the notion that man's exalted status was indicated both by his being created in God's image and also by the very fact that God deigned to disclose this information to him.[101] The phrase may also indicate that the murderer, by his act of homicide, had removed the "image of God" from himself and deserved to die.[102]

b. EXODUS

(1) *The Institution of Courts among the Israelites (Exodus 18:13–27)*

13. Next day, Moses sat as magistrate among the people, while the people stood about Moses from morning until evening.

101. Talmud, *Avot* 3:18; see Commentary of Rambam, *ad locum.*
102. Cassuto, *From Noah to Abraham*, p. 71.

14. But when Moses' father-in-law saw how much he had to do for the people, he said, "What is this thing that you have undertaken for the people? Why do you act alone, while all the people stand about you from morning until evening?"

15. Moses replied to his father-in-law, "It is because the people come to me to inquire of God.

16. When they have a dispute, it comes before me, and I judge between a man and his neighbor, and I make known the laws and teachings of God."

17. But Moses' father-in-law said to him, "The thing you are doing is not right;

18. You will surely wear yourself out, you, as well as this people. For the task is too heavy for you; you cannot do it alone.

19. Now listen to me. I will give you counsel, and God be with you! You act for the people on behalf of God: You bring the disputes before God.

20. And enjoin upon them the laws and the teachings, and make known to them the way they are to go and the practices they are to follow.

21. You shall also seek out from among all the people, capable men who fear God, trustworthy men who spurn ill-gotten gain; and set these over them as chiefs of thousands, hundreds, fifties, and tens.

22. Let them exercise authority over the people at all times; let them bring every major dispute to you, but decide every minor dispute themselves. Make it easier for yourself, and let them share the burden with you.

23. If you do this—and if God so commands you— you will be able to bear up; and all these people will go home content."

24. Moses heeded his father-in-law and did just as he had said.

25. Moses chose capable men out of all Israel, and appointed them heads over the people—chiefs of thousands, hundreds, fifties, and tens.

26. And they exercised authority over the people at all times: the difficult matters they would bring to Moses, and all the minor matters they would decide themselves.

27. Then Moses bade his father-in-law farewell, and he went his way to his own land.

(2) *The Giving of the Law at Mt. Sinai (Exodus 19:1–25)*

1. On the third new moon after the Israelites had gone forth from the land of Egypt, on that very day, they entered the wilderness of Sinai.

2. Having journeyed from Rephidim, they entered the wilderness of Sinai and encamped in the wilderness. Israel encamped there in front of the mountain.

3. And Moses went up to God. The Lord called to him from the mountain, saying, "Thus shall you say to the house of Jacob and declare to the children of Israel:

4. 'You have seen what I did to the Egyptians, how I bore you on eagles' wings and brought you to Me.

5. Now then, if you will obey Me faithfully and keep My covenant, you shall be My treasured possession among all the peoples. Indeed, all the earth is Mine.

6. But you shall be to Me a kingdom of priests and a holy nation.' These are the words that you shall speak to the children of Israel."

7. Moses came and summoned the elders of the people and put before them all the words that the Lord had commanded him.

8. All the people answered as one, saying, "All that the Lord has spoken we will do!" And Moses brought back the people's words to the Lord.

9. And the Lord said to Moses, "I will come to you in a thick cloud, in order that the people may hear when I speak with you and so trust you thereafter." Then Moses reported the people's words to the Lord.

10. And the Lord said to Moses, "Go to the people and warn them to stay pure today and tomorrow. Let them wash their clothes.

11. Let them be ready for the third day; for on the third day the Lord will come down, in the sight of all the people, on Mount Sinai.

12. You shall set bounds for the people round about, saying, 'Beware of going up the mountain or touching the border of it. Whoever touches the mountain shall be put to death:

13. No hand shall touch him, but he shall be either stoned or pierced through; beast or man, he shall not live.' When the ram's horn sounds a long blast, they may come up unto the mountain."

14. Moses came down from the mountain to the people and warned the people to stay pure, and they washed their clothes.

15. And he said to the people, "Be ready for the third day: do not go near a woman."

16. On the third day, as morning dawned, there was thunder and lightning, and a dense cloud upon the mountain, and a very loud blast of the horn; and all the people who were in the camp trembled.

17. Moses led the people out of the camp toward God, and they took their places at the foot of the mountain.

18. Now Mount Sinai was all in smoke, for the Lord had come down upon it in fire; the smoke rose like the smoke of a kiln, and the whole mountain trembled violently.

19. The blare of the ram's horn grew louder and louder. As Moses spoke, God answered him in thunder.

20. The Lord came down upon Mount Sinai, on the top of the mountain, and the Lord called Moses to the top of the mountain and Moses went up.

21. The Lord said to Moses, "Go down, warn the people not to break through to the Lord to gaze, lest many of them perish.

22. The priests also, who come near the Lord, must purify themselves, lest the Lord break out against them."

23. But Moses said to the Lord, "The people cannot come up to Mount Sinai, for You warned us saying, 'Set bounds about the mountain and sanctify it.'"

24. So the Lord said to him, "Go down, and come back together with Aaron; but let not the priests or the people break through to come up to the Lord, lest He break out against them."

25. And Moses went down to the people and spoke to them.

(3) The Decalogue (Exodus 20:1–18)

1. God spoke all these words, saying:

2. "I the Lord am your God who brought you out of the land of Egypt, the house of bondage:

3. You shall have no other gods beside Me.

4. You shall not make for yourself a sculptured image, or any likeness of what is in the heavens above, or on the earth below, or in the waters under the earth.

5. You shall not bow down to them or serve them. For I the Lord your God am an impassioned God, visiting the guilt of the fathers upon the children, upon the third and upon the fourth generations to those who reject Me;

6. But showing kindness to the thousandth generation of those who love Me and keep my commandments.

7. You shall not swear falsely by the name of the Lord your God; for the Lord will not clear one who swears falsely by His name.

8. Remember the Sabbath day to keep it holy.

9. Six days may you labor and do all your work;

10. But the seventh day is a Sabbath of the Lord your God: you shall not do any work—you, your son or daughter, your male or female slave, or your cattle, or the stranger who is within your settlements.

11. For in six days the Lord made heaven and earth and sea, and all that is in them, and He rested on the seventh day; therefore the Lord blessed the Sabbath day and hallowed it.

12. Honor your father and your mother, that you may long endure on the land which the Lord your God is giving you.

13. You shall not murder.
You shall not commit adultery.
You shall not steal.

You shall not bear false witness against your neighbor.

14. You shall not covet your neighbor's house: you shall not covet your neighbor's wife, or his male or female slave, or his ox or his ass, or anything that is your neighbor's."

15. All the people witnessed the thunder and lightning, the blare of the horn and the mountain smoking; and when the people saw it, they fell back and stood at a distance.

16. "You speak to us," they said to Moses, "and we will obey; but let not God speak to us, lest we die."

17. Moses answered the people, "Be not afraid; for God has come only in order to test you, and in order that the fear of Him may be ever with you, so that you do not go astray."

18. So the people remained at a distance, while Moses approached the thick cloud where God was.

Notes to Exodus 20:1–18

1. The Ten Commandments (or, more accurately, the ten statements or Decalogue) contain the basis of Jewish law, based upon the perception that a covenant was entered into between God and the Israelites. The relationship of the Decalogue to the other biblical norms has been the subject of much scholarly debate. Judaic legal tradition asserts that all of the other subsequent legal commandments in the Bible were also received at the same time[103] and are implicit in and spell out the basic norms of the Decalogue.

2. Note that the first five statements contained in verses 1 through 11 deal directly with the worship of God (honoring parents is regarded as an extension of honoring God). The remaining five statements deal with interactions among people. This numerical equality of treatment between the two groups of statements implies that norms regarding man are on an equal level with laws relating to God.

3. The first five statements contain radically novel concepts. The first two set forth the credo of absolute monotheism and the incorporeality of God, who is above, not part of, nature and who intimately supervises and absolutely controls human affairs ("who took you out of the land of Egypt"; "visiting guilt . . . upon the fourth generation"; and "showing kindness to the thousandth generation"). This is in sharp contrast with the prevailing beliefs in quarreling polytheistic, anthropomorphic deities. The notion of a human relationship with God, that people can love ("to those who love

me") instead of standing in abject terror of him, is also novel. The same is true with the institution of the Sabbath as a day on which all labor is to cease in acknowledgment that all creative powers are vested solely in God. The novelty of the first five provisions may be the reason why the first five statements are much lengthier than the last five terse statements concerning murder, theft, etc., which express concepts theretofore accepted throughout the Near East.

5. The style of the Decalogue is apodictic (phrased as direct commands), such as "Honor your father and your mother" or "You shall not murder." This reflects a direct communication from and personal relationship with God. This is different from the impersonal style of the Mesopotamian law codes, which are generally phrased, "If such and such occurs, then such and such disposition of the case shall be made." Note also that the Decalogue demands the performance of specified acts (e.g., "Honor your father and mother") as well as prohibiting other acts (e.g., "You shall not murder").

(4) *Injury to Persons or Property (Exodus 21:12–37)*

12. He who fatally strikes a man shall be put to death.

13. If he did not do it by design, but it came about by an act of God, I will assign you a place to which he can flee.

14. When a man schemes against another and kills him treacherously, you shall take him from My very altar to be put to death.

15. He who strikes his father or his mother shall be put to death.

16. He who kidnaps a man whom he held in his possession, shall be put to death.

17. He who curses his father or his mother shall be put to death.

18. When men quarrel and one strikes the other with stone or fist, and he does not die but has to take to his bed,

19. If he then gets up and walks outdoors upon his staff, (and the wound is healed,) the assailant shall go unpunished, except that he must pay for his idleness and his cure.

20. When a man strikes his slave or his maid, with a rod, and he dies there and then, he must be avenged.

21. But if he survives a day or two, he is not to be avenged, since he is his property.

22. If men wrestle, and one of them pushes a pregnant woman and a miscarriage results, but no other misfortune ensues, he shall be fined according as the woman's husband shall assess upon him through the judges.

23. But if a misfortune ensues, you shall give a soul for a soul;

---

103. See, e.g., *Torat Kohanim* to Lev. 25:1, Talmud, *Gittin* 60b, *Baba Batra* 15a, *J. Shekalim* 6:1; Rashi, Commentary on Exodus 24:12; S. Kasher, *Torah Shlemah*, vol. 16 (Jerusalem, 1962), addenda and pp. 207–08.

24. Eye for eye, tooth for tooth, hand for hand, foot for foot;

25. Burn for burn, wound for wound, bruise for bruise.

26. When a man strikes the eye of his slave, male or female, and destroys it, he shall let him go free on account of his eye.

27. If he knocks out the tooth of his slave, male or female, he shall let him go free on account of his tooth.

28. When an ox gores a man or a woman to death, the ox shall be stoned and its flesh shall not be eaten, but the owner of the ox is not to be punished.

29. If, however, that ox has long been a gorer, and its owner, though warned, has failed to guard it, and it kills a man or a woman—the ox shall be stoned and its owner, too, deserves to die.

30. Assessment shall be laid upon him to redeem his life.

31. So, too, if it gores a minor, male or female, [the owner] shall be dealt with according to the same norm.

32. But if the ox gores a slave, male or female, he shall pay thirty shekels of silver to the master, and the ox shall be stoned.

33. When a man opens a pit—or when he has dug a pit but has not covered it—and an ox or an ass falls into it,

34. The one responsible for the pit must make restitution; he shall pay the price to the owner, but shall keep the dead animal.

35. When a man's ox injures his neighbor's ox and it dies, they shall sell the live ox and divide the price; they shall also divide the dead animal.

36. If, however, the ox has long been known as a gorer, and its owner has failed to guard it, he must restore ox for ox, but shall keep the dead animal.

37. When a man steals an ox or a sheep, and slaughters it or sells it, he shall pay five oxen for the ox, and four sheep for the sheep.

Notes to Exodus 21:1–37

1. The norms contained in this chapter have been labeled "The Covenant Code" by many scholars because they are described as a covenant entered into between God, represented by Moses, and the people (see Exod. 24:8). In examining these norms, however, you should try to see whether they constitute a self-contained, complete body of laws, appropriate to govern even a simple agricultural or nomadic society. Are there any vital areas of human interactions that are omitted by these norms? Are the laws stated with sufficient clarity and precision? If not, how were these laws to be understood?

2. Verses 12 and 13 make a clear distinction between killing with *mens rea* and accidental death. In

the Bible killing is generally described by the word "*makeh*," which literally means "smites." The exact manner of killing is not usually described specifically as resulting from shooting a bow, poisoning, or the collapse of a faulty building. While Korngreen[104] feels that this illustrates the primitive state of biblical society, this conclusion seems unfounded. Specific modes of slaying, although at close range, are in fact described in Numbers 35:16–18, 22–23.

3. What means of execution were to be used for the capital punishment prescribed only in general terms by verses 12–20, "shall be put to death . . ."? Is there any significance in the deviation from the language of Genesis 9:6, "His blood shall be spilled . . ."?

4. *"You shall take him from My very altar to be put to death"* (Exod. 21:14). This verse reflects the perspective, rooted in antiquity, that a temple was also a sanctuary of refuge. The verse here is designed to counteract the notion that a place of worship could always serve as a sanctuary to protect against the infliction of penalties.[105]

5. *"When a man strikes his slave or his maid with a rod, and he dies, there and then, he must be avenged. But if he survives a day or two, he shall not be avenged, since he is his property"* (Exod. 21:20). Note the distinction between the killing of a slave and the killing of a free man in verse 12. What is the significance of describing the blow as being "with a rod," and why the difference in punishment if the slave dies immediately (instead of a day later), since in both cases he (the slave) is "his [the master's] property?" Is there a penalty implied if the slayer is somebody *other* than the slave's master? The Jewish legal tradition is that the slayer of a slave is punished equally with, and as severely as, the slayer of a free man. For an interpretation of the aforementioned biblical verses, see below, Part Two, Chapter VI, Section C 1.

6. *"If men wrestle, and one of them pushes a pregnant woman and a miscarriage results, but no other misfortune ensues, he shall be fined according as the woman's husband shall assess through the judges. If misfortune ensues, you shall give a soul for a soul; eye for eye, tooth for tooth, hand for hand, foot for foot; burn for burn, wound for wound, bruise for bruise"* (Exod. 21:22–25).

This rule is known as the *lex talionis*. Similar language is found in Leviticus 24:18–21, where the context makes it clear that the phrase refers to the payment of money only, for injury to the eye, and not to the physical mutilation of the tortfeasor (see below and Deut. 19:21). It should be noted that talmudic jurists

104. *Khuke Hamizrakh Hakadmon* (Tel-Aviv, 1944).
105. Compare "And Joab fled to the Tabernacle of God and held fast to the corners of the altar" (1 Kings 1:28).

claimed that these verses had never been understood, nor applied literally, to require an eye for an eye, but only obligated the payment of monies. The phrase was understood to mean that the tortfeasor might deserve to have his own eye plucked out in return but would be relieved of any penalty by payment of money damages in full for the injury and related losses, such as medical bills and loss of income (see verse 19, above).[106]

Verse 18 of this chapter of Exodus, which provides for the payment of money only in the case of tortious physical injury, substantiates this contention. Otherwise, mutilation should have been called forth there too.

It is noteworthy that the entire Bible with its many stories of killings and punishments covering nearly one thousand years, does not mention the punishment of an eye for an eye or a tooth for a tooth being applied in practice. (The only exception is Judg. 1:17, where a monarch who used to cut off the thumbs and toes of his captives was taken prisoner and had this penalty inflicted on him.)

7. The juxtaposition of the phrases "an eye for an eye" and "a tooth for a tooth" occurs also in Mesopotamian codes.[107] This may be because the eye was regarded as a person's most important and irreplaceable organ and the tooth the least important. The phrase would then connote that whether the most or least important organ was injured, damages had to be paid.[108]

8. For an interesting interpretation of the reasons for the order of the materials in verses 28 through 35, see Finkelstein, "Babel-Bible: A Mesopotamian View," Chapter II, Section F 2, below.

(5) *Theft and Other Tortious Damage (Exodus 22:1–26)*

1. If the thief is seized while tunneling, and he is beaten, and dies, there is no blood [guilt] in his case.

2. If the sun has risen on him, there is blood [guilt] in that case.—He must make restitution; if he lacks the means, he shall be sold for his theft.

3. But if what he stole—whether ox or ass or sheep—is found alive in his possession, he shall pay double.

4. When a man lets his livestock loose to graze in another's land, and so allows a field or a vineyard to be grazed bare, he must make restitution according to the top yield from that field or vineyard.

5. When a fire is started and spreads to thorns, so that stacked, standing, or growing grain is consumed, he who started the fire must make restitution.

6. When a man gives money or goods to another for safekeeping, and they are stolen from the man's house—if the thief is caught, he shall pay double.

7. If the thief is not caught, the owner of the house shall depose before the judges that he has not laid hands on his neighbor's property.

8. In all charges of misappropriation—pertaining to an ox, an ass, a sheep, a garment, or any other loss, whereof one party alleges, "This is it"—the case, of both parties shall come before the judges: he whom the judges declare guilty shall pay double to the other.

9. When a man gives to another an ass, an ox, a sheep, or any other animal to guard, and it dies of injuries or is carried off, with no witness about;

10. An oath before the Lord shall decide between the two of them that the one has not laid hands on the property of the other; the owner must acquiesce, and no restitution shall be made.

11. But if [the animal] was stolen from him, he shall make restitution to its owner.

12. If it was torn by beasts, he shall bring it as evidence; he need not replace what has been torn by beasts.

13. When a man borrows [an animal] from another and it dies of injuries, its owner not being with it, he must make restitution.

14. If its owner was with it, no restitution need be made; but if it was hired, he is still entitled to the hiring fee. . . .

17. You shall not tolerate a sorceress.

18. Whoever lies with a beast shall be put to death.

19. Whoever sacrifices to a god other than the Lord alone shall be proscribed.

20. You shall not wrong a stranger or oppress him, for you were strangers in the land of Egypt.

21. You shall not mistreat any widow or orphan.

22. If you do mistreat them, I will heed their outcry as soon as they cry out to Me;

23. and My anger shall blaze forth and I will put you to the sword, and your own wives shall become widows and your children orphans.

24. When you lend money to My people, to the poor who is in your power, do not act toward him as a creditor: exact no interest from him.

25. If you take your neighbor's garment in pledge, you must return it to him before the sun sets;

26. it is his only clothing, the sole covering for his skin. In what shall he sleep? Therefore, if he cries out to Me, I will pay heed, for I am compassionate. . . .

106. Talmud, *Ketubot* 38a; *Baba Kama*, 84a; Maimonides, *Guide for the Perplexed*, trans. Friedlander (reprinted New York, 1956), ch. 41, p. 344; see Chapter III, Section B 7, below.

107. See, e.g., Code of Hammurabi, secs. 196–201.

108. See David Hoffman, *Das Buch Leviticus*, trans. into Hebrew by Z. Har-Shefer and A. Lieberman (Jerusalem, 1967), p. 216.

Notes to Exodus 22:1–26

1. *"If the thief is seized while tunneling, and he is beaten to death, there is no blood [guilt] in this case* [literally, "he has no blood]" (Exod. 22:1). What is the rationale of this provision? What light does it shed on perspectives regarding self-help? What if the burglar has abandoned his attempt at tunneling and has begun to flee but is caught by the householder and killed? For the talmudic interpretation of "He has no blood," see Talmud, *Sanhedrin* 72b.

2. *"If the sun has risen on him, there is blood [guilt]"* (Exod. 22:2). What connection is there between the shining of the sun and "blood guilt"? This verse has been interpreted as prohibiting the killing of a burglar during the daytime, since, in an agricultural society in which the entire family would be out in the fields, the burglar would not have expected anyone to be at home at that time. The burglar presumably did not intend to kill any householder who resisted his attempts. One who attempted to burglarize at night, however, would be presumed to have murderous intent. This is the talmudic view,[109] which also interprets the verse as meaning that if it was as clear as the sun is by day that the thief had no intention to kill (as, for example, where the burglar was the father of a householder and would not therefore wish to kill his son), then, the householder who killed him would be guilty of murder.

3. Note the perspective reflected here that property (the items to be stolen) are not to be equated with life. The life of a burglar may *not* be taken to protect property—except in self-defense, where death is threatened by the burglar—and any life, even that of a burglar, is more important than property. These verses would then only exonerate one who killed a burglar if his own life was threatened (see below, Part Two, Chapter VI, Section C 1, for further exposition of this principle).

4. *"If the thief is caught, he shall pay double"* (Exod. 22:6). There is no provision for imprisonment of thieves (which became prevalent at a much later time), or for bodily mutilation of thieves, as expounded in the contemporaneous Mesopotamian codes of law. The claim is sometimes made that biblical law is like primitive law, which "runs much more heavily to tort, i.e., private wrong, than to crime, or public wrong,"[110] since there is no corporal punishment for wrongs to others, such as theft. Since, however, biblical law provides for courts and public officers to enforce monetary sanctions for theft, this demonstrates that the wrong is viewed as concerning the whole of society," so that 'crime' differs

from 'tort' not in kind, but in the effective predominance for purposes of administration, of the public and private elements, *both* of which are always present to some degree,"[111] although there is more public machinery available to deal with acts regarded as "crimes" than with "torts."

5. *"You shall not wrong a stranger or oppress him, for you were strangers in the land of Egypt"* (Exod. 22:20). This implies equal treatment for aliens who committed criminal offenses. The exhortation regarding equal treatment of strangers is stressed repeatedly throughout the Bible.

(6) *Carrying Out Justice, Obligations to the Poor, and Other Miscellaneous Norms (Exodus 23:1–12)*

1. You must not carry false rumors; you shall not join hands with the guilty to act as an unjust witness.

2. Do not side with the majority to do wrong, nor to act perversely; otherwise follow the majority.

3. Nor should you show deference to a poor man in his dispute.

4. When you encounter your enemy's ox or ass wandering, you must take it back to him.

5. When you see the ass of your enemy prostrate under its burden and would refrain from raising it, you must nevertheless raise it with him.

6. You shall not subvert the rights of your needy in their disputes.

7. Keep far from a false charge; do not bring death on the innocent and the righteous, for I will not acquit the wrongdoer.

8. Do not take bribes, for bribes blind the clear-sighted and upset the pleas of the just.

9. You shall not oppress a stranger, for you know the feelings of the stranger, having yourselves been strangers in the land of Egypt.

10. Six years you shall sow your land and gather in its yield;

11. But in the seventh you shall let it rest and lie fallow. Let the needy among your people eat of it, and what they leave let the wild beasts eat. You shall do the same with your vineyards and your olive groves.

12. Six days you shall do your work, but on the seventh day you shall cease from labor, in order that your ox and your ass may rest, and that your bondman and the stranger may be refreshed. . . .

(7) *The Covenant with God to Accept the Law (Exodus 24:3–8, 12–18)*

3. Moses went and repeated to the people all the commands of the Lord and all the norms; and all the

---

109. Abraham ben David (Ravad), Commentary on Rambam, Laws of Theft 9:9.
110. K. Llewellyn and E. A. Hoebel, *The Cheyenne Way* (Oklahoma City, 1949), pp. 47–48.

111. Ibid., 48. Furthermore, the Bible does provide for flogging for violations of biblical norms (see Deut. 25:1–3).

people answered with one voice, saying, "All the things that the Lord has spoken we will do!"

4. Moses then wrote down all the commands of the Lord.

Early in the morning, he set up an altar at the foot of the mountain, with twelve pillars for the twelve tribes of Israel.

5. He delegated young men among the Israelites, and they offered burnt offerings and sacrificed bulls as offerings of well-being to the Lord.

6. Moses took one part of the blood and put it in basins, and the other part of the blood he dashed against the altar.

7. Then he took the record of the covenant and read it aloud to the people. And they said, "All that the Lord has spoken we will do and hear!" Moses took the blood and dashed it on the people and said, "This is the blood of the covenant which the Lord now makes with you concerning all these commands. . . ."

12. The Lord said to Moses, "Come up to Me on the mountain and wait there, and I will give you the stone tablets with the teachings and commandments which I have inscribed to instruct them."

13. So Moses and his attendant Joshua arose, and Moses ascended the mountain of God.

14. To the elders he had said, "Wait here for us until we return to you. You have Aaron and Hur with you; let anyone who has a matter, approach them."

15. When Moses had ascended the mountain, the cloud covered the mountain.

16. The presence of the Lord abode on Mount Sinai, and the cloud hid it for six days. On the seventh day He called to Moses from the midst of the cloud.

17. Now the presence of the Lord appeared in the sight of the Israelites as a consuming fire on the top of the mountain.

18. Moses went inside the cloud and ascended the mountain; and Moses remained on the mountain forty days and forty nights.

Notes to Exodus 24:3–8, 12–18

1. *"All the things that the Lord has spoken we will do"* (Exod. 24:3); *"All that the Lord has spoken we will do and hear"* (Exod. 24:7). Jewish legal tradition has regarded these utterances as akin to the notion of a social contract, and as implying that the law is binding solely because the people willingly obligated themselves to accept it.[112]

2. Were the foregoing provisions of law adequate for an ordered society three thousand years ago? Does the chapter contain any provisions regarding the purchase or sale of houses and land or for their rental?

112. See Talmud, *Shabbat* 88a.

Such provisions are found in contemporaneous and earlier Mesopotamian codes, some of which preceded the Bible by hundreds of years, and in the records of transactions and court cases that have come down to us from those neighboring societies. Why are there no provisions for commercial documents, such as bills of sale, receipts, and promissory notes? What about provisions for marriage, divorce, or adoption of children? What of the treatment of employees? In short, does this section present a detailed code of laws adequate to order even a very simple society? If not, why doesn't it? Are the details clear concerning those provisions that *are* included in this section, or does the section seem to present only some very general rules, or perhaps the skeletal outline of a legal code? Are the norms in this section designed to be independent of the other norms in the Bible? It may be argued that the section is clearly to be supplemented by additional norms, and at best contains only the barest outline of a code, whose details and specific practices were well understood by the populace. This is, indeed, the talmudic view (see below, Part Two, Chapter V, Section B).

c. LEVITICUS

(1) *Avoiding Practices Abhorrent to God (Leviticus 18:27–30)*

26. You must keep my laws and my norms, and you must not do any of those abhorrent things, neither the citizen nor the stranger who resides among you;

27. For all those abhorrent things were done by the people who were in the land before you, and the land became defiled.

28. So let not the land spew you out for defiling it, as it spewed out the nation that came before you.

29. All who do any of those abhorrent things—such persons shall be cut off from their people.

30. You shall keep My charge not to engage in any of the abhorrent practices that were carried on before you, lest you defile yourselves through them: I the Lord am your God.

(2) *Attaining Holiness; Conduct toward One's Fellows (Leviticus 19:1–4, 9–18, 29, 32–37)*

1. The Lord spoke to Moses, saying:

2. "Speak to the whole Israelite community and say to them:

   You shall be holy, for I, the Lord your God, am holy.

3. You shall each revere his mother and his father, and keep My Sabbaths: I the Lord am your God.

4. Do not turn to idols to make molten gods for yourselves: I the Lord am your God. . . .

9. When you reap the harvest of your land, you shall not reap all the way to the edges of your field, or gather the gleanings of your harvest.

10. You shall not pick your vineyard bare, or gather the fallen fruit of your vineyard; you shall leave them for the poor and the stranger: I the Lord am your God.

11. You shall not steal: You shall not deal deceitfully or falsely with one another.

12. You shall not swear falsely by My name, profaning the name of your God; I am the Lord.

13. You shall not withhold wages of a hired person. You shall not commit robbery. The wages of a laborer shall not remain with you until morning.

14. You shall not insult the deaf, or place a stumbling block before the blind. You shall fear your God; I am the Lord.

15. Do not pervert the law. Do not favor the poor or show deference to the rich; judge your fellow person justly.

16. Do not deal basely with your fellows. Do not stand by the blood of your neighbor. I am the Lord.

17. You shall not hate your kinsman in your heart. Reprove your fellow persons and incur no guilt because of him.

18. You shall not take vengeance or bear a grudge against your kinsfolk. Love your fellow person as yourself! I am the Lord . . . .

29. Do not degrade your daughter, making her a harlot, lest the land fall into harlotry and the land be filled with depravity.

30. You shall keep My Sabbaths and venerate My sanctuary: I am the Lord. . . .

32. You shall rise before the aged and show deference to the old; you shall fear your God: I am the Lord.

33. When a stranger resides with you in your land, you shall not wrong him.

34. The stranger who resides with you shall be to you as one of your citizens; you shall love him as yourself, for you were strangers in the land of Egypt: I the Lord am your God.

35. You shall not falsify measures of length, weight, or capacity.

36. You shall have an honest balance, honest weights.

I the Lord am your God who brought you out from the land of Egypt.

37. You shall faithfully observe all My laws and all My norms: I am the Lord."

(3) *A People Apart in Holiness (Leviticus 20:22–26)*

22. You shall faithfully observe all My laws and all My regulations, lest the land to which I bring you to settle in spew you out.

23. You shall not follow the practices of the nation that I am driving out before you. For it is because they did all these things that I abhorred them.

24. And said to you: You shall possess their land, for I will give it to you to possess, a land flowing with milk and honey. I the Lord am your God who has set you apart from other peoples.

25. So you shall set apart the clean beast from the unclean, the unclean bird from the clean. You shall not draw abomination upon yourselves through beast or bird or anything with which the ground is alive, which I have set apart for you to treat as unclean. You shall be holy to Me, for I the Lord am holy, and I have set you apart from other peoples to be Mine. . . .

(4) *Tortious Injuries (Leviticus 24:17–22)*

17. If a man kills any human being, he shall be put to death.

18. One who kills an animal shall make restitution for it: a soul for a soul.

19. If anyone maims his fellow, as he has done so shall it be done to him:

20. Fracture for fracture, eye for eye, tooth for tooth. The injury he inflicted on another shall be inflicted on him.

21. He who kills an animal shall make restitution for it; but he who kills a human being shall be put to death.

22. You shall have one law for stranger and citizen alike: for I the Lord am your God.

d. Numbers

(1) *Cities of Refuge (Numbers 35:9–34)*

9. And the Lord spoke unto Moses, saying,

10. "Speak unto the children of Israel, and say unto them, When you be come over Jordan into the land of Canaan.

11. Then you shall appoint you cities to be cities of refuge for you; that the slayer may flee thither, who kills any person unawares.

12. And they shall be unto you cities for refuge from the redeemer; that the slayer shall not be put to death until he stands before the congregation for judgment.

13. And of these cities which you shall give, six cities shall you have for refuge.

14. You shall designate three cities on this side of the Jordan, and three cities shall you give in the land of Canaan, which shall be cities of refuge.

15. These six cities shall be a refuge, both for the children of Israel, and for the stranger, and for the sojourner among them; that every one that killeth any person unawares may flee thither.

16. And if he smite him with instrument of iron, so that he dies, he is a murderer: the murderer shall surely be put to death.

17. And if he smite him with a stone with which one can kill, and he dies, he is a murderer: the murderer shall surely be put to death.

18. Or if he smite him with a hand weapon of wood, with which one can kill, and he dies, he is a murderer: the murderer shall surely be put to death.

19. The redeemer of blood, himself, shall slay the murderer: when he meets him, he shall slay him.

20. But if he thrust him out of hatred, or hurl at him from ambush so that he die;

21. Or in enmity smite him with his hand that he die: he that smote him shall surely be put to death; for he is a murderer: the redeemer of blood shall slay the murderer, when he meets him.

22. But if he thrust him suddenly without enmity, or have cast upon him any thing without lying in wait.

23. Or with any stone, wherewith a man may die, seeing him not, and cast it upon him, that he die, and was not his enemy, neither sought his harm.

24. Then the congregation shall judge between the slayer and the redeemer of blood according to these laws.

25. And the congregation shall save the slayer from the hand of the redeemer of blood, and the congregation shall restore him to the city of his refuge, to which he fled: and he shall abide in it unto the death of the high priest, which was annointed with the holy oil.

26. But if the slayer shall at any time come without the border of the city of his refuge, whither he was fled;

27. And the redeemer of blood find him without the borders of the city of his refuge, and the redeemer of blood kill the slayer; he shall not be guilty of blood.

28. Because he must remain in the city of his refuge until the death of the high priest: but after the death of the high priest the slayer shall return into the land of his possession.

29. So these things shall be for a statute of justice unto you throughout your generations in all your dwellings.

30. Whoever kills any person, the murderer shall be put to death pursuant to the mouth of witnesses: but one witness shall not testify against any person to cause him to die.

31. Moreover you shall take no forgiveness monies for the life of a murderer, who deserves to die: but he shall be surely put to death.

32. And ye shall take no forgiveness monies for him that is fled to the city of his refuge, that he should come again to dwell in the land, until the death of the priest.

33. And you shall not pollute the land wherein you are: for blood defiles the land: and the land shall not be forgiven for the blood that is shed therein, but by the blood of him that shed it.

34. Defile not the land which you inhabit, wherein I dwell: for I the Lord dwell among the children of Israel."

Notes to Numbers 35:9–34

1. Note the extensive provisions for setting up a number of scattered cities of refuge, to which the accidental unpremeditated slayer could flee. This was designed not only to protect the accidental slayer, but to overcome the prevalent practice of feuding which resulted, in part, from the close feelings of kinship by all members of a clan and their feelings of responsibility for one another.[113]

2. *"That the slayer shall not be put to death until he stands before the congregation for judgment"* (Num. 35:12). This outlawing of mob violence or any non-judicial killings formed a vital foundation of Judaic criminal justice. This motion was elaborated considerably in the talmudic legal tradition.

3. Why is it that in verses 17 and 18 the death penalty is prescribed for one who kills with a stone or with wood "with which one can kill" (i.e., large and hard enough to kill), while in verse 16 there is a death penalty for one who kills with an iron instrument without the proviso that it be one "with which one can kill?" The implication is clear that it was felt that a blow with iron could be fatal, even if the iron implement was small, because of the sharpness and hardness of that metal, which had then only recently been introduced into the Near East (see above, Section A 7).

4. Compare the requirement in verse 17 that the wooden implement must be one with which one can ordinarily kill in order for the death penalty to be invoked, with the provision in Exodus 21:20 that one who strikes a slave "with a rod," causing his death, shall be killed if the slave dies that day, but escapes execution if the slave survives for a day or two. No conditions are placed there regarding the size, thickness, or sharpness of the instrument. A "rod" normally would be made of wood and would not ordinarily kill. The theory appears to be that striking a slave with a rod was commonly used to chastise him and would not be presumed to be employed with homicidal intent since a master would not wish to damage his extremely valuable property. This presumption would be rebutted if the beating were so severe that the slave died at once.[114]

113. See Robertson-Smith, *Kinship and Marriage*, pref. and ch. 2.
114. Rambam, Laws Concerning a Murderer and the Preservation of Life, ch. 2, sec. 14.

The presumption that a master would not wish to destroy his property would explain verse 17, "since he is his property." That verse sets forth the foregoing presumption as the rationale that relieves the master of the death penalty if the slave survives for a day, but not if he dies sooner. What if one kills someone else's slave? The distinction between murderous intent or malice aforethought and unintentional slaying is universal in American jurisdictions. (See, e.g., Michigan Comp. Law, Sec. 750.316 [1948]; 28 Michigan Statutes Annotated 548 [1972]; Title 18.2–32, Virginia Code of 1950 [Revised, 1975]; New Mexico Statutes of 1953, Chap. 40, Sec. 40 A–201 [Revised, 1972]. See also Deut. 19:11.)

5. *"The redeemer of blood shall slay the murderer"* (Num. 35:19). How is the execution of the murderer by the victim's "redeemer," or relatives, to be reconciled with the provisions for a court trial in verse 12: "The murderer shall not be killed before he stands before the congregation for judgment"? (See below for the talmudic understanding.)

6. *"And the congregation shall save the murderer from the redeemer of blood"* (Num. 35:25). This provision served talmudic jurists as a basic guideline that had profound ramifications concerning the function and purposes of courts. (See Talmud, *Rosh Hashannah* 26a, and see also below, Part Two, Chapter VI, Section C 2.)

7. *"And the congregation shall restore him to the city of refuge to which he fled"* (Num. 35:25). The simple meaning of this passage is that the accused murderer would not be tried by the court in the city of refuge but would be extradited to be tried by the court in the area where the murder had occurred. Only if he was found to have killed without intention was he escorted to the city of refuge to dwell in safety. Otherwise, if he was found to have intentionally murdered, he was to be executed.

8. In addition to the provisions in the Pentateuch, the role of the cities of refuge is described in the book of Joshua 20:1–6: "And God spoke to Joshua, thus, 'Speak to the children of Israel and say, Set aside the cities of refuge, that I spoke about to you, through Moses. A murderer who slays accidentally, without intention, can run there and these shall be a place of refuge from the redeemer of blood. He shall run to one of these cities and shall stand at the doorway of the gate of the city and speak to the elders of that city and tell his story. They shall gather him to them into the city, and give him a place where he shall live with them. If the redeemer of blood pursues him, they shall not turn over the murderer to him, because he killed his neighbor unintentionally, and did not hate him from beforehand. He shall dwell in that city until he stands before the congregation in justice, or until the death of the high priest of that time. Then, shall the murderer return and come to his city and house, to the city from which he fled."

Why does the death of the high priest serve as the date when the slayer may return home? (See Chapter III, Section B 2.)

9. *"Whoever kills any person shall be put to death pursuant to the mouth of witnesses: but one witness shall not testify against any person to cause him to die"* (Num. 35:30). This, too, is designed to prevent hastily imposed death sentences without adequate and convincing testimony. Clearly, it is often impossible to find two competent witnesses to a murder. What happens then?

This verse was the precedent for the requirement of two witnesses in the United States Constitution, Article III, Section 3, "No person shall be convicted of treason unless on the testimony of two witnesses to the same overt act."

10. *"You shall not take forgiveness monies for the soul of a murderer who deserves to die"* (Num. 35:31). This provision was designed to overcome the practice found in ancient societies whereby a murderer could escape death by the payment of money to the family or clan of the victim. The verse reflects the principle that murder is a crime not simply against the victim or his family but against God and the entire society. No human has the right to forgive it. The provision of not taking ransom "for a murderer, who deserves to die" should be contrasted with the provisions for monetary restitution in the case of one who caused a miscarriage (Exod. 21:22) or one whose ox killed a person (Exod. 21:30). In both of those cases the defendant was not guilty of premeditated murder and therefore did not "deserve to die."

11. *"And you shall not pollute the land wherein you are: for blood defiles the land: and the land shall not be forgiven for the blood that is shed therein, but by the blood of him that shed it. Defile not the land which you inhabit, wherein I dwell: for I the Lord dwell among the children of Israel"* (Num. 35:33–34). This principle should be compared with the Greek doctrine of the pollution of the land resulting from a murder.[115] Unlike Greek custom, however, the Bible bars the payment of money and exile in the case of a deliberate killing. Notice, too, the religious perspective that killing is a grievous sin, requiring forgiveness for the entire community, which is responsible for bringing the murderer to justice.

115. See D. M. MacDowell, *Athenian Homicide Law* (Manchester, 1963), pp. 141 ff.

e. DEUTERONOMY

(1) *Establishing Courts and Criminal Procedure
(Deuteronomy 16:18–20, 17:2–13)*

16:18. You shall appoint judges and officers for your tribes, in all of your settlements that the Lord your God is giving you, and they shall govern the people with due justice.

19. You shall not distort justice. You shall show no partiality; you shall not take bribes, for bribes blind the eyes of the discerning; upset the words of the just.

20. Justice, justice shall you pursue, that you may thrive and occupy the land that the Lord your God is giving you. . . .

17:2. "If there is found among you, in one of the settlements which the Lord your God is giving you, a man or woman who has affronted the Lord your God and transgressed His covenant.

3. Turning to the worship of other gods and bowing down to them, to the sun or the moon or any of the heavenly host, something I never commanded.

4. And you have been informed or have learned of it, then you shall make a thorough inquiry. If it is true, the fact is established, that this abhorrent thing was perpetrated in Israel.

5. You shall take the man or the woman who did that wicked thing out to the public place, and you shall stone them, man or woman, to death.

6. A person shall be put to death only on the testimony of two or three witnesses; he must not be put to death on the testimony of a single witness.

7. Let the hands of the witnesses be the first against him to put him to death, and the hands of the rest of the people thereafter. Thus you will sweep out evil from your midst.

8. If a matter is too baffling for you to decide, be it a doubt concerning homicide, civil law, or injury— matters of dispute in your gates—you shall promptly ascend to the place which the Lord your God has chosen.

9. And appear before the Levitical priests, and the one who shall be judge at that time. You shall inquire and they shall tell you the law.

10. You shall do whatever they tell you from that place which the Lord chose, and you shall be careful to do all that they shall teach you.

11. You shall act in accordance with the instructions given you and the law that they shall tell you; you must not deviate from what they tell you either to the right or to the left.

12. Should a man act defiantly and disregard the priest charged with serving there the Lord your God, or the judge, that man shall die. Thus you will remove evil from Israel.

13. All the people will hear and be afraid and will not act defiantly again.

Notes to Deuteronomy 16:18–20, 17:2–13

1. *"You shall appoint judges and officers for your tribes, in all your settlements"* (Deut. 16:18). This verse is indicative of the perspective that every sizable settlement had to have a court of its own. For the existence of a higher court, see note on Deuteronomy 17:8, below.

2. *"Then you shall make a thorough inquiry. . . . If it is true, the fact is established, that this abhorrent thing was perpetrated in Israel"* (Deut. 17:4). Similar language is found in Deuteronomy 13:15: "And you shall inquire and investigate, and ask well and if you find that it is true, the fact is established that this abhorrent thing was done in your midst." This was an obvious reference to the need for a very thorough inquiry before drastic penalties were to be meted out. As we shall see, talmudic jurists relied on these verses to insist upon an extremely careful inquiry concerning even the minutest details of the surrounding circumstances.[116]

3. *"A person shall be put to death only on the testimony of two or three witnesses. He must not be put to death on the testimony of a single witness"* (Deut. 17:6). A similar provision is found later, in Deuteronomy 19:15: "A single witness may not establish any guilt or blame against the person for any offense that may be committed. A case can be established only upon the testimony of two or three witnesses" (see also Numbers 35:30, above).

a. If two witnesses are sufficient, what is the significance of the additional phrase "or three witnesses"? Does it imply that the testimony of two witnesses is to be given the same weight as the testimony of three? What if the testimony of two conflicts with that of three other witnesses? With that of one hundred others?

b. Is circumstantial evidence acceptable where there are no witnesses? Can circumstantial evidence be utilized to fill out the evidence, which is *partially* established by two witnesses? What about testimony regarding all the facts by one witness, which is supported by circumstantial evidence?

4. *"Let the hands of the witnesses be the first against him, to put him to death, and the hands of the rest of the people thereafter"* (Deut. 17:7). Why should the witnesses carry out the execution instead of a professional executioner? How is this to be reconciled with the provision that the "redeemer of blood" should execute the murderer (Numbers 35:19, 21)?

---

116. Talmud, *Sanhedrin* 40a.

5. *"If a matter is too baffling for you to decide . . . you shall promptly ascend to the place which the Lord your God has chosen, and appear before the Levitical priests and the one who shall be judge at that time. You shall inquire and they shall tell you the law."* Does this indicate the existence of an appellate system? If not, which "baffling" issues were referred to the higher courts? (See Part Two, Chapter VI, Section B 2 *e* below.)

6. *"You shall promptly ascend to the place which the Lord your God has chosen. . . . You shall do whatever they tell you from that place which the Lord chose"* (Deut. 17:8–10). Is there any significance to the phrase "the place which the Lord has chosen," which is repeated twice? Could a higher court with supreme authority be established in any place at any time?

7. Do these verses indicate that the activities of the supreme authority were to be limited to cases or controversies that had already come before a court? Could they prescribe norms regarding matters that had not come up before any court?

8. *"You shall . . . appear before the Levitical priests and the one who shall be judge at that time"* (Deut. 17:8). Notice that there is no reference to appearing before a prophet to decide a controversy. Did prophets have any role in prescribing law or in deciding legal controversies? (See Part Two, Chapter V, Section A 2.)

9. *"You shall do whatever they tell you . . . and you shall be careful to do all that they shall teach you. You shall act in accordance with the instructions given and the law that they shall tell you. You must not deviate from what they tell you, either to the right or the left"* (Deut. 17:10–11). Why the unusual *fourfold* repetition of the warning to obey the word of the higher authority? Does it imply obedience even if their instruction is plainly *contrary* to the "plain meaning" of a biblical command? If so, does this imply their right to deliberately alter a preexisting biblical norm as they see fit?[117]

(2) Kingship (Deuteronomy 17:14–20)

14. If, when you have entered the land that the Lord your God has given you, and occupied it and settled in it, you decide, "I will set a king over me, as do all the nations about me."

15. You shall be free to set a king over yourself, one chosen by the Lord your God. Be sure to set as king over yourself one of your own people; you must not set a foreigner over you, one who is not your kinsman.

16. Moreover, he shall not keep many horses or send people back to Egypt to add to his horses, since the

117. See Maimonides, *Guide for the Perplexed*, ch. 41.

Lord has warned you, "You must not go back that way again."

17. And he shall not have many wives, lest his heart go astray; nor shall he amass silver and gold to excess.

18. When he is seated on his royal throne, he shall write a copy of this Torah before the Levitical priests.

19. Let it remain with him and let him read in it all his life, so that he may learn to revere the Lord his God, to observe faithfully every word of this Torah and these laws.

20. Thus he will not act haughtily toward his fellows or deviate from the instruction to the right or to the left, to the end that he and his descendants may reign long in the midst of Israel.

Notes to Deuteronomy 17:14–20

1. *"If . . . you decide, 'I will set a king over me, as do all the nations about me' "* (Deut. 17:14).

a. What light does this throw on the biblical perspectives regarding divine rights of kings?

b. From the limitations upon the king's power and status set forth in the foregoing verses, it is apparent that the reference was not to a despotic ruler such as the Egyptian pharaohs. The notion was closer to (though much more liberal than) the kings of the city-states in Syria-Palestine, Mesopotamia, and Asia Minor. Compare the functions of the king, in practice, in Judah and Israel with those of these other kings. Did the Jewish kings, in fact, adhere to the guidelines for royal behavior set forth in these verses?

2. *"He shall not keep many horses. . . . He shall not have many wives . . . nor shall he amass silver and gold to excess. . . . Thus he will not act haughtily toward his fellows* (Deut. 17:16, 17, 20). If the king's status was not to be elevated too much above that of the masses, what was the function of having the king?

3. *"He shall write a copy of this Torah before the Levitical priests. Let it remain with him and let him read in it all his life, so that he may learn to revere the Lord his God, to observe faithfully every word of this Torah and these laws"* (Deut. 17:18). Note that even the king was duty bound to obey the laws of the Bible and was not above the law. Compare the functions of the Jewish king in prescribing and applying the law to those of the kings in Syria, Palestine, Egypt, Mesopotamia, and Asia Minor. Is it significant that many of the Mesopotamian codes of law were compiled, recorded by, and named after kings, whereas among the Jews it was always the "law of Moses" (who, incidentally, was never referred to directly as a king) that was held to be binding? Consider too, in this regard, the function of the king in appointing and supervising judges and his relationship to and control of judicial officials. (See,

e.g., 2 Sam. 12:5–6, 15:2–4; 1 Kings 3:16; 2 Chron. 2:19; and see below, Chapter III, Section B 1 *b*.)

4. *"So that he and his descendants may reign long in the midst of Israel"* (Deut. 17:20).

a. This indicates the creation of a royal lineage with a king's son succeeding to the throne upon his father's death, rather than choosing a new king from among all of the most suitable candidates. Was it presumed that royal succession by descendants would lead to greater stability, or was rule by royal lineage an inseparable component of royal government? What was the actual practice in the ancient Near East, among Jews and non-Jews?

b. Note that the verses which immediately precede those that deal with the selection of kings in Israel provide that if a question of law arises which puzzles the local judges, "You shall promptly ascend to the place which the Lord your God has chosen. And appear before the Levitical priests, and the one who shall be judge at that time. You shall inquire and they shall tell you the law" (Deut. 17:8–9). Why do these verses not provide for submission of disputes to the king for a final judgment?

c. To whom does the verse "You shall appoint judges and officers in all of your settlements" (Deut. 16:18) apply? To the king? To the people as a whole? To the elders? Later in the Bible (2 Chron. 2:19) we find that the king did appoint judges.

(3) *The Unwitting Manslayer and False Witnesses (Deuteronomy 19:1–13, 15–21)*

1. When the Lord your God has cut down the nations whose land the Lord your God is giving you, and you have dispossessed them and settled in their towns and homes.

2. You shall set aside three cities in the land that the Lord your God is giving you to possess.

3. You shall prepare the way, and divide into three equal parts the territory of the country that the Lord your God has allocated to you, so that any manslayer may have a place to flee to.

4. Now this is the case of the manslayer who may flee there and live: one who has killed another unwittingly, without having been his enemy in the past.

5. For instance a man goes with his neighbor into a grove to cut wood; as his hand swings the ax to cut down a tree, the ax-head flies off the handle and strikes the other so that he dies. That man shall flee to one of these cities and live.

6. Otherwise, when the distance is great, the redeemer of blood, pursuing the manslayer in hot anger, may overtake him and kill him; yet he was not guilty of a capital crime, since he had never been the other's enemy.

7. This is why I command you: set aside three cities.

8. And when the Lord your God enlarges your territory, as He swore to your fathers, and gives you all the land that He promised to give your fathers.

9. If you faithfully observe all this instruction which I enjoin upon you this day, to love the Lord your God and to walk in His ways at all times—then you shall add three more towns to those three.

10. Thus blood of the innocent will not be shed, in the land that the Lord your God is allotting to you, to bring blood upon you.

11. If, however, a man who is his neighbor's enemy lies in wait for him and sets upon him and strikes him a fatal blow and then flees to one of these towns.

12. The elders of his town shall have him brought back from there and shall hand him over to the redeemer of blood to be put to death.

13. You must show him no pity. Thus you will purge Israel of the shedding of blood of the innocent, and it will go well with you. . . .

15. A single witness may not establish against a person any guilt or blame for any offense that may be committed; a case can be established only on the testimony of two witnesses or more.

16. If a man appears against another to testify maliciously and gives false testimony against him;

17. the two parties to the dispute shall appear before the Lord, before the priests or judges in authority at the time;

18. and the judges shall make a thorough investigation. If the man who testified is a false witness, if he has testified falsely against his fellow man;

19. you shall do to him as he schemed to do to his fellow. Thus you will remove evil from your midst;

20. others will hear and be afraid, and such evil things will not again be done in your midst.

21. Nor must you show pity: a soul for a soul, eye for eye, tooth for tooth, hand for hand, foot for foot.

Notes to Deuteronomy 19:1–13, 15–21

1. *"The elders of his town . . . shall hand him over to the redeemer of blood, to be put to death"* (Deut. 19:12). A few verses before this (Deut. 17:7), however, the text provides: "Let the hands of the witnesses be the first against him to put him to death, and the hands of the rest of the people thereafter." Do these provisions conflict? What happens if the victim has no relative who can act as "redeemer of blood," or if the relatives are unable or unwilling to carry out the killing?

2. *"You must show him no pity"* (Deut. 19:13). Does the need to warn sternly against having pity on a murderer and sparing his life reveal anything of the prevailing perspective concerning capital punishment? For similar warnings, see "And the land shall not be

forgiven for the blood which was spilled in it, except with the blood of the murderer" (Num. 35:33); "You shall not take forgiveness payment from a murderer who deserves to die, but he must be killed" (Num. 35:31).

3. *"If the man who testified is a false witness, if he has testified falsely against his fellow man, you shall do to him as he schemed to do to his fellow. Thus, you will rid yourselves of evil from your midst; others will hear and be afraid and such evil things will not again be done in your midst. You must not show pity; soul for soul, eye for eye, tooth for tooth, hand for hand, foot for foot"* (Deut. 19:18–21). In addition to serving as a deterrent to perjury, this provision reflects the prevalent notion of measure for measure: an evil deed deserves to be punished by inflicting the same type of evil upon the perpetrator. Compare the Mesopotamian codes of law for similar notions.

4. *"A soul for a soul, eye for eye . . ."* (Deut. 19: 21). Compare Exodus 21:23–24 and Leviticus 24:17–18, and see below, Chapter III, Section B 6.

5. *"You shall do to him as he schemed to do"* (Deut. 19:19). The use of the term "schemed" rather than "did," and the contexts of verses 17 and 18, indicates that the verse refers to a case where the judges had discovered the false testimony *before* carrying out the sentence desired by the false witness. Should it make any difference if the erroneous sentence had already been carried out? (See Talmud, *Hulin* 11b, *Makkot* 2b, for a distinction.) What do you think of the claim of Abarbanel, *ad locum*, citing Nissim Girundi (*Ran*) and Isaac Aramaah that penalizing the false witness at that late stage would undermine public confidence in the validity of court verdicts?[118] Ovadya of Bertanuro, *ad locum*, argues that some limit had to be placed on executions of witnesses on claims that they were perjurors, or else there would be a chain reaction, with relatives of executed witnesses successively testifying that the ones who incriminated their relatives were perjurors.

(4) *Absolution from Guilt for Homicide (Deuteronomy 21:1–9, 22–23)*

1. If, in the land that the Lord your God is giving you to possess, someone slain is found lying on the earth, the identity of the slayer not being known;

2. your elders and judges shall go out and measure the distances from the corpse to the nearby towns.

3. The elders of the town nearest to the corpse shall

then take a heifer which has never been worked, which has never pulled in a yoke;

4. and the elders of that town shall bring the heifer down to a rocky valley, which is not tilled or sown. There, in the valley they shall break the heifer's neck.

5. The priests, sons of Levi, shall come forward, for the Lord your God has chosen them to serve Him and to pronounce blessing in the name of the Lord, and to decide every dispute and issue of ritual impurity due to blemishes.

6. Then all the elders of the town nearest to the corpse shall wash their hands over the heifer whose neck was broken in the valley.

7. And they shall pronounce this declaration: "Our hands did not shed his blood, nor did our eyes see it done.

8. Absolve, O Lord, Your people Israel whom You redeemed, and do not let guilt for the blood of the innocent remain among Your people Israel."

And they will be absolved of blood guilt.

9. You shall remove from your midst guilt for the blood of the innocent, thereby doing what is right in the sight of the Lord. . . .

22. If a man is guilty of a capital offense and is put to death, you shall then hang him on a tree.

23. But you must not let his corpse remain on the tree, you must bury him the same day. For a hanging body is an affront to God and you shall not defile the land that the Lord your God is giving you to possess.

Notes to Deuteronomy 21:1–9, 22–23

1. *"The elders of the town nearest to the corpse shall then take a heifer which has never been worked . . . bring the heifer down to a rocky valley, which is not tilled or sown. There in the valley, they shall break the heifer's neck"* (Deut. 21:3–4). What is the symbolic significance of bringing a young heifer that has never worked to a spot that has never been tilled and then to kill it by breaking the back of its neck (in contrast to the normal slaughtering method of slitting the *front* of the throat)? Are these related to the untimely and unnatural death of the victim, before he could reach his full human potential? Is the violent death of the heifer a symbolic substitute for the punishment deserved by the entire community?

2. *"Then the elders of the town nearest to the corpse shall wash their hands . . . and they pronounce this declaration 'our hands did not shed this blood nor did our eyes see it done'"* (Deut. 21:6–7). Why was it necessary for the elders and leaders of the town to proclaim that *they* had not killed the victim? Would anyone suspect they had? Compare the notion of communal responsibility here with the emphasis on individual responsibility in other portions of the Bible (e.g., "Par-

---

118. See Commentary of Don Isaac Abarbanel (reprinted Jerusalem, 1954), and Isaac Aramaah, *Akedat Yitzhok* (reprinted Jerusalem, 1951); Talmud, *Makkot* 2b. D. Hoffman, Responsa *Melamed Le'Hoil* (Frankfort, 1926), sec. 3, no. 101; J. Loewe, *Beer Ha'Golah* (Jerusalem, 1971), p. 24.

ents shall not be put to death for children, nor children be put to death for parents. Each person shall be put to death only for his own crime") (Deut. 24:16).[119]

3. *"For a hanging body is an affront to God"* (Deut. 21:23). Why is this an affront to God? Consider the perspective that "in the image of God, was man created."

(5) *Individual Dignity and Responsibility (Deuteronomy 24:6–17)*

6. A handmill or an upper millstone shall not be taken in pawn, for that would be taking someone's life in pawn.

7. If a man is found to have kidnapped a fellow Israelite, enslaving and selling him, that kidnapper shall die; thus you will remove evil from your midst.

8. In cases of a scaly affection, be most careful to do exactly as the Levitical priests instruct you. Take care to do as I have commanded them.

9. Remember what the Lord your God did to Miriam on the journey after you left Egypt.

10. When you make a loan of any sort to your neighbor, you must not enter his house to seize his pledge.

11. You must remain outside, while the man to whom you made the loan brings the pledge out to you.

12. If he is a poor man, you shall not keep his pledge overnight.

13. You must return the pledge to him at sundown, that he may sleep in his pledged garment and bless you; and it will be to your merit before the Lord your God.

14. You shall not abuse a needy and destitute laborer, whether a fellow countryman or a non-citizen in your communities.

15. You must pay him his wages on the same day, before the sun sets, for he is needy and urgently depends on it; else he will cry to the Lord against you and you will incur guilt. . . .

16. Parents shall not be put to death for children, nor children be put to death for parents: each person shall be put to death only for his own crime.

17. You shall not subvert the rights of the stranger or the fatherless; you shall not levy on a widow's garment. Remember that you were a slave in Egypt and that the Lord your God redeemed you from there; therefore do I enjoin you to observe this commandment.

Notes to Deuteronomy 24:6–17

1. *"When you make a loan of any sort to your neighbor, you must not enter his house to seize his pledge. You must remain outside while the man to whom you made the loan brings his pledge out to you"* (Deut. 24:10–11). This provision regarding forbidden search and seizure by a creditor sheds light on the biblical perspective of each man's right to privacy and dignity, resembling the later aphorism, "A man's home is his castle." (See below, Part Three, Chapter IX, Section B 5, however, for later developments in Judaic law on this point.)

2. *"Parents shall not be put to death for children, nor children be put to death for parents. Each person shall be put to death only for his own crime"* (Deut. 24:16). This expresses the principle of individual, rather than collective, responsibility. The latter was prevalent throughout the ancient Near East and has persisted in many cultures including that of the United States (e.g., conspiracy and felony-murder laws, see below). Why was it necessary to repeat this principle *twice* in the same verse?

How is the principle of individual responsibility, enunciated here to be reconciled with Exodus 20:5: "He visits the sins of the fathers upon the children"?[120]

Note the provisions of Article III, Section 3, of the United States Constitution: "The Congress shall have power to declare the punishment of treason, but no attainder of treason shall work corruption of blood, or forfeiture except during the life of the person attainted." What is the reason for applying the biblical notions of individual responsibility (and its requirement for two witnesses) to treason, but not to other crimes? (For a detailed exposition of the biblical provisions for forfeiture in American law, see J. J. Finkelstein, "The Goring Ox," 46 *Temple Law Quarterly* [Winter, 1973]: 169.)

(6) *Limitations on Flogging (Deuteronomy 25:1–3)*

1. When there is a dispute between men and they go to law, and a decision is rendered declaring the one in the right and the other in the wrong;

2. if the guilty one is to be flogged, the judge shall have him bend over and be given lashes in the presence of the judges, by count, as his guilt warrants.

3. He may be given up to forty lashes, but not more, lest being flogged to excess, your brother be degraded before your eyes.

---

119. See also Talmud, *Shevuot* 39a and *Sanhedrin* 27b, regarding collective responsibility to "heaven" but not to man. For the very different treatment of the same case in other cultures of the ancient Near East, see S. Feigin, *Homicide in the Laws of the Ancient East*, vol. 32–33; *Ha'Tekufah*, pp. 740, 750; E. Neufeld, *The Hittite Laws* (London, 1951), p. 259.

120. See also "Will you also destroy the just with the wicked? "Will the judge of the whole world not do justice?" (Gen. 18:25); "If one man sins, will you be angry at the entire congregation?" (Num. 16:22); see text above discussing Deut. 21.

Notes to Deuteronomy 25:1–3

1. The limitation on the number of lashes was designed to prevent the offender from suffering grievous physical injury and from being unduly degraded.

2. *"Lest . . . your brother be degraded before your eyes"* (Deut. 25:3). In verse 2, the offender is called "the guilty one." Why is he here called, "your brother"? Note that since in this case a whipping was ordered by the judges, rather than simply a payment of money damages, the case must refer to a serious offense against another. Nevertheless, the perspective is that the offender should *not* be unduly degraded. This should be compared with the attitude and provisions in the contemporaneous Mesopotamian law codes, as well as the treatment of criminal offenders in the United States today.

(7) *Helping a Victim of Unjust Aggression (Deuteronomy 25:11–12)*

11. If men wrestle together, a man and his brother, and the wife of one approaches to rescue her husband from his assailant, and she stretches out her hand and grasps his genitals (literally, "his embarrassment"),

12. you shall cut off her hand. Do not have pity.

Notes to Deuteronomy 25:11–12

1. *"You shall cut off her hand"* (Deut. 25:12). Here, too, as in Deuteronomy 19:21 and Exodus 21:23–25, the provision was understood figuratively as requiring the payment of monetary damages, rather than a literal amputation of the hand. Why, however, was such a provision necessary, when it had already been provided for in Exodus 21:19, 21–25 (see notes, above)?

2. Isn't a wife justified in taking steps to protect her husband against an assailant? Does the provision refer to a case where the *extreme* action taken by the wife, which might emasculate or kill the assailant, was uncalled for by the circumstances? Notice the language used here, "If men shall wrestle together, a man and his brother." Compare to Exodus 21:22, "If men wrestle," where the word "together" and the phrase "a man and his brother" are omitted.

Are the imperatives "You shall cut off her hand. Do not have pity," addressed to the court, and do they refer to a penalty to be inflicted upon her *by the court, after* the incident, or do they counsel a *bystander* to take steps against the wife *during* her act, in order to prevent her from emasculating or killing the victim? To whom does the "you," in "You shall cut off her hand" refer—to the court or to a bystander? If the latter, would it indicate a perspective that any bystander is *obligated* to act to save one who is being attacked, even

if this meant harming the attacker? Might the phrase "Do not have pity" therefore require that anyone who is present is required to save the victim, even though this means harming the assailant, whose acts (like that of the wife here) might otherwise be looked upon with sympathy (see *Sifre, ad locum*)?

3. What type of society is reflected in the biblical laws? As mentioned previously, they contain no normative provisions regarding sales, credit, and leases of fields, which latter, particularly, were very prominent in the Mesopotamian codes. In fact, there is hardly any mention of commercial law in the Bible. Sales of land are usually mentioned in the context of one who is forced to sell his lands because of poverty, rather than for commercial purposes (Lev. 25:25), although the Bible does recount the purchase of land by Abraham and Jacob and the sale of Joseph as a slave. The Bible does not mention any commercial or legal documents, except for a passing reference to a bill of divorce. These documents were very widespread in Mesopotamia at that time. There is also no mention in the Pentateuch of laws regarding architects, physicians (except for the passing reference to the physician in Exod. 21:19), or the professional soldier. The procedure and requirements for marriage and divorce are not stated, nor is adoption mentioned in the Bible. The only social classes described are slaves and freemen (divided into priests, Levites, and Israelites). The Mesopotamian societies seemed to reflect a more complex economic and social structure that included nobles and semifree as well.

Is pentateuchal law suited only to a simple pastoral or agricultural society? Does it contain principles that would permit the ordering of a more complex, commercial and urbanized society, and was it so intended? If so, why are its laws formulated to reflect a simplified society? Would detailed norms appropriate for a complex, commercial society be intelligible to a people at a very early stage of societal development? (See below for the effect of conditions in biblical society on biblical law.)

E. *Studies in Nonbiblical Legal Documents*

1. CUNEIFORM LAW AND THE HISTORY OF CIVILIZATION
(By E. A. Speiser)*

I

Civilizations, like individuals, are known by their works. The most significant contributions of antiquity

*From *Proceedings of the American Philosophical Society*, vol. 107, no. 6 (1963).

are those that posterity took over and has kept alive. And nowhere is the survival span greater than with the legacy of the historic civilization of Mesopotamia.

Our cultural debt to that remote civilization is far more substantial and varied than is generally recognized. When we reckon today our years by the sun and our weeks by the moon, and call the days of the week after the planets; when we look at our time-pieces to tell the hours and the minutes and the seconds in conformance with the sexagesimal system of numeration; when we approach the "babel" of tongues with the tools of linguistic analysis; when we write our official records, our scholarly treatises, our literary creations, or our private letters; when we reaffirm our faith in laws impersonally conceived and in government that shuns autocracy—when we do these and many other things, we are utilizing, whether we know it or not, the results of an immemorial experiment in living in which ancient Mesopotamia played a leading part.

Two of these achievements in particular stand out above all others, namely, writing and law. Writing has been perhaps the greatest single factor in the advance of mankind to date; for though science may have overcome space, writing conquered time, by converting all history into a continuous and indelible record. Yet that particular contribution of Mesopotamia was but an incidental by-product, a surface feature rather than a basic element of the parent civilization. Law, on the other hand, was bound up intimately with the very fabric of the underlying society. Since Mesopotamian law was to emerge as the overriding cultural factor at home and a potent influence on other cultures near and far, a closer look at that institution should be of more than merely antiquarian interest. It can be shown, I believe, that the subject matter transcends regional, chronological, and inter-disciplinary boundaries.

With so much involved, it is fortunate that the pertinent sources are plentiful—indeed an embarrassment of riches. Our material ranges in time from the middle of the third to the end of the first millennium B.C., spanning thus the first half of all recorded history. And because there is at first nothing like it from any other land, the early legal records from Mesopotamia constitute the initial chapter in the history of jurisprudence in general. Geographically, the records stretch from Iran to the shores of the Mediterranean, and from Asia Minor to the borders of Egypt, thereby outstripping in each direction the boundaries of historic Mesopotamia. The languages involved include Sumerian, Akkadian, Elamite, and Hittite, among others. The total volume is literally incalculable, since much that has been dug up so far is yet to be published, and new texts are coming to light all the time. A single private home in the small provincial town of Nuzi, covering but a few gen-

erations, has yielded an archive of close to a thousand documents—almost three times as many as have come down to us from all of Egypt prior to the Persian era. As a result, we know that minor and out-of-the-way community from the middle of the second millennium B.C. more intimately than we know many a European capital at the time of Columbus.

The main thing, however, is that the legal tradition concerned is closely integrated in spite of the underlying differences in date, geography, political background, and language. The unifying factors outweigh all the divisive elements combined. One such common bond is the cuneiform script which was shared by all the languages and countries in question, so much so that even precision-conscious jurists speak today of "cuneiform law" rather than Mesopotamian law. And if pedants should demur on the ground that no discipline is wedge-shaped, and that such a label might be all too suggestive of sharp practices, they may be assured that the name is only a short-cut and that the practice was pursued with utmost propriety.

Another major unifying factor derives from the character and content of cuneiform law: wherever the system was in force, and whatever local modifications it may have exhibited, the fundamental concept was one and the same. This concept can be traced in each instance to its home base in southern Mesopotamia, the very region from which the script itself had fanned out as part of a broader cultural process. All in all, we have abundant material to study most of the periods and areas concerned, and thus gauge the grip that cuneiform law exercised on its host of followers throughout the long history of Mesopotamian civilization, as well as the effect that it had on later cultures.

II

Complex systems are often found to stem from deceptively simple principles. Cuneiform law is a case in point.

The basic premise of cuneiform law, the source to which the institution as a whole owed both its content and its vitality, may be summarized as follows: Law is an aspect of the cosmic order and hence ultimately the gift of the forces of the universe. The human ruler is but a temporary trustee who is responsible to the gods for the implementation of the cosmic design. Because the king is thus answerable to powers outside himself, his subjects are automatically protected against autocracy, and the individual has the comfort and assurance of certain inalienable rights.

Now if this is indeed the master key to the social history of Mesopotamia, it ought to operate with regularity regardless of time and place. The fact is that it does just that. The concept of law that has just been outlined is implicit in the very term that the Mesopotamians used for a comprehensive definition. In Akkadian, which merely reflects here the antecedent Sumerian, "law" is epitomized by the nontechnical phrase *kittum u mēšarum*, literally "truth and right." The two nouns are mutually complementary. In the Epilogue to his celebrated Code (from which the quotation at the beginning of this paper has been adduced) Hammurabi states explicitly that the sun god Shamash, patron of justice, bestowed on him the various forms of *kittum* (expressed in the pl. *kīnātim*), whereas the authority of the legislator was limited to *mēšarum*. A slightly earlier ruler of the nearby center of Mari goes even further. Shamash himself was not the source of *kittum* but only its guardian, for that boon, being eternal and universal, could not originate with gods, let alone mortals. An immutable aspect of the cosmic order, *kittum* is semantically the same as Biblical *'ᵉmet* (from **'amint*), the original force of which still survives in the common loan word "Amen." The independent function of a ruler, whether divine or human, is confined to *mēšarum*, that is, just and equitable implementation. In other words, *kittum* and *mēšarum* combined express eternal verities. Jointly, they spell law, but it is a broad and universally valid concept that is thus described, a system that is tantamount to a treasured way of life.

How the Mesopotamians arrived at such an affirmation is outside the scope of the present statement. What matters is that they did and that this approach was to have immensely fruitful consequences. At home, it made for order and stability under a state that was incompatible with autocracy, not just in theory but in actual practice; and the subjects, for their part, cherished the system, for it put even the lowliest among them on a par with the ruler in their common dependence upon higher powers. Abroad, various other lands proved eager to follow suit, however hostile they might be on other counts toward the political set-up in contemporary Babylonia.

Let us review briefly some of the major results in the central concept that has just been outlined, starting with internal developments.

1. Truths that are considered valid forever cannot vary with time or person. Hence the laws that embody or reflect such truths are both timeless and impersonal.

2. Interpretation of the law conceived in this fashion must not be left to lay parties. It has to be entrusted instead to professional judges.

3. In their effort to arrive at decisions in consonance with sanctioned norms, the judges were often obliged to look to established precedent. In this pursuit they were aided not only by compilations or codes, but also by comprehensive dictionaries of legal phrases and clauses, which had been compiled as early as 2000 B.C., some centuries before Hammurabi.

4. A professional judiciary and the validity of precedent go hand in hand with the paramount authority of the written document, its ubiquitous presence, and its reverent handling. This is why Mesopotamians were such ardent believers in texts, and more particularly the legal document, the written word serving as a tangible guarantee of the rights of the individual in society, and of harmony between society and the cosmos.

5. A commitment in writing was a commitment not merely to the other party or parties, but even more so to the higher powers from whom the law stemmed. This solemn obligation was underscored by the use of the cylinder seal. Attestation by means of a seal impression was markedly more binding than a signature or a sworn assurance. The cylinder was fundamentally a detachable surrogate for the person, a piece of oneself. In leaving its impression on a clay tablet, man surrendered himself to the powers of nature, who could then mete out due punishment in case of noncompliance. In exceptionally serious situations even this ominous pledge was insufficient; hence the still more personal imprints of fingernails, or impressions of the fringe of the garment worn at the time in question were either added or substituted. For the most part, however, the seal was deemed to be adequate. It identified the wearer as a responsible member of a civilized community, one who had been deputized, as it were, by the immortal stewards of the universe. As Herodotus was to remind us after the books on an independent Mesopotamia had already been closed at long last, no self-respecting Babylonian was likely to be seen without such a seal. And the Bible tells us that even distant cultural clients of Mesopotamia subscribed to the same beliefs and practices, as witness the incident of Judah and Tamar. The seal was thus in effect an isotope of Mesopotamia's cultural expansion and an index to that country's influence. All this gives new meaning to the term "Fertile Crescent," a meaning that was scarcely apparent to J. H. Breasted when he coined the phrase.

III

So much for the essential characteristics of Mesopotamian law in its domestic operation. Its strength derived from the premise that law on earth must be in harmony with cosmic law and order. It remains now to examine the dynamic capabilities of the Mesopotamian system as evidenced by its effect on Babylonia's neighbors, other societies of the ancient Near East, and finally the Classical world and hence ultimately also Western civilization.

To begin with, Assyria remained to the end the bitter political rival of Babylonia. As a society, however, Assyria was thoroughly Babylonianized—in language, religious and cultural traditions, and particularly in law. There is indeed the inherent probability that the spread of legal concepts was largely responsible in turn for the other instances of cultural and social colonization. The same holds true of Western Iran in so far as law and government were concerned. To be sure, both Assyria and Elam were ruled at one time or another from Southern Babylonia, which might have accounted for the nonpolitical influence as well. But there are other instances where no comparable political factors were at work. The Syrian city-state of Alalah, for example, was never dominated by Babylonia; yet it used Babylonian law and struggled with the Akkadian language as far back as the age of Hammurabi. Just so, the kingdom of Mitanni followed the same course at a time when Mitanni was the leading state in Western Asia. Similarly, Ugarit had its own dialect and employed a local alphabetic script for various administrative and literary purposes. When it came, however, to legal and diplomatic matters, Ugarit fell back on syllabic cuneiform and the Akkadian language, for such was the accepted practice in that part of the world. The Hittites, for their part, composed their legal code in their own distinctive kind of Indo-European or Indo-Hittite. Yet the very fact that the Hittites produced a law code altogether, one which reflects Mesopotamian influence not only in script but also in concept, places the product within the province of Mesopotamian jurisprudence.

It is thus apparent that one of the outstanding characteristics of Mesopotamian law was its strong appeal to other cultural centers. Where the exported goods still carry their original wrapping and labels—the script, the language, and the formal document—the ultimate source can be identified at a glance. But even where such identifying marks are absent, the content can still be traced to its home base. A primary case in point is furnished by the Bible.

This is not to dredge up once again the old pan-Babylonian heresy. On the contrary, it is now increasingly apparent that the Biblical process as a whole originated in a resolute protest against the religious orientation of Mesopotamia. But this does not imply by any means that the Biblical leaders renounced everything that stemmed from east of the Euphrates. There is scarcely a section of the Old Testament, especially in its early portions, that fails to reflect some form of influence from Abraham's homeland—which is precisely what one should expect in the circumstances. And nowhere is such influence more pronounced than in the general field of law.

Whether one takes up the Book of the Covenant in Exodus, the legal material in Leviticus, Numbers, or Deuteronomy, or pertinent passages in various narrative accounts, the most intimate kind of connection is immediately apparent to anyone who has dealt with both the Biblical and the Mesopotamian material. Yet mere correspondence in detail does not begin to define the closeness of the relationship involved. It is in the basic concepts of law and government that the strong ties between the Bible and Mesopotamia are especially prominent and significant.

In Israel, as in Mesopotamia, man was never the source of the law but only its servant. In both lands law was a gift from on high, a way of life that made all the difference between civilization and barbarism. The Bible epitomizes this approach in its term "Torah." If the Torah were no more than a collection of legalistic norms, Israel could scarcely have pointed the way to spiritual and social progress. Yet it was in Mesopotamia that the process got underway, thanks to the realization that *mesarum* without *kittum* (or *sedeq* without *'emet* in biblical terminology) would be but a blind alley.

As in Mesopotamia, moreover, so too in Israel the law was the real backbone of society. This is why legal analysis was taken up with renewed vigor in the Mishnah, and eventually attained its fullest scope in the Babylonian Talmud. This last achievement surely owed a great deal to the circumstance of its Babylonian locale. Although historic Mesopotamia had expired centuries earlier, her legal traditions were far from extinct. Small wonder, therefore, that the Babylonian Talmud teems with loanwords not only from the Akkadian but even from the antecedent Sumerian. Thanks to such interconnections, the Talmudic and the cuneiform sources have much to offer each other in terms of illustration and clarification; this enormously rich mine of information is as yet virtually untapped. To this very day, the orthodox Jew uses a Sumerian term when he speaks of divorce. And when he participates in the reading of the Torah lesson in the synagogue, he still touches the pertinent place in the scroll with the fringe of his prayer shawl, wholly unaware of the fact that he is thus re-enacting the scene in which the ancient Mesopotamian impressed the hem of his garment on a clay tablet, as proof of his commitment to the provisions of the legal record. The language and the persons and the circumstances have changed, the objectives are different, but the symbolism remains the same after some forty centuries.

Another case in point is the legal material in Old Aramaic. The papyri from Elephantine, at the southern extremity of Egypt, a small island manned by a Jewish garrison in the fifth century B.C., represent legal records that are unmistakably Mesopotamian in contents and phraseology. So strong was the underlying legal tradition that it could be maintained, in a different tongue and amidst a sharply dissimilar society, nearly two thousand miles from its ultimate center of origin.

There is further the instance of Islamic law. So many heterogeneous traditions converge in that vast conglomerate that to separate the component parts is a task calling for a combination of specialists. Nevertheless, the fact is plain that this discipline did not begin to thrive until Iraq—Mesopotamia's Arabian successor—had taken a hand in it. Devotion to law was evidently in the local air, or soil.

A brief word, in passing, about the situation in ancient Egypt. No country could have achieved Egypt's cultural record, and maintained it over a comparable period of time, without a solid framework of internal law. The only question, then, is the kind of law that prevailed there. The answer is not far to seek. The same article of faith that deified the pharaoh made it inevitable that he be also the source and master of all law. It is no surprise, therefore, that Egypt has yielded no evidence of any kind of legal code impersonally conceived, since the authority of such a code would have competed with the personal authority of the pharaoh. Nor can the virtual absence of legal records—there are fewer such witnesses from all of Egypt over a period of two millennia than there are from a single stray house in Mesopotamia representing no more than two centuries—be charged to pure coincidence. The obvious reason was the dominant concept of law in Egypt. By the same token, Egyptian law had scant appeal for outsiders. As suggested above, complex issues can sometimes be reduced to surprisingly simple explanations.

IV

There is thus abundant and compelling evidence that the legal tradition which originated in Mesopotamia had enough vitality to exceed its native limits in time as well as in space. It was a living and life-giving tradition because, in the final analysis, it sprang from man's hope to achieve harmony with the cosmos. The question that remains to be posed is whether these social attainments in the ancient Near East had any important bearing on the Classical world. The problem can be stated at this time only in barest outline.

A direct comparison of cuneiform and Classical law is all but ruled out by chronological considerations. Legal documents in Greek do not turn up until the sixth century B.C., and then only in a trickle. The Twelve Tables of the Romans are later still. Moreover, what little we do get at first is admittedly primitive, and hence reflects an early stage of development. In short, where formal law is concerned, the Classical lands got off to a relatively late start. By then, Assyria had already retired from history, and Babylonia was no longer a self-ruled country. Cuneiform law as such

had only a few centuries of reflex existence left to it. In these circumstances there is little opportunity to synchronize legal data from the outgoing East with those from the emerging West.

In their attempts at a comparative appraisal, nevertheless, some students have sought to trace the Twelve Tables and the prior legal material from Greece all the way back to the Code of Hammurabi. All such efforts are foredoomed to failure. Even in Hammurabi's time, legal imports from Babylon were adjusted to local needs and practices. Nor were Hurrian and Hittite and Biblical laws direct transcripts of Mesopotamian models. How, then, could there be a direct correlation between Classical law and Mesopotamian prototypes of far away and long ago?

The question, therefore, is not so much one of outright borrowing as of geographic and chronological links. In due course, Hellenism was to constitute a bridge between the Near East and Rome, which carried legal traffic among other kinds. To quote Paul Koschaker, himself a professor of Roman jurisprudence, "In my opinion there can be no doubt about the inclusion of oriental legal matter in Roman law—using the term 'oriental' in its broadest sense to include Hellenistic material as well." But the Hellenistic age cannot be pushed back past the middle of the first millennium B.C., let alone leave room for the required incubation period. The contacts, then, must be sought elsewhere and much earlier.

We know, of course, that the Phoenicians flourished at the turn of the second millennium, and that farther back the Hittites were a dominant power. Both peoples were in close touch with the Aegeans. Indeed, Hittite relations with the West were intimate enough to be reflected in Greek mythology and literature. Nevertheless, the case we are after does not have to be made abroad. Aegeans themselves have been positively identified in Syria in the fourteenth century B.C. In the port of Ugarit a special quarter was occupied by Minoans who had established there a merchant colony. Similar trading posts existed in all likelihood elsewhere along the Phoenician coast. Now trade was the one occupation above all others in which the written document was a necessity in all areas within the reach of cuneiform law. As was pointed out above, there are many business documents from Ugarit itself which were written, significantly enough, not in the local alphabet but in syllabic cuneiform and in the Akkadian language. The Minoan traders could not escape involvement in such written business transactions. In due time, they were bound to copy the process in dealings among themselves. As a matter of fact, samples of Minoan script have actually turned up in Ugarit, for law and literacy went hand in hand. The subsequent adoption

of the Phoenician alphabet by the Greeks was due undoubtedly to similar commercial intercourse. Thus it
was barter, not Homer, that made the Greeks literate.
Progress often travels by such devious paths.

Now when traders take over a script in compliance
with the legal demands of their profession, they have
been exposed not only to the juridical details but also
to the underlying concepts. Since the ideas that shaped
the law of the Mesopotamian pioneers promoted a way
of life that militated against autocracy in government,
it would be an anachronism to persist in the claim that
the Greeks' aversion to authoritarianism was wholly a
homegrown product.

When it comes to the development of Roman law,
there are many threads to disentangle. One has to
reckon with the influence of Greece, eventual contacts
with the Near East itself, and the growing administrative pressures of an increasingly unwieldy political
structure. Each of these factors must have had its effect
on Roman law. The results could scarcely be homogeneous. At a minimum, Rome was indebted to the Near
East, though indirectly rather than directly, for the law
code and the legal document. That these instruments
did not in the end prevent absolutism was due apparently to internal developments. But one cannot help
wondering, just the same, whether Rome's growing
familiarity with Egypt, the one Near Eastern exception
to an otherwise consistent anti-autocratic norm, did not
play its part in bringing absolute rule to Rome.

Today, though we freely acknowledge our manifold
debt to Greece and the Bible, we do not always appreciate the extent to which Israel and Greece contributed
to one of our fundamental affirmations, namely, that
truly constructive power is power vested outside the
agent who wields it. This abiding truth, however, was
discovered long before the start of the biblical and the
Greek experiences. It was first glimpsed in ancient
Mesopotamia; and once glimpsed, it was held on to
tenaciously as a source of strength at home and an example to others abroad.

In over-all retrospect, we are justified in adding to
the proverbial maxim *Ex Oriente Lux* a fitting twin
with the name of *Ex Oriente Lex*. The light in this instance is in many ways but another aspect of law. And
the region of the Orient which had much to do with the
progressive dissemination of both light and law was
ancient, but by no means outmoded, Mesopotamia.

Notes to Speiser, "Cuneiform Law and the History of Civilization"

Although Speiser notes that contemporary law is, in
general, indebted to cuneiform law, some details should
further be pointed out concerning the manner in which
the law of the ancient Near East affected other ancient

civilizations and ultimately shaped the course of our
own law today.

First of all, the law of the ancient Near East had an
effect on law in early Greece, and, through this medium,
it influenced subsequent legal systems and thoughts.[121]
Jewish law was affected by Mesopotamian law, and
many of the legal systems in Europe were in turn influenced by Jews who migrated there. Canon law, too,
was influenced by Judaic law.[122] Roman law, which
had a profound effect on European law, was also influenced by the law of ancient Greece, Canon law, Judaic law, and, in general, by the law of the Mediterranean world.[123] Islamic law was greatly influenced by
Jewish law and, in turn, had an influence upon European law, as well as North African law and Hindu
law.[124]

One must be cautious, however, in alleging cross-
cultural "influences" since alleged influences of the law
of one culture upon another are extremely difficult to
substantiate conclusively. Parallel development may be
responsible for what at first glance appears to be influence. Moreover, one may observe similar social institutions, such as the family and commercial transactions,
that exist in different cultures. Because of their comparable contexts, these institutions may receive similar
treatment in different societies.

Although of minor significance, it is nevertheless also
interesting to note the use of similar terminology in
many different legal systems, such as the use of the
biblical phraseology regarding "tunneling" under a
house by a burglar as expressed in the Bible (Exod.
22:1), the Vulgate, and Lex Saxonum of the eighth
century; the use of the phrase *"diatiki"* in the Talmud,
referring to a will and last testament, and the Greek
term *"ditheke"* used in the same connection; the similar
terms used for divorce in Hindu and Islamic law; and
the use of the term *"listim"* (robber, brigand) in Jewish
law, which appears derived from the Greek *"lestes."*[125]
These, of course, may only reflect the influence of form,
rather than content. So, too, the use of the water ordeal
in Europe in the ninth century (and in the Salem witch-
craft trials in Massachusetts) was predicated upon a
theory that the waters created by a monotheistic God

121. See C. H. Gordon, *The Common Background of Greek
and Hebrew Civilization* (London, 1962); M. C. Astour, *Hel-
lenosemitica* (Leiden, 1965).

122. J. Rabinowitz, *Jewish Law, Its Influence on the Development of Legal Institutions* (New York, 1956); R. Yaron,
"Jewish Law and Other Legal Systems of Antiquity," *Journal
of Semitic Studies* 4 (1959): 308–31.

123. H. Jolowicz, *Roman Foundation of Modern Law* (Oxford, 1957).

124. Jackson, "Evolution and Foreign Influence," pp. 383–
84.

125. Ibid., p. 376.

would reject the impure person and keep him afloat. This has been claimed to bear a resemblance to a similar ordeal in Mesopotamia,[126] which was based on the belief that the water itself was a deity or that a deity resided in the water.

These and other evidences of analogous forms, which have often been cited by scholars, are, however, far from strong evidence of important mutual influence of one legal system upon another. Similarly, the claims of other scholars that the law developed in all countries in fixed stages, determined by the underlying material cultures, which always develop in a distinct evolutionary pattern (the stage of food gatherers, stage of hunters, etc.),[127] has not been proven. All that one can say is that the material culture of a society significantly affects its laws.[128]

2. AUTHORITY AND LAW IN ANCIENT EGYPT
(By John A. Wilson)*

Any brief characterization of a history covering three thousand years will of necessity have to deal rather brusquely with the complexities of a changing organism. Further, the statement which follows may have certain dicta which seem to be competitive or mutually contradictory, such as the argument that the king of Egypt, as a god, was the sole source of law and authority, yet relied upon other gods for oracular direction and delegated great legal responsibility to the vizier and other officials. If such statements are paradoxical, it is because the Egyptian state retained the paradox of a dogma which insisted upon the divine absolutism of the monarch, along with a practice of government which utilized a number of responsible agents. Finally, the attempt to understand another culture in its own terms always has a semantic difficulty in the inexactness of the translation of concepts from one culture to the other.

Authority within the State

The basic proposition with regard to authority and the source of law in ancient Egypt is that the King of Egypt was a god. This may have been expressed in different ways in the course of Egyptian history, and this official dogma may have been imperfectly carried out in different periods, but there is abundant evidence from the beginning of the dynasties down to the Roman emperors that the central dogma of the state was that the ruler of Egypt was no representative or servant of the gods, did not rule by a divine right which came to him with his throne, but ruled because he was born a god, with the divine function of rule inherent in his physical and spiritual being. In the very first dynasty inscriptions designate the king as the god Horus, and some of the Pyramid Texts which exhibit an archaic type of writing and which apparently refer back to a predynastic situation insist upon his divine nature.

As the god who alone possessed and directed the state, the king of Egypt had certain divine attributes of rule. The most common are two, *hu* and *sia, or* sometimes three, *hu, sia,* and *ma'at*. We shall translate *hu* as "authoritative command," *sia* as "perception," and *ma'at* as "justice"; in other words, *hu*, the divine ability to create or recreate a situation by speech, *sia*, the divine recognition and understanding of situations, and *ma'at*, the maintenance of a divine order within society. All three attributes were deified by the Egyptians, Hu and Sia as gods and Ma'at as a goddess. To the king it was said: "Authoritative command is in thy mouth, perception is in thy heart, and thy tongue is the shrine of justice." Elsewhere, the king was said to have carried off authoritative command by conquest, to have gained control of perception. The first two, the ability to see and know a situation and the ability to meet that situation by command, are divine attributes which by themselves might work for good or evil; the third, justice or order or truth, is an attribute which imposes responsibilities upon the king, since it involves conformance with principles of the universe which come down from the creation or it involves right-dealing among humans. This *ma'at* is the most important of the divine attributes of the king, and we shall return to it later. Here it should be added that *ma'at*, in its sense of truth, order, or regularity, belonged to the world which the gods set up at the creation. Therefore, as the coronation of each king was a recreation for Egypt, the coronation texts insist that *ma'at* has been restored through the effective arrival upon earth of this eternal yet new god, the incoming king.

Nevertheless, the role of the king was not as arbitrary as most of the texts seem to claim. His brother gods recaptured a considerable share of the direction of specific acts of government. At the beginning of the Fifth Dynasty, the apparently unlimited authority of the king was checked by the abrupt rise in power of the sun-god Re. We cannot tell at what point in Egyptian history the gods began to express their desires through various kinds of oracles, but this agency becomes increasingly

126. See, e.g., Code of Hammurabi, sec. 2, in Pritchard, *Ancient Near Eastern Texts.* For a similar belief in Greece, see *The Iliad*, trans. Samuel Butler (reprinted New York, 1942), pp. 321–35.

127. See A. S. Diamond, *Primitive Law* (London, 1935), and Diamond, *The Evolution of Law and Order* (London, 1953).

128. See also the comprehensive theories of legal development, similarly unproven, set forth by Maine in *Ancient Law* (London, 1861) and *The Quest for Law* (London, 1941).

*From *Journal of the American Oriental Society*, April, 1959. Footnotes have been omitted.

clear as time goes on. The king himself, as a priest of all the gods, might visit a temple and lay a proposition before a god, as Ramses III sought the approval of Amon-Re for military campaigns. Thus the communication was directly between the god and the god-king. However, in other instances the god seems to have acted independently in affairs of the state, as when the god Amon-Re in sacred procession sought out an unimportant prince and indicated that this young man was to be the king whom we call Thut-mose III. Again, Hatshepsut refers to the dark period when Egypt lay under the foreign domination of the Hyksos conquerors: "They ruled without Re, and he did not act by divine command down to [the reign of] my majesty." That is, since the barbarian Hyksos did not use the sun-god in their government, that god refused to give oracular direction to the state throughout their rule and even later.

This brief notice of oracles is all that will be said here as an indirect reference to the authoritative role of the priests within the state. Their agency did not appear in the expressed dogma of the state, but it may nevertheless have been very effective.

The most important "civil" official in the sacred state of Egypt was the vizier, who at first had been selected from the king's family, but by the Fifth Dynasty might be unrelated to the king. From the same dynasty on, he enjoyed a subsidiary title, or perhaps an epithet, "the Prophet of *Ma'at*," that is, the priest who might speak for the goddess Truth or Justice. One official tells us of his appointment to be Prophet of *Ma'at*, with the proud boast: "I was a noble, the second of the king, the fourth of him who judged the Pair." This is remarkable language for one who was not a god: he claimed to be a partner of the king, as well as a partner of the god Thoth, who judged the pair of contesting gods, Horus and Seth. This is the clearest possible statement of the independent responsibility of this highest magistrate in the land, even though the accompanying text is careful to emphasize that this vizier acted only in strict conformance with the principles which the king had laid down for his office.

Those principles of just procedure and attitude will not be detailed here, but two points might be noted. First, in addition to the regular and formal hearing in his audience hall, when appellants might present their formal pleas, the vizier had to walk forth every day, so that poor or timid people might also have a chance to appeal to him for justice. Second, the king's charge to the vizier is very detailed, insists upon the strictest impartiality, and also directs that all of the vizier's judicial activity be carried out "in conformance with the regulations and that everything be done in conformance with the precedent therefor." This sounds as though the vizier had very little personal discretion, as though he

had to be scrupulous in maintaining justice according to known law, but essentially was merely the mouthpiece or the prophet for justice. The king uses the curious words to the vizier: "The place of refuge for the official is to act in conformance with the regulations." Despite the very sweeping range of functions laid upon the vizier, his individual authority was thoroughly limited by known precedents and procedures from the past. Perhaps, after all, only the king, who was a god, could dispense justice in terms of ethical principles, rather than customary procedures.

The Egyptian texts often relate how the king called together his counselors and sought their advice. This turns out to have no legislative force, since such a consultative assembly appears only in contexts where the king uses them as a sounding-board for his own ideas, or where the officials give a timorous advice which the king brusquely rejects in favor of his superhuman wisdom. This, to be sure, is a devise of propagandistic literature, in order to emphasize the higher qualities of the pharaoh, but it does indicate that the voice of the majority had no such weight in Egypt as it had in Mesopotamia.

Egypt is a land six hundred miles long, and the sole ruler could not exercise personal authority everywhere at all times. An elaborate bureaucracy was constructed, which dispensed justice and carried out administration in the king's name. As a matter of practical necessity, this included considerable local responsibility and therefore authority. The autobiographies of officials frequently assert this provincial independence in the claim that a noble has undertaken forthright action to keep his province free from disaster or that he had judged his people with impartiality. Thus, although the king was theoretically the sole source of law and authority, in practice he sought the backing of the gods, delegated a heavy responsibility to the vizier, and also delegated much local autonomy to the nobles in their own home districts.

The king was the god who dispensed rule, and the people were his materials to be ruled. He had a responsibility to maintain *ma'at* in his realm, and he had a proprietary responsibility to maintain his flock in a prosperous condition. But the people were only mortals, and they had no inherent right to justice. They could only be humbly grateful if they were nurtured toward prosperity and did receive an impartial and paternalistic justice. At one period in Egyptian history, the troubled times between the Old and Middle Kingdoms, there was a debate as to whether an ordinary Egyptian had a right to demand justice, but the normal situation in Egypt was that *ma'at*-justice was the king's offering to the gods, rather than a debt which the king owed to his subjects.

The Laws of the State

Egypt had neighbors in Asia who wrote down laws, arranged in such a systematic way and having such comprehensive coverage that it is customary to speak of codes of law in the Asiatic cultures. Despite all the written documents which have come down to us from ancient Egypt, we possess neither a body of law which is comparable to the Asiatic codes, nor any textual references to such laws elsewhere, nor even a later tradition about a king or official who was a law-giver or law-codifier until one comes down to the late tradition about King Bocchoris, who reigned about 700 B.C. We do have legal documents, such as testaments and transfers of property, as well as abbreviated records of court proceedings. These give us information about legal procedure but nothing about law. We do have specific legal regulations issued to cover specific situations, such as decrees exempting individual temples from the obligation to supply forced labor for the state, or a decree banishing a disloyal priest from his post. But these are decrees rather than law.

It is necessary to remove from consideration the former understanding of one Egyptian scene, with its accompanying text. When the Egyptian vizier sat in judicial hearing, forty objects were spread out on four mats in front of him, and it was formerly assumed that these were forty scrolls of law. The Egyptian word for these forty objects has now appeared in other contexts, and it seems that they were instruments used in punishment, such as leather straps. These then would be symbols of the punishing power of the state, and not the written, impersonal law toward which an appellant might stretch out his hand in supplication.

Since Egypt was blessed by having on earth a god as king, law proceeded from his mouth, always vitally renewed, and no codification was necessary or even proper. Of course legal procedure was followed in Egypt, but the specific practice must have stemmed from the customary law of the land before there was a unified state. It is even possible that such customary law differed in different parts of Egypt; that could well be within the divine understanding of the king as to what was good for his people.

Egypt had a word for a specific regulation or the law to cover a single situation, *hap*, but she had no word for law in general. The all-embracing term which applied to legal procedure and the spirit in which legal procedure was undertaken was *ma'at*, which in different contexts may mean: "order, right, right-dealing, rightfulness, righteousness, truth, justice." There was no distinction between "truth" and "justice"; both were covered by the term *ma'at*. Thus *ma'at* as "truth" involved right relations to "facts" as they were understood

in a sacred society, and *ma'at* as "justice" involved right relations between the governor and those who were governed as this was understood in a sacred society. The concept of *ma'at* definitely belonged to the religious order; it was the substance upon which gods fed; it was the daily offering of the king to the gods. It was thus a spirit which properly pervaded the civil carrying out of government and justice for the ends of religion.

The ancient Egyptians always shrank from the finality of carrying a series of concepts or a series of experiences on to their logical conclusions. They preferred to compromise or conciliate, to work things out on a topical basis, rather than to systematize experience into a set of working principles for the future. Crises could be met with flexibility of action, if one were not obligated to follow written principles such as lie behind a code of law. Further, each king was a newly reborn god, a new source of verbal law, and it would be unbefitting if he were to be made the heir to a long-standing code which came from outside of him.

Thus the picture which we get is that of a somewhat pragmatic order, governed only by the large and general principle of *ma'at*, which combined "truth," "justice," and "order." Certainly there was a recognition of the necessity and obligation for good management, but apart from that it is impossible to claim that ancient Egypt formulated any ethical basis for government and law. This "lawlessness" permitted a kind of flexible strength in allowing a dogmatically traditional society to meet the new situations of changing times. But it was also as inherent weakness of the society, and when the king ceased to function as a god and became the tool of priests, officials, and foreign rulers, Egyptian culture gradually disintegrated.

Notes to Wilson, "Authority and Law in Ancient Egypt"

In Egypt, the pharaoh himself was a god and the source of *ma'at*, justice, which only he could know and interpret. There was, therefore, no need for a written code, although the king did designate other officials to administer justice, presumably in accordance with tradition as this developed.[129] Justice was regarded as part of the cosmic order of the world. The same order that caused the seasons to follow each other caused men to respect their parents and the law. Peculiarly enough, although the pharaoh was divine, he too had to (eventually) respect *ma'at*. This concept was not then too different from the prevalent concept in Mesopotamia. In practice, however, the pharaohs tended to be more

129. M. Levi, *Political Power in the Ancient World* (New York, 1965), p. 2.

dictatorial, and were regarded with greater awe, than the Mesopotamian monarchs. (Compare also the plaint of Abraham in the Bible,[130] "Shall the ruler of all the land not do justice?" This indicates that even the God of the Bible was held to be bound by a concept of justice (see Part Two, Chapter V, Section C 1).

There are no records of the existence of any written legal code in Egypt until a much later time. This may be because the king himself was the law and also, perhaps, because it was feared that reduction of the law to writing might tend to circumscribe the power of the king. Similarly, we do not have much evidence regarding legal documents in use in Egypt until a much later time, although this may be due to the greater difficulty of preserving the perishable Egyptian papyri as compared to the Mesopotamian clay tablets. This dearth of legal codes and documents in ancient Egypt differs sharply from the situation prevailing in Mesopotamia.

3. EARLY LAW AND CIVILIZATION
(By E. A. Speiser)*

Introduction

It is a recognized fact that priceless records of pre-classical law have been neglected on the whole "by legal historians and students of jurisprudence." This is both puzzling and regrettable: puzzling because the history of a given discipline cannot fulfill its proper function until it has been carried as far back as the available sources permit; and regrettable because a deeper understanding of the neglected material could lend the whole subject added importance and dignity. Yet the legal historian has seldom had much time for anything earlier than Roman law. To be sure, he cannot ignore Greek law altogether; for the past fifty years, moreover, he has been obliged to make dutiful mention of Hammurabi. Yet to all intents and purposes he seems content to subscribe to this dictum of Sir Thomas Erskine Holland: "For the beginnings of the science which reduces legal phenomena to order and coherence the world is indebted to the Romans."

I wish to make it clear at the outset that this paper is in no way an apology for the romantic approach to antiquity. A venerable pedigree is not of itself a guarantee of intrinsic virtues. On the other hand, not to make adequate use of the contributions of the past is to squander valuable assets. We know now that the view of absolute Roman priority in the field of juris-

prudence can no longer be upheld with any degree of confidence. The question has been posed more than once whether the high level of Roman law was not due in part to the pioneering efforts of other and earlier civilizations. At all events, the prevailing view of Roman priority suffers from a palpable fault of perspective. Roman law, at a maximum, cannot be traced back much farther than about 400 B.C. But that date is no more than a half-way junction in the total of documented legal history. In other words, the student of jurisprudence who vaguely equates the Twelve Tables with his subject's Book of Genesis shuts off a whole half—the significant first half, at that—of his discipline. It is much like commencing the history of world civilization with the earliest testimony of the American Indians.

Nevertheless, correct perspective in the history of jurisprudence as such cannot be and is not the primary concern of the present account. No less important and constructive, and certainly more nearly within the competence of this writer, is the task of conveying some idea of the scope and sway of pre-classical law in a large part of the ancient Near East, where that law had come to enjoy supreme authority and had a prominent share in the advance of civilization. It is therefore to the role of law in the dynamics of early civilization that these remarks are directed in the main.

But before this task is attempted there are three further preliminary points that need to be clarified. First, my own approach to the subject is of necessity that of a humanist who has specialized in the experience of the Near East. And my excuse for poaching on juridical preserves is that for over a quarter of a century I have had to deal with ancient legal records, among other things, partly because there are many such records among the texts unearthed in the Near East, records which must be screened by the philologist in the first instance; and partly because the student of the Near East must not ignore the legal component if he wishes to understand the total civilization.

Secondly, in addressing myself to a non-orientalist audience I shall be obliged to touch, in passing, on some details which are common knowledge among the specialists. Yet some of the conclusions of this paper are by no means routine even with Near Eastern scholars. The orientalist has been just as neglectful of his legal sources, in the reconstruction of the history and culture of the region, as the jurist has been in tracing the background of his own discipline. In other words, what is here outlined is not in all details a consensus; rather it should be judged as a working hypothesis. A vast amount of work remains to be done, by orientalists and jurists in close co-operation, before the full import

---

130. Gen. 18:23–25; see also Num. 16:22 ("If one man sins, will you be angry at the entire congregation?") and Ps. 89:15 ("Righteousness and Justice are the Foundations of thy Throne").

*From E. A. Speiser, *Collected Writings* (Philadelphia, 1971).

of the judicial legacy of the Near East can be confidently evaluated.

Thirdly, the reader who ventures past these caveats will soon discover that the discussion centers mostly about cuneiform legal matters and that very little is said about the other legal systems of the area. No undue favoritism is thereby implied. For it so happens that cuneiform legal sources turn up earlier and in vastly greater numbers than juridical records in other scripts. Furthermore, the impact of cuneiform law is pervasive to an exceptional degree and gives the pertinent civilization a highly distinctive cast. Lastly, the influence of Mesopotamia, the home of the cuneiform medium, spread to several neighboring cultures. All in all, therefore, there are sound grounds for concentrating on cuneiform sources in an inquiry into pre-classical law.

Nature of the Cuneiform Legal Material

It was nearly ninety years ago that the subject of cuneiform law was first broached in modern times—in articles by the French savant Jules Oppert, who was not only one of the pioneers of cuneiform studies but also a man with prior training in jurisprudence. On the whole, however, there was little interest in the matter until the discovery of the stela of Hammurabi, in the winter of 1901–02, by another French cuneiformist, Père Scheil. This find came from the ruins of Susa, the capital of ancient Elam, in south-western Iran. Yet obviously it was not an Elamite relic, since the long inscription upon it had been composed in the language and name of the celebrated Babylonian ruler. The stela, then, had evidently been carried off to Susa as a trophy of war. The fact of its transfer to Elam is suggestive in itself. For the laborious transport of a heavy block of diorite (2.25 m. in height and with a circumference of 1.90 m. at the base and 1.65 m. at the top) over hundreds of miles of difficult terrain is striking evidence of the high regard in which the object must have been held even by an alien conqueror. Today, at a remove of close to three millenniums, we are in a good position to realize that the stela of Hammurabi was indeed an important milestone in the social history of mankind. The monument, in short, is priceless in more ways than one.

The text consists of a preamble, a body of laws, and an epilogue. Its archaic characters are beautifully engraved, and the composition—in the Old Babylonian dialect of Akkadian—is a model of grammar, precision of style, and inner logic. The number of laws involved was originally about three hundred; an exact count is now impossible because several columns, with perhaps one-sixth of the legal portion, have been effaced. The rest, however, is more than sufficient to demonstrate the kind of legal thinking involved and the extent to which law had come to permeate the entire structure of the local society.

Of special significance, in terms of the underlying social philosophy, is the fact that the powerful head of the Babylonian Empire was not the master but merely the humble servant of the law and strictly accountable to the gods for its just enactment. All in all, it would be difficult to conceive of a more penetrating, comprehensive and dependable introduction to an intricate civilization than we have in this document. A direct study of its contents can be far more revealing than scores of books *about* Hammurabi's Babylonia. And yet, this work, which we are fortunate to possess in the original rather than in some copy of much later date, was already utilized and revered about 1700 B.C. or approximately as many years before the age of Moses as separate the time of Columbus from our own day.

The term "code," it may have been noticed, has not been used at all in the preceding remarks. The omission is not accidental. The handful of jurists who have so far given their attention to this material seem agreed that what we have before us is not properly a code or digest, but "a series of amendments to the common law of Babylon." It is advisable, therefore, to speak here only of the "Laws of Hammurabi." The responsible authorities, then, were drafters rather than codifiers. Nor is the end product a pioneering effort, as many would still seem to believe. As far back as 1917, the distinguished German legal historian, Paul Koschaker, was able to show on internal evidence that the Laws of Hammurabi contain various interpolations and duplications—convincing proof that the document had a considerable history behind it. This deduction was supported by known fragments of laws which were the work of the Sumerians, who flourished in that area before the Babylonians and spoke a language that had no generic relationship with Semitic. On independent cultural grounds, moreover, some of us have long held that enactment comparable to the Old Babylonian laws must have been current back in the third millennium. For the legal structure was an integral phase of the historic civilization of Mesopotamia, and that civilization reaches in all its essentials well back into the third millennium. Accordingly, in a popular article written in 1949 and published in January 1951, I ventured to lay a representative legal scene in the twenty-first century B.C. We now have direct proof that such expectations were in no wise too sanguine.

As of this date we know of at least three collections of Mesopotamian laws which are anterior to Hammurabi's. In 1947, F. R. Steele discovered in the University Museum of Philadelphia new fragments of Sumerian laws which in conjunction with previously published specimens add up to the "Laws of Lipit-Ishtar," featuring a preamble, a central legal portion and an epilogue, precisely as in the case of Hammurabi. Lipit-Ishtar was a king of the South Mesopotamian city of Isin who ruled nearly two centuries before Hammurabi. Thus the famous Babylonian ruler had a solid precedent for his own legal project; not only is his arrangement the same as Lipit-Ishtar's, but there is an intimate relationship in contents wherever the individual enactments can be compared. In 1948 there was brought to light a still older body of laws, thanks to the efforts of A. Goetze of Yale in association with the Iraq Department of Antiquities. The place of origin was, this time, the city of Eshnunna, east of Baghdad. The language of the Laws of Eshnunna, however, is once more Akkadian rather than Sumerian, in spite of the antiquity of the text. Finally, S. N. Kramer of the University of Pennsylvania and its museum was able to announce in 1952 the discovery of a yet older body of laws, bearing the name of Ur-Nammu, the founder of the Third Dynasty of Ur. This gives us a second Sumerian legal work, alongside the two in Semitic. And the date of this particular collection is the twenty-first century B.C., or exactly as some of us had anticipated.

Aside from these early juridical works, which date from the end of the third and the early second millennium, there are collections of cuneiform laws from later periods. Extensive portions of the Middle Assyrian laws have come down to us on several clay tablets dating from the last quarter of the second millennium, and the following millennium is represented by a single clay tablet containing some of the Neo-Babylonian laws. As their names indicate, both these collections were phrased in respective dialects of Akkadian, which is the collective name for the principal Semitic speech of Mesopotamia. But cuneiform "codes" were not restricted to Mesopotamia proper. The Hittites, who employed the same form of writing in recording their own language, which has unmistakable Indo-European affiliations, had an analogous collection of laws of which two extensive tablets are now extant.

Legislative compilations, however, make up only a negligible part of the total cuneiform legal material that has been brought to light. Incomparably more numerous are the documents pertaining to the actual practice of law. Their total mounts up to countless thousands. They date all the way from the third millennium down through the first, and they cover a formidable array of legal types. Nor do they stem from Mesopotamia alone. Vast numbers of legal documents have come down to us from neighboring areas representing all sorts of eth-

nic groups and languages. Yet even here the cuneiform script became standard equipment and Akkadian the normal legal language. Thus the Hurians, who were linguistically and ethnically distinct from Sumerians, Semites and Hittites alike, resorted for official purposes to Akkadian, both in the region of modern Kirkuk and in their more widespread settlements in Syria. The Elamites—yet another distinct group—did likewise in their Iranian homeland. Thousands of cuneiform legal documents, written in Akkadian, have turned up in Cappadocia. Even Palestine has yielded material of the same kind.

What we have before us is a picture of unprecedented cultural expansion, which is especially vivid in its legal details. Invariably prominent in this picture are the following three features: a common script, a common language, and the obligatory employment of the legal document. The external criterion of writing permits us to apply to this community of cultural interests the designation "cuneiform culture," however incongruous this phrase might be on other grounds. The prevailing use of Akkadian, notably in the second millennium B.C., has more recent analogues in the use of Latin for legal purposes or of French in international diplomacy.

It would have been helpful to illustrate the main types of the extant cuneiform legal records, for no description can match the flavor and the impact of actual examples. But anything like a representative number of citations, together with the necessary minimum of explanatory notes, would carry us too far afield. Before we go on, however, to broader considerations, I may perhaps be allowed to adduce a single illustration in order to convey, to a very limited degree, something of the legal problems and procedures that these records reflect. The specimen which I have selected for translation (from the local dialect of Akkadian) has been taken from among the archives found in the area of Kirkuk, because these happen to reflect the spread of Mesopotamian concepts to adjoining regions and peoples. The document records a lawsuit. If it seems involved at first, it is mainly because many of the details were fully familiar to the parties concerned and required no elaboration. It will be noticed that the court was most careful in identifying the principals and in tracing the case, step by step, to its inception two generations earlier. The decisive bearing of the written records is brought out very pointedly. Incidentally, the tablet dates from the fourteenth century B.C., over a hundred years before the time of Moses. Yet it was not very long ago that critics doubted the possibility of complex legislation in the Mosaic age on the ground that those times were too primitive and that the knowledge of writing was as yet unequal to the task. Indeed, our perspective has changed radically within the past few decades.

Here is the translation of the first sixty-eight lines of the tablet:

Shurkitilla, the son of Tehiptilla, went to court before the judges with Taya, the son of Rimusharri. Thus Shurktilla:

'Kawinni, the son of Kunadu, and Ithapu, the son of Puhishenni, had adopted my father Tehiptilla for (the transfer of) two acres of land in the district of Shulmiya. Now Taya has sued me by swearing out against me a royal warrant, and has had me evicted from that land.'

Thus Taya: 'I have no connection (with the land) either by inheritance or by lot or in any other manner. (But) Hanate, the wife of Shanhari delegated me with these instructions: "Go and sue Shurkitilla by swearing out against him a royal warrant, and evict him from that land." So in accordance with Hanate's instructions I swore out against him a royal warrant and had him evicted from that land.'

Then the judges questioned Hanate, saying: 'Did you delegate Taya to swear out against Shurkitilla a royal warrant?' Thus Hanate: 'I sent Taya to Shurkitilla with these instructions: "Sue Shurkitilla by swearing out against him a royal warrant, and have him evicted from that land."'

Thereupon the judges dismissed Taya from the court proceedings. To Hanate the judges declared: 'Argue the case with Shurkitilla!'

Thus Hanate: 'When my husband Shanhari provided for me in his will, he deeded that land to me.' Then the judges examined Hanate's records of the will whereby Shanhari had deeded his land to his wife. But neither the name of Kawinni nor the name of Ithapu, who had adopted Tehiptilla, was inscribed in the records of Hanate.

Thereupon Hanate declared as follows: 'Kawinni died earlier; and later on Shanhari, in providing for me in his will, deeded that land to me.'

Then the registrars [whose five names are officially recorded] deposed before the judges: 'That land used to belong to Kunadu. Now Kawinni was Kunadu's eldest son and Kani was a younger son.' Then Hanate made this statement: 'That land did belong to Kunadu. Kawinni was Kunadu's eldest son, and Kani, the father of my husband Shanhari, was indeed a younger son.'

Whereas, therefore, Shanhari had deeded to his wife land that was not his, in that the names of Kawinni and Ithapu were not inscribed in his records, the judges ordered Hanate to surrender that land and assigned the land to Shurkitilla. And whereas she had a royal warrant sworn out against Shurkitilla, (evicting him) from his own land, the judges com-

mitted Hanate to Shurkitilla for the payment of one bullock as fine.

[The judges take certain additional steps to clear the title to the land under dispute. There follow the seals of the officials and the signature of the scribe.]

To get back to our main argument, how can one account for the unprecedented cultural influence of Mesopotamia, emanating as it did from a relatively small center in the South? It should be stressed that this expansion was by no means co-extensive with political authority. Even in Mesopotamia proper, the South and the North were traditional enemies. The Elamites and the Hurians on the fringe pursued their own political ways. The Hittites represented an independent power; nor were the various states of Syria and Palestine ordered about by a Mesopotamian power until the emergence of Assyrian might, in the first millennium. Yet all these diverse elements, in spite of their underlying differences, were drawn into the orbit of a single civilization, notably in such essentials as the concept and practice of law. Is there a plausible explanation for this phenomenon?

Law as the Touchstone of a Civilization

Legal systems not only help to implement but also serve to reflect the underlying concepts of government. In the ancient Near East state and religion were inseparable. The two interfused. Between them they embodied the individual society's way of life. Hence the pertinent legal systems have to be viewed in conjunction with the overall social philosophies which the respective societies had evolved.

The great impact of the legal thinking and practice of Mesopotamia on other parts of the Near East must be bound up, accordingly, with the kind of society that was characteristic of Mesopotamia. And, conversely, the failure of the other legal systems of the area to achieve similar prominence should be rooted in their respective sociocultural backgrounds.

The pre-classical Near East has left evidence of only one major juridical structure that may be said to have competed with that of Mesopotamia, namely, the Egyptian. To be sure, the effect of biblical law can hardly be overestimated; nor does Hittite law appear to have played a negligible role. These two systems, however, were not in competition with Mesopotamian law. On the contrary, they were related to it in several ways: the biblical in its framework, spirit, as well as in many individual provisions; and the Hittite still more closely by reason of the use of the cuneiform script and the stress on the written document. There is thus no genuine cleavage until we come to Egypt. The civilization of Egypt is found to be in sharp contrast with the cultural complex of that portion of Western Asia which has conveniently been designated as the Fertile Crescent. The contrast stems not so much from material ways as from differences in the way of life. And these differences are brought into sharp relief by the respective legal systems.

Readers of John Henry Wigmore's *A Panorama of the World's Legal Systems* may be still under the impression that the Egyptian system is the oldest known to man and that it can be documented as far back as 4000 B.C. The jurist repeated in this case an understandable error of earlier orientalists. Scholars have since been obliged to lower the date for the beginnings of recorded Egyptian history by about a thousand years. In the present context, however, the absolute antiquity of Egyptian law is not nearly as important as are its nature and place in the overall scheme of things. It is on these counts that the differences from the Mesopotamian system are most clearly apparent.

One highly significant point of contrast is noticeable at first glance. Egypt has not left to posterity a formal body of laws comparable to the Laws of Lipit-Ishtar or Eshnunna or Hammurabi, the Old Assyrian or the Middle Assyrian or the Neo-Babylonian systems, or the Hittite and Hebrew analogues. What is more, alongside the countless thousands of records relating to the practice of law in Mesopotamia and affiliated areas, there is barely a trickle from Egypt before the Persian and Greek periods. This is no mere argument from silence. The soil and climate of Egypt were kind to materials far more perishable than those that were employed for writing. The negative evidence of many centuries has in these circumstances a substantial cumulative bearing. Then there is compelling internal evidence. The local society was so constituted that it set far less store by the written legal document than could possibly have been the case in Mesopotamia. Nor is the reason for this Egyptian attitude far to seek.

In a paper read in 1940, and subsequently published and reprinted several times, I sought to sum up the situation as it presented itself to an assyriologist. We are on firmer ground today in that we can refer to a statement by one of our most distinguished egyptologists. In the lucid words of John A. Wilson's *The Burden of Egypt*, the pharaoh was the essential nucleus of the state:

> He, as a god, *was* the state. . . . To be sure, it was necessary for a new state to have rules and regulations for administrative procedures and precedent, but our negative evidence suggests that there was no codification of law, impersonally conceived and referable by magistrates without consideration of the crown. Rather, the customary law of the land was conceived to be the word of the pharaoh. . . . In later

times there was visible no impersonal and continuing body of law, like one of the Mesopotamian codes, until we come down into Persian and Greek days; the centralization of the state in the person of the king apparently forbade such impersonal law. The authority of codified law would have competed with the personal authority of the pharaoh.

In other words, since the pharaoh was regarded as a god, there could be no authority, personal or impersonal, superior to his own.

In sharp contrast to the authoritarian position of the pharaoh, the Mesopotamian ruler was viewed as an ordinary mortal who was accountable to the gods for his every move. His powers were further circumscribed, since the beginning of history, by the requirement that each major public undertaking must have the prior consent of the appropriate assembly, either of the elders or of the warriors. All this is intimately related to the Mesopotamian concept of the cosmos, that is to say, religion. State and religion were the two normative aspects of the way of life, just as in Egypt and elsewhere in the ancient Near East. What made the real difference in each case was the kind of religion and government involved. In Egypt the result was authoritarianism. In Mesopotamia the trend was towards democracy. And the mechanism whereby that democratic orientation was controlled and safeguarded made up the Mesopotamian legal system.

How such fundamentally opposed ways of life had arisen in two contemporaneous and otherwise related civilizations is a question that is altogether beyond the scope of this paper. Some of the answers, incidentally, are as yet concealed from us by deep layers of prehistory. At any rate, the fact is that these far-reaching differences existed and that they profoundly affected the historic careers of the two great civilizations. Although sundry details of these careers are still obscure, the principal features of the Mesopotamian experience fall into a clear pattern.

Since the kings of Mesopotamia lacked absolute authority—indeed even the Mesopotamian gods could not boast unlimited power—the position of the subjects was correspondingly enhanced. This shows itself with telling force in the ubiquitous recognition of private property and the prevailing respect for it. Nowhere is this lastnamed feature more sharply reflected than in § 7 of the Laws of Hammurabi:

> If a man has purchased or received for safekeeping either silver or gold or a male slave or a female slave or an ox or a sheep or an ass or anything whatsoever from the hand of a citizen or the slave of a citizen, without witnesses or a written contract, that man shall be put to death for he is a thief.

Time and practical considerations may eventually have modified this drastic provision. It is all too plain, however, that on more than one occasion possession of proper legal records was literally a matter of life or death. Small wonder, therefore, that the mounds which pockmark the landscape of Mesopotamia became repositories of hundreds of thousands of documents executed in strict conformity with the law of the land. The law rather than accidents of discovery and the use of a durable writing material accounts for the presence of all these tablets.

There is, furthermore, a strong probability that writing itself came to be invented in the first place in conjunction with age-old practices pertaining to temple and private economy. The cultivation of writing in turn —a highly intricate process before the introduction of the alphabet—has considerable bearing on the advance of other sciences. Progress was thus being registered on a broad front. But it was the law that remained the zealous guardian of the distinctive Mesopotamian way of life throughout the many centuries.

In passing, a few words may be in order concerning the Akkadian phrase which is used to express both the nature and the function of law. The reference in question is *kittum u mēsharum*. The first word means "that which is firm, established, true"; the third word (following the particle for "and") means "equity, justice." In other words, the whole phrase stands for something like "impersonal and immutable order tempered with equity and fairness." This is how Hammurabi describes his own legal effort. We could scarcely improve on it in seeking to characterize the whole legal philosophy of Mesopotamia.

The Dynamics of Mesopotamian Law

In the discussion so far I have spoken repeatedly of Mesopotamia, although this term stands for no ethnic, linguistic or political unit. Quite the contrary; for on all these counts the biblical tale of the Tower of Babel comes closer to the mark, in that it hints at a confusing variety of tongues and peoples. In the several millennia of its pre-classical history various mutually antagonistic peoples pass in review and several unrelated linguistic stocks are encountered. There is, however, an underlying cultural unity which transcends the conventional boundaries and gradually embraces the entire valley, to spread thence to adjoining areas. The composite product cannot properly be ascribed to any one people or center. It was, in effect, Mesopotamian.

The question was broached earlier whether this spectacular cultural dynamism can be explained. We have seen that characteristic legal features were the normal witnesses of the advancing Mesopotamian civilization: collections of laws and documents pertaining to legal

practice. Those features had come in their native vessels, so to speak: the cuneiform script and the Sumerian language, which soon gave way to Akkadian. It may be added in passing that an itinerant language is not the same thing as an international scientific formula. The language may be said to carry with it an accumulation of cultural genes. Thus the Hittites of Anatolia, in acquainting themselves with Akkadian and rudiments of Sumerian, exposed themselves not only to the appertaining laws but to religion, literature and the sciences as well. And so they proceeded to translate Akkadian myths and epics. Indeed, some Babylonian tales which had reached the Hittites through Hurian mediation turn up eventually in Greek mythology.

To get back, however, to the possible causes of this cultural expansion, it should be made clear that the problem is not capable as yet of a conclusive solution. In the nature of things, perhaps, some uncertainty will always attend any answer that may be attempted. The following remarks, which bring this paper to its conclusion, should be viewed therefore, as has already been indicated, as a working hypothesis. The test of such hypotheses has to be pragmatic. Let us see how this one works.

The outward signs of foreign dependence on Mesopotamian law are the script, the language and the document. Yet such formal indebtedness fails to reveal the secret of Mesopotamia's appeal. Magnetism on so large a scale would seem to suggest that content as well as form played here a substantial part. Nevertheless, the Hittites certainly did not simply adopt the laws of Hammurabi or the Old Assyrian laws. And the Hebrews remain even further apart; for they either never acknowledged the influence of the cuneiform script or they soon emancipated themselves from it in committing their own laws to writing. In content, then, there is nothing like a one-to-one correlation between the laws of Mesopotamia and Hittite or Hebrew law.

Yet too much store can be set, I believe, by this circumstance. Complete interdependence in details is not the only valid criterion of close substantive relationship. No less significant, I submit, would be affinity in ideas and spirit if that could be demonstrated and shown to be sufficiently far-reaching. Now law, as was pointed out earlier, serves to reflect the fundamental spirit of the given civilization. Mesopotamian civilization, by restricting the authority of the ruler, did much to emphasize and to protect the rights of the individual in relation to society and the cosmos. In this significant respect the social philosophies of the Hebrews and the Hittites had much in common with the Mesopotamian outlook on life. Their civilizations were related not only materially and intellectually but also, to a pronounced degree, spiritually. It is on this last count that the contrast between the Fertile Crescent and Egypt shows up in sharpest relief. And in each case the law is the key to the civilization.

It would appear, therefore, that the dynamism of Mesopotamian civilization was due in the last analysis to its distinctive way of life. We cannot tell at this time whether other civilizations found the Mesopotamian way appealing because it was similar to theirs, or whether they had first to be converted to that way under Mesopotamian influence. Be that as it may, we have now a better insight into what converted Mesopotamia itself into an integral cultural unit. We are no longer surprised by the fact that the stela of Hammurabi should have turned up at Susa. What is more, we have a clearer perspective on the characteristic biblical term *torah*. That term does mean "law," as it is commonly rendered. But it means also a great deal more than such a rendering would generally suggest. *Torah* corresponds also to the Babylonian *kittum u mesharum*, and beyond that, and more particularly, it stands also for a specific way of life. In addition, we are entitled to ask whether the remembrance of the bondage in Egypt, which runs through the Old Testament as a recurrent refrain, reflects no more than the experience of a small number of Hebrews during a relatively short period of their pre-history. In view of all that has been said so far, there is the inherent probability that the bondage in this instance was so exceptionally severe because it involved basic spiritual values and had resulted from a clash between fundamentally incompatible ways of life.

To be sure, we do not know, nor do I wish to assert, that the biblical estimate of the law as the key to a vital civilization was due to direct influence from Mesopotamia. It is significant, however, that the peak in the study of biblical law was reached, in later times, not in Palestine but in Babylonia, and was embodied in a major work which still bears the name of the Babylonian Talmud. Analogously, the most fruitful period in the development of Islamic law was witnessed when Baghdad was the capital of the Islamic world. The vitality of legal tradition in Mesopotamia survived thus by a number of centuries the end of the historic Mesopotamian civilization.

In conclusion, a word may be in order concerning the possibility that classical law may have owed some inspiration to oriental prototypes. With the unexpected expansion of juridical horizons as a result of recent discoveries, it was but natural that some writers should turn against the traditional views and seek to derive the classical law from Mesopotamia. But the leading workers in the field have refused to be driven to such extremes. Direct Roman borrowing from Mesopotamian legal sources is precluded, of course, by the fact that

the civilization of Mesopotamia had come to the end of its independent course before Rome became an oriental power. That specific cultural elements may have filtered through, by one route or another, from the Fertile Crescent to the classical world is quite another matter. And that legal items were not left out in the process is suggested by certain Babylonian loanwords in the West. The really important thing is that Mesopotamia had experienced more than two millennia of notable legal progress before classical civilization began. That experience could not have been without some effect on Europe. Finally, the kind of law which Mesopotamia evolved proved its capacity to serve as an aid to the democratic process. To the extent, therefore, that the Fertile Crescent as a whole contributed to the evolution of democracy, it placed under indebtedness not only ancient Greece but our modern western civilization as well.

4. CUNEIFORM CODES

a. THE CODE OF HAMMURABI
(Translated by Theophile J. Meek)

Hammurabi (also spelled Hammurapi) was the sixth of eleven kings in the Old Babylonian (Amorite) Dynasty. He ruled for forty-three years, from 1728 to 1686 according to the most recent calculations. The date-formula for his second year, "The year he enacted the law of the land," indicates that he promulgated his famous lawcode at the very beginning of his reign, but the copy which we have could not have been written so early because the Prologue refers to events much later than this. Our copy was written on a diorite stela, topped by a bas-relief showing Hammurabi in the act of receiving the commission to write the law-book from the god of justice, the sun-god Shamash. The stela was carried off to the old Elamite capital, Susa (the Shushan of Esther and Daniel), by some Elamite raider (apparently Shutruk-Nahhunte, about 1207–1171 B.C.) as a trophy of war. It was discovered there by French archaeologists in the winter of 1901–1902 and was carried off by them to the Louvre in Paris as a trophy of archaeology. All the laws from col. xvi 77 to the end of the obverse (from the end of § 65 to the beginning of § 100) were chiseled off by the Elamites, but these have been preserved in large part on other copies of the Code. The Prologue and Epilogue are written in semi-poetic style, marked by parallelism but not by regular metrical structure. . . .

*From J. Pritchard, *Ancient Near Eastern Texts Relating to the Old Testament* (Princeton, 1955). Accents have been deleted. Footnotes are from the original, renumbered.

The Prologue

(i)

When lofty Anum,[131] king of the Anunnaki,[132]
[and] Enlil,[133] lord of heaven and earth,
the determiner of the destinies of the land,
determined for Marduk,[134] the first-born of Enki,[135] (10)
the Enlil functions over all mankind,
made him great among the Igigi,
called Babylon by its exalted name,
made it supreme in the world,
established for him in its midst an enduring
    kingship, (20)
whose foundations are as firm as heaven and earth—
at that time Anum and Enlil named me
to promote the welfare of the people,[136]
me, Hammurabi, the devout, god-fearing prince, (30)
to cause justice to prevail in the land,
to destroy the wicked and the evil,
that the strong might not oppress the weak,
to rise like the sun over the black-headed
    [people],[137] (40)
and to light up the land.
Hammurabi, the shepherd, called by Enlil,
    am I; (50)
the one who makes affluence and plenty abound;
who provides in abundance all sorts of things for
    Nippur-Duranki;[138]
the devout patron of Ekur; (60)
the efficient king, who restored Eridu to its place;

(ii)

who purified the cult of Eabzu;
the one who strides through the four quarters of the
    world;

who makes the name of Babylon great;
who rejoices the heart of Marduk, his lord;
the one who throughout his lifetime stands
    responsible for Esagila; (10)
the descendant of royalty, whom Sin[139] begat;
the one who made Ur prosper;
the pious, suppliant one, who brought abundance
    to Egishnugal; (20)
the wise king, obedient to mighty Shamash;[140]
the one who relaid the foundations of Sippar;
who decked with green the *chapels* of Aya;
the designer of the temple of Ebabbar, which is
    like a heavenly dwelling; (30)
the warrior, he who spared Larsa;[141]
the one who rebuilt Ebabbar for Shamash, his helper;
the lord, who revived Uruk;[142]
who supplied water in abundance to its people; (40)
who raised aloft the head of Eanna;
who made riches abound for Anum and Inanna;
the shelter of the land, who collected the scattered
    people of Isin;[143] (50)
who makes the temple of Egalmah abound with
    affluence;
the monarch of kings, full brother of Zababa;[144]
the refounder of the settlement of Kish,
who has surrounded Emete-ursag with splendor; (60)
the one who has put the great shrines of Inanna in
    perfect condition;
the patron of the temple of Hursag-kalamma;[145]
the *terror* of the enemy;

131. The sky-god, the leader of the pantheon, worshiped especially in the temple of Eanna in Uruk along with the goddess Inanna.

132. In this inscription the Anunnaki are the lesser gods attendant upon Anum and the Igigi are the lesser gods attendant on Enlil.

133. The storm-god, the chief executive of the pantheon, worshiped especially in the temple of Ekur in Nippur in central Babylonia, modern Nuffar.

134. The son of Enki and consort of Sarpanit; the god of Babylon and in Hammurabi's time the god of the Babylonian Empire with the functions of Enlil delegated to him; worshiped especially in the temple of Esagila in Babylon.

135. Lord of the earth and the mass of life-giving waters within it, issuing in streams and fountains; the father of Marduk; worshiped especially in the temple of Eabzu in Eridu, in southern Babylonia, modern Abu Shahrein.

136. Lit., "to make good the flesh of the people."

137. The late-Sumerian expression for men in general.

138. Duranki, "bond of heaven and earth," was a time-honored Sumerian name of Nippur, the cult-center of Enlil, whose temple was Ekur.

139. The moon-god, the son of Enlil, father of Shamash, and consort of Ningal; worshiped especially in the temple of Egishnugal in Ur in southern Babylonia, modern Muqayyar.

140. The sun-god and the god of justice, the consort of Aya, worshiped especially in the temple of Ebabbar in Sippar in northern Babylonia, modern Abu Habba.

141. Another cult-center of Shamash, situated in southern Babylonia, modern Senkereh, with a temple also called Ebabbar. The city was captured by Hammurabi in the thirtieth year of his reign and its powerful dynasty brought to an end with the dethronement of its king, Rim-Sin. This event is set down as the formula for Hammurabi's thirty-first year, but the formula for the year always comes from an event in the preceding year; hence our year-numbers will be one less than those generally given.

142. An ancient and important city in southern Babylonia, the biblical Erech (Gen. 10:10), modern Warka, conquered by Hammurabi in the sixth year of his reign. It was the cult-center of Anum and Inanna, with its temple Eanna.

143. A city south of Nippur in southern Babylonia, conquered by Rim-Sin of Larsa in his twenty-ninth year, and then by Hammurabi in the sixth year of his reign. It was the cult-center of Ninkarrak, with its temple Egalmah.

144. A form of Ninurta, worshiped especially in the temple of Emete-ursag in Kish, northeast of Babylon, modern Tell el-Oheimir.

145. The temple of Inanna in Kish, where she was the consort of Zababa.

the one whom Erra,[146] his comrade, caused to attain
  his desire;   (70)

(iii)

who made Kutha preeminent;
who expanded every kind of facility for Meslam;
the fiery wild-bull who gores the foe;
the beloved of Tutu;[147] the one who brings joy
  to Borsippa;   (10)
the devout one, never neglecting Ezida;
god among kings, acquainted with wisdom;
the one who extended the cultivated land belonging
  to Dilbat;[148]   (20)
who stores up grain for mighty Urash;
the lord, adorned with scepter and crown;
the one whom the sage, Mama,[149] brought to perfection;
who laid out the plans for Kesh;   (30)
who makes sumptuous the splendid banquets for Nintu;
the solicitous, the perfect one,
who fixes the pastures and watering places for
  Lagash and Girsu,[150]   (40)
who provides bountiful sacrifices for Eninnu;
the one who seizes the foe; the favorite of Telitum;[151]
who fulfils the oracles of Hallab;[152]   (50)
the one who makes the heart of Ishtar[153] glad;
the illustrious prince, whose prayers[154] Adad[155]
  recognizes;
who pacifies the heart of Adad, the warrior, in
  Bet-karkar;   (60)
who always maintains the proprieties in Eugalgal;
the king, who granted life to Adab;[156]
the director of the temple of Emah;
the chief of kings, a fighter without peer;   (70)

---

146. The god of pestilence and war, often identified with Nergal. His temple, Meslam, was in Kutha in northern Babylonia, modern Tell Ibrahim.

147. Strictly a title of Marduk, but here applied to his son Nabum, the god of writing. His cult-center was Borsippa, near Babylon, with its temple Ezida.

148. A city not far from Borsippa, the cult-center of the god Urash.

149. A goddess worshiped in Kesh, near Lagash, in central Babylonia; also known as Nintu.

150. Lagash, modern Telloh, and Girsu were twin cities in central Babylonia. Ningirsu was the city god and his temple was Eninnu.

151. A title of Inanna.

152. A city in Babylonia as yet unidentified; a cult-center of Ishtar.

153. The Semitic name of Inanna.

154. Lit., "the lifting up of whose hands."

155. The weather-god, whose temple was Eudgalgal in Bet-karkar, a city as yet unidentified.

156. A city on the Euphrates in central Babylonia, modern Bismaya. Its deity was Mah and her temple was Emah.

(iv)

the one who granted life to Mashkan-shabrim;[157]
who provides abundance for Meslam;
the wise one, the administrator;
the one who plumbed the depths of wisdom;   (10)
the rescuer of the people of Malka[158] from trouble;
the founder of dwelling places for them in abundance;
the one who prescribed for all time splendid sacrifices
  for Enki and Damgalnunna,   (20)
who made his kingdom great;
the first of kings;
the subduer of the settlements along the Euphrates
  with the help of Dagan,[159] his creator;
the one who spared the people of Mera and
  Tutul;[160]   (30)
the devout prince, who brightens up the face of
  Tishpak;
the provider of splendid banquets for Ninazu;[161]
the savior of his people from distress,
who establishes in security their portion in the midst
  of Babylon;   (40)
the shepherd of the people, whose deeds are pleasing to
  Ishtar;
who installed Ishtar in Eulmash in the midst
  of Akkad[162] square;   (50)
who makes law prevail; who guides the people aright;
who returned to Ashur[163] its kindly protecting genius;
who silences the growlers;
the king, who made the name of Inanna glorious
  in Nineveh[164] in Emishmish;   (60)
the devout one, who prays fervently to the great gods;
the descendant of Sumu-la-el;[165]
the powerful son and heir[166] of Sin-muballit,   (70)

---

157. A city not far from Adab, modern Dshidr.

158. A city apparently on the middle Euphrates, conquered by Hammurabi in the ninth year of his reign and punished for a revolt in his thirty-fourth year. It was the seat of Enki and his consort Damgalnunna, also known as Damkina, the mother of Marduk.

159. The Dagon of the Bible; a west Semitic grain-god, early imported into Mesopotamia and worshiped chiefly along the middle Euphrates.

160. Two cities on the middle Euphrates. Mera may possibly be Mari, modern Tell Hariri, conquered by Hammurabi in his thirty-second year.

161. The god of medicine, worshiped particularly at Eshnunna in his temple Esikil. Tishpak was the chief god of Eshnunna.

162. An ancient city of northern Babylonia, founded by Sargon the Great as his capital; a seat of Ishtar, with her temple Eulmash.

163. The name of Assyria, of its ancient capital, modern Qal'at Shergat, on the upper Tigris, and of its national god. It is manifestly the city that is intended here.

164. The later capital of Assyria on the upper Tigris, modern Kouyunjik, an important seat of Inanna, with her temple Emishmish.

165. The second king of the Old Babylonian Dynasty.

166. "Son and heir," a single word in Babylonian.

(v)

the ancient seed of royalty, the powerful king, the sun
 of Babylon,
who causes light to go forth over the lands of Sumer
 and Akkad;[167]
the king who has made the four quarters of the
 world subservient; (10)
the favorite of Inanna am I.
When Marduk commissioned me to guide the people
 aright,
to direct the land,
I established law and justice in the language
 of the land, (20)
thereby promoting the welfare of the people.
At that time [I decreed]:

The Laws

1. If a seignior[168] accused a[nother] seignior and
brought a charge of murder against him, but has not
proved it, his accuser shall be put to death.[169]

2. If a seignior brought a charge of sorcery against
a[nother] seignior, but has not proved it, the one against
whom the charge of sorcery was brought, upon going
to the river,[170] shall throw himself into the river, and if
the river has then overpowered him, his accuser shall
take over his estate; if the river has shown that seignior
to be innocent and he has accordingly come forth safe,
the one who brought the charge of sorcery against him
shall be put to death, while the one who threw himself
into the river shall take over the estate of his accuser.

3. If a seignior came forward with false testimony
in a case, and has not proved the word which he spoke,
if that case was a case involving life, that seignior shall
be put to death.

4. If he came forward with [false] testimony con-

cerning grain or money, he shall bear the penalty of
that case.

5. If a judge gave a judgment, rendered a decision,
deposited a sealed document, but later has altered his
judgment, they shall prove that that judge altered the
judgment which he gave and he shall pay twelvefold
the claim which holds in that case; furthermore, they
shall expel him in the assembly from his seat of judgment and he shall never again sit[171] with the judges in
a case.

6. If a seignior stole the property of church or
state,[172] that seignior shall be put to death; also the one
who received the stolen goods from his hand shall be
put to death.

7. If a seignior has purchased or he received for
safekeeping either silver or gold or a male slave or a
female slave or an ox or a sheep or an ass or any sort
of thing from the hand of a seignior's son or a seignior's
slave without witnesses and contracts, since that seignior
is a thief, he shall be put to death.

8. If a seignior stole either an ox or a sheep or an
ass or a pig or a boat, if it belonged to the church [or]
if it belonged to the state, he shall make thirtyfold
restitution; if it belonged to a private citizen,[173] he shall
make good tenfold. If the thief does not have sufficient
to make restitution, he shall be put to death.[174]

9. When a seignior, [some of] whose property was
lost, has found his lost property in the possession of
a[nother] seignior, if the seignior in whose possession
the lost [property] was found has declared, "A seller
sold [it] to me; I made the purchase in the presence of
witnesses," and the owner of the lost [property] in turn
has declared, "I will produce witnesses attesting to my
lost [property]"; the purchaser having then produced
the seller who made the sale to him and the witnesses
in whose presence he made the purchase, and the owner
of the lost [property] having also produced the witnesses attesting to his lost [property], the judges shall
consider their evidence, and the witnesses in whose
presence the purchase was made, along with the wit-

---

167. Sumer was the ancient name of southern Babylonia and
Akkad of northern Babylonia, the two together constituting a
common name of the country as a whole.

168. The word *awelum*, used here, is literally "man," but in
the legal literature it seems to be used in at least three senses:
(1) sometimes to indicate a man of the higher class, a noble;
(2) sometimes a free man of any class, high or low; and (3)
occasionally a man of any class, from king to slave (see, e.g.,
CH, reverse xxvi, 39–44). For the last I use the inclusive word
"man," but for the first two, since it is seldom clear which of
the two is intended in a given context, I follow the ambiguity
of the original and use the rather general term "seignior,"
which I employ as the term is employed in Italian and Spanish, to indicate any free man of standing, and not in the strict
feudal sense, although the ancient Near East did have something approximating the feudal system, and that is another
reason for using "seignior."

169. With this law and the three following cf. Deuteronomy
5:20; 19:16 ff.; Exodus 23:1–3.

170. The word for "river" throughout this section has the
determinative of deity, indicating that the river (the Euphrates)
as judge in the case was regarded as god.

171. Lit., "he shall not return and sit."

172. Lit., "the property of god or palace."

173. The word is *muskenum*, which in the Code ordinarily
indicates a man of the middleclass, a commoner, but here and
in §§15, 16, 175, and 176 it manifestly refers to a private citizen as distinct from the church and state.

174. The laws on theft in the Code (§§6–13, 22, 23, 25, 259,
260, 265), do not agree among themselves, indicating that we
have laws of different dates in the Code. According to the
earliest laws (§§7, 9, 10, 22, 25) theft was to be punished by
death); later (§6) the death penalty was confined to the theft
of church or state property; later still severalfold restitution
(§§8, 265) or a fine (§§259, 260) came to be substituted for
the death penalty; see T. J. Meek, *Hebrew Origins* (1936), p.
61 f. For the Hebrew laws on theft see Exodus 20:15 (=Deut.
5:19); 22:1–4; Leviticus 19:11, 13.

nesses attesting to the lost [property], shall declare what they know in the presence of god, and since the seller was the thief, he shall be put to death, while the owner of the lost [property] shall take his lost [property], with the purchaser obtaining from the estate of the seller the money that he paid out.[175]

10. If the [professed] purchaser has not produced the seller who made the sale to him and the witnesses in whose presence he made the purchase, but the owner of the lost property has produced witnesses attesting to his lost property, since the [professed] purchaser was the thief, he shall be put to death, while the owner of the lost property shall take his lost property.

11. If the [professed] owner of the lost property has not produced witnesses attesting to his lost property, since he was a cheat and started a false report, he shall be put to death.

12. If the seller has gone to [his] fate, the purchaser shall take from the estate of the seller fivefold the claim for that case.

13. If the witnesses of that seignior were not at hand, the judges shall set a time limit of six months for him, and if he did not produce his witnesses within six months, since that seignior was a cheat, he shall bear the penalty of that case.

14. If a seignior has stolen the young son of a[nother] seignior, he shall be put to death.[176]

15. If a seignior has helped either a male slave of the state or a female slave of the state or a male slave of a private citizen or a female slave of a private citizen to escape through the city gate, he shall be put to death.

16. If a seignior has harbored in his house either a fugitive male or female slave belonging to the state or to a private citizen and has not brought him forth at the summons of the police, that householder shall be put to death.

17. If a seignior caught a fugitive male or female slave in the open and has taken him to his owner, the owner of the slave shall pay him two shekels[177] of silver.

18. If that slave has not named his owner, he shall take him to the palace in order that his record may be investigated, and they shall return him to his owner.

19. If he has kept that slave in his house [and] later the slave has been found in his possession, that seignior shall be put to death.

20. If the slave has escaped from the hand of his captor, that seignior shall [so] affirm by god to the owner of the slave and he shall then go free.

21. If a seignior made a breach in a house, they shall put him to death in front of that breach and wall him in.[178]

22. If a seignior committed robbery and has been caught, that seignior shall be put to death.

23. If the robber has not been caught, the robbed seignior shall set forth the particulars regarding his lost property in the presence of god, and the city and governor, in whose territory and district the robbery was committed, shall make good to him his lost property.

24. If it was a life [that was lost], the city and governor shall pay one mina[179] of silver to his people.[180]

25. If fire broke out in a seignior's house and a seignior, who went to extinguish [it], cast his eye on the goods of the owner of the house and has appropriated the goods of the owner of the house, that seignior shall be thrown into that fire. . . .

115. If a seignior held [a debt of] grain or money against a[nother] seignior and distrained (someone as) his pledge and the pledge has then died a natural death[181] in the house of his distrainer, that case is not subject to claim.

116. If the pledge has died from beating or abuse in the house of his distrainer, the owner of the pledge shall prove it against his merchant, and if it was the seignior's son, they shall put his son to death; if it was the seignior's slave, he shall pay one-third mina of silver and also forfeit everything else that he lent.

117. If an obligation came due against a seignior[182] and he sold [the services of] his wife, his son, or his daughter, or he has been bound over[183] to service, they shall work [in] the house of their purchaser or obligee for three years, with their freedom reestablished in the fourth year.[184]

118. When a male slave or a female slave has been bound over to service, if the merchant foreclosed,[185] he may sell [him], with no possibility of his being reclaimed.

119. If an obligation came due against a seignior and he has accordingly sold [the services of] his female slave who bore him children, the owner of the female slave may repay the money which the merchant paid out and thus redeem his female slave.

---

178. Cf. Exodus 22:2, 3a.
179. A weight of about 500 gr., divided into 60 shekels.
180. With §§23 and 24 cf. Deuteronomy 21:1 ff.
181. Lit., "in accordance with his fate."
182. Lit., "If with respect to a seignior [emphatic accusative of specification] an obligation has seized him."
183. The verb used here, *ittandin*, is IV 2 preterit with passive force, and not I 2 present, as regularly interpreted. For a discussion of this section and the following two, see T. J. Meek, *Journal of Near Eastern Studies* 7 (1948): 180–83.
184. Cf. Exodus 21:2–11; Deuteronomy 15:12–18.
185. Lit., "he caused (the time limit) to expire."

175. Lit., "he weighed out." In the time of Hammurabi coinage had of course not yet been invented and the money (usually silver, as here) was weighed out in bars.
176. Cf. Exodus 21:16; Deuteronomy 24:7.
177. A weight of about 8 gr.

120. If a seignior deposited his grain in a[nother] seignior's house for storage and a loss has then occurred at the granary or the owner of the house opened the storage-room and took grain or he has denied completely[186] [the receipt of] the grain which was stored in his house, the owner of the grain shall set forth the particulars regarding his grain in the presence of god and the owner of the house shall give to the owner of the grain double the grain that he took.[187]

121. If a seignior stored grain in a[nother] seignior's house, he shall pay five *qu* of grain per *kur* of grain[188] as the storage-charge per year.

122. If a seignior wishes to give silver, gold, or any sort of thing to a[nother] seignior for safekeeping, he shall show to witnesses the full amount that he wishes to give, arrange the contracts, and then commit [it] to safekeeping.

123. If he gave [it] for safekeeping without witnesses and contracts and they have denied [its receipt] to him at the place where he made the deposit, that case is not subject to claim.

124. If a seignior gave silver, gold, or any sort of thing for safekeeping to a[nother] seignior in the presence of witnesses and he has denied [the fact] to him, they shall prove it against that seignior and he shall pay double whatever he denied.

125. If a seignior deposited property of his for safekeeping and at the place where he made the deposit his property has disappeared along with the property of the owner of the house, either through breaking in or through scaling [the wall], the owner of the house, who was so careless that he let whatever was given to him for safekeeping get lost, shall make [it] good and make restitution to the owner of the goods, while the owner of the house shall make a thorough search for his lost property and take [it] from its thief.

126. If the seignior's property was not lost, but he has declared, "My property is lost," thus deceiving his city council,[189] his city council shall set forth the facts regarding him in the presence of god, that his property was not lost, and he shall give to his city council double whatever he laid claim to.

127. If a seignior pointed the finger at a nun or the wife of a[nother] seignior, but has proved nothing, they shall drag that seignior into the presence of the judges and also cut off half his [hair].

128. If a seignior acquired a wife, but did not draw up the contracts for her, that woman is no wife.

129. If the wife of a seignior has been caught while lying with another man, they shall bind them and throw them into the water. If the husband[190] of the woman wishes to spare his wife, then the king in turn may spare his subject.[191]

130. If a seignior bound the [betrothed] wife of a[nother] seignior, who had had no intercourse with[192] a male and was still living in her father's house, and he has lain in her bosom and they have caught him, that seignior shall be put to death, while that woman shall go free.[193]

131. If a seignior's wife was accused by her husband,[194] but she was not caught while lying with another man, she shall make affirmation by god and return to her house.

132. If the finger was pointed at the wife of a seignior because of another man, but she has not been caught while lying with the other man, she shall throw herself into the river[195] for the sake of her husband.[196]

133. If a seignior was taken captive, but there was sufficient to live on in his house, his wife [shall not leave her house, but she shall take care of her person by not] entering [the house of another].[197]

133a. If that woman did not take care of her person, but has entered the house of another, they shall prove it against that woman and throw her into the water.[198]

134. If the seignior was taken captive and there was not sufficient to live on in his house, his wife may enter the house of another, with that woman incurring no blame at all.

135. If, when a seignior was taken captive and there was not sufficient to live on in his house, his wife has then entered the house of another before his [return] and has borne children, [and] later her husband has returned and has reached his city, that woman shall return to her first husband, while the children shall go with their father.

136. If, when a seignior deserted his city and then ran away, his wife has entered the house of another after his [departure], if that seignior has returned and wishes to take back his wife, the wife of the fugitive shall not return to her husband because he scorned his city and ran away. . . .

---

186. Lit., "denied unto completeness."
187. Cf. Exodus 22:7–9.
188. I.e., 1⅔% since there were 300 *qu* in a *kur*.
189. This would seem to be the best translation of *babtum*, a feminine formation from *babum* "gate." Its use here is identical with that of *sa'ar* "gate," in Ruth 3:11; 4:10.

190. Lit., "owner, master."
191. Lit., "his slave." With this law cf. Deuteronomy 22:22.
192. Lit., "had not known."
193. Cf. Deuteronomy 22:23–27.
194. Lit., "If with respect to a seignior's wife (*casus pendens*) her husband accused her."
195. I.e. submit to the water ordeal, with the river as divine judge; cf. §2 above and note 170.
196. Cf. Numbers 5:11–31.
197. I.e. in order to live there as another man's wife.
198. I.e. to be drowned.

153. If a seignior's wife has brought about the death of her husband because of another man, they shall impale that woman on stakes.

154. If a seignior has had intercourse with his daughter, they shall make that seignior leave the city.

155. If a seignior chose a bride for his son and his son had intercourse with her, but later he himself has lain in her bosom and they have caught him, they shall bind that seignior and throw him[199] into the water.

156. If a seignior chose a bride for his son and his son did not have intercourse with her, but he himself has lain in her bosom, he shall pay to her one-half mina of silver and he shall also make good to her whatever she brought from her father's house in order that the man of her choice may marry her.

157. If a seignior has lain in the bosom of his mother after [the death of] his father, they shall burn both of them. . . .

192. If the [adopted] son of a chamberlain or the (adopted) son of a votary has said to his foster father or his foster mother, "You are not my father," "You are not my mother," they shall cut out his tongue.

193. If the [adopted] son of a chamberlain or the [adopted] son of a votary found out his parentage[200] and came to hate his foster father and his foster mother and so has gone off to his paternal home, they shall pluck out his eye.

194. When a seignior gave his son to a nurse and that son has died in the care[201] of the nurse, if the nurse has then made a contract for another son without the knowledge of his father and mother, they shall prove it against her and they shall cut off her breast because she made a contract for another son without the knowledge of his father and mother.

195. If a son has struck his father, they shall cut off his hand.[202]

196. If a seignior has destroyed the eye of a member of the aristocracy,[203] they shall destroy his eye.[204]

197. If he has broken a(nother) seignior's bone, they shall break his bone.[205]

198. If he has destroyed the eye of a commoner or broken the bone of a commoner, he shall pay one mina of silver.

199. If he has destroyed the eye of a seignior's slave or broken the bone of a seignior's slave, he shall pay one-half his value.

200. If a seignior has knocked out a tooth of a seignior of his own rank, they shall knock out his tooth.[206]

201. If he has knocked out a commoner's tooth, he shall pay one-third mina of silver.

202. If a seignior has struck the cheek of a seignior who is superior to him, he shall be beaten sixty (times) with an oxtail whip in the assembly.

203. If a member of the aristocracy has struck the cheek of a(nother) member of the aristocracy who is of the same rank as[207] himself, he shall pay one mina of silver.

204. If a commoner has struck the cheek of a[nother] commoner, he shall pay ten shekels of silver.

205. If a seignior's slave has struck the cheek of a member of the aristocracy, they shall cut off his ear.

206. If a seignior has struck a[nother] seignior in a brawl and has inflicted an injury on him, that seignior shall swear, "I did not strike him deliberately";[208] and he shall also pay for the physician.

207. If he has died because of his blow, he shall swear [as before], and if it was a member of the aristocracy, he shall pay one-half mina of silver.

208. If it was a member of the commonalty, he shall pay one-third mina of silver.

209. If a seignior struck a[nother] seignior's daughter and caused her to have a miscarriage,[209] he shall pay ten shekels of silver for her fetus.

210. If that woman has died, they shall put his daughter to death.

211. If by a blow he has caused a commoner's daughter to have a miscarriage, he shall pay five shekels of silver.

212. If that woman has died, he shall pay one-half mina of silver.

213. If he struck a seignior's female slave and has caused her to have a miscarriage, he shall pay two shekels of silver.

214. If that female slave has died, he shall pay one-third mina of silver.

215. If a physician performed a major operation on a seignior with a bronze lancet and has saved the seignior's life, or he opened up the eye-socket of a seignior with a bronze lancet and has saved the seignior's eye, he shall receive ten shekels of silver.

216. If it was a member of the commonalty, he shall receive five shekels.

199. Through a scribal error the original has "her."
200. Lit., "found out his father's house."
201. Lit., "in the hand."
202. Cf. Exodus 21:15. For the whole collection of laws dealing with personal injuries, §§195–214, cf. the similar collection in Exodus 21:12–27.
203. Lit., "the son of a man," with "son" used in the technical sense already explained in note 129 above and "man" clearly in the sense of "noble, aristocrat"; or it is possible that "son" here is to be taken in its regular sense to indicate a person younger than the assailant.
204. Cf. Exodus 21:23–25; Leviticus 24:19 f.; Deuteronomy 19:21.
205. Ibid.

206. Ibid.
207. Lit., "who is like."
208. Lit., "while I was aware of [it]."
209. Lit., "caused her to drop that of her womb [her fetus]." With this and the following five laws cf. Exodus 21:22–25.

217. If it was a seignior's slave, the owner of the slave shall give two shekels of silver to the physician.

218. If a physician performed a major operation on a seignior with a bronze lancet and has caused the seignior's death, or he opened up the eye-socket of a seignior and has destroyed the seignior's eye, they shall cut off his hand.

219. If a physician performed a major operation on a commoner's slave with a bronze lancet and has caused [his] death, he shall make good slave for slave.

220. If he opened up his eye-socket with a bronze lancet and has destroyed[210] his eye, he shall pay one-half his value in silver.

221. If a physician has set a seignior's broken bone, or has healed a sprained tendon, the patient[211] shall give five shekels of silver to the physician.

222. If it was a member of the commonalty, he shall give three shekels of silver.

223. If it was a seignior's slave, the owner of the slave shall give two shekels of silver to the physician.

224. If a veterinary surgeon[212] performed a major operation on either an ox or an ass and has saved [its] life, the owner of the ox or ass shall give to the surgeon one-sixth [shekel] of silver as his fee.

225. If he performed a major operation on an ox or an ass and has caused [its] death, he shall give to the owner of the ox or ass one-fourth its value.

226. If a brander cut off the slave-mark of a slave not his own without the consent of the owner of the slave, they shall cut off the hand of that brander.

227. If a seignior deceived a brander so that he has cut off the slave-mark of a slave not his own, they shall put that seignior to death and immure him at his gate; the brander shall swear, "I did not cut [it] off knowingly," and then he shall go free.

228. If a builder constructed a house for a seignior and finished [it] for him, he shall give him two shekels of silver per *sar*[213] of house as his remuneration.

229. If a builder constructed a house for a seignior, but did not make his work strong, with the result that the house which he built collapsed and so has caused the death of the owner of the house, that builder shall be put to death.

230. If it has caused the death of a son of the owner of the house, they shall put the son of that builder to death.

231. If it has caused the death of a slave of the owner of the house, he shall give slave for slave to the owner of the house.

232. If it has destroyed goods, he shall make good whatever it destroyed; also, because he did not make the house strong which he built and it collapsed, he shall reconstruct the house which collapsed at his own expense.[214]

233. If a builder constructed a house for a seignior and has not done his work properly so that a wall has become unsafe, that builder shall strengthen that wall at his own expense.[215] . . .

251. If a neighbor's ox was a gorer and his city council made it known to him that it was a gorer, but he did not pad its horns [or] tie up his ox, and that ox gored to death a member of the aristocracy, he shall give one-half mina of silver.

252. If it was a seignior's slave, he shall give one-third mina of silver.

253. If a seignior hired a[nother] seignior to oversee his field, and lending him *feed-grain*, entrusting him with oxen, contracted with him to cultivate the field, if that seignior stole the seed or fodder and it has been found in his possession, they shall cut off his hand.

254. If he appropriated the *feed-grain* and thus has starved the oxen, he shall make good twofold the grain which he received.

255. If he has let the seignior's oxen out on hire or he stole the seed-grain and so has raised nothing in the field, they shall prove it against that seignior and at harvest-time he shall measure out sixty *kur* of grain per eighteen *iku*.

256. If he was not able to meet his obligation, they shall drag him through that field with the oxen. . . .

265. If a shepherd, to whom cattle or sheep were given to pasture, became unfaithful and hence has altered the cattlemark or has sold [them], they shall prove it against him and he shall make good in cattle and sheep to their owner tenfold what he stole.

The Epilogue

The laws of justice, which Hammurabi, the efficient king, set up,
and by which he caused the land to take the right way and have good government.

I, Hammurabi, the perfect king,   (10)
was not careless [or] neglectful of the black-headed [people],
whom Enlil had presented to me,
[and] whose shepherding Marduk had committed to me;
I sought out peaceful regions for them;
I overcame grievous difficulties;   (20)
I caused light to rise on them.

---

210. The text has *uh-tap-da*, but this must be a scribal error for *uh-tap-pi-id*.
211. Lit., "owner of the injury."
212. Lit., "physician of an ox or an ass."
213. A measure equal to about 42 1/5 square yards.

214. Lit., "out of his own goods."
215. Lit., "out of his own money."

With the mighty weapon which Zababa and Inanna
    entrusted to me,
with the insight that Enki allotted to me,
with the ability that Marduk gave me,
I rooted out the enemy above and below;   (30)
I made an end of war;
I promoted the welfare of the land;
I made the peoples rest in friendly habitations;
I did not let them have anyone to terrorize them.
The great gods called me,   (40)
so I became the beneficent shepherd whose scepter is
    righteous;
my benign shadow is spread over my city.
In my bosom I carried the peoples of the land
    of Sumer and Akkad;   (50)
they prospered under my protection;
I always governed them in peace;
I sheltered them in my wisdom.
In order that the strong might not oppress
    the weak,   (60)
that justice might be dealt the orphan [and] the widow,
in Babylon, the city whose head Anum and Enlil raised
    aloft,
in Esagila, the temple whose foundations stand firm
    like heaven and earth,
I wrote my precious words on my stela,
and in the presence of the statute of me, the king of
    justice,
I set [it] up in order to administer the law
    of the land,   (70)
to prescribe the ordinances of the land,
to give justice to the oppressed.

I am the king who is preeminent among kings;   (80)
my words are choice; my ability has no equal.
By the order of Shamash, the great judge of heaven and
    earth,
may my justice prevail in the land;
by the word of Marduk, my lord,   (90)
may my statutes have no one to rescind them;
in Esagila, which I love, may my name be spoken in
    reverence forever!

Let any oppressed man who has a cause
come into the presence of the statue of me, the king of
    justice,
and then read carefully my inscribed stela,   (10)
and give heed to my precious words,
and may my stela make the case clear to him;
may he understand his cause;
may he set his mind at ease!
"Hammurabi, the lord,   (20)
who is like a real father to the people,
bestirred himself for the word of Marduk, his lord,

and secured the triumph of Marduk above
    and below,   (30)
thus making glad the heart of Marduk, his lord,
and he also ensured prosperity for the people forever,
and led the land aright"—
let him proclaim this,   (40)
and let him pray with his whole heart for me
in the presence of Marduk, my lord, and Sarpanit,
    my lady!
May the guardian spirit, the protecting genius,
the gods who enter Esagila, [and] Lebettum
    of Esagila,   (50)
prosper the wishes [made] daily
in the presence of Marduk, my lord, [and] Sarpanit,
    my lady!

In the days to come, for all time,   (60)
let the king who appears in the land observe
the words of justice which I wrote on my stela;
let him not alter the law of the land which I enacted,
the ordinances of the land which I prescribed;   (70)
let him not rescind my statutes!
If that man has intelligence
and is able to guide his land aright,
let him heed the words which I wrote on my stela,
and may this stela show him the road [and]
    the way,   (80)
the law of the land which I enacted,
the ordinances of the land which I prescribed;
and let him guide aright his black-headed [people]!
Let him enact the law for them;   (90)
let him prescribe the ordinances for them!
Let him root out the wicked and the evil from his land;
let him promote the welfare of his people!

I, Hammurabi, am the king of justice,
to whom Shamash committed law.
My words are choice; my deeds have no equal;   (100)
it is only to the fool that they are empty;
to the wise they stand forth as an object of wonder.
If that man heeded my words which I wrote on my
    stela,
and did not rescind my law,
has not distorted my words,
did not alter my statutes,   (10)
may Shamash make that man reign
as long as I, the king of justice;
may he shepherd his people in justice! . . .

Notes to the Code of Hammurabi

1. Note that homicide is dealt with in the Code of
Hammurabi in sections 153, 206, 210, 214, 218–219,
229–231, and 251–252.

The Middle Assyrian codes deal with homicide in sections 10 and 50–52.

The Hittite Code provides for homicide in sections 1–6 of the first part, and in sections 59 and 85 of the second part. Section 1 provides that a murderer should pay four men or women as compensation for the murder;[216] if a slain corpse is found in a field owned by no one, then the distance to the nearest village is measured from all sides of the corpse, with the nearest village paying compensation to the family of the victim.[217]

2. Notice the many florid phrases of self-flattery that King Hammurabi inserted in his Prologue: "the devout, god-fearing," "to rise like the sun over the black-headed people," "the efficient king," "the pious suppliant one, who brought abundance," "the wise king," "fighter without peer," "the one who plumbed the depths of wisdom," "the king who has made the four quarters of the world subservient," etc. Similarly, the inscriptions of the Egyptian pharaohs record their mighty deeds and praises but not their faults. These might be contrasted with the biblical perspective as reflected in this statement about Moses: "And the man Moses was humbler than any man on the face of the earth" (Num. 12:3); the many wrong-doings of Moses and other leaders are recorded in the Bible.

3. *"To cause justice to prevail in the land"* (Prologue, i, 31); *"who makes law prevail"* (iv, 51); *"I established law and justice in the language of the land, thereby promoting the welfare of the people"* (v, 19–21). These lines indicate the prevailing perspective, not different, in essence, from the view in our own Declaration of Independence, that it was the duty and function of the king to establish law and justice throughout the land and promote the welfare of the people. This perspective may have served as an effective limitation on the powers and authoritarian actions of the Mesopotamian king.

4. *"If a seignior accused another seignior and brought a charge of murder against him, but has not proved it, his accuser shall be put to death"* (Laws, 1). Note that the principle of *lex talionis*, or measure for measure, is employed here. This was a fundamental perspective in the concept of justice in the ancient Near East.

The inflexible application of this principle may lead to vicarious punishment, since "measure for measure" can also mean that if a child is killed, the child of the murderer shall be killed.[218] A similar notion, though not carried to the extremes prevalent in Mesopotamia, is found in the Bible:[219] "And you shall do to him as he schemed to do to his brother" (Deut. 19:19) and "As he did, so shall be done to him . . . An eye for an eye . . . Just as he inflicted a defect in a person, so shall it be inflicted in him" (Lev. 24:19–20). Jewish legal tradition, however, insists that this was not intended to be applied literally and was not applied in practice.[220]

5. Why does the Code of Hammurabi provide only that one who falsely accuses another of murder is to be put to death, but nowhere provides explicitly that he who murders another shall be killed?

6. *"The one against whom the charge of sorcery was brought . . . shall throw himself into the river"* (Laws, 2). Note that there apparently was no presumption of innocence applied here. The perception was that, in any event, if the accused were innocent, the river would demonstrate it. Compare, however, the first section of the laws, in which the guilt of the accused had to be proved.

7. *"If the river has then overpowered him, . . . if the river has shown that seignior to be innocent and he has accordingly come forth safe"* (Laws, 2). The theory seems to have been that if the man were innocent, the river god would protect him and would not permit him to drown. In other Mesopotamian societies, there was a reverse theory. If a man were innocent, the river god would "accept" him and permit him to sink. If he were guilty, the river god would "reject" him and would cause him to float on top of the river. The one who sunk down into the river was therefore innocent and would have to be pulled out quickly, before he drowned in its depths. This theory also was followed in medieval Europe and in the Salem witch trials in Massachusetts in 1692.

8. Many provisions of the Code of Hammurabi provide the death penalty for a thief, (e.g., sections 6, 7, 9, 10, 22, and 25); these appear contradictory to the provisions that thefts from a field were punishable by a fine (sections 256 and 259) and that thefts of animals required repayment in kind of many animals for each one stolen (sections 8 and 265). Whether the death penalty was actually carried out in practice is a subject of debate among scholars. It does seem, however, to reflect the perspective that a thief deserved the death penalty. Compare Exodus 22:6, which provides only a fine for all kinds of theft.

9. *"If a seignior made a breach in a house, they shall put him to death in front of that breach and wall him*

---

216. Compare to "Soul for a Soul" (Exod. 21:23).
217. Compare Deut. 21.
218. See Code of Hammurabi, sec. 230.

219. Compare "He who sheds the blood of man, by man shall his blood be shed" (Gen. 9:6).
220. Talmud, *Baba Kama* 84a; *Sanhedrin* 79b; see Rambam, Laws of Injuries and Damages, 1:3.

in" (Laws, 21). The language about a thief making a breach in a house in order to enter and burglarize it resembles somewhat the phraseology in Exodus 22:2 concerning a thief who is caught while "tunneling" into a house. In the Bible, however, the thief is not to be executed. If, however, in the course of battling with the burglar, the owner kills him, the householder is not guilty of murder.

In the Code of Hammurabi the execution of the thief "in front of that breach" is another reflection of the perspective that punishment was to be meted out "measure for measure." Here this took the form of execution at the place where the criminal offense was committed, or sealing up the breach in the wall with the thief's own body as punishment for his breaching the wall.

10. Section 23 of the laws of Hammurabi, requiring the locality to compensate the victim of a theft, is an ancient precursor of contemporary schemes to provide restitution for the victims of crimes. Such plans have been instituted in a number of jurisdictions in the United States. The Code of Hammurabi, however, reflects the notions both of communal responsibility and of compensation for life by the payment of money. The Bible, with its stress on individual responsibility for crimes[221] and on the sacredness and uniqueness of human life, makes it impossible to equate money with life (Num. 35:31) and has no provisions for communal payment of money to victims. Compare, however, the killing of the heifer by the adjoining community, required in the Bible in the case of a murdered person whose murderer is not caught,[222] and the notion in the Jewish tradition that "All of Israel are responsible for each other."[223] In the case of the unapprehended murderer, the Bible, requires the elders of the nearest city to wash their hands, slaughter a heifer, and affirm their innocence.[224] These acts do imply their responsibility to and for maintaining law and order in their community although in a human court of law, each person is answerable only for his own acts.

In documents recovered from the city of Nuzi, in Syria, there is an actual case in which the victim of a burglary sued the city for compensation. The city defended on the grounds that the items were not actually stolen, but it did not question the principle of compensation. This indicates that a rule similar to this provision of the Code of Hammurabi was in fact applied. It also may imply that rules similar to other provisions of the code were also applied in practice, even though

extant court records from that era do not refer to the Code of Hammurabi as the source or guideline for the law.

In what other respects does criminal law in the United States today reflect the notion of communal responsibility?

11. *"If fire broke out in a seignior's house and a seignior, who went to extinguish it, cast his eye on the goods of the owner of the house and has appropriated the goods of the owner of the house, that seignior shall be thrown into that fire"* (Laws, 25). Here, too, we have an extreme example of punishment "measure for measure," involving the taking of a life as a penalty for the taking of property. As indicated earlier, it is not known whether this was applied in practice.

12. Section 129 of the code provides that the life of a married adulteress may be spared by her husband. For a comparison with the biblical provisions, see Greenberg, "Some Postulates of Biblical Criminal Law," Chapter III, Section B 4 *a*).

13. Section 132 requires a married woman accused of adultery to go through an ordeal by throwing herself into a river to see whether she would drown. Compare the biblical provisions (in a similar case) for a rather harmless "ordeal," consisting of her swallowing water mixed with some earth from the Tabernacle floor. A document setting forth a curse upon adulteresses was immersed in the water (Num. 5:11–31).

14. *"If a seignior's wife has brought about the death of her husband because of another man, they shall impale that woman on stakes"* (Laws, 153). This implies a death penalty for the wife, even if she did not herself murder her husband but "brought about" his death at the hands of another. This offense, amounting to conspiracy, is not found in the Bible and was not carried over into later Judaic law. The crime of conspiracy would involve treating a conspirator as though he had committed the homicide that in fact had been carried out by his accomplice. This would be contrary to the biblical insistence on individual responsibility for one's own acts.[225]

15. Sections 194–197, again, reflect application of the perspective of "measure for measure" by inflicting the penalty upon the organ with which the offender committed the act, or upon an organ of the offender of the same type as the organ that was injured.

16. Sections 199 and 200, in referring to cases of assault in which an eye or tooth are destroyed, employ some of the same examples described in the Bible (Exod. 21:23–25; Lev. 24:19; Deut. 19:21). Why are

---

221. "Each man shall die for his own offense" (Deut. 24:16).
222. Deut. 21:1–9.
223. Talmud, *Shavuot* 39a.
224. Deut. 21:1–9.

225. "Each man shall die for his own offense," Deut. 24:16. See Talmud, *Kiddushin* 43a; *Sanhedrin* 77; Rambam, Laws Concerning a Murderer, ch. 2, rule 2 (Part Two, Chapter VI, Section C 1 *a*, below).

injuries to an eye and a tooth so prevalent in the Bible and Mesopotamian law codes as exemplars of tortious injury? It may be that these are intended to imply that the norms cover a wide spectrum ranging from injuries to an eye (considered as the most valuable and irreplaceable organ to injuries to a tooth, the least valuable.[226]

17. Section 207 refers to accidental death. There is only the payment of a monetary fine, but no mention of fleeing to a city of refuge. If the avenging of blood by a relative was a common practice,[227] one would expect it to be mentioned here.[228]

18. Section 218 holds a physician liable for the death of his patient ("they shall cut off his hand"). Does this conflict with section 207, which provides for monetary payment only for accidental death, rather than cutting off the hand of the assailant? Does section 218 refer to malpractice or gross negligence, which perhaps is treated more severely than death resulting unexpectedly from a blow? Compare Deuteronomy 25:12: "You shall cut off her hand." Here, too, Jewish legal tradition understood this as requiring a payment of money only.[229]

19. Section 229 holds a builder liable with his life for the death resulting when a house that he has constructed collapses. Liability for death, even where the victim was not killed directly by the defendant, is also reflected in Section 153. The Jewish legal tradition is contrary (see Part Two, Chapter VI, section C, below, and sources cited there).

20. Section 230 reflects a perspective that a child may be punished for the offense of his parents. For contrast with the biblical law, see Deuteronomy 24:16: "Each man shall be killed for his owns sins," and Greenberg, "Some Postulates of Biblical Criminal Law," Chapter III, Section B 4 *a*.

21. The owner of an ox that gores a person to death is only liable to a fine, even though he was warned (section 251). This leniency should be compared with the biblical prescription (Exod. 21:29) that initially provides death for the owner of the ox, although payment of money would act as a substitute for this penalty. This is the reversal of the normal treatment, since the Code of Hammurabi usually provides for a much more severe penalty than the Bible. What is the reason for this reversal of roles?

22. The Epilogue, rather than reflecting mere boasting (as in the Prologue), appears to represent the king's affirmation to the gods that he has carried out the duties incumbent upon him to establish law and to care for his people. Notice that the Epilogue expresses some of the same concerns as the Bible, such as to cause "the land to take the right way and have good government," (line 6–10); to make "an end of war," (line 31); to make sure "that the strong might not oppress the weak" and "justice might be dealt the orphan and the widow" (lines 58–60); "to prescribe ordinances of the land" and "to give justice to the oppressed" (line 70 ff).

23. *"Let any oppressed man who has a cause come into the presence of me, the king of justice, and then read carefully my inscribed stela"* (Epilogue, beginning of the second section). How many people during the reign of King Hammurabi were able to read? Was there free access to the temple where his code was inscribed? If not, what was the purpose of inscribing the code, and of these phrases of the epilogue?[230]

b. THE LAWS OF UR-NAMMU
(Translated by J. J. Finkelstein) *

Ur-Nammu (2112–2095 B.C.) was the founding ruler of the Third Dynasty of Ur, the builder of the best preserved ziggurat in ancient Mesopotamia, whose reign inaugurated the last great period of Sumerian literary creativity. Although some contemporary examples of this creative effort have begun to come to light in recent excavations at Nippur, most of the literary and scholarly production of this period is known only from copies produced in the scribal schools in Nippur and Ur some two to three hundred years later, i.e. between 1800 and 1700 B.C. This is true of the two extant manuscripts of of the Ur-Nammu Laws. Text A, Ni 3191, was copied in Nippur, and was edited by S. N. Kramer in *Orientalia*, XXIII (1954), 40 ff., with additional notes by A. Falkenstein, ibid., pp. 49 ff. This tablet originally contained eight columns of writing, four on each side, but less than half of the original content is preserved. Almost all of the obverse, the better preserved face, is devoted to the prologue, so that very little legal material is preserved in this text. Text B consists of two fragments, U.7739 and U.7740, of what was once a single tablet, but the two fragments do not join. They were found in Ur, and like text A, were written by a student scribe during the Old Babylonian period. This text was edited by O. R. Gurney and S. N. Kramer in *AS*, XVI (1965, the Landsberger Festschrift), 13–19. The editors thought that the tablet was intended to

---

226. See Hoffman, Responsa *Das Buch Leviticus* (Jerusalem, 1967), p. 216.

227. See Exod. 21:13; Num. 35:19, 21; Deut. 19:12.

228. Cf. Robertson-Smith, *Kinship and Marriage*, pref. and ch. 2.

229. ?, ad loc.; see Section B 3, above.

230. See S. Paul, "The Problem of the Prologue and the Epilogue to the Book of the Covenant," Section F 3, below.

*From J. B. Pritchard, *Ancient Near Eastern Texts Relating to the Old Testament* (Princeton, 1955). Accents have been omitted.

contain ten columns of writing—five on each face—of which only the obverse, one column on the reverse, plus one line on the next column were completed. The student scribe, for some unknown reason, stopped at that point, and failed to complete the tablet. As will be indicated below, the present translator believes that the tablet was originally intended to contain eight columns rather than ten (like the A text), of which the four of the obverse and the one on the reverse (col. v) plus one additional line were actually completed. (This opinion has since been confirmed by Dr. E. Sollberger of the British Museum, who has kindly provided the present author with photographs of the two fragments, and the information about their relative points of thickness, which precludes the possibility of an additional column.)

The present translation for the first time integrates both manuscripts into a single text as far as the extant material allows. The line count of text A as given by Kramer, while in need of some adjustment in the light of B, is retained here for the convenience of reference. The numeration §§ of text B is also retained here and cited within parentheses. The translation, while the responsibility of the present translator, is built upon that of S. N. Kramer in his original edition, and owes much besides to the enthusiastic cooperation of Professor Kramer while it was being prepared.

[lines 1–23 destroyed or fragmentary] (24–30) . . . [of] the land . . . , . . . monthly, he established for him 90 *kor* of barley, 30 sheep, and 50 quarts of butter, as a regular offering. (31–35) After An and Enlil had turned over the Kingship of Ur to Nanna, (36–40) at that time did Ur-Nammu, son born of [the goddess] Ninsun, for his beloved mother who bore him, (41–42) in accordance with his [i.e., of the god Nanna] principles of equity and truth, . . . [lines 43–72 destroyed or fragmentary].

(col. ii 73–74) He set up the seven . . . (75–78) Nammahni, the *ensi* of Lagash he slew. (79–84) By the might of Nanna, lord of the city [of Ur], he returned the Magan-boat of Nanna to the *boundary*[-*canal*], (85–86) [and] made it famous in Ur.

(87–96) At that time, the field[s] had been subject to the *nisqum*-official, the maritime trade was subject to the seafarers' overseer, (col. iii) the herdsman was subject to the "oxen-taker," the "sheep-taker," and the "donkey-taker."

[lines 97–103 destroyed] (104–113) Then did Ur-Nammu, the mighty warrior, king of Ur, king of Sumer and Akkad, by the might of Nanna, lord of the city [of Ur], and in accordance with the true word of Utu, establish equity in the land (114–116) [and] he banished malediction, violence and strife. (117–122) *By granting immunity in Akkad* to the maritime trade from

the seafarers' overseer, to the herdsman from the "oxen-taker, the "sheep-taker," and the "donkey-taker," he (123–124) set Sumer and Akkad *free*.

(125–129) At that time, the . . . . of Mar[ad] [and] Kazal[lu] *he* . . . . (130–134) [By] the might [of Nanna] [his] lord . . . . , he . . . . (135–142) The copper . . . , the [wooden] . . . [three lines missing], the copper . . . , the wooden . . . , [these] seven . . . , he standardized. (143–144) He fashioned the bronze *sila*-measure, (145–149) he standardized the one *mina* weight, [and] standardized the stone-weight of a shekel of silver *in relation to* one mina.

(150–152) At that time, the bank of the Tigris, the bank of the Euphrates . . . [153–160 destroyed] . . . (161) the king [or "owner"] provided a head gardener.

(162–168) The orphan was not delivered up to the rich man; the widow was not delivered up to the mighty man; the man of one shekel was not delivered up to the man of one mina.

[From line 169 to line 205, the A text is almost completely destroyed. It is likely that the series of law-cases began towards the lower end of col. iv on the obverse of the tablet, or at the very beginning of col. v on the reverse, since traces strongly suggest the beginning of a law-case with line 196, which will be considered here as § 1.]

2. (206–215) . . . . . . he shall plant for him, his . . . the planted . . . apple trees and cedars . . . [*he* . . .] without the owner's knowledge, . . . he shall bring in.

3. [216–221, destroyed]

4. (222–231 equals B § 1). If the wife of a man, *by employing her charms*, followed after another man and he slept with her, they [i.e., the authorities] shall slay that woman, but that male [i.e., the other man] shall be set free.

5. (232–239 equals B § 2). If a man proceeded by force, and deflowered the virgin (lit., "undeflowered") slave-woman of another man, that man must pay five shekels of silver.

6. (app. 240–244 equals B § 3). If a man divorces his primary wife, he must pay [her] one mina of silver.

7. (app. 245–249 equals B § 4). If it is a [former] widow [whom] he divorces, he must pay [her] one-half mina of silver.

8. (250–255 equals B § 5). If [however] the man had slept with the widow without there having been any marriage contract, he need not pay [her] any silver.

9. (equals 256–269 mostly destroyed)

10. (270–280). If a man had accused a[nother] man of . . . and he [i.e., the accuser] had him [i.e., the accused] brought to the river-ordeal, and the river-ordeal proved him innocent, then the man who had brought him [i.e., the accuser] must pay him three shekels of silver.

11. (281–290 equals B § 10). If a man accused the wife of a man of fornication, and the river[-ordeal] proved her innocent, then the man who had accused her must pay one-third of a mina of silver.

12. (291–301 equals B § 11). If a [prospective] son-in-law entered the house of his [prospective] father-in-law, but his father-in-law later gave [his daughter (i.e., the prospective bride) to] another man, he [the father-in-law] shall return to him [i.e., the rejected son-in-law] *two*-fold the amount of bridal presents he had brought.

13. (302–312 equals B § 12). [Only traces remain.]

14. (313–323, omitted in B). If [. . .] a slave-woman [*or a male slave fled from the master's house*] and crossed beyond the territory of the city, and [another] man brought her/him back, the owner of the slave shall pay to the one who brought him back *two* shekels of silver.

15. (324–330 equals B § 13 + § 21). If a [man . . .] cut off the foot [var., limb] of [another man *with his* . . .], he shall pay ten shekels of silver.

16. (331–338, omitted in B). If a man, in the course of a scuffle, smashed the limb of another man with a club, he shall pay one mina of silver.

17. (339–344 equals B § 22). If someone severed the nose of another man with a *copper knife*, he must pay two-thirds of a mina of silver.

18. (A 345–? equals B § 23). If a man cut off the [. . .] of [another man] with a [. . .] he shall pay [x shekels(?) of silv]er.

19. (B § 24 plus § 16). If he [*knocked out*] his to[*oth*] with [a . . .] he shall pay two shekels of silver.

20. [missing]. [There is a gap of close to 30 lines, which contained not more than three sections, including § 20, § 21, and the beginning of § 21'.]

21'. (B § 28). . . . he shall surely bring. If he has no slave-woman, he must surely pay ten shekels of silver. If he has no silver, *he shall pay him* [*with*] *whatever possessions he* [*owns*].

22'. (B § 29). If a man's slave-woman, comparing herself to her mistress, speaks insolently to her [or, him], her mouth shall be scoured with 1 quart of salt.

23'. (B § 30). If a man's slave-woman, comparing herself to her mistress, struck her . . [rest missing].

24'. [almost completely missing, possibly more than one section in the gap]

25'. (B § 34). If a man appeared as a witness (in a law suit), and was shown to be a perjurer, he must pay fifteen shekels of silver.

26'. (B § 35). If a man appeared as a witness (in a lawsuit), but declined to testify on oath, he must make good as much as is involved in that lawsuit.

27'. (B § 36). If a man proceeded by force, and plowed the arable field of a[nother] man, and he [i.e.,

the latter] brought a lawsuit [against him], but he [i.e., the squatter] reacts in contempt, that man will forfeit his expenses.

28'. (B § 37). If a man flooded the field of a[nother] man with water, he shall measure out [for him] three *kor* of barley per *iku* of field.

29'. (B § 38). If a man had leased an arable field to a[nother] man for cultivation, but he [the lessee] did not plow it, so that it turned into wasteland, he shall measure out [to the lessor] three *kor* of barley per *iku* of field.

[remainder of text largely destroyed]

Notes to the Laws of Ur-Nammu

The Laws of Ur-Nammu, unlike the laws of Hammurabi, contain provisions to standardize weights and measures and to grant protection from the tyranny of certain officials (lines 117–124, 143–149). King Hammurabi prescribed similar provisions in his *mesharum* edicts, but these were *not* included in his code.

c. LIPIT-ISHTAR LAW CODE
(Translated by S. N. Kramer)*

Like the Hammurabi Code, that of Lipit-Ishtar consists of three main sections: a Prologue; the legal text proper consisting of a large number of laws introduced by a Sumerian complex which is roughly the equivalent of the English word "if"; an Epilogue. The Prologue begins with a statement by King Lipit-Ishtar, the fifth ruler of the Dynasty of Isin, that after the leading Sumero-Babylonian deities Anu and Enlil had given the goddess Ninisinna[231] a favorable reign in her city Isin, and after they had called him, Lipit-Ishtar, "to the princeship of the land" in order "to bring well-being to the Sumerians and the Akkadians," he established justice in Sumer and Akkad. He then cites some of his achievements in regard to the welfare of his subjects: he freed "the sons and daughters of Sumer and Akkad" from slaveship which had been imposed upon them; he reestablished equitable family practices. The end of the Prologue unfortunately is destroyed; so, too, is the beginning of the legal text proper.

As for the legal body of the Lipit-Ishtar Code, the available text permits the restoration, wholly or in part, of some thirty-eight laws; practically all belong to the second half of the code, the first half being almost entirely destroyed. The subject matter treated in these laws is as follows: hiring of boats (laws 4 and 5); real

*From J. B. Pritchard, *Ancient Near Eastern Texts Relating to the Old Testament* (Princeton, 1955). Accents have been omitted. Footnotes are from the original, renumbered.

231. Ninisinna, "Queen of Isin," is the tutelary deity of Isin, just as Marduk was that of Babylon.

estate, particularly orchards (laws 7–11); slaves and perhaps servants (laws 12–17); defaulting of taxes (law 18 and probably 19); inheritance and marriage (laws 20–33); rented oxen (34–37). Immediately following the last of the thirty-eight laws extant wholly or in part, follows the Epilogue; because of the numerous breaks in the text, the latter is only partially intelligible. It begins with a reiteration by Lipit-Ishtar that he established justice in the land, and that he brought well-being to its people. He then states that he had set up "this stela," that is the stela on which the original code was inscribed,[232] and proceeds to bless those who will not damage it in any way, and to curse those who will.

The text of the code is reconstructed from seven clay tablets and fragments. Four of these are "excerpt tablets," that is, they are one- or two-column tablets which did not contain the entire code, but only small parts of it excerpted for scribal purposes. The remaining three pieces are all parts of a large, probably twenty-column tablet, which in its original state had contained the entire lawcode, including Prologue and Epilogue. Six of the seven tablets and fragments were excavated at Nippur and are now in the University Museum; one, of unknown provenience, is in the Louvre. All seven pieces date from the Early Post-Sumerian period, that is, they were actually inscribed sometime in the first half of the second millennium B.C. As for the first compilation of the code, it must have taken place sometime during the eleven-year reign of Lipit-Ishtar, who ruled probably during the first half of the nineteenth century B.C.; it thus antedates the Hammurabi Code by more than a century and a half. A scientific edition of the available text of the code, including copies of the unpublished material in the University Museum, was published by Francis R. Steele in *AJA*, LII (1948), 425–450; there, too, the relevant earlier studies are cited;[233] the present translation follows the Steele publication throughout.

Prologue[234]

[When] the great [Anu, the father of the go]ds, [and] [En]lil, [the king of all the lan]ds, [the lord who determines destin]ies, had . . . d to [Nini]sinna, [the daughter of A]nu the . . . *for* her . . . [*and*] the rejoicing . . . for her bright [forehead]; when they had giv[en h]er the kingship of Sumer [and] Akkad [and] a favorable

reign in her [city] Isin, the . . . established by Anu; when Anu [and] Enlil had called Lipit-Ishtar—Lipit-Ishtar, the wise shepherd whose name had been pronounced by Nunamnir [235]—to the princeship of the land in order to establish justice in the land, to banish complaints, to turn back enmity and rebellion by the force of arms, [and] to bring well-being to the Sumerians and Akkadians, then I, Lipit-Ishtar, the humble shepherd of Nippur, the stalwart farmer of Ur, who abandons not Eridu, the suitable lord of Erech, [king] of I[sin], [kin]g of Sum[er and Akkad], who am f[it] for the heart of Inanna, [estab]lished [jus]tice in [Su]mer and Akkad in accordance with the word of Enlil. Verily, in those [days] I *procured* . . . the [fre]edom of the [so]ns and daughters of [Nippur], the [so]ns and daughters of Ur, the sons and daughters of [I]sin, the [so]ns and daughters of [Sum]er [and] Akkad *upon whom* . . . slaveship . . . *had been imposed.* Verily, in accordance with . . . , I made the father *support* his children [and] I made the children [*support*] their father; I made the father sta[*nd by* hi]s children [and] I made the children *stand by* their father; in the father's house [and] [in the brother's] house I . . . . Verily, I, Lipit-Ishtar, the son of Enlil,[236] *brought* seventy into the father's house [and] the brother's house; *into* the bachelor's house I *brought* . . . *for ten months* . . . 10 . . . the wife of a man, . . . the child of a man. . . .[237]

The Laws

1. . . . which had been set up. . . .[238]

2. . . . the property of the father's house from its . . . .[239]

3. . . . the son of the state official, the son of the palace official, the son of the supervisor . . . .[240]

4. . . . a boat . . . a boat he shall . . . .

5. I[f] a man hired a boat [and] *set it on a* . . . *journey for him* . . . .[241]

6. . . . the gift . . . he shall . . . .

7. If he gave his orchard to a gardener to raise . . . [and] the gardener . . . to the owner of the garden . . . .[242]

232. The contents of our "code" tablet may be presumed to be identical with those of the original stela on which a scene similar to that on the Hammurabi stela may have been sculptured.

233. Cf. also Steele's preliminary announcement in *AJA*, LI (1947), 158–164.

234. For a brief comparative survey of the contents of the Lipit-Ishtar and Hammurabi codes, cf. Steele, *AJA*, LII (1948), 446–450.

235. Nunamnir is another name for the god Enlil; Lipit-Ishtar is frequently called "son of Enlil" in the relevant hymnal literature.

236. Cf. preceding note.

237. A break of more than two columns of text follows; at some point in this break the prologue ended and the laws began.

238. Remainder of the column destroyed.

239. Remainder of the column destroyed.

240. The remainder of this column and two additional columns are destroyed.

241. Remainder of column and beginning of following column destroyed.

242. Almost the entire remainder of the column destroyed.

8. If a man gave bare ground to [another] man to set out an orchard [and the latter] did not complete setting out that bare ground as an orchard, he shall give to the man who set out the orchard the bare ground which he neglected, as part of his share.

9. If a man entered the orchard of [another] man [and] was seized there for stealing, he shall pay ten shekels of silver.

10. If a man cut down a tree in the garden of [another] man, he shall pay one-half mina of silver.

11. If adjacent to the house of a man the bare ground of [another] man has been neglected and the owner of the house has said to the owner of the bare ground, "Because your ground has been neglected someone may break into my house; strengthen your house,"[243] [and] this agreement has been confirmed by him, the owner of the bare ground shall restore to the owner of the house any of his property that is lost.

12. If a slave-girl or slave of a man has fled into the heart of the city [and] *it has been confirmed* that he [or she] dwelt in the house of [another] man for one month, he shall give slave for slave.

13. If he has no slave, he shall pay fifteen shekels of silver.

14. If a man's slave has *compensated* his slaveship to his master [and] *it is confirmed* [*that he has compensated*] his master twofold, that slave shall be freed.

15. If a *miqtum*[244] is a grant of the king, he shall not be taken away.

16. If a *miqtum* went to a man *of his own free will*, that man shall not *hold* him; he [the *miqtum*] may go where he desires.

17. If a man *without authorization* bound [another] man *to a matter* to which he [the latter] had no knowledge, that man is not *affirmed*; he [the first man] shall bear the penalty in regard *to the matter to which he has bound him*.[245]

18. If the master of an estate or the mistress of an estate has defaulted on the tax of the estate [and] a stranger has borne it, for three years he [the owner] may not be evicted. [Afterwards] the man who bore the tax of the estate shall possess that estate and the [former] owner of the estate shall not raise any claim.

19. If the master of an estate . . . .[246]

20. If a man from the heir[s] seized . . . .[247]

21. . . . the house of the father . . . he [married], the gift of the house of *her* father which was presented to *her* as *her* heir he shall take.

22. If the father [is] living, his daughter whether she be an *entu*, a *natitu*,[248] or a heirodule, shall dwell *in* his house like an heir.

23. If the daughter *in* the house of [her] living father . . . .[249]

24. [I]f the secon[d wife] whom [he had] married bore him [chil]dren, the dowry which she brought from her father's house belongs to her children, [but] the children of [his] *first* wife and the children of [his] second wife shall divide equally the property of their father.

25. If a man married a wife [and] she bore him children and those children are living, and a slave also bore children for her master [but] the father granted freedom to the slave and her children, the children of the slave shall not divide the estate with the children of their [former] master.

26. [I]f his *first* [wife di]ed [and] [af]ter her [death] he takes his [slave] as a wife, the [children] of [his *first*] wife [are his he]irs; the children which [the slave] bore for her master shall be like . . . , his house they shall . . . .

27. If a man's wife has not borne him children [but] a harlot [from] the public square has borne him children, he shall provide grain, oil, and clothing for that harlot; the children which the harlot has borne him shall be his heirs, and as long as his wife lives the harlot shall not live in the house with his wife.

28. If a man has turned his face away from his *first* wife . . . [but] she has not gone out of the [house], his wife which he married *as his favorite* is a second wife; he shall continue to support his *first* wife.

29. If a son-in-law has entered the house of his [prospective] father-in-law [and] he made his betrothal [but] afterwards they made him go out [of the house] and gave his wife to his companion, they shall present to him the betrothal-gifts which he brought [and] that wife may not marry his companion.

30. If a young married man married a harlot [from] the public square [and] the judges have *ordered* him not to *visit* her, [but] afterwards he *divorced* his wife, money . . . .

31. . . . he has given him, after their father's death the heirs shall divide the estate of their father [but] the inheritance of the estate they shall not divide; they shall not "cook their father's word in water."[250]

---

243. That is, presumably, the broken-down house in the neglected grounds.

244. The meaning of the term *miqtum* (it is a Semitic, not a Sumerian, word) is unknown.

245. The rendering of this law is doubtful in many parts and its meaning is quite uncertain.

246. About ten lines destroyed.

247. About 34 lines destroyed.

248. Class of priestesses.

249. About 22 lines destroyed.

250. "Cook someone's word in water" seems to be an idiomatic expression for "disobey."

32. If a father while living has [set aside] a betrothal-gift for his eldest son[251] [and] [in] the presence of the father who was still alive he [the son] [married] a wife, after the father[’s death] the heir . . . .[252]

33. If it has been *confirmed* that the . . . had not divided the estate, he shall pay ten shekels of silver.

34. If a man rented an ox [and] injured the flesh at the nose ring, he shall pay one third of [its] price.

35. If a man rented an ox [and] damaged its eye, he shall pay one half of [its] price.

36. If a man rented an ox [and] broke its horn, he shall pay one fourth of [its] price.

37. If a man rented an ox [and] damaged its tail, he shall pay one fourth of [its] price.

38. . . . [he shall] pay.

Epilogue

Verily in accordance with the tr[ue word] of Utu, I caused [Su]mer and Akkad to hold to true justice. Verily in accordance with the pronouncement of Enlil, I, Lipit-Ishtar, the son of Enlil,[253] *abolished* enmity and rebellion; made weeping, lamentations, outcries . . . taboo; caused righteousness and truth to exist; brought well-being to the Sumerians and the Akkadians. . . .[254]

Verily when I had established the wealth of Sumer and Akkad, I erected this stela. May he who will not commit any evil deed *with regard to it*, who will not damage my handiwork, who will [not] erase its inscription, who will not write his own name upon it—be presented with life and breath of long days; may he rise high in the Ekur;[255] may Enlil's bright forehead *look down upon him*. [On the other hand] he who will commit some evil deed *with regard to it*, who will damage my handiwork, who will enter the storeroom [and] *change* its pedestal, who will erase its inscription, who will write his own [name] upon it [or] who, because of this [curse], will [substi]tute someone else for himself—[that man, whe]ther he be a . . . , [whether he] be a . . . .[256] may *he* take away from him . . . [and] bring to *him* . . . in his . . . whoever, may Ashnan and Sumugan,[257] the lords[258] of abundance, take away from him[259] . . . his . . . may he *abolish*. . . . May Utu, the judge of heaven and earth . . . take away . . . his . . . its

foundation . . . as . . . may be counted; let not the foundation of his land be firm; its king, whoever he may be, may Ninurta,[260] the mighty hero, the son of Enlil. . . .[261]

d. THE LAWS OF ESHNUNNA
(Translated by Albrecht Goetze)*

Texts: Iraq Museum 51059 and 52614 excavated at Tell Abu Harmal[262] near Baghdad by the Iraq Directorate of Antiquities in Pre-Hammurabi layers. . . .

1. 1 kor of barley is [priced] at 1 shekel of silver; 3 *qa* of "best oil" are [priced] at 1 shekel of silver; 1 seah [and] 2 *qa* of sesame oil are [priced] at 1 shekel of silver; 1 seah [and] 5 *qa* of lard are [priced] at 1 shekel of silver; 4 seah of "river oil" are [priced] at 1 shekel of silver; 6 minas of wool are [priced] at 1 shekel of silver; 2 kor of salt[263] are [priced] at 1 shekel of silver; 1 kor . . . is [priced] at 1 shekel of silver; 3 minas of copper are [priced] at 1 shekel of silver; 2 minas of refined copper are [priced] at 1 shekel of silver.

2. 1 *qa* of sesame oil *sa nishatim*—its [value in] barley is 3 seah; 1 *qa* of lard *sa nishatim*—its [value in] barley is 2 seah and 5 *qa*; 1 *qa* of "river oil" *sa nishatim*—its [value in] barley is 8 *qa*.

3. The hire for a wagon together with its oxen and its driver is 1 pan [and] 4 seah of barley. If it is [paid in] silver, the hire is one third of a shekel. He shall drive it the whole day.

4. The hire for a boat is 2 *qa* per kor [of capacity], 1 seah 1 *qa* is the hire for the boatman. He shall drive it the whole day.

5. If the boatman is negligent and causes the sinking of the boat, he shall pay in full for everything the sinking of which he caused.

6. If a man . . .[264] takes possession of a boat [which is] not his, he shall pay 10 shekels of silver.

7. The wages of a harvester are 2 seah of barley; if they are [paid in] silver, his wages are 12 grain.

---

251. "Eldest son" is expressed here by the words "son, big brother."

252. About 17 lines destroyed.

253. Cf. n. 5.

254. About 19 lines missing.

255. Enlil's main temple in Nippur.

256. About 7 lines destroyed.

257. Ashnan is the goddess of grain and Sumugan is the god of the "plain."

258. In more exact language "the lords" should read "the lady and the lord."

259. About 22 lines destroyed.

260. Ninurta, the son of Enlil, is the god of the South Wind; for some of the heroic feats ascribed to him, cf. *SM*, pp. 79–82.

261. Probably only a few lines missing.

*From J. B. Pritchard, *Ancient Near Eastern Texts Relating to the Old Testament* (Princeton, 1955). Accents have been omitted. Footnotes are from the original, renumbered.

262. Abu Harmal formed part of the kingdom of Eshnunna —the Diyala region east of Baghdad—which flourished between the downfall of the Third Dynasty of Ur (about 2000 B.C.) and the creation of Hammurabi's empire. Eshnunna was one of the numerous Amurrite-controlled states of the period. The city of Eshnunna itself is located at Tell Asmar which was excavated by the Oriental Institute of the University of Chicago.

263. The sign encountered here looks like the ideogram for "salt."

264. Possibly "(who finds himself) in *great peril*."

8. The wages of winnowers are 1 seah of barley.

9. Should a man pay 1 shekel of silver to a hired man for harvesting—if he [the hired man] does not place himself at his disposal and does not complete for him the harvest work everywhere, he [shall p]ay 10 shekels of silver. Should he have received 1 seah [and] 5 *qa* [of barley] as wages and leave the rations of [barley], oil [and] cloth[265] shall also be refunded.

10. The hire for a donkey is 1 seah of barley, and the wages for its driver are 1 seah of barley. He shall drive it the whole day.

11. The wages of a hired man are 1 shekel of silver; his provender is 1 pan of barley. He shall work for one month.

12. A man who is caught in the field of a *muskenum*[266] in the *crop* during daytime, shall pay 10 shekels of silver. He who is caught in the *crop* [at ni]ght, shall die, he shall not get away alive.

13. A man who is caught in the house of a *muskenum*, in the house, during daytime, shall pay 10 shekels of silver. He who is caught in the house at night, shall die, he shall not get away alive.

14. The fee of a . . .[267]—should he bring 5 shekels of silver the fee is 1 shekel of silver; should he bring 10 shekels of silver the fee is 2 shekels of silver.

15. The *tamkarrum*[268] and the *sabitum*[269] shall not receive silver, barley, wool [or] sesame oil from a slave or a slave-girl *as an investment*.

16. To a coparcener or a slave a mortgage cannot be furnished.

17. Should the son of a man bring bride-money to the house of [his] father-in-law—, if one of the two deceases, the money shall revert to its owner.

18. If he takes her [the girl] and she enters his house, but *afterward* the young woman should decease, he [the husband] can not obtain refunded that which he brought [to his father-in-law], but will retain the excess [in] his [hand].

18a. Per 1 shekel [of silver] there will accrue ⅙ shekel and 6 grain as interest; per 1 kor [of barley] there will accrue 1 pan and 4 seah as interest.

19. The man who gives [a loan] in terms of his retake shall make [the debtor] pay on the threshing floor.

20. If a man gives a loan . . . expressing the value of the silver in barley, he shall at harvest time receive the barley and its interest, 1 pan [and] 4[?] seah per kor.

21. If a man gives silver [as a loan] *at face value*, he shall receive the silver and its interest, one sixth [of a shekel] and [6 grain] per shekel.

22. If a man has no claim against a[nother] man, but [nevertheless] distrains the [other] man's slave-girl, the owner of the slave-girl shall [decla]re under oath: "Thou hast no claim against me" and he shall pay [him] silver in full compensation for the slave-girl.

23. If a man has no claim against a[nother] man, but [nevertheless] distrains the [other] man's slave-girl, detains the distrainee in his house and causes [her] death, he shall give two slave-girls to the owner of the slave-girl as a replacement.

24. If he has no claim against him, but [nevertheless] distrains the wife of a *muskenum* [or] the child of a *muskenum* and causes [their] death, it is a capital offence. The distrainer who distrained shall die.

25. If a man calls at the house of [his] father-in-law, and his father-in-law *accepts* him *in servitude*, but [nevertheless] gives his daughter to [another man], the father of the girl shall refund the bride-money which he received twofold.

26. If a man gives bride-money for a[nother] man's daughter, but another man seizes her forcibly without asking the permission of her father and her mother and deprives her of her virginity, it is a capital offense and and he shall die.

27. If a man takes a[nother] man's daughter without asking the permission of her father and her mother and concludes no formal marriage contract with her father and her mother, even though she may live in his house for a year, she is not a housewife.

28. *On the other hand*, if he concludes a formal contract with her father and her mother and cohabits with her, she is a housewife. When she is caught with a[nother] man, she shall die, she shall not get away alive.[270]

29. If a man has been made prisoner during a raid or an invasion or [if] he has been carried off forcibly and [stayed in] a foreign [count]ry for a [long] time, [and if] another man has taken his wife and she has born him a son—when he returns, he shall [get] his wife back.

30. If a man hates his town and his lord and becomes a fugitive, [and if] another man takes his wife—when he returns, he shall have no right to claim his wife.

31. If a man deprives another man's slave-girl of her virginity, he shall pay one-third of a mina of silver; the slave-girl remains the property of her owner.

32. If a man gives his son [away] for having [him] nursed and brought up, but does not give [the nurse] rations of barley, oil [and] wool for three years, he shall

---

265. The last two sentences are rather uncertain.
266. The *muskenum* is a member of a social class which at Eshnunna seems to be closely connected with the palace or the temple.
267. The undeciphered word must denote some kind of "money-lender" or "merchant."
268. The official "finance officer" who has a state monopoly on certain commercial transactions.
269. The woman to whom trade in liquor is entrusted.

270. The last sentence is contained only in IM 51059.

pay [her] 10 minas [of silver] for bringing up his son and shall take back his son.

33. If a slave-girl by subterfuge gives her child to a[nother] man's daughter, [if] its lord sees it when it has become older, he may seize it and take it back.

34. If a slave-girl of the palace gives her son or her daughter to a *muskenum* for bringing [him/her] up, the palace may take back the son or the daughter whom she gave.

35. Also the adoptant of the child of a slave-girl of the palace shall recompense the palace with its equivalent.

36. If a man gives property of his as a deposit to . . . and if the property he gives disappears without that the house was burglarized, the *sippu*[271] broken down [or] the window forced, he [the depositary] will replace his [the depositor's] property.

37. If the man's [the depositary's] house either collapses or is burglarized and together with the [property of the] deposit[or] which he gave him loss on the part of the owner of the house is incurred, the owner of the house shall swear him an oath in the gate of Tishpak[272] [saying]: "Together with your property my property was lost; I have done nothing *improper* or fraudulent." If he swears him [such an oath], he shall have no claim against him.

38. If one of several brothers wants to sell his share [in a property common to them] and his brother wants to buy it, he shall pay . . . .[273]

39. If a man is hard up and sells his house, the owner of the house shall [be entitled to] redeem [it] whenever the purchaser [re]sells it.

40. If a man buys a slave, a slave-girl, an ox or any other valuable good but cannot [legally] establish the seller, he is a thief.

41. If an *ubarum*, a *naptarum* or a *mudum*[274] wants to sell his beer, the *sabitum*[275] shall sell his beer for him at the current price.

42. If a man bites the nose of a[nother] man and severs it, he shall pay 1 mina of silver. [For] an eye [he shall pay] 1 mina of silver; [for] a tooth ½ mina; [for] an ear ½ mina; [for] a slap in the face 10 shekels of silver.

43. If a man severs a[nother] man's finger, he shall pay two-thirds of a mina of silver.

44. If a man throws a[nother] man to the floor in an *altercation* and breaks his *hand*, he shall pay ½ mina of silver.

45. If he breaks his foot, he shall pay ½ mina of silver.

46. If a man assaults a[nother] man and breaks his . . . , he shall pay two-thirds of a mina of silver.

47. If a man *hits* a[nother] man *accidentally*, he shall pay 10 shekels of silver.

48. And in *addition*, [in cases involving penalties] from two-thirds of a mina to 1 mina, they shall formally try the man. A capital offense comes before the king.

49. If a man is caught with a stolen slave [or] a stolen slave-girl, he shall surrender slave by slave [and] slave-girl by slave-girl.

50. If the governor, the river commissioner [or] an[other] official whoever it may be seizes a lost slave, a lost slave-girl, a lost ox, a lost donkey belonging to the palace or a *muskenum*[276] and does not surrender it to Eshnunna but keeps it in his house, even though he may let pass only seven days, the palace shall prosecute him for theft.

51. A slave or a slave-girl of Eshnunna which is marked with a *kannum*, a *maskanum* or an *abbuttum*[277] shall not leave the gate of Eshnunna without its owner's permission.

52. A slave or a slave-girl which has entered the gate of Eshnunna in the custody of a [foreign] envoy shall be marked with a *kannum*, a *maskanum* or an *abbuttum* but remains in the custody of its master.

53. If an ox gores an[other] ox and causes [its] death, both ox owners shall divide [among themselves] the price of the live ox and also the equivalent of the dead ox.

54. If an ox is known to gore habitually and the authorities have brought the fact to the knowledge of its owner, but he does not have his ox *dehorned*, it gores a man and causes [his] death, then the owner of the ox shall pay two-thirds of a mina of silver.

55. If it gores a slave and causes [his] death, he shall pay 15 shekels of silver.

56. If a dog is vicious and the authorities have brought the fact to the knowledge of its owner, [if nevertheless] he does not keep it in, it bites a man and causes [his] death, then the owner of the dog shall pay two-thirds of a mina of silver.

57. If it bites a slave and causes [its] death, he shall pay 15 shekels of silver.

58. If a wall is threatening to fall and the authorities have brought the fact to the knowledge of its owner, [if nevertheless] he does not strengthen his wall, the wall collapses and causes a free man's death, then it is a capital offence; jurisdiction of the king.

271. A part of the house at or near the door.
272. The main god of Eshnunna.
273. This expression, not yet fully understood, seems to imply a preferential treatment.
274. Social classes who seem to be entitled to a ration of beer.
275. See note 269.

276. See note 266.
277. Markings that can easily be removed.

59. If a man divorces his wife after having made her bear children and takes [ano]ther wife, he shall be driven from his house and from whatever he owns and may go after him who will accept him.

[60 and 61 badly mutilated and therefore incomprehensible]

e. THE MIDDLE ASSYRIAN LAWS
(Translated by Theophile J. Meek)*

The Middle Assyrian Laws are preserved to us, not on a stela as in the case of Hammurabi's laws, but on clay tablets, some of which are unfortunately badly broken, and the lacunae have not as yet been filled. The tablets were unearthed by German archaeologists in the course of their extensive excavation of ancient Ashur, modern Qal'at Shergat, from 1903 to the spring of 1914. The tablets themselves date from the time of Tiglath-Pileser I in the twelfth century B.C., but the laws on them may go back to the fifteenth century. . . .

The Laws

Tablet A[278]

1. If a woman, [whether] the wife of a seignior or the daughter of a seignior, has entered the temple of a god, has stolen something belonging to the sanctuary [from] the temple of the god, [and] it has been found [in her possession], when they have prosecuted [her] or convicted [her], [they shall take] the indictment and make inquiry of the god; as he orders [the woman to be treated], they shall treat her.

2. If a woman, whether the wife of a seignior or the daughter of a seignior, has uttered blasphemy or indulged in loose talk, that woman shall bear the penalty due her; they shall not touch her husband, her sons, [or] her daughters.

3. If, when a seignior was either sick or dead, his wife has stolen something from his house [and] has given [it] either to a seignior or to a lady or to anyone else, they shall put the seignior's wife to death along with the receivers as well. Also, if the wife of a seignior, whose husband is alive, has stolen [something] from her husband's house [and] has given [it] either to a seignior or to a lady or to anyone else, the seignior shall prosecute his wife and inflict the [proper] punishment; also the receiver who received [it] from the hand of the seignior's wife shall give up the stolen [property] and

they shall inflict on the receiver the same punishment that the seignior inflicted on his wife.

4. If either a male slave or a female slave has received something [stolen] from the hand of a seignior's wife, they shall cut off the nose [and] ears of the male or female slave, thus compensating for the stolen [property], while the seignior shall cut off his wife's ears. However, if he lets his wife go free, without cutting off her ears, they shall not cut off those of the male or female slave and so they shall not compensate for the stolen [property].

5. If a seignior's wife has stolen something from another seignior's house, exceeding the value of five minas of lead, the owner of the stolen [property] shall swear, "I never let her take [it]; there was a theft from my house," if her husband [so] desires, he may give up the stolen [property] and ransom her [but] cut off her ears. If her husband does not wish to ransom her, the owner of the stolen [property] shall take her and cut off her nose.

6. If a seignior's wife has made a deposit abroad, the receiver shall be liable for the stolen [property].[279]

7. If a woman has laid hands on a seignior, when they have prosecuted her, she shall pay thirty minas of lead [and] they shall flog her twenty [times] with staves.

8. If a woman has crushed a seignior's testicle in a brawl, they shall cut off one finger of hers, and if the other testicle has become affected along with it by catching the infection even though a physician has bound [it] up, or she has crushed the other testicle in the brawl, they shall tear out both her [eyes].[280]

9. [If] a seignior laid hands on the wife of a[nother] seignior, thereby treating her like a young child, when they have prosecuted him [and] convicted him, they shall cut off [one] finger of his. If he has kissed her, they shall draw his lower lip along the edge of the *blade* of an ax [and] cut [it] off.

10. [If] either a seignior or a lady entered a[nother] seignior's [house] and killed [either a man] or a woman, [they shall give] the murderers [to the next-of-kin[281]], and if he chooses he may put them to death, or [if he chooses] he may spare [them but] take [their property]. [However, if] the murderers have nothing at home [to give], either a son or [a daughter] . . . in the house . . . belonging to . . . .

11. [not preserved]

12. If, as a seignior's wife passed along the street, a[nother] seignior has seized her, saying to her, "Let me lie with you," since she would not consent [and] kept defending herself, but he has taken her by force

*From J. B. Pritchard, *Ancient Near Eastern Texts Relating to the Old Testament* (Princeton, 1955). Accents have been omitted. Footnotes are from the original, renumbered, with some omissions.
278. Schroeder, *KAV*, no. 1, pp. 1–14.

279. Cf. Tablet C + G, §9.
280. Cf. Deuteronomy 25:11 f.
281. Restoring *a-na bel nap-sa-a-te*, lit., "to the master of the life."

[and] lain with her, whether they found him on the seignior's wife or witnesses have charged him that he lay with the woman, they shall put the seignior to death, with no blame attaching to the woman.[282]

13. When a seignior's wife has left her own house and has visited a[nother] seignior where he is living, if he has lain with her, knowing that she was a seignior's wife, they shall put the seignior to death and the woman as well.

14. If a seignior has lain with the wife of a[nother] seignior either in a temple-brothel or in the street, knowing that she was a seignior's wife, they shall treat the adulterer as the seignior orders his wife to be treated. If he has lain with her without knowing that she was a seignior's wife, the adulterer is guiltless; the seignior shall prosecute his wife, treating her as he thinks fit.[283]

15. If a seignior has caught a[nother] seignior with his wife, when they have prosecuted him [and] convicted him, they shall put both of them to death, with no liability attaching to him. If, upon catching [him], he has brought him either into the presence of the king or into the presence of the judges, when they have prosecuted him [and] convicted him, if the woman's husband puts his wife to death, he shall also put the seignior to death, but if he cuts off his wife's nose, he shall turn the seignior into a eunuch and they shall mutilate his whole face. However, if he let his wife go free, they shall let the seignior go free.

16. If a seignior [has lain with a[nother] seignior's] wife at her invitation,[284] no blame attaches to the seignior; the [married] seignior shall inflict such punishment on his wife as he thinks fit. If he has lain with her by force, when they have prosecuted him [and] convicted him, his punishment shall be like that of the seignior's wife.

17. If a seignior has said to a[nother] seignior, "People have lain repeatedly with your wife," since there were no witnesses, they shall make an agreement [and] go to the river [for the water ordeal].

18. If a seignior said to his neighbor either in private or in a brawl, "People have lain repeatedly with your wife; I will prosecute [her] myself," since he is not able to prosecute [her and] did not prosecute [her], they shall flog that seignior forty [times] with staves [and] he shall do the work of the king for one full month;[285] they shall castrate him and he shall also pay one talent[286] of lead.

19. If a seignior started a rumor against his neighbor in private, saying, "People have lain repeatedly with him," or he said to him in a brawl in the presence of [other] people, "People have lain repeatedly with you; I will prosecute you," since he is not able to prosecute [him] [and] did not prosecute [him], they shall flog that seignior fifty [times] with staves [and] he shall do the work of the king for one full month; they shall castrate him and he shall also pay one talent of lead.

20. If a seignior lay with his neighbor, when they have prosecuted him [and] convicted him, they shall lie with him [and] turn him into a eunuch.[287]

21. If a seignior struck a[nother] seignior's daughter and has caused her to have a miscarriage, when they have prosecuted him [and] conv.cted him, he shall pay two talents thirty minas of lead; they shall flog him fifty [times] with staves [and] he shall do the work of the king for one full month.[288]

22. If in the case of a seignior's wife one not her father, nor her brother, nor her son, but another person, has caused her to take to the road, but he did not know that she was a seignior's wife, he shall [so] swear and he shall also pay two talents of lead to the woman's husband. If [he knew that she was a seignior's wife], he shall pay the damages [and swear], "I never lay with her." However, if the [seignior's] wife [has declared], "He did lie with me," when the man has paid the damages to the seignior, he shall go [to the] river, although he had no [such] agreement; if he has turned back from the river, they shall treat him as the woman's husband treated his wife.

23. If a seignior's wife, having taken a[nother] seignior's wife into her house, has given her to a man to lie with and the man knew that she was a seignior's wife, they shall treat him like one who has lain with a married woman and they shall treat the procuress as the woman's husband treats his adulterous wife. However, if the woman's husband does nothing to his adulterous wife, they shall do nothing to the adulterer or the procuress; they shall let them go free. However, if the seignior's wife did not know [the situation], but the woman who brought her into her house brought the man to her under pressure and he has lain with her, if when she left the house she has declared that she was ravished, they shall let the woman go free, since she is guiltless; they shall put the adulterer and procuress to death. However, if the woman has not [so] declared, the seignior shall inflict on his wife such punishment as he sees fit [and] they shall put the adulterer and the procuress to death. . . .

---

282. With §§12–17, 55, 56 cf. Deuteronomy 22:23–29.
283. Lit., "in accordance with his heart."
284. Restoring [ki-i] pi-i-sa, lit., "in accordance with her mouth."
285. Lit., "one month of days."
286. A talent contained 60 minas.

287. Cf. Leviticus 18:22; 20:13.
288. Other laws on the same topic are §§50–52 below, with all of which cf. Exodus 21:22–25; cf. also CH §§209–14.

50. [If a seignior] struck a[nother] seignior's [wife] and caused her to have [a miscarriage], they shall treat [the wife of the seignior], who caused the [other] seignior's wife to [have a miscarriage], as he treated her; he shall compensate for her fetus with a life. However, if that woman died, they shall put the seignior to death; he shall compensate for her fetus with a life. But, when that woman's husband has no son, if someone struck her so that she had a miscarriage, they shall put the striker to death; even if her fetus is a girl, he shall compensate with a life.

51. If a seignior struck a[nother] seignior's wife who does not rear her children and caused her to have a miscarriage, this punishment [shall hold]: he shall pay two talents of lead.

52. If a seignior struck a harlot and caused her to have a miscarriage, they shall inflict blow for blow upon him; he shall compensate with a life.

53. If a woman has had a miscarriage by her own act, when they have prosecuted her [and] convicted her, they shall impale her on stakes without burying her. If she died in having the miscarriage, they shall impale her on stakes without burying her. If someone hid that woman when she had the miscarriage [without] informing [the king] . . . .

54. [only a few signs preserved]

55. In the case of a seignior's daughter, a virgin who was living in her father's house, whose [father] had not been asked [for her in marriage], whose hymen had not been opened since she was not married, and no one had a claim against her father's house, if a seignior took the virgin by force and ravished her, either in the midst of the city or in the open country or at night in the street or in a granary or at a city festival, the father of the virgin shall take the wife of the virgin's ravisher and give her to be ravished; he shall not return her to her husband [but] take her; the father may give his daughter who was ravished to her ravisher in marriage. If he has no wife, the ravisher shall give the [extra] third in silver to her father as the value of a virgin [and] her ravisher shall marry her [and] not cast her off. If the father does not [so] wish, he shall receive the [extra] third for the virgin in silver [and] give his daughter to whom he wishes.[289]

56. If the virgin has given herself to the seignior, the seignior shall [so] swear and they shall not touch his wife; the seducer shall give the [extra] third in silver as the value of a virgin [and] the father shall treat his daughter as he wishes.

57. Whether it is flogging or . . . [of] a seignior's wife [that] is prescribed [on the tablet, [let it be done in the presence of the judges].

58. In all penalties, [whether tearing out (the eyes) or] cutting off [the ears] of [a seignior's wife], let the official be informed [and let him come] [and do] as [it is prescribed on the tablet].

59. Apart from the penalties for [a seignior's wife] which [are prescribed] on the tablet, [when she deserves it], a seignior may pull out [the hair of] his wife, mutilate [or] twist her ears, with no liability attaching to him.

The month of Sha-sarate, the second day, the eponymy of Sagiu.[290]

Tablet B

7. [If a seignior destroyed the house of his neighbor,] . . . as much as [the owner of the house] claims . . . for . . . and the value of the house . . . which he destroyed . . . twofold on the value of the house . . . he shall give to the owner of the house . . . ; for the one talent of lead they shall flog him five [times] [with staves] [and] he shall do the work of the king for one [full] month.

8. If a seignior has encroached on the more important bounded property of his neighbor, when they have prosecuted him [and] convicted him, he shall give up one-third as much field as he encroached on; they shall cut off one finger of his; they shall flog him one hundred [times] with staves [and] he shall do the work of the king for one full month.

9. If a seignior infringed upon the less important bounded property from allotment, when they have prosecuted him [and] convicted him, he shall pay one talent of lead [and] give up one-third as much field as he encroached on; they shall flog him fifty [times] with staves [and] he shall do the work of the king for one full month.

10. If a seignior dug a well [or] constructed a dike in a field not his, he lost title to his well [or] his dike; they shall flog him thirty [times] with [staves] [and] [he shall do] the work of the king for twenty days. The encroachment on the ground . . . in the . . . the dike . . . he shall swear, . . . "I did . . . I did not . . . the well; I did not . . . the dike"; the owner of the field . . . in . . . the well . . . and. . . .

11. . . . and . . . a creditor . . . to do . . . or . . . the creditor . . . the tablets . . . [the produce of] the labors . . . to do . . . the field . . . to the creditor . . . he shall give. . . .

---

289. Cf. Deuteronomy 22:23–27.

290. For this date in the reign of Tiglath-Pileser I of Assyria see E. F. Weidner, *AJO* 12 (1937): 48 f.

Tablet C + G[291]

1. . . . their master . . . and if the taker . . . which I *redeemed* . . . [he shall compensate for the male slave at the rate of] . . . talents of lead [and] for the female slave at the rate of four talents of lead. . . . However, if the receiver declares, . . . he shall [so] swear in the presence of god and he shall take as much as . . . .

2. [If a seignior sold] to another seignior [either a man of the aristocracy] or a woman of the aristocracy[292] who was living [in his house] as [security for] money or as [a pledge, or] he sold [anyone else] who was living in his house, [when they have prosecuted him], he shall forfeit[293] his money; he shall give [his equivalent in accordance with his value to] the owner of the property; they shall flog him . . . [times] [with staves] [and] he shall do the work of the king for twenty days.

3. [If a seignior] sold into another country [either a man of the aristocracy] or a woman of the aristocracy who [was living in his house] as [security for] money or as a pledge, [when they have prosecuted him] [and] convicted him, he shall forfeit his money; he shall give [his equivalent in accordance with his value to] the owner of the property; they shall flog him . . . [times] [with staves] [and] he shall do the work of the king for forty days. [If the man that he sold] died in the other country, he shall [compensate with a life]. An Assyrian man or an Assyrian woman [who] was taken [at the total value] may be sold into another country.

4. [If a seignior] sold [either an ox or] an ass or a horse or any beast not [his own which] was stabled in his house [as a pledge], he shall give [a beast like it in value], [but] he need not return the money. If [he did not give] a beast, he shall forfeit [his money]; the owner of the property whose [beast] was stabled [in the seignior's house] shall seize his beast, while the receiver [of] the beast [shall be reimbursed] for his money by the seller.

5. [If a seignior], upon stealing either an ox or an ass or a horse [or any other beast] from the pasture, [sold it] to a[nother] seignior at the proper price and the purchaser [paid the proper] price without knowing [that it was stolen], should it be found [in his possession], the seller shall compensate [in full] for the thing stolen, as much as it turned out to be.

6. [When a seignior found either a] . . . or a beast or any thing else [that was lost] and witnesses [saw it, if the seignior sold it and] the owner of that property recognized [his property] in the possession of [the purchaser] [and] seized [it], but the seignior [declared, "I] purchased it," the owner of the property shall [not] take his property [from his hand; he shall give it back and] get [it] from the hand of the seller and. . . . [Furthermore, the seignior] who bought the property and from whose hand [the owner of the property did take his property shall be reimbursed] by the seignior who sold [it] to him. [If the seller declares, "I did not [know] that his property was lost," [the witnesses who] saw [it] shall prosecute [him]; . . . .

6a. . . . he shall take and . . . which for money . . . two goats to the owner of the silver . . . has come forward and whatever . . . he shall not take from him. . . .

7. [If there was a] . . . or anyone who was living [in the house of] an Assyrian as a pledge [or as (security for) money] and the time expired . . . if he . . . the money for as much as his value, he shall take . . . ; if he did not . . . his money value . . . he shall acquire and take . . . he shall make known; the principal of the money . . . there is not . . . .

8. [If a seignior stole a] . . . or a beast or anything else, when they have prosecuted him [and] convicted him, he shall pay . . . [minas] of lead; they shall flog him fifty [times] with staves [and] he shall do [the work of the king for . . . days]. The judges of the *land* [shall give] this judgment. [If the stolen] [property] has reached [the value of] . . . [minas of lead] and [he has sold] the stolen [property], as much as he stole, [for the full price], small or great, the king shall inflict on him such [punishment] as he thinks fit.

9. [If, when a seignior] entrusted everything of every sort [either to his wife] or to a slave, [*something from the house*] was placed in deposit elsewhere [and the receiver], in whose house the deposit was made, did not report [*the deposit* to the seignior], who entrusted his house, [and the property] was found [in] his possession, [the owner of the property shall take his property], while that seignior shall be liable for the stolen [property].

10. [If a seignior] has overvalued [a trust] from his neighbor [and] has put [it] in writing, when they have prosecuted him [and] convicted him, since he is a thief, [he shall bear] the punishment which the king, [as he thinks fit], inflicts on him.

11. [If a seignior] has overvalued . . . [and] has put [it] in writing [so as to] make the creditors lose [their money], when they have prosecuted him [and] convicted him, [*because*] he wrote down [*too large an amount*], they shall flog him . . . [times] with staves . . . the hand of the creditors . . . the clerk and . . .

---

291. Schroeder, *KAV*, no. 6, p. 20 f., plus no. 143, p. 89. The two tablets are combined by Weidner, op. cit., Tafel III, no. 1.

292. Lit., "the son of a seignior or the daughter of a seignior," where "son" and "daughter" are used in a technical sense, meaning one who belongs to the class of seigniors.

293. Lit., "his hand shall go up from."

Tablet E[294]

1. . . . [when they have prosecuted him] [and] convicted him . . . which he paid back . . . they shall flog him; from . . . thirty minas of lead . . . and the rest of the fifteen minas . . . the sons of the king [and] the judges . . . which he paid back in accordance with what . . . which outside to the son . . . the king . . . .

2. [If] . . . he struck . . . to the head . . . which . . . one mina . . . him . . . .

3. [If] . . . everything, as much as . . . let him receive. However, if from . . . he seized and the work . . . he will not turn . . . his hire he shall not . . . the employer . . .

4. [If] . . . the doer . . . they shall deposit . . . of the former creditor . . . of the creditor . . . and . . .

Tablet F[295]

1. . . . to . . . the sheep which . . . . However, if [the seignior . . . and carried off] a sheep from the herd of his neighbor and changed [its ownership mark] and substituted his own ownership mark, [they shall flog] the seignior who carried off the sheep one hundred [times] with [staves] [and] they shall pull out [his hair]; [he shall do] the work [of the king] for one full month and he shall also be liable for the theft of the sheep.

f. The Hittite Laws
(Translated by Albrecht Goetze)*

The laws which have come down to us represent two tablets of a series called "If anyone." A label which is accidentally preserved (*ABoT*, 52) proves that there was a third tablet of which no text has become known as yet. . . .

Tablet I

1. If anyone kills a man or a woman in a quarrel, he has to make amends for him/her. He shall give four persons, man or woman, and pledge his estate as security.

2. If anyone kills a male or a female slave in a quarrel, he has to make amends for him/her. He shall give two persons, man or woman, and pledge his estate as security.

3. If anyone strikes a free man or woman and he/she dies, [only] his hand doing wrong, he has to make amends for him/her. He shall give two persons and pledge his estate as security.

4. If anyone strikes a male or a female slave and he/she dies, [only] his hand doing wrong, he has to make amends for him/her. He shall give one person and pledge his estate as security.

Later version of 3 and 4. [If anyone stri]kes [a woman] and she dies, [only] his hand doing wrong, [he shall give x minas of silver]; but if the woman is a slave, he shall give 2 minas of silver.

5. If anyone kills a Hittite merchant, he shall give 100 minas of silver and pledge his estate as security. If [it happens] in the country of Luwiya or in the country of Pala, he shall give 100 minas of silver and replace his goods; if [it happens] in the Hatti land, he has [also] to make amends for the merchant himself.

Later version of 5. If anyone kills a Hittite merchant for [his] goods, he shall give [x minas of silver] and shall make threefold compensation for [his] goods. [If] he had no goods with him, and anyone kills him in a quarrel, he shall give 6 minas of silver. But if [only] the hand is doing wrong, he shall give 2 minas of silver.

6. If a person, man or woman, dies in *another* town, he on whose property he/she dies shall set aside 100 *gipessar*[296] of his property and he shall receive it.

Later version of 6. If a man dies on the field [or] fallow of another man, in case he is a free man, he shall give field [and] fallow, house [and] 1 mina [and] 20 shekels of silver. But if there is no other man's field [and] fallow, a distance of three leagues in one direction and [a distance] of three leagues in the other direction [shall be taken] and whatever village is found to fall within it, he shall take those. If there is no village [within the area], he forfeits [his claims].

7. If anyone blinds a free man or knocks out his teeth, they would formerly give 1 mina of silver, now he shall give 20 shekels of silver and pledge his estate as security.

8. If anyone blinds a male or female slave or knocks out his/her teeth, he shall give 10 shekels of silver and pledge his estate as security.

Later version of 7 and 8. If anyone blinds a free man in a quarrel, he shall give 1 mina of silver. If [only] his hand does wrong, he shall give 20 shekels of silver.— If anyone blinds a slave in a quarrel, he shall give 30[?] shekels of silver. If [only] his hand is doing wrong, he shall give 10 shekels of silver.—If anyone knocks out the teeth of a free man, in case he knocks out 2 teeth or 3 teeth, he shall give 12 shekels of silver. If it is a slave, he shall give 6 shekels of silver.

---

294. Schroeder, *KAV*, no. 4, p. 19.
295. Schroeder, *KAV*, no. 5, p. 19.
*From J. B. Pritchard, *Ancient Near Eastern Texts Relating to the Old Testament* (Princeton, 1955). Accents have been omitted. Footnotes are from the original, renumbered, with some omissions.

296. A measure, probably a cubit.

9. If anyone batters a man's head, they would formerly give 6 shekels of silver; he who was battered would receive 3 shekels of silver, and they would receive 3 shekels of silver for the palace. Now the king has abolished the [share] of the palace and only he who was battered receives 3 shekels of silver.

Later version of 9. If anyone batters a man's head, the battered shall receive 3 shekels of silver.

10. If anyone batters a man so that he falls ill, he shall *take care* of him. He shall give a man in his stead who can look after his house until he recovers. When he recovers, he shall give him 6 shekels of silver, and he shall also pay the physician's fee.

Later version of 10. If anyone injures a free man's head, he shall take care of him. He shall give a man in his stead who can look after his house until he recovers. When he recovers, he shall give him 10 shekels of silver, and he shall also pay the physician's fee. If it is a slave, he shall pay 2 shekels of silver.

11. If anyone breaks a free man's hand or foot, he shall give him 20 shekels of silver and pledge his estate as security.

12. If anyone breaks the hand or foot of a male or a female slave, he shall give 10 shekels of silver and pledge his estate as security.

Later version of 11 and 12. If anyone breaks a free man's hand or foot, in case he is permanently crippled, he shall give him 20 shekels of silver. But in case he is not permanently crippled, he shall give him 10 shekels of silver.—If anyone breaks a slave's hand or foot, in case he is permanently crippled, he shall give him 10 shekels of silver. But in case he is not permanently crippled, he shall give him 5 shekels of silver.

13. If anyone bites off a free man's nose, he shall give 1 mina of silver and pledge his estate as security.

Later version of 13. If anyone bites off a free man's nose, he shall give 30 shekels[!] of silver and pledge his estate as security.

14. If anyone bites off the nose of a male or female slave, he shall give 30[?] shekels of silver and pledge his estate as security.

Later version of 14. If anyone bites off a slave's nose, he shall give 15 shekels[!] of silver.

15. If anyone mutilates a free man's ear, he shall give 15 shekels of silver and pledge his estate as security.

Later version of 15. If anyone mutilates a free man's ear, he shall give 12 shekels of silver.

16. If anyone mutilates the ear of a male or female slave, he shall give 6 shekels of silver.

Later version of 16. If anyone mutilates a slave's ear, he shall give 6 shekels of silver.

17. If anyone causes a free woman to miscarry—if [it is] the tenth month, he shall give 10 shekels of silver, if [it is] the fifth month, he shall give 5 shekels of silver and pledge his estate as security.

Later version of 17. If anyone causes a free woman to miscarry, he shall give 20 shekels of silver.

18. If anyone causes a slave-woman to miscarry, if [it is] the tenth month, he shall give 5 shekels of silver.

Later version of 18. If anyone causes *a slave-girl to* miscarry, he shall give 10 shekels of silver.

19 [*A*]. If any Luwian steals a person—man or woman—from Hattusa and carries him to the country of Arzawa, but his master traces him out, he shall forfeit his estate. [*B*]. If in Hattusa any Hittite steals a Luwian and carries him to the country of Luwiya, they would formerly give 12 persons, now he shall give 6 persons and place his estate as security.

20. If any Hittite steals a Hittite slave from the country of Luwiya and carries him to the Hatti land, but his master traces him out, he shall give him 12 shekels of silver and pledge his estate as security.

21. If anyone steals the slave of a Luwian from the country of Luwiya and carries him to the Hatti land, but his master traces him out, he shall give just the slave; there will be no compensation. . . .

49. If a *hipparas* man steals, there will be no compensation. If he is considered a felon, the community to which he belongs will make compensation. If one would indict them for theft, all of them were criminals or would have to be considered as thieves. Whether this [man] seize one [of them], or that [man] another, they would . . . (a penalty). . . .

57. If anyone steals a bull—if it is a weanling, it is not a bull; if it is a yearling, it is not a bull; if it is a two-year-old, that is a bull—they would formerly give 30 [head of] cattle. Now he shall give 15 [head of] cattle, [specifically] 5 two-year-olds, 5 yearlings [and] 5 weanlings and he shall pledge his estate as security.

58. If anyone steals a stallion—if it is a weanling, it is not a stallion; if it is a yearling, it is not a stallion; if it is a two-year-old, that is a stallion—they would formerly give 30 horses. Now they shall give 15 horses, [specifically] 5 two-year-old horses, 5 yearlings [and] 5 weanlings and he shall pledge his estate as security.

59. If anyone steals a ram, they used to give formerly 30 sheep. Now he shall give 15 sheep, [specifically] 5 ewes, 5 rams [and] 5 lambs.

60. If anyone finds a bull and removes the brand, [if] its owner traces it out, he shall give 7 [head of] cattle; he shall give [specifically] 2 two-year-olds, 3 yearlings [and] 2 weanlings and he shall pledge his estate as security.

61. If anyone finds a stallion and removes the brand, [if] its owner traces it out, he shall give 7 horses; he

shall give [specifically] 2 two-year-olds, 3 yearlings [and] 2 weanlings and he shall pledge his estate as security.

62. If anyone finds a ram and removes the brand, [if] its owner traces it out, he shall give 7 sheep; he shall give [specifically] 2 ewes, 3 rams [and] 2 lambs and he shall pledge his estate as security.

63. If anyone steals a plow-ox, they would formerly give 15 [head of] cattle. Now he shall give 10 [head of] cattle; he shall give [specifically] 3 two-year-olds, 3 yearlings [and] 4 weanlings and he shall pledge his estate as security.

64. If anyone steals a draft horse, its treatment is the same.

65. If anyone steals a *tamed* buck or a trained wild-goat or *tamed* mountain sheep, the compensation is as for a buck; and the compensation for it is the same.

66. If a plow-ox or a draft horse or a [milk-giving] cow or a brood ass-mare strays off to the corral, or if a *tamed* buck or a ewe or a ram strays off to the fold [and] its owner finds it, he shall receive the respective [animal]; there shall be no question of a thief.

67. If anyone steals a cow, they would formerly give 12 [head of] cattle; now he shall give 6 [head of] cattle; he shall give [specifically] 2 two-year-olds, 2 yearlings [and] 2 weanlings and he shall pledge his estate as security.

68. If anyone steals a brood mare, its treatment is the same.

69. If anyone steals a ewe or a ram, they used to give formerly 12 sheep. Now he shall give 6 sheep; he shall give [specifically] 2 ewes, 2 rams [and] 2 lambs and he shall pledge his estate as security.

70. If anyone steals a horse, or a mule or an ass and its owner traces it out, he shall receive the respective [animal]. In addition he [the thief] shall give it a second time and he shall pledge his estate as security.

71. If anyone finds an ox, a horse [or] a mule, he shall drive it to the king's court. If he finds it in the country, the elders may assign it to him and he may harness it. When its owner finds it, he shall receive the respective animal; there shall be no question of a thief. If the elders do not assign it [to him], he becomes a thief.

72. If an ox dies in anyone's field, the owner of the field shall give 2 oxen and pledge his estate as security.

73. If anyone disposes of a living ox [found on his property], he is as if he had committed theft. . . .

91. If anyone steals bees from a *swarm*, they would formerly give 1 mina of silver. Now he shall give 5 shekels of silver and pledge his estate as security.

92. If anyone steals two beehives or three beehives, formerly [it meant exposure to] bee-sting; now he shall give 6 shekels of silver. If anyone steals a beehive while no bees are therein, he shall give 3 shekels of silver.

93. If they seize a free man while breaking in before he has entered the house, he shall give 12 shekels of silver. If they seize a slave while breaking in before he has entered the house, he shall give 24 shekels of silver.

94. If a free man steals in a house, he shall give [back] the respective goods; they would formerly give for the theft 1 mina of silver, now he shall give 12 shekels of silver. If he has stolen much, they shall impose a heavy fine upon him; if he has stolen little, they shall impose a small fine upon him and he shall pledge his estate as security.

95. If a slave steals in a house, he shall give [back] the respective goods. For the theft he shall give 6 shekels of silver. They shall also cut off the slave's nose and ears and give him back to his master. If he has stolen much, they shall impose a heavy fine upon him; if he has stolen little, they shall impose a small fine upon him. If his master says: "I will make compensation in his stead," he may do so; but if he refuses, he will lose the slave.

96. If a free man steals in a granary and obtains grain in the granary, he shall fill the granary with grain and give 12 shekels of silver and he shall pledge his estate as security.

97. If a slave steals in a granary and obtains grain in the granary, he shall fill the granary with grain and give 6 shekels of silver and he shall pledge his estate as security.

98. If a free man sets a house on fire, he shall rebuild the house. Whatever was lost in the house, whether it is man, cattle or sheep, he shall replace as a matter of course.

99. If a slave sets a house on fire, his master shall make compensation in his stead. They shall cut off the slave's nose [and] ears and shall give him back to his master. But if he does not make compensation, he will lose that [slave].

100. If anyone sets a shed on fire, he shall feed his cattle and make amends in the next spring, he shall [also] give back the shed. If there was no straw therein, he shall just rebuild the shed.

Tablet II

101. If anyone steals vine or fruit branch, or . . . s, or onions, they would formerly give for 1 vine x shekels of silver, for 1 fruit branch 1 shekel of silver, for 1 . . . x shekel of silver, for 1 *bunch* of onions 1 shekel of silver, and they would strike him with the spear in the palace. Formerly they proceeded like this. Now he shall give, if a free man, 6 shekels of silver, and if a slave, 3 shekels of silver.

102. If anyone steals timber from a pond—if [it is] 1 talent of wood, [he shall give] 3 shekels of silver; if [it is] 2 talents of wood, he shall give 6 shekels of silver; if [it is] 3 talents of wood, [it is a case for] the court of the king.

103. If anyone steals freshly planted things—if [it is] 1 *gipessar*²⁹⁷ of planting, he shall replant it and give one shekel of silver; if [it is] 2 *gipessar* of planting, he shall replant it and give 2 shekels of silver.

104. If anyone cuts down *pomegranate* trees or *medlar* trees, he shall give x shekels of silver and pledge his estate as security.

105. If anyone sets a . . . on fire and [the fire] spreads to a fruit bearing orchard—if vines, fruit trees, *pomegranate* trees [or] *medlar* trees get burnt up, he shall give 6 shekels of silver for each tree; the planting he shall replant and he shall pledge his estate as security. If he is a slave, he shall give 3 shekels of silver.

106. If anyone makes fire on his field and sets another man's bearing field on fire, he who set the fire shall take the burnt-over field for himself and give a good field to the owner of the [burnt-over] field and [that man] shall reap it.

107. If a man turns [his] sheep into a vineyard under cultivation and they ruin it—if [it is] fruit bearing, he shall give 10 shekels of silver for each acre, but if [it is] bare, he shall give 3 shekels of silver.

108. If anyone steals tendrils from a *fenced-in* vineyard—if [there are] 100 trees, he shall give 6 shekels of silver and pledge his estate as security. But if they [are] not fenced-in and he steals tendrils, he shall pay 3 shekels of silver.

109. If anyone disposes of fruit from an irrigated [orchard]—if [there are] 100 trees, he shall give 6 shekels of silver.

110. If anyone steals plaster from a bin—however much he steals, he shall give the same amount a second time over.

111. If anyone . . . s plaster [mud] in [a . . .], it is sorcery [and a case for] the court of the king.

112. If they give [to a . . .] the field of a craftsman [which produces] grain, for 3 years he shall not perform socage, he will begin to perform socage from the fourth year on, and shall rank with the craftsmen.

113. If anyone cuts down . . . vine, that [man] shall receive the cut-down vine and give a good one to the owner of the vine and he will vindemiate. [Until] that man's vine [recovers, he keeps the offender's vine. Afterward] he takes [his own back].

[some sections mutilated or missing]

297. See note 296.

119. If anyone steals a bird from a pond or a trained . . . , they would formerly give x shekels of silver. Now he shall give 12 shekels of silver and pledge his estate as security.

120. If anyone steals . . . birds . . . ,—if (they are) ten birds, he shall give 1 shekel of silver.

121. If anyone, a free man, steals a plow and its owner finds it out, he shall put him upon the . . . and . . . . Formerly they proceeded in this way. Now he shall give 6 shekels of silver and pledge his estate as security. If he is a slave, he will give 3 shekels of silver.

122. If anyone steals a cart with all its accessories, they would formerly give 1 shekel of silver. . . . Now he gives x shekel of silver and pledges his estate as security.

123. If [anyone steals a . . . , it was formerly considered] a capital crime. [Now . . .], he shall give three shekels of silver and pledge his estate as security.

124. If anyone steals a *sisiyama*, he shall give 3 shekels of silver and pledge his estate as security. If anyone loads a cart, leaves it in the fields and [if] anyone steals it, he shall give 3 shekels of silver and pledge his estate as security.

125. If anyone steals a water *trough*, he shall give x shekels of silver. If anyone steals a *lash* or a *whip*, he shall give 1 shekel of silver.

126. If anyone steals a *zahrai* (emblem) in the gate of the palace, he shall give 6 shekels of silver. If anyone steals a bronze spear in the gate of the palace, he shall die. If anyone steals a copper *nail*, he will give one-half *parisu* of grain. If anyone steals *curtains* [to the amount] of 1 [bolt of] cloth, he shall give 1 bolt of wool cloth.

127. If anyone steals a door in a quarrel, he shall replace everything that may get lost in the house. He will also give 1 mina of silver and pledge his estate as security.

128. If anyone steals bricks—however much he steals, he shall give the same amount a second time over. If anyone steals stones out of a foundation, for two [such] stones he shall give 10 stones. If anyone steals a stone . . .-[. . .] or a stone *harmiyalli*, he shall give 2 shekels of silver.

129. If anybody steals the *reins*, the [leather] *annanu* . . . , the [leather] *gazzimuel* [or] the bronze *katral* of a horse [or] a mule, they would formerly give 1 mina of silver. Now he shall give 12 shekels of silver and pledge his estate as security.

130. If anybody steals the [. . .] . . . of an ox or a horse, he shall give x shekels of silver and pledge his estate as security.

131. If anyone steals a [leather] *happut* [. . .], he shall give 6 shekels of silver and pledge his estate as security.

132. If anyone, a free man, steals [a . . .], he shall give 6 shekels of silver and pledge his estate as security. If he is a slave, he shall give 3 shekels of silver.

133. If anyone, a free man, steals [a . . .], he shall give x shekels of silver. If he is a slave, he shall give x shekels of silver. . . .

188. If a man does evil with a sheep, it is a capital crime and he shall be killed. They bring him to the king's court. Whether the king orders him killed, or whether the king spares his life, he must not appeal to the king.

189. If a man violates his own mother, it is a capital crime. If a man violates his daughter, it is a capital crime. If a man violates his son, it is a capital crime.

190. . . . If a man violates his stepmother, there shall be no punishment. [But] if his father is living, it is a capital crime.

191. If a free man cohabits with [several] free women, sisters and their mother, with this one in one country and that one in another country, there shall be no punishment. But if [it happens] in one and the same place knowing [of their relationship], it is a capital crime.

192. If a man's wife dies [and] he marries his wife's sister, there shall be no punishment.

193. If a man has a wife and then the man dies, his brother shall take his wife, then his father shall take her. If in turn also his father dies, one of his brother's sons shall take the wife whom he had. There shall be no punishment.

194. If a free man cohabits with [several] slave-girls, sisters and their mother, there shall be no punishment. If blood-relations sleep with [the same] free woman, there shall be no punishment. If father and son sleep with [the same] slave-girl or harlot, there shall be no punishment.

195. If however a man sleeps with the wife of his brother while his brother is living, it is a capital crime. If a man has a free woman [in marriage] and then lies also with her daughter, it is a capital crime. If a man has the daughter in marriage and then lies also with her mother or her sister, it is a capital crime.

196. If his slave [or] his slave-girl commit a capital crime, they move them away and have them settled the one in this town, the other in that town; a sheep will be proffered in this one's stead and a sheep in that one's stead.

197. If a man seizes a woman in the mountains, it is the man's crime and he will be killed. But if he seizes her in [her] house, it is the woman's crime and the woman shall be killed. If the husband finds them, he may kill them, there shall be no punishment for him.

198. If he brings them to the gate of the palace and declares: "My wife shall not be killed" and thereby spares his wife's life, he shall also spare the life of the adulterer and shall mark his head. If he says, "Let them die both of them!" . . . the king may order them killed, the king may spare their lives.

199. If anyone does evil with a pig, he shall die. They will bring them to the gate of the palace and the king may order them killed, the king may spare their lives; but he must not appeal to the king. If an ox leaps at a man, the ox shall die, but the man shall not die. A sheep may be proffered in the man's stead and they shall kill that. If a pig leaps at a man, there shall be no punishment.

200 [A]. If a man does evil with a horse or a mule, there shall be no punishment. He must not appeal to the king nor shall he become a case for the priest.—If anyone sleeps with a foreign [woman] and [also] with her mother or [her] si[ster], there will be no punishment.

g. LAW IN THE ANCIENT NEAR EAST
(By J. J. Finkelstein)*

General

In this survey, the laws of the ancient cultures in Mesopotamia and neighboring countries will be discussed. That area will be designated hereafter as the "Near East." Ancient Egyptian law will not be included because collections of Egyptian law have not reached us yet. The concept of "law" in the Near East includes statutes, equity, and the practice of law. . . .

The laws that were collected in the legal codes of the ancient Near East are formulated to deal with imagined situations, and the relevant decisions to be followed for each code. . . .

Two expressions that are mentioned frequently in legal documents, although they are not distinct legal terms, are *kittum* and *mesharum*. *Kittum* means "truth and right": its main usage is not in the area of jurisprudence but rather in the area of religious thought. It is the cosmic and transcendental principle of right that transcends the actions of the lawgiver; The lawgiver is required to see to it that the deeds within human society shall conform to the principle of "right" (*kittum*). For this purpose he is to establish laws (*dinati*). *Mesharum* means "that which is characteristic of the principle of equity." When the principle of equity (*mesharum*) prevails over the human society, the principle of cosmic *kittum* ("right") is carried out in the realm of human society. The application of equitable principles is considered to be the duty of the king, who, from time to

*Free translation from *Encyclopedia Biblica* (Jerusalem, 1968), vol. 5, p. 587.

time, publishes edicts and decrees that are intended to bring about equity (*mesharum*). These prescriptions are called *mesharum*—edicts.

Their contents change from period to period and from reign to reign in accordance with the conditions. A king's *mesharum* edict was not intended to be applied forever but was, rather, a temporary ruling that sought to impose the principle of *mesharum* ("equity") in his kingdom by the correction of a specific social injustice. The custom of the kings was to publish ordinances like these at the beginning of their reign.

Types of Sources

Sources of ancient Mesopotamian laws are of two types: (1) legal documents, including correspondences of royal officials or of citizens, that discuss legal affairs; and (2) collections of formal laws (codes).

1. *Legal Documents.* To be considered in this source are the documents that reflect the practice of regulating the relationships within the society: for example, documents of real estate ownership, commercial contracts, monetary documents, and marriage contracts. Arrangements of this type were written in the form of a contract in which there was set forth the names of the parties who come into contractual agreement, the important details that both parties agreed upon, and the names of the witnesses. These also, generally, bore the seals of the parties in this venture and of the witnesses. Thousands of documents of this type have reached us, from all sectors and from all times in which cuneiform writing was used. Documents of another kind reflect the juridical procedure itself. They record laws and accounts of law cases between individuals. Most of them deal with litigation concerning the violation of obligations which stem from contracts or customary practices. There are fewer of these documents than there are contracts. They are, however, similar to contracts in some details; thus, for example, the names of the witnesses are included and generally the names of the judges are included with their seals. Documents from certain areas, such as those of the court of the city, Nuzi (the center of the Hurrian population in the middle of the second millennium B.C.E.), generally contain cases and accounts in detail, based upon the testimony of witnesses concerning the relationship between the litigants. From their contents we are able to discern the life of the society in question, its customs and laws. At any rate, the main importance of these records is that they are primary sources for the recognition of legal customs and institutions in Mesopotamia.

A third source for the knowledge of legal institutions are correspondences between citizens and officials,

among them letters that were written to kings or in the name of kings. Thus, for example, the correspondence of Hammurabi and his older contemporary Rim-Sin of Larsa, includes evidence of acts of corruption in the bureaucracy and descriptions of the royal acts for improving the situation, as well as a royal decree to put to death a convicted murderer. The correspondence by ordinary citizens frequently deals with the transfer of property from one to another in accordance with the common practice of court cases, most of which concerned money matters.

The documents just described are the sole source of information concerning the law that was applied in practice in Mesopotamia. Nevertheless, this rich material has not been utilized for the sake of comparison with biblical law. . . . The great majority of the material for comparisons with biblical law of which scholars have availed themselves stems only from the second type of sources, that is, the collections of laws (codes). There are a number of reasons for this. The codes are more similar in their contents and style to the biblical codes. The purpose of the Mesopotamian codes is similar to that of the biblical laws since they do not simply reflect the practice, but also the legal ideal that the lawgiver wishes to concretize. The codes of law both of the Torah and of Mesopotamia deal mainly with laws of damages and capital crimes that can easily serve as a basis of comparison. In contrast to this, the documents that would reflect the life of the law in practice during the biblical period have not been preserved. The Mesopotamian documents deal with the regulation of common human dealing; that is, they reflect the practices in business, family law and similar activities. The court decisions that have been preserved touch mostly upon these areas. Only the minority deal with injuries or damages. Rarest are those documents that deal with capital cases. All of the foregoing have brought about a situation in which most of the comparative study between Mesopotamian and biblical law deals only with the legal codes.

2. *Codes of Law.* From discoveries of recent years it has become clear that the tradition of the publication of the official law codes—for example, the laws of Hammurabi—is one of the oldest traditions in Mesopotamian literature. The earliest of the extant codes are from the end of the third millennium B.C.E. Below are listed the main codes according to their chronological order (according to the "middle chronology" of Sidney Smith, who sets the date of the reign of Hammurabi at 1750–1792 B.C.E.; the higher chronology makes his reign sixty years earlier and the former chronology makes it sixty years later). The following are the names of the major legal codes:

Name of the Collection	Era
Laws of Ur-Nammu	2100 B.C.E.
Laws of Lipit-Ishtar King of Isin	1950 B.C.E.
Eshnunna Laws	1900 B.C.E.
Laws of Hammurabi	1792–1750 B.C.E.
Assyrian Laws	1400–1100 B.C.E.
Hittite Laws	1400–1300 B.C.E.
Neo-Babylonian Laws	sixth century B.C.E.

The Legal Codes and Law Which Was in Practice

The laws in the codes that are extant deal with only a small portion of the sum total of subjects with which courts would occupy themselves. Broad areas of social activity and numerous subjects of injury and damages are not discussed at all in the codes. This applies to the largest code as well, the Code of Hammurabi. We may assume that the judges applied that which was the common practice and had received principles and laws that were never recorded in the official codes. There is no doubt that these principles were never considered to be the creation of a specific king or of a certain god but rather, they were believed to have existed from ancient times; indeed, from the time that all the orders, institutions and procedures were established for all time according to the doctrine of *kittum* and *mesharum*. The result was that, in the Mesopotamian mind, the source of the law was the traditional practice that was valid from antiquity. On the other hand, it is certain that those laws that were collected in the codes were considered to be the creation of the law-giving kings, at least from the literary point of view. The laws of Hammurabi, for example, were named after him, and many copies were made afterwards until the Neo-Assyrian period (as other literary works were copied). However, the question may be asked: "What was the influence of these laws from the legal point of view, that is, in what measure did they serve as actual law? A legal document, such as a court decision or contract written during the time of Hammurabi or afterwards, which would agree with one of the laws in the Code of Hammurabi could, presumably, serve as evidence that the judges, in practice, followed the laws of Hammurabi. In reality, however, we find private legal documents even from the period that preceded Hammurabi and are in agreement with his code. The more plausible conclusion, therefore, is that the judges made their decisions in accordance with the common practice and not according to a law recorded in a law code. That is to say, the law codes reflect the common practice and the common practice is not evidence for the authority of the law recorded in the codes, unless there is uncontrovertible evidence to the contrary. Thus, when a private legal document deals with a subject that is discussed in a formal code (the number of such documents is small, since the codes deal with a small percentage of subjects that would be raised in court), it generally becomes evident that the court decision that was followed actually contradicts the official law contained in the code. This is true as well for documents written during the reign of Hammurabi or his immediate successors. To explain this phenomenon, some assume that the Hammurabi laws (and similar codes) were not obligatory laws, but rather, laws for the general guidance of the judges, who were permitted to judge as they saw fit. Others assume that the judges were able to look away from the official law since there was no efficient way to enforce it. There is evidence, however, for another explanation: that the intention of the royal lawgivers was never that the laws should be put into practice. There are thousands of legal documents preserved from the period of Hammurabi, and his code is not mentioned in one of them, even when the decision is in agreement with the Code of Hammurabi. In addition, the Code of Hammurabi contains laws that are difficult to conceive as actually being carried out. For example, according to the Code of Hammurabi, sec. 230, the son of a builder is put to death when a house built by his father collapses and kills the son of the owner of the house. It is certain that when the builder does not have a son, this law cannot apply and another decision must be rendered. The result is that there is discrimination against a builder who has a son. It is, therefore, doubtful whether Hammurabi would have judged the case in accordance with his own law should the case have come before him. The main reason for this doubt, however, is that, in the epilogue, Hammurabi neither turns to the judges nor requests them to follow his code. He turns to the ordinary citizen and requests that he read his laws. Should the citizen find the law that would apply to his case, and thus be convinced that the king is concerned for the maintenance of justice, he would offer a prayer to Marduk on behalf of the king. At the end, Hammurabi addresses the kings who will succeed him. Thus, Hammurabi does not turn to the judges, but rather to the total citizenry of his land, in his generation and in subsequent generations as well. In the main, however, he turns to the gods. By means of his laws he seeks to win fame as a king who loves justice and law and to convince the gods of his loyalty to their command. For this purpose, Hammurabi inserts in the collection of his laws the accepted laws that were in existence prior to his time, since all of these laws seemed to him fine examples of the desired standard of justice. Even the strange laws that are inconceivable for practice fit the purpose of his code. They also serve as examples for ethical principles, for example, the principle of *lex talionis*. Although it is possible to discern here and there the influence of Hammurabi law upon traditional legal customs, one should not see in his novel law attempts to institute reforms in juridical procedure, but rather mere expressions of the ideal of justice. Perhaps the population welcomed this ideal with blessings. However, it appears that not only the population but the king, himself, did not intend to put it into effect. From the above discussion it seems reasonable that all of the legal codes from southern Mesopotamia that gave the impression of being the work of law-giving kings never functioned as law in actual practice and, moreover, their authors never intended to give them this status. One must see these codes as royal inscriptions of a particular kind, something like apologetic writings whose earliest extant example is the inscription with the reforms of Urukagina of Lagash (2350 B.C.E.). The epilogues of the laws of Lipit-Ishtar and Hammurabi, and the prologue of the code of Ur-Nammu as well, are similar to this inscription in both language and subjects, and the addition of laws formulated in casuistic formulation is only a stylistic development. Finally, it must be pointed out that Hammurabi published his laws towards the end of his life, when he began to be concerned for his good name in later generations; thus, it is now possible to find an explanation for the surprising fact that the publication of laws is never mentioned in the epithets of the forty-three years of his reign. It is known that the kings of the first dynasty of Babylonia would give a title to each year of their individual reign according to the most important event that occurred during that year. Hammurabi's publication of his laws was very important in the Mesopotamian culture of subsequent generations, who saw it as we see it today, as a literary model. To the contemporaries of Hammurabi, however, it was of minor value. The omission of the year of publication of the Code of Hammurabi from his year lists teaches us a lot. The publication of the *mesharum* edicts, which served the purpose of dissolving oppressive obligations, were considered as events important enough to be mentioned in the king's year lists. It is only in the epilogue, which is his last apology, that he declares himself to be a king of *mesharum* and hints of the economic reforms which he promulgated at the beginning of his reign.

The Influence of Social Order upon the Law Codes

As mentioned above there was an accepted legal practice and a common tradition in the ancient Near East. This is shown by the great similarity between the laws of different lands. This similarity, however, is no proof that the Mesopotamian laws directly influenced the laws of other lands. Only the codes of law of south-

ern Mesopotamia itself show dependencies upon one another. It is possible that there was influence only in isolated instances, as, for example, in the biblical case of the goring ox, which is very similar to the Mesopotamian law in both contents and formulation. On the other hand, the laws from different countries are not similar to each other in all respects since they reflect the peculiar social structure of that land. The laws of southern Mesopotamia (especially the laws of Hammurabi) testify to the sharp differences in social levels between the free man (*awelutum*) and the segment of the population dependent upon the state and required its protection (this group was called *mushkenutu*), and also the contrast between these levels and that of the slaves. This is particularly true in the laws of injury and damages and in matters of obligations between one and another. The distinctions between citizens and strangers (between natives and aliens) are, however, missing in the above laws. In all of Mesopotamian law there is no discussion dealing with religion except for one law in the Code of Hammurabi (the priestess who entered the tavern to drink beer, sec. 110). This law is included only as part of a group of laws dealing with taverns. Religious laws are rare in the Hittite Code and are completely absent in the Mesopotamian law codes. In contrast to Israel these nations did not see themselves as a kingdom of priests or as a holy nation. They would turn to a god through the king, who was the high priest, or through one of his priests who served as his substitute. The congregation had an insignificant part in the public cult. The yoke of commandments which obligated everyone did not exist for them and it is, therefore, natural that they saw no need to specify and enumerate these laws in a legal manner.

F. *A Comparison of Jewish and Cuneiform Cultural and Religious Perspectives*

1. BIBLE AND BABEL: A COMPARATIVE STUDY OF THE HEBREW AND BABYLONIAN RELIGIOUS SPIRIT
(By J. J. Finkelstein)*

One of the most absorbing aspects of the study of the civilizations of the ancient Near East, and especially of Mesopotamia, since the decipherment of cuneiform writing about a century ago, has been the continuous illumination it has thrown on the history, society, and religion of ancient Israel. These civilizations have, of

*From *Commentary Magazine*, November, 1958. Footnotes are from the original, renumbered.

course, a fascination in their own right, and the Assyriologists of today are not primarily concerned with the impact and implications of their work on the understanding of the Old Testament. But to the Western mind the Near East still represents the "Bible Lands" despite the current turmoil in the area occasioned by other interests; Egypt is still the land where the Israelites were in bondage, the land whence they emerged under Moses as a nation dedicated to a new religious idea, and Mesopotamia is traditionally the land of Abraham's birth, the land with which, by the testimony of the Bible itself, the Israelites continued to have important political and cultural contact throughout their history.

For the religiously oriented Westerner, Christian and Jew alike, it is naturally that part of the Babylonian record which has a direct bearing on the religious thought and literature of the Bible that attracts his most serious attention. Most of the West is committed in some degree to the belief that the monotheism of the Old Testament represents the highest level of theological perception yet attained by man, and that the religion of ancient Israel—or at least the religious thought of the prophetic age—embodies the most exalted spiritual conceptions ever attained by any ancient nation. When Babylonian religious and literary works were discovered, showing unmistakable relations with biblical counterparts, such as the Creation and Flood stories in Genesis, it was therefore inevitable that they should be very carefully scrutinized for the contrasts as well as for the parallels they displayed with the Biblical versions. Given the cultural background of the investigating scholars—many of them had in fact had a theological training and were committed to accepting the biblical word as divine inspiration—it was also inevitable that they would find the biblical stories superior in religious, ethical, and other qualities to their Babylonian counterparts. It may even be charged that this conclusion was a prior assumption, and that the investigation was undertaken with the implicit purpose of demonstrating the truth of this assumption.

On the surface the biblical versions of these stories do seem to exhibit a greater awareness of ethical values while lacking all the mythology of the Babylonian versions. Such considerations, when viewed against the larger background of the Babylonian religious system with its thoroughgoing polytheism, magic, astrology, and related religious institutions, served only to confirm biblical scholars and theologians late in the nineteenth century in their conviction that the monotheism of Israel was the superior theological concept, in that it provided the basis for an ethical rule of life unavailable to the polytheistic system of the Babylonians. In their zeal to uphold the superiority of the religion of the Old Testament these scholars ignored a body of substantial

evidence which might have cast a more favorable light on Babylonian religious thought. Numerous Babylonian religious texts such as hymns and prayers had already been published which reflected a high moral and ethical consciousness and a deep awareness of sin and retribution. There were indeed many Babylonian compositions that for moral and spiritual elevation could hold their own with some of the noblest passages in the Bible. The conclusions of these scholars, in brief, accorded scant justice to the Babylonian record, and little, as we shall see, to the biblical one.

It was therefore not surprising when the leading Assyriologist at the turn of the century, Professor Friedrich Delitzsch of the University of Berlin, in a series of three public lectures beginning in 1902, entitled "Babel and Bible," undertook to champion Babylonian religion and culture against the biblical scholars and theologians.[298] Although the declared purpose of the lectures was to synthesize the results of Mesopotamian archaeology and Assyriological study for the general public, the theme turned out to be nothing less than an all-out defense of the spiritual, ethical, and moral qualities of Babylonian culture and religion despite its obvious polytheism. It was at the same time an almost unrestrained attack on the claims made for the superiority of the religion of the Old Testament in these very same qualities.

Delitzsch epitomized his belief in the overall ethical superiority of Babylonian to Israelite civilization, apart from its obvious chronological priority, by giving Babel (Babylon) deliberate precedence over Bible in the title of his lectures. He compared the very same stories, including the Creation and Flood tales, which the biblical scholars had appealed to in support of their claim for the ethical superiority of the Bible, and purported to show that the Babylonian versions were superior in this respect. He went so far as to deprive the Israelites of the glory of having conceived of that unrivaled boon to Western living, the Sabbath, claiming instead that "there can therefore be scarcely the shadow of a doubt that in the last resort we are indebted to this ancient nation on the banks of the Euphrates and Tigris for the plenitude of blessings that flows from our day of Sabbath or Sunday rest." He even cast doubt upon the ultimate glory of Israelite religion by producing alleged evidence that the worship of Yahweh as the sole god was already known to "Canaanite" tribes who migrated to Mesopotamia before 2000 B.C.E. He also cited other texts which seemed to indicate that the Babylonians ultimately developed a monotheism centered on the god

298. The English translation of these lectures was published in this country in 1906 by the Open Court Publishing Co. in Chicago.

Marduk, the patron deity of the city of Babylon. Israelite religion was thus shorn of virtually all credit for
the major contributions to religious and ethical thought
which Judaism and Christianity had claimed for it.

Even a cursory reading of Delitzsch's lectures will
reveal that, together with a deep passion for his subject
and a justifiable resentment against the high-handed
manner with which biblical scholars often used it, he
harbored a deep antipathy to the religion of the Old
Testament. This last failing led him into errors of over-
statement, and even ignoring such parts of the records
on both sides as were prejudicial to his thesis. These
were, to be sure, common scholarly weaknesses to
which the biblical scholars had themselves succumbed.
Such weaknesses, however, might escape notice in the
work of defenders of the Bible, but they were likely to
stand out when displayed by someone on the other
side. Delitzsch himself provided his opponents with the
main weapons for their attack which followed on the
heels of his very first lecture.

The authorities of the Lutheran Church, and conservative theologians and biblical scholars of most Christian denominations, voiced violent objection to the
thesis of the lectures on purely doctrinal grounds. They
rightly regarded it as a direct assault on the fundamental Christian doctrine of the divine election of Israel,
and thus, by implication, on Christian teaching about
the ministry of Jesus. Delitzsch freely admitted that he
did not himself hold these beliefs, and in a private inter-
view with the Kaiser he admitted further that he did not
believe in the divinity of Jesus, nor that any passage in
the Old Testament foretold his coming. Wilhelm II
thereupon issued a lengthy statement dissociating himself and the German Lutheran Church (of which he
was the nominal head) from Delitzsch's views, pronouncing them a menace to public faith and morality.
To quote the famous theologian Harnack in approval
of the Kaiser's decision, it became "the talk of the
streets that 'the Old Testament no longer amounts to
much!' " Royal sponsorship was withdrawn from the
last lecture, and the public was exhorted not to take on
faith any of Delitzsch's opinions as they affected the
orthodox view of the Old Testament.

Such attacks from organized and conservative Christian quarters were to be expected, but scholars and
liberal theologians equally failed to come to grips with
the essence of Delitzsch's thesis. They contented themselves with pointing out Delitzsch's excesses and even
his misrepresentations; none was apparently moved to
reconsider the entire basis of the common belief in the
superiority of Israelite theology and ethics in the light
of the cogent evidence which Delitzsch adduced to show
that the Babylonians, despite their polytheism, similarly
reached high levels of ethical and spiritual thought.

The scholars were thus easily able to expose the
baselessness of Delitzsch's claim for the Babylonian
origin of the Sabbath. The basic facts are as follows:
the seventh, fourteenth, nineteenth, twenty-first, and
twenty-eighth days of every month were known as "evil
days" to the Babylonians, and of these days the nineteenth (which Delitzsch ignored for the obvious reason
that it did not fit into the Sabbath pattern) was considered the most baneful. These days were considered
dangerous for many kinds of activities, and for some
of them lamentation was prescribed. The Babylonian
term *shapattu*—possibly connected etymologically with
Hebrew *shabbat* (Sabbath)—was never applied to these
days as Delitzsch claimed, but only to the fifteenth day
of each month, which was never counted as one of the
"dangerous" days. The term *shappatu* did have a connotation of "ending" or "termination," but this did not
refer to any ceasing of work, but to the ending of the
first half of the month, or the time of the full moon.
Although it is still possible that the Hebrew term for
Sabbath is derived ultimately from the Babylonian term,
the character of the days to which the Israelites applied
it bears only the remotest relation to comparable Babylonian days.

Delitzsch's alleged evidence for the worship of Yahweh among certain "Canaanites" dwelling in Mesopotamia is more readily disposed of. It was not easily
refuted at the turn of the century because of the impre-
cise knowledge of dialectal Akkadian grammar current
in Delitzsch's day. The word which had been interpreted as referring to Yahweh we now know to be
nothing more than the first person possessive pronoun.
At all events, it is now commonly recognized that the
name Yahweh is excluded in all the cited occurrences.
We shall refer later to the texts which allegedly indicate
a tendency toward monotheism on the part of the Babylonians.

II

Many other details of evidence cited by Delitzsch in
support of his thesis were refuted in his day, and even
more can be discounted in light of our present knowledge. But the crux of Delitzsch's thesis raised a dilemma
which his critics virtually ignored. If it is true that
many Babylonian religious texts—not to mention the
implications of the great collection of the laws of Hammurabi discovered at the very time that Delitzsch's
lectures were in progress—reflected a deep consciousness of ethical and moral principles, wherein then lay
the reputed superiority of the monotheistic system of
Israel to the polytheistic system of Babylonia? Could
we not speak as appropriately of "ethical polytheism"
as we are wont to speak of "ethical monotheism"? It

certainly cannot be argued that monotheism per se represents a higher understanding of cosmological truth than polytheism does, especially if both conceptions are predicated on an ethical and moral order of the universe. The Chinese, after all, seem to have arrived at a moral and ethical conception of the universe without a theistic system at all.

But if the biblical scholars did not actually come to grips with this problem, they revealed an awareness of it. The superiority of the religion of Israel, they claimed, is manifested by the greater concern with ethical and moral considerations in the biblical record than in comparable Babylonian compositions. In other words, they grudgingly admitted the existence of ethical and moral motivation in Babylonian thinking, but claimed what might be described as a *quantitative* superiority for the ethical thought of the Old Testament. But this was precisely the level on which Delitzsch chose to fight. The debate was reduced to a sort of ethics contest, in which each side sought to prove the higher ethical content of its favorite. It might be instructive to follow the lines of the debate as it centered around the Babylonian and Biblical Flood stories, which interrelation is acknowledged on all sides, with the chronological priority of the Mesopotamian account being similarly unchallengeable.

There are, in point of fact, various Mesopotamian versions of the Flood episode, in the early Sumerian language as well as in the Semitic dialect of Akkadian, and there appears to be some organic connection among all of them. The best-known version is the latest and the most completely preserved one, the story of the Flood comprising the entire eleventh tablet of the most famous Babylonian literary work, the Epic of Gilgamesh. It is set in the form of a recounting by Utanapishtim—the Babylonian counterpart of Noah—of the circumstances of the great Flood, the means of his escape and the subsequent unique gift of immortality which the great god Enlil had bestowed upon him. The story is told to Gilgamesh who had finally sought out Utanapishtim at the end of a long series of journeys in search of the secret of immortality. By means of the recitation Utanapishtim seeks to convince his listener that this boon was granted only once to a mortal under unique circumstances and can never again be achieved by a mortal being. Here are the essential features of the episode as set out in this version:[299]

The great gods were prompted to produce a flood. The god Ea, lord of wisdom and the god most favorably disposed toward mankind, secretly warns Utanapishtim of the gods' plans and advises him to tear down his house and build a ship, to "Give up possessions, seek life; Despise property and keep the soul alive."

He is to take aboard the boat "the seed of all living things." The god also gives him the design of the boat, which is apparently to be in the form of an exact cube. When Utanapishtim wonders what to tell his fellow citizens when they see him at work on his strange project, Ea advises him to explain that he has to leave the city because Enlil, the chief of the gods, has taken a dislike to him, and that he is therefore going to live with Ea in the Apsu (the subterranean waters in Mesopotamian cosmology, which are the domain of Ea); a reply which was technically true, but purposely deceitful, for Enlil's dislike was of course directed against all of mankind. This deceit is underscored by the double meaning of the words of reassurance which Ea tells Utanapishtim to relay to his fellow citizens. He is to tell them that the gods will send down upon them a "rain of wheat"; but the word for wheat in Akkadian may also be understood as "woe." The context clearly indicates that the populace is expected to construe the message as a favorable one while Utanapishtim understands its true meaning. This subterfuge is apparently dictated by the desire to avoid having Utanapishtim tell an outright lie, especially on the advice of a god. The deceit clearly worked, the populace was touched by his explanation, and all apparently pitched in to help him get his ark ready by contributing equipment and supplies and aiding in the construction. He then loaded aboard all possessions, family, relatives, "the seed of all living things" and—in a characteristic Mesopotamian touch—a representative of each known craft.

The description of the ensuing storm is presented in mythological terms. Adad, the god of storm and rain, sends the flood-storm, preceded by twin destructive deities representing perhaps atmospheric disturbances such as the tornado; the major underworld god Nergal opens the dam on the subterranean waters; the war and irrigation god Ninurta breaches the dikes. The constant flash of lightning is described as the action of the host of earthly gods who "raised their torches to the sky, lighting up the land with their brightness." But the fierceness of the storm was such that even the gods became terrified, and they fled to the safety of the old sky-god Anu where they huddled crouching in fear "like dogs" beneath a wall. From this safe vantage point they observed the flood waters filled with the corpses of man and beast and were overcome with remorse for having consented to such destruction. Ishtar, the great mother goddess, gave loud voice to this grief with the words:

---

299. The most felicitous English rendering of the entire epic is by E. A. Speiser in *Ancient Near Eastern Texts Relating to the Old Testament* (Princeton, 1954). It forms the basis of the translations here.

How could I have ordered evil in the divine
   assembly,
Have ordered war to destroy my people,
When it is I myself who give birth to my
   people!

All the gods—with the apparent exception of Enlil, the chief of the pantheon—thereupon plunge into mourning. After raging for seven days, the flood subsided. In the words of Utanapishtim:

I then opened a vent [or: hatch] and light
   struck my face.
I looked about the sea; all was silence,
And all mankind had returned to clay.
The landscape was level as a flat roof.
I bent low and sat down weeping,
Tears running down my face.
I looked about in all directions for the ends of
   the sea;
At a distance of twelve [double hours] a
   mountain range emerged.
At Mount Nisir the ship came to a halt.

On the seventh day after this landing:

I sent forth the dove, setting her free.
The dove went forth and returned;
No resting-place appeared for her, so she
   returned.
I sent forth the swallow, setting her free.
No resting-place appeared for her, so she
   returned.
I then sent forth the raven, setting it free.
The raven went forth and saw the subsidence
   of the waters.
It eats, circles, caws, and does not return.
I let everything free to the four winds, and
   offered a sacrifice.
I poured out a libation on the top of the
   mountain.
Seven and seven vessels I set out.
Beneath them I heaped up cane, cedar, and
   myrtle.
The gods smelled the savor,
The gods smelled the sweet savor;
The gods gathered like flies around the
   sacrificer.

The goddess Ishtar arrives at the scene, vowing that she will never forget the Deluge, and attempts to prevent Enlil from sharing in the sacrifice, as it was he who brought on the Deluge "without reflection." When Enlil arrives, he sees the ship, and, realizing that some mortals had escaped destruction, he turns in anger on the rest of the gods. They then reveal to him that it was Ea who was responsible. Ea then addresses Enlil most eloquently:

O Valiant one, thou art the wisest of the gods.
How couldst thou without reflection bring on
   the Deluge?
On the sinner impose his sin; on the transgressor
   impose his transgression.
But be lenient lest he be cut off; be patient
   lest he [perish].

Ea continues by telling Enlil that (if it was his intention to punish mankind) instead of the Deluge he could have smitten mankind with attacks of wild beasts, famine, or pestilence, which would have served to "diminish" mankind, but not destroy it completely. Enlil is apparently overcome by this speech, and as a form of atonement blesses Utanapishtim, granting him and his wife the unprecedented gift of immortal life.

III

The parallels between this story and the Biblical Flood episode are fairly obvious. God decides to send down the Deluge because mankind has become evil and has corrupted the entire earth. Noah is to be spared because he is the only righteous person on earth. The dimensions of the ark which God commands Noah to build differ from those in the Babylonian account, but they are described in detail by God himself. He is to take aboard a male and female of each living species. In both versions the Deluge is the result of heavy rains and the simultaneous rising of subterranean waters. The traditional resting place of Noah's Ark, Mount Ararat in Armenia, is a notable variation from the Mount Nisir of the Babylonian story, which is in Southern Kurdistan. The most striking resemblances between the two stories occur at the end of the Flood, when Noah opens the window of the Ark, and sends forth the dove three times before it stays away for good; the biblical text at this point parallels the Babylonian almost word for word. Noah, like Utanapishtim, then offers sacrifices, and in a striking parallel to the Babylonian text we read: "God smelled the sweet savor" (Genesis 8:21), which prompts his decision never again to unleash such total destruction against the earth, "for the schemes of man's heart are evil from his youth, and I shall never again destroy all living things as I have done."

The dependence of the biblical story upon the Babylonian to some degree is granted by virtually all schools of thought. There can be no question about priority in time; the essential details of the Mesopotamian Flood story were already current by at least 2000 B.C.E. In evaluating the two versions, the Babylonian story is generally conceded the prize for its ingenuous human charm, which is enhanced by its being couched in poetic form. On the other hand, it has invariably come off a bad second in the test for moral and ethical content. John Skinner, for example, in his commentary on Genesis (1910) states: "The ethical motive, which is but feebly developed in the Babylonian account, obtains clear recognition in the hands of the Hebrew writers; the Flood is a divine judgment on human corruption; etc." There follows the expected invidious comparison between the "vindictive, capricious" and deceitful gods of the Babylonians and the one "almighty and righteous God—a Being capable of anger and pity, and even change of purpose, but holy and just in His dealings with men." A similar verdict, but in even more severe terms, is pronounced by the modern Assyriologist A. Heidel, in his book *The Gilgamesh Epic and Old Testament Parallels* (1949). He even quotes with approval an earlier contemptuous opinion of the Babylonian Flood story as "steeped in the silliest polytheism." It was just this kind of refusal to appreciate the merits of Babylonian religious thought and literature on their own terms by Biblical scholars that contributed to the violence of Delitzsch's reaction.

Granting for the moment the assumption made by virtually all Western theologians—which, say, an educated Chinese or Indian might conceivably not find so axiomatic—that monotheism is inherently a more advanced, elevated, and ethically superior form of religious conception than polytheism, what logical process dictates the further inference that the religious literature of a polytheistic society must of necessity be baser, cruder, or less moral in outlook than the literature of a monotheistic society? There is no doubt that the entire literature of the Old Testament, regardless of the age, character, or original function of its component elements, is made to conform with its over-all theme: the one God and his purposes, especially as they apply to man. But is it necessary to expect that the vision of ethical monotheism will transform every biblical episode in equal degree or be reflected in it? This is precisely what biblical scholarship implied by its uniform finding in favor of the biblical material whenever confronted with Mesopotamian parallels. It is doubtful, however, that an impartial observer would easily discern the higher ethical motivation inherent in the Biblical Flood episode, for example, as opposed to the Babylonian account. It is often pointed out in this connection that in the Babylonian story the gods decide to send down the Deluge without any apparent motivation, while in the biblical story the Flood is unleashed explicitly as a punishment for man's wicked behavior. The speech of Ea, however, after the Flood is over, is an indication that, to the mind of the Babylonians, the decision was in the first place prompted by man's evil behavior. The reason for its not being stated explicitly

is not necessarily due to the weak conception on the part of the Babylonian thinkers of the gods' concern for ethical conduct, to which it is often attributed. It must be remembered that the Babylonian story is presented as a recital by Utanapishtim of the significant events for the purpose of convincing Gilgamesh that his quest for immortality is vain; that his own immortal status was due to the unique circumstances of that ancient event, which can never again be repeated. It was not germane to this purpose to emphasize the causes of the Flood, nor would it have been appropriate for Utanapishtim himself to pass judgment on the alleged depravity of the whole race of his fellow men. The biblical narrative, on the other hand, is impersonal and its purpose is precisely to set forth God's actions and motives.

There exists, however, a much older version of the Babylonian Flood story than the one incorporated in the Gilgamesh Epic. Here the episode is part of a long impersonal narrative which was conceived as nothing less than a kind of history of mankind. This version of the Flood story is not often quoted in comparisons with the biblical story—although in numerous details it appears to be closer to the biblical version than the account in Gilgamesh—due to the fact that the text is still very fragmentary. But the vital point for us is that in this version the cause of the Flood is explicitly given:

The land became wide, the people became
    numerous.
The land hummed like a lyre [or: bellowed like
    wild oxen].[300]
The god was depressed by their uproar,
Enlil heard their clamour
And said to the great gods:
"The clamour of mankind has become oppressive,
Because of their uproar I want sleep."

There can be little doubt that the noise of mankind which disturbs Enlil's repose is only the metaphoric or mythological guise for what is clearly meant to be the wicked behavior of man. Biblical scholars will not be in a position to dispute such an interpretation, for these are precisely the terms in which the sinfulness of those most wicked of cities, Sodom and Gomorrah, is described in Genesis 18:20f. and 19:13. It is the noise and clamor of these cities which, having reached an intolerable pitch, impel God to send down a rain of "brimstone and fire." If the biblical "noise and clamor" can be interpreted as metaphor the same consideration

---

300. The ambiguity of the original Akkadian phrase presents this rather strangely contrasting pair of alternative renderings, but the sense of the simile is clear; humanity was setting up a constant din.

may be granted to the Babylonian use of the same terms. It is true that in the Biblical Flood story it is made explicit that Noah is to be spared because he was a "righteous man" while the rest of his generation was corrupt. Again it must be noted that we cannot fairly expect Utanapishtim to say this of himself in his narration to Gilgamesh. In the older text (usually referred to as the Atrahasis Epic, for this is the name of the Babylonian "Noah" in that version of the Flood episode) the section where such a statement might have been expected is missing. There is clear evidence, which we shall soon discuss, that Atrahasis is, in fact, thought to be righteous.

Returning to the reasons for the Deluge, neither the biblical version nor the Babylonian goes beyond generalizations in describing the alleged wickedness of man. From the biblical text alone it would appear that the behavior of mankind was no worse before the Flood than after it. It is only that later God becomes reconciled to the fundamentally evil "devisings of man's heart" (Genesis 8:21) and decides never again to resort to such extreme forms of punishment for it. Later Jewish rabbis, obviously not satisfied with this kind of motivation for the Flood, had recourse to midrash in order to supply appropriate grounds for such an extreme measure. They speculated on the nature of the wickedness, and imagined that it must have included various forms of sexual depravity, widespread homicide and robbery, or even all three. The ancient rabbis, as well as some modern scholars, were apparently also troubled by the lack of any indication in the biblical text that God had given mankind any warning of their impending doom, so as to allow them a chance for repentance.

Another disturbing feature was the apparently callous indifference of Noah to the doom of his fellow men. The proper task of a really righteous man (a *tzaddik*) would have been to warn them of the coming catastrophe and to exhort them to repentance. The rabbis proceeded to fill both these deficiencies by means of midrash. Thus God's decision to reduce the normal human life-span from the high hundreds of the pre-diluvian generations to one hundred and twenty—plainly an etiological tale meant to explain the still proverbial "one hundred and twenty years"—is interpreted by the rabbis as the period of grace during which mankind was given an opportunity to repent and reform its ways. Noah (together with Methuselah) exhorted his fellow men to repentance during this period, warning them of the divine punishment for their wickedness. In the same vein, the rabbis visualized the situation of Noah vis-à-vis his contemporaries when he began building his large and strange craft on dry land—a situation which, as we have seen, presented itself also to the mind of the

Babylonian writer—and they appropriately imagined Noah telling them the plain truth: God had decided to destroy all earthly life by means of a flood. The response of the populace, as imagined by the rabbis, was, as to be expected, derisive laughter. Now there is of course not the slightest warrant in the biblical text for any of these interpretations. Heidel, nevertheless, chooses to accept the midrashic period of grace as the literal meaning of the life-span episode together with the conception of Noah as preaching to his fellow men during this period. The moral justification for the Flood in the biblical text was evidently just as deficient to the sensibilities of modern scholars as it was to the ancient Jewish rabbis.

But if midrashic fancy may be exploited as a means of bolstering the moral basis of the Biblical Flood story, how much more justified is Delitzsch who, in championing the Babylonian version, points to the weeping of Utanapishtim when he beheld the aftermath of the Flood, a touch of human compassion absent in the biblical account. And on these grounds the case for Babylonia is even stronger than Delitzsch himself realized. For in the fragmentary late Assyrian revision of the Atrahasis Epic, in which the final Deluge is only the culmination of a series of lesser punishments, we find Atrahasis interceding with the gods in behalf of his fellow men in the two instances which are still preserved, a feature which is strongly reminiscent of Abraham's intercession with God on behalf of the people of Sodom. In other words, where the biblical story characterizes Noah as a *tzaddik*, but fails to illustrate it by deed, the Babylonian Flood tradition proves its hero's righteousness much more convincingly precisely by describing his deeds; what had to be supplied for the biblical account by rabbinic imagination is explicit in the Babylonian accounts.

The foregoing exposition is not, of course, designed as a defense of Delitzsch's thesis. It is meant rather to illustrate the hazardousness of attempting to prove the superiority of Israelite religion and ethics to the Babylonian on the basis of what are essentially trivial details. Parallel traditions, such as the treatment of the Flood legend in Babylonia and Israel, can be profitably compared only in the light of a full appreciation of the cultural and religious contexts of the respective civilizations. Such understanding is particularly vital when it is clear—as it is in our case—that the theme itself was an object of cultural borrowing. For it is obvious that the cultural content will determine to a great degree the treatment of the theme under observation. In civilizations with such greatly dissimilar religious orientations as Babylonia and Israel, the emphases and treatment of a common theme are bound to differ sharply. But once such differences are taken into account, value judgments based on comparisons will appear all the more meaningless.

IV

Now monotheism and polytheism—the most fundamental of the contrasts between Babylonian and Israelite theology—bear within themselves a series of cosmological implications which will channel the religious and philosophical responses of the followers of each approach along certain limited and inevitable lines. We cannot, of course, enter here into a lengthy discussion of all these implications, but we shall have to review, however sketchily, those that are basic to our present theme.

What is the essence of polytheism as a theological system? It implies the existence of a plurality of superhuman wills. This very condition precludes the absolute omnipotence of any one of these wills. Even if in the mind of a worshiper one or another of these wills, or deities, is thought to be the head of the pantheon, he must at all times be mindful of the purposes of the other deities which are potentially vitiating to his own designs. As in the case of Ea upsetting Enlil's plan for the destruction of all life by forewarning Utanapishtim of the coming Flood, even the chief deity may sometimes be tricked or deceived. The free expression of the will and personality of any one god is thus under constant threat of a clash with the will and personality of another god. In other words, the gods in a polytheistic system, though operating in an exclusive sphere, face much the same stresses and strains in their efforts at self-realization as man does on earth.

This has the further corollary that the gods cannot *consistently* act in accordance with a humanly conceived moral or ethical ideal. If the first thought of the gods, as that of man, must be "to look out for himself" vis-à-vis his fellow gods, moral and ethical considerations necessarily become secondary. From the point of view of mankind, therefore, the actions of the gods, especially as they affect man, may take on the appearance of caprice or wilfulness. But this does not mean, as has sometimes been stated, that gods act purposefully and wantonly to the detriment of man. On the contrary, to the mind of the Mesopotamian the gods stand in great need of and actually are dependent on the service of man. It is only that in the last resort the needs and welfare of man are of secondary importance in the gods' considerations; it may well happen that a course of action decided upon by the gods for good and sufficient reason to themselves may at the same time be catastrophic for man without his having done anything to incur such treatment. The people, such as the Babylonians, always viewed such misfortune as evidence of the gods' wrath and their own guilt. The profound

sense of sin and retribution of the Babylonians is amply attested to by their penitential prayers, which give moving expression to this feeling. But the crucial point is not that they possessed an awareness of sin, but that they had no assurance or hope that right conduct would insure their well-being. Sin and misconduct were sure to arouse the gods' anger, but there was no formula that could guarantee divine favor. No god was in a position to offer such assurance; he might at any time be compelled, for private reasons, to ignore such an agreement. For this reason even the concept of such an agreement is completely foreign to a polytheistic system. The gods, for their part, appreciated and even demanded moral and ethical conduct on the part of mankind, but they could offer no guarantees in return. Thus the Babylonian gods are often termed by modern writers (but rarely if ever by the Babylonians themselves) capricious, crafty, and treacherous. They are, to be sure, (for the most part) immortal, but in their needs, desires, and motivations, endowed with all of man's spiritual frailties; they are, in a word, only supermen. Mythology, which, in classical usage, involves the treatment of divine figures in human terms, is an inherent feature of any polytheistic system.

A monotheistic religion by virtue of its inherent characteristics tends, on the other hand, to become an ethical religion. There is no other being who is of the same essence as the single god; the possibility of a *real* rival is beyond conception. The will of this god is therefore incontestable. Though this god must always be conceived of in essentially human terms, man is conscious that this deity is in no way limited by any external forces which could restrict the full expression of his own personality; he has no peers to contend with, no rival wills to counteract. This feature alone renders him as fundamentally different from the gods of a polytheistic system, as from the condition of humanity itself. This god may then be conceived of as being motivated in his decisions by the highest ideals and never by the baser or selfish impulses which inhibit the realization of these ideals by man and polytheistic deities alike. He is therefore completely free to give his complete and unselfish attention to all that goes on in the universe.

By the same token he is in a position to lay down a mandate for man's behavior on earth in accordance with these ideals, and to guarantee man's well-being if his will is complied with, an advantage which, as we have seen, no polytheistic god could possibly enjoy. Man alone is capable of disregarding the divine will, but he does so only in full knowledge of the "Law" and of the inevitable consequences of his actions. The blueprint given by Yahweh to the Israelites for them to follow—the Torah—was conveyed with an unconditional guarantee of success if followed faithfully. Deuteronomy 30:11ff. states the situation with classic simplicity: "For this commandment which I command you this day is not too abstruse for you, nor is it too distant. Nor is it in heaven, that you might say 'Who will ascend for us to heaven to fetch it for us, to let us hear it, that we might observe it?' Nor is it across the sea that you might say 'Who shall go across the sea for us to fetch it for us, to let us hear it, that we might observe it?' For the thing is very near to you; it is in your mouth and in your heart to carry it out." The same text continues with the explicit guarantee of life and prosperity if the commands are faithfully obeyed and an unequivocal warning of extinction if they are disregarded. What is involved here is, in a word, a contract, or "covenant," the essence of which is the freedom of both parties to bind themselves to its terms. This condition could not obtain in a polytheistic system, in which the gods were not absolutely free; the concept of a "covenant" in a polytheistic society is inherently impossible.

The emphasis often placed on the "ethical" character of Israelite monotheism would in this light, therefore, appear to border on the tautologous. The god of Israel is "ethical" precisely because he is the sole deity. It is this uniqueness of Yahweh that carries with it the implication of absolute freedom which is basic to an organized and systematized ethic. Against this background there is little justification for the contempt in which Babylonian religious and ethical thought is often held, *given the polytheistic system under which they had to be conceived.* Nor is this polytheism itself a justifiable object of derision. The theological system of the ancient Greeks was in all essential features similar to that of the Mesopotamians, yet the Greeks have not suffered the abuse and scorn on this account which traditionally been the lot of the Babylonians. The Babylonians, did, after all, develop a practical system of ethics for human conduct, despite its ineffectiveness as a formula for ultimate salvation. But the wonder is not that their understanding of ethics, sin, and retribution was not as all-embracing or cosmologically anchored as it was in Israelite thought, but that they conceived of such values at all. Indeed, the record of the Babylonians may be of relevance to one of the great issues of our time, whether or not man can be committed firmly to an ethical rule of life that is not rooted in theology. The Babylonians deserve our sympathy perhaps, for their religious system denied them the possibility of coming to satisfactory terms with their universe, but even such an attitude must be tempered with admiration, for the three-thousand-year record of Mesopotamian civilization testifies at least to a remarkable human adaptation to a cosmos in which the future of man was viewed as hopeless.

The seeming preoccupation of biblical literature with the issue of sin and punishment is similarly a corollary of Israelite monotheism, and deserves no special praise on its own account. By their very possession of the "blueprint," the ideal norms of human behavior, the Israelites experienced a much more profound sense of human inadequacy and weakness than the Babylonians could. The latter had no standard on which they might pattern their lives. Their sense of guilt has a hopeless, almost amoral, character about it; there was always an awareness that their fate in the last resort did not necessarily depend on their guilt or innocence, but on the gods' private purposes. But the possession by the Israelites of such a standard afforded them not only a real perspective on their achievements, but a profound optimism as well; the goal or ideal is always in view, and is approachable if not easily attainable. To achieve salvation nothing more was required than to live up to an ideal that was always believed to have been revealed in the past by God and in force for all time to come. The Babylonians enjoyed no similar advantage. Only occasionally was a particularly favored individual—usually in legend—told what to do by a god, and even then it concerned only the immediate present. On the whole, however, the purposes of the gods were concealed, and were in any event usually prompted by immediate circumstances that could not be predicted far in advance.

The only recourse open to the Babylonians for determining the will of the gods was the process of divination, a procedure which could yield a "message" or "directive" only in the context of the moment, and which had to be instituted on every occasion when knowledge of the god's disposition—his motives were not of human concern—was vital for the undertaking at hand. It is of significance that the message or directive which the divinatory procedure was designed to disclose was called by the Babylonians *tertu*, a word cognate with Hebrew *torah*. The "torah" of the Babylonians, in a real sense, was something that had to be repeatedly elicited from the gods—virtually against their will—as the occasion arose, by the varied and devious means which constituted the elaborate pseudoscience of divination, of which astrology was only the latest and best-known form. Pathetic and barren as all this activity might appear to us today, there was no other method available to the Mesopotamians for ascertaining the will of the gods. The security offered by the monotheistic God of Israel, through a revelation valid for all times, was unavailable to the Babylonians, for their gods, as we have seen, were themselves in no position to grant it.

V

It will be clear then from the foregoing that most of the features of Babylonian religion which appear base or primitive to modern Western thought are only the inherent characteristics of a polytheistic theology. Western theology feels itself properly indebted to Israelite monotheism for having provided a rationalized basis for a coherent system of ethics offering a hopeful view of man's fate. Such a cosmic view could not have developed within Babylonian polytheism. Yet to hold Babylonian religious thought and ethics in contempt because of this is as legitimate as despising the elephant because he cannot outrace the horse.

In the contrast between a polytheistic system and all its implications and a monotheistic theology and all that it implies, lies the fundamental difference between Babylonia and Israel. But it must constantly be remembered that despite their gloomy view of man's condition, the Mesopotamians were compelled as a matter of practical necessity to organize their society in accordance with at least a *pragmatic* ethic. Men have always demanded ethical behavior on the part of their fellow men, failing at the same time to apply similar standards to their own conduct. The Babylonian gods too, although not themselves *bound* by moral or ethical principles, nevertheless appreciated them and expected man to live by them. The Babylonians, it would seem, fashioned their gods in their own image more faithfully than the Israelites did theirs. The appreciation by the Babylonians of morality and ethical conduct was as intense as that of any nation of the ancient world, and perhaps of the modern as well; their hymns, prayers, and wisdom literature, not to mention the vast and direct evidence of their law promulgations and untold thousands of surviving legal documents imply precisely this unending concern for justice and morality.

Bearing in mind the fundamental contrast in the theologies and world views of the Babylonians and the Israelites, we may return to the comparison of their respective treatments of material common to both of them, such as the Flood episode which we have used as the example in this essay. It will in the first place have to be recognized that the ethical motivations explicit in both versions do not do great credit to the highest concepts of either civilization. We should be in a particularly unfortunate position if we were compelled to deduce all the ethical implications of the Israelite cosmic view from the Flood episode, or, for that matter, from all the narratives in the book of Genesis. But once we are aware of these implications—from other biblical sources—we may detect their influence even in these portions.

We are struck, then, by the virtually complete absence in the Biblical Flood story of all the mythological byplay which permeates the Babylonian account. Where the biblical story, for instance, describes the action of the storm as extreme but natural meteorological manifestations, the Babylonian account portrays it in terms of actions by various gods. The biblical scholars have, of course, appealed also to this as evidence for the more "primitive" character of the Babylonian account. Yet if we recall that mythology, as we defined it earlier, is a corollary of a polytheistic theology and is excluded, by the same token, from a monotheistic one, we may view each version as self-consistent. Nor is there any need to imagine the early Israelite storytellers consciously editing the story they received from Mesopotamia by excising all the "offensive" mythological and polytheistic elements before it might be fit for "local consumption." The Israelite authors, rather, never really "heard" the story in its Babylonian form, for it would have been totally incomprehensible to them. If the notions of edition and excision are at all applicable, these processes must be thought of as unconscious; as the basic elements of the original tale were assimilated by Israelite tradition they were naturally and spontaneously harmonized with the Israelite cosmic view. Elements which were incompatible with this view disappeared of their own accord.

On the other hand, some elements which to modern theological sensibilities appear offensive, but are not intrinsically incompatible with monotheism, are found in the biblical as well as the Babylonian account. Thus we read in the biblical story that God locks the boat after Noah and his company are safely aboard, which contrasts with the Babylonian version in which Utanapishtim locks the door himself. Or again, at the end of the Flood we read that "God smelled the sweet savor," a clear echo of the Babylonian scene in which "the gods crowded like flies around the sacrificer." Neither scene in the one version can be said to be "more elevated" in conception than its counterpart in the other version. Yet both versions are internally consistent with their respective theological approach. The biblical scenes are not mythological, they are only extremely personal or anthropomorphized. What seems to be embarrassing to modern theological conceptions is at bottom only a matter of taste and degree. It can hardly be argued that personalization of the deity is incompatible with even the most exalted brand of monotheism. The God of Reinhold Niebuhr is, after all, identical in all essential respects with "De Lawd" of *The Green Pastures*. Numerous scenes of this type are found throughout the narrative and even the prophetical portions of the Old Testament. Such scenes are no more to be construed as vestiges of "crude" polytheism—as they often have been by biblical theologians—than are allusions to God's sight, hearing, or love. They are the natural consequence of the conception of a personal god, and are common to polytheism and monotheism alike.

When Delitzsch appealed to certain scenes in the Babylonian Flood story to support his contention that Utanapishtim is presented as a far nobler character than Noah—an argument for which we were able to cite even stronger evidence—it was apparent that he, as well as his critics, was not aware of the essential difference in approach between the two versions. In the Babylonian story the central character and focus of attention is Utanapishtim and the circumstances which enabled him to achieve immortality. It is the story of a human experience in which the role of the gods is secondary. The climax is the bestowal of immortality on the hero. Although the biblical tale opens with the statement "This is the story of Noah," it is really not the story of Noah; he is just the subject of the moment. The Flood episode, regardless of its original character, had already been recast to fit into a conscious progression of history in which the central theme is God and his dealings with mankind. The points of emphasis in the story are the wickedness of mankind, the contrasting righteousness of Noah, and his consequent exemption by God from the ensuing punishment. But the climax of the story is the covenant made by God never again to send a deluge against mankind, and in this climax—which is in fact the point of the entire story—Noah plays a small role indeed. The covenant made by God is not with Noah alone but with all earthly life. Having received his reward from God for his righteousness, Noah resumes his more modest role in the scheme of biblical genealogy.

The failure of the biblical narrative to demonstrate by detail the kindliness and saintliness of Noah is therefore neither an unfortunate omission nor a blemish on the ethical character of the narrative. Such details might have enhanced the artistry of the story, but their essential irrelevance to the theme would have obscured the focal point of the episode. The story thereby retains an austere and unadorned character by comparison with the Babylonian tale. It is significant, in this connection, that the rabbis felt these omissions as deficiencies, and proceeded to add just such midrashic embellishments as were explicit in the Babylonian account. But these are testimony only to the touching human qualities of the rabbis themselves, and serve to explain why the Babylonian Flood story is so much more appealing to our senses than is the Biblical version. And this contrast in focus between the two versions is again only the reflection of the contrasting theological approaches of the two civilizations. The gods of the Babylonians, though more human in attributes and qualities than Yahweh of the Israelites, are yet more remote from human approach and understanding; they do not normally reveal to man their wishes and their plans. What occurs on earth, though attributed to the will of the gods, cannot be described in terms of divine commands and compliance with them. Earthly events and institutions can only be described as the work of men. The famous laws of Hammurabi are, in the words of the prologue and epilogue to the laws, the work of the king himself. They are *not* received from Shamash, the god of justice. The god is conceived of as approving and demanding just action on earth, but he does not "reveal the Law" itself, as the Law of Israel is revealed by Yahweh himself. In the Flood episode, too, this difference is apparent. In the Babylonian account, although the flood is sent by the gods, the events are described from the human point of view; it is a tale of the experiences of human beings. The biblical story is but a chapter in a larger work, in which every episode is construed as a revelation by Yahweh of his will together with its earthly consequences. The perspective of the Biblical Flood tale is from the vantage point of the divine, and not that of man.

VI

Having set forth the view that most of the differences between Babylonian and biblical literature and thought can be attributed directly or indirectly to the contrast between polytheism and monotheism, we must deal at last with the alleged evidence that the Babylonians themselves ultimately approached the monotheistic conception. The text to which Delitzsch appealed in support of this proposition is a late one, in which the various gods are correlated with Marduk, the god of Babylon, in their several spheres of activity thus: Ninurta—Marduk of cultivation; Nergal—Marduk of war; Enlil—Marduk of dominion and counsel; Nabu—Marduk of fortune; Sin—Marduk as illuminator of the night; Shamash—Marduk of truth; Adad—Marduk of rain.

Since Delitzsch's time, similar texts have become known, one of which identifies the gods with the various parts of the body of the god Ninurta; another Assyrian text correlates the activities of the other gods with aspects of Ashur, the chief god of the Assyrians, and still another equates all the female deities with Ishtar, the great goddess of love and war. No serious student of the history of religion today would consider speculations of this kind as evidence for monotheism. They do indicate a common tendency towards syncretism, the identification of the different and independent personalities of the various deities as aspects of a single god.

This god is thereby perhaps magnified, but he is not basically transformed in any qualitative way. Such speculations are not monotheistic, for these other personalities continue to have their independent existence in the minds of the very same speculators, as was the case with the worship of Amon-Re during the Empire period in ancient Egypt. The worship of one god is itself not evidence of monotheism. It is best characterized as henotheism or monolatry, a system in which the existence *and effectiveness* of a plurality of deities is recognized within any one civilization although the attention of the worshiper for varying lengths of time and in different localities may be focused on a single one of these deities to the virtual exclusion of the others.

The tendency on the part of certain schools of thought to see in such manifestations tentative gropings toward monotheism is to be attributed in the first place to the tenacious hold which the evolutionary theories of the late nineteenth century still have on the religiously oriented Western mind. Anthropologists have long since discarded the theory of Tylor which postulated the progression of the religious development of the human race from animism to the belief in a supreme deity. And despite the patent absurdities in the "devolutionary" theory of Pater W. Schmidt and his school, the existence of true monotheistic beliefs in primitive cultures cannot be denied. The second reason for the tenacity of the evolutionary theory is the understandable desire of the educated layman to find a rational explanation for the development of monotheism in Israel in the midst of polytheistic surroundings. The evolutionary theory satisfied this desire by supplying the "missing link" of monolatry or henotheism. The fallacy inherent in the entire structure, which has been supported by the egocentricity of Western civilization, has been laid bare by Paul Radin, and need not be elaborated here.[301] Suffice it to say that factual anthropological data have demonstrated that the monotheistic conception of the cosmos can be, and, in fact, has been noted at all stages of social development side by side with the polytheistic conception. And although both views may be found concurrently in the same society, neither is prior to the other; they are in fact mutually exclusive and one cannot develop out of the other.

Monotheism, as Y. Kaufman recently said,[302] cannot be reached by the gradual reduction of the number of gods to one. Such a process has not been demonstrated in any society, present or past. At some time during the formative period of the Israelite nation, some individual *thinkers*, exactly as has been the case with individuals in primitive societies, viewed the cosmos in a way totally at variance with their co-nationals and contemporaries elsewhere in the civilized world. Following Radin, we may concede the possibility—perhaps the probability—that individuals in ancient Mesopotamia saw the universe in the same light. What is historically significant, however, is not the original conception, which can be found independently in various cultures, but that somehow in ancient Israel alone, this conception—as Radin has shown, usually a minority view—ultimately predominated over the other. The factors which contributed to the establishment of monotheism as the dominant theological view of the Israelites cannot have been inherent in the view itself. This is proved by its failure to take hold in other cultures. The success of monotheism in Israel must therefore be rooted in other conditions, which may be subsumed under the term environmental. To attempt to trace them would be outside the purpose of the present essay.

At all events, Delitzsch was justified, in the light of the prevailing view of the history of religion in his day, in appealing to such "monotheistic" Babylonian texts in support of his thesis. It was in fact an extremely telling point to which there could be no rejoinder. The orthodox theological approach of his critics had itself enthusiastically adopted the evolutionary view of the religious development of mankind, for it provided for the first time a scientific support for Christian apologetic. But if this evolution was possible within the religion of Israel, on what scientific grounds could it be excluded elsewhere? The text adduced by Delitzsch was meant to demonstrate that this "natural" process was not the exclusive property of the Israelites, but took place in Babylonia too, although it did not reach the level it ultimately attained among the Israelites. Against this kind of onslaught there was only one place of refuge, that of dogma; under the comfortable shelter of the belief in the divine election of Israel, all shades of opinion critical of Delitzsch took cover.

The syncretistic tendency manifested in the Babylonian texts alluded to above cannot properly, therefore, be considered even as a "stage on the road towards monotheism." When modern scholars evaluate such speculations as genuinely monotheistic, it is a manifestation only of the attraction that the evolutionary theory still holds for Christian theology. The Babylonian evidence indicates, in the first place, that the other gods did not cease to exist as a result of these speculations. The same thinkers, at other moments, could and did conceive of the separate aspects of the syncretistic deity in their original form, as individual wills and personalities. Secondly, far from approaching the attributes and conception of a true monotheistic god in all his transcen-

301. For a concise summary and evaluation of the entire question see Paul Radin, *Primitive Man as a Philosopher*, ch. 18.

302. *Great Ages and Ideas of the Jewish People*, edited by Leo W. Schwarz (New York, 1957).

dence and omnipotence, this deity remained in every essential characteristic the restricted deity of a polytheistic theology. Nothing has happened to him except that he has been aggrandized.

In summary, then, it may be said that no comparisons between Babylonian and biblical traditions can be undertaken without constant awareness of the polarity of the Babylonian and Israelite cosmic views, and of the profound effect this contrast had in the religious and cultural development within each civilization. Each system, to be sure, did experience an evolution, but these were internal evolutions; there was never a convergence of the two views towards each other, or, more exactly, a convergence of the polytheistic view towards the monotheistic one. Western man, as the heir of the Israelite tradition, feels that the monotheistic approach affords a firmer basis for his spiritual integration and reconciliation with the universe than was possible within the polytheistic cosmic view of the Babylonians. But this is hardly sufficient warrant for the abuse that the Babylonian experience has suffered at the hands of Western religious scholarship, whether in the form of unconscious condescension or as outright contempt. When Israel was born, civilization in Mesopotamia, based on a social order conceived in terms of high moral and ethical ideals, was already two thousand years old, and the material and intellectual products of this civilization had been diffused all over western Asia. Despite the profound difference of their cosmic orientation from that of the nations around them, the Israelites could and did assimilate with profit such social institutions, literary creations, and even religious usages which served as the practical basis of their own civilization, and which afforded them the institutional framework for the worship of their unique God.

Notes to Finkelstein, "Bible and Babel"

1. Professor Finkelstein appears to see the key distinctions between biblical law and Mesopotamian law as emanating from the contrast between Israelite monotheism and Babylonian polytheism. With regard to the treatment of murder and the criminal defendant, the Bible—in a radical departure from Mesopotamian perspective—holds that man is sacred and unique ("in the image of God") and has direct access to God through prayer and supplication because of this uniqueness. He does not require the intervention of any priest or religious hierarchy. Did these factors affect the treatment of murderers and other criminal defendants more than did simply monotheistic (as opposed to polytheistic) beliefs?

2. Finkelstein feels that polytheism leads to the view that the gods compete with one another and act out of expediency. This negates conduct according to an ethical ideal. The gods, therefore, cannot lay down a mandate for man. Is this persuasive? It should be noted that even the polytheistic pantheon had a god of justice who demanded righteous conduct from man. Nevertheless, despite the possibility that, as a matter of strict logic, polytheistic deities could act with consistent justice, in fact both Mesopotamian and Homeric mythologies record only gods who were capricious and morally indifferent.[303] Justice from the gods was regarded as a favor, not as a right. In the Mesopotamian view, there was an all-pervasive emphasis on the material, since both the cosmos and the gods issued from the same primeval element, which animated both man and gods. Accordingly, both could be subject to death, hunger, impotence, and sexual desires. In fact, even the gods were created through sexual cohabitation, and creation in polytheistic mythologies is always expressed in terms of procreation.[304] Similarly, in ancient Greece the word for god, *theos*, did not necessarily imply divinity but "meant first and foremost . . . any power, any force we see at work in the world, which is not born with us and will continue after we are gone, could thus be called a god, and most of them were," giving rise to such expressions as "love is *theos*" or "recognition between friends is *theos*."[305] Furthermore, Mesopotamia had a widespread belief in inherent primordial evil[306] and in the existence of cosmic evil forces that were beyond the control of deities so that the fate of man was not determined by his behavior. Therefore, the universe was purposeless, life had no meaning, and man was impotent.

The biblical perspective, on the contrary, held that morality, ethics, and justice were the essence of God's nature[307] and that God was the sole creator of nature, who controlled all cosmic forces and established categorical moral and ethical imperatives through a direct covenant with man. Each person bore individual responsibility for his acts,[308] and evil was a product solely

303. H. Frankfort, *Kingship and Gods* (Chicago, 1946), p. 277; M. I. Finley, *The World of Odysseus* (New York, 1959), p. 150; Sarna, *Understanding Genesis*, p. 17; Speiser, "Three Thousand Years of Biblical Study," in *Centennial Review* 4 (1960): 219.

304. Sarna, *Understanding Genesis*, p. 11; E. Vogelin, *Order and History* (Louisiana, 1956), p. 41; S. Moscati, *The Face of the Ancient Orient* (New York, 1962), p. 78.

305. G. M. A. Grube, *Plato's Thought* (London, 1835), p. 150; W. K. C. Guthrie, *The Greek Philosophers* (New York, 1960), pp. 10–11.

306. Sarna, *Understanding Genesis*, pp. 23–24.

307. See Gen. 18:25; Ps. 89:15; Deut. 32:41.

308. Note how Adam, Eve, and the serpent were each punished separately and differently for their transgressions (Gen. 3:11–21; see Deut. 24:16).

of human behavior.[309] The concept of sin and of moral culpability, introduced in the Bible, was alien to many ancient cultures, including those of the Greeks and Romans, who regarded such acts as merely unwise, rather than unethical, if disapproved by a deity whose power was superior to that of man.[310]

2. "BABEL-BIBLE": A MESOPOTAMIAN VIEW
(By J. J. Finkelstein)*

We must put before our mind's eye, the very peculiar relationship of Western thought to the Babel-Bible issue. What will be said here will probably strike most of us as an obvious truism. Yet the history of the Babel-Bible issue demonstrates plainly that it is a truism which is indeed so obvious, so all-pervading, that we no longer see it; we simply ignore it. And this is the incontrovertible fact that Western thought, primarily Western cosmology, is in every fundamental respect identical with the cosmic conception of the Bible; our approach to the Babel-Bible issue has been, in effect, a confrontation of the Mesopotamian world view with our own. Had we been regularly conscious of this relationship, the results of earlier analyses of the issue would have yielded more valid conclusions. As it is, we have been carrying on more or less of a polemic or medieval kind of debate with the Mesopotamian world under the delusion that we have been analyzing with detachment the relationship of two civilizations relatively removed from our own. . . .

This hard fact, the realization and awareness that in approaching the issue of "Babel and Bible" we are in effect speaking with the voice of one of the two protagonists, must be firmly established before we can proceed any further. We must constantly remind ourselves that while we understand the biblical view with relative ease and implicit sympathy, we can barely hope to penetrate beyond the most superficial levels of the ideological and conceptual world of Mesopotamian civilization. Yet even such awareness of our limitations will be sufficient to caution us against comparing isolated phenomena out of a conceptual nexus that we barely understand with parallel, or apparently identical, phenomena which we *automatically* evaluate against their relevant conceptual and cosmological background. The most serious flaw in the approach to "Babel-Bible"

in earlier years has been precisely the fact that comparable phenomena in the traditions of ancient Mesopotamia and Israel have been weighed in a single set of scales: the scale of Western values, which, by definition, is the scale of the biblical tradition alone.

Our next step, therefore, is to try to establish, however sketchily, some idea of the Mesopotamian cosmic conception, which must needs have affected the character of their social institutions, literature, and possibly even dictated their very structure. We may begin by stating that, broadly speaking, there are essentially two ways in which man tries to relate himself to the world of external experience, as an individual and as a society. For relate himself, he must; [for] in the most primitive societies, as well as in the most civilized, man is aware of his peculiar condition as being partly of the realm of the natural world and in certain other respects unique. The question then is to which of these two aspects will he turn for the explanation of his anomalous situation. Put another way, to which of his characteristics—those he shares with the rest of nature, or those which mark him as unique—will he attribute his significance? The biblical response is clear: Man's position is credited to his uniqueness; this uniqueness is not a liability but an advantage. In explaining this advantage to his own satisfaction, he arrives almost inexorably at an explanation of the cosmos, which we today —with our system of classification derived from another cultural complex—term monotheism—to us a theological notion, but to the ancient biblical thinkers the sum and substance of their cosmic apprehension. We may characterize the biblical cosmic orientation as "vertical"; its explanation of the cosmos is one of cause and effect—albeit according to a simple scheme—that is understood, like our own, in terms of time. Events and phenomena are not explained as answers to the questions "What" or "How"; everything that occurred after the act of Creation is understood as an explanation of "Why." The key word, especially in the book of Genesis is *toledoth*, of which the English rendering "generations" is now commonly misunderstood as genealogy, where it originally meant that which is generated, the consequences of certain antecedent events or persons. It is now quite properly being once again rendered as "history." By implication, finally, the premium and emphasis is put on the unique; for while the consequence embodies the antecedents, its essential character is that of something new and unprecedented. The one God is, so to speak, the embodiment, or the apotheosis, of the quality of uniqueness.

The Mesopotamian response to the problem of man and his environment had as its goal the *assimilation* of man to the natural environment. It saw the salvation

---

309. This is reflected in the Genesis episode relating to the Garden of Eden (Gen. 3); see also Lam. 3:38 ("From the one on high. there does not come forth evil or good").

310. J. Freund, *The Sociology of Max Weber* (New York, 1968), p. 190; see M. Weber, *The Sociology of Religion* (Boston, 1963).

*Read at the meeting of the American Oriental Society, Bryn Mawr, Pennsylvania, March 29, 1961.

of man in the suppression of those features which set him apart from the rest of nature, and in the attempt to harmonize him totally with nature. Its first and primary order of business, therefore, was to understand nature. Overwhelmingly, the bulk of intellectual thought in Mesopotamia was directed towards *explaining* the visible or conceptual universe; the implicit questions it set about to answer were "What" and "How"; rarely, and only very late, were there any serious "Why's." Experience and events have no transcendent significance in terms of time; whatever significance is inherent in them is due to certain intrinsic similarities that bind together groups of phenomena or events, whether these be physical or otherwise. The chief intellectual activity of Mesopotamian scholarship was the collection and *classification* of all experience primarily on the criterion of real or imagined similarity; this mode of apprehension of the universe may, by contrast with the biblical, be characterized as "horizontal." Their notion of cause and effect is not that of the Israelite conception of it but is rather the inherent or potential properties of phenomena in which the sequential factor is irrelevant; it is, of course, the very same method which later becomes basic in the natural sciences. Thus, behind the classification and ordering of stone, birds, fishes, animals, grammatical phrases, legal phrases, hypothetical events that we call "laws" and other events we call omens, there lies a single motivation and a single pattern of thought. It is the ordering of all experience on the basis of perceived similarities with a view to establishing a reliable degree of "predictability" which, in effect, affords man a measure of control over his environment. "Knowledge" in Mesopotamia may therefore be said to consist of the apprehension of the relationship existing between members of classes of the experienced universe. This relationship is impersonal and neutral. It is what we term magical, and the apprehension of the more abstruse relationships, as for instance in perceiving the similarity of events, is considered the height of "wisdom." We might compare this with the orthodox understanding of "knowledge" in the biblical view: it is "moral knowledge," the "knowledge of good and evil." The gods, in Mesopotamian thought, are little more than extensions of the apprehendable universe, arrived at either by personification of the major phenomena, such as the sky, air, the astral bodies, and the water, or by a kind of abstraction, such as the cattle and grain gods, or the deities representing crafts and institutions. They are supermen, not transcendent beings; they are subject to the same needs and passions as mortals, and, like mortals, they too—even the most powerful among them—must be at pains to discover the secret of the universe, the power of magic, except that as supermen, they are credited with the ability to mas-

ter such knowledge with greater facility than humans are. Finally, the gods themselves, as a class of experienced phenomena, are the object of learned classification along with the rest of the experiential universe. When, in the late Mesopotamian periods, we find what have been considered syncretistic attempts to subsume the role of a number of gods under the name of one of them, such as Marduk or Ninurta, such speculations are better understood as a new approach towards the same age-old goal. It does not herald a new cosmic orientation for mankind; it is at best, from the Mesopotamian point of view, a sophisticated refinement in the techniques for understanding or penetrating the nature of that class of phenomena known as deities, a new technique of classification. It is, in a word, conscious *theology*, a category of speculation which is altogether absent in the Old Testament.

I would emphasize here that in the Mesopotamian and biblical worlds we confront two totally contrasting modes of awareness, which cannot possibly evolve one out of the other. Neither can we say which is the more valuable or "loftier" conception. It is of course axiomatic to us that the Mesopotamian mode was unsuccessful in its attempt to integrate man into the scheme of nature; conversely the effectiveness and vitality of the biblical view is being demonstrated to this day. . . . On the other hand, we must not lose sight of the fact that in its confrontation of the natural universe, the empirical and predictive approach of the Mesopotamian thinkers broke the bounds of the irrational, of the realm of magic, in some categories, and advanced into the realm of true scientific method, most notably in the fields of mathematics and astronomy. To the degree that Western civilization considers itself "liberated" from nature, a substantial share of the credit for this aspect of its freedom is to be accorded to Mesopotamia as well as to Greece. In other words, if we grant that the condition of freedom implies a real understanding of the experienced universe and man's place in it, to the degree that the Western man has satisfactorily explained to himself the phenomenon of man, he is the heir of the biblical mode of thought; and to the degree that he feels himself in control of his environment, he is the heir of the Mesopotamian as well as the Greek orientation.

With this, then, I propose finally to submit to a brief analysis a group of phenomena common to the biblical and Mesopotamian traditions, in order to observe their points of similarity but, more importantly, to see whether the contrasting modes of apprehension of the two civilizations, as just sketched, could account for their divergences. I choose for this purpose the goring-ox rules out of the so-called law codes of Exodus on the one hand and of Eshnunna and Hammurabi on the other. I have deliberately chosen this set of rules precisely because the similarities among them are so noticeably strong that they have served as the parade example in the countless discussions of the relationship of biblical and Mesopotamian traditions. But such discussions have to my knowledge invariably approached the subject from the relatively narrow perspective of comparative legal practice, without deep concern for the ideological or conceptual factors involved, especially on the Babylonian side. Such considerations were reserved for comparisons of literary traditions, such as the Creation and Flood episodes, where cosmological factors were more obvious and explicit. But the expression of the cosmic orientation of a civilization even in the most mundane features of its social organization is no less real for being less obvious, and if we can detect its influence even in such a routine matter as the legal treatment of negligence, it would serve as warning that we had better probe more deeply into *any* sets of comparable phenomena of these two civilizations.

The goring-ox laws may now be reviewed quickly. The Laws of Eshnunna, beginning with paragraph 53, treat the following sequence of cases:

If an ox gores another ox and causes its death, the owners of the oxen shall divide between them the sale-price of the live *ox* and the *carcass* of the dead ox [emphasis added].

If an ox was a habitual gorer, the local authority having duly so notified its owner, yet he did not keep his ox in line, and it then gored a man, causing his death, the owner of the ox must pay ⅔ of a mina of silver [to the kin of the victim].

If it gored a slave to death, he must pay 15 shekels of silver.

There follow two sections which provide for the same damages when the animal is a vicious dog instead of a goring ox.

The Laws of Hammurabi deal with the situation as follows, beginning with section 250:

If an ox, while walking along the street, gored a man to death, there are no claims in that case.

But if the ox was a habitual gorer, the local authority having notified him that it was a habitual gorer, and yet he did not screen [or pad] its horns, nor had he kept his ox in line, and that ox then gored a free citizen [or the sons of a free citizen] to death, he must pay ½ mina of silver.

If it gored to death a man's slaves, he must pay ⅓ mina of silver.

The biblical rules beginning in Exodus 21:28 read as follows:

If an ox gores a man or a woman and he dies, the ox shall be stoned to death, its flesh may not be eaten, but the owner of the ox is innocent. But if the ox was a habitual gorer of long standing, its owner having been warned, and yet he had not kept him under guard, and then it killed a man or a woman, the ox shall be stoned to death, and the owner shall likewise be put to death. But if a ransom is imposed upon him, he shall pay the ransom for his life as much as is imposed upon him. Whether it has gored a son or a daughter [i.e., a minor], he shall be accorded the same treatment. If the ox gores a slave or a slavewoman, he must pay thirty shekels of silver to the owner [of the slave] and the ox shall be stoned to death.

After an interruption in which another kind of case is dealt with—and we shall soon return to the significance of this interruption—the writer returns to the goring ox, dealing with the case where the victim is another ox:

If the ox of one man gores the ox of his fellow and it dies, they shall sell the live ox and divide its price, and they shall divide the dead one also. But if it was known as a habitual gorer of long standing, and its owner had not kept him under guard, he shall make good ox for ox, and keep: the dead one for himself.

I should like to state at first that in all of this material I find really one clear instance which satisfies me that there is some relationship between the biblical and Mesopotamian rules, namely, the case in which one ox gores another ox; the biblical rule and the rule in the Eshnunna laws are stated identically almost word for word, and the rulings prescribed are identical. I have, however, no interest at present in exploring the kind of relationship involved, but will state simply my feeling that in general it has to do more with certain *literary* traditions in the ancient Near East than with legal ones. What does interest me, are the very striking divergences between the biblical and Mesopotamian rulings even when they are dealing with the identical hypothetical cases. Firstly, and most obvious, is the stipulation in the biblical laws that in all cases where the victim was a human, even a slave, the ox must be stoned to death, a detail not specified in any of the Mesopotamian laws, even when the ox was already known as a dangerous animal. There have been all sorts of explanations of the biblical provision, some going so far as to cite classical and medieval parallels where animals were put on trial for attacks on humans, and some using the comparison to demonstrate how particularly solicitous the biblical laws were of human life, and how crassly commercial the Babylonian practice was by contrast. All of such explanations are not only off the mark, but also beside the point. In the first place, if we were to be slavishly literal about the wording of laws—even real laws, and not these "pseudo-laws" of the Mesopotamian and biblical collections—we would have to conclude that our own societies are as callously inconsiderate of human life as the Mesopotamian. For in our own statutes, which generally include rules governing damages that might be assessed against owners of animals—and by most civil codes, dogs are not allowed a free bite out of humans even the first time—nothing is ever said about the destruction of the animal, for that is a *non-legal matter*, and will be done or not done purely at the discretion of, say, the local police, or on the basis of common sense. Students of primitive societies have consistently reported on the high level of common sense by which intrasocial disputes or differences are settled or extraordinary situations dealt with. It is also a matter of the most elementary common sense that in ancient Israel, when an ox gored a person to death, and the circumstances indicated that in some way or other the victim had been at fault in the first place, i.e., had been guilty of contributory negligence, the animal would certainly not have been destroyed. And conversely, in Mesopotamia, if it were clear that the attack of the ox had been clearly unprovoked, there would have been a demand for the destruction of the ox, purely on the grounds of public safety. But in either case these are extralegal considerations. What *is* of supreme interest is the *rationale*, the compelling ideological factor that made the destruction of the ox part of the explicit biblical provisions on the subject. Some scholars have of course seen that it is a religious provision, but mainly in terms of the objective guilt of the shedding of blood and the objective pollution thereby created, citing in this connection the Noachic law and the necessity for ritual expiation, even when a victim of an unknown homicide is found in a field, by the immolation of a calf. While this is nearer to the point, it is far from describing the whole case. It should be noted, for instance, that the specific means for the destruction of the ox is by *stoning*, and the contrast is particularly illuminating in the case where the owner is also liable to the death penalty—i.e., in the case where the ox had been known as a gorer—for in that case the text states that the ox must be stoned, but that the owner is just put to death (*mot yumat*), which certainly involves some *other* method of execution (probably by the sword). Now execution by stoning is specified in the Bible only for particular kinds of offenses: the violation of a religious order, or insurrection and sedition; indeed almost all the offenses incurring the penalty of stoning can be interpreted as forms of insurrection or sedition. But the shedding of the blood of one person by another is *not* among them; the execution of a convicted murderer is *never* by stoning. The specification for the *ston-*

ing of the ox must therefore be understood as a form of insurrection, an insurrection against the divinely ordained hierarchy of terrestial authority; man was ordained to rule over and dominate all earthly life, and the attack on man by an ox, in whatever circumstances, constitutes as much of an insurrection against the established order as cursing Yahweh, rebellion against one's parents, idolatry (rebellion against Yahweh)—all of which are offenses for which stoning is the specified method of execution.

Furthermore, the place these parallel sets of rules occupy in their respective documentary contexts, i.e., the place these groups of rules have in their respective schemes of classification, is particularly illuminating. Note first the place occupied by the goring-ox rules in the Laws of Hammurabi: It is the last subgroup in a larger series of rules whose main subject is oxen, beginning with paragraph 241; thus: oxen taken in distraint, the hire of oxen, the total loss of oxen through ravages of wild beasts or disease, and the death or injuries to oxen due to negligence or mistreatment by the person who hired it. All of this is then concluded by the rules of the goring-ox. The implications are clear: The phenomenon of a human gored to death by an ox is an incident which is no different *in essence* from other mishaps, or tortious situations that might commonly arise in connection with the use of oxen. In other words, the case of injury or death to a human is in no way a phenomenon or class apart; man is just one of the larger group of natural phenomena or elements most likely to be associated in untoward events connected with the use of oxen. The interest of the writer, furthermore, is not at all focused on the victim; as an incident, or phenomenon, his interest is strictly in determining the degree of negligence involved in the hypothetical case at hand. Where there could have been no presumption of negligence, there can be no award of damages; where there is a presumption of negligence, the guilty party, i.e., the owner of the ox, is liable for damages, and these, naturally enough, are determined objectively: the death of a free adult is a greater economic loss than the death of a minor, and the death of a slave a smaller loss than either. He has not the slightest *legal* interest in the ox; whether it should be destroyed or not would be decided on by the persons involved in the incident, but the essential point is that it is irrelevant to the whole context and purpose of the rule.

The Eshnunna group of rules, though far shorter than Hammurabi's, is oriented in the same way; the case where an ox gores another ox, which leads off the group, is fundamentally no different from the cases where the victim was a human, which follow upon it.

Like the Hammurabi rules, their interest is focused on the factor of negligence and the loss sustained in the incident.

It is far otherwise with the biblical group. The cases in which an ox gores a human follow immediately upon, and must be considered an extension of, the sequence of cases in Exodus 21 involving death or injury suffered by persons, beginning with the case of intentional homicide in verse 12. In harmony with the biblical mode of apprehension in which the entity of *man* is a category differentiated from the rest of the experiential universe, all that concerns man as a *legal* entity is a class apart as well. An incident is therefore not classified according to the similarity of circumstance but according to whether the victim is human or not. Thus, the case where an ox gores another ox is separated from the other goring-ox rules by the case in which an ox or an ass is killed by falling into an uncovered cistern. This separation is especially significant inasmuch as the case of the ox goring another ox is precisely the one in which the biblical rule and the Mesopotamian are virtually identical, in phraseology and ruling at the same time. The two cases are identical in ruling also precisely because the situation, not involving humans, is from the biblical point of view thus a purely civil tort, a status which, in the Mesopotamian view, also includes cases involving human victims. It is to be noted further that the biblical rules from this point on deal *exclusively* with tortious invasions, i.e., where no human victims are involved, with only one highly instructive digression in the case of larceny. While it is clear that larceny is treated in the Bible as a purely civil invasion (in contrast to the Mesopotamian view), the interest of the writer suddenly shifts to the person of the wrongdoer, when human life is involved. It operates on the principle that situations involving danger to human life lift an otherwise tortious case of burglary into another realm altogether; indeed the writer loses interest for the moment in the matter of compensation for the theft. Thus, he states only that if the victim of the burglary should slay the thief in a surreptitious entry, he—the victim of an unlawful invasion—is innocent. Is it not strange that this should have to be stated explicitly? But the whole point is cleared up by the opposite case, in which it is specified that where the burglary is being carried out in broad daylight, the victim may *not* slay the intruder, on pain of becoming legitimately liable to blood vengeance. In other words the victim of a burglary may protect his property at the expense of the life of the intruder *only* where there is a presumption of danger to his own life—the principle being, as it were, that a human life encumbered by a felony is less privileged than a human life without blame; but when there

is no such presumption the victim of a burglary *may not* be allowed to commit a privileged homicide even against invasion. It would be highly instructive to follow up this set of rules with the Mesopotamian rules relating to unlawful taking, but time does not permit.

From the foregoing brief analysis, I believe we may draw the following general conclusions: As with any problem involving possible institutional borrowing among two neighboring cultures, it is much more important to analyze the way in which the two cultures or societies utilize the material that is presumed to be common to both of them than to attempt to determine which owes what to the other. One obviously contributes nothing when one points out that Shaw and Shakespeare wrote about the same episodes in Roman history. The purely factual question of direct interrelationship of Mesopotamian and biblical phenomena cannot be decided with certainty in any individual instance. Again, as a purely historical detail, it would be my opinion that the goring-ox rules in Exodus—by virtue of identical details of phraseology—must somehow be related to the Mesopotamian rules, although there are no ways to establish the links for that connection. It is my view that to speak of a common law for all of the ancient Near East is absurd; what was common to the area was a community of literary traditions, or genres, which accounts for the widespread utilization of certain literary motifs, themes, idioms, and metaphors. The so-called codes of law constitute just such a genre; as they were never real "law" in their native milieus, they were certainly not "borrowed" as law in neighboring areas; but there *was* a community of literary expression of certain legal or social ideals, and these achieved something of a canonical status affecting the choice of the kinds of cases that would be included in such code documents and the phraseology in which they would be couched. In all of this, of course, Mesopotamia must be credited as the point of origin in the broadest sense. But for cultural significance all of this is at best secondary.

I would close with a quotation from something written by a member of this audience in another context: "Cultural phenomena must always be interpreted within the framework of the civilization in which they developed and exist. Every civilization has its own structure and it is the individual and distinctive, rather than the typical and general in which the historian is interested. . . . Identical or seemingly identical phenomena may in different civilizations have quite different meanings." As this observation is particularly pertinent to all the ramifications evoked by the issue "Babel and Bible," one can most appropriately close by saying "Amen."

Notes and Questions to Finkelstein, "Babel-Bible"

1. Does this article reflect the view that the basic distinction between biblical law and Mesopotamian law lies in the higher regard for human beings reflected in biblical law? If so, does this conflict with Finkelstein's view in his previous article, "Bible and Babel," that the key difference between biblical and Mesopotamian law emanates from the distinction between a polytheistic and monotheistic religion?

Does part of the difference also stem from the biblical perspective of an all-knowing God, whose awareness of a person's every thought and act accordingly requires man to follow the prescribed biblical standard strictly? Contrast this with the Mesopotamian view of gods as having only a generalized awareness of events. (Witness Utanapishtim, in the Mesopotamian Flood epic, who acts without the apparent awareness of the other gods.)

Does the higher status of man in the Bible also result in a higher standard of expected behavior by man?

2. Does monotheism imply a perspective of history as the unfolding of a divine plan? Is a philosophy of history easily developed in a polytheistic framework? Can the past (as a reflection of the unpredictable behavior of the gods contesting with each other) be a factor in understanding the present or in predicting the future?[311]

3. Is Finkelstein correct that Mesopotamian law is secular and that biblical law is religious in nature? May not Mesopotamian law, too, be religious in essence (even though there is no intermingling of ritual and "civil" laws, and delicts are not stated to be religious sins, etc.), since law must conform to eternal truths that are part of a cosmic order, with both the king and the general populace answerable to the gods for violations of their respective duties to promulgate and obey the law?

4. Does not Mesopotamian law, as reflected in the codes (and in the copies of court decisions which have come down to us), reflect the values of Mesopotamian society and an ethic of life? If so, is Professor Finkelstein correct that polytheism, unlike monotheism, cannot lead to "high" ethical standards? Were the ethical standards of Mesopotamia "high"? What is the definition of "ethical" and of "high," and by whose standards are these to be measured?

3. THE PROBLEM OF THE PROLOGUE AND EPILOGUE TO THE BOOK OF THE COVENANT
(By S. Paul)*

The object of this legal corpus [in the biblical book of Exodus], as has been seen, is to form a "holy nation." Law, moreover, is presented here not as a secular instruction but as a divine pronouncement. The biblical frame to the corpus refers law directly to God; hence, it derives its validity from being a revelation of the divine will. This is the decisive feature of biblical law and is the key to the understanding of its unique characteristics. For although the Israelite society was greatly indebted to its Mesopotamian predecessors for its deep respect for law, for the view of man not as the ultimate sources, but rather as the servant of the law, and for many legal prescriptions which eventually were adapted into biblical legal corpora, the basic concept of law in Israel was radically opposed to all other systems of jurisprudence.

Law in Israel has a divine authorship; it is not a "humanly authored safeguard of cosmic truth" [Greenberg, in Chapter III, Section B 3 a]. Since there is no metadivine sphere present in biblical thought, God does not receive any *kinatu* [cosmic truths] from a higher power for future dispensation. God alone is the ultimate source and sanction of law. The entire law is ascribed directly to him. "Here God is not merely the custodian of justice or the dispenser of 'truths' to man, he is the fountainhead of the law; the law is a statement of his will. . . . The only legislator the Bible knows of is God [Chapter III, Section B 3 a]. God, furthermore, is not merely the guarantor of the covenant, as the deities are in the epilogues to Mesopotamian legal collections and treaties; he is the author of the covenant who directly addresses his people.

In light of this, several characteristic traits of biblical law may be singled out:

1. Since law is an expression of the divine will, all crimes are considered sins, and certain offenses become absolute wrongs, incapable of pardon by human agency.

2. The whole of one's life is now directly related to the will of God. The distinction between *jus* [human law] and *fas* [divine law] known to Roman law is non-existent. Man's civil, moral and religious obligations all ultimately stem from God, and hence are interwoven within a single corpus of divinely given law. These three realms, which in extrabiblical societies would be incorporated respectively in law collections, wisdom litera-

---

311. See E. A. Speiser, "The Biblical Idea of History in Its Common Near Eastern Setting," *Israel Exploration Journal* 7 (1957): 201.

*From S. Paul, *Studies in the Book of the Covenant* (Leiden, 1970).

ture, and priestly handbooks, are here combined into one body of prescriptions.

3. Since God is the sole legislator, Israel is held responsible to him and not to any human ruler or legislative body.

4. Unlike Mesopotamia, where the king alone was chosen by the gods and granted the gift of the perception of the *kinatu*, God selects the entire corporate body of Israel to be the recipients of his law. His care and concern extend to all members of this community and not merely to one chosen individual. Thus everyone is held personally responsible for the observance of the law. This leads, in turn, to the concept of individual and joint responsibility. No longer is it the sole concern of the leader of the community (e.g., the king in Mesopotamia), to maintain justice and to protect the rights of his community. This responsibility is now shared by every member of the society; since the law was communicated to all, the responsibility for its observance rests on the people *in toto*. Each member of this community, then, has a dual responsibility: to observe the law personally and to see that the law is observed by the group. Each must see that justice is executed and that all crimes are punished—otherwise the community and its members are threatened with dire consequences. Faithful observance of the law, on the other hand, grants divine protection and reward to both the individual and the group. Law becomes the single most important factor in the life and destiny of Israel.

5. Publicity, not secrecy, is the hallmark of the law, which is proclaimed openly to the entire society and is not restricted to any professional class of jurists, lawyers, or judges. Exodus 21:1 makes this patently clear: "These are the norms that you shall set before them." Law publicly promulgated in advance is to be contrasted with the epilogue to LH [the Laws of Hammurabi] (LHXXVb:3–19), where the aggrieved party learns of the law pertaining to his case only after the crime has been committed. Law in Israel is prospective and prescriptive not retrospective and descriptive. Though LH was frequently copied in scribal circles, there is no mention in the collection itself of making the law part of the public domain. In the Israelite society, on the other hand, law was not only proclaimed publicly at the very outset, but, in addition, a renewed proclamation was required once every seven years.

6. Law, then, becomes a body of teaching directed to the entire community. Each member of the community knows prospectively of his individual and communal obligations. Since law serves as an instrument of education, a didactic aim is to be found only in biblical legislation. Thus, unlike most other ancient legal corpora, motive clauses are occasionally appended to both

apodictic and casuistic injunctions. These explanatory, ethical, religious, and historical comments appeal to the conscience of the people and pedagogically aid and motivate them to observe the law. God desires "men who confirm them inwardly."

7. Since man is conceived as being created in the divine image, the sacredness of a human being becomes a primary concern of the law. Thus, whoever destroys a human life must give a reckoning for it. Monetary compensation and property settlement, characteristic of extrabiblical legal corpora, are absent from biblical legislation. "Life and property are incommensurable" [Chapter III, Section B 3 a] in the Israelite system of law, where religious rather than economic values predominate. As a correlate the death penalty is now abolished for all crimes against property.

8. Whereas biblical legislation demands a "life for a life," brutal and multiple punishments frequently found in several extrabiblical legal collections are all but absent from Israelite law. The principle of individual culpability, moreover, predominates throughout the biblical legal corpora proper and leads eventually to the abrogation of vicarious punishment. Secular offenses are punished on the actual offender, not collectively or vicariously.

9. Since all men are created by God and thus stand equal before him, class distinction is rejected in the meting out of justice. This feature of Israelite law, absent from other legal compilations, is exemplified in the biblical version of *lex talionis*. Rather than being a primitive residuum, it restricts retaliation to the person of the offender, while at the same time limiting it to the exact measure of the injury—thereby according equal justice to all.

Notes to Paul, "The Problem of the Prologue and Epilogue to the Book of the Covenant"

1. Paul asserts that biblical law is religious, while Mesopotamian law is secular. For a contrary view, see M. Weinfeld,[312] who asserts the theory that there were two groups who made written records in Mesopotamia: the priests, who recorded the sacred literature dealing with prayers, stories of the gods, ritual texts, and similar material; and the scribes, who recorded works dealing with poetry, education, law, and the sciences.

Weinfeld claims that the works of the scribes, including those dealing with law and relations between men, were made public. The books of the priests, dealing with religious aspects, including the religious ramifications of crimes, were, however, kept secret. According

312. "Israelite and Non-Israelite Concepts of Law," *Bet Mikra* 17 (1964): 58–63.

to Weinfeld, this secrecy explains our lack of religious records dealing with law, although in his view crimes were also considered to be religious offenses in Mesopotamia.

Was the law in Mesopotamia, even if limited to those laws preserved in extant records, completely secular, or does it have religious overtones and underlying religious assumptions? How about biblical law—does it differ, essentially, from Mesopotamian law in this respect? Note that the Bible deals extensively with relations between man and God, as well as relations between men. See also Henry Maine, who maintains that ancient law was always intermixed with morality and religion.[313]

2. Paul claims that in biblical law, "class distinction is rejected in the meting out of justice." Is this true also with regard to a slave who is killed by a person (Exod. 21:21) or gored to death by an ox (Exod. 21:29–32)?

3. In addition to the distinctions between biblical and Mesopotamian law made here by Paul, the following distinctions mentioned by him elsewhere may be noted:

a. In the Bible, God is the direct author of the specific laws, not simply the enunciator of some generalized truths.

b. God himself is a direct party to the code, not just a guarantor.

c. The biblical code is in the form of a covenant. This is unique in ancient Near Eastern law.

d. Unlike the Mesopotamian codes, the Bible often gives justifying motives for norms, such as "because bribes blind the eyes of the wise" or "be holy, for I am holy."

e. The Bible imposes severe penalties for crimes against God (idolatry, blasphemy, and acts held to affect the holiness of the people, such as sodomy, and incest). At the same time, unlike the Mesopotamian codes, the penalties for other cases are less severe. Bodily mutilations (that is, cutting off arms, legs, or noses) were abolished, except for flogging, which was limited to forty strokes. The biblical expressions "an eye for an eye" and "you shall cut off her hand" have traditionally been taken to refer to a mode of expression only, rather than an actual practice (see Chapter II, Section D 3 *b*).

f. The Bible repeatedly demands protection for the stranger[314] and guarantees his equal treatment with the citizen. It also contains numerous rules and exhortations for the protection of the poor, widows, and orphans, including numerous specific provisions for their economic well-being.[315]

g. In the Bible there are liberal exemptions from military service (see Deut. 2).

h. The Bible prescribes harsh treatment for murderers, who must be killed; monetary composition is not tolerated.[316]

i. The style of the Mesopotamian codes is dry, using technical language, without literary overtones. By contrast, the style of the Bible is warm and emotional, appealing to the emotions as well as to reason, and attempting to persuade as well as instruct.

j. In the Bible the administration of justice and specific decisions were administered in the name of God. The tradition was therefore that judges were to sit in the sanctuary.[317] Mesopotamian court decisions do not refer directly to a code or to a divine law. Law was, however, regarded as part of the cosmic order.

k. Biblical crimes were held to pollute the purity of the community and of the land (Num. 35:33, 34).

l. In the Pentateuch crimes required expiation and forgiveness.

4. Although the Bible has many sharp distinctions from the Mesopotamian codes, it has certain similarities to treaties made by the Hittite kings; both utilized apodictic as well as casuistic styles; both were inscribed on large stones; both have long historical introductions (the book of Genesis and the first portion of the book of Exodus can be regarded as a long introduction); both contained formulas of blessings and curses; both were placed in a sanctuary; and both were read periodically in public.[318]

Despite sharp contrasts, there are numerous similarities in literary style, terminology, and legal provisions between the Bible and the Mesopotamian codes. Thus, for example, the provision in the Code of Hammurabi regarding assault (secs. 195–201, 206, 209, 211, 213, 218) are similar to the Bible in style, language, and even order. Both begin with norms dealing with the striking of a parent, followed by an assault resulting in the wounding of limbs (eye, tooth, etc.), followed by provisions regarding the striking of a pregnant woman, causing her miscarriage. The contents and thrust of the laws, however, are in marked contrast.

4. OTHER COMPARISONS BETWEEN BIBLICAL AND MESOPOTAMIAN LEGAL PERSPECTIVES

1. It is the consensus of scholars that the perspectives reflected in the Bible are much more similar to those prevalent in ancient Mesopotamia than in Egypt. Thus, both in Mesopotamia and Israel, the king, as well as

---

313. See his *Ancient Law*, pp. 14, 16, 28.
314. See Exod. 23:9; Lev. 24:22; Deut. 24:17.
315. See, e.g., Exod. 22:20–26; 23:11; 24:10–22.

316. Num. 35:31–34.
317. Talmud, *J. Makkot* 2:6; *Sanhedrin* ch. 11, Mishnah 6.
318. DeVaux, *Ancient Israel* (New York, 1965), pp. 143–50.

his subjects, was bound by the law. The authority of the king and of the elders was also similar. Many of the motifs in the Bible can only be understood clearly by reference to customs prevalent in Mesopotamian society—that is, the wife-sister motif mentioned in the Bible (Gen. 12:13, 26:7) by Abraham and Isaac; Esau's sale of his birthright to his brother, Jacob (Gen. 25:31–34); the relationships and interactions between Abraham, his wife Sarah, and their maid Hagar (Gen. 16); the taking of Laban's household gods by his daughter Rachel (Gen. 31:19, 30–35).

Why was Mesopotamia's influence much greater than that of Egypt, which was in much closer physical proximity?

2. Note the concept, which pervades both biblical law and the Mesopotamian codes, of "measure for measure," that is, penalizing an offender by inflicting upon him the same act that he committed. This was carried to extremes in Mesopotamia. Thus, in the Assyrian codes, if one rapes a virgin, the victim's father may rape the rapist's wife. Similarly, a penalty was commonly imposed on the *organ* with which the offense was committed. Thus, for homosexual rape, the penalty in the Assyrian codes is castration. The principle of *lex talionis* is also found throughout the Code of Hammurabi; thus, one who kisses without permission is punished by having his lips cut off. The Bible, too, repeatedly refers to "eye for an eye" (even though, traditionally, this was not applied literally) and has other similar provisions, such as "he who sheds the blood of man, by man shall his blood be shed" (Gen. 9:5).

3. For comparison between the Mesopotamian and biblical perspectives regarding communal responsibility for crimes and capital punishment for property crimes, see above, and see also Deuteronomy 21 and 13:13–19 and Exodus 22:2, 6.

4. Compare also the different forms of sanctions employed in the Bible and in the Mesopotamian codes. Thus, drowning, splitting an offender on a stake, and severing of limbs, all of which are prescribed in the Mesopotamian codes, are not found in the Bible as standard forms of punishment. These are, however, reflected in such literary phrases as "you shall cut off her hand" and "an eye for an eye" (Deut. 25:12), although

Jewish legal tradition holds that they were not intended to be, and were not, in fact, applied in practice.

It is interesting to note that in the Jewish legal tradition, strangulation and burning, two of the four forms of death penalty provided for, were to be performed in a manner calculated to leave little, if any, visible bodily mutilations (see Talmud, *Sanhedrin* 49b).

5. Some scholars claim that in Mesopotamia, in contrast with the biblical perspective, neither the gods nor the king prescribed detailed rules. If so, who originated the rules found in the Mesopotamian codes?

6. Is there any significance in the fact that in the biblical perspective God transmitted his thoughts and law directly to the people, while in the Mesopotamian perspective the gods did not communicate laws directly to the people but only through the king.

7. Compare the class discrimination in the Mesopotamian codes with the class distinctions in the Bible. Are they substantially the same or are there significant differences? What accounts for any differences?

8. The largest part of the Mesopotamian law codes is concerned with private property, and its protection. Is this true of the biblical codes? What is their main concern?

9. The Mesopotamian codes do not seem to have been applied in practice as the source or guide for court decisions. As J. J. Finkelstein (see above, Chapter II, Section E 4) and others have mentioned, *not one* of the thousands of legal documents that have been unearthed mentions the Code of Hammurabi. See below, Chapter III, Section B 6, however, for a case of an actual trial for adultery, in which a rule identical to one found in Hammurabi's Code was applied, as well as a recorded claim for compensation asserted against a town by the victim of a robbery. These accord with the provisions of the Code of Hammurabi. Moreover, even when the provisions of the codes are not explicitly applied, they can give us an idea as to the perceptions, if not practices, that were common in Mesopotamian society.

It is clear, on the other hand, that the biblical prescriptions were applied in practice. When lapses occurred, and they were numerous, they were duly decried by the prophets.

III. Biblical and Cuneiform Legal Systems in Operation: Authoritative Decision-Making in Biblical and Cuneiform Law

A. *The Making of the Law: Who Prescribed the Law?*

1. THE KING

a. THE MANNER OF THE KING
(By E. A. Speiser)*

The Terms *Shofet* and *Mishpat* and Their Meaning

The question at issue in this chapter is the basic concept of state in ancient Israel and, more particularly, the introduction of kingship as a replacement for the system previously in force. The answer to this question involves problems in the fields of linguistics, society, and cultural and political history. But the effort is justified, even in broad terms, for the results have an intimate bearing on the whole biblical way of life.

The biblical phrase that summarizes the question is *mishpat ha-melek* (1 Sam. 8:11). These two words together take in the underlying semantic issue in its entirety. The first is genetically related to *shofet*, the technical term for the chief official under the outgoing system of government; the second describes the head of state in the new scheme of things. The compound *mishpat ha-melek* thus underlines the transition from *shofet* to *melek*: the *shofet* was to give way to the king. But what did the former function actually imply? Strange as it may seem, this point is as yet far from settled.

The root *shpt* is the basis for some of the most intimate terms in the vocabulary of biblical society. Yet no vocable of like importance has been subjected to as monolithic a treatment at the hands of innumerable generations of translators, ancient and modern. Beginning with the Greek renderings, the pertinent verb has been given all too frequently the rigid meaning of "to judge." Accordingly, *shofet* became specialized as "judge." And since this technical value does not link up of itself with political leadership, modern scholarship has sought to establish the necessary bridge by explaining the *shofetim* as "charismatic judges." But this has merely served to compound an obscurity. The *shofet* as such was no more and no less charismatic than the *melek*. A Samson, for instance, until personal

*From *World History of the Jewish People*, vol. 3 (New Brunswick, 1970).

tragedy had humanized him, reflected little divine grace, let alone judicial conduct. If the position of the *shofet* was thought to be charismatic, it was not because of anything that was inherent in the meaning of the term. But if the *shofet* was something other than "judge," the translation of *shefatim* as "acts of judgment" must likewise be reconsidered, however felicitous it might appear to be on the surface.

When it comes to *mishpat*, it was evident from the start that "judgment" could not begin to suit all the occurrences. The familiar English translations, among others, recognize this fact by resorting to "justice, ordinance, rule, due, manner," and the like. Obviously, all these diverse meanings could not readily be traced back to an underlying connotation "to judge." Some other primary meaning of the root would thus seem to be indicated.

Etymological correspondences within a given linguistic family must always be evaluated with all due caution; they should never be permitted to override the evidence of actual usage. Yet such comparisons, if correctly adduced, can at least throw light on basic semantic values. In the case of *shpt*, we have now the independent testimony of the Mari texts. The new evidence is significant on several counts. For one, the pertinent Mari occurrences are unambiguous in their bearing. For another, they are not so much Akkadian as "Amorite," and hence that much closer to Canaanite. And for still another, the Mari texts date from the Old Babylonian period; they thus reflect earlier linguistic conditions than are to be encountered in the Bible. On all these counts, therefore, the Mari evidence in regard to *shpt* promises to be highly important.

We find, then, in Mari a functionary called *sapitum*; this term is an exact linguistic analogue of Hebrew *shofet*. The authority of the *sapitum* is described as *sapitutum*, his activity is indicated by the verb *sapatum* (Hebrew *shafot*), and the corresponding action noun is *siptum* (which would be *shefet* in Hebrew; cf. *shefatim*). Now the one thing that is clear at a glance is that *sapitum* is not "judge." For, as one literary text informs us, the god Shamash is *sapit ili u awelutim* "the *sapit* of gods and men" as well as *dayyan sakin napistim* "the judge of living creatures." In other words, the *sapitum* and the *dayyanum* perform separate functions; and since *dayyanum* is definitely "judge," *sapitum* must be something else. Elsewhere we learn that the *sapitum* was one who could issue and carry out the *siptum*, which in turn was a disciplinary warning or act. Normally such activities lay within the province of governors. But they could be delegated to special officials who then bore the appropriate title of *sapitum*.

The corresponding biblical terms are all of later date, but their basic meaning remains substantially the same. Thus *shefatim* refers unmistakably to "acts of discipline," hence "punishment" or the like. Accordingly, the *shofet* was originally someone with the authority to decide what administrative action was needed and, when necessary, to issue warnings and mete out punishment. He was arbiter or punitive officer, as the case might be, one whose duties were administrative rather than legal, although they naturally involved both judgment and devotion to justice. And if the analogy of Mari society is valid, the *shofet* was subject to higher authority as much as the *sapitum*. In the biblical instances, however, that authority was divine rather than human. In this respect the *shofet* was not unlike the Mesopotamian *issakku* or "governor."

As regards *mishpat*—which has not turned up at Mari—we should now expect it, theoretically, to mean something like "standard, regulation," and hence conduct, custom, manner, or characteristic behavior in general. In point of actual fact, the biblical uses of this term reflect every one of these nuances. The underlying connection may well have been "norm," based on a noun meaning "discipline," or the like, if not on a verb with the sense of "to regulate, administer." It may be noted in passing that the only Akkadian term which approaches the range of *mishpat* is *parsu*, which reflects the complex Sumerian concept of *m e*, approximately "norm, nature." Indeed, a recently published text from Alalakh speaks of a gift presented *kima paras* (URU) *Halab* (KI) "according to the custom of the land of Aleppo." In a Hebrew text this would have to be turned into *ke-mishpat halab*.

In summary, the semantic range of *shpt* is by no means oriented toward the legal concept "to judge." The strictly judicial aspect is here tangential or incidental at best.

The Nature of Kingship in Ancient Israel

Turning now to the matter of kingship, we find in the key passage about it in 1 Samuel 8 not only the noun form *mishpat*, but also the simple verb *shpt*, which occurs twice in the significant combination *melek le-shoftenu* (verses 5, 6). The obvious meaning in this phrase is not "a king to judge us," which clearly would be out of place, but "a king to govern us (like all the nations)," precisely what the foregoing discussion would lead us to expect. The next question before us is the exact force of *mishpat ha-melek* in the sequel. Does

mishpat refer in this phrase to the "rule, discipline" that the prospective king would impose? Or alternatively, is the sense "nature, habit, manner," that is to say, conduct habitual with kings? Since the term itself can have more than one meaning, we have to look to the context for the answer. But the context, too, happens to be ambiguous. Samuel is dealing with the *mishpat ha-melek* in order to warn the people against the king whom they had just requested; whether he is thus referring to the king's "rule," or to his "conduct," the picture remains just as grim. A possible hint of the intended meaning may be contained, however, in the related passage in Deuteronomy 17:14–20. There the subject matter is a list of various things that a king must be careful to avoid; it is a sort of negative *Fürstenspiegel*. Samuel on the other hand chooses to stress the things that the wrong kind of king is sure to do. In either instance the emphasis would thus seem to be conduct. On this basis, therefore, the traditional "manner of the king" may be said to strike the proper note.

In any case, however, there need be no doubt about the biblical concept of kingship in general. In deciding to be ruled by a king "like all the nations," Israel had a choice of two prevailing systems which had long been established in the neighboring lands. One was peculiar to Egypt; it featured a deified ruler, and hence an absolute form of government which made the king's authority supreme both in theory and practice. To Israel such a way of life could have meant only the most abject kind of surrender, spiritually as well as socially. Small wonder, then, that the Bible dwells constantly on the theme of Egyptian bondage in a manner that physical oppression alone would not have been sufficient to justify. Rather it was the horror of an utterly alien social system that made the memory of the Egyptian experience so acute and repelling. Thus "the manner of the king," as it is stigmatized in 1 Samuel 8:11–18, could just as aptly have been labeled in that context "the Egyptian manner." And it may safely be assumed that this is how the pronouncement was meant and understood.

The other system with which pre-monarchic Israel could not help being acquainted was at home throughout the Fertile Crescent. Its principal, and apparently original, exponent was Mesopotamia. Under that concept of state, the king was distinctly a mortal ruler whose authority was subject to two ever-present checks: one by the assembly of his elders, the other by the gods to whom the king was ultimately responsible for his acts. The law was impersonally conceived and it applied to the ruler and the ruled with equal force in guiding the king and safeguarding his subjects at one and the same time. To be sure, sporadic attempts were made in parts of Mesopotamia to invest the king with divine authority. But these were limited and short-lived in their effect. They failed to involve such strong personalities as Sargon of Akkad and Hammurabi, and they never spread to Assyria. The prevailing culture rejected all such pretensions as incompatible with the very spirit of the native civilization. And many other cultures found the basically democratic system of Mesopotamia attractive enough to copy its features and its numerous by-products.

Israel was on many basic counts a representative member of Fertile Crescent society. It would be very strange, therefore, if it failed to conform also on the all important issue of the fundamental concept of state. Nevertheless, one school of modern scholarship has been at pains to uphold the view that the idea of divine kingship was central to biblical thought. This interpretation however starts out with the demonstrably faulty premise that the ancient Near East as a whole shared the same ideology. Actually Egypt alone was thus involved, in sharp contrast with the rest of the region. The resulting ideological curtain proved to be a more formidable barrier than any conceivable physical obstacle.

There is, moreover, ample direct evidence to show conclusively that kingship in Israel was regarded as manmade in origin and limited in scope and authority. It was "the people" who "made Saul king" in Gilgal (1 Sam. 11:15). Following Saul's death, "the men of Judah . . . anointed David king over the house of Judah" (2 Sam. 2:4). This was later repeated when "the elders of Israel . . . anointed David king over Israel" (2 Sam. 5:3), except for one highly significant added touch: they first obtained assurance against autocracy in the form of a solemn "covenant." Later on, "all Israel" was prepared to approve Rehoboam as king following the death of Solomon (1 Kings 12:1). But when the people discovered that Rehoboam would oppose badly needed reforms, they promptly summoned Jeroboam before "the congregation" and "made him king over all Israel" (verse 20). In this passage the assembly plays the same decisive role that it enjoyed traditionally in Mesopotamia.

The authenticity of the instances just cited has never been disputed by the leading critical schools. The same cannot be said of Samuel's ominous warning about "the manner of the king," which gave the present chapter its title and starting point. For one reason or another, that passage has been assigned by the critics to a later period. It is wholly immaterial for our purpose whether this evaluation is right or wrong. What matters is that the spirit of the statement is fully in harmony with the other evidence concerning the nature of the Israelite kingship. The actual king-makers were the leaders of

the people; and such authority on the part of the people is literally "democracy."

The Introduction of Kingship in Israel

While there may thus still be some doubt as to the nature of Israelite kingship, no such uncertainty need exist concerning the reasons for the change from the previous system. The evidence on this point is both explicit and implicit, biblical and extra-biblical, but never really ambiguous. It remains only to view this evidence in its proper historical and cultural perspective.

The Philistines had arrived in the land from distant parts at the beginning of the twelfth century B.C.E. They evidently required several generations to establish themselves securely in the coastal plain. In any case, by the end of the eleventh century they were sufficiently entrenched and consolidated to make a bid for the control of neighboring areas farther inland. That expansion, however, was bound to run up against the counter-drive of the Israelites, who had been undergoing a similar process of settlement and consolidation for a slightly longer period than the Philistines. A head-on collision between these two dynamic forces was thus only a matter of time.

An important factor, however, in the impending struggle was the difference in the backgrounds of the respective opponents. The Israelites had started out as a number of separate tribes intent on taking up settled occupation of the land. They had a common body of religious beliefs and practices, but otherwise their interests and their prospects varied from place to place. Economic and political procedures had to be improvised and adjusted. And although a national consciousness had been solidifying for some time, the machinery to implement it was yet to be devised and developed.

The Philistines, on the other hand, had started out as a compact and well-organized social group. Otherwise they could not have embarked on a long journey across the sea, with the goal of conquest and settlement on their arrival. Such evidence about the Philistines as we do have points to a homogeneous social and political organization and an urban economy. All this was in sharp contrast with the unregimented ways of the Israelite tribes.

There was also one further factor which for a long time bade fair to outweigh all the others. This was the overriding technological factor at one of the decisive junctures in the advance of mankind. It falls under the heading of the Coming of Iron. The Iron Age had been ushered in only a bare few centuries earlier. It had a truly epochal impact on a very broad front. Industry and economy throughout the Mediterranean world were drastically affected; politics and warfare were revolutionized; large portions of the world's population were on the move. The so-called Sea Peoples put an end to the Hittite empire, overran Syria, and posed a mortal threat to Egypt. The incursion of Philistines into a land that was henceforward often to be called after them was but one of the innumerable reverberations of the advent of the Iron Age. Understandably, the newcomers were better schooled in the new vital iron technique than the older inhabitants. Indeed, a regretful tribute to Philistine superiority in this field has found its way into the Bible (1 Sam. 13:19–20). They had mastered the new art and were provident enough to treat it as their secret weapon while keeping that knowledge from potential enemies.

The inevitable clash between the Philistines and the Israelites thus loomed for the latter as a battle against seemingly impossible odds. They lacked the weapons and training, the social coherence and organization, to face this challenge to their very existence as a nation. The emergency called for heroic measures, for sacrifices and changes commensurate with the existing danger. And the common answer was embodied in the popular demand for a king, so that Israel might be put on a par with "all the nations."

What, then, did the introduction of kingship in this case actually imply? It could not mean the establishment of absolute rule, for the Israelite idea of kingship, as indicated above, involved a manmade ruler of an essentially democratic state. Nor was it simply a matter of changing from a theocratic to a secular regime. The old *shofet* was not appreciably more charismatic than the new *melek*. Nor is there much difference between these two terms, semantically speaking. If one has to give a workable translation to *shofet*, it would have to be something like "arbiter, person in authority," or just simply "leader." On the other hand, *melek* is etymologically no more than "counselor," as is abundantly clear from the uses of the corresponding verb, especially in Akkadian and Aramaic. It thus follows that the actual difference between these two terms was not so much one of kind as of degree. The same should also hold true of their respective functions.

In their former inchoate state the individual tribes were headed by chieftains set up by the more influential clans. Such heads bore the title *nasi*, which probably signified someone who had been "elevated" by the assembly of the leaders. When several tribes had to act in concert—in the face of a common danger, or for purposes of a joint religious undertaking—they would need an overall "arbiter" or "leader," in short, a *shofet*. This was necessarily a loose and casual set-up, with little if any governmental machinery. The arrangement would often not outlast the given emergency or joint enterprise. There was manifestly nothing permanent, let alone dynastic, in the concept of a *shofet*.

What "all the nations" had under their royal system was a head of state who was at the helm for life and would be succeeded by a logical representative of the same line. This applied not only to totalitarian Egypt but also to the antiauthoritarian systems of Mesopotamia, Syria, and Anatolia. And even where royal succession was not hereditary in theory, it was so normally in practice. The system was conducive to stability and efficiency. It meant proper administrative organization on a permanent basis, taxes, and personal services to the state, including military obligations. Inevitably, bureaucracy would encroach on personal liberties, and regimentation would tend to curb individualism. But these were the facts of political and economic life in an increasingly international world. They could spell the difference between survival and extinction.

Notes to Speiser, "The Manner of the King"

1. Note that neither Moses nor his successor, Joshua, were called kings. This was also true of the leaders who succeeded Joshua for the next few hundred years, until the people demanded a king in the time of Saul.[1]

2. The Bible repeatedly refers to the king as being subservient to the law and required to obey it.[2] Furthermore, there is no reference in the Bible to a king promulgating new laws in his own name. The Bible refers to the law as "the law of Moses my servant."[3] Contrast this with the Mesopotamian codes, which were named after kings: Code of Hammurabi, Code of Lipit-Ishtar, Laws of Eshnunna, and so on.

b. THE EDICT OF AMMISADUQA
(Translated by J. J. Finkelstein)*

It was the custom in Mesopotamia during the Old Babylonian period, but going back possibly to late Early Dynastic times, for the kings to proclaim an act of "justice" or "equity" . . . at the beginning of their reigns and at intervals of seven or more years thereafter. Such acts, concerned mainly with the remission of debts and other obligations, as well as the reversion of land holdings to their original owners, were known heretofore from allusions to them in royal year-names, and references to them in certain private legal documents. The Edict of Ammisaduqa, the tenth ruler of the Hammu-

1. See 1 Sam. 8.
2. Deut. 17:18, 20; 1 Sam. 8:4–22; 1 Sam. Chapters 9–12; 1 Kings 21.
3. Mal. 3:22; 2 Kings 23:25.
*From J. B. Pritchard, *Ancient Near Eastern Texts Relating to the Old Testament* (Princeton, 1955).

rabi Dynasty in Babylon (1646–1626 B.C.), represents the only extant substantial text proper of such an edict, the only other one known being a fragment of a similar edict issued by Samsuiluna (1749–1712 B.C.), the great-grandfather of Ammisaduqa. There is good reason to believe, however, that the early law "codes," such as those of Ur-Nammu, Lipit-Ishtar, the kingdom of Eshnunna, and the great "code" of Hammurabi, incorporate within their texts at least some of the provisions of the *misharum*-acts proclaimed by them during the course of their reigns, and it is likely that the well-known "reform" inscription of Urukagina, the last king of Lagash of the Early Dynastic period (*circa* 2350 B.C.), is a text of a closely related type.

[Text]

1. (Text C). The tablet [of the decree which the land was ordered] to hear at the time that the king invoked a *misharum* for the land.

2. (5) The arrears of the farming agents, the shepherds, the *susikku*-[agents][4] of the provinces, and [other] crown tributaries—the . . . of their *firm agreements* and the *promissory notes* . . . of their payments are herewith remitted. (10) The collecting officer may not sue the crown tributary for payment.

3. The "market"[5] of Babylon, the "markets" of the country[side], the *raibanum*[6] officer, which in the . . . tablet, are . . . *to* the collecting officer—(15) their arrears dating from the "Year in which King Ammiditana remitted the debts which the land had contracted [= year 21 of Ammiditana]" until the month of Nisan of the "Year: Ammisaduqa the king, Enlil having (20) magnified his noble lordship, like Shamash (Text A) he rose forth in steadfastness over his country, and instituted justice for the whole of his people [= year 1 of Ammisaduqa]"—because the king has invoked the *misharum* for the land, (25) the collecting officer may not sue the [. . .] for payment.

4. Whoever has given barley or silver to an Akkadian or an Amorite as an interest-bearing loan, or on the *melqetum* basis (30) [*or* . . .], and had a document executed—because the king has invoked the *misharum* for the land, his document is voided; (35) (Text C) he may not collect the barley or silver on the basis of his document.

5. But if, commencing with the month of Addar II

of the "Year in which King Ammiditana destroyed the wall of Udinim constructed by Damqiilishu" [= year 37 of Ammiditana], (40) he collected by constraint, he shall refund whatever he had received through collection. He who does not [thus] make a refund (45) in accordance with the royal decree, shall die.

6. Whoever has given barley or silver to an Akkadian or an Amorite as an interest-bearing loan or on the *melqetum* basis, and in the document which he executed (50) perpetrated a deception by having it drawn up as a sale or a bailment and then persisted in taking interest, he [i.e., the debtor] shall produce his witnesses, and they shall indict him [i.e., the creditor] for taking interest; because he had distorted his document, his document shall be voided.

(55) A creditor may not sue against the house of an Akkadian or an Amorite for whatever he had loaned him; should he sue for payment, he shall die.

7. (Text A) If anyone had given barley or silver as an interest-bearing loan and had a document executed, (ii 30) retaining the document in his own possession, and then stated: "I have certainly not given it to you as an interest-bearing loan or on the *melqetum* basis; the barley or silver which I have given you, I have given [as an advance] for purchases, or for the production of profit, or for some other objective," the person who had received the barley or silver from the creditor shall produce his witnesses to the wording of the document which the lender had denied, and they shall speak [their testimony] before god. (ii 40) Because he [i.e., the creditor] had distorted his document and denied the [truth of the] matter, he must pay [to the borrower] six-fold [the amount he had lent him]. If he [the creditor] cannot make good his liability, he must die.

8. (iii) An Akkadian or an Amorite who has received barley, silver, or [other] goods either as merchandise for a commercial journey, or as a joint enterprise for the production of profit, (5) his document is not voided [by the *misharum* act]; he must repay in accordance with the stipulations of his agreements.

9. Whoever has given barley, silver, or [other] goods to an Akkadian or an Amorite either [as an advance] for purchases, for a commercial journey, or as a joint enterprise for the production of profit, (10) and had a document executed, [but] in the document he had executed, the creditor stipulated in writing that at the expiration of the term [of the contract] the money would accrue interest (15) or if he made any [other] additional stipulations, he [i.e., the obligee] shall not repay on the terms of the [added] stipulations, but shall repay [only] the barley or silver [on the terms of the (basic) document]. The [obligations of the supplementary] stipulations upon the Akkadian (20) or the Amorite are remitted.

---

4. Semiofficial persons who received the cadavers of dead cattle and sheep from the herdsmen of the state herds, see sec. 12.

5. Akk. *karum*, lit. "port," "quay," but denoting in those instances (and secs. 10–11) the association of traders of each town, which primarily served palace or "state" rather than private interests.

6. An official whose main function appears to have been that of recruiting or overseeing the lower rank persons for military-feudal service to the crown, see sec. 22.

10. [. . .] . . . *to* Babylon, [the market of . . .], the market of Borsippa, [the market of . . .], the market of Isin, [the market of . . .], the market of Larsa, (25) [the market of . . .]as, the market of Malgium, [the market of Manki]sum, the market of Shitullum, [. . .] half [their] investment capital was given [*them*] [in the form of] merchandise out of the palace—the [other] half to be made up by them [i.e., the market associations of the named cities]—(30) *any* such merchandise shall be disbursed to them from the palace at the going price of the respective city.

11. If a [state] trading merchant, who customarily disposes of merchandise of the palace, made out a document in favor of the palace against the [collectable] arrears of crown tributaries as if he actually received [such] merchandise from the palace, and received [in turn] the [payable] document of the palace-tributary—thus no merchandise was actually given him from the palace in accordance with his document, nor did he receive [any funds] from the palace tributary (40) because the king has remitted the arrears of the palace-tributary, (iv) that merchant shall declare on divine oath: "[I swear that] I have not received anything in payment from the palace-tributaries as stated in this document." After having [thus] declared, (5) he shall produce the document of the palace-tributary, they [i.e., the authorities and the principals] shall settle the accounts jointly, and out of the merchandise stipulated in the document made out by the merchant in favor of the palace they shall remit in behalf of the merchant as much as was stipulated by the document made out by the palace-tributary (10) in favor of the merchant.

12. The *susikku*-agent of the land who (15) customarily receives [*the carcasses*] from the palace cattle-herdsmen, shepherds, and goatherds under divine oath, [and] who (21) customarily renders to the palace: For every cow carcass: one [quantity] of sin[ews] together with the skin; for every ewe-carcass: one-sixth . . . *barley*, together with the skin, plus 1¾ minas of wool; for every goat-carcass: one-sixth of [*a shekel*] of *silver* plus ⅔ of a mina of goat-wool,—because the king has instituted the *misharum* for the land, their arrears will not be collected. The . . . [*of*] the *susikku*-agent of the land (25) [*the quotas*] . . . will not be filled.

13. The arrears of the porter[s] which had been assigned to the collecting-agent for collection are remitted; they will not be collected.

14. (30) The arrears of the Suhu country[7] consisting of *sibsum*-rents[8] and/[or] half-share rents[9]—because

the king has instituted the *misharum* for the land, it is remitted; it will not be collected. (35) He [i.e., the collecting-agent] shall not sue for collection against the houses of Suhu [var.: the Suhian population].

15. The crop impost officer who customarily receives the impost proportions of fields [planted to] [barley,] sesame, or minor crops belonging to the palace-tributaries, the . . . , the crown dependents, the infantrymen, the sergeants, or other special feudatories—(v) because the king has instituted the *misharum* for the land, it is remitted; it will not be proportioned [i.e., the impost shares of each crop will not be collected]. [However,] the barley destined for sale or profit will be proportioned according to the customary ratio[s].

16. (5) The taverness[es] of the provinces who customarily pay silver [and/or] barley to the palace—because the king has instituted the *misharum* in the land, the collecting agent (10) will not sue for payment of their arrears.

17. A taverness who has given beer or barley as a loan may not collect any of what she had given as a loan.

18. A taverness or a merchant who [. . .] (15) dishonest *weight* shall die.

19. The infantryman or the sergeant who has leased [a . . . field] for three years does not perform the [. . .] service. (20) In the present [*year*], because the king has instituted the *misharum* in the land, the infantryman or the sergeant pays according to the [prevailing] ratio of his city . . . , a third or half [of the crop].

20. (25) If an obligation has resulted in foreclosure against a citizen of Numhia, a citizen of Emutbalum, a citizen of Idamaras, a citizen of Uruk, a citizen of Isin, a citizen of Kisurra, or a citizen of Malgium, [in consequence of which] he [placed] his own person, his wife (30) or his [children] in debt servitude for silver,[10] or as a pledge[11]—because the king has instituted the *misharum* in the land, he is released; his freedom (35) is in effect.

21. If a house-born slavewoman or male slave of a citizen of Numhia, a citizen of Emutbalum, a citizen of Idamaras, a citizen of Uruk, a citizen of Isin, a citizen of Kisurra, (vi) or a citizen of Malgium . . . whose price . . . , has been sold for money, or was (5) given over for debt servitude, or was left as a pledge, his freedom will not be effected.

22. (10) The *ra'banum* or regional governor who gives barley, silver, or wool to the "house" of an infantryman or a sergeant for harvest labor, or for the per-

7. A territory on the Middle Euphrates, below Mari.
8. A kind of rent due on tenanted fields, and payable in produce.
9. A rent in which the crop is divided equally between tenant and landlord, and operative usually where the landlord suppllied the seed corn and the farming equipment and animals.

10. Forcible seizure of a debtor or a member of his family (also of his chattels) by the creditor upon default on the debt.
11. Voluntary placement of a dependent or a slave by the debtor with the creditor on an antichretic basis covering only the interest on a debt.

formance of [other] labor, (15) as the result of force,[12] shall die. [That] infantryman or sergeant may [at the same time] keep [lit.: "carry off"] whatever had been given him.

Notes to the Edict of Ammisaduqa

1. Apparently, these reforms (*misharum*) were usually enacted toward the beginning of a king's reign. A formal text was not necessarily issued initially, although an official text would be drawn up later.[13] While the reforms in the edict seem to have been put into actual practice, the contracts referred to in the edicts are different from some of the forms of contract that have been unearthed through excavations.

2. With what aspect of societal life were the edicts concerned? Do they cover all aspects or were they limited to one area? The edicts that have been preserved indicate that they dealt primarily with economic reforms.

3. The reforms seem to have been of great importance. They are mentioned in letters of the period, and the years in which they were issued were celebrated as years of great accomplishment. Often the year of issue would be referred to officially as "the year in which the edict was issued."[14]

4. These reforms are our earliest indication of the recognition of the need to "adjust" the law to meet changed societal conditions.

5. There is also an extant record of an edict by King Urugakina of Lagash (*circa* 2500 B.C.E.) prohibiting the seizure of boats, donkeys, and other cattle by the "powerful ones," reducing the burial tax, abolishing the forced sale of animals at bargain prices to the king's officers, freeing prisoners, and making other necessary "adjustments" in the law. Urugakina did not rule for long, however, after issuing his reform edicts. There is speculation among scholars as to whether the ruling classes, which were the target of his reforms, deposed him.[15] There are Marxist scholars who maintain that the edict reflects a battle between the priests and aristocracy on the one hand and the rulers, jealous of their power, on the other hand.[16]

The references in the edict to prior times when women used to take two husbands has also aroused much controversy among scholars as to whether or not there actually was such an era of polyandry.[17]

2. THE COMMUNITY

a. PRIMITIVE DEMOCRACY IN ANCIENT MESOPOTAMIA (By Thorkid Jacobsen)*

Words which embody the hopes, the fears, and the values of generations are likely to lose in clarity what they gain in depth. One such word is "democracy," which denoted a form of government and now stands for a way of life. It may not be amiss, therefore, first to make clear in what sense we intend to use the word before we plunge in medias res.

We shall use "democracy" in its classical rather than in its modern sense as denoting a form of government in which internal sovereignty resides in a large proportion of the governed, namely in all free adult male citizens without distinction of fortune or class. That sovereignty resides in these citizens implies that major decisions—such as the decision to undertake a war—are made with their consent, that these citizens constitute the supreme judicial authority in the state, and also that rulers and magistrates obtain their positions with, and ultimately derive their power from, that same consent.

By "primitive democracy," furthermore, we understand forms of government which, though they may be considered as falling within the definition of democracy just given, differ from the classical democracies by their more primitive character: the various functions of government are as yet little specialized, the power structure is loose, and the machinery for social coordination by means of power is as yet imperfectly developed.

We should perhaps add that the contrast with which we are primarily concerned is the one between "democracy" as defined above, on the one hand, and "autocracy," used as a general term for forms which tend to concentrate the major political powers in the hands of a single individual, on the other. "Oligarchy," which so subtly merges into democracy and which so often functions in forms similar to it, can hardly, at the present stage of our knowledge of ancient Mesopotamia, be profitably distinguished.

12. I.e., the forcible hiring out of subordinates by their superior officers for harvest or other labor to third parties (on a profitable basis), even though their wages were being paid, cf. Code of Hammurabi, sec. 34. This section is not limited in force to the period of the *misharum*'s effectiveness, but is a statement against such an abuse of authority for permanent effect.

13. J. Finkelstein, "Amisaduqua's Edict and the Babylonian Law Codes," *Journal of Cuneiform Studies* 15 (1961): 91–104.

14. Ibid., p. 91.

15. See I. Stephens, "Notes on Some Economic Texts of the Time of Urukagina."

16. I. Diakonoff, in J. Hawkes and L. Wooley, *Prehistory and the Beginnings of Civilization* (New York, 1963), pp. 510–

13, 629–30; see idem, "Sale of Land in Pre-Sargonic Sumer," *International Congress of Orientalists* 23 (Moscow, 1945), p. 19 ff.

17. See E. R. Leach, *Polyandry, Inheritance, and the Definition of Marriage, Man,* vol. 55 (New York, 1955), p. 182; J. Renger, "Who Are All Those People?" *Orientalia* 264 (1973).

*From *Towards the Image of Tammuz* (Cambridge, 1970).

Autocratic Orientation in Historical Times

The political development in early historical times seems to lie under the spell of one controlling idea: concentration of political power in as few hands as possible.

Within small areas, in town and township, this principle had been realized—or was being realized—to a very substantial degree during the first centuries of Mesopotamian history. The country formed a mosaic of diminutive, self-sufficient, autonomous city-states, and in each such state one individual, the ruler, united in his hands the chief political powers: legislative, judiciary, and executive. Only he could promulgate and carry into effect new law; he alone was personally responsible by contract with the city-god for upholding justice and righteousness; as supreme commander of all armed forces, he led the state in battle; and, as administrator of the main temple complex, he controlled the most powerful single economic unit within the state.

But the momentum of the autocratic idea was still far from spent with the realization of this idea within small separate areas. It drove Mesopotamia forward relentlessly toward the more distant aim: centralization of power within one large area. Each ruler of a city-state was forever striving to subdue his neighbors, striving to become the one who would unite all of southern Mesopotamia into a single centralized state under a single ruling hand—his own. From before the dawn of history through the soldier-kingdoms of Lugalzagesi and the early Sargonids to the highly organized bureaucratic state of the Third Dynasty of Ur, we watch these efforts toward ultimate centralization steadily grow in power, in intensity, and in efficiency.

Democratic Institutions in the Judiciary in Post-Imperial Times

To find in a world so singularly autocratic in outlook, propelled in its domestic and foreign policies by the one urge for concentration of power, institutions based on diametrically opposite concepts, is somewhat unexpected. Yet in the judiciary branch of government, as a heterogeneous, unassimilated block, appear, even in the latest period of Sumero-Akkadian civilization, features of a distinct and democratic character.

Assyria. As a particularly striking example may serve the Assyrian merchant colonies in Asia Minor on the border of our cultural province. Here in early post-Imperial times (Isin-Larsa period) the highest judicial authority was not vested in any one individual but resided in a general assembly of all colonists: "the colony, young and old," as it is called. This general assembly was called into session by a clerk at the bidding of a majority of its senior members. Characteristically the clerk was not permitted to act at the bidding of any single individual and was severely punished if he did so.

The general assembly tried and decided lawsuits which arose in the colony, and even commissaries sent by the legal authorities of the mother-city Assur could not proceed, if they met with resistance on the part of a colonist, except by authority of this local assembly.

Babylonia. Turning from the "republican" Assyrian colonies to the Babylonia of Hammurabi as it is revealed some generations later in documents of the Old Babylonian kingdom, we are very naturally struck first of all by the degree to which royal power is there in evidence. Anybody can turn to the king with complaints; he looks into the matter and delegates the case to a suitable court for decision. At his service stands a corps of royal officials and "judges of the king," dealing out justice according to the "legal practice of the king."

But it is worth noting that alongside of, and integrated with, this judiciary organization centered in the king stands another having its center in the Babylonian city. The city as such deals out justice according to its own local ideas of right and wrong. Town mayor and town elders settle minor local disputes; other cases—perhaps the more especially difficult or especially important ones—are brought before the town as a whole, the "assembly," for decision. Our sources furnish a vivid and interesting picture of the workings of this assembly; we shall comment, however, on two significant points only—its composition and its competence.

That the Old Babylonian assembly comprises, as already mentioned, the citizens of a given town or village is apparent from the use of "town" and "assembly" as alternatives in our documents. In [one] text, . . . for instance, after a report has been made "in the assembly of [the town] Dilbat," the ensuing actions are carried out "as Dilbat commanded." The assembly of Dilbat is thus equivalent to the town itself. Similar evidence is given by [a] letter. . . . The writer of this letter needed a tribunal before which to compose a legal dispute; so he "assembled the town" (*a-lam u-pa-hi-ir-ma*). His phrase—since the act *puhhurum*, "to assemble," produces a *puhrum*, "assembly"—shows again that the town constitutes the assembly.

In interpreting this evidence, there is naturally some danger of going too far. Though citizens and therefore part of the *alum*, "the town," women are not likely to have participated in the assembly. Even the men may not always have put in an appearance in numbers which we should consider adequate representation of the citizenry. One inference, however, may be drawn from the fact that *puhrum* can alternate with the highly comprehensive term *alum*: participation in the *puhrum* and in the judicial functions which it exercised did not constitute the prerogative of some small favored class or group; it must have been open to the citizenry at large. And this is borne out by a Babylonian proverb which prudently, though with conspicuous lack of public spirit, warns:

> Do not go to stand in the assembly;
> Do not stray in the very place of strife.
> It is precisely in strife that fate may overtake you;
> Besides, you may be made a witness for them
> So that they take you along to testify in a lawsuit not
>   your own.

As will be readily seen, this proverb presupposes that anybody who happened along and has a mind to could "stand"—that is, participate—in the *puhrum*.

The competence of the Old Babylonian assembly is in general that of a court of law. A plaintiff may himself "notify the assembly" (*puhram lummudum*), or the case may be delegated to the assembly by the king or other high authority. The assembly investigates the case (inim-inimma igi-du$_8$), hears testimony, and may send one of the parties and his witness to some temple to prove their testimony by oath. Finally, it renders its decision (e or du$_{11}$ and *qabu*).

The cases tried by the assembly were, as shown by the records which have come down to us, both civil cases and criminal cases. The assembly had, as proved by one such record dealing with a case of murder, power to pronounce sentence of death. Occasional infliction of punishment in the assembly may represent a survival from times when the people met in assembly as both judge and executioner at the same time. The Code of Hammurabi decrees in paragraph 202 that "if a man has smitten the cheek of a man who is his superior (or "his senior"?) he shall be given sixty lashes with an ox whip in the assembly." It is also worth noting that if a judge has committed fraud in the carrying out of his duties he shall make twelvefold restitution, and "in the assembly they shall make him get up from his judge's seat not to return [ever] to sit in judgment with judges."

Of particular interest for the light it throws on the relation between these popular tribunals and the royal power is an Old Babylonian letter which shows that a man who had been arrested by a royal official for seditious utterances was placed before the assembly, where the charges were proved against him before he was committed to prison. Note also that the king, as already mentioned, may delegate cases to the assembly.

As will be readily perceived, the judiciary organization here outlined is democratic in essence. Judicial powers are vested in the community as a whole, in an assembly open to all citizens. Such institutions are manifestly not of a piece with the period in which they are found—a period dominated by the very opposite principle: that of concentration of powers in the hands of one single individual. The question then arises whether these institutions represent new ideas which are just beginning to gain momentum or something old which has been retained from earlier times.

The first alternative seems not very plausible, since the entire drift of Mesopotamian political life and thought in the historical periods is wholeheartedly in the other direction. Throughout we find no signs of growing democratic ideas. The second alternative, therefore, seems the more likely: these judiciary institutions represent a last stronghold, a stubborn survival, of ideas rooted in earlier ages.

Wider Scope of Assembly in Older Times

This inference is confirmed when we turn to the material which bears on earlier periods, for as we go back in time the competence and influence of the "assembly" appears to grow and to extend from judiciary functions to other, even more vital, aspects of government.

Tradition relating to times no farther back than those of the kings of Akkad already shows that the assembly deemed it within its authority to choose a king:

> In the "Common of Enlil," a field
> belonging to Esabad, the temple of Gula,
> Kish assembled
> and Iphurkish, a man of Kish,
> . . . .
> they raised to kingship.

When we consult still older tradition, tradition concerning Uruk in the time of Gilgamesh, beyond the border line of history proper, we find the ruler scrupulously refraining from action in the matter of peace or war until he obtains the consent of the assembly, in which, therefore, internal sovereignty of the state would seem to be vested.

The tradition in question relates that King Agga of Kish sent messengers to Uruk. Gilgamesh, lord of Uruk, is bent on resistance; but the decision apparently does not rest with him. He first approaches the senate, the elders of Uruk, to lay his proposal before them:

> Gilgamesh before the elders of his town
> spoke up. . . .

His address—urging reasons which are not yet entirely clear—ends in the plea:

> Let us not bow to the palace of Kish; let us smite [it]
>   with weapons!

The elders consider the proposal in their assembly:

> After an assembly had been established, the elders of
>   his town
> gave answer unto Gilgamesh concerning it.

This answer is in the affirmative, exactly repeating Gilgamesh's words and ending in the same exhortation. It greatly pleases Gilgamesh:

(As for) Gilgamesh, lord of Kullab,
. . . .
at the word of the elders of his town his heart
rejoiced, his liver was made bright.

But he is not yet through; the men of the town must be heard on the issue:

Next Gilgamesh before the men of his town
spoke up. . . .

His plea here is a word-for-word repetition of the plea before the elders, and the "men of his town," "after an assembly had been established," answer it. With differently worded reasons they urge the same course of action: "May you not bow to the palace of Kish; let us smite it with weapons." They add a declaration of confidence and faith, and Gilgamesh is again highly pleased:

On that day (as for) Gilgamesh, lord of Kullab,
at the word of the men of his town his heart rejoiced,
his liver was made bright.

Now the road is clear before him, and he immediately sets about arming for the coming conflict.

Here, then, we seem to have portrayed a state in which the ruler must lay his proposals before the people, first the elders, then the assembly of the townsmen, and obtain their consent, before he can act. In other words, the assembly appears to be the ultimate political authority.

Projections of the Old Assembly into the World of the Gods

Since the traces of this older, democratic form of political organization in Mesopotamia all point back to a time before the earliest historical inscriptions, it would normally be impossible to gain closer insight into its details and workings simply because we lack sources for the time when it was flourishing. A peculiar circumstance, however, comes to our aid.

The Sumerians and Akkadians pictured their gods as human in form, governed by human emotions, and living in the same type of world as did men. In almost every particular the world of the gods is therefore a projection of terrestrial conditions. Since this process began relatively early, and since man is by nature conservative in religious matters, early features would, as a matter of course, be retained in the world of the gods after the terrestrial counterpart had disappeared. The gods, to mention only one example, were pictured as clad in a characteristic tufted (sheepskin?) garment

long after that material was no longer in use among men. In similar fashion must we explain the fact that the gods are organized politically along democratic lines, essentially different from the autocratic terrestrial states which we find in Mesopotamia in the historical periods. Thus in the domain of the gods we have a reflection of older forms, of the terrestrial Mesopotamian state as it was in prehistoric times.

The assembly which we find in the world of the gods rested on a broad democratic basis; it was, according to the Adad myth in *CT* [Cuneiform Tablets] XV, 3, an "assembly of all the gods." Nor was participation limited by sex: goddesses as well as gods played an active part in its deliberations.

The assembly was usually held in a large court called Ubshuukkinna. As the gods arrived, they met friends and relatives who had similarly come from afar to participate in the assembly, and there was general embracing. In the sheltered court the gods then sat down to a sumptuous meal; wine and strong drink soon put them in a happy and carefree mood, fears and worries vanished, and the meeting was ready to settle down to more serious affairs.

They set [their] tongues [in readiness] [and sat down]
to the banquet;
They ate bread [and] drank[?] [wine].
The sweet drink dispelled their fears;
[So that] they sang for joy as they drank the strong
drink.
Exceedingly carefree were they, their heart was
exalted;
For Marduk, their champion, they decreed the
destiny.

The description is psychologically interesting. Here, as so often in Mesopotamian mythology, the important decisions originate when the gods are in their cups. In the toilsome earthbound life of the primitive Sumerians wine and beer were evidently necessary to lift the spirit out of the humdrum existence of everyday cares to original thought and perspective.

The leadership of the assembly belonged by right, it would seem, to An, god of heaven and "father of the gods"; but with him or alone appears also Enlil, god of the storm. An or Enlil usually broached the matters to be considered; and we may assume—our evidence does not allow us to decide the point—that the discussion which followed would be largely in the hands of the so-called *ilu rabiutum*, the "great gods" or, perhaps better, "the senior gods," whose number is said to have been fifty. In this discussion it was the intrinsic merit of a proposal which gave it weight: wise counsel, testifying to "intelligence, profundity, and knowledge," is much admired; and ability to make the others listen to one's words is a prized gift. Through such general discussion—"asking one another," as the Babylonians expressed it—the issues were clarified and the various gods had opportunity to voice their opinions for or against, at times espousing proposals which they later bitterly regretted. Such regrets befell Ishtar, who had supported the proposal to wipe out mankind with a flood, when she saw the results of the decision:

> Ishtar shrieks like a woman in birth pangs,
> The lovely voiced lady of the gods yells aloud:
> "The times before are indeed turned to earth,
> Because I myself in the gods' assembly
> Gave the ill counsel!
>
> How could I in the gods' assembly
> Give such ill counsel,
> To decree the fight
> For the destruction of my mankind?
> I alone gave birth to my mankind.
> Now they fill, like the spawn of fishes, the sea!"

A group of seven powerful gods, "the seven gods who determine destinies"—that is, whose word is decisive—had, it would seem, the final say, and when an agreement had at last been reached in this manner—voting is a technique of much later origin—it was announced by An and Enlil as "the verdict, the word of the assembly of the gods, the command of An and Enlil." The executive duties, carrying into effect the decisions of the assembly, seem to have rested with Enlil.

The functions of this divine assembly were in part those of a court of law. Here the crime of a man who destroys an inscription is taken up, and the deity to whom the inscription was dedicated speaks against him and "makes bad his case." Here sentence was once passed on all humanity because the constant noise which they made was obnoxious to divine ears. Another cause célèbre was against Enlil in his youth, when he was ostracized by "the fifty senior gods and the seven gods who determine destiny" for raping young Ninlil.

But the functions of the divine assembly which go beyond those of a court of law are the ones that command our greatest attention: the assembly is the authority which grants kingship. Once, we are told, great danger threatened: Ti'amat, the primeval waters, and her host of monsters planned war against the gods. The gods learned that:

> They are angry, they are plotting, they rest not night
>   and day;
> they have taken up the fight, they fume, they rage
>   like lions;
> they have established an assembly and are planning
>   the combat.
> Mother Hubur, who fashions all things,

has added [thereunto] irresistible weapons, has borne
  monster serpents
sharp of tooth, with unsparing fang;
she has filled their bodies with poison for blood.
Dragons grim she has clothed with terror,
has crowned them with glory and made them like
  gods,
so that he who looks upon them shall perish from
  terror,
so that their bodies shall rear up and their breasts
  not be turned back.

In this emergency young Marduk proved willing to champion the case of the gods, but he demanded absolute authority:

> If I am to be your champion,
> vanquish Ti'amat, and keep you alive;
> then establish an assembly and proclaim my lot
>   supreme.
> Seat yourselves together gladly in Ubshuukkinna,
> and let me when I open my mouth [have power to]
>   determine destiny even as you,
> [so that] whatever I frame shall not be altered
> [and] the command of my lips shall not return [void],
>   shall not be changed.

So the call to assembly went out, the gods gathered in Ubshuukkinna, and there, to meet the exigencies of the situation, they gave Marduk supreme authority:

> Thou carriest weight among the senior gods,
> thy status is unequaled, thy command is [like that of]
>   Anu.
> Marduk, thou carriest weight among the senior gods,
> thy status is unequaled, thy command is [like that of]
>   Anu.
> From this day onward thy order[s] shall not be
>   altered;
> to exalt and to abase—this shall be thy power.
> True shall be what[ever] thou dost utter, not shall
>   thy word prove vain [ever];
> none among the gods shall encroach upon thy rights.

They acclaimed him king and invested him with the insignia of royalty:

> They rejoiced [and] did homage, [saying:] "Marduk
>   is king!"
> They bestowed upon him the scepter, the throne, and
>   the *palu*;
> They gave him an unrivaled weapon to smite the
>   enemy, (saying:)
> "Go and cut off the life of Ti'amat
> May the winds carry her blood to out-of-the-way
>   places."

Then, having armed himself, Marduk led the gods to battle with Ti'amat.

As the assembly is the authority which grants kingship, it can also take it back. The Sumerians counted kingship as a *bala*, an office to be held by each incumbent for a limited period. Similarly kingship would be given for a time to one city and its god; then it would be transferred to another city and god. The period—to mention an example—during which Inanna's two cities, Kish and Akkad, held sway over Mesopotamia was "the term [*bala*] of Inanna."

The authority which determines when such a royal *bala* is to end is the assembly, as may be seen most clearly in a group of texts dealing with the fall of Ur. Under its famous Third Dynasty, Ur had dominated all of southern Mesopotamia. Its rule ended tragically in a savage attack by invading Elamites which all but wiped out the city. Among the texts which deal with this catastrophe we may first quote one in which the god of Ur, Nanna, is complaining to his father, Enlil, about what has happened. His complaint, however, evokes only a cool response:

> Enlil [answere]d his son Sin concerning it:
> "The deserted city, its heart, sobbing, wee[ps bitterly];
> in it [thou passest] in sobs the day.
> [But], Nanna, through thy own 'submission' [thou didst accept(?)] the 'Let it be!'
> By verdict, by the word [of] the assembly [of the] g[ods],
> by command of An and Enlil [. . .]
> [was the] k[ing]ship of Ur [. . . carried away].
> Since olden days when the country was founded [. . .]
> [are] the terms of kingship [constantly changed];
> [as for] its [i.e., Ur's] kingship, [its] term [has (now) been changed for a different term]."

Though the text here quoted has suffered considerable damage, the view which it takes of the fall of Ur stands out, fortunately, quite clearly: it was the normal end of Ur's—and of Nanna's—term of kingship; and it was brought about in the proper fashion, by a decision of the assembly of the gods.

This same view, that Ur's fall was a normal end to its term of reign, decided upon beforehand by the gods, underlies also [one] lament. . . . It finds, however, its most vivid expression in the long *Lamentation over the Destruction of Ur*, composed only a few generations after the disaster. There, toward the end of the fourth song, we are taken to the very assembly of the gods in which the decision was made and witness the passionate plea of Ningal, Nanna's consort, for mercy for the doomed city:

> Next unto the assembly, where the people were still [tarrying] on the ground,
> the Anunnaki gods being still seated after they had given the binding promise.

> did I verily drag [my] legs, did I verily stretch out [my] arms.
> I verily poured out my tears before An;
> verily I myself mourned before Enlil.
> "May my city not be destroyed!" I said indeed to them;
> "May Ur not be destroyed!" I said indeed to them;
> "May its people not be killed!" I said indeed to them.
> But An the while never bent toward that word;
> Enlil with a "It is pleasing; let it be!" never soothed my heart.
> The destruction of my city they verily gave in commission;
> the destruction of Ur they verily gave in commission;
> that its people be killed, as its fate they verily determined.

There can thus be no doubt that the assembly had power to revoke, as it had power to grant, kingship.

Conclusions

Our material seems to preserve indications that prehistoric Mesopotamia was organized politically along democratic lines, not, as was historic Mesopotamia, along autocratic. The indications which we have, point to a form of government in which the normal run of public affairs was handled by a council of elders but ultimate sovereignty resided in a general assembly comprising all members—or, perhaps better, all adult free men—of the community. This assembly settled conflicts arising in the community, decided on such major issues as war and peace, and could, if need arose, especially in a situation of war, grant supreme authority, kingship, to one of its members for a limited period.

Such a form of government is, it may be added, in no way unique but can be abundantly paralleled from elsewhere. We call attention especially to the early European material, for which we may quote two summaries by W. J. Shephard:

> Among all the primitive peoples of the West there seems to have been some kind of popular assembly which shared with the tribal chief or king and with a council of lesser chieftains the powers of social control.

Again, still more striking:

> The significant political institutions of the primitive Teutonic tribes who overran Western Europe were a folkmoot, or meeting of all the adult males bearing arms; a council of elders; and in time of war a war leader or chieftain. All important questions, such as peace and war, were decided by the folkmoot. The council of elders prepared questions to be submitted to the folkmoot and decided minor matters. It was a rude form of democracy in which government was

not differentiated nor law clearly distinguished from religious or social custom.

It need hardly be stressed that the existence of such close parallels in other societies lends strong support to the correctness of the reconstruction here proposed and promises valuable help in the interpretation of the fragmentary Mesopotamian data.

Notes to Jacobsen, "Primitive Democracy in Mesopotamia"

1. Jacobsen feels that prehistoric Mesopotamia was organized along democratic lines, while historic Mesopotamia was organized along autocratic lines. Speiser and Finkelstein, on the other hand, both feel that even in historic Mesopotamia, the king was not a deity and, apparently, was not a dictator, as evidenced by the active public assemblies.

2. The Mesopotamian view of the cosmic state was that, "just as a human state embodies many different subsidiary power structures at various levels—families, great estates, etc.—each with its own organization, but all integrated with the larger structure of the state, so, too, did the cosmic state. It, too, had such minor power groups, divine families, divine households, divine estates with stewards, overseers, servants, and other attendants. . . . Man's position in the state of the universe precisely paralleled that of the slave in the human city-state."[18]

3. Apparently, women had no share in the popular assembly in the Mesopotamian city-states.[19]

4. One should be careful not to conclude that the earthly state was "democratic" because it was modeled after the heavenly state of the deities that was conceived as run by an assembly. In fact, the sequence may have been just the reverse. Man's view of the heavenly state of the deities may have resulted from the prevalence of earthly rule by assemblies rather than by individual autocrats. As Aristotle pointed out, "Men imagine not only the forms of the gods but their ways of life to be like their own."[20]

B. *The Application of the Law*

1. INTRODUCTION

There were a wide variety of institutional appliers of the law in the ancient Near East. These, of course, included the kings.[21] Since kings were physically un-

able to judge all cases by themselves, they established royal courts. In addition, law was applied by priests as well as by popular assemblies. The latter often acted as courts in the Biblical Era (see above, Chapter III, Section A 2). Under Persian rule we find judicial functions assigned to local congregations.[22] They also acted as legislatures, prescribing rules. In addition, there were indigenous institutions, often stemming from tribal, clan, and family arrangements, that also applied the law.

The crucial role played by appliers of the law is obvious. Yet, it is well to remember the aphorism of Bishop Benjamin Hoadley (1676–1761), chaplain to George I: "Whoever hath an absolute authority to interpret any written or spoken laws, it is he who is truly the law-giver, to all intents and purposes, and not the person who first spoke or wrote them."[23]

2. THE COURTS

a. KING HAMMURAPI AS JUDGE
(By W. F. Leemans)*

In this contribution I shall try to clarify a point that seems to be of some importance: . . . the position of the king in the distribution of justice.

In research into the character of the Laws of Hammurapi two problems predominate: 1. Does the CH [Code of Hammurapi] contain laws or judgments? 2. Does the CH contain a codification or a reform of law? . . .

Basically the two questions find their answer in but one fact. The Old Babylonian king was an absolute monarch who however in his judicial capacity was not the source of law but only its agent. He maintained justice on behalf of his lord, the god of justice, the sun-god Samas. In this function he could give laws; laws emanated from him. As far as law was not expressly given, people lived under the virtue of customary law. But in that function the king was also the highest judge. This implies that judgments given by the king and laws promulgated by the king had the same force; both contained rules of law and, in fact, there was no practical distinction between the two. The king could give his judgments according to the customary law; in that case the "law" has the character of a codification; but the king could also give his judgment according to his own insights of justice; then the "law" has the character of a reform. . . .

18. T. Jacobsen, "The Cosmos as a State," in H. Frankfort, *Before Philosophy: The Intellectual Adventure of Ancient Man* (Baltimore, 1972), p. 162, 163, 196.

19. Ibid., p. 163.

20. Aristotle, *Politics* (Oxford, 1928), 125b; see Jacobsen, "The Cosmos as a State," p. 147.

21. See, e.g., 1 Sam. 8:5; 2 Sam. 8:15, 15:4; Ps. 72:1–2; 1 Kings 3:9, 28.

22. *The Book of Sirach* 1:30, 7:7, 23:24, 42:11; 45:17; see Z. Falk, *Hebrew Law in Biblical Times* (Jerusalem, 1964), pp. 56–59.

23. Bishop B. Hoadley, Sermon "On the Nature of Government" before King George, 31 March 1717.

*From *Symbolae Juridicae et Historicae Martins David Dedicatae* (Leiden, 1968).

The practice during the reign of King Hammurapi is known largely from the correspondence of the king with his high civil officers in the south, Sin-iddinam and Samas-hazir. Most of the cases are concerned with landed properties and rent or other exploitation rights of fields; CH secs. 27 ff. show that the law regarding land exploitation had Hammurapi's special interest.

If a litigant brought his case before the king, the case could be investigated and judged in three different ways:

1. The king tried the case himself and gave the final judgment,

2. The king gave a decision on the point of law and remitted the case for a decision on questions of fact to the local judges or authorities.

3. The king remitted the entire case to local judges.

The evidence for these three possibilities will now be given. [The names of the tablet collections have been omitted.]

Final Judgment of the Case

[Tablet no. 1]: Nabi-Sin had informed the king that his father's brothers had taken possession of a field and had exacted rent of a field which he and his brother had inherited from their father and which they had given to a tenant farmer. Hammurapi gave order to Samas-hazir and Marduk-nasir to "give them (evidently Nabi-Sin and his brother) the fields according to the certificate of assignment which they have legally made out before me" and to restore to them the barley which their father's brothers had exacted from the tenant farmer. Evidently, the facts were not in dispute and Hammurapi could decide the case immediately. The execution only was committed to Samas-hazir and Marduk-nasir.

[Tablet no. 2]: The *satammu* had delimited land for Lipit-Istar. During his absence a companion of Lipit-Istar had had Lipit-Istar's name erased and the field written in his name. This was proved and the king gave orders to Samas-hazir to hand over the field to Lipit-Istar and to send the *satammu* to the king (probably for punishment). Evidently the evidence was produced before the king and he gave the sentence, which Samas-hazir had to execute.

[Tablet no. 3]: The king wrote to Sin-iddinam that a field near Bad-tibira, which was an old possession of Enki-heutud, was by document stated to be his, and he ordered Sin-iddinam to restore it to the owner. It may be concluded that the King gave the judgment, which Sin-iddinam had to execute.

[Tablet no. 4]: Certain people informed the king that Samas-hazir and his colleagues had deprived them of a field that their lord (the king) had ascribed to them by a sealed tablet and now intended to give them a field elsewhere. Hammurapi orders Samas-hazir and some other officials to examine the sealed tablet and to give the plaintiffs a field according to that document and no other one. The king decided that the plaintiffs were entitled to the field mentioned in the tablet and the addressees had only to execute it. . . .

The King Decides the Point of Law and Remits the Case for a Decision on Questions of Fact to Local Judges or Authorities

[Tablet no. 9]: Sin-ismeanni of Kutalla, a grower of Tilmun dates, had informed Hammurapi that Samas-hazir had deprived him of a field of his paternal house and had given it to a [government official]. Hammurapi now asked Samas-hazir: Should a man ever be deprived of a permanent property? Investigate the case. If the field belonged to his paternal house, restore it to Sin-ismeanni. Consequently, the king decided that a man could not be deprived of a permanent property of his paternal house. But Samas-hazir had to examine whether the alleged facts were correct and in accordance with these facts to execute the king's sentence.

[Tablet no. 10]: This case resembles the preceding one. The sons of Ziiaki had informed the king that Samas-hazir had deprived them of a field of 6 bur belonging to their paternal house. The King ordered Samas-hazir and Marduk-nasir to investigate the case and, if the field of their paternal house was 6 bur, to give them 3 bur for their service; if it is 4 bur, 2 bur. According to this royal decision they had to give their decision.

[Tablet no. 11]: Certain officials informed the king that the [government officials] had revindicated the fields that were their old possession and that their fathers had used. Hammurapi wrote, probably to Samas-hazir, to examine the case and to decide according to his decision that one shall not reclaim fields which are an old possession and that the plaintiffs shall repossess their former possession as before. . . .

The King Remits the Entire Case to the Local Judges or Authorities

The letters of the king and the documents in which the cases are recorded are as a rule so concisely formulated that it is difficult to grasp the situation exactly. In the following instances the king remitted the case, but this does not imply in all instances that the king did not give a certain decision which we do not know but which contained directions for the suit which influenced the issue.

[Tablet no. 16]: Mar-irsitim and his brother had appeared before King Hammurapi and had alleged that their father's brother Ududu, a sutug of Ninlil, had given a field to their father. Evidently Ududu had revindicated the field after the father's death. The king ordered that the *puhrum* of Nippur should judge the case. The *puhrum* investigated the case and gave its judgment, viz. that the field had been given to the brother's father.

[Tablet no. 17]: Ibi-Adad informed the King that Sep-Sin, the son of Abiiatum, had revindicated a field of his paternal house which they (i.e., his family) had already long owned and that Samas-hazir, the town and the elders had investigated the case in court and had adjudged the field to him. Now Sep-Sin revindicated the field again and kept the barley from it. Hammurapi wrote to Samas-hazir: If Samas-hazir, the town and the elders have adjudged the field to Ibi-Adad, restore the field to him; if the case has not been examined and the field has not been adjudged to Ibi-Adad, let . . . the town and the elders, in the presence of the god, give the decision and restore the field according to its old status. . . .

Other examples, entering in all three categories may be found in the texts, especially in letters to and from the king, . . . but these cannot change the general picture. However, the information is too scanty for the drawing of any inference with regard to the question in which cases one or the other procedure was followed and with regard to the relative frequencies of the three categories. This might have differed under the different kings. It may be stated, however, that in a good many of his letters to Samas-hazir Hammurapi took the decision himself, while in most of his letters to Sin-iddinam he entrusted the decision to him and local judges. Probably Sin-iddinam was an official of higher rank than Samas-hazir.

In summing up the instances of royal judgments no attention has been paid to the question whether the King was applied to as first judge or in appeal. The case recorded in CT 29, 41–43 . . . has sometimes been taken to suggest the inference that appeal from the judgments of local judges was possible to the king. The question whether appeal was possible is closely connected with the nature of the judgments of the local judges; it has been amply discussed by J. G. Lautner . . . and it is too complicated to be considered afresh in this contribution.

It is an interesting feature that the king in the cases which he remitted to local judges, often asked for a report on the issue: The king wanted to be well informed about the justice done in his kingdom. In his government, the king was assisted by counsellors; it may perhaps be supposed that they took charge of his tasks during his absence in military campaigns. . . .

The procedure applied by Hammurapi was the same as that followed elsewhere in Mesopotamia before him

and there was no break at all with the past, as is sometimes supposed. . . .

The text published by Th. Jacobsen, An. Bibl. 12 (1959): 130 ff., records a murder case which was brought before king Ur-Ninurta of Isin. In this instance the king referred the case for trial to the *puhrum* of Nippur, which gave sentence of death. . . .

The purpose of this contribution is only to show the role of the King himself in the distribution of justice. Judges of the king administered justice in a similar way, sometimes taking the final decision themselves, other times taking only a decision in principle and remitting the case to a local court for the decision on the facts. . . .

The finding of the preceding investigation is that the ancient Mesopotamian kings were, in fact, personally concerned with the distribution of justice and that especially Hammurapi's activities in this domain are well attested; most of the instances mentioned date from his reign. He showed much diligence in the distribution of justice. He not only gave judgments himself but he desired to be informed of the judgments in remitted cases as well. By collecting all these judgments, the cases which occurred or could occur came out and in this way, together with earlier collections of laws, a basis could be laid for the compilation of his famous stela with laws. And in view of the king's interest in the distribution of justice, we need feel no surprise that it was Hammurapi who had this stela erected.

Notes to Leemans, "King Hammurapi as Judge"

1. Which cases were heard by King Hammurabi personally, and which did he assign to other judges, and why?

2. It should be noted that the Mesopotamian king constituted a court of appeals for his entire realm, independent of the cities.[24] At an early date the formula for oaths was made to include the king along with the gods. If an agreement was broken, or an oath falsely taken, the king was involved. He would then make it his business to uphold the rights of the injured party. This had an important effect upon the functions of the courts, since court decisions would be enforced pursuant to the authority of the king. Previously judges did not always have the power to enforce court decisions, and the litigant who did not have an influential patron could not receive satisfaction at court.[25]

24. H. Frankfort, *The Birth of Civilization in the Near East* (New York, 1955), p. 86.

25. Ibid.; *Kingship and Gods: A Study of Ancient Near Eastern Religion as the Integration of Society and Nature* (Chicago, 1948), p. 406; Jacobsen, "The Good Life," in *Before Philosophy*, p. 221.

3. In addition to the king's functions to uphold law and order internally and to punish evildoers, he was also expected to protect the state from external threats, to conduct wars, and sometimes to mediate disputes between city-states.

b. COURTS IN THE BIBLICAL ERA: THE JUDICIAL ROLE OF THE BIBLICAL KING

In the Biblical Era courts were required to be established in every district[26] to resolve disputes. Cases that baffled these district courts were to be brought to a higher court, which convened near the sanctuary.[27]

There are very few details in the Bible concerning the structure, functions, and powers of the courts. There is, therefore, considerable conflict among scholars on these matters.

There are scholars who believe that only members of the tribe of Levi could serve as judges. The sole evidence for this, however, are a number of isolated, ambiguous references in the Bible.[28] It appears more likely that there were many non-Levites who served as judges, since there are repeated references in the Bible to "elders" and to "the heads of patriarchal houses."[29] While the Bible refers repeatedly to courts composed of "elders of the city," the term "elders" refers to their functions as leaders in the community, rather than to their age. The Levites, who were not as a tribe given any land and whose sole occupation was specified work in the main sanctuary, were expected to devote themselves to the study of the Torah, to teach it as scholars, and to act as judges too.[30] It appears clear, however, that the chief leaders of the nation (and the leaders of individual tribes or groups of tribes) served as chief judges, to whom appeals could be addressed,[31] and su-

31. See Judg. 4:5; 1 Sam. 8:5; 2 Sam. 8:15, 15:4, 20:39, 2 Chron. 19.

pervised the operations of the courts throughout the land. It is unclear from the biblical texts whether the priests and Levites formed special tribunals or were part of the district courts.[32]

26. Deut. 16:18.
27. Deut. 17:8–13.
28. See, e.g., Deut. 17:9, 21:5; and 1 Chron. 23:3–4.
29. See, e.g., Deut. 1:15–16; 19:12; 1 Kings 21; see also, Asher Gulak, III *Yesode Ha'Mishpat Ha'Ivri* 4 (Berlin, 1922; reprinted in Tel-Aviv, 1927); I. Herzog, "The Administration of Justice in Ancient Israel," in *The Jewish Forum*, vol. 14, no. 3 (New York, 1931), p. 109; Falk, *Hebrew Law in Biblical Times*, (Jerusalem, 1964), p. 56.
30. Ezekiel 44:23, 24; see Mal. 2:68; see also Rambam, Laws of the Sabbatical and Jubilee Year, 13:12–13; Deut. 33:10; 2 Kings 17:27–28.
32. See Falk, *Hebrew Law in Biblical Times*, p. 56; and 2 Chron. 19:11; Herzog, *The Administration of Justice*, p. 109; see sec. c, below.

Although the Pentateuch does not specifically mention any judicial functions of the king,[33] in Israel the king took an active part in judicial functions. Thus, the Bible describes David in the following terms: "And David ruled over all of Israel, and David did justice and righteousness to all his people."[34] The well-known story of the rebuke of King David by the prophet Nathan also reflects the active role of the king in seeing to it that justice was done:

And God sent Nathan to David and he came to him and said, "There were two men in one city, one rich and one poor. The rich man had a great multitude of sheep and cattle. The poor man had nothing, except one small lamb that he had purchased, fed and raised together with him and his children. From his bread it would eat and from his cup it would drink and in his bosom it would sleep and was like a daughter to him. And a traveler came to the rich man and he would not take from his sheep or cattle to prepare a meal for the guest who had arrived, and he took the lamb of the poor man and he prepared it as food for his guest." And David became very angry with the man and he said to Nathan, "I swear by God that the man who does this deserves death, and for the lamb he shall pay fourfold because he did this thing and had no mercy."[35]

The establishment of courts by King Jehoshaphat is described in detail in the Bible:

He appointed judges in the land, throughout all of the fortified cities of Judah for every city. He said to the judges, "Consider carefully what you do, for you judge not for man but for God, who is with you in judgment. And now, let the fear of God be upon you; act carefully because there is no transgression, partiality, nor taking of bribes by God." Also in Jerusalem, did Jehoshaphat appoint Levites, priests, and some of the heads of families of Israel to judge for God and to decide disputes. They then returned to Jerusalem, and he commanded them thus, "You shall act in the fear of God, faithfully, with a complete heart. And with regard to every dispute that should come before you from your brothers, who live in the cities, concerning bloodshed, law, commandments, statutes and rules. You shall warn them so that they shall not be guilty before God and he

33. Deut. 17:14–20.
34. 2 Sam. 8:15.
35. 2 Sam. 12:1–6; see also 2 Sam. 14:4; 1 Kings 3:9 in which King Solomon prayed: "And give your servant a heart that will hear, to judge your people, to discern between good and evil, because who is able to judge your great nation"; see also the references to judicial function of the king in 2 Sam. 8:15, 15:4; Ps. 72:1–4, Jer. 22:15 and 1 Kings 3:28, 7:7.

shall not be angry with you and your brothers. Thus shall you do and you will not be guilty."[36]

We have little information about the actual operations of the Jewish courts[37] nor, whether they attempted solely to apply the law of the Bible, legal precedents, and custom; moreover, existing records do not indicate the extent to which they relied, if at all, on their own judgment on an *ad hoc* basis.[38]

c. APPLICATION OF THE LAW BY PRIESTS

In Mesopotamia priests often played an important role in the administration of justice.[39] The Bible also indicates that priests exercised judicial functions.[40] Note that priests, as well as elders, were stated in the Bible to be the ones before whom all quarrels were to be brought and who were involved in the ceremony to be performed when a corpse of a murder victim was found in a field.[41] It is recorded in 1 Chronicles 23:4 that six thousand Levites served as magistrates and clerks,[42] while the book of Ezekiel pinpoints priests as the judges in the future state to be established.[43] Nevertheless, the judiciary does not appear to have been limited to priests,[44] although they played a dominant role there. Teaching and scholarship were the functions to which priests were traditionally dedicated;[45] they were the ones who had the time to study the Torah, not having received land and being supported economically by the receipt of tithes from all crops that were grown. Furthermore, the priests were divided into twenty-four groups, each group serving in the temple twice a year, for one week each time. An individual priest in any group would serve only one day in each term in order to allow each one the opportunity to serve.[46] This left nearly the entire year free for study (see Section B 2 *b*, above).

36. 2 Chron. 19:1–10; see also DeVaux, *Ancient Israel*, pp. 150–52.

37. See De Vaux, *Ancient Israel*, pp. 155–57, who has attempted to piece together bits of information from various parts of the Bible into a very rough description of judicial procedure. The evidence, however, is too fragmentary to draw a complete and reliable picture.

38. See De Vaux, *Ancient Israel*, p. 150; Gulak, *Yesode Ha'Mishpat Ha'Ivri*, p. 5; U. Cassuto, *From Adam to Noah* (Jerusalem, 1944), p. 181.

39. Hawkes and Wooley, *Prehistory*, p. 497; DeVaux, "Ancient Israel," p. 154.

40. See Deut. 17:9, 19:17, 21:5, 31:9, 26; 33:10; Ezra 44:24; 2 Kings 17:27–28; Ezek. 44:23–24.

41. Deut. 21:5.

42. See also 2 Chron. 19:5–11, 34:13; Jer. 18:18; Mal. 2:6–8; DeVaux, "Ancient Israel," pp. 238, 354.

43. Ezek. 44:24; see also Micah 3:11.

44. See Deut. 17:9 ("You shall come to the Levitical priests and to the Judge . . ."); Herzog, "The Administration of Justice in Ancient Israel," reprinted in *Judaism: Law and Ethics* (London, 1976).

45. See Deut. 33:10; Ezek. 44:23–24; Mal. 2:68.

46. See Talmud, *Ta'anit* 27b; *Sukkah* 56a, b.

3. THE ROLE OF THE TRIBE AND FAMILY IN APPLYING CRIMINAL SANCTIONS

a. THE BIBLICAL CONCEPTION OF ASYLUM
(By Moshe Greenberg)*

The laws of the Bible treat of the right of asylum in three passages. In Exodus 21:12–14 it is promised that the accidental homicide will have a place appointed for him for flight. The nature of this place is not further defined, it being clear only that it is other than the altar of YHWH which is referred to in verse 14. For that verse says that the murderer is to be taken away for execution even from the altar; evidently, then, the aforementioned place is not that altar.

Numbers 35:9–34 says nothing of the altar, but prescribes that six Levitical cities, three on each side of the Jordan, are to be appointed as asyla—the term employed is [arei miklat] "cities of intaking"—for the accidental homicide. The "assembly"—a tribunal outside of the asylum—tries the fugitive manslayer, and if it finds him innocent of murder, it rescues him from the avenger and returns him to the city of refuge. There the manslayer must remain until the death of the high priest. If he leaves the city before, he may be slain with impunity by the avenger. No ransom may be accepted from the manslayer in lieu of his stay in the asylum.

The law of Deuteronomy 19:1–13 stresses the responsibility of the community to establish easily accessible asyla for the manslayer, and keep murderers from enjoying immunity in them. Nothing is said of the Levitical character of the cities of refuge, or of the requirement that the manslayer be detained in them until the death of the high priest.

The humanitarian purpose of these laws is obvious, and their aspiration to control vengeance by making it possible for public justice to intervene between the slayer and the avenger has long been recognized as an advance over the prior custom of regarding homicide as a purely private matter to be settled between the families of the two parties.

On the basis of this humanitarian and political understanding it has generally been assumed that the laws bear the following relation to each other: The law of Exodus, speaking of an altar, is compared with the flight of Adonijah and Joab into the tent sanctuary of Jerusalem, there to lay hold of the corners of the altar for protection from Solomon (1 Kings 1:50, 2:28). With good reason it is supposed that the law of Exodus reflects the earliest custom of seeking asylum at the local sanctuaries that filled ancient Palestine before the Josianic reform. The vague "place" of the Exodus law is accordingly interpreted to mean sanctuary site.

*From *Journal of Biblical Literature*, vol. 78 (1959), p. 125.

When the Deuteronomist proposed to abolish the local sanctuaries, "in order not to abolish the right of asylum along with the altars, he appoints special cities of refuge for the innocent who are pursued by the avenger of blood." The six cities of refuge are the Deuteronomist's means of replacing the local sanctuaries as asyla, for—it is argued—while the local altars and sanctuaries were in existence, what need was there of six special cities of refuge?

Inasmuch as Numbers also speaks of cities it is to be inferred that it followed Deuteronomy. The priestly interest reflected in the law of Numbers likewise is taken as a reflex of a later age. That the death of the high priest is the signal for the release of the manslayer signifies that "his death marks an epoch; it is when the high priest—not the king—dies that the fugitive slayer obtains his amnesty. . . . What now can be the meaning of this fact . . . but that the civil power has been withdrawn from the nation and is in the hands of foreigners?" In other words, the law reflects the theocratic organization of the Persian province of Judah. Again, the evidently punitive character of the manslayer's stay in the city of refuge, so foreign to the humanitarian interest of the early laws, bespeaks a later transformation of the entire concept of asylum.

Various details of this theory have been criticized. The altar, it has been pointed out, cannot have provided a permanent refuge for the manslayer, so that for the Deuteronomic provision of cities there was good practical ground even when many altars were available. The priestly law that the manslayer not be released until the death of the high priest has been interpreted alternatively—following ancient exegesis (see below) —as an expiation, which has nothing to do with the political importance of the high priest in post-Exilic times. But the inability of scholars to define convincingly either the nature of this expiation or its necessity has led to the general retention of the original, Wellhausenian position.

Now that position is open to question on several grounds. That a high priest's *death* should be the occasion of an amnesty is an odd idea. Amnesties, it has been observed, occur at the accession of new rulers, being a politic device for ingratiating themselves with the populace. Moreover, Wellhausen's interpretation disregards the whole tenor of the law: if there is anything characteristic of the priestly law of Numbers it is the insistence upon the absolute nature of the crime of homicide, and the impermissibility of mitigating its penalties by any human agency.

You shall not take a ransom for the life of a murderer who is liable to death, but he shall be put to death. And you shall accept no ransom for him who has fled to his city of refuge, that he may return to dwell in the land before the death of the high priest. You shall not thus pollute the land in which you live; for blood pollutes the land, and no expiation can be made for the land for the blood that is shed in it, except by the blood of him who shed it. (Num. 35: 31–33)

This would seem definitely to exclude the idea that any human authority was empowered to expunge the guilt of the homicide in a manner so savoring of political expediency as is implied by the notion of amnesty.

Indeed the Achilles' heel of the critical position is its failure to take into account adequately the religious presuppositions of the asylum law. The provisions of that law are not wholly accounted for on humanitarian or political grounds.

It must first be recognized that whenever an innocent man is slain the law considers the slayer guilty in a measure. Shedding an innocent man's blood, even unintentionally, involved blood guilt, and no manslayer was considered clear of this guilt. This appears, first, in the Deuteronomic law which does not regard as actionable the avenger's killing the manslayer on the way to the city of refuge. To be sure, the community is held responsible if the manslayer, who did not deserve to die, was caught owing to the failure of the people to make the city of refuge accessible (Deut. 19:10). Yet the avenger is not regarded as a murderer. Why? Because the manslayer was not guiltless. The law of Numbers makes this point explicit: if the avenger finds the manslayer outside the city of refuge and slays him, he shall not be guilty of bloodshed (35:27). The most striking legal expression of the objectivity of blood guilt—i.e., its incurrence even without criminal intent—is the law of Exodus 21:28 ff. concerning the homicidal ox. Here, where there can be no intent since the killer is a brute, the law nonetheless regards the animal as blood guilty and requires that it be stoned. Now this law is but the application of the principle of Genesis 9:5: "For your lifeblood I will surely require a reckoning; of every beast will I require it." And since that principle, laid down in a priestly passage, is incorporated in the Covenant Code—by universal agreement the earliest law collection—we are advised to pause before mechanically assigning ideas that occur . . . to late times.

The accidental homicide is, then, guilty, though not guilty of death. How is this guilt to be expiated? Illumination is thrown upon our subject from another quarter. In ancient Greece a strikingly parallel notion of the objectivity of blood guilt was held. Every bloodshed was polluting; a miasma lay on the slayer, as well as on the family and even the city of the slain, that had somehow to be purged away. The law of involuntary homicide of ancient Greece is set forth as follows by Demosthenes:

> The man who is convicted of involuntary homicide shall, on certain appointed days, leave the country by a prescribed route, and remain in exile until he is reconciled to one of the relatives of the deceased. Then the law permits him to return . . . it instructs him to make sacrifice and to purify himself, and gives other directions for his conduct. (*Against Aristocrates* [XXIII]. 72; trans. J. H. Vince, *Loeb Classical Library*)

Let us apply these concepts to ancient Israel. Condemnation to exile outside the country is not a penalty found in biblical law, for the reason that exile meant being cut off from YHWH, and, in the worst case, being forced to worship other gods (1 Sam. 26:19, Deut. 4:27 f.). The Israelite analogue to banishment could only have been the enforced exile of the manslayer from his home town. On the other hand, the punishment of homicide, as has been said, was not subject to human decision. The kinsman of the slain is not allowed to come to terms with the slayer, either in a monetary or any other fashion. He cannot pardon his act and expunge his sin. This is the explicit law of Numbers 35, but it is not a late idea of the priestly writer; it is a principle informing all of biblical law. Exodus 21:30 must specifically sanction the acceptance of ransom from the negligent owner of a homicidal ox because the rule is that homicides generally cannot be ransomed; an exception is here made only because the owner of the ox did not personally and with malice commit the slaying. Deuteronomy 19:12 f. has entirely replaced the right of the kinsman to dispose as he wishes of the murderer with the unconditional death penalty. True, the avenger is the executioner, but he has no say in the sentence; once the man has been convicted of murder the matter is out of his hands. It is the same in the case of the accidental homicide: the kinsman is not to say when his guilt is expunged.

Now the city of refuge, as conceived in Numbers, at once takes account of the whole situation in which the accidental homicide finds himself. In contrast with the temporary asylum provided by the altar, the city secures the life of the manslayer for an indefinite period. At the same time it provides for the expiation of his guilt: first, by an enforced detention—the manslayer may not buy his way out of the city of refuge. The punitive character of this detention was fully recognized by later writers. Both Philo (*De spec. leg.* III. 123) and Josephus (*Antiq.* 4.7.4) use the term [*phuge*] "banishment" to describe the stay of the manslayer in the city of refuge; tannaitic law uses the equally expressive [*galut*] "exile."

What is the meaning of the peculiar limit set to the term of banishment—the death of the high priest? Later Jewish jurists discussed the question in the following illuminating passage:

> *Mishnah*: If after [the slayer] has been sentenced as an accidental homicide the high priest dies, he need not go into exile.
> *Gemara*: . . . But is it not exile that expiates?—It is not exile that expiates, but the death of the high priest.
>
> (Bab. Talmud, Makkoth, 11b)

This interpretation accords fully with the biblical view of the incommutability of the penalties of homicide. "He who sheds the blood of man, by man shall his blood be shed, for in the image of God made He man" (Gen. 9:6). This statement, the ideological basis of the law's refusal to recognize the translatability of life into any other terms, occurs in the priestly writings. Again, however, it is no late conceit, but a principle that animated the earliest lawmakers of Israel as well. The clearest expression of this is the remarkable leniency with which property offenses are dealt with in biblical law. No crime against property is punished with death. The insistence of life for life, to the exclusion of monetary compensation—a severity unparalleled in ancient Near Eastern law—has its counterpart in the refusal to consider any offense against property worthy of the death penalty—equally unheard of in all Near Eastern systems but the Hittite. In biblical law life and property are incommensurable.

Taking life, then, imposes a guilt that cannot be expiated by any means short of death. But whose death can expiate the blood guilt of the manslayer who is not liable to capital punishment? A religious guilt such as blood guilt can be expiated only in religious terms. Can the Israelite manslayer offer—like his Greek counterpart—a purificatory sacrifice? The incommensurability of human with animal life forbids it. It is a remarkable fact that, while biblical, like Greek, law regards bloodshed as polluting, it does not prescribe a purificatory sacrifice to purge any slayer of guilt. And, although it is precisely for unintentional and unwitting sins that the sin and guilt offerings of Leviticus 4–5 and Numbers 15:22–29 are designed, the unintentional homicide is not required to make such a purgatorial offering. Only another human life can expiate the guilt of accidental slaying.

The sole personage whose religious-cultic importance might endow his death with expiatory value for the people at large is the high priest. During his life the priest expiates one type of religious guilt incurred by the people at large through the gold plate that he wears on his forehead: "It shall be on Aaron's forehead, and

Aaron shall bear the iniquity committed in the holy things, which the children of Israel shall hallow . . . and it shall always be upon his forehead, that they may be accepted before YHWH" (Exod. 28:36 ff.). By his death he expiates that guilt which can be expiated only through death, but which could not be so expiated before. A later jurist expresses the underlying conception thus: "Just as the clothing of the high priest expiates, so the death of the righteous man expiates."

It appears, then, that the city of refuge as conceived in Numbers is the necessary adjunct to, rather than a replacement of, the local altars. The altar gives temporary asylum from the immediate danger of pursuit by the avenger; the city alone provides for the expiation of blood guilt which every stratum of biblical law associates with homicide.

What, finally, is the relation of the law of Numbers to that of Deuteronomy? It has already been suggested that the six cities named in Joshua 20:7 f. as Levitical cities of refuge were the sites of important sanctuaries (this is certain for Hebron and Shechem) which had become popular refuges. The six were all part of Israelite territory only during the heyday of the united monarchy, shortly before and after the death of David. The united monarchy may also be considered a likely time for such a national program for regulating blood revenge to have been conceived, though the conception of asylum which it incorporates, apart from the specification of the six cities, is doubtless older. It is interesting, in passing, to note that the idea of punitive confinement to a city area coupled with a notion of special grace is also attested to at this time: Solomon's confinement of Shimei to Jerusalem on pain of death if he leaves is a sort of grim variation on the theme of the asylum (1 Kings 1:36 f.). In both cases persons are involved who, though they have committed a guilty act, are saved from the death penalty, the one by royal, the other by divine grace. The city of their confinement has at once the attributes of a prison and an asylum.

In perfect accord with pre-Josianic conditions, Numbers represents the cities of refuge as Levitical cities (35:6), a reflex of the fact that all were the sites of important priestly families who were the hereditary priesthoods of the local sanctuaries. The expiatory death of the high priest—it is left unclear whether of the city of refuge or of the slayer's home town—also accords best with a multiplicity of local priesthoods. Deuteronomy, on the other hand, has wholly transformed the ancient conception by effacing its sacerdotal side. The Levitical character of the cities of refuge (i.e., their being sanctuary sites) as well as the role of the high priest's death are ignored by Deuteronomy, whose doctrine of centralized worship entailed the virtual sec-

ularization of the concept of asylum. In Deuteronomy it does indeed become a purely humanitarian institution. But the law of Numbers, whatever be the date of its present formulation, preserves intact the cultic and expiatory features that are the earmarks of antiquity and that, indeed, are made necessary by the idea of the blood guilt of homicide which prevails in the earliest laws of Israel.

Thus, although there is no mention of cities of refuge outside of the laws, nothing stands in the way of assuming that the laws concerning them reflect the conceptions, perhaps even the custom, of the earliest age of Israel. The law of Numbers is to be understood as amplifying the vague "place" to which Exodus promises that the manslayer will be able to flee, and is designed as a final disposition of the fugitive who has fled for temporary protection to a local altar. Deuteronomy takes its departure from the law of Numbers, but by stripping the cities of their sacred status as sanctuary sites, and by its disregard of the religious-cultic provisions of Numbers, it is seen to be a later revision.

4. CRIMINAL SANCTIONS

a. SOME POSTULATES OF BIBLICAL CRIMINAL LAW
(By Moshe Greenberg)*

Among the chief merits of Professor [Yehezkial] Kaufmann's work must be counted the tremendous impetus it has given to the study of the postulates of biblical thought. The debt that the present paper owes to this stimulus and to the lines of investigation laid down by Professor Kaufmann is patent; it is a privilege to have the occasion to offer it to him in grateful tribute.

I

The study of biblical law has been a stepchild of the historical-critical approach to the Bible. While the law had been a major preoccupation of ancient and medieval scholars, in modern times it has largely been replaced by, or made to serve, other interests. No longer studied for itself, it is now investigated for the reflexes it harbors of stages in Israel's social development, or it is analyzed by literary-historical criticism into strata, each synchronized with a given stage in the evolution of Hebrew religion and culture. The main interest is no longer in the law as an autonomous discipline, but in what the laws can yield the social or religious historian. It is a remarkable fact that the last comprehensive juristic treatment of biblical law was made over a century ago.

*From *Yehezkel Kaufman Jubilee Volume* (Jerusalem, 1960).

The sociological and literary-historical approaches have, of course, yielded permanent insights, yet it cannot be said that they have exhausted all the laws have to tell about the life and thought of Israel. Too often they have been characterized by theorizing which ignores the realities of early law and society as we know them at first hand from the written records of the ancient Near East. Severities in biblical law are alleged to reflect archaic notions that have no echo in either ancient civilized, or modern Bedouin law. Humane features are declared the product of urbanization, though they have no parallels in the urban codes of Mesopotamia. Inconsistencies have been discovered and arranged in patterns of historic evolution where a proper discrimination would have revealed that the laws in question dealt with altogether separate realms.

The corrective to these errors lies ready to hand. It is that considerable body of cuneiform law—especially the law collections—which lends itself admirably to elucidate the meaning and background of the biblical law corpora. The detailed studies of these cuneiform collections, made chiefly by European scholars, furnish the student of the Bible with models of legal analysis, conducted without the prejudgments which frequently mar discussions of biblical law.

No clearer demonstration of the limits of literary-historical criticism can be found, for example, than that afforded by the studies made upon the laws of Hammurapi. Inconsistencies no less glaring than those which serve as the basis of analyzing strata in the Bible are found in this greatest corpus of Mesopotamian law. In this case, however, we know when, where, and by whom the laws were promulgated. We know, as we do not in the case of the Bible, that the code as we now have it was published as a whole, and intended—at the very least—as a statement of guiding principles for the realm of the king. When like discrepancies were pointed out in biblical laws it had been possible to defend stopping short with a literary-historical analysis by arguing that the discrepancies and inconsistencies of the present text were not found in the original documents that went into it. Attempts to interpret the biblical laws as a coherent whole were regarded as naïve and unscholarly. It was not possible to argue this way in the case of Hammurapi's laws. The discrepancies were there from the beginning, and though, to be sure, they may well have originated in earlier collections, the fact remained that they were, incorporated side by side in one law.

Two attitudes have been taken toward this problem in the code of Hammurapi. One, represented best by Paul Koschaker, is historical-critical. It aims at reconstructing the original laws which have gone into the present text and have caused the discrepancy; having attained this aim, its work is done. The other, represented by Sir John Miles, is that of the commentator, whose purpose is to attempt "to imagine how this section as it stands can have been interpreted by a Babylonian court." The commentator is compelled in the interest of coherence to look for distinctions of a finer degree than those made by the literary historian. Such distinctions are not merely the recourse of a modern harmonist to escape the contradictions of the text; they are, it would seem, necessary for understanding how an ancient jurist, how the draftsman himself, understood the law. It must be assumed that the laws of Hammurapi were intended as a consistent guide to judges, and had to be interpreted as they stand in as consistent a manner as possible.

The realization that careful discrimination between apparently contradictory laws is needed for this most carefully drafted ancient law corpus is highly pertinent for an understanding of biblical law. The literary-historical aim leads all too readily to a disregard of distinctions in favor of establishing a pattern of development. Only by endeavoring to interpret the laws as they now stand does one guard himself against excessive zeal in finding discrepancies which involve totally different subjects rather than a historical development. Adopting the method of the commentator, then, we are thrown back much more directly upon the laws themselves. Recourse to literary-critical surgery is resisted until all efforts at making distinctions have failed.

Another virtue of the commentator is his insistence on understanding a given body of law in its own terms before leaping into comparisons with other law systems. To do so, however, means to go beyond the individual rules; for it is not possible to comprehend the law of any culture without an awareness of its key concepts, its value judgments. Yet much of the comparative work done in Israelite-Near Eastern law has been content with comparing individual laws rather than law systems or law ideologies. But until the values that the law embodies are understood, it is question whether any individual law can be properly appreciated, let alone profitably compared with another in a foreign system.

In the sequence I shall attempt to indicate some instances of the gain accruing to the study of biblical law from the application of these two considerations: the insistence, first, upon proper discriminations, and second, upon viewing the law as an expression of underlying postulates or values of culture. The limitations of the sociological and literary-historical approaches will emerge from the discussion. My remarks are confined to the criminal law, an area which lends itself well to comparative treatment, and in which the values of a civilization come into expression with unmatched clarity.

II

Underlying the differing conceptions of certain crimes in biblical and cuneiform law is a divergence, subtle though crucial, in the ideas concerning the origin and sanction of the law.

In Mesopotamia the law was conceived of as the embodiment of cosmic truths (*kinatum*, sing. *kittum*). Not the originator, but the divine custodian of justice was Shamash, "the magistrate of gods and men, whose lot is justice and to whom truths have been granted for dispensation." The Mesopotamian king was called by the gods to establish justice in his realm; to enable him to do so Shamash inspired him with "truths." In theory, then, the final source of the law, the ideal with which the law had to conform was above the gods as well as men; in this sense "the Mesopotamian king . . . was not the source of the law but only its agent."

However, the actual authorship of the laws, the embodying of the cosmic ideal in statutes of the realm, is claimed by the king. Hammurapi repeatedly refers to his laws as "my words which I have inscribed on my monument"; they are his "precious" or "choice" words, "the judgment . . . that I have judged (and) the decisions . . . which I have decided." This claim is established by the name inscribed on the stele, and Hammurapi invokes curses upon the man who should presume to erase his name. Similarly, in the case of the laws of Lipit-Ishtar: Lipit-Ishtar has been called by the gods to establish justice in the land. The laws are his, the stele on which they are inscribed is called by his name. The epilogue curses him "who will damage my handiwork . . . who will erase its inscription, who will write his own name upon it." While the ideal is cosmic and impersonal, and the gods manifest great concern for the establishment and enforcement of justice, the immediate sanction of the laws is by the authority of the king. Their formulation is his, and his too, as we shall presently see, is the final decision as to their applicability.

In accord with the royal origin of these laws is their purpose: "to establish justice," "that the strong might not oppress the weak," "to give good government," "stable government," "to prosper the people," "abolish enmity and rebellion"—in sum, those political benefits which the constitution of the United States epitomizes in the phrases, "to establish justice, ensure domestic tranquillity, promote the general welfare."

In the biblical theory the idea of the transcendence of the law receives a more thoroughgoing expression.

Here God is not merely the custodian of justice or the dispenser of "truths" to man, he is the fountainhead of the law, the law is a statement of his will. The very formulation is God's; frequently laws are couched in the first person, and they are always referred to as "words of God," never of man. Not only is Moses denied any part in the formulation of the Pentateuchal laws, no Israelite king is said to have authored a law code, nor is any king censured for so doing. The only legislator the Bible knows of is God; the only legislation is that mediated by a prophet (Moses and Ezekiel). This conception accounts for the commingling in the law corpora of religious and civil law, and—even more distinctively biblical—of legal enactments and moral exhortations. The entire normative realm, whether in law or morality, pertains to God alone. So far as the law corpora are concerned there is no source of norm-fixing outside of him. Conformably, the purpose of the laws is stated in somewhat different terms in the Bible than in Babylonia. To be sure, observance is a guarantee of well-being and prosperity (Exod. 23:20 ff.; Lev. 26; Deut. 11:13 ff., etc.), but it is more: it sanctifies (Exod. 19:5; Lev. 19) and is accounted as righteousness (Deut. 6:25). There is a distinctively religious tone here, fundamentally different in quality from the political benefits guaranteed in the cuneiform law collections.

In the sphere of the criminal law, the effect of this divine authorship of all law is to make crimes sins, a violation of the will of God. "He who acts willfully [against the law] whether he belongs to the native-born or the aliens, is reviling the Lord" (Num. 15:30). God is directly involved as legislator and sovereign; the offense does not flout a humanly authored safeguard of cosmic truth but an explicit utterance of the divine will. The way is thus prepared to regard offenses as absolute wrongs, transcending the power of men to pardon or expunge. This would seem to underlie the refusal of biblical law to admit of pardon or mitigation of punishment in certain cases where cuneiform law allows it. The laws of adultery and murder are cases in point. Among the Babylonians, Assyrians, and Hittites the procedure in the case of adultery is basically the same. It is left to the discretion of the husband to punish his wife or pardon her. If he punishes his wife, her paramour also is punished; if he pardons her, the paramour goes free too. The purpose of the law is to defend the right of the husband and provide him with redress for the wrong done to him. If the husband, however, is willing to forego his right, and chooses to overlook the wrong done to him, there is no need for redress. The pardon of the husband wipes out the crime.

In biblical law it is otherwise: "If a man commits adultery with the wife of another man, both the adulterer and the adulteress must be put to death" (Lev. 20:10; cf. Deut. 22:22, 23)—in all events. There is no question of permitting the husband to mitigate or cancel the punishment. For adultery is not merely a wrong against the husband, it is a sin against God, an absolute wrong. To what extent this view prevailed may be seen in few extra-legal passages: Abimelech is providentially kept from violating Abraham's wife, Sarah, and thereby "sinning against God"—not a word is said about wronging Abraham (Gen. 20:6). Joseph repels the advances of Potiphar's wife with the argument that such a breach of faith with his master would be a "sin against God" (39:8 f.). The author of the ascription of Psalm 51—"A psalm of David, when Nathan the prophet came to him after he had gone in to Bath-sheba"—finds it no difficulty that verse 4 says, "Against thee only have I sinned." To be sure the law also recognizes that adultery is a breach of faith with the husband (Num. 5:12), yet the offense as such is absolute, against God. Punishment is not designed to redress an injured husband for violation of his rights; the offended party is God, whose injury no man can pardon or mitigate.

The right of pardon in capital cases which Near Eastern law gives to the king is unknown to biblical law (the right of the king to grant asylum to homicides in extraordinary cases [cf. 2 Sam. 14] is not the same). Here would seem to be another indication of the literalness with which the doctrine of the divine authorship of the law was held in Israel. Only the author of the law has the power to waive it; in Mesopotamia he is the king, in Israel, no man.

III

Divergent underlying principles alone can account for the differences between Israelite and Near Eastern laws of homicide. The unexampled severity of biblical law on the subject has been considered primitive, archaic, or a reflex of Bedouin vendetta customs. But precisely the law of homicide cannot be accounted for on any such grounds.

In the earliest law collection, the Covenant Code of Exodus, it is laid down that murder is punishable by death (Exod. 21:12 ff.). If homicide is committed by a beast—a goring ox is spoken of—the beast must be stoned, and its flesh may not be eaten. If it was known to be vicious and its owner was criminally negligent in failing to keep it in, the owner is subject to death as well as the ox, though here the law allows the owner to ransom himself with a sum fixed by the slain person's family (verses 28 ff.). This is the sole degree of culpability in which the early law allows a ransom. It is thus fully in accord with a later law of Numbers (35:31) which states, "You shall not take a ransom for the life of a murderer who is guilty of death, but he shall be surely put to death." A ransom may be accepted only for a homicide not committed personally and with intent to harm. For murder, however, there is only the death penalty.

These provisions contrast sharply with the other Near Eastern laws on homicide. Outside of the Bible, there is no parallel to the absolute ban on composition between the murderer and the next of kin. All Near Eastern law recognizes the right of the slain person's family to agree to accept a settlement in lieu of the death of the slayer, Hittite law going so far as to regulate this settlement minutely in terms of the number of souls that must be surrendered as compensation. Bedouin law is no different: among the Bedouin of Sinai murder is compensated for by a tariff reckoned in camels for any life destroyed. The Qur'an is equally tolerant of composition: "Believers," it reads (2:178), "retaliation is decreed for you in bloodshed: a free man for a free man, a slave for a slave, and a female for a female. He who is pardoned by his aggrieved brother shall be prosecuted according to usage and shall pay him a liberal fine."

In the Babylonian law of the goring ox, otherwise closely paralleling that of the Bible, no punishment is prescribed for the ox.

On both of these counts biblical law has been regarded as exhibiting archaic features. To speak in terms of legal lag and progress, however, is to assume that the biblical and non-biblical laws are stages in a single line of historical development, a line in which acceptance of composition is the stage after strict talion. This is not only incapable of being demonstrated, the actual history of the biblical law of homicide shows that it followed an altogether different principle of development from that governing Near Eastern law.

A precise and adequate formulation of the jural postulate underlying the biblical law of homicide is found in Genesis 9:5 f.: "For your lifeblood I shall require a reckoning; of every beast shall I requite it. . . . Whoever sheds the blood of a man, by man shall his blood be shed; for in the image of God was man made." To be sure, this passage belongs to a stratum assigned to late times by current critical opinion; however that may be, the operation of the postulate is visible in the very earliest laws, as will be seen immediately. The meaning of the passage is clear enough: that man was made in the image of God—the exact significance of the words is not necessary to decide here—is expressive of the peculiar and supreme worth of man. Of all creatures, Genesis 1 relates, he alone possesses this attribute, bringing him into closer relation to God than all the rest and conferring upon him highest value. The first practical consequence of this supremacy is set forth in 9:3 f.: man may eat beasts. The establishment of a value hierarchy of man over beast means that man may kill them—for food and sacrifice only (cf. Lev. 17:4)—but they may not kill him. A beast that kills a man destroys the image of God and must give a reckoning for it. Now this is the law of the goring ox in Exodus: it must be stoned to death. The religious evaluation inherent in this law is further evidenced by the prohibition of eating the flesh of the stoned ox. The beast is laden with guilt and is therefore an object of horror.

Babylonian law on the subject reflects no such theory as to the guilt the peculiar value of human life imposes on all who take it. Babylonian law is concerned with safeguarding rights in property and making losses good. It therefore deals only with the liability of the owner of the ox to pay for damages caused by his ox. The ox is of no concern to the law since no liabilities attach to it. Indeed, one could reasonably argue that from the viewpoint of property rights the biblical law is unjust: is it not unduly hard on the ox owner to destroy his ox for its first offense? Ought he to suffer for an accident he could in no way have foreseen and for which he therefore cannot be held responsible?

This view of the uniqueness and supremacy of human life has yet another consequence. It places life beyond the reach of other values. The idea that life may be measured in terms of money or other property, and *a fortiori* the idea that persons may be evaluated as equivalences of other persons, is excluded. Compensation of any kind is ruled out. The guilt of the murderer is infinite because the murdered life is invaluable; the kinsmen of the slain man are not competent to say when he has been paid for. An absolute wrong has been committed, a sin against God which is not subject to human discussion. The effect of this view is, to be sure, paradoxical: because human life is invaluable, to take it entails the death penalty. Yet the paradox must not blind us to the judgment of value that the law sought to embody.

The sense of the invaluableness of human life underlies the divergence of the biblical treatment of the homicide from that of the other law systems of the Near East. There the law allows and at times fixes a value on lives, and leaves it to the kinsmen of the slain to decide whether they will have revenge or receive compensation for their loss in money or property. Perhaps the baldest expression of the economic valuation of life occurs in those cases where punishment of a murderer takes the form of the surrender of other persons—a slave, a son, a wife, a brother—"instead of blood," or "to wash out the blood," or to "make good" the dead

person, as the Assyrian phrases put it. Equally expressive are the Hittite laws which prescribe that the killer has to "make amends" for the dead persons by "giving" persons in accord with the status of the slain and the degree of the homicide. The underlying motive in such forms of composition is the desire to make good the deficiency in the fighting or working strength of the community which has lost one of its members. This seems to be the meaning of Hittite Law 43: "If a man customarily fords a river with his ox, another man pushes him aside, seizes the tail of the ox and crosses the river, but the river carries the owner of the ox away, they (i.e., the authorities of the respective village or town) shall receive that very man." The view of life as a replaceable economic value here reaches its ultimate expression. The moral guilt of the homicide is so far subordinated to the need for restoring the strength of the community that the culprit is not punished but incorporated; this is the polar opposite of the biblical law that requires that not even the flesh of the stoned homicidal ox may be eaten.

That the divergence in law reflects a basic difference in judgments of value, rather than stages in a single line of evolution, would seem to be borne out by examining the reverse of the coin: the treatment of offenses against property. Both Assyrian and Babylonian law know of offenses against property that entail the death penalty. In Babylonia, breaking and entering, looting at a fire, night trespass—presumably for theft—and theft from another's possession are punished by death; Assyrian law punishes theft committed by a wife against her husband with death. In view of this, the leniency of biblical law in dealing with all types of property offenses is astonishing. No property offense is punishable with death. Breaking and entering, for which Babylonian law prescribes summary execution and hanging of the culprit at the breach, is punished in biblical law with double damages. If the housebreaking occurred at night the householder is privileged to slay the culprit caught in the act, though this is not prescribed as a punishment (Exod. 22:1 f.).

This unparalleled leniency of biblical law in dealing with property offenses must be combined with its severity in the case of homicide, just as the leniency of non-biblical law in dealing with homicide must be taken in conjunction with its severity in dealing with property offenses. The significance of the laws then emerges with full clarity: in biblical law life and property are incommensurable; taking of life cannot be made up for by any amount of property, nor can any property offense be considered as amounting to the value of a life. Elsewhere the two are commensurable: a given amount of property can make up for life, and a grave enough offense against property can necessitate forfeiting life. Not the archaicness of the biblical law of homicide relative to that of the cuneiform code, nor the progressiveness of the biblical law of theft relative to that of Assyria and Babylonia, but a basic difference in the evaluation of life and property separates the one from the others. In the biblical law a religious evaluation; in non-biblical, an economic and political evaluation, predominates.

Now it is true that in terms of each viewpoint one can speak of a more or a less thoroughgoing application of principle, and, in that sense, of advanced or archaic conceptions. Thus the Hittite laws would appear to represent a more consistent adherence to the economic-political yardstick than the law of Babylonia and Assyria. Here the principle of maintaining the political-economic equilibrium is applied in such a way that even homicides (not to speak of property offenses) are punished exclusively in terms of replacement. It is of interest, therefore, to note that within the Hittite system there are traces of an evolution from earlier to later conceptions. The Old Kingdom edict of Telepinus still permits the kinsman of a slain man to choose between retaliation or composition, while the later law of the code seems to recognize only replacement or composition. And a law of theft in the code (paragraph 23) records that an earlier capital punishment has been replaced by a pecuniary one.

In the same way it is legitimate to speak of the law of the Bible as archaic in comparison with postbiblical Jewish law. Here again the jural postulate of the biblical law of homicide reached its fullest expression only later: the invaluableness of life led to the virtual abolition of the death penalty. But what distinguishes this abolition from that just described in the Hittite laws, what shows it to be truly in accord with the peculiar inner reason of biblical law, is the fact that it was not accompanied by the institution of any sort of pecuniary compensation. The conditions that had to be met before the death penalty could be inflicted were made so numerous, that is to say, the concern for the life of the accused became so exaggerated, that in effect it was impossible to inflict capital punishment. Nowhere in the account of this process, however, is there a hint that it was ever contemplated to substitute a pecuniary for capital punishment. The same reverence for human life that led to the virtual abolition of the death penalty also forbade setting a value on the life of the slain man. (This reluctance either to execute the culprit or to commute his penalty created a dilemma which Jewish law cannot be said to have coped with successfully.)

Thus the divergences between the biblical and Near Eastern laws of homicide appear not as varying stages of progress or lag along a single line of evolution, but as reflections of differing underlying principles. Nor does the social-political explanation of the divergence seem to be adequate in view of the persistence of the peculiarities of biblical law throughout the monarchial, urbanized age of Israel on the one hand, and the survival of the ancient non-biblical viewpoint in later Bedouin and Arab law on the other.

IV

Another divergence in principle between biblical law and the non-biblical law of the ancient Near East is in the matter of vicarious punishment—the infliction of a penalty on the person of one other than the actual culprit. The principle of talion is carried out in cuneiform law to a degree which at times involves vicarious punishment. A creditor who has so maltreated the distrained son of his debtor that he dies, must lose his own son. If a man struck the pregnant daughter of another so that she miscarried and died, his own daughter must be put to death. If through faulty construction a house collapses killing the householder's son, the son of the builder who built the house must be put to death. A seducer must deliver his wife to the seduced girl's father for prostitution. In another class are penalties which involve the substitution of a dependent for the offender—the Hittite laws compelling a slayer to deliver so many persons to the kinsmen of the slain, or prescribing that a man who has pushed another into a fire must give over his son; the Assyrian penalties substituting a son, brother, wife, or slave of the murderer "instead of blood." Crime and punishment are here defined from the standpoint of the pater-familias: causing the death of a child is punished by the death of a child. At the same time the members of the family have no separate individuality vis-à-vis the head of the family. They are extensions of him and may be disposed of at his discretion. The person of the dependent has no independent footing.

As is well known, the biblical law of Deuteronomy 24:16 explicitly excludes this sort of vicarious punishment: "Parents shall not be put to death for children, nor children for parents; each shall be put to death for his own crime." The proper understanding of this requires, first, that it be recognized as a judicial provision, not a theological dictum. It deals with an entirely different realm than Deuteronomy 5:9 and Exodus 20:5, which depict God as "holding children to account to the third and fourth generations for the sins of their parents." This is clear from the verb [*yumat*], "shall be put to death," referring always to judicial execution and not to death at the hand of God. To be sure. Jeremiah and Ezekiel transfer this judicial provision to the theological realm, the first promising that in the future, the second insisting that in the present, each man *die* for his own sin—but both change [*yumat*] to [*yamut*] (Jer. 31:29; Ezek. 18:4 and passim).

The law is almost universally considered late. On the one hand, it is supposed to reflect in law the theological dictum of Ezekiel; on the other, the dissolution of the family and the "weakening of the old patriarchal position of the house father" that attended the urbanization of Israel during the monarchy. This latter reasoning, at any rate, receives no support from the law of the highly urbanized cultures of the ancient Near East. Babylonian, Assyrian, and Hittite civilization was surely no less urbanized than that of monarchial Israel, yet the notion of family cohesiveness and the subjection of dependents to the family head was not abated by this fact.

A late dating of the Deuteronomic provision is shown to be altogether unnecessary from the simple fact that the principle of individual culpability in precisely the form taken in Deuteronomy 24:16 is operative in the earliest law collection of the Bible. What appears as a general principle in Deuteronomy is applied to a case in the Covenant Code law of the goring ox: after detailing the law of an ox who has slain a man or a woman the last clause of the law goes on to say that if the victims are a son or a daughter the same law applies (Exod. 21:31). This clause, a long-standing puzzle for exegetes, has only recently been understood for what it is: a specific repudiation of vicarious punishment in the manner familiar from cuneiform law. There a builder who, through negligence, caused the death of a householder's son must deliver up his own son; here the negligent owner of a vicious ox who has caused the death of another's son or daughter must be dealt with in the same way as when he caused the death of a man or woman, to wit: the owner is to be punished, not his son or daughter. This principle of individual culpability in fact governs all of biblical law. Nowhere does the criminal law of the Bible, in contrast to that of the rest of the Near East, punish secular offenses collectively or vicariously. Murder, negligent homicide, seduction, and so forth, are punished solely on the person of the actual culprit.

What heightens the significance of this departure is the fact that the Bible is not at all ignorant of collective or vicarious punishment. The narratives tell of the case of Achan who appropriated objects devoted to God from the booty of Jericho and buried them under his tent. The anger of God manifested itself in a defeat of Israel's army before Ai. When Achan was discovered, he and his entire household were put to death (Josh. 7). Again, the case of Saul's sons, who were put to death for their father's massacre of the Gibeonites in

violation of an oath by YHWH (2 Sam. 21). Now these instances are not a matter of ordinary criminal law but touch the realm of the deity directly. The misappropriation of a devoted object—[*herem*]—infects the culprit and all who come into contact with him with the taboo status of the [*herem*] (Deut. 7:26, 13:16; cf. Josh. 6:18). This is wholly analogous to the contagiousness of the state of impurity, and a provision of the law of the impurity of a corpse is really the best commentary on the story of Achan's crime: "This is the law: when a man dies in a tent every one that comes into that tent, and every thing that is in the tent, shall be unclean" (Num. 19:14). Achan's misappropriated objects—the story tells us four times in three verses (Josh. 7:21, 22, 23)—were hidden in the ground under his tent. Therefore he, his family, his domestic animals, and his tent, had to be destroyed, since all incurred the [*herem*] status. This is not a case, then, of vicarious or collective punishment pure and simple, but a case of collective contagion of a taboo status. Each of the inhabitants of Achan's tent incurred the [*herem*] status for which he was put to death, though, to be sure, the actual guilt of the misappropriation was Achan's alone.

The execution of Saul's sons is a genuine case of vicarious punishment, though it too is altogether extraordinary. A national oath made in the name of God had been violated by a king. A drought interpreted as the wrath of God has struck at the whole nation. The injured party, the Gibeonites, demand life for life and expressly refuse to hear of composition. Since the offending king is dead, his children are delivered up.

These two cases—with Judges 21:10 f. the only ones in which legitimate collective and vicarious punishments are recorded in the Bible—show clearly in what area notions of family solidarity and collective guilt are still operative: the area of direct affronts to the majesty of God. Crimes committed against the property, the exclusive rights, or the name of God may be held against the whole family, indeed the whole community of the offender. A principle which is rejected in the case of judicial punishment is yet recognized as operative in the divine realm. The same book of Deuteronomy that clears parents and children of each other's guilt still incorporates the dictum that God holds children to account for their parents' apostasy to the third and fourth generation (5:9). Moreover it is Deuteronomy 13:16 that relates the law of the [*herem*] of the apostate city, ordaining that every inhabitant be destroyed, including the cattle. For the final evidence of the concurrent validity of these divergent standards of judgment the law of the Molech worshiper may be adduced (Lev. 20:1–5): a man who worships Molech is to be stoned by the people—he alone; but if the people overlook his sin, 'Then I," says God, "will set my face against that man, and against his family. . . ."

The belief in a dual standard of judgment persisted into latest times. Not only Deuteronomy itself, but the literature composed after it continues to exhibit belief in God's dooming children and children's children for the sins of the parents. The prophetess Huldah, who confirms the warning of Deuteronomy, promises that punishment for the sins of Judah will be deferred until after the time of the righteous King Josiah (2 Kings 22:19 f.). Jeremiah, who is imbued with the ideology of Deuteronomy, and who is himself acutely aware of the imperfection of the standard of divine justice (31:28 f.), yet announces to his personal enemies a doom that involves them and their children (Jer. 11: 22, 29:32). And both Jeremiah and the Deuteronomistic compiler of the Book of Kings ascribe the fall of Judah to the sins of Manasseh's age (Jer. 15:4; 2 Kings 23:26 f., 34:3 f.). Even Job complains that God lets the children of the wicked live happy (21:7 ff.). Thus there can be no question of an evolution during the biblical age from early to late concepts, from "holding children to account for the sins of parents" to "parents shall not be put to death for children, etc." There is rather a remarkable divergence between the way God may judge men and the way men must judge each other. The divergence goes back to the earliest legal and narrative texts and persists through the latest.

How anomalous the biblical position is can be appreciated when set against its Near Eastern background. A telling expression of the parallel between human and divine conduct toward wrongdoing is the following Hittite soliloquy:

> Is the disposition of men and of the gods at all different? No! Even in this matter somewhat different? No! But their disposition is quite the same. When a servant stands before his master . . . [and serves him] . . . his master . . . is relaxed in spirit and is favorably inclined(?) to him. If, however, he [the servant] is ever dilatory(?) or is not observant(?), there is a different disposition towards him. And if ever a servant vexes his master, either they kill him, or [mutilate him]; or he [the master] calls him to account [and also] his wife, his sons, his brothers, his sisters, his relatives by marriage, and his family. . . . And if ever he dies, he does not die alone, but his family is included with him. If then anyone vexes the feeling of a god, does the god punish him alone for it? Does he not punish his wife, his children, his descendants, his family, his slaves male and female, his cattle, his sheep, and his harvest for it, and remove him utterly?

To this striking statement it need only be added that not alone between master and servant was the principle of vicarious punishment applied in Hittite and Near Eastern law, but, as we have seen, between parents and children and husbands and wives as well.

In contrast, the biblical view asserts a difference between the power of God, and that of man, over man. Biblical criminal law foregoes entirely the right to punish any but the actual culprit in all civil cases; so far as man is concerned all persons are individual, morally autonomous entities. In this too there is doubtless to be seen the effect of the heightened stress on the unique worth of each life that the religious-legal postulate of man's being the image of God brought about. "All persons are mine, says the Lord, the person of the father as well as that of the son; the person that sins, he shall die" (Ezek. 18:4). By this assertion Ezekiel wished to make valid in the theological realm the individual autonomy that the law had acknowledged in the criminal realm centuries before. That God may impute responsibility and guilt to the whole circle of a man's family and descendants was a notion that biblical Israel shared with its neighbors. What was unique to Israel was its belief that this was exclusively the way of God; it was unlawful arrogation for man to exercise this divine prerogative.

The study of biblical law, then, with careful attention to its own inner postulates has as much to reveal about the values of Israelite culture as the study of Psalms and Prophets. For the appreciation of this vital aspect of the biblical world, the riches of cuneiform law offer a key that was unavailable to the two millennia of exegesis that preceded our time. The key is now available and the treasury yields a bountiful reward to those who use it.

Notes and Questions to Greenberg, "Some Postulates of Biblical Criminal Law"

1. Greenberg takes it for granted that the Mesopotamian law codes were intended as a statement of legal principles. Compare this with the view of Finkelstein in "Law in the Ancient Near East" (Chapter II, Section E 4 *g*). So, too, note the latter's disagreement with Greenberg's assumption that the Code of Hammurabi was intended as a consistent guide to judges.

2. Greenberg maintains that "if the housebreaking occurred at night the householder *is privileged* to slay the culprit caught in the act" (emphasis supplied). The wording of the biblical verse may, however, be taken to indicate not that slaying a burglar is a *privilege* of the householder but that the householder is not regarded as a murderer if he happens to kill the burglar during the struggle. ("If the thief is discovered in the tunnel and *is slain*, there is no blood guilt [Exod. 22:1], emphasis supplied.) Greenberg has followed here the

interpretation of the verse in the Talmud[47] that regards the householder as authorized to slay the burglar intentionally. Once the thief has turned to flee, however, he may not be killed, even according to the talmudic interpretation.[48]

3. Is Greenberg's explanation of the killing of Achan's family and Saul's sons convincing? Can these deviations from the traditional law have been due, instead, to the strong feeling that these were extraordinary circumstances requiring departure from the law in order to preserve the credibility and purity of the entire Jewish nation?[49]

4. Greenberg maintains, citing Leviticus 20:5, that when God himself punishes, he may extend his punishment to the family of the offender: "I will set my face against that man and his family. . . ." If this is so, why does God omit the punishment of the family when he also says, in Leviticus 20:4: "And I will set my face against that man and shall destroy him from the midst of his people"? Furthermore, if it is unjust for humans to kill one person for the offenses of another, how can God commit such injustice: "Will the judge of the whole world not do justice?"[50] It has been suggested that Exodus 20:5 may be interpreted as meaning, "who *annuls* the sins of the fathers *because of* the [acts of] the sons," instead of "who *visits* the sins of the fathers *upon* the sons."[51]

5. If, as Greenberg maintains, the execution of Saul's sons (2 Sam. 21:9) was an extraordinary departure from the common practice, why does the Bible not make any mention of this?

6. Greenberg refers to the provisions of the Assyrian and Hittite codes, that a murderer was required to hand over his own body, and sometimes the bodies of members of his family or servants, to the family of the murdered victim. The Hittite Code[52] even provides for the handing over of four persons to make up for the murder of one (see also paragraph 7, below). Can this throw any light on the biblical provisions of "a soul for a soul"?[53] That is, can the expression refer not to killing the murderer as punishment for his crime but, rather, to the perspective that the slayer ought to hand over a "soul" to become a slave to the family or community

of the victim to make up for their economic loss? Note that once the principle is established that economic compensation is sufficient (and that slaying of the murderer is not required), it is only a short step to have the murderer (instead of handing over himself, a member of his family, or one of his servants to become a slave to the victim's family) pay the monetary value of a slave. The immediately subsequent passage in Exodus 21, "an eye for an eye," could, then, also more readily be understood as requiring the payment of money only. This would accord closely with the tradition recorded in the Talmud that the verse "You shall give a soul for a soul, and eye for an eye" refers to the payment of money.[54]

7. Section 6 of the Hittite Code provides that if a man is found murdered in a field, the distance around the corpse shall be measured and the nearest city shall pay money for the murder. Deuteronomy 21:1–9, which also provides for measuring the distance around the corpse, does not provide for the payment of money by the nearest city because of its principle, "You shall not take ransom for the soul of a murderer" (Num. 34:31). Accordingly, in the Bible the elders of the nearest city wash their hands and pray for forgiveness (see Chapter II, Section D 2, above).

A later Assyrian tablet (*circa* 672 B.C.E.) records that a murderer was required to hand over his maidservant and her "family" as payment for the blood of the victim, thereby "washing off the blood."[55] Compare this phrase "washing off the blood" with the biblical washing of hands by the elders when someone is murdered and the assailant remains undetected.[56]

b. REFLECTIONS ON BIBLICAL CRIMINAL LAW
(By Bernard S. Jackson)*

In 1960 Professor Moshe Greenberg published an important essay in which he attacked the application of literary-historical techniques in the study of biblical law. All too often, he complained, apparent inconsistencies are arranged to produce historical sequences, when proper discrimination would show that the laws in question deal with altogether separate realms. Instead, he advocated the method of the commentator, who seeks to resolve apparent contradictions by making distinctions between the spheres of application of the laws concerned. Only when these efforts fail should

47. *Sanhedrin* 72a, b.
48. See Jerusalem Talmud, *Sanhedrin* 8:8.
49. See Rambam, Laws of the Sanhedrin, ch. 18; J. Ginsberg, *Mishpatim Le'Yisrael*; Z. H. Chajes, *Torat Ha'Neviim* (Hebrew; reprinted Jerusalem, 1958), pp. 27, 48.
50. Gen. 18:25; see above regarding the biblical perspective of individual responsibility.
51. See Y. Meklenberg, *Ha'ktav Ve'Ha'Kabala* (Hebrew; reprinted New York, 1946), ad loc.
52. See J. Pritchard, *Ancient Near Eastern Texts*, p. 189.
53. Exod. 21:23:

54. Talmud, *Ketubot* 38a; Note the view in the *Mekhilta*, ad loc., that while "an eye for an eye" refers to money, "a soul for a soul" refers to capital punishment.
55. See S. Feigin, "Homicide in the Codes of the Ancient Near East" (Hebrew), *Ha'Tekufa*, vol. 32–33, p. 740.
56. Deut. 21:1–9.
*From *Essays in Jewish and Comparative Legal History* (Leiden, 1975).

recourse be had to "literary-critical surgery." Such an approach might be thought to tend towards concentration on the details of particular formulations. Professor Greenberg insisted, however, that the process of interpretation must take account of "key concepts" and "value judgments," since law was "an expression of underlying postulates or values of culture." Further, valid comparisons between biblical law and other systems must take note of such values.

Two recent books on biblical law, by Shalom Paul and Anthony Phillips, adopt a similar approach. Both assert that there are "characteristic traits" or "leading features" which distinguish biblical law from the legal culture of the ancient Near East. Paul (but not Phillips) adopts also the method of the commentator in his annotations to Exodus 21:2–22:16.

It is hardly surprising that a new conservatism should emerge in the study of biblical law. Here as elsewhere a reaction to the extremes of higher criticism was inevitable. Roman law, too, has come to reject overzealous interpolation-hunting. It would be easy to accept the theory of this approach, and quarrel only with some of its applications. For Greenberg does not reject historical development outright. Nevertheless, I venture to suggest that his eminently reasonable formulation conceals some important shortcomings, and contains serious dangers for the unwary. I begin with some general considerations.

I

In advocating the approach of the commentator, Greenberg takes considerable support from developments in the study of the laws of Hammurabi (LH), where inconsistencies in the text have similarly required explanation. He maintains that the literary-critical approach, which attempts explanations in terms of historical strata, cannot provide the whole explanation. "We know . . . that the code as we now have it was published as a whole, and intended—at the very least —as a statement of guiding legal principles for the realm of the king. . . . It must be assumed that the laws of Hammurabi were intended as a consistent guide to judges, and had to be interpreted as they stand in as consistent a manner as possible." Hence, the approach of the commentator, as applied by Driver and Miles, must come into play. "The commentator is compelled in the interest of coherence to look for distinctions of a finer degree than those made by the literary historian. Such distinctions are not merely the recourse of a modern harmonist to escape the contradictions of the text; they are, it would seem, necessary for understanding how an ancient jurist, how the draftsman himself, understood the law." A similar approach, in Greenberg's view, is to be applied to biblical law.

These assumptions about the nature of the laws of Hammurabi are becoming increasingly doubtful. It is true that contemporary documents occasionally illustrate the application of some of Hammurabi's norms. But in no case so far known are the laws quoted or cited. Even if they were intended as a "consistent guide to judges," the nature of their authority is most unlikely to have been such as to require the judges to seek to harmonize apparent inconsistencies, especially such as appeared in provisions in widely separate parts of the corpus. Indeed, there are attested cases of judges clearly failing to apply the laws. It is noteworthy that neither the prologue nor the epilogue to the laws commends them to the use of the judges. In the epilogue it is the wronged litigant who is advised to take support from them, and future kings are asked not to change them. There is no evidence that the problem of deciding "how this section as it stands can have been interpreted by a Babylonian court" was encountered in practice.

It may be objected that even if the laws were not interpreted by courts, they must have been interpreted by someone. If no one else, then surely the draftsman of the official edition must have intended rational distinctions to be drawn between the materials drawn from his different sources? But though scribal activity certainly existed, juristic activity, which requires the existence of a legal profession, is not found in Old Babylonia. As for the draftsman himself, there are a number of possibilities. The first is that he was unaware of the inconsistencies. Such slips are not unknown in modern legal systems, and it is often left to litigation to bring them to light. As litigation apparently did not employ statutory interpretation, such inconsistencies may well have remained undetected. Alternatively, it may be that the draftsman was aware of them, but was unconcerned. The laws were an ideal pronouncement not of reason, but of justice. The commission of the draftsman was to establish justice "in the language of the land," not to reconcile earlier and later sources. A third possibility, in many cases the most likely, is that the draftsman saw no differences requiring reconciliation, since he conceived of the law in terms of cases rather than principles.

What has been said of the laws of Hammurabi applies with equal force to biblical law. Indeed, even were the approach of the commentator legitimate in the former case, it would not necessarily be so also in the latter. For we do not know, as Greenberg concedes, that biblical law was published contemporaneously as a whole, intended for use in legal practice. Later, of course, it came to be so regarded, and rabbinic exegesis —to which there is no parallel in the ancient Near East—is an admirable example of the approach of the commentator. But there is reason to believe that the

Torah was not so intended *ab initio*. A writer, be he a legal draftsman or not, adapts his style to the intended purpose of his document. Many of the characteristic features of biblical drafting illustrate not the religious nature of Israel's law, but rather the non-statutory nature of Israel's chief religious document. Some of its substantive provisions appear to be ideal, and the corpus as a whole, again like its ancient Near Eastern counterparts, may be best viewed as the components of a literary, rather than a primarily legal, tradition. But much of the content may still have been taken from the real legal world.

Greenberg also insists upon "viewing the law as an expression of underlying postulates or values of culture." He maintains that particular laws may only be understood as part of a total system of values, and that we should avoid comparison of individual biblical laws with individual laws from the ancient Near East. Both biblical law and ancient Near Eastern law, he suggests, have "inner postulates," which represent "divergent underlying principles" or "basic difference(s) in judgments of value," and it is to these that the comparatist should attend.

But is it really so, and, if it is, is there any reliable method of ascertaining such "inner postulates"? Greenberg takes support from the anthropologist E. A. Hoebel for the proposition that "it is not possible to comprehend the law of any culture without an awareness of its key concepts, its value judgments." But there is an enormous difference between anthropological field work and the analysis of ancient legal texts. In the former, express formulations of principle may be sought, if not spontaneously proferred, and the whole life of a people may be observed. Ancient legal texts, on the other hand, rarely provide express statements of principle, and are far from comprehensive in the information they provide as to the legal life of the people. Indeed, anthropological research has identified evolutionary trends which should make us wary of seeking general principles. Evolution is most commonly regarded as a process of increasing differentiation and integration. Differentiation may be observed not only in the functions of institutions, but also in the development of concepts. Applied to legal science, it means that fine distinctions are not to be expected in early phases of development. Integration refers to the degree of interdependence of social institutions. It too may be applied to the sphere of ideas. Legal norms appear less and less as isolated units and more and more as aspects of a system as the degree of integration increases. It may be noted that the greater the degree of integration, the easier it becomes to formulate principles encompassing more than a single norm. These observations do not imply acceptance of a nineteenth century unilinear evolutionary

concept, nor do they depend, for their present application, upon categorising biblical law as "primitive." They assume only that biblical law represents overall a less developed stage in the development of Jewish law than does Tannaitic law. This leads one to expect less of subtle distinction and formulation of principle in biblical than in Tannaitic law.

This judgment, it will be noted, is a relative one. I do not suggest that no principles existed in biblical law, any more than Greenberg suggests that the texts indicate no historical development. I do maintain that less importance ought to be accorded to underlying principles than Greenberg suggests, and stress the dangers to be encountered by those who seek them.

The search for such principles involves substantially the scholar's own legal, theological, or other preconceptions. In most cases it takes the form of generalization from a small number of concretely expressed laws and/or narratives. It is assumed that these sources reflect the alleged principles, which are implicit. All the scholar has to do is make them explicit. Sadly, the matter is not as simple. Different scholars may select for emphasis different aspects of the text, and hence construct different principles. Different views may be taken not only of the essential element deserving generalization, but of the level of abstraction at which the principle is to be pitched. For example, one might construct from Exodus 21:35 any one (and more) of the following: where a man's ox gores another man's ox to death, the value of the two oxen shall be divided; where a man's animal kills another man's ox, the value of the two animals shall be divided; where a man's animal kills another man's animal, the value of the two animals shall be divided; where the property of one man causes the death of another man's animal, the loss shall be divided; where one man's property causes damage to another man's property, the loss shall be divided; losses shall be divided.

I have avoided inserting issues such as "fault" and "strict liability" in these model principles, since their inclusion would illustrate another danger of this approach: the attribution to an early source of more abstract and sophisticated legal concepts of a later date. An example of this may also be taken from the law of oxen. Exodus 21:33–4 rules "And if a man will open a pit or if a man will dig a pit and will not cover it, and there falls into it an ox or an ass, the owner of the pit shall make good; silver shall he restore to their owner, and the dead (animal) shall be his." On this, Paul comments: "Damage caused to another's property through culpable negligence must be compensated in full." His formulation imputes to the law the abstract and sophisticated concept of "culpable negligence"— which simply is not in it. The law in fact imposes (what we might call) strict liability on the owner of an uncovered pit for the death of an ox or ass that falls into it. The owner of the pit may not have been in the least culpable in not covering the pit. He may have done his very best to guide the animal away. Nevertheless, according to the terms of the provision, he is liable.

The assumed implicit existence of postulates or principles of law raises more than methodological difficulties. It is of the utmost significance in evaluating the importance of such phenomena to observe whether they are implicit or explicit. Certainly, principles may exist under the surface, finding their expression in concrete situations. But it is only when they assume an explicit form that we can be confident (*a*) that they exist; (*b*) that they were consciously articulated; (*c*) that a certain minimum value, sufficient for their inclusion, was placed upon them; (*d*) that their range can be determined within reasonable limits. Biblical law does contain a number of principles of a higher level of generality than laws such as Exodus 21:33–4. Maxims such as "a life for a life" deserve primary, if not exclusive, consideration when postulates are sought.

There are also other dangers involved, when the interest in postulates assumes a comparative dimension. The desire to contrast two systems may lead to selectivity in the evidence adduced for each one. As for the ancient Near East, an all too ready tendency to find a common denominator for the purposes of contrast may exclude conflicting evidence from some area or epoch. It has become acceptable to speak of a single "cuneiform law." For some purposes this may be legitimate. For others, including Greenberg's postulates, it is not. When the concern is to view law "as an expression of underlying postulates or values of culture," it is misleading to classify together such diverse cultures as those appearing from the Middle Assyrian and the Hittite laws. It may be just possible that there was an historical period of which a unitary assumption would be justified. Some have looked to an original body of common Semitic custom. At least as plausible may be the view that the laws of the different groups converged as a result of prolonged contact. At best, the unitary assumption may be correct of but one historical period. Why should this be chosen for purposes of contrast, rather than any other? Similarly, it may be doubted that postulates remained constant throughout half a millennium or more of biblical law, or that different writers of the same period necessarily had the same postulates.

The role played by postulates also deserves critical attention. They appear to be regarded not merely as aids to the understanding of biblical law and to its proper differentiation from the laws of the ancient Near East. They assume an active role in the very creation of these differences. Greenberg is well aware that the dominant tendency today is to explain both similarities and differences in socio-economic terms. Beneath the surface there lurks here the question whether culture is determined primarily by material or by ideological factors. I do not propose to enter these murky depths, except to comment that Greenberg's expressed reason for rejecting the socioeconomic interpretation is not sufficient. He cites "the persistence of the peculiarities of biblical law throughout the monarchical, urbanized age of Israel on the one hand, and the survival of the ancient non-biblical viewpoint in later Bedouin and Arab law on the other" as evidence of the inadequacy of the social-political explanation of differences in the law of homicide. The argument is that if a law which developed in one socioeconomic climate survives in a different socioeconomic climate, its creation cannot have been due to that original socioeconomic climate. But such "survivals" have been familiar to anthropologists for more than a century.

Many of the difficulties here discussed result from the casuistic form of most biblical and ancient Near Eastern laws. The problem may be posed quite simply: "What principles may be inferred from these texts?" I have stressed already the relativity of principles. For the purposes of what follows, I may now define the term "principle" in expressly relative terms. A principle is any formulation of more general application than the text from which it is inferred. It is this problem that underlies the difficulties to be encountered by those who would use postulates to distinguish apparent inconsistencies. Moreover, this very same difficulty may sometimes invalidate the literary-historical approach.

II

One of Greenberg's postulates, wherein biblical law is distinguished from the laws of the ancient Near East, is that "in biblical law life and property are incommensurable. In the biblical law a religious evaluation; in non-biblical, an economic and political evaluation predominates." This judgment has since been taken up by both Paul and Phillips.

The postulate contains at least three elements, which deserve separate consideration. In Israel the death penalty is not imposed for property offenses, whereas in the ancient Near East it is; in Israel murder results in a mandatory death penalty, whereas in the ancient Near East it may be compounded by monetary payment; in Israel the values of the law are dominated by religious considerations, whereas in the ancient Near East the values are economic. At a higher level of abstraction these three merge into one: in Israel alone life and property are incommensurable.

I take first the proposition relating to property offenses. The "basic difference in judgments of value" is ascertained solely in terms of the penalties imposed. This is by no means an infallible test. The death penalty may be imposed for a number of reasons, not all of them related to moral or religious values. That for homicide, for example, may in some societies reflect demographic considerations. The punishment for infanticide may reflect either a "value of culture," or the interests of population growth, or a combination of these (and other) factors. Conversely, where euthanasia, in some form or other, is permitted, this may reflect a particular religious viewpoint as much as socioeconomic considerations. Nor does the imposition of the same penalty for different offenses necessarily imply the same value judgments of those offenses. The variation possible in the range of penalties is far less than the gradations of value. There was a time in English law when murder, theft, and treason were all capital offenses, but we may not assume from this that they were equal in the degree to which they offended the values of society. . . .

This consideration of the biblical evidence is sufficient to throw into doubt Greenberg's postulate that no property offenses are punishable by death in the Bible, and that this marks a difference between its underlying values, and those of the ancient Near East. It is not disputed that some property offenses are capital in the ancient Near East. But even here Greenberg's formulation shows the dangers of generalization and selectivity into which comparative postulate-hunting may lead. He writes: "Both Assyrian and Babylonian law know of offenses against property that entail the death penalty. In Babylonia, breaking and entering, looting at a fire, night trespass—presumably for theft—and theft from another's possession are punished by death; Assyrian law punishes theft committed by a wife against her husband with death." LH 25 does not necessarily deal with every looting from a fire. The offense is that of one who goes to extinguish the fire (a fireman?) but while there steals. LH 6–10 is nowhere generally enough formulated to justify a single conception such as "theft from another's possession." Middle Assyrian Laws (MAL) A3 does not punish any theft committed by a wife against her husband with death. It explicitly distinguishes the case where the husband is sick or dead from that where he is alive (and well). In the former case only is there a mandatory death penalty. In the latter, the husband appears to have a discretion. The formulation of LH 21 suggests strongly that the killing of the housebreaker is not a penalty, but rather a measure of self-defense, comparable to Exodus 22:1. The verb is active (*idukkusu*: they shall put him to death), unlike the passive formulation (*iddak*: he shall be put

to death) in the other theft laws. Laws of Eshnunna (LE) 12–13, Greenberg's "night trespass," may well be similarly explained. The formula there and in LE 28 is *imat ul iballut*, "he shall die, he shall not live." Elsewhere, the formula is *din napistim . . . imat*, "[it is] a case of life . . . he shall die." It is very plausibly argued that the import of *imat ul iballut* is to allow immediate self-help. Both in LE 12–13 and LE 28 the offender is seized *in flagrante delicto*, and the latter case is the *locus classicus* of permissible self-help, adultery caught in the act.

But the comparison is misleading for other reasons also. The laws of Hammurabi and those of Eshnunna are treated together as reflections of a single "Babylonian law," despite the political and geographical differences between them. If comparison is to be made, it should be made with each ancient Near Eastern society separately. The Laws of Eshnunna survive in only 59 sections, and the information on theft is far less than that in Hammurabi. The penalty for being caught in possession of a stolen slave was, at most, double, whereas a very similar case was capital under LH 19. As far as Eshnunna is concerned, there is no clear case of death for a property offense. Other legal systems are known from the ancient Near East, but are not mentioned by Greenberg. The Laws of Lipit-Ishtar of Isin (L-I) provide: "If a man entered the orchard of [another] man [and] was seized there for stealing, he shall pay ten shekels of silver," but there is also evidence of death (again, perhaps by way of self-help) for housebreaking. Above all, Greenberg omits Hittite Law, which contains a large number of theft offenses, all of them punished by penalties less than death, usually fixed payments or multiple restitution, save for the cases of theft of "a bronze spear in the gate of the palace" (sec. 126), and theft (by temple officials) of sacred objects, which are capital. We do not know what the practice was in Israel regarding theft of royal property, or what the penalty for kidnapping was in the Hittite Laws, but from what we do know it may be said that the underlying values of culture in the biblical and Hittite societies, in respect of their treatment of property offenses were relatively similar.

III

The law of composition for homicide is also adduced by Greenberg to show the incommensurability of life and property in Israel, but not in the ancient Near East.

The biblical evidence points, however, in two directions. There is the explicit prohibition of ransom (*KPR*) found in Numbers 35:31–2. But there are also laws in the Mishpatim which contemplate the use of composition. A historico-critical approach might distinguish between them by asserting that composition for homicide was (broadly) acceptable in the early period, but by the Priestly Code had been outlawed. Greenberg seeks rather to reconcile the texts, and does so by means of a principle: "A ransom may be accepted only for a homicide not committed personally and with intent to harm."

The provisions of the Mishpatim certainly fall far short of providing for, or even expressly contemplating, composition for homicide in general. Greenberg's principle is based on Exodus 21:29–30, where it has been made known to the owner of an ox that his beast is prone to gore, but he has not kept it in, and it has caused the death of a man or woman. The ox is stoned, and its owner, too, is liable to the death penalty. But the law goes on to regulate the possibility of ransom, requiring the owner of the ox to pay the whole of the sum claimed from him. . . .

The goring ox provision is the only one in the Mishpatim which mentions *KPR*. But there are other texts which envisage monetary payment as the consequence of homicide. In them the payment is not a ransom, since the relatives of the deceased have no right to demand the death of the offender. Nevertheless, these cases are relevant to Greenberg's contention that in biblical law the "taking of life cannot be made up for by any amount of property." In case of a miscarriage caused by men engaged in a fight, a sum of money is paid to the husband (Exod. 21:22). Though the sum is not *KPR*, the same phrase, of levying upon the victim, is used as in Exodus 21:30. Of course, here the victim is a foetus, not a living person in the normal sense. In Exodus 21:32, where the victim of the goring ox is a slave, a sum of thirty shekels is paid. Again, one might argue, the status of the victim is the significant feature. Exodus 21:20, with its ambiguous *NQWM YNQM* may well similarly involve a monetary payment, when a master beats his slave to death.

The import of the Mishpatim may be put thus. There is no explicit statement of general principle, whether allowing or prohibiting composition. There are certain cases, all of them special in some way, in which it is contemplated. No certain principle can be inferred, such as will tell us whether composition was or was not allowed in other cases. But the formulation of Exodus 21:30 suggests that *KPR* was not an unusual expedient, and this is confirmed by non-legal sources. . . .

The conclusion to be drawn from the biblical evidence is that there was a period in which composition for homicide was permitted, although we cannot know for sure whether this permission was restricted to certain cases, and, if so, where the dividing line was drawn.

A consideration of the ancient Near Eastern laws shows that the comparison is also less clear than at first appears. Greenberg maintains: "Outside of the Bible, there is no parallel to the absolute ban on composition between the murderer and the next of kin. All Near Eastern law recognizes the right of a slain person's family to agree to accept a settlement in lieu of the death of the slayer . . . ." Certainly, there is no parallel to Numbers 35:31, and the Middle Assyrian Laws at least know of the family's choice between death and property (A10, B2). But there is no mention of composition, in the sense of ransom (the biblical *KPR*) in the laws of Hammurabi. There, the penalties are fixed by law. No general statement of the law of homicide is found, but in the cases treated penalties of death, mutilation, or money are imposed according to the circumstances. The pecuniary cases are comparable to those of the Mishpatim. In LH 207 and 208 the homicide is unpremeditated (expressly). In LH 209 the victim is a foetus. In LH 212 and 214 she is of inferior status, the only variable distinguishing these two cases from LH 210. In LH 116, 219, and 231 also, the victim is a slave. The Hittite laws require substitution, rather than death, for homicide, but here too there is no general statement of the law of murder. The cases of substitution deal with unpremeditated and accidental killing. It is possible that substitution of persons was once known in Israel, though the evidence is not strong. Looking beyond the ancient Near East, we find that the growth of a repugnance towards ransoming the life of a murderer is not uncommon, and that the exclusion of the discretion of the kin in favor of penalties laid down by law is but a common reflection of the growth of state power. Of course, state power is generally considered to have been less developed in Israel than elsewhere. But Numbers 35:31–32 falls far short of creating real criminal law in Israel. Prosecution remained the responsibility of the family, which might still decide not to initiate proceedings. Only ransom was prohibited. Pardon remained possible, despite the theological objections to it (Num. 35:33–4). . . .

IV

The difference in underlying principles seen in the punishment of homicide and property offenses is interpreted by Greenberg as a reflection of different cultural values at the work in Israel and the ancient Near East respectively: "In the biblical law a religious evaluation; in non-biblical, an economic and political evaluation, predominates." Paul has found further applications of this distinction and considers it true of the respective systems generally.

The ascertainment of causal relationships in ancient law is an extremely hazardous business. Even in modern societies, with all the additional data and sociological techniques, the establishment of social causation is a highly complicated process. A rule is unlikely to be the result of a single influencing factor, and a decision as to which of a number of factors is dominant requires controlled experiment, such as is impossible when dealing with historical societies. Nevertheless, even if truly scientific conclusions cannot be reached, it is possible to formulate some criteria which may assist in discussing the problem.

First, explicit statements of the general policy of the law may sometimes be found. They will require careful interpretation, but even then deduction will be hazardous, since there is no certainty that a general policy necessarily produces its logical conclusions. Secondly, ideological or economic determinants may be inferred from the law itself. Such an inference can only be a hypothesis. It may be possible to ascertain from other explicit sources that such values were in fact held, or that such an economic situation actually did exist. The hypothesis may thereby be rendered plausible. But even such independent verification falls far short of proving that the law in question was the result of the proposed values or economic conditions. Thirdly, the reason for a law may even be stated alongside it. Of the three this may be the most reliable type of evidence, but it too is not conclusive. The reason may be a simplification, or represent a one-sided interpretation. It tells us what was the meaning assigned to the law by a particular person or tradition at a particular time, but that time may not represent the period of the norm's creation. The search for the ideological or economic causes of particular laws is even more difficult than the ascertainment of legal principles. When it ceases to be concerned merely with particular laws, and seeks contrasting causal principles underlying whole bodies of law, its value becomes highly doubtful. . . .

When comparing the biblical laws and the laws of Hammurabi, it now appears that we are dealing with two literary constructions, both representing only to a lesser or greater known extent the law as actually practiced. Moreover, we are, in one sense, comparing two religious literary texts, since the laws of Hammurabi, if not authored by a divinity, are offered to one in proof of the king's execution of his mandate. It is of interest to compare the values of these two documents and of their component parts. But we must not assume that we are thereby comparing two legal systems. . . .

In writing of the divergent postulates of biblical and ancient Near Eastern law, Greenberg was concerned, in part, to invalidate interpretations which, by assuming a unilinear evolutionary pattern, tended to view certain biblical rules as more archaic than those of Israel's neighbors. Several of the distinctions here discussed are such as would suggest to comparatists that it was biblical law which was the more advanced. Such a conclusion runs counter to general opinion. That, of

course, is no reason for rejecting these interpretations. They must be judged on their own merits. But as long as views of the relative advance of these various legal systems are seriously held, special care must be taken in handling the evidence for theories which run against them.

Important differences certainly exist both between biblical and cuneiform laws; and between cuneiform laws *inter se*. It has not been my purpose to paint a picture of dull uniformity. Such a view may reflect apologetic objectives just as much as one which asserts that Israel had a monopoly of humanity or wisdom. The differences may be easily ascertained, and will not mislead us as long as principles are not derived from them, or uniformity, whether of time or place, imposed where none exists. The differences may be easily determined. Their interpretation is more difficult.

The distinction between express and inferred principles is an important one, not merely in terms of evidentiary weight. Equally, it is essential that methodological assumptions be examined explicitly from time to time. Only by such discussion can precision be achieved, and progress made. By bringing these issues to the fore, Greenberg rendered a significant service to biblical scholarship.

Notes to Jackson, "Reflections on Biblical Criminal Law"

1. Note the extensive speculation and areas of uncertainty that one must face in dealing with a text as ancient as the Bible, as Jackson points out.

2. Toward the end of part III, Jackson insists that Numbers 35:31–32, barring "ransom," "falls far short of creating real criminal law in Israel. Prosecution remained the responsibility of the family, which might still decide not to initiate proceedings. Only ransom was prohibited. Pardon remained possible." Note, however, the explicit statement of the following verses:

> You shall not take ransom for the soul of a murderer who deserves to die, but he shall be killed. You shall not take a ransom for one who flees to a city of refuge to return to dwell in the land until the death of the priest. You shall not make wicked the land in which you dwell, because blood will taint the land, *and the land will not be forgiven for the blood which was spilled in it, except with the blood of the murderer.* You shall not contaminate the land in which you dwell and in which I dwell in its midst, because I am God who dwells among the children of Israel.
> (Num. 34:31–34; emphasis supplied)

3. See Part Two, Chapter V, Section A 3, below, regarding the drawbacks of attempting to interpret legal texts without reference to the unwritten legal tradition.

5. CASE STUDIES IN CRIMINAL LAW

a. MURDER AND ACCIDENTAL DEATH

(1) *Avenger of Blood*

(By Moshe Greenberg)*

Avenger of blood (lit. "redeemer of blood"), [mentioned in Num. 35:19, refers to] the kinsman (brother, son . . .) of a slain man who, as his redeemer . . . was duty bound to claim back his life from the slayer by killing him. . . .

In societies that lack a strong central authority the defense of private property and life is the task of the kinship group. The kinship group is both a defensive and an offensive unit: all are obliged to defend the right of any member, and all are accountable for the delict of any member. If a person is slain, his kin take vengeance for him upon the slayer, or on one or more of the slayer's kinship group. This in turn may give rise to counter vengeance, and a blood feud, terminating at times only with the extinction of a family, is set in motion.

In biblical Israel the sovereignty of the kinship group over matters affecting its private interest was just beginning to be superseded by communal authority. Biblical law still recognizes the kinsman as responsible for prosecuting homicide (Num. 35:19). However, it sanctions retribution only within the bounds of talion ("a life for a life"; Exod. 21:23) and only on the person of the culprit (Deut. 24:16 . . .). Moreover, the law seeks to control the redeemer through the agency of the asylum, which, by giving refuge to the homicide from the hand of the redeemer, makes it possible for the juridical organs of the community to interpose between them. Once the case has come before the public court, the redeemer has no more say in the matter. If the court finds the slayer guilty of murder, the law requires that he be put to death. To be sure, execution is still the prerogative of the kinsman (Deut. 19:12), but he is not free to pardon or accept a monetary composition instead (Num. 35:31 . . .). Though biblical law never replaced the private prosecutor for homicide with a public one, under the monarchy it appears that the king had the power to intervene and grant immunity to a slayer from the avenger (2 Sam. 14:8–11); to this extent, at least, even prosecution of the homicide had come under state control. However, the characterization of this procedure as guilty (verse 9) shows that the right of blood redemption was yet regarded as so sacred that no abridgment of it could be held guiltless.

The following instances of blood redemption occur: (*a*) Gideon slays the Midianite killers of his brothers (Judg. 8:18–21). Since the culprits are non-Israelite, this may not reflect normal practice, for (*b*) Joab's slaying of Abner for killing his brother in combat (2 Sam. 3:27,30) is not considered legitimate (1 Kings 2:5), whence it is to be inferred that slaying in combat does not normally privilege blood redemption. (This will account for David's failure to hold Joab guilty for killing Absalom.) (*c*) The Gibeonites secure the death of Saul's sons for his massacre of them (2 Sam. 21)— extraordinary for its being a vicarious punishment. . . . (*d*) A scrupulous refraining from vicarious punishment marks Amaziah's execution of his father's assassins (2 Kings 14:5–6). (*e*) Finally, there is the fictitious, but instructive, case of the Tekoite woman (2 Sam. 14:6–7), showing that redemption of blood was (paradoxically) carried out within a family as well—an internecine practice that sheds light on the fear of Rebekah in Genesis 27:45.

The kinsman's duty of redeeming blood is not to be confused with the actions of persons in authority undertaken to remove an imputed blood guilt: e.g., David's execution of Ish-bosheth's assassins (2 Sam. 4:11–12), and Solomon's execution of Joab (1 Kings 2:31–33; cf. verse 5 [RSV follows Luc. and OL reading the suffix "my" rather than the less pointed Hebrew "his"]). God's avenging of innocent blood is expressed by "avenge" (Deut. 32:43; 2 Kings 9:7); "require, exact vengeance (for)" (Gen. 9:5; Ps. 9:12; Ezek. 33:6). This expression, which refers to the kinsman's duty of redeeming family blood, is never used with God.

(2) *Banishment*

(By Moshe Greenberg)*

Banishment, [as referred to in the Bible, means] condemnation to exile since, to the Israelite, exile from his land meant being cut off from Yahweh (Hos. 9:3–5; cf. Gen. 4:14; Ezek. 11:15) and, in the worst case, being forced to worship idols (Deut. 4:27–28; 1 Sam. 26:19; Jer. 16:13), biblical law never prescribes it as a legal penalty. In Ezra 7:26, . . . "banishment" (cf. Vulg. *exilium*) or, better, "exclusion from the community" [is prescribed] (cf. 10:8). . . .

Voluntary exile was the last resort of hunted men: Jacob flees to Haran (Gen. 27:43), Moses to Midian (Exod. 2:15), David's parents to Moab (1 Sam. 22:3–4), David to Gath (1 Sam. 27:1–4), Absalom to Geshur (2 Sam. 13:38), Jeroboam to Egypt (1 Kings 11:40), Elijah to Phoenicia (1 Kings 17:9), Uriah to Egypt (Jer. 26:21–23). Taking asylum in another country was commonly practiced by political refugees

---

*From *Interpreter's Dictionary of the Bible*, ed. G. A. Buttrick (New York, 1962).

*From *Interpreter's Dictionary of the Bible*, ed. G. A. Buttrick (New York, 1962).

in the ancient Near East (cf. 2 Sam. 15:19; 1 Kings 11:14–25; Si-nuhe of Egypt; Idrimi of Alalakh); clauses dealing with the extradition of such fugitives are frequently found in Hittite treaties.

Since biblical law regards every homicide as guilty in some measure, the enforced stay of the accidental manslayer in the city of refuge may be considered a form of banishment (Num. 35:32; it is so regarded by Philo *On the Special Laws* III.123; *Jos. Antiq.* IV.vii.4; *M. Mak.* 2).

Roman law knew several forms of exile, from the severe *deportatio*, which was perpetual and involved confiscation of property and loss of citizenship, to the milder *relegatio*, by which a person was excluded from residence in a certain place, or confined to a particular place for a definite or indefinite period of time. A very common form was *relegatio in insulam*, which, according to early church tradition, was inflicted upon the author of Revelation (Rev. 1:9).

(3) *Blood Guilt*
(By Moshe Greenberg)*

Blood guilt, [as referred to in the Bible] (Exod. 22:2–3—H 22:1–2; cf. Num. 35:27), [concerns] guilt—not always liable to a legal penalty—incurred through bloodshed.

The most ancient view would appear to be exemplified by the Greek concept of the miasma (stain, pollution) of homicide, an automatic, objective state. Every bloodshed—even that committed in self-defense—pollutes and requires a purification. When criminal and non-criminal homicide were distinguished, this miasma nonetheless persisted. Plato still recognizes the need for purification even from the miasma caught inadvertently from a murderer. (*Laws* 916). It was not the killer alone, however, who was affected; until the wrath of the slain man's ghost was appeased, his family as well lay under a pollution which could be cast off only by exacting vengeance.

In Israel, too, blood guilt was defiling (Num. 35:33–34), but it was incurred only through slaying a man who did not deserve to die ("innocent blood"; Deut. 19:10; Jer. 26:15; Jonah 1:14). Killing in self-defense and the judicial execution of criminals are explicitly exempted (Exod. 22:2—H 22:1; Lev. 20:9; etc.). On the other hand, where there is "innocent blood," there is always blood guilt: for (*a*) intentional killing—including judicial murder (Judg. 9:24; 1 Sam. 25:26, 33; 2 Kings 9:26; Jer. 26:15)—as well as for (*b*) uninten-

tional (see below); for (*c*) being an indirect cause of death (Gen. 42:22), even if only through negligence or dereliction of duty (Deut. 19:10*b*; 22:8; Josh. 2:19). Finally, (*d*) persons in authority incur blood guilt for murder committed by those for whom they are responsible (1 Kings 2:5, 31–33).

While the law does not privilege the avenger of blood to take action against persons blood guilty under *c* and *d*, it does so in the case of murder and unintentional homicide. (Even a homicidal beast is considered blood guilty: he must be stoned and his carcass treated as taboo [Gen. 9:5; Exod. 21:28–32].) The avenger may slay the accidental homicide outside the asylum without incurring blood guilt (Num. 35:27), whence it may be inferred that the latter is not considered guiltless (this is borne out further by the character of the city of refuge). Yet insofar as the accidental manslayer is not deserving of death, the community is held blood guilty if it fails to provide him with an asylum (Deut. 19:10).

Since the bloodguilt of homicide lies on the entire community (Num. 35:33; Deut. 21:8–9), the communal interest and that of the avenger coincide insofar as both aim at eradicating the guilty party. When the criminal is known, his bloodguilt is expiable solely and entirely by his paying the legal penalty. No pecuniary composition or ritual expiation may be substituted for, or need be added to, this penalty: the murderer must die; the accidental homicide must serve out his term in the city of refuge (Num. 35:31–32; Deut. 19:13). However, if there occurs an untraceable murder in open country, the elders and priests of the town nearest to the corpse must perform a sacrificial purification—vicariously expiating life by life—accompanied by an avowal of innocence (Deut. 21:1–9).

Unexpiated bloodguilt is punished by God, the ultimate avenger (Gen. 9:5; 2 Sam. 4:11; 2 Kings 9:7; Ps. 9:12—H 9:13; Hos. 1:4). Unavenged blood cries to heaven for vindication—there is no trace of the idea that of itself it perils men (Gen. 4:10; Job 16:18; Isa. 26:21; Ezek. 24:7–9). As when God punishes idolatry (cf. Exod. 20:5; Deut. 5:9), here too he may exact retribution from the descendants of the bloodguilty person (2 Sam. 3:28–29; 21:1; 1 Kings 21:29; cf. 2 Kings 9:25–26; Matt. 27:25). The writer of Kings reckons the bloodshed of Manasseh as a cause of Judah's fall three generations later (2 Kings 24:4).

A peculiar extension of the idea is found in Leviticus 17:4: bloodguilt is imputed to one who slaughters a sacrificial beast at an unauthorized altar—as if to say that not even a brute's life might be taken except for divinely sanctioned purposes. The penalty for such bloodshed is "excising" (a divine punishment . . .).

---

*From *Interpreter's Dictionary of the Bible*, ed. G. A. Buttrick (New York, 1962).

(4) *City of Refuge*
(By Moshe Greenberg)*

City of refuge, [as referred to in the Bible] (Num. 35:11–12; cf. Josh. 20:4; Josh. 20:9), [concerns] one of the six Levitical cities appointed to receive and give asylum to accidental manslayers.

Among many peoples of antiquity (e.g., Phoenicians, Syrians, Greeks, Romans) certain shrines or sacred precincts were regarded as providing absolute security to fugitives. Innocent and guilty, criminals, runaway slaves, debtors, and political fugitives passed beyond the reach of revenge and justice alike upon attaining sacred ground and claiming the protection of the deity (cf. Tacitus Annotated III.60–63). In Israel as well, the altar of Yahweh afforded asylum to fugitives (1 Kings 1:50–53; 2:28–34). But biblical law restricted the right of asylum to the accidental homicide alone (Exod. 21:12–14; Num. 35:9–34; Deut. 19:1–13; Josh. 20 . . .). Its aim was to control blood revenge by making it possible for public justice to intervene between the slayer and the avenger of blood, "that the manslayer may not die until he stands before the congregation for judgment" (Num. 35:12). Ensuring the safety of the accidental homicide was in the vital interest of the whole community: "lest innocent blood be shed in your land . . . and so the guilt of innocent bloodshed be upon you" (Deut. 19:10).

As to the nature of the asylum, Exodus speaks vaguely of a "place" to which the accidental manslayer might flee, going on to say that the murderer must be taken even from the altar to execution (cf. 1 Kings 2:31–33). Numbers says nothing of the altar, but prescribes that six Levitical cities, three on each side of the Jordan, are to be appointed as asylums (Num. 35:6, 13–14). Deuteronomy 4:41–43 records that Moses designated the Transjordanian cities of refuge. Moses further ordered that three more be appointed in Canaan, with the eventual addition of yet another three contemplated when "all the land which [God] promised to give to your fathers" was conquered (19:1–10). That these are Levitical cities is not said in Deuteronomy. Joshua 20:7–8 lists the six cities of refuge as follows: Kedesh, Shechem, and Hebron in Canaan; Bezer, Ramoth-Gilead, and Golan in Transjordan—all priestly or Levitical cities (cf. Josh. 21:13, 21, 27, 32, 36; 1 Chr. 6:63).

Both the viewpoint and the procedure for dealing with the manslayer vary from source to source. In Numbers the "congregation"—a tribunal outside the asylum—tries the fugitive manslayer. If it finds him innocent of murder, it "rescues" him from the avenger

*From *Interpreter's Dictionary of the Bible*, ed. G. A. Buttrick (New York, 1962).

and "returns" him to the city of refuge, where he must remain until the death of the (local?) high priest. If he leaves before, he may be slain with impunity by the avenger. No ransom may be accepted from the manslayer in lieu of his remaining in the asylum (Num. 35:32)—his stay has, then, something of the nature of a punitive detention. Its termination at the death of the high priest was later interpreted—doubtless correctly—as a vicarious expiation of life by life (cf. T. B. Mak. 11*a*). The old idea of objective blood guilt dominates these laws.

Deuteronomy stresses the responsibility of the community to establish easily accessible asylums for manslayers, and to keep murderers from enjoying immunity in them. Should a murderer flee to a city of refuge, the elders of his home town must send for him and surrender him into the hand of the avenger. Nothing is said of an enforced detention or of a release at the death of the high priest.

Joshua 20 reflects both Numbers and Deuteronomy: the elders—here those of the city of refuge—pass upon the fugitive's right of asylum at his arrival; later the congregation tries him; if innocent, he must remain in the city until the high priest's death.

It is commonly held that the cities of refuge were conceived of by Deuteronomy (which is followed by Numbers)as a replacement of the local altars—abolished by the Deuteronomic reform—that had heretofore served as asylums. Yet even during the period of local sanctuaries provision must have been made for the prolonged protection of the manslayer, for whom the local altar afforded only a temporary refuge. Furthermore, the ancient notion that blood guilt is objective and defiles the land makes it necessary even for the accidental homicide to expiate his act. In Greece, where a similar notion of blood guilt prevailed, the unintentional homicide was punished with banishment until the kinsman of the slain person forgave him. Since banishment is not a biblical penalty, the Israelite analogue to this could only have been an enforced exile of the manslayer from his home town. Moreover, since the law does not permit the kinsman to compose the homicide in any way, another means of expiating the guilt had to be found. The city of refuge, especially as conceived of in Numbers, at once takes account of all these considerations: It secures the life of the manslayer for an indefinite period while at the same time providing for the expiation of his guilt, first by an enforced detention—tantamount to banishment from his home town—and then by the death of the high priest. Viewed in this light, the cities of refuge are necessary adjuncts, rather than later replacements, of the local altars.

The asylums were presumably priestly towns containing important shrines (this is certain for Hebron and Shechem) that had become popular refuges. The six cities were all part of Israelite territory only during the heyday of the United Monarchy, shortly before and after the death of David. The United Monarchy may also be considered the most likely time for such a national program for regulating blood revenge to have been conceived. Deuteronomy transformed the ancient conception by effacing its sacerdotal side: the Levitical character of the cities of refuge—i.e., their being temple cities—as well as the role of the high priest's death, is ignored by Deuteronomy, whose doctrine of centralized worship entailed the virtual secularization of the asylums. The law of Numbers alone, whatever be the date of its formulation, preserves the cultic and expiatory features that are the earmarks of antiquity. Thus, although there is no mention of the cities of refuge outside the laws, it appears likely that the laws take their departure from a living custom of the early age.

b. AN ANCIENT MESOPOTAMIAN TRIAL FOR HOMICIDE
(By T. Jacobsen)*

Introduction

The picture we can form of the early legal development in Mesopotamia and of the processes operative in it is gradually becoming clearer. From the oldest times, it would appear, justice was normally dispensed by local assemblies of villagers and townsmen, who judged according to a body of traditional unwritten common law with which everybody was familiar. How far the law that these assemblies administered was real law in the sense that it was backed by force or the threat of force is rather questionable. In certain cases involving capital punishment such backing may have been present since the assembly probably executed its own verdict by mob violence; in others it perhaps depended, for enforcement of its judgment, on some powerful individual in the community who had agreed beforehand to sponsor the weaker party, but in a great many cases it must have relied mainly on the general social pressure of public opinion. In large measure the early courts must therefore have had the character of mere courts of arbitration and they retained—except possibly for a brief period under the Third Dynasty of Ur—much of that character down to the time of Hammurabi and his successors.

Into the relatively static setup which we have described the political development projected in the Early Dynastic period a powerful instrument for legal change: the king. Kingship seems to have achieved a fair degree

of permanence and institutionalization in Mesopotamia during that period and the king—besides his central function of war leader—appears to have had from the beginning also certain general responsibilities for the peace and contentment of the society which he served. Old traditions preserved in myths and epics show that the king's aid could be enlisted in cases of grave wrong to individuals, and with the passing of time the king proved willing to make his power available more and more extensively to underpin justice. By the time of the Dynasty of Agade royal judgments were safeguarded by severe monetary sanctions, and the use of oaths by the name of the king in private contracts, which appears at the same time, can have had no other purpose than that of bringing royal punitive power to bear in the event of a breach. The same type of oath by the name of the king was used later, in the Isin-Larsa period, to shore up court decisions accepted by the parties, decisions which would otherwise have been without forcible sanctions. Also attested for the Isin-Larsa period is the characteristic function of the king as assigner of lawsuits brought to his attention to suitable courts for trial. This function almost certainly traces back to an earlier function as sponsor; the king's power made him the ideal person to induce courts to accept cases for which means of enforcing the decision would otherwise have been lacking.

By thus in various forms making his power and influence available as backing for decisions and commitments under the common law the king became a force contributing toward the gradual transformation of the nature of the common law from being essentially a body of ethical rules backed mainly by the pressure of public opinion to becoming more and more a body of legal rules in the true sense, backed by force and the threat of force.

The same vague original responsibilities of the king for peace and contentment among his subjects to which we traced his later activities in support of the common law were in all probability the source also of a different, not less interesting, royal function, that of modifying and changing the common law. At the beginning of a reign a new king would often promulgate a decree of "equity" (níg-si-sá, Akkadian *mîšarum*) which had for its aim the alleviation of social conditions felt to be unjust or unfair. Since such conditions were often hallowed by time and intimately connected with practices tolerated by the common law, an "equity" decree would frequently interfere with existing law, modifying or even abrogating it in the interest of the general welfare of the community. The earliest such decree known to us, the Reformtexts of Urukagina, appears as a contract concluded between the new king and the chief god of his city. However, since kingship in older times was

*From *Toward the Image of Tammuz and Other Essays on Mesopotamian History and Culture* (Cambridge, 1970).

an elective office it is reasonable to surmise that originally, in not a few cases, the content of such "equity"
decrees would reflect closely wishes and demands set
forth in the popular assembly which had chosen the
king. Due in great part to recent discoveries we can
now follow these decrees from Urukagina over Ur-
Nammu, Lipit-Ishtar, to Hammurabi and beyond. They
comprise what we traditionally call the Mesopotamian
law codes, including the most famous of them all, the
great Code of Hammurabi. But they are, of course, very
far from being codes in the proper sense of the word,
codifications of existing law; rather, they are the opposite: statements of desirable modifications and changes
in the law meant to compete with and to supersede it
with the help of royal authority. The degree to which
in individual cases they were successful and were able
to win out against the ingrained traditional concepts
and formulations of the common law is at our present
stage of knowledge very much an open question.

While our sources for the royal "equity" decrees, the
"codes," have increased significantly and gratifyingly
in recent years, giving us better insight into what we
must now see as a powerful influence at work on the
common law from the outside, as it were; our sources
for the common law itself, court records, contracts, and
other legal documents, have shown no comparable
spectacular and significant gains. This is in many respects to be regretted, for one would imagine that
increased knowledge would show that also inside the
common law forces for change and development were
at work and that royal decrees were not the only source
of new law. One would in this connection think first,
perhaps, of the popular assemblies which served as
courts and of the opportunities they must have offered
for discussion and divergence of opinion among the
laymen who constituted their membership. Here if any-
where, one would surmise, new popular concepts of
right and wrong would have had a hearing and the
opportunity of making themselves felt.

But though such discussions may be surmised our
actual sources have hitherto been disappointingly silent
on this point and the court records which have come
down to us deal almost exclusively with the establishing
of the facts of the case, never touching on points of
law. It is therefore particularly fortunate that at least
one example of a court record setting forth in some
detail a discussion about a point of law should now
have turned up, and it is further gratifying that the case
involved should be one of homicide. For homicide is an
offense very differently viewed at different stages of
legal development and a trial for homicide will therefore tend to throw special light upon development and
achievements.

Text and Translation

The tablet here published, 2N-T.54, was found in
the course of the excavations of the scribal quarter by
the Oriental Institute and the University Museum, Philadelphia, in the second season of the Joint Expedition's
work in Nippur. It was lying on the floor of a room
TB 10, in a private house which, to judge by the latest
of the dated documents found in that stratum (II 1)
should belong to the early years of Rim-Sîn of Larsa.
The tablet was unfortunately not intact, the upper left
hand corner had been broken off anciently, and it was
therefore a great satisfaction to discover later that a
duplicate existed and had been published years ago by
Chiera (*PBS* VIII 173). This duplicate, which came
from the earlier excavations at Nippur, is now in Philadelphia. Though relatively small it happens to preserve
exactly the parts which are missing in the tablet found
later and it is, to judge from the writing, of approximately the same age. Noteworthy is the fact that it
gives a fuller version of the text in some places. . . .

[Translation]
[EDITOR'S NOTE—The transliteration of the text
has been omitted.]

Nanna-sig son of Lu-Enzu
Ku-Enlilla son of Ku-Nanna the barber
and Enlil-ennam slave of Adda-kalla the orchardman
killed
5 Lu-Inanna son of Lugal-uru-du the nishakku.
After Lu-Inanna son of Lugal-uru-du
had been put to death
they told
Nin-dada, daughter of Lu-Ninurta,
10 wife of Lu-Inanna,
that Lu-Inanna, her husband,
was killed.
Nin-dada, daughter of Lu-Ninurta,
opened not her mouth, covered it up.
15 Their case was taken
to Isin before the king.
King Ur-Ninurta
ordered their case
to be accepted for trial in the Assembly of Nippur.
20 Ur-gula, son of Lugal-ibila,
Dudu, the birdcatcher,
Ali-ellati, the client,
Puzu, son of Lu-Enzu,
Eluti, son of Tizkar-Ea,
25 Shesh-kalla, the potter,
Lugalkam, the orchardman,
Lugal-a-zida, son of Enzu-andul,

and Shesh-kalla, son of Shara-HAR,
addressed [the assembly]:

30 "As men who have killed men
   they are not live men,
   the males [all] three of them and that woman
   before the chair of Lu-Inanna, son of Lugal-uru-du,
       the nishakku,
   shall be killed" they said.
35 Shuqalilum, the ERIN-GAL-GAL, sergeant of
       Ninurta, and
   Ubar-Enzu, the orchardman,
   addressed [the assembly] as follows:
   "Nin-dada, daughter of Lu-Ninurta,
   may have killed her husband;
40 but what can a woman do in [such a matter]
   that she is to be killed?" they said.
   In the Assembly of Nippur
   it [i.e., the assembly] addressed them as follows:
   "A woman who values not her husband
45 may give information to his enemy and thus
   he [i.e., the enemy] may [be able to] kill her
       husband.
   That her husband is killed
   he [i.e., the enemy] may [then] let her hear
   —why should he not thus make her keep silent
       about him?—
50 *She* [more than anyone else] killed her husband,
   her guilt is greater than [theirs:] that they killed a
       man"
   they said.
   In the Assembly of Nippur,
   the matter having been solved,
55 Nanna-sig, son of Lu-Enzu,
   Ku-Enlilla, son of Ku-Nanna, the barber,
   Enlil-ennam, slave of Adda-kalla, the orchardman,
   and Nin-dada, daughter of Lu-Ninurta, wife of Lu-
       Inanna,
   were delivered up to be killed.

60 Case accepted for trial in the Assembly of Nippur.

*Notes to "An Ancient Mesopotamian
Trial for Homicide"*

1. The first fourteen lines of the case record contain
a concise summary of the facts of the case. Note that
these facts are fashioned to reflect the conclusions of
the court *after* hearing the case.

2. The title of the victim, Nu-Es-Se indicates that he
was a high ranking priest.

3. One of the three defendants, Enlil-Ennam, was a
slave. It is interesting to note that he collaborated with
two free men and was tried together with them, apparently on an identical basis.

4. Note that the case was first brought before the
king, who assigned it for trial before the assembly.
Apparently, the king was in charge of the administration of justice and assigned cases for trial.

5. The accusations against the accused were made
by private citizens. There were, apparently, no official
prosecutors.

6. The decision, holding the wife guilty as an acces-
sory or conspirator although she did not directly kill
her husband, resembles section 153 of the Code of
Hammurabi. That section provides for execution by
impalement, but the records of the case simply state
that the wife was "delivered up to be killed," without
specifying the method of execution. There is also no
indication of who carried out the verdict, and no mention that the executioners or the accusers were relatives
of the victim.

7. The case was tried by assembly. In the Bible, too,
the assembly, or elders, wielded considerable power.
Thus, when Moses and Aaron first came to Egypt to
carry out their assignment by God to lead the Israelites
out of slavery, the first ones they spoke to were the
elders of Israel.[57] Similarly, mention is made of the
seventy elders who wielded influence and were granted
still greater authority by Moses.[58] In practice, an "assembly" in Israel also tried criminal cases and appears
to have included persons who acted as accusers and
defenders, as well as those who rendered the decision.[59]

The term "assembly," as used in the Bible, is also
utilized to refer to courts and other appliers of law, not
simply to gatherings of the local male population: "The
murderer shall not be killed until he stands before the
assembly for justice"; "The assembly shall save the murderer from the avenger of blood and the assembly shall
return him to the city of refuge in which he fled."[60]

6. RAPE, ADULTERY, AND SEDUCTION

a. SEX OFFENSES IN SUMERIAN LAWS
   (By J. J. Finkelstein)*

The first two contributions to the Landsberger Festschrift, *Assyriological Studies* No. 16 (1965), offer

57. Exod. 4:29.
58. Num. 11:16–29.
59. Jer. 26. Similar references are found in Ezek. 16:40;
23:40–47. See also Exod. 18:13–27; Deut. 16:18–13; Deut. 19:
11–21; also, Deut. 21:18–21, regarding a judgment by the
"elders of the city" for a rebellious son; Deut. 22:15, which
also refers to the "elders of the city", rather than to "the
judge"; and Deut. 25:1–3, Deut. 24:5–10, with its references
to the judicial function of the "elders of the city." See also
Jer. 34:8; De Vaux, *Ancient Israel, supra* 152–53.
60. Num. 35:12, 24, 25; See also, Amos 1:15; Zach. 8:16;
See also the trial of Susannah and the Elders, in the Book of
Susannah.
*From *Journal of the American Oriental Society* 86 (1966).

significant additions to two of the Sumerian law "codes" which have thus far been known only in fragmentary form. . . . The following study will limit itself to one of the fragments published by Civil. . . .

References to the cuneiform law-"codes" are abbreviated herein as follows: LUN = Laws of Ur-Nammu (main ed., Kramer, *Or* 23 [1954] pp. 40–48 with Pls. VI–VII); LLI = Laws of Lipit-Ishtar (main ed. F. R. Steele, *AJA* 52 [1948] 3–28, pls. I–VII); LE = Laws of Eshnunna (main ed. A. Goetze, *AASOR* XXXI [1956]); LH = Laws of Hammurapi (cited after Driver & Miles, *The Babylonian Laws*, vol. II [1955]); MAL = Middle Assyrian Laws (cited after Driver & Miles, *The Assyrian Laws* [1935]); HL = Hittite Laws (cited after Friedrich, *Die Hethitischen Gesetze* [1959]).

The Texts

We will first present here for convenience the transliterations and translations of the texts in question [EDITOR'S NOTE—The transliteration has been omitted], anticipating our conclusions by departing from the translations first given by the authors of the original publications, in favor of the rendering of the key terms to be advocated below:

Lipit-Ishtar § 33

If a man has declared that an undeflowered daughter of a [free-born] man has experienced sexual intercourse, and it is then proved that she had not experienced sexual intercourse, he [the accuser] must pay ten shekels of silver.

U. 7739 § 2

If a man proceeded by force, and deflowered the virgin [lit., undeflowered] slave-woman of a[nother] man, that man must pay five shekels of silver.

Contextual Evidence

. . . The extant law-"codes" are much concerned, on the other hand, with extramarital sexual behavior, particularly with the offenses of rape or seduction. These rules are pertinent to the present discussion, and are now reviewed here:

1. LE 26. This is the case where a young woman, engaged to be married (*terhatam ubil* "[the suitor] had brought the bride-price"), but still apparently living (until she would have come of age) in her parents' house, was raped and deflowered (*ittaqab/p-si*) by another man. Inasmuch as for legal purposes betrothal is as sacrosanct as a marriage already consummated, the violator is in this instance subject to the death penalty. This case is exactly paralleled by

2. LH 130. This case too is an act of rape (*ukabbilsi* "[the attacker] gagged her") upon a "married"

woman, who was still virgin (*sa zikaram la idu*) and still dwelling with her parents. In other words, the status of the woman is that of being betrothed, which, as in LE 26, renders the attacker liable to the death penalty. The difference between LE 26 and LH 130 is merely one of greater or lesser explicitness—LH 130 adding the details that the woman was still living with her parents, and that under the circumstances of the attack she is innocent of any blame, both of which are plainly implied in LE 26 as well—and in the choice of words to denote the virgin state of the woman before the attack. . . .

3. LE 31. "If a man has deflowered the slave-girl of a[nother] man, he must pay one-third of a mina [i.e., 20 shekels] of silver, the slave-girl remaining the property of her master." The existence of this rule proves that violation of young slave-girls of other persons was no less a matter of legal concern to the "jurists" of the Old Babylonian period and earlier than the rape of young women of free birth. As Goetze has already noted, the relatively high penalty imposed on the attacker must be construed as at least a partial compensation to the girl's master for the reduction in her value should her master have contemplated selling her or giving her away in marriage. . . .

4. M(iddle) A(ssyrian) L(aws) § 55. This case is one of rape of an unmarried and unbetrothed virgin. The girl's status, her physiological state before the attack, and the circumstances under which the attack occurred are set out by the "jurist" with the greatest of care, in the most explicit manner possible. . . . The girl is first described as a *batultu*, "virgin," an age distinction defining her as "pre-nubile" and only implicitly, therefore, untouched. She is then more explicitly described as not yet having been deflowered, nor taken in marriage. After further specifying that her father's estate had been under no obligation or lien—thus anticipating and heading off any possible justification on such a basis by the attacker—the text goes on to specify certain locations or circumstances in which the attack occurred: "whether in the city or in the open country; at nighttime in the public streets . . . ; in the public granary . . . ; or at the time of a town holiday. . . ." It will be shown below that the specification of these places and circumstances is not random, but is of juristic significance to the case. The last set of statements of the protasis of the case makes it explicit that the attack was a clear case of rape, and that there was no suggestion of consent on the part the girl. Inasmuch as the girl was unbetrothed at the time, the death penalty does not come into consideration as it did in the parallel rape cases in LE and LH. The heart of the penalty in the present instance provides for the forced marriage of the attacker—in the event that he was not

already married, and at the discretion of the girl's father —to the girl with deprivation of the right of divorce, or to pay the "virgin's third (of a mina of silver)" to the girl's father. In the event that the attacker was married only the second alternative was available. We may safely ignore—as a piece of typically Assyrian, moralistic "calculated frightfulness"—the further stipulation by which the wife of the attacker is to be handed over to the father of the raped girl for (sexual) degradation, then to be retained by him, either as a slave or concubine. Two of the elements in MAL 55, the specification of the places where the attack might have occurred, and the possibility of the forced marriage of the attacker to his victim as a consequence, immediately suggest that other extant "case laws" belong in the same context, namely,

5. YBT I 28 rev. v 3–25. . . . [EDITOR'S NOTE— The transliteration has been omitted.]

Section "a"

If [someone] deflowered the daughter of a free citizen in the street, and her father and her mother *did not know it*, and she/he [then] tells her father and her mother: ". . . . . ," her father and her mother may give her to him as a wife.

Section "b"

If [someone] deflowered the daughter of a free citizen in the street, [and] her father and her mother knew, and the "deflowerer" denied that he knew, [and] he [then], standing at the temple gate, swore . . . ." . . .

6. A Trial at Nippur, 3N-T403+T340. This text, together with two other fragments, T273 and T426, forms a "Sammeltafel" which includes the celebrated murder trial at Nippur. Professor Jacobsen has generously made available to me his transliteration and translation, which are utilized here [EDITOR'S NOTE—The transliteration has been omitted]:

Lugalmelam, son of Nanna'aramugi seized Ku(?)-Ninsubur, slave-girl of Kuguzana, brought her into the KI-LAM building, and deflowered her. After he had deflowered her, Kuguzana, her owner applied [for legal redress] to, and addressed the assembly of Nippur: "[*Lugalmel*]*am* seized my slave-girl, brought her into the KI-LAM building and deflowered her," he declared. Lugalmelam [then] addressed [the assembly]: "I did not *seize* his slave-girl, nor did I deflower her" he declared. His [i.e., Kuguzana's] witnesses appeared and confirmed it [i.e., the charge of Kuguzana]. The assembly of Nippur addressed [the litigants]: "Because he deflowered the slave-girl without [her] owner['s knowledge], Lugalmelam is to pay

½ mina of silver to Kuguzana her owner" *they* declared. The assembly instituted for them the judicial process. . . .

It is obvious that we have here an actual case of the type anticipated by U. 7739 § 2, and by LE 31. . . .

Equally of interest is the place where the offense was stated to have been committed, the e-KI-LAM, which seems to have been some kind of grain-storage building. This immediately calls to mind the *bit qarete* of MAL 55, as one of the likely places where such an attack could occur. It serves to reinforce our view that this trial, and the "code" cases discussed here, all belong to the same context.

From the juridical point of view it may be worth mentioning that the trial does not discuss the question of whether the slave-girl was raped or was a willing partner in the offense. This is unquestionably to be explained by the fact that in the eyes of Mesopotamian law, consent in such cases is immaterial; the slave-girl is not considered a legal person. Hence, her sexual violation, whether by rape, seduction, or even by her own solicitation, is exclusively considered as a tortious invasion against her owner, for which he may seek redress, if the act had been done without *his* consent or knowledge. Notable too is the wide discrepancy in compensation, between the half-mina of silver of the Nippur trial, which thus exceeds even the ⅓ mina prescribed in LE 31, and the nominal fine of five shekels of U. 7739 § 2. Unless the latter text is assumed to be in error in this respect, the explanation would lie in the fact that the Nippur case is one that came to trial, and that, furthermore, the defendant had denied his guilt, necessitating the calling of witnesses. For thus putting the court to greater expense, the damages the defendant was made to pay were probably augmented by a penal component designed to include "legal costs." The assessed sum may also have included an amount in compensation for loss of the potential "bride-price" to the girl's owner, as was the case in LE 31. The sum of five shekels in U. 7739 may represent, then, the fixed payment applicable in such instances when resort is not had to the law-courts, but settled privately.

The interpretation of YBT I 28 v, "a" and "b."

In my treatment of this text above, I postponed the coming to grips with the specific legal understanding of the two cases, and the differences between them. To these questions we may now return.

The specification that the offense occurred "in the street" is not a chance locution of the scribe; it must be understood as deliberate, and as bearing social and judicial implications. In dealing with this subject the other "law codes" similarly make explicit the circumstances of the offense. MAL 55 offers the most extensive catalogue of locales and circumstances: in town or out in the country; at nighttime in the public streets; in the town granary; during the town festival. What is the purpose of such a list of specifications? The answer leaves no room for doubt; these circumstances are meant to indicate that there could be no *a priori* presumption of rape on the part of the man or of consent on the part of the girl. Whether one or the other was the case must be determined on some other basis; the circumstances themselves are "neutral" in this respect, but would favor the man's claim of "mistaken identity" unless other facts indicated otherwise. That this view is the correct one is indicated by other cases in MAL. Thus MAL 12, concerning the rape of a married woman, starts out by stating that the woman was "passing along the street" (*ina rībēte tētetiq*). The writer, by so describing her deportment at the time of the attack, thus consciously indicates that the woman was engaged on a legitimate errand, that she was not "strolling" or "loitering" or in any other manner luring the stranger to her. The next section, MAL 13, by its very wording, suggests the opposite; here the woman had "gone out of her house" and gone to the house of another man. The circumstances themselves delineate the fact that the case is one of adultery, for which the woman will be put to death, and her paramour too, if it is proved that he knew her to be a married woman. The next rule, MAL 14, situates the offense in the street or at an inn, which, taken together, implies that the woman was intent on committing adultery, but sets up on the part of the man a valid plea that he was ignorant of the married status of the woman, which—if he could establish that fact—would exonerate him. An inn, or the street (in which the woman could be presumed to have been "loitering"), creates the opportunity for the chance encounter, in which the man might well have remained ignorant of the woman's status, a claim that would not have been very convincing if the offense occurred in the man's own house. . . .

It is only against this background that LH 141 and 143 may be understood. In 141, a woman bent on "going out of doors," while accumulating her private little "nest egg" at her husband's expense, may be divorced by him without settlement or turned into a slave. There is an implied suspicion of infidelity, but no clear proof was forthcoming. But if this propensity in the wife was aggravated by her refusing to her husband his conjugal rights, which is the case envisaged in LH 143, then she may suffer the death penalty; the presumption of adulterous conduct in this case on the part of the wife becomes more pronounced and decisive, even if positive proof of adultery is still absent.

It is quite clear that in the Mesopotamian view, Babylonian as well as Assyrian, the proper place for

women was in the home; for a woman to be out-of-doors, except on the most necessary business, or in the company of her husband, was to give occasion for suspicion and temptation. MAL 40, with its provision for the veiling of married women, including concubines and married hierodules, when they appear in public, and the simultaneous prohibition of this mark of respectability to bonafide prostitutes and the like, on pain of severe punishment, is but an index of the professed social concern for moral conduct on the part of respectable women. Yet despite these ideals, the practice often fell short of them—as is true of all societies. Especially young unmarried girls, even of good family, were given to going about in public—as the young town belles have been wont to do in all ages and places, despite the best intentions of parents. Such a propensity need not have been prompted in most cases by ulterior motives or desires, but only by a more or less innocent exuberance resulting from newly discovered vanity. That this was the case is shown by another section of the *ardat lilī* text cited above, Sm. 49+752 rev. i 5 ff. . . .

"The maid (i.e., the *ardat lilī*), who does not promenade along the roads and streets together with the [normal] maidens."

In other words, it was more or less expected that nubile young ladies would parade in public—with greater or lesser innocence of design—with or without their parents' approval. That this activity would on occasion result in a situation calling for legal adjudication was presumably also to be expected.[61] The goal of the law on such occasions is to determine the relative degree of culpability of either party. Was it a case of rape or one of consent on the part of the girl? Was the offending male guilty of deliberate seduction of an innocent young female, or could he legitimately claim

---

61. Witness what happened to Dinah, the daughter of Jacob who "went out to visit the daughters of the land" (Gen. 34: 1 ff.) a common enough situation that is not essentially different from that of the *ardat lili* passage just cited. Nor is it at all clear that Shechem really "attacked" her in a way that constituted real rape (cf. 2 Sam. 13:14, where Amnon "overpowered" Tamar—and, then—in predictable psychological terms—immediately "hated" her) for he wanted to marry her. The Midrashic authors were fully sensitive to the overtones of the verb *yasa* in this story, as their amplifications of it clearly show; see L. Ginzburg, *Legends of the Jews* I, 395; V, 298 f., 193, 313 f., 285.

It is noteworthy that at the end of the story, Genesis 34:31, Simon and Levi attempt to justify their massacre of the Shechemites by saying: "Should our sister have been treated like a whore?" which the Targum renders only here *nafqat bara*, literally "one who goes outside," revealing clearly an appreciation of the verb *yasa* of 34:1 by the Targum, in all its overtones. In Aramaic, then in postbiblical Hebrew, and colloquially, *nafqa'/h* is the precise term for "whore." Aram. *nafqa'* may therefore well be a direct reflex of Akk. *wasitum* in the Proto-diri text just cited.

that he had mistaken her for a prostitute? These are the circumstances which, in my view, constitute the basis of the two rules of YBT I 28, sections "a" and "b." As in the cases from MAL and LH just cited, it will be noted that the "jurist" tends to indicate the direction of the initial presumption by the very choice of phraseology used to describe the circumstances of the offending act.

The first fact, which prevailed in both cases, was that the girl was *in the street* at the time she was allegedly accosted and attacked. As in MAL 55, this factor establishes the basic ambiguity over whether the case was one of rape, seduction, or consent by the girl; the territory is "neutral" in this respect. The next factor to be considered is the knowledge or ignorance of some fact on the part of the girl's parents. It is here submitted that this factor is *the knowledge or ignorance by the parents that their daughter was out on the streets.* In section "a" it is established that the parents were ignorant of this fact, and this eliminates from consideration the element of possible contributory negligence on the part of the parents.[62] That this is not explicitly spelled out in the text may be attributed to the disjointed character of the text as a whole, or explained as an elliptical construction. In other words, the circumstances in case "a" must be understood as tending to establish the culpability of the seducer/attacker. Line 9 presents apparently insoluble difficulties in interpretation, but there can be no doubt that its force must be to similarly establish the culpability of the man. I therefore prefer to take it as a quotation of a statement made

by the girl to her parents to the effect that she was "raped." If the quotation is understood as something spoken by the man, then it can only be construed as a claim of extenuating circumstances, such as "mistaken identity," etc. But that would tend to establish a counterweight to the first circumstance as I have interpreted it, and this would go against all canons of hypothetical case statement in the Mesopotamian "law codes." For the circumstances of such cases are set out, not to test the ingenuity or perspicacity of the judge, or the adroitness of the "lawgiver"—which would have been the case if the factors tended to draw the judgment in opposite directions—but as cumulative reinforcement of the inevitable and unambiguously just decision. Thus in this case, the second factor—the declaration in line 9—must tend to reinforce the established factor of the innocence of the girl's parents of any contributory negligence, and the decision that goes with it: the parents may compel the seducer/attacker to marry the girl, which is precisely the same judgment as in MAL 55 when the attacker there was previously unmarried.

In section "b," the determining factors are the reverse of those in section "a." In the first place, the parents are here stated to have known [that their daughter was out on the streets]. This immediately sets up a circumstantial "climate" unfavorable to the girls' parents, for they thus become guilty of negligent conduct in permitting their daughter to be in the street. The second factor is a denial by the alleged attacker/seducer of certain knowledge. Here, I suggest, the ignorance claimed by the man is of the true status of the girl, i.e., that he did not know she was a virgin of good family, but had mistaken her for a prostitute. Once more this complete statement is not made explicit, but must be understood elliptically. It is in fact parallel to the decisive factor in MAL 14, 16, and especially 24, where the alleged adulterer established a legitimate claim of ignorance of the married status of the woman, in which case he is exonerated. In our section "b" the man must first swear an oath at the temple, upon completion of which—it will be noted that the text sets the oath procedure out as a series of preterite verbs, which implies that this condition was already fulfilled in that hypothetical case—it must be assumed that the man would be declared free of any obligation to the girl or her parents. This judgment is not included in the text; its omission may easily be explained this time as due to the nature of the tablet as a whole, as disjointed and consisting of loosely strung phraseology. This case too finds its parallel in MAL 24, where the man in whose home a married woman was found denied that he knew that his own wife had been harboring the runaway wife of another man. In these circumstances, the man will go free if he agrees to undergo the river ordeal.

62. From the series of goring-ox rules in LH 250–52, it can be demonstrated that Mesopotamian "jurists" were conscious of the principle of contributory negligence, although this has thus far remained unrecognized. Once more, the perception of the fact requires close attention to the wording of the case, in this instance § 250. Here the ox gored a man to death "as it was walking along the street." This specification is legally significant, but not in the sense in which Driver and Miles (I 442) attempt to interpret it "[the ox] has broken loose." It implies rather that the animal was behaving as it was supposed to, being marched along the road by whoever was in charge of it. It was the victim, by his own carelessness, who got in the animal's way, and was gored to death as a result. It is this fact of contributory negligence, then, that frees the owner of the ox of any possible liability, which would otherwise be inexplicable. And this interpretation is proved by the next rule, § 251, where it is the owner (or the one who was marching the animal) who is held liable for negligent conduct, in not having screened or padded the animal's horns, and for not having reined the animal to keep it marching directly along the road, which is the denotation of *sunnuqu.* This is proved by the LE parallel to this rule, § 54, where, at the end of text A iv, line 16, one must read GUD-*su la u⟨-se⟩-si-ir* "he did not keep his ox in the direct march," but presumably let the animal stray all over the street. The biblical parallel case, Exodus 21:29, "[the owner] did not guard him" (verb *samar*), while seemingly very general, may have had quite as specific a connotation in the context as the Mesopotamian rules.

We may now, therefore, conclude the discussion of the two rules in YBT I 28 rev. v 3 ff. by offering the following translations:

Section "a"

If [someone] deflowered the daughter of a free citizen in the street, her father and mother being ignorant [of the fact that she was in the street], and *she* [then] says to her father and her mother: "*I was raped*," her father and her mother may give her to him as a wife.

Section "b"

If [someone] deflowered the daughter of a free citizen in the street, her father and mother having known [that she was in the street], and her seducer [lit., "deflowerer"] denied that he knew [the girl to have been of free-born status], and swore an oath [to that effect] standing at the temple gate, [he shall be free of any obligation to the parents of the girl].

The distinction in judgment between the two cases may be understood in the following terms: case "a" is considered, on the basis of evidence and testimony, as tantamount to an instance of rape, hence the right of the girl's parents to insist on the marriage—it must also be tacitly understood that the parents, at their discretion, may request compensation for the "virgin's price" from the fellow in lieu of his marrying her, the alternative explicitly made available in MAL 55. Case "b," on the other hand, is adjudged as an instance of consent, in which the parents are presumed to have shared by their permissiveness in their daughter's being abroad, the case being clinched in favor of the man, by his declaration on oath that he was ignorant of the girl's true status. We assume, too, that the man is free of any monetary obligation towards the girl's parents, because of the factor of negligence contributed by them to the circumstances of the mischance. Apart from this element, this case will be seen to correspond to MAL 56. There, too, the case is one in which an unmarried, unattached virgin, "willingly gives herself to a man." In that case, as in our case "b," the man must swear an oath to this effect (i.e., to the fact of consent on the girl's part, and that he presumably could not have known her true status, and thus mistook her for a prostitute), upon satisfaction of which he is liable only for (thrice?) the "virgin's price." That the parents may still exact that compensation, as contrasted with our case "b," must be due to the absence of any fault on their part.

The Treatment of Sexual Offenses in the Law Codes

A synoptic view of all the extant "statutory" rules dealing with extramarital (hetero-) sexual activity will disclose a polarization of all the hypothetical cases along two axes of legal import: whether the woman involved was married or unmarried—and for penal purposes unmarried but betrothed virgins are classed with married women—and whether the woman involved was coerced into the act or whether she was a consenting partner. (As noted above, the second distinction does not apply in the case of slave-girls, where consent or coercion is immaterial to the assessment of damages.) The accompanying simple chart illustrates the distribution of these cases among the "codes," with which the biblical evidence is also cited for comparison.

It will, of course, not be surprising that the laws are unanimous in their concern about adultery, which is treated with the utmost gravity,[63] the death penalty often being faced by the adulteress, her lover, or both, depending on the circumstances. By contrast, even rape of an unmarried woman seems to have been treated as a relatively mild offense, and except for the talionic element in MAL 55—providing for the privileged raping of the attacker's own wife—was considered only an economic injury to the girl's father—or master, where the victim was a slave-girl. The only penal element that may come into force in such instances is the right of the girl's parents to insist that the attacker/seducer marry her with forfeiture of the future right of divorce, and the possibly penal assessment of triple the standard "bride-price."

Another index of the relatively lenient view taken in Mesopotamia of sexual 'misconduct' by and with unmarried women is the paucity of 'cases' of this sort in the earlier "codes"; LH, still the most extensive of the extant "law codes," allots no space whatever to incidents of this kind, even for the case of rape. Incidents and accusations involving married women are, by contrast, treated in great detail. LH 155, 156, treating of a man's sexual relations with his daughter-in-law, may be viewed both as cases illustrating this general concern with married women, and as belonging to the category

---

63. It being understood that "adultery" in Mesopotamia—as elsewhere in the ancient Near East—can only be an offense by the wife against her husband; illicit sexual relations by a married man with another woman is not an offense of "adultery" against the man's own wife, but against the husband of the other woman. LH 142 states what is probably the maximum legal remedy available to the wife whose husband has brought shame upon her by being a *wasi* "a gadabout" (although it is not impossible that this denotation may imply homosexual behavior, just as Aram. *nafeq* is the male counterpart to *nafqah* "prostitute"), namely, she may take her dowry and return to her father's house, i.e., she may divorce him. But this is certainly considered an extreme measure, set off at first by the wife's refusal to have sexual relations with her husband, which the local authorities must look into. The seriousness of the situation is better shown by LH 143, where it is the wife who is proved to be the "gadabout," . . . for which offense she is to be drowned.

FIGURE 1

Married Women (including betrothed)	Unmarried Women
Coercive (rape)	
LE 26	YBT I 28 Par. "a"
LH 130	U.7739 Par. 2*
MAL 12, 23b	LE 31*
HL II 83a	MAL 55
Cf. Deut. 22:25	Cf. Lev. 19:20*
LH 155—(incestuous class: coercion presumed)	Deut. 22:28 f.
	Exod. 22:15 (seduction, i.e., "statutory rape")
	*These cases involve a slave-girl, where consent is therefore legally immaterial.
Consentive	
U.7739 (LUN) Par. 1	YBT I 28 Par. "b"
LE 28	MAL 56
LH 129, 133b	
MAL 13, 14, 15, 16, 23a, c	
HL II 83b	
Cf. also Lev. 20:10	
Deut. 22:22, 23 f.	
Accusation only:	Cf. Deut. 22:20 (ex post facto disclosure)
U.7739 Par. 10	Accusation only:
LH 127, 131, 132	LLI 33 (N 1791)
MAL 17	

of incestuous relations, within which group of rules these two cases are placed. MAL emphasizes its recognition of the distinction in kind between sexual misconduct involving married women and those involving unmarried women, by isolating its two rules concerning the latter towards the end of the text (§§ 55–56), far removed from the group treating of married women.[64]

Accusations, especially when they are unsubstantiated, are a popular topos in the "code" since they serve so well to exemplify the "lawgiver's" zealous concern for strict justice: "You shall do to him exactly as he plotted to do to his brother."[65] The unsubstan-

tiated accusation of sexual misconduct becomes therefore a standard permutation in those groups of rules relating to sexual conduct, as, e.g., LH 131–32 and MAL 17–18, all concerning married women, and MAL 19, accusation of homosexuality against a man (cf. MAL 20). LLI 33 (N 1791) is the first occurrence of the case of such an accusation against an unmarried woman. In this instance the charge proved unfounded, for which the slanderer is assessed a fine of ten shekels. Deuteronomy 22:13 ff. provides the only parallel to this rule, but that case deals only with such an accusation brought ex-post facto by a husband against his newly married bride. The enormous fine of one hundred shekels which he must pay to the bride's father, and forfeiture of the right of divorce forever, if the charge is disproved—by comparison with which the ten shekel fine in LLI 33 seems almost trivial—is explained only as measure of the gravity of the charge, which, had it been proved true, would have resulted in the execution of the young bride. What punishment might have been meted out to the girl if the accusation had been sub-

64. This is but another indication of the greater juristic sophistication of MAL than all earlier "codes" including LH, which is more clearly exemplified by underscoring the criminal element in numerous cases which in earlier codes remain strictly within the realm of tort, by adding to the penalties a term of hard labor for the crown. (This is a remarkable provision when it is recalled that term sentences to prison or hard labor as specific punishments for crimes was an innovation in Western society only of the nineteenth century.)

65. Deuteronomy 19:19 f. Although not stated explicitly, as in the biblical statement, the same principle is implied in the juxtaposition of LH 3–4, following LH 1–2, involving false

witness in capital cases. Compare now U. 7740 §§ 34–5 (AS 16 pp. 17–18 obv. v. 34 ff.).

stantiated was probably not considered in the Lipit-Ishtar Laws, since this was a matter strictly within the discretion of her father, and not a matter of formal "law."

It will be observed also that the cases in all the "law codes" are derived from a comparatively limited repertory of circumstances (i.e., seduction, rape, consent) and statuses of the women involved (i.e., unmarried, betrothed, married, free, slave). The different "law codes" combine selected elements among these in constructing the hypothetical cases they choose to exemplify, but the fund always seems to be the same, whether the language used be Sumerian, Akkadian, and to a somewhat lesser degree, Hittite, and even the biblical "codes." None of the codes attempts to combine these elements in anything approaching an exhaustive series of possible permutations. The Middle Assyrian Laws treat the subject at greater length than the other collections, but this is due to the circumstance that the main extant tablet of these laws is just about completely devoted to the subject: "women" in various legal contexts, so that it is only natural that the topic of sexual offenses would play a greater role than it does in the other law "codes." Can therefore any principle be detected by which the several "codes" select some but not others of the possible sets of permutations? While for the most part it is difficult to detect any consistent principles governing these choices, it is possible to note certain tendencies, which apply not only in the case of sexual offenses, but for the construction of the "codes" in general. As already suggested above, the "codes" avoid presenting cases in which the attendant circumstances would tend to lead the verdict in opposite directions. While in day-to-day litigation ambiguity as to the right and wrongs of any given case was probably the norm, it is precisely the opposite of ambiguity of "the law" which the "codes" were intended to illustrate. These documents were not designed as exercises in legal casuistry, but as exemplifications of the meting out of justice, based on the presupposition or ideal that the "true" verdict is always hypothetically known or knowable, and that it requires only the dedication of the king and his officials, including the judges, to implement it whenever the occasion arises. . . .

If we turn once again to the chart of the "law-code" cases dealing with the sexual offenses, we may detect how the foregoing principle is exemplified in it. It will be noted that there is some sort of correlation between the two axes: married-unmarried, coercion-consent. Thus consent and unmarried women rarely occur together, the only totally unambiguous instance being MAL 56. The rape of unmarried women, on the other women, on the other hand—including "statutory" as well as actual rape—is more frequently dealt with, and

for this purpose, as we shall see, LH 130 and LE 26 must be grouped with the unmarried category. With married women, the correlation is reversed. Here instances of consent—understood as intentional adultery —appreciably outnumber cases of rape, especially if, as just suggested, LH 130 and LE 26 are removed from this group to that of unmarried women. What does this signify? The correlations, it would appear to me, are based on the experience of daily life. Unmarried women, even when betrothed, were usually minors, sexually speaking, since with the advent of their nubility they would soon have been married or, if already betrothed, have their marriage consummated. On strictly physiological grounds, therefore, it would have been unusual for a girl in this age group to seek sexual experience on her own initiative. In other words the combination of unmarried woman and the element of consent was a most unlikely one purely as an empirical matter. Young girls in this age group, however, were not immune to rape or seduction by strange men, especially under circumstances where men may have mistaken innocent coquetry for an invitation.

With married women, on the other hand, a consentive situation is more readily envisaged, whatever the safeguards established by the society to prevent its occurrence, as, e.g., veiling. Rape plays a lesser role, therefore, in such a situation, although it is by no means ruled out as a possible occurrence. The choice of cases in each of the "codes" dealing with the sexual offenses illustrates this fundamental dichotomy. Thus, it was noted earlier that LH ignores sexual offenses against unmarried women, and deals only with the rape of a betrothed girl. This choice is therefore dictated by two considerations: (*a*) the rape of unmarried, unbetrothed girls does not interest the drafter, since this would have been a trivial offense at best. (*b*) The drafter *is* interested in presenting an instance of rape. For this purpose he chooses a case in which the girl is betrothed— which turns the legal issue from that of a financial injury to the girl's father, to the more serious one of invasion of the domain of the future husband, entailing the death penalty for the attacker. (*c*) It is only by presenting an instance of this kind (where the raped woman was only betrothed) that the drafter may then neatly balance the picture by a selection of circumstances illustrating guilt on the part of the woman—the crime of adultery—which similarly entails the death penalty if substantiated, e.g., LH 129, 133b. . . .

. . . That a mere fine is assessed in LLI 33 is more readily understandable, since the case concerns an unmarried girl, and the offense would not have been grave even if the charge had been proved. The fine of 15 shekels against the false accuser in U. 7739 § 10, seems, however, surprisingly mild, for if the accusation had been substantiated, it would have entailed the conviction and death of the woman at one and the same time. But the interesting phenomenon is that even LH falls short of demanding the death penalty for the false accuser in this instance. Note that LH 3–4 establishes the doctrine that the penalty for false accusation will parallel the penalty that would have been paid by the accused had the charge been proved: the capital penalty in the capital case, pecuniary penalties according to the various possible claims. LH 1, dealing with the false charge of sorcery, and LH 2, dealing with criminal homicide, explicitly establish that doctrine for these charges. It is all the more significant, therefore, that LH tacitly excludes the death penalty in the case of an unproven charge of adultery, prescribing only, by § 127, the scourging of the accuser, and the shaving of his head-hair as a mark of ignomy, which is essentially duplicated for a similar charge by MAL 18. From this, I believe, we are authorized to conclude that however strongly the "codes," such as LUN, LE, LH, and MAL, express themselves on the subject of adultery, it was *de facto* not a capital crime, if indeed it was technically a "crime" at all, in the sense that the "state" would have undertaken the prosecution, as in the case of sorcery and at least some categories of homicide. For both LH 129 and MAL 15—and despite the apparently uncompromising wording of LE 26, 28—explicitly blunt the edge of their prescription of the capital penalty for the adultress by giving the husband the widest latitude in prosecution: by LH 129, if he spares his wife, then the state will spare the "other man"; MAL 15 allows the same latitude (restore, with Driver and Miles, *AL* p. 388 and in lines 56–1, respectively) but adds the privilege of mutilations (—an Assyrian characteristic, at least in words), and HL II 84 reflects a similar view in Anatolia. In other words, adultery, in ancient Mesopotamia was not quite the serious offense it would seem at first glance from a reading of the "codes." It was at bottom a civil invasion of a husband's domain, and it was left to him to take as serious or as lenient a view of the matter as he chose; in practice the inclination was towards the less severe view.[66]

Thus the assessment of a fine of fifteen shekels against the false accuser by Ur-Nammu's law is not at all extraordinary, and is probably a closer approximation of what actually was the prevailing practice in such instances than the penalties envisaged by the parallel rules in the other "codes."

We come back finally to the question of the sequence of the rules about sexual offenses in the Laws of Ur-Nammu. We cannot speak about what rules may have preceded U.7739 § 1, since the Nippur text is almost totally lost at that point. In other words, on the basis of the extant material we cannot be certain that LUN included a case of rape against a married woman, or against a virgin free-born woman. At all events, § 2, the rape of a slave-girl, apparently concluded the section about adultery and rape (i.e., consent: coercion), for the next group of rules deals with divorce, followed by about four sections of unknown content.[67] It is fairly clear then, that § 10, was not considered as a permutation of the class "adultery-rape," as it is in LH, but as belonging to a different class or subgroup of rules, perhaps one which was organized around the subject of false accusation requiring the ordeal, but since the extant material is again fragmentary following § 10, a more definitive assessment of the arrangement principle of the LUN rules relating to sexual conduct will have to await recovery of additional portions of the text.

b. A Textbook Case of Adultery in Ancient Mesopotamia
(By Samuel Greengus)*

. . . J. van Dijk republished a Sumerian document, earlier published by him in *Sumer* 15 (1959), 12–14, which records a divorce proceeding between a husband and wife. While both background events and court

---

66. In the statutory codes of most modern societies, adultery is not a crime, and even where it is, as e.g. the French Code Pénal, Art. 324 (quoted from W. Seagle, *The Quest for Law* 406 f. 2), and those codes based on it, the aim is primarily to justify as privileged the slaying of either party by the husband who catches them *in flagrante*, which more or less is the aim of MAL 15a, and is, *de jure* or *de facto*, an almost universal privilege; cf. E. A. Hoebel, *The Law of Primitive Man* 286. Apart from this—usually very circumscribed—privilege, adultery is usually no more than grounds for the husband to seek a divorce (which, in modern legal systems, is also a right of the wife against her husband), and in primitive law systems, an occasion for fines and/or compensations, to the "State" and to the injured husband, respectively; cf. P. Bohannon, *Justice and*

Judgment among the Tiv, p. 83 ff., and M. Gluckman, *The Judicial Process among the Barotse of Northern Rhodesia*, pp. 37, 64 f., 130 ff. and esp. 217: ". . . an adulterous woman (must) pay a fine (to the state) or go to prison, and thus be guilty by our standards of a 'crime'; while the adulterer pays higher 'civil' damages to her husband and is thus . . . guilty of a 'delict.' " Cf. in general; also Diamond, *Primitive Law*, p. 325.

67. § 5 is on the one hand a permutation of § 4, and a variation of LE 27 on the other. The rule states that a man who slept with a widow without (prior) contract need not pay her anything. This can mean only that the context is one of "divorce" and is contrasted with § 4, where a widow, who is divorced after a presumably legal marriage, is entitled to a half-mina of silver. The rule, in other words, is designed to illustrate the legal nullity of a "common-law" arrangement with a widow, by stating the consequence to the woman in the contingency of divorce under those circumstances, i.e., she would not be entitled to any claim for "divorce-money." The converse of this is the implication of LE 27–28, that in the event the woman then slept with another man, the "husband" could bring no charge of adultery against her.

*From *Hebrew Union College Annual* (1970).

proceedings are described in unusually vivid detail, the absence of gender determination in Sumerian raises the problem of determining just which of the parties is plaintiff and defendant. According to van Dijk, the text records how the husband, caught by his wife while engaged in a homosexual act, was brought before the court and penalized. The marriage was dissolved and the wife awarded divorce-money while the malfeasant husband was punished by having his pudendum shaven and being led naked through the streets of the city. According to van Dijk's interpretation, the document also records that the husband, prior to his being caught, had arranged for the support and maintenance of his wife and that he had also performed the marriage rites of anointing and veiling; these background events were recalled in the document allegedly to refute the husband's defense plea that he was in fact not legally married to his wife at the time of his crime. This interpretation of the case thus assumes that the husband is the defendant and that the wife is the injured party seeking redress.

It is our purpose in this article to offer another interpretation of the text which would reverse the picture: we would see a husband seizing his wife in *flagrante delicto* with another man; the wife, being an adulteress, is the defendant and the party suffering the penalties. We read the text as follows [EDITOR'S NOTE—The transliteration has been omitted]:

(1) Estar-ummi
        daughter of Ili-asu
        did Irra-malik
        take in marriage.
(5) In the first place,
        she burglarized his storeroom.
        In the second place,
        in his oil jar
        she made an opening and
(10)   covered it up with a cloth.
        In the third place,
        he caught her upon a man;
        to the body of the man on the bed
        he tied her
(15)   [and] carried her to the assembly.
        The assembly,
        because with a man upon her [sic]
        she was caught,
        his/her divorce money . . .
(20)   [they] decided;
        . . . [her] pudendum
        they shaved;
        they bored her nose with an arrow
        [and] to be led around the city

(25)   the king
        gave her over.
        It is a decision of the king.
        Isme-Dagan-zimu
        was deputy.

Lines 1–4 record the fact that Irra-malik, the husband, married Ili-asu; the meaning of these lines is the same regardless of whether one follows van Dijk's interpretation or our own. Lines 5–10, however, appear in our view to be a series of charges against the defendant rather than a sequence of marriage rites, whose recollection in this record would seem to be superfluous since lines 1–4 already state that Irra-malik married Ili-asu.

We see altogether (ll. 5–15) three charges against the defendant wife: the second more serious than the first and the third the most serious of all. The first offense (ll. 5–6) is the wife's breaking into the locked granary without her husband's permission. . . .

The second offense, ll. 7–10, is the charge of the defendant's clandestinely opening a storage jar of sesame oil and covering it with a cloth, giving it the appearance of not having been tampered with. . . .

Lines 11–15 record the third and most serious charge of lewd conduct. Van Dijk has taken these lines to describe the wife finding her husband engaged in a homosexual act. There is no evidence that homosexuality was a crime in ancient Sumer or Babylonia. The fact that the Middle Assyrian Laws (secs. 19–20) punish homosexuality does not bear on our period and place; the Assyrian Laws, moreover, do not treat homosexuality as a matrimonial offense but rather as a breach of general social decency. We have no knowledge as to whether or not homosexual behavior would serve as legal grounds for divorce.

In our view, these lines depict the husband finding his wife with another man, his tying them together in the bed, and carrying them off as evidence to the assembly. The husband's feat recalls the classic tale told of the god Hephaestus (Vulcan) who in a similar fashion trapped his wife Aphrodite in bed with Ares. In the Odyssey (viii 266 ff.), a minstrel tells the tale:

Now when Haphaestus heard the bitter tidings (of his wife's infidelity) he went his way to the forge, devising evil in the deep of his heart, and set the great anvil on the stithy, and wrought fetters that none might snap or loosen, that the lovers might there unmovably remain. Now when he had forged the crafty net in his anger against Ares, he went on his way to the chamber where his marriage bed was set out, and strewed his snares all about the posts of the bed, and many too were hung aloft from the main beam, subtle as spider's webs, so that none might see them, even the blessed gods; so cunningly were they forged. (Hephaestus then catches the lovers and summons the gods together to deliver judgement).[68]

We find this same story retold by Ovid in his *Ars Amatoria* (ii 577–81):

Vulcan set above and around her bed invisible nets, then pretended to go to Lemnos. The two lovers flew to their accustomed meeting place and both, naked as Cupid, were caught in the treacherous nets. Vulcan then called all the gods together and showed them the spectacle of the imprisoned lovers.[69]

The case of Irra-malik vs. Eštar-ummī involved a married woman who stood accused of adulterous conduct compounded by charges of her illicit use of her husband's goods. The combination of the charges of adultery and the unwarranted use of husband's goods is not unusual; they are likewise found together in the Code of Hammurabi, §§ 141–43. CH § 141 involves a wasteful and pilfering wife who behaves immodestly but who is not a proven adulteress; her husband may divorce her with no payment of divorce-money or he may reduce her to slavery and marry another woman. For a wasteful and immodest wife who brazenly states her wish to dissolve her marriage, CH § 143, suspecting the worst, prescribes drowning; only a chaste wife, whose husband is wasteful and loose, may according to CH § 142 leave her husband without penalty.

The cases of the Code do not imply that wastefulness was tantamount to adultery; the Code rather presents ideal, classic cases in which the defendant's blameworthiness is unambiguously clear: an immodest woman of poor reputation whose bad character can also be seen in her habits of household neglect and wastefulness. Our own text seems to describe this same classic situation: a wife, surprised in a tryst with her lover; a woman whose poor character is also proven by her unauthorized spending of her husband's goods and by her invasion of his locked storeroom.

Lines 16 ff. describe how the assembly proceeded to mete out punishment upon the faithless wife (the fate of the other man is not given). Lines 19 f. describe the payment or nonpayment of divorce-money. While divorce-money is usually paid by husbands to wives, the reverse is also possible. Another possibility is to . . . see here a decision of the court to deprive the wife of divorce-money. The latter restoration finds support

in the penalties of CH § 141, where the wife receives no divorce-money or any other quittance. . . .

Lines 21–26 describe further punishments meted out by the assembly: the woman was to be shaven, her nose pierced, and she was to be led in public humiliation around the city.

It is difficult to determine whether the shaving was for public humiliation alone or whether it was intended as a preliminary to enslavement. According to both CE § 28 and CH § 129, the penalty for an adulteress caught in *flagrante delicto* was death. CH § 141 allowed the husband to divorce an immodest and unchaste wife suspected of adultery or to keep her as a slave in his house. CH § 129 allows the outraged husband to save his wife from the death penalty but does not disclose her subsequent fate; from the phrase *u sarrum warassu uballat*, said apparently of her lover whom the king retains as a slave, we could infer that the wife, too, was kept as a slave in her husband's house, much as the wife in CH § 141. . . . Elsewhere, in CH § 143 and in other Old Babylonian marriage documents, a wife's divorce action is punished by death. There may thus be some justification in seeing slavery as an alternative to the death penalty, both in cases of adultery and divorce, where women were judged to have acted unchastely or brazenly. It is therefore possible that in our text the adulteress wife—shaven, mutilated, and humiliated—was to remain a slave in her husband's house.

. . . The associated penalties of mutilation and public exposure likewise almost invariably appear in contexts of public humiliation rather than enslavement. If we rely on the evidence of these other contexts which do not indicate slavery, then the likelihood of the wife's being degraded to slavery in our text is diminished; and we are dealing, more likely, with the punishment of adultery by mutilation and disgrace, much as in MAL A § 15. . . .

Lines 27–29 describe the case as a decision of the royal court; our text, however, is not similar to the Ur III court records studied by Falkenstein, van Dijk, Edzard and others but, rather, appears to belong to the group of "literary" legal decisions, similar to the homicide trial and to the rape of the slave girl trial treated by Jacobsen.[70] In each of these texts, the *puhrum*, or

---

68. *The Odyssey of Homer*, trans. S. H. Butcher and A. Lang (New York, 1950).

69. *Ovid's Art of Love: A New Prose Translation*, trans. R. Seth (London, 1953), p. 72.

70. For the homicide trial see T. Jacobsen, *Analecta Biblica* 12 (1959), 13 50; Jacobsen there (p. 134) noted the existence of two other cases: a dispute over offices and a case dealing with the seizure of a slave-girl. The text dealing with the slave-girl case was partially published by J. J. Finkelstein, *JAOS* 86:359, who reproduced Jacobsen's translation and transliteration. A possible fourth case belonging to this genre is *PBS* 8/1 100, which appears to deal with a dispute of heirs over a slave-girl.

assembly of Nippur, played a role similar to that of the *puhrum* in our case. All of these texts came from the same general period. Although there is no year date in out text, the name of the deputy in line 28, Isme-Dagan-zimu, indicates that our text is not earlier than the Isin-Larsa period; the Nippur tablets upon which the homicide and rape trials are written can be dated archaeologically to the Isin-Larsa period. The literary legal decisions are also characterized by the absence of witnesses and date, and by the duplicate copies in which these decisions appear. Duplicates of our text are not known, but it, nonetheless, clearly belongs to this genre.

Our study of the adultery case suggests a possible additional characteristic: the literary legal decisions can be related to cases in the Old Babylonian law codes. The homicide trial presages CH § 153; the rape trial, CE § 31; and our own case relates to CH §§ 141–143. While the Old Babylonian law may very well be collections of significant principles of adjudication selected for wider application to many related problems, there is no reason to deny the possibility of their dependence upon real cases in which these principles were ideally exhibited. The literary legal decisions appear to be records of such real cases from which general principles of adjudication could have been extracted. They appear to be famous cases of archetypal quality which the casuistic formulations of the codes summarize and abstract.

Could it be that we are dealing with fragments of a larger companion literature to the law codes, a literary collection of classic textbook cases, copied and studied along with the codes as part of the vast library of scribal lore?[71] While we cannot at this point assert that every paragraph of the law codes possessed a textbook "forerunner" or more detailed companion piece, we nevertheless do find sufficient evidence to suggest further exploration of this possibility.[72]

---

71. That the law codes are part of a literary, i.e., scribal tradition can be seen from (1) their duplicate copies and from copies made long after the era of their composition, promulgation, and application; (2) a comparison of Sumerian and Akkadian codes which show literary dependencies; (3) their formulation in *šumma* . . . clauses, typical of learned scribal compositions; and (4) evidences of literary endeavor (analogy, extrapolation, editing, variant readings, etc.) in their formulations. For recent discussions on this problem cf. F. R. Kraus, *Aspect du contact* . . . , 286–91, and J. J. Finkelstein, *JCS* 15 (1961): 101, 103 f.

72. The literary properties of the codes and of the "textbook cases" should not, however, prejudice one to deny the possible existence of an empirical core, actual cases, which would have underlain or inspired the scribal composition. In our case, for example, one may label the heroic act of tying the lovers to the bed and carrying them to court as a literary motif; but this may very well be only a literary embellishment of an actual case, a dramatic infusion of storytelling into a legal report. We

7. ASSAULT

a. AN EYE FOR AN EYE
(By A. S. Diamond)*

Most persons, if asked what they considered to be the outstanding characteristic of the law of wrongs in ancient Mesopotamia, would probably reply: "The cruel, bloody sanctions, and in particular the 'talionic' and 'sympathetic' punishments." This characteristic is too familiar to need examples. Of the 282 clauses of the Code of Hammurabi (CH), some 27 impose capital sentences for a wide variety of wrongs, including adultery and theft. Of the 'talionic' sanctions (those applying the principle of "an eye for an eye and a tooth for a tooth") one of the best examples is CH 229, 230: "If a builder has built a house for a man and his work is not strong, and the house he has built collapses and kills the owner, that builder shall be put to death. If the son of the owner is killed, they shall kill the builder's son." Clauses 196, 197 provide: "If a free man has injured the eye of a patrician, his own eye shall be injured. If he has broken the bone of a patrician, his bone shall be broken." Of the 'sympathetic' sanctions, examples are more familiar in the Middle Assyrian Laws (MAL), e.g., cutting off a man's lower lip for kissing a married woman (§ 9).

But in recent years earlier laws than these have become available from the same field, and they paint quite a different picture.

First, we may mention the laws now attributed to Lipit-Ishtar, King of Isin, though found sixty years ago —a Sumerian Code of an Akkadian king, dating from perhaps 164–75 years before the CH. They contain over one hundred laws of which very few are legible, and these are hardly relevant to the present purpose, save that one (§ 12) at least raises a doubt whether theft was capital in Isin as it was later in the CH.

Then there are the Laws of Eshnunna (LE) discovered in 1947, written in Akkadian, and perhaps to be attributed to Bilalama; laws of a kingdom which for a time held sway over most of the East Tigris region and part of Assyria. Homicide is apparently capital (see §§ 24, 48, 58; and contrast 54, 56), and so is adultery by a married woman, or rape of a married woman (§§ 28, 26) and burglary (§§ 12, 13), but for all personal injuries short of death the sanctions are always pecuniary (§§ 42–48), and so, too, in regard to theft (§ 49).

And now a fragment has been discovered of a still older Sumerian code of Ur-Nammu, founder of the third Dynasty of Ur, who began his reign some three

need not, however, doubt the essential historicity of the trial and the penalties.

*From *Iraq*, vol. 19 (1967).

hundred years before Hammurabi. Apart from the pro- logue, all that can be read are three laws, but happily they all provide for cases of serious personal injury (cutting off the foot, breaking bones, cutting off the [nose?]), and in every case the sanction is purely pecu- niary.

What is the explanation of this change? Dr. Kramer says of the Ur-Nammu laws: "These laws are of very special importance for the history of man's social and spiritual growth. For they show that, even before 2000 B.C. the law of 'eye for eye' and 'tooth for tooth'—still prevalent to a large extent in the biblical laws of a much later day—had already given way to the far more humane approach in which a money fine was substi- tuted as a punishment." Albrecht Goetze, in his com- mentary on LE, appears to share that viewpoint. He says the CH "retains the *jus talionis*; in the L.E. . . . it is replaced by fines." Professor Driver and Sir John Miles in *The Babylonian Laws* express a similar atti- tude. They say, for example: "The natural remedy for an assault is retaliation, and talion was a fundamental principle of early law and was only gradually replaced by a system, of fixed composition," i.e., pecuniary sanctions.

Goetze adds: "This archaism in the laws of Ham- murapi is remarkable." It certainly is, if it is archaism. It cannot be that the draftsman of CH had not heard of the "more humane approach" of the earlier laws. On nothing in this field are scholars more agreed than that successive legislators knew and made use of the work of their predecessors, and that legislators and codifiers all drew, as it were, on a common law and legal tradition of the area. For the same reason, the change cannot be explained by any difference between a Sumerian and a Semitic legal tradition. Hammurabi and Lipit-Ishtar both say they were legislating for Su- merian and Akkadian subjects alike, and these bodies of laws are written in either language and attributed to kings of both ethnic groups. It is strange that this par- ticular lawgiver and this code, admired and studied for so long an age thereafter, should have been guilty of such "archaism," or that the Middle Assyrians of sev- eral centuries later should have been equally archaic. It is also strange that in the CH this "archaism" is only fully applicable to the most serious assaults—namely, serious assaults on patricians. There appears to be no class distinction in the sanctions in the earlier laws, for example LE. On the other hand, in the MAL, some three centuries later than CH, not only are corporal sanctions numerous, but there is an additional type of corporal sanction, namely a period of forced labor—or is this also an archaism?

Judged, of course, by the data supplied by this field alone, without any preconception or assumption as to the course of development of **law** elsewhere, if we drew any general conclusions we should have to regard this change from pecuniary to corporal sanctions for the most serious wrongs as a sociological advance. It oc- curs in the later laws as against the earlier, and—still more important—it apparently occurs in the laws of the larger and more powerful and more centralized and economically more advanced states, where the codes and collections of laws are larger and richer in detail (CH and MAL) as against the smaller states, with their simpler economies and briefer collections of laws.

Whence, then, comes this view that talionic sanctions in the law preceded the pecuniary? It is an old view and probably dates from the period when the Hebrew Pentateuch (together with the Roman Twelve Tables) was considered the oldest surviving law. In the Penta- teuch the rule of "eye for an eye and tooth for a tooth" appears in the ancient code contained in the Book of the Covenant, but it is one of the plainest interpolations in the Pentateuch, being inconsistent with its immediate context; and it also occurs in the later book of Leviti- cus, so that *prima facie* it represents a late development in the law as against an earlier stage of pecuniary sanc- tions for wounding. It also occurs in the surviving fragments of the Twelve Tables, but here again it can- not be satisfactorily reconciled with another of those fragments.

What then is the present basis of this notion? Is it based on equally ancient or more ancient data than the Babylonian? But there are none. Is it then based on what we know of the course of history among the more primitive peoples known to us in the modern world? But all the evidence from primitive peoples indicates the reverse.

We have, in most cases, no knowledge of the history of the law of a particular primitive people over a long period of time. But there are outstanding exceptions. For example, we know the law, in this respect, of the primitive tribes of Germany in Tacitus' time, and can trace it forward in England and elsewhere over many centuries. Apart from such cases, in order to ascertain the course of history in the absence of a time-scale, we must be content with arranging the numerous primitive peoples known to us in the order of their material pro- gression towards civilization—in size, density of popu- lation, development of central organs of government, degree of economic specialization, extent of control over the natural environment. So arranged, we find a progression in law that is in outline universal.

When primitive courts emerge, and therefore law, properly so-called, appears—and this is generally at the emergence of a mixed pastoral and agricultural economy—the sanctions for the wrongs we have been considering are always pecuniary. They take, that is to say, the form of payments of animals or other goods or currency. This applies equally to homicide (intentional or unintentional) and wounding, adultery and rape of a married woman, and theft. Much later, at the beginning of civilization, these sanctions become corporal (that is to say, they take the form of death, mutilation and the like) but not all at the same time. First, adultery or rape of a married woman: a husband who catches his wife and her paramour in the act is entitled to put them both to death. Soon after this, intentional homicide becomes capital. Still later—by an extension of this last rule—the sanctions for the most serious woundings become corporal, and soon afterwards substantial theft becomes capital. We can see the same progress on a time-scale in England, where it is rapid.

There is another aspect of the change which goes far to explain it. Till the change occurs, all these wrongs —homicide, and even adultery, included—are civil offenses, that is to say, the community is satisfied if the wrongdoer has made his peace with the individual or group aggrieved, which he usually does by gifts. Now they are becoming criminal: the state is interested and its welfare is felt to be threatened. It is no longer satisfied that the next of kin should accept pecuniary compensation for murder, or the injured for a maiming. But the community cannot yet afford (and would not dream of providing) prisons where malefactors are nourished in idleness. Hence the death sentence for murder is inflicted by the next of kin, death for adultery by the outraged husband, corporal (including talionic or sympathetic) sanctions for serious wounding by the victim or his family, and death for theft by the owner or his family. Death and mutilations of all kinds have been frequent punishments for some little time, imposed by order of an irate king for political offenses against him, and there are a few other criminal offenses (mainly sacral) similarly punished; and these civil offenses are being added to the list of crimes, and during this process civil injury and crime are close together.

So, for example, 2000 years ago in Germany, the sanctions for all these wrongs were pecuniary, and they remained so in England from the beginning of the Anglo-Saxon occupation till the eleventh century. In England in 1100 A.D. adultery is criminal, and the husband is entitled to put to death his wife and the adulterer caught *in flagranti delicto*; and rape too is criminal and punishable by castration and blinding. In 1150 A.D. intentional homicide is criminal (as well as civil) and capital. The sanctions for wounding are still pecuniary, and also the sanctions for theft (except where a thief is found by night). Early in the thirteenth century serious wounding is criminal and the sanctions are mutilations, and by 1250 A.D. grand larceny becomes

criminal and capital. The LE (and the laws of Ur-Nammu, as far as they go) represent the legal situation in England in 1150 A.D. The CH represents England in 1250.

The MAL belong to a kingdom somewhat further to the north, and therefore towards the boundary of this old cultural field and nearer to the simpler cultures beyond, and though they are dated some three or four centuries later than CH, correspond to England of about 1225 A.D. The Hittite Laws, coming from Southeast Asia Minor at about the same time or a little later than the MAL, represent a far more backward stage, namely that of England in the eleventh century, when the sanction for homicide has not yet become capital.

It can be said with confidence that primitive courts must have been in existence in Babylonia at least several millennia before the LE and CH, and until the close of this period the sanctions for all these wrongs must have been pecuniary. Whether any written records of the law of this period will ever be found must depend on whether writing was in use so long ago for the purpose of recording law. At least we may hope to pierce by means of contemporary documents to the stage represented in England in the eleventh century A.D., and in Southeast Asia Minor in the Hittite Laws.

Notes and Questions to Diamond, "An Eye for an Eye"

1. Diamond's article is based upon his thesis that ancient society evolved in distinct stages.[73] This contention has been a matter of much dispute among scholars.[74]

2. Jewish tradition, as recorded in the Talmud,[75] is that the biblical passage "an eye for an eye" was always understood not to be taken literally but to require the payment of money only. While the tradition is alleged to have originated with the interpretation taught to Moses by God himself,[76] the talmudic rationale for this interpretation is that removal of the assaulter's eye would be unjust since it could lead to his death, whereas he had only injured an organ of the victim. Furthermore, the identical organs of two different persons might have quite different value statuses. For example, the assaulter might have only one eye to begin with, and its removal as a penalty would leave him completely blind, in a worse state than his victim. If an artist or concert pianist assaulted another and damaged his hand, the crippling of the artist-assaulter's hand in

73. See A. S. Diamond, *"Primitive Law"* (London, 1935).
74. See B. Jackson, "Evolution and Foreign Influence in Ancient Law," *American Journal of Comparative Law* 16 (1972): 385.
75. *Ketubot* 38a.
76. See Rambam, Laws of the Batterer and Damager, ch. 1, rule 6.

return would cause him grossly disproportionate harm. To boot, corporal punishment would not benefit the victim personally, whereas the receipt of monetary compensation would.

If the talmudic tradition is correct, why did the Bible state "an eye for an eye" instead of specifically requiring the payment of money damages? It may be, consistent with Diamond's reasoning, that this would equate a human organ with money and would play down the importance placed on the value of a human organ. It might, furthermore, imply that a person of means could with impunity cripple another's limb, knowing that he could make up for this fully by mere payment of money.[77] The implication of the biblical verse would then be that while the tortfeasor may deserve to have his limb destroyed, this cannot in fairness be imposed. What remains, therefore, is the obligation to compensate the victim by the payment of money, thereby also "relieving" the offender of the penalty that he really merited.[78]

The talmudic interpretation is supported by a suggested resolution of another problem. The biblical phrase "an eye for an eye" (which appears in three places in the Pentateuch)[79] seems at first glance to be inappropriate in both the first and last places that it is mentioned. Its first formulation appears in discussing the case of a pregnant woman who suffers a miscarriage when she is struck (apparently, on the belly, not the eye) by one of two quarreling men.[80] The formulation of the "eye for an eye" principle would seem more appropriate for the preceding case (Exod. 21: 18) in which two men quarrel and one injures the other's eye. Furthermore, the expressions "burn for burn" and "hand for hand, foot for foot" seem out of place in discussing the case of a pregnant woman who has been "pushed" (or struck).[81] The last formulation of the phrase[82] is in the context of punishing false witnesses. Since biblical law provides only for court sanctions imposed by death, flogging, or monetary fine, the expression "an eye for an eye" (etc.) seems singularly inappropriate.

It has been suggested that there was an ancient literary-judicial formula in the Near East of "soul for soul, eye for eye, tooth for tooth" that used to be applied literally in Mesopotamia. This expression, as well as other, well-established literary formulae, was utilized in the Bible,[83] although (as with many other changes in the Bible from preexisting customary practices) its meaning now was to require monetary compensation only. Once, however, the Bible utilized the expression "soul for soul" in dealing with the situation of the false witnesses (or the pregnant woman who died from her injuries), it continued with the rest of the traditional formula, "an eye for an eye, a tooth for a tooth,"[84] in accordance with the traditional literary mode of expression in the ancient Near East.

According to this theory, since the phrase "an eye for an eye" is utilized in the Bible only as a traditional literary expression, it could have been used without any longer being applied literally, according to its original meaning, as is the case with other traditional literary expressions. Furthermore, the apparently accidental striking of the pregnant woman, leading to a miscarriage, could not have been intended to lead to the literal taking of the life of the one who injured her, since that very section of the Bible[85] specifically negates the death penalty for accidental death. The expression "soul for soul" would, therefore, primarily mean monetary payment for the life taken.[86] The literal, original meaning of the phrase[87] would therefore not reflect actual biblical practice.

8. OTHER CRIMINAL TRIALS

a. RESULTS OF A TRIAL FOR CONSPIRACY (IN EGYPT)
(By J. Pritchard)*

The Twentieth Dynasty has provided us with a mass of legal material, particularly on the proceedings occasioned by the plundering of Theban tombs. We shall present here extracts from a document of different nature, dealing with a harem conspiracy and the plot to supplant Ramses III upon his throne by one of his sons. It is uncertain whether the conspiracy was successful to the point of taking the life of Ramses III. In that case, the court of inquiry and punishment will have

---

77. Compare the Code of Hammurabi (secs. 196, 198), which provides for blinding the assaulter if the victim was a member of the upper classes, but demands only a payment of money where the victim is a member of the lower classes. Compare also modern criminal law, which classifies assault and battery as a crime and entitles the victim to monetary compensation.

78. See Rambam, Laws of the Batterer and Damager, rule 3; see idem, *Guide for the Perplexed* 3:41.

79. Exod. 21:23; Lev. 24:20; Deut. 19:21.

80. Exod. 21:22.

81. Ibid.

82. Deut. 19:21.

83. See Talmud, *Berakhot* 31b, *Torah Kohanim*, Lev. 20:21 ("The Bible speaks in the expressions used by men").

84. The system of thought and expression, which moves from one topic to another, related only by similarity of words, was well established in the ancient Near East and is to be contrasted with the logical association of related subjects in Greek thought. See Cassuto, *From Adam to Noah*, ad. loc.

85. Exod. 21:13.

86. Cf. Talmud, *Baba Kama* 84a.

87. This would appear to be the way in which the Talmud would apply here its principle that "a biblical verse cannot be interpreted to negate its plain meaning" (*Yebamot* 24a; *Shabbat* 63a).

*From *Ancient Near Eastern Texts* (Princeton, 1955).

been constituted by Ramses IV in the name of his dead father. Alternatively, Ramses III survived the plot and himself constituted the court.

The manuscript is the Judicial Papyrus of Turin, dated to the end of the reign of Ramses III (about 1164 B.C.).

[Text]

. . . The abomination of the land. I laid the charge upon: the Overseer of the Treasury Montu-em-tawi; the Overseer of the Treasury Paif-ru; the Standard-Bearer Kar; the Butler Pai-Bes; the Butler Qedendenen; the Butler Baal-mahar; the Butler Pa-ir-sun; the Butler Thut-rekh-nefer; the Royal Herald Pen-Renenut; the Scribe May; the Scribe of the Archives Pa-Re-emheb; and the Standard-Bearer of the Garrison Hori, (5) saying: "As for the matters which the people—I do not know who—have said, go and examine them." And they went and examined them, and they caused to die by their own hands those whom they caused to die—[I] do not know [who—and they] inflicted punishment [upon the] others—[I] do not know [who] also. But [I] charged [them *strictly*], saying: "Be careful, guard against having punishment inflicted [upon] a [person] *irregularly* [*by an official*] *who is not over him*." So I said to them repeatedly. (iii 1) As for all that they have done, it is they who have done it. Let all that they have done come upon their [own] heads, whereas I am privileged and immune unto eternity, since I am among the righteous kings who are in the presence of Amon-Re, King of the Gods, and in the presence of Osiris, Ruler of Eternity.

I

(iv 1) Persons brought in because of the great crimes which they had committed, and turned over to the Place of Examination, in the presence of the great officials of the Place of Examination, in order to be examined by: the Overseer of the Treasury Montu-em-tawi; the Overseer of the Treasury Paif-ru; the Standard-Bearer Kar; the Butler Pai-Bes; the Scribe of the Archives May; and the Standard-Bearer Hori. They examined them. They found them guilty. They caused their sentences to overtake them. Their crimes seized them.

The great enemy Pai-bak-kamen, who had been Chief of the Chamber. He was brought in because he had been in collusion with Tiye and the women of the harem. He had made common cause with them. He had begun to take their words outside to their mothers and their brothers who were there, saying: "Gather people and stir up enemies to make rebellion against their lord!" He was placed in the presence of the great officials of the Place of Examination. They examined his crimes. They found that he had committed them. His

crimes laid hold upon him. The officials who examined him caused his sentence to overtake him.

The great enemy Mesed-su-Re, who had been butler. He was brought in because he had been in collusion with Pai-bak-kamen, who had been Chief of the Chamber, and with the women, to gather enemies and to make rebellion against their lord. He was placed in the presence of the great officials of the Place of Examination. They examined his crimes. They found him guilty. They caused his sentence to overtake him. . . .

(6) The great enemy Pa-tjau-emdi-Amon, who had been Agent of the Harem in the Retinue. He was brought in because he had heard the words which the men had plotted with the women of the harem, without reporting them. He was placed in the presence of the great officials of the Place of Examination. They examined his crimes. They found him guilty. They caused his sentence to overtake him. . . .

(v 1) The wives of the men of the gate of the harem, who had joined the men who plotted the matters, who were placed in the presence of the officials of the Place of Examination. They found them guilty. They caused their sentences to overtake them. Six women.

The great enemy Pa-iry, son of Rem, who had been Overseer of the Treasury. He was brought in because he had been in collusion with the great enemy Pen-Huy-bin. He had made common cause with him to stir up enemies and to make rebellion against their lord. He was placed in the presence of the officials of the Place of Examination. They found him guilty. They caused his sentence to overtake him.

The great enemy Bin-em-Waset, who had been Troop Commander of Ethiopia. He was brought in because his sister, who was in the harem in the retinue, had written to him, saying: "Gather people, make enemies, and come back to make rebellion against your lord!" He was placed in the presence of Qedendenen, Baal-mahar, Pa-ir-sun, and Thut-rekh-nefer. They examined him. They found him guilty. They caused his sentence to overtake him.

II

Persons brought in because of their crimes, because they had been in collusion with Pai-bak-kamen, Pai-is, and Pen-ta-Uret. They were placed in the presence of the officials of the Place of Examination, in order to examine them. They found them guilty. They left them in their [own] hands in the Place of Examination. They took their own lives; no penalty was carried out against them.

(5) The great enemy Pai-is, who had been Commander of the Army; the great enemy Messui, who had been Scribe of the House of Life; the great enemy Pa-Re-kamenef, who had been Chief [Lector Priest], the

great enemy Ii-roi, who had been Overseer of the Priests of Sekhmet; the great enemy Neb-djefa, who had been butler; and the great enemy Shad-mesdjer, who had been Scribe of the House of Life. Total: six.

III

Persons brought, because of their crimes, in to the Place of Examination, in the presence of Qedendenen, Baal-mahar, Pa-ir-sun, Thut-rekh-nefer, and Mer-usi-Amon. They examined them concerning their crimes. They found them guilty. They left them where they were. They took their own lives.

Pen-ta-Urt, he who had been called by that other name. He was brought in because he had been in collusion with Tiye, his mother, when she had plotted matters with the women of the harem about making rebellion against his lord. He was placed in the presence of the butlers in order to examine him. They found him guilty. They left him where he was. He took his own life.

The great enemy Henuten-Amon, who had been butler. He was brought in because of the crimes of the women of the harem, among whom he had been, which he had heard, without making report of them. He was placed in the presence of the butlers in order to exam-ine him. They found him guilty. They left him where he was. He took his own life. . . .

IV

(vi 1) Persons upon whom sentence was carried out by cutting off their noses and their ears, because they had abandoned the good instructions given to them. The women had gone. They had reached them at the place where they were. They had caroused with them and with Pai-is. Their crime seized them.

The great enemy Pai-Bes, who had been butler. This sentence was carried out on him: he was left, and he took his own life.

The great enemy May, who had been Scribe of the Archives.

The great enemy Tai-nakhtet, who had been Lieutenant of the Garrison.

(5) The great enemy Nanai, who had been Chief of Bailiffs.

V

Person who had been in common with them. He was rebuked severely with wicked words. He was left, and no penalty was carried out against him.

SUGGESTED READINGS

Albright, W. F. *Archaeology and the Religion of Israel.* Baltimore, 1942.

Bozeman, A. *Politics and Culture in the Ancient World.* Princeton, 1960.

Cassuto, U. *From Adam to Noah.* Jerusalem, 1976.

Daube, D. *Studies in Biblical Law.* Cambridge, 1947.

Driver, G., and J. C. Miles. *The Babylonian Laws.* Oxford, 1952.

Falk, Z. W. *Hebrew Law in Biblical Times.* London, 1964.

Frankfort, H., et al. *Before Philosophy: The Intellectual Adventure of Ancient Man.* Baltimore, 1972.

Gordon, C. H. *The Ancient Near East.* New York, 1965.

Hooke, S. J. *Babylonian and Assyrian Religion.* Oxford, 1962.

Kaufmann, Y. *The Religion of Israel.* Chicago, 1960.

Kramer, S. N. *The Sumerians.* Chicago, 1963.

Maine, H. *Ancient Law.* London, 1861.

Levi, M. A. *Political Power in the Ancient World.* New York, 1965.

Noth, M. *The History of Israel.* New York, 1958.

Pritchard, J., ed. *Ancient Near Eastern Texts Relating to the Old Testament.* Princeton, 1969.

Vaux, R. de. *Ancient Israel.* New York, 1961.

Wilson, J. A. *The Culture of Ancient Egypt.* Chicago, 1951.

Speiser, E. A., and M. Avi-Yonah, eds. *World History of the Jewish People.* London and New Brunswick, 1974–78.

Part Two

Talmudic Law
in the Eras of
the Second Jewish
Commonwealth,
Ancient Greece,
the Hellenist States,
Rome, and the
Early Middle Ages,
350 B.C.E.–630 C.E.

IV. Historical Introduction to Talmudic Law

A. *The Hellenist Milieu*

1. THE MACEDONIAN AND GREEK CONQUEST OF THE ORIENT

In about 326 B.C.E., Alexander the Great of Macedonia vanquished the Persian armies and captured all of the important centers of the Persian Empire, including Babylon, Susa, Persepolis, and Ecbatana. He thus became known as the "Great King of the Orient," ruler of a vast empire stretching from India to Greece and from African Nubia in the south to the Jaxartes River in the north. This area constituted practically the entire known world of that time, and contained all of its Jews.

A short time after his conquest, in 323 B.C.E., Alexander the Great died at the age of thirty-three. After his death his huge empire, was divided among his Macedonian generals, "diadochi."

At first the Macedonian generals were appointed as satraps, with each to govern one portion of a supposedly united empire. In practice, however, each satrap came to regard himself as independent, with unlimited authority over his territory, allegedly as a reward for his prior military service to Alexander. Soon Ptolemy, designated as governor of Egypt, proclaimed himself as king and extended his rule to Cyrene to the west and to Judah and parts of Syria to the northeast. Seleucus, a Macedonian general who was given Babylon as a satrapy, also had himself crowned as king and gradually extended his kingdom east to India and west to Asia Minor. His kingdom was therefore considerably larger than Ptolemy's. Extended and bitter strife subsequently ensued between these two former collegial generals, now satrap-kings, and between the other satraps in Asia Minor. During the strife Alexander's son and mother were murdered.

2. THE EXTERNAL POWER ALIGNMENTS OF THE HELLENIST STATES

The dominant motif of power conflicts in the third century B.C.E. was the intense rivalry between the Ptolemaic and Seleucid kingdoms. These states fought five long wars. The Ptolemies were victorious in the first four wars, but by 198 B.C.E. they were uprooted from Phoenicia, Judea, Samaria, and Trans-Jordan. These areas were then incorporated within the Seleucid kingdom.

The Seleucid kingdom, which was now nearly as large as Alexander's former empire, was poised to expand still further when it clashed with the new rising world power, Rome. The Romans fearing the expanded power of the Seleucid Empire, fought a number of battles with it, and eventually broke its power and the power of its allies in Macedonia as well.

In 169–168 B.C.E. Antiochus Epiphanes, the Seleucid king, invaded Egypt and conquered it. Before he could effectively annex Egypt to his kingdom, Rome stepped in and forced him to leave, ending forever the dreams of a mightly Seleucid kingdom. Legend has it that the Roman envoy drew a circle on the ground around King Antiochus and instructed him not to step out of it until he decided whether or not he would obey the dictates of Rome.

3. CULTURAL AND RELIGIOUS PERSPECTIVES IN THE HELLENIST NEAR EAST

The imperial Macedonian conquest of the Persian Empire resulted not only in widespread political upheaval, but also in great cultural and religious turmoil. The attack upon the Persian king and his associates, who were viewed as vice-regents of the gods, was regarded as an attack upon the gods themselves. There was also a purposeful attempt to spread Hellenism throughout the conquered world, and to substitute Greek theology and perspectives for those which had, theretofore, prevailed in the Near East. Hellenism included Greek language, names, literature, athletics, and even the political structure of the Greek *polis* (city-state). It also entailed a rational view of life and specific perspectives concerning the administration of government, the maintenance of armies, the conduct of economic life, and the intense pursuit of high personal status.[1] The victorious Greeks intended to transmit this entire cultural milieu to the conquered natives, who were regarded by the Greeks as barbarians with no culture at all. As a result of this psychological dehumanizing of the natives in the minds of the Greeks,

---

1. S. K. Eddy, *The King Is Dead—Studies in the Near Eastern Resistance to Hellenism* (University of Nebraska Press, 1961), pp. xviii, 34. See W. Tarn, *Hellenistic Civilization* (3d ed.; London, 1953).

the latter felt no compunction about exploiting the indigenous population.

Furthermore, to secure their political rule over the states in the Near East, Alexander's successors encouraged the large migration of Greeks and Macedonians there. Many came to find their fortunes and to exploit the riches and populations of the former Persian Empire. Accordingly, all of these factors encouraged a lust for power and riches and sanctioned aggressive and unscrupulous action by strength and cunning.[2]

The vigorous Greek proselytization resulted in the spread of Hellenist civilization over immense areas and in a fusion of elements of Hellenic and Eastern civilizations. At the same time, it also engendered considerable opposition from the local population. It was at this juncture, during the clashes and fusions between the Eastern cultures and Greek civilization (which was no longer at its peak), that the encounter and conflicts between the Greek and Jewish cultures occurred.

B. *Jewish History in the Hellenist Era: An Overview*

1. JUDEA UNDER THE PTOLEMIES AND SELEUCIDS

It should be noted that the Bible, the chief source for Jewish history until this period, closes with the books of Ezra and Nehemiah, which date to the fifth century B.C.E. For the next few hundred years there are few sources, the main one being Josephus' history, written in the first century B.C.E. Josephus, however, borrowed much from other sources and is not generally regarded as completely reliable. Many of the conclusions about the immediate postbiblical era are therefore a result of speculation and have been the subject of much scholarly dispute.

The incorporation of Judea into the empire of Alexander the Great in 322 B.C.E. was a major turning point in Jewish history. Until that time the social interactions of the Jews and their state were with the kingdoms of the Near East, such as Egypt, Assyria, and Persia. It was these states that determined the power status of the Jewish state and affected it culturally, as well. Alexander's conquests brought all of the previously Oriental civilizations of the Near East, including Judea, into the framework of the Western civilized world. The result was a combination and fusion of many diverse elements into a new cultural structure, as well as a serious reac-

tion throughout the Near East against Hellenist culture and domination.

Judea, under Ptolemaic reign, was permitted religious freedom and a Jewish "Council of Elders," consisting of priests and laymen, administered the city of Jerusalem. When the Seleucids incorporated Judea into their empire, they at first granted the Jews religious freedom and even undertook to pay for the expenses of the Temple at Jerusalem.

2. THE EFFECT OF HELLENIST CULTURE ON THE JEWS

As with other peoples, Hellenism had its affect upon the Jews, too. Many Jews joined, and others became acquainted with, the *polis*, the city-state in which the principle of free citizenship was established for the first time in the history of mankind. As mentioned above, full citizenship—that is, participation in government and legal administration—entailed worship of the city gods, which to the Jew meant apostasy.[3]

Many Jews participated in Hellenist athletics and physical fitness exercises. Some even decircumcised themselves in order to take part in the nude athletic events. Participation in athletics also necessarily, brought with it participation in Greek religious rites since all Greek athletic contests were under the patronage of the gods. Thus, even participation as a spectator involved a compromise with traditional Jewish belief.[4]

The *gymnasia*, many of which were set up in Judea by the high priest, Jason, were *ipso facto* opposed to the Jewish tradition. In the Hellenistic *polis*, of which there were some twenty-nine in Palestine, the students in the *gymnasia* regularly joined in religious processions, sang hymns to the gods, participated in the sacrifices, and in erotic homosexual associations with their teachers. Furthermore, the *gymnasia* displayed numerous busts of deities, particularly of Hermes and Heracles, the patron gods of the *gymnasia*.[5]

The thoughts and concepts of Greek philosophers were influential among Jews, especially outside of Judea. This was particularly true in Egypt. Many educated Jews in Alexandria, exemplified by Philo, the Alexandrian, sought to obtain a synthesis between Hellenism and Judaism. Of course, there was also much

3. Tarn, *Hellenistic Civilization*, p. 221.
4. Talmud, *Avodah Zarah* 18b.
5. L. Feldman, Review of Victor Tcherikover, *Hellenistic Civilization and the Jews*, in *Tradition* 2 (Spring 1960): 348; see H. I. Marrou, *A History of Education in Antiquity* (New York, 1956), p. 109; see also M. Hadas, *Hellenistic Culture: Fusion and Diffusion* (New York, 1959), which deals chiefly with the interaction of Judaism and Hellenism in the realms of religion, language, literature, and arts; M. Radin, *The Jews among Greeks and Romans* (Philadelphia, 1915); and K. G. Dover, *Greek Homosexuality* (Cambridge, Mass., 1979).

2. V. Tcherikover, "Hellenist Culture," in *World History of the Jewish People* (New Brunswick, 1972), pp. 34–35, 45; see idem, *Hellenistic Civilization and the Jews* (Philadelphia, 1959).

Hellenist influence in the social and economic life of the Jewish communities throughout the Mediterranean world.

As a result of the manifold Hellenistic influences, there were many Jews who sympathized with the Seleucids at the time of the Hasmonean revolt and who actively fought against Judah Maccabee (see Section B 3, below). These Jews turned out to be his bitterest enemies. They desired to realize Greek ideals and to participate in the universal culture. They viewed Judah Maccabee as an uncultured fundamentalist, blocking their access to the outside world.

The tolerant treatment of Jewish religious practices by the Seleucids changed, however, with the entry of Rome into the Near East. The military defeats of the Seleucids by Rome resulted in great insecurity in the Seleucid kingdom. Large portions of the Seleucid Empire revolted and tore themselves free from Seleucid rule, which was ultimately reduced to Syrio-Palestine, and portions of Mesopotamia. The situation was further exacerbated when King Antiochus IV, who assumed the title of "Theos Epiphanes" ("God Manifest"), conquered Ptolemaic Egypt but was immediately forced to withdraw because of Roman threats. Rome imposed a number of very substantial indemnities upon Antiochus IV, whose treasury was already depleted.

To help pay money for the Roman indemnity, Antiochus sold the high priesthood of the Temple at Jerusalem to the highest bidder. The candidates for this high office, who attempted to outbid each other, soon resorted to looting the Temple's treasury to pay the exorbitant prices demanded for the high priesthood. Eventually, Antiochus became aware of the source of the high payments to him and looted the Temple himself. This aroused great hostility among the Jews, and Jerusalem became the scene of an uprising, which was brutally repressed. Tension continued, and Antiochus ultimately forbade the practice of the Hebrew religion. Observances of such basic commandments as circumcision, the Sabbath, and dietary laws were punished by death, carried out in many savage ways. The Temple sacrifices were stopped, and Hellenic rites were imposed. Altars were set up all over the country. The populace was compelled to offer up Hellenic sacrifices and sometimes pigs, acts that were regarded by the Jews as abominations. While the reasons for this religious repression are not entirely clear, and appear irrational, Antiochus apparently believed that he could solidify his support by imposing a Hellenistic cultural unity upon the country. Additionally, and consistent with the cultural perspectives of that era, he treated all Jewish (and therefore *ipso facto* non-Hellenic) religious practices as personal disloyalty to him and as political treason.[6]

3. THE HASMONEAN REVOLT

These repressions gave rise to the revolt by Mattiyahu, a priest of the Hasmonean family. The fighting was led by his five sons, particularly Judah Maccabee. The revolt was not only against the religious repressions and a political battle against Seleucid tyranny, but it was also a reaction to the Hellenist culture and constituted a *kulturkampf* against it. During the revolt the Hasmoneans authorized military action on the Sabbath as a necessary step in order to save their lives, particularly in response to attacks by the Seleucids and Hellenized Jews. This was considered a great innovation in religious law at that time, although there was precedent for such actions.

Eventually the Hasmoneans, fighting against overwhelming odds, inflicted a series of crushing defeats upon the Seleucids. The Temple was reconquered, cleansed, and the candelabra there was rekindled. To commemorate this event, the holiday of Hanukkah was established, the first major religious holiday that was not authorized in one of the canonized books of the Bible.

Many battles continued to be fought, however, until complete political freedom, independence, and political rule by the Hasmoneans were obtained. In one of the battles Judah was killed, and his brother Jonathan succeeded him. Jonathan later supported the Seleucid Alexander in his attempt to become the Seleucid ruler, and he was rewarded by Alexander with the high priesthood. In 143 C.E. Jonathan even sent Jewish troops to the Seleucid capital, Antioch, to help Demetrius III, also a Seleucid, retain control. Thus, in an ironic turn of fate, Mattathias' son and successor, helped to keep Antiochus' successor on the throne.[7]

After Jonathan, too, was killed by assassination, another brother, Simon, became leader. In 140 B.C.E. Simon was designated as hereditary high priest, and proclaimed prince ("ethnarch") over Judea by a decree of "the priest, the people, the rulers of the nation and the dignitaries of the land."[8] Thus was established the Hasmonean dynasty. It should be noted that at that time possibly three-fourths of all Jews lived *outside* of Judea.[9]

Considerable fraternal strife occurred thereafter among members of the Hasmonean family for political domination. Eventually the necessity of political support by the Seleucids and the Hellenized elements, as

6. L. Ehrlich, *A Concise History of Israel* (New York, 1962), p. 99.

7. Eddy, *The King Is Dead—Studies in the Near Eastern Resistance to Hellenism.*

8. 1 Macc. 14:27.

9. See S. W. Baron, *Social and Religious History of the Jews* (2d ed.; New York, 1952), pp. 168–70.

well as the effects of Hellenistic cultural influences, resulted in the later generations of Hasmoneans becoming Hellenized. This aroused considerable opposition from the bulk of the population, which also could not reconcile itself to these alien practices, and to Jewish rulers who were not from the Davidic lineage.

4. ROMAN RULE OF JUDEA

The Hasmonean dynasty was continuously rent by bitter personal power struggles among its members. One of the later Hasmonean rulers, Alexander Jannai, proclaimed himself king (*circa* 103 B.C.E.). After his death his sons, Hyrcannus and Aristobolus, fought with each other to succeed him. Both appealed to the Roman general Pompey, who was then in Syria. This was the final step that drew Rome into direct participation in Judean affairs. Pompey and his armed forces came to Judea to "settle" the strife and besieged Jerusalem. When he captured it his soldiers massacred large numbers of the inhabitants. This was the end of the Hasmonean dynasty. Hyrcannus was appointed high priest, and a large part of Judea was placed under the rule of the Roman governor of Syria.

Subsequently Julius Caesar appointed Antipater (an Idumaean, whose people had been forcefully converted to Judaism by a prior Hasmonean ruler) as procurator, or governor, over Judea. Antipater appointed his son Herod to control of the northern province of Galilee. Eventually Rome appointed Herod as king of Judea, and he promptly exterminated all of the remnants of the Hasmonean family in order to eliminate all rival claimants to his throne. Herod, who was not a Jew (neither racially nor by religious beliefs and outlooks), governed as a merciless tyrant. His paranoid fears for his throne led him to murder his wife, his sons, many of his friends, and large numbers of the local population. Understandably, he was thoroughly hated and feared by all. He did, however, initiate considerable construction of cities. Most notably, he completely reconstructed the Temple at Jerusalem, turning it into a magnificent edifice of worldwide fame, his crowning achievement.

After Herod's death the Roman emperor, Augustus, incorporated Judea directly into the Roman Empire under a procurator. Internal administration, however, was left in the hands of the local population.[10] It was apparently in this period, during the governorship of Herod Antipas (the son of King Herod), who was Tetrarch of Galilee, and during the procuratorship of Pontius Pilate (26–36 C.E.), that the ministry of Jesus of Nazareth took place. This was later to have profound significance for the Jewish people.

10. Ehrlich, *A Concise History of Israel*, p. 131.

Eventually Herod's grandson, Aggrippa, was recognized by Rome as king of Judea, Samaria, and Idumaea. He was the last Jewish king of Judea; after his death in 44 C.E., Judea became a Roman province, ruled by a governor.

5. THE DESTRUCTION OF THE SECOND JEWISH COMMONWEALTH AND TEMPLE

Serious Roman mistreatment of the Jewish population followed. Onerous taxation was imposed, and the Roman procurator, Gennius Florus (64–66 C.E.), robbed the Temple and permitted his soldiers to plunder the city of Jerusalem. Consequently, the people revolted, led by extreme nationalists called Zealots, who wanted to drive out the Romans completely from Judea. After many years of fighting and much slaughter, the revolt was put down by Vespasian (who left in the midst of the war to become Roman emperor) and his son Titus. Hundreds of thousands of Jews were killed or died of starvation and disease during the fighting. Many thousands were taken as slaves to Rome and other parts of the Roman Empire. Jerusalem and the Temple were completely destroyed, as was the mountain fortress of Masada, whose inhabitants all committed suicide, rather than surrender to the Romans after a bitter three-year siege.

6. THE BAR KOKHBA REVOLT

After suppression of the revolt, there still remained a sizable number of Jews in the land, except in Jerusalem, where Jews were now forbidden to settle. Slowly the community began to rebuild itself. Harsh Roman rule continued however.

Despite the fresh memories of the recent national disaster, further widespread revolts of Jews occurred in about 115 C.E. in Egypt, Cyrene, Cyprus, and even portions of Mesopotamia. These revolts were repressed by the Romans with great bloodshed. When Hadrian became emperor of Rome, he decided on a policy of Pan-Romanism. With this motive, reinforced by his intense personal hatred of the Jewish religion and culture, he banned circumcision and other basic Jewish religious practices. These religious persecutions, together with the generally repressive Roman rule, led to a second major revolt in Judea, under the leadership of Bar Kokhba in 132 C.E. The fighting was intense, and numerous Roman legions were destroyed. The Roman defeats were so severe that Hadrian, in writing to the Roman Senate, omitted the customary opening greeting, "I and the legions are in good health."[11]

11. Dio Cassius, LXIX *Roman History*, 14; M. Grant, *The Jews in the Roman World* (New York, 1973), p. 253; cf. M. Fronto, *De Bello Parthico*, ed. Naber, p. 218.

Eventually General Julius Severus was sent to Judea from Britain. Slowly, and at great cost, he conquered the province. The bloodshed and destruction were enormous. According to one record, more than 580,000 people were killed, in addition to an even greater number that died from hunger and disease. Furthermore, nine hundred and eighty-five important villages reportedly were razed, as well as fifty of the most important fortresses in the country.[12] The city of Jerusalem was completely destroyed, and Jews were forbidden even to visit there. A new city, Aelia Capitolina, was erected nearby, and the name of the province was changed from "Judea" to "Syria-Palestine" (after the Philistines of antiquity, who had lived in portions of the land one thousand years before).

7. THE SPREAD OF CHRISTIANITY

Despite prolific research, the beginnings of Christianity remain shrouded in some obscurity. The earliest non-Christian historical sources date from a century after its origins, and even the first Gospels were written some decades after the death of Jesus. Josephus, the Jewish historian who lived in the first century C.E. and wrote in voluminous detail about many minor events in contemporary Judea, did not mention anything at all concerning Jesus.[13]

At first Christianity remained a small Jewish sect. It grew dramatically, however, under the energetic leadership of Paul. He stressed to the pagans the abandonment of what, to them, were the difficult and strange biblical norms of circumcision, dietary laws, and other religious observances. The waiving of these religious obligations, together with very active proselytization, garnered many more converts for Christianity than the very strict, uncompromising religion of Judaism. Judaism generally discouraged proselytization and took the position that it would not accept any convert unless the religious authorities were certain that the newcomer would abide by all of the strict requirements of Jewish religious law.

Christianity's most dramatic triumph came with the conversion of the Roman Emperor Constantine to Christianity before his death in 337 C.E. Following his conversion, Christianity became the official state religion of the vast Roman Empire. Within only a few subsequent decades, Christianity was transformed from the religion of a small minority of the Western world to the religion of the bulk of its population. This led to

a dramatic change in the status of Jews in the Roman Empire; they now became a minority in a Christian, instead of a pagan, world.

During the fourth and fifth centuries C.E., many of the early leaders of the Christian church—including St. Ambrose, St. John (Chrysostom), St. Augustine, and St. Cyril of Alexandria—actively propagated anti-Jewish feelings.[14] This caused bitter sectarian strife, particularly in Palestine, and led to active religious persecution of Jews once Christianity became the official religion of the Roman Empire. Drastic penal laws were gradually enacted by the civil authorities against the Jews, especially in the Eastern (Byzantine) Empire, after the Roman Empire split into east and west. The legal Codex of Theodosius II (438 C.E.) contained many restrictions on Jews, as did the Code of Justinian.

8. THE JEWS IN EGYPT

Beginning with the decline of the Judean state in the fourth century B.C.E., Jews migrated to Egypt in substantial numbers. This movement was given great impetus by the Antiochus persecutions. In Egypt, Jews gradually joined the Egyptian army and also became policemen, state officials, farmers, merchants, and craftsmen. Like the Greeks and other foreigners, they were often hated by the natives, who for a long time were mistrusted by the Ptolemaic rulers and were not given positions in the military or in the higher civilian bureaucracies.

In the middle of the third century B.C.E. the Bible was translated into Greek (the Septuagint version). This had a great effect upon the many Jews who no longer understood Hebrew. Consequently, this version was used by Jews in Egypt and the entire Greco-Roman world. It was also relied on by the church fathers and the authors of the New Testament.

Many of the Jews in Egypt, particularly Alexandria, were sympathizers of Hellenism who attempted to find a synthesis between the Hellenist and Jewish values and approaches to life. The existence of the Bible in a Greek version may have lessened the dependence of these Hellenist Jews upon the Jews of Palestine and may have led to a greater degree of separation between them.[15]

12. Ibid.
13. See W. H. C. Frend, *English Historical Review* 86 (1972): 345 ff., for a review of the literature; Grant, *Jews in the Roman World*, p. 105.

14. See, Grant, *Jews in the Roman World*, p. 287; Baron, *Social and Religious History*, vol. 2, p. 268.
15. See E. Bickermann, *The Historical Foundations of Post-Biblical Judaism*, in L. Finkelstein, *The Jews*, vol. 1 (New York, 1949).

C. *Internal Power Blocs in Judea during the Second Commonwealth*

There is much controversy among scholars concerning the identity and relative power of the participants in the decision-making processes in Judea during the Second Jewish Commonwealth. In general, however, the situation appears to have been as follows.

Under Ptolemaic rule many small tax farmers (who paid the government a set fee and then attempted to collect all that they could in taxes for their own profit) were replaced by one large tax collector for the entire area of Syria-Phoenicia. This individual wielded enormous power because of his tax-collecting authority, his wealth, and his friendship with the Ptolemaic kings. The situation changed when Judea was incorporated into the Seleucid Empire after the subsequent Hasmonean revolts.

There were six principal power groups that may be identified:

1. THE SUPREME JUDICIAL-LEGISLATIVE BODY

At the beginning of the Second Jewish Commonwealth (*circa* 500 B.C.E.) a decision-making body (*anshei k'nesset ha'gdola*—literally, "the people of the great assembly") was formed, consisting of one hundred and twenty members.[16] This group appears to have prescribed law and to have acted as a judicial body in applying law as well. Subsequently, for reasons not entirely clear, the size of the group was reduced to seventy-one members and was referred to as the Sanhedrin.[17] It was traditionally headed by two men, one of whom, the *nasi* (the exalted one), appears to have had a role in representing the Jewish community in its dealings with Rome.

Although the precise functions and scope of operations of the Sanhedrin is the subject of scholarly debate, it clearly was an important participant in decision-making during the Second Jewish Commonwealth, and for a considerable period thereafter.

2. THE PRIESTHOOD

The priests (a group limited to the descendants of Aaron, the first high priest) wielded considerable power

during much of the Second Commonwealth. At times the high priest had the authority to represent the community before the outside world and administered all state affairs, both religious and secular. Contemporary writers of the second century B.C.E., have recorded the great splendor of the Temple service in Jerusalem and the large numbers of priests who participated.

The Temple, which was run by the priests, was a source of power in the decision-making processes. It was, first of all, the holiest shrine in Judea and the center of religious worship. Those associated with it therefore acquired great respect in the eyes of the people. Their views weighed very heavily. Vast amounts of funds and treasures accumulated in the Temple, not only because Jews all over the world sent donations to the Temple but also because many used it as a safe depository for their funds. Control of these funds became an important factor when the Seleucid rulers introduced an informal bidding system, awarding the high priesthood to the highest bidder. These funds were, from time to time, utilized to pay the prices demanded to acquire this high office. Additionally, priests, whose main function was to teach the Torah, (the duty of any individual priest in the Temple being limited to short periods, a few times each year), became authorities on its norms, and often acted as judges and important decision-makers (see Part One, Chapter III, Section B 1 *c*).

The *gerousia* ("nobles of the people"),[18] a council of elders, played an important role in decision-making. It was probably composed of members of wealthier families and priests, modeled after the councils of nobles in Greece.[19]

3. THE PHARISEES

It also seems clear that, with the Hellenization of the high priesthood during the second century B.C.E., there emerged a strong and widespread group of scholars, called "scribes," who sought to counteract the influence of the Hellenist high priests and to dominate much of the decision-making processes. They were called Pharisees, (the Separatists), probably because they "separated" themselves from all that was unclean. They emphasized the observance of the Torah and its values, sought to set up schools in every town for its study in order to offset the influences of the *gymnasia*, which existed in every Greek settlement. They stressed the oral tradition, which augmented and explained the written Bible, and they concentrated their efforts on its study, self-improvement, and moral and ethical re-

16. This number may have been arrived at because it contained ten members—the traditional "congregation" for each of the twelve tribes (I. Herzog, *Judaism: Laws and Ethics* [London, 1976], p. 114).

17. See L. Honig, *The Great Sanhedrin* (New York, 1953); H. Mantel, *Studies in the History of the Sanhedrin* (Cambridge, 1961); A. Buechler, *Ha'Sanhedrin Be'Yerushalayim* (Hebrew; Jerusalem, 1976); Baron, *Social and Religious History*, vol. 2, p. 318.

18. See 1 Macc. 14:28.

19. Tcherikover, *Hellenistic Civilization and the Jews*, p. 111.

sponsibility. The Pharisees eventually became the most popular party and found substantial support among the lower economic classes. Some of the more famous early Pharisee leaders were Simon ben Shetah and Judah ben Tabai, both of whom fled to Egypt when King Alexander Jannai persecuted the Pharisees, and returned after his death. These two men were very active in ensuring a normative Judaism that would resist the changes brought about during the Hellenstic period and yet would apply the rules of the Torah to new situations while always attempting to achieve its basic goals.[20]

Simon ben Shetah tried to reduce the power of the Jewish king, Jannai, and compel him to submit to the power of the Sanhedrin. He (and the Sanhedrin) also prescribed reforms to help women by changing the economic arrangements required by Jewish law at the time of marriage so as to ensure support of widows and divorcees. Although the Pharisees were normally lenient in matters of punishment,[21] Ben Shetah acted rigorously when he felt it necessary and applied extraordinary provisions of law to execute many sorceresses. Hillel, too, authored many reformations of the law, most notably the *prusbul* (see below, Chapter V, Section C 4). In contrast with the other participants in the decision-making processes, the Pharisees generally were poor economically. Hillel is reported to have been a woodchopper, and Simon ben Shetah a seller of flax.[22]

4. THE SADDUCEES

Another group that participated in decision-making during the Second Jewish Commonwealth were the Sadducees. There is much controversy among scholars as to their precise identity, beliefs, and sources of support. The consensus of scholars is that they consisted primarily of priests and wealthy individuals who allied themselves to the powerful Hasmonean princes and who did not recognize the oral tradition as authentic in explaining and augmenting the norms and values of the Bible.[23]

5. THE ESSENES

Another group whose origin and role is also obscure is the Essenes. They were, apparently, a small semi-monastic community of ascetics who lived strictly supervised lives and who emphasized purity. There are many scholars who see connections between them and the Dead Sea communities, whose scrolls were unearthed in the late 1940s. There was perhaps some relationship between them and some of the early Christians.

In addition to the foregoing, there were other government officials and merchants who probably had some weight in decision-making. We do not have much information about the craftsmen, the "urban proletariat" and the power that they wielded, nor regarding the peasants who constituted a majority of the population.

6. THE ARMY

There was still another group that had an important role in the power processes: the paid professional army of the Hasmonean dynasty. After the Hasmonean revolt against the Seleucids, mercenaries replaced the civilian militia because of the long drawn-out nature of some of the military campaigns and the necessity for well-trained and equipped soldiers, who were required for the wars that constantly became more and more complicated, even at that time.

In short, many groups participated in the power processes and clashed with each other. In addition to the conflicts between the Pharisees, Hellenists, and Sadducees, there was also resistance by the masses of common people (most often represented by the Pharisees) against the authoritarian rule of the king. They reacted against the high priests appointed by the secular authorities, particularly where the appointees were Hellenists who deviated from traditional Jewish religious practices.

D. *The Jews in Babylonia: Demographic, Economic, and Cultural Conditions*

In contrast to the conditions of the Jews in Judea under Roman rule, the Jews of Babylonia (Mesopotamia) had a much more tolerable existence. The Jewish population of Babylonia was always very substantial. During the existence of the Second Jewish Commonwealth their numbers may have exceeded those of the Jewish population of Judea,[24] especially since augmented by continuous immigration of Jews from the Roman territories. They were also increased substantially by the general absence of religious persecution and by favorable economic conditions, including

20. S. Lieberman, *Hellenism in Jewish Palestine* (New York, 1950), p. 28 ff.; Buechler, "Studies in Sin and Atonement" (London, 1909).

21. Josephus, *Antiquities of the Jews*, 13:288–98.

22. Deut. Rabbah 3:5; see R. Marcus, "The Pharisees in the Light of Modern Scholarship," *Journal of Religion* 32 (1954): 153.

23. See Baron, *Social and Religious History*, vol. 2, p. 318. Grant, *Jews in the Roman World*, p. 39 ff.; see, however, B. Z. Katz, *Pharisees, Sadducees, Zealots, and Christians* (Tel-Aviv, 1948).

24. S. W. Baron, *The Jewish Community* (Philadelphia, 1942).

lighter taxation. Some scholars have even estimated that the Jewish population there grew from approximately one million to two million in the three centuries from 200 C.E to 500 C.E.[25] Regardless of the exact number of Jews there, it is clear that, first under Parthian and then under Persian rule (beginning 226 C.E.), the center of Jewish life and law moved from the Roman Empire to the Persian Empire.

One of the dominant factors in the cultural, religious, and decision-making activities of Babylonian Jewry was the existence there of Academies of law and religion. The chief ones were in Nehardea on the Euphrates River and further south in Sura. The most prominent heads in the history of these institutions were the two contemporaries Samuel and Rav (Abba Aricha), *circa* 226 C.E. Later on new academies were founded at Pumbedita and at Mehuza. Under the leadership of these academies there occurred a revival and flowering of learning and scholarship in Jewish law and religious studies. It was common for many thousands of Jews who worked in the fields by day to go to the academies or other centers of study at night to study the Torah. In the spring and in the fall, when little agricultural work was required, many thousands studied all day at these institutions.

In addition to providing an educated proletariat, these institutions trained many leading scholars and were a dominant feature in Jewish life and law for

25. Grant, *Jews in the Roman World*, p. 275.

nearly eight hundred years, until the middle of the eleventh century C.E.

Under the direction of a number of heads of these academies (notably Ashi and Ravina), the Babylonian Talmud (which was generally much more elaborate, detailed, and authoritative than its Palestinian counterpart) was codified and reduced to writing (*circa* 425 C.E.). The Babylonian Talmud not only constituted a vast repository of law, religious beliefs, practices, and traditions, but also served for nearly two millennia as a vital, unifying force for Jews all over the world, who studied it assiduously. They revered it and looked to it as the ultimate source of authority and inspiration. Its study also helped to detract the Jews from the vicissitudes of daily life in troubled times.

The language of the Jews of Babylonia at that time was Aramaic, which had been adopted as the official language of the Persian Empire. This was the tongue utilized to codify the Babylonian Talmud. The principal occupation of the Jews there was agriculture, and they were generally free to practice their religion without interference. Even here, however, there were intermittent persecutions by Zoroastrian Persian rulers. Intense religious persecutions also took place in the middle of the fifth century, when the Persian kings adopted Zendicism as their faith. These religious repressions were apparently an important factor in the revolt by the Jewish leader Mar Zutra, who succeeded in establishing an independent state at Mahuza for seven years, until it was conquered and he was crucified in 520 C.E.

V. Talmudic Law in General; The Effects of Cultural and Socioeconomic Conditions on Talmudic Law

A. General Conceptions of Law and Authority

1. THE TORAH BEFORE THE CREATION OF THE WORLD
(Babylonian Talmud, *Shabbat* 88b)*

. . . R. Joshua b. Levi also said: When Moses ascended on high, the ministering angels spake before the Holy One, blessed be He. 'Sovereign of the Universe! What business has one born of woman amongst us?' 'He has come to receive the Torah,' answered He to them. Said they to Him. 'That secret treasure, which has been hidden by Thee for nine hundred and seventy-four generations before the world was created, Thou desirest to give to flesh and blood!

. . . He [then] spake before Him: Sovereign of the Universe! The Torah which Thou givest me, what is written therein? *I am the Lord thy God, which brought thee out of the Land of Egypt.* Said he to them [the angels]. 'Did ye do down to Egypt; were ye enslaved by Pharaoh: why then should the Torah be yours? Again, What is written therein? *Thou shalt have none other gods:* do ye dwell among peoples that engage in idol worship? Again what is written therein? *Remember the Sabbath day, to keep it holy:* do ye then perform work, that ye need to rest? Again what is written therein? *Thou shalt not take [the name . . . in vain]:* is there any business dealings among you? Again what is written therein. *Honour thy father and thy mother,* have ye fathers and mothers? Again what is written therein? *Thou shalt not murder. Thou shalt not commit adultery. Thou shalt not steal*; is there jealousy among you; is the Evil Tempter among you? Straightway they conceded [right] to the Holy One, blessed be He.

Notes to "The Torah before the Creation of the World"

1. The talmudic tradition is that the Torah was created a long time before man and was a "secret treasure" that was hidden by God (who is called in the Talmud "The Holy One Blessed Be He" in the desire to avoid invoking the name of God in vain; see Exod. 20:7);

*Excerpts from the Talmud in English translation appearing in this work are from the Soncino Press translation (London, 1961) reproduced with minor changes. The translation has not been adapted to current language usage.

that the angels sought to keep it in the heavens and to prevent its being given to man; and that it is a "stored-up treasure in which Thou takest delight every day."[1] Compare with the Mesopotamian view that the *Kittum* was part of the cosmic order that existed before man and even before the gods.[2]

2. TALMUDIC LEGAL PERSPECTIVES

1. The foregoing talmudic selection reflects the perspective that the law is transcendental. This notion has been expounded very cogently by Rabbi Joseph B. Soloveitchik, one of the foremost Talmud authorities of our time, in his classic expositions of the talmudic perspectives concerning Judaic law.[3] The following is a combined summary, quotation, and paraphrasing (in the editor's own translation) of relevant portions of his quintessential Hebrew essay, "The Man of Law," in *Talpiot*, vol. 1 (1944–45).

In Soloveitchik's view, the transcendental nature of law results in the perception that:

The law has an *a priori* relationship, which has been established for all existence, with all its nuances, details, and tittles. The "man of law" [the person whose perspectives and practices accord completely with the traditions of Judaic law] approaches all of creation and examines it from the perspective of an ideal world reflected in his legal-cultural tradition. All the concepts of the law are *a priori* concepts and the "man of law" utilizes them to examine the entire world. His viewpoint is like that of a mathematician:

1. See *Shabbat* 89a, Soncino English trans. (London, 1961), p. 423.
2. See E. Speiser, "Cuneiform Law and the History of Civilization," Part One, Chapter II, Section C, above. For further discussion of the existence of the Torah before the creation of the world, see Talmud, *Avot* 3:14; Gen. *Rabbah* 1:2 (reprinted Jerusalem, 1969); Talmud, *Pesahim* 54a; Lev. *Rabbah* 19:1; *Avot De Rabbi Natan* 31, ed. Schechter (London, 1887); *Ben-Sirah* 1:1–5; Judah Ha-Levi, *Kuzari* (reprinted London, 1948), 3:73; Judah Loewe, *Netivot Olam* (reprinted London, 1968), 1:1; Isaac Aramaah, *Akedat Yitzhak* (reprinted New York, 1972), Gen. 1:1; M. Kasher, *Torah Shelema* (New York, 1950); Exod. *Mishpatim*. See, in general, A. J. Heschel, *Torah Min Hashamayim* (Hebrew; Jerusalem, 1962–65), pp. 8–32, for extensive citations to the literature of the ancient Near East, the Talmud, and the Middle Ages, and W. Harvey in *Encyclopedia Judaica*, 8:366 ff.
3. J. B. Soloveitchik, "Thoughts and Visions: The Man of Law" (Hebrew; New York, 1944–45), pp. 651 ff., 667–709; see also his works cited in footnotes 4 and 7, below.

a priori and ideal. Both the mathematician and the 'man of law' scrutinize the real world on an *a priori* and ideal level and utilize *a priori* terms and concepts, which establish beforehand their relationships to these phenomena. They examine the actual, relying on an ideal viewpoint . . . to ascertain whether the real phenomena accord to their idealistic conception: . . . The ideal creation, not reality, represents the yearning of the "man of law." . . . From this point of view . . . time is only an historical anomaly in the progress of the ideal law in its transformation into the real world . . . and as though it were not necessary to dwell on a transitory moment of deviation, which has established itself temporarily in our historical existence. . . .

Rabbi Soloveitchik's sometimes hyperbolical description of the law as independent of time, circumstances, or moral motivations[4] is not, apparently, meant to imply that law is really a closed system, isolated from developments in the human arena. This is stressed in the exposition of his thought by his son-in-law, Aharon Lichtenstein.[5] The law, although it is regarded as transcending time and space, is intended to operate within the confines of historical and spatio-temporal reality and is historically conditioned.[6] This motion is elaborated in the following condensations by others of public addresses by Rabbi Soloveitchik:

Halakhah [Jewish law], however is not always identical with common sense. The *Halakhah* system has its own methodology and manner of analysis and its own schemata and conceptualized rationale, similar to mathematical constructions. An analogy from the history of science will be helpful in explaining this point. Aristotelian physics proved faulty because it was governed by common sense. Objects fell, according to this approach, because they had weight. *Prima facie*, this is an eminently reasonable approach—conclusively disproved by Galileo and Newton. Galileo and Newton replaced a face-value understanding of natural phenomena with abstract scientific laws. They substituted a *logos* with conceptualization of reality for a common sense approach. Heat and sound and even matter are but configurations created by the human mind and expressed in mathematical terms which correspond to the external reality.

Similarly, the Oral Law has its own epistemological approach, divinely prescribed and conceptually understood, which only a scholar (*lamdan*) who has mastered its material and methodology can properly grasp. *Halakhah* has its own *logos*, its own method of thinking. It is more than a mere collection of laws, in the same way that Physics is more than an accumulation of laws. Both are autonomous, self-integrated systems. Consequently, the *Halakhah* need not conform to the dictates of common sense reasoning any more than mathematical or scientific conceptualized systems needs accommodate themselves to common sense. . . .[7]

One must not try to rationalize the norms of the Torah from without. One must not judge norms and laws (of the Torah) in terms of a secular system of values. Such an attempt, be it psychologism, or be it utilitarianism, undermines the very foundations of Torah and tradition, and leads eventually to the most tragic consequences of assimilation and nihilism. . . . One must not try to gear the *Halakhic* norms to the transient values of a neurotic society. . . .

But to say that the *Halakha* is not sensitive to problems, and is not responsive to the needs of people, is an outright falsehood. The *Halakha* is responsive to the needs of both the community and the individual. But the *Halakha* has its own orbit, moves at a certain definitive speed, has its own pattern of responding to challenge, its own criteria and principles. . . . To speak about *Halakha* as a fossil, Heaven forbid, is ridiculous. Those who study *Halakha* find it a living, dynamic discipline. . . . We are opposed to changes, but novelty is certainly the very essence of *Halakha*. Novelties must come from within the system, not from the outside. You cannot psychologize *Halakha*, historicize *Halakha*, or rationalize *Halakha*. These are foreign, extraneous. And not only *Halakha*. Can you psychologize mathematics? Let us take Euclidian geometry: I can give many psychological explanations why Euclid said two parallels don't cross. Would this change the mathematical postulate? . . .[8]

4. Emphasized also in his essay, "Mah Dodekh Midod" (Hebrew), in *Hadoar* 62 (1963): 39.

5. A. Lichtenstein, in *Great Jewish Thinkers of the Twentieth Century* (B'nai Brith Great Book series; New York, 1963), 3:281 ff.

6. See Maimonides (Rambam), *Guide for the Perplexed*, trans. M. Friedlander (New York, 1956), 3:27; D. Shapiro, "The Ideological Foundations of Halakhah," in *Tradition* 9 (Spring-Summer, 1967): 104, and footnote 30, below. See P. Wertheim, *Halakhah Ve'Halihut Ba'Hasidut* (Hebrew; Jerusalem, 1949), which attempts to show that halakhic decisions by Hasidim were influenced by their philosophic perspectives. Compare ". . . The Bible is God's anthropology rather than man's theology," in A. J. Heschel, *God in Search of Man* (Philadelphia, 1956), p. 412; see S. R. Hirsch, *Gesammelte Schriften* (Frankfurt, 1902), vol. 1; I. Leibovitz, "The World and the Jews," in *Forum* 4 (1965): 85.

7. J. B. Soloveitchik, "The First Rebellion against Torah Authority," in *Shiurei Harav: A Conspectus of the Public Lectures of Rabbi Joseph B. Soloveitchik* (New York, 1974), pp. 42–43. Since this work was written by students, it is not completely authoritative.

8. The last two paragraphs are from an address by Rabbi Soloveitchik at the 1975 convention of the Rabbinical Council of America, condensed by Dr. Isaac Hersh in "Surrendering to the Almighty," in *Light* (New York, 1976). The author possesses a tape recording of this address.

[While the law is transcendent],[9] yet at the same time Moses prevails over the angels who oppose the transmission of Law to man, by his argument,[10] 'What is written in it? 'Honor your father and mother.' Do you have a father or mother? What is written in it? 'You shall not kill'; 'You shall not commit adultery'; 'you shall not steal.' Is there jealousy among you, is the evil tempter among you?" In short, the contents of the law concerns itself with man and his activity, and is not appropriate for angels who inhabit a transcendental world.

This concern for human existence is reflected in the Talmudic principle that "The saving of a life is more important [literally, "pushes aside"] the entire Torah;"[11] "You shall live by them, but not die by them";[12] "Desecrate one Sabbath for him so that he should be able to keep many Sabbaths."[13] This principle is the slogan of Judaism. . . . In this point, there is revealed the antimony in the world view and in the spirit [of the "man of law"]. On the one hand . . . his shape and face resemble the scientist who employs, constructs, and compares his ideal concepts to the real world, as, for example, the mathematician. On the other hand, however, the "man of law" is not a prosaic cognitive type, who is not at all concerned with transcendental matters and is only subservient to temporal life. . . . He is a religious person, elevated and glorious. Yet, while the "man of religion" [the person whose perspectives and acts are determined solely by the stereotype of non-Jewish religious motivations, not by the perspectives of Jewish law] strongly desires to climb out of this vale of tears of reality to the Mountain of God, and to be taken out from the oppression of the senses into the broad spaces of transcendental existence, the "man of law" yearns to bring transcendentalism down into the "valley of death"[14] of our world, and to transform it into the world of life. At a time when the "man of religion" has pounding within him the yearning to run away and flee from reality . . . , the "man of law" draws a circle about himself in this world and refuses to emerge from it. He wishes to purify his world and not flee from it. . . . He desires to bring godliness and holiness down into space and time and into our finite earthly existence. The "man of law" is not like the "man of religion," who rebels against the rule of earthly existence and seeks a refuge in an ethereal world, and is not like the man of science, who has no contact with a transcendental existence. The "man of law" understands transcendentalism, but does not rise up to it, only brings it down to himself. In-

stead of raising the nether world to the upper world, he brings down the upper world into the lower world. . . .

In the Talmudic view, spiritual salvation is achieved by man interacting with other men, while strictly observing the laws of the Torah. The emphasis is upon temporal interactions, rather than transcendental relations. This view is symbolized by the biblical description of the descent of God on Mt. Sinai to give the Torah to the Israelite people.[15] Man can, therefore, reach the highest level of holiness, not by transcendental speculation, but by living a normal life, fully observing all of the given norms. Holiness is thus created primarily through the acts of man, rather than through the acts of God. The "descent of God" on Mt. Sinai, and the subsequent erection by the Israelites of the Tabernacle and Temple as places of holiness, symbolized both the transposition of the transcendental to earth and of the infinite God to a finite space. It is this which enables man to create holiness.

In short, the purpose of Jewish law, is to bring the spirituality of God down to earth. (This goal of the law is a very different view than that of Jewish mysticism, which views its objective as the freeing of man, as well as God, from any connection with the impure world). Jewish law is the method by which the infinite and formless transcendental spirituality, is transformed and applied to this finite world. The laws make the spiritual concrete, instead of permitting it to remain abstract. . . .

It might, therefore, be said that the basic methodology of Talmudic law is its quantitative function in establishing boundaries and limits for human action. This is reminiscent of Galileo's words that the book of nature is written in the letters of triangles, squares, circles, globes, and other mathematical shapes. It is the perspective of Judaic law that the law and religion can only have a significant effect upon man when they are concretized, so that they can be sensed with all the senses and are encountered by a person at all times. The law, therefore, takes the ephemeral spirituality of religion and quantifies it in fixed shapes through specific norms and legal principles. This may be compared to a scientist, who expresses the concepts of light, sound, and other aspects of physical existence in terms of mathematical relationships and objective formulas. The law, therefore, reflects both religion and God, in objective and concrete terms. In this respect, the law reflects God's essence in the same way that the earth and the heavens reveal something about the mystery of God. . . .[16]

In order to fully grasp the place of law in the Talmudic *Weltanschaung*, it is important to realize that in the Talmudic conception, man comes to

9. The following paragraphs are also paraphrased and translated from Soloveitchik's "Thoughts and Visions."
10. Talmud, *Shabbat* 88b.
11. Talmud, *Sanhedrin* 74a.
12. Talmud, *Yoma* 85b.
13. Ibid.
14. Paraphrasing Ps. 23:4.

15. Exod. 19:18, 20.
16. See Ps. 19:2.

know God and comes closer to Him by studying and fulfilling His Law. It is regarded as, perhaps, the best method to approach God. . . .

The shift of emphasis in religion and law, from the transcendental to the earthly, is also reflected in the Biblical and Talmudic scope of law, which covers all aspects of a person's personal and business life and is not restricted to ritual rules. In the Talmud rules concerning worship or the Temple do not occupy the central position in the Law . . .[17] [whose main purpose is to improve the material well-being of the individual and the community and to elevate the moral and intellectual status of man. See Maimonides, *Guide for the Perplexed*, part III, ch. 27].

2. The Talmudic conception of the goal of law, has been expressed more simply, by another prominent contemporary scholar, Dr. Samuel Belkin:

Our sages' chief concern was finding a system by which man, in his conduct, would apply the basic religious principles laid down in the Torah. . . . The underlying principles, and even the rules of procedure of Rabbinic law spring from profound religious and theological concepts, and are not based at all on social theories. The law pertaining to "crime," for example, often results from the religious concept of "sin," and the laws governing community life arise directly from the Talmudic concept of the sacredness of the individual personality. The laws of "the court of man" are seen as reflections of "the laws of heaven," and the norms for the conduct of man in his relations with his fellow man, are governed by man's relation to God. Human or social "practicality" was never accepted as a determining factor in Jewish Law. . . .[18]

Is the claim made in this last sentence true? Test this thesis in examining the materials in "Adjusting the Law to Meet Changed Conditions" (Part Three, Chapter IX, Section B).

3. The foregoing selection from the Talmud also reflects an additional aspect of its perspectives concerning the law. Law is regarded not merely as a tool for the proper ordering of a mundane society, to avoid misfortune and promote the general welfare, but as a

divine law of cosmic importance. Jewish mystics, therefore, in Talmudic times and subsequently, constructed metaphysical systems in which every aspect of the law and every detail has its proper niche in a cosmic framework.[19] The Torah is regarded as reflecting both God's transcendance and His immanence. Without the transcendental nature of the law, there would be no obligation to obey it. The immanence of God and His laws helps to determine the character of those laws, including its goal to order society in a manner that will bring it to its greatest possible perfection and to lift it up to the highest goals of eschatological fulfillment. This is regarded as an aspect of the will of God. In the talmudic view, this will is also imposed upon the physical world by the laws of nature.[20] Even more, "the law reflects not merely the will of God, but that which is identical with His will—His essence."[21] The laws, therefore, have both mundane as well as metaphysical goals that are not antithetical. They merely apply to different levels of personal or historical experience.[22]

It should also be realized that the non-law portions of the Bible and Talmud, dealing with its theological and metaphysical aspects, have also been regarded by talmudic decision-makers as intrinsic parts of the law, having a very significant influence in shaping it.

Accordingly, even those portions of the Torah that do not, on their face, contain legal norms are viewed as having great importance and as affecting law (in addition to their mystical connotations). No letter, jot, or title of the Torah is there by chance. Each has its importance for law throughout all generations.[23]

In the Judaic tradition, therefore, law is considered to be an aspect of the divine order for the entire cosmos. It relates to the ordering of human activity in the same way as the laws made for nature govern the activity of planets, of all creatures, and of the organic and inorganic worlds. Rabbi Joseph B. Soloveitchik has been quoted as follows:

---

17. See also the essay on Torah by Moshe ben Nahman (Ramban, also known as Nahmanides) in *Kal Kitvei Ha-Ramban*, ed. Shevel (Jerusalem, 1967), in which he seeks to establish that the Torah is unique compared to other documents and legal systems. See also Judah Loewe, *Tiferet Yisrael* (Hebrew; reprinted Jerusalem, 1970), esp. intro. and chs. 2 and 18; idem, *Discourse on the Torah and Discourse on the Commandments* (reprinted Jerusalem, 1971); idem, *B'er Ha' Golah* (Hebrew; London, 1960; reprinted Jerusalem, 1971), ch. 2; Abraham of Vilna, *Ma'Alot Ha'Torah* (Kapust, 1828; reprinted New York, 1946).

18. S. Belkin, *In His Image: The Jewish Philosophy of Man As Expressed in Rabbinic Tradition* (New York, 1960), intro.

19. Shapiro, "The Ideological Foundations of Halakhah," pp. 101–2.

20. "So, too, just as all creatures in the entire physical world obey God because of the law of nature which he has imposed upon them, man, too was given laws to order his life as another aspect of God's immanence" (ibid., p. 107). See Z. Shneur, *Tanya* (reprinted New York, 1960), ch. 5; see also Heschel, *Torah Min Hashamayim*, pp. 8–33.

21. Shapiro, pp. 108–9.

22. Ibid., p. 114. Since the law is held to reflect the essence of God, it has been asserted that the talmudic division of the laws of the Torah into positive commandments (requiring one to perform an act, such as helping another human in need) and negative commandments (prohibiting an act, such as murder) are reflective of God as a creator and as a divider (Gen. 1:4, 67). As such, he separates the permitted from the prohibited.

23. See Talmud, *Menahot*, 29b; see also Soloveitchik, "The Man of Law," p. 710.

Consider natural law. If a man decides to defy the law of gravity, and walks over a ledge, the law promptly exacts its claim on him and he falls down. We might call this "natural punishment." The punishment is built into the act; there is no need for extraneous punishment. If a person takes drugs, then, even if he repents, the organic and biochemical damage done to the body remains. God, as the Lord of nature, does not forgive.

Now, if this is true of natural law, it is also true of certain elements of moral law. A murder avenges itself on the murderer. If a man neglects to honor his parents, our sages say that his children, seeing the way he treats his parents, will not honor him. A person may turn to idol worship, but it will eventually be a means of his own self-destruction. If one does not observe the Sabbath, he will continue to lead a profane life without let-up. At no point does he come into the higher redeemed existence of the Sabbath as contrasted with the profane weekdays. . . . The basic moral law is contained in the Ten Commandments. The same God is the author of the natural and moral laws. Hence, promiscuity, theft, murder, perjury, idol worship, atheism, agnosticism, and so forth must all lead to disaster. At both the cosmic and moral level, it is impossible for any man to fight with God."[24]

4. Another fundamental notion and basic goal in the talmudic conception of law is human dignity. As Samuel Belkin put it:

Upon these twin principles—the sovereignty of God, and the sacredness of the individual—the religious philosophy of Judaism rests. Enunciated not merely as a theory, this philosophy is clearly reflected in the *Halakhah* [Jewish law]. In fact, only by properly understanding the Jewish concept of divine kingship and human worth can we fully understand many legal and spiritual institutions in Judaism. It is also true, however, that since Judaism is interested in practice, rather than in theory, only a close examination of Jewish Law can reveal its philosophic foundations.[25]

From this notion of the sacredness of the individual[26] flows the concept of man's freedom and his right to choose, just as the divinity he resembles possesses this ability. This freedom of choice is reflected in man's ability to choose good over evil[27] and is held to be a key element guiding the civil norms of the Talmud in the areas of contract, damages, torts, and other commercial dealings and relations between men:

In Jewish Law, commercial norms were not prescribed, based upon classic sociological, political, or economic perspectives. All of the rules that are arranged in *Hoshen Mishpat* [the standard Jewish commercial law code] concerning matters that people contract among themselves of their own volition and mutual agreement, consist only of a clarification of the intention and desires of the parties to the controversy, on the basis of the dealings between them. . . . It is a principal rule in the law of the Torah . . . that a person is the exclusive ruler of his possessions and treasures; not the law and not the judge decides the destiny of his possessions.[28]

As another contemporary authority has put it:

All of the norms of the Talmud and decision-makers regarding law, consist simply of the fathoming by the Torah of the real intention of people, that they intended a particular act or that they acted in a particular way. . . . This constitutes a crucial difference between Judaic law and other systems of law. In Judaic law, commercial norms are based upon considerations limited to the individual party covered by the law. . . .[29]

This implies that Judaic law emphasizes the role and freedom of the individual in deciding what to do with his possessions and what obligations he has undertaken, but that unlike other systems of law, which are guided mainly by considerations of public welfare, economy, and policy, it does not consider the impact of the decision on persons other than the immediate parties to the controversy. This, however, ignores considerations of public policy, which are prominent in Jewish law regarding commercial matters as well (see, e.g., the discussion in Section C 4, below, regarding the institution of *prusbul*).

5. Another important perspective of talmudic decision-makers is that each individual human is under the personal and distinct supervision of God who guides the individual's destiny, except for the choice to do good or evil, with due regard to his individuality. As the Talmud puts it, "No man lifts his finger unless it has been ordained by Heaven, and no individual grass grows unless it has also been so ordained."[30]

This notion of individual guidance and supervision of human affairs by God is applied in criminal law. Sanctions were not imposed on criminal defendants

---

24. Soloveitchik, "Aseret Hadibrot," in *Shiurei Harav*, p. 47.
25. Belkin, *In His Image*, intro.
26. See ". . . in the image of god, was man created" (Gen. 9.6).
27. Soloveitchik, "The Man of Law," p. 725.

28. Y. Abramsky, *Dinei Mamonot* (Hebrew; London, 1939), pp. 4, 6.
29. S. Y. Zevin, *Sofrim Ve'Sefarim* (Hebrew; Tel-Aviv, 1959), pp. 80–84; see also Loewe, *B'er Ha'Golah*, ch. 2; idem, *Tiferet Yisrael*, ch. 70, p. 218.
30. Talmud, *Hulin* 7b. Cf. Maimonides, *Guide for the Perplexed*, 3:17, in which he asserts that the destiny of all nonhuman creatures is viewed as not decided on an individual basis but, rather, on the needs of the entire species.

who had obviously committed criminal acts where important legal criteria had not been met (such as prior warning and the complex rules and standards regarding the eligibility of witnesses). In part, this was because reliance was placed upon God to deal with such criminal defendants, even if the human court would not penalize him (see Chapter VI, Section C, below).

6. Judaic law was also perceived as democratic in nature. This important perspective has also been dealt with by J. B. Soloveichik in his essay, "The Man of Law." The following is a combined summary and paraphrase (in translation) of a part of that essay dealing with this subject.

The talmudic perception of law, and of Judaism in general, is exoteric. Both belong to the entire nation, and all, regardless of status, are required to abide by their precepts. Neither law nor religion are the exclusive preserve of nobility, priesthood, or educated elite. This was held by talmudic authorities to be exemplified by the verse, "And you shall teach them to your children and you shall speak concerning them, when you dwell in your house, when you travel on the way, when you lie down, and when you arise." (Deut. 6:7; see Talmud, *Yoma* 72). This democratic notion, that the law and the Judaic religion in general belong to all of the people rather than to an elite group, is reflected in the talmudic position that any person can approach God and pray to him without the intercession of any priest. Similarly, the Talmud strongly opposes confession of sins to anyone except God, based upon the premise that anyone can directly ask God for forgiveness and change his evil ways.

As Rabbi Samuel Belkin put it,

It [Judaism] is a *Democracy* because, unlike any other legal system, the Rabbinic Code places all emphasis upon the infinite worth and sacredness of the human being. In Judaism the recognition of the *Demos*, the individual and the infinite worth of his personality, are but a necessary outgrowth of the acceptance of God's *theos* (rulership), a relationship succinctly summed up in the phrase "Democratic Theocracy."[31]

Compare the view of Josephus (a Jewish historian who lived in Palestine in the first century C.E. and played an important role in the Jewish revolt against Rome):

Some people have entrusted supreme political powers to monarchies; others, to oligarchies, and still others, to the masses. Our lawgiver, Moses, was attracted to none of these forms of policy, but gave his constitution the form which—if a forced expression is permitted—may be termed "theocracy" . . . [which] means placing all sovereignty in the hands of God.[32]

7. In addition to the basic goals and perspectives listed above, the following are additional articulated goals, expressed at a high level of abstraction, which flow from some of the aforementioned metaphysical perspectives, and have had a profound effect on Judaic law decisions: that the Law must act to benefit individuals and society, not to harm them; to do what is good and right; to strive for holiness; to walk in the ways of God and imitate his ways and acts; to seek peace; to aspire to the highest levels of piety; to extend oneself more than the measure of law requires; and to sanctify God's name.[33]

8. Another basic goal of Judaism is that man shall be creative, and one of the fundamental goals of the law was held to be to aid man in being creative in society, to improve society, and to correct inequities that may arise. Man's duty was viewed as requiring him to correct these defects that exist in society and were permitted to exist by God in order to leave room for man to act as His partner in creation.[34] The law was viewed as designed to increase holiness on earth in this manner and to procure God's immanence here. The transformation of God's transcendentalism into wordly immanence was held to be accomplished by the application of law in the mundane world, by man, who is regarded as being composed of a duality of godliness and chaos, which reflects in microcosm the same antinomy as exists in the macrocosm of the universe.

These basic goals and values were viewed as guides to decision-makers in prescribing and applying law and called for variations in law to meet new societal conditions in order to achieve these goals (see Part Three, Chapter IX, Section B).[35]

9. As a result of the perspectives that the Torah is sacred and that its study (including, of course, the Talmud) is one of the most sublime forms of divine worship, there has always been a tradition of remark-

31. Belkin, *In His Image*, intro.

32. Josephus, *Contra Apion* (London, 1907), 2:165.

33. Chajes, *Kal Kitvei*, p. 314; Shapiro, *"The Ideological Foundations of Halakhah,"* pp. 104, 115; see. Deut. 6:18, 12:28; *Sifre*, ad loc.; Talmud, *Baba Metzia* 16b, 108a; Lev. 19:2 and commentary of Moshe ben Nahman; Deut. 26:17; Talmud, *Gittin* 59b and *Baba Metzia* 30b, 83a.

34. Soloveitchik, "The Man of Law," pp. 710, 711, 714.

35. See W. S. Wurzburger, "Meta-Halakhic Propositions," in *Tradition* 2 (Spring, 1970): 211 ff. See also E. Rackman, *One Man's Judaism* (New York, 1970), p. 203, in which he describes his concept of the dialectic of the Halakhah as comprising conflicting values such as "freedom" and "sexual morality." Rackman maintains that the sages of each generation must adjust the law while remaining within the value framework of the Halakhah. See idem, "The Dialectic of the Halakhah," in *Tradition* 3 (Spring 1961): 131; and "The Future of Jewish Law" in *Tradition* 4 (Spring 1962): 32.

ably extensive and prolonged Torah study. This is exemplified by the incident reported in the Talmud of one noted decision-maker who studied with such intensity that he unconsciously crushed his fingers until they bled but remained unaware of his wounds.[36] A more recent example is told of a very prominent nineteenth-century scholar (Rabbi Akiva Eger of Poznan, Germany) who allegedly stopped off at an inn for the night, while on his way to his son's wedding. He asked the Jewish innkeeper if he could borrow any books of the Talmud or commentaries for the evening, and was finally given a volume of one of the classic commentaries. This, however, had some pages missing. The scholar then borrowed some paper, pen and ink. According to the story, the innkeeper, who continually scurried back and forth dealing with arriving and departing guests, noticed that the scholar was up the entire night poring over the volume and writing. In the morning, the book, with additional papers inserted, was returned to him by the scholar, who then thanked him and left. Some time later, when the innkeeper examined the volumes, he noticed that paper, written in by hand, had been inserted wherever there were original pages missing. Eventually, the innkeeper, compared these handwritten pages with another copy of the volume that he obtained and discovered that Rabbi Eger had handwritten the missing materials accurately, word for word. The innkeeper is then reputed to have said: "I am not surprised that Rabbi Akiva Eger knows the commentary by heart, word for word, and was able to accurately fill in the missing pages. Everybody knows that he is a brilliant scholar. What I am astonished at, however, is his love of Torah and studiousness in staying up the whole night, studying a work that he already knows by heart, word for word."

3. THE ORAL LAW
(By Moshe ben Maimon)

Following is a classical exposition of the traditional view of the role of Oral Law held by talmudic scholars. It analyzes the Oral Law into its component parts and discusses, among other matters, the oral tradition concerning the role and function of precedent in Jewish law, majority rule, the thirteen principles of interpretation of biblical texts, and the role of prophecy in the law. Its author, Moshe ben (i.e., the son of) (referred to by some as Maimonides), was one of the foremost talmudic scholars and Jewish philosophers of all times, as well as a noted physician. Although he lived in the Middle Ages (born in Spain in 1135 and died in Egypt

in 1204), the following essay succinctly summarizes the perspective concerning the oral law embodied in the Talmud.

The essay is taken from his introduction to his commentary on the Mishnah, which he composed in his youth. The author is more commonly referred to as Rambam, an acronym consisting of the first letter of his title *Rabbi Moshe Ben Maimon*, with the letter "a" added to provide vowel sounds. The translation is from the Hebrew version, which was based on the original Arabic.

You should know that every commandment which the Holy One Blessed Be He gave to Moses, our Teacher, he gave with its explanation. He would tell him the commandment and afterwards the explanation and its elements, and thus the rest of the Torah. The manner in which Moses taught Israel was thus (Talmud, *Erubin* 54b): Moses would enter his tent. Aaron would then enter first. Moses would tell him once the commandment that had been given to him and would teach him its explanation. Aaron would then turn and place himself to the right of Moses our Teacher. Afterwards Elazar and Itamar, his [Aaron's] sons, would enter. Moses would teach them that which he had already taught Aaron. They would then remove themselves. One would sit at the left of Moses and the other at the right of Aaron.

Afterwards the seventy elders would come in and Moses would teach them just as he taught Aaron and his sons. Then the multitude and all who sought the word of God would came. Moses would then put before them that commandment until they heard everything from him. The result is that Aaron heard that commandment from Moses four times, his sons three times, and the elders twice and the rest of the people once.

Moses would remove himself and Aaron would repeat and explain that commandment which he had learned and heard four times from Moses (as we described), for all who were present. Aaron would remove himself from there after his sons heard the commandment four times (thrice from Moses and once from Aaron). Elazar and Itamar, after Aaron left, would repeat the teaching of that commandment for all who were present and then, in turn, would remove themselves. The result was that the seventy elders heard the commandment four times, twice from Moses, once from Aaron, and once from Elazar and Itamar. Afterwards the elders, as well, would repeat the instruction of the commandment to the people once. The result was that all of the congregation heard the commandment four times, once from Moses, once from Aaron, once from his sons and once from the elders.

---

36. *Rava*, in Talmud, *Shabbat* 88a; for an analogous incident with Hillel, see Talmud, *Yoma* 35b.

All the people would then go to teach one another that which they heard from Moses and would record that commandment in scrolls. Officers would then spread out throughout all of Israel to teach and study until they would know verbatim the commandment so that they would be accustomed to reading it. Afterwards they taught the explanations of that law which was given by the Lord.

That explanation contained the fundamental principles. They would record the commandments and learn the tradition by heart. Our sages comment on the verse (Lev. 25:1) "The Lord said to Moses on Mount Sinai . . . 'in the seventh year there shall be a sabbatical rest for the land,' " were not all commandments given on Sinai? But this verse is intended to suggest the following comparison: How was it in the case of the law of the sabbatical year? Its general rules, its specific prescriptions and minute details were ordained on Mount Sinai? So, also, were all commandments with their general rules and their minute details ordained on Mount Sinai. . . .

Before his death Moses began to record the Torah in books. He wrote thirteen scrolls of the Torah. . . . He gave a book to every tribe to practice it and to follow its statutes. The thirteenth scroll he gave to the Levites and said, "Take this scroll of the law," etc. (Deut. 31). . . .

After he had died, that which he had transmitted to Joshua was studied by him and his contemporaries. Whatever Joshua or one of the elders received from Moses was never contested nor challenged. One who had not heard an explanation on a particular matter which had developed would evolve laws by reasoning with the thirteen principles [of interpretation, see below] that were given on Mount Sinai and by which the Torah was to be expounded. Among these newly evolved laws, there are some over which there was no disagreement but which were unanimously accepted. There were, on the other hand, some over which there was disagreement by those who entertained different opinions, for example, in the use of analogies. When this would happen, they would follow the majority opinion, as it is written (Exod. 23), "One is to follow the majority."

(You should know that prophecy is of no consequence in the explanation of the Torah and in the expounding of the commandments by means of the thirteen principles. The rational study and reasoning of Joshua and Phineas were identical to that of Rabina and Rav Ashi [prominent scholars who edited the Talmud]. . . . But in analysis, analogy, and examination of the norms of the Torah, he [the prophet] is like [any of] the sages who are like him but are not prophets. If he interprets a matter and one who is not a

prophet interprets it in a different manner, and the prophet says, "God told me that my interpretation is correct," one does not pay heed to him. Even if a thousand prophets, all [illustrious] like Elijah and Elisha interpret a norm in a certain way, while a thousand and one scholars interpret it in a different way, we "follow the majority" [Exod. 23:2] and we follow the opinion of the thousand and one scholars, not the opinion of the thousand [illustrious] prophets. . . . [The Torah] does not say, "You shall come [for judgment] to the prophet," but "You shall come [for judgment] to the Levitical priests and to the judge" [Deut. 17:9]. . . .)

Before he died, Joshua, May Peace Be With Him, taught the Elders the explanations that he had received [from Moses] and that which they had expounded in his time concerning laws over which there was no disagreement. . . . Afterwards these elders taught the prophets what they learned from Joshua and they in turn taught each other. There was no period when there was not any study or novel interpretation. The sages of every generation would place priority upon the statements of the predecessors. They would study them and expound upon them new interpretations. There was no dissent concerning the accepted principles until the period of the Great Synod, which consisted of Hagai, Zachariah, Malachai, Daniel, Hananiah, Mishael, Azariah, Ezra the Scribe, Nehemiah the son of Shealtiel. Joining them were the prophets, making a total of one hundred and twenty elders, some of whom were craftsmen, smiths, and of similar trades. They studied, as did their predecessors, and made enactments and ordinances. The last of that brilliant group was the first one of the sages mentioned in the Mishnah; he was Simon the Just, who was the high priest in that generation. When it came to the time of our master (rabbenu), the holy Rabbi [Rabbi Judah, the Exalted], May Peace Be With Him, who was unique in his time and the sole one in whom all the charm and excellent qualities were found so that his contemporaries deemed him worthy to be called, "Our Master (rabbenu), the Holy One," whereas his real name was Judah. He was perfect in wisdom and in virtue as it was said: "From the days of Moses our Teacher until Rabbi [Judah] we did not see scholarship and worldly prestige in one person" (Talmud, Gittin 59a). He was consummate in piety, humility, and in the abstention from pleasures. . . . He possessed clarity of language and was so expert in the holy language [Hebrew] that the sages learned explanations concerning their difficulties in Scriptures from the words of his servants and maids. . . . He collected the laws, words of the sages, and the controversies transmitted from the days of Moses our teacher, until his times. He himself was one of the receivers [of the tradition] for he received it from his father Simon . . . Simon from his father Gamaliel [and so on until Moses]. . . .

After collecting the opinions and decisions, he [Rabbi Judah] began to compose the Mishnah, which contains the explanations of all the commandments written in the Torah. Some are traditions that were transmitted by Moses. Some are opinions expounded by logic and do not contain any controversy. Some are opinions about which there are controversies concerning their bases. . . .

[There are] explanations transmitted by Moses, concerning which there is no dissent in any form. [For example], from then [the time of Moses] until the present time, we have not found a controversy among the sages in any period from the days of Moses up to the days of Rav Ashi [who edited the Talmud] that anyone claims that the eye of one who blinds another should be removed based on the verse "an eye for an eye," while another claims that the tortfeasor is only required to indemnify the victim by payment of money [all agree that only the payment of money is required]. . . .

Thus, laws [in the oral tradition] that are based upon the Torah, according to the principles discussed above, may be grouped into five divisions:

The first part contains explanations transmitted by Moses, which are alluded to in the Scriptures, and which can be deduced by means of logic. There is no dissent in this matter and as soon as one says, "It has thus been transmitted to me," it is accepted.

The second part consists of laws referred to as "laws received by Moses on Sinai," for which there is no proof, as we have mentioned; there is no disagreement concerning them as well.

The third part consists of laws that were expounded by means of logic. Differences of opinion are to be found in this area and the law was decided on the basis of majority opinion. These disagreements will occur as the result of change in intellectual examination. The Talmud thus says, "If it is a law, we shall accept it; if it is a logical inference, there is a reply to it" (*Yebamot* 76b). . . .

However, it is an error to assume that the laws concerning which there are differences of opinions were also directly received from Moses. In the same manner, it is wrong to believe that the differences resulted from an error in [transmitting] the laws themselves or forgetfulness, or because one received the laws correctly, and the opponent did not; or that one forgot or did not hear all the law from his teacher as he should have heard. It is equally improper to argue for this from the talmudic passage "When the number of unqualified disciples began to increase in the Schools of Shamai and Hillel, disagreement as well began to multiply and the Torah became like two Torahs (*Sanhedrin* 88b)."

This [contention] is very shameful and [these words] are the words of one who lacks understanding and knowledge of basic principles and who brings into question the integrity of the people from whom the law was received. That passage merely states that where knowledge and training are equal, disagreement will be rare. Insufficient knowledge and training caused the disciples to be inferior to their masters in matters of logical deductions. However, we cannot always expect scholars to be on the same level as their predecessors. We are nevertheless obligated to obey the scholars of every generation, as it is written, Deut. 17: "You shall listen to the judge who will be in that time." It is in this way that differences came about and not because of errors or because one tells the truth and the other not. . . .

The fourth part consists of restrictions that the prophets and sages in every generation enacted as preventive measures against the violation of biblical law. The Holy One Blessed Be He gave instructions for their enactment. This is what he said in His general statement, "You shall guard My Laws." The tradition received [interprets this as] "construct a guard for my guards" [enact measures to prevent a transgression of my laws]. The sages refer to them as edicts (*gezerot*). At times there would be disagreement concerning them. One sage would enact a restriction for a certain reason, while another sage would disagree. This is not an infrequent occurrence in the Talmud when it is said, "Rabbi A imposed the restriction for the following reason, whereas Rabbi B did not." When the restriction is agreed upon without dispute in any form, and this prohibition becomes widespread throughout Israel, one cannot oppose it. Even the prophets themselves were not permitted to suspend it. The Talmud states that Elijah, of blessed memory, was not able to abolish any one of the eighteen enactments issued by the School of Shamai and the School of Hillel. The reason given for this was that their prohibitions had spread throughout Israel.

The fifth part consists of the laws that resulted from discussions and were agreed upon as beneficial to men in matters of the Torah but do not add to or diminish from the (biblical) commandment. These were called ordinances (*takanoth*) and customs (*minhagim*). It is forbidden to transgress them. . . .

Thus, all the laws that are mentioned in the Mishnah are classified under the above five headings. They are: explanations received from Moses and which are hinted at in Scriptures or may be deduced by logical reasoning; laws that Moses received at Sinai (and which are not hinted at in Scriptures); those that resulted from reasoning from principles, wherein in some cases there may be disagreement; restrictions; and enactments. . . .

Notes to Moshe Ben Maimon, "The Oral Law"

1. Is Rambam's thesis convincing that there were no differences of opinion in the Talmud that were due to errors in transmitting the laws from one generation to the next? (For a similar assertion, see Abraham ben David (*Ravad*) in the introduction to his *Sefer Ha'Kabala* (reprinted Jerusalem, 1962).[37] Bear this thesis in mind as you examine the various aspects of Talmudic law dealt with in this book.

Why did Rambam take such an extreme position?

2. For further discussion see K. Kahana, *Kheker Ve'Iyun* (Hebrew; Tel-Aviv, 1960), p. 7ff; Judah Loewe (*Maharal, B'er Hagolah*, Jerusalem, 1971) chapter 2. See summary of his views in A. Karib, *Works of Maharal of Prague* (Hebrew; Jerusalem, 1958), p. 272 ff.

3. The complete oral law tradition was redacted and summarized in brief form by Judah Ha'nasi in about 200 C.E. and was then reduced to writing. It came to be known as the *Mishnah* (studies). Subsequent discussions and elaborations on the *Mishnah* were redacted by Rabbi Yokhanan and others in Israel circa 400 C.E. and a similar redaction in greater detail was completed in Babylonia by Rav Ashi and others at about 460–500 C.E. These discussions were reduced to writing and became known by the Aramaic term *Gemara* (studies). The compendium of the *Mishnah* and *Gemara* together are known as the *Talmud* (another Hebrew term for studies). References to the *Talmud* are generally to the Babylonian version. The Israel version came later to be known as the Jerusalem *Talmud*. A number of smaller works incorporating parts of the oral tradition were also redacted by others during this era.

Those portions of the compendiums dealing with legal issues came to be known as *Halakhah* (law), while the remaining portions dealing with biblical exegesis, ethics, theology, history, medicine, and numerous other disciplines, came to be known as *Agadah* (narration). The latter include mystic traditions (*kabbalah*) which were to be transmitted only to a select few.

The *Talmud* became the focus of the study of Jewish laws and other religious matters, and engendered a host of commentaries. Numerous codes of law were composed, attempting to summarize and decide among the various authorities on Talmudic law who disagreed on legal and ritual issues that arose over time. The most famous codes are that of Rambam (portions of which are reproduced below) and the code of Yosef Karo, with important additions and glosses by Moshe Isserlis

(both together known as the *Shulkhan Arukh*) drafted in the sixteenth century. These, in turn, generated numerous commentaries to expound and apply their provisions to the new issues and cases that continued to arise.

4. THE ORAL LAW AND ITS RELATION TO THE WRITTEN LAW*
(By Z. H. Chajes)

The Torah is divided into two parts, the written and the unwritten law. The former consists of the Pentateuch, which was divinely revealed to Moses at Sinai. The latter comprises expositions and interpretations that were communicated to Moses orally as a supplement to the former. Without them the scriptural texts would often be unintelligible since many of them seem to contradict others, and it is only by the aid of oral elucidation that their contradictions can be straightened out.

Many examples of such discrepant texts [have been noted]. . . . [For] instance. Scripture says, "Seven days thou shalt eat unleavened bread (Exod. 34:18), while elsewhere it say "Six days thou shalt eat unleavened bread" (Deut. 16:8). Again it says, "Seven days shall there be no leaven found in your house" (Exod. 12:19), while another verse reads, "The first day ye shall put away leaven out of your houses" (Exod. 12:15).

Furthermore, scriptural law is generally briefly worded and lacks detailed directions, so that even the most versatile scholar is often left in uncertainty and unable to arrive at definite decisions regarding points that are left indefinite.

The first of the 613 divine precepts [in the Torah] may be cited as an instance: "And God said unto them, 'Be fruitful and multiply'" (Gen. 1:28). Here it does not explicitly state whether this is a distinct command or merely God's blessing. And even if it is a definite command, other difficulties are bound to arise, such as whether the duty of reproduction is enjoined upon both man and woman or on the male alone. Again, what number of children is required (for the fulfillment of the command[ment]), or what happens if the children die? Or again, what happens if children (who have died) leave children, or if a son (who has died) leaves a daughter who gives birth to male children? Will they be regarded as his sons in connection with the fulfillment of the aforesaid command[ment]? Similar difficulties also arise in connection with the practice of other precepts which are worded in such general terms as to require further explanation and elucidation. The

---

37. For a detailed critique of this position, see H. Y. Bachrach, Responsa *Havat Yair* (Jerusalem, 1962), no. 192.

*Extracted from the annotated English translation of Z. H. Chajes' essay on the Oral Law by J. Shachter, entitled *The Student's Guide through the Talmud* (London, 1960).

rabbis, in fact, have argued from what is clear in one case to other cases which are not so clear, by means of the exegetical rulings by which the Torah is expounded. . . .

Allegiance to the authority of the said rabbinic tradition is binding upon all sons of Israel, since these explanations and interpretations have come down to us by word of mouth from generation to generation right from the time of Moses. They have been transmitted to us precise, correct, and unadulterated, and he who does not give his adherence to the unwritten law and the rabbinic tradition has no right to share the heritage of Israel. . . . [There are] interpretations of precepts which are worded vaguely in scripture [and] would remain obscure without the . . . elucidation [given by tradition]. . . . [Thus] in the verse [Exod. 13:16], "And they shall be frontlets [le'totafot] between your eyes," [scripture] does not give us any elucidation thereof.

And in the text, "And he shall serve him forever" (Exod. 21:6) referring to the piercing of the servant's ear, we should be in doubt whether "forever" is to have its usual meaning [of] "all his life," or whether it is limited to the "Jubilee" period [every fiftieth year, when all slaves were to be freed; see Lev. 25:40–41]. Explanations and interpretations answering all these doubts and questions have been transmitted to us orally.

Several of the interpretations which have been handed down to us [by the oral tradition] appear at first sight not to be in accordance with the literal meaning of the Scripture. The following are some examples. . . .

"Hand for hand, eye for eye" (Exod. 21:24) in its literal sense would mean actual retaliation in kind, i.e., to cause the offender exactly the same physical injury. Tradition, however, maintains that it is a matter of monetary compensation. So also the command "Then they shall hew off her hand" (Deut. 25:12) literally means the chopping off of the hand, whereas the oral interpretation requires only monetary compensation.

"And his owner also shall be put to death," according to the letter, means that he shall be killed, while the oral halakhah interprets it again to mean monetary compensation; and even where this compensation is not forthcoming, the owner is not liable to capital punishment. . . .

Another category of oral interpretation of the Torah precepts have come down to us which completely rescind the literal meaning of the text of Scripture, as is illustrated in the following expositions.

In the Torah we read, "Forty stripes he may give him" (Deut. 25:3). Yet by tradition this was reduced to thirty-nine. The rabbis have referred to this fact as evidence of the standing of rabbinic authority, remark-

ing, "How stupid the people in Babylon are who arise for a Scroll of the law but would not do so for Talmudic scholars." Actually, in the Torah forty (stripes) are prescribed, and the rabbis have reduced the number to thirty-nine. . . .

Raba (Talmud, *Yebamot* 24a) states that although it is generally accepted that we must not lose sight of the natural (that is, literal) sense of a passage, yet we see in the following passage that the rabbis have applied traditional principles of interpretation, although this may result in setting aside the literal meaning of the text. . . .

And so we see that (in some cases) the halakhah overrides the literal meaning of the passage. . . .

As for the class of interpretations mentioned above, although they were transmitted to us from Sinai, yet the rabbis have endeavored to give them biblical support, thus demonstrating that these Sinaitic laws also rest on Scripture, in accordance with accepted exegetical rules. . . .

We are thus led to recognize that, even without the above-mentioned methods of exegesis, these precise interpretations were already known as ancient traditions transmitted orally from Sinai, for how otherwise could such a law as the "taking" of the "fruit of a goodly tree" at the Feast of the Harvest have been given to Moses in general terms without instructing him in detail regarding the nature of the fruit and in what manner he should carry out the command, whether to take it to cover the *sukkah* [huts in which the Israelites were commanded to dwell during this festival] or to have it merely grasped by the hand. The same thing will apply in connection with the ordinance of the *tefillin* ("frontlets"). Surely, it could not be left in the bare form of Scripture [to command us to wear] "frontlets between your eyes" without adding further elucidation in detail as to what they consist of as well as the method of carrying out the command. Such explanatory details, therefore, must have been given clearly to Moses in connection with every precept, and this in spite of the fact that the rabbis endeavored to deduce them from Scripture by means of the exegetical rules. Surely, if their only source had been the biblical inferences quoted, one might justly ask, How were these precepts practiced before these exegetical rules were formulated? Was the precept of *tefillin*, for example, not properly practiced before these methods of biblical exposition were devised?

The fact is that neither Moses, Phineas, Joshua, Samuel, nor the elders had ever any doubt about the explanatory details of the written precepts because they were all handed down from generation to generation by oral tradition as received at Sinai; the rabbis merely sought to find biblical support for them. . . .

It is true that as far as scriptural norms regarding punishment are concerned, one is allowed to apply any of the exegetical methods of inference as long as it is supported by the authority of oral tradition; but in cases where the laws are clear and need only some written evidence, one may use even a far-fetched analogy, so long as it is applied in a scholarly way, to gain for these laws a basis in the written Torah. The reason why, indeed, the rabbis sought to establish methods by which they might give these accepted traditions a basis in the Pentateuch or in the other sacred writings, was that in ancient times it was not permitted to reduce the oral law to writing.

Since such [norms] were liable to be forgotten, the rabbis employed even strained and far-fetched biblical interpretations and supports to enable memory to retain them, as will be explained later at length. . . .

In view of all this, one should not be astonished at some of the homiletic expositions employed in support of clear and definite [norms], even if the literal meaning of the passages used appear to be far removed from the [norms] of which they are intended to serve as proof, because their main purpose was only to assist the memory in preserving [norms] transmitted orally and already practiced. . . .

Notes and Questions to Chajes, "The Oral Law and Its Relation to the Written Law"

1. With regard to the claim of Chajes that the laws in the Bible cannot be understood without a grasp of the oral tradition, examine the "covenant code" in chapter 21 of Exodus and the other biblical norms in Part One, Chapter II, Section D 2 above. Do they constitute a comprehensive code for ordering any society —even a primitive, simple one—or do they seem to constitute merely a bare-boned skeletal outline that requires "flesh and blood" details for practical application? Would this outline, (analogous, perhaps, to student notes taken of a lecture) require supplementation by a contemporaneous understanding of the missing details and of the meaning of the vague and ambiguous terms, that is, an Oral Law? See also the defense of the oral tradition in the seventeenth century by D. Nieto,[38] who cites extensive arguments for the existence of an oral tradition; he states that most of the biblical norms (including many of the most basic ones) are ambiguous and could only have been understood on the basis of an oral tradition.

2. Is an oral tradition a vital part of the American legal system today? Is it a necessary element of *any* system of law? See C. Tiedeman, *The Unwritten Con-*

stitution of the United States: A Philosophical Inquiry into the Fundamentals of American Constitutional Law (New York, 1890), and C. K. Allen, *Law in the Making* (London, 1964).

Are case law in the United States and in British common law analogous to the talmudic Oral Law? Is the notion of a constitutional right to privacy (see *Griswold v. Conn.* 381 U.S. 479, 1965), though not mentioned in the constitution, based upon an unwritten tradition? What of such "fundamental rights" as the right to travel, have a home, or a job? (See *Edwards v. Cal.* 314 U.S. 160, 1941; *Lindsey v. Normet*, 405 U.S. 56, 1972; *Roth v. Board of Regents*, 408 U.S. 564, 1972; (*Skinner v. Oklahoma ex rel. Williamson*, 316 U.S. 535, 541, 1942; *Loving v. Virginia*, 388 U.S. 1, 1967). Do terms such as "due process" and "bill of attainder" in the United States Constitution require an understanding of the tradition behind them in order to understand and properly apply them? (See Charles Black, *Structure and Relation in Constitutional Law* [Baton Rouge, 1969].)

3. If an oral tradition is a component part of any system of laws and is necessary for the proper understanding of legal terms (particularly when they are vague and sometimes apparently contradictory, as in the Bible), can biblical law be understood without reference to this oral tradition? If not, how seriously can one take the comments of Bible scholars and others who analyze the laws of the Bible but have no knowledge of this oral tradition? Would you downgrade any of the scholarly articles examined in part one of this book on this account? (Note that the ancient Near Eastern codes—even assuming that they are legal prescriptions—also contain large lacunae and leave much unstated.) Missing, for example, are provisions that murder is a crime (omitted from the Code of Hammurabi), the definition of theft, or of ownership. Accordingly, there must have been many assumptions and comprehensions of unwritten details by the people to whom these codes were directed.[39]

4. Chajes refers to interpretations of the Bible in the Talmud, which are either not implied in the plain meaning of the text, or which seem to contradict the text. It should be noted that the talmudic scholars exhibited an extraordinary sensitivity to subtle nuances of language, and therefore sometimes interpreted verses in a manner radically different from their, apparently, "plain meaning." This was particularly true of verses that contained ungrammatical or awkward phraseology.

Some scholars have even attempted to demonstrate that *every* talmudic interpretation of biblical texts that

---

38. In his *The Second Kuzari, Mateh Dan* (London, 1714; reprinted Jerusalem, 1958), pp. 11–15; see also J. J. Petuchowski, *The Theology of Haham David Nieto* (New York, 1972).

39. See Loewenstamm, "Law," in *World History of the Jewish People*, vol. 2 (New Brunswick, 1967), pp. 233–34.

does not seem to fit their simple meaning was, in fact, required because of the peculiar phraseology or context of the particular verse. Foremost among these was Malbim,[40] whose extensive commentary on the Bible, and his other works, is largely based upon this premise. Many of these startling and radical talmudic interpretations of biblical verses, have received support from other sources. Thus, the Hebrew word *totafot* (Exod. 13:16), commonly translated as "frontlets" and understood in the oral tradition as referring to boxes containing biblical selections to be worn on the arm and head, have now been discovered to be a word of old Sumerian origin meaning "four." This would explain the source of the talmudic tradition that the frontlet consists of four compartments, each containing a different selection from the Bible. Interestingly enough, the Talmud,[41] apparently unaware of the ancient Sumerian etymology, contains a discussion of the source of this tradition and indicates that the biblical word *totafot*, is a combination of two foreign words, each meaning "two" and together aggregating "four." Ancient Sumerian was already an ancient and unknown tongue in talmudic times, and it has only been recently rediscovered as a result of modern excavation.[42]

5. Chajes suggests another explanation for those interpretations of biblical texts in the oral tradition that do not seem to accord with their "plain meaning." He suggests that such interpretations sometimes were used as mnemonic devices to preserve these traditions at a time when Jewish law forbade recording them in writing. Sometimes these nonliteral interpretations were an attempt to find biblical support for an interpretation transmitted by the oral tradition. This was not meant to be simply a deliberate, misleading manipulation of authority symbols. Rather, it accorded with the perception that all matters were somehow hinted at in the Bible itself. Attempts were therefore made to find hints, albeit far-fetched, in the Bible for all the laws of the oral tradition.[43]

6. The prohibition mentioned by Chajes against reducing the Oral Law to writing[44] has the following principal rationale. Anything that is reduced to writing and is studied solely by examination of that writing is bound to be subject to different interpretations, no matter how carefully one attempts to formulate the writing with precision. This has been the common his-

tory of laws in many countries throughout history. Since the Oral Law was extremely complex and dealt with norms in very great detail, it was thought desirable to require that it be studied under the personal supervision of, and in direct contact with, a teacher who could listen to his students' expositions, correct mistakes, and be available for questions. The teacher's nuances of voice and facial expressions would also help to clarify his meanings. In this way an attempt was made to preserve the Oral Law with great accuracy and avoid conflict. It is arguable that this was an important factor in the apparent lack of legal interpretive conflicts, which later became so prevalent after the Oral Law was reduced to writing.[45]

Some of the additional reasons given for prohibiting the writing of the Oral Law is that it resulted from conflict with the emerging Christian sects and represented an attempt to prevent them from mastering the oral law in order to keep it as the exclusive preserve of the Jewish people.[46] A further reason is that preserving the law in its oral format preserves the flexibility of decision-makers to meet new situations that might arise from time to time.[47]

45. See Maimonides, *Guide for the Perplexed*, 1:71; cf. I. Twersky, "Religion and Law," in *Proceedings of the American Academy for Jewish Research* (New York, 1977), 44: 70, 76; see also Y. V. Katz, Introduction to *S'ma, Sefer Me'Irat Enayim* (Prague, 1606; numerous reprints); *BeHai*, Commentary to Exodus 34 (Jerusalem, 1968), pp. 355 ff.; *Ritva* to *Gittin* 60b (reprinted Jerusalem, 1967); *Ha'Meiri*, ad loc.; Nissim Gerundi (Ran), in Commentary to *Rif, Megillah* 4, 14a; Yosef Hazan, Responsa *Hikre Lev*, O.H. (Salonika, 1797), no. 56–57, p. 11; Loewe, *Tiferet Yisrael*, chs. 68–69; idem, *Discourse on the Torah*, p. 48 (his views are capsulized in A. Karib, "Works of the Maharal of Prague" [Jerusalem, 1968], 1: 269).

The prohibition against recording the Oral Law in writing is expounded in the Talmud, principally in *Gittin* 60b, *Temurah* 14b, and *Eruvin* 21b. For extensive discussions of the application of this rule in practice, see Y. N. Epstein, *Mavo Le-Nusah Ha-Mishnah* (Jerusalem, 1964), p. 699 ff.; S. Lieberman, *Hellenism in Jewish Palestine* (New York, 1962), p. 216; S. Albeck, *Mavoh La-Mishnah* (Jerusalem, 1959), pp. 113 ff.; see also C. Tchernowitz, *Toledoth Ha-Halakah* (New York, 1953), 1: 1–10; M. Elon, *Hamishpat Ha-Ivri*, (Jerusalem, 1973), p. 208; H. Zimmerman, *Binyan Halakhah* (Jerusalem, 1955), p. 1.

46. Midrash *Tanhuma, Ki-Tisah* 34; *Be-Hai*, Commentary to Exodus 34, p. 355 ff.; Epstein, *Mavo La-Nusah Ha-Mishna*, p. 694; Albeck, *Mavoh La-Mishna*, p. 114; A. Urbach, *Hazal, Pirke Emunoth Ve-Deoth* (Jerusalem, 1970), p. 271, and his "Halakhah U-Nevuah" (Hebrew), in *Tarbiz* 18 (1947): 1–27; Y. Behr, "Hayesodot Ha'Historiim Shel Ha-Halakhah" (Hebrew), in *Zion* 27 (1962): 118–30; see Loewe, *Tiferet Yisrael*.

47. Albo, *Ha-Ikarim* (reprinted Jerusalem, 1960), essay no. 3, ch. 23; H. Y. D. Azulai, Responsa *Birkei Yosef*, O.H. (Livarno, 1783), no. 49; S. Albeck, *Mishpahat Soferim* (Warsaw, 1903), pp. 24–25; H. Hirschensohn, in *Ha'Misderona* (Jerusalem, 1887), p. 129; M. Kasher, *Torah Shelemah*, Exod. 34, pp. 102–3. See also Elon, *Hamishpat Ha-Ivri*, p. 209; for other reasons, see also R. Margolis, *Yesod Ha'Mishnah Ve' Arihata* (Hebrew; Tel-Aviv, 1957); Elijah of Vilna, notes to *Shulhan Arukh*, O.H., sec. 49; Y. M. Katz, *Devarim She'Ba'al Peh Ee Ata Rashai Le'Omran Biktav* (Sinai, 1961), p. 264 ff.

40. An acronym of the first letters of Meir Leibish ben Yekhiel Michel, born 1808 and died 1879 in Kiev, Russia.

41. *Menahot* 34b.

42. The editor is indebted to Professor Sol Cohen, of Dropsie University, for this piece of scholarship.

43. See the last paragraph from Z. Chajes, *Kal Kitvei*, and Rambam, Introduction to the Mishnah; see Talmud, *Ta'anit* 9a.

44. Talmud, *Gittin* 60b, which relies on a nonliteral interpretation of certain biblical passages.

B. *Applying the Law: Principles of Legal Interpretation*

1. THE THIRTEEN CANONS OF SCRIPTURAL INTERPRETATION*

The thirteen rules of biblical interpretation were stated by Rabbi Ishmael ben Elisha and are taken from the introduction to the *Sifra,* a talmudic commentary to the Book of Leviticus. The author was killed as a martyr by the Romans in the year 135. The succinct explanation of these rules that follows, and their translation into English, is by Dr. Paltiel Birnbaum in his *Daily Prayer Book.*

Sifra, Introduction

Rabbi Ishmael says: The Torah is interpreted by means of thirteen rules:

1. Inference is drawn from a minor premise to a major one, or from a major premise to a minor one.

2. From the similarity of words or phrases occurring in two passages it is inferred that what is expressed in the one applies also to the other.

3. A general principle, as contained in one or two biblical laws, is applicable to all related laws.

4. When a generalization is followed by a specification, only what is specified applies.

5. When a specification is followed by a generalization, all that is implied in the generalization applies.

6. If a generalization is followed by a specification and this in turn by a generalization, one must be guided by what the specification implies.

7. When, however, for the sake of clearness, a generalization necessarily requires a specification, or when a specification requires a generalization, rules 4 and 5 do not apply.

8. Whatever is first implied in a generalization and afterwards specified to teach us something new, is expressly stated not only for its own sake, but to teach something additional concerning all the instances implied in the generalization.

9. Whatever is first implied in a general law and afterwards specified to add another provision similar to the general law, is specified in order to alleviate, and not to increase, the severity of that particular provision.

10. Whatever is first implied in a general law and afterwards specified to add another provision which is not similar to the general law, is specified in order to alleviate in some respects, and in others to increase the severity of that particular provision.

11. Whatever is first implied in a general law and is afterwards specified to determine a new matter, the terms of the general law can no longer apply to it, unless Scripture expressly declares that they do apply.

12. A dubious word or passage is explained from its context or from a subsequent expression.

13. Similarly, if two Biblical passages contradict each other, they can be harmonized only by [reference to] a third passage.

Illustrations

1. If, for example, a certain act is forbidden on an ordinary festival, it is so much the more forbidden on Yom Kippur; if a certain act is permissible on Yom Kippur, it is so much more permissible on an ordinary festival.

2. The phrase "Hebrew slave" (Exod. 21:2) is ambiguous, for it may mean a heathen slave owned by a Hebrew, or else, a slave who is a Hebrew. That the latter is the correct meaning is proved by a reference to the phrase "your Hebrew brother" in Deuteronomy 15:12, where the same law is mentioned (. . . "If your Hebrew brother is sold to you . . .").

3. (*a*) From Deuteronomy 24:6 ("No one shall take a handmill or an upper millstone in pledge, for he would be taking a life in pledge") the Rabbis concluded: "Everything which is used for preparing food is forbidden to be taken in pledge." (*b*) From Exodus 21:26–27 ("If a man strikes the eye of his slave . . . and destroys it, he must let him go free in compensation for his eye. If he knocks out the tooth of his slave . . . he must let him go free . . .") the Rabbis concluded that when *any* part of the slave's body is mutilated by the master, the slave shall be set free.

4. In Leviticus 18:6 the law reads: "None of you shall marry anyone related to him." This generalization is followed by a specification of forbidden marriages. Hence, this prohibition applies only to those expressly mentioned.

5. In Exodus 22:9 we read: "If a man gives to his neighbor an ass, or an ox, or a sheep, to keep, or *any* animal, and it dies . . ." The general phrase "any animal," which follows the specification, includes in this law all kinds of animals.

6. In Exodus 22:8 we are told that an embezzler shall pay double to his neighbor "for anything embezzled [generalization] for ox, or ass, or sheep, or clothing [specification], or any article lost" [generalization]. Since the specification includes only movable property, and objects of intrinsic value, the fine of double payment does not apply to embezzled real estate, nor to notes and bills, since the latter represents only a symbolic value.

7. In Leviticus 17:13 we read: "He shall pour out its blood, and *cover* it with *dust.*" The verb "to cover" is a general term, since there are various ways of cover-

*Paltiel Birnbaum, *Daily Prayer Book* (New York: Hebrew Publishing Co., 1973).

ing a thing; "with dust" is specific. If we were to apply rule 4 to this passage, the law would be that the blood of the slaughtered animal must be covered with nothing except dust. Since, however, the general term "to cover" may also mean "to hide," our present passage necessarily requires the specific expression "with dust"; otherwise, the law might be interpreted to mean that the blood is to be concealed in a closed vessel. On the other hand, the specification "with dust" without the general expression "to cover" would have been meaningless.

8. In Deuteronomy 22:1 we are told that the finder of lost property must return it to its owner. In a next verse the Torah adds: "You shall do the same . . . with his *garment* and with anything lost by your brother . . . which you have found . . ." *Garment*, though included in the general expression "anything lost," is specifically mentioned in order to indicate that the duty to announce the finding of lost articles applies only to such objects which are likely to have an owner, and which have, as in the case of clothing, some marks by which they can be identified.

9. In Exodus 35:2–3 we read: "Whoever does any work on the Sabbath shall be put to death; you shall not light a fire on the sabbath day." The law against lighting a fire on the Sabbath, though already implied in "any work," is mentioned separately in order to indicate that the penalty for lighting a fire on the Sabbath is not as drastic.

10. According to Exodus 21:29–30, the proprietor of a vicious animal which has killed a man or woman must pay such compensation as may be imposed on him by the court. In a succeeding verse the Torah adds: "If the ox gores a slave, male or female, he must pay the master thirty shekels of silver." The case of the slave, though already included in the preceding general law of the slain man or woman, contains a different provision, the *fixed* amount of compensation, with the result that whether the slave was valued at more than thirty shekels or less than thirty shekels, the proprietor of the animal must invariably pay thirty shekels.

11. The guilt-offering which a cured leper had to bring was unlike all other guilt-offerings in this, that some of its blood was sprinkled on the person who offered it (Lev. 14:13–14). On account of this peculiarity none of the rules connected with other offerings would apply to that brought by a cured leper, had not the Torah expressly added: "As the sin-offering so is the guilt-offering."

12. (*a*) The noun *tinshemeth* occurs in Leviticus 11:18 among the unclean birds, and again (verse 30) among the reptiles. Hence, it becomes certain that *tinshemeth* is the name of a certain bird as well as of a certain reptile. (*b*) In Deuteronomy 19:6, with regard

to the cities of refuge where the manslayer is to flee, we read: "So that the avenger of blood may not pursue the manslayer . . . and slay him, *and he is not deserving of death.*" That the last clause refers to the slayer, and not to the blood avenger, is made clear by the subsequent clause: "inasmuch as he hated him not in time past."

13. In Exodus 13:6 we read: "Seven days you shall eat unleavened bread," and in Deuteronomy 16:8 we are told: "Six days you shall eat unleavened bread." The contradiction between these two passages is explained by a reference to a third passage (Lev. 23:14), where the use of the new produce is forbidden until the second day of Passover, after the offering of the *Omer*. If, therefore, the unleavened bread was prepared of the new grain, it could only be eaten six days of Passover. Hence, the passage in Exodus 13:6 must refer to unleavened bread prepared of the produce of a previous year.

2. THE HERMENEUTIC PRINCIPLES AND THEIR APPLICATION
(By Bernard Rosenzweig)*

When the traditional Jew talks about the Torah and its binding character, he is discussing two Torahs which are in effect one: the Written Law (*Torah She-be-Ktav*) and the Oral Law (*Torah She-Baal Peh*). The Written Law consists of the Pentateuch which was divinely revealed to Moses at Sinai. The Oral Law, which makes equal claim to Sinaitic roots, embodies the expositions and the interpretations which were communicated orally to Moses as an elucidation of that Divine Law. In fact, the Oral Law is the soul of the Written Law, and invests it with individuality and uniqueness. The Rabbis tell us that God gave the Israelites the Written Law to make them become virtuous; and He gave them the Oral Law to distinguish them from the other nations. It is in this vein that Rabbi Yochanan said: "God made a covenant with Israel only for the sake of that which was transmitted orally."

In truth, one cannot obtain a knowledge of Judaism from a study of the Biblical text alone. Even a cursory reading of the Torah will demonstrate that without its authoritative exposition, many Scriptural texts would often be unintelligible, and would not suffice to meet the demand for clarification. There are many precepts worded vaguely in the Torah, which would remain obscure without the traditional elucidation. It stands to reason that, side by side with the Mosaic Code, there must have been an oral tradition which made explicit that which was implicit in the text.

*From *Tradition* 13 (Summer 1972): 49. Rosenzweig's transliteration of Hebrew terms and the use of capitalization have been retained.

For example, in discussing the laws of the Sabbath, the Torah sets down the principle: "But the seventh day is the Sabbath of the Lord thy God; in it thou shalt not do any work (*melakhah*) . . . ." What is meant by "work" in this connection? In the Written Law there is no exact definition of the concept of *melakhah*. Specifically, the Torah specifies a small number of forbidden acts on the Sabbath—ploughing, reaping, kindling a fire, and carrying from the private domain into the public domain. However, it is the Oral Law which defined thirty-nine major categories of "work," all of which are derived from the acts which were performed in the construction of the Tabernacle in the desert.

The Oral Law is divided into a number of categories. One of these primary groupings is defined as *Midot She-Ha-Torah Nidreshet Bahen*, i.e., "rules whereby the Torah is expounded." There is a mass of religio-legal material which is not found explicitly in the Holy Writ, but which was elicited therefrom by means of a set of hermeneutic rules for which Sinaitic origin is claimed. Through these principles of interpretation, the words of the Biblical text were subjected to extension, limitation, analogy, textual parallelism, logical inference, as well as other methods of interpretation which enable us to explain and to clarify many details in connection with the observance of the commandments.

There are three principal systems of hermeneutics found in rabbinic literature, namely those attributed to Hillel, Rabbi Yishmael and Rabbi Eliezer ben Rabbi Yose Haglili. Hillel was the first to formally set down and to enumerate a system of hermeneutics, consisting of seven basic principles. On the basis of Hillel's seven rules, Rabbi Yishmael projected the thirteen rules of interpretation which henceforth became the authoritative instruments of the midrashic method. The *Middot* attributed to Hillel and Rabbi Yishmael are generally utilized for halakhic exposition, whereas those of Rabbi Eliezer deal mainly with *Aggadic* interpretation, or the derivation from the text of some moral or ethical rule. Consequently, the thirty-two rules enumerated by Rabbi Eliezer do not play a significant role in our analysis of hermeneutic principles.

Let us discuss a number of *Middot* and demonstrate their application to the Biblical text.

Kal Ve-Chomer

The rule of interpretation which occupies primacy of place in the hermeneutic systems of Hillel and Rabbi Yishmael is termed *Kal Ve-Chomer*. The word *kal*, in this context, refers to that which is considered, within the framework of Jewish Law, to be less important, less stringent; while *chomer* defines that which is considered to be comparatively of greater halakhic weight, of greater importance, and, consequently, more stringent. In other words, the *Kal Ve-Chomer* characterizes a logical inference, an *a fortiori* argument, from the less stringent to the more stringent, from the minor to the major premise. At the same time, it also categorizes the syllogism which results from the movement in the other direction—from the more important to the less stringent, from the major to the minor premise.

Underlying the concept of *Kal Ve-Chomer* is the idea that if a certain restriction of the law is found in regards to a matter of minor importance, then we may logically infer that the same will certainly hold true of that which is of major importance. On the other hand, it stands to reason that if a certain leniency is detected in a law which is considered to be of major importance, we may properly conclude that the same leniency will certainly apply to that which is comparatively of minor importance.

Thus, for example, the Sabbath is regarded as weightier or of more importance than the Festivals, because every kind of work is forbidden on the Sabbath, while those acts which are necessary for the preparation of food are permissible on the Festivals. Now if a certain kind of work is permissible on the Sabbath, then we can infer that such a task is certainly permissible on the Festivals. In the tractate *Bezah*, for example, the school of Hillel contends, in opposition to the school of Shammai, that one may bring a burnt offering on the Festivals. In support of their position, the school of Hillel endeavored to develop an *a fortiori* argument. If, on the Sabbath, when it is forbidden to slaughter an animal in order to provide food for a layman, it is nonetheless permitted to offer up the public sacrifice for the Most High; then, it would surely seem to be logical, that on the Festivals, when it is permitted to slaughter on behalf of a layman, it should certainly be permitted to offer up a burnt-offering for the Most High. Here the new law for the minor premise is derived from the major one. On the other hand, if I find something which is forbidden on the Festivals, e.g., taking the heave (*Terumah*) which was to be given to the priest, then we can infer that this act would most certainly be forbidden to do on the Sabbath, which is weightier. Here we derived the more important from the less important.

The Rabbis discerned that in the Scripture the *Kal Ve-Chomer* was used. R. Yishmael taught that there were ten *a fortiori* arguments recorded in the Torah, which include the following:

(1) "Behold the money which we found in our sacks' mouths, we brought back unto thee"; does it not then stand to reason "how then should we steal out of thy lord's house silver or gold?"

(2) "Behold the children of Israel have not hearkened unto me;" surely all the more, "how then shall Pharaoh hear me?"

(3) "Behold, while I am yet alive with you this day, ye have been rebellious against the Lord," does it not follow then "and how much more after my death."

(4) "And the Lord said unto Moses: If her father had but spit in her;" surely it would stand to reason, "should she not hide in shame seven days."

The *Kal Ve-Chomer* is used throughout the Talmud, and covers many areas. In regards to the reading of *Megillat Esther* on Purim, the question arose whether the students of the Law should forsake their studies in order to hear the reading of *Megillat Esther*. We are told that the members of the house of Rabbi Judah the Prince desisted from the study of the Torah in order to come and hear the reading of the *Megillah*. They argued *a fortiori* from the case of the Temple service. The Temple service was suspended so that the priests, levites, and the Israelites at their station, could come and hear the reading of the *Megillah*. They reasoned that if the Temple service, which is so important, may be abandoned, how much more the study of the Torah?

In discussing the question of how far the responsibility of the borrower extends, the *Kal Ve-Chomer* was used in order to establish the limits. "If in the case of a paid bailee who is exempt from breakage and death, he is nevertheless liable for theft and loss; in the case of a borrower who is liable for breakage and death, would it not be all the more certain that he should be liable also for theft and loss?"

However, the *Kal Ve-Chomer* had certain restrictions. It could not be used in order to derive a law contrary to one set down in the Torah. The Torah tells us that if the intention of scheming witnesses is discovered, "then you shall do unto him as he purposed to do" to the accused. The very first Mishnah in the tractate *Makkot* indicates that the law of scheming witnesses does not strictly apply to the case of a priest accused of being the offspring of a divorced mother. Two witnesses, who are themselves priests, testify that a fellow-priest is a *chalal*, i.e., desecrated, and is, consequently, disqualified from priestly office. If these two priests are exposed as scheming witnesses (*Eidim Zomemim*), we do not say that each of them, in turn, becomes stigmatized as a *chalal*; instead, they each receive forty lashes.

Rabbi Joshua ben Levi derives this law from the interpretation of the Torah text. However, Bar Pada suggests that the sanction for this action may be obtained by means of a *Kal Ve-Chomer*. If a priest who is himself a desecrator of future generations by virtue

of his marriage to a divorcee, does not himself become desecrated, it follows that those who merely came to try and to desecrate another priest, but did not in fact desecrate him, should not themselves become desecrated. However, Rabina rejected this argument, because he indicated that if you accept this kind of deduction, you will in effect be nullifying the law of the Torah in regards to retaliation for scheming witnesses. We might argue that since the law declares that if the scheming witnesses were not discovered until after the execution of the sentence—the stoning of the accused —they were not punished by retaliation; then it is logical to argue that these witnesses who only intended to bring about the stoning of the defendant by their evidence, but did not succeed in stoning him, should not be stoned themselves! This *a fortiori* argument would undermine the law of the Torah and, consequently, cannot be properly advanced.

It is possible "to break" the *Kal Ve-Chomer* by demonstrating that the minor premise is not really minor, that it possesses a stringent side which is not found in the major premise, and therefore nothing can be derived from the major premise, since both premises are now of equal strength and stringency. The *Kal Ve-Chomer* can also be broken if we can show that the major premise is not as stringent as it appears, that it has a lenient side which is not found in the minor premise. Rabbi Simeon was of the opinion that no Biblical verse was required to forbid the eating of the first fruits outside the wall of Jerusalem because it is derived *a fortiori* from the law of the second tithe. If someone eats the second tithe, which is less restricted, outside the wall, he is flogged; then, it follows, that for eating the first fruits outside the wall a flogging is deserved. However, Raba refutes this *Kal Ve-Chomer*. In what respect is it assumed that the first fruits are more stringent than the second tithe? In that first fruits are forbidden to non-priests! But the second tithe is also a law of graver importance, because it is forbidden to an *onen*, to someone who is in mourning over a loved one who is still unburied. Consequently, the argument is unsound.

The Rabbis checked and limited the force of the *Kal Ve-Chomer* by applying the principle of *Dayyo*, i.e., that it is quite sufficient that the law in respect of the thing inferred should be equivalent to that from which it is derived. The origin for this principle is Biblical. When Aaron and Miriam spoke against Moses, Miriam became leprous, and Moses pleaded before the Almighty on her behalf. "And the Lord said unto Moses: If her father had but spit in her face, should she not be ashamed seven days?" How much more so then in the case of Divine reproof should she be ashamed fourteen days? Yet the number of days remains seven, for it is sufficient if the law in respect of the thing inferred be equivalent to that from which it is derived.

Finally, the principle has been firmly established that "no penalty is inflicted on the strength of a logical inference." In other words, no punishment, whether it be of a capital nature or lashes, can be inflicted in a law which is the result of a *Kal Ve-Chomer*. The reasoning behind this rule is meritorious. Since a *Kal Ve-Chomer* is something which a man is able to project on his own, and since it is the result of human reasoning, then there is always the possibility that the resulting inference can be logically broken; and, consequently, there can be no punishment.

Gezerah Shavah

We will define *Gezerah Shavah* as an analogy between two separate laws based on a similar word or phrase or root occurring in each. Hillel applied this rule in the following classical case: On one occasion, the fourteenth day of Nisan happened to fall on a Sabbath, and the *Bene Bathyra*, who were the religious heads of the Jewish community at that time, had forgotten whether the Paschal Offering overrides the Sabbath or not. Hillel, who had come from Babylonia, and who had studied under the two great masters of the time, Shemaia and Abtalion, was able to resolve their uncertainty. Among the arguments which Hillel advanced in support of permitting the Paschal sacrifice on the Sabbath was one based upon the rule of *Gezerah Shavah*. In regards to the Paschal Lamb we read: The children of Israel shall keep the Passover "*be-moado*," "in its appointed time." However, just as the expression "*be-moado*" in regards to the Daily Offering provides that it overrides the Sabbath, and that it was to be brought even on the Sabbath Day; similarly, the same expression, "*be-moado*," which is used in connection with the Paschal Lamb, also enjoins that this sacrifice be offered at the appointed time, even on a Sabbath day.

From this analogy, then, based on the word "*be-moado*" the Rabbis were able to formulate a most important *halakkhah*. The *Gezerah Shavah*, then, operates on two levels. It is an exegetical aid to determine the meaning of an ambiguous expression in the law, to give clarity to something already found in the Torah. At the same time, it creates new laws not found explicitly in the Torah, by construing laws with reference to each other, so that certain provisions connected with one of them may be shown to be applicable also to the other.

There is a *Gezerah Shavah* which acts as a form of clarification. In regards to the consecration of a woman for marriage we are told: "When a man takes (*yikach*)

a wife"; while in regards to the purchase of the cave of Machpelah, the Torah reads: "I will give the price of the field; take it (*kach*) of me." From this, the following *Gezerah Shavah* is developed: Just as the acquisition of the cave of Machpelah was achieved through money, similarly, the legal acquisition of a woman as a wife can be achieved through money. Here the concept of the consecration and acquisition of a wife is merely clarified through the use of the *Gezerah Shavah*.

On the other hand, there is a *Gezerah Shavah* which is used to create a new law. The *Mishnah* in *Yevamot* tells us that an uncircumcised priest may not eat *terumah* (the heave-offering). The *Gemara*, in commenting on the *Mishnah*, tells us: "A sojourner and a hired servant" were mentioned in connection with the Paschal Lamb; and "a sojourner and a hired servant" were also mentioned in respect of *terumah*. As the Paschal Lamb, in connection with which "a sojourner and a hired servant" were mentioned, is forbidden to the uncircumcised, so is *terumah*, in respect of which "a sojourner and a hired servant" were mentioned, forbidden to the uncircumcised.

The principle of *Gezerah Shavah* is subject to a number of limitations. Thus we are told, that even though a man may project a *Kal Ve-Chomer* on his own, no man may advance a *Gezerah Shavah* unless he has received it as a tradition from his teacher and his teacher from his teacher, all the way back in time to the Lawgiver, Moses. This obviously stands to reason. There must be this kind of restriction in regards to the *Gezerah Shavah* because, as Nachmanides points out, there are literally hundreds of words repeated in the Torah within different contexts; and if there were free license to make a *Gezerah Shavah* out of any two identical words, there would be the danger of introducing unauthorized laws or demolishing the basis of existing ones. This danger is not as apparent in the *Kal Ve-Chomer* because, at least, it must satisfy the self-limiting conditions of logical argument. On this basis, it becomes obvious that one can punish on the basis of a *Gezerah Shavah*, which has the force of tradition, and is not susceptible to the vagaries of logic.

It is of great interest to know which aspect of the *Gezerah Shavah* is the result of tradition. There are instances when the subject and the context are revealed by tradition, and it was left to the Rabbis to discover the words which substantiate this tradition. The *Mishnah* in *Ketubot* discusses the case of the fine which is imposed on the violator of a girl who had been betrothed and then divorced. Rabbi Akiva maintains that the girl is entitled to receive the fine and that the fine belongs to her. In defending his position, Rabbi Akiva explained that the Scriptural verse "That is not betrothed" is used as part of a *Gezerah Shavah*. In the case of an outrage it is said "that is not betrothed" and in the case of seduction it is also written "that is not betrothed." Just as in the case of an outrage, the fine is that of fifty silver coins, so will the fine be in the case of seduction; and, just as in the case of seduction the coins must be *shekels*, so in the case of outrage must they also be *shekels*.

However, the *Gemara* wonders what moved Rabbi Akiva to utilize the text of "that is not betrothed" for a *Gezerah Shavah*; why could he not have developed a *Gezerah Shavah* through the application of the word "*betulah*," virgin, which is found both in the verse in regards to seduction and that of outrage? In other words, the implication of this Talmudic discussion is that there was an accepted tradition that the cases of seduction and of outrage were the sources for a *Gezerah Shavah*, but there was no firm tradition as to which words were to be used in the construction of the *Gezerah Shavah*.

There are other situations in which the words which are to be used in the *Gezerah Shavah* were handed down by tradition, while their application had to be established by the Rabbis. When a Hebrew slave was freed, he was furnished with gifts. The question arose as to how much he was to be given. Rabbi Judah maintained that he was to be paid thirty *selaim*, and he derived his position on the basis of a *Gezerah Shavah* with the law of an injured heathen slave. In both instances, a form of the word "*netinah*," giving, is used. Just as in the case of a heathen slave, thirty *shekalim* is meant so, here too, thirty is meant. However, here the *Gemara* asks: Why should we not derive a *Gezerah Shavah* based upon the word "*netinah*" from the law in regards to the valuation of man, which would then make it a matter of giving the freed slave fifty *shekalim*? What seems to be clear from this discussion is that according to the tradition the word "*netinah*" in the verse on providing gifts for the freed slave was to be utilized as part of a *Gezerah Shavah*; the problem which the rabbis set about to resolve was from which particular law, using the similar word, was the *Gezerah Shavah* to be established, and the amount derived.

There is another important distinction in the application of the *Gezerah Shavah*. There is a definite difference in law, depending on whether only one word is redundant, i.e., whether only one of the two words in the analogy is disengaged and not being used for its own purposes and, consequently, superfluous and free for interpretation; or whether both words to be used in the *Gezerah Shavah* are redundant and superfluous, and free for interpretation in both texts. The practical difference between these two situations is reflected in the ruling that where only one of the words is free, then the *Gezerah Shavah* is subject to refutation; whereas a *Gezerah Shavah* in which both subjects are disengaged, cannot be refuted. It stands to reason that since both words are not used for themselves, and are, consequently, used only for the sake of the *Gezerah Shavah*, then it is considered as if the Torah had stated it explicitly, and it cannot be refuted. . . .

Notes and Questions to Rosenzweig, "The Hermeneutic Principles and Their Application"

1. Are these hermeneutic rules, such as *a fortiori*, very different than the rules of statutory interpretation applied in the United States and in other modern legal systems today? See, for example, the fourth rule and the widely utilized principle of *ejusdem generis*.[48]

2. Note, that a penalty could not be applied on the basis of a logical deduction, but could be inflicted based upon a tradition, which interpreted a phrase, applying the second of the hermeneutic principles (which is based upon the similarity of wording of an ambiguous phrase to that of another phrase, whose meaning is clear).[49] This reliance on tradition was premised, in part, upon the extraordinary concern which was taken to preserve the oral tradition accurately. Thus, one may find the Talmud citing a rule issued by a decision-maker, "While he was standing with one foot on a ladder,"[50] and other details, depicting precisely the circumstances in which the rule was issued. Note also Rambam's stance (Section A, above) that there was never an error in the transmission of such traditions.

This distrust of logic as the basis for inflicting penalties is based upon the view that logic may appear conclusive but still may be subject to refutation. In addition, some of the logical inferences included in the Thirteen Rules of Interpretation can be misapplied by formulating a proposition that is proper in form although its substance does not completely conform to logic. It may sometimes be difficult to detect such a flaw. A common example (which does have the obvious flaw of analogizing two intrinsically different substances) bandied about by talmudic students is the following takeoff on the inference of "*kal ve-khomer*" that is, *a fortiori*: "If fish, which can be eaten with a spoon, can be eaten more easily with a fork, then it follows that soup, which can comfortably be eaten with a spoon, can certainly be eaten with a fork." (See a similar example in the Talmud, *Kallah*, chapter 3, by

48. See M. McDougal, H. Lasswell, and J. Miller, *The Interpretation of Agreements and World Public Order* (New Haven, 1967).

49. Talmud, *Pesakhim* 6:1, 33a.

50. See principles of interpretation in U.S. Constitutional interpretation, in C. Black, *Structure and Relationship in Constitutional Law* (Los Angeles, 1970); idem, "The Unfinished Business of the Warren Court," *University of Washington Law Review* (1970–71): 3.

which one may "prove" that marriage is forbidden to all.)

3. There have been claims by scholars that many of the hermeneutic principles are similar to principles of Greek rhetoric and Roman legal practice.[51]

Shaul Lieberman, probably the greatest modern scholar in this field, claims that no one has been able to demonstrate definite Greek influence in the thirteen hermeneutic rules, except, perhaps, for the *kal vekhomer* (*a fortiori*) and *gezera shava* (analogy) utilized by the Alexandrian School. Lieberman does agree that a number of the rabbinic hermeneutic rules recur almost literally in Roman legal classics, such as those of Sabinus, Celsus, and Gaius. He asserts, however, that

> The Rabbis applied comparatively few rules to the *elaboration* of the legal parts of the Torah. They were the result of choice, discrimination, and crystallization out of many ways for the exposition of texts. In the *Aggadah* [the so-called, "non-legal" or moral, ethical, and exegetical portions of the Talmud], however, and in the *Asmahtot* [literally, "supports"; the citation of biblical verses to support legal principles or decisions] for the *Halakhah*, the rabbis resorted to well-established literary devices, which were current in the literary world at that time. Had the Rabbis, themselves, invented these artificial rules in their interpretations, the "supports" from the Bible would be ineffectual and strange to the public. But, as the utilization of instruments accepted all over the civilized world of that time, their rules of interpretation of the *Aggadah* (and their "supports" for the *Halakha* from scripture) were a literary affectation, which was understood and appreciated by their contemporaries.[52]

As indicated by Chajes, hermeneutic principles were sometimes applied to supply biblical support for the rulings of decision-makers, even when the rulings did not rely on hermeneutic principles that were part of the oral tradition. It should also be noted that these rules were sometimes applied to the interpretation of legal documents, as well as the Bible.[53]

4. Seven rules of exposition and interpretation of Scripture were listed by Hillel.[54] These rules, which were not originated by Hillel but were used prior to his time,[55] were formulated with greater particularity into thirteen rules by Rabbi Ishmael. There were also thirty-two rules of exposition formulated by Rabbi Eliezer, the son of Rabbi Jose, the Galilean. (These rules were added as an appendix to the printed version of the Babylonian Talmud following the volume *Berakhot*). These relate only to the exposition of verses that do not deal with legal decision making but, rather, confine themselves solely to Aggadah, that is, to moral, theological, or ethical concepts.

5. It should be noted that there were other principles of interpretation applied to talmudic law in addition to the thirteen. For example, the principle of "hekesh," inference by analogy (inferring a rule concerning one subject from the rules applicable to a similar subject),[56] is involved in the first three rules, though not completely incorporated therein.[57]

6. There were limitations on the use of the hermeneutical principles. For example, one could not apply the principle of analogy by similarity of wording (*gezerah shava*) unless one has been taught this as part of the tradition received from one's teachers. (See Talmud, *Pesakhim* 66a, and Moshe b. Nahman, Commentary to Rambam's *Sefer Hamitzvot*, "Root" 2, [Jerusalem, 1969].)

---

51. See S. Lieberman, *Hellenism in Jewish Palestine*, p. 54 ff.; see also J. Hadas's *Eshkol Ha'Kofer* (Constantinople, 1149), 124b; D. Daube, "Rabbinic Methods of Interpretation and Hellenistic Rhetoric," in *Hebrew Union College Annual* 22 (1949): 239 ff.; H. Strack, *Introduction to the Talmud and Midrash* (Philadelphia, 1931), pp. 95 and 288, n. 8. A. Schwartz has devoted six different books to this topic; see, e.g., his *Der Hermeneutische Syllogismus in Der Talmudischen Literature* (German; Vienna, 1901) and his subsequent works. See also L. Jacobs, "The Aristotelian Syllogism and the *Qal Va'Homer*," in *Journal of Jewish Studies* 4 (1953): 154; idem "The Talmudic Rule of Binyan Abh, and J. S. Mill's 'Method of Agreement,'" *Journal of Jewish Studies* 4 (1953): 59; C. Hirschensohn, *Berure Ha'Midut*, 2 vols. (Jerusalem 1929–31); M. Ostrowsky, *Hamidot She'Hatorah Nidreshet Ba'Hem* (Jerusalem, 1924); A. Kamina, *Mekharim* (Tel-Aviv, 1938), 1:172, and in *Jewish Quarterly Review* n.s. 30 (1939): 121; J. Teumin, *Ginat Veradim* and *Shoshanat Ha'Amakim* (Lublin, 1765; numerous reprints; Belkin, *Philo and the Oral Law* (Cambridge, 1940), p. 29 ff.; H. Wolfson, *Philo.* (Cambridge, Mass., 1946), 1:133 ff.; idem, *The Philosophy of the Church Fathers* (Cambridge, Mass., 1956), 1:31 ff.; M. Golding, "*Community, Covenant, and Reason: A Study in Jewish Philosophy*" (Ph.D. diss., Columbia University, 1959).

52. Lieberman, *Hellenism in Jewish Palestine*, pp. 54, 78.

53. Ibid., p. 62, citing to Tosefta, *Ketubot* 4:9 ff.; M. A. Amiel, *Ha'Midot Le'Kheker Halakha* (Jerusalem, 1939–45).

54. Introduction to *Torat Kohanim*, a midrashic exposition of the Book of Leviticus; see M. Zembe, *Otzar Sifri* (B'nai B'rak, 1967).

55. See Lieberman, *Hellenism in Jewish Palestine*, p. 58.

56. See Talmud, *Zevakhim* 46b.

57. See, in general, Hirschensohn, *Birurei Hamidot*. For further discussion of the talmudic principles of interpretation, see L. Jacobs, *Studies in Talmudic Logic and Methodology* (London, 1961); Daube, *Rabbinic Methods of Interpretation and Hellenistic Rhetoric*, in *Hebrew Union College Annual* 22 (1949): 239; H. Y. Lewin, "Al Yahas Ha'Halakhot Ve'Hadrashot" in *Weiss Jubilee Volume* (New York, 1954), pp. 407–39; A. Korhan, *Mevo Le'Torah She'Biktav U'Baal Reh'* (Tel-Aviv, 1956), p. 296 ff.; Y. I. Halevi, *Dorot Ha'Rishonim* (Berlin, 1923), 1:267 ff.; Amiel, *Ha' Midot Le'Kheker Halaha.*

It has also been suggested that hermeneutics were formulated in thirteen rules, corresponding to the same number of mercy and kindness attributes of God (see Exod. 34:6–8), to indicate that the exposition of biblical norms was to be performed in order to render mercy and kindness to those who would be affected by the expositions.

C. Adjustments in the Law to Meet Crises and Changed Conditions: Documentary Studies

1. THE LAW IS NOT IN HEAVEN
(Talmud, "*Baba Metzia 59b*")*

It has been taught: On that day R. Eliezer brought forward every imaginable argument, but they did not accept them. Said he to them: "If the *halachah* agrees with me, let this carob-tree prove it!" Thereupon the carob-tree was torn a hundred cubits out of its place—others affirm, four hundred cubits. "No proof can be brought from a carob-tree," they retorted. Again he said to them: "If the *halachah* agree with me, let the stream of water prove it!" Whereupon the stream of water flowed backwards. "No proof can be brought from a stream of water," they rejoined. Again he urged: "If the *halachah* agrees with me, let the walls of the schoolhouse prove it," whereupon the walls inclined to fall. But R. Joshua rebuked them, saying: "When scholars are engaged in a *halachic* dispute, what have ye to interfere?" Hence they did not fall, in honour of R. Joshua, nor did they resume the upright, in honour of R. Eliezer; and they are still standing thus inclined. Again he said to them: "If the *halachah* agrees with me, let it be proved from Heaven!" Whereupon a Heavenly Voice cried out: "Why do ye dispute with R. Eliezer, seeing that in all matters the *halachah* agrees with him!" But R. Joshua arose and exclaimed: "*It is not in heaven*" (Deut. 30:12). What did he mean by this?—Said R. Jeremiah: That the Torah had already been given at Mount Sinai; we pay no attention to a Heavenly Voice, because Thou hast long since written in the Torah at Mount Sinai, *After the majority must one incline.*

R. Nathan met Elijah and asked him: What did the Holy One, Blessed be He, do in that hour?—He laughed [with joy], he replied, saying, "My sons have defeated Me, My sons have defeated Me."

(Talmud, "*Baba Metzia 86a*")*

. . . he fled to Agama; there he sat upon the trunk of a [fallen] palm and studied. Now, they were disputing in the Heavenly Academy thus: If the bright spot preceded the white hair, he is unclean; if the reverse, he is clean (Lev. 13:1–3). If [the order is] in doubt—the Holy One, blessed be He, ruled, He is clean; whilst the entire Heavenly Academy maintained, He is unclean. "Who shall decide it?" said they.—"Rabbah b. Nahmani; for he said, 'I am pre-eminent in the laws of leprosy and tents.'" A messenger was sent for him, but

the Angel of Death could not approach him, because he did not interrupt his studies [even for a moment]. In the meantime, a wind blew and caused a rustling in the bushes, when he imagined it to be a troop of soldiers. "Let me die," he exclaimed, "rather than be delivered into the hands of the State." As he was dying, he exclaimed, "Clean, clean!" when a Heavenly Voice cried out, "Happy art thou, O Rabbah b. Nahmani, whose body is pure and whose soul had departed in purity!"

Notes and Questions to "The Law Is Not in Heaven"

1. The principle "The Law is not in Heaven" is another reflection of the symbiosis that exists in Jewish law between the perspective that law is transcendental and yet mundane. The conception that the power of decision was vested solely in human decision-makers, who could even overrule the will of God, is one indication (among others) of the strength of the "mundane" factors. (See Notes to Section A 1, above.)

2. How could the talmudic decision-makers and scholars, who were extremely God-fearing (many of whom were martyred by the Romans when they stubbornly insisted on continuing to profess their faith) disobey what they clearly admitted was the will of God and God's intention in drafting the biblical verse in questions? They clearly felt that it was God's will that humans should decide the law according to their own wisdom, rather than follow the dictates of "heaven," which admittedly reflected abstract "truth."[58]

3. Is there any practical significance in the above story for legal decision-making in Jewish law? Does it imply that human (rather than divine) decision-makers are required, because circumstances continually change and adjustments in the law by humans, who are familiar with the changed conditions, are indispensable? This is the contention of Levi Yitzhak of Berditchev,[59] who emphasized that only one who is alive, and therefore aware of all of the conditions presently existing in the world, is able to decide the law properly. Only such a person knows what decisions are necessary for the general welfare and for the individual benefit of the parties concerned. He concludes, accordingly, that the Talmud always refers to the Prophet Elijah, rather than Moses the lawgiver, as the one who will solve all of the legal problems remaining unanswered by the time of the coming of the Messiah, although Moses would also be resurrected at that time. He maintains that only a personage, like Elijah, could fulfill this function, since,

---

*Soncino Press translation (London, 1961).

58. See N. Gerundi, *Discourses*, no. 7, pp. 112, 114; Loewe, *Gur Arye* (Hebrew; Jerusalem, 1972) to Deut. 17:11, p. 83.
59. Levi Yitzkhak of Berditchev, *Kedushat Levi* (Hebrew; Muncazs, 1905), 108b.

according to the talmudic interpretation of Scriptures,[60] he never died but continues to mingle among men in human form. He is therefore familiar with circumstances as they change throughout time and recognizes the consequent need to change the law. Moses, who had died and was only to be resurrected at a much later time, would be unaware of the changed circumstances of men.[61]

Yosef Albo, a noted medieval Jewish philosopher, makes a related point:

> It is impossible that the law of God, blessed be He, shall be complete, so that it will be adequate for all times, because the novel conditions that constantly arise in the affairs of men, in laws and in deeds, are too numerous to count. There was, therefore, orally given to Moses on Sinai, general rules that were indicated briefly in Scriptures in order that the wise men of every generation should be able to apply them to new events.[62]

Although Albo lived in the Middle Ages, his views embody the concept of law found throughout the Talmud.

These adjustments in the law to fit changed circumstances were to be guided by the basic values and goals recognized by Jewish decision-makers (see Notes to Section A 1, above). Eliezer Berkovits has expressed this perspective as follows:

> *Halakhah* is a bridge over which Torah enters reality, with the capacity to shape it meaningfully and in keeping with its own intentions. *Halakhah* is the technique of Torah-application to a concrete contemporary situation. But while the Torah is eternal, the concrete historical situation is forever changing . . . *Halakhah* is not the law, but the law applied and by the manner of its application rendered meaningful in a given situation. . . ."[63]

4. The view expressed by Albo has its precedents in the thinking of the early Greeks. Plato expressed it this way:

> *Stranger.* Because the law cannot comprehend exactly what is noblest or most just, or at once ordain what is best for all. The differences of men and actions, and the endless irregular movements of human things, do not admit of any universal and simple rule. No art can lay down any rule which will last forever —that we must admit.
>
> *Young Socrates.* Certainly.
>
> *Stranger.* But this the law seeks to accomplish, like an obstinate and ignorant tyrant, who will not allow anything to be done contrary to his appointment or any question to be asked—not even in sudden changes of circumstances, when something happens to be better than what he commanded for someone.[64]

A similar thought is expressed by Aristotle,

> The reason is that all law is universal but about some things, it is not possible to make a universal statement which shall be correct. In those cases then, in which it is necessary to speak universally, but not possible to do so correctly, the law takes the usual case, though it is not ignorant of the possibility of error. When the law speaks universally then, and a case arises on it which is not covered by the universal statement, then it is right, when the legislator fails us and has erred by over simplicity, to correct the omission—to say what the legislator himself would have said had he been present and would have put into his law if he had known . . . and this is the nature of the Equitable, a correction of law where it is defective owing to its universality.[65]

5. For generally similar views, see Yitzhak Arama'ah,[66] who says that the rules of the Torah are designed for the majority of cases but will be inequitable in cer-

---

60. Kings 2:11.

61. See also a similar view by Moshe of Trani in his *Beth Elohim* (New York, 1972), ch. 60, p. 286; and I. S. Teichtal, *Em Ha-Banim SeMekha* (Budapest, 1943), pp. 161–64. See later in this section for additional materials concerning the need to change the law in accordance with changed circumstances.

62. Y. Albo, *Sefer Ha'Ikarim* (reprinted Jerusalem, 1960), discourse no. 3, ch. 23, p. 248.

63. "The Role of Halakhah," in *Judaism* 20 (Spring, 1971): 66, 72; see the examples that Berkovits sets forth, and the numerous examples in this book, below. See also Belkin, *In His Image*; Rackman, *The Dialectic of the Halakhah*; see also Jerusalem Talmud, *Sanhedrin* 4:2, "If the Torah had been given cut [i.e., formed in a rigid mode], we would have had no place to stand," and Babylonian Talmud, *Sanhedrin* 17a: "No one may be appointed to the Sanhedrin unless he is able to declare an insect to be pure [i.e., to "prove" that what is in biblical Law ritually impure, is pure]. This implies that, where necessary to meet changed societal conditions, the Sanhedrin may depart from the strict norms.

64. *The Statesman* (Jowett trans.), 294a.

65. *Nicomachean Ethics* 5:10; see also his *Politics* 3.20.1287.

66. Y. Arama'ah, *Akedat Yitzhok* (reprinted Jerusalem, 1961), "gate" 43, pp. 85b–86b; see also Y. Ginsberg, *Mishpatim Le-Yisrael* (Jerusalem, 1956), pp. 4, 131; M. Malbim, Commentary to Esther 1:28; Shlomo ben Aderet, *Responsa Rashba*, vol. 3, no. 393, and Isaac ben Sheshet, *Responsa Rivash*, no. 399, and the last comment of Shumel Edels (Maharsha) to the tractate *Yebamot* (appears in all standard editions of the Talmud) for discussions of the effect on norms of conditions of time, place, and other factors. See also R. Meir Stolwitz of Apta, *Ohr La'Shammayim* (Hebrew; Levov, 1850), commentary to Lev. 26, "The law should be decided according to the occasion and time." See Section 3, below, regarding adjustments in the law to meet changed conditions. See also Shapiro, "The Ideological Foundations of the Halakhah," in *Tradition* 9 (Spring–Summer, 1967): 104, regarding the effect of changed conditions in adjusting the law, and especially his footnotes; and see Y. Gilat, "The Halakhah and Its Relationship to Social Reality," *Tradition* 13 (Winter, 1972): 68, and

tain instances. In those cases the courts can use their discretion and decide even contrary to the rules.

6. Compare the view of divine natural law reflected in the above talmudic story with traditional natural law theories. Does Jewish law, as reflected here, completely conflict with natural law theory, or is it simply a different, if novel, version? If so, how?[67]

Note that in the Jewish tradition, God was the source of law. Once He transmitted the law to man, however, it was exclusively up to man to apply it. According to Aquinas, it is man's reason, not the divine basis of law, which makes law binding. This aided the Christian doctrine regarding the non-binding effect of Old Testament laws, while retaining a divine source (i.e., reason) for law. Note also the Platonic notion of the ideal law which is reflected only unclearly in the mundane world.

7. Many fundamentalist Talmud scholars have acknowledged that the above story was not an actual incident and is not to be taken literally.[68]

It is also accepted among traditional scholars that all of the stories, expositions, and other portions of the Talmud that do not deal specifically with any legal issues, are not necessarily meant to be taken literally.[69] Moshe Hayim Luzzatto,[70] maintains that the recording of these teachings in a form that is not to be taken literally was required in order to conceal its true meanings from the uninitiated when the Talmud was reduced to writing so that it would not be forgotten under the press of persecutions.[71]

8. Compare the perspective reflected in the above tale with the following opinion of an English judge:[72]

There is no law in England, but is as really and truly the law of God as any Scripture phrase, that is by consequence from the very texts of Scripture; for there are many consequences reasoned out of the texts of the Scripture; so is the law of England the very consequence of the very Decalogue itself; and whatsoever is not consonant to Scripture in the law of England is not the law of England. . . . Whatsoever is not consonant to the law of God in Scripture, or to right reason which is maintained by Scripture, whatsoever is in England, be it acts of Parliament, customs or any judicial acts of the court, it is not the law of England, but the error of the party which did pronounce it; and you, or any one else at the bar, may so plead it.

9. Regarding Rabbah b. Nahmani's death, note that the questions dealt with by the Heavenly Academy concerned human beings and not angels. This is consistent with the view that while heaven was the original source of the law, the law itself deals with the activities of man.

Also note that it is the decision of a living human being (Rabbah b. Nahmani) that governs the course of the law, not the opinion of members of the Heavenly Academy, who must ask a living person to decide the law.[73] Why, however was he then summoned to join the Heavenly Academy (that is, to die)? See Notes to Section A 1, above, regarding the perspective that the law is both transcendental and mundane in nature.

Interestingly, subsequent talmudic decision-makers decided the issue discussed by the Heavenly Academy *contrary* to the decision of Rabbah b. Nahmani, despite the fact that this was also the opinion of God and the fact that the Heavenly Academy had decided to resolve the issue according to Rabbah b. Nahmani. Did the talmudic decision-makers deliberately decide the matter in this way in order to demonstrate that "The Law is Not in Heaven"?[74]

14 (Spring, 1973): 52; B. Z. Katz, *Mizekenim Etbonen* (Tel-Aviv, 1964), and H. Soloveitchik, "Pawnbroking," in *American Academy for Jewish Research* 33 (1972): 203, 261 ff.; Y. Baer, "Historical Foundations of Jewish Law" (Hebrew), in 27 *Zion* (1962): 118.

67. See Aquinas' claim that natural law is known to all; that human law is derived from natural law and is binding only if it is in accord with reason; and that the law of the Old Testament is not binding when it is not reasonable, though it is of divine origin (*Summa Theologia* 1–2: q. 90, art. 1, 3; 91, 3; 94, 3, 4; 95, 2, 5; 98, 5; 103, 4; 104, 3). See L. Strauss, *Natural Right and History* (Chicago, 1953), pp. 81–82; M. Fox, "Maimonides and Aquinas on Natural Law," in *Dine Israel* (Tel-Aviv, 1972). See Cicero's statement that "True Law is Right Person in Agreement with Nature; it is of universal application, unchanging and everlasting" (*De Publica* 3.12.33; *De Legibus* 1.12.33).

68. Bezalel Ashkenazi, *Shita Me-Kubetzet* (reprinted Jerusalem, 1968), ad loc., citing Rabbenu Hananel; also S. Ashkenazi, *Yefe Mar'eh, Moed Kattan*, sec. 3 (Venice, 1590); *contra*, Elkana b. Yeruham, *Sefer Ha'Kanah* 6 (Koretz, 1784; written in the fourteenth century).

69. See Moshe ben Nahman in his public debate with Paulus, in J. Eisenstein, *Ozar Vikukhim* (New York, 1928), p. 89.

70. In his essay on the *Aggadot* of the Sages, in *Adir Bamarom* (New York, 1946), p. 241.

71. This principle, with minor variations, is also expressed in other places in the Talmud: See, e.g., *Temurah* 16a; cf. *Yebamot* 14a, *Erubin* 13b. See also the commentary of Tosefot,

ad loc.; Chajes, *Torat Ha'Neviim*, at the end of ch. 1, p. 17; idem, *Mavo La'Talmud*, chs. 27, 28, p. 333; Judah Loewe, *Hidushei Aggadot* (Hebrew; Jerusalem, 1962), ad loc., p. 29. See also *Milkhemet Hova*, cited in *Hidushei Gaonim*, Commentary to *Ein Yaakov* (New York, 1955), ad loc.; *contra Sefer Ha'Kana*.

72. J. Keble cited by C. K. Allen in *Law in the Making* (Oxford, 1964), p. 446.

73. See N. Gerundi, *Derashot Ha'Ran*, ed. A. Feldman (Jerusalem, 1974), discourse no. 7, pp. 113–14. See Z. H. Chajes, *Torat Ha'Neviim*, p. 184.

74. See Rambam, Laws of Impurity of *Tzaraat* 2:7, and J. Karo, *Kesef Mishnah*, ad loc.; M. Sofer, Responsa *Hatam Sofer*, O.H., no. 208; Z. Chajes, Addenda to *Torat Ha'Neviim*, no. 7, p. 184.

10. It should be apparent that Rabbah b. Nahmani's dying exclamation, "Clean, clean," not only answers the question posed by the Heavenly Academy but was also brought about to symbolize the notion that he lived a pure life until the very moment of his death.

11. The principle that the Torah is not in heaven and the perspective that the Heavenly Academy and God were forced to ask a human (in this case Rabbah b. Nahmani) to decide the legal question before them reflects the emphasis in talmudic law on the earthly rather than the transcendental. In this view, only human beings on earth have the sole control over the direction of law, not heavenly creatures, nor even God Himself. In fact the talmudic view is that even phenomena in nature can be affected drastically by decisions of the human court (Jerusalem Talmud, *Ketubot* 1:2; see also Talmud, *Avot* 5:11).

This perspective is also reflected in the talmudic rule[75] that a prophet may not decide questions of law on the basis of divine revelation, nor can he overrule decisions by human decision-makers. It is graphically illustrated in the talmudic saying (regarding the setting by the Jewish court of the date when a new month is to begin, which affects the dates when the religious holidays of that month will occur):

When the heavenly angels gather before the Holy One, Blessed be He, to ask, "When is Rosh Hashannah; When is Yom Kippur?" (when, according to the talmudic tradition, human destinies for the coming year are to be decided), the Holy One, Blessed Be He, says to them, "Do you ask *me*? You and I will both go together to the earthly *beth din* (the court)."[76]

Similarly, the talmudic view is that if the human decision-makers set a wrong date for a religious holiday, even through deliberate error, that date prevails.[77] This is true, even though in the talmudic perspective this requires God to decide human destinies on the date for Yom Kippur, which was selected in error rather than on the "correct" date when Yom Kippur would otherwise have been observed. These perspectives concerning the power of man to bind God are indicative of the extent to which talmudic law glorified man.[78]

It appears likely that another rationale for disregarding prophetic views or "voices from heaven" in decision-making was to avoid mistaken or false claims of divine communications.

12. The talmudic conception that man was granted exclusive control over law has an elevated place in the talmudic conception of religion and the cosmos. It implies that man can, and should, create new law. This places man (created in the "image" of God) alongside of God as a co-creator of the world, in view of the vital importance of law in the talmudic metaphysical view (see Soloveitchik, Section A, above). The Talmud expresses this in the saying[79] that "He who judges truthfully, becomes a partner with God in the creation of the world."

13. How does the talmudic perception that human decision-makers have the ability to change the law accord with its professed basic Jewish tenet of faith, that the law is immutable.[80] How can this basic dogma be reconciled with the talmudic perspective that the Torah was given to serve man forever, under all circumstances and conditions? Similarly, how does this alleged immutability of the law square with talmudic statements that make it clear that the laws of the Torah have been historically conditioned?[81] Can the ability to change the law be termed, an "immutable flexibility" with the basic goals, such as *imitio dio*, justice, helping one's fellow, remaining fixed, but their application changing to fit particular circumstances?

14. This talmudic tale, relating an apparent conflict between humans and God, with people as the victor, has provoked considerable comment over the ages. For a sampling of the rich literature relating thereto, see the talmudic dicta (*Midrash Rabbah*, Num. 19:20;

---

75. *Shabbat* 104a; *Safra*, Lev. 27:34.
76. *Rosh Hashanah*, 25a.
77. *Rosh Hashanah* 24, 25; ibid., Mishnah 2:9; *Midrash Tanhuma* 81:6.
78. See Sofer, Responsa *Hatam Sofer*, O.H., no. 208; also *Tanhuma*, Gen. 37:20; compare "the righteous person decrees and God fulfills" (H. Waxman, *Mishle Yisrael* [Jerusalem, 1933], no 3940).
   God is viewed as bound also by morality and "justice" (see Abraham's plaint, "Will the Judge of the whole world not do justice?" [Gen. 18:25]; A. Korn, "Ethics in Jewish Law," *Tradition*, 16 [Spring, 1976]: 201). There is a Hasidic tradition

that Rabbi Arye Leib of Spuler, acting on the complaint of a Jew that God had treated him unjustly, convened a court and held a trial in which God was the "defendant." After hearing plaintiff's contentions, and after announcing that he had communicated with God to obtain his defenses, the court ruled in favor of the plaintiff and against God! This illustrates the strength of the perception that God is bound by the Torah and by the decisions of humans who apply its norms. J. Rosenberg, *Tiferet Maharal* (Lodz, 1912), p. 158; for a similar tale regarding Rabbi Elimeleckh of Lizensk, see A. Kahan, *Ateret Ha'Tzadikim* (Warsaw, 1927), p. 18. Cf. Jerusalem Talmud, *Horiyot* 1:1, 2:2, which indicates the contrary; Azulai, *Shaar Yosef, Horiyot*, ad loc.; D. Hoffman, Commentary to Deuteronomy (Hebrew; Jerusalem, 1971), p. 315.
79. Talmud, *Shabbat* 10a.
80. See Rambam, Commentary to Mishnah, *Sanhedrin* 10.9, and his *Mishnah Torah*, 9:1.
81. See, for example, Talmud, *Arakhin* 29a; *Sanhedrin* 20b; *Negaim*, ch. 7, Mishnah I; *Sotah* 47a and b; *Avodah Zarah* 8b; *Zevahim* 112b; *Niddah* 61b; *Guide for the Perplexed* 3:37; Shlomo b. Aderet, Responsa *Rashba*, vol. 3, no. 393, and Isaac b. Sheshet, Responsa *Rivash*, no. 399; Shapiro, "The Ideological Foundations of Halakhah," p. 104, n. 20; Y. Karelitz, *Hazon Ish* (Jerusalem, 1950) *Yoreh Deah*, Rules of *Trefah*, sec. 5.

Jerusalem, 1969) that with regard to three matters God debated with Moses and conceded. In one of these, God agreed to apply "each man shall be killed for *his own* sin" (Deut. 24:16) instead of "visits the sins of the fathers upon the children" (Exod. 20:5); Nissim Gerundi, *Derashot Ha'Ran*, Discourse 3, 5, and 7; *Sefer Ha'Hinuh* (reprinted New York, 1960), commandment 408; Commentary of Nissim Gaon, *Berakhot* 19b; Moshe Bonems, *Mahadura Batra Le-Ha'Mahrasha*; ad loc.; Yosef Del Medigo, in *Ta'Almuot Hohma* (Venice, 1629) 22; Judah Loewe of Prague, *Be'er Hagola* (London, 1960), vol. 4, and *Aggadot Ha'Shass*, above, ad loc.; Z. Chajes, *Novellae*, ad loc.; Edmund Cahn, "Authority and Responsibility," *Columbia Law Review* 51 (1951): 838; J. Stone, *Human Law and Human Justice* (Stanford, 1965), p. 27, n. 89; E. Fromm, *Psychoanalysis and Religion* (New York, 1950), pp. 54 ff.; much of the literature is cited in I. England, "Majority Decision vs. Individual Truth," in *Tradition*, Spring 1975, p. 137 ff. See also the version in Jerusalem Talmud, *Mo'ed Katan* 3:1.

The views concerning this tale vary from an acknowledgment by God that he, too, is bound by the majority rule that he has propounded,[82] to the obligation of every individual to take responsibility for his decisions, even if this discomfits him. Some view the incident as a test set up by God to see if the rabbis would follow miracles, instead of human intellect and majority rule.

15. Compare this talmudic tale, nullifying the role of miracles in decision-making, with (*a*) the allegation in the Talmud (*Eruvin* 13b and *Yebamot* 14a) that a divine echo was accepted as deciding disputes between the Schools of Hillel and Shammai (see also *Makkot* 23b and *Yebamot* 79a); and (*b*) the "Responsa from Heaven" by Rabbi Jacob of Morois, in which the author claims that he posed questions to "Heaven" about legal and religious issues while asleep at night and would receive answers. These responsa were considered to be authoritative[83] (at least, no less so than Responsa by human decision-makers), although the decisions emanated from divine sources. See the thorough discussion by R. Margolis, in his introduction to Rabbi Jacob's *She'elot U'Teshuvot Min Hashamayim* (*Queries and Responsa from Heaven*; Jerusalem, 1962); H. Y. D. Azulai, *Shem Ha'Gdolim, Ma'Arehet Gedolim* (Livorno, 1774), pp. 47a–48b; Ovadya Yosef, I Responsa, *Yabia Omer*, O.H. (Hebrew; Jerusalem, 1960), no. 4,

42, p. 147 ff; Z. H. Chajes, *Torat Ha'Neviim*, ch. 1, p. 12 ff, ch. 5, p. 32, and Addenda, pp. 184–85; Mahari Ibn Haviv, *Tosefot Yom Kippurim* (Hebrew; Kusta, 1722), *Yoma* 75a.

2. MOSES AS THE SOURCE OF ALL LAW
(Talmud, *Menakhot* 29b)*

Rab Judah said in the name of Rab, When Moses ascended on high he found the Holy One, blessed be He, engaged in affixing coronets to the letters. Said Moses, "Lord of the Universe, Who stays Thy hand?" He answered, "There will arise a man, at the end of many generations, Akiba b. Joseph by name, who will expound upon each tittle heaps of laws." "Lord of the Universe," said Moses; "permit me to see him." He replied, "Turn thee round." Moses went and sat down behind eight rows [and listened to the discourses upon the law]. Not being able to follow their arguments he was ill at ease, but when they came to a certain subject and the disciples said to the master "Whence do you know it?" and the latter replied "It is a law given unto Moses at Sinai" he was comforted. Thereupon he returned to the Holy One, blessed be He, and said, "Lord of the Universe, Thou hast such a man and Thou givest the Torah by me!" He replied, "Be silent, for such is My decree." Then said Moses, "Lord of the Universe, Thou hast shown me his Torah, show me his reward." "Turn thee round," said He; and Moses turned round and saw them weighing out his flesh at the market-stalls. "Lord of the Universe," cried Moses, "such Torah, and such a reward!" He replied, "Be silent, for such is My decree."

Notes and Questions to "Moses as the Source of All Law"

1. How could Akiba ben Joseph refer to Moses as the source of a law when Moses himself did not even recognize it? Moreover, how was it possible that Akiba b. Joseph could expound "heaps of laws" upon each tittle, but Moses, the one who originally received the Torah with its tittles, could not? Why could not Moses, the original receiver of the law, at least follow the arguments of Akiba and his disciples, who after all were discussing the law of Moses?

Compare this tale with the proposition stated by the Talmud (*Megillah* 19b) that God revealed to Moses every novel exposition of the law that would ever be made by anybody in any later generation.

Might it be that the basic principles of the law were familiar to Moses, but not its later development and detailed application, which resulted from changed cir-

---

82. Compare Abraham's plaint, "Will the judge of the entire earth not do justice . . . " (Gen. 18:25), and the Mesopotamian view (see Part One) that even the gods were bound by *Kittum*.

83. See Isaac b. Sheshet, Responsa *Radvaz*, 1:10, p. 532; Benjamin the Physician, *Shibale Haleket* (Vilna, 1887), secs. 2:21, 1:4, 12.

---

*Soncino Press translation (London, 1961).

cumstances? (Note, however, that it is not clear in the story that the particular law, claimed by Rabbi Akiba to be one which Moses received at Sinai, was the very one which Moses did not recognize).

Could the law develop to a point where it would eventually be unrecognizable to its original authorities because of changed circumstances? Would Madison, Jefferson, and the other "founding fathers" of the United States recognize many of the decisions rendered by the U.S. Supreme Court during the past twenty years as implicit in the constitution that they wrote, and as they understood it? Compare Hayim Ibn Ittar (*Ohr Ha'Hayim*, Lev. 13:37), who asserts that Moses knew the particular part of the Oral Law expounded by Akiba but did not know *where* it was indicated in the Bible.[84]

2. Why did Moses sit behind eight rows of disciples (some versions have it as eighteen rows. See the commentary of Judah Loewe, ad loc.). The talmudic practice was for the best students to sit in the front row, while those who were less learned sat progressively further from the teacher.[85]

3. If Akiba was superior to Moses, why was the Torah given to Moses? Judah Loewe, in his commentary ad loc. maintains that this was because Moses was the man who lived in the mundane world, whereas Akiba reached a spiritual level in which he was, for all practical purposes, separated from the world. While this conforms to the notion that the Torah and its laws are meant for, and are to be controlled solely by, humans (Section A, above), it is generally recognized that Akiba ben Joseph was a very active participant, if not an organizer, in the major revolt of the Jews in Judea and throughout the Mediterranean world against Rome, *circa* 135 C.E.

3. THE POWER TO ABROGATE THE LAW
(Talmud, *Yebamot* 89b)*

R. Hisda sent to Rabbah through R. Aha son of R. Huna [the following enquiry]: Cannot the Beth din lay down a condition which would cause the abrogation of a law of the Torah? Surely it was taught: At what period of her age is a husband entitled to be the heir of his wife [if she dies while still] a minor? Beth Shammai stated: When she attains to womanhood; and Beth Hillel said: When she enters into the bridal chamber.

---

*Soncino Press translation (London, 1961).

84. For a very novel and interesting explanation of this portion of the Talmud, see Soloveitchik in *Hidushe Ha'Griz Al Ha'Shas*, pt. 3, p. 234; he contends, based on his interpretation of the Talmud, *Sanhedrin* 21, that the early scrolls of the Torah did not contain tittles.

85. See Talmud, *Baba Kama* 117a.

At all events it was here stated, 'He is entitled to be her heir'; but, surely, by Pentateuchal law it is her father who should here be her legal heir, and yet it is the husband who is heir in accordance with a Rabbinical ordinance!—*Hefker* by Beth din is legal *hefker*; for R. Isaac stated: Whence is it deduced that *hefker* by Beth din is legal *hefker*? It is said, *Whosoever came not within three days, according to the counsel of the princes and the elders, all his substance should be forfeited, and himself separated from the congregation of the capitivity*.[86] R. Eleazar stated [that the deduction is made] from here: *These are the inheritances, which Eleazar the priest, and Joshua the son of Nun, and the heads of the fathers' houses of the tribes of the children of Israel, distributed for inheritance* (Josh. 19:51). Now, what relation is there between *Heads* and *Fathers*? But [this has the purpose] of telling you that fathers may distribute as an inheritance to their children whatever they wish, so may the heads distribute as an inheritance to the people whatever they wish. . . .

. . . The other replied: With an abstention from the performance of an act it is different.

[90*b*] He, [on hearing the last reply] said to him: It was my intention to raise objections against your view from [the Rabbinical laws which relate to] the uncircumcised, sprinkling, the knife [of circumcision], the linen cloak with *zizith*, the lambs of Pentecost, the *shofar* and the *lulab*; now, however, that you taught us that abstention from the performance of an act is not regarded as an abrogation [of the law, I have nothing to say since] all these are also cases of abstention.

Come and hear: *Unto him ye shall hearken*,[87] even if he tells you, "Transgress any of all the commandments of the Torah" as in the case, for instance, of Elijah on Mount Carmel, obey him in every respect in accordance with the needs of the hour![88]—There it is different, for it is written, "*Unto him shall ye hearken.*" Then let [Rabbinic law] be deduced from it!—The safeguarding of a cause is different.

Come and hear: If he annulled [his letter of divorce] it is annulled: so Rabbi. R. Simeon b. Gamaliel, however, said: He may neither annul it nor add a single condition to it, since, otherwise, of what avail is the authority of the Beth din. Now, though here, the letter of divorce may be annulled in accordance with Pentateuchal law, we allow a married woman, owing to the power of Beth din, to marry anyone in the world! —Anyone who betroths [a woman] does so in implicit

---

86. Ezra 10:8.

87. Deut. 18:15, referring to a true prophet.

88. Where he offered a sacrifice on an improvised altar (v. 1 Kings 18:31 ff.) despite the prohibition against offering sacrifices outside the Temple.

compliance with the ordinances of the Rabbis, and the Rabbis have [in this case] cancelled the [original] betrothal.

Said Rabina to R. Ashi: This is a quite satisfactory explanation where betrothal was effected by means of money; what, however, can be said [in a case where betrothal was effected] by cohabitation! —The Rabbis have assigned to such a cohabitation the character of mere prostitution.

Come and hear: R. Eleazar b. Jacob stated, "I heard that even without [or contrary to] any Pentateuchal [authority for their rulings], beth din may administer flogging and [death] penalties; not, however, for the purpose of transgressing the words of the Torah but in order to make a fence for the Torah. And it once happened that a man rode on horseback on the Sabbath in the days of the Greeks, and he was brought before beth din and was stoned; not because he deserved this penalty, but because the exigencies of the hour demanded it. And another incident occurred with a man who had intercourse with his wife under a fig tree, and he was brought before beth din and flogged; not because he deserved such a penalty, but because the exigencies of the hour demanded it!"—To safeguard a cause is different.

Notes and Questions to "The Power to Abrogate the Law"

1. *"Abstention from the performance of an act . . is different.* What is the authority of the Talmud for this distinction? The implication is that it is based solely on logic, which has the force of a biblical injunction.[89]

2. *"The knife of circumcision."* A male child is required to be circumcised on the eighth day after his birth.[90] If the circumcision knife is not available, it may not be transported on the Sabbath, even though the transportation is forbidden only by a rabbinical prohibition, although this failure to circumcise would violate the biblical injunction to circumcise male infants on the eighth day after birth.

3. *"The Shofar."* The *shofar* (ram's horn) is required to be blown during the Rosh Hashannah[91] services and in the Jubilee Year. When Rosh Hashannah occurs on the Sabbath, the talmudic decision-makers decreed that it should not be blown out of fear that it might be transported, in violation of the biblical prohibition against transporting objects on the Sabbath. This resulted in the abolition of the blowing of the

shofar when Rosh Hashannah occurred on the Sabbath. The rule is followed to this day in traditional religious services.

4. *"The safeguarding of a cause is different."* "Safeguarding" (literally, "fencing-in a matter") is used in the sense of fencing in a dangerous beast or contagion to prevent its spread, or buttressing a wall that is in danger of crumbling.

Which situations are regarded by the Talmud as important enough to justify committing acts violating biblical norms in order to "safeguard a cause?" Although the exact definition is unclear, the incident cited here in the Talmud concerning the Prophet Elijah (who offered up a sacrifice in a place other than the Temple,[92] contrary to biblical prohibition),[93] would indicate that decision-makers could permit violation of biblical norms only if two conditions were met: (*a*) a great and pressing and (*b*) public need, such as the abolition of widespread idolatry, as was the case in the action by Elijah.[94]

5. *"Then let [Rabbinic law] be deduced from it."* How can the power of ordinary mortal decision-makers to abolish a law of the Torah be derived from the power of the Prophet Elijah to do this, since he presumably abolished the commandment because God specifically instructed him to do so in that case? The underlying rationale is that the Talmud holds[95] that even a prophet may not add or change any laws of the Torah. Accordingly, when Elijah suspended the norm prohibiting the offering of sacrifices outside the Temple, he did not act as a prophet *per se*, but only as an ordinary mortal decision-maker who took steps to meet the exigencies and needs of that time. If Elijah (who as prophet had no extraordinary power to change any biblical laws), could do this, then other human decision-makers could also change the law temporarily because of the needs of the hour.[96]

According to this interpretation of the talmudic statement here, it would follow that nonprophetic decision-makers have the same power as prophets to abolish a biblical law whenever there is a need to "safeguard a matter."[97]

The Talmud here, however, was interested in ascertaining the source for the authority to abolish a biblical law, even where the situation was *not* one of "safe-

89. See Chajes, *Torat Ha'Neviim*, p. 24; compare idem, pp. 37, 39.
90. See Gen. 17:12.
91. See Lev. 23:24, 25:9; Talmud, *Rosh Hashanah* 32a.

92. See 1 Kings 18:20–39.
93. Deut. 12:13–18.
94. For further comment, see paragraph 15, below; see also Y. Gershuni, *Shita Me'Kubetzet*, *Pesahim* (New York, 1960), 3:509, and Chajes, *Torat Ha'Neviim*, p. 24.
95. *Shabbat* 104a.
96. See Tosefot, *Yebamot* 90b, s.v. *Ve'Ligmar*.
97. See commentary of *Ritva*, ad. loc. See also Chajes, *Torat Ha'Neviim*, chs. 4, 5; A. Kook, *Mishpat Kohen* (Hebrew; Jerusalem, 1926), no. 144; I. Sender, *Beth Shraga* (Hebrew; New York, 1968), p. 103.

guarding a matter.'" Accordingly, it asserts here that the act of the Prophet Elijah is no authority for abolition in such a situation.

It should be noted, however, that the abrogation of a biblical law referred to here concerns only a *temporary* change in order to meet the "needs of the hour," not a permanent change. (See Part Three, Chapter IX, below, for the prolonged use of the power to make "temporary" changes in situations where changes of long duration in social conditions require the abrogation of the biblical law for indefinite or prolonged periods of time.)

6. *"If he annulled his letter of divorce."* Rabbi Gamliel had prescribed that no husband could cancel his agency or annul a bill of divorce once he had handed it to his agent for delivery to the wife. He could not do this even in the presence of another court, since the wife, unaware of the cancellation or annulment, might marry another man after the bill of divorce was physically delivered to her. This would make her a technical, though unwitting, adulteress and bastardize children of any second marriage contracted by her.

7. *"Anyone who betroths a woman, does so in implicit compliance with the ordinances of the rabbis."* The Talmud here assumes that the reasoning of note 8, below, applies.

8. *"This is a quite satisfactory explanation where betrothal was effected by means of money."* The marriage could then be annulled *ab initio* by application of the principle *hefker beth din, hefker*, literally, "whatever the court declares to be ownerless becomes thereby ownerless"; that is, the legal authorities have the power to expropriate anybody's money, including that used by the groom to betroth his bride. Since by this *ex post facto* expropriation, the money had not been his to give at the time of the betrothal, the marriage was invalid *ab initio*. This retroactive expropriation is a remarkable feat of legal *legerdemain*, employed to protect the wife and her potential offspring. This could not, however, effect an annulment *ab initio*, where the betrothal was effected by means other than money.[98]

9. *"The rabbis have assigned such a cohabitation the character of [mere] prostitution."* In biblical and talmudic law marriage is effected solely through the acts and mental intent of the man and woman. No sanction or authorization is needed from religious or secular authorities. Since the husband's agreement and consent are a *sine qua non* for the marriage, he may, in the talmudic view, condition his agreement here, just like any other contract, as he wishes. Traditionally, at marriage, every groom pronounces the formula, that he marries his wife "according to the laws of Moses and

of Israel"—interpreted here as intending to specifically *condition* the marriage on the continuous consent of the legal authorities. The Talmud here maintains that *every* groom conditions his betrothal and marriage on the continued consent of the legal authorities and that he, furthermore, impliedly agrees that, in the event the authorities are unhappy with the marriage and wish to terminate it, they may annul it *ab initio*. Since the marriage had been conditioned by the groom upon the continued consent of the legal authorities, they could annul it, *ab initio*, even without resort to the principle of *hefker beth din, hefker*. None of the past cohabitation of the couple, therefore, would have had the sanction of marriage and is, accordingly, referred to here as "prostitution." This *ex post factor* annulment of the marriage (which might have been entered into years earlier), based on a condition subsequent, is an extreme example of the use of conditional clauses to effect legal *legerdemain* in order to protect the wife and her offspring.

What if the groom specifically states during the betrothal that it is *un*conditional and that he does *not* betroth on condition that the legal authorities may terminate his marriage? Some authorities, nevertheless, hold that even then the legal authorities could annul his marriage *ab initio*, where such annulment is desirable because of his improper acts.[99]

Can the bride, too, condition her acceptance of the betrothal as she sees fit, since her consent, too, is necessary?

10. *'I heard that even without [or contrary to] any Pentateuchal [authority for their rulings] the beth din may administer flogging and penalties."* The expression "I heard" is unusual. Ordinarily statements in the Talmud either are made by a party who states the view to be his original view, or are specifically attributed to another authority. The expression "I heard" is commonly utilized in a situation where there was a prevalent belief as to a particular occurrence, but there was no specific authority that could be cited.

The unusual sanctions here were imposed in the aftermath of the Maccabean revolt against Hellenist-Syrian religious persecutions[100] (*circa* 150 B.C.E., see Chapter IV, above). At that time there was a major *kulturkampf* between the adherents of Hellenism and of traditional Jewish religious practices. The Hellenists stressed disregard for the Torah and all non-Greek

98. See Talmud, *Kiddushin*, Mishnah 1.

99. See Commentary of Tosefot, in Talmud, *Baba Batra* 48a.
100. See *Mehilta*, Exod. 20:5: "What are you being, taken out to be crucified?" "Because I circumcised my son. . . ." See the variant version of this execution in *Megilat Ta'anit* (a work composed in the Talmudic Era; reprinted Warsaw, 1874), ch. 6. This work cites other biblical verses as the source of authority to execute for the "needs of the hour."

culture, emphasized the human body and its natural functions, and demonstrably sought to display these perspectives. In reaction, the Jewish traditionalists sought to suppress these public demonstrations.

11. *"To safeguard a cause [literally, "to fence in the matter"] is different."* What is the authority that permits annulment of a biblical law in order to "fence in a matter," i.e., for the welfare of the public? Note that this authority seems to be taken for granted here, as reflected in the act of the Prophet Elijah on Mount Carmel.[101] The source of Elijah's authority is not, however, mentioned in the Talmud here and will be discussed later (see Part Three, Chapter IX, below).

12. The foregoing doctrines are extended even further in the Jerusalem Talmud.[102] In discussing this principle, it states as follows: "How far [may a Court go in punishing, even though not authorized by the Bible]? Rabbi Lezer, the son of Rabbi Yose, says "Even on the basis of hearsay." Rabbi Yose says, "When there were witnesses, but there was no forewarning" (commentary of David Frankel in his commentary, *Korban Edah*, ad loc.). It should be noted, however, that the precise meaning of these statements is the subject of controversy.

13. A concise summary of the talmudic understanding and the application of this doctrine was expressed by Rambam as follows:

The *Beth Din* may flog one who is not liable for flogging and may kill one who is not liable for the death penalty, not in order to violate the words of the Torah, but only in order to make a fence about the Torah. Once the *Beth Din* sees that the people commonly violate a law, they must "fence in" and strengthen the matter as they see fit for that time, but they should not establish such a rule permanently . . . And it happened that one rode a horse on the Sabbath in the times of the Greeks, and he was brought to the *Beth Din* and they stoned him. And it happened that Shimon Ben Shetah hung eighty women in one day in Ashkelon, even though there did not exist there the required methods of interrogation and questioning, and there was no forewarning nor clear testimony of eye-witnesses. It was only a rule "for the hour," according to what he saw as necessary. And so a *Beth Din*, in every place and at every time, may flog a person who has a bad reputation and about whom people talk say that he violates sexual prohibitions; provided, that these are constant rumors which continue and do not cease, as we have explained, and provided, that these are not known enemies of his, who wish to give him a bad name. They [the *Beth Din*] may likewise em-

barrass one who acquires a bad reputation and may speak badly of his parents in his presence. A judge may always expropriate money and give it to another as he sees fit, in order to fill in "breaches in the wall of faith" and to strengthen the "structure" or to penalize. . . . So, too, the judge may excommunicate one who is not liable to excommunication, in order to repair the "breaches in the fence" according to what he sees as appropriate and pursuant to the needs of the hour; but, he should state that he is excommunicating according to what he [the judge] feels appropriate. . . . Similarly, a judge may quarrel with one who deserves to be quarreled with, and may curse him, hit him, tear out his hair, and force him to take an oath to God against his will that he will do or refrain from doing a particular act. . . . Similarly, he may also tie him hand and foot and imprison him in prison, and push him and drag him on the ground, as it is said [Rambam here cites various biblical verses indicating that these sanctions, common among the Persians, were applied by Jewish authorities and the Talmud, *Mo'ed Katan* 16a, premises them as authority]. . . . All of these things may be done in accordance with what the judge sees as being appropriate and according to the needs of the hour. In all of these matters, he should act always for the sake of Heaven, and the dignity of people should not be light in his eyes because it [human dignity] is strong enough to set aside a rabbinical prohibition. Certainly, with regard to the dignity of the descendants of Abraham, Isaac, and Jacob, who keep the true law, one must be careful not to destroy their dignity but only to increase the dignity of God alone, because he who shames the Torah, will, eventually, be abused by people, but one who honors the Torah will be honored by people; and one can honor the Torah only by acting according to its rules and norms.[103]

Rambam states further that,

A *Beth Din* may set aside these things [rules made by prior decision-makers] temporarily, even though it is inferior to the earlier judges, because these rules cannot be more weighty than the words of the Torah itself, because even the words of the Torah may be set aside, temporarily, by a *Beth Din*. For example, a *Beth Din* which sees it as appropriate to strengthen the faith, may erect [fence] in order that the people should not violate the words of the Torah, [and] may flog and punish, even when not authorized by law; but they may not establish this exception to last for generations, and may not say "This is the law." Similarly, if they see fit, temporarily, to abolish a posi-

---

101. See Commentary, *Nimuke Yosef*, ad loc.
102. *Hagigah*, ch. 2, rule 2.

103. Rambam, Laws of the Sanhedrin, ch. 24, rules 4–10. See his *Guide for the Perplexed* 3:41; see also Saadya Gaon, *Book of Opinions and Beliefs*, trans. R. Rosenblatt (Jerusalem, 1948), p. 267.

tive commandment or to violate a prohibition, in order to return the people to the faith, or to save many in Israel from stumbling over obstacles in other matters, they may do whatever the hour requires. Just as a physician may amputate a hand or foot of a person in order that the entire [person] may live, so may a *Beth Din* rule at times, to violate some of the laws, temporarily, in order that the [entire] law may be preserved; as the early sages said, "Violate one Sabbath for him, so that he may observe many Sabbaths.[104]

Note that this formulation does not specifically premise the authority to inflict sanctions that deviate from traditional law on any specific biblical passage. It bases the authority upon public need and the logic of authorizing a minor violation of law in order to preserve the entire law.

14. The formulation of the doctrine in terms of meeting "the needs of the hour" has been held by some decision-makers not to limit deviation from a biblical norm to a temporary deviation. As long as the changed circumstances, which require deviation from the rule, continue, departures from biblical norms are permissible.[105]

15. It should be noted that since murder is prohibited in the Bible, the execution of a criminal defendant by a court, should also constitute murder, unless this execution is specifically authorized by the Bible. So, too, flogging or other corporal punishment carried out by the court without specific biblical authorization, would constitute assault, which is otherwise prohibited by the Bible.[106]

On what basis, then, did talmudic decision-makers feel that they were authorized to kill or inflict corporal punishment? The Talmud's reference to the precedent of the Prophet Elijah (*Yebamot* 90a) is not too persuasive, since his act of offering a sacrifice outside of the Temple compound would have been a transgression of considerably lighter consequence than unauthorized murder. Mere logic is also not sufficient authority to inflict penalties. (See Talmud, *Sanhedrin* 76a, and Section B 2, above.)

Talmudic authorities have, accordingly, constantly struggled with the problem of:

(*a*) The source of the *beth din*'s right and authority to execute a criminal in cases where the Bible does not

authorize this. Similarly, on what did the Prophet Elijah himself base his authority?[107] (See below for further elaboration and development of this point.)

(*b*) What limits, if any, apply to annuling biblical norms? Clearly, the absence of adequate guidelines can lead to radical innovations, extreme consequences, and abuses of the law (see Part Three, Chapter IX, below).

16. Despite the ambiguity, this selection from the Talmud reflects the explicit recognition by talmudic authorities of their right to alter biblical norms for public benefit, where this would result in attaining overriding, basic goals. This was forcibly put, in connection with the imposition of sanctions, by one of the foremost Jewish legal authorities of the Middle Ages,[108] who said: "If you apply the laws fixed in the Torah strictly, and do not punish except in accordance therewith . . . the world would become desolate . . . as the sages have said, 'Jerusalem was only destroyed because they based their laws upon the law of the Torah.' . . ." Compare the following statements:

(*a*) "Said Rabbi Yannai, if the Torah had been given immutably fixed (see David Frankel, *Karban Edah* [reprinted Jerusalem, 1973], ad loc.), society could not exist. . . . Moses said to the Lord, 'Advise me what is the Law.' He said to Him, . . . if the majority acquit, then acquit; if the majority find that he is liable, then, hold him liable. . . . Why is this? So that the Torah should be able to be expounded with forty-nine faces to find ritual impurity and with forty-nine faces for ritual purity" (Jerusalem Talmud, *Sanhedrin* 4:2). [See Yom Tov Ashvili (*Ritva*), Novellae *Eruvin* 13b, who cites Tosafot to the effect that God taught Moses forty-nine ways to permit any matter and forty-nine ways to prohibit any matter, leaving it to the decision-makers in each generation to decide as these issues came up. A similar notion of the flexibility of the law is cited by Shmuel Alkalai, Responsa *Mishpete Shmuel* (Venice, 1594), no.

104. Book of Judges, Laws of Recalcitrants (*Mamrim*), ch. 2, rules 4 and 5.

105. Z. Chajes, *Torath Ha'Neviim*, pp. 25, 40, 197; Ginsberg, *Mishpatim Le'Yisrael* (Jerusalem, 1956), pp. 45–55, 90.

106. Talmud, *Ketubot* 35a, 35b; Rambam, Laws Concerning a Batterer, 5:1; Aderet, Responsa *Rashba*, no. 127; see Talmud, *Ketubot* 32a, and Rashi, ad loc., s.v. *"Ve'i Memona"*; Rambam, Laws of Sanhedrin 16:12; David Ibn Zimra, *Radvaz*, Commentary on Rambam, Laws of *Mamrin* 2:4.

107. See S. Yisraeli, *Amud Ha'Yemini* (Jerusalem, 1965); Tosefot, *Sanhedrin* 89b, s.v. *Elijah*; Ha'Meiri, *Beth Ha'Behira*, *Yebamot* 90b, and Yom Tov Ashvili in *Ritva*, ad loc.; Shlomo b. Aderet in *Rashba*, ad loc.

108. Responsa *Rashba*, vol. 3, no. 393, cited by J. Karo in *Beth Yosef, Tur Hashen Mishpat* (reprinted New York, 1945), sec. 2; see Talmud *Gittin* 4:2; Abraham ben David, *Ra'avad*, *T'mim De'im* (Lvov, 1812), no. 203; Tosefot *Yebamot* 88a, s.v. *Mitah* 90b, s.v. *Kivan*, and 110a, s.v. *Le'Fikah*; Tosefot, *Nazir* 43b, s.v. *Ve'Hai*; Tosefta, *Berahot* 16a, s.v. *Ve'Hotem*; *Nedarim* 90b, s.v. *Hazvu*; and Shlomo b. Aderet, *Rashba*, ad loc.; *Tosefot, Baba Batra*, 48b, s.v. *Tinah*; *Avodah Zarah* 13a, s.v. *Et Susehem*. See also S. Zucrow, *Adjustment of Law to Life in Rabbinic Literature* (Boston, 1928), who attempts to set forth numerous instances of changes made in Jewish law to meet new circumstances. Many of his claims, however, are disputable. See also Y. Gilat, *Beth Din Matnin La'Kur Davar Min Ha'Torah, Bar-Ilan University Yearbook* (Hebrew; Ramat Gan, Israel, 1970), p. 117.

9, and by Shlomo Algazi, *Halikhot Olam* (Venice, 1639), p. 88b.]

(*b*) "One is not appointed to the Sanhedrin unless he knows how to 'prove' that a [dead] insect is ritually pure," [that is, that it does not make one who touches it ritually impure, although it is basic that such insects do in fact defile ritually under biblical law (*Sanhedrin* 17a)].

(*c*) "It is better that one letter [i.e., one commandment] of the Torah be uprooted, so that the [entire] Torah should not be forgotten." [Talmud, *Temurah* 14b; see *Yebamot* 89a; *Makkot* 23b. See also Z. H. Chajes, *Torat Ha'Neviim*, in *Kal Sifrei Ma'Haratz Hayot* (Jerusalem, 1958), ch. 6, pp. 34 ff, 190 ff, 194 ff; and the rejoinder of M. Sofer in Responsa, *Hatam Sofer*, O.H., no. 208; see also Judah b. Asher, Responsa *Zikhron Yehuda*, no. 79.]

4. THE INSTITUTION OF THE *PRUSBUL* BY HILLEL

(Talmud, *Gittin* 36a)*

Hillel Instituted the Prusbul. We have learnt elsewhere: a *prusbul* prevents the remission of debts [in the sabbatical year]. This is one of the regulations made by Hillel the Elder. For he saw that people were unwilling to lend money to one another and disregarded the precept laid down in the Torah, *Beware that there be not a base thought in thine heart saying . . . The Seventh Year is Approaching . . . And You Will Give Him Nothing* (Deut. 15:9). He therefore decided to institute the *prusbul*. The text of the *prusbul* is as follows: 'I hand over to you So and So, the judges in such and such a place, [my bonds]. So that I may be able to recover any money owing to me from So and So at any time I shall desire;' and the *prusbul* was to be signed by the judges or witnesses. . . .

Come and hear: Samuel said: This *prusbul* is an assumption on the part of the judges; if I am ever in a position, I will abolish it. Rabbi Nahman, however, said: I would confirm it. Confirm it? Is it not already firmly established? What he meant was: I will add a rule that even if it [the *prusbul*] is not actually written it shall be regarded as written.

Notes and Questions to "The Institution of the Prusbul *by Hillel*"

1. Note that Rabbah (see *Gittin* 36b) maintains that Hillel's *Prusbul* was instituted as as a result of the principle permitting expropriation of property (*hefker beth din, hefker*). The implication is that human decision-makers may annul a biblical norm by this technique and may compel either abstention from an act mandated by the Bible or performance of an act prohibited by the Bible.

2. *Evasions of Law and Legal Fictions.* Was Hillel's institution of the *prusbul* an evasion of biblical law? In the talmudic perspective it was not. The objective of the biblical institution of debt-remission during the Sabbatical Year was to help the poor. In Hillel's time, however, the remission of debts harmed the poor, because it discouraged people of means from lending them money out of fear that the debt would be cancelled because of the Sabbatical Year, and would never be repaid. Accordingly, the adverse effects of debt remission on the poor, eventually greatly exceeded the benefits to them. The institution of the *prusbul* was designed, in part, to help the poor, by encouraging the extension to them of credit, which would otherwise have been unavailable. Hillel's *prusbul* was thus viewed as an attempt to achieve the identical goal (of aiding the poor) that had been intended by the biblical norm of debt remission, yet circumventing the actual remission of debts while preserving the technical form of that biblical norm. Preservation of traditional legal forms has the advantage of providing the desired appearance of the stability of law, which is so desired by society. "Constant changes would tend to disturb the whole system of the law, and would lead people to believe that the law is not of Divine origin. . . ."[109]

In the talmudic perspective, adherence to the letter of the law has the additional asset of preserving the mystical (kabbalistic) and metaphysical purposes that would have been accomplished by the original biblical norm of debt remission. Biblical norms were viewed as having mystical and metaphysical consequences, in addition to their apparent utility in regulating human behavior.[110]

3(*a*). Would you term Hillel's *prusbul* a "legal fiction?" A commonly accepted definition of that term is by Henry Maine: "Any assumption which conceals, or affects to conceal, the fact that a rule of law has undergone alteration, its letter remaining unchanged, its operation being modified."[111] Did the *prusbul* "conceal" an alteration of a rule of law?

Can the term "legal fiction" apply to the general principles (Section 5, above) that decision-makers may annul biblical norms and that they may flog and penal-

---

109. Maimonides, *Guide for the Perplexed*, trans. Friedlander, 3:41, p. 347; see J. Frank, *Law and the Modern Mind* (New York, 1931), pp. 5–31, 118–47. See also R. Pound, *Interpretations of Legal History* (Cambridge, Mass., 1923).

110. See Shapiro, *"The Ideological Foundations of the Halakhah,"* p. 101 ff.; Moshe ben Nahman (Ramban), intro. to his Commentary on the Bible, ed. Shevel (Jerusalem, 1975), p. 436.

111. H. Maine, *Ancient Law* (London, 1861), p. 25.

ize, although contrary to biblical Law? Are these evasions of the law or concealment of changes therein?

3(b). Maine also claims that law in its early stages is rigid and cannot change. According to him, law develops gradually, however, by use of legal fictions, followed by utilization of equity jurisdiction to establish a new set of norms, which then coexist with the ancient law. Finally, in its last stage, changes in law are affected by legislation (ibid., p. 29). Is this theory borne out by the foregoing selections from the Talmud, Yebamot and Gittin?

4. Note that Samuel maintained that the prusbul was too extreme a measure, which should be abolished, while Rabbi Nahman desired to extend it even further and apply it, even if made orally (see Talmud, Gittin, 36a and 36b).

5. Compare the authority of the beth din to expropriate property for the benefit of a private individual under the doctrine of hefker beth din, hefker, with the power of eminent domain under the Fifth Amendment of the U.S. Constitution, which may be exercised only for a "public purpose."[112]

6. For extensive discussions of the prusbul and similar institutions, see Chajes, Torath Ha'Neviim, above, p. 34 ff.; Chernowitz, II Toledot Ha'Halacha, p. 132 ff.; Elon, Ha'Mishpat Ha'Ivri, p. 418; K. Kahana, p. 18 ff.; 41 ff.; M. Silberg, Talmudic Law and the Modern State (New York, 1973), p. 22 ff. See also Talmud, Pesahim 9a; Betza 11b; Shabbat 139b.

7. For a similar circumvention of a biblical norm, which was instituted in order to keep within the form of traditional law while not frustrating its basic purpose, consider the heter iska (permit to do business), which was designed to circumvent the biblical prohibition regarding the taking of interest on loans. The use of a heter iska became widespread in the middle ages.[113]

Numerous principles of law evolved in order to permit both interest-bearing business loans, necessary for the economic livelihood of many Jews in the Middle Ages, and non-business loans to the poor, who required the money for the necessities of life.

8. The institution of the prusbul by Hillel was, according to one view in the Talmud, a prime example of the application of the principle hefker beth din, hefker in prescribing law. This is to be contrasted with its more common utilization by courts to decide monetary disputes. In addition to the many instances in the Talmud that rely on it as a basis for decisions in commercial law,[114] it is also applied in other areas,[115] such as sacerdotal law.[116]

9. The principle of hefker beth din, hefker was one of the most widely used bases for prescriptions and application of law throughout the long history of Judaic law. It was held to be applicable at all times and was not limited to a requirement of a great public need.[117] It was also extensively utilized in prescriptions made by Jewish communities through their lay representatives and leaders, who claimed the right to exercise this power.[118] It has been claimed that this principle, and that of dina de'malhuta dina, "the law of the state is the law" (see Chapter VI, Section A 3, below) are both simply different aspects of the same norm.[119]

10. In summary, then, the foregoing selections from the Talmud reflect the talmudic perspective that authorized decision-makers could contravene biblical norms under the following circumstances, based upon the indicated rationales:

(a) A court, or other authoritative decision-maker, may expropriate money or property from any party and transfer title to another in its discretion. This authorization, based on the doctrine of hefker beth din, hefker, was claimed to be applicable at all times. This legal principle contained the potential for changes in law in nearly all areas of societal activity, since it related to the ownership of property, which permeates nearly all facets of commercial life, and often sacerdotal practices.

112. See Shlomo b. Aderet in Rashba, Novellae to Gittin 36b. See also Isaac b. Sheshet, Responsa Rivash, no. 399, and S. Luria in Yam Shel Shlomo, Yebamot 10, 19; Rambam, Laws of Sanhedrin, ch. 24, rule 6; contra B. Ashkenazi, Shita Mekubetzet (Metz, 1764); Baba Kama 100a; Moshe Trani, Responsa Mabit (Lvov, 1861; reprinted New York, 1968), vol. 2, no. 128. See Ginsberg, Mishpatim Le'Israel, p. 39–40, n. 297, for citation of additional authorities and further discussion; Yaakov Karliner, Keren Orah (Vilna, 1852); Yebamot 90b. See Section 3, above, for citations to other authorities.
113. See H. Soloveitchik, "Pawnbroking: A Study in Ribbit and of the Halakhah in Exile," Proceedings of the American Academy for Jewish Research 38–39 (1972): 203; S. Z. Auerbach, "Concerning Evasions Regarding Interest" (Hebrew), Ha' Neeman 27, no. 32 (1966): 1–8; S. Atlas, "Legal Evasions in the Talmud" (Hebrew), in L. A. Ginsberg Jubilee Volume (New York, 1946), pp. 1–24. Another prominent example of circumvention of a biblical norm is the selling of leaven to non-Jews before Passover and its repossession immediately after Passover in order to satisfy the commandment that "Seven days shall leaven not be found in your homes" (Exod. 12:19; Tosefta Pesahim, ch. 2; S. Y. Zevin, Ha'Moadim Ba'Halakha [Jerusalem, 1952]).

114. See Talmud, Yebamot 89b, Gittin 78a; Gerundi, Novellae Ran, and Ashvili, Ritva, Novellae, ad loc.; Gittin, 37b. See also Talmud, Sanhedrin 5a, which relies on this principle to permit one-judge courts to operate.
115. See, for example, Tosefta, Shekalim 1:3; Mishnah, Shekalim 1:2; Peah 5:1; Gittin 55a, Rashba, ad loc.; Terumot 2:2, Yebamot 67a and b, and Rashba, ad loc.; Zevahim 8:7.
116. Shlomo b. Aderet, Novellae Rashba to Talmud, Shabbat 18b.
117. See Yosef Habiba, Novellae, Nimuke Yosef to Talmud, Yebamot 90b; Ashvili, Novellae of Ritva, ad loc.
118. See Shlomo b. Aderet, Responsa Rashba, vol. 5, no. 126; vol. 4, no. 142; Elon, Hamishpat Ha'Ivri, p. 421.
119. A. Kahana-Shapiro, Responsa D'Var Avraham (Warsaw, 1906), 1:1.

(*b*) Any person could be ordered to "sit and do not commit the act," that is, to refrain from performing an act prescribed by the Torah. This was also regarded as applicable at all time, within the discretion of authoritative decision-makers.

(*c*) One could be compelled to violate a biblical norm either by way of performing an act contrary to biblical law, or refraining from performance of a biblically required act in order "to safeguard a cause" (literally, "to fence in the matter"). This power was alleged to be applicable where there was a great and compelling public need. This included the authority of the *beth din* to have a defendant executed even though this was not authorized by traditional biblical norms. Some authorities claimed that only the "Great Court" (the Sanhedrin) had this power.[120] (See, however, Part Three, Chapter IX, Section B 2, below.)

(*d*) A marriage could also be annulled *ab initio*, based on the rationale that "anyone who betroths a woman conditions it on the consent of the rabbis." This presumption that every groom conditions the continued validity of his marriage upon the continued consent of authorized decision-makers was also alleged to apply at all times. As mentioned above, it may be applied even when the groom specifically or impliedly does not so condition his marriage. Decision-makers could also apply the principle of *hefker beth din, hefker* to annul marriages, where the betrothal was effected by means of a gift of money to the bride. As noted, these are extreme measures since they authorize decision-makers to dissolve a marriage *ab initio*, many years after it was effected.[121]

In the aggregate, the aforementioned legal doctrines permitted the adjustment of law in practically all areas of human activity, as detailed hereafter. In addition, there were still other doctrines that were utilized for such purposes. (See Part Three, Chapter IX, Section B 3, below.)

11. As noted above, the Talmud, in enunciating the principle that offenders could be killed or flogged, even contrary to the apparent rules of the Bible, did not cite any biblical authority for this (nor for the principle that one could be required to remain passive and thereby violate a biblical injunction). What made the talmudic decision-makers so certain that they could kill in such situations? It is important to realize that talmudic decision-makers were deeply religious and would

not act to transgress so fundamental a biblical precept as killing or maiming a criminal defendant, unless they perceived biblical authorization to do this. It should be noted that floggings, when not authorized by the Bible, are regarded as tortious battery, prohibited by the Bible,[122] while an unauthorized killing by a court would be a violation of the biblical norm "Thou Shalt Not Kill."[123] (For the actual practice in imposing sanctions contrary to biblical norms, and the principles, rationales, and precedents relied on, see Part Three, Chapter IX, Section B, below.)

5. ADJUSTMENTS IN FAMILY LAW

During the Talmudic Era, Palestinian Jews were dispersed all over the known world. There were intense Roman persecutions and constant warfare between the Romans, Parthians, and Persians, with continuous military incursions and brigandage. Consequently, there arose many tragic family separations and other unfortunate situations, with particularly devastating impact upon wives. Jewish decision-makers attempted to come to their aid with a number of far-reaching legal innovations. Some of the most important ones were the following:

1. The Talmudic decision-makers established a rule that a marriage was invalid where the woman was kidnapped, or was otherwise coerced, in order to force her to marry. It made no difference that later, at the marriage ceremony, she voluntarily consented to the marriage. In either case the marriage, technically valid according to biblical law, was invalidated by the talmudic decision-makers in order to deter such acts, which were becoming more prevalent.[124]

In these cases the women, although considered married under biblical law, were nevertheless permitted to marry other men without divorce—an act that otherwise would constitute adultery. This was a very far-reaching exercise of authority by talmudic decision-makers since both the Bible and the Talmud were extremely strict with regard to chastity by married women. It was openly acknowledged that these decisions annulled biblical law and that decision-makers

120. See Maimonides, *Guide for the Perplexed* 3:41; Chajes *Torat Ha'Neviim*, pp. 196–97; see also Sofer, Responsa *Hatam Sofer*, O.H., no. 208; Habiba, Novellae, *Nimuke Yosef to Sanhedrin* 52b; Gerundi, Novellae *Ran, Sanhedrin* 46a.

121. See Ha'Meiri, *Yebamot*, ad loc.; for further discussion, see Auerbach, in *Torah She'Baal Peh* (Jerusalem, 1956); O. Yosef, ibid., p. 56.

122. See Talmud, *Ketubot* 35a and b; Rambam, Laws of the Sanhedrin, ch. 16, rule 12; Laws Concerning a Batterer, 5:1. See Arye Leib, *Turei Even* (Metz, 1791), *Megillah* 27a; Talmud, *Shabbat* 128b; Shlomo b. Aderet, Responsa *Rashba*, 1:252, 257; Y. Babad, *Minhat Hinuh* (Lvov, 1869), no. 48; S. Zalman, *Shulhan Arukh Ha'Rav* (Kapust, 1814), sec. 5, Rules of Injury, subsec. 4.

123. See Section 3 C, above; see also Isaac b. Sheshet, *Radvaz*, Commentary to Rambam, Laws of *Mamrin*, ch. 2, rule 4; Chajes, *Kal Kitvei*, p. 197 ff.; S. Yisraeli, *Amud Ha'Yemini*.

124. Talmud, *Baba Batra* 48b; *Yebamot* 110a. See Ashvili, Commentary *Ritva, Yebamot* 91b; Habiba, *Nimuke Yosef*, ad loc.; Elon, *Ha-Mishpat Ha'Ivri*, pp. 427–28.

had the authority to invalidate biblically valid marriages.[125]

2. The Bible requires the testimony of two eye witnesses to prove a matter.[126] Accordingly, when a husband disappears, his wife is not permitted to remarry until his death is established by two witnesses. This norm led to great difficulties, particularly during the many Jewish wars and revolts against Roman rule in the first two centuries of the Christian Era. Accordingly, talmudic decision-makers ruled that a woman who testified that her husband had died could remarry, even without corroborating testimony by other, unrelated witnesses.[127] The Talmud records that this principle was originally established in the case of a woman whose husband was bitten by a snake and who died while he was harvesting wheat in the company of other men. His wife came to testify to the court about his death. The court investigated and concluded that he had indeed died. The court was impressed by the fact that the other men who were with him at his death did not come to notify the court and might, later, have become unavailable as witnesses. A new rule was therefore established that a woman who testified as to her husband's death could remarry. This norm was eventually further extended.

These are the matters in which [the members of] the School of Hillel changed their mind and ruled like the School of Shamai: the woman who came from across the sea and said, "My husband died" may remarry; ... The School of Hillel had said, "We only heard this rule where she comes from the harvest" [the case mentioned above, where witnesses might still be available]. The School of Shamai said to them, "It makes no difference whether she comes from the harvest of wheat, or whether she comes from harvesting olives, or whether she comes from across the seas. They only spoke about the harvest of wheat, because those were the facts in that case." The School of Hillel thereupon changed their mind and ruled like the School of Shamai.[128]

3. This deviation from the biblical norm was still not sufficient to solve the problem of wives who desired to remarry following their husbands' disappearance. Men would often disappear or die during the many wars and turbulences of that era without the wife being personally present at the husband's death, and where two witnesses were not available.

Said Rabbi Akiva, when I traveled to *Neharda'a* [in Babylonia] to establish a leap year [which could not be performed in the land of Israel because it was forbidden under Roman religious persecutions], I found Nehemia of D'li. He said to me, "I heard that the only one in the land of Israel who permits a woman to marry on the testimony of only one witness, is Rabbi Yehuda ben Baba." I said to him, "This is correct." He said to me, "Tell them in my name, 'You know that the country is racked by armed bands [and I cannot come to testify; also, those who witness a husband's death may not be able to come to testify either]. I have received a tradition from Rabbi Gamliel, the Elder, that one may permit a wife to marry on the testimony of one witness.'" When I (i.e., Rabbi Akiva) came and I set these words before Rabbi Gamliel [the Younger], he was very happy about my words and said, "We have found a companion to Rabbi Yehuda ben Baba." Because of these words, Rabbi Gamliel then recalled that there were many who had been killed at Tel-Arza and Rabbi Gamliel, the elder, had authorized their wives to marry on the testimony of one witness. From that time on, it became established to permit (wives) to marry upon the testimony of one witness.[129]

Rambam, however, explains the tradition of dispensing with the requirement of two witnesses, by saying:

Do not be perplexed that the sages permitted this weighty matter of [which would, without Talmudic authorization, be] adultery, on the testimony of a woman, a slave, maid or [based on hearsay testimony concerning] the tales told by a gentile who is not [himself] testifying, or on [other] hearsay, or on written evidence, and without thorough investigation and interrogation, as we have explained. The Torah was not scrupulous in requiring the testimony of two witnesses and the other laws of evidence, except where it was not possible to clearly establish a matter without testimony of witnesses who, for example, would testify that one man killed another, or that he lent money to him. But with regard to a matter which can [eventually] be clearly established without the testimony of this witness and this witness cannot evade us if the matter is not true (as, for example, where he testifies that someone has died), then, the Torah was not scrupulous [in requiring two witnesses] with regard to him, since it would be far-fetched that he would testify falsely. Accordingly, the sages were lenient in this matter and believed a single witness, or a maid, or a writing, without investigation and interrogation, in order that Jewish women should not remain tied down [to a husband who had disappeared and had never returned].[130]

---

125. Jerusalem Talmud, *Gittin* 4:2; see also p. 495, regarding the ordinance of Rabbi Gamliel.

126. Deut. 19:16; see, however, Talmud, *Gittin* 2b; Tosefot, *Yebamot* 88a, s.v. *Mitokh*.

127. Talmud, *Yebamot* 116b.

128. Talmud, *Ediot*, ch. 1:12; *Yebamot* 15:2.

129. Talmud, *Yebamot* 16:7.

130. Rambam, Laws of Divorce, ch. 13, rule 29. See, how-

According to this view, the Bible does not always require two witnesses, despite its provision that "according to two witnesses . . . shall a matter be established."[131] Can persuasive circumstantial evidence, then, be admissible in criminal cases if there is good policy justification, just as it is admitted to establish death of a husband? (See Chapter VI, Section C, below.)

The permissible use of circumstantial evidence is also intimated by the biblical verse[132] "and they shall spread the sheet . . ." (of the connubial bed, i.e., to be used as proof of virginity, in the case of a husband who accused his bride of not being a virgin). The Talmud, too,[133] interpreted this as meaning, "until the matter is established [by witnesses] as clearly as by exhibiting the sheet." Thus, the testimony of witnesses is required to meet the higher (in this case) standard of circumstantial evidence.

4. The public policy behind the law in these cases is often described in the Talmud as "because of the need to prevent her from becoming a 'tied-down' wife [tied to a husband, who had disappeared and might never return], the rabbis were lenient."[134] This leniency was also reinforced by the premise that the wife's credibility in these cases was greater than usual. It was felt that the wife would not remarry, unless she was sure that her husband was dead, since, if he were alive, it would eventually come to light. She would then be forced to leave her second husband, and any children of the remarriage would be stigmatized as bastards.[135] Although a number of talmudic commentators felt that this logic was sufficient to satisfy the biblical requirement of two witnesses (since the testimony of the wife, in this case, was as persuasive as the testimony of two witnesses),[136] the preponderant opinion is that this leniency of permitting the wife to remarry (based on her own testimony or based on the testimony of one witness, even where the wife has no independent knowledge regarding the husband's death) was based upon the power to set aside biblical norms. As one of the most authoritative commentators said, "Even though the sages did not have the power to uproot a rule of the Torah by authorizing performance of an act [which violates a biblical norm], yet, where there is a reason and logic, everybody agreed that they do have the power to uproot."[137]

This view is supported by the fact that permission for the wife to remarry here does not seem to have been effected by the accepted technique of annulling the marriage *ab initio*, which purports to conform to biblical law. In that case, she should not be forced—as she is here—to leave the second husband, if the first husband reappeared.[138] Perhaps, however, this penalty was retained as a threat, in order to make sure that the wife would check carefully before she remarried.[139]

5. The rule permitting the wife to remarry, although the death of the husband was not established by the testimony of two witnesses, was extended to many other circumstances, including hearsay testimony, rumors, and other inconclusive evidence of death.[140]

6. For adjustments of the law in other noncriminal areas, see Talmud, *Pesahim* 91b, 92a, 92b, and commentary of S. Yitzhaki, Rashi, ad loc., and Tosefot, ad loc.; Talmud *Betza* 8b, and Y. T. Ashvili, *Ritva*, above, and Shlomo b. Aderet, *Rashba*, above, ad loc.; Tosefot, *Eruvin* 26b; Talmud, *Rosh Hashannah* 32b, and *Ritva*, above, ad loc.; Meir of Lublin, Responsa *Maharam* (Lublin), no. 20; Tosefot, *Zevahim* 65a, s.v. *Minyan*; Talmud, *Parah* 7:6; Tosefta *Niddah* 1:3; Jerusalem Talmud, *Niddah* 1:4; *Berakhot* 16a and Tosefot, ad loc., s.v. *Vehotem*; *Avodah Zarah* 13a and Tosefot, ad loc., s.v. *"Amar Abaye"*; *Baba Metzia* 32b, s.v. *midivrei*; Talmud, *Sukkah* 42b; *Megillah* 4b, *Rosh Hashannah* 29b; Nissim Gerundi, Novellae, *Ran, Nedarim* 90b, and Tosefot, *Yeshanim*, ad loc.; Rashi, *Shevuoth* 45a, s.v. *Takkanat*; Mishnah, *Keritot* 5a, and Rashi, ad loc.; Tosefot, *Gittin* 54b, s.v. *Shelo Yomar*; Tosefot, *Ketubot* 11a, s.v. *Ger Katan*.

---

ever, *Sifri*, Deut. 19:15, sec. 154, which derives the exception from that biblical verse. See also Tov Ashvili, Novellae *Ritva, Yebamot* 88a; Tosefot, *Yeshanim*, ad loc.; Shimon Duran, Responsa *Tashbatz* (Lvov, 1791), vol. 1, no. 85; Isaac b. Sheshet, Responsa *Rivash*, no. 195; Ezekiel Landau, Responsa *Noda Be'Yehuda*, E.H., vol. 1, no. 33.

131. Deut. 19:15.

132. Deut. 22:17.

133. *Ketubot* 46a; the Talmud often regards a strong inference from circumstances (referred to by the term "*Anan Sahadi*"—"We, the court, testify") as the equivalent of testimony by two witnesses. See, e.g., Talmud, *Baba Batra* 35b; Tosefot, s.v. *Ve'i Dali*.

134. Talmud, *Yebamot* 88a.

135. See Talmud, *Yebamot* 87b, 25a, 93b, 115a, 116b.

136. See Ashvili, Novellae *Ritva, Yebamot* 88a. This is analogous to the thesis of Rambam, note 130, above.

137. Tosefot, Talmud, *Nazir* 43b and *Yebamot* 88a. See, however, Sofer, Responsa *Hatam Sofer*, O.H., no. 208; Chajes, Duran, Responsa *Tashbatz* (Lvov, 1791), vol. 1, no. 85; Isaac b. Sheshet, Responsa *Rivash*, no. 195; Landau, *Noda Be'Yehuda*.

138. See Mishnah, *Yebamot* 87b.

139. See Elon, *Ha'Mishpat Ha'Ivri*, p. 433, n. 147.

140. See Mishnah, *Yebamot* 6 and 16:7; Jerusalem Talmud, *Yebamot* 16:7; Y. Kahana, *Sefer Ha'Agunot* (Jerusalem, 1954).

VI.   The Legal System in Operation

A. *Jewish Loss of Power and Exile: The Impact on Jewish Law of Existing in an Alien Authority and Power System*

1. NON-JEWS AS THE SOURCE OF POWER FOR JEWISH DECISION-MAKERS: CHANGES FROM A HIERARCHICAL AUTHORITY AND POWER SYSTEM TO A DUAL–CO-ARCHICAL SYSTEM

With the Roman takeover of Judea (*circa* 60 B.C.E.), the elimination of the Jewish Hasmonean monarchic dynasty, and, even more, the termination of the Second Jewish Commonwealth (*circa* 70 C.E.), the Romans became the ultimate source of power and authority for decision-making. Nevertheless, with relatively brief interruptions, the Jewish community was still permitted to maintain a judicial system and otherwise make decisions for the internal ordering of Jewish society there.

The result was a dual authority system in which both Roman and Jewish officials participated. Jewish decision-makers acted by virtue of Roman authorization and were often religious figures who were regarded by tradition as authorized to make decisions. Such dual authority systems were not new to the Jewish community. Yet the existence of Rome as the seat of power for many centuries thereafter had very significant effects on decision-making.

A similar situation existed in Babylonia, which contained a very substantial Jewish community that rivaled and sometimes overshadowed, the Palestinian one. There, too, the non-Jewish rulers permitted the Jews a substantial amount of autonomy and power in the internal affairs of Jewish society. In order to understand the consequences of dual authority, it is necessary to briefly sketch the history and background of such co-archical systems in the two leading Jewish communities of that era: Palestine and Babylonia.

2. THE INTERNAL POWER STRUCTURE: AUTHORITATIVE DECISION-MAKING AFTER THE SECOND JEWISH COMMONWEALTH; INSTITUTIONAL PATTERNS AND PARTICIPANTS

Jewish decision-making following the destruction of the Second Jewish Commonwealth was extremely com-

plex. Like many other facets of Jewish Law, it has existed in many varied contexts and stages of societal development, ranging from semicapitalist and, later, semifeudal Rome and nearly feudal Persia, through thoroughly feudal medieval Europe, the commercial and industrial revolutions, and the rise of the modern state and postindustrial society. Jewish decision-making functioned during these decisive stages of society in a myriad of cultural and religious milieus, including polytheism, Hellenism, dualistic Zoroastrianism, monotheistic Christianity, humanism, and the age of science. The institutional patterns and participants of decision-making varied from epoch to epoch and from place to place. Accordingly, no attempt will be made here to examine in detail decision-making in all countries at all times. Instead, the patterns will be sketched in outline, with more detailed study of selected portions.

A rather arbitrary distinction will also be drawn between formal institutional decision-makers and patterns, on the one hand, and individual and class participants in decisions, on the other hand. In practice, of course, there is considerable overlap, and firm bounds are artificial.

In order to understand the roles and identities of the various institutional and class participants in Jewish decision-making, it is first necessary to grasp the contexts and constitutive processes operating in the Jewish communities. A brief overview of contexts of Jewish communal decision-making is, therefore, sketched herein. A more detailed examination of the roles played by the major participants will be detailed thereafter.

The authoritative Jewish institutional participants in decision-making during the Second Jewish Commonwealth, and thereafter, may arbitrarily be grouped for the purpose of examination, as follows:

A. *Trans-Local and Regional*
   1. The king
   2. Courts and judicial networks
   3. The *gaonite* and other academies of law and religion
   4. Lay councils and religious synods
   5. The exilarchate (*resh galuta*) in Babylonia, the patriarchate (*nasi*) in Palestine, and similar institutions in other countries
   6. Regional rabbinates
B. *Local-Communal*
   1. Local communal polities and bureaucracies,

including communal heads, officers, executive committees, and electorates

2. Courts
3. The rabbinate
4. Trade and social organizations

The principal classes of Jewish participants in the foregoing institutional patterns of Jewish decision-making included:

1. Those claiming royal descent from King David
2. Scholars educated in the Jewish law and religion
3. Plutocrats
4. The lay electorate and taxpayers
5. Non-taxpaying residents

Non-Jewish organs of power, both secular and religious, and their officials, were of course crucially important for Jewish decision-making, as detailed herein.

It should be noted that there was considerable overlap in the aforementioned categories, with one person often belonging to a number of classes and serving in more than one institutional pattern. Furthermore, the breakdown of decision-making into institutional patterns and classes is artificial and is only made here to facilitate examination. Sometimes, too, local and regional participants were closely intertwined. Accordingly, examinations of different institutional patterns and classes of decision-makers, and sometimes local and regional elements as well, will be interwoven in the following discussion. The extent of the authority and control exercised by these institutions and participants in decision-making, varied, of course, from community to community and underwent substantial change in the various epochs of Jewish history. The role of Jewish decision-makers remained crucial for a period of nearly two millennia. It was drastically reduced with the collapse of Jewish autonomous self-government in the aftermath of the French Revolution, and the gradual incorporation of Jews in the social and political life of the countries in which they resided.

3. JEWISH DECISION-MAKING IN A DUAL AUTHORITY SYSTEM

a. EARLY PALESTINE AND BABYLONIA

As far back as the Biblical Era, Jewish municipalities in Palestine had considerable independence because of perennially weak central governments and the lack of an authoritarian, centralized, religious bureaucracy. Cities and towns were largely self-sufficient economically, and frequently differed very widely from one another in their geographic setting. All of these factors fostered local independence and the development of local agencies to supervise and provide needed munici-

pal services, particularly administration, religious worship, a judiciary, and education.

When the bulk of the Jewish population was exiled to Babylonia, (*circa* 600 B.C.E.), it appears that the Jews there eventually organized themselves into the same type of self-sufficient communities, which provided for their essential needs in much the same fashion as they had formerly done in Palestine. This pattern of local self-government continued when the Jewish Commonwealth was reestablished in Palestine some time later. This was true even during the period of Roman rule of Palestine, and it remained substantially unchanged even after the destruction of the Temple and Second Jewish Commonwealth, (*circa* 70 C.E.).

b. REDUCTION IN JEWISH POWER RESULTING FROM THE DESTRUCTION OF THE SECOND JEWISH STATE AND TEMPLE

Although the Romans had dominated Judea since about 60 B.C.E., they had permitted its internal power structure to continue essentially unchanged. However, the destruction of the Temple and the Jewish State (*circa* 70 C.E.) brought with it profound power changes in the relationship of the Jewish people to the external world, and among themselves. The state of Judea ceased to exist and became just another province in the Roman Empire. Because of the long and bloody revolts (the first by any people, as a whole, against Roman domination), all activity in the province was carefully watched and scrutinized by the Roman overlords. Nevertheless, the bulk of the population of both Judea and Galilee remained Jewish, and it was as a Jewish province that it related and interacted with Rome and the other provinces of the Roman Empire.

Internally, the elites of the monarchy and of the priesthood ceased. The Romans did, however, permit Yohanan ben Zakai to found an academy for the study of law and religious subjects at Yavneh. This academy, and others that were subsequently established elsewhere, were supported by voluntary contributions of Jews throughout the land.

Ben Zakai attracted and trained numerous outstanding scholars who were eventually appointed to a reconstituted Sanhedrin. Now, however, the main criteria for membership in the Sanhedrin were learning and piety, rather than wealth or political influence. The scholars of the Academy attained great eminence, and consequently crucial importance, in the decision-making processes. They decided on all questions of Jewish religious law, which encompassed the entire spectrum of human activity. These decisions dealt with all social relations between people, such as marriage, divorce, commercial transactions, and assault. With Roman sanction, courts were gradually reestablished in towns throughout the land to decide disputes in accordance with traditional Jewish law, the Sanhedrin acting as a superior court.

There was thus, in effect, a dual system of government: The Romans controlled external affairs and certain internal civic matters (including road-building and taxation), while the Jewish courts and the academies, with overlapping membership, controlled many other areas of individual and societal activity, promulgated prescriptions, and decided disputes. Under this system Jewish legal and religious scholarship began to flourish once more, although the larger part of the case law and legal traditions remained oral. While summaries of the law were reduced to writing by a number of scholars, these were utilized only privately and were not made for publication or wide circulation. Among the most influential scholars and decision-makers of the era were Rabbi Eliezer ben Hyrcanus, Rabbi Yehoshua ben Perachya, and Rabbi Akiba and his disciples, particularly Rabbi Meir. This power condition of the Jewish people did not last long, however, and was soon altered drastically by the Bar Kokhba revolt.

The unsuccessful Bar-Kokhba revolt against Rome (*circa* 135 C.E.) resulted in wholesale carnage that decimated the Jewish population and led to the sale of many thousands of Jews as slaves throughout the Roman Empire. The Jews became a minority in their own land; henceforth, they were "strangers in a pagan world."[1] The destruction in Judea, the southern part of the country, was so complete that the center of the Jewish life that remained shifted to Galilee. The Academy was moved from Yavneh in Judea, to Usha in Galilee, and the Sanhedrin, too, was transferred there. Its powers apparently were reduced further, although it had already ceased to inflict capital punishment approximately one hundred years prior to that move.

The practice, as well as teaching of the Jewish religion and law in Judea, was banned by the Romans on the pain of death. Nevertheless, many Jews, including Rabbi Akiba (who had supported the Bar Kokhba revolt), defied the ban and were martyred by the Romans. The latter taxed their ingenuity to devise the cruelest ways to put these martyrs to death. Crucifixion was one of the mildest means utilized.

The importance of the country as a center of Jewish life declined drastically. The religious persecutions were accompanied by economic poverty and were magnified by the imposition of additional onerous local taxation, as well as by prohibitions placed upon Jews in other countries against sending tithes to support the academies, the Jewish poor, and other institutions in Palestine. There was even a claimed decline in the rainfall of the area.[2] The ban on the practice and teaching of the Jewish religion and law was later repealed by the Emperor Antoninus Pius in 138 C.E. This eased somewhat the plight of the Jewish peoples.

c. ROMAN PALESTINE: THE PATRIARCHATE

In 140 C.E. the Roman Emperor Antoninus Pius appointed Shimon ben Gamliel as "ethnarch" of the Jews in Palestine, apparently in an attempt to pacify them after the bloody Bar Kokhba revolt. The Jews called this leader *"nasi"* ("exalted one"), later translated into Latin as "patriarch."

The occupant of this position possessed much wealth and land and had great decision-making powers enforced by the Roman authorities. This afforded him great political and economic powers.[3]

The patriarch was in charge of the collection of revenue for the state, for his own support, (including his administrative assistants and bodyguard), for the Academy of Law, which he maintained, and other expenses. One-half shekel was contributed to him yearly by Jews throughout the Roman Empire as a continuation of their donative practices during the existence of the Temple at Jerusalem. The *nasi* acted as the representative of the Jewish community in its dealings with Rome and, in addition, served internally as the leader of the Jewish community in both religious and civil affairs. Simultaneously, he occupied a position as co-leader of the Sanhedrin, assisted by the *av beth din* ("head of the court"). He had the right to appoint and depose any Jewish communal officer, including judges, to whom he also awarded exemption from personal liability for errors in judgment.[4] In addition to heading the Jewish Academy of Law (which, too, analyzed and decided difficult cases, and promulgated ordinances), he also reserved for himself the important function of fixing the Jewish calendar. This involved determining which months should have twenty-nine and which thirty days, and also whether an additional month should be added to any particular year to form a leap year. The fixing of the calendar was crucial to Jewish religious observance since it determined the dates upon which the Jewish religious festivals and holidays would occur.

2. C. Roth, *A Short History of the Jewish People* (London, 1953), p. 117.

3. See the story related by Jerome of an upper-class Roman who was allegedly executed for stealing some papers of the *nasi*, Gamliel; S. Baron, *The Jewish Community* (Philadelphia, 1942), p. 141.

4. Talmud, *Gittin* 59a, *Sanhedrin* 32b.

1. E. Schurer, *History of the Jewish People in the Time of Jesus*, ed. N. Glatzer (New York, 1961), p. 308; M. Grant, *The Jews in the Roman World* (New York, 1973), p. 270.

A key element in the authority accorded to the *nasi* was his claimed descent from King David (normally via Hillel). This caused him to be regarded by the Jews as a semi-monarch who continued the Davidic royal dynasty. This notion appears to have been in accordance with the expectation of the Jews, based upon various biblical verses,[5] that they would always be ruled by one of David's descendants.

Judah *Ha-Nasi* (*circa* 200 C.E.), under the spur of the harsh Roman rule and the economic decline and turmoil in the land, departed from long tradition and codified the Oral Law and expositions of the Bible (henceforth called the Mishnah, literally "studies") and reduced it to writing.[6] (It is interesting to note that this codification of Jewish law took place at about the same time as the codification of the law of Rome under the Emperor Septimus Severus, *circa* 200 C.E.). Eventually, the Roman Emperor Caracalla, in his Constitutio Antoniniana, decreed that all non-slave inhabitants of the Roman Empire (including Jews) were Roman citizens (212 C.E.). This served to further improve the position of Jews under Roman rule.

The power of the *nasi* to impose severe physical sanctions is described in a letter of Origenes, one of the early Church fathers, to Julius Africanus (*circa* third century C.E.),

You ask, "How do they [the Jews] judge capital cases [while they are] in captivity?" To this one may say, that the matter is not perplexing, because great nations that are subjugated, have been permitted by the king to live in accordance with their laws, even though they are in captivity, and to keep their own courts. Even now, that the Romans rule [in Palestine], and the Jews pay them a tax of two drachmas, the Ethnarch [the Jewish *nasi* in Palestine] has such power concerning the Jews, that it is as though with the Caesar's consent, there is no distinction between him and one whom he would place to rule upon them, since trials are conducted according to the [rules of] the Torah in private, and some are condemned to death, but not, however, completely in public, but yet, not without the knowledge of Caesar. This matter I have learned and investigated when I lived in their land for a long time.[7]

As long as the institution of the patriarchate continued, its occupant was the most powerful Jewish decision-maker in Palestine. The institution was, however, abolished by the Roman emperor at the death of the patriarch Gamliel in 425 C.E. The special contributions made by Jews all over the world for his support were confiscated by the emperor, who insisted that the tax be continued for his own benefit.[8]

d. PERSIAN AND PARTHIAN BABYLONIA: THE EXILARCHATE

The Jewish community in Babylonia constituted, perhaps, the largest and most influential Jewish community in the world from at least the first to eleventh centuries C.E. Its influence was felt in the entire Jewish world, including the land of Israel. The most important single participant in the decision-making process in Babylonia was the exilarch (called "*resh galuta*," or, head of the Jews in exile). While there is much scholarly debate regarding the beginnings of this institution, it seems clear that it became one of the most durable institutions in human history, lasting for more than one thousand years. Some trace it as far back as the exile of King Yehoyahim of Judah (*circa* 580 B.C.E.), who was exiled to Babylonia, jailed there, and, allegedly, later released and made the head of the Jewish community in Babylonia.[9] Others trace it to Zerubavel (one of the major figures in the biblical book of Ezra), who lived at the beginning of the Second Jewish Commonwealth, *circa* 500 B.C.E.[10] Although sources concerning this institution during the Second Jewish Commonwealth are practically nonexistent, the institution is often mentioned in the Talmud, with regard to the epoch following the destruction of the Second Jewish Commonwealth.[11]

The exilarch was an appointee of the king and ranked very high in the state hierarchy, being a member of the king's Council of State, advising on non-Jewish, as well as Jewish matters. The occupants of this office claimed direct descent from King David, wore princely attire, held court, and were immensely wealthy. They

5. Gen. 49:10, 2 Sam. 7:16. See Talmud, *Sanhedrin* 5a; S. Assaf, *Tekufat Ha'Gaonim Ve'Safruta* (Jerusalem, undated), p. 24; Y. Falk Kohen, *Perisha, Hohen Mishpat*, sec. 3.

6. There are numerous scholarly controversies as to whether Judah was the one who reduced it to writing, or whether he only reformulated and rearranged it systematically. See, e.g., H. Albeck, *Mavo La'Mishnah* (Jerusalem, 1959), p. 109; Y. Epstein, *Mevo'ot Le'Safrut Ha'Tanaim* (Jerusalem, 1957), p. 18; M. Elon, *Ha'Mishpat Ha'Ivri* (Jerusalem, 1973), p. 860 ff.; *R. Sherira Gaon Igeret*, ed. B. H. Levin (Haifa, 1921; reprinted Jerusalem, 1972), p. 17.

7. Origenes, *Epistuga ad Africanum*, sec. 14; cited and translated in M. Elon, *History of the Jews* (Jerusalem, 1953–56),

p. 112; see A. Gulak, *Yesode Ha'Mishpat Ha'Ivri* (Tel-Aviv, 1967), 4:27; see, however, Origenes' statement in another place that the right to execute was removed from the Jews (Y. Ba'er, *Zion* 21 [1956]: 24), and J. Mann, "*Skira Historit al Dinei Nefashot Bazman Hazeh*," in *Hatzofeh LeKhakhmat Yisrael* 10 (1926): 200, 202.

8. S. Baron, *The Jewish Community*, p. 145.

9. *Sedar Olam Zuta* (Kushta, 1517), apparently written in Babylonia at the beginning of the ninth century.

10. See M. Baer, *The Babylonian Exilarchate in the Arsacid and Sassanian Periods* (Tel-Aviv, 1970); J. Neusner, *History of the Jews in Babylonia*; Assaf, *Tekufat Ha'Gaonim*, p. 25.

11. See Talmud, *Horiyot* 11b; Jerusalem Talmud, *Kelaim* 9:4; *Ketubot* 62b; *Sanhedrin* 5a.

were regarded by the Jewish community there as a part and continuation of the Davidic royal dynasty. This resulted from the perspective that even after the termination of royal rule by David and his descendants, and after the destruction of the Temple and the Second Jewish Commonwealth, Jews were obligated to appoint a leader who was a descendant of King David, and who should be obeyed by the people, much as his ancestor, David had been.[12]

The exilarch had many vital functions. First, and perhaps, foremost, he represented the Jewish community before the non-Jewish king. While there are few sources attesting directly to this function, it seems well substantiated by the evidence that we have regarding the political structures in Babylonia[13] and from letters that have been preserved appointing a Nestorian communal leader, whose position regarding his religious community was analogous to that of the exilarch.[14] From the point of view of the non-Jewish king, however, the exilarch's most important function, was the collection from the Jewish community of the poll tax, which was imposed upon every ethnic group. Similarly, he was charged with collecting the extraordinary taxes which were often imposed by the Persian kings who ruled over Babylonia, in order to finance their extended wars with Rome.[15] Without the revenues collected by the exilarch, many state activities, especially warfare, and construction, would be impossible. He was also extremely influential in the supervision of commercial activity by Jews, with responsibility for preventing fraud (principally, checking the accuracy of the weights and measures used by the merchants). He had authority to regulate the prices charged for merchandise, hours of work, and many other important activities. He could even give certain individuals priority in selling their merchandise.[16] Control of these vital economic functions, gave him, of course, great power within the Jewish community.

Like his religious counterpart among the Nestorians, the exilarch was authorized by the king to settle disputes among the various Jewish communities, and to see to it that justice prevailed and that the weak were protected. He, accordingly, established and supervised courts, which decided controversies involving damages and commercial suits,[17], and also apparently purely

religious law and ritual, as well.[18] Sometimes, where an exilarch was learned, he might, himself, act as judge.[19] There were, however, other Jewish courts in Babylonia which were not controlled by the exilarch, and coexisted with his court. This resulted, in effect, in two distinct sets of Jewish courts. These non-exilarch courts, were established and maintained by the Jewish Law Academies, whose head (called *Rosh Yeshiva*, i.e., "Head of the Academy") often commanded great respect, and even awe, among the Jewish communities.[20]

Possibly included in the wide-ranging powers of the exilarch, was the right to impose capital punishment and sanctions of various kinds. There is a record of the blinding of an offender.[21] This incident has, however, been taken by many authorities to refer to a severe financial penalty which would make the offender's life "dark" thereafter.[22] The exilarch and his assistants were able to freely imprison or confiscate property.[23] Often, they were very high-handed and ruled with an iron hand.

Apparently even those judges who did not serve in the exilarch courts, were generally required to obtain the permission of the exilarch to serve as judges, even though they were ordained in the Law Academies to act as judges.[24] This was the functional equivalent of the professional certification today. The Talmud, however, indicates that some of the judges did not receive any certification by the exilarch, and that they asserted that it was not necessary.[25] In any case, authorization of the exilarch to act as judge was extremely important. Without it, a judge would be powerless to implement his decision and could even be unable to compel a litigant to appear in his court. Additionally, he might be liable personally if he ruled erroneously.[26]

Furthermore, the members of the Jewish Law Academies, and the judges appointed by them, were often dependent in varying degrees, upon the exilarch. He often had the power to appoint the Heads of the Academies and was repeatedly called upon to support the

12. See the statement of Rabbi Nissim, in *He'Halutz* (Vienna, 1888), 8:110; Baron, *The Jewish Community*, p. 576; Assaf, *T'Kufat Ha'Gaonim*, p. 24.
13. M. Baer, *The Babylonian Exilarchate*, pp. 44, 54.
14. Ibid., pp. 44, 54, 56.
15. Ibid., p. 118.
16. See Talmud, *Baba Batra* 22a, and Jerusalem Talmud, *Baba Batra* 8:1.
17. Baer, p. 77.

18. See Moshkin, *Ozar Ha'Gaonim*, p. 23, n. 3, and Talmud, *Mo'ed Katan* 3.
19. See Talmud, *Mo'ed Katan* 16b; Baer, *The Babylonian Exilarchate*, p. 75.
20. See text immediately following and Talmud, *Sanhedrin* 5a.
21. Talmud, *Sanhedrin* 27a.
22. See A. Harkavy, *T'Shuvot Ha'Gaonim* (Jerusalem, 1955), p. 183; *contra* M. Abulafia, *Yad Ramah* (Salonika, 1798), ad loc., and Y. Eibschutz, *Urim Ve'Tumim* (Karlsruh, 1775; reprinted Jerusalem, 1972), sec. 2; see also H. Tauyish, *Ozar Ha'Gaonim, Sanhedrin*, pp. 22–24.
23. Talmud, *Baba Kama* 59a; Jerusalem Talmud, *Baba Batra*, at the end of ch. 5; *Gittin* 14a and b.
24. Gulak, *Yesode Ha'Mishpat Ha'Ivri*, 4:23.
25. Talmud, *Sanhedrin* 5a.
26. Ibid.; M. Baer, *The Babylonian Exilarchate*, p. 117.

many hundreds of students from his own personal funds (since the exilarchs were extremely wealthy), or, perhaps, from the taxes collected from members of the Jewish community. The Law Academy in Pumbedita eventually set up its own system for collecting funds, and became, therefore, more independent of the exilarch in this respect.[27] It should be noted, however, that often judges did not receive salaries from any source, except for their lost earnings as a result of the demands on their time. These expenses, were often shared by both litigants.[28]

In addition to the exilarch's economic strength due to his wealth, his power to assess and collect taxes, his authority to regulate manifold commercial activities, and his right to appoint judges in the Jewish communities, his stronghold on economic life was also aided by the semifeudal land tenure system. Any landowner who did not pay the required tax (generally one-sixth to one-third of the crop) could be deprived of use of the "king's land" by the exilarch, acting as agent of the king. He could replace the owner with any person who was willing to pay the tax arrears. The new occupant of the land was also entitled to hold the defaulter in bondage.

As a result of all of these factors, Jewish communities in Babylonia were run in an extremely authoritarian manner by the exilarchs, who were usually the predominant Jewish power and authority figure there.

e. Comparisons of Decision-Making Powers of the Exilarch and the Nasi

The exilarch in Babylonia generally was authorized by the king to act in many more spheres than his counterpart, the *nasi*, in Palestine. This was due to a number of reasons. First of all, the Persian, and later Islamic, rulers in Babylonia had a consistent policy to maintain the autonomy of each ethnic group in their realms in order to facilitate administrations of their states and to minimize local discontent. In Palestine, by contrast, under the Roman and later Byzantine) rule, there was considerable persecution of the Jewish community for political reasons (and later for religious motives, due to the zealousness of the Christian Byzantine rulers and the Church). Furthermore, in Babylonia the Jews were concentrated in a few urban centers and were heavily engaged in commerce. It was, therefore, natural, to invest the exilarch with those powers to regulate commerce that were commonly entrusted to various government officials in the country. In Palestine, however, there were far fewer Jews living in commercial centers or engaged in commerce. The task

of supervising and regulating commerce was therefore commonly given to non-Jews, because of the ethnic-centered philosophy of government then prevalent. Additionally, the semifeudal nature of Babylonian land tenure, the closely regulated economy, and the great stature of the exilarch in the Babylonian state, all served to give him greater power than his counterpart in Palestine, the patriarch.

In the Jewish religious perspective (even in Palestine), the exilarch was generally also regarded as superior to the *nasi*. This was due to two reasons. Firstly, the exilarchs were regarded as being more directly descended from King David (and from his male heirs) than the holders of the title *nasi* in Palestine. Although the *nasi*, too, was required to be of Davidic lineage, this could be by descent from female heirs.[29]

The exilarch's prime qualification for office was his direct descent from King David. This resulted in greater community acceptance of his right to govern as a successor in the Davidic line of royalty than was accorded to the *nasi*. Rambam[30] accordingly summarizes the view of the Talmud as implying that one who receives authorization from the exilarch to act as judge could do so even in the land of Palestine, but that one who received such an authorization from the *nasi* in Palestine could not act as a judge outside of that land.

Secondly, based on biblical verses, the exilarch was regarded by the Jews as a ruler, while the *nasi* was in theory, considered primarily a scholar. The *nasi*, in the early years of this institution, was expected to be one of the more prominent and learned scholars of his time.[31]

The position of the exilarch exemplified the explicit recognition accorded in Jewish decision-making processes to the roles of both authority (here, the expectation of the community that the exilarch would be a descendant of King David, and thereby his successor as chief decision-maker), and of control (since the power of the exilarch was vested in him by the non-Jewish rulers).

---

27. Ibid., p. 104 ff.
28. Talmud, *Bekhorot* 4:61; Baer, p. 117.
29. See Talmud, *Sanhedrin* 5a, and *Tosefot*, ad loc.; Talmud, *Kilayim* 9:4, *Ketubot* 62b; see also Rambam, Commentary to the Mishnah, *Bekhorot* 4:4. See Y. Eibschutz, *Tumim*, H.M., sec. 2; Y. Gershuni, Ha'Samhut Shel Rosh Galuta," in *Ha'-Pardes* (New York, 1957), vol. 31.
30. Commentary to the Mishnah, *Bekhorot* 4:4; ibid., Laws of the Sanhedrin 4:14; See Talmud, *Sanhedrin* 5a.
31. See Talmud, *Sanhedrin* 5a; Abulafia, *Yad Ramah*, ad loc., and Eshtor Ha'Parhi, *Kaftor Va'Perah* (reprinted Jerusalem, 1956), ch. 12; also Talmud, *Horiyot* 11b, where the superiority of the exilarch over the *nasi* is detailed. See also Gershuni, *Ha'Samhut*; M. Baer, "The Exilarchate in the Talmudic Era" (Hebrew), *Zion* 28 (1963): 3; idem, "The Religious Communal Functions of the Exilarchs in the Talmudic Era," in *Fifth World Congress of Jewish Studies* (Jerusalem, 1972), 2:84; Y. S. Zuri, "Exilarchate Rule," in *The History of Hebrew Public Law* (Tel-Aviv, 1939), p. 320.

f. The Effects of Non-Jewish Authority Systems on Jewish Law

(1) *The Exilarchate and Patriarchate*

The Babylonian exilarch was supposedly designated for the post by the Jewish community, then officially appointed by the king and subsequently confirmed by the Jewish community.[32] Often, however, the masses of the Jewish community, and even its leaders, were unable to resist the king's choice for this post. Sometimes the appointment was made to whoever paid the highest price.[33] At other times plutocrats close to the king were able to influence the appointment of their candidate as exilarch or to cause his discharge. The heads of academies, and the candidates, themselves, were periodically involved in rivalries with each other, or united together to influence the selection, or firing, of an exilarch.[34]

Despite the non-Jewish origins of his appointment, the exilarch wielded great influence in the application of Jewish religious law. First of all, he and his appointees acted as judges; they could, and did, execute offenders, imprison them, or impose other forms of corporal punishment, particularly flogging. Unless specifically sanctioned by the Bible, such killing, confinement, or beatings violate basic biblical norms (see Chapter V, Section C, above). Nevertheless, it was his appointment by the non-Jewish king that gave the exilarch the authority in Jewish eyes to impose these penalties, which were recognized as perfectly adequate in Jewish law.[35]

Similarly, the exilarch and his judicial appointees often rendered decisions in commercial disputes, based upon the talmudic principle of *hefker beth din, hefker.* This permitted them to confiscate and reallocate people's wealth as they saw fit. Although appropriation of property by a private individual would constitute theft and robbery, it was regarded as perfectly proper when done by the *resh galuta* (the exilarch) and his judges. The exilarch further intervened in purely ritual matters, including his function in publicizing (and perhaps help-

ing to authorize) the fixing of the Jewish calendar. This included the determination of when the Jewish months should commence, which in turn determined the dates on which all of the Jewish religious holidays would be observed.

Furthermore, decisions and prescriptions of the exilarch concerning any matter could sometimes acquire the force of Jewish religious norms by the very fact of his appointment by the gentile king to make decisions and prescriptions. These would be accepted by all Jewish religious decision-makers, based upon the Jewish legal principle *dina de'malkhuta dina* ("the law of the state is the law"), a principal whose bounds have not always been consistently applied or defined.[36]

Additionally, the exilarch appointed (or could influence the designation of) the heads of the academies of law.[37] These, in turn, prescribed and applied all areas of Jewish law, including ritual, family law, and commercial issues. (Saadya Gaon, for example, aggressively asserted his right to fix the Jewish calendar and determine when the Jewish months, and consequently the Jewish religious holidays, would fall. See also the many prescriptions of the *gaonim*.)[38] The exilarch's control regarding the heads of the law academies greatly extended his decision-making influence throughout the entire Jewish world.

In short, although the exilarch's power and authority stemmed from a non-Jewish king, he and his academic and judicial appointees played an important role in Jewish decision-making, including those that touched on basic biblical norms relating to corporal punishment, commercial matters, interpersonal relations, and ritual. The decision-making power and authority granted to the exilarch by the king were vested in him in the first place and were sustained to a vital extent because of his acceptance as a leader by the Jewish community as a result of his Davidic descent. The presence of these two factors, which provided him with both authority and control, established his ability to play his vital role in Jewish legal decision-making over such a long period of time.

Some of the same effects occurred with regard to the *nasi* in Palestine. His appointment by the Romans gave

32. See Rambam, Commentary to the Mishnah, *Bekhorot* 4; M. Baer, *The Babylonian Exilarchate.*

33. Epistle of Rav Sherira Gaon (Levin ed.), p. 92.

34. Ibid.; Baron, *The Jewish Community*, p. 577; M. Baer, *The Babylonian Exilarchate.*

35. See Shlomo b. Aderet, Responsa *Rashba*, vol. 1, no. 637, and vol. 2, no. 290; Gerundi, *Ran*, Novellae to *Sanhedrin* 27a and 46a; Isaac b. Sheshet, Responsa *Rivash*, no. 271. Compare Rashi, *Sanhedrin* 5a, and Ha'Meiri, *Beth Habhira, Baba Mezia* 83b; Shimon b. Tzemah Duran, Responsa *Tashbatz*, vol. 1, nos. 158–62; Shlomo b. Shimon Duran, Responsa *Rashbash*, no. 533; Jacob b. Asher, *Tur, Hoshen Mishpat*, sec. 3:12; Y. Eibschutz, *Urim Vetumim* (Warsaw, 1882), sec. 3; Y. Karo, *Shulkhan Arukh, Ho. M.*, sec. 3, and, particularly, the gloss of M. Isserlis, ad loc.

36. See S. Shilo, *Dina De'Malhuta Dina* (Jerusalem, 1975), pp. 433–41, 457; Talmud, *Baba Batra* 55a; M. Baer, *The Babylonian Exilarchate*, p. 90; Gulak, *Yesode Ha'Mishpat Ha'Ivri*, 4:28–29.

37. Epistle of Rav Sherira; Rambam, Commentary to the Mishnah, *Bekhorot* 4:4; Y. Baer, *Zion* 21 (1956): 145.

38. See Part Three, Chapter VIII, Section B 1 *b*, below, and Y. Schipansky, Takkanot Ha'Gacnim," in *Ha'Darom* 24 (1967): 135; H. Graetz, *History of the Jews* (Philadelphia, 1891–98), 3:254, and M. Baer, *The Babylonian Exilarchate*, p. 104. See, in general, Tzur, *Shilton Reshit Ha'Golah Ve'Hayeshivot* (Hebrew; Tel-Aviv, 1939); also M. Baer, "The Religious Communal Functions of the Exilarchs in the Talmudic Era."

him the power to appoint judges and influence prescriptions, and he played a crucial role in setting the Jewish calendar and the dates of the religious holidays. Although, the Jewish community had (at least at times) a voice in his selection[39] (and the *Nasi* was traditionally the son of the prior holder of this office), it was the Romans who had the final say in making the appointment. Accordingly, non-Jewish sources of power and authority attained significance and acceptance by the Jewish community in Jewish decision-making.

(2) Incorporating Non-Jewish Norms into Jewish Law

There was another important effect of the loss of Jewish power and its replacement by non-Jewish power and authority systems. This was the incorporation into Jewish Law of non-Jewish norms and prescriptions. While this phenomenon first became formalized as a principle of Jewish law in the third century C.E. (*Dina De'Malkhuta Dina*, the Law of the Kingdom is the Law),[40] it had been implicitly recognized before that time, and even claimed to be a widespread phenomenon existing from antiquity.[41]

Many different rationales were advanced as the basis for the adoption of non-Jewish norms in order to demonstrate the compatibility of their acceptance, with traditional principles of Jewish Law. The more common rationales were: the necessity to adopt non-Jewish rules because of the king's naked power to enforce his norms[42] and the authorization of this adoption by Jewish decision-makers, applying the principle of *hefker beth din, hefker*[43] (see Chapter V, Section C, above); and the biblically recognized right and obligation of non-Jewish authorities to promulgate and enforce norms,[44] and their rights to do this as counterparts of

the recognized right of Jewish kings to act in this capacity.[45] These norms would then be binding upon their Jewish, as well as non-Jewish, subjects; there was also posited a social contract between the king and his subjects, including the Jews.[46]

While ostensibly, non-Jewish norms were not to be adopted to permit matters that were prohibited by the Bible or by rabbinic decree,[47] this was not always the case in practice, in regard to sanctions that related to the maintenance of public order.[48] Thus, a number of prominent talmudic decision-makers were employed as officials by the Roman authorities and sought out Jewish law violators to be put to death by the Romans,[49] although those arrested were not liable to capital punishment under Jewish law. While not constituting outright murder in Jewish law (see, Section C, 1, infra), such arrests clearly raised the issue of whether or not they were prohibited by the Bible. So, too, in the Middle Ages, Jewish officials were at times, authorized by Jewish religious authorities to act as agents of the king in having various offenders put to death, and even to act, themselves, as hangmen.[50] Similarly, the exilarch (and other officials in various countries) were authorized by the non-Jewish authorities to inflict corporal sanctions,[51] to act in a number of areas relating to Jewish religious prohibitions,[52] and to ap-

39. See Talmud, *Berakhot*, ch. 27; A. Orenstein, *Ha'Nesiyut Be'Yisrael* (Hebrew; Tel-Aviv, 1956); H. Albeck, "The Sanhedrin and Its Patriarch" (Hebrew), in *Zion* 8 (1943): 165; Y. Henkin, "The Law of Patriarch and King" (Hebrew), in *Ha'Darom* 31 (1970): 50; H. Mantel, "The Patriarchate" (Hebrew), in *Mahanaim* (Tel-Aviv, 1972), p. 164.

40. Talmud, *Baba Batra* 54b, 55a; *Baba Kama* 113a and b; *Gittin* 10b, *Nedarim* 28a.

41. Talmud, *Gittin* 1:5; *Baba Kama* 10:1; see especially, Y. Antoli, *Melamed Letalmidim* (Berlin, 1866), pp. 71–72. See also A. Roth, "Dina De'Malkhuta Dina," *Ha'Soker* (Hebrew; Budapest, 1937), 5:110 ff.; S. Shilo, *Dina De'Malkhuta Dina* (Jerusalem, 1974), pp. 22, 34, 38.

42. Nissim Gerundi, Novellae to *Nedarim* 28a; Shlomo b. Aderet, Responsa *Rashba*, attributed to Rambam, no. 22; Meir b. Baruch, Responsa *Maharam* of Rothenberg (Prague ed.), no. 1001; R. Asher, *Piskei Ha'Rosh, Nedarim* 3:11; see Shilo, *Dina De'Malkhuta Dina*, p. 62 ff.; R. Hayim Responsa *Maharam, Ohr Zarua*, no. 110.

43. Jonah Gerundi, *Aliyot De'Rabbenu Yona, Baba Batra* 55a; A. Kahana-Shapiro, Responsa *D'Var Avraham*, no. 1; A. Agus, Responsa *Baale Ha'Tosefot* (New York, 1954), no. 12.

44. Rashi, Commentary to *Gittin* 9b, s.v. *Kesherin*, ff.; M. Ha'Meiri, *Baba Kama* 113a; *Ritva*, Novellae to *Baba Batra* 55a,

s.v. *Hani Tlat*; M. Sofer, Responsa *Hatam Sofer*, H.M., no. 44; Shlomo b. Aderet, Responsa *Rashba* 3:109; Moshe b. Nahman, Novellae *Ramban, Baba Batra* 55a, and his commentary to Deut. 17:15; H. Hirschensohn, *Malki Ba'Kodesh* (St. Louis, 1919), vol. 2, nos. 2:2, 5; I. Z. Meltzer, *Even Ha'Azel* (Jerusalem, 1955), also *Money Damages*, 8:5.

45. Shlomo b. Aderet, Responsa *Rashba* 3:109; Moshe b. Nahman, Novellae *Ramban, Baba Batra* 55a; Antoli, *Melamed Letalmidim*, pp. 71–72; Sofer, Responsa *Hatam Sofer*, H.M., no. 44; M. Trani, *Kiryat Sefer*, "Rules of Armed Robbery," ch. 5; also, S. Z. Auerbach, *Ma'Adane Aretz* (Hebrew; Jerusalem, 1960), 20:12.

46. Shlomo b. Meir (Rashbam), *Baba Batra* 54b, s.v. *Ve'-Ha'Amar Shmuel*; Rambam, Laws of Armed Robbery and Lost Property, 5:18; see Y. T. Ashvili, *Ritva*, Novellae to *Baba Batra* 55a, s.v. Hani; J. Karo, *Shulhan Arukh*, H.M., sec. 369:2.

47. Shimon Duran, Responsa *Tashbatz*, 1:158–62; Elon, *Ha'Mishpat Ha'Ivri*, pp. 167–68.

48. With regard to the issue of whether acquisition of title to property or enforcing a money judgment pursuant to non-Jewish norms would otherwise be considered as "theft" when Jewish legal principles would have led to a different result, see Shimon Duran, *Tashbatz*, ibid.; S. Shkup, *Sha'are Yosher* (Jerusalem, 1965), "gate" 5, ch. 1.

49. Talmud, *Baba Mezia* 83b; ibid. and 84a. See also Jerusalem Talmud, *Terumot* 8:4; *Niddah* 61a; N. Gerundi, Novellae to *Sanhedrin* 46a.

50. Asher b. Yehiel, Responsa *Rosh*; Shlomo b. Aderet, Responsa *Rashba*, vol. 2, no. 290; Assaf, *Jewish Hangmen*; E. Halevi, Responsa, *Zekan Aharon* (Jerusalem, 1970), no. 3.

51. See text at Section *d*, above.

52. Baer, "On the Religious Communal Functions of the Exilarch in the Talmudic Era," p. 84.

point judges[53] to decide matters in religious as well as commercial areas.

Nevertheless, attempts were made, where possible, to limit the scope of adoption of non-Jewish norms to areas of commerce,[54] and by some decision-makers, to relations with the government.[55] The theory has even been asserted that non-Jewish norms were merely recognized by Jewish law but did not become a "part" thereof![56] Attempts at such limitations seem to have become more prevalent with the decline of the power and size of the Jewish community in Babylonia,[57] which became marked in the tenth century, and the growth at that time of Jewish communities throughout Europe and North Africa. An important motive for these efforts to exclude non-Jewish norms was the fear that they would displace traditional Jewish law.

What is clear, however, is that loss of Jewish power and its displacement by non-Jewish power and authority systems, with Jews as a minority community, gave added impetus to the outright incorporation into Jewish law of many non-Jewish norms and prescriptions.[58]

(3) *Religious Perspectives Concerning the Authority of a Jewish Royal Agent to Impose Biblically Prohibited Sanctions*

As indicated above, Chapter V, Section C, 2, homicide, mutilation, or wounding are viewed as violating the most fundamental biblical norms, unless authorized by the Bible. Nevertheless, there has been a long history of sanctions imposed and condoned by leading Jewish religious authorities on the grounds that as Jewish agents of a king (even non-Jewish), they had the right to do so. Prime examples are the cases of two of the most prominent talmudic decision-makers, Rabbi Eliezer ben Rabbi Shimon and Rabbi Yosi ben Ishmael (*circa* 200 C.E.). Acting on behalf of the Romans, they tracked down Jewish thieves and other violators of law and turned them over to the Romans for punishment, including the death penalty. This was explained by them on the grounds of *"hurmena de-malka"* (the order of the king). Although the Talmud records that they were both rebuked by their colleagues for this, the Talmud does not conclude that they had acted wrongly, and indicates that they were certainly not morally guilty

of murder in turning over these violators of law for execution.[59]

As one of the principal talmudic commentators explained:

Here [in the case of Rabbi Eliezer and Rabbi Yosi], although they judged without witnesses and without forewarning, in a time when there was no Sanhedrin, this was different, because they were acting as agents of the king, and it is part of the laws of the kingdom to kill without witnesses and forewarning in order to preserve the world, as we saw in the case of [King] David,[60] who killed the Amakelite convert [who had admitted slaying King Saul] and an agent of the king counts like him [the king]. Nevertheless, in a place where the king is not permitted to do this under the laws of the kingdom, then, his appointee is not permitted [to do this, either], and if the king tells him to do it, he must let himself be killed but not violate [the biblical command, "Thou shalt not kill"].[61]

This was later applied in practice to permit the Babylonian exilarch to maim[62] and even to allow Jew-

53. Talmud, *Sanhedrin* 5a; see M. Baer, *The Babylonian Exilarchate.*

54. Talmud, *Baba Batra* 54b.

55. Talmud, *Nedarim* 28a, *Baba Kama* 113b; see *Sefer Ha'-Terumot* 46, 8.5; Meiri, *Baba Kama* 113b.

56. Elon, *Ha'Mishpal Ha'Ivri*, p. 59.

57. Ibid., p. 54.

58. See Y. Katz, *Ben Yehudim Le'Goyim* (Jerusalem, 1961); S. Goren, "Dina D'Malhuta Be'Yisrael," in *Ohr Ha'Mizrah* 1 (1954): 27; S. Yisraeli, *Amud Ha'Yemini* (Tel-Aviv, 1956), sec. 8, p. 63 ff.; E. Waldenberg, *Hilhot Medina* (Jerusalem, 1952), "gate" 3:6, p. 180 ff.

59. Talmud, *Baba Mezia* 83b, 84a; Ha'Meiri, *Beth Ha'Behira*, ad loc.; see Shlomo b. Aderet, Responsa *Rashba*, vol. 2, no. 290.

60. 2 Sam. 1:16–17.

61. Y. T. Ashvili, *Ritva*, Commentary to Talmud, *Baba Mezia* 93b, cited in *Shita Mekubetzet*, ad. loc. Midrash Rabba, above, Genesis, sec. 94 and at Lev. 19; David Halevi, *Toreh Zahav, Yore Deah*, sec. 157, no. 8; Z. H. Chajes, *Torat Ha'-Neviim*, p. 45.

Contra Menahem Ha'Meiri (the classical talmudist), in his commentary *Beth Ha'Behira*, to the Talmud, *Baba Mezia* 83b, which states: "Scholars, saints, and men of good deeds, should, nevertheless, keep themselves far from working for the government. This is certainly so with regard to accepting any kind of an appointment to seek out thieves and robbers and other wicked people, and to turn them over to be killed. This would cause the death of many souls under the laws of the state, which do not accord to the laws of the Torah. Whoever causes a death not in accordance with the laws of the Torah is considered a heretic (*Min*) and an informer, as was said to one of their famous ones [to Rabbi Eliezer, in Talmud, *Baba Mezia* 83b], 'Until when will you deliver the nation of our Lord to be killed?' Even though he excused himself concerning this and said, 'I am removing thorns from the vineyard,' his colleagues retorted, 'Let the owner of the vineyard [God himself] come and remove his thorns.' Even though you might reply that he [Rabbi Eliezer ben Shimon] used to let them go, unless he was convinced they were guilty under the laws of the Torah, he would, in that case [if he would let them go] have violated the laws of the state. This, too, is forbidden, as another such famous person [Rabbi Yose ben Yishmael, ad loc.] said, 'What shall I do? It is a rule of the king.' Accordingly, it is appropriate to keep distant from such activities and anything resembling them and to try with all one's strength (to do this). As was said to one of those officials, 'Your father fled to Lodacia. You, flee to Asia.'"

For accord, see David Bonfils, cited in Nissim Gerundi, Novellae *Ran to Sanhedrin*, 27a and 46a; Shlomo b. Aderet, Responsa, *Rashba*, vol. 2, no. 290.

62. See Talmud, *Sanhedrin* 27a; *Baba Mezia* 24.

ish hangmen to continue on their jobs, executing both Jews and non-Jews for the king.[63]

This startling rationale implies that a non-Jewish king has the same power in Judaic law as a Jewish king (see section C, 1, below) to kill as he sees fit for the benefit of public order. His appointed agents, including Jews, may likewise kill without violating the biblical postulate "Thou shalt not kill." This reasoning, however, seems obscure, since an agent for a non-Jewish king has not been held to permit performance by a Jew of any other acts violative of biblical norms, such as desecrating the Jewish Sabbath.

It is conceivable that the rationale is the talmudic principle of the Noahide "*dinim*,"[64] which are held to impose certain fundamental biblical requirements upon non-Jewish societies and to require them to institute a rational form of government and legal system (including, sanctioning norms). This is viewed as obligating Jews, as well as non-Jews, to carry out government norms that relate to maintenance of minimum public order, including the execution of offenders. This reflects the basic perspective that both the Jewish, as well as non-Jewish, communities had the right (based on the general need) to inflict sanctions (including executions) to maintain public order and could authorize their king, or other representatives, to prescribe sanctions for them[65] (see section B, 1, below).

It is also arguable that talmudic decision-makers regarded Rabbi Eliezer ben Shimon as a Jewish judge authorized to apply Jewish law, although appointed by the (non-Jewish) king. As a judge applying Jewish law, he could then utilize the rule, cited below, that a *beth din* could execute, even though not in accordance with biblical law (see Chapter V, Section C, 2, above).

(This view, too, would reflect the far-reaching effect on Jewish law of non-Jewish power and authority systems, in permitting appointment of a Jewish judge by a non-Jewish king, with the judge thereafter able to inflict "extralegal" sanctions, even if this meant nullifying traditional law).

The Talmud, however, in describing the application of "extralegal" sanctions, always says, "a *beth din* may

flog and punish. . . ." This implies that only a court (normally composed of at least three persons), not an individual, could invoke this principle (see also Part Three, Chapter IX, Section B 2, for application of the *rodef* [murderer pursuer] principle to these cases).

In any case, whichever rationale is correct, it is clear that talmudic decision-makers openly recognized that non-Jewish power sources could profoundly affect Jewish decision-making in many areas of basic Jewish religious norms. This included appointment to office by non-Jewish officials of the exilarch and other Jewish agents and subagents of the king. These, not infrequently, inflicted extraordinary nonbiblical corporal sanctions or confiscated and gave title to property, contrary to biblical norms and prescribed norms that were *ipso facto* accepted as Jewish religious norms.

g. NOTIONS OF AUTHORITY AND CONTROL

The foregoing are a few examples of the effect of non-Jewish power factors on Jewish religious law and of the perceptions regarding the necessity for effective law to operate on the basis of both control (actual power of coercion under the threat of imposing sanctions or indulgences) and of authority (decisions by persons whom the community expects to make decisions, in accordance with community expectations). Without this authority, "Laws repugnant to the notions of right of a community, or to its practical requirements are likely to be defeated by passive resistance and by the difficulty of constant supervision and repression."[66]

It should be noted that in addition to the two factors of actual control and authority, both the Babylonian exilarch, and the local community councils, acted as representatives of the entire Jewish community. There was a pervasive notion that the community as a whole, whether through its king, courts, or community council, was capable of prescribing and applying any kind of necessary norms, even if not in conformance with the biblical or talmudic principles normally applied (see Section C 1 *a*, below).[67]

63. Responsa, E. Halevi, *Zekan Aharon*, no. 3; S. Assaf, "Talyanim Yehudim," in *Mekorot U'Mehkarim Be'Toldot Yisrael* (Jerusalem, 1946), p. 252.

64. Talmud, *Sanhedrin* 56b, interpreting Gen. 9; Moshe Isserlis, Responsa *Rama*, no. 10; Sofer, Responsa *Ha'Tam Sofer*, vol. 6, no. 14. See Talmud, *Shevuoth* 35b; Antoli, *Malemed Letalmidim* pp. 71–72.

65. For citations, see notes 40–46, Section 3 *f* (2), above, regarding incorporation of non-Jewish norms into Jewish law. See also I. Cohen, *Sefer Me'Irat Eynayim* (printed in standard editions of the *Shulhan Arukh*), H.M., sec. 2, citing Rambam; Talmud *Shevuoth* 35b; Sofer, Responsa *Hatam Sofer*, O.H. no. 208 and vol. 6, no. 14; N. Z. Y. Berlin, *He'emek She'Lah*, sec. 20; M. S. Ha'Cohen, *Ohr Sameakh*, Laws of Kings 3:6.

66. P. Vinogradoff, "Customary Law," in C. G. Crump and E. Jacobs, eds., *The Legacy of the Middle Ages* (Oxford, 1928), p. 287. See Y. Rosannes (*Persahat Derahim*, discourse no. 12), who examines the question of whether a king who loses actual power remains king in the eyes of Jewish law. This seems in part to concern the issue of whether authority and actual control are necessary elements of law. According to some authorities, this is the problem alluded to in the Jerusalem Talmud, *Horiyot*, ch. 3, rule 2, *Rosh Hashanah*, ch. 1, rule 4; see Commentary of Ha'Me'iri, *Horiyot*, ch. 3; and the Babylonian Talmud, *Horiyot*, p. 14, *Sanhedrin* 5a; see Rashi and Tosefot, ad loc.; Isaac b. Sheshet, Responsa *Rivash*, no. 271; Y. Eibschutz, *Tumin* (Warsaw, 1882), sec. 2; A. Bornstein, Responsa *Avne Nezer* (Pietrokov, 1912), no. 312; Y. Gershuni, *Ha'Pardes* (New York, 1956); idem., *Mishpat Ha'Melukha* (New York, 1959), pp. 26–27.

67. In medieval Europe, unlike Babylonia, the kings did not appoint an individual to be head of the Jewish community.

Judges appointed by the exilarch were also regarded as authoritative decision-makers since they had control, which they exercised as subagents of the king, as did the exilarch himself. This actual control itself appears to have vested the *resh galuta* and his judicial appointees with the necessary authority, in terms of community expectations, to make authoritative decisions. One of the reasons why the king did not appoint Jewish judges directly (and instead appointed an exilarch, who in turn then appointed Jewish judges) was the desire to satisfy community expectations that its judges would be Jewish, rather than mere appointees of a non-Jewish ruler.

It was felt that judges appointed directly by the non-Jewish king would lack the necessary authority and acceptance by the Jewish community, since the population would not regard them as Jewish judges acting in accordance with Jewish law. On the other hand, judicial appointees of the exilarch were regarded as authoritative, since the exilarch was normally a descendant of King David, and was himself regarded as an authoritative ruler, decision-maker, and the proper personage to appoint judges.

Nevertheless, there were eras when a judge appointed by the exilarch did not decide cases on his own without direct community participation in decision-making:

> When he [the judge appointed by the exilarch] reaches his destination [a particular community], he chooses two of the important men of the town to sit with him. . . Now, if that judge is straight in his ways and clean in his judgment, the heads of the community will write to the *resh galuta*, (the exilarch), and praise him. But if there is something evil in him or if they find some imperfection, they write to the *resh galuta* and to the heads of the academies: How cruel are his deeds and how ugly are his ways. And they [the exilarch and the academies] remove him and appoint someone else in his stead.[68]

Furthermore, judges were required to be "*savir*" (wise) and "*gamir*"[69] (trained in law). Otherwise judi-

cial appointments might be considered invalid, since they would be unacceptable to the community at large. Here, too, there was recognition of the notions of both authority as well as control in legal decision-making.

As noted earlier, the notion of authority was also recognized in explicitly requiring that no prescription could be promulgated by the *beth din*, unless they first ascertained that the prescription was acceptable to the community. Furthermore, any existing prescription was recognized as becoming invalid, if its disregard by the public became widespread.[70]

Conversely, once a practice, initiated without prescription, became widespread, no one, "Not even Elijah, the Prophet" could abolish it.[71]

B. *Participants in the Legal Process: Decision-Making by Prescribers and Appliers*

As outlined above(Section A 2 and Chapter IV, Section C), there were a number of participants in decision-making in the Jewish community during the Second Jewish Commonwealth and the Talmudic Era. The functions of some of the more important participants will now be examined in greater detail.

1. THE KING

The function of the king in Jewish intracommunal decision-making is shrouded in obscurity. There is no clear picture regarding his participation in the decision-making processes in either the First or Second Jewish Commonwealth, and the extent of his involvement in prescribing and applying law is unknown. It seems certain, however, that there was often tension between the king and the courts.[72]

In the Talmudic Era, although there were no longer any Jewish kings, there existed very definite perspectives regarding the decision-making functions that were proper for a king. These views were not purely theoretical since they helped to shape the roles played by institutions that represented a continuation or replacement of the monarchic institution.

It was widely held that the king had the ultimate responsibility for maintaining public order. Accordingly, if the judiciary could not, or did not, maintain such order by penalizing offenders, it was believed to be the

---

Instead, in accordance with medieval notions of government (see Part Three, Chapter VIII, Section A 2, below), the Jewish community as a whole would often receive a certain amount of autonomy from the king in acting to maintain order among the Jewish population. The community, as a communal polity, would thereupon enact numerous ordinances. These were held to be binding, even though they were not in accordance with biblical or talmudic rules. Here, too, their validity were held to be governed by some of the same principles that had been invoked with regard to the decisions and judical appointments of the Exilarch. See Sections 3 *b* and 3 *f* (2), above, and Part Three, Chapter VIII, Section A, below.

68. R. Nathan Ha'Babli, in Y. Neubauer, *Seder Ha'Hamim VeKorot Ha'Yamim* (reprinted Jerusalem, 1958), p. 86; S. Assaf, *Batei Ha'Din Ve'Sidreihem* (Jerusalem, 1924), p. 38.

69. See Talmud, *Sanhedrin* 5a; Gulak, *Yesode Ha'Mishpat Ha'Ivri*, 4:21 ff.

70. Talmud, *Avodah Zarah* 36d; see Rambam, Laws of *Mamrim*, ch. 2, no. 4.

71. Talmud, *Yebamot* 66a; Jerusalem Talmud, *Yebamot* 12:1, *Shabbat* 108a.

72. Talmud, *Sanhedrin* 19a; Josephus, *Antiquities of the Jews*, XIV, 9, 3.

king's function to do this. It was recognized that talmudic criminal law would shackle the judiciary in imposing sanctions (because of such stringent requirements as forewarning and qualified witnesses). Biblical norms, too, provided only for monetary payment, not imprisonment for such crime as theft, assault,[73] etc. (see Exod. 21:19 and 37). Accordingly, the king was viewed as having a very active role in the sanctioning process and was expected to impose whatever sanctions he felt necessary for public order, regardless of their illegality under the norms applied by the courts.[74] In the same way, he was to take any other steps necessary for public welfare. In essence, then, these views called for a dual legal system, with the king regarded as having broad equity and executive corrective functions,[75] in the same manner as non-Jewish kings.

In the same way, once the Jewish monarchy was terminated the king's functions were viewed as transferred to the *beth din*,[76] the exilarch, the patriarch, and perhaps as reverting to the community,[77] itself (as was the case before the monarchy was instituted),[78] for the king was perceived as essentially the representative of all of Israel (as was the *beth din*).[79] These transferees could therefore also exercise their power to impose sanctions and otherwise act for the public good, without regard to the traditional biblical and talmudic norms that were binding on the courts.[80]

This perspective helped to set the stage for Jewish courts and communal organizations to inflict sanctions not authorized by the norms that ordinarily applied, and to put aside the strict talmudic safeguards for criminal procedure.

2. THE JUDICIAL SYSTEM

a. THE HIGH COURT (SANHEDRIN) DURING THE SECOND JEWISH COMMONWEALTH

In addition to the nobility, the priesthood, and the army, power was also institutionalized in the Sanhedrin. At the beginning of the Second Jewish Commonwealth the Jews had a "Great Assembly" of one hundred and twenty members.[81] This was the central and highest decision-making body, both in prescribing and applying the law. There is much scholarly dispute concerning its functions and powers and even the precise era in which it existed. At some time, however, it gave way (or was transformed into) a body later called the "Great Sanhedrin," a term probably of Greek origin.

There are some who believe that at different (and perhaps overlapping) times, there were three different bodies that were called by this name: a court of law that decided questions of ritual; a court composed of priests, who formulated rules for the Temple service and decided on religious problems that arose there; and a council composed of laity and priests, acting as the supreme administrative, and perhaps prescriptive, organ for all civil matters.[82]

What is clear is that there were constant struggles and bitter rivalries among the Jewish power groups (the nobility, the important priestly families, the Pharisees, the Sadducees, etc.) for control of the Sanhedrin.

73. Exod. 21:18–19, 37; 22–26; M. Ginsberg, *Mishpatim Le'Yisrael*, p. 136 ff.

74. Talmud, *Sanhedrin* 20b; Rambam, Laws of Kings, 1:1 ff., and 3:5, 10; idem, Laws Concerning a Murderer, 2:4; N. Gerundi, *Derashot Ha'Ran*, discourse nos. 11, 189, 191; Y. Horowitz, *Shne Lukhot Ha'Brit*, vol. 3, Commentary to Deut. 16:18, p. 18a; Isaac Abarbanel, Commentary to Deut. 16:18 and intro. to Judges; S. Federbush, *Mishpat Ha'Melukha Be'-Yisrael* (Jerusalem, 1973), p. 44. Others have denied a dual system and claimed that the king did not apply the "royal law" himself, but authorized the Sanhedrin to do so; Z. H. Chajes, *Torat Ha'Neviim*, ch. 7, p. 46 ff.; Ginsberg, *Mishpatim Be'Yisrael*, pp. 136, 137; Waldenberg, *Hilkhot Medina*, 3:5, pp. 159, 171.

75. M. Simha Ha'Kohen, *Ohr Sameah* (reprinted Jerusalem, 1960) to Laws of Kings 3:10 and to Laws Concerning a Murderer, ch. 2; Gershuni, "Dine Sanhedrin Ve'Dine Malhut," in *Torah She' Baal Peh* (Jerusalem, 1974), pp. 92, 96, 97 ff.

76. N. Gerundi, *Derashot Ha'Ram*, p. 191; Abarbanel, Commentary to Deut. 16:18; Horowitz *Shne Lukhot Ha'Brit.* See J. B. Soloveitchik, essay on *Kiddush Ha'Khodesh*, dealing with the function of the *beth din* as representative of the Jewish community. See also I. Sender, "Beth Din Ha'Gadol U'Beth Din Shel Shivim Ve'Ehad," in *Ohr Ha'Mizrah* 25 (1976): 39, 44, reprinted in I. Sender, *Ohel Rivkah* (Chicago, 1979), p. 204.

77. Talmud, *Sanhedrin* 5a (re the exilarch); Ha'Meiri, *Beth Ha'Behira* (Jerusalem, 1971), *Sanhedrin* 52b; Rambam, Laws of Sanhedrin, 4:13; A. Kook, *Mishpat Kohen* (Jerusalem, 1937), no. 144.

78. See Horowitz, *Shne Lukhot Ha'Brit.*

79. Moshe ben Nahman in *Mishpat Ha'Herem*, Responsa Rashba, attributed to Ramban (reprinted Warsaw, 1894), no. 285; Chajes, *Torat Ha'Neviim*, ch. 7, p. 46 ff.; Kook, *Mishpat Kohen*; Jerusalem Talmud, *Horiyot* 3:2; Sofer, Responsa, O.H., no. 208.

80. See Section C 1, below, and Sofer, Responsa, O.H., no. 208.

81. Possibly consisting of ten (i.e., a "congregation") for each of the twelve tribes; I. Herzog, "The Administration of Justice in Ancient Israel," in *Judaism: Laws and Ethics* (London, 1976), p. 114; see also Y. I. Halevi, *Dorot Harishonim* (Berlin, 1923); Y. Greenwald, *Le'Toledot Ha'Sanhedrin Be'-Yisrael* (New York, 1950); H. Mantel, *Studies in the History of the Sanhedrin* (Cambridge, 1961); H. Tchernowitz, *Toldot Ha'Halakhah* (New York, 1950), p. 215 ff.

82. A. Buechler, *Ha'Sanhedrin Be'Yerushalayim* (Jerusalem, 1975); Rambam, Laws of *Mamrim*, 1:1 ff.; S. Hoenig, *The Great Sanhedrin* (New York, 1953); see Gulak, *Yesode Ha'-Mishpat Ha'Ivri*, 4:14 ff. See also Sender, *Beth Din Ha'Gadol*, who distinguishes between a "Great Court" and a "Court of Seventy-One," each of which had distinct functions; see also Goren, "The Struggle over the Sanhedrin during the Second Jewish Commonwealth," in *Torat Ha'Moadim* (Hebrew; Tel-Aviv, 1964), pp. 511, 515–16, 523 ff., 537 ff.; and idem, "The Structure and Functions of the Sanhedrin after the Destruction of the Second Temple," ibid., p. 523 ff.

Ideally, according to the Talmud,[83] new appointments to membership in the "Great Sanhedrin" were made by members of that body themselves, from among the members of a "Smaller Sanhedrin," a twenty-three judge court that sat on the Temple Mount, or from other twenty-three judge courts that were located in various towns. In theory, this cooptation would assure that the new members would continue to represent the perspectives of their predecessors and would have considerable experience and expertise in the law. Perhaps in this way they would also come from important families from all parts of the land. The Great Sanhedrin would then be a more or less representative body of judges learned in the law.[84] In practice, however, it is clear that pressures exerted by the kings, the nobles, the high priest, and members of various factions among the Jews often resulted in appointments of members who had the backing of whichever group or coalition of groups was most influential at that time.

There is also much obscurity regarding the role actually played by the Sanhedrin.[85] It appears to have had multiple functions: to act as representative of the community in vital decisions, such as initiating wars; as supervisor of the lower courts and as the highest judicial authority; as a board of higher education, supervising religious and legal education; and probably also as a prescriber of ordinances and as an executive body. Considerable confusion also reigns concerning its overlap with the *gerousia* (*elders*), its relations with the king, and the role of the high priest, who was sometimes vested with the "*protasia*" (the right to represent the people before the authorities).

Until the advent of the Hasmonean dynasty (*circa* 150 B.C.E.), the high priest appears to have acted as head of the Sanhedrin; thereafter leadership of the Sanhedrin was by "pairs." with one person serving as *nasi* (leader) and another serving as *av beth din* (the head of the court). Both were members of the Sanhedrin, but their precise roles and functions are a matter of much scholarly debate. Perhaps the most famous of

these pairs were Hillel and Shammai, who were contemporaries of Herod Antipatis. Possibly this change in the leadership of the Sanhedrin was due to its reduced political influence, but this is not at all certain.[86]

The consensus of scholarly opinion is that the decision-making power of the Sanhedrin became greatly diminished toward the end of the Second Jewish Commonwealth, and its functions as a court of first instance were probably limited to capital cases involving important political personalities.[87] It also issued ruling on cases that puzzled the lower, twenty-three judge courts. It also had the additional function of training and educating future judges. This task was performed, in part, by having rows of disciples attend court hearings regularly and even participate in the court deliberations.[88]

The high court also acted as a court of second instance. It is important to note that this function of the Sanhedrin does not seem to have been by way of an appeal from decisions rendered by courts of inferior jurisdiction. Instead, it related to cases that a lower court had *not* yet decided because it was puzzled as to the law. The lower court itself (rather than dissatisfied litigants) would then send the matter to the high court for an authoritative ruling. It should also be noted that the Sanhedrin did not apparently hold hearings in order to determine the facts of these cases, nor did it hear the contentions of both litigants. It's sole function seemed to be to determine the law on the basis of the facts as passed on to it by the lower court.

Even those cases that were brought to the Sanhedrin from the lower courts did not go there directly. They apparently were first screened by two courts, which sat, respectively, on the Temple Mount and near the gate of the Temple. These determined whether those questions had already been decided. Only cases for which there was no precedent (and which perhaps were regarded as important enough for the high court to decide) were passed on to the court for a ruling.[89] When the case was passed on to the Sanhedrin, the litigant and a lower court emissary, as well as the members of the two screening courts, would attend the hearings of the Sanhedrin to hear their deliberations and

83. *Sanhedrin* 88a; see Rambam, Laws of Sanhedrin, 2:8. Compare Abarbanel, Commentary to Deut. 16:7; Eibschutz, *Urim Ve'Tumim*, sec. 7.

84. See Tosefta, *Sanhedrin*, ch. 7. While the Levites traditionally served on the Sanhedrin (see Deut. 17:9), this was no longer the case during the Second Commonwealth (Talmud, *Yebamot* 86a); there was also a separate court of priests (Talmud, *Ketubot*, ch. 12), but its precise functions are also unclear (Talmud, *Midot* 5:4; Federbush, *Mishpat Ha'Melukha Be'Yisraeli*, p. 46; Herzog, "The Administration of Justice in Ancient Israel," p. 109).

85. Goren, pp. 515, 516, 523 ff.; J. B. Soloveitchik, "Kiddush Ha'Khodesh"; H. Soloveitchik, *Ha'Griz*, Commentary on *Rambam* (Jerusalem, 1965), Laws of Kings, *Sanhedrin*, 4; Federbush, *Mishpat Ha'Melukha Be'Yisrael*, p. 92; Moshe b. Nahman, Commentary *Rambam* to *Sefer Ha'Mitzvot*, no. 153.

86. See Gulak, *Yesode Ha'Mishpat Ha'Ivri*, p. 15; Z. Frankel, *Gerichtliche Beweis Nach Moses-Talmud Recht* (Berlin, 1846), p. 2; Graetz, *History of the Jews*, pt. 2, ch. 17.

87. See Josephus, *Antiquities of the Jews*, XV, 173; XIV, 3–5, 9; Talmud, *Sanhedrin* 19.

88. See Talmud, *Sanhedrin* 37a; *Shevuot* 31; Tosefta, *Sanhedrin*, ch. 1, sec. 34, and in ch. 8. According to Rambam, this was true only of the "Smaller Sanhedrin"; see his Laws of Sanhedrin, 1:7.

89. These two screening courts, then, fulfilled a function similar to that of a court proposed for the United States to screen cases that may be worthy to go to the U.S. Supreme Court for final appellate review.

final decision. These would then be taken into account in future cases that might arise.[90]

Apparently, even after the destruction of the Second Jewish Commonwealth and the later abolition of the Sanhedrin, the aforementioned procedure for requesting an authoritative review by a higher court was in general followed. A court that desired further clarification regarding the law would send a written inquiry to a higher court, which, in turn, would then issue a decision based solely on the question posed to it in writing.[91]

In short, the Sanhedrin probably would act as a court of first instance only in capital cases involving important political figures. It would act as a court of second instance where the lower court, on its own initiative, would send an issue to the Sanhedrin for clarification. This would occur in regard to issues that puzzled lower courts or issues upon which there was a division of opinion there. Its role in prescribing ordinances is obscure.[92]

In addition to the Great Sanhedrin, it appears that each tribe had its own central tribal Sanhedrin, to which other lower tribal courts would refer difficult matters.[93] The precise relationship of these tribal Sanhedrins to lower courts, to each other, and to the Great Sanhedrin, remains unclear.

b. JEWISH COURTS AFTER THE DESTRUCTION OF THE SECOND JEWISH COMMONWEALTH

After the destruction of the Second Jewish Commonwealth (70 C.E.), the "Small Sanhedrins," consisting of twenty-three judge courts, were abolished. (It is possible that this may have occurred even before the destruction, since the primary jurisdiction of these courts was in capital cases, which had been abolished some time before the end of the Second Jewish Commonwealth.)[94] Nevertheless, the Great Sanhedrin and the local courts, consisting of three judges, remained.

The prime function of these three-judge courts was to decide civil suits, while the Great Sanhedrin (called, with increasing frequency, the "Great Court") supervised the activities of these lower courts, prescribed regulations, and concerned itself with religious practices and many other areas, except for capital cases and similar subjects.[95] The operation of these courts, including the Great Sanhedrin, continued to receive the sanction of the Roman authorities.[96]

Under the reign of the Roman Emperor Hadrian (circa 140 C.E.), however, there occurred a profound change that was to have lasting effects on the Jewish legal system. As part of brutal religious persecutions, Jewish courts were entirely abolished. To enforce this, the Romans decreed that any person who granted ordination (the rite entitling the grantee to be a judge) should be killed, together with the one ordained, and that, furthermore, the entire situs of the ordination should be razed.[97] This posed the most serious threat to the continuation of Jewish law, precisely the effect that the Romans intended.

Despite the official provision of Roman law outlawing formal Jewish courts, there were intermittent periods in which Jewish courts were permitted to operate by the Romans. Thus, Origenes, one of the early Church fathers, asserts in his epistle to the Africans, section 14, third century C.E., that there was a court in Palestine that heard capital cases and carried out executions, although these were performed without publicity.[98]

c. LOWER COURTS OF TWENTY-THREE JUDGES AND OF THREE JUDGES

Here too, we do not have enough information to form a clear picture of the structure and operations of the Jewish courts. Consequently, only a general sketch will be presented, based on the information available.

While the Talmud makes repeated references to courts of twenty-three and of three members,[99] the historian Josephus, one of our chief sources of information for this era, makes a number of references to courts composed of seven members.[100] This has given rise to many conflicting views among scholars on the number of judges customarily sitting in the Jewish courts.[101]

90. Gulak, *Yesode Ha'Mishpat Ha'Ivri*, p. 19; see R. Margolis, *Margoliot Ha'Yam* (Jerusalem, 1962), pp. 18–20.

91. Talmud, *Sanhedrin* 31; Jerusalem Talmud, *Sanhedrin*, ad loc.

92. See Goren, "The Struggle over the Sanhedrin," p. 515; idem, "The Structure and Functions of the Sanhedrin," p. 523 ff.

93. *Sifri* to Deut. 15; Talmud, *Horiyot* 5a; Moshe b. Nahman, Commentary *Ramban* to Deut. 15; R. Be'Hai, ad loc.; Herzog, "The Administration of Justice in Ancient Israel," p. 136.

94. Talmud, *Sanhedrin* 41a, *Avodah Zarah* 8b, *Shabbat* 15a; Federbush, *Mishpat Ha'Melukha Be'Yisrael*. See Goren, "The Structure and Functions of the Sanhedrin," p. 523 ff.; Buechler, *Ha'Sanhedrin Be'Yerushalayim*; Gulak, *Yesode Ha'Mishpat Ha'Ivri*, pp. 23 ff., 39 ff.; Elon, *History of the Jews in the Land of Israel in the Mishnaic and Talmudic Eras*, p. 114 ff.; N. Orater, "Bitul Ha'Sanhedrin Ve'Hasmikha" (Hebrew; Jerusalem, 1971).

95. Cf. Gershuni, "Beth Din Ha'Gadol Be'Yerushalayim U'Beth Din She'Be'Yavne, in *Ohr Ha'Mizrah* 2 (1956): 11.

96. See Talmud, *Ediot* 7, Mishnah 7; see citations in note 94, above.

97. Talmud, *Sanhedrin* 130b.

98. See Chapter VI, Section A 3 c and notes thereto, above.

99. E.g., Talmud, *Sanhedrin* 2a; Tosefta, *Sanhedrin*, ch. 7; *Sifri*, Deut. 25.

100. *Antiquities of the Jews*, IV, 8, 14; VI, 8, 38; *Wars of the Jews*, II, 20, 5.

101. See E. Schurer, *History of the Jewish People* (New York, 1961), vol. 2, sec. 23; J. L. Saalschutz, *Das Mosaiche*

The traditions recorded in the Talmud, however, by experts in the law (many of whom had acted as judges for long periods of time, and all of whom faithfully attempted to preserve tradition) are much more reliable than the statements of Josephus—if, indeed, there is a conflict between them. The Talmud does make reference to "seven good men of the town" who provided leadership for the community.[102] It has been speculated that during the numerous wars of the Jews with the Romans, the continuous Roman persecutions, and the Roman abrogation of the right of Jews to try capital cases, these seven lay readers of the communities sometimes took over the functions of courts and attempted to resolve squabbles, particularly those involving claims of money.[103] In any case, the repeated talmudic references and legal discussions concerning courts of twenty-three and courts of three, rather than seven, members appear to be reliable evidence regarding the number of judges in the courts throughout the land.

Three-judge courts were located in all of the towns of Israel and heard suits involving claims of money.

It should be noted that even suits involving claims of money only, or minor infractions, were heard and decided by three-judge courts, rather than by a single judge. While a scriptural basis is adduced in the Talmud, it was also due to a well-entrenched perspective that "there is only one [i.e., God] who judges alone,"[104] and that one human judge alone would err more frequently than three. It should be remembered that no compensation was paid to the judges, so that having more than one judge to hear cases did not impose a financial burden on the community.

In many of the towns, however, there were also courts consisting of twenty-three judges (the "Small Sanhedrin"), until these were abolished by the Romans. Their chief function was to hear capital cases. It may be, however, that they also acted as the chief decision-makers of the community in all civil and civic matters, and that they had developed from the earlier, long-standing institutions of the "elders" and "heads of patriarchal families" that had existed in every community. This would explain the need to have courts consisting of so many judges, since these "judges" may have included representatives of all of the important families and clans in the area, who acted as the deci-sion-making body.[105] There are numerous implications in the Talmud that often only two of the members of the twenty-judge courts were learned in the law[106] and that the members of these courts were customarily chosen from among the residents of the areas in which they sat.[107] These two phenomena, while possibly due to other reasons as well, lend support to this thesis.[108]

Each of the local twenty-three judge courts had one member, the *mufla*, whose function it was to scrutinize the actions of the other members of the courts and advise them if they erred in the law.[109] This, too, may indicate the lack of expertise in the law that often existed among members of these courts. Another important function of the *mufla* was to analyze legal problems to which the court did not know the answer, and to present these problems before the higher court in Jerusalem.

> If one of them needed [to know] the law, he went to the court in his town. If there was no court in his town he would go to the court that was nearest to his town. If they had heard [what the law was], they would tell them. If not, he and the "*mufla*" among them would go to the court that was on the Temple Mount [in Jerusalem]. If they heard [what the law was], they would tell them. If not, he and the "*mufla*" among them would go to the court that sat near the gate [of the Temple]. If they heard [what the law was], they would tell them. If not, all of them would go to the court that sat in the Chamber of Hewn Stone [part of the Temple structure].[110]

The "*mufla*," therefore, had a dual function: he would help the members of the twenty-three judge courts to clarify the legal issues involved in the cases that they heard, and to arrive at a correct conclusion. This was very important where these courts consisted of mixed groups, with few legal experts (due to the widespread Roman killings and persecutions) and often many laymen who were not well versed in the law. Additionally, he acted as the link between the twenty-three judge court with which he was associated and the higher courts in Jerusalem, presenting puzzling local legal issues for decision, so that the law would

---

Recht (Berlin, 1848), vol. 1, sec. 4; I. Weiss, *Dor Dor Ve'Dor-shav* (Vilna, 1804), sec. 1, ch. 21; Gulak, *Yesode Ha'Mishpat Ha'Ivri*, p. 7.

102. Talmud, *Megillah* 26a; *Baba Batra* 7b.

103. Gulak, *Yesode Ha'Mishpat Ha'Ivri*, p. 8; Herzog, "The Administration of Justice in Ancient Israel," pp. 118 ff., 122 ff.

104. Talmud, *Avot* 4:8; cf. *Tosefot, Sanhedrin* 5a; s.v. *Ke'-gon.*

105. Gulak, *Yesode Ha'Mishpat Ha'Ivri*, p. 9; *contra* Herzog, "The Administration of Justice in Ancient Israel," p. 138.

106. Tosefta, *Sanhedrin* 8; Talmud, *Sanhedrin* 17b; Rambam, Laws of the Sanhedrin, ch. 26; *contra* Herzog, ibid., p. 138 ff.

107. Talmud, *Sanhedrin* 88a.

108. Gulak, *Yesode Ha'Mishpat Ha'Ivri*, p. 9; *contra* Herzog.

109. Talmud, *Horiyot* 4, and Talmud, *Sanhedrin* 16b; see the view of Rashi and *Tosefot* to *Horiyot* 4, that he was not a member of the court.

110. Tosefta, *Sanhedrin* 87a.

be applied uniformly by the various courts throughout the land.[111]

d. ONE-JUDGE COURTS

Alongside the lay courts and informal arbitration bodies (see Section *h*, below) that developed subsequent to the destruction of the Second Jewish Commonwealth, there were also formal courts consisting of one professional judge. These existed in Babylonia and in Palestine during the intermittent periods when Jewish courts were tolerated by the Romans.[112]

While the origins of one-judge courts are unclear, they may have first made their appearance in Babylonia, where a limited Jewish autonomy, including the exilarchate and a system of Jewish courts were well established. Consequently, even the courts consisting of one professional judge were held in wide esteem by the population and had the necessary powers of coercion, backed by the exilarch and, ultimately, by the ruling Persian authorities.[113] Nevertheless, particularly in Palestine, there was a widespread feeling that only God was fit to judge alone.[114] There were talmudic authorities who maintained that a one-judge court could not be regarded as an authorized judicial body under biblical norms.[115] The institution declined during the Middle Ages, until it was practically abandoned,[116] except in cases where both litigants agreed to accept the ruling of a one-judge court. Prominent individual scholar-decision-makers, however, continued to receive requests (usually in writing) from professional courts and others to resolve intricate questions of law that arose. The decisions of these individuals generally were widely accepted. Functionally, these respected scholar-decision-makers operated as the professional one-judge courts.

e. APPELLATE REVIEW

Appellate review of court decisions appears to have become well established by at least the middle of the Talmudic Era (*circa* 300 C.E.). Local courts were required, upon request, to set forth their decisions in writing so that these could be reviewed by the "Great Court" or by the courts of the larger cities, whose members were generally more erudite, and held in greater esteem than the judges of the local courts.[117] There were even cases involving suits predicated on written documents in which a defendant who had lost the case and had paid the amount of the judgment was able to reinstitute suit against the successful plaintiff in order to recover the judgment that he had paid.[118] Decisions of one-judge courts were subject to review[119] of the factual findings, and cases could be reopened on the basis of new evidence.[120] Time limits were often placed upon the reopening of decided cases.[121]

Some scholars also claim that the Sanhedrin occasionally acted as an appellate court, reviewing decisions already handed down by lower courts and overturning them if warranted.[122] It is also possible that when issues were referred to the Sanhedrin by the lower courts, it would, in effect, prescribe new law by laying down a new legal principle where it thought that existing precedent was not applicable. This might be done on the basis of one of the accepted hermeneutic rules. It also allowed the Great Court to promulgate adaptations to changing social conditions as the need arose.[123]

In sum, there existed a right to appeal, although this was not uniform in all eras and places and might, in practice, be limited or qualified.

f. OTHER SUPERIOR COURTS

During the time that the Great Sanhedrin existed, it acted as a superior court, supervising the activities of the lower courts that were scattered throughout the land of Israel. It also established policy and formulated legal principles that were appropriate for society,

---

111. Gulak, *Yesode Ha'Mishpat Ha'Ivri*, p. 13; see R. Margolis, *Margoliyot Ha'Yam* (Hebrew; Jerusalem, 1958), p. 18 ff.
112. See Talmud, *Sanhedrin* 5a; cf. Tosefot, ad loc., s.v. *"Kegon."*
113. Gulak, *Yesode Ha'Mishpat Ha'Ivri*, p. 36.
114. Jerusalem Talmud, *Sanhedrin* ch. 1; *Avot* 4:8.
115. See Talmud, *Sanhedrin* 2b, 3a, 5a.
116. Rambam, Laws of the Sanhedrin, chs. 12, rule 11, and ch. 5, rule 18; Moses Isserlies, *Rama, Ho. Mis.*, sec. 3, subsec. 2. See also Y. Lorberbaum, *Netivot Ha'Mishpat*, and A. L. Ha'Kohen Shein, *Ketzot Ha'Hoshen* (both reprinted numerous times, including in the *Shulhan Arukh* [New York, 1967]).

117. Talmud, *Sanhedrin* 31a; *Baba Kama* 112b; Rambam, Laws of *Mamrim*, 1:4; see Asher b. Yehiel (Rosh), ad loc. *Baba Metziah* 69b, sec. 45; *Shulhan Arukh, Ho. Mis.*, sec. 14, subsec. 4; R. Y. Hazan, *Hikre Lev*, H.M. (Kusta, 1760), vol. 1, sec. 85–86; H. Hirschenson, *Malki Ba'Kodesh* (St. Louis, 1919–23), vol. 1, no. 1; vol. 2, p. 62, vol. 4, p. 14; Gulak, *Yesode Ha'Mishpat Ha'Ivri*, p. 182. See Part Three, below, concerning appellate courts in the Middle Ages.
118. See Talmud, *Sanhedrin* 32; Rambam, Laws of Loans, ch. 14, rule 3; *Shulhan Arukh, Ho. Mis.*, sec. 25, and J. Kohen, *Me'irat Aynayim*, sec. 58, subsec. 1, and sec. 82; S. Kohen, *Sifse Kohen* (in standard editions of *Shulhan Arukh*), sec. 22, sec. 88, subsec. 25; Gulak, *Yesode Ha'Mishpat Ha'Ivri*, p. 183.
119. Talmud, *Sanhedrin* 33a.
120. Mishnah, *Sanhedrin* 3:8; 4:1.
121. See materials cited in note 117, above; cf. A. J. Silverstein, "The Right of Appeal in Talmudic Law," *Case Western Reserve Journal of International Law* 6 (1973): 33 ff.
122. Gulak, *Yesode Ha'Mishpat Ha'Ivri*, p. 19.
123. See Talmud, *Sanhedrin* 32a, regarding the appellate function of the Sanhedrin; A. Buechler, *The Sanhedrin* (Jerusalem, 1970); H. Mantel, *Studies in the Sanhedrin* (Cambridge, Mass., 1970); cf. Silverstein, "The Right of Appeal in Talmudic Law," p. 33.

as conditions changed. It also promulgated prescriptions, where necessary.[124]

After the abolition of the Great Sanhedrin, its place was taken in practice by the "Great Court" of the patriarch in Palestine, the academies of law in Palestine and Babylonia,[125] and by the courts under the aegis of the exilarch (see Section *i*, below), whose permission was, at many times, required in order for anyone to act as a judge.

There is also mention of a "Court of the Place of Assembly" ("*makom ha'vaad*"), which apparently consisted of all of the judges of the region, who assembled to consider important matters.[126] Later, during the Middle Ages, when such formal superior courts did not exist, a prominent rabbi or decision-maker of the region would often exercise a supervisory function over the Jewish courts. His ability to do so was generally based not on formal authorization by the non-Jewish powers but, rather, on the esteem with which he was held, and the deeply felt religious perspectives of the members of the Jewish community.

In addition to the supervisory and prescriptive functions of the superior courts, these also sometimes acted in still another capacity. A litigant who could sometimes insist that the case be heard by a superior court instead of the local court[127] (see Section *f*, above). However, numerous restrictive rules were often placed in the way[128] (see also Section *i*, below, regarding superior Jewish courts in Babylonia).

g. Courts of Special Jurisdiction

There is evidence in the Talmud that there were a number of courts of special jurisdiction operating simultaneously during the Second Jewish Commonwealth. There is mention of a "Court of Priests," whose precise function is a matter of scholarly debate. Its function was probably limited to ritual, and perhaps also civil, matters that especially concerned priests. (These were mainly matters unique to members of the priesthood, such as regulating religious services in the Temple or the setting of a different standard of support for widows and divorcees of priests.)[129]

There was also a court whose judges were called "*dayane gezerot*" or "*dayane gezelot*," meaning, respectively, prescribing judges and judges of robbery.[130] Its function appears to have been to act as a criminal court, dealing primarily with theft and prescribing laws in this area.[131] Possibly the judges of these courts were appointed by the Roman authorities and judged criminal cases in accordance with Roman law, rather than traditional Jewish law.[132] These courts should be contrasted with some of the Jewish courts in Europe during the Middle Ages, which also passed upon criminal cases and applied non-Jewish law in certain respects, particularly with regard to the sanctions imposed (see Part Three, Chapter IX, Section B 2). Other scholars maintain that the members of this court were in fact appointed by the Roman authorities but did judge in accordance with traditional Jewish law.[133] The Romans may also have authorized individual judges to prescribe laws concerning robberies and torts, and perhaps even to supervise commercial activities and prescribe laws in this area too.

h. Lay Courts

After the abolition of Jewish courts by the Romans (*circa* 140 C.E.), the Jewish court system survived but temporarily assumed a different form. Apparently Jewish litigants, in the absence of Jewish courts and unwilling to resort to Roman courts for resolution of controversies, would voluntarily submit their controversies to two laymen (one of whom was chosen by each of the parties). These two laymen would then select a third person to join them. The three would act together as an informal court of arbitration, to which the Romans apparently did not object. They would then hear the case and hand down a decision, which at first was technically unenforceable under Roman law. In practice, however, resort to these informal lay courts and obedience to their decisions were compelled by the social pressures within the Jewish communities and by the intense religious feelings and nationalistic perspectives of the litigants themselves. In this way, a Jewish court system continued and the Roman decree was circumvented. This was the foundation of the institution that was to persist for thousands of years and came to be called the "*beth din shel borerim*" (literally, the "court of the selectors," that is, the litigants).[134] The first mention of this institution in the Talmud is by

124. See Elon, *Toldot Ha'Yehudim*, p. 132 ff.
125. Gulak, *Yesode Ha'Mishpat Ha'Ivri*, p. 38; see Elon, *Toldot Ha'Yehudim*.
126. See *Sanhedrin* 31a; Tosefot, *Baba Kama* 112b; Rambam, Laws of the Sanhedrin, ch. 6, rules 6–9.
127. See Talmud, *Sanhedrin*, 31a; *Baba Kama*, 112b.
128. Talmud, *Sanhedrin* 31a, and Jerusalem Talmud, *Sanhedrin* ch. 3, rule 32. See, in general, Herzog, "The Administration of Justice in Ancient Israel," p. 117 ff.
129. See Talmud, *Ketubot* 104b, 105a; and Jerusalem Talmud, *Sanhedrin*, ch. 3, rule 32; Weiss, *Dor Dor Ve'Dorshav*, sec. 1, ch. 21; Talmud, *Kiddushin* 76b; Gulak, *Yesode Ha'Mishpat Ha'Ivri*, p. 20; Herzog, "The Administration of Justice in Ancient Israel," p. 109; cf. Talmud, *Rosh Hashanah* 22a.

130. Talmud, *Ketubot* 104b, 105a; *Baba Kama* 58a.
131. See Talmud, *Ketubot*, 104b, 105a.
132. See N. Krochmal, *More Nevokhay Ha'Zeman* (reprinted Jerusalem, 1961), sec. 13; but see Weiss, *Dor Dor Ve'Dorshav*, sec. 1, ch. 21.
133. See Gulak, *Yesode Ha'Mishpat Ha'Ivri*, p. 22.
134. Gulak, *Yesode Ha'Mishpat Ha'Ivri*, p. 25.

Rabbi Judah, who lived in that era and was secretly ordained.[135]

According to Rabbi Judah, these lay courts were composed of one scholar who had some training in the law and two laymen who might be completely unlearned but who possessed common sense.[136] Even the one "learned" lay judge who joined the other two unlearned laymen to form a lay court was often not as learned, or as trained, as the expert judge who sat (often with his unlearned colleagues) in the professional courts, when these were permitted to function.[137]

Resort to lay courts was ordinarily held to be prohibited, and they were not to be regarded as courts according to the talmudic interpretation of biblical norms. Because of the public need for them, however, they were permitted to function by application of the principles of *hefker beth din, hefker,* and on the theory that the ordained (and therefore authorized) decisionmakers of an earlier era, had authorized nonordained (including lay) courts to function as agents of the ordained authorities.

These courts may at first have handled only matters that did not require legal analysis.[138] It has been claimed that this combination of one person trained in the law and two untutored laymen is somewhat reminiscent of the twenty-three judge courts in the various cities of Palestine, which may also have contained unlearned laymen.[139] Eventually, however, these lay courts became so adept that they handled many complex legal questions and decided them by resort to traditional Jewish law and precedent, not by the application of common sense.[140] They heard controversies regarding commercial transactions, loans, inheritances, and torts, but apparently not serious offenses involving deliberate violence, such as assaults and robbery.[141]

Lay courts also acquired the power and authority to coerce litigants to appear before them when there was no court of professional judges in the area.[142] In such cases, if one of the litigants would ask three laymen to serve as judges, they could compel the other party to the controversy to appear before them and could hear and decide the case, unless the defendant wished to have the case heard by a court of professional judges.[143] Furthermore, lay judges would be liable in the event that they handed down an erroneous decision that caused financial loss to one of the litigants. This was not so if both litigants had voluntarily agreed to submit their controversies to these lay judges.[144] In addition to these now formalized lay courts, there were also, apparently, informal lay courts of arbitration that had no coercive powers.

The institution of lay courts was eventually recognized by the Roman authorities themselves, following an edict of the Emperor Honoreous (398 C.E.). The *Codex Theodoseanus* (and later, with slight modifications, Justinian's *Corpus Juris Civilis*) provided as follows:

> The Jews live in accordance with Roman and general law with regard to those details that do not concern their religion so much, but which relate to the order of the state, and its law. The established courts are open before them, and they sue and are sued in accordance with Roman law. Nevertheless, if, according to a compromise resembling arbitration, they shall desire to be judged by Jews or their Patriarchs, in accordance with the agreement of the parties, and then, only in monetary matters, the laws of the state do not prevent them from going to their courts, and the decisions of these [courts] shall be carried out by the judges of the provinces as though they were issued by courts of arbitration.[145]

While this informal court resembled Roman arbitration procedures, it had a distinctively Jewish format. Under Roman law, one judge was normally chosen by the parties to a controversy, to litigate the matter. Only in unusual cases would two or more arbitrators be chosen.[146] The Jewish arbitration court was different. Continuing the Jewish tradition of the formal three-judge courts, the Jewish court of arbitration consisted of three persons, one selected by each of the parties, with the third selected by the first two arbitrators.[147] (In the event that the first two arbitrators could not agree on a third person, the leaders of the community would designate the third arbitrator.) The three arbitrators would then decide the matter, either in accor-

---

135. Talmud, *Bekhorot* 36b, 37a; see *Sanhedrin* 3a.

136. Talmud, *Bekhorot,* ibid.; *Sanhedrin* 3a; and Novellae of R. Nissim, ad loc.; cf. Herzog, "The Administration of Justice," p. 120.

137. See Talmud, *Sanhedrin* 5a, and commentary of *Rosh,* ad loc.; *Shulhan Arukh, Hoshen Mishpat,* sec. 3, and J. F. Kohen, *Me'irat Enayim,* sec. 2; and S. Kohen, in *Sifse Kohen,* sec. 25, subsec. 9; Gulak, *Yesode Ha'Mishpat Ha'Ivri,* p. 35.

138. Talmud, *Nedarim* 77a.

139. Gulak, *Yesode Ha'Mishpat Ha'Ivri,* p. 34; Talmud, *Sanhedrin* 36.

140. See Talmud, *Bekhorot* 28a; *Sanhedrin,* 3a, 5a, 36, and Tosefot, ad loc.

141. Gulak, *Yesode Ha'Mishpat Ha'Ivri,* p. 34.

142. See Talmud, *Sanhedrin* 3a, 5a, Tosefot, s.v. "*Dan,*" and commentary of R. Asher (Rosh), ad loc.; see also Yaakov b. Asher, *Tur, Hoshen Mishpat,* sec. 3, and Y. Karo, *Shulhan Arukh, Hoshen Mishpat,* sec. 3.

143. *Sanhedrin* 5a; Gulak, *Yesode Ha'Mishpat Ha'Ivri,* p. 34.

144. Talmud, *Sanhedrin* 5a. See, however, Kohen in *Sifse Kohen, Hoshen Mishpat,* sec. 25, subsec. 15.

145. *Codex Theodoseanus* 2. 2. 10; *Corpus Juris Civilis, Codex Justinianus* 2. 1. 9. 8. The Justinian Code had substituted the phrase *"communis pactio"* (the general agreement) for *"per compromissum"* (according to a compromise).

146. See Ulpianus, *Dig.* 4:17.

147. Talmud, *Sanhedrin* 23a.

dance with strict Jewish traditional law, or by a decision that came close to it. It became customary for the litigants to execute a document of arbitration, in which they agreed to abide by the decisions of the arbitrators.[148]

Once the institution of lay courts became well-established, it received recognition and continued to flourish thereafter. These lay courts operated even after the Romans later lifted their prohibitions upon the existence and operations of Jewish courts, since there were often very few professional judges or scholars who could serve as judges, because of the remoteness of an area or because of the wholesale slaughters and death in the aftermaths of the Jewish rebellions, mass enslavement, and emigration of large portions of the population. The use of lay courts was widespread throughout the Talmudic Era and continued in the Middle Ages.[149] It is interesting to note that the lay court, consisting of one person learned in the law and two unlearned laymen, was also found among the ancient Germans, who called the institution "*Schoffengerricht*."[150]

Where there were formal courts to hear and decide cases in strict conformance to traditional Jewish law, either of the litigants in a case brought before a lay court could insist that the case be presented to the formal Jewish courts.[151]

i. JEWISH COURTS IN BABYLONIA

In Parthian and Persian Babylonia, where a major portion of world Jewry resided, the situation was quite different, even after the destruction of the Second Jewish Commonwealth. The non-Jewish authorities permitted Jewish courts to exist and to decide cases in accordance with traditional Jewish law. The judges there were appointed by (or at least received "permission" to officiate as judges from) the exilarch, the head of the Babylonian Jewish community (see Section VI, A 3, above). At a later date some judges were appointed by the heads of the academies of law. The Jewish court in Babylonia reached an extremely high level under the leadership of Samuel of Nehardea and Rav of Sura, both of whom headed prominent academ-

emies of law in their respective cities. The judicial system there included three distinct superior courts that supervised the activity of the many local Jewish courts: the court of the exilarch[152] and the courts that were maintained by each of the two most prominent academies of law.

There is some indication in the Talmud that the court of the exilarch also applied Persian law, but the matter remains the subject of conflict among scholars.[153]

3. THE ACADEMIES OF LAW AND RELIGION HEADED BY THE GAONIM

Because of the traditionally great respect for Jewish learning and religious leadership, and the widely held perspective that decision-making and leadership should be provided by those who were learned in the Torah and steeped in piety, academies of law and religion, led by their heads and their academic staffs, exercised an important influence in decision-making. Some of these academies, led by outstanding legal and religious scholars, attracted many students, sometimes even from foreign lands. A number of academy heads were not paid salaries but supported themselves by engaging in various occupations, including agriculture and trade.[154]

The academies participated in decision-making in a number of ways. They convened synods, initiated prescriptions, participated in the application of the law as judges in important cases, and authored many responsa and influential legal treatises. They educated thousands of students and inculcated them with perspectives that became widespread in the Jewish community and exercised an important impact on decision-making. Often, too, their leading students would, ultimately, occupy key rabbinical, and sometimes lay, positions in important Jewish communities.

Additionally, the heads of academies, or *gaonim*, in Babylonia were at times able to appoint judges and, after the Talmudic Era, to influence the selection and deposition of exilarchs. Unlike the situation in medieval Europe, however, the academy staffs did not serve as community rabbis but confined their official positions to acting as heads and members of academies. Normally the Babylonian Academies were controlled by their respective heads, but they were subject to the influence of the academy staffs.

In Palestine, from the second to the fifth century, the patriarch, who acted as the lay head of the Jewish

---

148. Talmud, *Baba Batra* 167a, Jerusalem Talmud, *Mo'ed Katan* 3:3, where the document of arbitration is called "*compromisium*."

149. See Tosefot, *Sanhedrin* 5a, s.v. "*Dan*"; Rambam, Laws of the Sanhedrin, ch. 2, rule 10, and ch. 4, rule 1; R. Asher, Commentary of *Rosh* to Talmud, *Sanhedrin* 5a; Yaakov b. Asher, *Tur Hoshen Mishpat*, sec. 3, and Y. Karo *Shulham Arukh, Hoshen Mishpat*, sec. 3, and Kohen, *Sifse Kohen*.

150. Gulak, *Yesode Ha'Mishpat Ha'Ivri*, p. 35.

151. See also the ordinances of Jewish religious leaders of twelfth-century France and Germany, under the leadership of Rabbi Jacob Tam, in Finkelstein, *Jewish Self-Government in the Middle Ages* (New York, 1924) p. 153; *Shulan Arukh, Hoshen Mishpat*, sec. 13, subsec. 3.

152. See Talmud, *Baba Batra* 55a.

153. See Talmud, *Baba Kama* 58b, *Shevuot* 34b, *Baba Batra* 55a; Ba'er, *Roshe Ha'Gola*, Gulak, *Yesode Ha'Mishpat Ha'Ivri*, p. 28–29.

154. See Talmud, *Ketubot* 105a, 106; *Gittin* 60b; *Berakhot* 28a.

community there, also served as head of the academy and appointed new members. He was, in general, able to control the academy, although there was at least one revolt against the patriarch Gamliel. This may, however, have occurred before the establishment of the institution of the patriarchate.[155]

4. LAY DECISION-MAKERS

a. PERSPECTIVES CONCERNING DECISION-MAKING BY THE LAY COMMUNAL POLITY

The constitutive scheme of Jewish decision-making, as recorded in the Talmud, deals primarily with the institutional patterns of decision by royalty (or equivalent national figures), and by the religious leadership acting through assemblies, Sanhedrin, or *beth din*. The Talmud deals only minimally with lay decision-makers who were not religious leaders. Even the notions regarding the role of royalty in the legal processes are not dealt with very extensively in the Talmud, but were amplified by medieval Jewish scholars such as Rambam, Nissim Gerundi, and Isaac Abarbanel.[156]

It is clear, however, that beginning with approximately the fourth century C.E., and certainly from the tenth century on (see Part Three), there was a widespread perspective among Jews that individual Jewish lay groups and communities had wide-ranging rights to prescribe for their members and residents in nearly all areas of human activity.

The extensive powers envisioned for each individual community, could have led to wide variations in communal decision-making in the different communities, but for the uniform legal tradition, and the wide influence of rabbis and heads of academies who participated very actively in communal leadership, and helped to shape local lay decisions everywhere to conform to the same Jewish legal norms. Other powerful stimuli to uniformity were the rule of the exilarchate and patriarchate in Babylonia and Palestine, respectively.

Underlying the far-reaching development of decision-making by lay communal polities was the perspective that communal participation was essential for decision-making and the notion that the views of laymen were of crucial importance in the prescriptive processes. It was accepted, for example, that no religious prescription could be promulgated by rabbis or by a *beth din* if the ordinance was not likely to be accepted by most laymen. These unpopular prescriptions were not to be prescribed initially, and if prescribed were not regarded

as valid[157] Even a prescription that had widely been observed for many years, but was subsequently disregarded *en masse*, was also regarded as invalid.[158]

These democratic notions were also reflected in the talmudic aphorism, "No officer may be appointed without first consulting the people."[159] In other words, current community expectations were a *sine qua non* for prescriptions to be regarded as law.[160]

Much more important than this passive role of laymen was their active participation in prescriptive decision-making. Prescriptions by the lay community as a whole are rooted in antiquity and were recognized as binding in Jewish law, at least as far back as the third century C.E.[161] They appear to have emerged from the large measure of communal autonomy that existed in many areas of the ancient Near East and Mediterranean lands. Communal legislation became a vital factor in permitting Jewish communities to adjust to the new social, economic, and political reality.

The following talmudic statement is one of the earliest postbiblical Jewish legal sources concerning lay prescriptions:

> The people of a town can force each other to build a synagogue for all of them and to purchase a scroll of the Torah and prophets. The people of a town may set conditions concerning prices, regarding measures (used by merchants), regarding the wages of workers and may enforce these. The people of a town may say, "One who informs concerning another, shall pay so much and so much", and, "whoever shall inform to the government shall pay so much and so much"; and "whoever's cow shall graze among the plants, shall pay so much and so much," and may enforce these. . . . The wool dealers and the dyers may say, "If any items to be purchased are brought to the town, we shall be partners regarding them." The bakers may arrange for [alternate] times of work [for themselves]. The donkey drivers may say, "Whoever's donkey dies, we will supply him with another donkey." If it dies from neglect, they do not have to supply him with another donkey. If it dies without

155. Baron, *The Jewish Community*, vol. 1, p. 150. See Talmud, *Sanhedrin* 5a.
156. See also Baron, *The Jewish Community*, vol. 1, p. 217.

157. Talmud, *Avodah Zarah* 36a; Jerusalem Talmud, ch. 2, rules 8, 16, and 1; ch. 2, rules 4, 9, and 41; Rambam, Laws of *Mamrim*, 2:6.
158. Rambam, ibid., 2:5–7; see also Tosefta, *Sotah* 15, 10; M. Roth, Responsa *Kol Mevasser*, vol. 1, no. 3; M. Bloch, *Sha'Arei Torat Ha'Takkanot* (reprinted Jerusalem, 1971), intro., sec. 7.
159. Talmud, *Berakhot* 55a; cf. M. Kasher, *Torah Shelemah* (Jerusalem and New York, 1927) vol. 15, pp. 187–89.
160. See M. McDougal's views on the role of community expectations in law, in M. McDougal, H. Lasswell, and J. Miller, *Interpretation of Agreements and World Public Order* (New Haven, 1967).
161. Y. Baer, "The Foundations and Beginnings of Jewish Communal Organizations in the Middle Ages" (Hebrew), *Zion* 25 (1940): 1.

neglect, they must supply him with another donkey. If he says, "Give me [money] and I will buy one for myself," they do not listen to him, but purchase one and give it to him. The shipowners may say, "Whoever's ship is lost, we will supply him with another ship." If it is lost because of neglect, they are not required to supply him with another ship. If he sails to a place where people do not sail, they do not have to supply him with another ship.[162]

Although the Talmud does not specify any biblical authority for democratic communal decision-making, it seems clear that, even in antiquity, the community had always been regarded as having the power to prescribe and apply binding norms, and that it was recognized that community decision-making was a basic element in the biblical perspective of law. It has also been contended that prescriptions of kings, both Jewish and non-Jewish, in prebiblical as well as postbiblical times, were regarded as binding primarily, because kings were deemed to be acting for, and representing, the community.[163] Consequently, when there was no king, or with regard to minor communal civil matters that did not concern the king, the community as a whole was always recognized as having the authority to decide for itself.

A number of scholars have sought to find the so-called "legal" basis of communal enactments (which later became of overriding importance in medieval Jewish decision-making) in a modified theory of social contract or covenant, i.e., that the residents of a community have voluntarily agreed to be bound by communal enactments and have even waived the application of strict biblical and traditional Jewish law.[164]

Use of this legal fiction would not, however, fully explain the recognition accorded to communal ordinances during the Middle Ages by appliers of traditional Jewish law, for many of these ordinances provided for flogging, imprisonment, or even capital punishment. According to traditional principles of Jewish law, a person does not have the control, in a legal sense, over his own body and may not authorize another to wound, kill, or even imprison him.[165] The theoretical "consent" would therefore be of no avail. Furthermore, consent could not be the exclusive rationale behind community ordinances since, in many communities, those who were not wealthy, or were not taxpayers or property owners, had little or no voice in elections or community prescriptions.[166] Similarly, many communal ordinances were aimed at non-residents or strangers, who certainly had never agreed to these communal enactments that gave preferences to local residents. Also, there is, of course, the objection that ordinances should not, under this theory, be binding either upon those born in the community or those who arrived there, subsequent to the enactment of the ordinances.

It is arguable that from the perspective of Judaic scholar–decision-makers, the right of the community to prescribe the foregoing countertraditional enactments was predicated not on the theory of consent or covenant but on the perspective that the needs of a community were superior to the needs of any individ-

---

162. Tosefta, *Baba Mezia* 11, 23; see also *Baba Batra* 8b. Compare with current insurance policy provisions.

163. Gerundi, *Derashot Ha'Ran*, discourse no. 11; Ha'Meiri, *Beth Ha'Behira* (Jerusalem, 1977), *Sanhedrin* 52b; Sofer, Responsa *Hatam Sofer*, O.H. (Vienna, 1882), no. 208; Kook, *Mishpat Kohen*, no. 144; Chajes *Torat Ha'Neviim*, pp. 46–47; Sender, *Beth Din Ha'Gadol* in Ohr Ha'Mizrah 25 (1976) 39, 44, reprinted in Sender, *Ohel Rivkah* (Chicago, 1979), p. 204. See Elon, *Ha'Mishpat Ha'Ivri*, vol. 2, p. 561; Rambam, Laws of Kings, ch. 5; Soloveitchik, "Kiddush Ha'Khodesh." Note, however, that the Talmud indicates that the decision-making authority of a king or *beth din* is predicated upon biblical verses.

164. Elon, *Ha'Mishpat Ha'Ivri*, p. 517; M. Goldin, "The Juridical Basis of Communal Associations in Mediaeval Rabbinic Legal Thought," p. 77; see Israel Isserlis, Responsa *Terumat Hadeshen* (reprinted Warsaw, 1882), no. 342; Epstein, *Arukh Ha-Shulhan*, Ho. Mis., 7. See also Rambam, Laws of Armed Robbery (*Gezelah*) 5:18, and S. Y. Zevin, *Le'Ohr Halakhah*, p. 333 (reprinted Jerusalem, 1968), vol. 7, p. 22; Chajes, *Torat Ha'Neviim*, pp. 46–47.

It should be noted, however, that Rousseau apparently did not contemplate a real consent in his theory of social contract. As G. H. Sabine has remarked, "The word 'contract' was about

as misleading as any that Rousseau could have chosen" (see his *A History of Political Theory* [New York, 1955], p. 587).

For a survey of the positions of the social contract theorists regarding the theory of associations, see O. Gierke, *Natural Law and the Theory of Society*, trans. by E. Barker (Boston, 1957), pp. 62–92. See also K. K. Kahana, *Three Great Systems of Jurisprudence* (London, 1955), pp. 75–78, for a hypertechnical interpretation of the theory of social contract in Jewish law as an agreement that results in creating for the participants and their successors a right *in rem*, not a right *in personam*. See S. Atlas, "The General Will in Talmudic Jurisprudence," in *Hebrew Union College Annual* 26 (1955): 1–38, on the subjection of the individual to the community in Jewish law. See also Shlomo b. Aderet, Responsa *Rashba*, vol. 3, no. 411, in which he discusses this problem in the context of questioning why biblical and talmudic laws should bind subsequent generations. He relates this issue to the talmudic proposition that any matter accepted pursuant to an oath is binding upon one's descendants. See Jerusalem Talmud, *Pesahim* 4:1: "The consent of the members of the local community, just like the consent of the Israelites at Sinai, has the status of an oath or vow." See also Solomon Di Medina, Responsa, *Zikne Yehuda* (reprinted Jerusalem, 1956), sec. 1, no. 35; sec. 4, nos. 228, 230; Moshe ben Nahman in *Mishpat Ha'Herem*, in Responsa *Rashba* attributed to Ramban (Warsaw, 1883), sec. 285, p. 122.

See also Abarbanel Commentary to Deut. 29: "On this issue (regarding the obligation of the law upon those who did not stand at Sinai), the sages of our generation in the kingdom of Aragon marshalled in battle; see I. Perfet, Responsa *Rivash*, no. 399.

165. David ben Zimra, Commentary *Radvaz* to *Rambam*, Laws of Sanhedrin, 18:6.

166. See Part III, Chapter VIII, below.

uals. It was perceived that the failure or inability of a community to promulgate these enactments to govern and regulate life there, would endanger the well-being, and even existence, of the entire community. It is this superior need that justified extreme community actions.

This perspective overlaps with the theory regarding a pursuer (*rodef*) who, if he attempts to kill, may be killed by anybody (not simply by the intended victim; see Section C, below). The *rodef* theory was extended to authorize sanctions against acts, such as moving into a community that are not *malum in se* or inherently immoral. The same perspective seems to have been behind the feeling that a king could prescribe enactments and apply the law, even contrary to traditional legal principles, since royal enactments would generally benefit a community.[167] This perspective was also applied by talmudic decision-makers in recognizing the ordinances promulgated by non-Jewish governments and kings; these were held to be binding on Jews (see the principle of "the law of the Kingdom is the law," Section A, above, and the discussions there concerning the imprisonment and execution of violators of the law, by Jewish agents of non-Jewish kings). Belief concerning the right to bind those born subsequent to the enactments, was reinforced by the view, predicated on biblical verses, that oaths and bans could bind those born thereafter. Consequently, communal ordinances were commonly issued in the form of oaths or bans.[168]

The need for, and legitimacy of, lay communal enactments was recognized by medieval scholar–decision-makers whose rulings and advice were always sought after to legitimize or contest community decisions. Whether queried by communities that wished to enact ordinances or individuals who disputed their right to legislate, rabbinic decision-makers uniformly upheld the right of the organized Jewish community to promulgate valid and binding ordinances:

> It is clear that the public may enact ordinances and make agreements as it deems fit and these laws exist as rules of the Torah. The public can fine and punish all who violate these enactments. . . . Each and every community may do this and fine and penalize not according to the laws of the Torah . . . and so all the Holy communities have been accustomed to do and no one ever raised doubts about this. . . .[169]

We have found that the sages gave the power and strength to every community to promulgate ordinances for themselves, and no other community may abolish them, as we learned, 'The people of the

town may set conditions regarding measures. . . . Rabbi Isaac said, "How do we know that *beth din* may expropriate?' . . . and we learned, Rabbi Eliezer said, "I heard that a *beth din* may flog and punish, even when not authorized by the Torah' . . . from this you may deduce that the *beth din* of every community may issue edicts for their community in their discretion to meet the needs of the hour. . . . When [the members of] a community make an ordinance among themselves and [issue an] edict, how can any *beth din* untie it? This would open all bonds. If so, every one would remove himself from taxation and from all ordinances of the *Beth Din*. . . .[170]

Each and every community is, in its place, like the *Gaonim* and all of Israel, who promulgated a number of ordinances for all, which apply for all of Israel. . . .

Whenever the majority agree and enact an ordinance and take it upon themselves, do not listen to the words of the individual; because the majority of each and every town, in relation to individuals, are like the great *beth din* in relation to all of Israel; if they have promulgated, their edicts are binding, and whoever violates them shall be punished.[171]

In fact, the community, represented by its leaders who were elected by the members of the community, was sometimes pictured as having absolute power over all internal matters of the community and its members. "Nothing can resist the will of the community" was the way this perspective was expressed by one of the leading decision-makers of that era.[172]

Since the communities were regarded as having the same power to prescribe enactments as the ancient *beth din*,[173] they utilized the same traditional principles of law as the *beth din* to enforce their enactments, including the right to expropriate, the right to penalize, even

167. Chajes, *Torat Ha'Neviim*, pp. 44–48.
168. See Moshe ben Nahman (Ramban), in *Mishpat Ha'-Herem*, sec. 285, p. 122 of Responsa *Rashba*, attributed to Ramban (Warsaw, 1883).
169. Shlomo b. Aderet, Responsa *Rashba*, vol. 4, no. 185.

170. Meir of Rothenberg, Responsa *Maharam* of Rothenburg (Lvov ed.), no. 423.
171. Shlomo b. Aderet, Responsa *Rashba*, vol. 1, p. 729; vol. 3, pp. 411, 417; Responsa of Yehudai Gaoim, Lewin, *Ozar Ha'Gaonim* (Haifa-Jerusalem, 1928–43), *Nedarim*, p. 15; *Mordecai, Shevuot* (printed in standard editions of the Talmud), ch. 3, no. 755; *Responsa of the Sages of France and Lothair* (Vienna, 1881), no. 24; Y. Miller, p. 13; Tzemah Duran, Responsa, *Yachin U'Boaz*, vol. 2, no. 20.
172. Shlomo Yitzhaki, Rashi, Responsa, p. 287, no. 246; p. 289, no. 247. See also Y. Baer, "Origins of the Organization of the Jewish Community of the Middle Ages," in Zion, 15 (1950): 33; Shlomo Yitzhaki, Responsa *Rashi*, p. 313, no. 277; p. 350, no. 345; p. 274, no. 241; p. 313, no. 277; p. 350, no. 345; p. 258, no. 231; p. 290, no. 248; p. 188, no. 165; p. 175, no. 154; p. 179, no. 107; p. 282, no. 242; Meir b. Baruh, Responsa of *Maharam* of Rothenberg (Prague ed.), no. 941; Responsa of *Maharam* (Lemberg ed.), no. 423; *Mordecai, Baba Batra*, no. 481.
173. See Hananya Gaon, in *Hayim Modai*, Responsa of the Gaonim, *Sha'Are Tzedik* (Jerusalem, 1966), vol. 4, sec. 4, no. 16, p. 126; Responsa of Rabbenu Gershom, no. 67 (Eidelberg ed.; New York, 1956), p. 154; Shlomo b. Aderet, Responsa

when not authorized by biblical norms, and the principle "the law of the Kingdom is the law."[174] It is claimed that Jewish law recognized the right of non-Jewish courts (representing the community), as well as Jewish courts, to expropriate. Such recognition would then form the basis of the principle, "the Law of the state is the law." This would, however, tend to limit application of this principle to commercial and financial matters.[175]

b. Lay Communal Decision-Making in the Roman Empire

After the destruction of the Second Jewish Commonwealth, there was a substantial Jewish population scattered throughout the Mediterranean lands. Traditional Jewish communal self-government continued in all these areas, although with varying degrees of independence. In Rome, Jews, like other people, were permitted to form corporate groups. Although this was later revoked by Julius Caesar and Augustus, "ancient" groups were still permitted to continue their corporate existence, and the Jewish community there qualified as "ancient." It is estimated that there were thirteen different Jewish congregations in Imperial Rome, each of which constituted a separate community. Additionally, there were many others scattered throughout the various Roman provinces, including the Balkans, Italy, Sicily, Spain, Hungary, Cyrennica, and Gaul.[176]

Each of these diaspora communities was sovereign and generally followed the structure and format of the many Hellenic associations that existed during the Greco-Roman era. The communities were headed by councils of elders, called *zekenim* or *gerousia* (the counterpart of the Greek *presbyteroi*). There was usually also an executive committee (*archontes*), whose members were elected for one year, a secretary (*grammatew*), and a *hazzan* or sextant. Like the Hellenic associations, officers were elected annually and all members had equality in theory. In practice, however, wealth procured influence. From time to time synods were gathered for both religious and social purposes.[177]

Each recognized congregation possessed wide sovereignty, which permitted it to adjudicate litigation between its members. This right was accorded to Jewish congregations by pagan Rome, even after the destruction of the Second Jewish Commonwealth. In fact, the Roman authorities often executed sentences imposed by the courts of the Jewish communities. Major crimes, however, such as those calling for capital punishment, were handled exclusively by Roman authorities. They felt that such violations of law threatened public order and Roman rule, requiring these matters to be handled directly by Roman authorities. The Jewish communities (as was the case with other recognized communities) were also authorized to tax their members. The powers of the Jewish communities were so great that they were accused, from time to time, of having been granted more autonomy than other communities.[178]

When the Roman Empire became Christian, following the reign of Constantine (*circa* 395 C.E.), the powers of its Jewish communities were severely curtailed. This was due both to intense anti-Jewish feelings which prevailed, and in order to discourage inhabitants of the Roman Empire from converting to Judaism, which was still regarded, at that time, as a serious threat to Christian supremacy. Nevertheless, synagogues were still protected from seizure and destruction by mobs or Christian clerics.[179] Jews could still bring their civil litigation to Jewish decision-makers, who would act as arbiters. Their decisions could be referred to provincial Roman judges for enforcement. It may be that the right of enforcement was even greater than was usually accorded to arbiters.[180]

Among the powers vested in Jewish communities in the various provinces of the Roman Empire, particularly in Palestine, was the right to fix prices and supervise the markets, including the accuracy of the weights and measures utilized.[181] The purchaser was entitled to a refund if the overcharge (termed *Ona'a*) exceeded one-sixth of the value. In the communities in Babylonia, these regulations extended to hours of work and the protection of creditors and weaker members of the community.[182]

c. Lay Communal Decision-Making in Roman Palestine

In Palestine, as in the rest of the Roman Empire, each Jewish community was governed by a council,

Rashba, vol. 3, nos. 411; 417; vol. 1, no. 709; vol. 7, no. 490; vol. 4, no. 142, Isaac b. Sheshet, Responsa *Rivash*, no. 399; Israel Isserlin, Responsa *Terumat Hadeshen* (B'nai B'rak, 1971), no. 214, and Tzemah Duran, *Yahin U'Boaz*, vol. 2, no. 20.

174. See Abraham K. Shapiro, *Devar Avraham*, vol. 1, sec. 1, subsec. 7, pp. 59, 66.

175. See Responsa of Rabbenu Gershom, no. 67; Responsa of Yosef Tuv-Alem, in Responsa of *Maharam* of Rothenburg (Lvov ed.), no. 423; Shlomo b. Aderet, Responsa *Rashba*, vol. 1, p. 729; vol. 3, p. 411; Y. Antoli, *Malemed Letalmidim*, p. 71.

176. S. Baron, *The Jewish Community* (Philadelphia, 1942), p. 81.

177. Ibid., p. 90.

178. Ibid., p. 111.

179. See the communication of the Emperor Theodosius I in 393 C.E., which ordered steps to be taken to check the over-zealousness of Christians in despoiling and razing synagogues (ibid., p. 113).

180. See Theodosian Code 2.1.10; see also, Code of Justinian 1.9.8; Baron, *The Jewish Community*, pp. 113, 115.

181. "No one outside the Jewish faith shall fix prices for Jews" (Theodosian Code 16. 8. 10; Decree of Theodosian of 396 C.E.; Code of Justinian 1. 9. 9).

182. Jerusalem Talmud, *Baba Batra*, Mishnah V, 15a and b, 89a; also *Baba Metzia* 41a.

traditionally consisting of seven males, called the "best men,"[183] or *hever ha'iyer*,[184] unlike the Greek *polis*, which usually had several hundred men sitting in its ruling council. All Jewish residents who had resided in the community for at least twelve months were members, and rules were formulated with regard to those with shorter term residencies.

There appears to have been continual tension between plutocrats and other members of the ruling classes, on the one hand, and the rabbi-scholars (who, at that time, came from all social and economic classes, and plied various crafts), as to who should be the ultimate authority in governing the community.[185] Partly, in an attempt to gain the upper hand, the rabbis promulgated a prescription that no town ordinance could be valid without the consent of the leading scholar-decision-maker of the town.[186]

In order to foster the study of the Torah, and to prevent its commercialization by paid officials, the rabbi-scholars favored exemption from taxes of scholars who devoted the major part of their time to the study of the Torah.[187] "According to a usage still persisting in Judea, not only among us, but also among the Hebrews, those who meditate day and night on the Law of the Lord, and have no portion in this earth, except God alone, are maintained by the services of the synagogues and the rest of the world. This is done out of a sense of justice, lest some people live in well-being and others in care; but (instead) that the superfluity of the former should alleviate the misery of the latter."[188]

C. *Documentary Studies in Criminal Law*

1. GENERAL ATTITUDES: THE SANCTITY AND DIGNITY OF LIFE

a. LAWS CONCERNING A MURDERER AND THE PRESERVATION OF LIFE
(By Moshe ben Maimon)*

Chapter 1

1. If one slays a human being, he transgresses a negative commandment, for Scripture says, *Thou shalt not murder* (Exod. 20:13). If one murders willfully in the presence of witnesses, he is put to death by the sword, for when Scripture says, *He shall surely be punished* (Exod. 21:20), we have learned from tradition that this means death by the sword. Whether one slays another with an iron weapon or burns him in fire, he is put to death by the sword.

2. The redeemer of blood is commanded to slay the murderer, for Scripture says, *The redeemer of blood shall himself put the murderer to death* (Num. 35:19). Whoever is eligible to inherit from another is deemed the redeemer of blood. If the redeemer of blood is unwilling or unable to put the murderer to death, or if the victim has no redeemer of blood, the court must put the murderer to death by the sword.

3. If a father kills his son, the rule is as follows: If the murdered son has a son of his own, the latter must slay his own grandfather, because he is the redeemer; but if there is no son, none of the brothers may become the redeemer of blood with the duty of killing his father, rather the court must put him to death. The law of the redeemer of blood applies to men and to women alike.

4. The court is warned against accepting ransom from a murderer, even if he offers all the money in the world and even if the redeemer of blood agrees to let him go free. For the life of the murdered person is not the property of the redeemer of blood but the property of God, and Scripture says, *Moreover ye shall take no ransom for the life of a murderer* (Num. 35:31). There is no offense about which the Law is so strict as it is about bloodshed, as it is said, *So shall ye not pollute the land wherein ye are; for blood, it polluteth the land . . .* (Num. 35:33).

5. If a murderer kills willfully, he may not be put to death by the witnesses or the spectators before he is brought to court and condemned to death, for Scripture says, *That the manslayer die not until he stand before the congregation for judgment* (Num. 35:12). The same rule applies to anyone who is liable for death at the hands of the court because he has transgressed and committed a crime. He may not be put to death until he is sentenced by the court.

6. The above rule applies when the offender has already transgressed and committed the crime for which he is liable for the death penalty at the hands of the court. But if one person is pursuing another with the intention of killing him, even if the pursuer is a minor, it is the duty of every Israelite to save the pursued, even at the cost of the pursuer's life.

7. Thus, if one has been warned but still pursues the other person, he may be killed even if he does not accept the warning, seeing that he continues to pursue. If it is possible to rescue the pursued at the cost of one of the pursuer's limbs, such as by striking him with an arrow or a stone or a sword and cutting off his hand or breaking his leg or blinding his eye, this should be done. If, however, it is impossible to judge exactly and

183. See Josephus, *Wars of the Jews* II, 20; V, 70.

184. Mishnah, *Megillah* 1:3; see *Baba Batra* 8b.

185. See, in general Buechler, *The Political and Social Leaders of the Jewish Community of Sepphoris in the Second and Third Centuries* (London, 1909).

186. Talmud, *Baba Batra* 8b.

187. Ibid.

188. Saint Jerome, *circa* 406 C.E., *Adversus Vigmataxitium* 13 at end, and *Adversus Juvinal Annum* 1, 25; A. Migne, *Patrologia Latina*, vol. 23, pp. 246, 350.

*The translation is from the Yale Judaica Series, trans. H. Klein (New Haven, 1954).

the pursued can be rescued only if the pursuer is killed, he may be killed even though he has not yet killed anyone, for Scripture says, *Then thou shalt cut off her hand, thine eye shall have no pity* (Deut. 25:12).

8. Concerning this rule there is no difference either between the private parts (cf. Deut. 25:11) and any other part of the body (injury to which) may endanger one's life, or between a man and a woman. The intent of the above scriptural passage is that if one intends to deal another a death-blow, the pursued should be saved at the cost of the pursuer's hand. If this is impossible, he must be saved even at the cost of the pursuer's life, for Scripture says, *Thine eye shall have no pity* (*ibid.*). . . .

10. The rule is the same whether one is pursuing another to kill him, or whether he is pursuing a betrothed girl to ravish her. For Scripture says, *For as when a man ariseth against his neighbor and slayeth him, even so is this matter* (Deut. 22:26), and says further, *The betrothed damsel cried and there was none to save her* (ibid., 22:27), intimating that if there is someone to save her, he should save her by any possible method, even by killing the pursuer.

11. The same rule applies to all other forbidden sexual contacts, apart from offenses with animals. In the case of homosexuality, however, the one pursued should be saved (even) at the cost of the pursuer's life, as is the rule concerning all other sexual offenses.

If, however, one pursues an animal to lie with it, or is bent on doing prohibited work on the Sabbath, or on committing an act of idolatry—although the laws concerning the Sabbath and those concerning idolatry involve basic principles in the religion of Israel—he may not be killed until he has committed the transgression, whereupon he must be brought to court and duly tried and then put to death.

12. If one pursues a woman forbidden to him, seizes her, lies down with her, and commences coition, he may not be killed until after his trial, even though he has not completed the act. If one is pursuing a woman forbidden to him, and others are pursuing him to save her, and she says to them, "Let him alone so that he will not kill me," they may not grant her request but should confound him and prevent him from coition by injuring his limbs, or, if they cannot do this at the cost of his limbs, then even at the cost of his life, as we have explained.

13. If one is able to save the victim at the cost of only a limb of the pursuer, and does not take the trouble to do so, but saves the victim at the cost of the pursuer's life by killing him, he is deemed a shedder of blood, and he deserves to be put to death. He may not, however, be put to death by the court.

14. If one person is able to save another and does not save him, he transgresses the commandment, *Neither shalt thou stand idly by the blood of thy neighbor* (Lev. 19:16). Similarly, if one person sees another drowning in the sea, or being attacked by bandits, or being attacked by wild animals, and although able to rescue him either alone or by hiring others, does not rescue him; or if one hears heathen or informers plotting evil against another or laying a trap for him and he does not call it to the other's attention and let him know; or if one knows that a heathen or a violent person is going to attack another and although able to appease him on behalf of the other and make him change his mind, he does not do so; or if one acts in any similar way—he transgresses in each case the injunction, *Neither shalt thou stand idly by the blood of thy neighbor* (*ibid.*).

15. If one sees someone pursuing another in order to kill him, or sees someone pursuing a woman forbidden to him in order to ravish her, and although able to save them does not do so, he thereby disregards the positive commandment, *Then thou shalt cut off her hand* (Deut. 25:12), and transgresses two negative commandments, *Thine eye shall have no pity* (*ibid.*), and *Neither shalt thou stand idly by the blood of thy neighbor* (Lev. 19:16).

16. Although there is no flogging for these prohibitions, because breach of them involves no action, the offense is most serious, for if one destroys the life of a single Israelite, it is regarded as though he destroyed the whole world, and if one preserves the life of a single Israelite, it is regarded as though he preserved the whole world.

Chapter 2

1. If one person kills another himself, such as by striking him with a sword or with a deadly stone, or by strangling him, or by thrusting him into a fire, he must be put to death by the court, seeing that he himself killed another in some manner.

2. If, however, one hires an assassin to kill another, or sends his slaves to kill him, or ties another up and leaves him in front of a lion or another animal and the animal kills him, and, similarly, if one commits suicide, the rule in each of these cases is that he is a shedder of blood, has committed the crime of murder, and is liable for death at the hand of Heaven; but there is no capital punishment at the hands of the court.

3. How do we know that this is the rule? Because Scripture says, *Whoso sheddeth man's blood by man shall his blood be shed* (Gen. 9:6), referring to one who commits the murder himself and not through an agent; *And surely your blood of your lives will I de-*

mand (Gen. 9:5), referring to suicide; *At the hand of every beast will I demand it* (*ibid.*), referring to one who places another before a wild animal for it to devour; *And at the hand of man, even at the hand of every man's brother, will I demand the life of man* (*ibid.*), referring to one who hires others to kill someone. In these last three cases, the verb *demand* is explicitly used to show that the judgment is reserved for Heaven.

4. Regarding any of these or similar murderers who are not subject to being condemned to die by verdict of the court, if a king of Israel wishes to put them to death by royal decree for the benefit of society, he has a right to do so. Similarly, if the court deems it proper to put them to death as an emergency measure, it has the authority to do as it deems fit, provided that circumstances warrant such action.

5. If the king does not kill them, and the needs of the time do not demand their death as a preventive measure, it is nevertheless the duty of the court to flog them almost to the point of death, to imprison them in a fortress or a prison for many years, and to inflict severe punishment on them in order to frighten and terrify other wicked persons, lest such a case become a pitfall and a snare, enticing one to say, "I will arrange to kill my enemy in a roundabout way, as did So-and-So; then I will be acquitted."

6. Whether one kills an adult or a day-old child, a male or a female, he must be put to death if he kills deliberately or exiled if he slays inadvertently, provided that the child is born after a full-time pregnancy. But if it is born before the end of nine months, it is regarded as a miscarriage until it has lived for thirty days, and if one kills it during the period of thirty days, he may not be put to death on its account.

7. Whether one kills a healthy person or a dying invalid or even a person in his death throes, he must be put to death on this account. But if the death throes are humanly caused, for example, if one who has been beaten to the point of death is in his throes, the court may not put his slayer to death.

8. If one kills another who suffers from a fatal organic disease, he is legally exempt even though the victim ate and drank and walked the streets. But every human being is presumed to be healthy, and his murderer must be put to death unless it is known for certain that he had a fatal organic defect and physicians say that his disease is incurable by human agency and that he would have died of it even if he had not been killed in other ways.

9. If such an organically defective individual kills a person, he must be put to death, for Scripture says, *So shalt thou put away the evil from the midst of thee* (Deut. 19:19), provided that he kills in the presence of a court. However, if he kills before witnesses, he is exempt, for the witnesses might possibly be proved to be conspirators, in which case they could not be put to death since they would have plotted to kill someone afflicted with a fatal organic disease. Now evidence that cannot possibly be subject to the law concerning conspiracy is not deemed valid in capital cases.

10. Whether one kills an Israelite or a Canaanite slave, he must be put to death on his account, or—if he slays inadvertently—he must go into exile.

11. If an Israelite kills a resident alien, he does not suffer capital punishment at the hands of the court, because Scripture says, *And if a man come presumptuously upon his neighbor* (Exod. 21:12). Needless to say, one is not put to death if he kills a heathen. Whether one kill's another's slave or his own, he must be put to death on the slave's account, seeing that a slave has taken upon himself the yoke of the commandments and is added to God's people.

12. The difference between one's own slave and another's slave is that one has the right to flog his own slave. Consequently, if one deals his slave blows sufficient to kill him, and the slave is dying but lives for twenty-four hours and then dies, he should not be put to death on the slave's account even though the latter dies as a result of the flogging. For Scripture says, *He shall not be punished for he is his property* (Exod. 21:21). By *a day or two* in the same verse is meant a day that is like two, namely, twenty-four hours.

13. But if one strikes a slave not his own, then since he has dealt the slave a blow sufficient to kill him he is condemned to die on the slave's account as he would be in the case of a freeman, even if the slave dies as a result of the blow several days later.

14. In my opinion, if one strikes his slave with a knife or a sword or a stone or his fist or in any similar manner, and the slave's injuries are declared to be fatal and he does die, the law of survival for *a day or two* does not apply; rather the master must be put to death on his slave's account even if the slave dies after a year. For Scripture says, *With a rod* (Exod. 21:20), because the Law grants his authority merely to strike his slave with a rod or a stick or a strap or the like, but not to deal him murderous blows.

Notes and Questions to Moshe ben Maimon,
"Laws Concerning a Murderer and the
Preservation of Life"

Chapter 1

Rambam's Code of Laws (formulated in twelfth-century Egypt) represented the most thorough and systematic attempt that had ever been made to summarize talmudic norms, principles, and rationales. It is a classic work, drafted with extraordinary care and precision, and it has engendered more commentaries than any other single work, with the exception of the Talmud itself. Although composed in the Middle Ages, it reliably reproduced in succinct fashion the perspectives and practices of the Talmudic Era. Its wording and ordering of norms should be scrutinized with care.

1. *Rule 2*

(*a*) "The Redeemer of Blood is obligated to kill the slayer . . ." This reflects the feelings of clan kinship in which each person is to concern himself with the welfare of his relatives. This perspective is not confined to homicide. A similar attitude is reflected in the biblical provisions[189] that relatives were obligated to redeem one whose poverty had forced him to sell himself as a slave and to redeem ancestral lands sold because of impecunity.[190] The practice apparently arose to attempt to ensure that no one would be completely isolated in society, exposed to physical harm by an enemy or to dire poverty. The accidental slayer was required to flee to one of the many cities of refuge (see Num. 35). The ratios for this were atonement, to avoid feuds with him by the victim's relatives, to save the slayer from being killed by them, and to penalize him for his negligence.[191]

The practice of "redeeming blood" of a murder victim is a very ancient one in human society. Remnants of the practice are still found today among some of the tribes of Arabia, and the memories of this are preserved in portions of Southern Europe, especially the Balkans (see Robertson-Smith, cited above, particularly the preface and ch. 2).

This institutional practice commonly involved killing the murderer as well as members of his family or clan. The Bible attempted to severely restrict this institution by limiting the punishment to the murderer (thereby insulating his family),[192] by requiring a court trial for the one accused of murder,[193] and by providing cities of refuge for accidental murderers.[194]

Echos of the institutional practice of "redeeming blood," may also be found in the Bible in the vengeance

of Gideon upon the murderers of his brothers,[195] the slaying of Abner by Joab in revenge for the murder of his brother,[196] and Absalom's killing of Amnon for raping Tamar, his sister.[197] The practice is referred to, specifically, in a tale related to David.[198]

This institutional practice is alluded to in other ancient Near Eastern sources. In Ugaritic mythology Anath avenges her brother Baal, and Pa'at attempts vengeance for the slaying of her brother Akhat. Some have claimed it to be echoed in the Code of Hammurabi[199] and in the Assyrian Code,[200] which grant the husband or other relative the right to decide whether or not a malefactor should be put to death.[201]

The institutionalized killing of manslayers by relatives of the victims appears to have become non-existent by the time of the Second Jewish Commonwealth. It has been speculated that the institution disappeared when the central state authority became strong enough to prosecute all cases of murder, doing away with the necessity of action by relatives of the victims.[202]

Nevertheless, some talmudic authorities have asserted that the institution of "redeeming blood" continued in the post-Talmudic Era.[203]

(*b*) How would you reconcile the provision here for the killing of the manslayer by the relatives of the victim with the provisions of rule 5, below, that a slayer may not be killed until he has been tried and found guilty by a court? The talmudic perspective, codified

189. Lev. 25:47:54.
190. Lev. 25:25–28.
191. See Halevi, *Ha'Hinuh* (reprinted Jerusalem, 1958), no. 410; Y. Z. Yaskowitz, *Amvuha De'Sifri* (reprinted Jerusalem, 1967); Num., ch. 35; Y. Kopperman, *Arey Miklat* (Jerusalem, 1972).
192. "Fathers shall not be killed for sons and sons shall not be killed for fathers. Each man shall be killed for his own sins" (Deut. 24:16).
193. Num. 35:12.
194. Num. 35:11–15; Deut. 19:7–10.

195. Judg. 5:18–21.
196. 2 Sam. 3:26–27.
197. 2 Sam. 13:23.
198. 2 Sam. 14:6.
199. Sec. 129.
200. Tablet 1, secs. 10 and 15; tablet 2, sec. 2.
201. See also W. Robinson–Smith, *Religion of the Semites* (London, 1889), pp. 112, 272, 417, 420; and idem., *Kinship and Marriage in Early Arabia* (reprinted Boston, 1970), particularly the pref., p. 25 ff., and ch. 2.
202. R. Jackson, "Evolution and Foreign Influence in Ancient Law," *American Journal of Comparative Law* 16 (1968): 386.
203. See Moshe b. Nahman (Ramban), Commentary to *Sefer Ha'Mitzvot* of Rambam, no. 13; Y. Perlow, Commentary to *Sefer Ha'Mitzvot* of Saadya Gaon (reprinted Jerusalem, 1973), negative commandment 274; R. Yeruham, *Misharim* (Venice, 1553), at the end of his *Netivim*, 32:3, expresses the view that certain aspects of the institution should continue to apply today. Note the view of Eibschutz (*Urim, Hoshen Mishpat*, sec. 2), that every person is potentially a "redeemer of blood" (this follows from the Talmud, *Makkot* 12, that every person may kill a murderer where the court is physically unable to do so) but that, except for extraordinary circumstances, the principle of "redeeming blood" does not apply today. *Contra* A. Shein, *Ketzot Ha'Hoshen*, sec. 2 ad loc.; Bachrach, Responsa *Havat Yair* (reprinted Jerusalem, 1973), no. 146; Y. Trunk, *Yeshuat Yisrael* (reprinted New York, 1948), *H.M.*, no. 2. See also Rambam, Laws of Sanhedrin 4:8. The foregoing views are based upon these scholars' understanding of the Talmud's tradition regarding this matter, rather than upon extra-talmudic historical sources.

here by Rambam, is that the institution of the "redeemer of blood" was not a form of legalized lynching by relatives but was, rather, the utilization of relatives as official executioners by the court, *after* it had tried and found the slayer guilty.[204] *Rambam*, accordingly, provides at the end of rule 2, that if the "redeemer of blood" was unable or unwilling to perform the execution, the court would then appoint someone else.

(*c*) Although a number of the biblical passages referring to the "redeemer of blood" appear in the context of the killing of an *accidental* murderer by relatives of the victim, Rambam here cites the passage in Numbers ("The redeemer of blood shall be the one to kill the murderer"), which appears in the context of *deliberate* murder. This supports his conclusion that the institution of the "redeemer of blood" was utilized in cases of intentional murder, as well as in cases of accidental murder.[205]

2. Rule 4

Note that the rationale of Rambam for this rule is that the life of the victim belongs to God, not to the relatives or to the "redeemer of blood." Contrast this with the interpretation of this norm by Moshe Greenberg (Part One, Chapter III, Section B 4), that the rationale for this rule is that human life and money or property are not to be equated. Would *Rambam*'s rationale permit the inference that human life and property could sometimes be equated?[206]

3. Rule 5

Notice the broad sweep of the prohibition against the taking of human life, except by court order, following a trial (see, however, note 4, below).

Can a trial be held with the defendant *in absentia*? Notice the phraseology, "before he is brought to court and condemned to death," which indicates an absolute ban on such trials.

4. Rules 6 and 7: The Rodef (Pursuer)

(*a*) Rambam's reliance on the biblical verse, "You shall cut off her hand. Do not have mercy" (Deut. 25:12) as asserting a right and obligation to kill a *rodef* (apparently based on the interpretation of this verse in *Sifri*, ad loc.) may be predicated on the following: The biblical command "And you shall cut off her hand" is phrased in the second person singular rather than in the third person plural (i.e., "*They* shall cut off her hand"), unlike other commandments, such as Deut. 25:1–3 and 24:16). This may indicate that the verse is directed at *any* person who happens to be a bystander and is not addressed solely to the court. Furthermore, since the verse was understood in the Talmud to require payment of money by her for the injuries that she caused, and not to require a literal *lex talionis*,[207] it would merely duplicate the similar norm in Exod. 21:19, unless it also served to set forth the *rodef* norm.

The reason for this extreme biblical command is that the woman in the biblical verse at issue had overreacted and had unjustifiably seized the genitals of the man with whom her husband was quarreling, thus endangering his life.[208] The verse, accordingly, sets forth by way of concrete example (the common mode of expression in the Bible and all of the ancient Near East) the principle that every bystander is obligated to act against an assailant to save the life of a person in danger, even if this requires injuring the assailant. The additional biblical phrase, "You shall not have mercy," is viewed as justifying rescue actions on behalf of the victim, which are even more extreme than cutting off the hand of the assailant, and authorizes killing the assailant if this is necessary.[209] Although the passages cited by Rambam here (dealing with a threat to life) would not justify killing a *rodef* who was intent upon rape (rather than killing), the Talmud[210] cites other biblical passages justifying actions against the *rodef* in this case, too.

The Talmud[211] does not rely on the biblical verse utilized in the *Sifri*, and cites a number of other verses that require bystanders to come to the assistance of those threatened by a *rodef*.

---

204. See Num. 35:12, 19, 21, 24; Deut. 19:12. Additionally, the "redeemer" may have acted as a citizen-prosecutor, bringing the homicide to the attention of the court for trial, and advancing arguments for conviction. See N. Gerundi, Novellae *Ran* to Sanhedrin 45b; R. Margolis, *Margaliyot Ha'Yam*, 2: 180.

205. See the commentary of Y. Rozanis, *Mishna Le'Meleh* (printed in standard editions of Rambam's code). See Talmud Sanhedrin 45b; Moshe b. Nahman (Ramban), Commentary to *Sefer Ha'Mitzvot*, no. 13.

206. See the biblical verse, "If forgiveness money shall be assessed upon him . . ." (Exod. 21:30; Talmud, *Sanhedrin* 15b; Jackson, "Some Reflections on Biblical Law," Part I, Chapter III, Section 3 *b*, above).

207. *Sifri*, Exod. 21:30.

208. See Rambam, at the beginning of rule 8, and M. Trani, *Kiryat Sefer*, ad loc., citing Talmud, *Baba Kama* 28a. Note the language of the verse, "If men shall quarrel *together, a man and his brother*," indicating lack of a murderous intent by the men. Note also the juxtaposition with the prior case in the Bible which provides, "If brothers shall dwell together" (Deut. 25:5). This is in contrast to identical language in another verse, "If men shall quarrel . . ." (Exod. 21:22) that does not contain the additional phrase, "together a man and his brother." The verse in Exodus is held to refer to a case of murderous intent and accordingly concludes, "You shall give a soul for a soul" (Exod. 21:23). See Meir Ha'Cohen, *Meshehk Hokhma* (Jerusalem, 1946), ad loc.

209. See Rambam at the end of rule 8.

210. *Sanhedrin* 73a.

211. Ibid.

It is interesting to note that Rambam, however, bases the *rodef* principle upon the interpretation in the *Sifri* of the biblical verse "You shall cut off her hand. Do not have mercy," instead of the other verses relied on by the Talmud. Utilization of the verses relied on by the Talmud may result in different legal consequences than are implied by the verse applied by Rambam.[212] The Talmud, too,[213] in citing five different biblical verses as supporting the *rodef* principle, indicates the additional norms implied by each verse.

(*b*) What is the rationale that permits anyone present to kill the assailant and forms a broad exception to rule 5, which prohibits the killing of a slayer unless tried and convicted by a court? The rationale clearly appears to be predicated on the need to save the life of the intended victim, and not to punish the assailant.[214] The *rodef* rule, accordingly, applies even where the assailant lacks *mens rea* and would not have been condemned to death had he been tried by a court. A minor (i.e., non-adult) assailant may therefore also be killed by any bystander.[215]

This rationale also clarifies the reason why the *rodef* norm does not apply if the crime has already been committed.[216] It also explains why the *rodef* principle applies only where the crime is against another person and is not applied to prevent commission of other capital offenses, such as idolatry:[217]

If a person is about to commit a crime, we may prevent it by killing him. Only in two cases is this permitted; viz., when a person runs after another in order to murder him, or in order to commit fornication; because in these two cases, [the offense] once committed, cannot be remedied. In the case of other sins punished with death by the Court of Law, such as idolatry and profanation of the Sabbath, by which the sinner does no harm to another person, and which concern only his own principles, no person may be killed for the mere *intention*, if he has not carried it out [emphasis supplied].[218]

Other scholars maintain[219] that the primary ratio for the *rodef* principle is to save the "soul" of the *rodef* by preventing him from committing the crime.[220]

(*c*) Notice that every bystander, not only the intended victim, is absolutely *required* (not merely permitted) to stop the assailant, even if this means killing him. Compare this with the "Good Samaritan" norms prevalent in American and British Law;[221] also compare the notorious Kitty Genovese case in Queens, New York, in 1965, in which some thirty-eight persons failed to intervene or even to call the police when they heard the screams of a woman who was stalked near an apartment building, repeatedly stabbed over a substantial period of time, and finally killed.[222]

(*d*) Must a bystander risk his life to save another person from an assailant, from robbers, or from drowning? Does the requirement in rule 7 to strike the *rodef* with a sword if feasible (based on, "You shall cut off her hand"), imply that one must approach the *rodef* at close quarters, thereby necessarily incurring some risk? Does the other biblical verse cited by Rambam, "Do not stand by the blood of your brother," also imply this? Rambam's position on this point is not clear. Notice the phraseology in rule 14, in which the examples given of possible ways to save somebody from robbers, all reflect steps which do not indicate any taking of risk, such as calling for help, or notifying the intended victim of the impending attack.[223] Compare:[224]

212. David of Navahrdik, Responsa *Galya Masehet, Y.D.* (Vilna, 1845), sec. 5, pp. 91, 73; Margolis, *Margaliyot Ha'Yam*, p. 79, no. 4.

213. *Sanhedrin* 73a.

214. See Rashi, *Sanhedrin* 72b.

215. See Talmud, *Sanhedrin* 72b.

216. See rule 12, below, and Rambam, Laws of Battery and Damages, ch. 8, rule 11, which is phrased in the context of the *rodef* norm stated in rule 12, immediately thereafter; see commentary of Joseph Karo in *Magid Mishnah* (printed in standard editions of Rambam's code).

217. See rule 11, below; see, however, Ha'Meiri, *Beth Ha'-Behira, Sanhedrin* 72a, p. 268, to the effect that a burglar is treated as a *rodef* and that an attempt should, therefore, be made to kill him with a sword. The prescription for killing a *rodef* with a sword (the form of execution most commonly employed by the court) indicates that the killing of a *rodef* is treated as an execution by a court and implies, perhaps, that he is to be killed as a punishment, rather than simply to save the intended victim. Cf. Margolis, *Margaliyot Ha'Yam*, vol. 2, p. 79, no. 2, and G. Fishman, *Simhat Ha'Hag* (Belgaraya, 1936), sec. 17, attempting to prove a punishment ratio from the requirement of Rambam, that a *rodef* must first be warned; see Rambam, Laws of Murderers, ch. 1, rule 7; and Laws of the Batterer and Damager, ch. 8, rule 10; Landau, Responsa *Noda Be'Yehuda* (reprinted New York, 1955; 2nd ed.), *Hoshen Mishpat*, secs. 9 and 60. The need of forewarning does not, however, prove that the rationale of the *rodef* norm is punishment. The forewarning may simply be needed before taking such a serious step as killing the *rodef*.

218. Rambam, *Guide for the Perplexed*, trans. by Friedlander (reprinted New York, 1956), 3:40, pp. 342–43.

219. See Abulafia, *Yad Ramah*, and *Sanhedrin* 73a.

220. See also Rashi, *Sanhedrin* 72b, and commentary of N. Gerundi (Ran) to 73a; Margolis, *Margaliyot Ha'Yam*, p. 79, no. 1; Rozanis, in *Mishnah Le'Meleh*, Laws of the Sabbath, ch. 24, rule 7; Landau, Responsa *Noda Be'Yehuda* (2nd ed.), *Hoshen Mishpat*, no. 60; Azulai, *Mahzik Beraha, O.H.* (Livorno, 1795), no. 339, sec. 5. See the explanation of Halevi, *Hinuh*, commandment 601 for the rule of *rodef*, and the Rambam, *Sefer Ha'Mitzvot*, negative commandment no. 293.

221. See J. M. Ratcliffe, ed., *The Good Samaritan and the Law* (New York, 1965).

222. See *New York Times*, 12 March 1965, pp. 35, 37. See A. Rosenthal, *Thirty-Eight Witnesses* (New York, 1965).

223. J. Karo, in *Kesef Mishnah*, to Rambam, rule 14, cites the Jerusalem Talmud that one is required to take action against a *rodef*, even if this involves *some* risk, but not if the risk is substantial. These terms are of course incapable of pre-

You have asked me . . . if the ruler told a Jew, let me cut off one of your organs (which would not be fatal), or else I will kill some other Jew. Some say that he must let them cut off his organ . . . [In my opinion] This is unlike the Sabbath [which one may not violate to save an endangered organ, although one may violate the Sabbath to save a life], since there the misfortune arises from heaven. . . . But that one should bring a misfortune upon himself for his companion's sake, we have never heard this. Additionally, perhaps by cutting off his organ, even though it is not a vital one, he may lose a lot of blood and die . . . and if there is a doubt [about this and he does sacrifice his organ], he is a pious fool, because a doubt concerning him is better than a certainty concerning his companion.

His conclusion is, therefore, that one is not required to have his organ cut off, to save the life of his companion.[225] Is there a difference between this case and that of the *rodef*? Is it significant that in the case of a *rodef* one acts against a wrongdoer, not against himself, and that the harm to the rescuer is not inevitable?

(*e*) A variant of the *rodef* theory is applied in the case of a burglar. The biblical passage regarding the slaying of a burglar[226] states literally that "he has no blood." This is commonly understood as, "There shall be no blood *guilt*."[227] The Talmud, however, interprets the phrase quite differently. It views the text as meaning that the burglar is regarded as if he had no blood, that is, as if he were no longer a living person. (The "he" in the verse would therefore refer to the burglar, not to the slayer). This leads the Talmud to the con-

clusion that the householder (or any bystander) may *initially* slay the burglar, who is no longer regarded (for this purpose) as a living human being. The Jewish Publication Society translation would simply imply that if the burglar was in fact slain, the slayer could not be penalized after the fact. This, however, is far from implying that anyone had the right to slay the burglar.[228]

The Talmud,[229] in discussing the reasons why a burglar may be slain, says, "It is understood that a person would not quietly stand by while his money is being taken. The thief, accordingly, thinks 'If I go to his house, he will stand and oppose me (to prevent the burglary) and if he does oppose me, I will kill him.' " The ratio for this norm, then, is that the burglar is a potential *rodef* because of the substantial possibility that he will be discovered by the householder (or bystander), who (in the talmudic view) is certain to resist and may be killed in the process.

According to the talmudic interpretation, then, the Bible explicitly condones slaying an assailant in the case of a burglar-*rodef*.[230] Why, therefore, does Rambam (rule 7) rely instead on the passage, "You shall cut off her hand. Do not have mercy," which does not, on its face, clearly deal with a *rodef* situation?

Rambam's reasoning appears to be that the killing of the burglar is only justified, (that is, relieves the slayer of liability) but is not required. The option always exists to permit him to accomplish his burglary and leave. The verses in Exodus are therefore limited to *permitting* the householder, or any bystander, to slay the burglar (Note the phraseology of the verse, "And he shall be smitten," that is, if it turned out that the burglar was in fact slain by the householder or by anyone else).[231] By contrast, however, the imperative verse relied on by Rambam, "And you shall cut off her hand. Do not have mercy," imposes an *obligation*, to take action against the assailant, and to kill him, if necessary, in order to save the life of the intended victim.[232]

(*f*) Why is it that a burglar *may* be killed, while there is an absolute *obligation* to act against a *rodef*

cise definition. See Karo, in *Beth Yosef, Hoshen Mishpat,* sec. 426, and S. Cohen in *Sifse Cohen,* ad loc.; Talmud, *Ketubot* 61b; see also Margolis, *Margaliyot Ha'Yam,* no. 9; David b. Zimra, Responsa *Radvaz* (reprinted New York, 1967), vol. 2, no. 218; Rambam, *Sefer Ha'Mitzvot,* negative commandment no. 297 and positive commandment no. 247; and Aharon Alfandri *Markevet Ha'Mishnah* (Izmir, 1755), commentary to Laws Concerning a Murderer, ch. 1, rule 7.

224. David B. Zimra (*circa* 1550) Responsa *Radvaz,* vol. 3, no. 627, p. 126. See also regarding the issue of whether one may save one's own life by means of destroying another's property, in Talmud, *Baba Kama* 60b; Rambam, Laws Concerning a Batterer, ch. 8:4, and commentary ad loc. of Abraham b. David (Ra'avad); Rosanis, *Perashat Derachim* (Warsaw, 1871), ch. 19, p. 156; Talmud, *Ketubot* 19b.

225. Cf. M. Simha in *Ohr Sameah,* Laws Concerning a Murderer, ch. 7, rule 8, who cited *Radvaz* as holding to the contrary. For a thorough discussion of this and other aspects of the Good Samaritan problem, see A. Kirschenbaum, *The "Good Samaritan" and Jewish Law,* Dinet Israel (Tel-Aviv, 1976), p. 7.

226. Exod. 22:1: "If the thief is discovered in the tunnel and is killed, he has no blood."

227. See, e.g., Shmuel b. Meir in his commentary *Rashbam,* ad loc., and the translation by the Jewish Publication Society, which interprets the "he" in the phrase "He has no blood" in the original Hebrew text as referring to the *slayer.*

228. See Talmud, *Sanhedrin* 72a, and Rashi's commentary, printed in standard editions of the Talmud, ad loc.

229. Ibid.

230. Talmud *Sanhedrin* 72a, interpreting the biblical verse as meaning, "If the thief is found in the tunnel, is smitten and dies, he has no blood" (Exod. 22:1).

231. See also Rashi's commentary to *Sanhedrin* 72a, indicating that in the case of the burglar one only has the right to kill him, but not the obligation.

232. See also the passage cited by the Talmud, *Sanhedrin* 73a, regarding a betrothed woman who is raped, ". . . and no one helped her," which, according to the Talmud, indicates that there is a positive obligation to take premeditated action against her assailant. See Margolis, *Margaliyot Ha'Yam,* p. 74, no. 7.

and to kill him, if necessary. It is likely that the burglar is treated more lightly since his primary intention is to burglarize, not to kill, whereas the *rodef* intends to kill. Furthermore, the burglar is regarded by the Talmud as intending to kill only if attacked by the householder (or bystander), who may attempt to kill the burglar. As a result, the burglar would then, in a sense, be the intended "victim" of a householder—a *rodef*.[233] The different treatment accorded to the burglar and the *rodef* is also implied by the passive phraseology in the Bible dealing with the burglar (Exod. 22:1), "And he *is smitten* and dies," indicating no obligation to slay him. This should be contrasted with the imperative language interpreted to apply to a *rodef* who intends to kill—"You *shall* cut off her hand. Do not have mercy"—relied on by Rambam.[234]

The *rodef* principle expounded by Rambam here illustrates the painstaking care with which talmudic scholars scrutinized every word of the Bible. Each of the many biblical terms and verses cited in the Talmud relating to the case of a *rodef* was understood as having a precise meaning. Great differences in applying the *rodef* principle would, accordingly, result from reliance upon one, rather than another, biblical verse.

(*g*) If a bystander attempts to kill a *rodef*, who then kills the bystander, is this killing punishable? Is the *rodef* now regarded as the intended "victim" of the bystander, and is the bystander now regarded as a *rodef*, who may be killed by his intended victim? Y. Rozanes is of the opinion that the bystander-rescuer, who is obligated to take action against the *rodef*, cannot himself be regarded as a *rodef* who may be killed. Accordingly, if the bystander-rescuer is killed by the *rodef*, the *rodef*'s action is punishable as murder.[235]

What if a householder or bystander attempts to slay a burglar (pursuant to Exod. 22:1) and the burglar, in self-defense, slays the householder? Does the same result follow? Here, as indicated above note 1(*e*) the householder is not under an obligation to kill the burglar but is merely entitled to do so. Can the burglar, then, be regarded as the intended "victim" and the householder be regarded as transformed into a *rodef*? Similar reasoning was utilized in the Talmud[236] regarding another case in which there was a right, but not an obligation, to kill.

(*h*) Must the intended victim of a burglary, or of a *rodef* intent on slaying, wait until "pressed to the wall" before killing his assailant or burglar? Must he first attempt to escape, if necessary, or permit the burglar to successfully carry out his intentions? This is the predominant rule in American and English Law.[237] The talmudic statement[238] regarding a burglar is, "The Torah said, 'If one comes to kill you, arise to kill him.' " The term "arise" implies not only that the householder may, with premeditation, slay the burglar[239] but also that he may "arise" (that is, go forward), to meet the burglar and slay him without waiting for the burglar to attempt to kill him.[240]

Ha'Meiri[241] applies the *rodef* concept to justify an attack against an entire nation, resulting in the probable death of many persons who do not individually have any *mens rea*. What is the modern justification for war by a democratic state, which may also cause thousands of innocent people to suffer or die?

5. *Rule 7*

(*a*) Rambam here formulates the rule that the *rodef* must be forewarned before being killed.[242] Y. Rozanis[243] asserts that the intended victim himself (since he is distraught by the impending attack, and is the one most concerned with saving his life), need not forewarn the attacker before killing him. In the case of a burglar, however, it has been maintained that neither a householder nor bystander needs to forewarn the burglar before killing him.[244]

(*b*) So, too, the intended victim is not required to take the care necessary to wound the attacker instead of killing him, although a bystander is required to exercise this care.[245]

233. See the commentary of N. Gerdundi (Ran) to Talmud, *Sanhedrin* 73a; also Hayim Al'Gazi, *B'Ne Haya* (Urta, Kyuva, 1712), *Sanhedrin*, ad loc.

234. See Y. Etlinger, *Aruh Le'Ner* (Altona, 1850), *Sanhedrin* 72b.

235. See his *Mishnah Le'Meleh* (printed in standard editions of Rambam's Code of Laws) to rule 15, herein.

236. *Sanhedrin* 82a; see also D. Frankel, commentary *Shiyure Karban* to Jerusalem Talmud, *Kiddushin*, ch. 8, rule 9; and Margolis, *Margaliyot Ha'Yam*, vol. 2, p. 79, no. 2 (printed in standard editions of the Jerusalem Talmud).

237. See W. Prosser, *Law of Torts* (3rd ed.; St. Paul, 1964), p. 112.

238. *Sanhedrin* 72a and b.

239. See Rashi, *Sanhedrin* 72b, and Rambam, "Every one has the right to kill him . . . ," in Laws of Theft, 9:7.

240. See Ha'Meiri, *Beth Ha'Behira*, who cites the talmudic *Midrash Tanhuma*, which interprets Num. 25:17, "Trouble the Midianites, *because* they (will) trouble you . . ." as authorizing a preemptive attack on the Midianites in order to head off an expected assault. According to M'eiri, this is the biblical source for the talmudic statement permitting a householder to initiate aggressive action against a potential attacker; see Margolis, *Margaliyot Ha'Yam*, p. 78, no. 10.

241. Ibid.

242. See Laws of the Sanhedrin, ch. 12, rule 2.

243. In his *Mishnah Le'Meleh*, Laws of the Batterer and Damager, ch. 8:10.

244. See, e.g., N. Z. Y. Berlin, in *Merome Sadeh* (Jerusalem, 1965), *Yoma* 85, asserting that the meaning of the phrase "arise to kill him" (Talmud, *Sanhedrin* 72a, regarding a burglar) indicates that the householder may kill him without forewarning.

245. Rozanis, *Mishnah Le'Meleh*, Laws of the Batterer and Damager 8:10; see Rambam, rule 7: ". . . at the cost of one of the pursuer's limbs . . ."; see also Isaac b. Sheshet, Responsa

See, however, the case of Abner,[246] who killed (instead of wounding) his pursuer. The Talmud[247] maintains that Solomon agreed that Joab was justified in killing Abner for this (see Section C, 2, below).

In the case of a burglar there seems to be a consensus that no attempt need be made to wound him instead of killing him.

(*c*) Furthermore, the rule permitting killing of a burglar indicates that he may be killed, even if there is doubt as to whether or not he would kill anyone who stood in his way.[248]

Since there is always some doubt as to whether a burglar will be discovered and would thereupon kill anyone who resists him, the burglar exemplar in the Bible has been held to indicate that an intended victim (or perhaps even a bystander) may similarly kill a non-burglar *rodef*, even if there is doubt as to whether or not the *rodef* would kill him. The intended victim need not wait until he is certain.[249]

Why the greater permissiveness in killing a burglar (who, after all, is only a potential *rodef*) than in killing an actual *rodef*, who now intends to kill?

6. *Rule 12*

(*a*) When the intended victim of a rape, fearful for her life, implores her would-be rescuers to desist, why are her wishes to be ignored? Is this position consistent with traditional Jewish law and morality? (See the Talmud[250] regarding the controversy in this matter between Rabbi Judah and his colleagues). Some scholars maintain that all are agreed that it is the desires of the hostage that should determine the issue.[251] The conflict

in the Talmud, however, revolves around the issue of whether the hostage desires most of all to survive, even if this means being raped, or whether she would really rather die, despite her statements brought out by hysteria.

Does the same rationale and morality apply to a hostage who is not being held for rape, but only until the demands of the captor are met? What about a captive's request not to attempt his rescue where this inaction might encourage subsequent attempts by others to take hostages?

(*b*) With regard to the sacrifice of one (or a few) person(s) in order to save many, there is a biblical precedent in the handing over of Sheva ben Bichri to his pursuers for execution in order to save the other people of the city from death.[252] Talmudic decision-makers have held this up as a model to be followed.[253] Consider the spate of airline high-jackings in recent years and the holding of children and other innocents as hostages at Ma'alot, Israel and elsewhere. The Israeli government has always taken the position that the captors should be attacked, captured, or killed in order to deter hostage-taking in the future, without regard to the desires of the captives. Is this position consistent with traditional Jewish law and morality?

7. *Rule 13*

The rule here that the slayer of a *rodef* is not liable to a sanction if the *rodef* could have been stopped by a mere wounding is based on the Talmud.[254] See Section C, 2, below for the talmudic elaboration of the discussion between Joab and Abner, regarding the latter's slaying of Joab's brother, who had attempted to slay Abner, and the subsequent discussion between Solomon and Joab as to why the latter had killed Abner in revenge.

8. *Rules 14 and 15*

Why does Rambam state that one who fails to save another, who is drowning or being attacked by robbers, violates the biblical commandment "Do not stand by the blood of your companion," while he states that he who fails to save another from attack by a *rodef* violates this verse as well as the verses, "You shall cut off

Rivash, no. 238; *contra* Rashi, commentary to *Sanhedrin* 57 and 74; see H. Benebashti, *Hamra Ve'Haya* (Livorno, 1802), *Sanhedrin* 72a.

246. 2 Sam. 8:32.

247. *Sanhedrin* 49a.

248. See Y. Babad, *Minhat Hinuh* (Lvov, 1869), commandment 296, who cites the view of Rabbi Ishmael, in Talmud, *Yoma* 85a. The latter derives from the case of the burglar (whose life may be taken to preserve the life of the householder, thus overriding the norm "Thou shalt not kill") the rule that even where there is a *doubt* of a threat to life the Sabbath, too, can be violated in order to preserve life. *Rava,* however, maintains that the case of the burglar involves a *certainty* of murder in the event that the householder resists.

249. See Eliezer Landau, *Yad Ha'Melch* (Levov, 1826) to Rambam, Laws Concerning a Murderer, ch. 1; Schipansky, "Studies in the Law of *Rodef*" (Hebrew), in *Ohr Ha'Mizrah* 20 1971): 15, 20.

250. *Sanhedrin* 73b.

251. See Yehiel Heller, Responsa *Amude Ohr* (Koenigsburg, 1858), sec. 87, no. 12. With regard to a person's right to decide matters concerning his body, including the right to die, compare David ben Zimra, commentary *Radvaz* to Rambam, Laws of the Sanhedrin, 18:6; Talmud, *Baba Kama* 91b; Rambam, Laws Concerning a Murderer, ch. 2, rule 3. In American jurisdictions, the notion of the right to privacy has been ap-

plied to find that one has a right to commit suicide. (See, Griswold v. Connecticut, 85 S. Ct. 1678, 1965; Matter of Quinlan, 355 Atl.2d 647, 1976.)

252. 2 Sam. 20:22. Note also that King David handed over Saul's innocent sons to be killed by the Gibeonites, upon their demand (2 Sam. 21:9). See also Judges 15:13 detailing how the Israelites handed Sampson over to the Phillistines. Talmudic decision-makers do not appear to have criticized this. See Talmud, *Yebamot* 79a.

253. Tosefta, *Terumot,* ch. 7; Jerusalem Talmud, *Terumot,* ch. 7.

254. *Sanhedrin* 74.

her hand. Do not have mercy"? Furthermore, is there any additional norm inferred from the phrase "Do not have mercy" that would not be implied if the Bible had simply provided, "You shall cut off her hand?" Apparently, "You shall not stand by the blood of your companion" is taken to imply simply an obligation to help, such as by throwing a rope to a drowning person, or distracting robbers who are about to attack somebody else, or by calling for help. It does not necessarily authorize wounding or killing an assailant. The verse "Cut off her hand" is taken to imply this additional authorization to wound, and "Do not have mercy" to even kill if necessary. (As to whether a bystander must risk his life, see 4(*d*), above.)[255]

Chapter 2

1. *Rule 2*

The rule here implies that conspiracy is not a crime. This contrasts with the law in other ancient Near Eastern lands.[256] In talmudic law only the agent or co-conspirator who carries out the slaying is punishable (overruling Shammai, who cites a contrary view of the Prophet Hagai, the author of one of the books of the Bible). The Talmud[257] explains this on the theory that the agent should realize that "[if] the words of the Master [conflict with] the words of the disciple [the principal, or co-conspirator], whose word should one listen to?" The agent should therefore be aware that he must always obey the higher law of God's command, rather than the instructions of his principal.

Why, however, is the principal insulated from capital punishment?[258] This norm is predicated upon the principle of individual responsibility for crimes: "Each man shall be killed for his own sin."[259] In the United States and other western countries, however, each con-

spirator is held equally punishable for a crime committed by any of the conspirators in the course of the conspiracy, a form of collective responsibility. Is this consistent with our notions of individual worth and democracy? What of the "felony-murder" rule that if a murder is committed in the course of perpetrating a felony, all the participants in the felony are punishable for the homicide?

2. *Rule 3*

Rambam here interprets each of the fourfold repetitions of the biblical stricture against bloodshed to refer to a distinct case. This is in line with the general talmudic perspective that every word and letter of the Bible has a specific purpose, and that none are superfluous. (See Chapter V, Section C 2, above, regarding the story of Akiba and Moses, and the inferring of numerous teachings from the jots and tittles of the letters in the Bible.)

3. *Rules 4 and 5*

(*a*) This section indicates the perspective that there were parallel structures existing side by side for the application of law and the maintenance of minimum order by the king, and by the *beth din*. From where does the king derive his authority (as distinct from his power and ability) to kill those who do not, technically, deserve the death penalty? Why is this not considered murder? Where there is no king, is there any other public authority that may have the same powers?[260]

(*b*) Are the powers cited here for the king and the *beth din*, coextensive? Notice that the *beth din* can only act in this way by a "temporary ruling" to meet the needs of the hours (see the end of rule 4 and beginning of rule 5), while the king's authority to act is described as being permissable "under the laws of the kingdom, and for the public benefit."[261]

---

255. On the *rodef* principle in general, see Ginsberg, *Mishpatim Le'Yisrael* (Jerusalem, 1956), pp. 177, 180–83, 192–93, 337, etc.; Sofer, "The *Rodef* Who Can Be Stopped by Being Wounded" (Hebrew), in *Ha'Ohel* (Israel, 1957), vol. 3; Schipansky, "Studies in the Laws of *Rodef*" (Hebrew), in *Ohr Ha'Mizrah* 20 (1971): 15 ff.; E. Hazan, "The Rule Regarding the Death Penalty Where a *Rodef* Can Be Stopped by Wounding," in *Ha'Pardes* 37, no. 2 (1953): 14–16; S. D. Shapiro, "Concerning a *Rodef*" (Hebrew), in *Ohr Ha'Mizrah* 20 (1969): 21.

256. See Code of Hammurabi, sec. 153.

257. *Kiddushin* 43a and *Sanhedrin* 76–77. See Y. Kanevsky, *Kehilat Yaakov* (B'nai B'rak, 1963), *Kiddushin*.

258. See also Rambam, Laws Concerning a Murderer, ch. 3:10, 11.

259. Deut. 24:16. Note, however, that certain facets of the notion of collective responsibility do appear in Jewish law: e.g., the obligation of all persons of the nearest town upon the finding of a murder victim, where the identity of the slayer is unknown (Deut. 21); Cain's query, "Am I my brother's keeper?" with the implication that God felt that he was; "All Israel are guarantors (i.e., responsible) for one another" (Talmud, *Shavuot* 39a); and the obligation to stop a *rodef* (ch. 1 of Rambam, above). These, however, apply to responsibility before God, not before man. Note, however, Rambam, Laws

---

Concerning a Murderer ch. 2:5, which provides that sanctions, otherwise underserved, may be imposed solely in order to deter *others*. Is the offender here being punished in effect for the future crimes of others?

260. See N. Gerundi, in *Derashot Ha'Ran*, discourse no. 11, who asserts that when there is no king the powers are transferred to the *beth din*; see Rambam, Rules of Armed Robbery, 5:18; Sofer, Responsa *Hatam Sofer, O.H.*, no. 208, and vol. 6, no. 14; Ha'Kohen, *Ohr Sameah*, Laws of Kings, 3:10; Isserlis, Responsa *Rama*, no. 10; N. Z. Y. Berlin, Responsa *Meshiv Davar* (Warsaw, 1894), vol. 1, no. 44. For a detailed discussion of this issue, see Chapter VI, Section B 4 *a*, below, "Perspectives Concerning Decision-Making by the Lay Communal Polity."

261. See Gershuni, "The Norms of the Sanhedrin and The Norms of the Kingdom," in *Torah She'Baal Peh* (Hebrew; Jerusalem, 1974), p. 92; see also Rambam, Laws of the Sanhedrin, 18:6, Laws of Kings, 3:10, and Ha'Meiri, *Beth Ha'Behira, Shabbat* 56. The king was held to be permitted to kill even innocent persons if necessary for a great public need. (See Talmud, *Yebamot* 79a.)

(c) Why was it necessary to invest the *beth din* with such extraordinary sanctioning powers? Are these due to the numerous requirements that must be fulfilled before a capital sentence may be imposed, and which make it extremely difficult to convict? (see Section C 2, below.)

(*d*) Note Rambam's view that the purpose of these extraordinary sanctions is solely to deter others from committing crimes, rather than the other purposes of sanctions discussed below (Section C). Does punishment, in fact, deter? There is a growing literature on the subject.[262]

4. *Rule 6*

(*a*) The underlying rationale of this rule is that the victim must be a viable person in order for the murderer to forfeit his life. An infant born prior to nine months of gestation is not regarded as having established his viability. Accordingly, the murderer of such an infant could not be executed.

In cases of doubt as to the period of gestation that has elapsed, the Talmud cites a rule of thumb: If the infant is born with hair on his head and fully developed nails on its fingers and toes, this indicates that nine months of gestation have passed.

(*b*) Contrast this ruling with the prosecutions of physicians for homicide in a number of American jurisdictions for permitting an aborted embryo to die outside of the womb. Would such prosecution also run counter to the norm set forth in rule 2, above?[263]

5. *Rules 7 and 8*

(*a*) One who is in *extremis* as a result of wounds is regarded, for this purpose, as though he were dead already. Consequently, the law regards it as though a "dead person" had been "killed," and the slayer is not subject to capital punishment. The Talmud relies upon its interpretation of a biblical verse to distinguish between one in *extremis* because of illness (and is still regarded as "living") and one who is dying because of blows and is regarded as already "dead" for this purpose. No reason is given in the Talmud for this distinction.

Why is a distinction made between the killing of a victim who is on the verge of death because of illness and the killing of somebody who is dying because of blows previously inflicted upon him? What is the distinction between one who is dying from an illness, such as cancer, whose murderer would not be killed, and one who has a hole in one of his vital organs, which makes it certain that he will die within the year (see rule 8)?

There are authorities who claim[264] that one who is dying from an illness may yet recover. Consequently, his murderer is regarded as having killed a viable person. A person who is in *extremis* because of wounds inflicted upon him or because of a hole in one of his vital organs is, it is claimed, more certain to die shortly. Consequently, his murderer is not regarded as having killed a viable person. This is similar to the rationale of rule 6 regarding the killing of an infant who is born before nine months of gestation have elapsed. This view is troublesome, however, since there does not, in fact, seem to be a statistical difference in the probability of death between any of these cases. Furthermore, judicial notice appears to be taken in Jewish law of the proposition that most persons who are on the verge of death do die, regardless of whether the person is in *extremis* as a result of illness or wounds.[265] One commentator[266] maintains that the degree of probability of death is not the distinction between the first two cases cited. His view appears to be that if the victim had already been dying of wounds inflicted by someone else, and was then killed by still another blow, the blame for the killing must be apportioned among the persons who inflicted the wounds that brought him to *extremis* and the one who delivered the final blow, causing death. The death penalty is traditionally avoided when a number of persons jointly inflict blows resulting in death.[267]

(*b*) It has been contended that the rationale of regarding a person as "dead," thereby relieving his killer of the death penalty, can be applied to the cases of the *rodef* and burglar. Since these persons, too, may be killed by anyone in order to save the intended victim (of the assailant or burglar), the *rodef* and burglar are regarded as functionally "dead." Accordingly, one who kills them is not subject to the death penalty.[268] This reasoning would also exempt from the death penalty one who killed a *rodef* whom he could have stopped by wounding. This exemption from the death

---

262. For views that it does, see G. Tullock, "Does Punishment Deter Crime?" in *The Public Interest* 36 (Summer 1974), p. 103 ff.; I. Erlich, "The Deterrent Effect of Capital Punishment," *American Economic Review* 64 (1974). M. Plattner, "The Rehabilitation of Punishment," *The Public Interest*, 44 (Summer 1976): 104.

263. See also Ashvili in his commentary *Ritva* to Talmud, *Kiddushin* 43, intimating that one may not be sentenced to death unless he has performed an "act" resulting in the death, not (e.g., as in conspiracy) by merely uttering words. Under this reasoning, would neglect of an aborted embryo (i.e., a failure to act) constitute an "act"?

264. Benebashti, in *Hamra Ve'Haya, Sanhedrin* 78a.

265. See Tosefot, *Sanhedrin* 78a, and *Yebamot* 120b.

266. Chajes, Commentary to Talmud, *Nazir* 4b (printed in standard editions of the Talmud).

267. See also Margolis, *Margaliyat Ha'Yam*, p. 92, no. 5; and Y. Rosen, Responsa *Tzafnat Pa'Aneah*, sec. 1, no. 54, and Responsa *Helkat Yoav, Y.D.*, no. 27.

268. Novellae of I. Soloveitchik (Jerusalem, 1973), pp. 137–38. To the same effect, see Zevin, "Addenda to *Mishpat* Shylock," in *L'Or Ha'Halakhah* (Jerusalem, 1957), p. 335.

penalty applies even when the slaying of the *rodef* was not intended to, and does not in fact, result in saving the intended victim.

6. *Rule 9*

The essence of the rationale for this rule is as follows: Witnesses in capital cases are not qualified to testify unless their testimony is given under the threat that if it is proven that they testify falsely, they themselves may be executed for this.[269] Such a threat does not exist in the case of witnesses who testify that a person with a fatal defect killed somebody. Here, even if their testimony is proven false, they have at most attempted to bring about the death of a fatally defective person. They cannot, in such event, be in a worse position than if they had killed such person with their own hands, in which case, they could not be killed (see rule 8).[270]

Note that witnesses in capital cases, whose testimony is proven to have been deliberately false, face the death penalty (see Deut. 19:19). This is the exception to the principle (rule 2) that no one may be executed unless one has murdered with one's own hands. False witnesses do not kill with their own hands but attempt to bring about the death of the defendant through execution by the court.

7. *Rule 10*

This rule is predicated upon the perspective that an idolator was, in general, regarded as a barbarian, without qualities of mercy and kindness. It was not, therefore, viewed as appropriate for a court of human beings to take the life of his murderer, but it was more fitting to let God himself inflict the sanction.[271]

A non-Jew, even a slave, who did not worship idols and followed at least the principles of minimum human decency and kindness, was treated in the same way as a Jewish victim. His murderer could be executed (see rules 10 and 11).

---

269. See Deut. 19:19.
270. See J. B. Soloveitchik, *Beth Ha'Levi* (reprinted New York, 1965), sec. 3, no. 4.
271. See *Mehilta*, Exod. 21:13. For use of a similar perspective, see Talmud, *Shabbat* 16b, which states that the Sanhedrin ceased to judge capital cases forty years before the destruction of the Temple at Jerusalem, leaving the punishment of murderers in the hands of God. Also see *Sanhedrin* 37b regarding an accused murderer (found with a bloody knife in his hand immediately after the murder), who could not be executed because there were not two eye-witnesses to the act. Similarly, rule 11 concerning the killing of one who has a fatal defect and ch. 1, rule 13, concerning one who killed a *rodef*, when he could have stopped him by wounding, and all of the protective rules detailed in the Talmud and in Rambam's Laws of the Sanhedrin, below. In all these instances the appropriate punishment for the murderer is left to God. See Loewe, *Be'er Hagolah*, ch. 2; see also Epstein, *Torah Temimah* (reprinted New York, 1967) at Exod. 21:13.

Why does Rambam call this chapter "Laws Concerning a Murderer and the Preservation of Life"?

2. CRIMINAL PROCEDURE: RIGHTS OF THE CRIMINAL DEFENDANT

a. Selections from the Talmud, Sanhedrin, Chapter 1
(Mishnah IV)*

Capital cases are tried by a court of twenty-three. A beast that commits an unnatural crime, or a beast that suffers an unnatural crime, is tried by a court of twenty-three, because it is written (Lev. 20:16): "Thou shalt slay the woman and the beast"; and it is written again (Lev. 20:15): "And ye shall slay the beast." [The case of] an ox to be stoned is dealt with by a court of twenty-three; for it is written (Exod. 21:29): "The ox shall be stoned, and its owner shall be put to death," which implies: [the law regarding] the death of the owner likewise applies to the death of the ox. The wolf, the lion, the bear, the leopard, the panther, and the serpent are sentenced to death by a court of twenty-three. Rabbi Eliezer says: "Whoever kills them before [they are brought to trial] has acquired merit." Rabbi Akiba says: "They must be sentenced to death by a court of twenty-three."

Notes and Questions to Selections from the Talmud, Sanhedrin, Chapter 1, Mishna IV

1. What is the rationale of bringing an animal to court, solemnly sentencing it to death, and having the execution supervised by the court? This was not done in order to punish the animal.[272] Rather, the basic notion appears to be that no life, not even that of an animal, is to be taken as a *sanction* without what we term today as "due process." The rationale for this may have been the fear that the imposition of capital sanctions upon animals without due process could lead to lawlessness in the imposition of capital sanctions upon humans.

The sentencing by a court of the man-killing animal also reflected the gravity with which the animal's taking of a human life was viewed.

2. The initial trial procedure for animals was similar to that employed for human defendants only with regard to the requirement of trial in the presence of the defendant and to sentencing by the court after duly

---

*This translation is from H. L. Goldin, *Hebrew Criminal Law and Procedure* (New York, 1952).
272. Maimonides, *Guide for the Perplexed*, Book III: 40. Compare, "From every beast, will I demand it . . ." (Gen. 9:5), that verse was, however, interpreted to refer to the case of one who murdered by placing his victim in front of a wild animal (see Rambam, Laws Concerning a Murderer, 2:3).

weighing the facts of the case and establishing that the accusation had been proven. The judicial tilts in favor of human defendants (see Section *e*, below) were not applied to animals.[273]

3. The scriptural basis adduced in the Talmud to support the principle that a formal judicial proceeding is required before executing a homicidal animal is found in Exod. 21:29: "The ox shall be stoned, and its owner shall be put to death." The juxtaposition and comparison in the verse of the death of an ox that killed a human being and the death of its owner is understood to refer to the general principle that whenever an ox or other animal is to be put to death by man, it shall be under the same general procedures that apply to the death of man by a court.

4. The reference in the Mishnah to the killing of a wolf, lion, bear, etc., is to the case where one of these animals, which is kept as a pet, kills someone. There is no such prohibition about killing these animals in their wild state, since they are then clearly dangerous.

5. The Talmud[274] derives its principle that men and women are to be treated alike in criminal cases and in

273. Talmud, *Sanhedrin* 360.

274. *Kiddushin* 34a. "The trial of animals was carried to extremes in Medieval Europe. Among the more interesting facets of medieval legal processes were the frequent criminal prosecutions of animals. The courts had Biblical authority for these remarkable trials: according to the Mosaic code, if an ox killed a man, it was to be stoned to death; if a man committed bestiality, both man and beast were to be executed; and God cursed the serpent in the Garden of Eden.

In 1456, a pig was sentenced to be burned in the Rhineland for having killed and eaten a small child. Another pig died for the same offense in Amsens in 1463—also at the stake. Sometimes the animals were first put to torture: according to one theory, so their grunts and squeals could be interpreted as confessions, but according to another, only because torture had become an integral part of any legal proceeding. The *lex talionis* was usually observed: if a dog bit a man, the dog was held down and the man allowed to bite him back, and so on.

Animals—even insects—were allowed to have lawyers. The insects (usually fleas, lice, or locusts) had to be given three days' notice before trial and some representatives brought into court, duly notified, and then freed to effect service upon others. The main issue during the trial was whether the creatures were simply obeying the will of God ('I will send wild beasts among you which shall destroy you and your cattle and make you few in number.'), or whether they had criminal intent. This was always a difficult matter to prove and was a source of much judicial consternation.

To emphasize the anthropomorphic nature of the offense, the animal was sometimes dressed in clothes and tied in a sitting position during the trial. In 1386, a pig in Falaise, Normandy, that tore the face and arm of a small child was dressed in clothes and sentenced to be maimed in the same manner as the child. In 1685, a wolf in Austria that had killed several people was dressed in clothes, wig, and beard. His snout was cut off and a human mask tied over it during trial. He was sentenced to be hanged.

If a man committed bestiality, true to Biblical precedent, both he and the creature were killed. Cotton Mather describes the death of a Mr. Potter in New Salem, Connecticut, who in

the imposition of sanctions from the equation of men and women in the aforementioned verse (Exod. 21:29) regarding an ox that "shall kill a man or woman."

b. SELECTIONS FROM THE TALMUD, SANHEDRIN, CHAPTER 4
(Mishnah I)*

Both civil and capital cases require investigation and examination of witnesses, as it is written (Lev. 24:22): "One manner of judicial law shall ye have." What difference is there in point of law between civil and capital cases? Civil cases are decided by a court of three and capital cases by a court of twenty-three; in civil cases the opening argument may be either in favor of the defendant or against him, and in capital cases the opening argument must be for acquittal and not for conviction; in civil cases a verdict may be reached either in favor of the defendant or against him by a majority of one vote, but in capital cases a verdict for acquittal may be reached by a majority of one vote, and a verdict of conviction may be reached only by a majority of no less than two votes; in civil cases verdicts may be reversed either for the purpose of declaring the defendant not liable or to declare him liable, but in capital cases verdicts may be reversed [from conviction] to acquittal, but not [from acquittal] to conviction; in civil cases all are permitted to argue either for the defendant or against him, but in capital cases all are permitted to plead for acquittal, but not all are permitted to argue for conviction; in civil cases he who had argued against the defendant may thereafter argue in his favor, and he who had argued in his favor may thereafter argue against him, but in capital cases he who had argued for conviction may thereafter argue for acquittal, but he who had argued for acquittal may not thereafter argue for conviction; in civil cases the merits of the case are discussed in the daytime, and the verdict may be reached during the night, but in

1662 kept a harem of a cow, two heifers, three sheep, and two sows. His harem were first hanged before his eyes, a sight that reduced Potter to tears, and then Potter suffered the same fate.

The courts, as time passed, gradually grew more reasonable in their treatment of accused animals. An Austrian dog that bit a man was sentenced to only a year in jail in 1712. In 1750, Jacques Ferron of Vanvres, France, and his she-donkey were arrested for bestiality. The court reluctantly agreed to hear testimony of character witnesses, and the she-donkey was lucky enough to have a good one. The prior of a convent pointed out that the donkey has 'always been virtuous and well-behaved and never given occasion for scandal. This is clearly a case of rape.' The court agreed and only the unfortunate Ferron was hanged."

—From Daniel R. Mannix, *The History of Torture* (London, 1970).

*From H. L. Goldin, *Hebrew Criminal Laws and Procedure* (New York, 1952).

capital cases the merits are argued in the daytime and
the verdict must be reached in the daytime; in civil
cases the merits of the case may be discussed and a
verdict may be reached the same day, either in favor
of the defendant or against him, but in capital cases a
vedict of acquittal may be reached the same day, but
a verdict of conviction not until the following day; for
this reason, trials involving capital cases may not be
held on the eve of the Sabbath or of a festival.

(Mishnah II)

In civil cases and in cases concerning uncleanness
and cleanness, they begin by taking the votes of the
senior judges, but in capital cases they begin by taking
the votes of those that sit on the side (i.e., the junior
judges). All are qualified to hear and determine civil
cases, but not all are qualified to hear and determine
capital cases, but only priests, Levites, and Israelites
that may give [their daughters] in marriage into the
priestly stock.

(Mishnah III)

The Sanhedrin was arranged in a semicircle so that
they all might see one another. Before them stood two
clerks of the court, one on the right and one on the
left, and they recorded the opinion of those that argued
for acquittal, and the opinion of those that argued for
conviction. Rabbi Judah says: "There were three clerks;
one recorded the opinion of those that argued for acquittal, and one recorded the opinion of those that
argued for conviction, and the third recorded both
opinions."

(Mishnah IV)

And before them were three rows of students, and
each knew his proper place. If it became necessary to
appoint a new judge, they promoted one from the first
row, and one from the second row came into the first
row, and one from the third row came into the second row; and they chose yet another from the congregation and set him in the third row. He did not sit in
the place of the former, but he sat in the place that was
proper for him.

Notes and Questions to Selections from the Talmud, Sanhedrin, Chapter 4, Mishna I–IV

Mishnah I

1. The rules set forth in this and the following Mish-
nahs, reflect the Talmudic perspectives that it is the
duty of the court (and, in fact, of every individual) to
attempt to find some defense or excuse for the criminal
defendant. As support for this view, the Talmud[275] cites

the biblical verse, "And the congregation shall save the
murderer" (Num. 35:25). The legal process is therefore to be tilted in favor of the defendant.

In non-criminal cases, however, the court must act
in an even-handed manner toward the plaintiff and
defendant, since a tilt toward one would prejudice the
rights of the other.[276]

2. *"In capital cases . . . he who had argued for acquittal may not, thereafter, argue for conviction."*

(*a*) The talmudic rationale for this is that the judge,
who is not permitted to change his previous argument
for acquittal, would thereby be encouraged to find additional support to maintain his view for acquittal.[277]

(*b*) Another reason for preventing a judge who had
argued for acquittal to subsequently argue for a conviction was that later arguments might help to convince
his fellow judges. Part of the process of tilting the judicial procedure in favor of the defendant was to minimize, wherever possible, argument for convictions.[278]

3. *"Capital trials may not be held on the eve of the
Sabbath or of a festival."*

(*a*) The trial could not commence on Friday, suspend for Saturday, and continue on Sunday for fear
that the judges would, in the interim, forget some of
the points that they had considered.[279] This was true,
even though the court clerks would record the substance of the testimony and arguments of the prosecution and defense. Furthermore, it was feared that one
who speaks rarely expresses orally all of his thoughts
and reasonings concerning any matter.[280] Accordingly,
even though the scribes would accurately record the
reasoning that was expressed orally, they would necessarily fail to record other reasonings and nuances that
were not verbally expressed. Accordingly, it was feared
that the judges would forget their own reasonings, or
those expressed by the defense, if the trial were unduly
prolonged.

What of the complex criminal trials in the United
States today, especially the so-called "political" trials,
which last for many months, with thousands of pages
of testimony? Would the availability of complete short-
hand, stenotype, and videotape transcriptions of all the
proceedings make any difference in Jewish law?

Another rationale was based on the possibility that
the trial might be concluded on the same day with a
verdict of guilty. The defendant's execution would then
have to be postponed until after the Sabbath or festi-

---

275. See *Sanhedrin* 2a ff.

276. See commentaries of Tosafot and Ha'Meiri, *Beth Ha'-
Behira,* ad loc.
277. Talmud, *Sanhedrin* 34a; Rashi, ad loc.
278. Margolis, *Margaliyot Ha'Yam,* vol. 1, p. 143, no. 4.
279. Talmud, *Sanhedrin* 35a.
280. Abulafia, *Yad Rama,* and Margolis, *Margaliyat Ha'-
Yam,* vol. 1, p. 148, no. 11.

val, causing him the extreme mental anguish of prolonged waiting for death.[281]

Mishnah II

(*a*) One of the reasons why members of the Sanhedrin could not come from parents whose marriage
was prohibited under biblical law (that is, certain close
relatives) may have been to ensure that their judgment
and decisions should receive widespread acceptance by
the community. The judge who, for example, was a
bastard, might be faced with strong public reaction
and intolerance of his decisions, in view of the strongly
held feelings, common in the Talmudic Era, concerning the importance of lineage.

A related rationale was that service on the Sanhedrin
was considered the equivalent of service in the Temple
by the priests and Levites. These could not serve if
afflicted with a physical defect,[282] because their participation would adversely affect the dignity of the proceedings, given the perspectives prevalent at that time.
Aged and childless judges were also disqualified for
fear that they might be overly strict.

(*b*) Although converts were disqualified from sitting
as judges in capital cases for the aforementioned reasons, they could nevertheless act as judges if they were
preeminent in learning or wisdom. Accordingly, two
converts, Shemaya and Avtalyon, whose erudition was
unparalleled, were appointed as heads of the Sanhedrin.[283]

Mishnah III

1. *"So that they all might see one another."*

(*a*) The semicircle also permitted all of the judges
to face all of the witnesses and to clearly observe them,
as well as each other.[284]

(*b*) Rashi maintains that both clerks reported the
contentions of those who argued for acquittal and those
who argued for conviction. Their records could then
be compared with each other to ensure accuracy. Rambam, however, maintains that one clerk recorded the
arguments for conviction and the other, the arguments
for acquittal.[285]

2. *"Rabbi Judah says, 'there were three clerks.'"*
Rashi maintains that Rabbi Judah felt that it was burdensome for each clerk to record the contentions for
both conviction and acquittal. Accordingly, one clerk
recorded only the contentions for conviction, while the
other recorded only those for acquittal. The third clerk,
however, recorded all contentions, and his records were
used to verify the accuracy of the records kept by the
other two clerks. Rambam maintains that the third
clerk was necessary (as part of the functional "due
process" requirements) because the biblical requirement of two witnesses demanded that there would be
two clerks to attest to (and assure accurate reflection
of) the contentions of those who were for acquittal and
those who were for convictions.

Mishnah IV

There were trainees who sat in three rows in front of
the "Smaller Sanhedrin." Each row contained twenty-
three persons, the same number as in the rows occupied by the judges. New appointments to the court
would be made from these trainees, who were seated
in the order of their training and ability.

c. SELECTIONS FROM THE TALMUD, SANHEDRIN,
CHAPTER 4
(Mishnah V)*

Mishnah. How were the witnesses inspired with awe?
Witnesses in capital charges were brought in and in-
timidated [thus]: Perhaps what ye say is based only on
conjecture, or hearsay, or is evidence from the mouth
of another witness, or even from the mouth of a trustworthy person: perhaps ye are unaware that ultimately
we shall scrutinize your evidence by cross examination
and inquiry? Know then that capital cases are not like
monetary cases. In civil suits, one can make monetary
restitution and thereby effect his atonement; but in capital cases he is held responsible for his blood [the accused's] and the blood of his [potential] descendants
until the end of time, for thus we find in the case of
Cain, who killed his brother, that it is written: "The
bloods of thy brother cry unto me": not the blood of thy
brother, but the bloods of thy brother, is said—i.e., his
blood and the blood of his [potential] descendants. (Alternatively, the bloods of thy brother, teaches that his
blood was splashed over trees and stones.) For this
reason was man created alone, to teach thee that whosoever destroys a single soul of Israel, scripture imputes
[guilt] to him as though he had destroyed a complete
world; and whosoever preserves a single soul of Israel,
scripture ascribes [merit] to him as though he had preserved a complete world. Furthermore, [he was cre-

---

281. See Talmud, *Yebamot* 6b.
282. See Responsa *Hatam Sofer, O.H.*, no. 12; Rambam,
Laws of Sanhedrin, 11:11.
283. Riva, in the commentary of the *Baale Ha'Tosefot*, Exod.
21; Benebashti, *Dina De'Haya*, positive commandment no. 97;
Azulai, *Bire Yosef, Ho. Mis.*, 7, no. 6; cf. Judah Loewe of
Prague in *Dereh Hayim* (reprinted Jerusalem, 1971), who
maintains that Shemaya and Avtalyon were not themselves
converts but were descendants of converts. See also Y. T. Lipp-
man-Heller, *Tosefot Yom Tov* (printed in standard editions of
the Mishnah), *Avot* 1:10.
284. Rashi, ad loc.
285. Laws of the Sanhedrin, 1:9.

*Soncino Press translation (London, 1961).

ated alone] for the sake of peace among men, that one might not say to his fellow, "My father was greater than thine," and that the *minim* might not say, "there are many ruling powers in heaven"; again, to proclaim the greatness of the Holy One, blessed be He: For if a man strikes many coins from one mould, they all resemble one another, but the Supreme King of Kings, the Holy One, blessed be He, fashioned every man in the stamp of the first man, and yet not one of them resembles his fellow. Therefore every single person is obliged to say: The world was created for my sake.

Perhaps ye will say: Why should we incur this anxiety? [Know then:] Is it not already written, "And he being a witness, whether he hath seen or known, if he do not utter it?" And should ye say: "Why should we bear guilt for the blood of this [man]":—surely, however, it is said, "When the wicked perish, there is joy"!

Gemara. Our Rabbis taught: What is meant by *based on conjecture?*—He [the judge] says to them: Perhaps ye saw him running after his fellow into a ruin, ye pursued him, and found him sword in hand with blood dripping from it, whilst the murdered man was writhing [in agony]: If this is what ye saw, ye saw nothing.

It has been taught: R. Simeon b. Shatah said: May I never see comfort if I did not see a man pursuing his fellow into a ruin, and when I ran after him and saw him, sword in hand with blood dripping from it, and the murdered man writhing, I exclaimed to him: Wicked man, who slew this man? It is either you or I! But what can I do, since thy blood [i.e., life] does not rest in my hands, for it is written in the Torah, *At the mouth of two witnesses etc., shall he that is to die be put to death?* May He Who knows one's thoughts exact vengeance from him who slew his fellow! It is related that before they moved from the place a serpent came and bit him [the murderer] so that he died.

Notes and Questions to Selections from the Talmud, Sanhedrin, Chapter 4, Mishna V

1. There were many procedures followed in criminal trials that resulted in an overall tendency to tilt the scale in favor of the defendant (see Section *b*, above and *f*, below). Admonishing the witnesses to be very careful about the accuracy of their testimony and placing them in "awe," (although, also designed to procure accurate and reliable testimony), is one of them.

In American and British courts the attempt to place the witnesses in "awe" is effected by requiring them to take an oath, or affirmation, that their testimony will be truthful. In traditional Jewish law witnesses were not required to take an oath and, in fact, may have been disqualified as witnesses if their testimony was

considered unreliable without an oath.[286] In medieval Europe, as a result of intercultural influences, Jewish witnesses came to share the perspective prevalent among non-Jews that they were not required to testify truthfully unless put under oath. Accordingly, the practice arose to require witnesses to take an oath.[287]

2. *"Whosoever destroys a single soul of Israel . . ."* In the oldest accurate manuscript available, the word "Israel" does not appear.[288] The word "Israel" is also omitted in the other reference to this statement in the Talmud.[289] The statement of the Mishnah would therefore apply to any person. (The word "Israel" does appear, however, apparently in error, in Rambam, Laws of a Murderer, ch. 1, rule 16, but not in Rambam, Laws of the Sanhedrin, ch. 12, rule 3.) The context of the statement in the Mishnah supports its application to all people, since the Mishnah derives its conclusion from the creation of Adam, who was not an Israelite.

3. Although there is some question as to the extent to which Jewish courts, in practice, applied the many defendant-biased rules of capital cases (see Section *e*, below), the incident related here by the Talmud, concerning Simeon ben Shetah, indicates that the disqualification of circumstantial evidence[290] was applied in actual practice. Why did not Simeon ben Shetah apply one of the "extraordinary" procedures that were available to punish criminals? Note that Simeon ben Shetah himself utilized some of the "extraordinary" steps.[291]

4. Implicit in Simeon ben Shetah's statement is that not all punishments of criminal activity must come

286. See Talmud, *Kiddushin* 43b and Tosefot, ad loc.
287. Isaac b. Sheshet, Responsa *Rivash*, nos. 170, 176; Shimon b. Tzeman Duran, Responsa *Tashbatz*, vol. 3, no. 15; Karo, *Shulhan Arukh, Hoshen Mishpat*, sec. 27, subsec. 1, and Moshe Isserlis, *Rama*, ad loc.; J. F. Cohen, *Me'irat Eynayim*, sec. 16; cf. Sofer, Responsa *Hatam Sofer, Hoshen Mishpat*, p. 207.
288. See N. Rabinowitz, *Dikdukei Soferim, Sanhedrin* (Munich, 1868), ad loc., and *Baba Batra* 11a, no. 5.
289. *Avot* of Rabbi Nathan (printed in standard editions of the Talmud), chap. 31; and in Rambam, Laws of the Sanhedrin, ch. 12, rule 3; see Kirschenbaum, *The "Good Samaritan" and Jewish Law*, p. 17, note 37, for a detailed discussion of the versions of this *phrase* appearing in various editions of the Talmud.
290. The disqualification is based upon the verse, "according to the testimony of *witnesses* shall they slay the murderer" (Num. 35:30, emphasis added). Another view is that the disqualification is based on the verse "according to the testimony of two or three witnesses, shall a matter be established" (Deut. 19:15); see Mintz, Responsa (Maharam Mintz) (Salonika, 1802), no. 23, and below for the function of witnesses in a trial.
291. See Mishnah, *Sanhedrin* 7:4 and 45b; Plotzki, *Hemdat Yisrael* (Pietrakov, 1927; reprinted New York, 1965), p. 162 ff., and p. 28 ff. of the addenda.

from man and that God would inevitably punish criminals. It is possible that this, too, was the ratio of Rabbi Akiba and Rabbi Tarfon,[292] who sought to eliminate capital punishment by courts (see Section *e*, below).

5. *"The world was created for my sake."* The sense of this statement is that the humanity of the accused was of such immense importance that it would be calamitous if he were executed by inaccurate testimony. It was also an appeal to the witnesses not to debase *themselves* and degrade their value as human beings by false testimony. Thus the court tried to persuade the witnesses to testify truthfully and accurately, based on an appeal both to their nobility as human beings, and on the threat that their false testimony would be discovered and they would be punished (a "carrot-and-stick" approach).

d. THE TALMUDIC PROTOTYPE OF RODEF
(*Sanhedrin* 49a)*

Then Joab was brought before the Court, and he [Solomon] judged and questioned him, "Why didst thou kill Abner?" He answered, "I was Asahel's redeemer of blood." "But Asahel was a pursuer!" "Even so," answered he; "but he [Abner] should have saved himself at the cost of one of his [Asahel's] limbs." "Yet perhaps he could not do so," remonstrated [Solomon]. "If he could aim exactly at the fifth rib," he retorted, ("even as it is written, *Abner with the hinder end of the spear smote him at the waist*; concerning which R. Johanan said: It was at the fifth rib, where the gall-bladder and liver are suspended.)—could he not have aimed at one of his limbs?" Thereupon [Solomon] said: 'Let us drop [the incident of] Abner; . . .

. . . *And Joab took him aside into the midst of the gate to speak with him quietly.* R. Johanan said: He judged him according to the law of the Sanhedrin. Thus he asked him: "Why didst thou kill Asahel?"—"Because Asahel was my pursuer." "Then thou shouldst have saved thyself at the cost of one of his limbs!" "I could not do that," [he answered]. "If thou couldst aim exactly at his fifth rib, couldst thou not have prevailed against him by [wounding] one of his limbs?"

Notes to "The Talmudic Prototype of *Rodef*," Sanhedrin 49a

The elaboration here of the killing of Abner by Joab[293] reflects the extreme scrutiny with which each word of the Bible was examined by Talmudic sages. Here Joab's taking of Abner "into the midst of the

gate" is held to indicate a court setting, since courts in the Biblical Era commonly sat at the gates of the city. Otherwise, it would have been more reasonable for Joab to attempt to murder Abner quietly, without public notice. It also indicates the talmudic belief that every single word in the Bible has a purposeful meaning and that no word is superfluous. Additionally, it reflects the view that the "heroes" of the Bible were not common murderers.

The talmudic elaborations[294] of the discussions between King Solomon and Joab regarding the latter's killing of Abner appears to form the basis of Rambam's conclusion[295] that one who could have stopped a *rodef* by wounding him, but killed him instead, could not be executed by a court but might, in turn, be killed by the *rodef*'s "redeemer of blood." Note that Abner could have stopped Asael by merely wounding him, and that Joab qualified as a "redeemer" of his brother Asael.

e. OBSTACLES TO, AND VIEWS CONCERNING, CAPITAL PUNISHMENT IN TALMUDIC LAW
(*Makkot* 6b)*

R. Jose[296] observes that a malefactor is never put to death unless two witnesses had duly pre-admonished him. . . . Said R. Papa to Abaye: Is this really R. Jose's view? Do we not learn: R. Jose says, An [avowed] enemy is executed, because he is, as it were, attested and already pre-admonished?—To this Abaye replied that the authority of that cited Mishnah was R. Jose b. Judah, as it is taught [explicitly elsewhere]: R. Jose b. Judah says, a scholar needs no pre-admonition, because pre-admonition was introduced only as a means for discriminating between the inadvertent and deliberate offender.

Another interpretation of the words, at the mouth of two witnesses . . . , is that the Sanhedrin shall not hear the evidence from the mouth of an interpreter. Certain foreigners came [with a suit] before Raba and he appointed an interpreter. How could he do that? Do we not learn that *the Sanhedrin shall not hear the evidence from the mouth of an interpreter?*—Raba understood well enough what they said, only he did not know how to reply.

(*Makkot* 7a)

A Sanhedrin that effects an execution once in seven years, is branded a destructive tribunal; R. Eliezer b. Azariah says: Once in seventy years. R. Tarfon and R. Akiba say: Were we members of a Sanhedrin, no

---

292. Talmud, *Makkot* 7a; see also Loewe, *Be'er Ha'Gola*, ch. 2.
*Soncino Press translation (London, 1961).
293. 2 Sam. 3:27.

294. *Sanhedrin* 49a.
295. Laws Concerning a Murder, ch. 1, rule 13.
*Soncino Press translation (London, 1961).
296. Usually = R. Jose b. Halafta, but R. Jose b. Judah.

person would ever be put to death. [Thereupon] Rabban Simeon b. Gamaliel remarked, [yea] and they would also multiply shedders of blood in Israel!

A Sanhedrin that effects an execution once in seven years is branded a destructive tribunal; R. Eliezer b. Azariah says, once in seventy years. The question was raised whether the comment [of R. Eliezer b. Azariah was a censure, namely] that even one death-sentence in seventy years branded the Sanhedrin as a destructive tribunal, or [a mere observation] that it ordinarily happened but once in seventy years?—It stands [undecided].

R. Tarfon and R. Akiba say, Were we members of a Sanhedrin, no person would ever be put to death. How could they [being judges] give effect to that [policy]?—Both R. Johanan and R. Eleazar suggested that the witnesses might be plied with [intimate] questions such as, "Did you take note whether the victim was [perchance] suffering from some fatal affection or was he perfectly healthy?" R. Ashi [enlarging on this] said: And should the reply be, "Perfectly healthy," they might further be embarrassed by asking, "Maybe the sword only severed an internal lesion?"

Notes and Questions to "Obstacles and Views Concerning Capital Punishment in Talmudic Law," Makkot 6b and 7a

1. Rabbi Jose elaborates the principle that a criminal defendant may not be put to death unless he has been warned *before* committing the crime that his proposed act was a capital offense. He holds that the forewarning must be given by the witnesses themselves, not by a third person. He bases this view on the biblical passage (Deut. 17), "Out of the mouths of two witnesses, the matter shall be established." He interprets this verse to mean that *all* of the elements of guilt, including the required forewarning, must be established by the testimony of the two witnesses, themselves.

2. Rabbi Jose ben Judah (not the same R. Jose of the preceding paragraph) maintained[297] that the whole purpose of the forewarning was to insure that the defendant was fully aware that his act would be a capital crime. In other words, ignorance of the law *is* a valid excuse. Accordingly, a scholar who is well-versed in the law needs no forewarning. Another purpose of the forewarning is to make certain that the killing was intentional, not accidental. As a result, forewarning would not be necessary in the case of a defendant who killed his avowed enemy since it is regarded as highly unlikely that the act was accidental. Other talmudic authorities maintain that every person requires forewarning.

297. But see Jerusalem Talmud, *Makkot*, ad loc.

3. The ban on the use of interpreters in court is based on the rationale (the functional equivalent, in a sense, of the American "due process" requirement) that an interpreter might mistranslate or omit some proper nuance of language of the testimony. Additionally, judges who understand the testimony without the intervention of an interpreter are able more effectively to cross-examine the witnesses and litigants. The ban resulted in the norm that no one could be appointed a member of the Sanhedrin unless he was fluent in all of the "seventy" languages in use at that time.[298]

4. The Talmud's question concerning R. Eliezer is obscure. The translation here follows the interpretation by Menahem Ha'Meiri in his *Beth Ha'Behira, Makkot* (Sofer ed. [Jerusalem, 1965], p. 37). In any case, unclarity remains about the actual frequency of executions by the Sanhedrin.[299]

5. Rabbi Simeon ben Gamliel apparently was more concerned than Rabbi Akiba and Rabbi Tarfon that the court's lenient treatment of accused murderers would encourage more people to commit crimes. It should be noted, however, that even Akiba and Tarfon agreed that, where the court felt it necessary, it should deter criminal activity by imprisonment, or more severe sanction.[300] It is possible that the conflict between these scholars revolved around whether it was more important to save the innocent from execution, or to protect the public by eradicating individuals who were most probably—but not beyond the shadow of the slightest doubt—criminals.[301]

6. Although the failure of the witnesses to answer the questions posed by Rabbi Akiba and Rabbi Tarfon would not disqualify their testimony, these might serve to confuse them sufficiently so that their testimony would be inaccurate in vital portions.[302]

6. Is it conceivable that Rabbi Simeon ben Gamliel's position as *nasi*, with responsibility to the Romans for maintaining public order, was more reason for him to be concerned about the occurrence of crimes than Rabbi Akiba and Rabbi Tarfon?

7. The views of Akiba and Tarfon came close to advocating the abolition of the death penalty completely. Leading Talmud commentators feel, however, that they desired to abolish it in most, but not necessarily in all, cases.[303]

298. *Sanhedrin* 17a.
299. See Loewe, *Be'er Ha'Gola*, ad loc.
300. See Mishnah, *Sanhedrin* 9:5, and the commentary of Chajes to Talmud, *Makkot*, ad loc.
301. See commentary of Ha'Meiri, *Beth Ha'Behira*, p. 37.
302. See commentary of *Tosefot, Makkot* 7a, and Ha'Meiri ad loc.
303. See Tosefot, and Chajes, commentary, ad loc.

f. THE TRIAL OF A CAPITAL CASE
(Moshe ben Maimon)*

The following selections from Rambam's Code of Laws codifies talmudic law regarding some of the procedures in the trial of criminal cases. Although some of these provisions have already been included in the preceding selections from the Mishnah, they are repeated here because of the many additions made by Rambam and the framework in which he incorporated them.—A. M. S.

Chapter 9

1. If in trying a capital case all the members of the Sanhedrin forthwith vote for conviction, the accused is acquitted. Only when some cast about for arguments in his favor and are outvoted by those who are for conviction is the accused put to death.

2. In case there is a difference of opinion among the Small Sanhedrin with respect to a capital charge, twelve voting for acquittal and eleven for conviction, the accused is acquitted. If twelve vote for conviction and eleven for acquittal, or eleven for acquittal, eleven for conviction and one is undecided, even if twenty-two vote for acquittal or for conviction and one is undecided, two more judges are added. The one who is undecided is as though he were nonexistent because he cannot afterward argue for conviction. There are therefore, after the addition has been made, twenty-four judges besides the one who is undecided. If thirteen vote for acquittal and twelve for conviction, he is acquitted. If eleven vote for acquittal and thirteen for conviction, he is convicted, even if one of the original twenty-three is undecided, because there is a majority of two for conviction. If, however, twelve are for acquittal, twelve for conviction, and one is undecided, two more judges are added. This process of increasing the number of judges goes on, until those who are for acquittal constitute a majority of one, in which case the accused is acquitted, or until those who are for conviction constitute a majority of two, in which case the accused is convicted. If the vote is tied, while one judge is undecided, the number of judges is increased, until the tribunal comprises seventy-one.

When this number is reached and thirty-six are for acquittal and thirty-five for conviction, the accused is acquitted; if thirty-six are for conviction and thirty-five for acquittal, the two sides argue the case until one changes his opinion and the accused is either acquitted or convicted. If no one changes his opinion, the presid-

ing judge announces, "We have reached an impasse," and the accused is acquitted. If thirty-five are for conviction, thirty-five for acquittal, and one is undecided, he is acquitted. If thirty-four declare for acquittal, thirty-six for conviction, and one is undecided, the accused is convicted, because there is a majority of two for conviction.

3. If a difference of opinion arises among the members of the Supreme Court—whether the difference is one bearing on a capital charge, or on a monetary matter, or on any question of law—the number of judges is not increased. They argue the case one with the other and the decision favored by the majority is followed. If the difference is one with respect to a capital charge, the same procedure is followed until the accused is either acquitted or convicted.

Chapter 10

1. Any judge in a capital case, whose vote—either for acquittal or for conviction—voices not his own carefully considered opinion but that of a colleague, transgresses a negative command. Concerning him Scripture says: *Neither shalt thou bear witness in a cause to turn aside* (Exod. 23:2). It has been learned by tradition that this injunction means, "Do not say when the poll is taken, it is good enough if I follow So-and-so; but give expression to your own opinion."

2. This negative command also forbids the judge who argued in favor of acquittal to argue later for conviction, as it is said: *Neither shalt thou bear witness in a cause to turn aside.* This rule holds good only as long as the case is still in the stage of discussion. But at the time when the verdict is about to be handed down, he who argued for acquittal may change his opinion and vote for conviction.

3. If one of the disciples who has spoken in favor of the accused dies, he is regarded as (though alive and) standing by his opinion.

4. If one of the disciples says: "I have a statement to make in favor of the accused," and then becomes speechless, or dies before he makes his statement and gives the reason for his opinion, his declaration is disregarded.

5. If two judges deduce the same argument from two scriptural verses, they are counted as one only.

6. It has been learned by tradition that in capital charges we do not begin with the opinion of the most prominent judge—lest the others not considering themselves competent to differ with him accept his opinion. It is mandatory that everyone should voice his own view.

7. Moreover, in capital cases, the opening statement (of the judges) must be one of encouragement and not

---

*From the Yale Judaica Series, trans. A. D. Hershman (New Haven, 1949).

of discouragement; that is, the judges say to the defendant, "If you have not committed the offense with which you are charged by the witnesses, you have no cause to fear the outcome."

8. If in a capital charge one of the disciples says, "I have a statement to make against the accused," he is silenced. But if he says, "I have a statement to make in his favor," he is brought up and seated among the Sanhedrin. If there is substance in his argument, he is listened to [and is allowed to vote], and he does not descend from there any more. If there is no substance in his argument, he does not descend from there all that day. Even if the accused himself says, "I have a statement to make in my favor," he is listened to, provided there is anything of substance in what he says.

9. If the court has erred in a capital case, declared guilty one who is not guilty, and rendered a verdict for conviction, and later discovers a reason for setting aside the decision—a reason which would give the accused a chance to clear himself—it revokes its decision and tries him again. But if it has erred in that it acquitted one who is liable to death, its decision is not revoked and the case is not reconsidered. This applies only to an error in a law which the Sadducees do not admit. But if the court has erred in a law which even the Sadducees admit, the decision is reversed for condemnation. . . .

Chapter 11

1. In what respects do civil cases differ from capital cases? Civil cases are tried by three judges, capital cases by twenty-three. In civil cases, the judges open the debate with either a favorable or an unfavorable statement; in capital cases they open the debate with a favorable statement, not with an unfavorable one, as has already been stated. In civil cases, the decision either for acquittal or for conviction is by a majority of one; in capital cases by a majority of one for acquittal, by a majority of (at least) two for conviction. In civil cases the verdict may be reversed either for acquittal or for conviction; in capital cases only for acquittal but not for conviction, as has already been stated. In civil cases, both the judges and the disciples may argue either for acquittal or for conviction; in capital cases, all may argue for acquittal, but only the judges may argue for conviction. In civil cases, the judge who has argued for conviction may subsequently argue for acquittal and the judge who has argued for acquittal may subsequently argue for conviction; in capital cases the judge who has argued for conviction may afterward argue for acquittal, but the judge who has argued for acquittal may not afterward argue for conviction, except at the time when the verdict is about to be pronounced, when he has the right to range himself on the

side of those who are for conviction, as has been stated before. In civil cases the trial is held in daytime and the verdict may be reached at night; in capital cases the trial is held in daytime and the verdict must be reached in daytime. In civil cases the verdict, whether of acquittal or of liability, may be reached on the same day; in capital cases the verdict of acquittal may be reached on the same day, but a verdict of conviction may not be reached until the following day.

2. Therefore, capital cases are not tried on the eve of a Sabbath or on the eve of a festival, for should the accused be found guilty, he could not be executed the following day, and it is forbidden to delay execution of the sentence until after the Sabbath. Therefore, he is kept in prison till Sunday, when his trial begins.

3. According to biblical law, civil suits may be tried any day, as it is said, *And let them judge the people at all seasons* (Exod. 18:22). The Rabbis, however, ordained that no trials be held on Fridays.

4. The rules obtaining in capital cases obtain also in cases involving flogging and those involving banishment. The only respect in which a case involving flogging differs from a capital charge is that the former is tried by three judges. None of these rules is operative in the trial of "an ox to be stoned" save that it is tried by a tribunal of twenty-three.

5. The rules followed in other capital cases are not followed in the case of an enticer. In his case, witnesses are put in hiding. No forewarning, required in other cases of those who are put to death by order of the court, is required. If the court has pronounced him not guilty, and someone says, "I have a statement to make against him," the enticer is brought back (to court). If he has left the court adjudged guilty, and someone says, "I have a statement to make in his favor," he is not brought back. There is no plea made on his behalf. On the tribunal trying his case are appointed a very aged man, a eunuch, and a childless man, because these are not likely to show him compassion. For stern treatment, meted out to those who mislead the people to go after things of nought, is clemency to the world at large, as it is said *that the Lord may turn from the fierceness of his anger, and show thee mercy* (Deut. 13:18).

6. In monetary matters and cases of uncleanness and cleanness, the court begins with the opinion of the most eminent judge, hearing what he has to say. But in capital cases, the court begins with the opinion of those on the side (benches) and the opinion of the most distinguished is heard last. . . .

Chapter 12

1. What is the procedure in capital charges? When the witnesses appear in court, stating, "We saw So-and-so commit such-and-such a transgression," the questions

are put to them, "Do you know him (the accused)?" "Did you warn him?" If they say, "We do not know him," or "We are in doubt as to his identity," or if they did not warn him, he is exonerated.

2. Whether the accused be a scholar or an ignorant man, forewarning is a prerequisite, as the purpose of warning is to make it possible to distinguish between the unwitting and the presumptuous transgressor, for there is the possibility that the accused committed the offense unwittingly.

How is he warned? He is told: "Abstain, or refrain, from doing it, for this is a transgression carrying with it a death penalty," or, "the penalty of flagellation." If he abstains, he is exonerated. So too, if he remains silent, or nods his head, he is exonerated. Even if he says, "I know it," he is not culpable, unless he surrenders himself to death, saying, "I know full well (the nature of the offense and the penalty it involves), nevertheless I will commit it." If such be the case, he is put to death. Moreover, he is not liable unless the offense is committed by him immediately after the warning, that is, within an utterance. But if the interval is longer than an utterance, another warning is required. Once warning was given him—whether by one of the witnesses or by someone else in the presence of witnesses, even if the admonitor was a woman or a slave, aye, even if he heard the admonition but did not see the admonitor, even if the warning was uttered by himself —he is put to death.

3. Once the witnesses say: "We gave him due warning and we know him," the court gives them a solemn charge. How are they charged in a capital case?

The court addresses them thus: "Perhaps what you are about to say is mere conjecture or hearsay, based on secondhand information, on what you heard from a trustworthy person. Perhaps you are unaware that we will in the course of the trial subject you to inquiry and query. Know that capital cases are unlike monetary case. In a monetary case, one may make restitution and his offense is expiated; but in a capital case (the witness) is accountable for the blood of the man and the blood of his (potential) posterity until the end of time. Thus with respect to Cain it is said: *The voice of thy brother's bloods crieth* (Gen. 4:10)—that is, his blood and the blood of his (potential) descendants. For this reason, but a single man was created, to teach us that if any man destroys a single life in the world, Scripture imputes it to him as though he had destroyed the whole world; and if any man preserves one life, Scripture ascribes it to him as though he had preserved the whole world. Furthermore, all human beings are fashioned after the pattern of the first man, yet no two faces are exactly alike. Therefore, every man may well say, 'For my sake the world was created.' And perhaps you will say, 'Why borrow this trouble?' It is said: *He being a witness, whether he hath seen or known, if he do not utter it, then he shall bear his iniquity* (Lev. 5:1). And perhaps you will say, "Why should we incur guilt for the blood of this man?' It is written: *And when the wicked perish, there is joy* (Prov. 11:10)."

If the witnesses stand by their evidence, the oldest of them is called and is subjected to inquiry and query, as will be set forth in the Treatise on Evidence. If his testimony is unshaken, the second is called and examined likewise. Even if there are a hundred witnesses, each is subjected to inquiry and query. If their evidence tallies, the debate is opened with words of encouragement (to the accused), as has already been stated. He is advised not to be afraid of what the witnesses have said, if he knows that he is not guilty. Then the trial proceeds. If he is found not guilty, he is set free. If he is found guilty, he is held in custody till the following day. In the meantime the judges meet in pairs to study the case, eat but little and drink no wine at all; all night each judge discusses the case with his colleague or deliberates upon it by himself. The following day, early in the morning, they come to court. He who was in favor of acquittal says, "I was for acquittal and I hold to my opinion"; he who was for conviction says, "I was for conviction and hold to my opinion," or "I changed my opinion and am now for acquittal." Should there be any mistake as to the identity of those who were in favor of conviction or of acquittal for the same argument (deduced from two scriptural verses), in which case the two count only as one, as has already been stated, the judges' clerks, who have a record of the reason given by each for his vote, call attention to this fact. The discussion is renewed. If (after the final vote is taken), the accused is found not guilty, he is set free. If it becomes necessary to add to the judges, the addition is made. If those for conviction are in the majority and the accused is pronounced liable, he is led forth to be executed.

The place of execution was outside the court, far away from it, as it is said: *Bring forth him that hath cursed without the camp* (Lev. 24:14). It seems to me that it was approximately six miles distant from the court, corresponding to the distance between the court of Moses, our teacher—the court located at the entrance of the Tent of Meeting—and the [outer limit of the] camp of Israel.

4. Once the verdict of conviction has been rendered, the culprit is executed on the same day without delay. Even if the culprit is a pregnant woman, it is not permitted to wait until she has given birth. She is struck against the womb so that the embryo is killed first. But if she had already sat on the birth stool, the execution is delayed until she has given birth. . . .

Chapter 13

1. He who is condemned to death is led forth from the court while one with a signaling flag is stationed at the door of the court and another, at some distance from him, is mounted on a horse. A herald precedes the culprit, announcing, "So-and-so is going forth to be executed by such-and-such a death, because he committed such-and-such an offense in such-and-such a place at such-and-such a time, and So-and-so and So-and-so are the witnesses against him. Whoever knows anything in his favor, let him come forward and state it." If one says, "I have something to say in his behalf," the signalman waves his flag, and the horseman runs and brings the culprit back to court. If he is found not guilty, he is set free; otherwise, he is led forth to be executed. Should the accused himself say, "I have something to say in my favor," although there may be no substance in what he has to say, he is returned once, aye, even a second time, because it is possible that, overwhelmed by fear, he was unable to marshal his arguments and that on being brought back to court (once again), he might regain his composure and offer a plausible plea. If after he has been returned to court no substance is found in what he said, he is once more led to the place of execution.

Should he assert a third time that he has a statement to make in his own behalf, if there is some cogency in his statement, he is brought back. This is done even many times. For this reason two scholars accompany him that they may listen to what he says. If they find that there is substance in his statement, he is brought back; otherwise, he is not brought back. If nothing is found in favor of acquittal, the execution is carried out. The duty of executing the culprit by the mode of death prescribed for him rests upon the witnesses. But in case of one convicted of murder, if the witnesses do not put him to death, others are bound to do so.

When he is about ten cubits away from the place of execution, he is told to make confession, for it is incumbent on all who are condemned to death to make confession. Everyone who does so has a portion in the world to come. If he knows not how to confess, he is instructed: "Say, 'May my death be an expiation for all my sins.'" Even if he knows that the evidence on which he is convicted is false, he uses this form of confession.

2. After he has confessed, he is given a cup of wine containing a grain of frankincense to induce a state of stupor and then he is executed by the mode of death prescribed for the offense of which he is guilty.

3. The wine, the frankincense, the stone with which the culprit is stoned, the sword with which he is beheaded, the cloth with which he is strangled, the tree on which he is hanged, the flags which are waved in the case of those who are executed by order of the court, the horse which runs that he might be delivered (from death)—all these are provided out of public funds, but if any individual offers to donate them, his offer is accepted.

4. The members of the tribunal must not follow the bier of one who is condemned to death. They are forbidden to eat food on the day of the execution. The latter prohibition is included in the injunction *Ye shall not eat with the blood.* (Lev. 19:26). Neither is a meal of comfort prepared for the near of kin of one who is executed by order of the court, because of the negative command *Ye shall not eat with the blood.* These things are forbidden; but the disregard of them does not involve the penalty of flagellation.

5. If one charged with a capital offense is found guilty on any of the intermediate days of a festival, the judges study carefully his case, eat and drink (all that day), give their final decision when the sun is about to set, and have him put to death.

6. No mourning is observed for those who are executed by order of the court. After the execution, the relatives come and greet the witnesses and the judges, as if to say that they harbor no ill feeling against them, for the judgment given by them was a true judgment. But though they do not observe mourning rites, they grieve for the executed, for grief is a matter of the heart.

*Notes and Questions to Moshe ben Maimon,
"The Trial of a Capital Case"*

Chapter 9

1. *Rule 1*

(*a*) This rule, which has been the cause of much discussion, is based on the following statements in the Talmud.[304] "Rabbi Kahana said, 'A Sanhedrin, all of whose members felt that he was guilty, [must] acquit him. What is the reason? We have learned that the judgment must be postponed [overnight] to search for a defense, and these will no longer see [one] for him.'" The common understanding of this talmudic dictum is that part of the "due process'" accorded to a criminal defendant in Jewish law was that after the deliberations of the court, and before any judgment was reached, the judges were required to spend the night together in pairs, searching for a possible defense for the criminal defendant.[305] Here, since all the judges of the Sanhedrin unanimously felt that the defendant was guilty, they would no longer actively search for a possible defense in his behalf. Accordingly, he was deprived of this "due

---

304. *Sanhedrin* 17a.
305. *Sanhedrin* 5:1.

process" requirement. He could not, therefore, be convicted and had to be acquitted. This rule would then reflect the extreme lengths to which Jewish law would go to accord a criminal defendant "due process."

(*b*) There have been many attempts to explain the obvious difficulties of this ruling. In the sixteenth century, Rabbi Loewe of Prague[306] explained the rule on the basis of the perspective that God would punish any criminal whom the court acquitted. There was no problem therefore, according to him, of a guilty criminal going unpunished. Nevertheless, the human court could not execute a criminal who was clearly guilty unless the trial was free from all defects. Since there was a "due process" failure here, the defendant was acquitted and his punishment left to God.

Compare the "Miranda" and "Poisoned Fruit" doctrines in the United States, which prevent the imposition of sanctions upon defendants who clearly appear to be guilty of crimes, where the police have engaged in acts that violated the defendants' constitutional rights.

(*c*) Z. Chajes[307] maintains that it is always possible for a judge to find some defense, such as insanity, for a criminal defendant. Since none of the judges here could advance any defenses at all in behalf of the defendant, even for the purpose of argument only, they were clearly incompetent or prejudiced. The defendant should therefore be acquitted.

Others have attempted to interpret the rule in a similar vein. A literal translation of the rule, as formulated by Rambam, is: "A Sanhedrin, all of whom opened the proceedings in capital cases, by first talking about his guilt, acquits him." It has been argued, therefore, that Rambam's reference here is not to a unanimous decision by a court after due deliberation but, rather, to an immediate conclusion by the Sanhedrin of "guilty" at the very opening of the trial, without due deliberation, without attempting to find any defense on the defendant's behalf, and without even permitting him to advance defenses. In such a case, the defendant is to be acquitted by the court. He cannot, thereafter be retried by another court because of the trauma that he suffers from the guilty verdict of the first court.[308] According to this view, the use of the phrase "all opened the proceedings . . ." indicates that the rule refers to an expression of the guilt of the defendant by the judges at the very beginning of the trial.

(*d*) A completely different interpretation of the foregoing statement in the Talmud (*Sanhedrin* 17a) is

attributed to Meir of Mehrin.[309] He is alleged to have interpreted the Talmud as saying that the defendant is "executed forthwith," rather than "acquitted forthwith," if the Sanhedrin unanimously found him guilty. It should be noted, however, that Meir of Mehrin, in his commentary *Yad Ramah*, does not set forth this view and, in fact, indicates the reverse.[310]

(*e*) This rule, in addition to its obvious difficulties in permitting the release of the defendant who was clearly guilty, is also apparently contradicted by the rule in the Talmud[311] that a person with a fatal defect who killed somebody in the presence of the court could be convicted, although his act could readily prejudice the court and would make it unlikely that its members would endeavor assiduously to find some defense for the accused.

It is quite possible that this rule applied also in other (nonhomicide) criminal offenses where less severe sanctions may be imposed, since Rambam ruled that the same norms that apply to capital cases apply also to the trial of these other offenses.[312]

2. Rule 2

(*a*) "*The one who is undecided is as though he were non-existent . . .*" If that is so, how can Rambam state in the very next sentence, "If thirteen vote for acquittal and twelve for conviction," since there are now only twenty-four participating judges (with the two who were added to the court)? Apparently, even the judge who was undecided may thereafter vote for acquittal, but may not vote for conviction.[313]

(*b*) Compare the possibility of conviction in Jewish law by a plurality of two with the prevalent rule in the United States requiring conviction by a unanimous jury or by a substantial majority. Should it make any difference that in Jewish law the judges pass both on the facts and on the law, while juries pass only on the facts? Consider also that the right of appeal in Jewish law may be more limited (see Section B 2 *e*, above).

Chapter 10

1. Rules 1–2

The biblical verse[314] cited by Rambam as the source of these two rules is interpreted to mean "Neither shalt

306. Loewe, *Be'er Ha'Golah*, ch. 2.
307. In his commentary to *Sanhedrin*, 17a.
308. Shimon Duran, *Rashbatz*, in his *Milhemet Mitzva* (Levov, 1857); Margolis, *Margaliyat Ha'Yam*, vol. 1, p. 72, no. 19.

309. Cited by Al-Gazi, in his *Halihot Olam*, sec. 643, and in Benebashti, *Hamra Ve'Haya*, addenda at end of Commentary to *Sanhedrin* 17a. See also Babad, *Minhat Hinuh*, no. 73; Trani, *Kiryat Sefer*, ad. loc.; Margolis, ibid., no. 24.
310. See his *Yad Ramah* (Warsaw, 1895) commentary to *Sanhedrin* 8b.
311. *Sanhedrin* 78a; see also Rambam, Laws of the Sanhedrin, beginning of ch. 3.
312. Rambam, Laws of the Sanhedrin, 11:4.
313. See Karo, *Kesef Mishnah*, ad loc.
314. Exod. 23:2.

thou . . . turn aside" to follow the view of others, or to turn aside from your previous view.[315]

2. *Rule 3*

The reference here to a "disciple" is to one who is temporarily added to the court and becomes a member thereof.[316]

The disciple who advanced an argument in favor of the accused and died was counted as a judge and was considered to have voted in favor of acquittal.[317]

3. *Rule 5*

A literal translation of rule 5 should read, "If two deduce the same argument, even, from two scriptural verses, they are counted as one only." This implies that if they deduced their arguments from the same verse, they are also counted as one.[318]

If two judges agree on a legal principle, and on its source in a biblical verse (that is, if both feel that he has violated the commandment, "Thou shalt not kill"), why should their opinions not count? Must each of the judges voting for conviction adduce a separate verse for his ruling? Some authorities, accordingly, claim that the word "even" is a scribal error and should not appear.[319]

It is arguable, however, that rule 5 here also refers to the case, referred to in rules 3 and 4 immediately preceeding, of a *disciple* who advances an argument for the defense and is elevated to the court (see rule 8, below). Two disciples who advance the same defense (both basing it upon one biblical verse) are both elevated to the court but have only one vote. Any two or more of the original judges, however, may base their legal argument upon the same scriptural verse.[320] The word "even" is then appropriate in that two disciples who advance the same argument do not receive two votes in the court, although they utilize two different scriptural verses as the basis for the argument.

The rule should then read, "If two deduce the same argument . . . ," referring to discussion by the disciples. The word "judges" should not, then, appear.

The reasoning for this rule, however, in the Talmud (*Sanhedrin* 34a) is that no passage in the Bible is superfluous. Accordingly, two different passages cannot appear for the purpose of teaching only one rule. Since two passages are cited by two persons for the same

rule, one of them must be mistaken. The two votes are, accordingly, counted only as one.[321] This reasoning seems applicable to judges as well as disciples.

4. *Rule 6*

Any judge may, and is required to, differ with the chief judge, since even a disciple may venture an opinion contrary to that of the judges.[322]

5. *Rule 7*

The words "encouragement" and "discouragement" in the Yale University translation are the translator's own additions and should be omitted. Instead, the phrase should read, "Capital cases are not opened with [discussions of] guilt, but [of] innocence."

Rule 7 is based on the Mishnah, *Sanhedrin* 4:1. The phraseology of this rule indicates that the judges must commence their deliberation of the case by considering defenses rather than the evidence for guilt.[323]

6. *Rule 8*

Note the extremes taken to encourage acquittals of criminal defendants. This rule reflects one of the easiest ways for a judicial trainee to be elevated to the court. It would also cause members of the court to be defendant-oriented.

The beginning of rule 8 in the Yale University translation should more properly read: "If, in capital cases, one of the disciples says, 'I have an argument to make for his guilt,' he is silenced. But if he says, 'I have an argument to make in his favor,' he is brought up and seated among the Sanhedrin . . . Even if the accused himself says, 'I have an argument to make in my favor . . . .' "

The elevation to the court of disciples who successfully advanced arguments for the defendant, occurred only in the case of the "Small Sanhedrin" of twenty-three members. The "Great Sanhedrin," consisting of seventy-one members, was not increased by adding disciples.[324]

7. *Rule 9*

Note the clinical training of law students and future judges by encouraging them to participate in court proceedings.

(*a*) The first lines of the rule should more properly read: "If the court has erred in a capital case, and declared guilty one who should have been acquitted,

315. David b. Zimra, Commentary, ad loc. (printed in standard editions of Rambam's code).

316. Talmud, *Sanhedrin* 33b, 34a, 43a; N. Gerundi, Commentary *Ran*, ad loc.; Margolis, *Margaliyot Ha'Yam*, vol. 1, p. 142, no. 14, p. 173, nos. 10–12; see rule 8, below.

317. Margolis, ibid., vol. 1, p. 143, no. 5.

318. See Karo, *Kesef Mishnah*, ad loc.

319. Response of M. Hagiz, in Responsa *Shte Ha'Lehem* (Vandzbak, 1733), sec. 19.

320. Margolis, *Margaliyot Ha'Yam*, p. 144, no. 10.

321. See Rishi's commentary, ad loc.

322. See rule 8; Habiba, *Nimuke Yosef, Sanhedrin* 36a; Rashi, Commentary to *Sanhedrin* 32a; N. Gerundi, Commentary *Ran*, ad loc.; David b. Zimra, Responsa *Radvaz*, vol. 1, no. 308.

323. See Rashi, Commentary to *Sanhedrin* 32a.

324. Ha'Meiri, *Beth Ha'Behira, Sanhedrin* 33a.

and rendered a verdict for conviction, and later feels that it should set aside the decision, it revokes the decision and tries him again."

(*b*) The latter portion of this rule is probably the earliest known precedent for the constitutional rule of "double jeopardy." The court may also set aside a "guilty" decision and acquit the defendant without a new trial, if it deems this proper.[325]

Chapter 11

1. *Rule 1*

(*a*) The third line should more properly read as follows: "In civil cases, the judges open their deliberations by considering matters either favorable or unfavorable to a litigant; in capital cases, they open their deliberations by considering matters in the defendant's favor, not in his guilt."

(*b*) "*In capital cases . . . by a majority of (at least) two for conviction.*" Note, however, that in the "Small Sanhedrin" of twenty-three judges there could be no conviction by a majority of two unless one of the judges could not reach a conclusion and additional judges were added;[326] e.g., if twelve voted for conviction and eleven for acquittal, there was only a majority of one. If thirteen voted for conviction and ten for acquittal, there was a majority of three, not two. In the Great Sanhedrin of seventy-one members, the same situation existed (that is, for example, thirty-six for conviction and thirty-five for acquittal would only constitute a majority of one, whereas thirty-seven to thirty-four would be a majority of three, not two), except according to Rabbi Judah, who maintains that the Great Sanhedrin had only seventy members. A vote of thirty-six for conviction to thirty-four for acquittal was therefore possible.[327]

(*c*) This rule emphasizes that the judicial "tilt" in favor of a defendant, was applied in all "criminal" cases, that is, those in which corporal punishment or exile could be imposed as a sanction. The "tilt" included not only the procedural rule mentioned above but also important "substantive" rules, such as requiring forewarning of a defendant by two witnesses, etc.[328]

The judicial "tilt" in favor of a criminal defendant is predicated upon the sanctity and dignity of human life, including that of a criminal defendant. This "tilt" is not applicable to the hearing held in the case of an animal that has killed a human being (see Section C 2 *a*, above).

2. *Rule 5*

(*a*) The beginning of this rule should more properly read, "The rules followed in other capital cases are not followed in the case of an enticer to idolatry. In this case, unlike other capital cases, witnesses may be put in hiding, and no forewarning is required. If the court has pronounced. . . ."

(*b*) Since an idolator was considered to be a barbarian, capable of any and every social evil, and whose actions therefore were an affront to God, one who attempted to entice others to become idolators was considered to be one of the greatest threats to society. The Bible,[329] in an unusual threefold repetition, forbids any

329. Deut. 13:7–11.

mercy in this case. The Talmud derives from this that the application of the law was to be tilted against him, rather than in his favor, as with the ordinary defendant.[330]

(*c*) Note, however, Rambam's language, "For stern treatment . . . is clemency to the world at large." This takes a "hard-line" position that those guilty of offenses should be dealt with sternly. The statement that such sternness is "clemency to the world" indicates his view that mercy to one who harms other individuals is, in effect, cruel to others, who may suffer at his hands if he is not dealt with adequately. This is consistent with the view that society should be more concerned with the victims of crimes than with the mild treatment of offenders. Note, in this connection, the talmudic dictum, "Whoever is kind to the cruel, will end up by being cruel to the kind."[331] This is predicated upon the thesis that cruelty, or lack of mercy, by society is desirable in dealing with serious crimes and that the execution of those guilty of capital offenses is not murder but is justified as a form of self-defense. It is also an expression of society's abhorrence of the crime and may further have an educational effect on the members of society in shaping their attitudes toward such offenses.

(*d*) Rambam supports his statement concerning stern treatment of serious offenders by citing a biblical passage that does *not* deal with an enticer. The passage cited comes after an extraordinary biblical provision that if the inhabitants of a town become idolators, they are to be killed. (This provision caused no end of difficulties for talmudic decision-makers, who declared it theoretical only since it never had been, and never

---

325. Abraham De Butan, *Lehem Mishnah* (printed in standard editions of Rambam's code), ad loc.
326. See Talmud, *Sanhedrin* 40a.
327. Ibid., 17a.

328. See Karo, *Kesef Mishnah,* ad loc. See also, Rashi, Commentary to *Sanhedrin* 81b; cf. Shlomo b. Aderet, Responsa *Rashba*, vol. 4, no. 109; Moshe Mintz, Responsa (Maharam Mintz), no. 12; Roth, Responsa *Kol Mevaser*, vol. 1, no. 35, sec. 6–8; Margolis, *Margaliyot Ha'Yam*, vol. 2, p. 99, no. 12.
330. *Sanhedrin* 67a.
331. *Yalkut Shimoni* (reprinted Jerusalem, 1960), 1 Sam., no. 121, p. 723.

would be, applied in practice).[332] After the Bible commands the killing of all the inhabitants (an apparently extremely cruel act on its face), it provides, "In order that God turn away from his wrath, and show you mercy."[333] Although the reference here to "mercy" seems ironic, Rambam understood the term "mercy" as appropriate, since cruelty to offenders could be merciful to the world at large. The sense of the verse's wording would then be as follows: If the Israelites were to obey God and show mercy to society (by being cruel to offenders), God, in return, would show them mercy.

(*e*) Note that entrapment, permitted in the case of an enticer, is prohibited in all other criminal cases.[334]

(*f*) The biblical provision for the unusually harsh treatment of the idolatrous town has been held to be a precedent and exemplar for the imposition of extraordinary sanctions by later decision-makers for the good of society.[335]

Chapter 12

1. Rule 1

(*a*) "*Do you know him?*" The question, in essence, is whether the witnesses recognize the defendant. Other talmudic commentators interpret the rule differently.[336]

2. Rule 2

(*a*) "*Unless he surrenders himself to death . . . .*" Rambam utilizes a similar expression with reference to killing an informer[337] and a *rodef*.[338] Contrast this with the rationale of Ibn Zimra[339] that a person may not be executed based on his confession because he does not have the right to cause his own death.[340]

(*b*) Clearly, under the requirements set forth here, a murderer could not be executed unless he knew that he was certain to be caught and executed. Such a murder normally would only be committed by a sane person if he had such an intense hatred for the victim that he was willing to lose his own life, as long as he could deprive the victim of his. Apparently, it does not refer to the case of a murder for the purposes of robbery or for any other motive that did not involve a motive so intense that the slayer was willing to lay down his life for it. What, then, of these other murderers? Would they go free for lack of proper forewarning? Presumably they would be penalized in some other way under the discretionary powers of the court in order to deter future murders.[341]

Under the foregoing rule, what proportion of murderers were handled by the traditional laws regarding homicide, and what proportion by the extraordinary powers vested in the court's discretion? Note that in the United States most murders are claimed to be crimes of passion, committed by friends or relatives. These would seem most likely to be the kind that were processed in Jewish courts by applying the ordinary norms.

(*c*) Is the foregoing rule, requiring a forewarning immediately prior to the commission of the crime, realistic for preserving minimum order in society? If, in fact, it could result in a conviction only in an infinitesimally small percentage of homicides, what was the purpose of such a restricted rule? Unfortunately, we do not know the number of homicides handled by Jewish courts in Israel during the Second Jewish Commonwealth, nor the percentage of these to which this tradi-

---

332. Talmud, *Sanhedrin* 71a.

333. Deut. 13:18.

334. Talmud, *Sanhedrin* 57a. See Kirschenbaum, "Double Jeopardy and Entrapment in Jewish Law," *Israel Yearbook on Human Rights* 3 (Tel-Aviv, 1973): 202.

335. Chajes, *Torat Ha'Neviim*, p. 50 ff.

336. See Rashi, Commentary to Talmud, *Sanhedrin* 40a; Rabbenu Hananel (printed in standard editions of the Talmud), ad loc., *Sanhedrin* 40b.

337. Laws Concerning a Batterer and Damager, 8:10.

338. Ibid. 8:12.

339. See his Commentary *Radvaz* to Rambam, Laws of the Sanhedrin, 18:6. See also his commentary to Laws of Kings, 9:4; Yisraeli, *Ha'Torah Ve'Hamdina* (Hebrew; Jerusalem, 1954), 5–6:107.

340. See Yisraeli, ibid.; David b. Zimra (commentary *Radvaz* to Laws of Kings, 9:4) utilizes the rationale than one must surrender oneself to death, to explain Rambam's ruling (Laws of a Murderer, 1:13) that one who killed a *rodef* when he could have stopped him by a mere wounding is not subject to capital punishment. David b. Zimra explains this as resulting from the fact that the *rodef* "surrendered himself to death." This may not contradict David b. Zimra's view that one does not have a

right to cause one's own death, since it may be that he was not referring to a "waiver" of life; see Zevin, "Addenda to *Mishpat* Shylock," p. 335, citing R. Akiva Eger, Novellae to *Ketubot* 33b, who explains "surrendered himself to death" here as involving a ratio similar to that advanced by Y. Soloveitchik, *Ha'Griz*, Novellae (Jerusalem, 1973, p. 137) namely, that since a *rodef* may be slain by the intended victim or by a bystander, he is not deemed to be a "viable" person. Consequently, he has thereby "surrendered himself to death," since his slayer is not liable to capital punishment. (See Rambam, Laws Concerning a Murderer, ch. 2, rule 6.) This ratio would not be applicable in our case, however, where a murderer was being tried by the court.

Zevin in addenda to "*Mishpat* Shylock," above extends this reasoning to explain why a *rodef* may be killed without acknowledging orally that he "surrenders himself to death" (as required by Rambam in rule 2). Zevin claims that since the *rodef* was subject to being killed by the victim or bystander, this fulfills the requirement of an oral "surrendering himself to death." If Zevin's ratio were correct, it should apply to do away with the oral, overt "surrender himself to death" requirement for every accused slayer, since every accused slayer was necessarily a *rodef* in the moments before he killed the victim! According to Zevin, every *rodef* impliedly "surrenders himself to death," since the defendant and every bystander is required to stop him, by death, if necessary.

341. See *Rambam*, Laws Concerning a Murderer, 2:4–5.

tional rule applied. Some scholars have concluded that rules such as the foregoing were purely theoretical and were never applied, nor meant to be applied, in actual practice.[342] It is also conceivable that some of the rules protecting criminal defendants were developed to protect them against the harsh Roman rulers of Judea, who would turn over brigands and revolutionaries to the Jewish courts for trial and execution.

3. *Rule 3*

(*a*) See note to rule 1, above.

(*b*) Note that the Sanhedrin could not render a verdict of guilty until their members had spent an additional night attempting to find a defense for the accused (see rule 1, above).

4. *Rule 4*

(*a*) The reason for executing the convict immediately was to save him the pain and suffering of awaiting his execution. This consideration for the suffering and dignity even of convicts emanates from the basic perspective that every human, including a convict, must be treated with great consideration, since he is as important as "an entire world" (see rule 3, above) and is created "in the image of God."[343] Additionally, the perspective, "You shall love your neighbor as yourself"[344] was applied in the Talmud[345] to the execution of criminals.

Compare the long time (sometimes years) that convicts in the United States must wait for execution, especially where it is delayed until the final outcome of the numerous appeals that are permitted. Note, however, that in Jewish law, no appeal from a conviction in a capital case was ordinarily possible.

Chapter 13

1. *Rule 1*

"Is stationed at the door of the court . . ."

(*a*) The flag bearer stands at the door of the court house, so that if any member of the court (or a member of the public who comes there) says, "I have something to say in his favor," he could then signal the horseman to stop the proceedings. This would be effective only if the horseman was still in sight. Other authorities claim that the flag bearer did not remain at the court house but mingled with the crowd, at some distance from but following, the accused. If any member of the public claimed that he had a defense for the accused, the flag bearer could then immediately signal the horseman, who would stop the proceedings.[346]

(*b*) *"The signal man waves the flag, and the horseman runs and brings the culprit back to court."* Note that the hearing regarding the new defense is not held on the spot because the convict (on his way to the execution, followed by crowds of people) might be overwhelmed by fear and unable to marshall his arguments. Instead, he is brought back to court. This, of course, could delay the proceedings for a considerable time.[347]

(*c*) Note that the witnesses against the accused are required to carry out the execution with their own hands. This is based upon the scriptural verse, "The hand of the witnesses shall be first against him to kill him."[348] This may sometimes have the effect of deterring false testimony, since the witnesses know they will have to bloody their own hands.

2. *Rule 2*

Note that the convict was first put into a state of stupor and then executed, so that he would feel no pain and would avoid some of the anguish of awaiting execution.

3. *Rule 3*

"If any individual offers to donate them, his offer is accepted." The Talmud[349] states: "The most respected women of Jerusalem used to donate and bring the wine and frankincense."

D. *The Rationale of Sanctioning*

The talmudic view of the rationale of punishment is ambivalent and has given rise to varying interpretations:

1. PUNISHMENT AND DETERRENCE
(Maimonides, *Guide for the Perplexed* 3:41)*

The punishment of him who sins against his neighbor consists in the general rule that there shall be done unto him exactly as he has done: if he injured anyone personally, he must suffer personally; if he damaged the property of his neighbor, he shall be punished by loss of property. But the person whose property has been damaged should be ready to resign his claim totally or partly. Only to the murderer we must not be lenient because of the greatness of his crime; and no ransom

---

342. See Chapter VI, Section E, below.
343. Gen. 1:27, 9:6.
344. Lev. 19:18.
345. *Ketubot* 37b.
346. Ha'Meiri, *Beth Ha'Behira, Sanhedrin,* 40b.

347. Cf. Rashi, Commentary to *Sanhedrin* 42b, indicating that the procession was stopped and the hearing held on the spot; see Margolis, *Margaliyot Ha'Yam,* vol. 1, p. 170, no. 6.
348. Deut. 17:7. In the case of homicide, it is the redeemer of blood who has the prior obligation to carry out the execution.
349. *Sanhedrin* 43a.
*The translation is by M. Friedlander (New York, 1956).

must be accepted of him. "And the land cannot be cleansed of the blood that is shed therein but by the blood of him that shed it" (Num. 31:33). Hence even if the murdered person continued to live after the attack for an hour or for days, was able to speak and possessed complete consciousness, and if he himself said, "Pardon my murderer. I have pardoned and forgiven him," he must not be obeyed. We must take life for life, and estimate equally the life of a child and that of a grown-up person, of a slave and of a freeman, of a wise man and of a fool. For there is no greater sin than this. . . . It is right that the more frequent transgressions and sins are, and the greater probability of their being committed, the more severe must their punishment be, in order to deter people from committing them; but sins which are of rare occurrence require a less severe punishment. For this reason one who stole a sheep had to pay twice as much as for other goods, i.e., four times the value of the stolen object; but this is only the case when he has disposed of it by sale or slaughter (Exod. 21:37). As a rule, the sheep remained always in the fields, and could, therefore, not be watched so carefully as things kept in town. The thief of a sheep used, therefore, to sell it quickly before the theft became known, or to slaughter it and thereby change its appearance. As such theft happened frequently, the punishment was severe. . . . The law concerning false witnesses (Deut. 19:19) prescribes that they shall suffer exactly the same loss which they intended to inflict upon another. If they intended to bring a sentence of death against a person, they are killed; if they aimed at the punishment of stripes, they receive stripes; and if they desire to make a person pay money, they are sentenced to pay exactly the same sum. The object of all these laws is to make the punishment equal to the crime; and it is also on this account that the judgments are "righteous" (Deut. 4:8). . . .

Preliminary Remark.—Whether the punishment is great or small, the pain inflicted intense or less intense, depends on the following four conditions.

1. The greatness of the sin. Actions that cause great harm are punished severely, whilst others that cause little harm are punished less severely.

2. The frequency of the crime. A crime that is frequently committed must be put down by severe punishment; crimes of rare occurrence may be suppressed by a lenient punishment, considering that they are rarely committed.

3. The amount of temptation. Only fear of a severe punishment *restrains* us from actions for which there exists a great temptation, either because we have a great desire for these actions, or are accustomed to them, or feel unhappy without them.

4. The facility of doing the thing secretly, and unseen and unnoticed. From such acts we are deterred only by the fear of a great and terrible punishment.

[These same thoughts are expressed in his code, "Laws Concerning a Murderer" 2:5; see also 2:9.—A. S.]

2. ATONEMENT
(S. R. Hirsch, *Commentary on Genesis* 9:6)[*]

Behind the judicial punishment ordained by the Torah, there is neither the idea of deterrence nor of retaliation, the so-called *jus talionis*, much as one thought one could deduce the former from, "And all Israel shall hear and see" (Deut. 13:11) and the latter from, "An eye for an eye" (Exod. 21:24). The fact that, in the laws of Jewish traditional punishments, no circumstantial evidence whatsoever, and no self-confession is accepted; that in cases of capital or corporal punishment, only such evidence may be admitted, of witness who not only saw the crime committed, but who had warned the accused at the moment of the occurence, of the letter of the law and of the penalty it would incur, a state of affairs which in any premeditated crime could easily be avoided; the further fact that in most crimes against property, even for robbery, no punishment at all, not even a fine, but only restitution, was incurred; already these striking peculiarities of Jewish jurisprudence definitely refute any idea that legal punishments are based on the principal of deterrence. (The author then adds, that deterrence could not have been the rationale for sanctions, since there are only four cases in which the Bible provides that punishment had to be publicized in order to deter would-be violators of law, all of these cases being unusual and rare circumstances, in which punishment would not ordinary be regarded as necessary) . . . just as little is the *jus talionis* to be deduced from the eye for an eye etc. of the Jewish law. Tradition teaches that thereby only a calculated amount of money is imposed, and, at the same time, points out how the taking of this legal canon, literally, in the sense of "an eye for an eye," would be morally impossible for any idea of equity. But even from the text itself, it is evident that by "an eye for an eye," only the exact reckoning in money of the amount of indemnification to be paid, is meant. Just before, it says (Exod. 21:24) "An eye for an eye"; it has already said in verse 19 that compensation in money is to be paid for inflicting wounds. . . . To the intelligent, all punishments are atonements, . . . not atonement of the offended principle, but atonement,

*The translation is by I. Levy (New York, 1965).

rehabilitation of himself. The future life of even the criminal, who suffers capital punishment, is taken to extend beyond the short span if his earthly existence. If he has paid for the damage he has done to the principle of Law by the loss of his existence here, he goes on to meet a new existence with regained purity. 'In the image of God, he made man.' In this sentence of the higher God-like nature of human beings, the motives . . . may well be given.[350]

[The foregoing overview is based in part upon the Talmudic principle that those who are executed by the *Beth Din* receive atonement for their crimes (*Sanhedrin*, 47a). Note that the ratio for capital punishment of a murderer in the statement "Because in the image of the Lord, was man made" (Gen. 9:6) may refer to the ratio of punishment, atonement, or both.[351] Regarding the atonement attained by execution or flogging, see Talmud, *Sanhedrin* 43b, 47a and b, and *Makkot* 23a. —A. M. S.]

E. *An Appraisal of the Function of the Judiciary in Maintaining Public Order and Imposing Criminal Sanctions*

How was public order maintained and how were criminal acts deterred in the Talmudic Era, in view of the pronounced judicial bent in favor of accused persons? These included the provisions that accused criminals could not be convicted without express forewarning, which had to be acknowledged orally by the accused, in the presence of two unrelated witnesses; the ban against admissibility of confessions and circumstantial evidence, acquittal in the event of unanimous conviction, and the many procedural requirements, discussed below. These would appear to make it well-nigh impossible ever to convict any criminal. Unfortunately, we lack hard data on how many persons were tried and convicted under these norms during the Second Jewish Commonwealth and the Talmudic Era.[352] Accordingly, it has been argued that these norms were ideal only and were never intended to be utilized in actual practice.[353]

The nature of Jewish trial law may be reflected in the fact that there was no attempt made to weigh the credibility of witnesses. Once two persons qualified as witnesses, their testimony was given the same weight as the testimony of one hundred witnesses who testified to the contrary.[354] Even if it was suspected that the testimony might be false, it might still be accepted and relied upon.[355] Similarly, women and relatives could not qualify as witnesses (regardless of whether they testified for the benefit of, or adverse to, the related party), despite their unquestioned credibility.[356] Similarly, the court could not decide on the basis of circumstantial evidence, no matter how overwhelming, and required the testimony of two witnesses.[357] Furthermore the Sanhedrin voluntarily moved out of the Temple Mount forty years before its destruction (Talmud, *Avodah Zarah* 8b) in order to avoid sentencing murderers to be executed (murderers could only be tried there, see Talmud, *Sanhedrin* 14b, 52b; *Shabbat*, 16b; Mekhilta, ed. D. Z. Hoffman (Berlin, 1905), p. 126; Rambam, *Sefer Hamitzvot*, "Root" 14) because incidents of murder proliferated. This does not accord with the notion that the function of a court is to maintain public order.[358] (See also Rambam, Laws of *Mamrim*,

350. See also A. Buechler, *Studies in Sin and Atonement* (London, 1928). Note also the talmudic view that a thief who confesses to his crime before witnesses come to testify against him is relieved of paying any penalty, other than the value of the stolen property (*Baba Kama* 14b, 74b).

351. Compare H. Cohn, "The Penology of the Talmud," *Israel Law Review* 5 (Jerusalem, 1970): 53.

352. Talmud, *Makkot* 7a.

353. See G. F. Moore, *Judaism* (Cambridge, 1927–30), vol. 2, p. 186; Z. Ginsberg, *On Jewish Law and Lore* (New York, 1970), p. 6.

354. Talmud, *Yoma* 83a, *Makkot* 5b; see, however, Tosefot, *Yebamot* 87a, s.v. *Asa*, that testimony would not be accepted if it contradicted facts known to all; see S. Cohen, *Sifse Kohen*, H. M., sec. 46:8.

355. See Jerusalem Talmud, *Sanhedrin* 6:3, where evidence of witnesses in a capital case was allowed to stand, even though they were suspected of perjury. There were, however, other factors present in that case. See, however, Talmud, *Sanhedrin* 32b; Talmud, *Shevuoth* 30b; Rambam, Laws of the Sanhedrin ch. 24:1 and 3, and particularly, commentary of David b. Zimra (Radvaz), ad loc.; Talmud, *Yebamot* 88a and *Tosefot* s.v. *Asa* ad loc. The law in this entire area is murky and requires clarification. See also Talmud, *Baba Batra* 31a; Rambam, Laws of Testimony, 22:1 and idem, Laws of the Foundations of the Torah, 7:7.

356. Jerusalem Talmud, *Yoma* 6.1, Jerusalem Talmud, *Sanhedrin* 3:9; Rambam, Laws of Testimony, 9:2, 13:1, 15; *Shevuot* 30a, *Baba Kama* 88a; *Sanhedrin* 27b. Epstein, *Tosafot, Zevakhim*, 103a, s.v. *Aivi*; Shlomo ben Aderet, *Responsa Rashba Attributed to Rambam*, no. 74; Talmud, *Levush Mordecai, Gittin* (Jerusalem, 1948), sec. 5.

357. Talmud, *Sanhedrin*, 37b. See, however, the selection from Rambam, Laws of Divorce set forth in Chapter V, Section C 5, above and Yom Tov Ashvili (Ritva), Novellae *Yebamot* 88a and as cited by Yosef Habiba, *Nimuke Yosef, Yebamot* ad loc. There is also a general principle that the testimony of one witness is sufficient (Talmud, *Yebamot* 87b), except in a case in which a defendant could be found liable by the court to pay monies to the plaintiff, or in which he could be subject to a sentence of death or flogging, or where the presence of witnesses was required for the legal validity of an act by the parties, such as divorce or levirate marriage. (*Sifri*, Deut. sec. 188 as per the reading of the text by Elijah of Vilna; Y. I. Halevi, *Dorot Ha'Rishonim* in *Sefer Zikaron*, ed. A. Auerbach; Bnai Brak, 1964, p. 142; see Y. Katz, *P'nai Yehoshua, Gittin* 2b.)

358. It has also been theorized that the Sanhedrin moved away because many of the murders were committed at the

1:1, and Laws of Coming Into the Temple, 6:11, which indicate that the preoccupation of the Sanhedrin was with ritual law and with educating the populace, not with criminal trials [Talmud, *Avodah Zarah* 8b]).

It may be that criminal trials in Jewish law were in essence a mode of divine service, or ritual, whose function was to attain atonement for the convict, and not necessarily to fathom the truth.[359] While the protective norms may be viewed as implying that talmudic criminal law was ideal only, and not meant to be applied in practice to maintain public order, this raises many questions. It is difficult to maintain that talmudic criminal law was ideal only, since a tremendous amount of discussion in the Talmud is devoted to very detailed discussions of these norms. Furthermore, some of the incidents recorded in the Talmud purport to report the application in practice of these rules; for example, Rabbi Simon ben Shetah's inability to bring a murderer to trial, despite the existence of strong circumstantial evidence,[360] the mishnaic statements that courts would execute criminals only once in seven (according to some versions, seventy) years,[361] and other similar reports.

Some scholars have maintained that while the judiciary was expected to apply the aforementioned norms in practice, these were effective only in a peaceful society, not prone to violence. When criminal activity became widespread and the norms were ineffective, the king (or another ruler or community leader, or otherwise, the court) was expected (and was viewed as authorized) to apply whatever means were thought

necessary to control criminal behavior.[362] Once monarchy ceased, the courts took over decision-making in this area and imposed whatever sanctions they felt appropriate, regardless of the traditional judicial norms.[363]

To the extent that king and court imposed sanctions to maintain public order, it is arguable that both were viewed as deriving their authority from the people and that they carried out their functions as representatives of the community.[364] Acting partly on this perspective, the Jewish communal organizations in the Middle Ages often carried out public order functions, imposed sanctions, and otherwise acted without regard to ordinary traditional norms.

It may also be conceivable that some of the norms protecting criminal defendants were designed to thwart Roman efforts to utilize the Jewish courts to punish brigands and other revolutionaries. There is, however, no concrete evidence to sustain this view.

In sum, there remains considerable ambiguity regarding both the perspectives and practices of Jewish decision-makers in applying criminal law during the Talmudic Era.

For adjustment of criminal law to meet changed societal conditions, see Part Three, Chapter IX, Section B, below.

---

behest of men of power whom the Romans exempted from penalty by the Sanhedrin. The Sanhedrin moved out of the Temple to avoid acting only against those who were too weak politically or militarily or too poor to acquire Roman insulation from the legal process. See Y. I. Halevi, *Dorot Ha'Rishonim*, pp. 146 ff.

359. See Shlomo b. Aderet, *Responsa Rashba Attributed to Ramban*, no. 74; Hirschensohn, *Malki Ba'Kodesh* (Jerusalem, 1923–26), no. 4, p. 27; see Chapter VI, Section D, below, "The Rationale of Sanctioning." See Talmud, *Sanhedrin* 43b, 47a and b, and *Makkot* 23a.

360. Talmud, *Sanhedrin* 37b.

361. Talmud, *Makkot* 7a.

362. N. Gerundi, *Derashot Ha'Ran*, discourse no. 11; Abarbanel, Commentary to Deut. 17:18 and to Judg. 17, 18:7, citing "There, were established seats of justice, seats for the house of David" (Ps. 122:5) as reflecting the dual functions of king and courts; I. Horowitz, *Shnei Luhot Ha'Brit* (reprinted Jerusalem, 1972), vol. 3, pp. 186–87; see also Ginsberg, *Mishpatim Le'Yisrael*, p. 134, n. 171, for extensive discussion. See Loewe, *Be'er Hagola*, ch. 2.

363. See Rambam, Laws Concerning a Murderer, chs. 4 and 5, which implies that both king and courts so acted at the same time.

364. Rambam, Laws of Armed Robbery, 5:18. See also Shmuel ben Meir (Rashbam), *Baba Batra* 54b; N. Gerundi, Novellae to *Nedarim* 28a; Chajes, *Torat Ha'Neviim*, ch. 7; Kook, *Mishpat Kohen*, no. 144; Zevin, Addenda to "*Mishpat Shylock*," p. 335; Yisraeli, *Hatorah Ve'Ha'medina*, 107; J. B. Soloveitchik, "Kiddush Ha'Hodesh," in *Ha'Pardes* (1944); Moshe Isserlis, Responsa *Rama*, no. 10; Sofer, Responsa *Hatam Sofer*, O.H., no. 208, and vol. 6, no. 14; Sender, *Ohel Rivkoh*, (Chicago, 1979), p. 204.

SUGGESTED READINGS

Allen, L. *Comparisons between Talmudic and American Law.* New York, 1960.

Avi-Yonah, M., ed. *World History of the Jewish People,* vol. 7: *The Herodian Period.* New Brunswick, 1975.

Baron, S. *Social and Religious History of the Jews.* Philadelphia, 1952–69.

Belkin, S. *In His Image.* (New York, 1960)

Chajes, Z. H. *The Student's Guide through the Talmud.* Trans. J. Schacter. London, 1960. A translation into English of Chajes' classic *Mavo La'-Talmud* (Introduction to the Talmud).

Cohen, H. "Secularization of Divine Law," *Scripta Hierosolymitana,* vol. 16 (1966).

Daube, D. "Rabbing Methods of Interpretation and Hellenistic Rhetoric," *Hebrew Union College Annual,* vol. 22 (1949), p. 239.

Elon, M. *The Principles of Jewish Law.* Jerusalem, 1975.

Falk, Z. W. *Introduction to Jewish Law of the Second Jewish Commonwealth.* Leiden, 1972.

Herzog, I. *Main Institutions of Jewish Law.* London and New York, 1965.

Herzog, I. *Judaism: Law and Ethics.* London, 1976.

Hirsch, S. R. *Horeb.* London, 1962.

Hoenig, S. B. *The Great Sanhedrin.* Philadelphia, 1953.

Kirschenbaum, A. *Self-Incrimination in Jewish Law.* New York, 1970.

Kirschenbaum, A. "The 'Good Samaritan' in Jewish Law," *Dinei Israel,* vol. 7 (1976), p. 7.

Lieberman, S. *Hellenism in Jewish Palestine.* New York, 1962.

Mantel, H. *Studies in the History of the Sanhedrin.* Cambridge, 1965.

Moshe ben Maimon. *Mishneh Torah: The Code of Maimonides.* Yale Judaica Series; New Haven, 1949 and thereafter in seriatum.

Moore, G. F. *Judaism in the First Century of the Christian Era.* Cambridge, 1927–30.

Neusner, J. *Foundations of the Babylonian Talmud.* Leiden, 1970.

Neusner, J. *History of the Jews in Babylonia.* Atlantic Highlands, N.J., 1966–70.

Schalit, A., ed. *World History of the Jewish People,* vol. 6: *The Hellenistic Age.* New Brunswick, 1972.

Schimmel, H. *The Oral Law.* Jerusalem, 1971.

The Talmud. (Soncino Press English translation.) London, 1935–52.

The Talmud with English Translation and Commentary. (The "El Am" Talmud.) New York, 1965 and thereafter in seriatum.

Part Three

Jewish Law in the Middle Ages (post 630 C.E.)

VII. Political and Social Contexts of Jewish Decision-Making in the Middle Ages

A. *Jews in Christian and Islamic Countries*

Beginning with the Edict of Toleration of the Emperor Constantine (313 C.E.), the governmental view concerning the Jews changed gradually from that of "a distinguished religion, certainly permissible"[1] to a "sacrilegious gathering" and even a "nefarious sect."[2] This attitude led to many restrictions against Jews, which were enshrined in various legal codes, such as the Code of Theodosius and the Code of Justinian. This situation continued after the division of the Roman Empire into its Western and Eastern units (*circa* 300 C.E.).

After the conquest of much of Christian Europe by the Germanic tribes and the establishment of Germanic states as successors to the Western Roman Empire, the condition of the Jews there improved temporarily. In many ways, these states followed the traditional German juridical systems, under which broad toleration was granted to religious minorities, who were free to follow their ancestral traditions. The "Breviary" of Alaric modified much of the anti-Jewish legislation of the Theodosian and Justinian codes.

Visigoth Spain, however, was different. There the intensive drive for the unification of the country, plus the extreme views held by the local Catholic clergy, resulted in the persecution of ethnic minorities and harsh measures taken against them. This included both Jews, Moslems, and heretical Christians.[3]

There was a substantial Jewish population in the Byzantine Empire, which stretched from southern and central Italy through the Balkans and Asia Minor, and was one of the most powerful states in the period from the eighth to the tenth centuries. It was marked by a vigorous economy, whose prosperity was based to a significant degree upon trade and efficient government administration.

The status of Jews in Byzantium was a mixed one. On the one hand, the Second Counsel of Nicaea ruled against forced conversion. The *Basilica* (the legal compendium of that era) continued to recognize the Jewish community and its rights,[4] including the right to refrain from labor on the Sabbath. On the other hand, Jews suffered from many other restrictions and were excluded from the army and the vast civil service.

Their status was never very secure, particularly in the face of the near-pathological anti-Jewish attitudes of some of the emperors and leading personalities. The sharpness of the anti-Jewish feelings among the Christian Roman emperors in the Eastern (Byzantine) Empire is exemplified in the remark made by the Emperor Zeno (474–491 C.E.), who, upon hearing that the bones of Jewish dead had been consumed in a fire at the synagogue at Antioch, exclaimed, "Why did they not burn the living Jews along with the dead?"[5] A common attitude among Church leaders and emperors was that the Jews should forever suffer because of their alleged participation in the killing of Jesus and that they should become permanent wanderers and aliens.

Among the anti-Jewish acts was the abolition of the Jewish patriarchate (see Part Two, Chapter VI) in Palestine in 429 C.E. This greatly reduced the scope of Jewish communal decision-making there. The widespread discrimination and anti-Jewish attitudes were also important factors in the continued migration of Jews from the Byzantine Empire to Babylonia, where the generally lenient Persian treatment led to the flowering of the Jewish community and of Jewish law and scholarship.

Eventually the Emperor Heraclius ordered that every Jew in the Roman Empire should be baptized and completely outlawed the practice of Judaism (629 C.E.). This edict could not be fully enforced, however, because invading Arab armies suddenly burst forth from the Arabian peninsula. Headed by the caliph Omar, they conquerd all of Palestine and the entire Persian Empire as well (*circa* 636 C.E.). Omar's conquest of Palestine was also aided significantly by the Jews of Jerusalem, who looked to him as a savior from Byzan-

1. See S. Baron, *The Jewish Community* (Philadelphia, 1942), p. 228; M. Grant, *The Jews in the Roman World* (New York, 1973), pp. 282–87.

2. A. Sharf, "The Jews in Byzantium," in *World History of the Jewish People*, vol. 11 (New Brunswick, N.J., 1974), p. 57; C. Roth, *A Short History of the Jewish People* (London, 1953), p. 138.

3. B. Blumenkranz, "The Roman Church and the Jews," in *World History of the Jewish People*, vol. 11, pp. 69–70.

4. Sharf, "Jews in Byzantium," pp. 57–61, 65. See also Codex Theodoseanus 2.2.10; Corpus Juris Civilis, Codex Justinianus 2.1.6.8.

5. Grant, *Jews in the Roman World*, p. 287.

tine persecution. The anti-Jewish attitude of the Byzantine emperors and Church leaders was a forerunner
of the treatment that was later to be accorded to the
Jews in Europe under Christendom.

After its conquest of these vast territories and populations, most of which were forcefully converted to
Islam under the threat of death, Islamic rulers gradually became somewhat more tolerant. They permitted
Jews and other religious minorities to practice their
religion, subject, however, to a number of discriminatory practices. These were mainly the payment of poll
taxes, the wearing of special dress, and the prohibition
from bearing arms or riding on horseback. Islamic
rulers permitted the institution of the exilarchate (*resh
galuta*) to continue in Babylonia and to wield great
power within the Jewish community. The heads of the
academies in Babylonia (who began to be called *gaonin*,
"Exalted Ones," at about this time) also exerted great
influence in Jewish decision-making (see Chapter VIII,
Section B 1 *b* below).

In the wake of the Arab conquests of North Africa
and Spain, many Jews left the Near East, seeking
better economic conditions in the conquered territories.
Substantial Jewish populations proliferated thereafter
all along the North African coast and in Spain. Most
of the Jews in these countries were farmers, artisans,
and merchants. Many of them, particularly in Spain,
became physicians, and some even obtained positions
of great diplomatic importance. Most of the Jews in
these countries became thoroughly Arabicized, speaking the Arabic language and emulating Arab learning
and poetry. In the Islamic countries there was a great
growth in Jewish intellectual life, *belles lettres*, and in
Jewish religious and talmudic studies. There were, however, intermittent periods of persecution, particularly
by the Berbers in the portions of Spain that they had
conquered from the Christians toward the end of the
eleventh century, and by the Berber Almohade dynasty
in 1146, which forced all Jews either to convert, be
killed, or leave the country. As a result, thousands of
Jews left the Berber realms at these times.

Nevertheless, because of the relatively tolerant treatment, many Jews moved to Islamic countries. These
soon contained the bulk of the world Jewry in numbers
and was the center of Jewish learning. The relatively
tolerant conditions of the Jews in Islamic countries is
to be contrasted with the position of the Jews at that
time in Christian countries, where their status gradually
deteriorated.

B. *The Church and the Jews in Western Europe*

Despite the encouragement of Jewish settlement in
Western Europe by sovereigns such as Charlemagne,
Louis the Pious, and many of the Carolingian and
Capetian rulers (who realized the importance of Jews
to the economic development of their lands), many of
the early Church leaders there harbored hostile anti-
Jewish attitudes. The Church was, furthermore, constantly and intensely preoccupied with encouraging
Jews to convert to Christianity and feared Jewish pros-
elytizing among Christians and pagans. This led to
periodic violent riots, with much killing and destruction, forced baptism, and wholesale expulsion of Jewish
communities. These were common in Spain, France,
and Lombardy in the seventh century and periodically
thereafter. Additionally, many restrictions were imposed upon Jews by various Church councils, including
prohibitions against the possession of Christian slaves,
the building of new synagogues, the holding of public
office, and serious restrictions on the ownership of land
and engaging in trade.

There was a curious bifurcation between the attitudes
and actions of the Church toward Jews in medieval
Europe. Despite the many persecutions in practice (including massacres, expulsions, assaults, forced baptism,
and various discriminations and indignities), led by
local clergymen or encouraged by the Church in Rome,
the official Church position was that Jews in Christian
society should be extended a limited toleration. In
theory at least, they were to be allowed to exist as a
subject people, albeit with many inequalities and mis-
treatments, in order to demonstrate the superiority of
Christianity. This was much the same as the Muslims
treated religious minorities. Nevertheless, while the
Church at Rome ordinarily did not actively urge massacres, expulsion, or forced conversion of Jews, it did
not often protest such acts either. Neither did it curb
local clergy who instigated them, nor limit church activities that would inevitably lead to such excesses.

While there were theoretical objections to converting
Jews by force,[6] these were not applied in practice. No
sanctions were imposed upon those who used force to
convert Jews, nor did the Church define the meaning of
"force." Consequently, children, especially, were converted forcibly under the claim that these conversions
were consensual. Furthermore, the Church insisted that

---

6. See, e.g., the Council of Toledo in 633; Letters of Gregory
the Great; B. Blumenkranz, "The Roman Church and the
Jews"; Baron, *The Jewish Community*, vol. 1, p. 216.

those who had been converted forcibly to Christianity were required to remain Christians.[7]

The prevailing perspective in medieval Europe was that the Jews were a lower class who were in effect serfs, subject to the whim of either Church or lay princes. The very right of Jews to dwell in any locality depended upon the will of these masters. Consequently, despite the common expulsions of entire Jewish communities from localities or states throughout the Middle Ages, there is no record of any Jew or Christian ever contesting the right to decree such expulsion.

The attitude of the various popes, individually, toward the treatment of Jews was not consistent. Most often, they were satisfied to leave this to the whims of local ecclesiastical authorities. Pursuant to the traditional official position of the Church, most popes since Calixtus II (1119–1124) confirmed by papal bull, *Sicut Judaets*, the privileges of the Jews of Rome to remain there and engage in normal activities. While the bull was directed only to the Jews in Rome, it could, and often did, serve as an example to all of Christendom. So, too, a number of popes came out officially against forced baptism or assaults, often, however, without attempting to enforce these positions. Those who were in fact forcefully converted were required to remain Christians under official Church rule. Pope Leo VII even explicitly authorized the forcible conversion of Jews. A number of popes, such as Honorius III in 1221, issued anti-Jewish bulls that ordered the razing of synagogues.

Rampant discrimination against Jews was often encouraged by the Church. Innocent IV (1250) prohibited Jews from employing non-Jews or from living near Christians, and required them to wear clothing identifying them as Jews.[8] Jewish communities were often compelled to send representatives to debate in public the merits of Christianity. The Church also disqualified Jewish witnesses from testifying in Christian courts. This, however, had the effect of relegating Jewish litigation to Jewish courts, and it strengthened the powers of Jewish decision-makers. The Church also instituted a vigorous censorship of Jewish books and periodically organized episodes of Jewish book-burning. These actions had the effect of impeding the spread of Jewish learning and scholarship, with many valuable religious and legal works being lost forever.[9] At the same time,

they tended to unify members of the Jewish community in reaction against a hostile world.

In this anti-Jewish atmosphere entire communities might be penalized, at the urging of local clergy, by onerous fines or even expulsion because of the alleged anti-Christian acts of any individual Jew. Church intervention on behalf of Jews was not common. As a result, there was vigorous activity on the part of Jewish communities to prevent and curb activities by any individual Jew that could endanger the entire community. This was particularly true with regard to informers who might denounce individual Jews or an entire community to the authorities. In turn, these curbs resulted in great and extreme powers being vested in the hands of Jewish communal decision-makers. (For the effects on Jewish law of the fear of informers, see below, Chapter IX, Section C 2.)

C. *Changes in the Jewish Condition in the Early Middle Ages*

1. ECONOMIC CHANGES AND JEWISH POPULATION SHIFTS

During the eighth to eleventh centuries profound changes took place in the condition of Jewish communities thoroughout the world. Perhaps the most basic change of all was the gradual movement of the centers of Jewish population from the Near East (including the Mediterranean lands) to northwestern Europe. There had been numerous Jewish settlements in Europe from very early times, principally as a result of the sale of Jewish slaves by the Romans and the establishment of Jewish mercantile centers. Now, however, there was a gradual shift of Jewish population to these areas, so that they ultimately contained the bulk of world Jewry as well as the main centers of Jewish scholarship and leadership. The main factor in the dramatic increase in Jewish population in the West appears to have been economic conditions that spurred gradual migration of small groups of Jews from the East. The policies of the Moslem conquerors of the East gradually drove Jews and Christians into crowded urban slums, which made life very unattractive, both economically and socially. At the same time, increased trade and prosperity in the West, with new areas of Europe being constantly opened to settlement and trade, attracted many Jews there.[10]

The Moslem invasions and the division of the Mediterranean world in the seventh to ninth centuries re-

7. See, e.g., Regulations of the Council of Toledo in the years 633, 653, 655, 681, 693, 694, etc.

8. See also, the Regulations of the Third Lateran Council, 1179, and of Pope Paul IV, in 1558.

9. Baron, *The Jewish Community*, 1:216–17. See also S. Schwarzfuchs, "France and Germany under the Carolingians," in *World History of the Jewish People*, vol. 11, p. 143; C. Roth, *Short History of the Jewish People*, p. 146 ff.

10. See C. Roth, in *World History of the Jewish People*, vol. 11, pp. 3, 18–19.

sulted in great upheavals in the European economy. They spurred a surge of economic activity toward the northern portion of Europe, away from Moslem threats. Commerce expanded rapidly along the valleys of the Meuse and Rhine rivers, which became the nerve centers of western European trade. It was the bright economic picture in these areas that drew large numbers of Jews to settle there.

Another stimulus to Jewish immigration to France and Germany in the ninth and tenth centuries was the common practice of local areas to invite Jews to settle there in order to stimulate commercial activities and the development of cities. The emperor, or the local bishop or noble would grant Jews protection from the "insolence of the populace"[11] and would give them land for houses. The "privileges" granted by the emperor or bishop also protected their property and, purportedly, insulated them from forced baptisms. Jewish communities were also granted the right to appoint communal authorities with the authority to conduct civil, and even penal, trials.

The Jews commonly would settle voluntarily in a quarter of the town that centered around the synagogue. A wall was often built around that quarter to protect them from a hostile population. This voluntary settlement in one area later degenerated into the coerced confinement of Jews in ghettos.

By the end of the eleventh century there was a substantial Jewish population in Germany, the size of which is a matter of scholarly debate.[12]

2. THE GROWTH OF JEWISH LEGAL AND RELIGIOUS CULTURE IN THE WEST

Until the tenth century the center of Jewish learning was situated in Babylonia. Subsequently, along with the shift of the center of Jewish population to the West (aside from the simple increase in population), a similar transference of cultural and legal influence occurred. The causes of the apparently sudden emergence of learning and legal scholarship in the West remain obscure. There is even a legend of four learned emissaries from a Jewish academy in Babylonia, sent to Europe to collect contributions, who were captured by pirates and sold to various parts of North Africa and Spain. There they allegedly set up academies of their own and trained many disciples, who subsequently played leading roles in Jewish religious and legal affairs.

What is clear, however, is that, beginning with the tenth century, most of the leading talmudic scholars

who played a crucial role in decision-making (particularly in the prescription and application of norms) were found in the West. Such noted decision-makers as Isaac Al-Fasi, Gershom ben Yehudah ("The Light of the Exile"), who was active in the prescription of many regulations that profoundly affected Jewish life, Rabbi Shlomo Yitzhaki (commonly known as Rashi and noted for his classic, detailed commentaries on the Bible and nearly the entire Talmud), the French and German scholars (known collectively as the authors of the incisive *tosefot* commentaries to the Talmud), all lived and were active in the West. This activity corresponded with the growth of many elementary and higher schools of Jewish religious and legal studies throughout the West, particularly in France and Germany, leading to what was perhaps the highest level of Jewish education ever achieved by Jewish communities. The main center of talmudic and Jewish legal studies was in France and Germany, while philosophy and *belles lettres* flourished more in Spain.

3. THE URBANIZATION OF JEWISH LIFE IN EUROPE

By the tenth century Europe, including its Jewish communities, had become increasingly urbanized. In the East, under Islam, most Jews were peasants, craftsmen, and inhabitants of small villages. In Europe, however, most of the Jews were city dwellers by the eleventh century. There were many factors that contributed to this trend.

The increasingly numerous prohibitions upon Jews to own land in many places, their exclusion from the feudal rural society (which was tied together by a common faith and religious oaths), and their fear of living in isolated rural areas in hostile environments that were physically dangerous as well as inhibiting to Jewish religious practices (such as communal prayer) led to the gradual concentration of Jews in urban areas. This movement was also greatly stimulated by the attractions of urban centers as foci of commerce and learning.

Another important factor was the opening of new trade routes, which attracted Jewish settlers because they offered commercial possibilities. Thus, Jewish urban concentrations developed all along the major trade routes from the coasts and up through the river valleys in Italy, France, and Germany.[13]

The rise of cities in medieval Europe had a substantial effect on the legal status and economic activities of the Jewish communities. The cities were centers of industrial and commercial activity. This led to rivalry between the Christian townsmen and the Jews, who

11. Blumenkranz, "The Roman Church and the Jews," p. 162.
12. Ibid., p. 165.

13. Roth, in *World History of the Jewish People*, p. 43.

were engaged in competitive activities in large numbers, particularly after they were driven from agriculture. At the same time, it led to much economic and eventually cultural, contact between Jews and Gentiles.

The struggles of the cities for liberation from royal rule and for autonomy encouraged the Jewish communities to strive for the same ends. The populations of the towns formed associations and communes, which eventually were recognized by grants from the feudal lords. These communes may have followed the models of the earlier Jewish communal structure, the *kahal*.[14] On the other hand, once the cities received autonomy, they sometimes regulated Jewish commercial activities more closely than a larger territorial unit could hope to do. The economic rivalries, added to the intense anti-Jewish feelings generated by religious and other factors, caused many cities to expel their Jewish populations. The proliferation of cities, therefore, often meant more frequent and thorough Jewish expulsion. All of the foregoing activities, of course, affected the scope of operations of Jewish communal leaders and decision-makers.[15]

4. INCREASED JEWISH COMMERCIAL ACTIVITY

During the eighth through the tenth centuries Jews played an increasingly important role in trade, particularly international trade, in which they had a number of unique advantages. The former unity of the Roman Empire, which had formed one political, economic, and cultural unit with two predominant languages—Latin and Greek—was shattered by the Moslem conquests in the East. International merchant travelers no longer found the same way of life, law, or religion existing in every country that they visited. While the adoption of the Arabic language throughout the Islamic East was not an insuperable barrier to trade, the hostile attitudes there toward Christians and toward the West in general, plus the different cultural and legal perspectives and practices, did obstruct trade.[16]

In these changed circumstances Jews had unique advantages in trade. They were universally educated and could communicate in writing with Jews in foreign lands since all understood Hebrew. The religious persecutions of Jews and the numerous discriminatory practices against them resulted in a solidarity of feeling among Jews. They were received sympathetically by

their co-religionists in other countries, who would often go to great lengths to help them. There was a similarity of cultural outlook among Jews everywhere, and, of crucial importance, talmudic law was applied by Jews in all countries. Jewish merchants could therefore plan their transactions with certainty as to the legal consequences, and they were assured of a prompt and equitable resolution of any conflicts that might arise in their mercantile dealings. All these factors are thought to have resulted in the prominent participation of Jews in international trade.[17]

5. THE POLITICAL AND POWER STATUS OF JEWS IN MEDIEVAL EUROPE

The Jews occupied a unique and unfortunate power position in the early Middle Ages. On the one hand, the spread of Christianity and hostile anti-Jewish feeling against them placed them in an inferior power position. In addition, the feudal structure of the Middle Ages, based heavily on a common religious faith, had no place for the Jew. On the other hand, many of the royal sovereigns of Europe at first encouraged Jewish immigration to their lands in order to foster and stimulate commerce and also looked to them as a fruitful source of taxation to finance royal wars and construction, the principal activities of royalty in the Middle Ages. Thus the Jews became, in effect, royal serfs and vassals of the kings.

This role was fortified by the practice of the Jewish communities to pay to the king the taxes that they had traditionally paid to the Roman Empire. The result was that the kings often protected the Jews in order to preserve them as tax-producing assets. At the same time, the kings exercised minute control over the Jewish communities, regulating their internal affairs, taxing them arbitrarily, and using them as a source of income whenever money was needed, especially on short notice. The status of Jews as vassals of the king also meant that the king could confiscate their property, alienate all of their rights, and expel them without warning from his lands. This situation led to many tragic consequences for a period of more than one thousand years.

D. *The Crusades*

The Crusades inaugurated a prolonged era of unprecedented martyrdom and religious persecution of Jews in Europe.[18] The first Crusades of major impor-

---

14. See E. Petit-Dutailles, *Les Communes Francais: Caracteris et Evolution des Origins au XVe Siecle* (Paris, 1947), pp. 12–38; Schwarzfuchs, "France and Germany," p. 150.

15. Baron, *The Jewish Community*, 1:274–77.

16. P. Grierson, "Commerce in the Dark Ages: A Critique of the Evidence," in *Transactions of the Royal Historical Sociey*, 5th series, 9 (1959): 123–40.

17. Baron, *The Jewish Community*; Roth, in *World History of the Jewish People*, p. 29.

18. See, in general, A. M. Haberman, *Sefer Gezerot Ashkenaz Ve'Zarefat* (Tel-Aviv, 1946); S. Runciman, *History of*

tance were the Crusades to Spain in 1063, aimed at regaining that land from the Moslems. On their way the Crusaders turned on the Jewish communities, whom they regarded as anti-Christian. With great religious fervor, they massacred the Jewish populations of many communities and forcefully converted others.

In 1095, during the long series of mass Crusades that engulfed nearly all of Europe, the Crusaders attacked numerous Jewish communities in the course of their trek to the distant Holy Land. The result was widespread mass slaughter. The victims could sometimes escape death only by forced conversion to Christianity. Nearly all of the Jews, however, chose to be killed rather than to relinquish their faith. Thus the entire Jewish community at Worms was killed. Similar occurrences took place at Prague, Cologne, and many other communities. Often, in anticipation of an attack by the Crusaders, the Jews of a community would all dress in white burial shrouds and march to the cemetery in prayer. There they would be killed when they refused to be baptized. Other communities committed suicide *en masse*, sometimes with parents and children, husbands and wives, killing each other, instead of waiting to be tortured or killed by the crusading mobs. Typical also was the behavior at Xanten where:

> there was also a pious man called "The Rabbi of France." He said to all of them, "This is what is done our country." Digging a pit, he pronounced the ritual blessing, cut his own throat, and died before the Lord.[19]

Thus, wholesale suicides and self-immolation by entire communities became common during the violent persecutions that accompanied the many Crusades. When the Crusaders finally reached and conquered Jerusalem in 1097, they herded all of the Jews of the city into a synagogue, set fire to it, and burned them inside, along with the sanctuary.

Similar massacres occurred during subsequent Crusades, including innumerable massacres at London and other parts of England. Also during the Crusades, numerous false blood libels were spread against Jews, accusing them of kidnapping Christian children and drinking their blood as part of religious ceremonies. These accusations, too, often led to violent outbreaks. During episodes of widespread disease, particularly the

outbreak of the bubonic plague ("the Black Death"), to which approximately one-third of the population of Europe succumbed, the Jews were again blamed, leading to widespread slaughter, forcible conversion, and expulsions.

It should be noted that in the eleventh century the power of the crown had expanded considerably in many lands. Accordingly, when kings now expelled the Jews from their lands, or issued edicts against them, these had a much wider and more serious effect than similar occurrences just a century earlier, which were often limited to much smaller areas.

Following the Church's Lateran Council of 1215, which took a very strong anti-Jewish stand, persecution of Jews in Europe increased further. Thus, Edward I of England had Jews tortured to extract money from them to replenish his finances. Many of the survivors were massacred. When those that remained eventually became too poor to pay taxes to the crown, he expelled them from England.

In France, Louis IX made serious attempts to enforce the decrees of the Lateran Council, and he ordered all copies of the Talmud burned. In 1249 he ordered all Jews expelled from France. This latter decree was not, however, fully carried out. Not long afterward, Phillip the Fair had all of the Jews of his realm arrested, confiscated all of their property, and expelled them. This terminated Jewish life in France, including the noted centers of Jewish learning there, which had been preeminent for approximately four hundred years. (Thereafter some Jews were permitted back intermittently, only to be expelled again at a later date.) Similar fates met the Jewish communities in Germany and parts of Italy.

E. *The Effects of the Crusades*

1. CHANGES IN THE ECONOMIC POSITION OF THE JEWS

In the wake of the Crusades, the increase in hostile anti-Jewish sentiment affected all areas of Jewish economic activity. The resulting discrimination against Jewish merchants, made commercial ventures, particularly in foreign countries, dangerous for Jews. This, together with the closer ties that emerged between the West and East and the protection achieved for Christian traders in the Mediterranean and Middle East, led to a drastic decline in the role of Jewish merchants in international trade in the twelfth century and thereafter.

Jewish craftsmanship and local commercial ventures were also seriously affected. Medieval European commercial and craft guilds were social bodies with important religious aspects, including their own religious

the Crusades (Cambridge, Eng., 1951–55); H. Graetz, *History of the Jews* (New York, 1941).

19. Blumenkranz, "The Roman Church and the Jews," p. 162, citing S. Salfeld, *Das Martyrologium Des Nurenberger, Memorbuches* (Berlin, 1898). See also the prayer *"Av Ha'-Rakhamim,"* incorporated in the Sabbath prayers, and the dirges, *"Ha'Kharishu Mimeni Ve'Adabera," "Mi Yiten Roshi Mayim,"* and *"Amarti She'v,"* commemorating the massacres at Speyer and Mainz, incorporated in the religious services for Tisha Be'Av.

services, processions, and often, chapels. They were run on sentiments of uniformity, and sought to protect each other against foreigners, including Jews, who were regarded as aliens. The guilds, therefore, had no place for Jews.

With the spread of prohibitions against Jews on hiring non-Jewish assistants (e.g., the Third Lateran Council of 1179), combined with the exclusion of Jews from the craft guilds and numerous other restrictions placed upon Jews engaged in manufacturing and handicrafts, the number of Jews in these occupations also declined dramatically.

Often the only economic activity open to Jews from which they could earn a livelihood, was money-lending. Their participation in this activity was spurred by a number of additional factors. Wars, construction, and increased commercial trade, the hallmarks of medieval Europe in the post-Crusade era, required extensive financing. At the same time, the Church took a very strong position against usury (e.g., the Third Lateran Council of 1179). This led many Jews in Christian countries to become occupied, directly or indirectly, in money-lending. In fact, nobles who wished to lend money, but to avoid Church criticism, utilized Jews as conduits to lend money, the true identity of the real creditor being kept secret. The demand for funds was also increased dramatically by the change in the European economy of that era from a barter to a money economy.

By the middle of the thirteenth century, however, the money-lending business proved too lucrative and attracted many non-Jewish usurers. Because of the numerous restrictions and discriminations against them, Jews could not compete successfully with their non-Jewish competitors. Consequently, in a short time the Jews were reduced to petty lending, amounting to pawnbroking (lending small sums of money, secured by pledges of personal property). Nevertheless, the Jews continued to earn universal odium as usurers.

This was true despite the fact that in the south and east of Europe, where the discriminatory restrictions upon Jews were commonly ignored, the Jews were largely and preeminently engaged in the dying and weaving of silk and were heavily involved in handicrafts, particularly as goldsmiths and silversmiths in Spain, southern Italy, Sicily, and other areas.

2. THE DEGRADED SOCIAL POSITION OF THE JEWS

The Church's Third Lateran Council of 1179 prohibited Christians from lodging among or near Jews. This laid the foundation for the ghetto system, which became prevalent at a later time. These regulations, together with the prohibitions against associating with or working for Jews, degraded them socially, in addition to greatly restricting their ability to earn a livelihood in commerce and industry.

Among the many anti-Jewish provisions adopted by the Fourth Lateran Council of 1215, under the auspices of Pope Innocent III, was the forced wearing of a special mark of identification by Jews. Commonly this was a yellow or crimson cloth, or a special type of hat. The wearing of these marks stigmatized the Jews, leaving them open to constant insults, assaults, and massacres. The persecutions and uncertainty of life caused degrading child betrothals to become common, out of fear that the parents would die and leave their children, particularly the girls, destitute.

Jewish isolation also encouraged Jewish religious studies as a haven from a hostile world. But, in this poisoned atmosphere, burnings of the Talmud and other Jewish books occurred regularly. Perhaps the most famous burning was in Paris in 1242, when twenty-four wagon loads of Jewish books—precious and rare, especially in that preprinting era—were burned. The burnings were so common and thorough that today only one complete European handwritten manuscript of the Talmud (the so-called, "Munich" manuscript) exists.

Fortunately, however, there were times when the regulations were ignored, although they were enforced periodically. For example, although Jewish physicians were prohibited from treating non-Jews, many of the kings, and even popes, had Jewish physicians.

F. *The Growth of Jewish Communities in Poland*

Spurred by the continuous persecutions in Western Europe, many Jews, particularly those of Germany and France, moved to Poland. That country had been devastated by the Tartar invasions of 1240–1241, and the Polish sovereigns established a policy of attracting merchants and craftsmen. In 1264 King Boleslav issued a charter of protection and liberties for the Jews there. This was enlarged in 1354, by Casimir the Great, who prescribed that disputes involving Jews could be heard only by the crown (to insure impartiality) and that Jews were permitted to rent estates from the nobility. The authority of Jewish communities and their right to regulate internal Jewish affairs were established by successive edicts promulgated by a number of Polish kings.[20]

20. See, in general, I. Heilpern, in *Beth Yisrael Be'Polin* (Tel-Aviv, 1946); S. Dubnow, *History of the Jews in Russia and Poland* (Berlin, 1923).

Despite occasional flare-ups from the peasants, the number of Jews in Poland grew rapidly. It has been estimated that there were at least 50,000 Jews there by the year 1500, and there were at least 600,000 there by 1648. They were engaged in all kinds of handicrafts and commerce, were active at the trade fairs, and served as tax farmers and financial agents for the nobility and crown. These latter activities aroused great hostility on the part of many peasants and led to great tragedy later.

G. *The Spanish Inquisition and Expulsion from Spain*

The Jewish communities in Spain flowered intermittently until the middle of the fourteenth century, when mass slaughters and forced religious conversions occurred repeatedly.

In 1478 a new institution—the Inquisition—was established by Pope Sixtus IV. Its first head in Spain was Torquemada (who, ironically, was himself a descendant of converted Jews). Its principal task in Spain was to investigate religious lapses among the Christians. The Inquisition soon introduced a period of mass interrogations, torture, and violent death. At least 30,000 persons, principally converted Jews (often called "Marranos," which probably meant "pigs") were put to death, while hundreds of thousands were sentenced to other penalties. The death penalty was carried out publicly by an *"auto da fe"* (literally, "an act of faith"), in which the victim, standing before huge mobs (sometimes numbering many thousands of persons who came in from the countryside especially to witness the spectacle) was asked to publicly repent and accept the Christian faith. Upon refusal, the victim would be tied to a stake and burned to death. Often death was preceded or accompanied by many other horrible tortures, including boiling in oil. The Inquisition not only repressed the practice of Judaism in Spain but also spread to other parts of Europe, where it helped to spark a strong reaction in the Reformation movement against the Catholic Church.[21]

In 1492 King Ferdinand and Queen Isabella (who by their marriage united the kingdoms of Castile and Aragon) ordered all Jews in Spain to either convert to Christianity or leave. At least 150,000 Jews, and perhaps many more, opted to go into exile rather than forsake their religion. While thousands took passage to lands where they thought they might be granted entry,

there was widespread exploitation and charging of exorbitant transportation rates by unscrupulous ship captains. Many of those who sailed were seized by the ships' crews and sold as slaves in Africa, and their possessions were stolen by the crews. Many were thrown overboard into the sea, while numerous overcrowded and unseaworthy ships sank, together with their entire crews and passengers. Many of those who did reach lands where they were admitted, such as Sicily and Sardinia, were subsequently expelled from there in the following few years and had to go into exile once again. The majority of about 100,000 Spanish Jews went to Portugal, where the king gave them eight months to quit the country. However, the Portuguese king, Manuel, desirous of marrying the daughter of Isabella and pleasing her, seized all Jewish children between the ages of four and fourteen and forcibly baptized them. He then declared their parents to be slaves unless they agreed to be converted. Large numbers complied.

Many of those who did not travel to Portugal settled along the North African coast, where they formed their own groups within the established Jewish communities there and kept up their Spanish traditions and language.

Perhaps the main area where Jews were freely admitted without subsequent religious persecution was Turkey, which had been ruled by the Turks since the capture of Constantinople (and the fall of the Christian Byzantine Empire) in 1453, some forty years earlier.

Another important area where Jewish refugees from Spain resettled was Palestine. Many noted scholars emigrated there, and the city of Safed, in the Galilee, became a center of Jewish religious studies, notably Kabbalah (mysticism) and Jewish law. It became the home of Rabbi Isaac Luria and Rabbi Joseph Karo, who were world famous in these respective fields.

A number of Jews settled in Holland when it later freed itself of Spanish rule, and many ended up in Poland, which was seeking to attract Jewish immigrants in order to develop the country (see above, Section F).

Substantial numbers of Marranos immigrated to the western hemisphere, particularly the West Indies and Brazil. In fact, Columbus's expeditions, which found and explored the New World, were financed by Marranos and Jews; all of his ships' doctors and many of their officers were Marranos, and his interpreter, the first man to set foot in the New World, was also a Marrano. Many of these New Christians became very active in the commercial trade that developed between the New World and Europe, particularly commerce with tobacco, sugar, coral, and foreign exchange. It has been speculated that one of the unexpected results of the Inquisition in Spain was to spur the transfer of the center of world commerce from southern to north-

---

21. See, in general, Y. Baer, *History of the Jews of Christian Spain* (New York, 1971); A. Neuman, *History of the Jews of Spain* (New York, 1960); Roth, *A Short History of the Jewish People*, pp. 307, 357 ff.

ern Europe as a consequence of the activity of the Marranos.[22]

H. *Effects of the Renaissance and the Reformation on Jewish Life*

The Renaissance, with its emphasis on learning, *belles lettres*, and the arts, had its effects on Jewish life, particularly in Italy. There was greater tolerance for Jews and increasing interaction, intellectually and socially, among Jews and non-Jews there, with many Jews making important cultural contribution, particularly in the areas of philosophy and poetry.

The Protestant Reformation, while primarily directed against the Catholic church, led indirectly to anti-Jewish agitation. Martin Luther, who sparked the Protestant Reformation against the Catholic Church, had at first hoped to convert the Jews to Christianity and was sympathetic with their plight at the hands of the church. His translation of the Bible relied heavily on Jewish commentators. When, however, he realized that, even after the reforms that he introduced, the Jews were not embracing Christianity, he became a bitter Jew-hater and preached the burning of synagogues and mass expulsion of Jews.

The Protestant Reformation movement brought anti-Jewish measures from many quarters. Protestant leaders became bitterly disappointed in the Jews when they did not convert to Christianity. The Catholic church's counter-reformation movement, seeking to battle and contain the effect of Protestantism, often held Jews responsible for the Reformation and sought to suppress Jews along with Protestants.

---

22. See, in general, the citations in footnote 21.

I. *The End of Jewish Communal Autonomy and the Imposition of the Ghetto*

The Chmielnicki massacres in Poland in the middle of the seventeenth century decimated and weakened Jewish life there and were a prime factor in the disintegration of the Jewish autonomous communal governments, including the Jewish Council of Four Lands and the Council of Lithuania (see Chapter VIII, Section A 1 *d*, below). Another fatal blow to Jewish autonomy occurred in the 1700s as a result of the gradual lifting of the restrictions of ghetto life.

In the wake of the Napoleonic conquests, the ghetto walls were torn down. In France the National Assembly made Jews equal citizens. With the spread of the French Revolution and its emphasis on liberty, equality, and fraternity, the ghetto walls came tumbling down in Venice, Rome, the Rhineland, Frankfurt, and many other areas.

The end of Jewish isolation and the integration of Jews into the non-Jewish world was a death blow to Jewish autonomous government. This, in turn, ended the communal application of traditional Jewish law in Europe, which had been backed by the sanctions of government force and authority. Although Napoleon reconstituted a Sanhedrin in France, this was short-lived and of lesser duration than his reorganization of the Jewish communities (1807–1808). Even this, had only minor impact on government-sanctioned application of Jewish law.

Thus the French Revolution, and the resultant emancipation of Jews and their integration into the non-Jewish community, resulted in the loss, with one blow, of the physical control and authority of Jewish decision-making institutions and the continued vigorous development of applied Jewish Law.

VIII.   The Jewish Legal System in Operation

A. *Jewish Communal Autonomy and Decision-Making**

1. SOCIETAL CONTEXTS OF JEWISH COMMUNAL DECISION-MAKING

The key factor that determined the extent of Jewish communal authority and decision-making in the Middle Ages was taxation:

The legal recognition and support of Jewish autonomy was in more or less direct ratio to Jewish fiscal contribution. It was at its highest where Jewish taxes played the most significant role in the state's budgetary system, as in north-central Europe during the Middle Ages and at its lowest in the Byzantine Empire or the areas of resettlement, where the Jews paid little more than their Christian neighbors.[1]

Local community decision-making in medieval Europe came to be made more and more frequently by the lay community council rather than, as heretofore, by the *beth din* or by individual scholar–religious leaders. This was due to a coalescence of many diverse factors. There was an economic, political, and population decline in Babylonian Jewry, which had occupied a central position and which formerly had a controlling voice in Jewish decision-making all over the world. The scattered Jewish European communities in the early Middle Ages did not have a central decision-making body. Yet decisions were urgently required to meet the new exigencies of life, including increasingly complex commercial transactions and radical changes in economic and social conditions. These varied from place to place.[2]

The institution of the salaried rabbi did not become widespread until about the fifteenth century. At the same time, many of the lay leaders were extremely well versed in Jewish law and were consequently viewed as appropriate persons to act as decision-makers. All of these factors led to a pronounced increase in local communal decision-making by laymen. Even when the practice later became common to hire community rabbis as salaried employees, the extent of lay decision-making remained substantial since the Rabbis were subject to lay supervision and dependent upon laymen for their livelihood (see Section B 1 *c*, below).

Coinciding with the need for, and the spread of, Jewish communal decision-making by laymen in early medieval Europe, was the phenomenon of wide grants of autonomy to Jewish communities by non-Jewish rulers. These attained their apogee in medieval Europe because of the coalescence of a number of diverse factors.

Feudal Europe was divided into a hierarchy of discrete corporate bodies, each with its own political status and distinct economic function. In agriculture there were classifications into serfs, tenants, and nobles, while in the towns and cities there were divisions into different crafts and trades. This breakdown of society into distinct layers and units appeared natural to the medieval mind.

Accordingly, it was only natural for Jews also to constitute a separate unit in society.[3] The Church, too, adhering to Christian tradition, recognized the Jewish community as a separate unit, distinct from the rest of society. This view was reinforced by the prevalent medieval attitude toward the Jews as being misguided and different than anyone else. The result was a policy of letting the Jews do as they wished, since they were wrong anyway.[4]

The revenue needs of the medieval states were important spurs in their recognition of Jewish communal autonomy. All Jews were, in effect, regarded as the serfs of the various princes (or of the Church), in whose realms they dwelled. Consequently, Jews were required to pay a separate tax to the state. This tax became a crucial element in financing the constant wars and other state activities during the Middle Ages, which required perennial infusions of fresh funds. The Jewish communities were regarded as more efficient units than the state for the collection of such taxes, and they were given considerable autonomy in this respect. Indeed, the administrative weakness of the medieval principali-

---

*See "Lay Decision-Makers," Part Two, Chapter VI, Section B 4.

1. S. Baron, *The Jewish Community* (Philadelphia, 1942), 1: 282.

2. See Y. Baer, *History of the Jews in Christian Spain* (New York, 1971), pp. 28–29; M. Elon, *Ha'Mishpat Ha'Ivri* (Jerusalem, 1973), 2:562.

3. See H. Ben-Sasson, *Chapters in the History of the Jews in the Middle Ages* (Hebrew; Tel-Aviv, 1969), p. 90; Baron, *The Jewish Community*, p. 209.

4. Ben-Sasson, *Chapters*, p. 90.

ties, which were unable to service the needs of the various groups in society, was an important factor in the recognition of separate groups in that society, each with its own distinct needs. The collection of the Jewish tax by the Jews themselves, was also thought to ensure the ability of the state to collect such taxes since even if an individual taxpayer fled the land, the Jewish community would still be held responsible.

While the tax payment was very onerous, the taxes were sometimes regarded as a distinct advantage by the Jews themselves. "Taxes are our protectors," exclaimed one Jewish leader,[5] since Christian rulers otherwise might have no compunction in expelling the Jews from their territories at the slightest whim.

At the same time, this Jewish communal responsibility for assessing and collecting these taxes helped to bind the members of the Jewish community together and to strengthen the hand of its leadership.

It should be noted that in some parts of early medieval Europe, there was considerable hostility by feudal lords toward urban communal associations. Like the non-Jews, the Jews formed secret associations and at first met in cellars and graveyards.[6] As discussed, however, there eventually evolved universal recognition of the right of Jewish communities to act autonomously with regard to their internal affairs and to decide controversies among themselves in accordance with traditional Jewish law. In some parts of Europe such rights were not new but had existed during the times of the Roman Empire and were often simply continued by many of the subsequent rulers.

There was also, perhaps, a feeling among non-Jewish medieval rulers that permitting the Jews to have their own leadership would ensure their obedience to the laws of the land. These leaders would in effect be hostages, liable to severe punishment in the event of violation of the laws by any members of the Jewish community.

The Jewish communal structure was further fortified by the strong Jewish tradition of communal self-rule, with each community constituting a distinct cell, economic unit, and family-type grouping, which decided its own destiny in many areas (see Section B 1, below). Jews, therefore, commonly demanded and received from the gentile rulers grants of local autonomy and exclusion from the feudal structure as a condition of settlement and residence.[7] At the same time, each Jewish community was also regarded by Jews as an integral portion of the larger mystical community of Israel, bound to it by intense religious ties.[8] The communal ties forged by this perspective were further strengthened by the common religious activities and beliefs of Jews everywhere.

Another factor that fostered local Jewish communal decision-making was the restriction of Jews to only a few areas of economic activity. This bound Jews together with strong ties of economic self-interest. They were forced to act in unison to regulate some of these economic activities, in order to protect these circumscribed sources of livelihood for the members of the community. Similarly, the intense animosity of the outside world bound the Jews together and forced them to take common counsel and action against a hostile world. Constant alertness was required since the acts of any individual Jew could be perceived by hostile neighbors as anti-Christian in some way and could often bring tragedy upon the entire community. The necessity for quick and vigorous action in this regard tended to result in increased powers for the leadership of the Jewish community. The imposition of the ghetto system, in which all Jews were required to dwell in one quarter, reinforced the perspective that the Jewish community was, in effect, a state within a state.

At the same time, Jews, rather than Gentiles, were the prime decision-makers who applied the law governing internal regulation and settled disputes among Jews during the Middle Ages. In addition, Jews were discouraged from resorting to non-Jewish courts by an ancient Jewish tradition that such action amounted to renunciation of the Torah and to the elevation of non-Jewish law and ideals above that of Judaism.[9] Furthermore, the Church disqualified Jewish witnesses from testifying in state courts. This forced Jewish litigants to bring their disputes to Jewish courts.

More important, perhaps, was the fact that Jewish law was highly developed, both because of its intense study throughout the centuries for religious reasons, and because of its exposure to, and development under, varied societal conditions. These included semi-capitalist Hellenist and Roman centers, the semifeudal conditions in Christian Rome and Persia, and the expanded economic activities of the Islamic caliphate and the port cities of Southern Europe and Byzantium. This made Jewish law well equipped to deal with the varied litigation that arose in lands with different economic and social conditions. By contrast, the law prevailing in the

5. Asher ben Yehiel, in *Rosh*, Talmud, *Baba Batra* 8a; see also the similar views of Netira, a Jewish plutocrat, below.

6. Shlomo Yitzhaki, Responsa *Rashi* (Jerusalem, 1962), p. 258, no. 231; E. Petit-Dutailles, *Les Communes Françaises*, pp. 82–86.

7. A. Agus, "The Autonomous Rule of Jewish Communities in the Middle Ages" (Hebrew), *Talpiot*, vol. 5 (New York, 1951), pp. 176, 189.

8. See Ben-Sasson (*Chapters*, p. 84), who claims that this basic Jewish religious concept helped to distinguish the Jewish community during the Middle Ages from the individual towns and cities of gentiles.

9. See, e.g., Talmud, *Gittin* 8:2.

courts of illiterate early medieval Europe was often primitive. It should be recalled that as powerful an emperor as Charlemagne was able to write only one letter of his name, while the other letters preceding and following it had to be filled in by professional scribes.[10] Furthermore, the uniformity of Jewish law in all countries ensured similar court decisions in similar cases, inspiring confidence and permitting activities to be planned, based on reasonable predictions of the way they would be treated by the courts.

All of the foregoing factors led to the recognition by the authorities in medieval Europe of the autonomy of the various Jewish communities, and to their authorization to both prescribe and apply law, as well as to enforce their own decisions.

These functions were taken over largely by Jewish laymen. The structure of Jewish communities was uniform throughout medieval Europe as a result of strong tradition and of the uniform standards of the Christian Church of Europe regarding the Jewish communities. In many ways, therefore, these Jewish communities became self-contained states and effective substitutes for the Jewish state that had existed in Judah many centuries before.

From the point of view of the state, however, the main task of the autonomous Jewish communities was to collect the lump-sum tax that was placed on every Jewish community and to allocate the burden among the members.

a. THE MEDITERRANEAN LANDS IN GENERAL

The condition of Jews and the contexts of Jewish decision-making in the Middle Ages were different in the countries of southern Europe that bordered the Mediterranean (Byzantium, southern Italy, southern France, the Iberian Peninsula) than in northern Europe. Jewish settlements in the south were rooted in antiquity, having predated the advent of Christianity. The traditions and institutions of Roman law, which recognized Jewish communal autonomy, self-rule, and decision-making, were largely continued. These lands were closer to Islamic countries and were influenced by the attitudes in favor of autonomy and greater tolerance for minorities that generally prevailed there.[11]

b. SPAIN

In the early Middle Ages the Christian rulers in Spain often valued Jews as allies and soldiers in their battles with Islam for control of the Iberian Peninsula. Their

value was considered so great that at times they were prohibited from emigrating from the country. The kings, accordingly, sought to protect them. Nevertheless, the Jews in time came to be looked upon as royal "treasure," or "property." Initially, Spanish rulers also encouraged the use of Jewish courts by Jewish litigants, in accord with the perspective that each group should be judged by its own laws. This afforded Jewish communal decision-makers wide latitude in the prescription and application of the law. Gradually, however, the prerogatives of Jewish decision-making were reduced. In 1315 the Jews of Majorca were placed under the local non-Jewish civil law and judiciary. This was extended to Barcelona (by Pedro IV) in 1377, and in 1380 the Jews were prohibited from adjudicating criminal law matters in Castile by King John I. Civil as well as criminal jurisdiction was removed from the Jews and Moors by John II in 1412. This practice was extended by subsequent rulers, particularly King Ferdinand and Queen Isabella in 1476, and it soon spread to the entire Iberian Peninsula.[12]

c. NORTHERN EUROPE

The condition of the Jewish communities, and consequently of Jewish decision-makers, in Northern Europe was different in a number of respects from that in Southern Europe. First of all, there was no strong tradition of Roman law, with its recognition of civic equality. The influence of similar Muslim perspectives was also nonexistent. The feudal divisions of society into autonomous corporate groups were very extensive, and Jews could not usually become a part of any of these groups. In Germany primitive Teutonic legal systems were still influential, with their notion of different (inferior) treatment for aliens. In medieval Europe the Jew was certainly "alien" and, hence, did not receive equal treatment with non-Jews.

As a result of the autonomous corporate division of feudal Europe, Jewish life was regulated on different levels by the imperial, royal, ducal, episcopal, and municipal rule, which affected the lives of communities and individuals.[13] The Jews, however, not belonging to any of the feudal divisions of society, eventually came to be regarded as royal serfs and had to pay large annual taxes to the king for the privilege of simply remaining in his realm. As feudal possessions, they were often prohibited from leaving a land without permission of the king, and they were sometimes extradited from other states to which they had moved.[14]

10. Baron, *The Jewish Community*, 1:211.
11. Ibid., 1:227.

12. Ibid., 1:238–39.
13. Ibid., 1:248.
14. E.g., by Louis IX, 1230; see ibid., 1:246.

Nevertheless, there was a tradition, inherited from the Franks, of Jewish autonomy in communal self-government that was incorporated in many "privileges," such as the privileges granted in 1090 to the Jews of Worms by Henry IV, and extended to Jews in all of Germany by Frederick II in 1230. These privileges allotted much power to Jewish communal decision-makers, including the Jewish judiciary. The royal grants of Jewish autonomy were also influenced by the notion that it would be easier to raise taxes from the Jews by having these collected by their own chosen chiefs.[15]

Following the Crusades, which generated intense anti-Jewish feelings (see Chapter VII, Section E, above), Jewish communities suffered a series of mass expulsions (i.e., from England in 1290, from France in 1306 and 1397, from many German and Italian localities in 1348–50, and from Spain and Portugal in 1492 and thereafter). These, of course, ended Jewish autonomy there and severely curtailed Jewish decision-making activities, other than those concerned solely with ritual and sacerdotal practices. Beginning in the sixteenth century, however, the trend began to be reversed and the legal and economic status of Jews became generally more stable (with less frequent, though, violent exceptions) in Germany, Italy, Holland, and particularly Poland. Marranos (Jews who were forcibly converted to Christianity but secretly remained Jews) emigrated to many areas in western Europe and founded numerous communities there. The relative security enjoyed by the Jewish community during this epoch encouraged the development of Jewish communal institutions and Jewish autonomy. This, in turn, meant wider powers for Jewish decision-makers.

However, the relative stability also had its drawbacks. It "tended to crystalize communal evolution at a stage achieved in the sixteenth century. There were few subsequent creative innovations," even during the intense Shabbatian controversies and the spread of Jewish religious movements of the seventeenth and eighteenth centuries.[16] Apparently, without a powerful stimulus to change, Jewish communities tended to continue in their traditional ways.

d. POLAND AND LITHUANIA

During the Middle Ages many of the countries in Central and Eastern Europe were extremely desirous of attracting Jewish settlers in order to help develop their countries economically and to increase their populations. As a result, King Boleslav of Poland granted "privileges" to Jews, assuring them of the right to en-

gage in commercial activities and to run their own affairs (1264). Similar steps were taken by rulers in Austria, Bohemia, and Hungary.

Jewish autonomy probably reached its zenith in Poland during the sixteenth and seventeenth centuries. King Sigismund Augustus issued an edict in 1551, permitting the Jews to select a chief rabbi and to appoint judges with the authority to apply traditional Jewish law. These officials were to be answerable only to the king. This has often been regarded as the "Magna Carta" of the Jews in Poland.

The Jewish communities of Poland henceforth proceeded to select these officials, as well as representatives to local community councils, which regulated internal Jewish affairs. At the yearly Polish commercial fairs, particularly those at Lublin and Jaroslav, representatives of the different Jewish communities would meet to decide on the apportionment of the tax burdens placed upon the Jews by the king and to resolve disputes between communities. These resembled the Jewish synods that were convened in Franco-Germany in the eleventh century, but they had much greater powers and wider effect in Poland. These intercommunity meetings eventually developed into a *va'ad* ("council") known as the Council of Four Lands (consisting of "Greater Poland," "Little Poland," Podolia, and Volhynia). There was a separate council for Lithuania.

The Council of Four Lands acted as a parliament for the Jews of Poland. It enacted much legislation, including regulations prohibiting ostentatious and expensive dress and entertainment. It resolved disputes between communities, acted to prevent undue competition among Jewish merchants, and served as a court of appeals for difficult, protracted litigation. It apportioned the royal taxes among the Jewish communities, enforced royal edicts, and even sent representatives to attend the meetings of the Polish parliament (the *Sejm* or *Diet*) at Warsaw. (For details, including the allocation of decision-making powers in the *va'ad*, see Section A 2 *b* [3], below.)

Many Jews immigrated to Poland because of the attractions there, in contrast to the intense persecution and massacres in western Europe during the Crusades. Spurred by these royal privileges, the Jews eventually came to be regarded as *servi camerae*, or "servants of the treasury," that is, the king. This reflected a semi-contractual relationship in which the king was to provide the Jews with royal protection. In return, they were to pay annual taxes to the king and perform various other duties, including cleaning the king's mills, watching for thieves, and other civic functions. The privileges and protection granted by the king allowed the Jews communal autonomy, backed by the power of the king.

---

15. See Ben-Sasson, *Chapters*, p. 90.
16. Baron, *The Jewish Community*, 2:121.

Gradually, however, royal power in Poland was eroded, and the country was transformed into what amounted to a republic of nobles. The Polish parliament, consisting of representatives of the upper and lower nobility, exercised increasing control. Pursuant to the Constitution of 1539, the king waived his right to income from those Jews who lived on the so-called "private lands" that belonged to the nobles, rather than to the king. Many Jews thus fell under the rule of the local nobles.[17]

e. THE NEAR EAST UNDER ISLAM

With the conquest by Islam of the Persian Empire, the eastern Mediterranean lands, all of North Africa, and Spain (632–713), nearly all of the Jewish communities in the world were subject to the rule of either Islam or Christianity, which latter had prevailed in the Roman Empire some three hundred years before. The rule of Jewish communities by Christendom and Islam thus replaced the dualistic governance of Jewish communities by Rome and Persia.

Islam adopted the "protection" system in which Jews (as well as Christians and Zoroastrians) were regarded as "protected people," with inferior status but with the right to religious and ethnic self-determination. This was, in many ways, similar to the policy that had been followed by Rome. In return, these minorities had to pay a tribute, principally in the form of poll and land taxes, and they were subject to indignities, which in those times were regarded as tolerable. The collection of taxes from Jews was entrusted by the government to the Jewish community on the theory that it would be a more efficient tax collector. This was because it was more familiar with local facts regarding the census, the wealth of the various taxpayers, the determination of who was a scholar (to be exempted from taxation under Jewish tradition and in accordance with Muslim tradition as well), and other factors that were required to be considered in the collection of revenues.[18] The effect of all this on the populous Jewish communities of Babylonia was the continuation of the Persian system of an autonomous Jewish community headed by an exilarch.

While the payment of taxation because of religious beliefs could be onerous, it is interesting to note that there were many Jews who felt that the payment of taxes made them more secure from persecution and expulsion. Netira (an influential Jewish banker who lived toward the end of the ninth century) argued against a proposed abolition of these taxes by the caliph, saying that "through the tax, the Jew insures himself" and that its abolition "would give free rein to Arabs to shed Jewish blood."[19]

(1) *Jewish Authoritarian Leadership*

The Islamic perspective that communities should be ruled by individuals led to authoritarian, and occasionally despotic, communal rule by individual Jews. The authority and power of Jewish communal decision-makers tended to be further strengthened under Islamic rule because these decision-makers were regarded by Islamic authorities as key government functionaries, whose power should be supported because they performed the vital tasks of tax collection.

Their control was reinforced by their authority to regulate the markets, which could crucially affect the livelihood of any individual. Additionally, Jewish communities maintained courts to resolve litigation among Jews, pursuant to the principle of Muslim law that each person was to be judged in accordance with his own law. The unity of the Jewish community was further enhanced by its authorization to maintain *waqf* ("sacred property") and its power to inherit the estates of those who died without heirs.[20]

The authoritarian Jewish communal leadership is reflected in the complaint by a Karaite against the allegedly exploitative Rabbanite leaders, to the effect that:

> They rule with an iron hand and "whosoever putteth not into their mouths, they even prepare war against him" [paraphrasing Micah 3:5]. They elevate themselves and suppress the people through bans, anathemas, and the assistance of gentile officials. They punish their poor and force them to borrow money on usury, in order that they give it to the officials, so that their rule may be perpetuated.[21]

His accusations probably are greatly exaggerated since he was a bitter opponent of the Rabbanites, against whom he waged religious polemics.

It is clear, however, that in Islamic lands, with their tradition of absolutist regimes, many individuals (both laymen and rabbis) and small groups rose to positions of great influence. This was especially true in Babylonia, Egypt, Turkey, and Spain. The exilarch in Babylonia, and later the *nagid* in Egypt, were authorized by

17. M. Balaban, *Bet Yisrael Be'Polin*, ed. I. Halpern (Jerusalem, 1956), 1:44–45; Baron, *The Jewish Community*, 1:267–71.

18. Baron, *The Jewish Community*, 1:158–60.

19. A. Harkavy, "Netira and His Sons" (Hebrew), in *Festchrift for A. Berliner* (Berlin, 1903), pp. 19, 36, 39; similarly, Asher ben Yehiel's view that "taxes are our protectors" in his Commentary *Rosh, Baba Batra* 8a.

20. Baron, *The Jewish Community*, 1:160–61, 170–72.

21. Sahl B. Masliah, *Sha'Are Zedek*, vol. 3, nos. 6, 7, fol. 240.

the caliphs to serve as leaders of the various Jewish communities and were vested with great powers.[22]

(2) *The Exilarchate and the Gaonate (Deanship of the Law Academies)*

Under Islam the institution of the Babylonian exilarchate was continued from the Persians. The exilarch continued to be appointed by the head of state, who usually respected the wishes of the Jews. The exilarch continued to wield vast powers and was able to tax Jewish merchants, regulate the markets, and appoint and depose the heads of academies and local judges.

The selection of a candidate for the position of exilarch was commonly made at a Jewish public assembly, led by the two *gaonim* (heads of the two academies of law in Babylonia).[23] The exilarch was regarded by the Jews as a king and successor to the throne in the Davidic royal dynasty. Accordingly, it was accepted as dogma that no one could become exilarch unless he was a descendant of David. Nevertheless, the choice of a specific candidate often led to strife. As with the ancient Davidic royal rulers, the office would ordinarily pass from father to the oldest son,[24] but often it would pass to a brother, uncle, or others, since Islam did not approve of the principle of primogeniture, and the principle of hereditary succession was not always followed.[25] There was often much conflict between candidates who desired the office and among their sponsors, particularly the heads of the academies, who had an important say, if not a veto, on the appointment. Thus, when the exilarch Rav Huna died (*circa* 485), his son-in-law bribed the Persian king and was appointed exilarch.[26] Frequently, the candidate who bribed the king with the greatest sum of money would be appointed exilarch.[27]

Under Islam the *gaonim* continued to be an important power factor in decision-making. As before, their power was due to their almost complete monopoly over the value of enlightenment (i.e., the mastery of the norms and legal principles of the Torah and their domination of the scholars of the academies). The immense prestige and respect that this brought them, augmented perhaps by the increased influence accorded to scholars in the Islamic world, eventually resulted in their playing a leading role in selecting candidates for the position of exilarch and made them a crucial factor in deciding who was to succeed him. They were sometimes very influential with the plutocrats, who wielded great influence with the caliph; and they could, and sometimes did, have exilarchs appointed or deposed.[28]

Furthermore, the *gaonim* eventually succeeded in establishing their right to appoint judges for many of the communities in Babylonia. This further enhanced their decision-making powers, as well as their income, since all litigants were required to pay judicial fees. Additionally, the heads of the academies controlled considerable lands belonging to the academies through direct contribution, or purchased with donations sent by Jews all over the world.

The academies and their heads remained influential until the eleventh century, when their influence declined markedly following the death of Hai Gaon in 1040. The institution of the gaonate continued, however, for at least two centuries thereafter. As long as the exilarchate and gaonate institutions lasted, however, the latter constituted a serious check on the power of the former, and a constant power tug-of-war between them resulted.

Beginning in the twelfth century, with the weakening of the Baghdad caliphate and the consequent independence, in practice, of many areas of the Near East, a number of local exilarchs were appointed by various local gentile rulers, and they served simultaneously. This fragmentation of the exilarchate was impelled by practical political factors. The exilarch appointed by the caliphate at Baghdad could no longer exercise influence for the benefit of the Jews in some of the semi-independent areas, such as Egypt and Syria. Furthermore, the obedience of Jews in those lands to the exilarch of Baghdad would be regarded as treason and as opposition to the assertions of independence by local rulers.

The appointees in these local areas were sometimes called "*resh galuta*" (exilarchs) and at other times "*nagid*" (literally "prince"), or "*nasi*" ("patriarch" or "leader"). Local Jewish leaders with these titles existed in Egypt, Spain, and portions of North Africa. In Egypt a *nagid* occasionally served simultaneously with a member of the family of the Babylonian exilarch who had come to Egypt. The latter was called "*nasi*" and exercised spiritual leadership. The *nagid* would often defend

22. David Ibn Zimra, Responsa *Radvaz*, vol. 3, no. 622.

23. *Seder Olam Zuta* (London, 1910); S. Assaf, *Tekufat Ha-Gaonim Vesafruta* (Jerusalem, 1967), 39.

24. There were some exceptions, e.g., Bustenai, who was appointed exilarch by the Arabian conquerors of the Persian Empire in 637 C.E. but was not a descendant of the previous exilarch, although he was from the Davidic line; Assaf, *Tekufat*, pp. 29–30, 38; contra *Seder Olam Zuta*; see Assaf, *Teshuvat Ha-Gaonim* (Jerusalem, 1942), no. 57; H. Tykocinski, "Bustenai, The Exilarch" (Hebrew), in *Devir* (Berlin, 1923), 1:145.

25. R. Levy, *An Introduction to the Sociology of Islam* (London, 1929–1931), 1:292.

26. See *The Epistle of Rav Sherira Gaon*, ed. B. Levin (Jerusalem, 1960), p. 92.

27. Y. Baer, *History of the Jews*, p. 34; *Epistle of Rav Sherira Gaon*.

28. Assaf, *Tekufat Ha-Gaonim*.

the *nasi* and would occasionally even ask his authorization before accepting the post as *nagid*.[29]

ƒ. OTHER SOCIAL CONTEXTS OF JEWISH DECISION-MAKING

In addition to the societal contexts of Jewish decision-making set forth above, decision-making by both communal groups and religious leaders was influenced by numerous factors, including economic, social, and even climatic.

The role of these factors has been acknowledged by traditional, leading Jewish decision-makers and scholars. It can be observed, for example, in the application in medieval Europe of the biblical prohibitions regarding lending at interest. Decisions on these matters were shaped by economic and social conditions (particularly discriminatory prohibitions upon Jews from engaging in other occupations) to such an extent that decisions might sometimes be regarded, from the point of view of traditional technical legal doctrine, as "an *halakhic* outrage" and "truncated nonsense."[30] Numerous other social conditions[31] affected legal traditions and norms, including the lighting of the Hanukkah menorah,[32] business dealings with non-Jews,[33] the remission of loans at the end of the Sabbatical year,[34] the "fictitious" sale of leaven before Passover,[35] extinguishing fires on the

Sabbath,[36] leniency in accepting evidence concerning the death of a missing husband thereby permitting a wife to remarry,[37] the legal liability of women in commercial litigation,[38] and prohibitions against polygamy.[39] It is also possible that many of the medieval decisions concerning religious dietary laws were influenced by the lack of Jewish slaughterhouses[40] and bakeries.[41] (See Part Two, Chapter V, Section A 1, regarding the effect of historical conditions on the law.) The focus of this book will be mainly on those factors that affected sanctioning and criminal law perspectives.

2. DOCUMENTARY STUDIES OF AUTONOMOUS JEWISH COMMUNAL DECISION-MAKING

a. AN OLD MEDIEVAL FORM FOR APPOINTING A JEWISH COMMUNAL LEADER AND DECISION-MAKER*
(By Judah Al-Barceloni)

We, the elders and heads of the community of the city of _____, who are signed hereunder (declare that the circumstances giving rise to this document were) as follows: that because of our many sins we have become lowered and few, reduced until we remain only a few from many, like a lone sentry on top of a mountain, and like a flag on a hill; the members of our community have remained without a head, without a *nasi*, without a chief judge, and without a leader, until we became like sheep without a shepherd; some of the members of our community go without clothing; some of them speak profanity; some intermingle with the Gentiles, eat their bread, and become like them, so that

29. Ibid., pp. 36–37.

30. H. Soloveitchik, "Pawnbroking: A Study in *Ribbit* and of the *Halakhah* in Exile," in *Proceedings of the American Academy for Jewish Research* (New York, 1972), pp. 203, 263. This study is a penetrating one of the role of economic factors in certain aspects of Jewish decision-making. See the detailed listing of source materials on this subject by Soloveitchik, in *Law and Economics in the Middle Ages* (Hebrew; Jerusalem, 1972); in "Can Halakhic Texts Talk History?" (dealing with medieval Jewish commerce in wine), *Annual, Jewish Studies Association*, vol. 8 (Waltham, 1978); and in *Relations between Law and Circumstances* (Hebrew; Jerusalem, 1972). See also S. Stein, "The Development of the Jewish Law of Interest from the Biblical Period to the Expulsion from England," in *Historia Judaica* 17 (1955): 3; J. Rosenthal, *Mehkarim U'Mekorot* (Jerusalem, 1966), 1:253 ff.

31. See Z. H. Chajes, "Darke Hora'ah," in *Kal Sifre Maharatz Hayot* (Jerusalem), ch. 2, pp. 224–25.

32. E. Katzenellenbogen, *Kenesseth Yehezkel, O.H.* (Jerusalem, 1968), no. 17.

33. Responsum of Gershom ben Yehuda (Germany, *circa* eleventh century), in Assaf, *Simhoni Memorial Volume* (Jerusalem, 1950), p. 120; Eliezer of Metz, *Sefer Yereim* (Vilna, 1901), no. 270, p. 257. For the effects of intensive Jewish involvement in viticulture and wine trade in medieval France, see L. Rabinowitz, *Social Life of the Jews in Northern France in the XII–XIV Centuries* (London, 1939), p. 43; Gershom ben Yehuda, in *Teshuvot Hahamei Zarfat Ve'Lothar* (ed. Y. Miller, Jerusalem, 1967), nos. 90–92; H. J. Zimmels, *Ashkenazim and Sephardim* (London, 1958), p. 207 ff.

34. Deut. 15; see I. S. Kahana, *Shemittat Kesafim* (Hebrew; Jerusalem, 1945), p. 161 ff; M. Kolon, Responsa *Mahari Kolon*, no. 92.

35. See S. Zevin, *Ha'Moadim Ba'Halakha* (Jerusalem, 1963), p. 220 ff.

*From Judah Al-Barceloni, *Book of Documentary Forms*, written in Spain, *circa* late eleventh and early twelfth centuries (reprinted Jerusalem, 1967), pp. 7–8; English translation by the editor.

36. M. Isserles, Gloss to *Shulhan Arukh, O.H.*, sec. 334:26a; Meir of Rothenberg, Responsa *Maharam* (Prague ed.), no. 140; Zimmels, *Ashkenazim and Sephardim*, p. 220 ff.

37. I. Perfet, Responsa *Rivash*, no. 378.

38. Talmud, *Baba Kama* 87a; *Raavan, E. H.* (Prague, 1610), no. 115; Mordecai b. Hillel, Commentary to *Baba Kama*, no. 88.

39. Jacob Emden, Responsa *She'ilat Ya'avetz* (Lemberg, 1894), 2:15; Samuel DiMedina, Responsa *Y.D.*, no. 109. See also Y. Horowitz, *Yad Ha'Levi* (Berlin, 1733), commandment no. 175, pp. 143–44, regarding other changes in legal decision-making concerning women.

40. See B. Katz, *Mizkenim Etbonan.*

41. Jacob ben Asher, *Tur*, Y.D., sec. 112; Mordecai ben Hillel, Commentary to *Avodah Zarah* 4, no. 844; see C. Tchernowitz, "Toldot Ha'Shulkhan Arukh Vehitpashtuto," vol. 4, in *Ha'Shiloah* (1898) 400; Zimmels, *Ashkenazim and Sephardim* (New York, 1971), p. 210. See also A. Katznelsohn, *Ha'Talmud Ve'Khokhmat Ha'Refuah* (Jerusalem, 1971), p. 172; D. Sperber, "Flight and Title by Adverse Possession" (Hebrew), in *Bar-Ilan Year Book* (Ramat-Gan, 1972), p. 290 ff; idem, "On Social and Economic Conditions in Third-Century Palestine," in *Archiv Orientalni* (1970), p. 1 ff.

there is no difference between them, except the name "Jew" alone.

Since we saw this, we became disgusted and took it upon ourselves and gathered with all of the members of our community and discussed and considered and saw that this matter is an embarassment to us and to the members of our community.

[Accordingly] we have agreed, in the presence of the members of our community, and from small to large, we have persuaded Mr. _____, a member of our city [to become our leader] because he is wise, understanding, fears the Lord, and is a person of substance who hates bribery. He has accepted our appointment—may the Lord consider this as a good deed for him—and we have requested him to guide us in the proper way and to teach us the law of our God (may his name be blessed forever, and may his rememberance be exalted eternally); to judge us as he will be guided from Heaven, and to force all the people who speak profanity [to cease], to flog them, excommunicate them, and [to do likewise to] those who intermingle with the Gentiles, in order to guide them in the proper way, to remove them from their crooked ways, and to teach them; [because of this] perhaps the Lord will have mercy on us and will forgive our sins when we listen to his rebukes.

In the presence of all of the members of our community, we have agreed upon and have completely accepted and taken upon ourselves and our generation as an acceptance, an oath and a vow that nobody will have permission, neither us nor our children, forever, to veer from his rebukes, teachings, and words;

Every Jew from our community who will depart from his words, or violate his commands, will be deemed excommunicated; his children, bastards; his bread, the bread of a *kuti* (peoples who settled in Palestine after the destruction of the first Temple and with whom intermarriage and social intercourse were prohibited—see 2 Kings 17:27–41); his wine, wine that was poured before idols; he shall not be buried in a Jewish grave, and his children shall leave school; no son of his shall be circumcised; and anyone who departs from his word, changes the way, or makes crooked the straight, shall be under the anathema of Joshua, the son of Nun,[42] and the curse of Elisha, the son of Shafat,[43] and the ban of Rabbi Yehuda bar Yehezkel.[44]

Anyone who will be appointed [henceforth as leader] of our community, whether from those who are here today, or those who are not here today, may the Lord of the world bless him and grant him, etc.

Whatever we and the members of our community have agreed together to write and to sign on the _____ day of the year _____, we have written and have signed, etc.

(And the reason that we wrote this document of ordinances here, not that this is its place—rather, its place belongs together with the [other] Documents of Appointment—but we wrote it here because it was found in an ancient draft form among the documents.)

[EDITOR'S NOTE—Observe that it was the members of the community themselves, not an outsider, who selected the leader and who reduced their agreement and selection to writing.]

b. REGIONAL AND TRANS-COMMUNAL DECISION-MAKING

In all of medieval Europe there was a trend for the larger Jewish communities to make decisions that would be binding upon the smaller communities and rural areas adjacent to them. This resulted both from pressures of the state government and also from the wishes of the Jewish communities themselves.

The central government, which was primarily interested in the Jewish communities because of the revenues they yielded, found it easier to collect taxes by concentrating responsibility in a few hands. Furthermore, following old traditions, cemetery land would be granted to individual Jewish communities and would be designated as exclusive burial grounds for an entire region. Since cemetery grants to communities were very infrequent, Jews living within the region were permitted to bury their dead only in the regional cemetery, even if they resided a great distance away. Burial in the regional cemetery, however, required the permission of the community that had received the exclusive cemetery rights. These cemetery communities often utilized their burial monopoly to impose their will on all communities that utilized their burial grounds and insisted on collecting and allocating the tax burdens for the entire district. In the same way, they frequently appropriated the right to make decisions for the outlying communities.

The concentration of power in a regional center was frequently desired by the small Jewish communities themselves because this tended to unify Jewish communal endeavors and to provide needed supervision. Affiliated regional communities could more easily establish and support courts of appeal, could prescribe and enforce ordinances that required area wide acceptance, and could negotiate with the central government more effectively.[45]

42. See Josh. 6:26.
43. See 2 Kings 9.
44. See Talmud, *Kiddushin* 70a.

45. Baron, *The Jewish Community*, 1:283–84.

Besides the trend to concentrate power in one urban center for all of the communities existing within a region, there was also occasional concentration of decision-making in the hands of one person appointed by the state to head all of the Jewish communities. This was particularly true in the Orient, with its authoritarian tradition of individual rulers. Such power was often concentrated in the hands of a single person, exemplified by the exilarch in Babylonia, the *nasi* in Palestine, and the *nagid* in Egypt.

In Europe, where it was typical for church officials to supervise large regions, sometimes even an entire land, and also to convene loosely organized synods and assemblies, both of these forms of concentrated decision-making were emulated among the Jewish populations there. While Jewish transcommunal decision-making powers in Europe were usually concentrated in communal bodies, there were occasions in which decision-making was centralized in one person, usually, a religious leader.

(1) *Southern Europe*

(*a*) Portugal

The most concentrated Jewish transcommunal decision-making in all of Europe existed in Portugal. King Alfonso III and John I (*circa* 1250 and 1390) issued regulations concerning the Jewish communities and established a Jewish hierarchy, with most of the power concentrated in the hands of a chief rabbi (*Arraby Moor*). This official, like the Babylonian exilarch, was responsible for the collection of taxes for the state, as well as the orderly management of the Jewish community.[46] It is probable that he was nominated by the Jews themselves. Unlike Babylonia, however, where the powers of the exilarch were counterbalanced by the powers of the heads of the academies, it appears that the Portuguese chief rabbi was less subject to such check. He appointed overseers for the seven different districts in Portugal. These overseers, in turn, controlled the selection of local officials who governed their communities. This resulted in undemocratic and autocratic decision-making on the model of the Portuguese state government itself. The overseers, in addition to their administrative functions, also served as intermediate courts of appeal, with the chief rabbi acting as the final court of appeal. The chief rabbi was empowered to institute criminal proceedings against violators of the law, to arrest lawbreakers, and to cause them to be severely punished. He also appointed local rabbis and teachers for the various Jewish communities.[47]

(*b*) Spain

In Spain a lump-sum tax was imposed on all of the Jewish communities within an entire district. This sum was then to be allocated among the various Jewish communities, with each locality allocating its share among the individuals residing there. These tax districts became the basic Jewish communal units. Agreements were made between various Jewish communities for cooperation in a number of fields, and a serious attempt was made to establish a permanent parliament for all of the Jews in Aragon in 1354. Although a conference was held at Barcelona for this purpose, a centralized legislature did not materialize, mainly because of petty jealousies. This attempt anticipated the more successful venture by Polish Jewry some two centuries later.

A number of synods were eventually convened by various Spanish Jewish communities, the most famous being the one at Valladolid, Castile, in 1432. These enacted a number of important prescriptions, including those attempting to restrict individual Jews from using their influence with the king and nobility to procure appointments as rabbis, scribes, and other communal officials.[48] Some of these are reproduced on the following pages.

The kings of Aragon, Castile, and Navarre appointed chief rabbis to supervise and lead Jewish communities. Some were invested with powers over Jews in individual provinces, while others were occasionally put in charge of all the Jewish communities in the entire country. These rabbis of the court (*rab de la corte*) acted as the allocators and collectors of the taxes imposed on the Jewish communities, in addition to serving as chief judges, rabbis, and spiritual leaders.[49]

The Spanish Aragonese kings, who controlled Sicily and Naples for a time, attempted to impose centralized control on Jewish community affairs there as well. This attempt was not long-lived, mainly, because of intense Jewish opposition. The attempted centralization was finally abolished in 1447.[50]

(*c*) The Ordinances of the Synod at Valladolid, Spain (1432)*

[Following are selections from the synod of the Jewish communities in Castile, Spain, in 1432. These reflect the wide scope of communal regulations. They were written in Spanish but utilized Hebrew characters.]

---

*Selections translated by L. Finkelstein in *Jewish Self-Government in the Middle Ages* (New York, 1924), with minor changes by the editor.
48. L. Finkelstein, *Jewish Self-Government in the Middle Ages* (New York, 1924), p. 367 ff.
49. Baron, *The Jewish Community*, 1:287–89.
50. Ibid., p. 294. See also A. Lev, "The Ordinances of the Jewish Communities of Castilia" (Hebrew), *Ha'Asif* 30 (1887): 133.

---

46. Ibid., 1:285.
47. Ibid.

(At the command of the King, the Rabbi of the Court, Don Abraham, invited the communities) to send trusted men from their communities who would keep the paths of righteousness and with whom he could take "sweet counsel." And the communities did as he commanded and some of them sent letters to the said Rabbi confirming and accepting everything which he would command and ordain, and some sent trusted representatives to represent them. The princes of the people were gathered together, the people of the God of Abraham, in the Court of our Lord, the King, in the city of Valladolid. And in the last ten days of the month of Iyyar of this, the above-mentioned year 5192 [1432 C.E.] in the said city of Valladolid, we, the undersigned, were present in the great synagogue, which is in the Jewish Quarter of the Community of Valladolid, when there gathered (in the presence of the honored prince, Don Abraham, the Rabbi of the Court of our lord, the King), various scholars who came from various communities, worthy men clothed with authority, certified by credentials from the different communities of the domain of our lord, the King, which they presented before us, the undersigned. And there were present also some worthy men who go to the Court of our lord, the King. They held meetings among themselves in regard to a *takkanah* (ordinance) which they decided was to deal with certain definite subjects and other matters, which are for the service of the Creator, the glory of the holy Torah, the service of the King, and the success and welfare of the communities. This ordinance was agreed upon unanimously without anyone dissenting, and it was completed on the first day of Sivan of the above-mentioned year, 5192. The text of the *takkanah* follows immediately on our signatures.

In witness whereof we have signed our names to it:

Isaac Ha-Kohen / Ben Joseph Ha-Kohen / Ben Crispini / Baruch Ben Abraham / Ibn Sahl.

In previous times there were ordained in the holy communities of the dominion of our lord the King, general *takkanot* and regulations which were to be observed by all the communities and those who were at their head, so that they might establish *takkanot* and choose proper paths in which all the people of the communities might walk. Thus was the Torah established on its proper foundation and every community was settled in quiet. For some time past, however, for various reasons, no general *takkanah* has been enacted by means of which the communities might be led, as a result of which much harm has befallen the communities and there has come about disorder in their management. Therefore, have we, the aforementioned delegates by virtue of the authority given by our lord, the King, to the worthy Rabbi, Don Abraham, and by

virtue of the authority given us by our sages to attend to the arrangements of our own communities and by the authority given us by the communities, established this ordinance and agreement that we have divided into five chapters as will be explained, the following being the text:

I

"This is the gate of the Lord, the righteous shall enter into it."[51]

The first of our decisions and the beginning of our *takkanot* has for its object the maintenance of the students of our Torah. For it is upon the Torah that the world is founded, as the Sages say: "On three things the world stands, on the Torah, on divine service, and on kindly acts."[52] Whereas we saw that the hands of the students of the Torah have slackened in most places, and that they obtain their livelihood only with extreme pain, and that for this reason the pupils are becoming constantly fewer, and even the children of the primary school are idle in many places because their parents cannot afford to pay the salary of those who might teach them the Torah, and the Torah would almost have been forgotten in Israel because of these reasons, and in order to "bring back the crown to its ancient glory"[53] and that there may be found scholars in Israel and that the students may increase in the communities; therefore, do we ordain that each of the communities of the whole kingdom of Castile shall be obliged to establish and provide a Voluntary Fund for *Talmud Torah* [the study of the Torah] in the following manner: For every head of big cattle that is slaughtered as kosher among them and for them, they should pay for *Talmud Torah* five *maravedis*; . . . For each jug of wine which is sold at retail . . . they should pay to the *Talmud Torah* three pence per jar . . . .

Primary School Teachers

Every community of fifteen families shall maintain a proper teacher for the children of primary school age who shall instruct them in Scripture. They shall allow him a reasonable salary according to his needs. The fathers of the children shall pay the teacher each according to their means, and if the amount paid by the fathers is insufficient for the maintenance of the teacher, the community shall be obliged to pay the remainder necessary for his livelihood.

Rabbis

A community having forty families or more shall be obliged to endeavor, so far as possible, to maintain

51. Ps. 118:20.
52. Talmud, *Avot* 1:5.
53. See Talmud, *Yoma* 69a.

among themselves a rabbi who will teach them *halakhot* and *aggadot* [laws and nonlegal religious matters]. The community must maintain him reasonably. His salary shall be paid from the income of the tax on meat and wine and the income from the *Hekdesh*, if there is any, or from the *Talmud Torah* Fund, so that he should not have to beg his livelihood from any of the leaders of the community, and so that he may reprove them and guide them in all things which pertain to the service of the Creator, blessed be He. If the community and the rabbi can come to no agreement as to the amount of the salary, they shall be obliged to give him the income of the *Talmud Torah* of the locality and then to increase the amount as may be ordered by the rabbi of the court.

Talmudic Academy

Moreover, we ordain that each rabbi shall maintain a Talmudic Academy, where those desirous of learning may study the *halakhah* (law). He shall lecture at such hours as the rabbis are wont to lecture.

Number of Pupils per Teacher

Whereas according to the Talmudic law no teacher is permitted to teach more than twenty-five pupils,[54] unless he has an assistant, therefore, we ordain that no teacher shall teach Scriptures to more than twenty-five children, but that if he has an assistant he may teach forty in accordance with the law of the Talmud. A community having fifty children shall be obliged to maintain two teachers; the same law is applied to any number above forty.

Prayers

Moreover, we ordain that they should take heed in the synagogue that no one lift his hand against his neighbor to smite and to insult his neighbor. Therefore, we ordain that if any Jew strike his neighbor in the synagogue or in a place fixed for prayer, whether he strike him in the face or hit him with his fist, or catch him by the hair of his head or of his beard, or draw a weapon in the synagogue wounding his neighbor in the hand or in any other part of the body, he shall pay for each time he assaulted him two hundred *maravedis*, one half of which shall be given to the *Talmud Torah* Fund and the other half shall be distributed among the poor as charity, or in such a way as the judges shall designate. If he wounded his neighbor with a knife, a stone, or any other implement that can cause death, he shall pay in each instance three hundred *maravedis*, which shall be distributed in the manner described. These punishments are to be understood to be only the penalties for the profanation of the synagogue.

54. See Talmud, *Baba Batra* 21.

II. *The Election of Judges and other Officers*

Whereas the number of scholars has become small, and those who are fit to act as judges have become few, so that there are only a few communities in the kingdom which have a court of three who are fit to act as judges in these times in accordance with Talmudic law; and whereas our forefathers were constrained because of this to go beyond the law of the Talmud in their ordinances concerning the election of judges, and since unless there are authorized judges in each city to try claims and complaints and to punish transgressors, there will be chaos so that neither men nor women will be safe; for the world depends on three things: on justice, on truth, and on peace,[55] and where there is no true Torah, there is no peace; therefore have we ordained and agreed that in each community they shall choose judges to decide their cases as has been said and the members of the community shall accept them as judges. But they shall choose the most fit and the most worthy that can be found in the locality, for the Torah often warns us in regard to this matter; therefore, do we ordain that any community which at present has no judges shall be obliged to assemble in the usual meeting place according to the customary announcement, within ten days from the day when this *Takkanah* is read. In those places where there are judges, they shall be obliged to gather within ten days before the completion of the term of the incumbent judges, and elect new judges for the coming year. They shall follow this rule every year so long as this ordinance shall be in force. An anathema shall be pronounced binding all those who are choosing the judges to consider only what will be pleasing to "Him who dwelleth in Heaven. . . ." The electors shall choose those who are most worthy and fit in the community for this office and the same refers to all other officers, such as investigators and treasurers and those who look into the public needs and any other officers which the community will choose. As soon as the *herem* (anathema) has been pronounced they shall begin to discuss the matter and if they agree, so much the better. If they do not agree they shall deliberate for the following three days and no one shall leave the meeting except for the purpose of eating or drinking or some other essential matter. If they do not agree within three days they shall remain for eight days, day and night, in that place, none of them leaving it except to eat or drink or for some necessary reason as described. If they cannot come to any agreement within the said time they shall notify the Rabbi of the Court, who shall select judges, and the community and their judges shall be obliged to carry out the order of the Rabbi of the Court. This procedure

55. Talmud, *Avot* 1.18.

shall be followed in the election of judges or of any other officials; and such official shall hold his position for the whole year.[56]

We further ordain that no officer may appoint any judge or any other officer without the consent of the community, or the majority thereof, and that the proposed officer must be mentioned by name (before the electorate). Any election held in any other way than that prescribed is hereby declared void.

Duties and Powers of Judges

We further ordain that whoever is appointed in each community shall have the power as long as this *Takkanah* is in effect, to judge any dispute, contentions or quarrels which may arise between man and man, according to Talmudic law. They shall have the power of imposing fines and punishment with the consent of the rabbi and three of the most worthy of the "Best Men" of the city. They shall, however, keep in mind the privilege granted by our lord, the King, to the said Rabbi of the Court, Don Abraham. Moreover, anyone who feels himself too severely dealt with may appeal to the said Rabbi for redress.

Qualification of Judges

We further ordain that the judges of the community must not be related to each other. . . .

Rules of Procedure

We further ordain that the judges shall fix a place for trying cases three days in the week, and that they shall observe the rules concerning judges, that they shall compel the defendant to come before them and do justice to the plaintiff. The litigants shall be obliged to come on the summons of the judges; and should either fail to appear, he shall pay to the Charity Fund for the first offense a gold piece, for the second offense three gold pieces, and for the third offense ten gold pieces, besides such punishment as the judges may inflict on him.

Cases Where Judges Are Litigants

We further ordain that if any Jew or Jewess have a complaint against any judge or any judge has a case against any member of the community, that judge shall be obliged to appear with his opposing litigant before one of the judges, his colleagues. If there is no other judge in the community, the community shall be obliged to provide for them one or more judges. The same procedure shall be followed if the judges are relatives of one of the litigants or friends or enemies to one of them

in the sense of Talmudic law. No judge shall be permitted to try any case in which he, personally, or one of his relatives is involved, unless the litigant has accepted him in the prescribed manner.[57]

Judges to Have No Jurisdiction over Tax Lists

We further ordain that no judge shall be empowered to interfere by means of his judicial authority in the matter of the tax lists or in the distribution of the taxes, but he may try cases arising among the members of the community in regard to taxes.

Special Judges

We ordain that if a community feel that they do not want to entrust the differences arising among them to their judges, and there are differences among them requiring the attention of another judge, and they petition the Rabbi of the Court to send them judges, declaring that to be the desire of the majority, counting both by persons and by wealth, and if it appear to the Rabbi to be an emergency, which, if not met, will result in harm to the community, he shall choose a God-fearing man, for the time for which the community request him, and the community shall be obliged to accept his decisions. But if the majority of the community do not make such a petition to the Rabbi of the Court, he shall not send any judge against the will of the community.

Appeals

Regarding appeals, every judge shall be obliged to grant an appeal to the Rabbi of the Court within reasonable time to the party demanding it. The appellant shall give guarantees that he will cover the expenses incurred and shall take an oath that he makes the appeal because he feels himself misjudged, and not merely to delay the execution of justice.

Written Briefs

Since, if one of the litigants were permitted to write down his grievances and bring them to court, he would probably write more than is necessary, perhaps even indulging in insults, which would result in more expenses and disputes, and whereas those who instruct others to plead in certain ways are included under the rule that he who teaches another what to plead injures the community and he who teaches them to plead falsely is a sinner; therefore, have we decreed that no litigant shall submit written briefs to the court without having received permission from the local judge. Even in cases in which a brief is permitted, it must be in keeping with propriety, without injurious words or insults against anyone, and must be signed by the person

56. For a similar procedure, see the Responsum of Meir ben Barukh, quoted in *Responsa Maimoniyot*, Laws of *Kinyan* chap. 27.

57. See Talmud, *Sanhedrin* 3:2.

who drew it up and state that no one else drew it up for him. Any brief presented in any other way will not be accepted by the judge. We further ordain that no one shall give a litigant any arguments or causes to plead, unless he is given permission in writing by the court to do so. Whoever will, without permission of the court, help a litigant who is not a relative of his, with arguments, shall lose his stipend from the *Talmud Torah* Fund if he is a scholar; and if the pleadings suggested were false, he shall be proclaimed an evil counselor. If he is a man who does not receive any stipend, he shall be fined as much as appears just to the court and to the rabbi.

Taking Testimony against Judges

Every communal scribe shall be obliged to record and take the evidence which anyone may give against the *dayyan* (judge) or against anyone else who is not involved in the suit which is pending before the *dayyan* between the day when the suit is brought and the third day following, including the whole of the latter, and if the defendant is not willing to make a reply within the given time, the suit is to be decided in favor of the plaintiff as not contested; and he should write in the record that the defendant was not willing to make any reply, and hence he shall be obliged to summon the *dayyan* or the party against whom the said evidence has been given, and he shall have another witness with him on each of the said three days. If the scribe disregard the foregoing, he shall pay as a fine twenty *maravedis* for each time he disregards it.

Bodily Apprehension

We ordain that no judge shall order a Jew or Jewess to be seized bodily, except by order in writing signed by himself and witnesses; and that when the crime for which the person is apprehended is not defamation or a capital crime, the reason shall be stated in the writ.

Serving a Writ

We further ordain that if anyone obtains a writ from the Rabbi of the Court and does not present it to the opposing party within fifty days in the presence of witnesses, or place it in front of his door in the presence of one of the adult members of the family or in the synagogue at the morning prayers in the presence of those who are praying, he shall no longer be permitted to serve it or make any use of it, and it shall cease to have any value.

III. *Denunciations*

No Jew or Jewess shall bring his or her neighbor, whether a Jew or Jewess, before any judge, ecclesiastic, or secular who is not of our faith, although such a judge should decide in accordance with the law of Israel, unless it be a matter of payment of taxes or imposts or coinage or other rights of our lord, the King, or of our lady, the Queen, or the money or rights of the Church or of a lord or lady of a place. Whoever transgresses this law is to be declared anathema and excommunicated, and no one shall have any dealings with him; he shall not be buried among Jews, his bread shall be like the bread of a *kuti*, his wine shall be considered like that of libations to the idols. For each transgression he shall pay one thousand *maravedis* to the Jew who suffered by the denunciation, or to whomever the Rabbi of the Court will order that it should be paid. But if any Jew refuses to come to a Jewish Court after being summoned three times, the Rabbi and the Judges of the Community may give the plaintiff permission to apply for redress to the Gentile Courts.

Any Jew or Jewess denouncing another Jew or Jewess in such a way that harm may result to the Jew or Jewess, even though no gentile is present, shall be fined for each time he or she used defamatory language one hundred *maravedis* (half to be paid to charity and half to whomever the judges designate), and shall be imprisoned for ten days. If any harm results from the denunciation, the guilty one shall be compelled to pay, in addition to the above, all the damages that have been suffered because of the denunciation. If the denunciation speech was made in the presence of gentiles, the punishment is imprisonment for twenty days and a fine of two hundred *maravedis*. If any harm results in this case, the denouncer shall be compelled, in addition to undergoing the said punishments, to make recompense for all damage suffered through the denunciation, and he shall be excommunicated for ten days. If any bodily harm results to the denounced one because of the words of the denouncer, the offender shall receive corporal punishment to the extent ordered by the rabbi.

If any Jew or Jewess is alleged to have caused the apprehension of another or the seizure of his property by some gentile man or woman, but the matter is not substantiated by witnesses, being merely supported by the weight of circumstantial evidence, the judge shall have the duty with the counsel of the rabbi, to order the denouncer apprehended and punished bodily in accordance with what seems proper to the scholars, so far as they may (legally).

If the alleged denunciation is confirmed by one witness as well as incriminating circumstances, or if he confesses to it, there shall be branded on his brow the word *malshin* (informer).

If the crime is proven through the testimony of two witnesses, the denouncer shall receive for the first offense one hundred lashes, and be driven from the city in accordance with the decision of the rabbi and the judges and the leaders of the city above-mentioned. If he is guilty of a third offense, as established by the testimony of two proper witnesses, the Rabbi of the Court may, in accordance with Jewish law, order his death through the judiciary of our lord, the King.

If he cannot be put to death, or branded on the brow, or flogged in the above-mentioned manner, they shall denounce him in every place as an informer and a denouncer so that all Jews may keep aloof from him. He shall be declared in all Israel as the "Man of *Belial*, the man of blood,"[58] no one shall permit him to marry his daughter nor shall he be accepted in the Congregation of Israel for any religious matter so long as he resists the execution of justice as here ordained.

This punishment shall not apply to one who gives information to our lord, the King, for his benefit even though that brings harm on some Jew. Such a one is not to be called either a denouncer or an informer since it is the duty of all Jews to look after the service of the King.

If, however, the informer of the King makes false accusations against another Jew, he is to be punished severely because he lied to the King, and he is a false witness and a defamer. For this reason every possible punishment should be inflicted upon him.

Appeal to Jewish Courts for Safety

If any Jew or Jewess demands from any judge or judges of the communities that he set a truce between him and any other Jew or Jewess, one or many, the judge or judges shall be obliged to compel the person or persons to grant the truce in order to put a temporary end to the quarrels. Each party shall be expected to keep the agreement and whoever breaks it shall be liable for suit according to the laws of the kingdom with the advice of the rabbi. If the judge or judges refuse to interfere in the matter, the petitioner shall have the right to proceed before the gentile courts.

Forced Betrothals or Marriages

No one shall have the right to use a writing from our lord, the King, or our lady, the Queen, or any other lord or lady, or any other person, whether by persuasion or intimidation, to compel a Jewess to accept a Jew, or to compel a Jew to accept a Jewess, in betrothal or marriage. Whoever transgresses this ordinance shall be declared anathema and excommunicated, his bread the bread of *kutis*, and his wine the wine of libations, he shall not be buried among Jews, and he shall pay a fine of five thousand *maravedis* according to the order of the Rabbi of the Court.

Whereas it happens at times that some enter the houses of Jews perforce with the help of Gentiles and

58. See 2 Sam. 17:7.

compel daughters of Israel to accept money or valuables as *kiddushin* (betrothal) or they force a ring on a woman's finger, and there thus arise cases of doubtful marriage, and whereas all of this represents a laxity in the matter of marriage, and there has always been an ordinance among the Castilian communities in regard to this, therefore do we ordain that no marriage shall be performed except in the presence of ten adult Israelites, one of them being a relative of the bride. If the father or the brother of the bride is in the neighborhood, they must be present to give their consent. The minister of the Congregation must recite the benedictions of the marriage. Whoever will transgress this law shall be declared anathema and excommunicated and incapacitated to act as witness. He shall receive one hundred lashes and pay a fine of ten thousand *maravedis* as the Rabbi of the Court will order.

No one is permitted to act as a witness to a marriage that is not performed in accordance with the above-mentioned ordinance, even though the bride has become engaged to the man with the consent of her father. If anyone knowing the intentions of the bridegroom acts as witness in violation of this ordinance, and his guilt be made certain, he shall be punished in the same way as the bridegroom himself.

Intimidation of Judges

No Jew or Jewess shall be permitted to bring a gentile man or woman in order to threaten or intimidate a judge, an investigator or any other officer of the Jewish community. If a gentile man or woman threatens a Jewish community on behalf of any Jew or Jewess who denies that the Gentile came at his or her request, it shall be the duty of the Jew or Jewess to see to it that the Gentile abandons his threat in such a way that no harm may befall any individual or the community. If he refuses to obey and prevent the Gentile from carrying out his threat and draws any advantage from the said threat or intimidation on the part of the Gentile, it shall be looked upon as if proven by two witnesses that he brought the Gentile to help him. If the community or any member of it has to undertake any expenditure because of the threat, the judges, acting on the advice of the rabbi, may take of the property of the transgressor and give it to whomever they please. If the Gentiles are influential persons and prevent the execution of justice against the transgressor, the judges of the locality shall be obliged to bring the matter to the attention of the Rabbi of the Court so that he may see that justice is done. If, however, the person on whose account the Gentile interfered requests the Gentile to desist, he shall be liable to no punishment. . . .

No person of the children of Israel shall have the right to avail himself of any letter of grace or privilege or other order, whether written or oral, of our lord, the King, or our lady, the Queen, of any other lord or lady, to have himself appointed rabbi or to obtain any agreement or emolument from any of the communities, or to be appointed clerk, or ritual slaughterer or minister or teacher or messenger of the court; or to obtain any other office in the gift of the communities, without the consent of the communities or the community in which the office is to be held. Nor may he win the agreement of the communities or the appointment through threats or intimidation by Gentiles or any one Gentile. Whoever transgresses this ordinance shall be declared anathema and excommunicated. . . .

Right of Redress for Individuals

Whereas certain communities have made very rigid ordinances providing that all the expenses and taxes of the community should be distributed among all the inhabitants and that everyone without exception should be obliged to pay and no one is permitted to enjoy the right to be free from taxes, and as the tax assessors often cause serious and evident wrongs, therefore we ordain that henceforth no such ordinance shall be made; and in regard to those already made, we ordain that a general meeting be held of all the members of the community in accordance with the custom, so that they may release the *herem* (the anathema; i.e., repeal the ordinance) and be free to make such ordinance in regard to exemption from taxes as the rabbi of the city may suggest, or if there should not be any in that city, according to the suggestion of the rabbi of the nearest city.

No community shall henceforth have the right to forbid any individual to make known such grievances as he may have against it. . . .

Announcement of Community Meetings

In many Communities there are officers, like investigators and community leaders, who publish the announcements in such an astute manner that the public meeting is only sparsely attended, only those being invited whom they choose, and they ordain whatever they please to ordain. As a result of this practice many scandals have arisen, and, moreover, this is contrary to the law of the Talmud which provides that an ordinance is not binding unless accepted by the whole or the majority of a community. We therefore ordain that any ordinance passed in the aforesaid manner shall be void. If it be an ordinance levying taxes, there must be present a majority of the taxpayers of the past three tax lists, nearest the time of the ordinance, as well as a majority by wealth of those who would pay the proposed tax. . . .

Conclusion

We agree that this *Takkanah* shall be established over all the Holy Communities of our lord, the King, and over each one of them just as it has been drawn the first day of *Sivan* of this year and for the coming ten years. All the communities shall act in accordance with it. Every one of these communities shall act similarly in accordance with it from the day on which it is read to them and announced until the end of the said ten successive years. No man shall raise objections to it either in whole or in part. Whoever transgresses or causes another to transgress or raises any objection so as to annul it as a whole or in part, shall be declared anathema and excommunicated in accordance with our judgment since this ordinance was established by the authority given the worthy Rabbi Don Abraham.

(2) *Northern Europe*

(*a*) Synods and Chief Rabbis: France, Germany, and England

Jewish communities in northern Europe convened a number of important regional synods, probably in emulation of the Catholic Church synods there. This was particularly true where there was no other effective areawide Jewish leadership. These synods were attended both by prominent rabbinical and lay figures. It should be noted that in medieval Europe the latter were usually quite learned in Jewish law and religious practices. The assemblies dealt with religious problems, social welfare, and political matters, particularly relations with non-Jews. There is a tradition that the earliest synod was convened by Rabbi Gershom in the tenth century, but there is no concrete evidence for this. The earliest synod for which we have clear evidence was that convened by Rabbi Jacob Tam and his brother Samuel at Troyes in 1150. This was attended by one hundred and fifty rabbis and elders and appears to have dealt mainly with attempts by some Jews to have non-Jewish officials interfere in Jewish communal matters. Jews in this area of Europe had become especially sensitive to non-Jewish interference following the first Crusades of 1099, with the attendant persecutions of Jews.

A second synod was convened at Troyes in about 1160, and other important gatherings were convened by the three communities of Speyer, Worms, and Mayence (known as the Ordinances of *SUM*, an acronym formed by the first letters of the Hebrew names of these communities) during the beginning of the thirteenth century. Synods were also convened from time to time in a number of other communities of Western Europe, most notably at Frankfurt, Germany, in 1603, where some very far-reaching ordinances were enacted.

In a fashion somewhat resembling the pattern in Spain and Portugal, a Jewish *procureur général* was appointed by the French king, Philip the Fair, at Rouen in 1297. The position continued until 1394, when the Jews were expelled from France. Additionally, a chief rabbi and judge were selected by the Jewish communities of France and confirmed by the king in 1359.

In England, too, King John appointed Jacob of London as the "Presbyter of all the Jews throughout England . . ." in 1199. Probably, however, this official had little, if any, spiritual functions.[59]

It is possible that German Jewry also had a chief rabbi, in the person of Barukh b. Meir of Rothenburg,[60] who was, perhaps, followed in this office by his disciple, Asher ben Yehiel.[61]

It is clear, however, that in the Holy Roman Empire there were a series of appointments made by various sovereigns to leadership of the Jewish communities there. King Ruprecht (1400–1404) appointed one, Israel of Krems, as chief Jewish *hochmeister* over "each and every Jewish master, Jew, and Jewess of the German lands." This appointment was forcibly imposed upon the Jews, who staunchly resisted it. Israel was promptly excommunicated by the majority of German rabbis, but the king threatened severe action against anyone who attempted to enforce the ban. Similar appointments were made by the Emperor Zigismund and other kings, but the post instituted by the German kings did not last long. Eventually it degenerated into a semi-official position, its most notable occupant being Josel of Rosheim in the sixteenth century.

Attempts at centralization of Jewish communal rule in the Holy Roman Empire gradually weakened as the empire itself disintegrated in the continuous religious wars of that era. In the seventeenth and eighteenth centuries most of the provincial rabbis in Germany were selected by provincial Jewish councils and exercised authority in conjunction with them.[62] It should be noted that in Germany, as in France, a rabbi, not a layman, was appointed as head of all the Jews there. This was probably due to the perspectives of that epoch, modeled after the fashion of the Catholic Church, in which prominent church officials also served as secular heads of regions.

Italian synods, attempting to exercise centralized Jewish communal control, were also convened in southern Italy in 1421 and, most notably, at Ferrara in 1554.

Eventually, however, both the German and Italian regional assemblies were discontinued. In the milieu of intensely anti-Jewish feelings, the assemblies aroused government suspicions that the Jews were hatching antigovernment plots. The kings also became persuaded that the assemblies were not financially productive in raising revenues for the government. At the same time, the cohesiveness of the Jewish communities began to dissolve with the rise of the commercial revolution.[63]

(*b*) The Ordinances of the Franco-German Synod at Troyes (*circa* 1150)*

[The Introduction, which is in the usual style of the French rabbis of the period, recites the serious troubles that had come upon the Jews because of denunciations. Some had defamed their fellows in secret, others had committed the crime in public, with equally dire results. The ordinance continues thus:]

Therefore have we taken counsel together, the elders of Troyes and her sages, and those of her vicinity, the sages of Dijon and its vicinity, the leaders of Auxerre, and of Sens and its suburbs, the elders of Orléans (?) and the vicinity, our brothers, the inhabitants of Chalon-sur-Saone, the sages of the Rhine country, and our masters of Paris and their neighbors, the scholars of Melun and Etampes, and the inhabitants of Normandy, and the shore of the sea, and Anjou and Poitiers, the greatest of our generation, the inhabitants of the land of Lorraine; of those mentioned here, some have already agreed and from some we have not yet heard, but since the matter was pressing, we were confident (in their agreement) knowing that they are great men who listen to their inferiors, and knowing that the decision is a correct one, which if it were not written down, ought to be written down.

1. We have voted, decreed, ordained, and declared under the *herem* ("ban") that no man or woman may bring a fellow Jew before gentile courts or exert compulsion on him through Gentiles, whether by a prince or a common man, a ruler or an inferior official, except by mutual agreement made in the presence of proper witnesses.

2. If the matter accidentally reaches the government or other Gentiles, and in that manner pressure is exerted on a Jew, we have decreed that the man who is aided by the Gentiles shall save his fellow from their hands and shall secure him against the Gentiles who are aiding him, so that the Jew may not be harmed nor even be in apprehension because of the Gentiles, nor shall he lose his claim or his property. He shall see to it that his fellow shall be in no fear of them, and he shall make satisfaction to him and secure him in such a

59. Baron, *The Jewish Community*, 1:296–98.
60. He was referred to as *Supremus Magister* in a decree of the Emperor Rudolf I in 1288.
61. Baron, *The Jewish Community*, 3:70–71.
62. Ibid., 1:298–99.

*Translated by L. Finkelstein in *Jewish Self-Government in the Middle Ages* (New York, 1924), with minor changes by the editor.
63. Ibid., 1:320.

manner as the "seven elders" of the city will ordain. If there is no such board in his town, he shall act on the order of those of the nearest city in which such are to be found.

3. He shall not intimidate the "seven elders" through the power of Gentiles. And because the masters of wicked tongue and informers do their deeds in darkness, we have decreed also excommunication for indirect action unless he satisfy him in accordance with the decision of the "seven elders" of the city.

4. It was further decreed that he should apply to them [to the "seven elders"] on the first possible day and that he should return the damage in accordance with all that they decree to him.

5. No man shall try to gain control over his neighbor through a king, prince or judge in order to punish or fine or coerce him, either in secular or religious matters, for there are some who play the part of saints and do not live up to ordinary standards.

6. He who transgresses these three decrees of ours shall be excommunicated, all Israel shall keep apart from him, those who sign (this decree) as well as those who do not sign, their pupils, and the pupils of their pupils, their comrades, great and small.

7. As for he who transgresses our decree, his bread is that of a *kuti*, his wine is that of libations, his books are as those of the magicians, and whosoever converses with him is like unto him; and he shall be in excommunication like him. But he who takes these matters to heart and is apprehensive of the words of our Creator and our words, will find our words good and upright. There is an old ordinance against *malshinim* (informers) and those who tell tales in secret; if a man sin against man, let him be judged by proper judges, but let not the hand of a stranger pass among them, and let them behave themselves with sanctity and purity, separating themselves from the people of the land; then shall each come to his destination in peace.

8. If because of the fear of the government, a man speak to the informer occasionally, this excommunication shall not fall on that man, provided he does not use this pretext to multiply words with him. This is an application of the principle given in regard to the fasting of pregnant and nursing women on fast days other than Yom Kippur and Tisha B'Av: "They need not fast, but yet they must not indulge in delicacies; they may only eat and drink for the sake of the child."

9. If one refuses to come to court and there are proper witnesses in regard to the matter and the plaintiff collects a claim through the power of Gentiles, our excommunication will not apply.

10. We, the undersigned, request all those that are in touch with the government to coerce through the power of Gentiles anyone who transgresses our commandments, in order that the scriptural injunction, "to

observe very much and to carry out" what they are commanded, may be fulfilled. And righteous action leads to peace.

> Samuel ben Meir
> Jacob ben Meir
> Samuel ben Jacob
> Isaac ben Solomon Troyes

(c) *Takkanot* [Prescriptions]
(By M. Elon)*

The Kenesett ha-Gedolah ("Great Assembly" [500–300 B.C.E.])

One of the principal tasks of the men of the Great Assembly was to make legislation ". . . and make a fence around the Torah" (Avot 1:1). Talmudic tradition attributes to the times of Keneset ha-Gedolah numerous *takkanot* in different fields of *halakhah*—benedictions and prayers (Ber. 33a; BB 15a), family law (incest in the second degree—Yev. 2:4; Yev. 21a). *Takkanot* pertaining to procedural rules and other fields of the *halakhah* are attributed to Ezra the Scribe (BK 82a; TJ, Meg. 4:1, 75a).

The Sanhedrin and the Period of the Tannaim [300 B.C.E.–220 C.E.]

The Great Sanhedrin fulfilled the function of a legislative body. The *takkanot* it enacted in the Temple period, as well as those enacted by the *nasi* and his *beth din* after the destruction of the Temple, are of material importance and served to prescribe the modes for the development of the *halakhah*, fashioning its character and evolutionary path for generations to come. A very substantial part of these *takkanot* are embraced in the different fields of Jewish law—civil, criminal, and public. The overwhelming majority of the *takkanot* of the Sanhedrin have come down anonymously, having been ordained by the Sanhedrin as a legislative body. In restricted cases the name of the halakhic scholar heading the Sanhedrin is recalled—for instance Simeon b. Shetah (in *takkanot* concerning family and criminal law, etc.—Shab. 14b–16b; Ket. 82b; TJ, Ket. 8:11, 32c), Hillel the Elder (concerning the prosbul . . .), Gamliel the Elder (particularly in the area of family law—Git. 4:2–3, and concerning the *agunot* . . .), Johanan b. Zakkai, Gamaliel of Jabneh, and so on. The aforementioned *takkanot* were also enacted by the Sanhedrin as a body, but they have been traditionally transmitted in the name of the contemporary head of this body. Around the middle of the second century the Sanhedrin sitting at Usha in Galilee enacted a number of *takkanot* known as the *"Takkanot Usha."* This was

*From *The Principles of Jewish Law* (Jerusalem, 1975). Prescriptions in Jewish Law are generally referred to as *takkanot*, if they impose a duty, and as *gezerot*, if they prohibit specified acts.

a time of warfare and hardship following on the decrees of the emperor Hadrian, and it brought in its train a certain disintegration of family life. A large number of the Usha *takkanot* are concerned with the determination of different family law directives in the area of rights and obligations between spouses and between parent and child (Ket. 49bf.; BK 88b; BB 139b). There are also *takkanot* dating from the end of the Tannaitic period attributed to particular scholars, such as Yose b. Halafta of Sepphoris and Judah ha-Nasi.

A decisive majority of the *takkanot* known to have been enacted until the end of the Tannaitic times have not come down in the names of the bodies or scholars who enacted them. Consequently it is difficult, as regards a large proportion of the *takkanot*, to establish their exact stage of enactment during this long and significant period. These anonymous *takkanot* embrace whole areas of Jewish law, such as family law, property and obligations, labor law, torts, procedure and evidence—in which fields the directives thus laid down constitute basic principles of the aforesaid legal system.

[These served as precedents for the medieval prescriptions.]

(3) *Poland and Lithuania*

In Poland the centralization of Jewish communal activity achieved greater and longer term importance than in any other land. The Polish kings at first appointed a series of elders for the Jewish communities, their main function being the supervision of tax collections. Under pressure from the Jewish communities, the Polish kings agreed reluctantly to confirm the appointments of Jewish regional leaders who were selected by the Jewish communities themselves. Accordingly, in 1518 and 1519 two chief rabbis were appointed for Poznan. In 1527 the king ratified the selection of Rabbi Samuel Margolies and invested him with very wide powers:

> As long as he may live, to judge in matters pertaining to law, to recognize, bind or absolve, to impose censures and bans in accordance with the ritual and custom of Mosaic Law, and to exercise all forms of authority in spiritual matters with respect to all the Jews residing in the land of Great Poland and the Duchy of Mazovia. It is, hereby, expressly stated, and, as the said Jews have declared before us, has been observed as an ancient usage, that, if any Jew should venture to take lightly the censures and bans imposed upon him by the aforementioned Doctor Samuel, and make no attempt to extricate himself therefrom within one month, such a person, after being denounced to us, shall be beheaded and all his property confiscated for our treasury.[64]

In 1522 Judah Aaron, and subsequently the famous Shalom Shakna of Lublin, were appointed as chief rabbis.

At the same time, the conflicting desires of the king and the Jewish communities regarding the selection of communal leaders led to the eventual establishment of regional councils that were selected by the Jews but confirmed in office by the king.[65] (The provincial chief rabbis were also selected by the Jewish electorate.) These permanent communal Jewish bodies, elected by the Jews and recognized, but not controlled, in their detailed operation by the Polish government, emerged as a compromise between the conflicting desires of the state and the Jewish communities. The central government, which was primarily interested in collecting the maximum revenues from its Jewish population, thought it desirable to concentrate this function in a few hands for maximum and most efficient collection but desired to retain ultimate control. At the same time the Jews, who desired autonomy, received the power to select their own leaders.

The Jewish communities desired the existence of transcommunal councils for a number of very good reasons. Massive immigrations to Poland from various parts of Germany and other lands resulted in cultural conflicts regarding religious observances, and sometimes different perspectives and varying methodologies in commercial dealings. Since Jewish merchants traded with, and often traveled in many communities, a central authority, transcending any one community, was necessary to regulate affairs for the benefit of Jewish merchants and tradesmen. Furthermore, because of favoritism, traditional Jewish law prohibited community leaders from sitting in judgment on matters involving individual members of their own community, or their community as a whole. It was therefore necessary to be able to obtain judges from other communities on a regular basis to adjudicate intercommunity disputes.

Relations with non-Jews were another important factor impelling Jews to establish intercommunal councils. Hostile measures against individual Jews or Jewish communities came up on the horizon periodically. These had to be met and checked, promptly and efficiently. Jewish craftsmen also had to contend with the restrictions against them imposed by the non-Jewish guilds in many different areas of Poland and Lithuania.

Strict regulations were also required for the economic activities of those Jews who competed with the nobles (particularly in activities such as tax farming and the export of grains) in order to obviate hostile measures taken or instigated by such nobles. Additionally, it was continually necessary for Jewish communities to nego-

64. I. Halpern, *Beth Yisrael Be'Polin* (Tel-Aviv, 1946), p. 39.

65. Baron, *The Jewish Community*, 1:301.

tiate with officials of both the central and provincial Polish parliaments. This could best be handled by a central organization that could draw upon the resources of the various Jewish communities all over Poland. Furthermore, it was vital to defend the rights of Jewish merchants who traveled to the large commercial fairs, and also to meet the needs of the Jewish poor and refugees, who often moved from community to community. These, as well as the intercommunal needs regarding education and copyrights for religious books, which were sold all over Poland, gave rise to the desires of the Jews in Poland to establish intercommunity regional councils.

Such Jewish regional councils were formed and were recognized and invested with authority by King Casimir the Great in 1334. In the main they emulated the Polish Sejm (parliament), which arose out of the gathering of the provincial Polish nobility. The royal privileges for Jewish councils were subsequently expanded.[66]

In 1533 a Jewish national tribunal was established to adjudicate intercommunal litigation. In 1540 the seat of the tribunal, which consisted of two rabbis from each of the larger communities of Cracow, Poznan and Lvov was moved to Lublin. Parallel with these developments, councils were formed by Jewish representatives of three of the major regions of Poland, e.g., Lesser Poland (i.e., Cracow and Lublin); Greater Poland (i.e., Poznan); the then so-called "Red" Russia (i.e., Lvov); and, later, the Lithuanian area of Brizsc. Later, certainly by 1623, a separate council was formed for Lithuania. The two councils had separate treasuries, separate tax assessments, and separate internal organizations which existed, although the areas in which both councils operated were in one country.

The Jewish council of Poland, commonly called the Council of Four Lands, consisted of some thirty delegates, including a number of leading rabbis from the four major communities, and was recognized as a supreme court for all the Jews of Poland. It commonly met twice a year, its first meeting coinciding with the large fairs at Lublin and Jaroslav, to which most of the Jewish merchants, lay leaders, and rabbis frequently traveled for both economic reasons, and for social and religious intercourse. Unfortunately, the record books of the Polish Council were burned, but a significant number of its actions and deliberations are mentioned in the records of other communities and in many Responsa. The Lithuanian Council, which convened more irregularly, consisted of from six to nine members, later increasing to twelve to fifteen delegates.

Each council had a chairman (*parnas*), who received a salary. These tended to be selected from leading patrician families, which resulted in a tendency toward oligarchy and cooptation. In Poland only laymen were selected for the chief post, while in Lithuania, the first and probably most prominent chairman, was a rabbi.[67]

The Jewish councils in both Poland and Lithuania were very active and performed vital decision-making functions, both in the prescriptions of many ordinances concerning communal affairs and in maintaining an appellate court system for the adjudication of litigation, particularly litigation in which a community as such was a party.

As far as the Polish government was concerned, the importance of the Jewish council was mainly in its collection of taxes. In 1500 it collected 20,000 zlotys. This tax collection increased to 220,000 zlotys by 1717. This increase is all the more remarkable since it was far greater than the increase in the Jewish population of Poland during that period, and it occurred during the catastrophic economic decline in Poland during that era.

Some of the major ordinances prescribed by the regional Jewish councils represented attempts to obviate the undesirable competition between Jews and Polish noblemen regarding the farming of state revenues. The councils also prescribed ordinances regulating interest rates and bankruptcies, the enforcement of debt collections, forms of loan instruments, and the methods and procedures for elections of communal officers in the Jewish communities. They prosecuted criminals who fled from other lands and took action against defaulting debtors from other countries who entered Poland. They gave all kinds of assistance, financial as well as political, to Jewish communities in need, including those outside of Poland. Also, the council intervened, on request, in attempts to settle quarrels within other communities and to heal intercommunal rifts. They tried to institute and enforce copyrights on books, issued approvals and disapprovals of the publication of specified books, and supervised educational and charitable activities.[68]

On a reduced scale, there were also other transcommunal provincial councils and provincial chief rabbis, operating in smaller regions. These paralleled the activities of the Central Council and the court of the Council of Four Lands, and the Lithuanian Council. These subregional councils also allocated the tax burdens, maintained a judiciary, and engaged in other activities similar to those of the interregional councils.

Jewish communal organization and decision-making in Poland, both regional and local, fell into a sharp

---

66. Ibid., 1:324.

67. Ibid., 1:325–26; see Dubnow, *Pinkas Ha'Medinah* (Jerusalem, 1969).

68. Balaban, *Beth Yisrael Be'Polin*, pp. 60–62; Baron, ibid., 1:330–31.

decline following the terrible Cossack massacres and the Swedish-Muscovite invasions of 1648–1657, which resulted in mass slaughter and destruction. The tax burdens placed on these councils were too onerous, since they had to pay the increasingly burdensome taxes imposed by the state in addition to the many necessary "gifts" to local nobles, members of the central and provincial Polish parliaments, the church, and others. Because of the drastic economic declines that set in following the Cossack massacres and wars, it has been estimated that the communal indebtedness of Polish Jewry in 1764 was approximately ten million florins.[69]

It appears likely that the Jewish transcommunal councils in Poland lasted as long as they did, despite their staggering debts, because of the support of members of the Polish nobility and of the clergy. Many of them had invested considerable sums of money as loans to the Jewish communities at high rates of interest, and they were desirous of protecting their investments. It has been estimated that 30 percent of the debt of the Jewish communities in Poland was owed to nobles, and 35 percent to the clergy, including monasteries and entire clerical orders.[70]

The breakdown and decline of Jewish communal autonomy and decision-making was further intensified by their frequent inability to take action. This was caused largely by the veto power that individual communities could exercise, in emulation of the *liberum veto* of the Polish *Sejm*. Representatives of individual communities who disagreed with the proposed actions of their council could paralyze it simply by absenting themselves from meetings. The councils attempted to deal with this by enacting regulations requiring the attendance of representatives at meetings under threat of fines, but this was often ineffective.

The councils also lost much of their support among the Jewish masses because of increasing oligarchic control of decision-making by plutocrats and interrelated members of a few leading families. This led to grave abuses that were deeply resented by the masses. It is possible that this disaffection also helped to spur the spread of Hasidism, the fervent Jewish religious movement that began in the late eighteenth century and appealed largely to those in the lower social and economic classes; it may even have fed the semi-revolutionary Frankist movement.

Eventually the Polish *Sejm* dissolved both the central and provincial Councils in 1764 because of its dissatisfaction with the amount of taxes collected by these Jewish communal organizations.[71] The political partition of Poland in 1772 sealed the coffin of the Jewish transcommunal councils.

(4) Central Europe

A regional organization of Jewish communities existed in Moravia in the early part of the sixteenth century and was well-established by the seventeenth century. This region had many vigorous chief rabbis who were active in Jewish communal affairs, including Judah Loewe (1553–1573; later the rabbi of Prague), Yom Tov Heller (1625–1626), David Oppenheim (1690–1718) and Samson R. Hirsch (1847–1851).

The ordinances of Moravia were compiled and revised by Rabbi Menahem Krochmal in 1681–1682 and published as "The Three Hundred and Eleven Ordinances" (see Section B 2, below, for selections). The regional organization of the Jewish communities of Moravia existed, although in modified form, for four hundred years, until the end of World War I.

There was also a regional communal organization centered at Prague and a German intercommunal organization established by a conference at Frankfurt, Germany, in 1603. The latter attempted to establish a permanent central organization, uniform system of taxation, and district courts for a number of cities in the region, including Frankfurt, Worms, Mayence, Horn, Friedberg, Fulda, Schneitoch, Gunzberg, and others. However, this attempt was not successful.

(5) Summary

In Islamic lands the Islamic tradition of leadership by authoritarian individuals was replicated in Jewish communal leadership as well. Individuals were appointed as leaders and as chief rabbis of large regions, such as the exilarch in Babylonia and the two gaonic heads of academies there, the patriarch (*nasi*) in Palestine, the *nagid* in Egypt. There may also have been Islamic influence in the appointments of the chief rabbis in Spain. Even here, the influence of the national lay Jewish leaders was often counterbalanced, at least in part, by the scholar–decision-makers and heads of the academies of law.

Europe, with its own social and political milieu, did not generally carry on the hierarchic form of hereditary leadership as in the Babylonian exilarchate or the Palestinian patriarchate. Instead, Jewish communal leadership followed the pattern, which had existed during the Christian Roman Empire, of a theoretically free and egalitarian communal structure. There was little formal concentrated leadership in the hands of authoritarian individuals. Communal government made notable ad-

69. I. Shipper, "The Financial Ruin of the Central and Provincial Autonomy of the Jews in Poland, 1650–1764" (Yiddish), in *Yivo Studies in Economics*, vol. 2 (Warsaw, 1932).

70. Ibid.

71. Baron, *The Jewish Community*, 1:336.

vances with the establishment of regional transcommunal decision-making bodies.

Nevertheless, in time, oligarchic tendencies and even economic exploitation arose. These ultimately helped to undermine the strength of both the intercommunal and intracommunal structures.

During the hundreds of years of their existence, however, Jewish communal and intercommunal institutions played a vital role in decision-making and affected nearly all areas of Jewish life.

B. *Participants in Jewish Decision-Making*

1. THE CONSTITUTIVE SCHEME OF JEWISH COMMUNAL DECISION-MAKING: PARTICIPANTS AND INSTITUTIONS

a. LAY COMMUNAL DECISION-MAKING

(1) *Perspectives Concerning Limitations on Communal Authority*

As detailed above (see Section A, above), the perspective was widespread, particularly during the Middle Ages, that Jewish communities should organize and were the proper vehicles to regulate societal activities and make the necessary decisions in nearly all areas of human interactions, and that they could depart from traditional legal principles to carry out this function.[72]

Nevertheless, there were certain basic principles to which community governments were bound, in theory. They were viewed as unauthorized to act unfairly toward an individual, or to allocate community burdens in a capricious manner, since such acts were held to constitute "robbery" and were not the legitimate acts of a governing body.[73] Decisions were to be made by majority vote, and there was considerable scholarly conflict concerning the rights of minorities.[74] Commu-

nal enactments might sometimes be regarded as invalid either because they violated biblical law[75] or even simply because they were too onerous to be borne by the community[76] or would be adverse to public morality.[77]

Despite these theoretical restrictions, which sometimes affected practice, the local Jewish communities effectively made and enforced decisions in nearly every area of human activity, and they were in many ways the most important Jewish decision-making institutions in Europe during the Middle Ages.

(2) *The Scope of Communal Decision-Making*

(a) Taxation and Economic Regulation

The most important single decision-making task of Jewish communities was probably assessing and collecting the amount of tax to be paid by each individual in the community. As John Locke remarked, "Who determines taxation, seems even more fundamental than who determines legislation."[78] This authority, of course, gave the communal organization and its officers great powers.

Taxes normally were assessed according to a graduated scale of income as well as capital. The monies raised went not only to pay the government taxes and "gifts" to the provincial officials and members of the nobility, but also for maintenance of the synagogue, help for the poor, maintenance of a ritual bath, and, especially in the later Middle Ages, the occasional maintenance of a hospital, an inn for wayfarers, payments of the salaries of school teachers, ritual slaughterers, sexton, and rabbi (when these latter became paid professionals).

In Babylonia and Palestine, the Jewish community had a long tradition of exercising important economic regulatory functions, including taxation, controlling prices, hours of work, competitive and monopolistic practices, and other vital areas of commerce.[79] Similar close economic regulation was practiced by Jewish communities in the Middle Ages, as well.[80]

72. Meir ben Barukh, Responsa *Maharam* of Rothenberg (Lvov ed.), no. 213, 423; Shlomo ben Aderet, Responsa *Rashba*, vol. 1, nos. 680, 729, 811; vol. 3, nos. 398, 411, 417; vol. 5, nos. 126, 127, 184, 250, 272. Also Shlomo Yitzhaki, Responsa *Rashi*, no. 246, pp. 287–89; and ibid. quoted in Commentary of Mordecai ben Hillel to Talmud, *Shevuot* 2:758. See the citations and examples in Chapter IX, Section C, below.

73. Hayim ben Yitzhak, Responsa *Maharah Ohr Zarua*, no. 222; Shlomo ben Aderet, Responsa *Rashba*, 5:185; Meir ben Barukh, Responsa *Maharam* of Rothenberg (Prague ed.), no. 106; ibid. (Lvov ed.), no. 371; M. Isserlis, Responsa *Rama*, no. 73; Responsa of Hanina Gaon, in Responsa of the *Gaonim*, *Sha'are Tzedek* (Jerusalem ed.), vol. 4, sec. 4, no. 16, p. 126.

74. See A. Freiman, "Majority and Minority in the Community," 2 *Yavneh* (Hebrew; Jerusalem, 1948); Mordecai ben Hillel, Commentary to *Baba Kama*, p. 179, citing Rabbi Jacob Tam; Meir ben Barukh, Responsa *Maharam* of Rothenberg (Crimona ed.), no. 230. For additional citations, see Section B 1 *a* (5), below.

75. Meir ben Barukh, Responsa *Maharam* of Rothenberg (Lvov ed.), no. 423; Shlomo ben Aderet, Responsa *Rashba*, vol. 2, no. 289; vol. 5, no. 287; vol. 7, no. 108.

76. Shlomo ben Aderet, Responsa *Rashba*, vol. 3, no. 411; vol. 7, no. 108; Agus, Responsa of *Ba'ale Ha'Tosafot* (New York, 1954), p. 39.

77. Shlomo ben Aderet, Responsa *Rashba*, vol. 2, no. 279; see also S. Atlas, "The General Will in Talmudic Jurisprudence" (Hebrew), in *Hebrew Union College Annual*, vol. 26 (Cincinnati, 1955), sec., pp. 1–38.

78. John Locke *Treatise on Civil Government* (London, 1690).

79. See Part Two, Chapter VI, Section A 3, above; Talmud, *Baba Batra* 8a, 55a, 89a. For other communal activities in Babylonia, see Talmud, *Baba Batra* 3a (acquisition of weapons, hiring guards, maintaining the water supply), and Assaf, *Tekufat Ha'Gaonim*, p. 19.

80. Agus, Responsa of *Ba'ale Ha'Tosefot*, p. 178 ff.

(*b*) Exclusion of Newcomers

Another area of communal decision-making important in early medieval Europe was in determining who should be permitted to live in a community. The perspective was that all "citizens" of a Jewish community were entitled to dwell in the community and receive protection. Citizenship was often procured only by birth or by official community admission. Non-citizens could be excluded from residing or doing business in a community. This was known as the *herem* or *hezkat ha-yishuv* (the "ban," or the "right of settlement"), which allegedly originated in a prescription of Rabbi Gershom's synod.[81] However, Rabbi Jacob Tam (*circa* 1150) limited the rights of Jewish communities to exclude newcomers to those who were suspected of denouncing Jews to the authorities or of refusing to pay their taxes.[82] The right of exclusion, nevertheless, was frequently practiced at the discretion of Jewish communal leaders.[83] As late as the seventeenth century, the Lithuanian Council prescribed ordinances requiring that Jews from other lands be driven out of Lithuania.[84]

Some communities, fearful of the loss of community resources, even forbade the *outward* emigration of residents and would tax parents if their daughter married and left the city.[85]

Restrictions on travel and trade were much less prevalent in Mediterranean countries, such as Spain and Italy, where capitalism flourished. In fact, some of the Jewish communities in mercantile centers, such as Bologna, maintained hostelries for visiting merchants.[86] Some even attempted to attract commerce by granting immigrants immunity with regard to prior crimes.[87]

(*c*) Miscellaneous Prescriptions

The scope of communal lay enactments ranged over nearly the whole of Jewish law. In addition to prescrip-

tions concerning taxation, criminal law, and civil procedure, communities sometimes enacted ordinances that concerned themselves directly in sacerdotal areas, such as ritual law, marriages, and divorces—areas which in theory were regarded as the exclusive preserve of rabbinic decision-makers. For example, a number of communities promulgated ordinances that all future questions of law, including those concerned with rituals and religious prohibitions, were to be settled by following the views of Rambam or of Josef Karo.[88]

Some communities took the far-reaching step of declaring void marriages that were not performed in the presence of ten adult males, the quorum prescribed by rabbinic law.[89] In such cases, the wife was thus permitted by these communities to remarry without a divorce. Permitting the remarriage of such women, who were deemed as still validly married under Biblical law, was a momentous step, since preservation of the sanctity and inviolability of marriages was regarded as fundamental to Jewish religious law and life. Some scholar–decision-makers were strongly opposed to such lay communal enactments,[90] while others upheld the rights of communities to prescribe that all questions of law, including rituals and religious prohibitions, should be decided in accordance with the view of a particular rabbinic authority.[91]

(*d*) Changes in Traditional Law

Just as the *beth din* was regarded as empowered to change biblical norms to meet changing circumstances, so, too, individual lay communities were recognized as having similar powers. Ultimately they, also, enacted numerous changes in traditional Jewish law when they felt it appropriate. In addition to voiding biblically valid

81. Germany, *circa* 1000 C.E.; see Talmud, *Baba Batra* 21a and b; commentaries of Rabbenu Gershom and Asher b. Yehiel, *Rosh*, ad loc.

82. See *Tosefot*, ad loc.; see also Judah the Pious, in *Sefer Hasidim*, nos. 130, 160; Y. Z. Kahana, "*Hezkat Ha'Yishur*, in *Mekhkarim Be'Safrut Ha'Teshuvot* (Jerusalem, 1973), p. 445. Rabinowitz, "The Talmudic Basis of the Hebrew *Herem Ha'-Yishub*," in *Jewish Quarterly Review* 37 (1937–38): 217.

83. Baron, *The Jewish Community*, 2:543; Agus, Responsa of *Ba'ale Ha'Tosefot*, pp. 178–79.

84. See Dubnow, *Pinkas*, no. 47 ff, of the year 1623; no. 202 of 1628; nos. 500, 516, of 1655; no. 600 of 1667; no. 602 of 1670; Halpern, *Miluim*, no. 40.

85. Shlomo ben Aderet, Responsa *Rashba*, vol. 3, no. 406; Baron, *The Jewish Community*, 3:103, n. 10.

86. Ibid., 2:49.

87. S. D. Luzzatto, "Responsum of the Roman Scholars addressed to the Scholars of Paris" (Hebrew), in *Beth Ha'Ozar* (Levov, 1847), 1:57a, 60a, dealing with a letter dating from 1184 that states, "We have never heard of such a practice . . ." in regard to a query about denying newcomers the right to settle.

88. Nissim Gerundi, Responsa *Ran*, no. 62; Isaac ben Sheshet, Responsa *Rivash*, nos. 21, 105, 345, 478, 493; J. Karo, Responsa *Avkat Rohel*, no. 32; see Communal Ordinances of Toledo, Spain, of 1305, cited in Baer, *The Jews in Christian Spain* (New York, 1929), 1:949; Y. Z. Kahana, "Polemics Concerning the Establishment of Decision-Making According to *Rambam*," in *Sinai* (Hebrew; Jerusalem, 1955) 36:402, M. Zakuto, *Shuda De'Daina*, below.

89. Shlomo ben Aderet, Responsa *Rashba*, vol. 1, no. 551; Issac ben Sheshet, Responsa *Rivash*, no. 399; H. Benebashti, *Knesset Ha-Gedolah*, no. 32.

90. See Yosef Benlev, Responsa *Mahari* ben Lev (Jerusalem, 1959), vol. 1, sec. 12, no. 75, pp. 183, 263; Shlomo ben Aderet, Responsa *Rashba*, vol. 1, no. 253.

91. "The Ordinances of the Community of Mantova, Italy," in Zakuto, *Shuda De'Daina*, below. For a contrary view regarding the scope of lay communal decision-making, see the blanket statement of Elon, who accepts at face value the assertions of some talmudic scholars that lay communities did not have the right to inject themselves into matters of ritual law or religious prohibitions. See his *Ha'Mishpat Ha'Ivri*, 2:574–75; cf. Karo, Responsa *Avkat Rohel*, no. 32. See also M. P. Golding's valuable study, "Juridical Basis of Communal Associations in Medieval Rabbinic Legal Thought," in *Jewish Social Studies* 28, no. 2 (1966): 71.

marriages not performed in the presence of ten males (see above), they inflicted corporal and even capital sanctions not authorized by biblical law (although, as detailed in Part Two, Chapter V, Section C 3, above, such sanctions would be regarded as murder or illegal maiming, unless there was perceived authority therefor), permitted relatives and other interested parties to qualify as witnesses, contrary to traditional talmudic law;[92] and enacted far-reaching deviations from traditional talmudic law in other areas of criminal law, including procedure, and evidence.[93] Judges who were related to the litigants, or who were members of the community involved in litigation, were also permitted to adjudicate cases, contrary to accepted talmudic law.[94] So, too, the attestation of a town scribe was substituted for the attestation of two qualified witnesses.[95]

In the same fashion, the taxing powers of Jewish communities were not restricted by the traditional principles of Jewish law.[96] Communities were also held authorized to deviate from the law in other civil matters.[97]

Among the important sanctioning areas in which changes in traditional law were effected were the frequent prescriptions for the imprisonment of debtors who did not pay their debts when due. This was done despite the explicit provisions of the Bible and of talmudic law.[98] Many Jewish communities enacted ordinances permitting the imprisonment of such debtors,[99]

and in Lithuania and Poland it became a very widespread practice.[100]

An important spur to the departure from application of principles of traditional Jewish law by lay communal bodies and by scholar-religious leaders was the acceptance of the notion that "the law of the land is the law."[101] Without this concept Jewish life would have been extremely difficult in an alien, hostile environment. This principle permitted Jewish decision-makers to adopt various non-Jewish civil norms that prevailed in their lands and whose violation would have aroused the ire of non-Jewish rulers. Accordingly, these non-Jewish norms helped to shape Jewish commerce and other activities and often played an important role in Jewish decision-making.[102]

(3) *The Relationship of Lay Communal Decision-Making to Traditional Jewish Decision-Making*

Widespread recognition has been accorded to the view of Sir Henry Maine[103] that when a legal system becomes rigidified and unable to change to meet new socioeconomic conditions, rival legal systems (such as the English Courts of Equity) arise, which apply different rules more suited to the changed conditions. While it may be argued that the Jewish communal ordinances in the Middle Ages were an example of this phenomena, Maine's reasoning may not be appropriate here. As discussed below (Chapter IX, Section C 2), scholar–decision-makers in the Middle Ages, both in their Responsa and in their capacity as communal judges, attempted to solve competing claims in the face of radically changed conditions by making many adjustments in the law, based on many well-established talmudic legal principles. These adjustments were, notably, the power of the court to expropriate as it saw fit, the power to impose sanctions not authorized by biblical law as normally applied, and even the power to nullify completely a biblical law when the need arose.[104]

There were established perspectives calling for a community role in decision-making. Lay communal ordinances were, at least in theory, prescribed in reliance on traditional principles similar to those utilized

92. Shlomo ben Aderet, Responsa *Rashba*, vol. 1, nos. 680, 811; vol. 2, no. 107; vol. 5, nos. 184, 250, 273, 285; Asher ben Yehiel, Responsa *Rosh*, vol. 5, no. 4; vol. 6, no. 21; Responsa *Hikre Lev, Ho. Mis.* (Salonika, 1817), no. 23; Jacob ben Asher, *Tur, Shulkhan Arukh, Ho. Mis.*, sec. 37, subsec. 18; Talmud, *Baba Batra* 43a; *Sanhedrin* 23a; *Hagiga*, 22a.

93. See Responsa *Zikhron Yehuda*, no. 58; Jerusalem Talmud, *Hagiga* 2:2; *Tur, Shulkhan Arukh, Ho. Mis.*, no. 2. Responsa *Ritva*, no. 131.

94. Shlomo ben Aderet, Responsa *Rashba*, vol. 6, no. 7; Josef Karo, *Shulkhan Arukh, Ho. Mis.* sec. 37, subsec. 12; Benebashti, *Kenesset Ha'Gedolah, Ho. Mis.*, sec. 7, subsec. 22; Elon, *Ha'Mishpat Ha'Ivri*, 2:597–98.

95. Moses ben Nahman, Responsa *Rashba*, attributed to *Ramban*, no. 65; Shlomo ben Aderet, Responsa *Rashba*, vol. 2, no. 111; vol. 3, no. 438.

96. Shlomo ben Aderet, Responsa *Rashba*, vol. 3, nos. 398, 406; vol. 4, no. 260; Meir ben Barukh, Responsa *Maharam* of Rothenburg, nos. 106, 915 (Prague ed.); Mordecai ben Hillel, Commentary *Mordecai* to *Baba Batra* 522, 595.

97. See Meir ben Barukh, Responsa *Maharam* of Rothenberg, no. 213, (Lvov ed.).

98. Exod. 22:24–26; Deut. 24:6, 10–13; *Rambam*, Laws of Lenders and Borrowers, 2:1–2; see Elon *Ha'Massar*, pp. 171–201; cf. commentary of Rashi to Talmud, *Pesahim* 91a; see also A. Gulak, *Yesode Ha'Mishpat Ha'Ivri*, 2:124–27.

99. Isaac ben Sheshet, Responsa *Rivash*, no. 484; Gulak, *Otzar Ha'Shatarot* (Jerusalem, 1926); Elon, "The Sources and Nature of Jewish Law," *Israel Law Review* (1968) vol. 3, no. 1, p. 110; see Talmud, *Ketubot* 86a.

100. See the Ordinances of the Lithuania Council of 1637, no. 333; A. Ankava, in *Kerem Hamar*, vol. 2, no. 22, p. 4a. See also Elon, "An Analysis of Communal Ordinances in Jewish Law" (Hebrew), in *Legal Studies in Honor of Rosenthal* (Jerusalem, 1964); 1:22 ff; S. Tal, "Legal-Halakhic Principles on Which Communal Prescriptions Are Based" (Hebrew), in *Dine Israel* 3 (1972): 36 ff.

101. Talmud, *Baba Batra* 54b, 55a.

102. Baron, *The Jewish Community*, 1:214; see in general, S. Shilo, *Dina De-Malkhuta Dina: The Law of the State Is the Law* (Jerusalem, 1974).

103. In his *Ancient Law* (London, 1861).

104. See Part Two, Chapter V, Section C 3 above.

by the *beth din* and individual scholar–decision-makers. The proliferation of medieval lay communal prescriptions to meet societal needs does not appear to have been due to the need to supplant a fossilized legal structure. It seems, rather, to have stemmed from the prevalent medieval notions that it was appropriate for community laymen, who were intimately familiar with local conditions and needs, to enact appropriate prescriptions in order to deal with new societal situations. This only continued an ancient tradition and served to complement a long series of religious-lay regional synods in early medieval Europe.

It should also be noted that in early medieval Europe, which did not have professional salaried rabbis, there was no sharp dichotomy between laymen and religious leader–scholars since the latter were also laymen.[105] Perspectives concerning the ancient roots of communal enactments can be seen in the fact that the Talmud cites a communal prescription that it attributes to Joshua and his associates (including, apparently, lay leaders) as the source of the legal principle that a court may expropriate property in its discretion.[106] As detailed above, Jewish communal decision-making was also well established in the Roman Empire and in Babylonia.[107] Lay decision-making was particularly appropriate in early medieval Europe. Trained scholars and religious leaders were in short supply, and often there was no full-time *beth din*. Rabbis were not salaried communal employees but were active as community laymen.

Since scholar–religious leader decision-makers viewed communal decisions and prescriptions as being within the traditional framework of Jewish decision-making,[108]

they attempted to apply to communal prescriptions, the same legal principles that governed the enactments of the *beth din*: that prescriptions must adhere to "fundamental" principles of government and not harm public morality and discipline;[109] that decision-makers were required to ascertain whether proposed enactments could be borne by the public without undue burden and to appraise the extent to which existing prescriptions were observed. Proposed enactments that were unbearable would be aborted, and those already in effect would be annulled. So, too, "unfair" enactments that unduly penalized individuals would be cancelled.[110] Communal decisions, like those of the court, were required to be made by majority vote,[111] and the community could expropriate property in the same manner as a court.[112]

(4) Takkanot ha'Kahal [*Communal Prescriptions*]
   (By M. Elon)*

The *Takkanot ha-Kahal* [communal prescriptions] embrace that part of legislation in Jewish law which is enacted by the public or its representatives in contradistinction to the *takkanot* enacted by a halakhic authority, i.e., by the court and halakhic scholars. The enactment of legislation by the public is already to be found in ancient *halakhah*. Thus it was stated that the *benei ha-ir* ("townspeople") have authority to pass enactments obliging all residents of their town in matters such as the prices of commodities, weights and measures, and laborer's wages, and to impose fines on those transgressing their enactments (Tosef. BM 11:23; BB 8b). The same sources (Tosef. BM 11.24–26) disclose that legislative authority was entrusted also to more restricted bodies, such as various artisans' and traders' associations within the town, such regulations obliging only the members of the particular association.

For as long as a single Jewish center, first Erez Israel and later the Babylonian Jewish center, exercised hegemony over the entire Diaspora, there was little legislative activity of a local nature, both from the aspect

---

105. Accordingly, it appears unwarranted to make a sharp dichotomy between enactments by scholar-religious leaders and communal prescriptions. See *contra* Elon, *Ha'Mishpat Ha'Ivri*, pp. 391, 558 ff.

106. Talmud, *Yebamot* 89; *Gittin* 36b; see also Agus, "The Autonomous Rule of Jewish Communities," p. 194 ff.

107. See Part Two, Chapter VI, Section A 3 above.

108. "Just as all communities are subjected to the high court or the *nasi*, so is every individual subjected to his local community" (Shlomo Yitzhaki, Responsa *Rashi*, vol. 1, no. 769). See also the views of *Rashi*, cited in the commentary of Mordecai ben Hillel to Talmud, Shavuoth, vol. 2, no. 758, and to *Hulin* 711; see *Kal Bo* (Naples, 1490), no. 142, author unknown; Meir ben Barukh, Responsa *Maharam* of Rothenberg, nos. 10, 165, 230 (Crimona ed.); nos. 46, 104, 106, 245, 383, 708, 716, 934, 940, 941, 994 (Prague ed.), nos. 108, 248 (Lvov ed.); Agus, "The Autonomous Rule of Jewish Communities," p. 177; B. Lipkin, "Prescriptive Jurisdiction of the Community" (Hebrew), in *Sinai* 20 (1949): 233; idem, "The Views of the Early Authorities Concerning Communal Enactments" (Hebrew), in *Ha'Torah Ve'Ha'Medina* (Jerusalem, 1940), 2:41; Tal, "Legal-Halahaic Principles," p. 31; Elon, "An Analysis of Communal Enactments in Jewish Law" (Hebrew), in *Legal Studies in Honor of A. Rosenthal* (Jerusalem, 1964), p. 1; numerous studies of Y. Schipansky concerning Commu-

nal Prescriptions, in *Ha'Darom* (New York, 1966, 1967, 1968), vols. 22, 24, 28, and in *Ohr Ha'Mizrah* 28 (1969): 180.

109. See, e.g., Shlomo ben Aderet, Responsa *Rashba*, vol. 2, no. 279, nullifying on this ground the abolition of the office of an inspector of communal affairs.

110. Moshe Isserlis, Responsa *Rama*, no. 73; Meir ben Barukh Responsa *Maharam of Rothenburg*, no. 106 (Prague ed.).

111. See Section I *a* (4), below, for other principles that applied equally to communal enactments and decisions of the *beth din*. See Meir ben Barukh, Responsa *Maharam* of Rothenberg, no. 230 (Crimona ed.). See Section B 1 *a* (1), above, for additional citations.

112. "*Hefker tzibur hefker*," a term that parallels the expression concerning courts, "*hefker beth din, hefker*"; Shlomo ben Aderet, Responsa *Rashba*, vol. 4, no. 142; Isaac ben Sheshet, Responsa *Rivash*, no. 399.

*From *The Principles of Jewish Law* (Jerusalem, 1975).

of quantity and in the degree of authority carried. The great impetus to legislation by the public came at the end of the tenth century with the emerging stature of the Jewish community. The community enjoyed a substantial degree of autonomy. It had its own internal governing bodies, saw to the social and educational needs of its members, maintained a *bet din* possessing jurisdiction in the areas of civil, administrative, and ritual law, and to some extent also criminal jurisdiction. It also imposed and collected taxes, both to satisfy the fiscal demands of the ruling power and to finance communal services. The legal order governing the fulfillment of these manifold tasks was in large measure derived through the enactment of *takkanot* by the community. To ensure that the communal enactments be capable of fulfilling their envisaged objectives, the halakhic scholars saw the need to found these *takkanot* on principles belonging to the sphere of the public law and, from the aspect of their legal validity, to free them from the requirements and restrictions found in the private law. In consequence the scholars evolved basic principles in the area of Jewish public law constituting an impressive part of their wide legal creativity in this field, against the background of the social and economic realities of Jewish autonomy.

(5) *Procedures and Institutions in Lay Decision-Making*

(*a*) The Lay Electorate

In the Jewish communities throughout medieval Europe the practice gradually developed to periodically convene plenary assemblies in order to elect communal officers and members of the community council, and sometimes to vote on proposed ordinances. As a rule, only the male heads of families could vote, with women and single persons being excluded.

In theory, communal decisions were to accord with the will of the majority. In practice, however, there were numerous modifications.[113] There often were property qualifications for voting, or decision-making power was frequently weighed in favor of persons with means. This was justified by the argument, "Why permit those with no money to decide how to spend the money of those who had it?" Accordingly, fiscal decisions by plenary assemblies often required a majority of those with wealth.[114] The members of the community were

sometimes divided into a few (usually three) parts, according to wealth. Each class was then given a stipulated (usually equal) number of votes, as in Valencia, Spain, Rome, Italy, and Frankfurt, Germany.[115] This, of course, favored the wealthy. Often those who did not pay a stipulated minimum amount of tax were not given the right to vote or to hold office (for example, in Lvov and Moravia). Sometimes the poor could not vote but could be elected to office, as in Avignon.[116]

The meetings were generally held in the synagogue, with decisions usually by majority vote of the qualified electorate.[117]

(*b*) Communal Officials

The elected Jewish communal officers and members of the community council were generally the most prominent individuals. In France and Germany, during the early Middle Ages, these were most often the scholars and religious leaders,[118] and later they were the wealthier males in the community. Nearly always, however, at least one scholar of Jewish law and religion was included. In Poland all communal prescriptions were usually drafted by and required the consent of the local rabbi.

The selection of Jewish communal officials was frequently interfered with by the state, however, and in Poland by the local nobility as well. This interference was especially common in Poland and in Mediterranean countries where authoritarian Muslim tradition survived. In Poland the Jews resisted and eventually won the right to select officers of their own choosing, subject to confirmation by the provincial governor. There was usually no sharp state opposition to this, since the process soon deteriorated into the payment of a substantial "gift" to the governor in return for his confirmation. Similar situations prevailed in a number of communities in Germany.[119]

Although Jewish communities in Palestine during the Second Jewish Commonwealth, and in Babylonia for

113. See, in general, A. Freiman, "Majority and Minority Principle in Community," in *Yavneh* (Hebrew; Jerusalem, 1948); Agus, *The Autonomous Rule of Jewish Communities*, p. 190; Baer, "The Elements and Beginnings of Organized Jewish Communities in the Middle Ages" (Hebrew), in *Zion* 15 (1950): 1.

114. See Karo, *Shulkan Arukh, H.M.*, no. 103, sec. 3; Moshe Isserlis, *Rama*, ad loc.; and Joshua Falk Kohen, *Sema*, ad loc.;

Israel Isserlin, *Terumot Ha'Deshen*, no. 344; Joseph Katz, *She'-Erith Yosef*, no. 18; M. Krochmal, *Tzemah Tzedek*, nos. 1, 18–19; Jacob Reisher, Responsa *Shevut Yaakov*, vol. 1, no. 72. Compare the slogan of the American Revolution, "No taxation without representation."

115. Baron, *The Jewish Community*, 2:28–30, 38.

116. Ibid., 2:28–30, 38, 39.

117. See the two sections immediately following for detailed discussion of majority rule; see also Meir ben Barukh, Responsa *Maharam* of Rothenburg, no. 918 (Prague ed.); Hayim ben Zvi, *Maharah Ohr Zarua*, no. 222; Karo, in *Beth Yosef, Tur, O.H.*, no. 53, citing Eliezer ben Yoel; Finkelstein, *Jewish Self-Government*, pp. 33 ff, 49 ff, 107, 121, 132; Isaac B. Sheshet, Responsa *Rivash*, no. 457–461.

118. Agus, "The Autonomous Rule of Jewish Communities," p. 182, n. 38; Tal, "Legal-Halakhic Principles," p. 34 ff.

119. Baron, The Jewish Community, 2:34–35.

many centuries thereafter, had traditionally been governed by "seven good men,"[120] many of the medieval Jewish communities in Europe were administered to by one to five communal officers. Often, however, they were still referred to as the "seven good men." Many communities had large numbers of officers in the governing council. For example, at times Rome had sixty and Cracow had twenty-three. Others had fewer officers.

In medieval Poland there were three, often overlapping, levels of officers. These emulated the three-tiered levels of Polish government adopted pursuant to the Laws of Magdeburg. An officer on the uppermost tier was called either *rosh* ("head"), *rosh ha'Kahal* ("head of the community"), or *parnes* (the ancient title used by the leaders of the communities in the Near East). In Poland there were usually three to five "heads" of communities who acted together as a community council. Customarily, one of these "heads" would serve for an entire month, and then be succeeded, in rotation, by another. During his month of service, each would be known as the "head of the month." These communal leaders took an oath of allegiance to the king, and their appointment required the consent of the king's provincial governor.

Communal officers were sometimes required to donate or "loan" money to the community for the privilege of serving, were liable for fiscal wrongdoing, and would frequently be held responsible by the non-Jewish authorities for crimes of individual members of their communities.[121]

The "head of the month" supervised the meetings of the community council and was also in charge of both the assessment of taxation and the activities of the courts during that period. He would also prepare the budget of the community and lists of those permitted to live there. His decisions in any of these areas could vitally affect the interests of one or all members of the community.

The middle level officers in Poland, the *tovim* ("good men"), usually consisting of from three to five persons, would assist the community heads and often fill in for them in their absence. They would also sit in a special court with the Polish official, known as the "judge of the Jews," who was appointed to hear cases in which Jews litigated with non-Jews.

The lower level of communal officers in Poland, often referred to as members of the *edah* (congregation) or *kahal* (community) generally acted in administrative capacities to carry out various communal functions and often served on subcommittees. These would deal with the keeping of the communal books and records, the supervision of courts, the checking of weights and measures used by community merchants, the supervision of street cleaning, assessment of property, the distribution of charity, and the redemption of captive Jews. In addition, each association of tradesmen or craftsmen had its own *parnes*, or "head."

Usually officers in all three tiers were elected for one year only.[122]

The Polish communal officers would often also set ceilings for the rental of apartments and even establish the number of rooms permitted for each family. Additionally, they supervised the moral standards of the community and attempted to protect creditors in the face of bankruptcies. On occasion their activities could be dictatorial, as in Poznan, where the poor were prohibited from marrying without the specific authorization of communal officers. This was done so that their families would not become a community burden.[123]

The officers' other important functions in community decision-making were their maintenance of internal order, their roles in the drafting of ordinances, the regulation of communal and individual behavior, and the supervision of the local court system and serving as lay judges for the resolution of conflicts in a number of very important areas (see Section 2 *h*, below). They also influenced communal decisions by their participation in the many committees that dealt with specific services, such as sanitation, education, and charity for the poor. Normally officers served without pay.

Local community decisions were enforced by various sanctions, to be described later, notably social ostracism, excommunication, appeals to the government, corporal punishment, and often imprisonment in community prisons.

b. THE ROLE OF THE ACADEMIES IN DECISION-MAKING

Academies of law and religion often played important roles in medieval Jewish decision-making, particularly in Babylonia. The two chief academies of law there, at Sura and at Pumpedita (the successor to the academy that had previously existed in Nehardea), exerted a crucial influence in decision-making during their approximately eight hundred years of existence (from the third to the eleventh centuries C.E.). Their influence was not limited to Babylonia but extended to Jewish communities throughout the world, including those in Christian Europe, and was exerted in many ways.

120. Talmud, *Megillah* 26a; Jerusalem Talmud, *Megillah* 3:2.
121. Baron, *The Jewish Community*, pp. 52, 55, 61, 63.
122. Balaban, *Beth Yisrael Be'Polin*, pp. 46–47.
123. Ibid., p. 49.

(1) *Education*

The Babylonian academies had an important educational function in training thousands of future judges, rabbis, and influential lay leaders who came there to study from all over the world. Classes were also conducted for many thousands of Jews from adjacent areas who spent a full month of study at the academies in the fall, and again in the winter of each year (when they were free of their agricultural work).

The educational activities of the academies extended their sway way beyond the confines of Babylonia. Many of their students came from all over the known world, including Persia, Media, Palestine, Egypt, North Africa, Italy, Spain, and other parts of Europe. Some had to travel many months before they reached the academies. (There was even a legend of a student who lived so far away that it took him six months to reach the academy, where he spent one day and thereupon had to return home. He was then dubbed "the one-day scholar.") Many of these disciples would later often occupy very important positions as judges, heads of academies, or communal leaders, with important input in local decision-making and in religious observance and perspectives. The influence of the academies was, accordingly, greatly expanded by the presence of these disciples from many lands.

(2) *The Academy Courts*

The academies also exercised a direct voice in decision-making. First of all, they, eventually, came to serve as superior courts.[124] During the last few centuries of their existence, decisions made by the exilarch and his court required certification by the heads of the academies and their courts. The academies, therefore, acting through their courts, played an important role in applying the law throughout the areas of their jurisdiction.

Furthermore, beginning in about the seventh century C.E., the academies expanded their jurisdiction and appointed judges to sit and hear cases outside of the academies, in many of the localities in Babylonia. These judges could be removed by the academies at any time for cause. This further increased the crucial role played by the academies in the application of the law.

(3) *The Gaonic Responsa, Treatises, and Prescriptions*

Another crucial and far-reaching method of academy decision-making for Jewish communities all over the world was by way of Responsa. Jewish communities and individuals from many lands, including decision-makers faced with puzzling cases (in some cases former

students of the academies) would submit written queries to the Babylonian academies regarding difficult issues that had arisen. These concerned all areas of societal activities, including religious practice and rituals, conflicts between individuals, communities, or both; family law, criminal law and sanctions, the collection of taxes, the organization and administration of Jewish communities, and intricate legal issues concerning commercial transactions and relations with non-Jews. The written replies by the heads of the academies (called *gaonim*) were known as Responsa.

An additional influence in Jewish communal decision-making was exerted by the academies as a result of their composition of many legal treatises. These summarized and analyzed the complex issues that arose in many areas of law. The heads of the academies were particularly prolific in publishing legal tomes dealing with the multitude of commercial transactions that took on varied and complex forms as society and commerce developed during the Middle Ages.

Another crucial method by which the heads of the academies and their staffs intervened in the decision-making processes with far-reaching effects was in the promulgation of new prescriptions. From time to time the heads of the two most prominent academies would meet with the exilarch (and members of the various courts maintained by the academies and the exilarch) to decide on new prescriptions to meet changing economic and social conditions. Copies of new prescriptions that were promulgated were sent to Jewish communities all over the world and were accepted and followed there, giving the *gaonim* and the Babylonian academies crucial, worldwide influence in Jewish decision-making.

These gaonic prescriptions covered many areas. They were often radical departures from traditional law but were made in order to achieve basic, overriding goals in the face of changing societal conditions. For example, divorce was the sole prerogative of the husband, at least in theory. He could terminate the marriage by handing his wife a duly drafted, executed, and witnessed Bill of Divorce. Moreover, divorce could not be effected in any other way. Widespread resentment of this situation by wives began to increase during the Middle Ages. In a number of cases, wives who desired divorce, but were unable to obtain it, deserted their husbands and ran off, sometimes with non-Jewish men. Accordingly, the *gaonim* and their assembled associates and staff promulgated a prescription that every husband was obligated to hand his wife a Bill of Divorce if she so requested.[125] This was a revolutionary departure

---

124. See Responsa of the *Gaonim* (Harkavy ed.; Berlin, 1887), nos. 198, 371; Assaf, *Batei Ha'Din*, p. 45.

125. See Isaac Alfasi, Commentary to *Ketubot* 63a; Karo, *Tur, Shulkhan Arukh, E. H.*, sec. 77; Gulak, *Yesodei Hamishpat Ha'Ivri*, vol. 3, sec. 12:4, pp. 28–29.

since well-established talmudic precedent had been firm in holding that with the exception of a few cases set forth in the Talmud, divorce could be effected only on the husband's initiative and that a divorce was invalid where the husband had been coerced into handing his wife a Bill of Divorce. The fundamental and revolutionary nature of the new prescription can be appreciated from the fact that it permitted one who theretofore would have been deemed to be a "married woman," to marry another man under a procedure that had previously been illegal and, moreover, would otherwise have made the woman guilty of adultery and liable to capital punishment. This particular prescription, however (unlike many gaonic innovations), met with widespread resistance, particularly in France and Germany, where it was later abandoned.

In the first few centuries following the destruction of the Second Jewish Commonwealth most of the Jews in Babylonia possessed real property or were farmers. Personal possessions were of relatively little importance. Accordingly, under traditional talmudic law[126] a widow could only collect her *ketubah* (an amount which her husband obligated himself, at the time of marriage, to pay for her economic support in the event of widowhood or divorce) from real property but not from chattels. Similarly, a creditor who desired to collect his debt from the heirs of the deceased debtor, could collect only from real property. Economic and social conditions changed radically, and most Jews did not possess real property any longer. This imposed great hardship on widows and creditors as well as, indirectly, on debtors (since creditors were now reluctant to lend, for fear they could never collect their debt). In about the sixth century the *gaonim* and their staffs prescribed that widows and other creditors could collect and levy upon personal property inherited from the deceased husband or debtor.[127] This prescription was widely accepted, despite its radical nature.[128] Although there was some precedent for this in the Talmud,[129] the widespread acceptance of this prescription was due primarily to the esteem with which the heads of the academies were held throughout the Jewish world.

This diminution of land holdings by Jews in the Middle Ages also led to other gaonic prescriptions, such as that permitting the acquisition of legal title to chattels, even where the parties to the transaction did not own any real property.[130]

Similarly, when serious economic decline set in among Jewish communities in the Middle Ages, the heads of the academies prescribed that debtors who claimed that they had no assets with which to repay their debts were required to take an oath to this effect. This, too, was contrary to the talmudic tradition, which looked askance at the proliferation of oaths, which were regarded as a taking of the name of the Lord in vain.[131]

In summary, then, the heads of the academies prescribed many fundamental and far-reaching changes in Jewish law by promulgating new prescriptions that affected Jewish life in communities throughout the world. The universal significance of these prescriptions should be contrasted with those made later by the Jewish synods in Europe (such as those convened in Franco-Germany by Rabbi Gershom, Rabbi Jacob Tam, and other rabbis in Spain and Poland), whose effect was limited to portions of Europe only.[132]

Undoubtedly, however, the most far-reaching significance of the academies of Babylonia on law and the decision-making process was in the redaction of the Babylonian Talmud (*circa* 300 C.E.) by Rav Ashi, the head of the academy at Sura, and other leading scholars who assisted him. This massive work then became the primary source book of Jewish law, accepted by Jews throughout the world as the most authoritative guide. It ultimately became the subject of literally thousands of commentaries, with enormous and unquestioned authority.

(4) *The Academies versus the Exilarchate*

In time the academies of Babylonia gradually emerged as counterpoises to the power of the exilarch. The heads of the academies (*gaonim*) acquired such great prestige that they were at times able to challenge the power of the exilarch, and even have him deposed. Accordingly, there was a continual tension and interplay of force between the heads of the academies and the exilarch, with sometimes one and sometimes the other dominating. The extent of their power depended upon many factors, particularly the various personalities involved and the degree of influence of their respective supporters (see Section [6], below). By the tenth century, however, the position of the heads of the academies had become so strong *vis-à-vis* the exilarch that the latter's legal decisions required certifica-

---

126. Gulak, ibid., vol. 1, sec. 57, p. 154; vol. 3, sec. 25:5, p. 62.

127. Responsa of the *Gaonim, Hemda Genuza* (Jerusalem, 1862), no. 65.

128. See Rambam, Laws of Creditors and Debtors, 11:11; Laws of Marriage, 16:8.

129. *Ketubot* 86a.

130. Responsa of the *Gaonim* (Assaf ed.; Jerusalem, 1927),

vol. 1, no. 105, departing from talmudic precedent (*Baba Metzia* 46a).

131. See Responsa of the *Gaonim*, Assaf ed., vol. 1, sec. 130; Rambam, Laws of Creditors and Debtors, ch. 2.

132. Assaf, "The Academies in Babylonia" (Hebrew), in *Tekufat Ha'Gaonim*, p. 64.

tion by the heads of the academies.[133] This led to additional strife between the exilarch and the *gaon*.[134]

(5) *Sources of Income of the Babylonian Academies*

Although many of the heads of the Babylonian academies received no compensation as such and supported themselves financially by agriculture and trade,[135] the academies received considerable financial aid from Jewish communities in a number of ways. Each member of a Jewish community, except for the poor, was required to pay a yearly tax for the support of the academy.

Furthermore, contributions were sent by Jewish communities all over the world for the support of the academies. Contributions often were sent together with written requests to the academies for guidance with regard to specific issues of law that had arisen in various communities. The senders of these inquiries felt it only proper that they who received the requested guidance from the academies should make financial contributions to support the activities of the academies. This practice eventually led to the active solicitation of legal inquiries by the academies when they were in need of funds.[136] Additionally, it appears that many of the communities as a whole contributed annually for the support of the academies.[137] Various emissaries of the academies were dispatched periodically to many countries to augment the fundraising efforts.

Further support also came from bequests and devises, from the receipt of monies collected as fines by the Jewish courts throughout the world and, at times, from the ownership of real property acquired by the academies.[138]

It should be noted that even after the decline of the Babylonian academies in the eleventh century, and their eventual disappearance a few centuries later, their function was taken over by the heads of prominent academies of law in many countries of North Africa and Europe and, still later, by many erudite professional rabbi–scholars, who engaged in all of the varied decision-making activities of the Babylonian *gaonim*. Even where the non-Jewish authorities did not often give these rabbi–scholars the power to enforce their decisions, their influence in the decision-making processes could still be enormous. This was due to the wide es-

teem in which they were held and to the deep religious convictions of Jews throughout the world who felt obligated to abide by their decisions.

(6) *The Final Decline of the Exilarchate and Gaonate*

The ultimate decline of the exilarchate and the gaonate was due in the final analysis to events in the non-Jewish world. With the disintegration of the caliphate into many independent realms (with rival caliphates being established in Baghdad, Cordova, and Cairo), the exilarch appointed by the Baghdadian caliphate could no longer wield authority or control in any of the lands not ruled by his appointer. The conquests of Babylonia by the Mongols in 1258 and thereafter caused widespread destruction and were important factors in the economic decline of western Asia. This contributed to the impoverishment of many Jews there and to intensive emigration to North Africa and Europe. All of these events eroded the exilarchate and weakened the academies, too, reducing the numbers of students as well as the sizes of financial contributions.

It is noteworthy, however, that the Babylonian exilarchate was the longest lived dynasty in the history of mankind, having existed for more than one thousand years.[139]

c. THE SCHOLAR–RELIGIOUS LEADER AS DECISION-MAKER

Perhaps, the most important single participant in Jewish decision-making in the Middle Ages was the scholar–religious leader, who might act as academy head, community rabbi, judge, or lay leader.

Despite continuous discriminatory practices and intermittent persecutions during the Middle Ages, the Jewish communities of western Europe, notably in France and Germany, established centers of learning where Jewish scholarship (mainly Jewish religious and legal studies) flourished. In the early Middle Ages these scholars and heads of academies were not salaried professional rabbis. Nevertheless, they taught extensively and acted as judges, without pay, following talmudic tradition.[140] It was common for them to work for their livelihood either in industry or commerce and to receive no pay from the community.

As discussed above, Jewish communities in medieval Europe were commonly granted almost complete autonomy in internal life by the non-Jewish authorities. The scholar–religious leaders had a decisive voice in community decisions of all kinds, including the regu-

133. Responsa of the *Gaonim*, no. 555 (Harkavy ed.).
134. Assaf, *Tekufat*, p. 23.
135. See Talmud, *Ketubot* 105a, 106a; *Gittin* 60b; Assaf, *Tekufat*, p. 67.
136. See, for example, The Letters of Rav Sherira Gaon, in *Jewish Quarterly Review*, n.s., 9 (1919): 147; Assaf, *Tekufat*, pp. 48, 68.
137. Ibid., p. 69.
138. Ibid., p. 70.

139. Baron, *The Jewish Community*, 179–86.
140. Talmud, *Bekhorot* 4:6, *Ketubot* 105a, *Horiyot* 10a.

lation of economic and social affairs, because they were held in the highest esteem, in accordance with deeply rooted tradition. It was universally felt that they should lead the community, which should conduct its affairs in accordance with traditional talmudic laws as far as possible.[141] (See Section B *a* [4], above, for details concerning the view that community enactments could depart from, or even be contrary to, traditional talmudic laws.) Of course, these spiritual leaders also decided religious issues, which, in the Jewish perspective, covered the entire ambit of human activities. They also authored many written Responsa in reply to questions of all kinds submitted to them by individuals and communities from near and far. Many of them, particularly Rabbi Gershom of Mainz, Germany, and Rabbi Jacob Tam, convened synods, where important regulations ("*takkanot,*" see Section A 2 *b* [2], above) were promulgated concerning the conduct of Jewish communities and individuals.

A number of crucial societal activities also were regulated by these transcommunal synods led by scholar–religious leaders. For example, in the standard prenuptial *ketubah* agreement, the agreed sum to be paid by the husband to ensure the wife's economic support in the event of his death or divorce was set by synod at an amount seventy-five times greater than the amount that had traditionally prevailed in the Biblical Era, and some six hundred times greater than the standard amount utilized in Babylonia. The increase was, of course, due to the greater prosperity of the Jews of western Europe. This regulation was of particularly great social and economic importance for the status of women throughout the Middle Ages.

A strict ban was placed on polygamy in the eleventh century, by a synod that was allegedly headed by Rabbi Gershom. This prohibition was induced, in part, by the hostility that the Jewish practice of polygamy purportedly aroused in Christians, and probably because of cross-cultural influences. Simultaneously, as a corollary to this ban (and partly to prevent its evasion by the husband, who might divorce his wife in order to marry another woman), divorce of a wife without her consent was also prohibited. Subsequently, to avoid coerced consent by the wife, the consent of the three communities of Speyer, Worms, and Mainz (the principal communities that participated in the ban) was also required for divorce. These bans had a profound effect upon the relative positions of husbands and wives, since a wife might be able (pursuant to a prior prescription by the Babylonian *gaonim*, which was sub-

sequently abandoned in Europe) to coerce her husband to divorce her, whereas a male was powerless to divorce his wife against her will. This completely reversed their previous respective power positions regarding divorce.

There were numerous other important regulations, including those concerning majority rule in communities, the payment of tax money to communities in the event of a dispute, and many additional areas.[142]

Despite the crucial function of lay leaders in communal decision-making, community rabbis played a very significant role, particularly in prescriptions. The rabbi was often the driving force behind the proposal and adoption of the prescriptions. He was the one who commonly drafted their wording and whose consent was normally required in order for the prescription to become effective. The rabbi was also active in the application of law, as a judge and author of Responsa, deciding specific cases. He might often serve as the head of an academy of law. In general, the rabbi served as a vital check upon the authoritarian rule of lay oligarchies. In all of these areas the rabbi's power stemmed from the universal reverence for learning among Jews, and the accepted principle, and ancient tradition, that the scholar–religious leader should be the head of the community. The rabbi, at least in theory, was the leading figure in the community, overshadowing the plutocrats and other leading laymen.

(1) *The Payment of Compensation to Scholar–Religious Leaders*

Traditionally scholar–religious leaders were not salaried community employees but were engaged in various other occupations for their livelihood. However, in the gaonic era in Babylonia (beginning in about the seventh century) there is increasing evidence of scholars of Jewish law and religion who were supported financially by a community and who, in turn, devoted all of their time to teaching, deciding questions of law, and supervising the proper execution of the procedures necessary for marriage, divorce, and other transactions that required a particular form in accordance with religious dogma.[143] The Spanish rabbi, Judah Al-Barceloni (*circa* eleventh-twelfth century) asserted:

---

141. See Agus, "Autonomous Rule in Jewish Communities," pp. 190–91.

142. See Y. Schipansky, *Takkanot Harishonim,* in *Ha'Darom* 28 (1969): 154; idem, *Takkanot Shum,* in *Ha'Darom* 26 (1968): 173; idem, *Takkanot Rabbenu Gershom,* in *Ha'Derom* 22 (1963): 103; idem, *Takkanot Ha'Geonim,* in *Ha'Darom* 24 (1965): 135; M. Bloch, *Shaare Torath Ha'Takkanot* (reprinted Jerusalem, 1971); I. Epstein, *The "Responsa" of Rabbi Solomon Ben Aderet* (London, 1925), p. 48.

143. Responsa of the *Gaonim* (Koronel ed.; Vienna, 1871), sec. 82; A. Neubauer, *Seder Ha'Hahamim* (Oxford, 1888–1893), pp. 85–86; Assaf, *Be'Ahalei Yoakov* (Jerusalem, 1943), pp. 40–41; Abraham ben David, *Sefer Ha'Kabbalah.*

Most places have instituted a practice to establish a fund for the courts, out of which they pay the monies necessary to support the courts . . . and they collect monies (for this fund) at the beginning, or at the end of the year. This is not considered to be bribery or the payment of money (to procure a decision) because all Israel is obligated to support its judges and sages. . . . An amount is assessed upon the community and is collected at a specified time as other taxes, so that the funds will be collected and ready, and the judge would not have to be beholden to anybody for its collection.[144]

Although the practice of scholars accepting money in order to devote their time to studying the Torah or to sitting as judges was sharply condemned by Rambam,[145] it continued nevertheless, although causing pangs of conscience in the hearts of many of the recipients.[146] In the thirteenth century, although a number of communities still followed the principle of not paying any money to judges,[147] the payment of such salaries became quite prevalent.[148]

Although the payment of compensation to community judges and rabbis appears to have proliferated more rapidly in Spain, it was also practiced in Germany and other portions of Europe, where it apparently took longer to become entrenched. A number of the most prominent spiritual leaders refused to take any compensation from the community, and supported themselves by sundry activities, including active marriage match-making.[149] The main reason for the prevalence of community-supported rabbis and judges lay in the reduced economic opportunities for self-support by these individuals, and perhaps the need for full-time rabbis and judges due to the increasing complexity of economic and social activities and the growth in the size of Jewish communities. These induced a greater number of complex legal and religious problems and an increasing need for full-time religious leadership.

Nevertheless, despite the communal payment of compensation, there was often a lack of formal institutionalization of the scholar's role as spiritual leader, judge, and supervisor of the necessary religious procedures required for marriages and divorces. Occasionally a scholar might be engaged in these activities for many years, only to have another scholar move into town and engage in similar activities. This was often not regarded as reprehensible, since the very notion of performing these activities for pay was frowned upon. At the same time it was felt that the more scholars that resided in a town, the better. Accordingly, many of the leading scholars and spiritual leaders in Germany, such as Jacob Weil and Israel Isserlin, justified Israel Bruna in his move to Regensburg, even though a certain Rabbi Anshil was already acting as spiritual leader there.[150]

By the sixteenth century the trend was clear: The general practice in the Jewish communities of Europe was for the rabbi to receive a fixed compensation from the community.[151] At the same time, the position of community rabbi gradually became more formalized, so that where a community had appointed a rabbi, no one else could enter the community to perform any of the standard rabbinical functions without the expressed permission of the local rabbi. In 1632 the Lithuanian Council provided that no rabbi could supervise marriages in another town.[152]

(2) *Sources of Income of the Salaried Community Rabbis*

One of the main sources of income of the salaried community rabbi in medieval Europe was a fixed salary from the community. The funds needed to pay such salaries either were levied as a special tax upon the community[153] or sometimes were paid from special collections made during the religious festivals.[154] While the amounts of these salaries varied from community to community,[155] they were often very generous, particularly in the larger communities.[156] Nevertheless, there sometimes were complaints that they were woefully inadequate.[157]

In the smaller communities, which were frequently poverty-stricken, the salaries paid to community rabbis were often extremely meager.[158] This was also true in

144. Cited in Yaakov ben Asher, *Tur, Ho. Mis.*, sec. 9.

145. See his commentary to the Talmud, *Avot*, ch. 4, Mishnah 5.

146. See the Last Will and Testament of Judah ben Asher, published in *Beth Talmud* (Vienna, 1791), pp. 373–77, vol. 4; Simon Duran, Responsa *Tashbatz*, vol. 1, no. 142; see Assaf, *Be'Ahalei Yaakov* (Jerusalem), p. 42.

147. Asher ben Yehiel, Responsa *Rosh*, sec. 55, subsec. 5; see also sec. 6, subsec. 16; Simon Duran, Responsa *Tashbatz*, vol. 1, secs. 142, 147, 148.

148. Isaac ben Sheshet, Responsa *Rivash*, secs. 60, 192, 445.

149. Moshe Mintz, Responsa *Maharam Mintz* (Jerusalem, 1969), sec. 74; see *Minhage Maharil* (Remona, 1558); Assaf, *Be'Ahalei Yaakov*, p. 43.

150. Y. Weil, Responsa *Mahari Weil* (Jerusalem, 1959), sec. 151; Israel Isserlin, *Pesakim* (B'nai B'rak, 1971), sec. 126.

151. Baron, *The Jewish Community*, 1:81.

152. See Dubnow, *Pinkas Ha'Medinah*, sec. 226 and 613.

153. E.g., in Babylonia; with regard to judges, see: "The Tale of Nathan the Babylonian," in A. Neubauer, *Seder Ha'-Khakhamim* (Jerusalem, 1907), and "The Travels of Petahia of Regensburg" in *Sibbuv* (ed. L. Gruenhut; Jerusalem, 1905).

154. Yitzhak ben Moshe, *Ohr Zarua* (Zhitomir, 1862), sec. 1, subsec. 113; Yaakov Berav, S. DiMedina, Responsa *Maharashdam* (reprinted New York, 1964); *Yora Deah*, sec. 227.

155. See the detailed figures in Assaf, *Be'Ahalei Yaakov*, pp. 45, 46.

156. Assaf, *Be'Ahalei Yaakov*, p. 46.

157. Shlomo El'Ami, *Egeret Ha'Musar*, pp. 29, 30. The book was written in 1415, republished in Vienna, 1872.

158. See ibid.

larger communities following wars or economic declines. Some communities even conditioned the hiring of a rabbi on his supplementing his income by engaging in commerce or other activities.[159]

In addition to a fixed salary, the community rabbi had a number of other sources of income. Most important of all was the fee that he collected for acting as judge. This sum was contributed in equal amounts by both litigants. In many places the amount was not fixed but depended solely upon the generosity of the litigants.[160] In other places, however, it was fixed according to a sliding scale, depending upon the amount of the suit.[161]

Another important source of income to the rabbi was the supervision of marriages and divorces. There were fixed fees for these activities, and, in isolated instances, the rabbi might even collect a fixed percentage of the dowry.[162] In cases of divorce, rabbis would sometimes exact very large fees, allegedly in order to discourage husbands from divorcing their wives.[163] The practice of imposing inordinately large fees for supervising divorces led to much sharp criticism by some prominent decision-makers. Ovadiah of Bartenuro expressed his dismay at the fact that

> the ordained rabbi, head of the academy, is not embarrassed to take ten gold pieces in order to spend one-half hour supervising the writing and delivery of the Bill of Divorce. . . . In my eyes, this rabbi is nothing but a robber and highwayman . . . and I fear that this divorce is invalid.[164]

Still another source of rabbinic income was the fee received by him for granting to qualified applicants the title of *"morenu"* ("our teacher"), which authorized the recipient to decide questions of law and *"khaver"* ("colleague," a lesser title). In some cases, payment of such fees led to the feeling that these titles had been purchased, rather than awarded on merit.

There were, in addition, gifts customarily given by laymen to the rabbi on the occasion of various religious festivals of the year.[165] These activities sometimes led to a lowering of the esteem of the rabbis in the eyes of many. Some even felt that positions as rabbis were sought after because of the prospect of wealth.[166] Many of the most prominent rabbis, however, refused to take any kind of gifts, or even fees for services, and they died penniless.[167]

(3) *The Community Rabbi as Decision-Maker*

Before the twelfth century there was no prevalent institution of a rabbi who was formally appointed by a community to lead and guide its spiritual life.[168] Until then spiritual guidance was provided by the many members of the community who were erudite and trained in religious practices and law. These persons would resolve questions concerning religious rituals and conflicting claims that arose from commercial transactions if there were no professional Jewish courts available.[169]

The institution of the salaried community rabbi became more common in the fifteenth century, due in part to the resolutions of regional Jewish synods that required every community of minimum size to appoint a spiritual leader.[170] The occupant of this position played a crucial role in medieval community decision-making. In theory at least, the local rabbi was the sole decision-maker regarding any religious questions (of which there were many) that might arise, and he also had to decide all disputes arising from commercial transactions. In some of the larger communities commercial suits were handled by special courts, which were, however, under the general supervision of the rabbi. A prominent rabbi would commonly receive numerous queries from other communities, asking him to decide not only difficult questions of religious ritual and sacerdotal matters but, more often, difficult questions arising from commercial lawsuits and the delicate area of family law.[171]

Another crucial role of the rabbi was his overall supervision of the election of community leaders, officials, and the officers in charge of the various local associations, including all of the trade and charitable groups. Furthermore, because of the great deference

159. See H. N. Dembitzer, *Kelilat Yofi* (Cracow, 1898) in his introduction and p. 55b; also the Records of the Community of Bamberg, pp. 12, 24–25.

160. See in Dubnow, *Pinkas Ha'Medinah*, the Records of the Lithuanian Council, sec. 622.

161. See the Records of the Community of Bamberg (pp. 21, 23) and of Dusseldorf, Cracow, and other communities, in Assaf, *Be'Ahalei Yaakov*, p. 46.

162. See the Records of the Community of Bamberg; David Ibn Zimra, Responsa *Radvaz*, sec. 622.

163. See *Minhage Maharil*. Another device to discourage divorce was incorporated in the ordinances of the towns of Speyer, Worms, and Mainz. These provided that a husband could not divorce his wife, unless he obtained the consent of two of these communities, excluding the one in which he resided.

164. See his commentary to *Bekhorot*, ch. 4, Mishnah 6.

165. See Nathan Hanover, in *Yeven Mezula* (Venice, 1653), sec. on Torah.

166. See Assaf, *Be'Ahalei Yaakov*, p. 48, citing *Zera Baruh Shelishi, Berachot.*

167. Zelig Margolis, Introduction to *Hibure Likutim* (Venice, 1715); see also the preface to *Zera Baruh Shelishi* by the head of the Council of Four Lands, testifying that the author had never taken any fees for acting as judge.

168. See Assaf, "Le'Korot Ha'Rabanut," in *Be'Ahalei Yaakov* p. 27; Jacob Tam, *Sefer Ha'Yashar* (Berlin, 1893), p. 81a; Yitzhak ben Moshe, *Or Zarua*, sec. 2, subsec. 42.

169. See Weil, Responsa *Mahari Weil*, no. 151; *Pesakim* of Israel Isserlin, sec. 126.

170. See the Records of the Community of Mehrin, sec. 528, in Assaf, *Be'Ahalei Yaakov*, p. 56.

171. Ibid.

formally accorded to him, the rabbi commonly played a leading role in community decision-making regarding issues of all kinds. Community ordinances were normally drafted by him and were not considered as binding unless signed by the rabbi.[172]

Additionally, the rabbi would often maintain an academy of legal and religious studies, with consequent influence in decision-making. The rabbi was frequently also charged with supervising certain commercial activities of the community, particularly making sure that prices did not rise too steeply or suddenly, that weights and measures were accurate, and that there were no other fraudulent practices.

As a result of all of these important functions, the medieval rabbi was, in many cases, the leading decision-making figure in his community. Often his influence would extend beyond the confines of his own community, because of his participation in regional synods, his written Responsa deciding cases and issues that arose in other communities, the influence he exercised through the disciples from other communities that he trained in his academy, and through the influential books on law and religion that he authored, that might receive widespread acceptance. This was especially true in Poland and adjacent areas, where, it was said, "without him [the rabbi], no man lifted his hand or foot; he commanded and it was obeyed. He held in his hand a staff and a strap to smite and flog, to punish and to humiliate those who transgressed and [had the power] to promulgate ordinances."[173] The Polish rabbi could not only enforce his decision by use of the terrible weapon of excommunication but could, at least in theory, utilize the right given in the 1669 Charter of the King of Poland (King Michael Vishnevski) that, "Those that disobey him [the rabbi] shall be punished by the government court with death, and their possessions shall be forfeited"; or the rabbi could have the recalcitrant fined, flogged, or jailed.[174]

In short, the community rabbi was, at least in form, the leading individual decision-maker in the community. The rabbi's role in community decision-making was also enhanced by the honors and prestige accorded him. These included numerous signs of deference during the prayer services, his exclusive presiding at weddings, circumcisions, and funerals, and even his universal exemption from taxation.[175]

By the time the institution of the salaried community rabbi became more common in the fifteenth century,

there no longer existed the "semikha" ("ordination") that prevailed in the Talmudic Era. Attaining semikha authorized the recipient to decide all questions of law, including the infliction of penalties and death.[176] A rabbi in Europe was expected, instead, to have received some sort of authorization from a recognized scholar to decide questions of law that might arise in commercial transactions or in religious rituals.[177] In fourteenth century Germany such authorizations were reduced to writing, and the recipients were entitled to be called "morenu" ("our teacher"). This formalization of authority to decide questions of law was apparently instituted by Meir Ha'Levi of Vienna because of the great shortage of scholars of the law following the bubonic plague that had spread through Europe.[178] The receipt of such titles was much sought after, not only because the holder could serve as rabbi of a community, but also because it entitled him to many other privileges, including active participation in choosing the communal rabbi and professional judge, and often exemption from taxation. It also assured him an active part in other community affairs, as well as communal honors.[179] In a relatively short while the granting of such titles became very common, and in some towns in Poland where there were only fifty men, twenty of them would allegedly have the title "morenu" ("Our Master") or "khaver" (literally "colleague").[180]

The influence of the medieval European rabbi as the leader in Jewish communal decision-making was offset by a number of factors. Until about the fifteenth century, scholars and spiritual leaders usually supported themselves by various crafts or trades and were not salaried community rabbis.[181] Thereafter, once the scholar became a community rabbi, dependent upon the community for his livelihood, his powers and independence often decreased. Furthermore, with the flourishing of capitalism in Italy, Poland, and elsewhere at that time, there was a substantial rise in the number of Jewish plutocrats who wielded great influence in the communities. In Italy some of these soon sought to replace the rabbis as community leaders. As commer-

172. Based upon Talmud, *Baba Batra* 8a.

173. See in general, N. Hanover, *Yeven Metzulah*; see also Assaf, *Be'Ahalei Yaakov*, p. 53.

174. Assaf, ibid.

175. See the Will and Testament of Judah Ibn Tibbon, in Assaf, *Be'Ahalei Yaakov*, p. 50; Records of the Council of Lithuania, sec. 607, Shimon Duran, Responsa *Tashbatz*, vol. 1,

sec. 143; Yisrael ben Hayim, Responsa *Mahari Bruna* (reprinted Jerusalem, 1960), sec. 102; see, in general, Assaf, *Be'Ahalei Yaakov*, pp. 48–50.

176. See Talmud, *Sanhedrin* 13b.

177. Isaac ben Sheshet, Responsa *Rivash*, sec. 271.

178. Assaf, *Be'Ahalei Yaakov*, p. 28.

179. See Yisrael ben Hayim, Responsa *Mahari Bruna*, sec. 278; Responsa *Leket Yosher*, Yosef ben Moshe (Berlin, 1903–04), vol. 1, sec. 3; Ephraim Luntshitz in *Olelot Ephraim* (Lvov, 1894), secs. 359, 366.

180. See Hanover, in *Yeven Metzula*; Don Isaac Abarbanel, *Nahalat Avot* (Kusta, 1505), ch. 6, sec. 2.

181. Baron, *The Jewish Community*, 1:81; *contra* S. Zeitlin, "Rashi and the Rabbinate," in *Jewish Quarterly Review* 31 (1940–41): 1–58.

cial transaction became ever more complex, beginning with the commercial revolution in the fourteenth century, laymen who were familiar with the customs and practices of merchants began to be selected as judges. This occurred, for example, in Rome in 1536 and in other parts of Europe. Lay leadership by plutocrats often tended to become oligarchic and authoritarian, giving rise to bitter complaints by rabbis and scholars.[182]

The short tenure (commonly one to three years) that became usual for rabbis throughout Europe increased their dependency upon local plutocrats and lay leaders. By the nineteenth century, however, permanent rabbinical positions became more prevalent,[183] while Jewish communal autonomy and decision-making had been drastically reduced. Despite the availability of positions with long-term tenure, there was still a larger turnover in rabbinic posts, with rabbis often voluntarily leaving their communities to assume better paying or more prestigious positions elsewhere.

Even in Poland, however, where perhaps the influence of rabbis in decision-making reached its zenith, the rabbis did not have sole judicial authority in the application of the law. In many of the communities laymen participated as judges in the courts, sometimes in dominant positions. Thus, elder lay communal leaders often acted as judges in applying the law in dealing with crimes, assessment and collection of taxes (including tax evasion), other areas of public law, and a number of areas of commercial law, such as landlord-tenant affairs.[184] Lay heads of guilds ruled on all intra-guild matters, which constituted an important portion of the commercial activities of a community.[185] The only area in which the rabbi had supreme decision-making powers was in questions regarding religious ritual and food restrictions, marriages, and divorces. Even here, laymen occasionally intervened, sometimes enacting ordinances directly affecting those areas.[186]

(4) *Selecting the Community Rabbi*

In Babylonia the professional judges who supervised the spiritual activities of their communities were ap-

pointed by the exilarch or the heads of the two academies. In Europe, however, beginning at about the fifteenth and sixteenth centuries, the community rabbi was chosen by the local community itself.[187]

There was no completely uniform practice as to which members of the community should participate in selecting the rabbi. There were some communities in which all taxpayers had a voice in the selection. In others participation was limited to those who paid large amounts of taxes, together with those who were recognized as scholars of the law.[188] By the seventeenth and eighteenth centuries the general practice was for the rabbi to be selected by the wealthy, the scholars, and the other "important" personages in a community. The bulk of the population would have little say in the selection.[189] In some communities, the group of selectors was even more narrow—only the officers of the community and those who had received the titles "*morenu*" or "*khaver*" participated.[190] In some cases a screening committee was set up to select a number of candidates and the "important" people in the community would then, by secret ballot, select one of these to be rabbi.[191] After the selection it was then customary to send an official "Letter of Appointment as Rabbi" to the successful candidate, a copy of which was normally duly recorded in the records of the community. The new rabbi would often send back a letter of acceptance and greetings to the community.

Often, however, there existed important factors that prevented the community, or its leaders, from selecting the candidate whom they felt to be most suitable. It was not unheard of for candidates for positions of rabbi, anxious for the power, respect, or income of the post, to bribe or otherwise attempt to influence a king or local nobleman to force their appointment. This led to the adoption of strict prohibitions upon this practice by various synods, but to no great avail.[192]

---

182. See the complaints of Leo of Modina about dictatorial lay leaders in S. Bernstein, ed., *The Divan of Leo of Modina*, vol. 24, p. 113 ff; Y. de Modina, Responsa *Ziknei Yehudah* (Jerusalem, 1957), p. 24.

183. See the assertion of Moshe Sofer, "None ever heard nor saw in these lands that a rabbi should have been deposed, and one ought never to do such a thing," in Responsa *Hatam Sofer, O.H.*, no. 206, in connection with Karo, *Shulkhan Arukh, H.M.*, sec. 339, no. 3; *Y.D.*, no. 334, no. 42.

184. See also the Moravian Ordinances, Section 2 *a* below.

185. See Weil, Responsa *Mahari Weil*, no. 146; E. Landau, *Derushe Ha'Tzlah* (Warsaw, 1899), folio 7b; Baron, *The Jewish Community*, 2:88.

186. See Chapter VIII, Section B 1 *a* (2), above; cf. Elon, *Ha'Mishpat Ha'Ivri*, p. 574 ff.

187. See Weil, Responsa *Mahari Weil*, sec. 146; Yisrael ben Hayim, Responsa *Mahari Bruna*, sec. 233; Samuel De Medina Responsa *Maharashdam, Y.D.*, sec. 220; Yosef Kolon, Responsa *Mahari Kolon*, sec. 227; Isaac ben Sheshet, Responsa *Rivash*, secs. 270, 271; and Last Will and Testament of Judah ben Asher, published in *Beth Ha'Talmud*, vol. 4.

188. M. Krochmal, Responsa *Tzemah Tzedek* (Lvov, 1861), secs. 1, 2.

189. Assaf, *Be'Ahalei Yaakov*, p. 32. See also Agus, "Autonomous Rule in Jewish Communities," p. 190.

190. Rashi Fein, *Kirya Ne'Emana* (Vilna, 1860), pp. 40, 128; see in general, Yom Tov Heller, *Megillat Evah* (Lodz, 1924).

191. The minutes of the community of Berlin, Germany, for the year 1772, in Landshut, *Toldot Anshe Shem* (Berlin, 1884).

192. See Meir ben Barukh, Responsa *Maharam* of Rothenburg (Prague ed.) for the ordinance adopted by the twelfth-century synod headed by Jacob Tam Shmuel b. Meir (Rashbam) and 150 other rabbis. It also appears in Finkelstein,

In the fifteenth century the German King Ruprecht attempted to impose his own candidate as chief rabbi of all the Jewish communities. The Jews, however, refused to accept the royal appointee. The king thereupon issued an edict imposing severe sanctions on anyone who would not obey his decision, but the designee soon resigned from this position. Thirty years later, in 1437, there was a second attempt, which also failed. Similar unsuccessful attempts were made in Poland in the sixteenth century.[193]

Yet in some cases the efforts of the kings or noblemen were successful. The candidates whom they appointed were often incompetent.[194] In Poland a number of the kings specifically provided in the charters that they gave to the Jewish communities, that these communities could choose their own rabbi.[195] Nevertheless, local Polish noblemen, who often obtained great powers and acted as semi-independent local sovereigns, occasionally interfered in the selection of communal rabbis. In the seventeenth and eighteenth centuries, particularly, these noblemen were extremely active in attempting to enlarge their revenues by accepting large sums of money from candidates who wished their appointments forced on various local Jewish communities.[196]

Accordingly, these non-Jewish noblemen and other persons of influence, who often had a crucial part in the selection of a Jewish rabbi, played indirect but important roles in Jewish communal decision-making. Many of the decisions that were later taken in these communities were either made by or influenced by the rabbis, whose selection was often shaped by influential personages.

Attempts were sometimes made by rabbinical candidates to give "gifts" or bribes to Jewish lay leaders.[197] In Poland the intercommunity Council of Four Lands

repeatedly enacted provisions (e.g., in 1587, 1590, 1597, and 1640) prohibiting such bribes, and even required a public anathema to be publicly proclaimed at the opening of every session of the council. The necessity for the council to publish new ordinances to this effect at relatively short intervals indicates the pressing nature of the problem.[198] The ordinances were not very effective, and, at a somewhat later time, Rabbi Yom Tov Lippman Heller succeeded in getting many of the local Jewish councils in Europe to renew the prohibition against purchasing a position for money, to place a ban on this practice, and to order that the ban be read in public whenever a rabbi was to be selected by a community.[199] This demeaning procedure evidences the pervasiveness of the undue influence utilized in these matters.

The Lithuanian Council also felt it necessary to prohibit such acts. Typical is the following provision:

> If a Rabbi be elected because of a loan or a bribe, the amount so advanced shall be confiscated by the Province, he shall be forbidden to assume office, and the recipient shall be permanently expelled and barred from holding office. Before the Rabbi-elect preaches his first sermon, according to custom, he shall be required to appear before his Provincial Chief Rabbi and shall state under a ban [i.e., accept an anathema upon himself to take effect in the event that he lied] that he is assuming his office lawfully.[200]

The problem became exacerbated still more after the massacres in 1648 and 1649 (see Chapter VII, Section I, above), when the Jewish communities in Poland became impoverished because of the mass slaughters and destruction that occurred. Many of them were therefore anxious to retain rabbis who could support themselves in whole or in part, or who would even contribute monies to alleviate the financial plight of these communities. Large communities, such as Poznan and Vilna, engaged rabbis on this basis.[201]

Another element affecting the selection of the most qualified candidate by the communities was the bias in favor of relatives exerted by wealthy and powerful individuals in a community. Not infrequently they would

Jewish Self-Government, p. 154; see also the Responsa *Maharam* of Rothenburg, sec. 137.

193. Assaf, *Be'Ahalei Yaakov*, p. 34, citing Graetz-Shefer, *History of the Jews*, 6:100–108, 313–16; and Harkavy, *Hadashim Gam Yeshanim* (St. Petersburg, 1897), pp. 7–8.

194. Shlomo ben Aderet, Responsa *Rashba*, vol. 1, sec. 475; see also Shimon Duran, Responsa *Tashbatz*, vol. 1, sec. 158.

195. See the Charter of King Kazmir, in 1334, published in Graetz-Shefer, *History of the Jews*, 5:326; the Charter of King Zigmund Augustus in 1551, ibid., 7:323; and the Charter of King Michael Vishnevski in 1669, ibid.

196. See Meir Eisenstadt, in Responsa *Panim Me'Irot* (Lvov, 1891), vol. 2, sec. 152; Shaul ben Moshe, *Givat Shaul* (Zalkava, Poland, 1474), intro. See also the letter sent by the community of Lissa to the city of Frankfort, Germany, in Assaf, *Be'Ahalei Yaakov*, p. 36.

197. *Mahari Weil, Pesakim*, nos. 68, 129, 255; see, particularly, the bitter denunciation of the wealthy by Jona Landsofer in his introduction to *M'il Tzedaka* (Prague, 1700). See also Margolis, Introduction to *Hibure Likutim* (Venice, 1715), and Isserlin, *Pesakim*, Nos. 68, 255.

198. Y. Perles, "Urkunden Zur Geschichte Der Judischen Provinzial-Synoden in Polen," in *Monatschrift for Geschichte and Wissenschaft des Judentoms* (1867), pp. 222, 223; Harkavy, Graetz-Shefer, 7:17, 20; Assaf, *Be'Ahalei Yaakov*, p. 37.

199. Heller, in *Megillat Evah*; Perles, *Geschichte Der Juden in Pozen* (Berlin, 1865), pp. 67, 222–26.

200. Dubnow, *Pinkas*, Ordinance of 1694; see also Rabbi Loewe of Prague, in his *Netivot Olam*, Section on Law (Zhitomir ed., 1967), p. 95, who raises the question of whether rabbis are (*ipso facto*) disqualified to be judges, since they are so dependent upon lay communal leaders.

201. See R. Fein, *Kirya Ne'Emana*, p. 270; and R. Kaufman in *Monatschrift*, vol. 39, pp. 38–46, 91–96. See also Y. Emden, *Edut Be'Yaakov*, p. 48; Assaf, *Be'Ahalei Yaakov*, p. 39.

throw their weight to secure the appointment of a son, son-in-law, or other relative as rabbi.[202] Many communities prescribed ordinances barring a son or son-in-law of a community member from being appointed as rabbi and occasionally applied the prohibition to all relatives of community residents.[203] Even such a well-known scholar as Yair Bachrach, one of the most erudite rabbis of his time, was unable to succeed his father as Rabbi of Worms, despite the request made by his father during his last illness.[204]

In the city of Brest-Litovsk, Lithuania, however, a son and three sons-in-law of Saul Wahl, a Jewish nobleman, served as rabbis in the sixteenth century. Incidentally, the last three rabbis of that community (until its destruction by the Nazis in World War II) were, successively, father, son, and grandson. All three, however, were extraordinarily gifted scholars of saintly character, who pioneered new methods of talmudic legal analyses and accepted the post as rabbi because of their poor financial circumstances.

d. CONFLICTS AND SHARING OF DECISION-MAKING POWERS BETWEEN RABBIS AND LAY LEADERS

Throughout Jewish history there have been conflicts between scholar–rabbis and lay leaders in allocating decision-making powers. These were reflected in the struggles in Babylonia between the exilarch and the heads of the Jewish academies of law (and to a lesser extent, in Palestine) with sometimes one and sometimes the other getting the upper hand. The same conflicts occurred in the Jewish communities in Europe during the Middle Ages. These struggles sometimes assumed great importance in lands such as Spain and Poland, where the Jewish communities were given great autonomy and widespread powers, including the power to impose sanctions of various kinds, and occasionally even the death penalty. The base of power of the scholar–rabbis was their dominance of legal and religious knowledge, their control of the education processes, and, most crucially, the prevalent community view that societal life should be guided by Jewish law and religious values, as determined by the scholar–rabbis. The power base of laymen was largely economic and also resulted from their influence with non-Jewish power figures.

Despite the tensions between rabbis and laymen, there was overall agreement in many areas. Scholars and rabbis approved, in general, of the role of commu-

nity laymen in enacting and administering certain ordinances, even where these deviated from traditional Jewish law. As detailed above, this attitude regarding lay decision-making had its origins in ancient tradition and in the widespread recognition of the need and appropriateness of lay decision-making in the medieval setting. This was particularly true regarding taxation[205] and the imposition of sanctions.[206]

(1) *Rabbi–Scholar Approval and Veto of Lay Communal Prescriptions*

Although rabbis generally approved of lay communal prescriptions, there was often tension and considerable scholar–rabbi opposition to specific communal prescriptions, particularly those that dealt with ritual law and religious prohibitions[207] and the imprisonment of debtors.[208] There was also always the fear that lay communal prescriptions, although recognized as necessary to meet the exigencies of changing societal conditions, might deviate from fundamental goals and postulates of traditional Jewish law.[209] Rabbis and scholar–decision-makers attempted, therefore, to impose a requirement that lay communal enactments had to obtain the consent of a scholar who was well versed in Jewish law and religious perspectives.[210] Lay prescriptions were also felt to be a threat to the prestige and influence of scholar–decision-makers if made without the authorization of scholarly authorities.[211]

These concerns were reflected in some communal ordinances specifically providing that they would be invalid unless consented to by the local or regional rabbi.[212] Gradually, however, laymen succeeded in es-

---

202. Isaac ben Sheshet, Responsa *Rivash*, secs. 268, 270.

203. See the Ordinances of Pozen, in Perles, *Geschichte der Juden in Pozen*, p. 87; Assaf, *Be'Ahalei Yaakov*, p. 40.

204. See his *Klalle Etz Hayim*, printed at end of his *Havat Yair* (Lvov, 1894).

205. See Section B 1 *a* (2), above; see also Isserlin, Responsa *Terumat Hadeshen*, no. 342.

206. See ibid and Shlomo ben Aderet, Responsa *Rashba*, vol. 3, no. 393; vol. 4, no. 311; Asher ben Yehiel, Responsa *Rosh*, sec. 1, no. 1, sec. 5, no. 4; Moshe ben Nahman (Ramban), Responsa of *Rashba* attributed to *Ramban*, no. 220, Meir ben Barukh, Responsa *Maharam* of Rothenburg, no. 220 (Berlin ed.); no. 383 (Prague ed.); Karo, *Shulkhan Arukh, Ho. Mis.*, secs. 37, 22.

207. Josef ben Lev, Responsa *Mahari Ben Lev*, (Jerusalem, 1959), vol. 2, sec. 12, no. 75, p. 183.

208. See J. Eibschutz, *Urim Ve'Tumin*, no. 97; Asher ben Yehiel, Responsa *Rosh*, no. 68, subsec. 10; Isaac ben Sheshet, Responsa *Rivash*, no. 373; Karo, *Shulkhan Arukh, Ho. Mis.*, sec. 97, subsec. 15.

209. See Elon, *Ha'Mishpat Ha'Ivri*, 2:607.

210. Based upon Talmud, *Baba Batra* 9a; see Yom Tov Ashvili, Novellae of *Ritva*, and Moshe ben Nahman, Novellae of *Ramban*, ad loc.

211. Ashvili, Novellae of *Ritva*; see Isaac ben Sheshet, Responsa *Rivash*, no. 399; Shlomo ben Aderet, Responsa *Rashba*, vol. 4, no. 185; Asher ben Yehiel, Commentary *Rosh* to *Baba Batra* 9a.

212. Halpern, Ordinances of Moravia, pp. 57, 96, 110–11; see view of Yosef Migash, cited in B. Ashkenazi, *Shita Me'Kubetzet, Baba Batra* 9a.

tablishing their right to prescribe without the authorization of any local scholar or rabbi.[213]

In practice, nevertheless, there was substantial involvement of local rabbis or scholars in the prescription processes in many Jewish communities, particularly in Poland. Scholars would commonly be the ones who drafted communal ordinances, and after the establishment of a paid professional rabbinate in medieval Europe by the fifteenth century, community prescriptions often would not be regarded as valid unless signed by the local rabbi. As a paid professional, dependent upon the community for his livelihood, the rabbi was often subject to intense lay pressure (see Section [4], below).

(2) *Rabbinic Nullification of Communal Enactments; Majority Rule and Minority Rights*

Rabbi–scholars could often effectively veto lay communal enactments, and this was a potent weapon in the recurrent tugs-of-war for control of the decision processes. The immense prestige and esteem that many rabbi–scholars possessed resulted in appeals made to them by individuals who felt aggrieved as a result of community enactments. From time to time, acting on such appeals, or even on their own initiative, these scholar–decision-makers declared lay communal prescriptions to be invalid. Their great prestige often ensured that their decisions would be followed.

Many different reasons were cited by scholars for nullifying lay communal prescriptions. Sometimes the scholar–decision-makers claimed that lay communal enactments violated biblical law[214] or were too difficult or onerous to be borne by the community.[215] At other times the prescriptions were held to be improper and in violation of basic goals of Jewish law, since they were inequitable and amounted to "robbery,"[216] violated the basic rights of individuals,[217] or constituted

an unequal allocation of community burdens.[218] For these purposes, they could rely on talmudic precedent, which expressed some of the overriding, basic goals of law in terms of high-level abstractions. These included the necessity to do what is "just and good"[219] to avoid quarrels and unpleasantness,[220] including those between Jews and Gentiles[221] and, in charitable giving, to prefer a neighbor over those who reside further away,[222] that is, residents of a town over non-residents.[223]

One of the most important goals and perspectives that governed community rule was that the wishes of the majority should prevail. On the one hand, this perspective, predicated on the biblical verse "tend towards the majority . . ." (Exod. 23:2),[224] negated one-man authoritarian rule, at least in theory. On the other hand, this perspective could also be carried to extremes and applied to entirely disregard the wishes of the minority.[225]

The right of the community minority not to be coerced by the majority was upheld by Rabbi Jacob Tam in the eleventh century.[226] A number of other scholars —including Moshe ben Maimon (Rambam), Eliezer of Metz, Barukh of Rothenburg, Asher ben Yehiel and his son Jacob (author of the authoritative law code, *Turim*)—accepted this view.[227] However, most of the Jewish medieval scholars—including Shlomo Yitzhaki (Rashi), Eliezer Ha-Levi, Moshe ben Nahman (Ramban), and Shlomo ben Aderet (Rashba)—agreed that, except in unusual cases, the community minority was

---

213. Y. Sirkis, New Responsa *Bah*, no. 43; Sofer, Responsa *Hatam Sofer, Ho. Mis.*, no. 116; *contra* decisions from prior eras; e.g., Shlomo ben Aderet, Responsa *Rashba*, vol. 4, no. 185; vol. 5, nos. 125, 245; vol. 7, no. 108; M. Abulafia, *Yad Ramah*, *Baba Batra* 9b; Elon, *Ha'Mishpat Ha'Ivri*, pp. 607–14; idem, "Sources and Nature of Jewish Law," pp. 97 ff.

214. Meir ben Barukh, Responsa *Maharam* of Rothenburg, no. 423 (Lvov ed.); Shlomo ben Aderet, Responsa *Rashba*, vol. 2, no. 289; vol. 5, no. 287; vol. 7, no. 108.

215. Shlomo ben Aderet, Responsa *Rashba*, vol. 3, no. 411; vol. 7, no. 108; Agus, Responsa of *Baale Ha'Tosefot*, p. 39.

216. Hayim ben Yitzhak, Responsa *Ohr Zarua*, no. 222; Shlomo ben Aderet, Responsa *Rashba*, vol. 5, no. 188; Responsa of Meir Abulafia in Yehuda ben Asher, *Zikhron Yehuda*; Meir ben Barukh, Responsa *Maharam* of Rothenburg, no. 106 (Prague ed.); Moshe Isserlis, Responsa *Rama*, no. 73; Landau, Responsa *Noda Be'Yehuda* (2nd ed.), *Ho. Mis.*, no. 40.

217. Moshe Isserlis and Meir of Rothenburg, ibid.

218. Responsum of Hananya Gaon, in Responsa of the *Gaonim*, vol. 4, *Sha're Tzedek* (Salonika, 1792; reprinted Jerusalem, 1966), sec. 4, no. 16 at p. 126; Ashvili, *Ritva*, Novellae to *Avodah Zarah* 36b; Y. Bachrach, Responsa *Havat Yair*, no. 81; Elon, *Ha'Mishpat Ha'Ivri*, pp. 614 ff.

219. Deut. 6:17–18; Tosefta *Shekalim* 2,2; Talmud, *Baba Metzia* 108a; Elon, *Ha'Mishpat Ha'Ivri*, p. 513.

220. Talmud, *Kiddushin* 63a; *Ketubot* 58b, 47a; *Yebamot* 15a; *Gittin* 59a.

221. Talmud, *Avodah Zarah* 26a; *Baba Metzia* 32b; Jerusalem Talmud, *Ketubot*, ch. 9, rule 4.

222. *Baba Metzia* 71a.

223. Talmud, *Baba Metzia* 71a: "The poor of your town come first." See Moses ben Nahman, Commentary *Ramban* to Deut. 6:18.

224. See Talmud, *Sanhedrin* 3b, 52a; Freiman, "Majority and Minority in the Community," p. 1.

225. See Alfasi, Responsa *Rif* (Leiter ed. Pittsberg, 1954), no. 13; Finkelstein, *Jewish Self-Government*, 49.

226. Mordecai ben Hillel, Commentary *Mordecai* to *Baba Kama*, no. 179, *Baba Batra*, no. 480; Meir ben Barukh, Responsa *Maharam* of Rothenburg, no. 230 (Crimona ed.); *Tshuvot Maimoniut* (medieval Responsa by miscellaneous authors, printed as an addendum to standard editions of *Rambam*, Laws of Judges, ch. 10.

227. See citations in note 226 and Meir ben Barukh, Responsa *Maharam* of Rothenburg, no. 968 (Prague ed.); Mordecai ben Hillel, Commentary *Mordecai* to *Baba Batra*, no. 481.

required to accept the decisions of the majority.[228] This latter view gradually prevailed and was generally followed by scholar–decision-makers.[229] Similarly, it came to be accepted that a republican form of government satisfied the basic goals of Jewish law. The representatives of the community could therefore promulgate enactments on behalf of the entire community,[230] and the specific consent of residents was not necessary for each new prescription. Nevertheless, the basic rights of minorities was to be protected against arbitrary and unwarranted majority action.[231]

It should be noted that despite the theoretical principle of democratic majority rule, substantial portions of community residents were disqualified from voting (or otherwise discriminated against) because communal governance was weighted in favor of, or based upon, wealth, property ownership, and scholarship, and because of oligarchic tendencies as well. Control by small elites became commonplace.[232] Accordingly, one must conclude that, in practice, Jewish communal decision-making often had many undemocratic features, although the reasons and precedents for this might be quite persuasive. Claims that Jewish communal decision-making was always thoroughly democratic must be treated with great skepticism. For a realistic comprehension of Jewish law, the actual practices in Jewish society must be studied, not simply the theoretical principle of majority rule that was enunciated by the scholarly authorities but not practiced in real life.[233]

(3) Interpretation of Communal Prescriptions by Rabbis and Scholars

Rabbinic and scholarly influence on lay decision-making was exerted in still another important way. When there was a dispute as to the interpretation of a particular ordinance, or when there was no set custom or ordinance governing a matter at issue, there was a widespread view that this was a "legal" issue to be referred for decision to the local rabbi or to an eminent scholar of the law.

Ambiguities in ordinances or customs could often be asserted, and each case normally would have some facts that were different than other prior cases. Consequently, the power to "interpret" the ordinances and to rule on disputed issues vested the rabbis and scholars with great powers. They could thereby blunt the thrust of an ordinance or effectively nullify it. As a result of the continuous tension and conflict, there gradually arose an intricate system of checks and balances in allocating decision-making powers between the lay leaders, the rabbi–scholars, and the professional judges of the communities. The relative strengths of each of these participants in the power processes varied, of course, with the different constellations of factors that affected decision-making in each community during different epochs.

Nevertheless, there were considerable polemics concerning the sharing of power between scholars and laymen, particularly when laymen intervened in applying the law. For example, the practice developed for lay leaders to decide cases within their jurisdiction on the basis of communal or state ordinances, custom, or simply lay feeling regarding right or wrong, rather than upon the precedents or principles of Jewish law.[234] This practice affected medieval Jewish courts as well as lay bodies. A number of factors caused this phenomenon: lay participation in some of the courts, the selection of judges by the litigants themselves on condition that they act as arbitrators (rather than as appliers of traditional law), and the tendency of many of the professional Jewish judges to attempt to work out amicable settlements between the parties, following ancient Jewish traditions discussed in the Talmud.[235] Occasionally, where specialized knowledge of a particular trade was required, rabbis were dispensed with completely, and lay arbiters were used exclusively. This was the case regarding complex commercial transactions and the evolution of the law merchant in Italy and Germany.

Such lay intervention in the decision-making processes provoked sharp reactions. One scholar described this situation by saying:

> Because of the needs of the hour, our sages, of blessed memory, said that a court could flog and punish, even, when not authorized by the Torah; not however, to violate the words of the Torah, but to make a fence around the Torah. Consequently,

228. See Hayim ben Yitzhak, Responsa *Ohr Zarua*, no. 222; Isaac ben Sheshet, Responsa *Rivash*, no. 249; Shlomo ben Aderet, Responsa *Rashba*, vol. 2, no. 279; vol. 5, nos. 242, 270; Moshe ben Nahman, Responsa of Rashba attributed to Ramban, nos. 65 and 280; idem, Responsa *Ramban* (Freiman ed.; Jerusalem, 1934), no. 111; Shlomo Yitzhaki, Responsa *Rashi*, as cited in Mordecai ben Hillel, Commentary *Mordecai* to *Shevuot* 2:758. See, in general, Elijah Mizrahi, Responsa, no. 57; Binyamin Z'Ev, Responsa (Lvov, 1860), nos. 290, 296, 298–300; Asher ben Yehiel, Responsa *Rosh*, no. 6:5, 7; *Kal Bo*, nos. 142, 116.

229. See Sofer, Responsa *Hatam Sofer, Ho. Mis.*, no. 116.

230. Shlomo ben Aderet, Responsa *Rashba*, vol. 3, no. 443; Hayim ben Yitzhak, Responsa *Ohr Zarua*, no. 65; M. Trani, Responsa *Mabit*, 1:84.

231. See citations in footnotes 226–230, above.

232. See Section B 1 *a* (5), above. See also Agus, "Autonomous Rule in Jewish Communities," pp. 190–91.

233. Contra Elon, *Ha'Mishpat Ha'Ivri*, pp. 580–87, 591–94.

234. Asher ben Yehiel, Responsa *Rosh*, cited in *Terumath Ha'Deshen*. See Kolon, Responsa *Mahari Kolon*, no. 169; Weil, Responsa *Mahari Weil*, no. 76; Isserlin, *Pesakim*, no. 267; Mintz, Responsa *Mahari Mintz*, no. 46, 93.

235. Baron, *The Jewish Community*, 2:209.

it has been established that in every city, the [lay] leaders of the community should judge in accordance with the nature of the matter and the ordinances. These are called the "Decisions of Laymen." There are also towns in which there are no scholars. In order that they should not resort to non-Jewish judges, it was permitted for them to have Jewish judges, who were not learned in the law. This continued generation after generation until they forgot the laws of the Torah, and even where there was one who was learned, they would appoint [as judges] persons who were not learned out of respect for them, and they would rule as they wished, sometimes because of honor and sometimes because of love or fear. One sin drags in another, and this caused conflict in Israel, because each one wished to rule over his neighbor, and desired that his neighbor not rule over him. It has been written in the name of one sage, who also objected to laymen's decisions, and said, "In my eyes, they are worse than the decisions of the non-Jews, since they have an order in their rulings, while the decisions of the laymen are without order and they sometimes find for and sometimes against [in the same case]; sometimes deliberately intending to harm somebody and sometimes unintentionally." Even the scholars of the Torah, who are learned in the law, when they sit together with the [lay] leaders, judge in accordance with their wish, contrary to the Torah. With my own eyes, I have many times seen that their decisions were distorted because of their own selfish interests, and the one who lost the case cries, "This is contrary to the laws of the Torah, as set forth explicitly in the *Shulhan Arukh* [the Jewish code of laws]," but nobody pays attention to him. Sometimes, they impose sanctions upon him, humiliating him or requiring him to pay fines on these matters, and who can tell them what to do?[236]

In many of the Jewish communities in Italy wealthy lay leaders often acted as judges in ordinary commercial disputes. This led to bitter attacks by rabbis, who claimed that this practice had brought about the decline of the Jewish courts, and wholesale resort by Jewish litigants to non-Jewish courts.[237] David Openheim, a well-known medieval rabbi, wrote:

> Truth is a witness for itself, and matters of common knowledge need no corroboration, that in the holy community of Venice, there is no judgment in ac-

cordance with the Torah, and no established court of well-known scholars of the law . . . poverty, penury, a melting of the heart has occurred among the scholars of the Torah, because of their fear of those who are rich and powerful and their need to rely on them for their livelihood. These have caused the law to retreat.[238]

(4) *Bases of Lay Power*

In general, the influential community laymen were the ones who selected the community rabbi. Their approval was also required for renewal of his contract of employment. Such contracts normally provided for a term of three to five years and were negotiated in each case by the individual community and rabbi. There was no central organization that set the terms of employment and tenure. Consequently, the power not to renew a contract was the most powerful weapon that was used by laymen in their conflicts with the community rabbi. If the contract was not renewed, the rabbi's position was terminated, and he had to look for a new post. This weapon was sometimes exercised against even the most famous rabbis and scholars. Rabbi Yair Bachrach, one of the leading Jewish scholars of Europe in his time, was compelled to leave his position in Koblentz when his contract was not renewed.[239]

The strife that resulted from failures to renew these employment contracts was reflected in the ordinances of the Lithuanian Council providing that no notice was required to be given to a rabbi in order to terminate his term. The fact that he was not rehired was to be sufficient notice.[240] Five years later, however, in 1728, the council modified this ordinance to provide (§ 726) that if the rabbi was not given a one-half year notice of intention not to renew his contract, his term would be renewed for the same period of time for which he had originally been hired. This was not always carried out in practice, however, as evidenced by the fact that this ordinance had to be promulgated again some years later.

In Germany, where there was no strong regional council, some of the individual communities inserted similar conditions in their contracts with the rabbi.[241] The last rabbi of the city of Vilna, Lithuania, was discharged from his position by the lay leaders of the

---

236. Yehuda L. Puhwitzer, *Kene Khakhma* (Frankfurt-Am-Main, 1682). See also *Khemdat Ha'Yamim*, vol. 2, p. 38a (Livorno, 1763), the authorship of which is a matter of scholarly conflict; Weil, Responsa *Mahari Weil*, sec. 146; Landau, *Derushe Ha'Tzlakh* (Warsaw, 1878), p. 6a.

237. See the sharp criticism by Judah A. De Modina published in L. Blau ed., *Kitvei Rabbi Yehuda Arya Modina* (Budapest, 1906), pp. 166, 171.

238. Published by Z. Dushinsky in *Hazofe Lekhakhmat Yisrael* (Budapest, 1913), 6:162.

239. Introduction to his *Kellale Etz Ha'Hayim*. For examples of brutal economic pressures against community rabbis by local plutocrats, see Y. Y. Reines, in *Khotam Takhnit* (Jerusalem, 1934), pp. 18, 19, 23 ff.

240. Dubnow, *Pinkas Ha'Medinah*, Records of the Lithuanian Council, sec. 48.

241. See Records of the City of Bamberg, pp. 13, 22–24.

community, despite the fact that he had received a contract hiring him as rabbi for his entire life (an unusual provision in those days). His removal from office was not, however, fully effective.[242] If a community rabbi behaved in scandalous fashion, as happened from time to time, he could then be removed summarily from office by the chief rabbi of the district or by a well-known Rabbi in the general area, whose decision would be accepted by the community because of his eminence, due to his well-known erudition and piety.[243]

In the power tensions between the communal rabbi and laymen, much depended, of course, upon the personality of the particular rabbi, the extent of the pressures to which he was subject, and many other factors.[244] As Israel Lipkin of Salant is reputed to have said, "Any rabbi whom the community does not constantly wish to fire is no rabbi, but any rabbi that it does fire, is not a *'mensh'* [socially adept person]."

On the other hand, an important counterweapon of the rabbi in his struggles with laymen was his ability to leave his position and accept an offer in another community. Rabbis who were learned were often in great demand, and many communities would regard it as an honor if such a person would accept a position there. Many of the leading rabbis, particularly those who were unafraid to criticize influential laymen, often resigned their position to serve elsewhere. For example, Yoel Sirkish, Yom Tov Lipman Heller, Tzvi Ashkenazi, Shimon Auerbach, Yonatan Eibschutz, Meshulem Igra, and Ya'akov Yehoshua are only a few of the most eminent rabbis—famous to this day—who frequently left positions to serve elsewhere, often because of sharp conflicts with community laymen.[245]

On the other hand, when a community was well satisfied with its rabbi, it would often do all in its power to prevent him from leaving to become rabbi of another community. Occasionally, laymen might even abuse and manhandle the representatives of the successful community who came to escort the rabbi to his new position. In extreme cases the rabbi might have to sneak secretly out of a town in order to escape his virtual "imprisonment" by his community, which refused to permit him to leave them.[246]

(5) *Communal Prescriptions for the Allocation of Power among Laymen and Rabbis*

Power conflicts between laymen and rabbis were reflected in many ordinances (both intercommunal and intracommunal), which often limited the powers of the community rabbi. One of the earliest such limitations —that on his power to excommunicate—was imposed by a synod of more than one hundred and fifty prominent rabbis of many communities in France and Germany in the twelfth century (see Section A 2 *b*, above). It should be noted that the rabbis at that synod were not salaried by communities and were, in effect, scholar-laymen who engaged in all types of occupations. Sometimes neither a rabbi nor a community was authorized to excommunicate any person without the consent of the other.[247]

Other limitations on the powers of the community rabbi were often inserted by individual communities in their contracts with him. Some contracts provided, for example, that the rabbi should not interfere at all in any community affairs concerning the collection of taxes or exclusive franchises (a very important and lucrative source of income in the Middle Ages) and other specified matters. Often community ordinances provided that even in matters where the rabbi had the right to act, his view should only be regarded as the view of one person, equal to, but not superior to, the opinion of any other individual layman, except in the case of a tie vote. A rabbi who might also be a participant in regional councils was sometimes prohibited from signing any council decisions that would adversely affect his own community, unless he first notified his community leaders.[248] The community of Vilna did not even permit its rabbi to ordain anybody as a "rabbi" (or even as a "colleague") unless the lay heads of the community concurred and joined in the ceremony.[249]

These limitations indicate the extent to which the rabbi's power was often circumscribed, and it is possible that his role was at times still more limited in actual practice. Of course, the personality of the rabbi and of the leading laymen, the extent of the crises, and

242. See I. Klausner, *"The Internal Controversy in the Community of Vilna"* (Hebrew; Jerusalem, 1942). For the firing of other well-known rabbis, see Assaf, in *Kiryat Sefer*, vol. 14, pp. 551–52; vol. 15, pp. 113–19.

243. See, for example, I. Bruna, Responsa *Mahari Bruna*, secs. 277, 281, 282.

244. See Margolis, Intro.

245. See also Assaf, "Lekorot Ha'Rabanut," in *Be'Ahalei Yaakov*, p. 59.

246. See Y. Lifschitz, *Toledot Rabbi Yitzhak Elhanam Spector* (Warsaw, 1896); Assaf, "Lekorot Ha'Rabanut," p. 61.

247. Meir ben Barukh, Responsa *Maharam* of Rothenburg (Prague ed.), no. 155; Y. Bruna, Responsa *Mahari Bruna*, no. 188; Asher ben Yehiel, Responsa *Rosh*, sec. 43, nos. 8 and 9; Isserlin, *Maharil, Minhagim*, last paragraph. See also the public burning of a Declaration of Excommunication, recorded in the Records of the Community of Frankfort, in *Ohr Ha'Yashar* (Amsterdam, 1859); also the Records of the Community of Cracow, in *Ozar Ha'Safrut*, vol. 4, sec. 4, p. 594.

248. See, e.g., Fein, *Kirya Ne'Emana*, pp. 39–40, regarding the city of Vilna.

249. Ibid.; see also the Ordinances of Moravia, below, which placed limitation on both rabbis and lay leaders.

the many other surrounding circumstances influenced the exact balance of power in any community.

It is interesting to note in this connection that, although the twelfth century synod of French and German rabbis circumscribed the powers of rabbis to excommunicate, regional synods of fifteenth and sixteenth century Poland and Lithuania, in which laymen predominated, often sided with the rabbis in their disputes with laymen. Thus, the Lithuanian Council prohibited any community from circulating any letter (setting forth its decisions or urging action) to other areas, without the express signature of the community rabbi,[250] and that "in the event of a difference of opinion between the rabbis and the [lay] leaders as to who should assess [the community taxes] and in which manner [the taxes should be assessed], the view of the rabbis shall prevail."[251] These regional ordinances did not, however, apply where any community had specified a different provision in its contract with the rabbi. The limitations that were placed upon the power of the rabbi by these contracts were recognized by the council as valid.[252]

The pro-rabbi leanings of the Lithuanian Council may have been influenced by the fact that its head was often a rabbi and that a number of rabbis were extremely active in organizing and administering the council. Another factor may have been the proliferation of academies, which stressed the pre-eminent place that scholar-rabbis should have in communal decision-making. These academies exercised a considerable influence in shaping the perspectives of their students, many of whom became influential laymen.

The most common allocation for the sharing of power was for the lay leaders to decide all matters that involved the possible imposition of sanctions, taxes, regulation of mercantile practices, the right to settle in the community, the acquisition of exclusive franchises to engage in certain types of business, particularly tax farming, the administration of the estates of noblemen,[253] and often the right to sell liquor. The rabbis and professional judges were to decide commercial litigation, religious ritual, including dietary laws, and family law questions. A similar division of authority

existed in many parts of Germany as well.[254] Where laymen were authorized to impose severe sanctions, they would, in practice, often consult with a leading rabbi before inflicting the death penalty or other severe punishment.[255] In all areas of law, decisions of laymen were occasionally struck down by scholars on the grounds that they violated fundamental values and goals of Jewish law. In addition, decisions were subject to interpretation by scholars in the event of dispute (see Section B 1 *d* [3], above).

The division of decision-making powers in the application of the law is reflected in the ordinances of the Lithuanian Council:

> The leaders of the community shall decide in cases of quarrels, conflicts . . . fines and punishments, while the judges of the community shall decide commercial cases. The [lay] leaders should not involve themselves in commercial matters, and the judges should not involve themselves in matters that do not concern them.[256]

In Poland and Lithuania, however, the rabbis, professional judges, and scholars of the law apparently often had the upper hand, at least in outward appearance. The rabbis in those countries played an extremely active role in community affairs and were regarded with very high esteem because of their great erudition and piety. This reflected the strong influences that enlightenment and rectitude had upon power positions. The ordinances of many communities specifically prohibited lay leaders from interfering with or overruling decisions reached by the professional rabbi-judges.[257] Professional courts in Poland could act on their own to compel a litigant to attend court hearings and could enforce their decisions without recourse to the lay heads of the community.

In medieval Germany, although the rabbis were also held in great esteem, their role in decision-making was somewhat smaller than in Poland. They were often not formally given the power to enforce their decision or to compel attendance at court hearings. For this they would sometimes have to resort to the lay leaders and

250. Records of the Lithuanian Council, sec. 153, in Dubnow, *Pinkas Ha'Medinah*; see also Mintz, Responsa *Maharam Mintz*, sec. 6, and Talmud, *Baba Batra* 9a, for a similar view.

251. Records of the Lithuanian Council, sec. 716.

252. Ibid., sec. 918.

253. Asher ben Yehiel, Responsa *Rosh*, sec. 7, no. 11; Isserlin, Responsa *Terumath Ha'Deshen*, sec. 342; Joseph Ibn Ezra, in *Ma'asa Melekh* (Salonika, 1601), p. 64b. See also *Jahrbuch der Judishe Literarischen Gesellschaft*, pp. 322 and 331, which provided that even cases of theft were to be decided by the lay leaders; see the ordinances of the Lithuanian Council, nos. 66 and 364; the Records of the Community of Dubnow, in *Sefer Dubnow Rabati*, p. 50, and in Assaf, "Le'Korot Ha'Rabanut," p. 55.

254. See also Shlomo ben Aderet, Responsa *Rashba*, vol. 2, no. 290, which indicates that in Toledo, Spain, the lay leaders decided cases of capital punishment.

255. See, e.g., Asher ben Yehiel, Responsa *Rosh*, sec. 18, no. 13; Judah ben Asher, Responsa *Zikhron Yehuda*, sec. 58; Assaf, *Ha'Onshin* (Jerusalem, 1922), pp. 18–21.

256. Dubnow, *Pinkas Ha'Medinah*, sec. 364. This ordinance was adopted in 1599. See also the Ordinances of Moravia, below.

257. See, e.g., the Ordinances of the City of Cracow, in *Jahrbuch der Judisch Literarischen Gesellschaft*, vol. 10, pp. 326, 332. This was also the case in the community of Zalkava; see S. Buber, *Kirya Nisgava*, pp. 96, 111.

request them to compel obedience to the court's process.[258]

In Moravia, where the institution of Jewish courts was well established, the courts would hear all cases involving commercial disputes. In the smaller communities, however, where there were no courts, such disputes would be heard by lay leaders. Here, too, the power of the rabbis was less than in Poland and a suit by an individual against the head of a small community could be heard by the lay leader of the district in which it was located. Similarly, any two litigants had the right to have their case heard by the lay leader of the community instead of by the professional court. In actual practice, nevertheless, a compromise developed between lay leaders, communal rabbis, and professional judges in the sharing of power. The result was that the Moravian ordinances provided that a lay leader of a community could not hear a case unless he was joined by the rabbi or professional judge. Conversely, the rabbi could not hear any case alone and was required to be joined by two of the lay leaders of the community. Even the Jewish High Court of Moravia consisted of two lay leaders and the chief rabbi, or sometimes four lay leaders and the rabbi. In some of the other countries, too, the practice developed for professional judges not to decide any cases at all, unless one of the lay leaders was present.[259] In Italy (see Section 2 *h*, below), the laity usually ruled supreme.

Even in countries where scholarly influence predominated, the decision-making powers of lay leaders in the application of the law was great in many of the smaller communities that did not have a rabbi. There the lay leaders decided all commercial cases.[260]

(6) *The Role of the Community Proletariat in Decision-Making*

As a result of the various factors discussed above, the lay members of Jewish communities also exercised a crucial function in decision-making. In local communities, particularly in Europe during the Middle Ages, the residents elected community officials, voted for the passage, rejection, or retraction of ordinances in nearly every area of activity, and had a say (although often only through their elected representatives) in the selection of the rabbi, judge, or other hired officials of the community. In the same way, they also had a voice in the selection of representatives to regional synods and councils, which would promulgate important ordinances and would hear many of the important cases arising in that region.

From time to time there were sharp conflicts between the leaders of a community and members of the lower classes, particularly craftsmen. The conflicts often arose as a result of complaints by members of the lower socio-economic classes that the leaders of the communities were imposing too great a tax burden upon them while lightening the tax burden on the wealthier individuals. Occasionally craftsmen objected strongly to restrictions of dress imposed upon them—for example, prohibitions against wearing fur hats to the synagogues on the Sabbath.[261]

Thus there was a fourway tug-of-war for power between the rabbi, the professional judges, the lay officers, and the members of the community—particularly those who had a hand in choosing the persons to fill these positions—complicated by the interventions of the scholars who headed the academies of law and by the plutocrats. These conflicts led to continual tensions and accommodations in the Jewish communities throughout the Middle Ages regarding the sharing and allocation of decision-making power. As was to be expected, sometimes one individual, institution, or group would predominate, and sometimes another. At times power would be vested in more or less "equal" divisions among the various parties.

(7) *Communal Control by Lay Oligarchies*

In time the position of the communal rabbi appears to have been gradually whittled down in favor of lay oligarchies, although a scholar–rabbi with a strong personality might still predominate in his community.

Many Jewish communities adopted regulations designed, in theory, to prevent oligarchic rule, such as limiting terms of election to one year and prohibitions against reelection to office.[262] Nevertheless, this antioligarchic goal was often frustrated by a coalescence of a number of factors.

Balloting ordinarily was not by direct, secret votes of equal weight. Often there was no free choice of officers by the citizens of a community because of provisions for selection by lot (as in Spain, Gerona, and Leghorn) and limitations on those who were eligible for office (commonly only men of wealth could qualify, as in Cracow, Poznan, and many other communities), restrictions on the right to vote (often only those with

258. See the Records of the Community of Bamberg, p. 13; the Records of the Community of Hesse, in the *Jubilee Volume in Honor of Hildesheimer*; *Revue des Etudes Juives*, vol. 19, p. 126; and the Records of the Community of Hildesheim, published in *Ha'Eshkol* (Cracow, 1904), vol. 6, pp. 236–40.

259. Asher ben Yehiel, Responsa *Rosh*, sec. 97, no. 1; Responsa *Rambam*, in *Pe'er Ha'Dor* (Lvov, 1859), secs. 211, 214.

260. Shlomo ben Aderet, Responsa *Rashba*, vol. 2, no. 290.

261. See "The Revolt in the Communities of Grodna, Vilna, and Minsk in the Eighteenth Century," in the *Historische Schriften Fun Yivo*, vol. 2, p. 590; also Assaf, "The Inner Life of the Jews of Poland" (Hebrew), in *Be'Ahalei Yaakov*, p. 75. See below for oligarchic rule in Jewish communities.

262. See the Ordinances of Moravia, below, no. 98.

property or those who paid a specified minimum amount of tax could participate). There was a common practice of indirect voting in which a number of electors would be selected. These, in turn, would select a smaller group of electors. The latter would then choose the various officers of the community for the coming year.

In Cracow, for example, those who would "bear the burdens and taxes of the community" would select nine of their members. These nine would, in turn, choose five members, who would then select the officers of the community.[263] In Lithuania only fifteen "elders" cast ballots for electors. In many communities there was cooptation by existing officials in the appointment of new communal officials.[264] In many communities all key offices were held by the members of one family, whose position would pass from father to son. Thus, in Frankfurt, Germany, the community was ruled by one single family (the Kann family and its offshoots, the Bing, Haas, Stern, and Beer families) for over two centuries, from 1550 to 1754.[265] It should be noted that this tendency toward oligarchic rule paralleled the political developments in Europe at that time, when most cities were under the sway of aristocratic families.[266] The effect of these limitations on participation in communal decision-making was oligarchic rule by the wealthy and the members of a few interrelated families. These could be as authoritarian as the exilarch of Babylonia or the patriarch in ancient Palestine.

Interestingly, the glorification of scholarship in the Jewish community led oligarchic plutocrats to pride themselves on their own learning. They would also attempt to marry off their daughters to scholars, whom they would support in order to enable them to continue their studies. The traditional Jewish emphasis upon learning and scholarship attracted many of the best minds and characters in the Jewish community to devote themselves to the study of Jewish law and religion and produced a very large number of extraordinarily fine and saintly personalities.[267] In turn, the rabbis' superior learning brought immense power and influence to this educated elite. Some of the outstanding rabbis obtained such preeminence that their "utterances became axioms, judgments became binding precedents, (their) writings authoritative sources for judicial practice . . . due to the recognition of their intellectual acumen, sincerity, and piety."[268]

Accordingly, community rabbis were often able to contest the oligarchic rule by plutocrats. The rabbis came from all economic classes of society and, in accordance with Jewish cultural traditions, were held in the highest esteem because of their learning and piety. While they did not attempt to monopolize knowledge (endeavoring, on the contrary, to spread religious education as much as possible), their possession of this value served to give them great powers. They could, and often did, utilize their powers to check the authoritarian rule of oligarchs, and they were often unafraid to denounce in very plain language misuses of power by plutocrats. As one of the influential decision-makers of this so-called "aristocracy of learning" wrote,

> On account of our sins, a calamity has befallen most communities, in as much as the elders oppress and despotically govern the people. Bent upon private selfish gains, rather than the glory of Heaven, they lessen their own (tax) burdens, and shift it upon the shoulders of the unfortunate masses.[269]

In short:

> Jewish communal rule in medieval Poland gradually led to the rise of communal oligarchy . . . and a powerful bureaucracy. The relative stability (toward the end of the Middle Ages) enabled a few families in each community to retain wealth and political connections for periods unprecedented in the medieval period proper.[270]

Once plutocrats and bureaucrats obtained control, they often attempted to retain it by use of all means, whether legal or improper. Although democratic forms persisted, the majority of the population, especially in the larger communities, often had little or no influence in community decision-making.

Although members of the communal officialdom could theoretically act as a counterweight to the plutocracy, their own self-interest often led them into unofficial and informal alliances with plutocrats in order to retain their offices and powers. The only ones who were in a position to combat authoritarian rule, and who often did, were the rabbi-scholars. They were, however, afflicted with the crucial weakness of being hired for periods of a few years at a time. They were dependent for their positions and livelihoods upon the oligarchies that ruled the community. Their desperate need for oligarchic approval for renewal of their contracts often led them to cooperate with oligarchic elites.

In the long run, however, this oligarchic authoritarian management of the Jewish communities led to its own ultimate downfall, as was the case in the larger non-

263. Balaban, *Ordinances of Cracow* (reprinted Jerusalem, 1969), p. 47.
264. Hayim Yitzhak, Responsa *Ohr Zarua*, no. 65.
265. Baron, *The Jewish Community*, 2:46, 47, 51; 3:141–42, n. 73.
266. Ibid., 2:51.
267. See ibid., 2:94, 181–82.
268. Ibid., 2:244.

269. Weil, Responsa *Mahari Weil*, no. 173.
270. Baron, *The Jewish Community*, 2:812.

Jewish authoritarian states of Europe. The spread of the Hasidic movement, which catered to members of the lower economic classes and selected its own spiritual leaders, ignoring the official rabbis, may have been spurred by alliances of rabbis with authoritarian communal leaders. Also, too, the support of Jewish oligarchic tendencies by non-Jewish rulers (in order to more easily control and deal with the Jewish communities) was essentially destroyed by the collapse of public support and the change in secular governmental rule following the French Revolution.

2. JEWISH COURTS IN THE MIDDLE AGES: A DOCUMENTARY STUDY

In the more than 1700 years that elapsed following the destruction of the Second Jewish Commonwealth in 70 C.E. until the French Revolution in 1786, non-Jewish rulers in nearly all countries permitted the Jewish communities to maintain their own Jewish courts and to decide disputes in accordance with Jewish law. Jewish officials throughout the ages made constant attempts to preserve this decision-making power and to prevent resort by Jews to non-Jewish courts for the resolution of their disputes. Those Jews who did turn to non-Jewish courts were regarded as renegades and traitors to the Jewish nation and its religion.[271]

It was also strongly felt by Jewish religious leaders and decision-makers that the maintenance of active Jewish courts that applied Jewish law would clarify the law and help its development. Study of the law without practical application would only lead to obscurity and ignorance of the law.[272]

With few exceptions, the exclusive resort by Jews to Jewish courts was preserved. Achievement of this result was aided by the fact that non-Jewish courts were often regarded as being untrustworthy and as relying upon false testimony.[273] "Certainly, their judgment is no judgment, because they sentence to death without trial, even with regard to themselves, and certainly [with regard to] Jews, and they rely on their witnesses who are all false witnesses."[274] Furthermore, they were regarded as often being influenced by intense anti-Jewish feelings.[275] An interesting seventeenth-century conversation has been recorded between Duke Karl Ludwig, and the Rabbi of Mannheim, in which the Duke complained that Jews were corrupting his judges through extensive bribery, which violated biblical laws as well as the laws of the realm. The Rabbi responded:

> It is known, that there is no hatred as intense as religious hatred. . . . When a Jew and a non-Jew come to court, then, without a doubt, the judge sides with the non-Jew, and suspects the Jew of lies and trickery. Accordingly, when any Jew who has a dispute with a non-Jew, comes before the court, he fears that he will lose, because of the natural sympathies that the judge has for his non-Jewish adversary. He, therefore, attempts to right the scales of justice (and) even (them), by bribing the judge, not to distort justice, but, on the contrary, to see that it remains righteous, and to preserve it from distortion.[276]

There was also a feeling that litigation in non-Jewish courts could drag on for protracted periods—for example, the complaint of a widow that it had taken her seven months to get the court to hand down a decision.[277] Jewish courts on the other hand, were very scrupulous about handing down decisions within a very short time, since inordinate delay was considered scandalous and a great injustice.[278] In fact, the honesty, good judgment, and prompt decisions of the Jewish courts often attracted many non-Jewish litigants to utilize their facilities.[279]

In Poland there was another factor that contributed to the exclusive resort by Jews to Jewish courts. There was always the widespread ignorance of the Polish language among the Jewish population, which put them at a great disadvantage before the non-Jewish courts. This, of course, did not apply to the Jews in countries like Italy, France, Spain, Germany, North Africa, and Western Asia, who were generally fluent in the languages of those countries.

Other factors preventing Jewish use of the non-Jewish courts, were the repeated anathemas and excommu-

271. Talmud, *Gittin* 88b; Rambam Code of Laws, Rules of the *Sanhedrin*, 26:7; Tzemah Duran, Responsa *Yahin U'Boaz* (Jerusalem, 1970), sec. 1, no. 6; see Ordinance of Rabbi Jacob Tam, in Finkelstein, *Jewish Self-Government*; Shimon Duran, Responsa *Tashbatz,* sec. 2, no. 292; Haim Benebashti, Responsa *Baye Hava*, sec. 21, no. 58; Asher ben Yehiel, Responsa *Rosh*, sec. 68, no. 13; Shlomo ben Aderet, Responsa *Rashba* cited in Karo, *Beth Yosef, Tur Orah Haim*, sec. 26; Assaf, *Batei Ha'Din Ve'Sidrehem* (Jerusalem, 1924), p. 11.

272. See Responsa *Rambam* to Rabbi Pinhas, a judge in Alexandria, in *Pe'er Hador*; Samuel Avuhab, *Sefer Ha'Zikhronot* (Prague, 1650), p. 68a, and the intro. to his Responsa *Devar Shmuel* (Venice, 1702).

273. Y. Miller, Responsa *Gaonei Mizrah U'Maariv* (Berlin, 1888), no. 179.

274. See Responsa of the *Gaonim* (Harkavy ed.), no. 278.

275. See Bachrach, Responsa *Havat Yair*, no. 136.

276. Ibid.

277. Responsa of Hai Gaon, in *Ginzei Kedem* (Jerusalem, 1922), no. 1, p. 77.

278. See Talmud, *Avot*, ch. 5, Mishnah 9; *Yebamot* 6b; the Ordinances of Rabbi Jacob Tam in Finkelstein, *Jewish Self-Government*; The Records of the Lithuanian Council, sec. 67; Ordinances of the City of Cracow, Poland, in *Jahrbuch der Judisch Literarischen Gesellschaft*, 10:332–33; Moshe Zakut, *Shuda De'Daine*, below; Assaf, *Batei Ha'Din*, p. 15.

279. Shlomo ben Aderet, Responsa *Rashba*, vol. 3, no. 76; vol. 4, no. 16; Epstein, Intro., *Arukh Ha'Shulkhan, Hoshen Mishpat* (Pietrokoff, 1893).

nications placed upon those who attempted to litigate there. These excommunications could make social and commercial life impossible and were an extremely effective weapon.[280]

While few Jews in Poland and the Balkans attempted to utilize non-Jewish courts during the Middle Ages, they were apparently, used widely in Majorca and Italy.[281] The fact that the Jews in Germany had to repeatedly pronounce bans on the use of non-Jewish courts may indicate that there were serious lapses in this respect there, too. Applications to non-Jewish courts were also made by many of the Jewish Marranos who fled Spain and Portugal because of the Inquisition there, and who attempted to continue their practice of referring their suits to non-Jewish courts.[282] Many efforts were made to correct such practices. These included barring the facilities of the Jewish courts to such recalcitrants in other matters where they might need the aid of the Jewish courts.[283]

In those instances where the Jewish courts were powerless to dispense justice and to compel attendance, there often was resort to non-Jewish courts. Frequently, however, permission to do so was first required to be obtained from the Jewish courts.[284] Jewish restrictions on resort to non-Jewish courts, began to break down in Europe in the eighteenth century, when Jews were granted greater liberties to participate in the social and economic life of the larger society. This was particularly true in Germany:

> I have seen it here in the holy community of Metz, and it is so in the other communities in Germany, that the ordinances of the communities have permitted litigants in disputes over checks, to submit their disputes to non-Jewish courts. Who permitted this to them? . . . This practice appears very evil to me, but I do not have the power to abolish it, be-

cause it has become ingrained because of this ordinance.[285]

a. COMMUNAL PRESCRIPTIONS FOR JUDICIAL SYSTEMS

The roles of local and regional lay officials, rabbis, and professional judges in the Jewish decision-making processes in medieval Europe are reflected in transcommunal prescriptions regarding civil court procedure. These shed light on the power sharing and on the structure of checks and balances among the various local and transcommunal decision-makers.

Following are representative selections (translated from Hebrew by the author) from prescriptions in central Europe and in Italy in the later Middle Ages.

(1) *The Ordinances of the Jewish Community of Moravia (Sixteenth and Seventeenth Centuries)*

These prescriptions were arranged and recorded in the records of the Moravian community by Rabbi Menahem Krochmal in 1651. Most of these ordinances are from prior periods, many of them from the time of the famous Rabbi Judah Loewe, who was Rabbi of Nicholsburg from 1557–1577 and later Rabbi of Prague. These appear in S. Assaf, *Batei Ha'Din Ve'Sidrehem Akhare Khatimat Ha'Talmud* (Jerusalem, 1924), and Y. Halperin, *Takkanot Medinat Mehrin* (Jerusalem, 1952).

Section 60

If one of the heads of the province [one of the Jewish lay communal leaders, who also served as heads of local districts; the two terms, "head of province" and "head of district", are therefore used interchangeably] shall invite any of the people in his province to court, he may do so [under the law], and if the man shall fail or refuse to heed the head of that district, or shall refuse to do anything commanded of him, then the head of that district has the right to excommunicate him, and to fine him up to the sum of five Reichsthaler, but never more. Whoever supports the excommunicated one, or treats lightly the excommunication by the head of the district, shall likewise be excommunicated and fined like him in the sum of five Reichsthaler. In any case, however, the head of the province may not demand more than five Reichsthaler as security (in those cases) when he may (under the law) demand security.

Section 61

If the head of a province disqualifies somebody [from holding office or from testifying as a witness] for a specific time, or has rendered a sentence or verdict, the

280. See Chapter XI, Section B 1, below. See Assaf, *Batei Ha'Din*, p. 18 regarding the anathemas pronounced by Rabbi Gershom in Germany; those of Rabbi Jacob Tam in Meir ben Baruch, Responsa *Maharam* Rothenburg, at end (Prague ed.), and cited in Mordecai ben Hillel, Commentary *Mordecai* to Baba Kama, at end; and the anathemas pronounced in various synods in Germany through the Middle Ages (see Nathan Hanover, *Yeven Me'Tzula, supra*, in the Section on Law).

281. Assaf, *Batei Ha'Din*, p. 17; J. Mann, *The Jews in Egypt and in Palestine under the Fathimid Caliphs* (New York, 1970), vol. 2, no. 173; David Ibn Zimra, Responsa *Radvaz*, sec. 1, nos. 109, 115, and 1190.

282. Samuel DiMedina, Responsa *Maharashdam, Hos. Mis.*, supra, no. 327; Benebashti, Responsa *Baya Hayia*, sec. 1, no. 155.

283. Menahem of Merzberg, *Nimukei*, published at the end of Weil, Responsa *Mahari Weil*; Isserlis, Responsa *Rama, Ho. Mis.*, sec. 26.

284. Sherira Gaon, in Responsa of the *Gaonim* (Harkavy ed.), no. 233; Hayim Palagi, *Hukot Hayim* (Izmir, 1791), sec. 6; Assaf, *Batei Ha'Din*, p. 24.

285. See Eibschutz, *Urim Ve'Tumim*, sec. 26. See also Asher ben Yehiel, Responsa *Rosh*, sec. 18, no. 20, regarding the practice in thirteenth-century Spain.

new head who succeeds him [in office] may not relieve him of that penalty or fine without the consent of the three preceding heads, i.e., those who previously sat in judgment of that man, and their concurrence is necessary to relieve him [of the sentence or verdict].

Section 62

Whoever has an established residence and pays tax in one of the communities of one of the provinces, but is [also] a tax-farmer or owns a concession in a city or town in a different province, and somebody [there] has a controversy with this man—the plaintiff shall have the right to request him to appear before the head of the district which is nearest to him, and the defendant cannot excuse himself by saying, "I will go to the head of the district of the community to which I pay taxes." The head of the district that is nearest to the city or town where he conducts his tax-farming or his concession can coerce him to appear in judgment before him, but this is only where he will sit with him in judgment before a rabbi or [professional] judges, as provided for in the ordinance.

Section 63

The head of a province has no power nor authority to judge or punish the people in the [local] community, where he lives. Instead, they shall follow [i.e., are to be judged by] the other head of the province. In any case, if occasionally the heads and officials of the local community wish to coerce one of the householders in that community by pronouncing an excommunication upon him if he does not appear before them for trial, and that person excuses himself by saying, "I will go to the head of my district and I will prevail there," and the local heads or officials do not pay any attention to him, then the head of that province has the right to prevent them from pronouncing an excommunication upon him until that head of the district hears the matter. That householder shall be given enough time so that he can go to the head of the district and return. Similarly, if they wish to coerce him [to appear for trial] with other means of coercion, the head of the province has the right to prevent this, if he sees fit, until he goes to the head of the district and returns.

Section 64

If one has a claim against another regarding money matters, he does not have the right to subpoena him to appear before the head of the district, but is required to go to the court in his own community, before the judges or the chief judge [normally, the rabbi] if that community has an established rabbi or judges. But if no rabbi or judges have been established for that community, then the plaintiff has the right to subpoena him to [appear before] the head of the district, if the claim is for more than five gold pieces. If, however, the claim is less than five gold pieces, then he must go to trial with him in his own community, before the noble judges, or community lay leaders, or officials, may God preserve them.

Section 65

If one has a claim against the head of the local community, then if the claim is for five gold pieces [or less], he is able to, and may, subpoena him to trial to the head of the district, even though that community has established judges or a rabbi; this is certainly true if the claim is for more than five Reichsthaler. If the claim, however, is less than five Reichsthaler, he must go to trial with him before the rabbi of the community, or before the noble judges.

Section 66

If the head of the province subpoenas somebody to [appear for] trial before him, when he is permitted to do so, and there is a rabbi in the community where he lives, he must include with him [as judge] only the [aforementioned] rabbi of that community, and not any other rabbi.

Section 67

The judges of a community shall only judge money [i.e., commercial] matters. However, suits to recover for humiliation, slander, loss of earnings, medical bills, and like matters shall be judged by the lay heads and officials of the community, together with the rabbi, the chief judge of the community, if there is a chief judge in that community. If there is no chief judge [ordinarily, the community rabbi] there, then the lay leaders and officials, together with the judges, shall hear the matter. Nevertheless, neither the lay leaders or officials, nor the rabbi or judges, can fine one person more than five Reichsthalers, unless they are joined by the rabbi of the province, may he be preserved, in which case they may fine him up to twenty Reichsthalers, but not more. Similarly, the lay leaders and officials or judges cannot disqualify any person [from holding office, or being a witness] without being joined by the rabbi of the province, and then only if he sits with them as a judge. The consent of the head of the district shall be to no avail if given after they have disqualified him but before he had sat with them in judgment. If there is a head of a province in the community, they shall join him with the head of the district, both for imposing fines of twenty Reichsthalers, or in order to disqualify him as mentioned above.

Section 68

The head of a province may not judge [a matter] without the rabbi, even though the parties to the controversy come to him by themselves, or he comes to some place or community for purposes other than this case. If the rabbi is not there, he shall join a judge with him. If there are no judges there, he must join with him, someone else to be selected. Similarly, a rabbi of a community shall not judge a case alone but should join with him, the lay head of the community or [other] officials of the community, even in a place where there are no established judges. In a place in which there are established judges, he must have two judges join with him.

Section 69

Two heads of provinces that join together with one rabbi to sit in judgment have the rights and the powers of a council and are able to subpoena anyone who lives in that area and may punish and excommunicate anybody who refuses to come to them. . . .

Section 70

If it becomes known that within two weeks there will be [a session of] a council, even a small council, consisting of two heads of provinces, together with one rabbi, to judge between men, then even a defendant may, and has the power to, say, "I will go to the great court" [consisting of] two heads of provinces and one rabbi because of the biblical provision, "Justice, justice shall you pursue" (Deut. 16:20).

Section 71

The head of a province who subpoenas someone, in a case where he may subpoena him, to appear in judgment before him is not permitted to subpoena him, except to [appear in] the community in which the head of the province resides. If, however, the head of the province is in a different community, he may not subpoena anybody from another community to [appear in] that community unless it is before two heads of provinces, as set forth above. Then they are able to subpoena all of the people of that area, as set forth above.

Section 72

Regarding the expenses to be borne by one who subpoenas another to [appear before] a council, if he subpoenas him for judgment before a "complete" council, such as [consisting of four] heads of provinces and certainly all of them, he is not required to post security for the expenses. If he subpoenas him unjustly, they will perceive [and decide] how much the plaintiff shall pay for expenses [of travel]. If, however, he subpoenas him to a small council, that is, two heads of provinces

and one rabbi, the plaintiff is required to post security with the rabbi or the sexton [of the community] for the expenses of the defendant in the event that the subpoena is [held to be] unjust. If, however, it happens that the plaintiff is poor and has no security [to post], he shall present the matter before the head of the district, and if the head of the district thinks that there is substance to his claim, and that he does not have security [to post], the head of the district may give him a writing, signed by him, to the effect that his adversary is required to come, pursuant to the subpoena, even though he does not post security.

Section 73

Unless the claim is for at least five Reichsthaler, no person may subpoena another [to appear] before the complete council of five heads of provinces. Similarly, if the matter [claim] is one concerning humiliation, fines, quarrels, and disputes, Heaven forbid; similarly, with regard to a council of four heads of provinces, which is also called a "complete council."

Section 74

Every half year two heads of the district must convene a council in their district in one of the communities in which they wish to establish seats of justice to decide between men. They shall join any rabbi with them, and they shall notify all of the communities in their district, which have quarrels or disputes, in order that they shall know to come to judgment at the appointed day to the council. If, in that place, there is one who is selected [to be on the council], they are obligated to join him, as well as to sit with them in judgment. The head of the district is obligated to announce [this] every half year in the synagogue in every community in the area. Whoever has any case against another, shall present his matter before the head of the district. They shall also announce whether they [the litigants] are obligated to pay judgment fees for their [the heads of the provinces, etc.] expenses, or not; and, in general, they [the heads] shall not incur any expenses for the province [with regard to] this council. If, however, any community or individual is able to prevail upon the rabbi of the province to join the two heads of the district in their area, then the two heads of the district are obligated to send to the rabbi of the province [inviting him] to join them in that district.

Section 75

If any community requests that one or two heads of the district shall come to them, they are required to come and hear their cases, on the condition that they shall be joined by a rabbi and that all of the expenses shall be borne by that community.

Section 76

If it shall be found that anyone acted improperly, that he did not deal in good faith, or that he disgraced God in any matter, or acted in any way improperly, the head of the district is required to subpoena him to appear before him, and to rebuke him, to punish him and fine him as much as he is worth [provided he is] joined by one rabbi or one learned judge, as set forth above. He shall not, however, issue any decision on any matter out of his presence, nor even to require him to post security on any matter, unless he subpoenas him to appear in judgment before him. If he refuses to go, or evades coming, then he may *excommunicate* him, or *fine* him because of this, even though he is not present [emphasis added].

Section 77

In any council of the noble heads of a province, may they be preserved, whether a complete council or whether a small council, they may join with them only one rabbi, but not two, and certainly [not] more. However, without one rabbi with them, they are not permitted to convene at all to judge between one man and another, but the rabbi of the province must be with them in the complete council and [any] rabbi in the small council, or even [any] rabbi in the complete council, if the rabbi of the province, may God preserve him, is not there.

Section 78

If one has a complaint concerning one of the noble former heads of a province, that is, one who was a head of a province in the preceding three years, he must go for judgment with him in his city before the [professional] judges, if it is a claim of money, or before the heads and officials of the community, together with the rabbi or established judges, if it is a claim concerning humiliation or quarrels, Heaven forbid. If, however, the plaintiff wishes to subpoena him to appear before the head of the province, he may not, and is not able to subpoena him unless they convene at least three heads of provinces and one rabbi with them, whether it be a claim for money or other matters. Any former head of a province who was not head of a province in the preceding three years, is to be treated like any other man and has no greater privileges than they.

Section 79

If the head of a province shall penalize anyone in his district for any reason, [such as one] who is not behaving properly or [if] a judgment was rendered [in a case concerning] another and him, and that man opened a big mouth unjustly against him, then *the head of the province is able, and may, do with that man as he desires and excommunicate him, imprison him, or fine him*. In any case he can, and may, decide on his own—provided, however, that the head of a province should conduct himself gently with the people and shall not treat them disrespectfully, since perhaps, Heaven forbid, the head of the province may [act so as to] cause one to open a big mouth against him, and no man may be held [to account] for [any acts that he commits because of] his anguish. If it shall be found that the head of the province acted wrongly against an individual and excommunicated him, fined him, or otherwise punished him unjustly, if this shall be established, then a well-publicized public announcement shall be made in that community that the excommunication was never valid, and the fine shall be returned to him out of the pocket of the head of the province. The noble officers, the heads of the provinces, may the Lord protect them, shall issue a decision concerning the head of the province who did this and shall not, Heaven forbid, defer to that head of a province [emphasis added].

Section 80

All of the fines levied by the noble heads of provinces, may God protect them, whether by all or some or one of them, shall be recorded in a just and true fashion, and they shall render an account as to how the fines (monies) were disbursed.

Section 81

When the head of a district shall excommunicate anybody in his area, for whatever reason, and the excommunicated one shall not pay any attention and remains excommunicated for eight days without repenting from his evil ways, in order to evade the excommunication, then that great excommunication shall be communicated to his associates, the noble heads of provinces in other areas. They are obligated to also pronounce an excommunication upon him in all of these areas. Whoever will permit the excommunicated one to enter his house, after the announcement was made in the communities as set forth above, or any head of a community that permits him to attend the synagogue in his community, shall be fined with a very huge fine, and shall be punished with excommunication and ostracism, as set forth above.

Section 82

Every place shall judge cases in accordance with the ordinances, and a head of a district who comes to a community for other purposes may subpoena litigants to appear before him and a rabbi or judge. If one sues another before a [joint session of a] head of the province and rabbi, then the defendant cannot have the case heard by another head of a district, or by the rabbi of the province, may God preserve him, and certainly not by the council, unless the council is to be convened [anyway] within two weeks from the date that he demands that he come to court. The foregoing, however, applies only to a suit by one individual against another. If, however, there is a quarrel among the members of the community concerning the affairs of the community, regarding appointments [of officials], or regarding the income of the community, or regarding the ordinances of the community, or the selection of a rabbi, a cantor, a sexton, and other communal matters, whatever they may be, or if an individual has a quarrel with a community, whether he is the plaintiff or defendant, and [the claim] is for more than ten [gold pieces], or there is a quarrel between the community and the rabbi of the community, whatever it may be, this is a judgment for the great [ones] and even an individual or rabbi may say, "I will go to the great court and have the case judged before the two heads of the district, together with the rabbi, or by the rabbi of the province together with the head of the district"; and certainly the members of a community may say this. The man who says, "I will go to the great court" is required to prevail upon one head of a district, or upon the rabbi of the province, to come within thirty days to one of the communities in that area to judge between them. This need not be in their own community, as long as it is in that district. Those who sit in judgment shall decide who shall bear the expenses of the second head of the district, or of the rabbi of the province, may God preserve him, or whether one, or both, adversaries shall bear them, as they see fit. . . .

Section 213

None of the noble heads of provinces are able, or permitted, to change any judgment of the head of the court [the rabbi] or [of] the judges and the head of the court, or [of] the judges or head of the community, unless the fee for the appeal ("*appilazian*") has been paid, and he will see it written and sealed that the fee for the appeal ("*appilazia*") [*sic.*] has been paid, and unless he also sees their claims and answers.

Section 214

A judgment for a sum of less than ten gold pieces cannot be appealed at all, even if it is a judgment of judges who sat without a rabbi. On a judgment that is for ten gold pieces or more, it is possible to appeal, but the execution of the judgment shall not be held back by this [appeal]. The defendant [appellant] must carry out the judgment, but the plaintiff [appellee] must post a certain and sufficient surety that if the judgment is overturned, then the money will be returned to the

defendant completely. If he [the plaintiff] does not have a sufficient and certain surety, then the sum that the defendant is required to pay shall remain with the court. If the defendant is not able to fulfill his obligation to carry out the judgment, *the court shall coerce him to carry out the judgment*, in accordance with the ordinances, *by excommunication or imprisonment*, as *appropriate*. Nevertheless, although the defendant is not able to carry out the decision of the court, he does not lose his right to appeal because, since the court can coerce him [to carry out its decision it is certain that] he [will] fullfill the decision [emphasis added].

Section 215

The appellate procedure shall be as follows: If the decision shall be by one of the judges without a rabbi, an appeal cannot be taken unless an appellant posts cash security of one Reichsthaler with the noble judges within two days (or posts security in the form of property if he does not have cash). The judges shall then give him a writing, setting forth the decision of the court, with the arguments of both parties, well and truly clarified. The case shall then be heard by two heads of the district, together with one rabbi. If the decision [of the lower court] shall be found to be in error, the decision shall be overturned, and the monies posted for the appeal with the judges shall be returned to the appellant.

If the decision [to be appealed] was from a rabbi and judges, then the appeal money in the sum of two Reichsthalers shall be posted within two days; that is, two gold pieces for the rabbi and one gold piece for the judges. This, however, only applies in the case of a rabbi who maintains an academy of law for [at least] six youths. If the decision [to be appealed from] was by one head of a province together with a rabbi, then appeal money in the sum of four Reichsthalers shall be posted within two days, and the case shall be heard on appeal only before a complete council, that is, at least four heads of provinces, together with one rabbi, if the rabbi of the province is not present. If the decision appealed from shall be found to be in error, it shall be overruled, and the appeal money posted shall be returned. If the appellant loses on appeal, he is then required to pay his adversary all of his damages and expenses [resulting from the appeal].

Section 216

If the decision [of the lower court] required an oath [of one of the litigants], whether simple or weighty, the one required to take the oath may not post appeal money [and take an appeal, thereby avoiding the oath] but is required to fulfill the decision of the court. His adversary may, however, post appeal money [and take an appeal], even where his opponent is required to take the oath.

Section 217

There shall be no appeal from decisions [awarding damages] for humiliation and slander. The decision shall be carried out.

Section 218

No head of a district may issue a writing [required] for an appeal to a community, unless he has ascertained that money or property has been posted as security for the appeal, pursuant to the ordinances. . . ."

(2) The Ordinances of the Jewish Community of Mantova, Italy (1677)

[EDITOR'S NOTE—The following selections from the Ordinances of the Jewish Community of Mantova, are translated from Hebrew by the author. They are from the writings of Moshe Zakut, a noted medieval Jewish scholar–decision-maker, in his *"Shuda De'Daine"* (literally, "The Discretion of the Judges"), published in 1678 in Mantova. A new edition by Judge Ya'akov Bazak appeared in *Matitya*, the Tenth Anniversary Volume of the Yeshivat B'nai Akiba (Jerusalem, 1972).

These ordinances, adopted in 1677, represent an excellent example of carefully thought out and well-written Jewish medieval ordinances, designed to govern litigation and appeals for the types of controversies that were common at that time. These ordinances are noted for their clarity and their willingness to depart from traditional Jewish law in order to meet the needs of litigants of that era. Rabbi Zakut lived in a period of rapidly expanding and increasingly complex commercial activities, and he designed the ordinances to be appropriate to the circumstances existing at that time. Societal conditions then were in many ways different from those that had existed during the period of the redaction of the Talmud (see Bazak, pp. 49, 51).]

The following is a copy of the language of the agreement of the general council [the representatives of the members of the community, who acted as a legislative body] of all of the population of the holy communities, both those who pay taxes and those who do not pay [previously, those who did not pay taxes had not been able to participate in the general council].

[Dated] this third day of February 1676, after announcements in all of the synagogues, and after all of the officials had notified by letter all of the cities in this state that they should come and be present in the city at the aforementioned time. All of this was done at the request of our master, Rabbi Moshe Zakut, may the Lord watch and preserve him, who expounded and proved with logical arguments, convincing to those with

understanding, the great need for the people of this state to institute procedures and establish rules in order to eliminate the quarrels that continue to arise daily between men regarding money matters and to preserve the truth and peace among them. They agreed, by vote of one hundred and twenty "yeas" to thirteen "nays," that the members of the small council [which acted as an executive board], together with the honorable aforementioned sage, shall present and establish for the future those general rules that are just in their eyes. They shall decide on the rules that they see fit, both general and detailed, regarding the drafting of all types of documents and writings, including their validation and cancellation and, similarly, regarding any transaction or matter that might arise (there being nothing that is not included under this general heading), and regarding all quarrels, both relating to their procedure and substance. And all of the rules that they shall establish, and the laws that they shall decide, and the methods of procedures that they shall set forth by majority vote shall be laws and statutes forever, never to pass away. (All of this, after obtaining the necessary authorization for the Honorable Exalted One [the Duke of Mantova], may the Lord preserve him).

Introduction

I [Rabbi Moshe Zakut] paid close attention to this matter . . . to draft various ordinances regarding money matters, which (ordinances) are proper, planned out, great, and reliable. I derived wisdom from the elders [of preceding eras] who had promulgated many ordinances, even contrary to the laws,[286] as the ordinance of Rabbi Gershom, *Me'Or Ha'Golah* [an eminent eleventh-century rabbi in Germany], all in accordance with their wise discretion. . . .

In order to transform my thoughts into deeds, I expressed my views to the heads of the community, people of substance and exaltation . . . and when they heard my advice, they unanimously agreed with my views. . . . Then, in accordance with their instructions, all of the residents of this holy community were called together, and their call went out to all of the residents of the district, who were all gathered here together. They notified them concerning what they had agreed to, in order that their rules would be effective for their quiet, peace, and tranquility in all sorts of commercial ven-

---

286. Editor's note: See, e.g., the Responsum of Rabbi Gershom in Responsa *Khakhme Zarfat Ve'Lotar*, sec. 97, which concludes with the words, "Therefore, whatever the communities have done, their ordinances are (valid) ordinances, and their acts are (valid) acts . . ." See also Chapter VIII, Section A 1, above. Some of the important changes in traditional law effected by the ordinances of Mantova are pointed out briefly in the "Editor's notes" herein.

tures and transactions. And they, nearly all of them
. . . agreed and accepted the proposal of their leaders,
and voted to accept their words, because they relied
upon me and upon their exalted leaders to promulgate
whatever was necessary . . . At that happy hour the
leaders hurried to request the permission and aid of our
exalted lord, the duke, may the Lord preserve him. . . .
We, therefore, assembled for a number of days, and
they debated all of the recorded topics that I placed
before the honorable and wise members of the small
council, and by a great majority, agreed to them. . . .
We all, therefore, command and ordain that all those
who dwell in our community and provinces shall from
today on be careful to follow, fulfill, and validate all
of the aforementioned rules . . . all of which will be
recorded and will be sweet and pleasant to those who
love quiet, will destroy quarrels, and keep away causes
of damage and hatred. . . .

I. . . . We have concluded and stated that in all
transactions that may be undertaken from today on
regarding money matters, no defendant may support
his case by claiming, "I possess established [precedent
that I follow"].[287] In every case where the *Shulkhan
Arukh*[288] rules on a matter it shall be followed, and it
shall be so, even though there are other authorities who
disagree with his ruling. . . .[289]

IV. In the event that the weight of legal authority
on both sides is evenly divided, the matter shall be
decided by the sages of the *yeshiva*[290] in accordance
with the majority opinion, from which no one may
depart.

V. The following shall be done at all times, when
there is a puzzling matter, whether in financial affairs
or concerning ritual or sacerdotal matters. All of the
decision-makers shall gather together, discuss the matter, and after debate the truth shall be clarified (and
shall be established) according to the majority.

VII. For righteousness and justice, the rabbi and the
small council, may the Lord preserve them, shall supervise the truthful appointment of two types of judges,
divided (recorded) into two lists: one, of scholars of
the law, and the second, of laymen.[291] They shall send
and call for all those who appear to be fit to be chosen,
and when any man appears before them, they shall
alert and urge him to accept willingly an appointment
[as judge] among his brethren to help the Lord in the
fulfillment of his laws for an extended period of time,
for the benefit of the members of this holy community,
may the Lord preserve them. Whoever accepts upon
himself the yoke of Heaven shall be remembered for
good and shall sign a document that shall be placed in
the list appropriate for him. The two lists shall be maintained in the house of the rabbi, and from that time on
everyone [recorded in those lists] is required to serve
in his appointed duty, whenever his turn shall arrive.
They shall not be able to evade [service] by excuses,
unless they give an appropriate excuse for such avoid-
ance. . . .

If there shall be a dispute between people regarding
any matter, and if they both agree to select two judges
in accordance with the accepted procedure of selection,
they may choose whomever they wish. If both, or one
of them, wish [to select] one of those recorded in the
lists, the rabbi shall select two or one of them. If the
plaintiff shall select his judge but the defendant shall
refuse and shall not make his choice [for judge], the
rabbi shall send the sextant three times to warn him to
hurry [to make the selection]. If he still refuses, he shall
be publicly declared to be one who refuses [to heed
the courts].[292] If, despite this, he is still not chastised,
the rabbi shall select one judge from the list and shall
subpoena him one time, with a warning that the matter
will be heard *ex parte*, with the court listening only to
the claims of the other litigant. If he still refuses and
does not appear, the plaintiff shall receive a proclamation of excommunication [against the defendant], and
they shall give him [the plaintiff] a decision of the court,
to do with him as necessary. This is done to him because he persists in his rebellion and stupidity.

VIII. If the defendant will demand of the plaintiff,
"Advise me as to the nature of your quarrel with me,"
the plaintiff must then advise him only as to what type
of claim or claims [he has], without [being required to]
advise him as to any proof; [he is] only [required to
give him] some very general information, so that the
defendant will be able to select a judge, as appropriate.[293]

287. Editor's note: I.e., that there is legal authority relied on
by the plaintiff, contrary to the prevailing authorities relied
on by a court hearing the case.

288. Editor's note: The authoritative Jewish Code of Laws,
written by Joseph Karo (Chapter IX, Section B, below).

289. Editor's note: The claim of a litigant that his position
was supported by a legal authority, despite prevailing legal
opinion by others, had often blocked the rendering of decisions
in legal disputes. See Y. Bazak, *"Shuda De'Daine"* in Matitya
(Jerusalem, 1972), p. 57, n. 4; Isserlin, Responsa *Terumat
Ha'Deshen*, sec. 310; Benebashti, *Keneset Ha'Gedola, Ho. Mis.*,
sec. 25; Epstein, *Arukh Ha'Shulkhan*; and Y. Lorberbaum, in
Netivot Ha'Mispat to *Shulkhan Arukh, Ho. Mis.*, sec. 25, subsec. 13.

290. Editor's note: The designated name in Mantova for the
Upper Court.

291. Note the similarity to the British jury system, in which
the judge determines the law while the jury, consisting of the
parties' peers, determines the facts.

292. Editor's note: He could then be excommunicated or
subjected to other penalties; see Kolon, Responsa *Maharik*,
cited in Isserlis, *Darke Moshe to Tur, Ho. Mis.*, sec. 11, subsec. 1.

293. Editor's note: See the Responsa of Moshe Zakut, the
author of these ordinances, in his Responsa *Ramaz* (Venice,

IX. Since, according to law, the plaintiff may appoint someone to represent him in his stead, and it is customary to select someone who is clever and sharp, and sometimes the defendant is simple, not knowing what to ask [or contend], or how to read his documents, or make his calculations; the defendant shall, therefore, also be permitted to appoint a representative [in his stead (i.e., a lawyer)] who will be able to carry out his agency properly. See Chapter IX, Section C 2 c (3), below.

X. The court shall have the power to render a compromise judgment, even without an act of the parties which evidences their assent (to such compromise) . . . whenever they [the judges] see fit, or in a matter which cannot be clarified, and so on. This includes judges selected by the parties to decide the matter, who may also effect a compromise, on condition that this shall be upon the advice of the just members of the *yeshiva* [the high court in Mantova].

XI. In any controversy, whenever the parties execute a Document of Compromise, called "*compromiso*," in which they state under oath that they will not demand, "Show me the legal principle on which you based your judgment of my case,"[294] then any decision that the judges shall render shall be valid and binding, and no one shall set aside their decision. But, if there was no written oath to this effect, even if they both agreed to this, then, if one of the litigants shall seek to dispute the court decision, he shall come before the members of the *yeshiva* within eight days, but not more. They shall send for the judges to advise them [of] the principles upon which they based their decision. If their decision was correct, it shall be certified [by the members of the *yeshiva*], and if it departed from justice, they shall overrule it. All that they decide, shall be done. . . .

XII. If two persons agree to litigate with each other, and shall select their choices [to hear the case], or shall accept [a judge for the case] voluntarily, even a single judge, then, even though they did not execute a document [of compromise] selecting judges, and did not perform any acts evidencing their consent, they cannot change their minds after one, or both of them, have presented and completed their contention before them or him. . . .

XIII. If two judges sit on a case and disagree, one saying, "This one shall prevail" and the other saying, "He shall lose," they shall add a third party as judge, as is customary. If, after they have discussed the matter, only two of them shall agree with each other, the decision shall not state that there was a difference of opinion. All three must sign the written decision.[295]

XIV. Furthermore, if, after they have heard the contentions of the litigants, one of the three judges says, "I do not know," it is not necessary to bother to add still another judge. They shall simply say to him, "Go to the *yeshiva* and ask the decision-makers, and follow their decision."

XVII. . . . From now on we decree and clarify that, with [regard to] all types of gifts and testamentary wills, whether it is established by two reliable witnesses that the donor or testator has orally stated that it is his desire and wish, out of his own free will and [out of] his decision to benefit the donees that he names, in such case, whatever he desires, shall be valid and shall not be voided because of claims [that something was amiss], whether in the phraseology utilized, the manner of acts performed,[296] or in the types of rights, for whomever he wishes and whatever he wishes on any matter. Whatever he states orally shall be valid and binding, even if it is contrary to legal precedent.[297]

XVIII. Furthermore, all of the members of our community shall be qualified and deemed reliable to testify as witnesses or to act as judges in any matter, even though they are personally concerned, since the matter is one which may benefit the community [and which may, therefore, indirectly benefit them, too] with regards to estates, gifts, and charitable donations to the poor or to scholars of the law and others; unless, however, they are disqualified because of near relationship, or because of their violation of law publicly announced; and provided, further, that they do not have any personal benefit from the matter for themselves. Similarly, if there shall be a dispute between communities, it shall not be necessary to select judges from a different place, but they shall be permitted to select judges from their midst, as they desire, and they shall not have to resort to people from other places.[298]

1661), sec. 14. He explains that certain legal issues are commonly decided by reference to precedent, while other issues are decided in accordance with the customs and practices of the marketplace. The defendant must, therefore, be aware of the precise issues involved, so that he can select the proper judge, either a scholar or lay businessman, as appropriate. Compare to the bill of particulars in the American legal system.

294. Editor's note: A right traditionally accorded to every litigant in a court of law; see Karo, *Shulkhan Arukh*, sec. 14, subsec. 1.

295. See Moshe Zakut, Responsa *Ramaz*, sec. 31; Bazak, *The Judge in Hebrew Law* (Hebrew; Jerusalem, 1961), p. 30. This should be compared with American judicial practice, in which minority, dissenting opinions are specified and their authors identified.

296. Editor's note: Certain acts were necessary in traditional Jewish law to certify or establish the acquisition of title.

297. Editor's note: This provision follows the principle that decision-makers may change established biblical rule regarding money matters; see Part Two, Chapter V, Section D 8.

298. Editor's note: This provision, too, represented a change from traditional Jewish law; see Chapter IX, Section A 2, below.

XIX. All documents, including all types of documents of sale or loan, or other transactions, shall not require the scribes to extend themselves to include all of the detailed provisions and practices that were customary until now. If they desire, they may include a provision in short form that the document was made in accordance with all of the necessary conditions and practices that were customary, pursuant to the agreement of both parties. This will be of great aid.

XX. Furthermore, any document that the rabbi of the communities signs in place of one witness, or if two witnesses sign and the rabbi authenticates it, shall be deemed authenticated as though by a court of three judges.

XXI. All documents that are sold by one person to another, whether promissory notes of Jews or promissory notes of non-Jews, shall be transferable by delivery alone;[299] provided, however, that the seller who transfers such document will execute an assignment called the *girota*, as is customary among merchants. It is not necessary to write out, "This document, and all property upon which it is a lien, is acquired by you," since the transferor intends this. . . .

XXIII. . . . With regard to any written [obligation] that the obligor admits was written by him, he shall not be believed to say, "I paid it," even though he swears to this. Indeed, a handwritten document and a document that was authenticated by a court shall be equal[ly enforceable], in order not to close the doors [of credit] in the face of borrowers.[300]

XXIV. Any man who has children and who, before his death, desires to order that his wife shall manage all of his property, shall not be able to do this unless he orders that two trustees shall be joined with her. If he does not do this, then the members of the small council shall be obligated to appoint them after his death, and they shall have powers like trustees who are appointed by the decedent. This will grant help for the orphaned heirs, and will always benefit them.

XXV. At the order of the rabbi and the small council, a trustworthy and skillful man shall be appointed to be the town clerk. They shall arrange for him to have a record book in which the total number of pages shall be recorded, and at the bottom of each page the rabbi shall sign his name. In that book the clerk shall record all of the detailed provisions of agreements [between grooms and brides] or of *ketubot* [prenuptial agreements made by husband and wife at the time of

their marriage], so that, if they shall be lost at any time, they [the husbands] shall not remain with their wives without a *ketubah*.[301] Also, whoever desires can order the clerk to copy documents of sale or admissions of obligation, or obligations, gifts, wills, or the form of notes, policies, and court decisions. Any type of writings that are recorded there shall be deemed authenticated and established as valid, even for relatives of the clerk. This is so even though, under the law or religion, they would be invalid because of the language utilized, or because of the absence of any of the provisions required by our sages or by our religion, which require authentication. There shall not apply here the rules regarding invalidation of a document by its holder,[302] nor the cancellation of debts as a result of the passage of a Sabbatical Year.[303] The validation and drafting [of these instruments] shall be without any argument or contention [disputing their validity] at all. When anyone needs a copy of any writing recorded there, he shall go to the clerk, who shall copy it and attest to its validity with his signature, and his signature shall be relied upon.

XVI. This is the Book of Ordinances upon which we have agreed, all being established as necessary for our benefit, in order to quiet disputes and to preserve our faith. Our attention is focused upon the future, and not on the past. We hereby notify all of the people of our city and district that, by the power given to us by the residents of our community, we retain the power, together with the head of our *yeshiva*, to clarify any doubt that may occur in the wording of our ordinances, and also the right to add to them if we think it fit to do so, so that they shall be for our good and benefit for as long as it shall be the will of our exalted lord [the Duke], may his honor be increased . . . and all is established and validated with our signatures. . . .

(Signed by fifteen representatives of the community)

b. The Selection and Approval of Jewish Judges

In Palestine, as long as the institution of the patriarchate (*nasi*) existed, the patriarch appointed whomever he thought proper as judges. Similarly, the exilarch (*resh galuta*) in Babylonia appointed judges for the various Jewish communities there. However, beginning at about the ninth century, the heads of the Jewish

299. Editor's note: Without the necessity of an additional writing, evidencing the transfer as traditionally required; see Karo, *Shulkhan Arukh, Ho. Mis.*, sec. 66, subsec. A.

300. Editor's note: Contrary to traditional law, which requires that every document for any obligation be authenticated by a court; see Karo, *Shulkhan Arukh, Ho. Mis.*, sec. 46, subsec. 1.

301. Editor's note: Cohabitation without physical possession of the *ketubah* document is prohibited under traditional law in order to protect the economic rights of the wife, which are provided for in such marriage agreements; see Rambam, Laws of Marriage, 10:10.

302. Editor's note: Because the holder admits that part of the loan set forth therein has been paid, see Karo, *Shulkhan Arukh, Ho. Mis.*, sec. 84.

303. See Deut. 15:2. The foregoing provisions, too, changed traditional Jewish law.

academies of law in Babylonia (*gaonim*) acquired "jurisdiction" over certain of the communities there and selected and appointed the judges.[304] Subsequently, the heads of the academies acquired the exclusive right, at times, to select and appoint judges for all of the Jewish communities in Babylonia. At other times this right was retained by the exilarch.[305]

It is interesting to note, however, that during much of the latter portion of the gaonic era, a judge, whether appointed by the exilarch or the head of the academy, did not sit in judgment alone. It was, instead, traditional for him to select two of the prominent members of the community to sit with him as judges in all cases.[306] This apparently gave the judgments of the court greater acceptance and authority in the eyes of the members of the community. Similarly, the heads of the communities would write back to the exilarch (or head of the academy) rating the judge on how well, or poorly, he performed his functions. If they were severely critical of him, he would often be removed by his appointors.[307] Local communities, in effect, exercised a modified power of veto and recall over the judges selected.[308]

There was sometimes specific provision for the recall of a judge in the middle of his term because of complaints by the community. In the Spanish communities this was done by the "royal rabbi" (*rab de la corte*) if he received a written request from the majority of taxpayers and residents of a community.[309] In other communities the judges could be removed by the heads of the communities.[310]

In Europe and North Africa each community would select its own judges,[311] and in many communities judges were selected each year for a term of one year only.[312]

In Eastern Europe, while the judges were selected by the local community, this was not done in a completely democratic way (see Section B, above, with regard to election of other community officials). In the community of Cracow, Poland, for example, twenty-three selected members of the community (including fourteen members of the executive council, four "heads," and five of the "good persons" (see Section B 1 *a* [5], above; would each write down the name of his preferred candidate on a piece of paper. The papers were then placed in a box and a secretary would draw nine of these. These men would then select five "electors," who would, in turn, be cloistered in a room day and night until they chose the persons to fill all of the community positions, including judgeships. The number of judges chosen by the various communities would depend on the size of the community, with some choosing five[313] or more,[314] some two or three, and others choosing only one.[315]

Though it appears that normally only qualified candidates were chosen as judges, this was not always the case. There are recorded complaints that the "heads" and other prominent persons in the community who participated directly in selecting judges would often engage in "log-rolling" and would choose their own friends and relatives.[316] The need for judges to be selected annually often resulted in their feeling completely dependent upon the good will of the officers of the community who made the selections. This, too, could lead to great favoritism.[317] Apparently, however, this was not very widespread; it was not rare, however, judging by the repeated admonitions made against such practices.[318]

In medeval communities there were always a number of men, learned in talmudic law and known for their piety, who had the title, "*rav*" (rabbi), "*khaver*" (colleague), or "*morenu*" (our teacher). Such titles were

304. See Harkavy, *Tshuvot Ha'Gaonim*, pp. 355–56; Report of Natan Ha'Bavli, in A. Neubauer, *Seder Ha'Khakhamim, Ve'-Korot Ha'Yamim* (reprinted Jerusalem, 1967), sec. 2, p. 86. Compare A. Aptowitzer, *Jewish Quarterly Review*, n.s. 4, vol. 31.

305. See The *Travels of Benjamin of Tudela* (ed. A. Asher, New York, 1927); the Travels of Petahia of Regensberg in *Sibbuv* (ed. L. Gruenhut, Jerusalem, 1905); Assaf, *B'ate Ha'-Din Ve'Sidrehem* (Jerusalem, 1924), p. 39.

306. See Natan Ha'Bavli, in Neubauer, *Seder Ha'Khakhamim*.

307. Ibid.

308. Surprisingly enough, Assaf (*B'ate Ha'Din*, p. 41) cites this practice as evidence that the judge was completely independent of the communities where he performed his duties!

309. In Finkelstein, *Jewish Self-Government*, Ordinances of Valladolid, p. 359; see also pp. 356–57.

310. Y. Al-Barceloni, *Sefer Ha'Shtarot* (reprinted Jerusalem, 1957), p. 131.

311. This was, apparently, the case in Palestine after the termination of the patriarchate; see Harkavy, *Tshuvot Ha'-Gaonim*, sec. 180; Al-Barceloni, pp. 7, 131.

312. See the Ordinances of the Jewish communities of Cas-

tilia at the Synod of Valladolid in 1432, in Finkelstein, *Jewish Self-Government*, pp. 356–57; Shlomo ben Aderet, Responsa *Rashba*, vol. 3, secs. 417, 422–25; vol. 5, sec. 284; Isaac ben Sheshet Perfet, Responsa *Rivash*, secs. 214, 228. Similar provisions are found in the records of the community of Zalkava, Poland, in Buber, *Kirya Nisgava* (Cracow, 1903), pp. 94–107; in Lithuania, as recorded in Fein, *Kirya Ne'Emana*, p. 41; and in Cracow, Poland, as recorded in the records of that community. See Assaf, *Bate Ha'Din*, p. 44.

313. Isaac ben Sheshet Perfet, Responsa *Rivash*, no. 228.

314. See Section *d*, below; D. Shohet, *The Jewish Court in the Middle Ages* (New York, 1931), 159.

315. Shlomo ben Aderet, Responsa *Rashba*, vol. 3, no. 385, 388.

316. J. L. Puhavitzer, *Diveri Ha'Yamim* (Hamburg, 1692), ch. 23; Luntshitz, *Amudei Shesh*, Section on Laws.

317. Ibid.; Judah Loewe of Prague, *Netivot Olam* (Prague, 1595), sec. on "Laws," ch. 2.

318. See, e.g., Zelig Margolis, Introduction to *Khiburei Likutim*, (Venice, 1715).

also found in the communities in the Near East.[319] It was from among persons with these qualifications, especially those with the title "rabbi," that professional judges were chosen. See, however, Section B 2 h, below, for the common practice in Europe for lay community leaders to serve as judges. Many of these laymen were learned and were the recipients of scholarly titles.[320]

c. THE COMPENSATION OF JUDGES

Traditionally there was always opposition among Jews to judges receiving compensation (whether from the litigants or otherwise), out of fear that this would lead to corruption.[321] Accordingly, the judges were ordained scholar–laymen who took time out from their occupations to hear cases. Nevertheless, judges in both Palestine and Babylonia during the first few centuries C.E. were paid for the time that they lost in their occupations or trade while acting as judges.[322]

Beginning in about the ninth century, the Jewish communities in Babylonia were taxed in order to support the professional judges.[323] The spread of the practice of compensation for judges appears to have been retarded by the strong positions taken by Rambam against the practice of utilizing knowledge of the Torah to obtain compensation.[324]

In Poland and Germany, particularly from the fifteenth century on, Jewish judges received compensation from fees paid by both litigants. Often the judges would have no other income. Initially the size of these fees was dependent upon the good will of the litigants, and the judge was not expected to demand outright payment of a fee in any amount. Apparently, however, enough judges violated this expected behavior for the Lithuanian Council to promulgate an ordinance in 1673 that "No court in the world may specifically demand the payment of a fee for hearing the case [by saying] "give such and such sum"; only, whatever the litigants contribute voluntarily, they should accept."[325]

The practice eventually became widespread in many communities for the litigants to pay a fixed fee, set in accordance with the size of the suit.[326] The practice of judges to accept fees directly from the litigants aroused great opposition among many of the eminent rabbis and scholars because it resembled bribery too closely. It might, in fact, lead to the payment of an extra "fee" by one of the litigants in an attempt to unduly influence a judge.[327]

A few rabbis and judges who disapproved of this practice voluntarily renounced the acceptance of any kind of fee for sitting as a judge. Sheftel Horowitz[328] relates that his father, one of the most eminent and pious Jewish scholars in seventeenth-century Germany, regretted the fact that he had accepted judicial fees in his younger days and ceased this practice when he became older. His letter of appointment as Rabbi of the City of Frankfurt, in 1606, specifically provided that he voluntarily relinquished receipt of any judicial fees.

There appears to be little question that an independent judiciary, not forced to accept fees from individual litigants in the cases before it, would have adhered to higher standards of justice than those which, in fact, sometimes prevailed in Jewish courts.[329] The economic status of the Jews in Poland and Lithuania, however, declined brutally, particularly in the aftermath of the periodic massacres and invasions there. To avoid poverty, judges and rabbis were forced to accept fees to act as judges. They avoided the traditional restrictions on such practices by relying on technical distinctions, such as that most of their judgments were based upon compromises between the litigants, rather than upon a strict interpretation of the law. Compromise judgments, they maintained, were not encompassed by the traditional opposition to the acceptance of judicial fees.[330]

d. THE COMPOSITION AND NUMBER OF JUDGES OF JEWISH COURTS

There were a number of different types of courts existing in Jewish communities throughout the Middle

319. Hanover, *Yevan Metzula*, sec. on "Torah"; Mann, *The Jews in Egypt and Palestine Under the Fatimid Caliphs* (New York, 1970) 1:264; see Harkavy, *Tshuvot Ha'Gaonim*, sec. 233.

320. See also Avuhab, *Sefer Ha'Zikhronot*; Assaf, *Bate Ha'-Din*, p. 47; see also Section 2 a, above, for the selection of judges by the litigants themselves in certain instances.

321. See Talmud, *Bekhorot*, ch. 4, Mishnah 6.

322. Assaf, *Le'Korot Ha'Rabbanut*, in *Be'Ahalei Yaakov*, p. 44.

323. See the testimony of Natan Ha'Bavli, in Neubauer, *Seder Ha'Khakhamim*; N. Koronil, *Tshuvot Ha'Gaonim* (Vienna, 1871), sec. 82; the assertions of Judah Al-Barceloni, cited in Yaakov ben Asher, *Tur, Hos. Mish.*, sec. 9.

324. See his commentary to the Talmud, *Avot* 4:7.

325. Sec. 622 of the Ordinances of the Lithuanian Council in Dubnow, *Pinkas Ha'Medinah*; for a similar provision in the

city of Zalkava, Poland, see Buber, *Kirya Nisgava*, sec. 49 of the section "Judicial Procedure."

326. See the records of the community of Bamberg, pp. 21, 23; the records of Cracow in *Jahrbuch*, 10:331–32.

327. See Ephraim Margolis, in *Amude Shesh*, who charged that this practice led to all sorts of gross corruption and miscarriages of justice; see also, H. N. Dembitzer, *K'Lilat Yofi* (Cracow, 1888), sec. 2, p. 35.

328. Sheftel Horowitz, in *Vave Ha'Amudim* (Livorno, 1837), sec. on "Judgment"; see M. Horowitz, *Frankfurter Rabbinen*, (reprinted Jerusalem, 1972), sec. 2, p. 58.

329. See Ephraim Margolis, in *Amude Shesh*.

330. Y. Sirkis, Responsa *Bakh*, sec. 58; Y. Raisher, Responsa *Shevut Yaakov*, sec. 2, no. 142; Meir Eisenstadt, Responsa *Panim Me'Irot*, sec. 2, no. 159.

Ages. They ranged from courts in which cases would be heard by one or more professional judges together with one or more persons—not necessarily professional judges—selected by each of the parties, to courts where only community leaders acted as judges. Courts had different, and sometimes overlapping, jurisdictions.

The most traditional and recognized type of court was one in which cases were heard by three professional judges. Traditionally, hearings by one judge only were frowned upon.[331] Occasional indications in the Talmud that a professional judge could decide cases alone[332] were held to apply only to scholars who received wide recognition.[333] Both in Babylonia, where judges were chosen by the exilarch or by the heads of the academies, and in Europe or other areas, where the communities themselves chose judges, the most widespread form of Jewish court was a court of three professional judges.[334] In Poland and Lithuania (particularly, from the middle of the seventeenth century on) a number of the larger communities, where there was considerable litigation, selected a panel of judges to serve simultaneously for a term of one year in a number of three-judge courts.[335] The same was true in Prague, Bohemia.[336] Sometimes these courts would serve during alternate weeks, as in Zalkava and Lvov.

In Cracow, where there were three courts (each, with three judges), one court would serve as a lower court with jurisdiction in suits involving up to ten gold pieces and other minor suits of various types. This court was not obligated to follow technical legal precedent or the strict rules of evidence, and it operated in a fashion analogous to small claims courts in the United States. The second (or "intermediate") court had jurisdiction in all cases in which the sum demanded was from ten to one hundred gold pieces while the third (or "high") court decided cases involving demands for more than one hundred gold pieces.[337]

e. THE COMMUNITY RABBI AS JUDGE

In the large communities in Poland, law suits involving demands for money were normally heard by professional judges, not by the community rabbi. Sometimes, however, a community rabbi would act as co-judge when the litigants requested it, and he would, in general, supervise the operation of the courts to see that justice was done. His opinion might also be requested in difficult matters in which the professional judges would desire such advice. In the smaller communities, which had no professional judges, the rabbi might serve as sole judge in money suits.[338] This was the case in a number of communities in Germany, where suits involving small amounts would be heard by the rabbi acting as sole judge.[339] The rabbis of larger communities, particularly those whose legal erudition was widely esteemed, spent much of their time responding to inquiries from near and far, especially concerning legal issues that arose in commercial transactions.[340] In some communities in Germany, notably Frankfurt-am-Main, suits involving large sums of money, were decided by the rabbi of the city, rather than by the professional judges.[341] Smaller commercial lawsuits were heard by judges and sometimes by community lay leaders.

Normally, however, the community rabbi rarely acted as professional judge. His main function was spiritual guidance and the supervision of educational activities.[342]

f. JEWISH COURTS IN SUBURBAN AND RURAL AREAS

In medieval Europe only those urban areas with large Jewish communities maintained Jewish courts on a permanent basis. Most of the Jews in Germany and Poland during that time lived in rural areas, subject to administrative rule by the larger urban centers nearby, and thus the rural residents were required to utilize the courts of the urban community exclusively. If a rural area was located near more than one urban center, it was normally included within the jurisdiction of that center which provided it with most of its religious needs, especially the cemetery where it buried its dead.[343] In fact, throughout much of the Middle Ages,

331. Talmud, *Avot* 4:6; *Sanhedrin* 5a; H. Modai, *Tshuvot Ha'Gaonim, Sha'are Tzedek* (reprinted Jerusalem, 1966), vol. 4, secs. 35, 37; Eshtor Ha'Parkhi, *Kaftor Va'Ferakh* (Berlin, 1851), ch. 12.

332. See, e.g., *Sanhedrin* 5a.

333. *Ibid.*; see Modai, *Tshuvot Ha'Gaonim, Sha'are Tzedek* vol. 7, secs. 37, 38; see in general Shohet, *The Jewish Court in the Middle Ages.*

334. See Y. Miller, *Tshuvot Gaone Mizrakh U'Maariv* (Berlin, 1888), pp.152–53; D. Kassel, Responsa *Gaonim Kadmonim* (Berlin, 1848), pp. 135, 144, 146, 147, and especially 133. See, however, David Ibn Zimra (in his commentary to Rambam, Laws of the Sanhedrin, 2:11), who records an ancient tradition in Egypt to have one-judge courts.

335. For Vilna and Horudna, Poland; see Fein, *Kirya Ne'-Emana*, pp. 41, 270, 272. For Lvov and Lissa, see Levin, *Geschichte der Juden in Lissa*, in Assaf, *Bate Ha'Din*, p. 49.

336. Assaf, *ibid.*, p. 49.

337. See Kochmal, Responsa *Tzemah Tzedek*, no. 15.

338. See Fein, *Kirya Ne'Emana*, p. 39.

339. See D. Kaufman, *Pinkas* of Bamberg, in *Kovetz Al Yad*, vol. 7, p. 12; M. Horowitz, *The Rabbis of Frankfurt*, vol. 1, p. 58; Eibshutz, *Urim Ve'Tumim, Hoshen Mishpat*, sec. 3.

340. Assaf, *Bate Ha'Din*, p. 53.

341. M. Horowitz, *The Rabbis of Frankfurt*, p. 58.

342. Assaf, *Le'Korot Ha'Rabbanut*, in *Be'Ahalei Yaakov*, p. 51.

343. Meir ben Barukh, Responsa *Maharam* of Rothenburg (Prague ed.), p. 113; Isserlin, *Pesakim*, sec. 65; *Pinkas* of the Lithuanian Council, in Dubnow, *Pinkas Ha'Medinah*, sec. 829.

exclusive franchises for the use of land as cemeteries were zealously guarded by communities for this reason, as well as others.[344] The residents of rural communities were occasionally required to transport their dead over very large distances, despite poor roads and bad weather, in order to bury them in the cemetery allotted to their community.[345]

Even when a small rural community succeeded in establishing its own court, the larger urban centers would often attempt to preserve their influence by insisting that all law suits for large sums were required to be brought in the urban center. To this end, they applied pressures made possible by their exclusive cemetery franchises and by the taxing authority granted them by the central non-Jewish government, or regional intercommunity Jewish councils.[346] Such litigation restrictions were placed upon the community of Zalkava in Poland, by the city of Lvov.[347] The Council of the Four Lands and the Lithuanian Council decided numerous cases regarding conflicting claims of jurisdiction among urban centers and outlying communities.

g. APPELLATE COURTS

In the Middle Ages there was widespread provision among many Jewish communities in Europe for appealing the decisions of Jewish courts. This practice had precedent in Jewish judicial history.[348] It is possible that the existence of the right to appeal also may have been influenced by the existence of the right in many contemporaneous non-Jewish legal systems.

In Castile, Spain, Abraham Benebashti, the Royal Rabbi (*Rab de la Corte*), organized a synod of the rabbis and representatives of many of the Jewish communities in 1432. This synod provided, among other things, that any litigant who was dissatisfied with a decision of a Jewish court could appeal to the royal rabbi, provided that he posted security to cover the expenses of the appeal. Every Jewish judge was, upon

demand, required to give a written copy of his decision, together with its reasoning, to every litigant.[349] In Portugal, too, litigants could appeal the decision of Jewish courts to the chief rabbi of the land.[350]

In Aragon, Spain, there was no official chief rabbi. Many of the important communities in this country selected a number of judges who heard appeals from the Jewish courts. Thus there are records of such appellate systems in the important communities of Saragossa, Hueska, and Calatayud, where the appellate judges were known as "Silukin judges," i.e., judges who presided over cases that were "removed" from the jurisdiction of the lower court.[351]

Although all of the known records regarding the existence of appellate Jewish court systems in Spain date from the fifteenth century, it is likely that provisions for appeals existed prior to that time as well.[352]

The tradition among Spanish Jewry of the right to appeal was carried over with them to Turkey, where many of these Jews found refuge after the expulsions from Spain. Here, too, each of the major Jewish communities set up a special appellate court.[353] Apparently, however, not many appeals were taken in Turkey, as evidenced by the lack of any record regarding such appeals in the medieval Responsa literature from that country. This was possibly due to the expenses involved.

The right of appeal also existed in Jewish communities in Italy, as evidenced by the incorporation of such rights in the ordinances drafted by Moshe Zakut, which were adopted by a number of Jewish communities.[354] The perspective that a litigant who lost a case should be able to appeal to a higher court is also expressed by Ovadia Superno, a medieval Italian rabbi, in his commentary to Exodus 18:21.

In medieval Moravia there was a well-established system of Jewish courts that were reorganized by Rabbi Judah Loewe, later of Prague. In the ordinances (gathered together by Rabbi Menahem Krochmal in the seventeenth century), specific provision was made for

---

344. Isserlin, ibid.

345. Assaf, *Bate Ha'Din*, pp. 64, 65.

346. Assaf, *Bate Ha'Din*, pp. 66–67; see, however, Hanover, in *Yeven Metzula*, who indicates that litigants in Poland had a choice of utilizing the Jewish courts in their city, or going to that of a nearby area or even to the "higher court" for the entire area.

347. Buber, *Kirya Nisgava*, pp. 84–85.

348. See Part Two, Chapter VI, Section B 1, above; Talmud, *Sanhedrin* 31b, 33a (see Shlomo Yitzhaki, Commentary *Rashi*, ad loc., *s. v. yesh gadol*); *Baba Kama* 112b; Asher ben Yehiel, Commentary *Rosh*, ad loc. and at *Baba Metzia*, 69b, sec. 45. See, however, Y. R. Hazan, Responsa *Hikre Lev, Ho. Mis.*, vol. 1, sec. 85–86; Shabse Cohen in *Sifse Kohen, Ho. Mis.*, sec. 19; Joshua Falk Kohen, in *Me'irat Enayim, Ho. Mis.*, sec. 19; Y. Katz, in *Shita Mekubetzet* to *Baba Kama* 12a; H. Hirschensohn, in *Malki Bakodesh*, 2:62–64, and 4:14–16.

349. Finkelstein, *Jewish Self-Government*, pp. 359–60; Baer, *History of the Jews in Christian Spain* (Philadelphia, 1966).

350. See also Assaf, *Bate Ha'Din*, p. 75.

351. Perfet, Responsa *Rivash*, nos. 227, 381, 393, 494, 506, 413.

352. Assaf, *Bate Ha'Din*, p. 77. Note, however, the query of King Pedro III in the thirteenth century as to whether or not Jewish law permitted appeal from a decision of a Jewish court. See Baer, in *Dvir* (Berlin, 1924), vol. 2, p. 312, 1181.

353. See the letter of Rabbi Yaakov Meir, the Chief Rabbi of the Sefardi Spanish Jews in Palestine, formerly Rabbi in Salonika (which for many years was part of Turkey before it reverted to Greece), claiming that appellate courts had "always" existed in Constantinople, in Hirschensohn, *Malki Ba'-Kodesh* (St. Louis, 1919–22), 4:14.

354. See M. Zakut, in *Shuda De'Daina*, sec. 36, reproduced in Chapter VIII, Section B 2 *a* (2), above.

appeals within forty-eight hours to an appellate court, consisting of two lay leaders and one rabbi (and, in certain instances, four lay leaders and one rabbi). No appeal was permitted in suits for libel and slander.[355]

In Bohemia there was also an appellate system. In its chief city, Prague, there were four different Jewish courts, one of which sat as a court of appeals to hear cases brought from the other three courts. In the other communities in Bohemia appeals were taken to the lay leader of the community.[356] Even during the times when Prague had only two courts, one of them acted as a court of appeals.[357] The judges of these appellate courts in Bohemia were commonly called "*appilantim*," and many of the most prominent scholars of the area sat as judges there. Even in Germany, where there was no well-established system of Jewish appellate courts, there is evidence of this practice.[358] Appeals were sometimes taken to prominent rabbis, whose decisions were accepted because of the widespread esteem in which they were held.[359]

A limited right of appeal existed in medieval Poland. In the event that one of the judges dissented from the decision of a lower court and, if the case involved substantial penalties (including the possible removal of a defendant from office), such appeals were taken to the council itself, which commonly appointed committees to hear the appeals.[360] Interestingly, disagreement with a decision of the lower court by the rabbi of the community was not sufficient to permit an appeal. The dissenting vote of one judge was also required. In contrast, any new ordinance enacted by a community could not go into effect without the consent of the rabbi, who, at least in theory, exercised a veto power.[361]

The right of appeal existed in Lithuania, and the ordinances of the Lithuanian Council specifically provided for a limited right of appeal.[362] There is also evidence of a practice in Poland and Lithuania for a litigant who lost a case to turn to the lay heads of the community with a demand that they appoint additional judges and have the case heard anew.[363]

In "White Russia" (as it was called in the seventeenth century) many of the communities provided for the right of appeal when the sum involved exceeded a specified amount.[364] It is possible that appeals in cases involving large sums were also permitted in Poland and Lithuania, as well as in "White Russia" and Moravia, where community ordinances make specific provision for such appeal.[365]

Ezekiel Landau, who was rabbi in a number of towns in Poland and later in Prague, wrote in his Responsa:[366]

> Regarding your question as to whether a judge is required to advise the litigant as to the reason for his decision: you ruled quite correctly, that even though there is no reason to suspect the judge, he must, nevertheless, set forth the contentions of the parties and his decision in writing, if the hearing was compelled upon the litigants. Any time that the two litigants do not appear before the court voluntarily, but, instead, one of them sent the sextant to request his [adversary's] presence, it is regarded as a compelled hearing. This requires that the judgment and the contentions be set forth in writing, so that a litigant may apply to the higher court to find out if the judge did not err. This is certainly true in our times, when errors are common . . . It is also elementary that the judge or the rabbi must sign the writing [court decision], and no rabbi is suspected by me of refusing to do this, unless he is certain that the decision is wrong, whether by error or deliberately, and is embarrassed to admit his mistake.[367]

There is also evidence that appeals were permitted in other parts of Europe, such as Austria-Hungary.[368] The same was true of the many Jewish communities in Bulgaria.[369] The common practice of denying the right to appeal where the sums involved were small (on the theory that these were not worth the effort and time involved) tended to discriminate against the poor, whose litigation usually involved only small amounts of money.

In summary, despite doubts as to the scope of appellate practice in biblical or early talmudic tradition, the right to appeal a court decision to a higher authority became well-established and was widely practiced in numerous communities in Europe, at least as early as the thirteenth century.

355. See Section B 2 *a* (1), sections 213–18, above.
356. Assaf, *Bate Ha'Din*, pp. 80, 81.
357. Ibid., citing Fodibrar-Fogis, *Alterthumer der Prager Josefstadt*, p. 159.
358. Meir ben Barukh, Responsa *Maharam* of Rothenburg, no. 523 (Prague ed.); Mordecai Yaffa, *Levush Malhut* (Lublin, 1690), sec. 14; Isserlis, Responsa *Rama, Ho. Mis.*, sec. 14, no. 6; Isserlis, Responsa *Rama, Ho. Mis.*, sec. 14, citing Mordecai ben Hillel and *Hagaot Maimuni*.
359. See also the ordinances of the community of Bamberg, in D. Kaufman, *Kobetz Al Yad*, 7:30, 37, 38.
360. Balaban, in *History of the Jews in Russia* (Moscow, 1915), 1:213.
361. Assaf, *Bate Ha'Din*, p. 84.
362. See sec. 426 in Dubnow, *Pinkas Ha'Medinah*.
363. R. Zvei Hirsh, *Ateret Zvi, Hoshen Mishpat*, sec. 87 (Jasnitz, 1722).

364. See Assaf, *Bate Ha'Din*, p. 85.
365. See also the provisions for appeals in Hanover.
366. *Noda Be'Yehude, Ho. Mis.* (1st ed.), sec. 1.
367. See also Y. Epstein, in his *Arukh Ha'Shulkhan, Ho. Mis.*, secs. 11, 13, and 14.
368. Assaf, *Bate Ha'Din*, pp. 82–83.
369. See David Pepino, Responsa *Hoshen Ha'Afudi, Hoshen Mishpat* (Sofia, 1915), sec. 42.

h. LAY COURTS

The existence of courts whose judges were laymen, rather than professionally trained and ordained judges, appears to have originated during the era inaugurated by the Emperor Hadrian's prohibition against the existence and operation of Jewish courts and the ordaining of Jewish judges (see Part Two, Chapter VI, Section B, above). The first mentions of this institution in the Talmud are by Rabbi Judah, a contemporary of Rabbi Meir, both of whom lived at that time and were ordained secretly.[370] Apparently, in the absence of official Jewish courts, Jewish litigants who were unwilling to resort to Roman courts to resolve their controversies either chose courts of arbitration (where the judges were commonly learned scholars) or, when these were not available, presented their controversies to laymen who acted as judges.[371] Apparently the Romans did not ban such lay courts. Accordingly, the practice developed for each litigant to choose one lay judge, and those two judges would then select a third one to join them. Thus the lay courts continued the tradition of a Jewish judical system in which cases were decided by three judges rather than by one. There is reason to believe that the institution of lay courts of that era existed as a common practice only in Palestine, but not in Babylonia, where the Jewish courts always received government sanction and support.

At any rate, in the very extensive medieval Responsa literature from Babylonia, there is hardly any mention of lay courts[372] or of any tradition regarding them. Similarly, lay courts did not apparently exist in medieval Spain, where Jewish courts operated with government sanction.[373]

Lay courts, however, were common during the Middle Ages in Germany and Italy, where the institution of Jewish courts was not always well-established. In Poland lay courts also existed, even in a number of communities that had professional judges.[374] This was true even in a large community like Cracow, which had three different courts composed of professional judges. Nevertheless, litigants had the right to choose their own lay judges, each judge then choosing a third to form a lay court.[375]

It should be noted, however, that even where the court consisted of non-professional judges, a litigant would normally choose as a judge only someone who was well-versed in Jewish law. Some communities even formally required a lay judge to at least have the title of *"morenu"* ("our teacher"), a form of certification conferred by the rabbi and leaders of the community.[376]

Following talmudic precedent, the lay judges selected by each of the litigants during the Middle Ages would, in turn, commonly select a third person to join them, forming a lay court of three.[377] The third person would normally be the rabbi of the community.[378] This gave lay courts greater acceptance and authority in the eyes of the litigants. In a number of communities the custom was for each litigant to choose two lay judges, with the four judges selected by the litigants choosing still a fifth one.[379] Still another variation, which was common in Poland, Germany, and Prague, was for lay judges to first meet together and see whether they could arrive at a joint decision. Only if they were unable to do this would they select another party to join them and, in effect, decide the issue.[380] Occasionally the lay leaders of the community would select the third lay judge in the event that the first two judges selected by the litigants could not arrive at any decision.[381]

Originally the lay judge selected by each litigant was supposed to act impartially. This eventually degenerated into the practice of each selectee becoming, in effect, a lawyer for his selector and attempting to secure a decision in favor of his client at all costs. This normally went hand in hand with the selector paying an additional fee (beyond the normal court fee) to the "lay judge" that he had selected. This practice aroused violent opposition and contempt of many rabbis and decision-makers who labeled it as corrupt.[382] Nevertheless, the practice became prevalent and even accepted as fair by the litigants themselves, who felt it advantageous that they have learned counsel who could help

370. Talmud, *Bekhorot* 37a.

371. See Talmud, *Sanhedrin* 5a.

372. Assaf, *Bate Ha'Din*, p. 54.

373. See, however, Al-Barceloni, *Sefer Ha'Shtharot*, p. 14; and the edicts of King Pedro III, published in *Revue des Etudes Juives*, vols. 60–70, *Regne, Catalogues des Actes*, no. 1435.

374. Y. Reisher, Responsa *Shevut Yaakov, Ho. Mis.*, no. 142; Responsa *Shev Yaakov, Ho. Mis.* (Jerusalem, 1972), no. 1.

375. Assaf, *Bate Ha'Din*, p. 55; *Jahrbuch der Judisch-Literarische Gesellschaft*, 10:333.

376. See Section 2 *d*, above; Meir Kartzenellenbogen, Responsa *Maharam* of Padua (Cracow, 1892), no. 53; the Ordinances of the Community of Hamburg-Altona, printed in the *Mitteilungen der Gesellschaft fur Judische Volkskunde*, no. 90, 1903.

377. See Jacob ben Asher, *Tur, Ho. Mis.*; and Karo, *Shulkhan Arukh*, sec. 13, for discussions of this procedure.

378. Reisher, Responsa *Shevut Yaakov*, Responsa *Shev Yaakov*.

379. An odd number of judges was, of course, required to prevent split decisions; see Talmud, *Sanhedrin* 3b; Tosefta *Sanhedrin*, ch. 3; Landau, Responsa *Noda Be'Yehuda* (1st ed.), *Ho. Mis.*, no. 2.

380. Landau, Responsa *Noda Be'Yehuda* (1st ed.), *Ho. Mis.*, no. 3; and ibid., *Derushe Ha'Tazlah*, 16a.

381. Isserlis, Responsa *Rama, Ho. Mis.*, no. 13.

382. Eisenstadt, Responsa *Panim Meirot*, sec. 1.

them advance arguments to further their cause. This perspective was influenced by similar practices in the operation of many of the non-Jewish contemporary legal systems of Europe.[383]

One of the advantages of resort to lay judges (called *"borerim"*), was that their proceedings were more informal, speedy, and less bound by legal precedents. They could also resolve disputes by effecting compromises, instead of ruling according to technical legal doctrine.[384] Because of this last factor, it was accepted that no litigant could coerce his adversary into having the case heard by lay judges instead of the professional courts.[385] It should be noted that even the professional courts often effected compromises. These, however, were not supposed to depart too greatly from the decision that would have been rendered under traditional law and precedent. In practice, it became impossible to measure the extent to which the compromise decision departed from the law.[386]

i. Merchant and Guild Lay Courts

In the long evolution of Jewish communal society in Europe, another form of lay court developed in some of the Jewish communities. This was a court of laymen who were either merchants or craftsmen, and who decided cases involving their fellow merchants or artisans. In Venice, for example, there was a court of merchants to which all traders would bring their litigation.[387] Although this practice aroused considerable opposition from rabbis (see Section B 1 d [3], above), many rabbis and Jewish professional judges did not regard it as a threat, since the lay judges were intimately familiar with, and were guided in their decisions by, the customs common among merchants, who planned their transactions with these practices in mind.[388] In 1536 Jewish financiers of Rome selected a number of persons to rule on all disputes among their members.[389] There is even some speculation that the merchants' court in Venice consisted of non-Jewish judges.[390]

In many of the Jewish communities in Europe, particularly in Poland, there were associations consisting of artists or craftsmen of one particular trade, such as associations of goldsmiths, bookbinders, and tailors. These often had their own synagogues. In many cases these associations were required to choose one of the professional judges of the community to hear all disputes involving members of the association, but a number of communities permitted the associations to select their own judges to resolve disputes among their members.[391] This was true in such cities as Cracow, Lvov, and Slutzk.[392]

j. Intercommunity Courts for Communal and Private Disputes

In addition to the vital function of the Jewish national councils of Poland, Lithuania, and Moravia in prescribing the law in the sixteenth to eighteenth centuries, these councils were also quite active in establishing institutions for the application of law.

Large commercial fairs were held annually in a number of important centers in Europe, such as Leipzig, Lublin, and Jaroslav. The fairs were extremely important, both for intranational commerce and for international trade, and they would attract merchants from all parts of the country and from many foreign lands, as far away as Turkey and the Near East. This was particularly true of the commercial fairs in Poland and Lithuania. The fairs attracted not only merchants with all sorts of wares but also many thousands of rabbis, heads of academies, students, and laymen. Hence, the fairs served as important centers for social and intellectual intercourse and, not unimportantly, for the arrangement of marriage matches between Jews from all parts of Europe. Sometimes thousands of marriages were "arranged" at these annual fairs.[393]

These fairs also served as important meeting places for the representatives of various Jewish communities in Eastern Europe in their attempts to resolve their communal disputes and arrange for the common good. Claimants would also come there to litigate disputes with persons from other parts of the country or from foreign lands, thereby avoiding the laborious and time-consuming journey to the place of residence or business of the ones whom they sought to sue.

In order to arrange for the expeditious disposition of litigation between merchants from different commu-

383. See Y. Epstein, *Arukh Ha'Shulkhan, Ho. Mis.*, sec. 13.

384. See Karo, *Shulkhan Arukh, Ho. Mis.*, sec. 13.

385. Ibid.; Gershon Ashkenazi, Responsa *Avodat Ha'Gershuni* (Lvov, 1861), no. 47.

386. See Assaf, *Batei Ha'Din*, p. 61.

387. Kohen, Responsa *Maharshakh* (Salonika, 1592), vol. 2, no. 229.

388. Kohen, Responsa *Maharshakh*, vol. 1, no. 164; Benebashti, Responsa *Baya Hai, Ho. Mis.*, vol. 1, no. 19; vol. 2, no. 158.

389. Fogelstein and Rieger, *Geschichte der Juden in Rom* (Berlin, 1905), vol. 2, pp. 416–17.

390. See Assaf, *Batei Ha'Din*, p. 62.

391. See Dubnow, *Pinkas*, sec. 817; *Jahrbuch der Judisch-Literarischen Gesellschaft*, 13:133–36.

392. P. Wettstein, in *Ha'Measeh* (Petersburg, 1902), p. 131; Shlomo ben Aderet, Responsa *Rashba*, vol. 3, no. 63; Assaf, *Bate Ha'Din*, pp. 63–64.

393. Hanover, *Yeven Metzula*.

nities and countries, the practice developed for the leading communities to send a number of their professional judges to the fairs, where special tribunals were established, consisting of judges from various communities. The communities of Poznan, Cracow and Lvov would each send two judges to, and the communities of Brisk, Horodna, and later Pinsk, alternated in sending one judge each to the fairs at Lublin and Yaroslav. Other communities would be represented at fairs held elsewhere.[394] The various communities would often send some of their most prominent judges to participate in these intercommunity courts at the fairs.

The substantial amount of litigation at the fairs gradually became a very lucrative source of income for the judges, who would collect fees from both litigants for hearing the cases. Some communities then decided to even out the annual earnings of judges from judicial fees by sending only judges who did not serve in judicial positions in the communities.[395] Some judges even attempted to increase their incomes by retaining fines that they levied on some of the defendants, while others attempted to impose special taxes on every merchant who participated in the fairs. This naturally aroused great opposition.[396]

Because of the short duration of the commercial fairs, the tribunals hearing cases at the fair were required to decide the cases as expeditiously as possible. Their decisions could be enforced by impounding the merchandise brought to the fairs by a judgment debtor, or by prohibiting him from participating in all future fairs. Occasionally, he might even be imprisoned until the completion of the fair.[397] All of these methods could be extremely effective.

Since the fairs were regarded as extremely important for both commercial, social, and communal affairs, steps had to be taken to permit unfettered attendance by all, including those who feared they would be sued there by claimants. Accordingly, severe restrictions on such suits were imposed by the Council of the Four Lands and the Lithuanian Council, and only a limited number of exceptions were permitted.[398]

Jewish community councils in medieval Europe were also active in applying the law themselves in certain important cases. These usually involved conflicts be-tween two communities, or complaints by an individual against one of the important urban communities. Individual complaints against the smaller communities were normally heard by the court of the urban center of the region. These intercommunity councils also heard and decided cases on appeal from decisions of the courts of individual areas.[399]

The Council of Four Lands in Poland, which normally consisted of about thirty representatives from the chief communities there, would select a number of persons from these communities to act as judges of a higher court, to hear the aforementioned types of cases. These judges were known as "national judges" (*dayane medina*). Most of those selected would be the more prominent rabbis and scholars in those communities, but a number of prominent laymen were also included in this higher court.[400] The Lithuanian Council also followed a similar procedure, appointing members, including prominent laymen, to the higher court.[401]

The high court of the Council of Four Lands would ordinarily, meet once, and in its later years twice, a year. Accordingly, it required litigants who desired to appear before it to give their adversaries six months notice.[402] The high court of the Lithuanian Council, which met much more frequently, followed a different procedure. It would not entertain litigation unless the plaintiff first presented his case before the leaders of two principal communities represented in the Lithuanian Council. These, if they saw some merit in the complaint, would issue a subpoena requiring the defendant to attend the next session of the high court.[403] Similarly, complaints of individuals against their communities would first be heard by the rabbi of the plaintiff's community, who would then issue the appropriate subpoena if he saw merit in the complaint, and if the community persisted in its refusal to provide the necessary rectification.[404]

It should be noted that complaints of individuals against communities would not be heard by the high court unless the complaint set forth a case of illegal coercion or use of force against the plaintiff. No claims for money only would be heard unless the complaint demanded a sum in excess of a specified amount. If the defendant did not appear before the high court, a default judgment would not be issued. Instead, the court

394. See Ordinances of the Lithuanian Council, secs. 414, 422, 818, 829, in Dubnow, *Pinkas Ha'Medinah*; Assaf, *Batei Ha'Din*, p. 59.

395. L. Levin, *Jahrbuch*, 2:5.

396. See S. Luria, *Yam Shel Shlomo, Baba Kama*, ch. 8, sec. 9.

397. Assaf, *Bate Ha'Din*, p. 61.

398. *Pinkas* of the Lithuanian Council, sec. 819. For analogous norms, see Talmud, *Baba Kama* 113a; these resemble provisions to this effect, which are common in American jurisdictions.

399. Hanover, *Yeven Metzula*; see "Appellate Courts," Chapter VIII, Section B 2 g, above.

400. Hanover, ibid., and see the records of the city of Pozen, in L. Levin, *Jahrbuch*, vol. 3, sec. 39, p. 100.

401. Records of the Lithuanian Council, sec. 776, in Dubnow, *Pinkas*.

402. L. Levin, *Jahrbuch*, vol. 2, pp. 110–11.

403. Assaf, *Bate Ha'Din*, p. 71.

404. Ordinances of the Lithuanian Council, secs. 16, 113, 683, 539, in Dubnow, *Pinkas*.

would resort to excommunications and other penalties.[405]

Interestingly enough, the calendar of the high court gave priority to complaints of individuals against communities. Only when these were completed, would the court entertain suits between communities against each other. Even then, preference was given to claims by the chief communities, and suits by the smaller communities against each other would be heard last.[406]

k. COMPELLING COMPLIANCE WITH COURT
   SUBPOENAS

Jewish courts in medieval Europe were often either unable or unwilling to resort to the non-Jewish authorities in order to compel a defendant to appear in their court. To effect attendance, however, they resorted to a variety of devices.[407] Foremost among them was the authorization to the plaintiff to stop the religious services in the synagogue until the defendant agreed to appear in court. This practice was recognized in an ordinance attributed to Rabbi Gershom in eleventh-century Germany, although it is also mentioned in the Talmud.[408] This interruption of religious services would result in intense social pressure being brought by the congregation upon the recalcitrant defendant, including ostracization and other pressures. The practice became very widespread,[409] and it was quite effective since few defendants could bear the intense humiliation and loss of face. Nevertheless, the practice was the subject of severe criticism because of the quarrels and disturbances in synagogue decorum to which it led, and because of the excesses in its use.[410] Accordingly, numerous restrictions were instituted regarding this practice,[411] and many communities enacted ordinances barring it.[412]

Another extremely effective form of social pressure was the anathema or excommunication imposed with varying severity upon the recalcitrant defendant. This might prevent anyone from speaking to him or doing business with him, and it would prevent his attendance at religious services. In the closed Jewish societies of the Middle Ages, this could often be tantamount to death.[413] Still another form of social pressure and humiliation was to post the name of the defendant in the synagogue. In addition to the embarrassment that ensued, the defendant was thereby disqualified from holding any position in the community.[414]

Economic sanctions were also employed. Again, where the Jewish communities were endowed with the power by the secular non-Jewish authorities, the defendant could be fined. In Germany, Poland, and Lithuania, as well as in Turkey, Palestine, and other countries in the Near East, a Jewish court would often issue an order that anybody who owed monies to the defendant or possessed his goods should not repay the debt or return the chattels.[415] While this extreme sanction was first utilized by the Jewish communities to enforce the payment of taxes by community members,[416] its use was thereafter extended to compel attendance at court.[417]

A variant of this sanction in Poland was to impound the merchandise brought by the defendant to the annual commercial fairs at Lublin and Jaroslav, which practically all merchants attended since it generated a substantial portion of their income. This extreme application was utilized to compel payment of community taxes.[418] Scholar–decision-makers, however, criticized the use of this sanction to compel attendance in court as an unwarranted extension of a talmudic principle permitting attachments of the property of a judgment debtor.[419] One court compelled a woman defendant to appear in court by threatening to forbid her husband

405. Ibid., sec. 336.

406. Ibid., sec. 668.

407. See Chapter XI, Section B 5, below, regarding sanctions imposed by Jewish decision-makers. Many of these penalties were employed to compel compliance with court subpoenas.

408. Jerusalem Talmud, *Peah,* ch. 1, rule 1.

409. See Shlomo ben Aderet, Responsa *Rashba,* sec. 4, no. 66; Eshtor Ha'Parakhi, *Kaftor Va'Perakh* (Lunz ed.), no. 583; Judah Ha'Hasid, *Sefer Hasidim* (reprinted Jerusalem, 1973), no. 1712; Hayim ben Yitzhak, *Ohr Zarua,* Rules of the Sabbath, no. 45.

410. See Judah Ha'Hasid, no. 462; S. E. Luntshitz, *Amudei Shesh,* section on "Prayer."

411. See Rosenthal, in the *Jubilee Volume in Honor of Azriel Hildesheimer* (Berlin, 1890); and Finkelstein, (*Jewish Self-Government,* pp. 113, 129), who, among other data, discusses the ban on this practice instituted by a twelfth-century synod in Troyes, France, headed by Rabbi Jacob Tam, in which 150 leading rabbis from France and Germany took part.

412. See, for example, the community of Zalkava, Poland, as recorded in Buber, *Kirya Nisgava,* p. 88. See Chapter IX, Section B 5 *k,* below.

413. Assaf, *Batei Ha'Din,* p. 25; Assaf, *Ha'Onshin,* pp. 49–50, 3132; Samuel and Moshe Bakhrakh, Responsa *Hut Ha'-Shani* (Lvov, 1899), no. 28. See Chapter IX, Section B 5 *i,* below.

414. See the Ordinances of the Community of Hesse, in the *Jubilee Volume in Honor of Hildesheimer;* Assaf, *Batei Ha'Din,* pp. 32–33. See Chapter IX, Section B 5 *m,* below.

415. See Cohen, *Sifse Kohen, Hoshan Mishpat,* sec. 73, 35; Trani, Responsa *Mabit,* sec. 2, no. 33; Isserlin, Responsa *Terumat Ha'Dashen,* no. 305; Kolon, Responsa *Maharik Kolon,* no. 109.

416. See Duran, Responsa *Tashbatz,* no. 506.

417. Asher ben Yehiel, Responsa *Rosh,* sec. 73, no. 1; Isserlin, Responsa *Terumat Ha'Dashen,* no. 305; Weil, Responsa *Mahari* Weil, no. 21.

418. Assaf, *Batei Ha'Din,* pp. 30–31.

419. See Talmud, *Ketubot* 19a; Isserlin, Responsa *Terumat Ha'Deshen;* Kolon, Responsa *Maharik Kolon;* M. Azarye of Pano, Responsa *Rama Mi'Pano* (Venice, 1600), no. 51.

to permit her to stay in his house.[420] Another method was to deny the facilities of the Jewish court to the defendant in other disputes in which he might be involved until he complied with the subpoena.

Where the aforementioned sanctions proved ineffective, the court might permit the plaintiff to resort to a non-Jewish court. Occasionally it would hear the complaint in the absence of the defendant and thereafter, if it deemed the complaint to be meritorious, would issue a default judgment. Default judgments, however, were generally in great disfavor.[421]

l. EX PARTE HEARINGS

In traditional Jewish law, hearings could not ordinarily be held without the physical presence of the defendants in court.[422] In the Middle Ages, however, hearings were occasionally held *ex parte*, if the defendant was an informer or was an individual with suffi-

cient power to frighten off potential witnesses.[423] These exceptions were based on statements in the Talmud permitting such hearings when the defendant or his witnesses were sick, or the witnesses desired to go abroad and the defendant failed to attend a court hearing, although requested to.[424]

Although there were a number of talmudic authorities who disputed the availability of such hearings under traditional talmudic law,[425] a number of communities enacted ordinances providing for such *ex parte* hearings.[426] This was also applied in Moravia and by the chief rabbinate in twentieth-century Palestine.[427]

420. See Buber, *Anshe Shem*, p. 232.

421. See Jerusalem Talmud, *Sanhedrin*, 3:9; J. F. Kohen, *Me'irat Enayim, Hoshen Mishpat*, sec. 18.

422. Talmud, *Baba Kama* 112b; *Sanhedrin* 19a.

423. Yehiel ben Asher, Responsa *Rosh*, sec. 17, no. 1; Perfet, Responsa *Rivash*, no. 238; Isserlin, Decisions, sec. 175.

424. See also comment of Y. Boaz Barukh, *Shilte Ha'Giborim*; Mordecai ben Hillel, Commentary *Mordecai* to *Baba Kama*, ch. 10; M. Isserlis, Responsa *Rama, Ho. Mis.*, sec. 28.

425. Hayim Benebashti, Responsa *Baya Haya, Hoshen Mishpat*, sec. 1, no. 17. M. Shick, Responsa *Maharam Shick, Ho. Mis.* (Munkatch, 1891), sec. 2; compare Shlomo ben Aderet, Responsa *Rashba*, sec. 2, nos. 192 and 344; Karo, *Shulhan Arukh, Ho. Mis.*, sec. 18.

426. See, e.g., Buber, *Kirya Nisgava*, p. 110, regarding the community of Zalkava; see Zakut, *Shuda De'Daina*, regarding the practice in Italy.

427. Assaf, *Batei Ha'Din*, p. 37.

IX. Adjusting the Law to Meet Changed Conditions

A. *The Development of New Legal Institutional Practices*

The precarious existence of Jewish communities in Europe, living in a hostile environment as vassals of the king and subject to his every whim, gave rise to the gradual development of new Jewish legal institutions, which reflected both this condition and the increased urbanization and mercantile activity. Some of these factors affected Jewish decision-making in Jewish communities in North Africa and Western Asia as well.

There were fundamental innovations regarding the institutions and processes of Jewish decision-making in the Middle Ages, such as the growth of Jewish communal autonomy in decision-making, the development of judicial systems, the roles of the community rabbi and of the laity, communal prescriptions and departures from traditional law, including, capital and corporal sanctions and imprisonment of debtors, discussed elsewhere herein in detail. A number of the more notable of these developments will now be described.

1. CHANGES IN FAMILY LAW

Many fundamental innovations in family law were made during this period, usually for the benefit of women:

a. A ban on polygamy in the eleventh century attributed to Rabbi Gershom's synod[1] in Franco-Germany.

b. A ban on divorcing a wife without her consent, instituted by the same synod.

c. A prescription by Jewish decision-makers in Babylonia that a wife could force her husband to divorce her for any reason.

d. The institution of the rule that a husband could not inherit from his wife if she died in the first year after their marriage, and that he was required to return the dowery that she had brought. If she died during the second year of her marriage, the husband was required to return one-half of the above amounts. Under traditional talmudic law, the husband inherited from his wife, even if she died immediately after their wedding.[2] This came to be regarded as unfair, particularly in the Middle Ages, when it became a widespread practice for brides to receive large doweries from their parents, due in part to improved economic conditions. The changes were included in the ordinances of the three cities of Speyer, Worms, and Mainz (the principle Jewish communities of Germany in the early Middle Ages) and later spread to all of the Jewish communities in Germany and Poland. This occurred despite a report that Rabbi Jacob Tam, in his old age, had changed his mind about this ordinance.[3]

e. Another change in inheritance law, was that a deceased wife's property should be inherited jointly by her husband and her children. This was initiated despite the strong talmudic view that the Bible required that a husband be the sole heir of his wife. The reason for the change was to encourage fathers to give their daughters as much property as they gave to their sons, without having to fear that their sons-in-law, rather than their own descendants, would be the beneficiaries.[4] This change was instituted, and followed, in Spain.

f. In some instances changes were made that adversely affected the rights of wives. According to modifications instituted in Spain, a widow whose husband had left a small estate could no longer collect more then one-half of the estate in fulfillment of the provisions of her *ketubah* (the prenuptial agreement which fixed the amount to be paid by the husband to support her in case of widowhood or divorce). If, however, the husband's estate was large, his children had the option to permit the widow to collect all of the amount specified in her *ketubah*, but the entire balance of the estate would be inherited by them. This, of course, would be to their advantage, where the remainder was substantial.[5] In a number of North African communities the woman's rights were reduced still further in 1584, apparently in emulation of the practices among the Islamic population there.[6]

---

1. See L. Finkelstein, *Jewish Self-Government in the Middle Ages.*

2. See Talmud, *Ketubot* 48b, 83, 84; *Baba Batra,* 111.

3. See Tosefot *Ketubot* 46b, *s. v. "Katav La"*; Israel of Kremez, *Ha'Gaot Ashri* (printed in Standard ed. of the Talmud) *Ketubot,* ch. 4, sec. 9; *Nakhlat Shiva* (Warsaw, 1893), secs. 9 and 10; Finkelstein, *Jewish Self-Government,* pp. 163–64, 166.

4. Shimon Duran, Responsa *Tashbatz,* vol. 2, sec. 292.

5. Asher ben Yehiel, Responsa *Rosh,* sec. 55; see Jacob ben Asher, *Tur, Even Ha'Ezer,* sec. 118.

6. Shimon Duran, Responsa *Tashbatz,* vol. 2, sec. 292, vol. 3, sec. 15.

2. JUDICIAL PROCEDURE

Changes in social and economic conditions resulted in many changes in judicial procedures. In addition to those discussed elsewhere herein, there were numerous minor changes exemplified by the novel requirement that witnesses should take an oath in court. This was contrary to the talmudic principle that a witness who cannot be believed without an oath is disqualified.[7] The reason for this change was that it was the custom among non-Jews to require witnesses to take an oath. Consequently, Jewish witnesses also came to feel that they would not violate Jewish religious law in testifying falsely unless they were under oath.[8]

Despite the talmudic principle that relatives of litigants, women, and minors were not qualified to be called as witnesses to testify in court,[9] Rabbi Jacob Tam and his colleagues in Franco-Germany (circa twelfth century) prescribed that such testimony would be acceptable in cases involving assaults, quarrels, and humiliations and, further, that the victim of an assault or murder (if the victim lived long enough to testify) and his relatives would be qualified. The change applied also to charges against informers. The reason for the prescription was the difficulty of obtaining qualified witnesses in these instances.[10] Similar exceptions were also extended to cases dealing with the "right of settlement," without which a Jew could not settle in specific areas,[11] and later even to commercial litigation.[12]

3. RESIDENTIAL AND MERCANTILE PROTECTIONS AND RESTRICTIONS

Utilizing a perspective analogous to the protectionist outlook of the medieval guilds, Jewish decision-makers promulgated and enforced bans on the right of newcomers to settle in existing mercantile colonies and other communities. This was done to protect the status of the earlier settlers from being undermined by more recent arrivals.[13] The issue bears some similarity to the zoning restrictions imposed in many American communities to prevent the influx of newcomers, particularly, those from lower economic or different social and racial classes.[14]

The activities of Jewish merchants and traders were protected by numerous regulations which were promulgated to strengthen and enforce the jurisdiction of the Jewish courts. This was important so that Jewish defendants in law suits could be brought to trial before Jewish courts, and the court decisions enforced. This gave added protection to Jewish merchants who traveled or did business with Jews in other communities.

The recognition of the ma'arufiya, or the exclusive right to do business with certain commercial clientele, was recognized by Jewish decision-makers in Europe, although it probably originated in the East.[15]

Resort to self-help by Jews in mercantile disputes was limited by prohibitions upon the retention of chattels by bailees who had claims against the bailors.[16] Jews were also forbidden to acquire property that had been lost by other Jews whose ship had sunk and whose cargo was thereafter pillaged.

Institutions such as these may have had greater effect than simply the protection of rights of Jews in urban communities and of Jewish commercial enterprises. They may also have spurred Jews who were limited by these restrictions to move elsewhere to new lands or to seek out other clients. In any case, these legal institutions certainly had important economic effects.[17]

4. LAW ENFORCEMENT OFFICIALS

An additional novelty in the application of the law in Spain was the selection in some communities of

7. Tosefot, *Kiddushin*, 43b.

8. Shimon Duran, Responsa *Tashbatz* ibid; I. Perfet, Responsa *Rivash*, secs. 166, 170, 176; Responsa *Mahari ben Lev.*, vol. 4, sec. 1.

9. *Sanhedrin*, ch. 3; Eliezer ben Nathan Commentary *Rivan* (New York, 1964); Hayim ben Yitzhak, *Ohr Zarua*, and Mordecai ben Hillel, Commentary *Mordecai*, ad loc.; M. Perlmutter, Responsa *Even Ha'Shoham* (Petersburg, 1907), no. 17.

10. The text of the ordinance is in Finkelstein, *Jewish Self-Government*, and in Meir ben Barukh, Responsa *Maharam Rothenberg* (Prague ed.), sec. 622; and in the *Kalbo* (author unknown); see also Menahem of Merzburg, *Nimuke Maharam* of Merzburg, published at the end of the Y. Weil, Responsa *Mahari Weil*. For similar provisions in Spain, see Shlomo ben Aderet, Responsa *Rashba*, vol. 1, nos. 680, 811; vol. 2, no. 107; vol. 5, nos. 184, 250, 272, 285.

11. See Meir ben Barukh, Responsa *Maharam* of Rothenberg, published in standard ed. of Rambam, Laws of Judges, at end, sec. 13; see also Shlomo ben Aderet, Responsa *Rashba*, vol. 4, no. 185.

12. See Ordinances of the Community of Mantova, above.

13. See, e.g., the regulation attributed to Rabbi Gershom of Mainz, in Finkelstein, *Jewish Self-Government*, pp. 111, 376. L. Rabinowitz, "The Talmudic Basis of the Hebrew *Herem Ha'Yishub* (Jewish Quarterly Review, 1937–1938) 37: 217.

14. *Southern Burlington County NAACP v. Township of Mt. Laurel*, A.2d (New Jersey, 1975); see also Meir ben Barukh, Responsa *Maharam* of Rothenberg, printed in standard ed. of Rambam, at end of Laws of Judges, sec. 13; Shlomo ben Aderet, Responsa *Rashba*, vol. 4, no. 185. See also Chapter VIII, Section B 1 a (2), for further details.

15. Y. Miller, Responsa of the Sages of France and Lothar, no. 87; Hayim ben Yitzhak, *Ohr Zarua*, B.M. 10a, no. 28; D. Kassel, Responsa *Gaonim Kadmonim*, no. 151; S. Luria, Responsa (Jerusalem, 1969), nos. 35, 36.

16. Miller, Responsa of the Sages of France and Lothar, nos. 87, 88; see Rabinowitz, the *Herem Hayishub* (London, 1945); Finkelstein, *Jewish Self-Government*.

17. See Finkelstein, ibid.; S. W. Baron, *The Jewish Community* (Philadelphia, 1942); C. H. Ben-Sasson, *Perakim Be'Toldot Hayehudim* (Tel-Aviv, 1969).

"*berurim*," officials whose task it was to seek out and to penalize those who violated the laws (including the ordinances adopted by the Jewish communities). There was evidence that Jewish communities demanded (and apparently their demands were granted) that the king permit these officials to impose severe sanctions upon violators of the law, including monetary fines and corporal punishment.[18]

The foregoing are only a few examples of some of the innovations in Jewish law in the Middle Ages. There were many others.[19]

B. *New Forms of Authoritative Prescriptions and Decisions for a Dispersed Jewry*

1. THE SHULHAN ARUK: ENDURING CODE OF JEWISH LAW

(By Isadore Twersky)*

Shulhan 'Aruk, a term taken over from early rabbinic exegesis in the Midrash[20] and applied to one of the most influential, truly epochal literary creations of Jewish history, has a double or even triple meaning, and its use therefore necessitates precise definition or description. *Shulhan 'Aruk* is the title given by R. Joseph Karo (1488–1575) to a brief, four-part code of Jewish law which was published in 1565–66, just over four hundred years ago. *Shulhan 'Aruk* also designates a composite, collaborative work, combining this original text of R. Joseph Karo, a Spanish emigré from Toledo (1492) who lived and studied in Turkey and finally settled in Palestine in a period of turbulence and instability and apocalyptic stirrings, with the detailed glosses—both strictures and supplements—of R. Moses Isserles (c. 1525–1572), a well-to-do Polish scholar, proud of his Germanic background, who studied in Lublin and became de facto chief rabbi of Cracow in a period of relative stability and tranquillity. This unpremeditated literary symbiosis then generated a spate of commen-

taries and supercommentaries, brief or expansive, defensive or dissenting, from the *Sefer Me'irat 'Enayim* of R. Joshua Falk and the *Sefer Siftei Kohen* of R. Shabbetai ha-Kohen to the *Mishnah Berurah* of R. Israel Meir ha-Kohen; and the term *Shulhan 'Aruk* continued to be applied to this multi-dimensional, multi-generational, ever-expanding folio volume—a fact which attests the resiliency and buoyancy of the Halachic tradition in Judaism. A person must, therefore, define his frame of reference when he purports to glorify or vilify, to acclaim or condemn—or, if he is able to avoid value judgments, to describe historically.[21] The genuinely modest purpose of the following remarks is, first, to chronicle the emergence of the *Shulhan 'Aruk*, especially in its first and second meanings, and then to describe a few of its salient literary and substantive characteristics. "The rest is commentary," which we should go and study.

I

In the year 1522,[22] R. Joseph Karo, a young, struggling, volatile and ascetic scholar, having settled temporarily and discontentedly in Adrianople, Turkey, launched a massive literary project that would preoccupy him, sometimes at a frenetic pace, for over thirty years—twenty years in the composition and about twelve years in editorial revision and refinement.[23] The stimulus was provided by the worrisome decline in scholarship—"and the wisdom of their wise men shall perish"—[24] coming in the wake of the rigors and vicis-

---

18. Shlomo ben Aderet, Responsa *Rashba*, vol. 4, sec. 311.

19. See, e.g., S. Assaf, *Ha'Onshin* (Jerusalem, 1922), pp. 12–15; Ginsberg, *Mishpatim Le'Yisrael* (Jerusalem, 1956), Intro. See "Other Social Contexts of Jewish Decision Making," Chapter VIII, Section A 1 *f*; also "Miscellaneous Prescriptions" and "Changes in Traditional Law," Chapter VIII, Section B 1 *a* (2).

*From *Judaism* 16 (Spring 1967). The transliteration has been left intact, although it differs somewhat from that appearing elsewhere in this volume.

20. *Mekilta* on Exodus 21:1, ed. J. Z. Lauterbach (Philadelphia, 1935), vol. 3, p. 1. " 'And these are the ordinances which thou shalt set before them.' Arrange them in proper order before them like a set table (*shulhan 'aruk*)." See Rashi on this verse, who adds, "like a table set before a person with everything ready for eating." . . .

21. Contemporaries would sometimes criticize the *Shulhan 'Aruk*, even stridently, but it was left for modern, post-Enlightment writers to vilify it. See, for example, the references in L. Greenwald, *R. Joseph Karo u-Zemano* (New York, 1954), pp. 174–176; B. Cohen, *Law and Tradition in Judaism* (New York, 1959), pp. 66–68; R. J. Z. Werblowsky, *Joseph Karo* (Oxford, 1962), p. 7; *Jewish Encyclopedia*, III, p. 588.

Actually, there is no need even for devotees of the *Shulhan 'Aruk* to indulge in meta-historical panegyrics, for supernatural phenomena carry no weight in Halachic matters. The *Shulhan 'Aruk* is not a revealed canon, nor is it a hypostasis of the Law. In the long, creative history of the Oral Law, it is one major link connecting R. Hai Gaon, Maimonides, Nahmanides and R. Solomon ibn Adret with R. Elijah Gaon of Vilna, R. Akiba Eiger, and R. Yosef Rosen. It is a significant work which, for a variety of reasons, became a repository and stimulus, a treasure and inspiration for Halachah, both practice and study.

22. What follows is based essentially on the authors' own, often autobiographical narratives; R. Joseph Karo's introductions to the *Bet Yosef* and R. Moses Isserles' introduction to the *Darke Mosheh*, which can conveniently be found in the Jerusalem, 1958 reprint of the *Turim*. I have interpolated historical or other explanatory comments, but have not seen fit to burden the reader with cumbersome references. I wanted simply to recount their tale.

23. He came to Palestine and settled in Safed in the year 1536. See Professor Z. Dimitrovsky in *Sefunot*, VII, p. 62, n. 137.

24. The verse is Isaiah 29:14 and is quoted in similar con-

situdes of exile, the endless turbulence of history, and the increasing human imperfection.[25] The need was great for a comprehensive as well as authoritative guide, which would stem the undesirable and almost uncontrollable proliferation of texts and provide a measure of religious uniformity in this period of great turmoil and dislocation. This would be accomplished, however, not by producing another compact, sinewy manual—a small volume such as the *Agur*, which R. Karo treats pejoratively[26]—but by reviewing the practical Halachah in its totality. The oracular type of code, containing curt, staccato directives and pronouncements, was neither adequate nor reliable. It did not provide for intellectual stimulus and expansion of the mind, nor did it offer correct guidance in religious practice.

R. Joseph Karo's ambitious undertaking in the field of rabbinic literature, entitled the *Bet Yosef (House of Joseph)*,[27] was thus motivated by the need to review "all the practical laws of Judaism, explaining their roots and origins in the Talmud" and all the conflicting interpretations concerning them. No extant work answered to this need. In order to avoid duplication or reduce it to a bare minimum, he decided to build his own work around an existing code that was popular and authoritative. He selected the *Turim* of R. Jacob b. Asher (1280–1340) rather than the more famous and widespread *Mishneh Torah* of R. Moses b. Maimon, because the latter was too concise and monolithic, presenting, on the whole, unilateral, undocumented decisions, while the former was expansive and more interpretive, citing alternate views and divergent explanations. At this stage, then, the text of the *Turim* was only a pretext for

his own work.[28] His method was to explain every single law in the text, note its original source, and indicate whether the formulation found in the *Turim* was the result of consensus or was subject to dispute. He would, furthermore, explain the alternate interpretations and formulations which the *Turim* referred to but rejected. In addition, he would introduce and elucidate those views which the *Turim* had totally omitted from consideration. As a purely theoretical increment, he promised to examine and explain those views of predecessors —especially Maimonides—which were problematic or remained obscure despite the availability of such commentaries as the *Maggid Mishneh*.[29] He would, incidentally, correct the text of the *Turim*, which suffered many scribal corruptions. That he intended his encyclopedic review of Halachah to be used as a study-guide is indicated by his promise always to give exact bibliographical references in order to enable his readers to consult original texts or check quotations in their original contexts. However, having completed this panoramic presentation and almost detached, academic analysis of a law, he would regularly indicate the normative conclusion, for the "goal is that we should have one Torah and one law." The function of this massive work is thus twofold: to flesh out the bare-bones codifications which are too brief and uninformative, but preserve their sinewiness and pragmatic advantage by unequivocally stating the *pesak*, the binding regulation, in each case.[30] Certitude and finality are among the top-priority items that will be guaranteed.[31]

In connection with this, the author lays bare his juridical methodology, a methodology that was to be vigorously contested, as we shall see. The judicial process was complex. A Talmudist could arrive at the normative conclusion by critically reviewing and appraising all arguments and demonstrations marshalled by his

---

text by Maimonides, introduction to the *Mishneh Torah*. The correlation of political adversity and intellectual decline becomes a constant theme and appears almost as a stereotype justification for Halachic abridgements or codifications. Difficult times necessitate the composition of books which would facilitate the study and perpetuate the practice of Halachah. Note, for example, the introduction to the *Turim*. See my *Rabad of Posquières* (Cambridge, 1962), pp. 133–134, n. 9.

25. This reflects the widespread attitude of humility, even of self-effacement, expressed in the Talmudic dictum: "If those before us were sons of angels, we are sons of men, and if those before us were sons of men, we are like asses" (*Shabbat*, 122b; *Yoma*, 9b). It is typical of the deep-rooted veneration traditionally displayed by later scholars to early masters. However, it did not, as we shall see, restrict independence of mind or stifle creative innovation. Fidelity and freedom were felicitously combined.

26. Why this small work, written by R. Jacob Landau at the end of the fifteenth century, is singled out for special criticism is not clear. . . .

27. He thus incorporated his first name into the title—again, pretty much standard literary procedure. There is, however, an added homiletical explanation: just as the house of Joseph in Egypt supplied bodily nourishment, so this book will supply spiritual nourishment.

28. Actually, the *Mishneh Torah*, with its theoretical approach, which included all laws and concepts, even those temporarily devoid of practical value, would not have been consonant with R. Joseph Karo's practical orientation, while the *Turim*, with its limited scope, did coincide with the latter goal. Another reason for selecting the *Turim* could have been the fact that the *Turim* was the most popular textbook at the time.

29. This foreshadows his later work, the *Kesef Mishneh*, in which he reveals himself as an astute, sympathetic and resourceful student of the *Mishneh Torah*.

30. Later commentators—e.g., the authors of the *Sefer Me'irat 'Enayim* and the *Bayit Hadash*—felt that R. Joseph Karo's ultimate codificatory aim vitiated his commentatorial one and that the former prevailed at the expense of the latter. Their own works, which were intended exclusively as faithful text commentaries, were thus urgent desiderata. Contemporaries such as R. Solomon Luria (*Yam shel Shelomoh, Hullin*, introduction) note the extraordinarily wide bibliographic coverage and unusual erudition of the *Bet Yosef*.

31. His striving for a powerful, central authority is unmistakable (and, incidentally, something he shared with his Sephardic teachers and colleagues—e.g., the great R. Jacob Berab). . . .

predecessors and then selecting the most cogent, persuasive view. His guide would be examination of underlying texts, relying, in the final analysis, upon his autonomous judgment and not on appeal to authority.[32] This independent, assertive approach is unqualifiedly repudiated by R. Joseph Karo for two reasons: 1) it would be presumptuous to scrutinize the judgment of such giants as R. Moses b. Nahman, R. Solomon b. Adret, R. Nissim, and the Tosafists and then pass judgment on them—we are not qualified or competent; 2) even if the task were not beyond our powers and capacities, the process would be too long and arduous. Forcefully underscoring his subservience and *apparently* forfeiting his judicial prerogatives, he chose to arrive at the normative conclusion in each case by following the consensus or at least the majority rule of the greatest medieval codifiers—R. Isaac Alfasi (d. 1103), Maimonides (d. 1204), and R. Asher ben Yehiel (d. 1328).[33] Contemporary legislation, innovation, and native usage are given no role whatsoever—almost as if the law were all logic and no experience. In other words, in the realm of commentary, R. Joseph Karo was bold and resourceful, while in the realm of adjudication he was laconic, almost self-effacing.

At about the same time, in entirely different circumstances and with a totally different motivation, R.

Moses Isserles, born into comfort and affluence,[34] son of a prominent communal leader who was also a gentleman scholar and (for a while) son-in-law of the greatest talmudic teacher in Poland (R. Shalom Shakna), also began to compile an exhaustive commentary on the *Turim*. He reveals the immediate stimulus which led to his project: having been persuaded by friends to assume rabbinic duties in Cracow—his youth, immaturity, and unripe scholarship notwithstanding—he found himself deciding many Halachic problems and issuing numerous judicial opinions. It was his practice to turn directly to the Talmud and consult its authoritative expositors, among whom he mentions R. Isaac Alfasi, R. Moses b. Nahman, and R. Asher b. Yehiel. He found, however, that he was repeatedly subjected to criticism for having ignored the rulings of the most recent scholars (e.g., R. Jacob Weil, R. Israel Isserlein, R. Israel Bruna) who were really the progenitors of contemporary Polish Jewry and gave it its creative and directive vital force. They introduced, *inter alia*, many preventive ordinances and stringent practices which tended to nullify earlier decisions, and as a result no picture of Halachah could be true to life which did not reflect these resources, motifs and developments. This put R. Moses Isserles in a bad light, and he and his colleagues were, therefore, subjected to much severe criticism, the validity of which he fully appreciated and accepted, as we shall see.

Impromptu, ad hoc review—and judicious, instantaneous application—of all this material, this panoply of interpretations and traditions, would be cumbersome, if not impossible. It therefore occurred to R. Moses Isserles that the way out was to prepare a digest and anthology of all opinions and record them alongside of a standard code. The best book was the *Turim*, for its arrangement was very attractive and useful, and it was easily intelligible to all. He set out, with great determination and commensurate perseverance, to implement this literary plan (he vividly describes his frenetic, indefatigable activity, without ease and without quiet). At a rather advanced stage of his work, he was electrified by the news that "the light of Israel, head of the exile" R. Joseph Karo had composed a comparable commentary on the *Turim*, the *Bet Yosef*, the excellence of which was immediately evident. R. Moses Isserles' anxiety was indescribable; just as he neared the hour of consummation, it appeared that his efforts and privations would turn out to be a wearying exercise in futility. He acknowledges—with what seems to be a blend of modesty and realism—that he could not hold a candle to R. Joseph Karo. However, shock did not lead to paralysis. His peace of mind and momentum were

32. The following passage from Benjamin Cardozo, *The Nature of the Judicial Process* (New Haven, 1921), p. 10, comes to mind: "What is it that I do when I decide a case? To what sources of information do I appeal for guidance? In what proportions do I permit them to contribute to the result? . . . If a precedent is applicable, when do I refuse to follow it? If no precedent is applicable, how do I reach the rule that will make a precedent for the future? If I am seeking logical consistency, the symmetry of the legal structure, how far shall I seek it? At what point shall the quest be halted by some discrepant custom, by some consideration of the social welfare, by my own or the common standards of justice and morals?"

The most forceful contemporary exponent of this approach was R. Solomon Luria, as exemplified in his *Yam shel Shelomoh*. He was preceded in this by R. Isaiah of Trani. See, generally, my *Rabad of Posquières*, pp. 216–19.

33. This distinguished triumvirate was already recognized as authoritative before the time of R. Joseph Karo, as he himself implies. Explicit confirmation is found in the *Responsa* of R. David b. Zimra (Radbaz), v. IV, n. 626. R. Moses Isserles (introduction to *Shulhan 'Aruk*) and R. Joshua Falk (introduction to *Sefer Me'irat 'Enayim*) suggest that the Sephardic view would automatically prevail inasmuch as Alfasi and Maimonides would always coalesce to determine the majority view. The truth is that R. Asher b. Yehiel was not fully representative of the Tosafistic school of France and Germany and was at a very early date accepted in Spain, to the exclusion of other Tosafists. This was noted in the introduction to the commentary *Ma'adane Yom Tob* and also in an anonymous responsum in R. Joseph Karo's *Abkat Rokel*, n. 18, which refers to R. Asher as a "Spanish rabbi." See the literary study by José Faur in the *Proceedings of the American Academy for Jewish Research*, XXIII (1965).

34. See his *Responsa*, nn. 45, 95, 109, and others.

restored when, reassessing the situation, he realized that the field had not been completely preempted and that he was still in a position to make a substantive contribution.

There were three areas in which he could realign his material and operate creatively and meaningfully:

1) He would compress the material, almost encyclopedic in its present proportions, and present a more precise formulation of the law. Length, as Maimonides notes, is one of the deterrents of study.[35] Nevertheless, R. Moses Isserles is somewhat apologetic at this point, because he was fully aware of the pitfalls of excessive brevity; indeed, it had been the codificatory syndrome —the rigidities and inadequacies of delphic manuals— that initially impelled him to disavow the methodology of existing codes. As a compromise, he determined to cite—not to reproduce or summarize—all sources, so that the inquisitive or dissatisfied but learned reader will be able to pursue matters further, while the less sophisticated and less talented reader will still benefit and not be able to argue that the material is too lengthy and complicated.

2) The *Bet Yosef* was too "classical," somewhat remote, for Germanic-Polish Jewry: it failed to represent equally the more recent codifiers and commentators. His work, the *Darke Mosheh*, would do justice to them by incorporating their positions. It would reflect the historical consciousness of R. Moses Isserles and his colleagues who looked upon themselves as heirs and continuators of the Ashkenazi tradition. On one hand, therefore, the *Darke Mosheh* would be an abridgement of the *Bet Yosef*, and, on the other, it would expand its scope. Clearly, R. Moses Isserles had taken the words of his earlier critics to heart.

3) Perhaps the most radical divergence between the two works appeared in the methodology of *pesak*, formulating the normative conclusion and obligatory pattern of behavior. Unlike R. Joseph Karo, who cautiously claimed to follow the *communis opinio*, or majority rule, of early codifiers, and unlike those who would freely exercise independent judgment in arriving at practical conclusions, R. Moses Isserles adopted a third stance: to follow most recent authorities—*halakah ke-batra'e*.[36] This method would preserve established

precedent and respect local custom. It is reflected stylistically in R. Moses Isserles' habit of underwriting the most valid view by adding "and this is customary" and then identifying the source or by noting candidly "and so it appears to me."[37] He is thus more independent and resourceful than R. Joseph Karo, though less so than R. Solomon Luria.[38] In short, as R. Moses Isserles puts it in a rhetorical flourish, "And Moses took the bones of Joseph"[39]—he adapted and transformed the essence of the *Bet Yosef* and abandoned the rest.

This ends the first chapter of our story in which R. Joseph Karo made it to the press before R. Moses Isserles and forced the latter to revise his initial prospectus in light of a changed literary reality. What is, of course, striking is the remarkable parallelism and similarity of attitudes between these two Talmudists, both seeking to push back the frontiers of Halachic literature, both convinced of the need to review individual laws in their totality and not rely upon delphic manuals, and both selecting the same code (*Turim*) as their springboard.

II

Ten years later, in the course of which the *Bet Yosef* spread far and wide and his authority was increasingly respected, R. Joseph Karo came full cycle in his own attitude towards the oracular-type code. Having previously and persuasively argued against the utility and wisdom of the apodictic compendium, he now conceded its need and efficacy. He himself abridged the voluminous *Bet Yosef*—"gathered the lilies, the sapphires"— and called his new work the *Shulhan 'Aruk*, "because in it the reader will find all kinds of delicacies" fastidiously arranged and systematized and clarified. He was persuaded that the *Shulhan 'Aruk* would serve the needs of a diffuse and heterogeneous audience. Scholars will use it as a handy reference book, so that every matter of law will be perfectly clear and the answer to ques-

35. The reference is probably to the *Guide for the Perplexed*, I, 34 (tr. S. Pines [Chicago, 1963], p. 73): "For man has in his nature a desire to seek the ends; and he often finds preliminaries tedious and refuses to engage in them."

36. In formulating this principle, R. Moses Isserles relies— with good effect—upon the authority of R. Isaac Alfasi. See *Darke Mosheh*, introduction, and *Yoreh De'ah*, 35:13. An anonymous contemporary, writing against R. Joseph Karo, advances the same position; *Abkat Rokel*, n. 18. Note R. Joseph Karo's important discussion in *Kesef Mishneh, Hilkot Mamrim*, II:1.

37. It is noteworthy that R. Hayyim b. Bezalel, a former classmate and colleague of R. Moses Isserles, took him to task for not going far enough in his vindication of local custom. The *Wikkuah Mayyim Hayyim* is built on this premise. This work is significant also in that it opts for still another possibility of juridical methodology. The author's contention is that a code should simply review all the different opinions and arrange them systematically but leave the final determination to the specific rabbinic authority that is responsible for a given decision. He protests forcefully against "levelling" books which tend to obliterate the distinctions between scholar and layman and implicitly undermine the authority of the scholar. A code should be an auxiliary manual for the judge and scholar, not an explicit, monolithic work.

38. See n. 13. R. Solomon Luria also displays an anti-Spanish, especially anti-Maimonidean, animus or polemicism, which is not found in R. Moses Isserles.

39. Exodus 13:19, with a play on the word "bones" (*'azmot*), which may be interpreted as essence (*'azmut*).

tions concerning Halachic practice will be immediate and decisive. Young, untutored students will also benefit by committing the *Shulhan 'Aruk* to memory, for even rote knowledge is not to be underestimated.[40]

When the *Shulhan 'Aruk appeared*, it elicited praise and provoked criticism; the former could be exuberant, and the latter, abrasive. Some contemporaries needed only to resuscitate R. Joseph Karo's initial stance and refurbish his arguments against such works as the *Agur*. R. Moses Isserles' reaction moved along the same lines which had determined his reaction to the *Bet Yosef*.[41] He could not—like R. Solomon Luria or R. Yom Tob Lipman Heller—take unqualified exception to the codificatory aim and form,[42] for he had already, in his revised *Darke Mosheh*, aligned himself in principle with this tendency and had eloquently defended it. He could, however, press his substantive and methodological attack on Karo: the latter had neglected Ashkenazic tradition and had failed to abide by the most recent rulings thereby ignoring custom which was such an important ingredient of the normative law.[43] Moreover, just as R. Joseph Karo drew upon his *Bet Yosef*, so R. Moses Isserles drew upon his *Darke Mosheh*;[44] both, coming full cycle, moved from lively judicial symposium to soulless legislative soliloquy. If R. Joseph Karo produced a "set table," R. Moses Isserles spread a "tablecloth" over it.[45] It is certain that the "table" would never have been universally accepted if it had not been covered and adorned with the "tablecloth." R. Moses Isserles' glosses, both strictures and annotations, were the ultimate validation of the *Shulhan 'Aruk*. The full dialectic has here played itself out, radical opposition to codes giving way to radical codification, almost with a vengeance; for the *Shulhan 'Aruk* is the leanest of all codes in Jewish history—from the *Bet Yosef* to the *Shulhan 'Aruk*, from the baroque to the bare.

It is not this dialectical movement *per se* which is novel or noteworthy, for this characterizes much of the history of post-Talmudic rabbinic literature. Attempts to compress the Halachah by formal codification alternate with counter-attempts to preserve the fulness and

richness of both the method and substance of the Halachah by engaging in interpretation, analogy, logical inference, and only then formulating the resultant normative conclusion. Any student who follows the course of rabbinic literature from the Geonic works of the eighth century through the *Mishneh Torah* and *Turim* and on down to the *Shulhan 'Aruk* cannot ignore this see-saw tendency. The tension is ever present and usually catalytic. No sooner is the need for codification met than a wave of non-codificatory work rises. A code could provoke guidance and certitude for a while but not finality.[46] *'Arvak 'arva zarik*—"your bondsman requires a bondsman." A code, even in the eyes of its admirers, required vigilant explanation and judicious application. The heartbeat had constantly to be checked and the pulse had to be counted. It became part of a life organism that was never complete or static. What is striking, therefore, in the case of the *Shulhan 'Aruk* is that the dialectical movement plays itself out in the attitudes and achievements of the same person—"surfing" on the "sea of the Talmud," rising and falling on the crests of analysis and thoughts of argumentation, and then trying to "gather the water into one area," to construct a dike that would produce a slow, smooth flow of its waters. The *Shulhan 'Aruk* thus offers an instructive example of the dialectical movement in rabbinic literature as a whole.

This whole story is important, I believe, because it expands the historical background against which the *Shulhan 'Aruk* is to be seen and cautions against excessive preoccupation with purely sociological data, with contemporary stimuli and contingencies. It makes the *Shulhan 'Aruk* understandable in terms of the general history of Halachic literature and its major trends. It provides an obvious vertical perspective—i.e. literary categories seen as part of an ongoing Halachic enterprise—to be used alongside of an, at best, implicit horizontal perspective—i.e. historical pressures and eschatological hopes—for an explanation of the emergence of the *Shulhan 'Aruk*.[47] This is strengthened by the striking parallelism between the literary careers of R. Moses Isserles and R. Joseph Karo; their historical situations, environmental influences, social contexts (in a phrase of contemporary jargon, their *sitz-im-leben*)

---

40. See *Berakot*, 38b. It is interesting that Maimonides also intended his *Mishneh Torah* to be used by "great and small," learned and simple.

41. See *Rabad of Posquières*, p. 113, and pp. 96–97.

42. A helpful review of these attitudes can be found in H. Tchernovitz, *Toledot ha-Poskim*, v. III. The rationale of this position is eloquently stated by the Maharal of Prague in *Netibot 'Olam, Netib ha-Torah*, ch. 15. I say "unqualified exception" because the fact is that R. Moses Isserles' contribution to the *Shulhan 'Aruk* is significantly more expansive than that of R. Joseph Karo.

43. See, e.g., *Orah Hayyim*, 619; *Yoreh De'ah*, 381, 386.

44. See his *Responsa*, nn. 35, 131.

45. The imagery is provided by R. Moses Isserles himself. The "table" was bare and uninviting without his "tablecloth."

46. See B. Cardozo, *The Nature of the Judicial Process*, p. 18: "Justinian's prohibition of any commentary on the product of his codifiers is remembered only for its futility."

47. This important vertical perspective is usually left out of the picture. See e.g., R. Werblowsky, *Joseph Karo*, pp. 7, 95, 167. There can be little doubt that R. Joseph Karo was preoccupied with eschatological hopes and that he saw the catastrophic nature of his period as having messianic significance. This is attested, *inter alia*, in the introduction to *Sefer Haredim*.

are so different, but their aspirations and attainments are so similar.

III

When we come to gauge and appraise the impact of the *Shulhan 'Aruk*, it is idle to speculate whether R. Joseph Karo intended the *Shulhan 'Aruk* to circulate and be used independently, as a literary unit sufficient to itself, or to be used only as a companion volume together with the *Bet Yosef*. His intention has been disputed and variously construed. Some condemned those who studied the *Shulhan 'Aruk in vacuo*, thereby acquiring superficial acquaintance with Halachah, claiming that this contravened the author's intention. Others treated the *Shulhan 'Aruk* in a manner reminiscent of R. Joseph Karo's original attitude as found in the preface to the *Bet Yosef*. In this case, however, the original intention of the author is eclipsed by the historical fact, abetted or perhaps made possible by R. Moses Isserles' glosses,[48] that the *Shulhan 'Aruk* and not the *Bet Yosef* became R. Joseph Karo's main claim to fame, and its existence was completely separate from and independent of the *Bet Yosef*. Commentators such as R. Abraham Gumbiner in the *Magen Abraham* effectively and irreparably cut the umbilical cord which may have linked the *Shulhan 'Aruk* with the *Bet Yosef*. What some literary critics have said about poetry may then be applied here: "The design of intention of the author is neither available nor desirable as a standard for judging the success of a work of literary art."[49] In our case, consequently, we should simply see what are some of the characteristics of the *Shulhan 'Aruk* and some of the repercussions of its great historical success.

Perhaps the single most important feature of the *Shulhan 'Aruk* is its unswerving concentration on pre-

scribed patterns of behavior to the exclusion of any significant amount of theoretical data. The *Shulhan 'Aruk* is a manual for practical guidance, not academic study. This practical orientation is discernible in many areas and on different levels.

First of all, by initially adopting the classification of the *Turim*, R. Joseph Karo capitulated unconditionally to the practical orientation. The import of this becomes more vivid when we contrast the two major codes on this point. The *Mishneh Torah* is all-inclusive in scope, obliterating all distinctions between practice and theory, and devoting sustained attention to those laws and concepts momentarily devoid of practical value or temporarily in abeyance because of historical and geographical contingencies. Laws of prayer and of the Temple ceremonial are given equal treatment. Laws concerning the *sotah*, the unfaithful wife (abrogated by R. Johanan b. Zakkai in the first century), are codified in the same detail as the ever practical marriage laws. The present time during which part of the law was in abeyance was, in Maimonides' opinion, an historical anomaly, a fleeting moment in the pattern of eternity. The real historical dimensions were those in which the Torah and its precepts were fully realized, that is, the time after the restoration of the Davidic dynasty, when "all the ancient laws will be reinstituted . . . sacrifices will again be offered, the Sabbatical and Jubilee years will again be observed in accordance with the commandments set forth in the Law."[50] The Oral Law was, therefore, to be codified and studied exhaustively. The *Turim*, on the other hand, addresses itself only to those laws that are relevant, to those concrete problems and issues whose validity and applicability are not confined either temporally or geographically. For while both Maimonides and R. Jacob b. Asher were of one mind in abandoning the sequence of the Talmudic treatises and seeking an independent classification of Halachah, they differed in their goals: Maimonides sought to create a topical-conceptual arrangement that would provide a new interpretive mold for study and would also be educationally sound, while R. Jacob b. Asher was guided only by functionality and as a result was less rigorous conceptually. It involved a lesser degree of logical analysis and abstraction, and did not hesitate to group disparate items together. A code, according to this conception should facilitate the understanding of the operative laws and guide people in translating concepts into rules of conduct.

The *Shulhan 'Aruk* adds a further rigorism to the practicality of the *Turim*. The *Turim*'s practicality expresses itself in the rigid selection of material, in the

---

48. The fact is that R. Moses Isserles' strictures are very radical, but low-keyed and disarmingly calm. They are free of the stridency and impetuosity which punctuate the glosses of R. Abraham b. David on the *Mishneh Torah*, but are nevertheless uncompromising in their criticism. While they contain explanations, amplifications and supplements, most were designed simply to supersede R. Joseph Karo's conclusions. It is only the harmonious literary form that avoided an overt struggle for Halachic hegemony such as occurred in other periods—for example, in the thirteenth century when Spanish students of the great Nahmanides attempted to impose their customs and interpretations on Provence. There was no dilution of diversity in this case, either, but there was at least a formal fusion of Ashkenazi and Sephardi Halachah in one work. Sephardim continued to rely on R. Joseph Karo, pointing to the verse, "Go unto Joseph; what he saith to you, do" (Genesis 41:55); Ashkenazim continued to rely on R. Moses Isserles, adapting the verse, "For the children of Israel go out with upraised hands" (*beyad ramah*—and "Ramah" was the acrostic for R. Moses Isserles).

49. W. K. Wimsatt and M. C. Beardsley, "The Intentional Fallacy," *Sewanee Review*, LIV (1946), 468.

50. *Hilkot Melakim*, XI:1. See Rabbi J. B. Soloveitchik, "Ish ha-Halakah," *Talpiyot*, 1944, pp. 668 ff.

circumscribed scope, but not in the method of presentation, which is rich, varied, and suggestive, containing as it does much textual interpretation and brief discussion of divergent views, while the functionality of the *Shulhan 'Aruk* is so radical that it brooks no expansiveness whatsoever. The judicial *process* is of no concern to the codifier; exegesis, interpretation, derivation, awareness of controversy—all these matters are totally dispensable, even undesirable, for the codifier.[51] In this respect, the *Shulhan 'Aruk* has greater affinities with the *Mishneh Torah*, which also purports to eliminate conflicting interpretations and rambling discussions and to present *ex cathedra* legislative, unilateral views, without sources and without explanations. The fact is that the *Shulhan 'Aruk* is much closer to this codificatory ideal than the *Mishneh Torah*, which, after all, is as much commentary as it is code. One has only to compare, at random, parallel sections of the *Turim* and *Shulhan 'Aruk* to realize fully and directly, almost palpably, the extent to which the *Shulhan 'Aruk* pruned

the *Turim*, relentlessly excising midrashic embellishments, ethical perceptions, and theoretical amplifications. It promised to give the "fixed, final law, without speech and without words." It left little to discretion or imagination.

There is yet another area in which this austere functionality comes to the surface—in the virtually complete elimination of ideology, theology, and teleology. The *Shulhan 'Aruk*, unlike the *Mishneh Torah* or the *Sefer ha-Rokeah*, has no philosophical or Kabbalistic prolegomenon or peroration. The *Shulhan 'Aruk*, unlike the *Mishneh Torah* or the *Turim*, does not abound in extra-Halachic comments, guiding tenets and ideological directives.[52] While, as I have tried to prove elsewhere, the *Mishneh Torah* does reveal the full intellectualistic posture of Maimonides,[53] the *Shulhan 'Aruk* does not even afford an oblique glimpse of the Kabbalistic posture of R. Joseph Karo, who appears here in the guise of the civil lawyer for whom "nothing was more pointless, nothing more inept than a law with a preamble."[54] He was concerned exclusively with what Max Weber called the "methodology of sanctification" which produces a "continuous personality pattern," not with its charismatic goals or stimuli, the ethical underpinning or theological vision which suffuse the Halachah with significance, guarantee its radical, ineradicable spirituality and thereby nurture the religious consciousness. The *Shulhan 'Aruk* gives the concrete idea, but omits what Dilthey called *Erlebniss*, the experiential component. In the *Shulhan 'Aruk* the Halachah manifests itself as the *regula iuris*, a rule of life characterized by stability, regularity, and fixedness, making known to people "the

51. This is, of course, a codificatory utopia, never achieved. First, all the author's protestations not withstanding, the *Shulhan 'Aruk* is not a mechanical, scissors-and-paste compilation. For all his veneration and authority and his *a priori* declaration of subservience to the three great medieval codifiers, the author writes selectively and discriminatingly. Already his contemporary, R. Hayyim b. Bezalel, observed (in the *Wikkuah Mayyim Hayyim*) that Karo did not really follow the standards he outlined theoretically. Similarly, R. Moses Isserles in the introduction to the *Darke Mosheh* called attention to inconsistencies and discrepancies between the statement of intention and actual performance. There are many examples which show how subtly but steadily the author of the *Shulhan 'Aruk* modified positions and expressed his own judgment. This is often indicated by the deletion of a phrase or addition of a word in what is otherwise a verbatim reproduction of a source. Note *Yoreh De'ah* 246:4, which is almost an exact quotation of Maimonides. *Hilkot Talmud Torah*, I:11, 12. The author has, however, expunged the sentence which makes philosophy (*pardes*) an integral, even paramount component of the Oral Tradition, for this statement obviously caused him more than a twinge of discomfiture. R. Moses Isserles reinserts this reference less conspicuously and more restrainedly toward the end of his gloss. The author's censure of the writings of Immanuel of Rome (*Orah Hayyim*, 307:16) is an example of a novel, emphatic addition.

Second, all the author's statements about certitude, finality, and unilateral formulations notwithstanding, there are many paragraphs which cite multiple views. Sometimes reference is even made to the authorship of these divergent views. See, e.g., *Orah Hayyim*, 18:1; 32:9; 422:2 and many others. This area of indecision is one of the major concerns of the nineteenth-century work, *'Aruk ha-Shulhan* by Rabbi Y. M. Epstein, and such earlier works as *Halacha Aharonah we-Kuntros ha-Re'ayot*.

Third, there is a sparse amount of interpretive and exegetical material. See, e.g., *Orah Hayyim*, 6:1, which contains the explanation of a liturgical text. Note also 11:15, 14:1, 14:3, 15:4, 17:1 and many others where reasons are briefly adduced or the Halachic process is traced. What is more, even the self-sufficiency of the work is weakened when, for example, the author says (*Orah Hayyim*, 597), "this is explained well in the *Tur* in this section."

52. One striking illustration is provided by the prologue of the *Turim* to the *Hoshen Mishpat*, where the instrumental role of positive law is expounded. The point of departure is the apparent contradiction between two statements in the first chapter of *Pirke Abot*. One reads: "Upon three things the world stands, upon Torah, upon divine service, and upon acts of lovingkindness." The other reads: "By three things is the world sustained, by justice, truth, and peace." These are means; the others are ends. The author of the *Shulhan 'Aruk* omits all preambles and plunges directly into the legal-institutional details. Compare the two also at *Orah Hayyim*, 61, 125, 242 (introduction to the laws of Sabbath) and others. At *Yoreh De'ah*, 335 (visitation of the sick), the *Turim* starts unhurriedly with a midrashic motif used by Nahmanides at the beginning of his code *Torat ha-Adam*, while the *Shulhan 'Aruk* plunges *medias in res*. It has no time—or need—for adornment.

53. In my article "Some Non-Halakic Aspects of the Mishneh Torah," which is scheduled to appear soon in *Medieval and Renaissance Studies*, ed. A. Altman (Cambridge, 1967).

54. J. W. Jones, *The Law and Legal Theory of the Greeks*, p. 8. R. Moses Isserles fleshed out a good number of the lean formulations in the *Shulhan 'Aruk*, introducing many Kabbalistic motifs and explanations. See, for example, *Orah Hayyim*, 426 (on New Moon), 583 (on Hoshanah Rabbah), 664 (on *kapparot*), and others. See also 290, in comparison with the *Turim*. He is thus much less reserved and less reticent than his Sephardic counterpart.

way they are to go and the practices they are to follow" (Exodus 18:20). These specific, visible practices are not coordinated with invisible meaning or unspecified experience. One can say, in general, that there are two major means by which apparently trans-Halachic material has been organically linked with the Halachah proper: 1) construction of an ideational framework which indicates the ultimate concerns and gives coherence, direction and vitality to the concrete actions; 2) elaboration of either a rationale of the law or a mystique of the law which suggests explanations and motives for the detailed commandments. The *Shulhan 'Aruk*, for reasons of its own, about which we may only conjecture, attempts neither.

IV

This restrictive, almost styptic trait of the *Shulhan 'Aruk* was noticed—and criticized—by contemporaries, foremost among whom was R. Mordecai Jaffe (1530–1612), disciple of R. Moses Isserles and R. Solomon Luria, and successor of R. Judah Loewe, the famous Maharal, of Prague. It is worth re-telling the story of the composition of his major, multi-volume work, known as the *Lebush*, inasmuch as it zeroes in on the radical functionality of the *Shulhan 'Aruk* and also briefly reviews the tense dialectic surrounding codification which we discussed above.

R. Mordecai Jaffe, a very articulate, sophisticated writer who was well acquainted with the contemporary scene, describes the enthusiastic reception accorded to the *Bet Yosef* because people imagined it would serve as a concise, spiritual compendium, obviating the need for constant, wearisome recourse to dozens of rabbinic volumes in order to determine the proper Halachic course. He shared this feeling and heightened anticipation, but enthusiasm gave way to disillusionment as he realized that the *Bet Yosef* was anything but concise. Inasmuch as a comprehensive and compact compendium remained an urgent desideratum, he began a condensation of the *Bet Yosef* that would serve this purpose. External factors—an edict of expulsion by the Austrian emperor, which compelled him to flee Bohemia and settle in Italy—interrupted his work. In Italy, where so much Hebrew printing was being done, he heard that R. Joseph Karo himself had made arrangements to print an abridgement. Again he desisted, for he could not presume to improve upon the original author who would unquestionably produce the most balanced, incisive abridgment of his own work. R. Jaffe adds parenthetically—but with remarkable candor—that there was a pragmatic consideration as well: even if he persisted and completed his work, he could not hope to compete publicly with such a prestigious master as R. Joseph Karo—and to do it just for personal consumption, to satisfy his own needs, would be extravagant.

However, upon preliminary examination of the *Shulhan 'Aruk*—in Venice—he noted two serious deficiencies. First, it was too short and astringent, having no reasons or explanations—"like a sealed book, a dream which had no interpretation or meaning." He describes it as "a table well prepared with all kinds of refreshments, but the dishes are tasteless, lacking the salt of reasoning which makes the broth boil and warms the individual"—i.e., lacking a minimum of explanatory and exhortatory material to embellish and spiritualize the bald Halachic directives. Second, it was almost exclusively Maimonidean, or Sephardic, and Ashkenazic communities could not, therefore, be guided by it—an argument that had been tellingly and uncompromisingly put forward by both his teachers (Isserles and Luria). Again he started work on a new composition which would fill the gap, and again he abandoned his plans in deference to R. Moses Isserles who was reported to have undertaken this task. When the full *Shulhan 'Aruk* appeared—the text of R. Joseph Karo and the glosses of R. Moses Isserles—he quickly realized that only the second deficiency had been remedied, that Ashkenazic Halachah had found a worthy and zealous spokesman, but the first deficiency remained—and this was glaring. Some measure of explanation was as indispensable for law as salt was for food. So, for the third time, he turned to producing a code which would a) strive for a golden mean between inordinate length (the *Bet Yosef*) and excessive brevity (the *Shulhan 'Aruk*); and b) would explain, motivate, and spiritualize the law, often with the help of new Kabbalistic doctrines.

In effect, R. Mordecai Jaffe—whose code was a potential but short-lived rival to the *Shulhan 'Aruk*—addressed himself to the problem which great Halachists, ethicists, philosophers and mystics have constantly confronted: how to maintain a rigid, punctilious observance of the law and concomitantly avoid externalization and routinization. On one hand, we hear the echoes of Maimonides, R. Eleazar ha-Rokeah of Worms, and R. Menaḥem b. Zerah (author of the *Zedah la-Derek*), who attempt to combine laws with their reasons and rationale, as well as R. Bahya ibn Pakuda, R. Jonah Gerondi, and R. Isaac Abuhab, to mention just a few of his predecessors. On the other hand, this tone continues to reverberate in the *Shulhan 'Aruk* of R. Shneur Zalman of Ladi, as well as in the writings of R. Isaiah Hurwitz and R. Moses Hayyim Luzzato, to mention just a few of his successors. The common denominator here is the concern that the Halachic enterprise always be rooted in and related to spirituality, to knowledge of God obtained through study and experience. All difficulties notwithstanding, it was generally felt that even when dealing with the corpus of practical, clearly definable law, an attempt should be made to express the—perhaps incommunicable—values and aspirations of religious experience and spiritual existence.

V

However, when all is said, it would be incorrect and insensitive to assert unqualifiedly that the *Shulhan 'Aruk,* that embodiment of Halachah which Jewish history has proclaimed supreme, is a spiritless, formalistic, even timid work. Its opening sentence, especially as elaborated by R. Moses Isserles, acts as the nerve center of the entire Halachic system and the fountain of its strength.

> A man should make himself strong and brave as a lion[55] to rise in the morning for the service of his Creator, so that he should "awake the dawn" (Psalms 57:9)[56] . . .
> "I have set the Lord always before me" (Psalms 16:8). This is a cardinal principle in the Torah and in the perfect (noble) ways of the righteous who walk before God. For[57] man does not sit, move, and occupy himself when he is alone in his house, as he sits, moves, and occupies himself when he is in the presence of a great king; nor does he speak and rejoice while he is with his family and relatives as he speaks in the king's council. How much more so when man takes to heart that the Great King, the Holy One, blessed be He, whose "glory fills the whole earth" (Isaiah 6:3), is always standing by him and observing all his doings, as it is said in Scripture: "Can a man hide himself in secret places that I shall not see him?" (Jeremiah 23:24). Cognizant of this, he will immediately achieve reverence and humility, fear and shame before the Lord, blessed be He, at all times.

Law is dry and its details are burdensome only if its observance lacks vital commitment, but if all actions of a person are infused with the radical awareness that he is acting in the presence of God, then every detail becomes meaningful and relevant. Such an awareness rules out routine, mechanical actions; everything must be conscious and purposive in a God-oriented universe, where every step of man is directed towards God. Ha-

lachah, like nature, abhors a vacuum; it recognizes no twilight zone of neutrality or futility.[58] It is all-inclusive. Consequently, every action—even tying one's shoes[59]—can be and is invested with symbolic meaning. Nothing is accidental, behavioral, purely biological. Even unavoidable routine is made less perfunctory. The opening paragraph of the *Shulhan 'Aruk* is thus a clear and resounding declaration concerning the workings and the searchings of the spirit. Its tone should reverberate throughout all the subsequent laws and regulations. It provides—as does also paragraph 231, which urges man to see to it that *all* his deeds be "for the sake of heaven"—an implicit rationale for the entire Halachah, but it is a rationale that must be kept alive by the individual. It cannot be passively taken for granted; it must be passionately pursued.

What I am saying, in other words, is that to a certain extent the *Shulhan 'Aruk* and Halachah are coterminous and that the "problem" of the *Shulhan 'Aruk* is precisely the "problem" of Halachah as a whole. Halachah itself is a tense, vibrant, dialectical system which regularly insists upon normativeness in action and inwardness in feeling and thought.[60] It undertook to give concrete and continuous expression to theological ideals, ethical norms, ecstatic moods, and historical concepts but never superseded or eliminated these ideals and concepts. Halachah itself is, therefore, a coincidence of opposites: prophecy and law, charisma and institution, mood and medium, image and reality, the thought of eternity and the life of temporality. Halachah itself, therefore, in its own behalf, demands the coordination of inner meaning and external observance —and it is most difficult to comply with such a demand and sustain such a delicate, highly sensitized synthesis.[61]

There can be no doubt that R. Joseph Karo, the arch mystic passionately yearning for ever greater spiritual heights, could not have intended to create a new concept of orthopraxis, of punctilious observance of the law divorced, as it were, from all spiritual tension. While this may indeed have been one of the unintended repercussions of the *Shulhan 'Aruk*—while it may un-

---

55. See *Pirke Abot*, V: 23.

56. This verse, meaning that man "awakens the dawn and not that dawn awakens man," is elaborated in the Palestinian Talmud, *Berakot*, ch. 1 and is cited by the *Turim*.

57. What follows is part quotation, part paraphrase from the *Guide for the Perplexed*, III, 52. Maimonides refers in this context to the Talmudic saying in *Kiddushin*, 31a forbidding a person to "walk about proudly, with erect stature," because of the verse, "the whole earth is full of His glory." He concludes: "This purpose to which I have drawn your attention is the purpose of all the actions prescribed by the Law."

58. See Maimonides' definition of futile action in *Guide for the Perplexed* III, 25: "A futile action is that action by which no end is aimed at at all, as when some people play with their hands while thinking and like the actions of the negligent and the inattentive."

59. *Orah Hayyim*, 2:4.

60. See the brief discussion of this in my article in *Tradition*, V (1963), pp. 144–45. For a clear, almost unnoticed example of this correlation, see *Yoreh De'ah*, 335:4 where it is stated that the external action of visiting a sick person without the concomitant feeling of compassion and inward action of prayer for his recovery does not constitute the fulfillment of a *mizvah*.

61. See in this connection G. Van der Leeuw, *Religion in Essence and Manifestation* (Harper, 1963), II, p. 459 ff; Joachim Wach, *Sociology of Religion* (Chicago, 1944), p. 17 ff.

knowingly have contributed to the notion, maintained by a strange assortment of people, that Judaism is all deed and no creed, all letter and no spirit—its author would certainly discountenance such an interpretation and dissociate himself from it. If the *Shulhan 'Aruk* only charts a specific way of life but does not impart a specific version or vision of meta-Halachah, it is because the latter is to be supplied and experienced independently.[62] The valiant attempt of so many scholars to compress the incompressible, imponderable values of religious experience into cold words and neat formulae, alongside of generally lucid Halachic prescriptions, did not elicit the support of R. Joseph Karo. Halachas could be integrated with and invigorated by disparate, mutually exclusive systems, operating with different motives and aspirations, as long as these agreed on the means and directives. I would suggest that R. Mordecai Jaffe's parenthetical apology for his expansive-interpretive approach to Halachah—that every person spices his food differently, that every wise person will find a different reason or taste in the law, and this reason should not be codified or legislated—may well be what prompted R. Joseph Karo, generally reticent about spiritual matters, to limit his attention to the concrete particularization of Halachah. This could be presented with a good measure of certitude and finality, but its spiritual coordinates required special and separate, if complementary, treatment.[63]

As a personal postscript, or "concluding unscientific postscript," I would like to suggest that, if the Psalmist's awareness of "I have set God before me continually" (Psalm 16:8)—the motto of the *Shulhan 'Aruk*—is

one of the standards of saintliness,[64] then all "*Shulhan 'Aruk* Jews," all who abide by its regulations while penetrating to its essence and its real motive powers, should be men who strive for saintliness. But strive they must, zealously, imaginatively, and with unrelenting commitment.[65]

Notes and Questions to Isadore Twersky, "The Shulhan Aruk"

1. Did the *Shulhan Aruk* rigidify and "fix" the law, making it less able to meet the needs of a changing society, or did it, on the contrary, standardize Jewish legal norms, and take cognizance of historical developments in the law, thereby facilitating their application in Jewish communities all over the world?

2. ORIGINS AND DEVELOPMENT OF THE RESPONSA
(By S. Freehoff) *

When a legal system has not yet been clearly codified, but is still to a large extent a mass of unorganized tradition, then those who are the carriers of the tradition attain a special status. The average man is, under the circumstances, unable to learn the law independently, as he could if it were codified. He has to turn to those who are the repositories of the tradition. "The priest's lips should keep knowledge, and they shall seek the law at his mouth" (Malachi 2:7). The priest was the transmitter of the old traditions and, since there was no clear code, the only way for a person to know the law was to ask him.

Such personal inquiries were the rule in many legal systems at the stage when they carried a body of unorganized or half-organized traditions. Besides, the greater the reliance upon a non-professional judge—so that the judgment of the average person, sitting as a member of a jury, was the source of decision—the greater was the need for special legal guidance. The amateur judge needed someone to whom to turn with an inquiry in cases of special difficulty.

These personal inquiries inevitably take the form of correspondence when the people under the legal system involved live scattered over a large area or in various countries. There is almost certain to develop some system of asking and receiving opinions from an expert who dwells in the metropolis or in the mother country from which the colonists had spread. Such were the

62. The introduction to the *Shulhan 'Aruk* should perhaps be re-examined at this point. After stating that this compendium will serve the needs of the veteran scholar and the uninitiated student, the author refers to the pleasures which the *maskilim*, the wise men, will derive from his work. *Maskilim* is a common epithet for Kabbalists, for mystics proficient in esoteric lore. "The wise will shine like the brightness of heaven when they shall have rest from their travail and the labor of their hands." Does this suggest that the *Shulhan 'Aruk* will provide a compass with the help of which the *maskilim* will be able to chart their own course in the lofty spiritual realms?
It should also be noted that R. Joseph Karo is for the most part uncommunicative about his inner world, his spiritual *Anschuung*, and even about such contemporary issues in which he was deeply involved, as the attempted re-institution of ordination in Safed. I would add that even in the *Kesef Mishnah* he remains remarkably reticent (see, e.g., *Hilkot Talmud Torah*, I:11, 12), and only occasionally is a subdued comment forthcoming (e.g., *Yesode ha-Torah*, I:10; *Teshubah* III:7; X:6).
The introduction to the *Bet Yosef* has a single laconic reference to the *Zohar*. R. Moses Isserles is more expressive in this respect; see n. 33.
63. See the balanced remarks of Werblowsky, pp. 290–92; also pp. 146–47.

64. S. Schechter, *Studies in Judaism* (New York, 1958), p. 147.
65. See R. Moses Hayyim Luzzatto, *Mesillat Yesharim* (Philadelphia, 1948), pp. 3–4.
*From Solomon Freehoff, *The Responsa Literature* (Philadelphia, 1955).

circumstances which prevailed in earlier Roman history. The Law itself, originally in the keeping of the priest, was imperfectly codified. Also, the judge, the *iudex*, was not generally a professionally trained lawyer. Thus there emerged a group of people who specialized in the knowledge of the traditions and forms of the Law. These were known as "Consultants in the Law" (*iuris consulti*), or the "Wise Men of the Law" (*iuris prudentes*). The answers which they gave to the questions asked of them were known therefore as *responsa prudentium*, "the answers of the learned." In later Roman Law these responsa attained considerable authority. The Emperor Augustus, for example, gave certain jurists the right to issue responsa which carried the emperor's authority. The right to answer legal questions officially fell into disuse by the end of the third century of the present era, but in the meantime a body of responsa had accumulated which had considerable legal authority.

Similar conditions prevailed in Mohammedan Law. The Mohammedan world was widespread and the Law was still largely in the form of unorganized tradition. Hence there developed the Moslem *fatwa* as an important element in Moslem Law. The bases of Islamic Law, in addition to that found in the Koran, are the decisions and statements made by Mohammed himself. These were handed down by tradition. These traditions were variously collected and organized into different systems of law. Moreover, since the judge, the *cadi*, was not a professionally trained lawyer, there was constant need for experts who could be approached for opinions. Thus there was a *mufti* in every community who gave *fatwas*, or responsa, as to what the law was. These *fatwas* were generally not discussions, but merely brief answers to the questions before him, sometimes merely "yes" or "no." The sultan in Constantinople appointed a supreme *mufti* who answered questions which the Palace presented to him.

In the American legal system, there is also some need for what might be described as responsa, or law set forth in correspondence. This is chiefly due to the fact that the amount of new legislation is always large; and it is frequently important, before undertaking certain business enterprises, to know what the implication of the relevant laws may be. Hence the attorney general of most states, and also the attorney general of the United States with regard to Federal laws, will issue opinions which constitute a definition of the meaning of a law. While they do not always have the effect of law itself or that of a case decided in the courts, these "responsa" of the attorneys general have great weight in the development of law. This parallels exactly the place and influence of responsa in Jewish Law.

The factors mentioned above—the inchoate nature of the tradition, resort to non-professional judges, distance from a central authority, risk involved in relying on unofficial interpretation—operated toward the development of the responsa in Jewish Law. The Law was largely a tradition. That which was written in Scripture had been amplified and explained by the Oral Law taught in the schools in Palestine and later in the schools of Babylonia. There was constant need for the opinion of experts as to what the Law implied or intended. Furthermore, in Jewish Law the judges were often laymen selected as arbitrators by the parties to the dispute and therefore they frequently needed guidance and advice. Perhaps the most important factor was the fact that Jewry was widely scattered almost from the very beginning of the development of the postbiblical Law. The amplifications of Scripture which gradually found their way into the Mishna had to be made known to the populous Jewry which remained in Babylonia. Hence we find already in the talmudic literature evidences of the development of law by correspondence, through messages sent from Palestine to Babylonia.

There was, however, a special difficulty which hindered the development of Jewish Law by correspondence. This lay in the fact that it was forbidden to put the Oral Law into written form. The part of the Law which was written, namely, the Bible, could always be copied; but that which was oral had to remain oral, to be taught by word of mouth and not be recorded. How then was it ever possible to send legal advice by correspondence? This problem is taken up in the Talmud. The question arises incidentally in a discussion about the sacrifices offered in the Temple, specifically as to whether the libations could be offered at night as well as by day. "When Rav Dimi went up (that is, came to Palestine from Babylonia), he found Rabbi Jeremiah lecturing in the name of Rabbi Joshua ben Levi as follows: 'Whence do we derive the fact that the libations which accompany a sacrifice can be offered only by day.'" Rav Dimi heard Rabbi Jeremiah prove this law on the basis of an interpretation of a biblical verse. The discussion then continues as follows: "He (Rav Dimi) said: 'If I could have found a messenger, I would have written a letter and sent it to Rabbi Joseph in Babylonia (telling him of what Jeremiah here in Palestine had said).'"

The Talmud then continues to discuss the statement of Rav Dimi that he would have sent a letter to Babylonia if he had found a messenger. It says: "If he *had* found a messenger, could he have written such a letter at all? Did not Rabbi Abba in the name of Rabbi Johanan say that those who write down the traditional (the oral) teachings are like those who actually burn the Torah and that he who learns the Oral Law from such writings receives no reward?" (In other words, how could he write a letter on a question of Oral Law when the Oral Law may not be written down?)

The answer which the Talmud gives is that perhaps the case is different in regard to *new* interpretations (that is, new ideas may perhaps be written down). Furthermore, it is better that one letter of the Torah should be uprooted than that the whole Torah should be forgotten. In other words, it is better occasionally to give up the old prohibitions against writing down the Oral Law than to run the risk that the expanding Law, growing through the accumulation of new ideas, should become too vast for the memory to hold and thus be forgotten.

Because the Oral Law could not possibly be remembered as it expanded and developed, the old prohibition against writing down the Oral Law lapsed and soon much of it to that date was written down in the Mishna. From then on there was less objection to new questions in the Law being dealt with by correspondence. Thus, for example, Rabbi Johanan in Palestine wrote to Rab and Samuel in Babylonia; while at another time Samuel sent to Rab Johanan thirteen scrolls full of questions and discussions as to the ritual unfitness of certain animals or birds. Once, when Judah ben Ezekiel in Babylonia was discussing a matter of trespassing, Rab Kahana said to him: "I will bring a letter from the west (that is, from Palestine) that the law is not according to Rabbi Simon (whom you are following)." Clearly these letters from Palestine were considered authoritative. There are frequent references in various tractates of the Talmud to Rab Abin, a Babylonian who went to Palestine and sent letters from there giving the opinion of the Palestinian authorities. Thus, in a discussion as to the rights of a widow to be sustained by the estate of her late husband, Rab Pappa says, "If it were not for the fact that Rab Abin had spoken of it in the letter that he sent, I would not know the law, etc." . . .

In addition to the exilarch, who was virtually a king over the Babylonian community, and his officially appointed judges, there were the great Babylonian schools, those of Sura and Pumpeditha, whose chief teachers had the title of "Gaon" (Eminence). . . .

To the gaonim questions began to come from every land where Jews were settled. The gaonim encouraged the sending of these questions for a number of reasons: their sense of duty to Judaism, a consciousness of their own authority in Jewish life and, no doubt also, because each inquiry was generally accompanied by a contribution for the maintenance of their schools. As the Jews of the diaspora in the earlier centuries had

maintained the Temple, so from the sixth to the eleventh centuries they maintained the schools of Babylonia by means of these and other contributions.

The answers, the responsa, of the gaonim accumulated in the course of those centuries. While, presumably, tens of thousands of them have been lost, many hundreds remain and form the first great body of Jewish laws-by-correspondence. Cairo in Egypt was the natural distribution point for the answers sent to the western lands—to northwest Africa, Spain and elsewhere—and these answers were often copied in Cairo and a copy kept there. Hence, when the great *Geniza* ("the lumber room") in Cairo was uncovered by Solomon Schechter a generation ago, perhaps the greatest treasure discovered there was the hoard of gaonic responsa. The Cairo *Geniza* gave a new impetus to the study of these early legal letters.

The gaonic responsa were generally brief and direct. We wish they were a little more elaborate. It would have been better if they began, as in later responsa, with more (there are some) honorific salutations to the writer and to the people of his community. Perhaps, then, the addressee and the address would have been preserved. Mostly, however, they are not preserved, and the only introduction we have in most of the responsa is, "as for your question, etc." Had they been preserved we would know the names and the status of many Jewish communities and have a far clearer idea than we now have of the distribution of the Jews in those days. The answers were rarely long. Sometimes the questioner asked for an interpretation of a difficult passage in the Talmud and the answer had to be somewhat elaborate; but generally it was a direct, concise response to a specific question.

A large proportion of the questions dealt with the procedure and customs of worship. With the Jews scattered far and wide, different synagogue customs quickly developed and the gaonim felt the necessity of bringing order into this situation.

A gaonic responsum will often simplify a rather complex law in a terse, almost epigrammatic way. . . .

A large number of the gaonic responsa answer questions which ask for the meaning of talmudic passages. Some of the questions are rather simple, such as a student might ask of his teacher. But in the days of the gaonim many of the communities were just beginning to become acquainted with the Talmud and there were no available commentaries.

The gaonim, thus, regulated synagogue customs, clarified complicated questions in the Law and interpreted and explained the Talmud to inquirers in many lands. Their interpretations of the laws became the basis of later codes and later responsa, and their explanatory comments on talmudic passages the basis of later talmudic commentaries.

Although one of the later gaonim might refer in a responsum to responsa of his predecessors, there is no evidence that the gaonim themselves collected their responsa or considered them as a separate branch of Jewish literature that would need to be preserved as such. To the gaonim, their decisions were simply decisions. Sometimes the decision required some elaboration; sometimes they gave expository commentaries on a portion of a talmudic text. But these were not preserved any more than most people preserve a copy of their correspondence. The recipients, however, did preserve them. Collections of gaonic responsa have therefore come down to us; and in the age of printing many of them were published. To the gaonim themselves, their responsa thus represented their legal correspondence; but to the scholars of the diaspora, the responsa were the source and the foundation for their own study of the Talmud and for their own commentaries as well as compendia of law.

The knowledge of the Talmud, helped and fostered by the activity and guidance of the gaonim, eventually began to flourish in the western lands. Soon competent local authorities emerged in western North Africa (in what is now Tunis and Algiers), in Spain, in France and in the Rhineland. Since it was always difficult and expensive to send inquiries by land and sea all the way to Babylonia, it was natural that more and more questions, which might earlier have been addressed to the gaonim, would now be directed to the local scholars. These scholars answered as they had been taught to answer in the responsa of the gaonim—briefly, directly and with a minimum of explanation. The responsa of the early diaspora scholars were also to a large extent in Arabic (the universal language of the Islamic lands), as were many of the responsa of the gaonim. Since they were not yet considered an independent branch of Jewish legal literature, but merely answers to inquiries or decisions on problems, they were not preserved by their writers but by others. In fact, many of the decisions of those scholars who lived at the time of the later gaonim were often preserved amid collections of gaonic responsa. Thus, the responsa of Kalonymus of Lucca and of his son, Meshullam in Germany, and the responsa of Rabbenu Hananel of Kairouan in North Africa, were preserved in other books. For a century or so after the gaonim, the western scholars felt no need to preserve their own responses. Isaac Alfasi, the great authority of the eleventh century in Spain, and Maimonides, in the following century, wrote their responsa mostly in Arabic. Their brief, unelaborated decisions were not made available as separate collections for many centuries after their death, and certainly many hundreds of their responsa have been lost. So, too, in northern France, Rashi, the chief authority of his day, did not gather or preserve his responsa. All we have are scattered references to his decisions in the books of his disciples.

Not until the respondents began to write elaborate responsa, each responsum being virtually an essay, not until the responsa were in Hebrew or in the Aramaic-Hebrew of the Talmud, not until the author himself began to feel the necessity of preserving his responsa, can the responsa be said to have arrived at the status where they constituted a separate branch of rabbinic literature. This status was arrived at in northern France in the responsa of Rabbenu Tam (1100–1171), Rashi's grandson; and in Spain in the responsa of Solomon ben Adret (1235–1310).

The reason for this elevation of responsa to a separate branch in Jewish literature at this period can be explained chiefly by the changing status of talmudic knowledge. In the time of the gaonim, the knowledge of the Talmud was well established and widespread only in Babylonia. The great semi-annual assemblies and the permanent schools kept the tradition unbroken from the days of the Talmud itself. In the diaspora, this huge and difficult work was largely unknown. But through the influence of the gaonim, the knowledge of the Talmud spread first among their correspondents, and later, through the efforts of these scattered scholars who established schools. In time there were thousands of students competent in talmudic law. When that stage was attained, the answer to a legal inquiry assumed an entirely different character.

In the earlier period, inquiries had dealt in large measure with the meaning of talmudic passages. Such inquiries were no longer needed. The meaning of the text was taught directly in the Talmud schools. In the earlier period, inquirers had been after decisions in the specific disputes in which they were involved, and the decisions were given. Now that the inquirers were likely to be talmudic scholars themselves, a mere "yes" or "no," or "permitted" or "prohibited," no longer served as an answer. Now the questions and answers took on the nature of correspondence between approximate equals, and a respondent had to give an elaborate talmudic justification for his answer, the questioner being in a position to evaluate the reply. Even in the responsa of Alfasi and Maimonides this distinction is to be noticed. When the inquirer was a scholar, the answer was elaborate; while the answer to most inquirers was brief, sometimes only one word.

In northern France, where the analytical study of the Talmud flourished first and developed the *Tosafot*, we find that Rabbenu Tam, the greatest of the Tosafists, gave virtually every responsum the form of a well-rounded rabbinic essay. Solomon ben Adret's responsa, in Spain, a century later, were generally likewise full rabbinic essays. From then on, responsa were nearly all written in Hebrew, preserved by their authors and copied and made available to a larger group of students. There was now a widespread talmudic world. The average questioner was himself a scholar. The responsa were no longer, as in the time of the gaonim and the earliest respondents, merely decisions, but full discussions of the law. Thus the responsa came into their own as a specific type of literature, with fixed characteristics destined to be maintained in all the centuries that followed.

The only differences between the later responsa and those of the twelfth and thirteenth centuries were incidental. Though their content and background may differ, the proportion of subject matter varying from time to time and place to place, their style and structure have remained essentially the same. First comes a statement of the case, usually in the question, which was generally printed together with the responsum. Then the responsum begins by indicating what at first appearance would seem to be the law as recorded in one or the other of the codes. Then follows a discussion of difficulties, due to contradictory opinions in the codes on this or on related questions, which compel the respondent to go back to the basic talmudic discussion from which the law in question ultimately derives. This in turn is followed by an analysis of passages in the Talmud that may possibly yield a principle relevant to the case at hand. The principle is tested by being subjected to real or apparently contradictory opinions in the Talmud; and, having withstood the test, it is applied to the case in hand. In some countries there was more and in some countries there was less of such internal talmudic discussion. In some centuries one code was referred to, in other centuries another. But the responsa have retained essentially this classic form.

As Jewish life developed in the various countries, historical, political and economic changes raised new questions. As the number of talmudic scholars, teachers of *yeshibot*, communal rabbis, increased, so did the number of resonsa writers. There are by now about fifteen hundred books dealing with responsa alone and perhaps five hundred more which deal primarily with other branches of rabbinic literature but also contain a number of responsa.

To obtain a bird's-eye-view of this vast literature, it is necessary to deal with historical circumstances as well as the literary products of certain types of personality.

There were some famous Jewish communities which contributed greatly to this literature, and others, equally famous, which produced very little. So, too, there were renowned scholars who became respondents of world-wide fame, and others, equally great, who wrote almost no responsa at all. . . .

The geographical and chronological distribution of responsa writing is rather remarkable. One country suddenly emerges as a center of responsa literature, only to fade out even though its Jewish population may still be large and its Talmud scholars still numerous. As suddenly, another country arises as a center, remains the premier land for responsa for a century or two, and then in turn sinks into obscurity. Often there are two great centers simultaneously, as North Africa and Germany in the fourteenth to the fifteenth centuries, and Turkey and Poland in the sixteenth to the early seventeenth centuries. In order to present a broad view of the important lands of responsa writing, only those respondents will be mentioned who have become sufficiently well known to be read beyond the land of their origin and whose decisions form the basis of later responsa and may even be embodied in the codes which summarized Jewish law from time to time.

Germany and Spain to the Fifteenth Century

Jacob ben Meir (Rabbenu Tam, 1100–1171), the grandson of Rashi, was, next to his grandfather, the greatest master of the Franco-German school. He organized his learned correspondence in what is the second volume of his *Sefer ha-Yashar* ("The Book of the Upright"). He was the greatest among the tosafists (the writers of additional notes to the Talmud). The tosafists noted the difficulties in every part of the Talmud and then explained them brilliantly away. It was these deeper analyses, the discovering of difficulties and the harmonizing of them, that Rabbenu Tam brought into the responses in his *Sefer ha-Yashar*, so that this procedure became thereafter a part of every classic responsum. Up to now, as has been pointed out, the responsa of the gaonim, of Maimonides, of Alfasi, had been primarily decisions. These newer responsa were debates, discussions, learned conversations.

Rabbenu Tam was followed in Germany by Meir of Rothenburg (1215–1293), whose many responsa, extant in numerous collections and quoted in other works, are a permanent part of the structure of the legal tradition. In the next generation in Germany, at the end of the fourteenth and the beginning of the fifteenth centuries, there were Jacob Moellin (Maharil) and Israel Isserlein of Neustadt, Vienna, and somewhat later, their disciples, Jacob Weil and Israel Bruna.

In the same period there flourished in Italy the prime respondent in all the history of Italian Jewry, Joseph Colon (1420–1480). His responsa are likewise among the classic works in the field. He was influenced largely by the German school of Talmud study, but was a bridge with the Jewry of the Mediterranean.

Incidentally, Jacob Moellin, who was as famous for his notes on customs and ceremonies (*minhagim*) as for his responsa, indicates how vitally important he considered this type of legal decision to be as a source of authority. He says to a correspondent: "As for your statement that one should not rely upon responsa; on the contrary, I say, they are practical law and we should learn from them more than from the codifiers who, after all, were not present at the time when the decision was made." In other words, whereas the codes may summarize the decisions of various responsa or of the talmudic debates, a responsum, which arose from an actual case submitted, should be the prime source of authority. Jewish Law is in this regard like the Anglo-Saxon Law, more emphatically case-law than code-law.

While these authorities flourished in France and Germany, a great light in the field of responsa arose in Spain, Solomon ben Adret (1235–1310). He wrote, according to some reports, seven thousand responsa, of which three thousand are extant. His works are authoritative throughout the Jewish world down to our day.

Soon after his time, Jewish life in Spain began to break up under the blows of persecution. Spanish Jewry scattered from the Iberian peninsula and during the next three centuries established new and creative communities. Their first place of creative resettlement was northern Africa, chiefly in the areas which today are Tunis and Algiers, where the earliest talmudic schools in the diaspora had developed to which the gaonic responsa had first been sent in the west.

It was almost inevitable that the responsa literature should have flourished in the new North African-Spanish Jewish communities. The native Jews differed greatly from the new immigrants. Their learning, Jewish and secular, was far inferior to that of the newcomers; their economic development was backward; and many of their religious customs were peculiar to themselves. The misunderstandings and communal disputes between the native African Jews ("the wearers of the turban") and the Spanish newcomers ("the wearers of the biretta") required adjudicament and harmonization. Furthermore, many of the Jews who had remained in Spain had been forcibly converted to Christianity and, during the next century or so, numbers of them escaped to the African communities. Their status presented immediate problems. Many of them had married in the church.

Was their marriage valid as Jewish marriage? And what of their children? Did they need to be reconverted? These vexing problems of the escaped converts, added to the tensions due to the differing customs and manners of the communities themselves, required immediate solution. This was no time for leisurely theoretic studies. The immigrant Spanish scholars were besieged with urgent questions, and so the responsa literature achieved a rapid development through their efforts.

Thus, three and a half centuries after Rabbenu Hananel, the correspondent of the gaonim, had flourished in Kairouan, North Africa, from which scholars like Alfasi had moved to Spain, the reverse current began. It was led chiefly by Isaac bar Sheshet (Ribash; 1326–1408), whose great volume of responsa soon became a classic. His younger colleague and sometime rival, Simon ben Zemach Duran (*Tashbetz*), likewise was the author of a great volume of responsa. Simon's son, Solomon ben Simon (Rashbash), who succeeded him as rabbi of Algiers, and two of his grandsons published jointly a work of responsa that won a permanent place in this literature. Its curious title, *Yakhinu-Boaz*, borrows for these two sons of Rabbi Solomon the names of the two columns beside the bronze "sea" in the Temple built by King Solomon. With these two scholars in the early part of the sixteenth century, the fame of the North African community as a source of decision came to an end; and, although the study of the Talmud continued in North Africa, it produced in later times only one more writer of responsa whose works were known beyond the confines of his own country, namely, Judah Ayyas (1690–1760). The contemporary school in Germany likewise lost its creativity, although it experienced a revival some generations later.

Turkey and Poland, Sixteenth and Seventeenth Centuries

Although Algerian primacy in the responsa literature had ceased, the ex-Spanish Jews were destined to write a new chapter in the history of responsa. But another century was to elapse. From about 1400 C.E. to 1500, the two great centers were virtually silent: Germany, because the effects of the persecutions resulting from the Black Plague broke up communities and crushed the creative spirit; Spain, because the persecutions rising toward the climax of the expulsion in 1492 left no energy for cultural discussion. While German Jewry would wait for at least two centuries before reviving sufficiently to produce world-famous respondents, Spanish Jewry would, after somewhat less than a century, begin once more to produce responsa which became a permanent part of the literature. Spanish Jewry, especially after the expulsion in 1492, moved eastward. It was at the eastern end of the Mediterranean—in Egypt, in Palestine and in Turkey—that it began to flourish anew. As with German Jewry and Spanish-Algerian Jewry in the earlier period, this efflorescence in the Turkish Empire was one of a pair of two great centers. Almost exactly at the same time, Polish Jewry achieved its greatest development. As Spanish Jewry, exiled to the east, revived in Turkey, so German Jewry, exiled to the east, came to a new flowering in Poland.

As with Algerian-Spanish Jewry a century or so earlier, the needs of time and place almost compelled the scholars to undertake the practical task of responsa writing. In the Turkish Empire, as had been the case previously in North Africa, there was an urgent communal problem. The Spanish exiles found Greek-Jewish congregations already established in the cities and towns to which they came. To complicate matters, the exiles themselves established a number of separate congregations, the immigrants grouping themselves according to their home cities or districts in Spain. There immediately arose questions of jurisdiction. Bans were frequently proclaimed forbidding members to leave their present congregation in order to join another congregation. How valid were these bans? What was the "Jewish community"? Was it the entire Jewry of the city, or was it each separate congregation? Many questions were asked and responsa written on these difficult and often acrimonious questions of communal organization. These were the first questions which arose; then other questions were added, and soon a flourishing responsa literature developed.

In Poland the problems were somewhat different, but they were analogous. Poland was a new and undeveloped country. There were no preexisting communities. The Jews immigrating westward from Germany and Bohemia had to build their life upon new foundations. They soon developed talmudic schools, regulated problems of trade and taxation and planned nation-wide councils. The rabbis were required to lay down the legal basis for a network of new communities whose individuals were working out their careers in a new environment. The practical problems required specific answers to specific questions. Responsa literature inevitably expanded in this new home.

In Palestine, in Salonika and Constantinople, and also in Cairo, Egypt, the Spanish exiles produced at least a dozen great respondents whose works are still in use, besides a host of lesser lights who likewise wrote responses. Most, though not all of these, were exiles from Spain. Some of them had been brought out of Spain as children by their parents. Some had been born in exile. The most famous of these was Joseph Caro, the great codifier, the author of the *Shulhan Arukh*.

His immense commentary on the *Tur*, a legal code compiled in Spain in the fourteenth century, *Bet Joseph* ("The House of Joseph"), is a veritable treasure-house of the responsa of all the past ages, Spanish and German. While his own books of responsa, the collection of *Abkat Rokhel*, and his responsa on marriage laws were not outstanding, his *Bet Joseph* made the responsa a permanent and determining factor in the codes of Jewish law. One might well say that the responsa of the past became part of the intellectual apparatus of all succeeding decisors by virtue of their decisions being cited in Caro's great commentary.

His contemporary, David ben Solomon ibn Zimra (Radbaz, 1479–1589), passed most of his life as rabbi of Cairo. His responsa are in the first rank of this literature. Elijah Mizrahi (1455–1525), rabbi of Constantinople, was somewhat older. He was not of Spanish, but of Italian origin. David Cohen (Radak) was rabbi of the island of Corfu in the early sixteenth century. Samuel ben Moses Medina (Rashdam, 1505–1589), was rabbi in Salonika. Moses of Trani, Joseph Trani and Joseph ibn Labi (Leb), rabbi in Salonika and Constantinople; Jacob Berab, likewise an exile from Spain, famous for having made the attempt to revive the old form of Mosaic ordination, and his great opponent, Levi ibn Habib (1480–1555), rabbi of Jerusalem, both of them exiles from Spain—all these men transcended the region of their activity. Their books are quoted by scholars of Jewish Law in every land.

Simultaneously with the Turkish productivity, Polish Jewry had its time of greatness. The chief respondents were Moses Isserles of Cracow (Rama), his kinsman, Solomon Luria of Lublin, and, somewhat later, Meir of Lublin (Maharam).

The Polish and the Turkish schools did not need to wait for future generations to unite them in the common treasury of Jewish legal literature. The two luminaries, Joseph Caro of the Turkish group, and Moses Isserles of the Polish, moved together and, as twin stars, shone upon Jewish legal literature. Joseph Caro had written his great code, the *Shulhan Arukh* ("The Set Table"). This work, for all its clarity and succinctness, would never have been accepted by German and Polish Jewry had Moses Isserles not written his notes to it, embodying the customs of the north European Jews. Together the book and the notes became one work, and the one work has ever since been the predominant governing code in Jewish religious life.

After this high tide of responsa writing, there was again a subsidence; and while, of course, some responsa were always being written, no great respondent arose for almost a century. The next writer destined to make a permanent contribution was the German, Yair Hayyim Bacharach (1639–1702), the rabbi of Worms. His somewhat later contemporary was Z'vi Ashkenazi (Hakham Z'vi, 1660–1718), rabbi of Amsterdam and Altona; and then Ashkenazi's son, the famous Jacob Emden (1697–1776). It was almost a century thereafter that two great centers once more arose to exist side by side. The forerunner of the new time of creativity was Ezekiel Landau (1713–1793), rabbi of Prague, a many-sided talmudist, famous chiefly as author of the responsa, *Noda bi-Yehudah*. He was followed in Prague by Elazar Fleckeles (1754–1826), and in Nickolsburg, Moravia, by Mordecai Benet (1753–1829). It seems strange that these three men constitute almost the only responsa writers in the great Bohemian-Moravian community. There were many great and creative rabbis of Prague before them, but not one became widely known as a writer of responsa. Somewhat older than Ezekiel Landau was the well-known Jacob Reisher (*Shebut Ya'acob*), rabbi of Metz, who died in 1733. A contemporary of Ezekiel Landau, but not comparable to him in greatness or fame, was Joseph Steinhart (*Zikhron Joseph*, 1720–1776), rabbi of Fuerth. Of this group in Bohemia and in Germany, only Ezekiel Landau and perhaps Jacob Reisher were of first rank. However, they were soon followed by the great development of responsa in Hungary and in Galicia in the early nineteenth century.

Hungary and Galicia, the Nineteenth Century

Jewish life remained fairly static for another century. Very few new religio-legal problems arose. The great responsa collections of the Turkish and Polish rabbis of the sixteenth and early seventeenth centuries contained the answers to most questions that would arise. But in the beginning of the nineteenth century, vast and rapid changes took place. The modern era was dawning over the mass settlements of eastern Europe. New modes of business developed. New and closer relationship with the Gentile world grew up. New inventions brought new questions. New ideas of worship were advocated. The old communities of Galicia and Hungary, being west of the Czarist "iron curtain," came face to face with modernity. The new adjustment, the resistance to or compromises with modernity, brought a renewed flowering to the historic responsa literature.

Both these centers produced, at the same time, a galaxy of famous respondents. First and foremost in Hungary was Moses Sofer of Frankfort-on-the-Main, who spent most of his career as head of the *yeshiba* in Pressburg, Hungary (now Slovakia). Before his day there had been only one well-known respondent in Hungary, Meir Eisenstadt (*Panim Meirot*, 1670–1744). Moses Sofer (1763–1839), an indefatigable respondent

and brillian talmudist, inspired his contemporaries and a host of successors. A somewhat older contemporary was his second father-in-law, Akiba Eger (1761–1937), of Posen. Among his younger contemporaries was Judah Assad (*Yehuda Ya'aleh*, 1794–1866); Meir Ash (*Imre Esh*, died 1861); Moses Schick (1807–1879); Abraham Samuel Sofer (*K'tah Sofer*, 1815–1872), the son of Moses Sofer; Eliezer Deutsch of Bonyard (1850–1916), and many others.

Equal creativity occurred simultaneously in Galicia. Ephraim Zalman Margolis of Brody (*Bet Ephraim*, 1762–1828), was followed by Solomon Kluger, one of the most prolific of rabbinic authors (1783–1869); his great contemporary, Joseph Saul Nathanson of Lemberg (1808–1875); Chaim Halberstam (1793–1876), who represented a fine combination of hasidic mysticism and legal learning; Isaac Aaron Ettinger of Lemberg (1827–1891); and, later, Isaac Schmelkes of Lemberg, whose *Bet Yitzhak* contains a vertible mountain of responsa.

While this great creativity took place in Hungary and in Galicia, the part of Poland which was within the Russian Empire, the other lands in Russia and Lithuania produced very few respondents. Mention might be made of the famous head of the *yeshiba* in Volozhin, Naftali, Z'vi Berlin (*Meshib Dabar*, 1817–1893), and Menachem Mendel of Lubovitch (*Zemah Zedek*). But, considering the vast population of Jews in the Russian Empire and the tremendous amount of Talmud study which went on there, one would expect a much greater activity in this field. This strange paucity of responsa in Russia, when the two adjoining lands were so active, is partially explained by the fact that in Hungary and in Galicia most rabbis had small *yeshibot* in their own communities; and their disciples, when they later came to congregations of their own, would each send questions to his teacher. In Russia, great nationwide *yeshibot* were established whose scholars were not in contact with the active problems of the rabbinate.

Another explanation may be the different degree of westernization in Russia and the other two lands. Russia was, even in those days, behind an "iron curtain" of isolation; whereas Galicia and Hungary were both part of the Austro-Hungarian Empire and therefore in the main stream of western life. The great changes which modernity brought—new ideas, reforms, new inventions—had to be faced by every rabbi in Hungary and Galicia. Therefore there were innumerable new, practical problems to cope with. Whereas in Russia, new invention was slow to penetrate and the new ideas in those days, while they manifested themselves in the writings and in the lives of a few, never resulted, as in Hungary and Galicia, in attempts to capture the old communities. Thus the vast learning in Russia and Russian-Poland continued to confine itself to theoretical discussions of talmudic problems. Many of the books published as responsa were really not responsa at all, but an exchange of *hiddushim*, talmudic analyses, between learned scholars. A large volume of responsa by a Russian scholar might contain ten or fifteen questions, each exhaustively dealt with, generally on a theoretical basis; whereas a volume of the same size by a Hungarian or Galician contemporary might have three to four hundred responsa, the overwhelming percentage of which dealt with practical, urgent matters.

The old and largely isolated life of Jewry in the Russian Empire suddenly broke up, not because of the impact of outer forces as in the Austro-Hungarian Empire, but due to the inner desire of millions of Jews to leave Russian oppression and run away to the New World. In the latter half of the nineteenth century, a large proportion of Russian Jewry moved westward. Thus inevitably the honored rabbis of the old homeland became part of the memory and a source of religious authority for Jews scattered all over the world. By the centrifugal force of immigration, certain great Russian rabbis became world figures. Naftali Z'vi Berlin, in his *Meshib Dabar*, already indicated how many questions had been sent to him from America. Isaac Elhanan Spektor (1817–1896), rabbi of Kovno, quickly became known all over the vastly expanded Jewish diaspora. Within Russia, too, Jewish life was affected by the changes now attempted by the Russian government. It interfered with the old type of Jewish education and the training for the rabbinate; also the emigration of millions created a problem for many wives whose husbands disappeared without a trace (*agunot*). Isaac Elhanan Spektor suddenly was confronted with a host of urgent, practical problems. He had the ability and the will to cope with them, and his responsa, *En Yitzhak* and *Be'er Yitzhak*, came to be among the best known books in this field.

Simultaneously with the rise of Isaac Elhanan Spektor, and to the same extent for similar reasons, Galicia developed a great authority, in the latter half of the nineteenth century, in the person of Sholom Mordecai Shwadron of Berzun. Six volumes of his responsa have been published and many other responsa still await publication. He and Isaac Elhanan Spektor were by far the greatest respondents at the close of the last century.

In the early part of the twentieth century, there were no respondents who attained worldwide fame. Perhaps one of the best known is David Hoffmann (1843–1921). He represents a rather unusual type of respondent. Born in Hungary, a pupil of Moses Schick, he became rector of the great Rabbinical Seminary for Orthodox Judaiism in Berlin. Thoroughly trained in modern scientific method, he nevertheless was an active and widely-sought respondent. His book of responsa, *Melamed le-Ho'il* ("Teaching to Benefit," based upon the verse in Isaiah 48:17, "Who teacheth thee for thy profit"), shows a new style in the long history of responsa writing. Although he cites past authorities and analyzes the Talmud, which is the classic procedure in responsa, his style is exact and his responsa read like scientific essays. A similar change in style is found in the responsa of the contemporary chief Sephardi rabbi of Palestine, Benzion Uziel (*Mishp'te Uziel*). His responsa are a model of system and clarity. After stating the subject, he lists all the subproblems involved and takes them up one by one, dealing with them in unadorned and lucid style. Perhaps the fact that Hebrew had become a living language in Israel converted his, as it has done with other responsa, from the old, rather difficult, rabbinic style to readable modern writing.

The history of the responsa literature reveals a steady development from the terse decisions of the gaonism through the complicated talmudic analysis of Rabbenu Tam. There was shifting of dominant themes, revealing changes in history and in social living. It flourished in certain countries, generally in two countries simultaneously, fading away into generations of sterility and and rising again to periods of creative splendor. It is, of course, not possible to explain completely the ups and downs of this development. Sometimes a new efflorescence was due to the personality and authority of some individual, and sometimes even where there was a need for practical decisions, responsa writing nevertheless did not develop for want of adequate, authoritative scholars. In such circumstances, the most urgent questions were sent to rabbis in distant lands. Thus, Joseph Hayyim ben Elijah, rabbi of Bagdad in the nineteenth century (*Rab Pe'alim*, Jerusalem, 1901), responded to questions from Singapore, Bombay and Calcutta.

But, generally, the circumstances evoked the needed scholarly labors and the literature developed when there was special need for it. Wherever a new community was being built, as in Algiers, Turkey and sixteenth-century Poland, or wherever new influences created new situations and where these requirements were able to call upon a broad, Jewish, scholarly competence, there the responsa literature awoke to a new springtime. So, too, as the problems of the modern day impinge upon the historic Jewish faith, there will be need for more and more responsa writing. This unique type of Jewish legal literature may well be at the beginning of a new development, especially in Israel where a Jewish society must seek to achieve a harmony with a long Jewish tradition.

Notes and Questions to S. Freehoff, "Origins and Development of the Responsa"

1. What were the relative effects of the Responsa and the *Shulkhan Arukh* on the development and application of law? Were the two contradictory or complementary?

C. *Adjusting Criminal Laws to Crises and New Conditions in the Talmudic Era and Middle Ages*

1. DOCUMENTARY CASE STUDIES OF EXTRAORDINARY SANCTIONS IN THE TALMUDIC ERA UNCALLED FOR BY NORMAL LEGAL DOCTRINES

Since medieval Jewish decision-makers cited a relatively small number of talmudic passages as precedents for imposing extraordinary sanctions, a few of the better known talmudic passages on these issues are reproduced below.

a. THE HANGING OF THE WITCHES
(Sanhedrin 45b)

Whereupon R. Eliezer said to them: But did not Simeon Ben Shetah hang women at Ashkelon? They retorted: (on that occasion) he hanged eighty women, notwithstanding that two (malefactors) must not be tried on the same day.

b. AMPUTATING THE ARM OF AN ASSAULTER
(Sanhedrin 58b)

Resh Lakish said: He who lifts his hand against his neighbor, even if he did not smite him, is called a wicked man, as it is written, "And he said unto the wicked man, 'Wherefore wouldst thou smite thy fellow?'" (Exod. 2:13). "Wherefore hast thou smitten" is not said, but "Wherefore wouldst thou smite," showing that though he had not smitten him yet, he was termed wicked. . . .

R. Huna said his hand should be cut off, as it is written, "Let the uplifted arm be broken" (Job 38:15). *R. Huna cut off the hand* [of one who was accustomed to strike other people—emphasis added]. . . .

c. BLINDING A MURDERER
(Sanhedrin 27a–27b)

[As we find] in the case of Bar Hama, who committed murder. The *Resh Galutha* said to R. Abba Ben Jacob: "Go and investigate the matter; if he is definitely the murderer, dim his eyes."

d. EXECUTION WITHOUT TRIAL BY A COURT: DEATH BY FEEDING; EXECUTION BY THE TEMPLE PRIESTS
(Sanhedrin 81b)

MISHNAH. He who was twice flagellated [for two transgressions, and then sinned again,] is placed by *beth din* in a cell and fed with barley bread, until his stomach bursts.

MISHNAH. One who commits murder without witnesses is placed in a cell and fed with "Bread of Adversity and water of affliction."

MISHNAH. If one steals the Kiswah, or curses the Lord by enchantment, or cohabits with a heathen (lit., Syrian) woman, he is punished by Zealots. If a priest performed the Temple service whilst unclean, his brother priests do not charge him therewith at *beth din*, but the young priests take him out of the Temple Court and split his skull with clubs. . . .

Notes and Questions to Sanhedrin *81b*

1. *"Is placed . . . in a cell."* The Talmud (*Sanhedrin* 81b) explains that this cell was so narrow that the prisoner would only be able to stand, and not lie down. This penalty appears to have been borrowed from the contemporary Roman and Persian practices.

How did the talmudic decision-makers know that they had a right to cause the death of the transgressor? Some authorities[66] assert that although this right is not set forth in the Bible, it is part of the oral tradition handed down from Moses. Others,[67] however, term it a prescription of the "scribes" (i.e., rabbis).

The Jerusalem Talmud and Rambam[68] quote the language of the Mishnah as being, "He who kills *people*" (emphasis added; i.e., he who has killed *more* than once) is placed in the cell.[69]

Why is it that the Mishnah here provides that one who kills without two qualified witnesses being present, or who is a recidivist of lesser (but still serious) crimes, is executed in a more painful way than one whose slaying is properly witnessed? Note that the only one who could be executed in the traditional manner by a *Beth Din* was one who was forewarned, still stubbornly as-

66. Shlomo Yitzhaki, Commentary *Rashi*, 81b, *s.v. "Ve'-Haikha"*; Moshe ben Nahman, Commentary *Rambam* to *Sefer Ha'Mitzvot*, general principle no. 2, N. Gerundi, Novellae *Ran*, *Sanhedrin* 81b, ad loc.
67. Rambam, in *Sefer Ha'Mitzvot*, ibid.; M. Abulafia in his *Yad Rama*, *Makkot* 7a; cf. his statements in his *Yad Rama*, *Sanhedrin* 81a; Isaac ben Sheshet, Responsa *Rivash*, no. 251; see also M. D. Plotzki, in *Khemdat Yisrael* (Pietrokoff, 1903), Positive Commandment no. 13.
68. Rules Concerning A Murderer, 9:8.
69. For additional and detailed discussion regarding imprisonment in such cell, see M. D. Plotzki, in *Kli Khemda*, sec. 156, no. 2, and Joseph B. Soloveitchik, Responsa *Beth Ha'Levi* (Jerusalem, 1976), vol. 2, sec. 39, nos. 3–4.

serted that he would nevertheless commit the murder, and who then proceeded to do it in the presence of witnesses (see Part Two, Chapter VI, Section C 1, above). This could only occur when the passions of the slayer were aroused to an unusually high pitch. This presumably would only occur where the victim had grievously harmed him. It may be that a slayer of this type was not thought likely to repeat the crime against anyone else. Where, however, the slayer had already killed many persons or had repeatedly committed serious transgressions, despite many floggings, he was thought likely to continue in his ways and was regarded as a danger to others. In order to eliminate him as a threat to society, and to deter others from committing similar acts, it was felt he should be put to death in an extremely painful manner.[70]

It has been claimed that murder was the only capital crime for which one could be imprisoned in a cell and put to death in the manner described in the Mishnah. None of the other capital crimes set forth in the Bible resulted in such a severe sanction.[71]

2. *"If one steals."* Note that in the four cases listed in this Mishnah sanctions are not imposed by the court but by bystanders. This may be termed a form of legalized lynching. Why were such mob actions sanctioned, and why did the *beth din* itself not deal with the offenders. Note Rashi,[72] who remarked that these cases are part of the oral tradition from Moses, for which no rationale was set forth in the Bible or given orally.

Note that if a zealot asks the court whether he may kill the offender, he is told that he may not.[73] Note, also, that zealots may act only if they strike while the offense is being committed or immediately thereafter.[74] These restrictions tend, of course to limit zealous acts.

The Talmud limits zealot action in the case of cohabitation with a heathen women to a case in which both the woman and her father are idolators. A child conceived of a union with such a woman was thought likely to become an idolator, and an Israelite male who cohabited with her was suspected of being similarly influenced.[75]

If a woman cohabits with a heathen male, may she, too, be punished by zealots in the same manner as a male offender? Some commentators hold that the rule does not apply to a woman since the offense is less grave. The reason for this is that the child that she may conceive will be considered a Jew to be raised by her, since Jewish law follows the maternal line in cases of mixed parentage. The child would presumably not be brought up as an idolator[76] by the mother.

According to the Talmud, all three cases listed in the Mishnah in which zealots may act against the offenders relate to offenses that are affronts to the majesty of God, *viz.*, stealing sacred implements of worship from the Temple; cursing God, when this is accompanied by the attribution of magical powers to a source alleged to be superior in this respect to God;[77] or sexual cohabitation, which involves intimate association with, and results in increasing the number of, committed idolators.[78] It should be noted, in this connection, that the word "zealous," used in the Mishnah to describe those who act against the detractors of God, is commonly, utilized in the Bible as a trait of God, when indicating His intense dislike of idolatory (see Exod. 20:5).

3. *"The young priests take him out of the Temple."* The reference here may be to those priests who are under the age of twenty, at which age their Temple service customarily begins. Priests who actually served in the Temple would not take part in the killing, in order not to defile themselves and thus be excluded from performing the Temple worship.[79]

Note that a priest who performed the Temple service while impure could only be punished by his fellow priests, not by any "zealot."[80]

4. *"And split his skull with clubs."* The reason why clubs (literally, "pieces of wood") were utilized instead of swords or knives was because of the great affront committed by the perpetrator to the honor of the priests.[81] Another reason may be that this non-court killing was condoned only when carried out in the heat of passion by seizing any available implement, immediately following the commission of the offense. Pieces of wood were plentiful in the Temple since they were used to burn the sacrifices. It is also possible that swords or knives were not used, since it was forbidden to bring

70. R. Margolis, *Margaliyot Ha'Yam* (Jerusalem, 1958), p. 101, no. 26.

71. Rambam Laws Concerning a Murderer, 4:9; Menahem Ha'Meiri, in *Beth Ha'Bekhira*, ad loc.

72. Ad loc., *s.v.* "Ve'Haikha."

73. See Talmud, *Sanhedrin* 82a.

74. See Menahem *Ha'Meiri*, in *Beth Ha'Bekhira*, ad loc.; David Ibn Zimra, Responsa *Radvaz*, vol. 2, no. 631; H. Benebashti, *Hamra Ve'Khaya*, *Sanhedrin* 81b.

75. See Shlomo Yitzhaki, Commentary *Rashi*, and Ovadya Bartenura, ad. loc.

76. See Moshe ben Nahman (Rambam), in *Milkhamot* chap. 8, *Sanhedrin*, at end; Y. Al'Gazi, in *Kehilot Yaakov* (Salonika, 1786), no. 77; and E. Landau, Responsa (first ed.), *Ev. Ha.*, no. 150; cf. Mordecai ben Hillel, Commentary on *Mordecai Yebamot*, ch. 4:108, and Y. S. Nathanson, Novellae, ad loc.; R. Margolis, *Margaliyot Ha'Yam*, vol. 2, p. 101, no. 29.

77. See Talmud, ad loc. 81a.

78. See David Ibn Zimra, Responsa *Radvaz*, ibid.

79. R. Margolis, *Margaliyot Ha'Yam*, p. 100, no. 34, citing Abraham ben David, Responsa *Ravad*, and Asher ben Yehiel, Responsa *Rosh* to *Tamid* 45a; and Hillel Gelbstein, *Mishkenot L'Avir Yaakov* (Jerusalem, 1896), ad loc.

80. See Gerundi, Responsa *Ran*, ad loc. and David Ibn Zimra, Responsa *Radvaz*, sec. 2, no. 631.

81. David Ibn Zimra, Responsa *Radvaz*, sec. 2, no. 631.

them into the Temple area, both because they were deemed an affront to the dignity of the Temple and of the persons who possess them, and because the use of implements of war (and consequently of any iron implement)[82] was prohibited in the Temple.[83]

Some authorities[84] maintain that the three cases in which any zealots may kill, as well as the fourth case in which a priest may be killed by his fellow priests, are not part of the oral tradition derived from Moses but are instances in which the scholar–decision-makers, on their own initiative, permitted the offenders to be killed, since the offenses were considered grave, as evidenced by the biblical provisions that the perpetrators deserved death (albeit by God rather than man).

Despite the existence of the norm authorizing zealots to act, there are strong undertones of disapproval by Jewish decision-makers. The Jerusalem Talmud[85] indicates that the act of Phineas in slaying Zimri for cohabiting with the Midianite woman[86] (the precedent-setting example of the norm permitting punishment by zealots) was disapproved of by the scholar–decision-makers of the time, who desired to penalize him for this homicide.[87] Furthermore, even under the accepted norm, homicide by zealots, while permissible, is not obligatory.[88]

The dissatisfaction with zealots taking the law into their own hands is further indicated by the fact that a court may not authorize a zealot to act if he requests permission; furthermore, if the offender turns on the zealot and kills him, he cannot be penalized. The zealot is regarded as a *rodef*, since his act is not obligatory and is committed to take revenge, rather than to rescue a potential victim. Under this reasoning, an ordinary (i.e., non-zealot) *rodef* who kills a would-be rescuer who tries to slay him, is guilty of murder, since the attempted slaying by the rescuer *was* obligatory.[89]

The norm of the Mishnah, permitting homicide by zealots, was pointedly omitted from the *Shulhan Arukh*,

the standard code of Jewish Laws,[90] because punishment by zealots is permissible only if there is a Sanhedrin sitting in the Temple at Jerusalem. This situation, of course, no longer exists. It should be noted that the law's toleration of zealots, acting in the heat of passion to avenge an affront to God, resembles the biblical toleration of the "redeemer of blood," acting to avenge the death of his relatives.[91]

Note also that a similar norm[92] permitting any individual to dispose of a troublesome informer or sectarian (a type of individual who, in the Talmudic Era, commonly denounced Jews to the authorities and caused harm in other ways) by, for example, pushing him into a pit to die, is another example of authorized non-court sanctions.

The effect of community perspectives on Jewish law is reflected in the position taken by a number of leading decision-makers that tolerance of vigilante actions by zealots is not applicable today, in view of the radically changed perspectives of society.[93]

I believe that the norm permitting one to push an informer or sectarian into a pit [to die], applies only during times when God's close supervision [of activities on earth] is apparent, as in the times when miracles were common, echos from Heaven were utilized, and the righteous of the generation were clearly under the special supervision and protection of God; scoffers were then extremely evil in inclining towards their passions and libertinism. At such times, removal of the wicked helped the progress of the world, since everybody realized that incitement of the generation [to sin] would bring tragedy to the world and would result in pestilence, sword, and hunger in the world. Today, however, when God's supervision is not noticeable and the faith has been cut from the poor of the nation, pushing [informers and sectarians into pits] does not repair the breaches [in the "fences" of the world], but adds 'breaches,' since this seems in people's eyes as destructive and as use of brute force, Heaven forbid. Since the whole purpose [of the norm] was to "repair," this rule does not apply at a time when it does not serve to repair and when we must get people to repent, but only with 'chains of love,' and place them under a ray of light, as is in our power.[94]

---

82. See Talmud, *Shabbat* 6:4.

83. Exodus 20:22; *Mekhilta*, ad loc.; 1 Kings 6:7.

84. David Ibn Zimra, Responsa *Radvaz*. For further extensive discussion of other aspects of punitive measures by zealots, see Y. F. Perlow, Commentary to *Sefer Ha'Mitzvot* of Saadya Gaon, (reprinted Jerusalem, 1973), sec. 3, no. 25, S. Yisraeli, Kanaim Pogin Bo, in *Herzog Memorial Volume* (New York, 1962), p. 272.

85. *Sanhedrin*, ch. 9 at end.

86. Num. 25:7–8.

87. See Y. Rozanes in *Mishnah Le'Melekh* (printed in standard editions of Rambam's Code of Laws), Laws Concerning a Murderer, ch. 1 at end, rule 15.

88. Cf. Rambam, Laws of Forbidden Sexual Relations, ch. 12, rule 4; see also Gerundi, Novellae to *Ran*, ad loc.

89. See Talmud, *Sanhedrin* 82a; Gerundi, Commentary *Ran*; M. Abulafia, *Yad Ramah*, ad loc.; Y. M. Harlap in *Beth Ze'Vul* (Jerusalem, 1942), sec. 2, no. 2, subsecs. 8–11.

90. See Joseph Karo, *Shulkhan Arukh, Ev. Ha*, sec. 16, subsec. 104; see also Moshe of Brisk, Commentary *Khelkat Me'-Khokek*, ad loc.; R. Margolis, *Margaliyot Ha'Yam*.

91. Num. 35:10–29; see Part Two, Chapter VI, Section C 1, above.

92. Talmud, *Avodah Zarah* 26a.

93. See Y. Eibschutz, *Tumim, Ho. Mis.*, sec. 3; and Yehoshua Trunk of Kutna, in *Yeshuot Yisrael* (Warsaw, 1870), ad loc.

94. Y. Karelitz, *Khazon Ish* (Jerusalem, 1942), Y. D., sec. 13.

Are self-help and vigilante sanctions ever justified? Do they have a place in the constitutive scheme of a modern humanistic society?

It is possible that all of the practices of non-court sanctions (the three cases where zealots may act, the killing by fellow priests, the disposal of informers and sectarians), as well as the non-traditional sanctions imposed by the courts (incarceration and death by improper feeding), and the imposition of traditional sanctions by the court in non-traditional sanctions (i.e., for one who rode on a horse on the Sabbath) all represented the resort to self-help by those who cared about the basic values of Jewish society, which were being violated with increasing frequency. Legitimization of these practices may have reflected a great measure of desperation in the face of the inability of the existing legal system and traditions to cope with the growing violations of basic goal values. This situation was probably exacerbated by the limitations placed by the Romans on the penalties that Jewish courts could impose, and by the increased violations of basic norms, resulting from changing cultural outlooks and mores under Greco-Roman cultural influences.

In the eyes of talmudic decision-makers, these self-help measures resembled the biblical institution of self-help by the "redeemer of blood." That practice, too, apparently originated when there was no strong central government to act effectively against murderers.

If this thesis is correct, the foregoing practices cited in the Mishnah would indicate an example (not uncommon in other societies, too) of a society which, under stress, adopts increasingly extreme measures and departs from long-established traditions, in order to survive.

We do not know the extent to which any or all of the foregoing self-help principles were actually utilized in practice, although it appears likely that non-court disposals of informers and sectarians may not have been uncommon. We also do not know the extent to which these measures succeeded, although continuation of these extreme measures against informers during the Middle Ages might indicate that these steps were at least thought to be effective.

2. DOCUMENTARY CASE STUDIES OF EXTRAORDINARY SANCTIONS IN THE MIDDLE AGES

The following selections are from medieval Responsa and law codes by leading Jewish decision-makers, dealing with actual cases, and from Jewish communal ordinances in Poland and Germany.

a. IMPOSING SANCTIONS NOT AUTHORIZED BY LAW*
(By Josef Karo)*

The *Rashbah* (Rabbi Shlomo Ben Aderet, 1235–1310, Spain) wrote in a Responsum: "It appears to me that if the witnesses are believed by the chosen judges, they (the judges) may impose monetary fines or corporal punishment as seems fit to them. This is in order to preserve the world (society). For should you establish everything according to the laws of the Torah, and act only in accordance with how the Torah punished, in cases of injury and similar cases, the result would be that world society would perish, for we would need witnesses and forewarning. As the Talmud says, "Jerusalem was destroyed only for they established their decisions in accordance with biblical Law." Certainly, outside of Israel where we do not try cases where a monetary penalty is involved, the result would be that light-minded people would "make a breach in the fence of the world" [open the way to lawlessness.]. The result would be that the world be barren [desolate]. The (Rabbis) of Blessed Memory have already penalized. . . . [Here the Responsum cites a number of talmudic precedents, listed in Chapter VII, above.]

Therefore, if these chosen judges, seeing the need and the requirement of the period, sentence one either to corporal punishment or to pay a fine in order to reform society, it is in accordance with the law of the Torah. This is certainly true should they have authority from the king, as was the case of Rabbi Elazar the son of Rabbi Simeon in the beginning of the chapter *Hapoalim* (Talmud, *Baba Metzia* 83b). Nevertheless, the chosen judges must weigh the cases carefully, act in accordance with the laws of the country, and for the sake of Heaven.

In another Responsum, he [Shlomo ben Aderet] wrote: "In cases of capital punishment, they [the judges] must be careful to act in agreement with the elders of your city in order that they may react to the great need [of the time] and after careful deliberation. See the Responsa of *Rambam* (Rabbi Moses Ben Nachman, 1194–1270, Spain and Israel), No. 240, where he wrote about the law that one may be lashed and punished not in accordance with the law. . . . He further wrote in No. 279, concerning a community that selected and appointed judges to [punish] transgressors and had written in the ordinances established by agree-

*From Josef Karo (b. 1488, Spain; d. 1575, Israel), Commentary, *Beth Yosef* to Jacob ben Asher's *Tur, Hoshen Mishpat*, Laws Concerning Judges, section 2. Karo was the sixteenth-century author of the standard Jewish code of Laws, the *Shulkhan Arukh*, and one of the foremost Jewish legal authorities of all time. The following free translation is by the editor.

ment that they [the selected judges] are empowered to discipline and impose fines as they see fit, based upon the testimony of witnesses who are related or upon hearsay testimony, or from other similar [otherwise inadmissable testimonies], which appears to them to be true, and they are able to judge and impose fines.

The need for proper witnesses applies only to biblical law. However, when one transgresses the ordinances of the state, the need of the hour must be done. If you do not say so, they [the authorities] will not impose penalties, and will not judge in matters . . . such as theft and injury. They would also be required to forewarn the would-be offender [before he commits the offense]. They [Rabbis] did indeed say "[offenders] are lashed and punished, [though] not in accordance with the law, not to violate biblical law, but rather to make a fence" [to preserve the Torah by these measures].

Also the *Rosh* [Rabbi Asher ben Yehiel,] wrote in a Responsum, No. 18, concerning a widow who became pregnant by a Gentile. Since this affair was well known, the sender of the question had in mind to scar her face by cutting off her nose, since she adorned herself in the presence of her lover and by [requiring her to] pay a fine to the authorities of the city. They asked him [Rabbi Asher] if he agreed to this punishment. He replied, "You have judged well. May her nose be cut off to scar her and make her repulsive to her paramours. This matter should be carried out immediately so that she may not become depraved. It is also advisable to fine her according to her wealth."

b. INFORMERS

(1) *The Practice Concerning Informers*
(By Moshe ben Maimon)*

Sec. 10. It is permissible to kill an informer in every place, even nowadays, when we do not judge capital cases. It is permissible to kill him before he informs, as soon as he says, "I will inform concerning so and so, whether with regard to [endangering] his body or his property, and even regarding unimportant property, he has permitted himself to be killed. One is obliged to kill him, and whoever kills him first merits.

Sec. 11. If the informer carried out his plans and informed, I believe that it is forbidden to kill him, unless he is established as an informer, [whereupon] he may be penalized, lest he inform on others. It is an occurrence in every era in the cities of the west [i.e.,

Spain] to punish informers that are known to inform concerning property, and to turn the informers over to non-Jews to punish them, to beat them, and to imprison them in accordance with their evilness. So, too, whoever vexes the congregation and causes them pain, one may hand him over to non-Jews to beat him, to imprison him, and to fine him. But on account of an individual's pain, it is forbidden.

(2) *Disposing of an Informer*
(By Asher ben Yehiel)*

Question: May our Master instruct us: what may be done with a man who was exposed as an informer to the gentile rulers about individual Jews and the community? He continuously threatens each day that he will go and slander individual people and communities of Jews to the Gentiles regarding matters that would cause [the Jews] physical harm or property damage. The [Jewish] community is extremely fearful of this man since he serves every night in the court of one of the powerful Gentiles.

The Jews are now given the jurisdiction by the king to try him in secrecy and execute him if he is found to be guilty and deserving of the death penalty. It is concerning this that the heads of the communities assembled and set up a court to investigate the matter. Should the aforementioned accusations be borne out by the testimonies [of witnesses], they [the court] will rule according to what will seem to them to be just.

Now, may our Master guide us, what is his verdict? May he be judged as a *rodef* [an aggressor who attempts to kill] since he continues to threaten while Don Pedro is present here although he has been reproached? Is it permissible to save oneself at the expense of his life as was the case of Rav Kahana in the last chapter, *Hagozel* [Babylonian Talmud, *Baba Kama*]?

Responsum: Although the four modes of capital punishment entrusted to the courts were abolished with the Sanhedrin's going into exile, this implied only that a person may not be tried for a capital offense. Since the Sanhedrin were not functioning, no man has the power to try another for a capital offense. However, in those situations enumerated in the tractate *Sanhedrin,* chapter *Sorer Umoreh,* executions were not abolished. For example, an aggressor who attempts to murder may be killed as a preventive measure, to save the life of the intended victim. [The reason is] that their deaths are not dependent upon the [presence of] an *Edah* [congre-

---

*From Code of Laws, Laws Concerning a Batterer, 8:10–11. The translation is by the editor. Moshe ben Maimon was born in Spain in 1135 and died in Egypt in 1204.

*From Responsa *Rosh*, no. 1:1, by Asher ben Yehiel (b. 1250, Cologne, Germany; d. 1327, Toledo, Spain). The free translation is by the editor.

gation of Israel, represented by the court] and witnesses, but rather upon an individual who, on witnessing the attempted murder or bodily injury, is obligated to kill the aggressor. The biblical basis is "Thou shall not stand by the blood of your neighbor" (Lev. 19:16).

One who attempts to hand over the property of a neighbor to gentile [authorities] has been equated by the Sages to one who pursues another with the intention of killing him. As Scripture says: "Your sons have fainted; they lie at the head of every street like an antelope in a net" (Isa. 51:20). This means: as this antelope receives no compassion when it falls into the net, similarly, when the property of a Jew falls into gentile hands, no one is moved [to help]. Today, they [the Gentiles] take part [of the Jew's property], tomorrow the whole [property], and finally he is handed over [to gentile authorities] and is put to death in an attempt to get him to admit to having more wealth. Therefore, he [the informer] is a *rodef* [pursuer to commit murder] and forfeits his life in order to save [the victim].

The present case of which you have written: that witnesses have testified that when Don Pedro was there, he threatened to inform; that one of the authorities of the community had spoken to him to cease and desist from the threats, but he refused, is entirely the same as the case of Rav Kahana in the latter chapter *Hagozel*: "Someone who wanted to point out [to Gentiles] the location of his neighbor's straw. Coming before Rav, he was told, "Don't point it out." He replied, "I will point it out. I will indeed." Rav Kahana who was sitting there, arose and "tore the man's windpipe out of him."

Here, as well, as soon as one of the community authorities told him to desist and he refused, he surrendered his life to every Jew. Whoever kills him first has served Heaven. Certainly, if they ordered him killed by non-Jews, it would be permissable. Sectarians and informers may be pushed down (into a pit from which they cannot escape), even when they are not in the act of informing. Although Rabbi Abahu wrote that they are not directly put to death, but rather are left to die, directing a Gentile to put him to death is the same as pushing him into the pit, since he does not partake in the [direct] act [of killing him]. I have also seen this [opinion] in a Responsum: it is permissible to hire a non-Jew to kill an informer, even while he is not informing.

Now, certainly in our case, where according to the testimony of the witnesses, he threatened [harm], was warned but refused to heed, he is to be considered in the act of [informing]. Permission is therefore granted to everyone to kill him. It is also not necessary to receive the testimony in his presence. Even when it is not

a case of [him being killed] in the act, since they pass sentence to have him killed by a Gentile, it is unnecessary to receive the testimony in his presence. [The reason is] that the matter is well known: A person who has the status of being an informer (*masor*) is befriended by the Gentiles for their own sake. If it were necessary to receive the testimony in his presence and to cross-examine in his case, it would never be possible to carry out the sentence. He would always be saved by his gentile friends. Since when he, himself, is not in danger, he informs on individuals or groups, certainly when he feels personal danger, he would inform and reveal community secrets and endanger all of the Jews.

Thus, the practice in the entire Diaspora has been, that when one has the status of being a *masor* or informer by informing or delivering Jews or their property three times to Gentiles, [the practice is] to seek counsel and methods on how to have him "removed from the world" as a precautionary measure, so that others may also learn from this, thereby reducing the number of informers, and to save every persecuted Jew from him.

Therefore, in this case when witnesses testified that he had the status of being an informer and *masor*, and he was in the act [of informing], they [the community authorities] did well in sentencing him to be hanged. Thus may all of God's enemies be destroyed and those who love Him may be like the splendor of the sun.

The opinion of Asher
the son of Rabbi Yechiel of Blessed Memory

(3) *A Case Concerning an Informer*
(By Shlomo ben Aderet and Meir ben Baruch of Rothenberg)*

[The manuscript containing the Responsum has the following introduction, added by an unknown scribe:] This epistle, our great master Rabbi Shlomo Ben Aderet, may his memory be blessed, sent concerning an informer, in the city of Barcelona in his days. He was from [one of] the important families there and had many and important relatives. [The Jewish] communities sentenced him to death [and he was executed by] being made to bleed from both arms in the street that was in front of the cemetery in Barcelona. After the death of the great communal leader, Yosef Abrabalya, may his soul rest in Eden, there arose friends of that informer, who said that he had been sentenced to death contrary to law. There then arose the aforemen-

---

*The following Responsa by Shlomo ben Aderet (1235–1310, Spain) and Meir ben Baruch of Rothenberg (1215–1293, Germany) were published by D. Kaufmann in the *Jewish Quarterly Review* 8 (1895–96): 228. The translation is by the editor.

tioned Rabbi [Shlomo Ben Aderet], may his memory be blessed, and sent this letter to the rabbis of France, to advise them concerning the case and the transgressions of that informer, in order to quiet the quarrels caused by his relatives and to seal their mouths, so that no wing should flutter, and no beak should twitter [paraphrasing Isa. 10:14] concerning him and the brothers Yosef and Moshe, of the Abralaya family, who hold positions in the government, and who had caused and brought about the death of that informer, upon the advice of the holy communities, all of whom had agreed concerning the sentence and his death.

[The Responsum of Shlomo ben Aderet, addressed to the rabbis of France, requests them to take the necessary steps to preserve order in society, details the facts of the case and the great reluctance of the author to issue an advisory opinion to the king as to whether he should execute the offender. The Responsum then continues as follows:]

After much toil and many expenditures, we were forced to tell our Lord, may his glory be elevated, that which appeared [proper] in our eyes, [namely,] that he could act in accordance with the proper verdict, and that, in our view, he deserved death. If he [the King] wished, he could execute him, according to what he, [the accused] himself, had testified before us, and according to the testimony that had been given concerning him in all of the various courts [in the different communities]. [This is] aside from what he could be presumed to have done [based upon his previous conduct]. I am sending you herewith copies of the testimony that was given in part in his presence, in part, before the one whom he appointed to act in his stead and to receive the testimony, because he was tied in chains, and in part, [the testimony given] before his agents and the agents of the communities in every city.

After all of this, our Lord the King, may his glory be elevated, sent the aforementioned judge to decide the case, according to what we advised. He [the accused] again asserted that he had additional contentions. The aforementioned judge permitted him to set forth his contentions with the representatives of the communities and we left. In the meantime, that aforementioned judge of the king died, and after many days, the king sent one of his assistants to kill him, and he did so. . . .

One of the brothers thereupon arose and acted as an informer in his place and said to one of the King's judges that we had advised improperly, contrary to [Jewish] law, because we have no authority to judge capital cases, and certainly not outside of the land of Israel, and that all of the testimony must be received in the presence [of the defendant] . . . But he failed, attempted to minimize his embarrassment, tried to make

an about face, and tore his garment. Nevertheless, in order that another informer should not arise and attempt to undermine and dig under the wall [the structure of law and authority], permitting some to enter the breach, . . . I am writing [to advise] on what we relied in giving our advice to our Lord the King, may his glory be elevated.

And you our Masters, it is up to you to repair the fence [of the law] in the face of [threatened depredations by] the lion, lest he come and inherit the land. . . . If we do not go forward to meet them with staffs, . . . lest sinners multiply. . . .

First of all, we concluded that he [the accused] was a *rodef* and a *rodef* may be killed in every epoch, both in the land of Israel and outside it, and even without a court, as is indicated from the incident with Rabbi Shila (Talmud, *Berakhot* 58a) and since [King] David said to [King] Saul [when the latter pursued him]. "According to the Bible, it is permitted to kill you. Why? Because you are a *rodef* and the Bible says, 'He who comes to kill you, arise to kill him'." (See Talmud, *Sanhedrin* 72b). [This norm applies] even to one who is a *rodef* who threatens one's money [rather than bodily harm or imprisonment], as can be seen from the incident with Rabbi Kahana (Talmud, *Baba Kama* 117b), who said [to one who threatened to inform] "Do not point out [to the authorities the location of property hidden to avoid taxation]," and he replied, "I will certainly point it out." He [Rabbi Kahana, thereupon] tore out his gullet. One who is not known to [repeatedly] do so, [i.e., to inform] cannot be killed, until he acts. One who, however, is known to do this [i.e., constantly inform] can be killed, both while he acts, and after he acts, and whoever does this first [to him], deserves merit in killing those who are accustomed to cause harm, as we learned in [the Talmud] *Avoda Zara* 26b, "Sectarians, informers, apostates, and scoffers, can be pushed down [into a pit] and may not be raised [therefrom]." Even to kill them [directly] with [one's own] hands [is permissible], because they are like a snake . . . and as we studied in the Mishnah of *Baba Kama* (1:4), "A snake is always presumed to cause damage." Therefore, a snake, whoever kills it first, has merited [a reward]. . . . So the *Gaonim*, may their memory be blessed, ruled, and so it is done in practice. An informer who is known to inform, is killed directly in many places in Israel. So wrote and testified *Rambam* in his work (*Mishneh Torah*, Laws Concerning a Batterer and Damager 8:11), that this is the practice in all the cities of the West [Spain]. This is the everyday practice in the land of Castilia, and it was customary to do this before [with the knowledge and sanction of] the great ones of the generation that were there. Such is also the practice in the Kingdom of Aragon. So, too, there were [similar] incidents in Catalonia, in the generation before us, and also in this generation.

Even if the law would be weak in our hands [even if the traditional legal principles would not clearly authorize this], we would not be able to act in accordance with what the earlier authorities did and what the later authorities continue to hold. Even though they are not prophets, they are the sons of prophets [paraphrasing Talmud *Pesakhim* 66b)]. The Jerusalem Talmud said, "Whenever there is a law which is weak in your hands, and you do not know its nature, go out and see how the community acts, and [you should] act likewise."

Who is presumed [to be] an informer? Whoever is so known in public, not [necessarily] that it was so found by a court of twenty-three judges, before whom testimony was received. If this would be required there would never be one who is presumed to be so [an informer] today, since we do not have a court of experts [who are ordained]. Yet, the wise scholars, authors of many treatises, testified and wrote that an informer who is known to be such, is killed [in practice] in every epoch. He who becomes modest or has mercy on him, is cruel to the people of his generation, as was said in the Talmud (*Gittin* 56a), "They wished to kill him [an informer, who tried to libel the Jewish communities as rebels against Rome] in order that he should not tell [the Romans]. Said Rabbi Johanan, the modesty of Rabbi Zaharia, the son of Avtolus [who refused to permit the informer to be killed, since there were absent the prerequisites for traditional trial, conviction, and execution], burned our Temple, and destroyed our chapel, and exiled us from our land." Furthermore, because of the sins of our generation, a number of people have begun to learn this corrupt trade [denouncing and informing], and there is no trait which holds so much evil as this one, because it is the mother of the death of all the living [paraphrasing Gen. 3:20].

Whenever the hour requires it, one may smite and punish, [although] not according to law, in every place and in every time, in order to fence in a matter [to preserve the public from grave harm], like he who rode on a horse on the Sabbath in the days of the Greeks, and who was brought before the court and stoned (Talmud, *Sanhedrin* 46a) and like the incident with Shimon ben Shetah, who hung up eighty women in Ashkelon (Talmud, *Sanhedrin* 6:6) even though one may not hang women, and two persons cannot be judged in capital cases in one day. So it is done in practice every day in every place and so the *Gaonim* [recognized scholarly authorities] wrote. In these cases and those like them, one does not insist upon a court of twenty-three judges who are ordained, and [it is not necessary] to receive testimony before use [judges] nor [do we insist on] all

matters that are [ordinarily] required in capital cases. In these matters, we only go after [desire to ascertain] the truth, and to remove harm, and to erect fences in the face of breaches. These are like the rulings of Rav Huna, who amputated the arm [of an assaulter; Talmud, *Niddah* 13b] and the exilarch who said to Rabbi Aha Bar Yaakov, "Go out and, look, and examine. If he certainly killed a person, dim his eyes" (Talmud, *Sanhedrin* 27a). . . .

In our case, we did not judge him, but we were asked our advice by the King, may his glory be exalted, [who requested that we] examine the matter with our eyes, and to tell him our advice, in accordance with what he [the informer] did. We advised him [the King] that he was able to kill him, [the informer] because all of these [requirements of Talmudic laws] were only necessary when [judgment was to be made in accordance with] the laws of the Sanhedrin, who acted according to biblical law. However, [in a case that is decided according to] the law of the [non-Jewish] kingdom, one does not pay attention to all of these [Talmudic rules] . . . , since their [the Spanish state] law is only concerned with ascertaining the truth. One may be killed under the laws of the kingdom, even pursuant to the testimony of relatives, or pursuant to his own confession, and without forewarning, and without [a court of] twenty-three [all required by Jewish law] because the law of the kingdom [is only concerned with] ascertaining the truth. [Otherwise] if you do not say this, but you establish everything in accordance with the laws of the Torah, according to the laws of the Sanhedrin, the world would be desolate, because murderers and their associates would multiply; as Rabbi Akiva said, "If I would have been in the Sanhedrin, no person would ever have been killed" (Talmud, *Makkot* 1:10), and as they said, "Every Sanhedrin that executes two times is called a murderous [court]."

In our case, once this [the facts] was known in truth, even though the testimony was not taken in his presence, and . . . not before a court of twenty-three judges, [the verdict is still proper], since all of these [Talmudic] rules have no relation whatsoever to ascertaining the truth. [But] the law of the kingdom is only interested in ascertaining the truth from whoever said it, even if he [the accused], himself, said it, or others so testified, not in his presence nor before a court.

More than this was said [this principle was extended further], since Rabbi Eliezer, the son of Rabbi Shimon, used to seize thieves and the wicked, in accordance with the order of the Roman kingdom, and used to punish and kill them. So, too, Rabbi Yishmael, the son of Rabbi Yose [acted in this way]. Even though Rabbi Yehoshua ben Karha said to him, "Vinegar, the son of wine. Until when will you turn over the nation of our

Lord to be killed?" (Talmud, *Baba Metzia* 83b). So, too, Elijah said the same thing. Nevertheless, we cannot make [out] Rabbi Eliezer and Rabbi Yishmael to be completely erroneous in [regard to] explicit laws. Instead, [they were rebuked, since] because of their saintliness, they should have refrained from killing in instances where the Torah did not require the death penalty. Similarly, when he called them "vinegar, the son of wine," he meant to say that they did not conduct themselves in a saintly manner, as their parents had done. If they would have been completely in error, and had acted against the law, he would not have called them "vinegar, the son of wine," but "erroneous, and completely wicked [persons]." Far be it from the great ones of Israel and [for] elevated, and saintly persons like them [to be wicked wrongdoers]. Furthermore, Rabbi Eliezer, the son of Shimon, had examined himhelf and found himself to be as pure as gold (Talmud, *Baba Metziah* 83b). There is further proof for this, since Rabbi Yishmael said to Elijah, "What shall I do? It is the law of the king." And Elijah answered, "Your father ran away to Asia. You [should] flee to Ludakia." If it would have been completely forbidden [to act as Rabbi Yishmael had acted], why did he tell him, "It is a law of the king." He should have let himself be killed rather than violate [the laws of the Torah]; like he to whom it was ordered, "Kill so and so. If not, I will kill you" (Talmud, *Sanhedrin* 84a). Also, Elijah should have said to him, "Why do you see that your blood is redder than his?" (see Talmud, *ibid.*). But certainly, it is as I have said, that whoever is so appointed by the king, may judge and perform in these cases all of the laws of the kingdom, because with these laws, the king establishes the land. . . . The king, in his laws, does not need all of these matters which are utilized by the Sanhedrin to judge, at least, [not] a court of twenty-three judges . . . [nor] eye witness testimony, nor all of the other rules.

Shlomo ben Aderet

[The following reply was written by Rabbi Meir ben Barukh of Rothenberg, Germany. He was the leading Jewish decision-maker in Franco-Germany of his time and was the teacher of Rabbi Asher ben Yehiel, who subsequently fled to Spain and who was a contemporary of Shlomo ben Aderet.]

"Concerning informing, it is a custom of our ancestors and a rule in all places of Israel that we have seen and heard, to permit that whoever is first, merits to kill those informers who are known to inform and are accustomed thereto, until it becomes to them as though it were permissible, if there are witnesses to this matter. [This is true] even though there was no testimony taken in their [the informers'] presence but it was established

through witnesses. Although *Rambam*, may his memory be blessed, wrote as follows, "If the informer has done what he planned, I believe that it is forbidden to kill him," and we learned from him [that] the reason why it was permitted to kill an informer who informed concerning a small amount of money . . . , [was] that he was [regarded as] a *rodef* [and it is, therefore, permitted] to kill him . . . Just as an antelope when it falls into a net, they [the hunters] do not have mercy on him, so, too, a Jew, when his falls into the hands of a Gentile, they do not have mercy on him, and it is as though he informed upon him to kill him. It is, therefore, permitted to save the intended victim, even at the cost of the life of the *rodef*. When, however, he had already carried out [his informing], he is no longer considered a *rodef* who still threatens to kill. This is [true] only concerning one [for] who it was not established that he had informed on three [different] occasions. But if it was established that he had done this three times, it is presumed [that he will do this again] and if we have not seen in him any sign of atonement, then, whoever is first to kill him has merited. . . . And all is as our Master [Rabbi Shlomo ben Aderet] has written. If one is established as an informer, it is permissible to destroy his body, but not his possessions . . . And the words of our master are straight and true concerning [the laws] regarding informers and it is not [necessary] to dwell at length on this matter.

Peace be to our master and peace be to his teaching, and to all [the members of] his academy. With a soul that turns to his teachings, his true servant.

Meir, the son of Barukh

Notes and Questions to A Case Concerning an Informer

1. At first glance, the rationale permitting Jewish courts, and even individuals, to kill informers without meeting the traditional strict legal requirements of trial, testimony, and thorough questioning of witnesses seems extremely puzzling. The reason commonly advanced (as by Asher ben Yehiel and Shlomo ben Aderet) that an informer is regarded as a *rodef* (even when he informs only about tax evasion, which would not result in the death of the alleged evader) does not seem completely persuasive. Furthermore, an informer can be treated as a *rodef* and killed where he merely *threatens* to inform, whereas, technically, one who simply threatens to become a *rodef* may not yet be treated as such until he acts.[95]

Other legal scholars have analogized the informer to the case of the burglar mentioned in the Bible,[96] who

---

95. See Rambam, Laws Concerning a Batterer, 8:5, in Chapter XI, Section C 1 *a*, above; also Y. Bachrach, Responsa *Ha'Vat Yair*, sec. 65.

96. Exod. 22:1. The biblical phrase "He has no blood" is

"tunnels" under a house in order to burglarize it. He may be killed, since he is viewed as a potential *rodef* because he may kill the householder. The Talmud regards the biblical norm, which authorizes the householder to kill the burglar as an example of the traditional principle, "He who comes to kill you, arise and kill him (first)."[97]

This analogy to an informer is unsatisfactory, since a burglar may be killed, only if he is encountered in a tunnel on his way to commit a burglary. He may not be killed when he merely threatens to burglarize at some time in the future.[98] An informer, on the other hand, may be killed even when he is not in the act of informing and only threatens to do so.[99]

It seems reasonable, therefore, that the unusually stringent rules applied to informers (including their summary execution without trial) were influenced by a number of unique conditions. This may be deduced, in part, from the fact that there is no mention in the Talmud of the rule permitting the killing of informers, with regard to the era prior to the destruction of the Second Temple and Jewish Commonwealth in 70 C.E.[100] This may indicate that this principle originated or, at least, received widespread application, following that destruction. According to talmudic tradition,[101] the destruction of the Second Temple and Commonwealth was caused by Jewish informers who provoked violent Roman action against the Jews. This destruction was accompanied by mass slaughter, and the dispersion of Jews throughout the world as a helpless minority, without sovereignty or power. The Jewish community, its consciousness seared by these traumatic events, thereafter sought, at all costs, to avoid similar tragic results in the future by encouraging extraordinary actions against informers.

Another unique condition also contributed powerfully to the development of the Jewish attitude towards informers. Christian sects, which grew greatly in numbers and influence in the first century following the destruction of the Second Temple and Jewish Commonwealth, became increasingly hostile to their former Jewish compatriots. As early as the Jewish revolt against Rome (led by Bar Kokhba, *circa* 135 C.E.), members of Christian sects earned the hostility of many Jews by refusing to participate in the revolt.[102] The aftermath of that bloody revolt, with its huge toll of death and destruction, left the Jews with very bitter memories. As time went on, moreover, there was increasing friction between Christians and Jews in Palestine, with Jews claiming that there were frequent denunciations to the Roman overlords by Christians who accused both individual Jews and the Jewish religion as such, of hostility to the Romans. This, too, allegedly, often led to imprisonment, death, exile, or confiscation of property. The hatred of informers was exacerbated with the Christianization of the Roman Empire. Many onerous restrictions were then placed on Jews and on the practice of their religion.[103]

It is the difficulties caused by sectarians that probably led to the rule[104] that they could be pushed into a pit (by any individual who had the opportunity to do so without getting caught), and left there to die. This provision appears to have been aimed only at those who were active in informing against individual Jews or against the practice of Judaism in general, and who thereby caused many harsh repressions to be brought upon the Jewish people. Talmudic decision-makers did

---

understood by the Talmud as referring not to the lack of "blood guilt" on the part of the householder who kills the burglar but, rather, to the fact that the burglar is regarded as though he had no blood, i.e., he is not a person. His life may therefore be taken with impunity. Cf. Commentary of Shmuel ben Meir, *Rashbam* (printed in many Hebrew editions of the Bible) to Exod. 22:1. The verse may have both meanings simultaneously. See Abraham ben David (Raavad), Commentary to Rambam Laws of Theft 9:9.

97. See Talmud, *Sanhedrin* 72a; Shlomo Yitzhaki, *Rashi*, Commentary to Exod. 22:1 and to Talmud, *Baba Kama* 117a; Commentary (by an unknown editor) printed at end of standard editions of Rambam, *Hagaot Maimuneot* to Rambam, Laws of Theft, at end.

98. See Rambam, Laws of Theft, 9:7–12.

99. See Rambam, Laws of Assault, ch. 8; see, however, Responsa of Meir of Rothenburg, published in *Teshuvot Maimuneot*, printed at the end of the Laws of Damages of Rambam's Code of Laws, sec. 15. See also Karo, *Shulkhan Arukh, Ho. Mis.*, sec. 388; and Commentary of S. Kohen, in *Sifse Kohen* ad loc., subsec. 56.

100. See Israel Shipansky, *"Ha'Minim Ve'Hamalshinim"* (Heb., *Jubilee Volume in Honor of S. Federbush* (Jerusalem, 1961), p. 342.

101. *Gittin* 56a.

102. An examination of the works of the early Church Fathers cited by B. Z. Katz, in his *Prushim, Zedokim, Kanaim, Notzrim* ([Tel-Aviv, 1948], p. 371), does not, however, reveal any basis for his claims that Christians informed against Jews to the Roman authorities and revealed many of their military secrets.

103. This sectarian strife resulted in the addition, during this era, of a most unusual section to the main portion of the daily prayers, the *"Amidah"*. While, without exception, all of the eighteen portions of this prayer requested God to provide aid that was beneficial (such as healing the sick, granting wisdom, etc.) and would harm no one, the new section added was quite unique. It consisted of a bitter denunciation of "sectarians" and of informers, with a plea to God to utterly destroy them. The "sectarians" referred to were probably the early Christians, who were mentioned in one breath with Jewish informers because it was believed that both denounced Jews to the gentile authorities. The sectarian informers, however, added a new element to informing by their attempts to denounce the Jewish religion, itself, and bring it into disrepute with the gentile authorities. This often led to persecution directed at the Jews in general, not simply against any particular individual. See Schipansky, *Ha'Minim Ve'Hamalshinim*, pp. 346, 349.

104. Talmud, *Avodah Zarah* 26a.

not apply this principle of law to those who merely refused to accept all or portions of the Jewish religion and who violated its tenets.[105]

It is with this background in mind that one can understand the bitter feeling against informers, based on the widespread perception that they had been a prime cause of the destruction, slavery, exile, and persecution, which ultimately dragged on for millennia.

Accordingly, informing was regarded as a serious threat, not only to individual Jews but to the continued existence of the Jewish nation as a whole. The intensity of this feeling continued during the Middle Ages when Jewish communities often had a very precarious existence and were repeatedly expelled from many countries, often without warning, leading to much death, wanderings, and misery.[106]

Nevertheless, the legal rationale for legitimizing individual vigilante action against informers continuously troubled decision-makers. As indicated in the Responsa of Asher and Aderet, the authorization to act against informers under Jewish law has sometimes been cast in the format of the *rodef* doctrine on the theory that it applies to informers and others who may be a threat to the life of an individual person[107] or, perhaps, who

endangered the entire Jewish community. For a lengthy discussion of the punishment of informers in Jewish law, see Isaac ben Sheshet, Responsa *Rivash*, no. 79.

c. MURDER

(1) *Sanctions for Homicide*
(By Judah ben Asher)*

Responsum: [To] the wise [men] of great achievement, the honorable elders who are in Cordova, may their Rock and Creator guard over them. May the Keeper of the Truth keep you forever, as is your wish and the wish of the one undersigned below who greets you with well-being.

Your letter containing: [the description of how] Saul struck Isaac; the testimonies produced against him in the incident; the counterclaims of Saul against the witnesses; the testimonies produced against [his character]; the arguments in his favor that deal with the other transgressions of which he has been accused, had reached me. However, the actual testimony against him that deals with other transgressions did not reach me; per-

---

105. Schipansky, *Ha'Minim Ve'Hamalshinim*, p. 345; see also Talmud, ibid.

106. The role of the informer in medieval Spain has been described as follows: "The most dangerous criminal in the Spanish *Juderia* was the informer, or *Malsin*. He was despised as a traitor and dreaded as an enemy of society. The hatred which he inspired can be explained only by the panicky state of mind of a community which lived in constant dread of lurking danger. The informer, *Malsin*, was essentially one who betrayed his people by denouncing the community or its representatives to the general authorities; but the term was broadened to include anyone who reported a violation of law, actual or alleged, to the government officials and thereby jeopardized the person or property of his fellow Jew. The truth or falsity of the charge was not always material, nor even the good or bad faith of the informer. The flagrant offense lay in dragging in an outside jurisdiction, which notoriously had no sense of mercy or justice where Jewish life and property were involved. . . .

"The curse of the informer plagued the life of the *Juderia* throughout its history and followed the unhappy exiles in their wanderings after the final expulsion (of Jews from Spain, in 1492). No one was too highly placed to be beyond his poisoned fangs. Men of leading importance in their communities—Jewish bailiffs, court physicians, diplomats and ministers of finance; distinguished rabbis who were universally beloved and revered, like Alfasi, Nissim Gerundi, Barfat, and Hasdai Crescas—were the targets of venomous denunciations. They were thrown into prison, their lives were in grave danger and, with their fate, the existence of their communities was at stake. . . . (A. Neuman, *The Jews in Spain* [Philadelphia, 1948], 1:130, 132).

107. Z. H. Chajes, *Torat Ha'Neviim*, ch. 7, "The Law of the King of Israel," p. 48. See D. Kaufman, "Jewish Informers in the Middle Ages," *Jewish Quarterly Review* 8 (1895–96): 221. For claimed precedents, where the welfare of the nation was threatened, compare King David's handing over of Saul's sons to the Gibeonites for killing (2 Sam. 8:9) and Talmud, *Yeba-*

mot 79a, and the Israelite preemptive attack on the Midianities (Num. 25:1). See S. Luntshitz, *Kli Yakar*, ad loc. See below for further discussion of the legal rationales. Compare Rabbi Isaac ben Shmuel, reproduced in Abraham ben David, *Temin De'Im* (Warsaw, 1897), no. 203: "My lord wondered how (we could authorize) the destruction of life of a Jewish informer, concerning money . . . This is not surprising, because there is a very important reason. Sometimes, it (informing) can threaten the life of many people, as, for example, when he is known not to have any regard for the life of his friend and it is suspected that he would rob and kill him when he can. Even if we don't know this for certain, yet, since most of those who act the way he does are suspected of this, it is permitted (to kill, even when he is not in the act of "pursuing"), and it is possible that there is a biblical verse (which authorizes) this. Even if there is no such verse, the sages have the power to uproot a rule of the Torah, even by requiring an act (which violates a rule of the Torah) according to all authorities, when there is some reason to permit it, for then, it is not like an "uprooting." Even when it says (Talmud, *Yebamot* 89a) that a rule forbidding an act (which is required by the Torah) is different, but with regard to requiring performance of an act, (which is prohibited by the Torah), they (decision-makers) do not have the power to uproot—that is only where there is no reason that is very persuasive to make it appropriate to uproot a rule. This is the way I explain the matter, that where there is a good reason, all agree that a (biblical) rule may be uprooted and there is much proof to support this. Their rationale is that in such case, it is not an uprooting."

The foregoing selection also reflects the view that the Torah itself authorized and expected departures from traditional law, where necessary. Compare M. Elon, *Mamishpat Ha'Ivri* (Jerusalem, 1973), p. 435.

*From Responsa *Zikhron Yeduha*, no. 58, by Judah ben Asher (b. 1270, Germany; d. 1327, Spain). See also Responsum No. 79, which deals with corporal punishment and amputations. Judah's father was the author of the Responsum in Section 2 *b* (2), above.

haps it was an error. It seemed to you [as proper] to consult with me in this matter, and [you] requested of me that I write you what appears to me should be his punishment. [You seek my opinion as well whether] you have to investigate and verify Saul's written charges disqualifying the witnesses against him, and, should they prove to be true, whether their testimony would be null and void. Although I am not worthy that you send your question to me, nevertheless I am fulfilling your command and will not turn you away.

It is well known that from the day the Sanhedrin went into exile from the Chamber of Hewn Stones, capital punishment was abolished in Israel. Whatever [capital punishment] is carried out at the present time, is only a precautionary measure for safeguarding against current breaches in the law. Blessed is the Lord who gave the thought to the kings in this land, of giving the Jews the power to prosecute and to do away with evildoers. Were it not for this, the Jews would not be able to exist in this land. Many Jews, as well, who would certainly be doomed to death by the gentile judges, were saved by being tried by Jewish judges. The laws we follow in these capital cases are not all by the authority of biblical law. I will, therefore, write down for you what seems to me to be just according to what I see in the trials of this city.

At the beginning we must investigate whether Saul's charges against the witnesses are true. You cannot require anyone under the threat of excommunication to testify whether each witness is suspected of committing transgressions. This would be an "inquisition" which should not be directed against any person! However, should men come before you and testify concerning any one of them, you may make them testify the truth under [threat of] a ban and you may accept their testimony.

Now, concerning your question as to what appears to me [to be proper], it is that he sinned exceedingly by striking the Jew with a cruel blow. It is so, since it is plain that he died from the blow struck by him; this is well known; he admitted to it; his fleeing is also evidence against him; he also paid out money for his medical treatment. I have carefully examined the testimony of the witnesses and have found that Moses Peselez and Abraham Chalul testified that they saw him strike the fatal blow. Joseph ben Avid and Isaac ben Yom Tov testified that they saw them quarreling, then going away and later returning again. They also saw Isaac lying on the ground, wounded in his head, with the blood flowing. The testimony of the remaining witnesses is insufficient on the subject of what happened at the time of the wounding. Joseph Avid and Isaac Yom Tov are cousins and are considered as one witness. The testimony of the other witnesses is not disqualified by it [their being

related]. That which is said, "If it is found that one of the witnesses is a relative or disqualified, all the testimony is invalidated" (Talmud, *Sanhedrin* 9a), applies only if the witnesses come on their own. However, when they testify because of a man, where all of them must come to testify, that testimony is not invalidated should it be found that one of them is a relative or disqualified; thus did my father (Rabbi Asher ben Yechiel of Blessed Memory) write.

Concerning the punishment for Saul, it seems to me that it should be in one of the following five ways according to the usual way of handling capital cases: (1) Should the testimony of Moses and Abraham be sustained, he [Saul] should be put to death; (2) Should the testimony of one of them be sustained with the testimony of Joseph or Isaac, both of his hands should be cut off; (3) Should the testimony of one of them [Moses or Abraham] be sustained and the testimony of Joseph and Isaac invalidated, his right hand should be cut off—on the basis of the testimony of Moses or Abraham alone, and the [information] known that he struck him with a fatal blow; (4) Should the testimony of Moses and Abraham become invalidated and the testimony of Joseph and Isaac [sustained], his left hand should be cut off—on the basis that we have one witness that he struck him with a fatal blow; (5) Should all of the testimonies be invalidated, he should be banished [from the community] to fulfill [the requirement]: "You shall remove the evil from your midst" (Deut. 13:6).

Rabbi Judah, the son of Rabbi Asher

(2) *Criminal Procedure*
(By Rabbi Isaac ben Sheshet Perfet)*

To the elders of Tirol, who sit in judgment and march along the paved road, the way to justice and holiness, in order to establish justice firmly in the land and the city upon its foundation, to smite with sticks those fools who have caused harm, and with scorpions, those who refuse to heed. . . .

Your letter reached me with its list of queries concerning the man . . . who shouted in public and in the streets lifted his voice and opened his mouth unlawfully. His opponent contended before you and requested that he be judged as an informer and sentenced to death. You have many doubts about this case, out of which you constructed five questions concerning some of the details about the judgment, but not the fundamental correctness of the judgment itself. It seems that your view is that if the allegations are correct, and it is proven through witnesses that the defendant did those

*From Responsa *Rivash*, no. 234–36, by Rabbi Isaac ben Sheshet Perfet (b. 1326, Spain; d. 1408, Algeria). The translation is by the editor, as are the section headings.

things claimed, as his opponent set forth in his contention, then the defendant is punishable by death as an informer. Nevertheless, you are not sure how to inquire into the facts, whether solely through witnesses or also through his confession; and if both, which should come first; and whether his confession may be accepted, and concerning other issues which are set forth in the five questions that you have set forth.

Although you have not inquired concerning the fundamental issues of whether or not he is punishable by death as an informer—assuming that he uttered the words claimed by his adversary—still, I will advise you of my views in this matter, even though it is not proper manners to respond to a question which was not posed. I am obligated to do as our sages said in the Talmud, "How do we know that a disciple who sits before his teacher and thinks of a defense for the poor man or a legal contention against the rich, should not remain silent? It is written (Exod. 23:7), 'Keep far from falsehoods.' " If this is true with regard to financial matters, then it is certainly so with regard to taking of a life.

First, however, I will advise you of my opinion regarding your questions, on the assumption that he is punishable by death for his deeds, as you think. I shall then explain why an informer is punishable by death under biblical law, and how. The conclusion will be that this man is not punishable by death.

(*a*) Admissibility of Confessions

First: You were in doubt as to whether the confession of the informer could be accepted before hearing the testimony of the witnesses against him, and whether or not accepting his confession mattered.

Response: There is no doubt that in civil suits, the testimony of witnesses is heard only after the defendant has replied to the contentions of the plaintiff. This is because if the defendant confesses, he will be obligated to pay, since the confession of a defendant is as valuable as the testimony of one hundred witnesses. If, however, the defendant denies the claim of the plaintiff, the testimony of witnesses is then needed and is received. Accordingly, why should the *beth din* be bothered to hear the testimony of the witnesses before hearing the response of the defendant to the plaintiff's claim? Perhaps the testimony will not be needed because the defendant will admit to the claim of the plaintiff. Our sages have said in a number of places in the Talmud "The *beth din* should not be bothered for nothing." Therefore, the testimony of witnesses in civil suits is not received until the defendant denies the claim of the plaintiff. With regard to witnesses in a criminal case however, one who examines them very thoroughly is praiseworthy as we learned in the Talmud, *Sanhedrin*, "Whoever examines extensively is praiseworthy. It hap-

pened that Ban Zakki examined concerning the stems of the fig tree." [Where witnesses had testified that the defendant had murdered the victim under a fig tree, they were questioned as to whether the stems of the figs were thick or thin.] It therefore appears that, at first, it is proper to receive the confession of the defendant before receiving the testimony of the witnesses, so that they can examine the witnesses concerning the details supplied by the defendant. If, however, it was not done in this way, and the testimony of the witnesses was received first, it is not important and the confession of the defendant can be received thereafter.

Connected with the aforementioned question is the issue of whether the receipt of the confession smacks of a trial [prior to the presentation of a complaint]. It appears to me that you raised this question because of the law in Aragon that one may not commence a trial interrogation [before a complaint is presented]. I believe that since there is a complainant here, the law has been followed. The law only applies to prohibit interrogations where there is no complainant, but since there is a complainant here, receipt of the defendants confession is not a prohibited interrogation. I have many times seen here that the representative of the community receives the confessions of a criminal as long as there is a complainant. Do not, however, rely on me in this matter because this is not my field, since it is not part of our Torah. Ask the non-Jewish scholars, since if you fear this law, it is their law and will be decided by them. So, too, with regard to your inquiry as to whether the seal of the king is sufficient for you to conduct the inquiry or not, without endangering the *beth din* or the community, this, too, is in their province.

(*b*) Providing an Attorney for a Defendant

Second: Whether the *beth din* is obligated to provide an attorney for the informer to arrange his contentions, or to appoint a representative for him? And if it is the law that he be provided with an attorney, should this be done before he confesses or afterwards, since he requested that he be given an attorney, just as the complainant has an attorney?

Response: In monetary suits there is a controversy among the *Gaonim* as to whether the defendant can appoint an *antler*, that is, an attorney or representative who would plead for him at the *beth din*. There are some who say that if the defendant wishes not to appear before the *beth din*, he may appoint an agent in front of witnesses, who (the agent) would plead on his behalf before the *beth din*. They bring proof from the question asked in the Jerusalem Talmud in *Sanhedrin*. . . . We therefore see that even a defendant can appoint an *antler*, and this is the view of the author of the [*Shulkhan*] *Arukh*. However, Rabbi Alfasi wrote in a Responsa that the defendant may not appoint an *antler*, and this is also the view of the Rabbi Saadiah. In the Jerusalem Talmud it is [explained that the reason is] because of the dignity of the High Priest, but for other people— "No." Yet, it seems to me that this is only in monetary suits, where it is possible to distinguish between the plaintiff and the defendant. The plaintiff, as long as he authorizes another person [to act for him] on his claim and says, "Go sue, and keep for yourself what the court will award," it is as though the agent became a party to the suit. The defendant cannot [then] say to him [the assignee of the claim], "I have nothing to do with you." But with regard to the defendant, however, who has nothing to assign, it is possible that he may not appoint an *antler*, since the plaintiff can say to him, "You are not my adversary and I will not litigate with you, since I have had no dealings with you."

In capital trials, however, if they may be distinguished, it seems that the opposite is true . . . since we need, "The congregation shall judge . . . and the congregation shall save" [see Num: 35:24, 25; i.e., the community must do all it can to assist the defendant], and we learn (Talmud, *Sanhedrin* 32b), "In capital cases, all may advance defenses on his behalf but not all may express arguments to convict him." The defendant, therefore, can appoint an *antler* to plead for him and advance defenses on his behalf, since we listen to all who come and say, "I have a defense for him" (Talmud, *Sanhedrin* 40a). Even after the trial has ended and he is brought out to be stoned, if somebody says, "I have a defense for him," he is returned [for further trial]. And certainly, if the complainant has an *antler* who advances arguments for conviction, then the defendant can also appoint somebody to advance defenses. Now, however, that they are accustomed to accept confessions, if the *beth din* sees fit to receive his confession before he appoints an attorney to plead on his behalf, in order that he should not teach him to plead falsely, in order that they render a true judgment, they have the right to do so.

(*c*) Freeing a Defendant on Bail

Third: Does the *beth din* have the right to take Simeon, the informer, out from prison on the basis of secured guarantors, a huge sum, and [the threat of] penalties, with the guarantors being liable to all that the informer would be liable, if the allegations concerning the informing are established?

Response: There is no doubt that whenever there is a possibility of capital punishment, the *beth din* is obligated to arrest him and incarcerate him in a prison until it becomes clear to them that there is no possibility of capital punishment, only a monetary judgment. They may not free him on the basis of guarantees, because

the criminal, if he sees that he will be convicted by the court, will immediately flee. What can the *beth din* do to the guarantors, and what will they accomplish if they penalize them when they have not committed any crime? "Tuviah has sinned and Zigud will be flogged?" And although they obligated themselves for this, a person cannot obligate himself for something for which he is not liable, except in monetary matters, but not for capital punishment. Furthermore, the criminal will go scot-free without any punishment, and we will be unable to fulfill "And you shall remove the evil from your midst." Furthermore, it is not fitting that one who has committed a crime and who may possibly be liable for capital punishment, should go and stroll in the streets while the *beth din* is still looking into and examining his case. . . . Therefore, if the *beth din* sees that the complainant has a case and that if his case is proven, then the criminal will be subject to execution or other capital punishment, they should not free him on the basis of guarantors.

(*d*) Accepting Testimony in the Absence of the Accused

Fourth: Must testimony be received only in the presence of the litigants, or [can it be received] even in their absence?

Response: It is a firm rule that the testimony of witnesses cannot be received except in the presence of the party [concerning whom they testify], even in monetary suits. . . . The authorities have agreed that even after the fact, if testimony was received in the absence of the parties, the testimony does not count. This is certainly the case in capital trials, which follow stricter rules. So, too, in [the Babylonian Talmud,] *Sanhedrin*, [it is related that] a slave of King Yannai murdered somebody. They [the *beth din*] sent to King Yannai, "You should also come here, as it says [in the Bible], 'And they shall testify concerning the owner [of the ox] that he did not watch him' (Exod. 21:29). The Torah said, 'Let the owner of the ox come and stand [i.e., be present during the testimony] about his ox.' He came and sat down. Said Rabbi Shimon ben Shetah, 'King Yannai, stand on your feet and let them testify concerning you. . . !'" So, too, is the language of Rambam, "Also in monetary suits, testimony can only be received in the presence of the party." The word "also" indicates that this is certainly true in capital cases. This is also implied in his explanation of the Talmud, *Sanhedrin*, that the *beth din* said to the defendant, "If you did not kill, do not be afraid." [do not fear the testimony of the witnesses, indicating that defendant hears their testimony]. Therefore, in capital cases, testimony can only be received in the presence of the party, that is, criminal defendant.

I have, however, found in a Responsum of Rabbi Asher, the German, that with regard to testimony concerning an informer, who is to be judged according to the laws of the non-Jews, that there is no need to receive the testimony in his presence since "It is a known fact that whoever is known to be an informer giving falsehoods, the non-Jews are friendly to him for their own benefit. If it were necessary to receive testimony in his presence, and to examine and scrutinize his case, it would never be possible to punish him, because he would be saved by the non-Jews. This is so since even when he is not in danger he informs on individuals and on the public. Certainly, if he sees himself in danger of bodily harm, he will inform and disclose the secrets of the public and endanger all of Israel. It is, therefore, customary in all of the areas of the exile, where one has become held to be an informer by informing three times about Jews or their money to non-Jews, that they look for a way or scheme to remove him from the world, in order to "fence-in the matter" so that others will take heed and informers will not multiply in Israel. Also to save all of the Israelites who are pursued by him."

In this connection the foregoing does not seem to apply here, since he has not informed on previous occasions. It also does not appear that he is a powerful and stubborn person. It is, therefore, fitting that testimony be received in his presence, unless the judges fear that this would be dangerous. In that case, because of the needs of the hour, the *beth din* then has the right to act contrary to the law, in order to make a fence around the Torah. This, too, was done by Shimon ben Shetah who hung eighty women in one day. However, whether the charter [given to the Jewish community] by our Lord, the king, may his splender increase, is sufficient for this, or not, you must inquire about this from the non-Jewish scholars.

(*e*) The Legal Rationale for Capital Punishment

Now I will explain to you why an informer is killed under the laws of our Torah and how. Know, that an informer is not killed under the law because of what he did, since even if he informed in a matter causing danger and death, which actually resulted in the death of somebody, the informer cannot be killed under the law. The reason is that a murderer is not killed by the *beth din*, except where he kills with his own hands. Where, however, he orders or causes [another] to kill, such as, if he incites a dog or snake [to bite] he is only subject to death at the hands of Heaven. [So, too, the informer did not kill with his own hands, but only caused the authorities to kill.] This is certainly true if the informer merely informed concerning another's money but did not endanger his life, then the informer should certainly not be executed for this.

The reason why an informer is killed under the law, is because of what is to happen in the future. For example, where he has not yet informed but threatens to inform, he is then killed as a *rodef* [pursuer] in order to save the intended Jewish victim. This is because whenever a Jew is reported to the non-Jews, even regarding a [minor] matter [such as hay or straw], there is a danger [to life], since, whenever a Jew falls into their hands, they have no mercy upon him. . . . This is the incident with Rabbi Kahana (Talmud, *Baba Kama* 117a). . . . Now, Rabbi Kahana did not kill this informer for his prior informing, because this would have only obliged the informer to pay back the money losses that he caused. He killed him because, after Rav warned him that he should not repeat his wrongdoing, he persisted in his defiance and said, "I will certainly point out" [the alleged tax evasion, to the authorities]. This [authorization to kill an informer] applies even where the informer informs about money and there is no danger to life. Therefore, Rabbi Kahana arose and acted zealously and as Phineas (see Num. 25:7).

Although the authority of the *beth din* to inflict capital punishment had already been abolished at that time, and although Rabbi Kahana was not a judge, but sat before Rav as a student before a teacher, he still killed him, because it is a commandment and an obligation upon every person to save a victim from the hands of a *rodef*, even at the expense of the life of the *rodef*. As it says, "You shall not stand by the blood of your comrade" (Lev. 19:16). Here, too, it is necessary to warn him, if there is an opportunity, before killing him, just as in the incident with Rabbi Kahana, where he warned him. . . . So, too, Rambam (Laws Concerning a Batterer, 8:9) wrote that one warns him and says, "Do not inform," and if he is temeritous, and says "No. I will, nevertheless, inform," it is a commandment to kill him, and whoever is first, is meritorious."

We find this in the Talmud, *Berakhot* 58a, with Rabbi Shila. A certain man said to the king, "There is a Jewish man who sits as a judge [without permission]." He [Rabbi Shila] did not kill him. When, however, he threatened to inform to the king [about another matter], he [Rabbi Shila] then said, "He is a *rodef*, and the Torah said, "He who comes to kill you, arise and kill him." Rabbi Shila thereupon killed him. Here, too, it is possible that Rabbi Shila warned him even though this is not mentioned in the Talmud, or that he had no opportunity to warn him. It is also possible that an intended victim, who comes to save himself at the expense of the life of the *rodef*, is not required to warn the *rodef*, because he is agitated concerning the danger to his life and is attempting to save himself. One is not obligated to warn in such a case, but as soon as he sees that somebody comes to kill him, he should arise and attack the *rodef*. But if a third person comes to save him, he must warn the *rodef* before killing him, if there is an opportunity. Also in the Talmud, *Sanhedrin* 72b, Rabbi Hana maintains that it is permissable to save a victim at the expense of the life of the *rodef* and that it is not necessary to warn the *rodef*. It is sufficient to tell him, "He is a Jew. He is a member of the covenant." It is only necessary to warn one who will be liable to execution at the hands of the *beth din*. So also wrote Rambam. In the name of Rabbi Ahron Halevi, I have found [it written] that even those who hold that one must warn a *rodef* [hold that] this only applies to a third person who comes to save the victim. All are agreed, however, that the victim himself need not warn. . . . So, too, [regarding] an informer, since the obligation to kill him arises because he is regarded under the law as a *rodef*, [the law is as follows:] before he commits an act, every person may kill him, in any place and at time in order to save the pursued. Where, however, he has already committed an act and has informed, he may not be killed but must be brought before the *beth din* to be punished as called for by law, or, even more severely, in order to "fence-in the matter" in accordance with the needs of the hour. He is also then required to pay the victim the amount of his loss, as is established through witnesses. If, however, he is accustomed to [inform] and has a reputation that he has informed on Jews three times, he is then regarded as a [perpetual] *rodef*, and every person may kill him in any place and at any time, both through a *beth din* or without a *beth din*, in order to save Jews from his hand so that he should not inform upon them, since he is accustomed to and has a reputation for informing. This is as we learned in the Talmud, "Sectarians and informers are pushed into pits and are not raised up." The term "informers" means that they are accustomed to and have a reputation for informing, as Rambam (Laws Concerning a Batterer, 8:9) says, "If the informer performed his intentions and informed, I believe that it is forbidden to kill him unless he is known to be accustomed to inform. He may then be killed so that he should not inform upon others. It is a daily occurence in the cities of the west [Spain] to kill informers who are known to inform constantly regarding the money of Jews, and to turn over these informers to non-Jews to kill them, smite them, or imprison them according to their crimes." . . . Rabbi Hannanel explained that the term "They are pushed into a pit" means that they are pushed into a pit so that they cannot climb out and will die there by themselves. To kill them outright, however, is forbidden. Rambam, however, does not agree to this,

since he says, (Laws Concerning a Murderer, 4:10) "One is obliged to kill them. If he is able to kill them in public, he should do so. If not he shall employ various stratagems until he causes their death." Even according to the view of Rabbi Hannanel, as long as a *beth din* sentenced him to death and turned him over to the officers of the kingdom to kill him, this counts as though they were pushed into a pit, and it is not as though the *beth din* killed them with his own hands. So, too, wrote Rosh [Asher ben Yehiel]. The foregoing is what appears to me to be the law regarding an informer, and why he is killed and how.

Accordingly, with regard to Shimon, who is being held by you, even though it is established that he said the things which it is claimed, he is not subject to a death penalty according to biblical law. Even if what he says counts as informing, since he already committed the act of informing, he is not subject to the death penalty, unless he was accustomed and known to constantly inform on others and has done this three times as I have written above.

Furthermore, we must determine whether the words he uttered count as informing or not. After the aforesaid Reuven and his son were suspected of the theft and were held for some time in the hands of the Secretary [an official appointed by the king who had wide-ranging authority to act and to supervise the activities of the Jewish community] and the representatives of the community, and there is no doubt that this was well known, if Shimon, because of his great anger concerning the theft from his sister (and perhaps because the Secretary did not bring the suspects to judgment) complained that the trial should have been held before the Secretary and the Jewish representatives, this is not really informing. Although he said that Reuven and his son are thieves, and should be put to death because of the theft, this is not informing since they were already held publicly by the Secretary and it was clear that whether the trial would be held before the city officials, or before the Secretary, everything would proceed in accordance with the law.

Even the utterances that he made against the Jewish community representatives cannot be called informing, since they could not be punished despite his complaints, because the Secretary [who was a highly influential, non-Jewish representative of the king] participated in their acts.

Nevertheless, since his acts caused damages and expenses to the community and legal proceedings against the elders and leaders of his people, Shimon could not escape being a troublemaker for the community in uttering those words. He should be punished for this as the *beth din* sees fit, whether by flogging, excommunication, fines, or incarceration; as Rambam wrote, "Whoever causes trouble and pain for the community, it is permissible to hand him over to non-Jews to hit him, to imprison him, or to fine him. It is, however, forbidden to so hand him over if he has only caused trouble for an individual." So, too, if the *beth din* sees that there are "Breaches in the wall" during that generation, that there is no limit to their temerity and to their informing, and that they do not put any lock on their mouths, they [the *beth din*] have the right to punish them more than the law would require in order to "fence-in the matter" according to the needs of the hour. This is what is written in the Talmud, *Yebamot*, Said Rabbi Eliezer ben Jacob, 'I have heard that the *beth din* may smite and penalize not in accordance with the law; not in order to transgress on the words of the Torah, only to make a fence about the Torah.' And it happened during the days of the Greeks that one rode upon a horse on the Sabbath, and he was brought before the *beth din* and stoned. This was not because the law so provided, but because the hour needed it. There was another incident with one who had sexual relations with his wife under a fig tree [in public] and he was brought before the *beth din* and flogged. This was not because that was the law, but because the hour needed it." The conclusion of the Talmud there was that this was done to "fence-in the matter". . . .

(3) *Representation by Attorneys in Jewish Courts*

The question of representation by an attorney in Jewish courts involved two issues: whether the personal appearance of the litigants in court was required and whether assistance of counsel would be permitted.

Jewish courts traditionally insisted that the litigants appear before them in person, rather than through a representative. In criminal cases, where capital punishment was a possibility, this was held required by express biblical provision: "The slayer shall not be killed until he shall stand before the congregation in judgment . . ."[108] Even in civil cases, however, Jewish courts insisted that both plaintiff and defendant should appear in person, and not send a representative to appear in their stead. This position of the courts was predicated upon a number of factors. A litigant who was not physically present before the court could not be cross-examined, nor be put under oath, in order to ascertain the true facts of the case. There was also a fear that while a defendant who had direct dealings with a plaintiff might not have the temerity to falsely deny a claim, his representative would not be restricted by such inhibitions. Furthermore, the litigants' personal

knowledge of the facts and their interest in the case would help to ensure that all of the facts, as well as the legal arguments, would be advanced before the court, leading to an appropriate decision.

With regard to the issue of permitting assistance by counsel, there was a fear both of distortion and manipulation of the law by attorneys, and attempts by them to have their clients either lie, withhold the truth, or testify in a manner designed to bring about a miscarriage of justice. There was also apprehension that an attorney might wield undue influence with the communal or non-Jewish authorities, or would be so cunning that he would be able to wrongfully influence the course of the decision.[109] The issue of representation in court by an attorney was often regarded as an evil practice, which could lead to serious distortion of the law and miscarriage of justice.[110]

In time, these two issues: assistance by counsel and representation of a litigant by a person who would appear in his stead, became intertwined, and both were severely frowned upon. Gradually, however, the courts' attitude changed.

An important factor in overturning the aforementioned negative attitudes was the growth of international trade and travel. Plaintiffs would often be unable, or unwilling, to travel to a foreign land where a defendant resided, in order to appear personally in court in suits to recover monies. The practice arose, therefore, of permitting a plaintiff to appoint a representative to appear at court in his stead to assert his claim.[111] Permitting a plaintiff to sue via a representative was also thought to be helpful to the flow of credit to foreign borrowers and to purchasers of goods on credit, since otherwise the inability to sue debtors in foreign lands would deter the extension of credit.

None of these policy reasons, which operated to benefit creditors, applied to dispense with personal appearances by debtors, who continued to be required to appear in court, although plaintiffs might send representatives to appear on their behalf. There was still another reason for the distinction between debtors and creditors with regard to personal appearances. The legal theory permitting a plaintiff to appear by representative, was that the plaintiff had assigned all of his interest in the claim to the representative, who was then the real

---

108. Num. 35:12.

109. See Talmud, *Shevuot* 31c; Assaf, *Batei Ha'Din* (Jerusalem, 1924), 95.

110. Talmud, *Avot* 4:10.

111. See Jacob ben Asher, *Tur, Ho. Mis.*, sec. 123; and Karo, *Beth Yosef, Ho. Mis.*, sec. 124. See in general, A. Kirschenbaum, "Representation in Litigation in Jewish Law," *Dinei Israel* (Tel-Aviv, 1975), vol. 6, p. xxv; N. Rakover, *Ha'Shelikhut Ve'Harsha'ah Ba'Mishpat Ha'Ivri* (Hebrew; Jerusalem, 1922).

party in interest to the claim. The defendant, however, had no such "asset" to assign to a representative.[112]

Eventually, however, the distinction between the rights of plaintiffs and defendants to representation became eroded, and both were permitted to select representatives to appear in court in their stead.[113] This development, in turn, appears to have affected the stance in the related issue of assistance by counsel in cases where the defendant or plaintiff did appear in person. Eventually the practice became widespread of permitting assistance of counsel to both plaintiff and defendant, regardless of personal appearances by the litigants.[114]

Representation and assistance by attorneys became particularly widespread in medieval Spain, where some merchants retained attorneys on an annual (or other periodic) basis, to represent them in court in all litigations in which they were involved.[115] Some of the attorneys were retained on a long-term basis and paid for their time, whether or not they won or lost the cases.[116] Representation by attorneys, who appeared in court together with plaintiffs and defendants, later became quite widespread in Italy, too.

Nevertheless, there remained intense opposition to the employment of counsel in Jewish courts. Negative views regarding attorneys were widespread in non-Jewis circles, too. There were claims that attorneys often lied and used other unethical practices in order to win their cases, and even that whoever was a liar and trickster was, *ipso facto*, a more successful attorney[117] (a

claim often heard today, in the United States, as well).

Additional opposition arose from the practices of some attorneys who attempted to pressure Jewish courts into applying the non-Jewish "law of the land" (in lieu of Jewish law) when this was favorable to their clients. Implied threats by attorneys to report to non-Jewish authorities that the Jewish courts were applying laws that were, allegedly, directly contrary to the law of the land and in violation thereof smacked of informing and engendered much revulsion.[118] A number of courts in Italy, accordingly, decided to permit counsel to assist plaintiff or defendant, only if they were closely related by blood or marriage. Some communities completely prohibited the appearance of counsel in all cases.[119] There were similar bans on representation by counsel in Cracow, Poland, but less so in Germany.[120]

In some parts of Germany, where counsel was permitted, minimum qualifications were set for them, and they were required to have at least the title of *"Khaver"* (literally, "colleague"), which was conferred by the rabbi upon those who had established both their piety and erudition in law.[121]

In cases where the defendant was liable to capital punishment by a Jewish court (as in some Jewish communities in Spain in the thirteenth century; see above), the defendant was always permitted to retain counsel to assist him in presenting his defense.[122]

Compare these restrictions on the use of counsel with the provisions regarding the right to counsel in the United States Constitution, and with the practice in England with regard to criminal (as contrasted with civil) cases.

It has also been claimed that if a defendant did not have counsel to assist him, the Jewish courts would provide one for him, sometimes at no cost to the defendant, if he were poor.[123] If this is correct, then the Jewish courts in Spain provided free counsel to the poor

---

112. See Responsa of Isaac b. Sheshet; Responsa, *Rambam* in Responsa *Zera Anashim* (Husiatin, 1902), sec. 8; and Asher ben Yehiel, Commentary on *Rosh* to *Shevuot*. See also the conclusion of Isaac Alfasi in his *Rif*, ad loc. with regard to the statement in that section of the Talmud. Impermissibility of a defendant to utilize a representative to appear for him was also concurred in by Saadya Gaon, Hai Gaon, and Samuel ben Hafni Gaon; see *Sefer Ha'Itur*, p. 62a (Lemburg ed., 1874); A. Harkavy, Responsa of the *Gaonim*, (Berlin, 1887), sec. 180; Karo, *Shulkhan Arukh, Ho. Mis.*, sec. 124.

113. See Eibschutz, *Urim Ve'Tumin, Ho. Mis.*, sec. 124; Weil, Responsa *Mahari Weil*, sec. 109.

114. Assaf, *Batei Ha'Din*, p. 96. For variant practices in different communities, some of which insisted that a plaintiff who did appear personally in court should argue in person and not by an attorney, see the commentaries to sec. 124 of *Shulkhan Arukh Hoshen Mishpat* of Joshua Falk Cohen, *Me'Irat Enayim*, and Shabse Kohen, in *Sifse Kohen*, both works appearing in standard editions of the *Shulkhan Arukh, Hoshen Mishpat* and Y. Sirkis, *Bayit Khadash*, to Jacob ben Asher, *Tur, Ho. Mis.*, sec. 124.

115. Shlomo ben Aderet, Responsa *Rashba*, vol. 2, nos. 393 and 404; vol. 3, no. 141.

116. Responsa of Moshe ben Nahman, cited in Jacob ben Asher, *Tur, Ho. Mis.*, sec. 123, and in Karo, *Beth Yosef*, ad loc.; Weil, Responsa *Mahari Weil*, sec. 109.

117. Isaac ben Sheshet, Responsa *Rivash*, sec. 235; Karo, *Beth Yosef, Ho. Mis.*, sec. 124; Zakut, in *Shuda De'Daina*, reprinted in Chapter VIII, B 2, above; Benebashti, in Responsa

Baya Haya (Jerusalem, 1970), *Ho. Mis.*, sec. 2, no. 90; see also the commentary of Isaac Abarbanel to Exod. 23:1.

118. A. H. Rodriguez, in Responsa *Orakh La'Tzadik* (Livorno, 1780).

119. David Pipino, Responsa *Khoshen Ha'Efod*, (Sofiia, 1895), sec. 43; Shlomo ben Aderet, Responsa *Rashba*, vol. 5, no. 288. See similar provisions in the ordinances of the city of Constantinople and other communities in Turkey and Egypt, published in A. Halevi, Responsa *Ginat Veradim, Ho. Mis.*, sec. 6, no. 1; Benebashti, Responsa *Baya Haya, Ho. Mis.*, sec. 1, no. 12, subsec. 25.

120. *Jahrbuch der Judisch-Literarische Gesellschaft* 10:334; Y. Isserlin, Responsa *Terumat Ha'Deshen*, sec. 354; Weil, Responsa *Mahari Weil*, secs. 101 and 109.

121. See the ordinances of the communities of Altona and Hamburg, 1726, published in *Mitteilungen zur Judischen Volkskunde* (1903).

122. Isaac ben Sheshet, Responsa *Rivash*, sec. 235.

123. Ibid.; see Assaf, *Batei Ha'din Ve'Sidrehem* (Jerusalem, 1924), p. 99.

some seven hundred years before the United States Supreme Court required this in *Gideon v. Wainright.*[124]

d. PUNISHING A BLASPHEMER
(By Asher ben Yehiel)*

Question: Let it be known to our teacher, may he be well, that here in Cordova a very serious incident took place. The ears of all those who hear of it become "singed." A certain debased person was detained on charges by Gentiles. He settled with them by paying money. Some of his acquaintances later went to console him. He went out [to welcome them] and stood at the entrance of his yard. They calmed him in this matter, one of them saying, "Blessed is he who frees the imprisoned." Nevertheless, he, turning upward [to heaven], blasphemed and reviled his King and God. . . . About ten of the community notables, men of action, with this honorable [man] Rabbi Judah, and local sages, with the city elders [decided] to do away with him. Learning of this, relatives of the guilty person went with bribes, it seems, to the great royal dignitary, Don Juan Manuel whom we received in our area as the procurator for his majesty, the king. . . . This lord agreed that the guilty one should remain in his prison until the Responsum of my teacher, may he be well, will arrive instructing [us] what to do. . . .

Response: May the delightful pious and charming notables accept [the blessing of] abundant peace! Your asking me concerning capital cases is rather strange. In all of the lands that I have heard of they do not try capital cases except in this land of Spain. When I came here I was very astonished. How were they able to try capital cases without the *Sanhedrin?* They replied that it is by royal authority. The assembly [of judges] also judges in order to save [lives], since greater amounts of blood would have been spilled if they were tried by the Gentiles. I permitted them to continue with their practice. However, I never agreed with them on any loss of life.

Nevertheless, I see that all of you are of the opinion to remove this evil from your midst. He certainly did desecrate the name of heaven in public and it was already heard by the Gentiles, who view with seriousness anyone who speaks against their religion and beliefs. The desecration would be increased if no act of vengeance would be taken against him. We do find that in order to sanctify the name of God they raised their hands against princes on behalf of proselytes [see 2 Sam. 21:8–9] and let their [the princes'] corpses hang overnight. [We also find] that in order to check lawless-

ness they stoned to death a person who had ridden a horse on the Sabbath [see Talmud, *Yebamot* 90b]. It is also proper that God's name should be sanctified by the loss of this wicked person, and so as you see fit.

If I were present at your contemplations, my opinion would have been that they should pull out his tongue and cut off the major portion necessary for speech thereby silencing his lips. In this way they would mete out [punishment] to him according to his deed. This is a well known vengeance which is witnessed daily.

You, however, do according to what seems proper in your eyes. I do realize that your intentions are that God's name should be sanctified.

The opinion of the writer, Asher
the son of Rabbi Yehiel of Blessed Memory

Notes to Asher ben Yehiel, "Punishing a Blasphemer"

"This incident is typical of the religious conception that was common in the Christian environment concerning crimes like these. It is known that Louis IX, the King of France, zealous for his god, ordered on many occasions that the tongues of blasphemers should be cut out. The Jews, too, conducted themselves in this way" (Y. Baer, *History of the Jews in Christian Spain* [Hebrew; Jerusalem, 1965], p. 188).

e. PUNISHING A FORNICATOR
(By Asher ben Yehiel)*

Question: When I was in Kuka with Don Juan, may the Lord preserve him, I was advised by some Jews there that a certain widow had become pregnant from a Muslim, that "her belly was now between her teeth," and that there were continuously rumors concerning her. I examined the matter and inquired as much as I could concerning this matter among the Jews to ascertain whether there was clear testimony of eyewitnesses concerning this, so that the facts could be definitely established. I did not find any Jew who could give definite testimony to them that [her pregnancy] was from the Muslim. . . . My suspicions were placed before Don Juan, may the Lord preserve him, concerning the Muslim, and he replied that this was not a matter for him [to decide] since she was a Jewess, but that we should judge her according to the laws of our Torah. . . . Therefore, I beg you . . . to guide us how I should judge her, in order that the laws of our Torah should not be treated lightly and scornfully in the eyes of the non-Jews . . . we should be harsh, as you will advise me . . . because all of the communities in the vicinity of Kuka tell tales that the knowledge concerning this prostitute will spread among the non-Jews, who will look scorn-

---

124. 372 U.S. 335, 83 S. Ct. 792 (1963).
*From Responsa *Rosh*, no. 17:8, by Asher ben Yehiel. The translation is by the editor.

*From Responsa *Rosh*, sec. 18, no. 13, by Asher ben Yehiel. The translation is by the editor.

fully at our laws, and in order that the women should hear and not be like her. It occurred to me that since the matter received so much notoriety, that she should be duly punished by destroying the shape of her face [apparently by destroying her nose; see Section a, above], which she prettied up for her paramour, and that she pay the Lords of the city some money. And now, if you desire and see fit to be even harsher with her, or to punish her in a different manner, so I will do . . .

Yehudah ben Yitzhak Wakir

Response: . . . You have judged well to duly punish her so that she would become disgusting to her para-mour, and this matter should be carried out suddenly, and she should be fined in accordance with her wealth. Peace be to you and all yours.

Asher ben Yehiel

Notes to Asher ben Yehiel, "Punishing a Fornicator"

Under the prevailing law of non-Jewish courts at that time in Spain, the widow could have been sentenced to be burned to death.[125] Accordingly, the sentence imposed by the Jewish courts and approved by *Rosh* was viewed as resulting in a "lighter" penalty for her![126]

f. IMPRISONING A THIEF ON CIRCUMSTANTIAL EVIDENCE
(By Shimon ben Tsemah Duran)*

Question: Reuben was blind and travelled with Simon as a companion. Blind Reuben had some diamonds sewn into his garment; Simon would join him on trips and sleep near him. When Reuben looked for the dia-monds and did not find them, he suspected that Simon stole them since he was an evildoer. When Reuben made the claim against him, he denied it. What is the law in this case?

Responsum: It is known that a thief does not steal in the presence of witnesses. Should we go and judge in such a case on the basis of witnesses, the cause of justice would suffer. The authority is, therefore, given to all judges in every generation to set up precautionary measures and safeguards in these matters and the *Gaonim* have done so in laws that pertain to fines.

Even on the basis of Talmudic law, it is permissible to enact these reforms. "We may flog and impose pun-ishments not on the basis of strict law in order to enact

safeguards and precautionary measures" (*Yebamot* 90b). We may certainly do it to help the wronged from the hand of the wrongdoer and the humiliated from the hand of the arrogant. We find in the Talmud that on the basis of a plausible reason, they tied up a man until he admitted to a theft (*Baba Metzia* 24a): "From the host of Mar Zutra, a silver goblet was stolen. He [Mar Zu-tra] saw that student wash his hands and wipe them on the cloak of his friend. He [Mar Zutra] said, "It is he, since he does not care about his friends possessions. They tied him up until he confessed." In the chapter *Get Pashut* (*Baba Batra* 167a), there are two cases where they tied one up until he confessed.

Here, there appears to be a plausible reason. This victim is blind and when he joined up with "Ahazyahu" (a wicked king of Israel) the Lord made a breach in his works (see 2 Chr. 20:37); leaving him in a place of bears and lions.

It is sound judgment that he be threatened and in-timidated with specific actions to be taken against him should he not confess. It is so written in Tur *Khoshen Mishpat* in chapter 64 (citing a responsum by his father, the *Rosh* of Blessed Memory).

I have already imprisoned here a Jew against whom a wayfarer from Nefussa made a charge that he stole. On the basis that "one recognizes words of truth," I imprisoned him. There was no governor or official who would free him. Afterwards the object stolen was found in his possession. The entire community—may their Rock keep and protect them!—[thanked me] for my alertness in this matter.

g. COMMUNAL CRIMINAL LAW PRESCRIPTIONS

Following are selected Jewish medieval communal prescriptions, which illustrate the type of behavior reg-ulated and the range of sanctions imposed for deviance, by Jewish communities in medieval Europe.

(1) *Ordinances of the Jewish Community of Cracow, Poland* (circa *1595* et seq.)

1. ". . . Whoever informs about [and thereby endan-gers] the money, and certainly [if he endangers] the body of one Jew, and certainly, many [Jews], to non-Jews, . . . every Jewish man knows the law, and it is not necessary to promulgate a new ordinance in this matter. We have only come to warn and decree that every Jewish man who hears or sees an act of this kind, whether it concerns him personally or not, is obliged, under threat of a grave excommunication, and under penalties applied to an informer, himself, to come within three days and to testify about what he saw or heard, to whichever two lay leaders he desires, who

---

125. See Y. Baer, *History of the Jews in Christian Spain* (Philadelphia, 1966); Y. Raisher, Responsa *Shevut Yaakov*, vol. 2, sec. 82.

126. See Assaf, *Ha'Onshin*, p. 69, no. 58.

*From Responsa, *Tashbatz*, sec. 3, no. 168, by Shimon ben Tsemah Duran, (b. 1361, Majorca; d. 1425, Algeria). The trans-lation is by the editor.

have no connection with the informer. These two leaders shall do whatever they have to do [in this matter]. If the informer is powerful, and it is not possible to do anything with him at that time, then, the rabbis, heads, and officials of the Jewish community shall record his name in a Book of Remembrances, so that afterwards, they shall not circumcise his child, shall not perform marriages for his children, or [perform] any other matter that relates to the holiness of Israel. The rabbis, lay leaders, and officials shall watch him carefully in order to fulfill, "and on the day that I will visit [punishment upon him], then I will visit [this punishment, too], upon him. . . ."[127]

[Note the unwillingness in the first sentence to spell out the authorization for any Jews to kill an informer. The ordinance only hints at this, probably, because the Jewish community was not authorized to impose capital punishment.]

2. ". . . Every householder who does not pay tuition for his child by the end of the semester, shall be coerced into doing so by imprisonment, by excommunication, and by the taking of security. It shall be announced in the synagogue that no teacher may take his child to teach him for the coming semester, until he pays the teacher for the past semester. . . ."[128]

3. ". . . The youth, Tzvi Hirsh ben Zanvil . . . has admitted that he took part in the theft that occurred in the house of the noble. The decision was rendered by the honorable community, may they be protected, that he shall forfeit his right of residence here, and he shall not return here all the days of his life. He shall not be seen nor found here. He shall also be flogged by the night watchman in front of the gate of the synagogue, and they shall escort him when he leaves the city, until he is outside the city. If he shall ever return here, his sentence is recorded that, his ears shall be amputated, in addition to other punishment that shall be inflicted upon him. To strengthen the validity [of this sentence], the foregoing youth has, himself, signed this verdict [accepting it]. . . ."[129]

[It is a matter of speculation, whether the mutilations threatened ("his ears shall be amputated") were actually practiced or were simply hyperbole. See also below for other communal prescriptions imposing severe sanctions for prohibited behavior.]

(2) *Sanctions Imposed by the Portuguese Jewish Community in Hamburg, Germany, (1655–1670)**

[These selections illustrate some of the more moderate sanctions imposed by Jewish communities in Western Europe. Why, do you suppose, were they milder than those of the community of Cracow? The following selected synopses have been culled from the records of the Portuguese Jewish community, whose members had emigrated to Hamburg, Germany, from Portugal in order to be able to freely worship as Jews. In Hamburg the Portuguese Jewish community, was vested with considerable autonomous powers to maintain public order. No Jews were permitted to remain in Portugal, after the sixteenth-century expulsions (see Chapter 1, Section C, above), and all were forced to either convert to Christianity or leave. Those who converted under pressure but worshipped secretly as Jews were liable to the death penalty (often by public burning) or torture by the Inquisition.]

1. "Yaakov Haluah is ordered not to leave his house until further orders. . . ."[130]

2. "The aforesaid is permitted to leave his house for one morning to go to the court, to which he was subpoenaed. He is, however, to return directly to his house afterwards and not to leave it. . . ."[131]

3. "Mr. Linada, who attempted to coerce David Haluah to marry his cousin, under a threat of death, and who also humiliated the sexton of the community, was ordered to remain in his house until the following Sunday and then to leave the city, and never to have any other transactions with David Haluah . . ."[132]

4. "The lay leaders of the community hereby decide to initiate discussions with the manager of a city factory, to arrange for juvenile delinquents to be sent to work at the factory for a period from two to four weeks. The support for these youngsters, so penalized, will be paid for by the community. . . ."[133]

5. "Shlomo Sanka Perverizka was notified to leave the city voluntarily, within fifteen days, or be forced to do this. . . ."[134]

6. Elijah Avuhab is to be excommunicated. No one shall speak to him, unless he receives a specific permit. . . .[135] Rafael Milano and Sarah Abarbanel are to

---

*Transcripts of these records may be found in *Jahrbucher der Judisch-Literarischen Gesellschaft*, vols. VI–XII (Frankfort, 1908–1917), and S. Assaf, *Ha'Onshin Akhare Khatimot Ha'Talmud* (Jerusalem, 1922).

127. Exod. 32:34; i.e., action shall be taken against him when the opportunity arises. The Ordinance of the Council of Four Lands, cited in the Ordinances of the Community of Cracow, Poland, in Balaban, *Jahrbuch*, vol. 10, p. 309; Assaf, *Ha'Onshin*, p. 130.

128. *Jahrbuch*, vol. 11, p. 100.

129. P. Wettstein, *Ozar Ha'Safrut*, vol. 4, p. 614.

130. Ibid., vol. 9, p. 323.

131. Ibid., vol. 9, p. 333.

132. Ibid., vol. 10, p. 251.

133. Ibid., vol. 10, p. 284.

134. Ibid., vol. 12, p. 64.

135. Ibid., vol. 12, p. 70.

be notified not to speak with Mr. Avuhab within the confines of the city of Hamburg. If she does wish to speak with him, she must do this outside of the boundaries of the city. . . ."[136]

7. "The rabbi of the city notified the community council that some people were conducting themselves in an immoral and untraditional manner. They are to be notified that unless they correct their ways, the community council will utilize the power given to it by the rulers of the city to banish them from the city. . . ."[137]

8. "The community leaders announced that young people who continue to misbehave, and are not controlled by their parents, will be penalized with corporal punishment, imprisonment in jail, and banishment from the city. . . ."[138]

9. "Because of the repeated misdeeds of Abraham Dek Asiris, his mother is to be requested to send him out of the city for a period of two years. . . ."[139] After his mother notified the community leaders that she did not have the necessary monies in order to pay for his journey to another land, the community council passed a resolution to lend her one hundred marks for this purpose. . . ."[140]

3. PRECEDENTS, PRINCIPLES, AND RATIONALES FOR EXTRAORDINARY SANCTIONS AND ADJUSTMENTS IN THE LAW

a. BIBLICAL AUTHORITY

With reference to the question of what made Jewish decision-makers think that they had the right to kill or mutilate contrary to traditional norms, usually applied, it is important to note that Talmudic decision-makers were deeply religious persons who often became martyrs for their faith. Consequently, they would certainly not transgress fundamental biblical precepts, such as prohibitions against killing or flogging, unless they perceived clear biblical authorization to do so.

The main talmudic precedents in which extraordinary sanctioning was employed are set forth above (Section C 1). While these precedents were relied on in the Middle Ages, they were not completely satisfactory, since these precedents were postpentateuchal. Talmudic decision-makers asserted that all biblical laws had to be derived from the Pentateuch not even from later sections of the Bible.[141] The various claims of biblical

justification and authority to kill, maim, and otherwise impose sanctions on convicted criminals, contrary to normal legal norms, may be classified as follows:

1. The Talmud (*Yebamot* 90b) cites the biblical precedent mentioned above, of the Prophet Elijah, who acted in violation of a biblical injunction in order to meet the special "needs of the hour."[142] This is not completely satisfactory authority, however, since the precedent is postpentateuchal, and, furthermore, it did not deal with so basic a norm as homicide.

2. Ravad (Abraham ben David) maintains that the authority relied on the verse, "It is time to act for God, since they have set aside your Torah" (Ps. 119:126). This verse is often relied on in the Talmud as the authority to deviate from traditional biblical norms.[143] The verse is interpreted to mean, "It is time to act for God, *and* to set aside your Torah," or "they (decision-makers) have set aside your Torah *because* it is time to act for God." Reliance on this verse also raises problems since it, too, is postpentateuchal.

3. *Megilat Taanit*, a work dating from the Talmudic Era (Warsaw, 1874), chapter 6, cites as authority the biblical verses "and you shall remove the evil from your midst" (Deut. 17:7), and "So that all Israel shall hear and see" (i.e., shall be deterred; Deut. 13:12). The Talmud, (*Sanhedrin* 78a) also relies on the passage, "And you shall remove the evil from your midst" as the basis for executing a person with a fatal defect who murders another in the presence of a court. (Without the authorization of this verse, such a murderer would have escaped the death penalty pursuant to ordinary biblical law, as interpreted in the Talmud; see Rambam, Laws Concerning a Murderer, 2:9. This verse is relied on in *Megilat Taanit* for the *beth din* to impose sanctions not otherwise authorized by the Bible.[144]

4. Moshe ben Nahman relies on the verse in Leviticus 27:29, "Anyone devoted by men . . . shall be put to death," which he interprets as authorizing extraordinary sanctions.[145]

5. "You shall observe scrupulously all their instructions to you" (Deut. 17:10) is cited by Rabbi Nissim[146] as the authority that vests decision-makers with extraordinary powers to deviate from traditional norms.

---

136. Ibid.
137. Ibid., vol. 12, p. 89.
138. Ibid., vol. 12, p. 89.
139. Ibid., vol. 12, p. 89.
140. Ibid., vol. 13, p. 113.
141. Talmud, *Baba Kama* 2b; *Khagiga* 10b; Rambam, Laws of the Foundations of the Torah, 9:1, 4; Z. H. Chajes, *Torat Ha'Neviim*, ch. 1, p. 12.

142. See also, Rambam, Laws Concerning a Murderer, 2:4, and Karo, *Kesef Mishnah*, ad loc.; Rambam, Laws of the Foundations of the Torah, 9:3.
143. See Talmud, *Temurah* 14b.
144. See M. Ha'Meiri, *Beth Ha'Bekhira*, ad loc., and comment of A. Sofer, the editor, thereon.
145. See his Commentary Ramban, ad loc., and his *Mishpate Ha'Kherem* in Responsa *Rashba*, attributed to Ramban, no. 285; also M. Sofer, Responsa *Hatam Sofer, Orah Hayim*, no. 209.
146. *Derashot Ha'Ran*, no. 11.

6. Isaac Arama'ah premises the authority on the verse (Deut. 17:11), "You shall not deviate to the left or the right"[147] (from the laws that the judges tell you). He understood this verse as authorizing judges to *deliberately* deviate from established principles. General principles, he argued, could only be appropriate in the usual case, but would be inappropriate in certain particular instances that require deliberate deviation in order to achieve just results.

7. Rivash (Isaac ben Sheshet) premises the authority on a passage in the Book of Joshua,[148] which the Talmud also relies on for the principle *"hefker beth-din, hefker."* This passage also faces the objection that it is postpentateuchal.

8. Moshe Sofer[149] premises this authority upon the verse in Deuteronomy 19:10, "The blood of the innocent shall not be shed . . . And you shall have no blood guilt upon you." This implies, according to him, taking action to avoid the shedding of innocent blood, including the punishment of criminals in order to deter further criminal acts.

9. Yeruham Perlow cites the verse, "And you shall guard my ordinances."[150] This verse is cited in the Talmud as authorizing decision-makers to prescribe norms designed to ensure compliance with biblical commandments, but is not cited there as authorizing deviation from norms and imposing extraordinary sanctions.

The lack of clarity and divergent views as to the precise biblical verse that authorizes deviation from accepted norms of punishment reflect the fact that none of the verses quoted *specifically* authorizes extraordinary punishments contrary to the biblical norms and principles that ordinarily apply.

b. LEGAL PRINCIPLES

The authority to impose extraordinary sanctions and to otherwise deviate from traditional law in order to deal appropriately with a current situation has been formulated into a number of legal principles in Jewish law.

1. Some authorities maintain that the power to impose extraordinary sanctions on criminals and other deviants is part of the implied power and authority granted in the Bible to a king and to communal leaders, and that it is implied in the verse, "Ye shall place a king upon you."[151]

Since the authority of a king was regarded as derived from the community, it followed that the *beth din*, acting as representative of the entire community, was also authorized by the community to do whatever was necessary for public order, including the execution of criminals.[152]

An analogous doctrine viewed a non-Jewish king as having similar powers and permitted Jews to carry out extraordinary sanctions on the king's behalf.[153]

2. A similar view regarding the power of the community to authorize extraordinary actions has been held to be implied in the principle[154] *"dina de'malhuta dina"* ("the law of the kingdom is the law").

3. Another talmudic principle should also be noted to the effect that even after the traditional ordination and the *Sanhedrin* were abolished, subsequent decision-makers were authorized to exercise the same penal powers as the *Sanhedrin* had possessed, on the grounds that the latter had authorized subsequent decision-makers in all future times to act as their agents in this regard.[155]

4. The right, if needed, to impose extraordinary sanctions because of changed conditions, and to otherwise deviate from biblical norms, has been expressed in the Talmud in a number of other legal principles. The Talmud does not, however, specify a pentateuchal source for these principles, some of which appear to be based purely on logic.

a. "It is time to work for God and to set aside your laws."[156]

b. "It is better that one letter of the Torah shall be uprooted, so that the (entire) Torah should not be forgotten from Israel."[157]

c. "Sometimes, the abolition of the law results in its establishment."[158]

d. "Desecrate one Sabbath for him so that he will be able to observe many Sabbaths."[159]

---

147. See his commentary *Akedat Yitzkhak* to Exod., ch. 21.
148. 19:51. See his Responsa, no. 399; see also Talmud, *Yebamot* 89b; David Friedman, *Emek Berakha*, sec. 1.
149. In his Responsa *Hatam Sofer, O.H.,* at the end of Responsum no. 208.
150. Lev. 18:30. See his commentary to *Sefer Ha'Mitzvot* (Jerusalem, 1973), Intro., nos. 16 and 17, pp. 103–04.
151. Deut. 17:15; Rabbi Nissim, *Derashot Ha'Ran,* no. 11; Abraham Kook, Responsa *Mishpat Kohen,* sec. 144, no. 15.

152. Ibid.
153. See Talmud, *Baba Metzia* 83b, 84a; Y. Tov Ashvili, Commentary *Ritva,* ad loc., and Gerundi, Commentary *Ran,* to p. 46a; Asher ben Yehiel, Responsa *Rosh,* no. 17:8; Shlomo ben Aderet, Responsa *Rashba,* vol. 2, no. 290.
154. Talmud, *Baba Batra* 54b, 55a; *Baba Kama* 113a & b; see Rambam, Laws of Theft, 5:11, and Shmuel ben Meir, Commentary *Rashbam* to Talmud, *Baba Kama* 55a; see also E. Waldenberg, *Hilkhot Medina* (Jerusalem, 1952), "gate" E, 6. For the authority of a non-Jewish king to authorize a Jew to kill, see Part Two, Chapter VI, Section A 3 *e,* above.
155. Talmud, *Gittin* 88b; see Moshe ben Nahman, Novellae *Ramban,* to *Yebamot* 46b; Y. Lorberbaum, *Netivot Ha'Mishpat, Ho. Mis.,* sec. 1.
156. The phraseology of this principle, as well as its alleged source, is the verse in Ps. 191:126; Talmud, *Temurah* 14b.
157. Ibid.
158. Talmud, *Menakhot* 99b.
159. Talmud, *Yoma* 85b.

This latter phraseology has been utilized to permit the desecration of the Sabbath in order to save a life.

5. The Talmud interpreted the biblical verse, "And you shall live with them [my commandments]" (Lev. 18:5), as implying, "but shall not die because of them."[160] This requires desecration of the Sabbath in order to save a life.

c. RATIONALES

A number of overlapping rationales have been advanced at various times by Jewish decision-makers to explain the reasons behind the foregoing principles of law and biblical verses legitimizing the imposition of extraordinary sanctioning and other deviations from traditional norms.

1. A number of authorities[161] premise the authority to impose extraordinary sanctions on the need to preserve public order and prevent anarchy. They claim that it is a matter of "logic" to permit the community to take whatever action is necessary to preserve minimum public order and achieve basic societal goals, regardless of the adverse effects of such actions upon minority deviants. (Compare the utilitarian views of Jeremy Bentham and J. S. Mill.)

Since this rationale is not premised on any specific biblical verse, and is claimed as a matter of "logic" to be applicable at all times, it has been held to have been applicable in the pre-Biblical Era, as well.[162] This is in addition to the authority to establish laws and public order, which are[163] claimed to be included in the Noahide laws.

2. This "need" has sometimes been cast in the form of the legal fiction of a social contract: namely, that all people, including those who later became criminal defendants, had "agreed" to accept the consequences of societal rules and had "authorized" human decision-makers to make them.[164] This is open to the objection that in Talmudic law a person does not "own" his life

and is not considered empowered to authorize anyone to kill him.[165]

3. The principle of self-defense. The criminal or deviant is regarded as a *rodef*. Just as one who is about to kill an individual may be slain to save the intended victim, so, too, one who constitutes a threat to the *entire community* may be slain in order to preserve the community. Similarly, if his acts serve to encourage others to commit crimes, he may be slain to deter further criminal acts by others which threaten the societal fabric.[166]

All of the foregoing rationales and legal principles seem, in the final analysis, to come down to the basic proposition that the community has the power to kill to protect itself and its public order, since these constitute society's most basic values, without which civilized societal life cannot exist.

All of the legal principles above, utilized by Jewish decision-makers, also reflect the fundamental premise that societal decisions must be predicated on basic value choices designed to effectuate society's basic goals, regardless of the existence of contrary legal principles. This has been stressed by a number of modern jurisprudential scholars.[167] Thus, thousands of years ago, Jewish decision-makers explicitly recognized the need for what Karl Llewellyn called a "juristic method" that would result in "the creation of techniques that efficiently and effectively solve the problems posed . . . so that the basic values of the society are realized through the law, and not frustrated by it."[168] Jewish decision-makers, accordingly, employed the aforementioned legal principles and rationales to achieve the basic societal goals of minimum public order and the preservation of the faith.

Although talmudic decision-makers cited the aforementioned various principles and rationales of law to justify the setting aside of biblical laws, it seems clear that their decisions were also based upon the perspective that the Bible *itself* expected and authorized this, where departure from the law was necessary in order to meet basic, overriding goals. We have noted the difficulty that Jewish decision-makers have had in pinpointing the specific biblical verses that authorized such

160. Talmud, *Sanhedrin* 74a.
161. Rambam, Laws of *Mamrim*, 2:4–5; Shlomo ben Aderet, Responsa *Rashba*, vol. 4, no. 311, and Moshe ben Nahman, in Responsa *Rashba*, attributed to Ramban, no. 279; see also Responsa of Benjamin Ze'ev, no. 290, and Isaac Alfasi.
162. Sofer, Responsa *Hatam Sofer, Orah Hayim*, no. 208; see Isaac Sender, "The Seven Noachide Commandments Prior to the Giving of the Torah" (Hebrew), in *Ha'Me'Ayin*, (Jerusalem, Tamuz, 1974), pp. 53, 59; *Be'er Avraham, Yitro*, ch. 1, sec. 9.
163. Talmud, *Sanhedrin* 56a.
164. See M. Ha'Me'iri, in his *Beth Ha'Bekhira, Baba Kama* 84; Rabbi Abraham Kook, *Mishpat Kohen*, sec. 144, no. 15. One of the clearest formulations of this perspective is by Chajes, *Torah Ha'Neviim*, in Kol Sifrei (Jerusalem, 1958), ch. 7, pp. 47–48. See also Duran, Responsa *Tashbatz*, sec. 3, nos. 159, 168; Alfasi, Responsa *Rif*, no. 36; Waldenberg, Responsa *Tzitz Eliezer*, sec. 2, no. 22; Mordecai Yaffe, *Levush Malhut, Ho. Mis.*, sec. 2.

165. David Ibn Zimra, Commentary *Radvaz* to Rambam, Laws of Sanhedrin, 18:6; see Chajes, ibid.; S. Y. Zevin, Addenda to "*Mishpat Shylock*," in *L'Or Ha'Halakha* (Jerusalem, 1957); S. Yisraeli, *Amud Ha'Yemini* (Tel Aviv, 1966).
166. Chajes, *Torath Ha'Neviim*; see Part Two, Chapter VI, Section C 1, above.
167. See the many published works of Professor Myres M. McDougal and his "The Ethics of Applying Systems of Authority: The Balanced Opposites of a Legal System," in H. Lasswell and H. Cleveland, eds., *The Ethics of Power* (New York, 1962), p. 221.
168. E. A. Hoebel, *Law of Primitive Man* (Cambridge, 1954), p. 281.

departures. Nevertheless, it is clear in both theory and practice that traditional legal principles may be overriden to attain basic goals.

Consequently, many of the early rulings and prescriptions cited in the Talmud, which set aside biblical norms, are simply stated in the Talmud without any justification, other than a bare reference to the factual circumstances that created a need for deviations from biblical law. It was accepted that human decision-makers had the power and authority to set aside the law when necessary.[169]

This premise was expressed as follows in a classic talmudic commentary by Shmuel Edels.[170] In attempting to answer the question of why this tractate of the Talmud ends with the saying of Rabbi Elazer, in the name of Rabbi Hanina, that "the scholars of the Torah promote peace in the world," he says:

Because in this tractate, there are many perplexing matters which appear as though a law of the Torah was being uprooted; as . . . it asks, "And can the *beth din* arrange to uproot a rule of the Torah" with regard to many matters? And it answers [that it can]; *Tosefot* . . . has written, "And this is not uprooting a rule of the Torah, since it appears to be a reasonable matter . . ." This, however, is [a] very unsatisfactory [answer]. Also, in our matter, how were they [the talmudic authorities cited in *Yebamot*, able to be] lenient with a married woman [and permit her to remarry with an uncorroborated claim that her husband had died, and thereby] to uproot a rule of the Torah, which requires investigation and interrogation [of witnesses]? Also in the first chapter [where the traditional rules require that the husband, in that case, must divorce his wife, the talmudic authorities said], "What shall we do? Should we have them be divorced, then they [the divorced wives] will be looked upon with disgust by men." And if you will say, "Let them be disgusting," [the Bible provides that] "Its [the Torah's] ways are the ways of pleasantness and all its paths are peace" (Prov. 3:17). And, similarly, we find (*Yebamot* 87b) that the Talmud does not require a woman who has remarried, to go through a Levirate rejection by her deceased first husband's brother [although required by biblical law, Deut. 25:5–10], since this would lower her es-teem in the eyes of her second husband, contravening, "Its ways are ways of pleasantness." At first glance, this seems puzzling, shall we relieve her of the obligation of a Levirate rejection [required by the Bible] upon the [flimsy] grounds of the verse that, "Its ways are ways of pleasantness" [which does not deal with this issue]? This can only be due to an accepted tradition that [the principle] "Its ways are ways of pleasantness" [require us to take steps] to prevent her second husband from looking down at her and divorcing her?

For this reason [to answer the foregoing questions], this volume of the Talmud ends with this statement that "scholars of the Torah promote peace in the world," which means that the foregoing [decisions] do not uproot rules of the Torah, because these matters concern peace . . . [and these decisions were made] in order to avoid Levirate rejection which can lead to quarrels, since he [the brother of the wife's deceased first husband] may not want to go through the required rejection ceremony [which refusal would, under biblical law, prevent her from marrying someone else] and she may not desire him. This would lead to her being tied down to him, [and unable to marry another man, until he consented to go through the rejection ceremony], which is not peace . . . . Therefore, this is not uprooting, but it is a matter of peace that she should not be tied down. And it says, "Its ways are ways of pleasantness." [This implies] that she should not become disgusting in the eyes of her [present] husband; and if he [the brother of her first husband] rejects her, these are not "the paths of peace". . . .

This tractate of the Talmud, therefore, ends with "God will give strength to his nation" (Ps. 29:11), to tell us that this [a decision of this type] is not uprooting a rule of the Torah, because our God gave the strength and power to his nation, that is, (to) the scholars, to be lenient in this matter, because God will bless his people with peace, as it says, "And all its paths are peace" and there will not be peace if she will be tied down . . . In this way, the verse provides, "God will lift his face to you and give you peace" (Num. 6:26), i.e., even if you uproot a rule of the Torah, God will give you peace. . . ."

The foregoing appears to reflect the view that there are appropriate adjustments in the law that may appear to uproot biblical norms but do not really do so. They are, in fact, authorized and expected by the Bible, in order to fulfill its overriding goals of peace and happiness.[171]

169. See Elon, *Ha'Mishpat Ha'Ivri*, pp. 412–13; Y. Gilat, *Beth Din Matnin La'Akor*, in *Bar-Ilan Year Book* (Ramat-Gan 1969–1970), p. 118; E. Berkovitz, *Hagdorat Koah Hahamin La'akor Davar Min Ha'Torah* (Heb.) (Sinai, Av-Elul 1974), p. 227; idem, "The Role of *Halakhah*," in *Judaism* (New York, 1971), vol. 20, p. 66; E. Rackman, "*A Challenge to Orthodoxy*," in *Judaism* 18 (New York, 1969): 143; W. Wurzburger, "Meta-Halakhic Propositions," in *Tradition* (New York, 1960), p. 211.

170. *Circa* 1600, in the final portion of his classic commentary, *Maharsha*, to the Talmud, *Yebamot*.

171. See Responsum of Rabbi Isaac ben Shmuel, reproduced in Abraham ben David *Temin De'Im*, no. 203: "Even if there is no such Biblical verse, the sages have the power to uproot a rule of the Torah according to all authorities, when there is some reason to permit it, for then it is not like an uprooting."

4. THE IMPOSITION IN PRACTICE OF EXTRAORDINARY SANCTIONS CONTRARY TO TRADITIONAL NORMS

The foregoing selections are representative of the extraordinary sanctions and procedures accepted by Jewish decision-makers during the Talmudic Era and the Middle Ages. In the eyes of talmudic and medieval decision-makers, these extraordinary steps had a long history going back to the Biblical Era and were well established in Jewish law.

Following, is a more detailed list, of major instances during the Biblical Era (pursuant to the talmudic interpretation of the Bible) and during the Talmudic Era and the Middle Ages in which severe and extraordinary sanctions or procedures actually were imposed, although they were not called for (or were even contrary to) the biblical norms as normally applied. In each case, talmudic decision-makers viewed the sanctioners as being well aware of traditional norms, but as acting to meet a pressing, public need, which permitted the use of these extraordinary sanctions.

a. THE BIBLICAL ERA

1. Zimri was killed by Phineas for fornicating with a Midianite woman (not a capital offense), and the slaying was viewed by God as justified.[172]

2. Akhan was stoned to death by Joshua for stealing chattels that had been consecrated to God. Jewish legal tradition regarded this as contrary to normal law since there were no two witnesses[173] to the act. Although Akhan confessed, traditional Jewish law holds that no man may be executed on the basis of his confession.[174]

3. The Israelite tribes made war on the tribe of Benjamin[175] and nearly exterminated it for not punishing the persons who raped and killed a concubine at Givah. This was held to have been based upon the principle that the *beth din* may punish even contrary to biblical law.[176] Technically, under traditional law, the people of Benjamin were not punishable for their malfeasance in not penalizing the perpetrators.[177]

4. The Jewish population of the cities of Succot and Penuel were attacked by Gideon,[178] and many were killed for refusing to provide his army with provisions.

5. The inhabitants of the village of Yavesh Gilead were slain for not coming to a meeting established for them.[179]

6. King David executed an Amalekite, based on his confession that he had killed King Saul. Traditional Jewish law regarded confessions as inadmissible in evidence.[180]

7. King David ordered the killing of the two brothers who had boasted of killing Ish-Boshet, the son of former King Saul. David further ordered their hands and feet cut off and hung their corpses by the reservoir of the city of Hebron.[181] In this he went contrary to traditional doctrine in many respects, in inflicting a penalty pursuant to confession, and also in executing them, mutilating their corpses, and displaying them for a lengthy period. This was contrary to the biblical commands, including those requiring two witnesses[182] and prohibiting a corpse from hanging overnight.[183]

8. King David handed over seven of King Saul's children to be killed by the Gibeonites who sought revenge for the acts of King Saul. This was contrary to the express provision of the Bible.[184] "And sons shall not be killed because of their parents; each man shall die for his own sins." Similarly, David permitted their bodies to hang on a tree for many days, contrary to the biblical rule.[185]

9. King David ordered that one who (he thought) had stolen an only lamb from a poor man should be killed.[186] The Bible[187] provides only a monetary penalty for theft, not capital punishment.

10. King David commanded Solomon to kill Joab,[188] who was not liable for the death penalty under traditional doctrine.

11. Ezra threatened[189] to kill anyone who disobeyed his rule, pursuant to the authorization of the Persian King.[190]

12. Other biblical precedents claimed are: the slaughter of all the inhabitants of the city of Shechem by the children of Jacob,[191] the death sentence by "burning" passed upon Tamar by Judah,[192] and the slaughter of the Ephraimites by Yiftah.[193]

---

172. See Num. 25:8–13.
173. As required by Deut. 17:6, 19:15.
174. Rambam, Laws of the Sanhedrin, 18:6.
175. Judg. 19.
176. Moshe ben Nahman, Commentary *Ramban* to Gen. 19:8.
177. Ibid.
178. Judg. 8; see Isaac Abarbanel, ad loc.

179. Judg. 21:10; see Moshe ben Nahman, Responsa *Rashba*. Attributed to the *Ramban*, no. 288.
180. See 1 Sam. 1:15–16; Rambam, Laws of Sanhedrin, 18:6; see Talmud, *Sanhedrin* 44a.
181. 2 Sam. 4:2, 12.
182. Deut. 16:6.
183. Deut. 21:23.
184. Deut. 24:16; 2 Sam. 21:9.
185. Deut. 21:23; see Talmud, *Yebamot* 79a.
186. 2 Sam. 12:1.
187. Exod. 22:1–3.
188. 1 Kings 2:5; see, however, Talmud, *Sanhedrin* 49a.
189. Ezra 7:26.
190. See Talmud, *Mo'ed Katan*, 16a.
191. Gen. 34:25.
192. Gen. 38:24.
193. Judg. 12:6.

Chajes[194] asserts that the Pentateuch itself illustrates the use of extraordinary punishments when the need arises, in its prescriptions (Deut. 13:13–19) for the "*Iyr Ha-Nidakhat*" (a city, the bulk of whose inhabitants began to worship idols. Such a city was to be destroyed totally, together with all of its population)[195] and for the "Rebellious Son" (Deut. 21:18–21)[196] who was to be killed if he refused to heed his parents, and was a glutton, although he had not, as yet, committed any capital crime. In both cases the traditional safeguards and requirements of criminal law were to be dispensed with in order to meet a pressing, overriding need to achieve a basic goal. This assertion is, of course, based upon the talmudic interpretation of these two biblical cases.

b. The Talmudic Era

1. A man who rode a horse on the Sabbath contrary to a rabbinical ordinance[197] was executed; a man who copulated with his wife in public was flogged.[198]

2. Shimon ben Shetah hung eighty sorceresses in one day contrary to traditional law, which required forewarning and trial, and which limited executions to one per day and did not utilize hanging as a means of execution.[199]

3. In a sharp departure from the normal practice, murderers and certain other offenders were sometimes executed by confinement in a narrow cell, where they were fed only barley and water until their intestines burst. This was done where technical requirements regarding witnesses and forewarning were not met, but there was felt to be a "need" to punish. The talmudic language implies that this was the actual practice,[200] not just theory.

4. Any priest who served in the Temple at Jerusalem while he was ritually impure would be taken out by his younger colleagues, who would kill him by splitting his skull. The language used by the Talmud indicates that this used to happen in practice. Similarly, one who was caught fornicating with a non-Jewish woman, could be killed by zealots—in effect, a legally sanctioned form of "lynching."[201]

5. Rabbi Kahana killed a man who threatened to inform the authorities that his neighbor owned property that was subject to taxation.[202]

6. The Talmud cites two different cases where daughters of priests were executed for fornication. They were enveloped with branches and burned to death. This was contrary to traditional norms, under which the court, in those instances, lacked jurisdiction to execute (since executions could only be authorized as long as the Temple at Jerusalem existed and the *Sanhedrin* convened there.[203] At the time of one (and perhaps both) of these incidents, the Temple and the *Sanhedrin* had long ceased to exist. Additionally, executions were not normally performed in the manner described).[204]

7. A married woman and her paramour, who were caught hugging and kissing, were killed although there was no evidence of sexual intercourse.[205]

8. A murderer was blinded on orders of the exilarch (head of the Jewish communities of Babylonia).[206] This penalty was inflicted although the crime was not witnessed by two qualified witnesses.[207] Some authorities maintain that the Talmud here does not refer, literally, to a blinding, but, rather, to some other severe punishment.[208] Since blinding could result in death, it has been theorized that blinding here might have been carried out by shining bright lights into the eyes of the assailant.[209]

9. Rabbi Huna amputated the arm of a chronic assaulter.[210]

10. A recidivist thief was given a harsher monetary penalty than called for by biblical law.[211]

11. An adulterer and adulteress were killed by one who witnessed the adultery. The slayer's act was regarded as entirely proper,[212] although there was no

---

194. *Torat Ha'Neviim.*

195. See Deut. 13:13–19.

196. Deut. 21:18–21.

197. Talmud, *Yebamot* 90b; one view in the Jerusalem Talmud, ad loc., regards it as a biblical prohibition.

198. See Shlomo ben Shimon Duran Responsa *Rashbash*, no. 510, who cites a variant version that the latter, too, was executed.

199. See talmudic discussion, *Sanhedrin* 45b.

200. Talmud, *Sanhedrin* 9:5, 81b.

201. Ibid.

202. Talmud, *Baba Kama* 117b; see also Talmud, *Berakhot* 58a, for another case where a talmudic scholar killed an informer.

203. Talmud, *Sanhedrin* 52a and b, Mishnah. Talmud, *Sanhedrin* 52b; Talmud, *Shabbat* 15a; Talmud, *Avodah Zarah* 5b; Mekhilta, Exod. 21; Rambam, *Sefer Ha'Mitzvot*, positive commandment no. 176, and ibid.; Rambam, Laws of the *Sanhedrin*, 14:1.

204. See commentaries, ad loc., of Menahem Me'iri in *Beth Ha'Bekhirah* (Jerusalem, 1971), and Shlomo Luria in *Khakhmat Shlomo* printed in standard editions of the Talmud.

205. Talmudic incident cited by Karo in his commentary to *Hoshen Mishpat*, sec. 2.

206. Talmud, *Sanhedrin* 27a.

207. See Meir ben Gedalya, Responsa *Maharam* of Lublin, no. 138.

208. See Rabbi Hananel, commentary (in standard editions of the Talmud) ad loc.; *contra* commentary of Shlomo Yitzhaki, *Rashi*, and Rabbi Yona Gerundi, ad loc.; and Rabbi Yeruham, *Mesharim*, sec. 2, no. 51.

209. See Eibschutz, *Tumim*, sec. 2.

210. Talmud, *Niddah* 13b. See *Sanhedrin* 58b.

211. Talmud, *Baba Kama* 96b.

212. *Zohar Hadash*, Ruth, ch. 4.

court trial and the adultery was not witnessed by two persons.

12. Two noted talmudic sages, Rabbi Eliezer ben Shimon, and Rabbi Ishmael ben Yose, acted as policemen for the Roman governor. They caught thieves and other violators of law and turned them over to the Romans to be imprisoned and killed, although the offenders were not subject to capital punishment under Jewish law.[213]

13. "It happened that a pious man was walking on the road and he saw two men copulating with a female dog. They said, 'We know that this pious man will go and testify about us, and our master, David, will kill us.' "[214] This *may* indicate a fear of being executed based on the testimony of the pious man, despite the biblical rule requiring two witnesses. Furthermore, the traditional principle was that one witness was not only insufficient to convict, but was also not even permitted to testify. If he did, he would be flogged.[215] It is quite possible, however, that these two offenders did not know the law.

14. See Section 5, below, regarding flogging, imprisonment, and other lesser sanctions imposed, although not called for by ordinary biblical norms. For other examples of departures from biblical norms, see Talmud, *Avoda Zara* 13a, and commentary of *tosefot* ad loc.; commentary of Joseph Karo in *Kesef Mishnah* to Rambam, Laws of Vows, 3:9; Z. H. Chajes, *Ho'Raat Sha'ah*, in his *Torat Ha'Neviim*, p. 40, and in his Introduction to the Talmud, ibid., ch. 3; Naftali Zvi Yehudah Berlin, *He'Emek She'Elah*, no. 58, section 14; Elon, *Ha'Mishpat Ha'Ivri*, p. 437; see also N. Zucrow, *"Adjustments of Law to Life in Rabbinic Literature"* (Boston, 1928). See in general, Y. Ginsberg, *Mishpatim Le'Yisrael*, pp. 1 ff.

5. SANCTIONS IN THE MIDDLE AGES

a. CAPITAL PUNISHMENT

It should be noted that, according to talmudic legal principles, the death penalty could not be inflicted unless there was a Sanhedrin sitting in their chamber at the Temple in Jerusalem, sacrificial rites were still being performed there, and the judges imposing the sentence had been ordained by judges who had themselves been ordained in a direct line of ordination originating with Moses.[216]

Furthermore, ever since the latter portion of the Second Jewish Commonwealth (*circa* the first century c.e.), Jewish communities were not normally given the power by non-Jewish rulers to inflict capital punishment. Instead, they utilized other sanctions, such as flogging, ostracism, or permanent excommunication,[217] even where the offender had committed murder. Thus, for example, capital punishment does not seem to have been applied by Jewish communities in North Africa, as reflected in their astonishment at claims that some Jewish communities elsewhere did resort to it.[218] While claims have been made that Jewish communities in Italy employed capital punishment,[219] the factual accuracy of these assertions is open to question.

In a few countries of Europe, however, particularly Spain, capital punishment was inflicted by Jewish courts and decision-makers, as reflected in the decisions reprinted above. A more detailed list of the leading instances of executions, mutilations, and other severe sanctions imposed in practice, follows:

1. Yosef Ibn Avitor reported that his great-grandfather (*circa* 990 c.e.) had inflicted capital punishment in a number of instances in Spain.[220] Even if true, it is clear, however, that he was the only one at that time who was regarded as able to take it upon himself to impose such severe sanctions.

2. An informer was killed pursuant to the order of Rabbi Joseph Halevy Migash[221] (Spain, 1077–1141 c.e.). The execution was allegedly performed on Yom

213. Talmud, *Baba Metzia*, 83a. See, however, commentary of Yom Tov Ashvili, *Ritva*, ad loc., that these two sages were justified, since one may kill if he acts as an agent of the king. See, to the same effect, Shlomo ben Aderet, Responsa *Rashba*, cited in Karo, *Beth Yosef, Ho. Mis.*, sec. 388, and, to similar effect, commentary of Gerundi, *Ran*, to *Sanhedrin* 27a and 46a. Compare, however, commentary of Menahem Ha'Meiri, *Beth Ha'Bekhirah*, to Talmud, *Baba Metzia* 83a, that these two talmudic sages acted wrongly in handing over criminals to the Roman government for execution, since they were not liable to capital punishment pursuant to the laws of the Torah. He claims, furthermore, that the acts of these two saviours constituted a species of "informing" against members of the Jewish community. See also Shlomo Duran, Responsa *Rashbash*, no. 533, on this same subject; Shlomo ben Aderet, Responsa *Rashba*, sec. 4, no. 311; Responsa published in *Jewish Quarterly Review* 8 (1895–96): 217; and Moshe ben Nahman, Responsa *Rashba*, no. 279, attributed to Ramban; Yaakov Reisher, Responsa *Shevut Yaakov*, sec. 1, no. 130. See Part Two, Chapter VI, Section A 3 *e*, above.

214. Jerusalem Talmud, *Sanhedrin* 6:3, 27:1.

215. See Talmud, *Pesakhim* 113b.

216. Talmud, *Shabbat* 15a, *Sanhedrin* 14b, and *Tosefot* ad loc.; Rambam, Laws of Sanhedrin, ch. 4; see I. Herzog, "The Administration of Justice in Ancient Israel," in *Judaism, Law and Ethics* (London, 1977), p. 141.

217. Responsa of the Gaonim, *Khemda Genuza*, sec. 20; Hayim Mudai, Responsa *Sha'are Tzedek*, vol. 4, sec. 38; A. Epstein, *Ma'ase Ha'Gaonim* (Berlin, 1910), p. 73; Assaf, *Ha'-Onshin*, p. 47. See Commentary Rambam to Mishnah, *Khulin*, ch. 1; Anan, *Sefer Ha'Mitzvot*, 16, in Assaf, ibid.

218. Assaf, ibid., p. 18.

219. See Ahimaetz, *Megiliat Yukhsin*, in A. Neubauer, *Seder Ha'Khakhamim* (Jerusalem, 1967), vol. 2, p. 14.

220. See A. Marmorstein, in *Revue Etudes Juives*, vol. 120, pp. 101–04; see also J. Mann in *Jewish Quarterly Review*, n.s. 11 (1921): 456.

221. Rabbi Judah ben Asher, Responsa *Zikhron Yehuda*, no. 75.

Kippur (the holiest and most solemn day of the year), which fell on the Sabbath (making it an even holier day) during the closing prayer of *Ne'ilah*, (the most solemn time of the day, when mundane acts, and certainly the taking of a life, would ordinarily be regarded with horror). It is possible that the date and time alleged for the execution are not to be taken literally, but that they simply utilized a recognized literary expression[222] to reflect the perspective that doing away with informers was a "holy" and meritorious act.

3. Moshe ben Maimon (Egypt, 1135–1204) said, "And it is an everyday occurence in the cities of the west (Spain and northwest Africa) to kill informers who are known to constantly inform regarding Jewish money, and to turn over the informers to non-Jews to be killed or beaten, and imprisoned, according to their wickedness".[223] In the editions of the Maimonidean Code that were not censored by the Christian Church, the word "killed" was changed to "punished."[224] Note that the killing and punishment were allegedly carried out by non-Jews, apparently because the non-Jewish rulers do not grant the Jews the authority to inflict such punishments.[225]

4. Meir (*Maharam*) of Rothenberg (Germany, 1215–1293) ruled that an informer is regarded as a pursuer (*rodef*) who can be killed by all. If it is possible to deter him in another way, however, this should be done.[226]

5. *Maharam* also ruled that if an informer is not in the act of informing, he may not be killed.[227]

6. Shlomo ben Aderet (known as *Rashba* (Spain, 1235–1310) authorized the killing of criminals; the nature of the crime is not stated.[228]

7. *Rashba* also authorized corporal punishment where necessary, and apparently also capital punishment.[229]

8. *Rashba* also authorized, by implication, the execution of thieves who disgraced the Jewish community by their acts.[230]

9. *Rashba* also participated in the issuance of a verdict for the execution of an informer and asserted that there was a common practice of killing informers in Barcelona, Castille, Saragosa, Aragon, and Catalonia.[231] Meir of Rothenberg (*Maharam*) agreed with *Rashba* that this was the proper penalty.

10. *Rashba* also authorized whatever corporal punishments, and impliedly executions, decision-makers felt appropriate, even if contrary to biblical law.[232]

11. Asher ben Yehiel (known as *Rosh*; Spain, 1250–1304) authorized the execution of Jewish informers:

It is, therefore, the practice in all parts of the diaspora, that where there is an informer who is known to inform regularly, since he informed to non-Jews concerning Jews or their money, [that] they should seek counsel or a stratagem to rid the world of him; this is in order to "fence in the matter," and in order that others will be deterred, so that informers will not increase in Israel, and also to save all Jews who are persecuted by him. Accordingly, in this case, where witnesses testified that he constantly informed, and he was in the act of informing, they did well to sentence him to be hung.[233]

12. Asher ben Yehiel (*Rosh*) also authorized:

(a) the killing of one who blasphemed God.[234]

13. (b) The fining and, if necessary, killing of one who refused to follow his rulings.[235]

14. (c) The killing of other informers.[236]

15. Judah ben Asher (Spain, 1270–1327) ordered the execution of a murderer,[237] and amputation of the hands of an assaulter.

222. See also Mann, *"Skirah Historit Al Dine Nefashot Bazman Hazeh," Hatzofeh Le'Hakhmat Yisrael* (1926), vol. 10, p. 200 and in *Jewish Quarterly Review*, n.s. 10 (1920): 120–30; Ginsberg, *Mishpatim Le'Yisrael*, p. 23, f.n. 158; Talmud, *Pesahim* 49b, ad loc.

223. Rambam, Laws of Tortious Injury, ch. 8, sec. 11. See also his commentary to the Mishnah, *Khulin* 1:2.

224. See Ginsberg, *Mishpatim Le'Yisrael*, p. 25, n. 186, and S. Frankel ed. of Rambam, Laws of Tortious Injury, 8:11 (Jerusalem, 1975), ad loc.

225. See also Rambam, ibid., ch. 8, sec. 10, stating that an informer could not be killed by a Jew unless he was first warned and knowingly disregarded the warning.

226. Responsa *Maharam* of Rothenberg (Rabinowitz ed.), sec. 2, no. 247. See also Responsa *Maimonius* appearing at the end of Rambam, Book of Torts, no. 15, and Mordecai ben Hillel, Commentary *Mordecai to Baba Kama*, ch. 10, no. 195.

227. Responsa *Maharam* of Rothenberg, sec. 1, "gate" 2, no. 137. See also his Responsa, sec. 3, no. 231, 232 (Crimona ed.), and his Responsa in sec. 1, "gate" 1, no. 317 (Berlin ed.).

228. Responsa *Rashba*, vol. 5, no. 238.

229. Ibid., vol. 3, no. 393.

230. Responsa, vol. 5, no. 243. See Moshe ben Nahman, Responsa *Rashba*, no. 279, attributed to Ramban, in which he also authorized corporal punishment but did not mention the death penalty.

231. Letter of Shlomo b. Aderet (Rashba) to Meir of Rothenberg in 1279, reproduced above. The letter was published by Kaufman in the *Jewish Quarterly Review* 8 (1895–96): 223. See Ginsberg, *Mishpatim Le'Yisrael*, p. 25; Assaf, *Ha'Onshim*, p. 65–66; and Regne, *Catalogue Des Actes De Jaime I, Pedro III et Alfonso III*, nos. 725, 728, 752, and 262, 315.

232. Shlomo b. Aderet Responsa *Rashba*, vol. 3, no. 393, also cited in Karo, *Beth Yosef, Tur, Ho. Mis.*, sec. 2; cf. Responsa *Rashba*, vol. 2, no. 26; vol. 5, no. 243, and Responsa *Rashba*, cited in Karo, *Beth Yosef, Tur, Ho. Mis.*, sec. 388; Rambam, Responsa *Maimonius*, Book of Torts, nos. 14, 15.

233. Responsa *Rosh*, sec. 17, no. 1; see also nos. 6, 8, and 85, and p. 892.

234. Ibid.; sec. 17, no. 8.

235. Ibid., sec. 17, nos. 8, 9.

236. Ibid., sec. 17, nos. 1, 6, 8.

237. Responsa *Zikhron Yehuda*, nos. 58, 75. Compare his Responsa, no. 79, in which he refused to authorize execution due to a lack of sufficient witnesses. For other reports of assaults, murder, and punishments, see Regne, *Catalogue Des*

16. Isaac ben Sheshet (*Rivash*) (b. Spain 1326; d. Algeria, 1408) authorized the execution of two men who ambushed and killed their enemy.[238]

17. Shlomo Duran (*Rashbash*) (Algeria, 1400–1467) held that whoever kills an informer merits a reward from Heaven.[239]

18. Menahem of Merzberg (Germany, *circa* fourteenth century) authorized the hiring of a non-Jew to kill an informer.[240]

19. David Ibn Zimra (*Radvaz*; b. Egypt, 1479; d. Israel, 1573) ruled that an informer may be killed.[241]

20. Elijah Halevi (Turkey, *circa* 1550) maintained that all informers may be killed, even after they have completed informing.[242]

21. Meir of Lublin (Poland, *circa* 1600) ruled that a murderer could be killed even on the basis of hearsay testimony.[243]

22. Abraham Rappaport (Poland, *circa* 1650) authorized the killing of an informer.[244]

23. Shlomo Cohen (lived in Turkey and Salonika, *circa* sixteenth century) ruled that every informer may be killed.[245]

24. Yosef Almoshnino (lived in Salonika, Israel, and Belgrade, 1642–1689) reports an incident in which an informer was dragged out of the synagogue in Lvov, Poland, on Yom Kippur Eve and thrown into the river to drown.[246]

25. Elijah Ha-Levi, (Turkey, *circa* sixteenth century) reports of an informer who was choked to death.[247]

26. There are a number of other miscellaneous reports of informers being killed, as late as the eighteenth and nineteenth centuries.[248]

27. Many Jewish communities, particularly in medieval Spain (such as Catalonia, Aragon, and Valencia), formally decided to take steps (including requesting the permission of the king) to dispose of informers.[249] The resolution concerning informers adopted by the Great Synod of 1432, at Valladolid (consisting of representatives of important Jewish communities in Castille, Spain, reprinted in Chapter VIII, Section A 2 *b*, above)[250] is representative.

28. Similar ordinances were adopted by the communities of Tunis, Morocco, and Algiers in 1391.[251] Isaac ben Sheshet Perfet recounts that it was the practice to kill informers in Castille, Aragon, Valencia, and Catalonia.[252]

29. The perspectives regarding capital punishment for murder in sixteenth-century Poland are vividly expressed in the following responsum of a noted decision-maker of that era.

> Nowadays it is the need of the hour [to execute a murderer], because in all the places and communities, there has been an increase of informers. Last week, we were advised by messengers sent by the community at Sharigrad, that an informer there had falsely libelled the entire Jewish community. Also, the inhabitants of the community of Bar, sent [a

---

Actes De Jaime, 1, Pedro III et Alfonso III, nos. 268, 307, 444, 452, 485, 522, 563, 644, 653; Assaf, *Ha'Onshin*, p. 78.

238. Responsa *Rivash*, no. 251. See also no. 238, 239, and addenda thereto; and Duran (Algeria, *circa* 1390) in Responsa *Tashbatz*, sec. 2, no. 26, and sec. 3, nos. 158, 191.

239. Responsa *Rashbash*, no. 177.

240. *Nimukei* of *Maharam* of Merzburg, in Weil, Responsa *Mahari Weil*, p. 175b.

241. Responsa *Radvaz*, sec. 3, no. 536.

242. Responsa *Zekan Aharon*, no. 152.

243. Responsa *Maharam of Lublin* (reprinted Jerusalem, 1973), no. 138, see also addenda thereto.

244. Responsa *Etan Ha'Ezrahi*, no. 55.

245. Responsa *Maharshah* (Salonika, 1581), sec. no. 29.

246. Responsa *Edut Be'Heyosef* (Juta, 1711), vol. 1, no. 34. See also Mann, "Historical Overview of Capital Punishment 'Today' " (Heb.), *Hazofeh Le'Hahmat Yiesrael* (Budapest, 1926) vol. 10, p. 200, and in *Jewish Quarterly Review*, n.s. 10 (1920): 128; Ginsberg, *Mishpatim Le'Yisrael*, p. 23, n. 58; Talmud, *Pesakhim* 49b, 117; Alfasi, *Rif.*, ad loc. 16b; see also David Kahana Shapiro (Poland, *circa* 1925), who maintains that the talmudic principle "the law of the kingdom is the law" permits corporal punishment, and apparently the death penalty as well, to be inflicted by Jews, pursuant to state law. Responsa *Devar Avraham*, sec. 1., no. 1, subsec. 2, and no. 11, subsec. 11. See also, to same effect, Shlomo ben Aderet, Responsa *Rashba*, in Kaufman, *Jewish Quarterly Review* 8 (1896): 228, Y. Antoli, *Malemed La'talmidin*, (Berlin, 1866), p. 71b; and in Karo, *Beth Yosef, Ho. Mis.*, sec. 388, at end.

247. Elisha Halevi, Responsa *Zekan Aharon* (reprinted Jerusalem, 1970), no. 95; see nos. 11, 75; see also nos. 142, 152, 164.

248. S. Federbush, *Mishpat Hamelukha* (Jerusalem, 1973), 77; *Monatschrift*, vol. 14; I. Alfassi, in *Encyclopedia Judaica* (Jerusalem, 1971), vol. 14, p. 527 regarding the murder of two Jewish informers in 1838, allegedly authorized by Rabbi Israel Friedmann, founder of the famous Hasidic dynasty of Ruzhin. There is a record of one informer who was sentenced to death by the rabbi of Strassburg, Germany. He was handed over to a Christian judge there and was killed by being drowned in the river, apparently the prevailing method of execution in that locale. (See N. Koronil, *Khamisha Kuntresim* [Vienna, 1924]; see also Graetz, *History of the Jews* (transl. Shefer, Warsaw, 1900, 7:14–15). There is some doubt, however, concerning the reliability of this record, which also claims that the rabbi, as a result of subsequent informing against him, was forced to flee Germany to Babylonia, where a ban of excommunication was then issued against the informers.

249. See Finkelstein, *Jewish Self-Government*, p. 330.

250. The synod was convened under the leadership of the "Rabbi of the Court", Abraham Benebashti. See Finkelstein, *Jewish Self-Government*, pp. 349 ff., which contains a somewhat different translation of the text.

251. Responsa *Rivash*, sec. 79.

252. Ibid., no. 79.

notice] to advise us about [the existence of] informing in the community of Marahvy. In addition, because of our sins, there has been an increase of
thieves and robbers, until recently, Moshe, the son-
in-law of Henekh, was killed by his Jewish wagon
driver. Accordingly, there is no greater breach [in the
"walls" of society] than this.

It is, therefore, reasonable to sentence him to death
in order to fence in the breaches of the past and for
the future. But I did not have the heart to issue this
sentence, because the *Nimuke Yosef* [Yosef Habiba]
had written that nowadays we do not have the power
to kill or sentence to death. It was my view to agree
to sentence him to have his limbs amputated, to cut
out his nose, tongue, and his hands . . . I changed
my mind, and I decided to sentence him to death. . . .

You spent a lot of money to redeem him [from
prison] because he claims that he wishes to repent.
This is a disgrace to God, since people will say that
the crime of shedding blood is not considered a
wrongdoing by Jews. Accordingly, if a non-Jew
would, God forbid, murder a Jew, they will also not
avenge it. I constantly scream like a rooster about
the practices of this generation, that [when] any thief
or sinner is placed in jail, many attempts are made
to redeem him by means of bribes. This thing, because of our many sins, multiplies misdeeds and
thefts. . . . Therefore, God forbid, do not give a
penny to redeem him from death. If he wishes to
forsake his religion and convert, as the priests constantly tried to persuade him [to do], and thereby
desired to relieve him of the death penalty, for this,
I worry and for this we are required to bribe them
so that they *should* wreak vengeance upon him, and
[so that] his apostasy should not help him. Otherwise, every evildoer will do as he wishes, and will
then go and convert. . . ."[253] [emphasis supplied.]

b. THE MANNER OF INFLICTING THE DEATH PENALTY

Under ordinary talmudic legal principles, the Jews
in the Middle Ages did not have the right to inflict the
death penalty.[254] Accordingly, when capital punishment
was nevertheless imposed by Jews during the Middle
Ages, it was usually inflicted by methods that were
different than those traditionally provided for in talmudic law.[255] Nevertheless, traditional methods of exe-

cution (though perhaps differing in some details) were
sometimes applied.[256]

Usually, however, all kinds of untraditional methods
were used. Thus, one informer was killed by stabbing
him in the arms so that he bled to death.[257] Most commonly, where the laws of the state authorized this, the
culprit would be turned over to non-Jewish officials for
execution by whatever bethod prevailed at that time.
This was true in Spain, where under state law the convict would be turned over to state officials for execution.[258] The state government used this procedure as a
source of income. For every such execution, the Jewish
community would be required to pay to the state the
sum of one thousand dinars.

In 1380 the Jews of Castille lost the right to inflict
the death penalty as a result of an incident in which
the king was misled into authorizing capital punishment.
This was then carried out by the Christian police chief,
together with two Jews, who entered the house of an
informer and killed him. Thereafter the two Jews who
carried out the execution and one judge were executed.
The police chief who participated in the execution had
one hand amputated.[259]

Some of the early Polish kings also provided for execution by the state of those condemned to death by the
Jewish community. This was similar to the practice of
the Christian Church, which would not itself carry out
corporal punishments but would hand offenders over
to the state.[260]

c. PERMISSIBLE SLAYING OF "INNOCENT" PERSONS

Another extraordinary authorization for homicide,
more poignant and tragic than usual, sometimes occurred during the Middle Ages. Homicide was held to
be authorized to forestall the execution of a threat of
imminent and forcible religious conversion, especially
of children. There were numerous incidents, especially

253. Maharam Zak, in Abraham Shrensilsh, Responsa *Etan
Ha'Ezrahi*. See also Responsa *Maharam* of Lublin, sec. 15 and
379, which appears only in the Venice ed.; see also the decision
of Isserlin, *Pesakim*, sec. 92; and Y. Bakhrah, Responsa, *Havat
Yair*, sec. 139.
254. See Chapter IX, Section B 2, above.
255. See Meir of Lublin, Responsa *Maharam* of Lublin, no.
138.

256. Thus, an informer was stoned to death at the order of
Halevi Ibn Migash, Responsa of Judah ben Asher, in *Zikhron
Yehudah*, no. 75; see also Mann, in *Jewish Quarterly Review*,
n.s. 10 (1920): 128–30. There is also a report of an informer
who was choked to death, Elijah Ha'levi, Responsa *Zekan
Aharon*, no. 95. Both of these modes of execution resemble
the traditional forms.
257. Responsa of Shlomo ben Aderet, reproduced at Chapter III, Section B 2 *b*, above. See also Judah ben Asher, Responsa *Zikhron Yehudah*, no. 75.
258. See, for example, the resolutions of the synod at Valladolid, Spain, in 1432, reproduced at Chapter VIII, Section
A 3 *b*, above; see also Isaac ben Sheshet, Responsa *Rivash*, nos.
234–39, and Asher ben Yehiel, Responsa *Rosh*, Chapter III,
Section B 2 *d*, above; Assaf, *Ha'Onshin*, p. 21.
259. See Assaf, *Ha'Onshin*, ibid.
260. See canons 20 and 23 of the Second Lateran Council
of 1139 and canon 18 of the Fourth Lateran Council of 1215.

during the Crusades, when entire Jewish communities, faced with this threat, committed suicide *en masse*. Sometimes the adults would kill themselves and their younger children, as well as killing other adults (including, parents, spouses, and siblings) who flinched in the face of taking their own lives. A few of the best known instances are the mass suicides-homicides at York, England, and in Mainz, Speyer, and Worms, Germany.[261]

There were instances in which teachers killed the young pupils who were in their charge in the face of such imminent threat.[262] One noted medieval Jewish decision-maker reported the case of a man "who slaughtered his wife and their four children," at their request, during "the mass murders at Coblenz, the city of blood," in order to forestall their forcible conversion. "He, too, wished to kill himself after their death, but the Lord saved him, through non-Jews." In the course of the responsum, he notes that "We heard that many great ones used to slaughter their sons and daughters, and also our Rabbi Klonimus did this, as recorded in the dirge. . . ."[263]

There are a number of other instances in which "innocent" persons have been slain and the homicide has been regarded as justified. A detailed analysis is beyond the scope of the present work. Since their analysis and ramifications are extremely complex, they will, however, be sketched very briefly. Although they overlap, these instances can arbitrarily be classified into two general categories for the purpose of analysis.

(1) *In Order to Sanctify (or, Not to Disgrace) the Lord, or to Strengthen the Faith*

a. This is exemplified by the following sanction: *King David's handing over the sons of King Saul to be killed by the Gibeonites, who demanded retribution for Saul's alleged wrongs against them.*[264] The surrender of these completely "innocent" persons to a certain death was viewed by talmudic jurists as justified in order not to "disgrace the name of heaven" by demonstrating that the Israelites kept their oath.[265] This incident allegedly led many thousands of heathens to convert to Judaism.[266]

b. The biblical case of the "Wayward City,"[267] *all of whose inhabitants became idolators.* The Pentateuch provides that they were all to be killed and the city destroyed. This imperative included the slaying of children and even the few innocent adults who might dwell there.[268] The Talmud does, however, indicate that this norm is purely theoretical, there never having been, nor ever would be, a case that would meet all the conditions required for the application of the foregoing norm. The rationale behind this imperative was to strengthen the faith by inflicting extraordinary sanctions upon those who high-handedly violated the basic tenet of Judaism. The purpose of the sanction was not, allegedly, simply to punish.[269]

c. The case of the "Seven Nations" of the land of Canaan, who were all to be killed, if they did not flee or accept basic monotheistic precepts.[270] The rationale given by the Bible was that this was in order that the Israelites should not be led back to idolatry by them.[271] See Numbers 31:15–18; Rambam, Laws of Melakhim, 5:4.

The Talmud[272] also records an instance in which a perjured witness was executed contrary to traditional norms, in order to demonstrate to the Saducees that their interpretation of the Bible was incorrect.

(2) *Choice of Life Situations, or the Preservation of Many Lives*

This is exemplified by the following situation:
a. The permitted slaying of a minor rodef (or of a foetus), although there is no mens rea, *in order to save*

---

261. See Chapter VII, Section D, above. There was precedent for this in the instances of mass suicide-homicides recorded in the Talmud, including that at Masada. See Part Two, Chapter IV, Section B 5, above.

262. See J. Karo in *Bedek Ha'Bayit*, Y.D. (Salonika, 1605), sec. 157; Y. Tov Ashvili (*Ritva*), Novellae *Avoda Zara*, ch. 1. *Daat Zekenim* (printed in many standard editions of the Hebrew Bible) by the authors of *Tosefot*, report in their comments on Genesis 9:5; that "it happened that one teacher slaughtered many children during a time of forced conversion, because he feared that they would be converted. There was one rabbi there with him, who was terribly angry with him, and called him 'murderer', but he did not pay any heed; and that rabbi said, 'If I am right, then you will be killed in an unnatural manner'. And so it was, that he was seized by non-Jews, who tore off his skin and placed sand between the skin and the meat. Then the decree (of forced conversion) was cancelled, and if he had not slaughtered those children they would have been saved." See also, *Midrash Rabbah*, Lamentations (Jerusalem, 1961), no. 53 which records the story of Hannah, who instructed her seven children to let themselves be killed rather than worship idols. See also Talmud, *Gittin*, 57b.

263. Meir of Rothenberg, Responsa (Bloch edit. Berlin, 1891), pp. 346–47; see also a similar incident recorded by Menahem (*Maraham*) of Merzburg, in *Nimukei*, last paragraph (published together with Responsa *Mahari Weil*, Jerusalem, 1959); and also Y. Bazak, "The Law of Homicide in the Responsa Literature", 68 Sinai (Heb.; Jerusalem, 1971), pp. 275, 276.

264. II Sam. 21:9.

265. Talmud, *Yebamot* 89a.

266. Talmud, ibid.

267. Deut. 13:13–20.

268. Deut., ibid.; Talmud, *Sanhedrin*, 111b, 112a; Rambam, Laws of Idolatry 13:13.

269. Rambam, *Guide for the Perplexed* (Friedlander transl., New York, 1956), 3:41; Z. H. Chajes, "Torat Ha'Neviim," *Kol Sifre*, p. 50.

270. Deut. 7:2; 20:7.

271. Deut. 20:18.

272. *Khagiga* 16b.

the intended victim or the mother (see Part Two, Chapter VI, Section C 1, above).[273]

b. The slaying of one person in order to save the lives of many persons. This class is exemplified by the biblical incident in which Sheva ben Bihri, who revolted against King David, took refuge in a city that was then besieged by David's soldiers. Upon the threat of the besiegers to destroy the entire city and all its inhabitants, the residents killed him and handed his corpse over to the besiegers.[274] This was applied in the Talmud[275] as a precedent for any case in which an armed band demands the surrender of a designated individual, under a threat to kill all if the demand is not met.

The Jerusalem[276] Talmud records one view (Rabbi Yohanan) that even one who was not guilty of a capital offense could be surrendered to save the lives of the group, as long as the person to be surrendered had been selected by the would-be killers. If, however, the choice was left to the group threatened with death, they were to refuse to select a "victim" (by lot, or otherwise), even if this meant that they would all die. This subject is obviously an extremely complex one, which has arisen to plague decision-makers throughout history.[277]

The problem has arisen recently in the contexts of demands for extradition made upon the state of Israel by the United States, concerning persons accused of having committed crimes in the United States and who then fled to Israel.[278]

c. Another subgroup is the case in the Talmud,[279] recorded of one who was ordered, "Kill X or we will kill you." The hapless victim of the threat then inquired of a talmudic decision-maker what he was to do. He was told, "Why do you view your blood as redder [than his]. Perhaps, his blood is redder [than yours; i.e., "You

may not kill him, even if this means that you will be killed, instead"]. It has been maintained, however, that if, instead, the threat is, "Kill X or we will kill you *and* X," the one threatened may kill "X"; then only one life would be lost, whereas refusal to comply would result in two deaths.[280]

d. Another subgroup of cases is posed in the Talmud concerning "two who were traveling in the desert," where only one of them had water, which was sufficient only to sustain him. If he were to drink all of it himself he would probably survive. If both were to share the water, both would probably die.[281] There are conflicting views in the Talmud as to the proper course of action to be followed in such case.

Among the ramifications of this prototype situation is the case of a hospital that has only one kidney (or other organ) available for a transplant, but a number of patients clamoring for it.[282]

e. The extraordinary imperative[283] was to exterminate the nation of Amalek (these were the first to attack the Israelites after the exodus from Egypt; see Exodus 17:8), including women and children.[284] This imperative has been attributed to the necessity of deterring attacks on Jews by threatening such would-be attackers with these terrible consequences.[285] If so, it might be regarded as a variation of the "choice of life" or self-defense *rodef* situations set forth above.

f. Battle commands to soldiers in war time, which are likely to result in death, have also been regarded as permissible.[286]

d. GOUGING OF EYES AND AMPUTATION OF LIMBS

A study of the records of sanctioning by Jewish decision-makers in the Middle Ages discloses the wide-

273. *Talmud Sanhedrin*, 72b; Cf. David Ha'Levi, in *Tore Zahav*, Y.D., (printed in standard editions of the *Shulkhan Arukh*), sec. 157:8.

274. II Sam. 20.

275. *Terumot* 7:12.

276. *Terumot*, ch. 8.

277. See E. J. Shochet, *A Responsum of Surrender* (Los Angeles, 1975). See also the two lifeboat cases, in which some passengers were thrown out of lifeboats or refused admission, in order not to overload the boats; Queen v. Dudley and Stephens, L.R. 14 Q.B. Div. 273, 1884; United States v. Holmes, 1 Wall. 1, 26 Fed. Cas. 360, No. 15383, E.D. Pa.; 1842; J. Hall, *General Principles of Criminal Law* (New York, 1947), pp. 377–426; L. Fuller, "The Case of the Speluncian Explorers", in *Problems of Jurisprudence* (Brooklyn, 1949), pp. 2–27; see also *Torah She'Baal Peh* (Jerusalem, 1972), vol. 12.

278. See Y. Gershuni, "May the State of Israel Hand Over A Law-Breaker to Another Nation?" (Heb) in *Ohr Ha'Mizrah*, vol. 20 (1972) 69; B. Rabinowitz-Tumim, "Extradition to Non-Jews for Imprisonment" (Heb.) in *Noam* (Jerusalem, 1956), vol. 7, p. 336.

279. *Sanhedrin*, 72b, see also *Torah Sha'Book Peh* (Jerusalem, 1972), vol. 12. The entire volume is devoted to this issue.

280. See *Rashi*, ad loc. Yom Tov Ashvili, *Ritva, Pesakhim* 25a; J. Karo, on this issue in *Kesef Mishna*, Laws of Foundations of the Torah 5:5 and regarding the requirement to risk one's life to save another; see also A. Enker, *Duress and Necessity in Criminal Law* (Heb.; Ramat-Gan 1977), ch. 7, p. 188. I. Unterman, "Parameters Regarding the Rescue of Many" (Heb.; *Ha'Torah Ve'Hamedina*, Jerusalem, 1955–56), vol. 718, pp. 29 ff.; and S. Israeli, ibid, 32; I. Unterman, "Parameters Regarding the Sanctification of the Name of Heaven" (Heb.; *Torah She'Baal Peh* 1972), vol. 14, p. 10; Y. Weinberg, Responsa *Sridei Esh* (Jerusalem, 1977), vol. 4, no. 78; see also *Midrash Rabba*, Genesis ch. 94; the Biblical Book of Judges (15:9–13), regarding the surrender of Samson to the Philistines.

281. Talmud, *Baba Metzia*, 62a.

282. See Y. Gershuni, *"Mutav She'Yishtu Shneihem"* (Ohr Hamizrah, 1976), vol. 23, p. 162; See also Y. Karelitz, *Khazon Ish, Sanhedrin*, no. 25 (B'nai Brak, 1964); ibid, commentary to Rambam, Laws of Foundations of the Torah, 5:4.

283. Deut. 25:17–19.

284. I Sam. 15:3.

285. Rambam, *Guide for the Perplexed*, 3:41, p. 349.

286. See Deut. 20, 21:10; Talmud, *Sanhedrin* 2a, 20b, See N. Z. Y. Berlin, *He'Emek Davar*, Genesis 9:5; Deut. 20:8; M. Zemba, *Zera Avraham* (Warsaw, 1937), no. 24.

spread use of amputations and sundry mutilations (see section 6, below, for an examination of the factors leading to this phenomena). Following is a list of some representative examples:

1. Tezemah Gaon (Babylonia, *circa* ninth century) cites the practice in the land of Israel of amputating the finger of a *kohen* (priest) who married a divorcee (contrary to biblical law; see Lev. 21), in order to prevent him from raising his hands to bless the people with a priestly blessing. (A priest with a missing limb would not be permitted to bless the congregation.)[287]

2. Rabbi (Jacob) Tam (France, *circa* twelfth century) allegedly ruled that one who hits another should have his hand amputated.[288]

3. Meir (Maharam) of Rothenberg (Germany, thirteenth century) also authorized the amputation of the arm of a wife-beater if other measures proved unsuccessful in curbing his assaults.[289]

4. Asher ben Yehiel (known as *Rosh*; Spain, *circa* thirteenth century) authorized the killing of a blasphemer but advised the Jewish authorities to cut out his tongue and added the comment that "this is a common punishment that we see everyday."[290] It is possible that the phrase "that we see everyday" does not refer to a common practice of inflicting such a penalty. It may simply refer to the fact that if this punishment were to be carried out, the sanction would constantly be in evidence, since people would continually see that the blasphemer had no tongue.

5. Asher also ordered the amputation of the nose of a widow who consorted with, and became pregnant by, a non-Jew.[291]

6. Yehuda (Spain, early fourteenth century), the son of Rabbi Asher, ordered the amputation of the arms of a murderer.[292]

7. Yehuda also ordered the amputation of both arms of a murderer if there was only one qualified witness to the slaying.[293]

8. One who waylaid and beat up a judge (who had ordered him to pay a tax) was sentenced to have both of his arms amputated at the suggestion of the leaders of the community. This sanction was endorsed by the community rabbi, who felt that a similar sentence would be appropriate, even if the victim were not a judge. The fact that the suggestion was made by many community leaders and approved by the rabbi indicates that this sanction was not uncommon.[294]

9. Rabbi Yerukham B. Meshulam (Germany, *circa* fourteenth century) authorized amputating the arms and blinding one who was guilty of repeated assaults.[295]

10. Rabbi Nissim (Spain, *circa* fourteenth century) authorized knocking out the teeth and blinding the eyes of those who lent money at interest. This phrase can, however, be taken in a figurative, rather than a literal, sense, following Exodus 21:26–27.[296]

11. Menakhem of Mertzberg (Germany, *circa* fourteenth century) authorized amputating the arm of one who assaulted others.[297]

12. Jacob Weil (Germany, *circa* fifteenth century) concurred with the suggestion made to him to gouge out the eyes of one who had desecrated the Sabbath and Yom Kippur. The very fact that a letter was addressed to Weil (*Mahari*), inquiring whether eye-gouging was permissible, indicates that the practice was not unknown.[298]

13. Solomon Luria (Poland, *circa* sixteenth century) cites a responsum that authorized the amputation of a limb of a murderer.[299]

14. Luria also maintained that a murderer could either be killed, have one of his limbs cut off, be flogged, be exiled, or be imprisoned on bread and water (apparently, for life).[300]

15. A particularly extreme example of the amputation sanction was that carried out by Shakhna, the Rabbi of Lublin, Poland, one of the most famous scholar–decision-makers of the sixteenth century. He ordered that a particular violator of the law should have his tongue amputated and both eyes gouged out.[301] The convict thereafter converted to Christianity and married. He and his children subsequently caused considerable harm to members of the Jewish community by denouncing them to the authorities and by other means.[302] This

---

287. Decision of Tzemakh Gaon, *Halakhot Pesukot*, sec. 84 (cited in *Shaarei Tshuva*, sec. 177. See also Responsa *Hai Gaon* (Babylonia, *circa* 1050), no. 231, and Karo, *Beth Yosef*, E. H., sec. 6, who cites the same practice in the name of Natronai Gaon. See Ginsberg, *Mishpatim Le'Yisrael*, p. 27, no. 187; Talmud, *Sanhedrin* 58b.

288. Asher of Lunil, *Orkhot Khayim* (Pavo, 1403), p. 101b.

289. Meir ben Barukh, Responsa *Maharam* of Rothenberg, (Prague ed.), nos. 81, 926.

290. Asher ben Yehiel, Responsa *Rosh*, sec. 17, no. 8.

291. Ibid., sec. 18, no. 13.

292. Yehuda ben Asher, Responsa *Zikhron Yehudah*, no. 77.

293. Ibid., no. 58.

294. Ibid., no. 79.

295. Yerukham *Sefer Meshorim* (New York, 1968), sec. 1, no. 1, and sec. 23, no. 5; Yaffa, *Levush Iyr Shushan*, sec. 2. To the same effect, see Meir ben Barukh, Responsa *Maharam* of Rothenberg (Prague ed.), nos. 81, 296; Isaac ben Sheshet, Responsa *Rivash*, no. 251.

296. Gerundi, Responsa *Ran*, no. 41.

297. *Nimuke*, printed at end of Weil, Responsa *Mahari Weil*, p. 174a.

298. *Pesakim*, (Decisions) printed at end of Responsa *Mahari Weil*.

299. *Maharshal, Yam Shel Shlomo*; Talmud, *Baba Kama*, sec. 8, no. 6.

300. Ibid., *Baba Kama*, 8:7.

301. Meir of Lublin, Responsa *Maharam of Lublin*, no. 138.

302. Ibid.; Luria, *Yam Shel Shlomo, Yebamot*, ch. 10, sec. 20.

tragic experience deterred later Jewish judges from imposing similar sentences. Death, with its permanent eradication of a public enemy, was felt to be a more prudent sanction.[303]

16. It may not have been unknown in Poland to cut off the two ears of a thief who had been banned from a Jewish community but who returned there nevertheless. This is indicated by a resolution of the community council of Cracow, Poland, in 1659.[304]

17. It appears to have been an acceptable practice in fifteenth century Poland and Germany to gouge out eyes and cut off tongues. Thus, a verdict was handed down by a Jewish court to gouge out the eyes of a murderer, and he accepted this verdict.[305]

18. Self-mutilation: "It happened with our teacher, Rabbi Mordecai, that he hit another Jew with his fist. He said, 'The arm that hit a Jew should be broken.' He then placed his hand in a hole in which there was a brick, and broke it."[306]

Notes to Extraordinary Sanctions

There are really three basic issues that must be examined in attempting to understand the extraordinary sanctioning processes utilized by Jewish decision-makers in the Talmudic Era and in the Middle Ages:

1. Why did Jewish decision-makers in these eras depart so sharply from the traditional principles of Jewish criminal law? These had emphasized such remarkable protection for criminal defendants, and had purportedly tilted the entire criminal trial processes in the defendant's favor, so that capital punishment would be nearly impossible? What happened to the sustained Jewish humane tradition that purported to minimize corporal punishment and mutilations? In this connection, it is interesting to note that in the Bible, which records human activities over a period of more than one thousand years, and which details innumerable offenses, there is no mention of Jewish decision-makers ever inflicting such penalties, as gouging out eyes, cutting off tongues, or amputating noses or other limbs.[307] In

fact, as discussed above, biblical law represented a shift away from the imposition of such sanctions.[308]

2. How were the earlier talmudic decision-makers able to sustain a society with minimum public order when it would have been practically impossible to convict anyone under the rigorous evidentiary and procedural rules, set forth above?

3. What made Jewish decision-makers think that they had the *right* to kill, mutilate, and inflict severe corporal punishment? What authoritative legal principles did they utilize to justify these extraordinary sanctions, which, if not authorized by the Bible, would constitute murder or prohibited mayhem (see Part Two, Chapter V, Section D 5, above)? It should be realized that the decision-makers who inflicted, and justified, these sanctions were deeply religious and ready to die for their religion if need be. Many were in fact martyred. They would not, therefore, have violated fundamental biblical norms unless they were persuaded that their actions were biblically authorized.

For more discussion of these issues, see section 6, below.

e. BRANDING

1. The Bible (Gen. 38:24) records that Judah ordered that his daughter-in-law, Tamar, should be taken out and "burned." Some have interpreted the verse to mean branding her face with a mark to stigmatize her as a prostitute, rather than burning her to death.[309] This resolves the problem raised by some talmudic authorities of how Tamar could have been killed since she was not then a married woman.[310] The simple meaning of the verse, and it is so interpreted in the Talmud, is that Judah ordered her to be killed.[311]

2. Although there is no record that branding was actually ever carried out by Jews in the Middle Ages, the ordinances of the community representatives of Castille, Spain, at Valladolid in 1423,[312] provided, "If the informing has been established by the testimony of one witness or circumstance, or by a confession of the informer himself, or in accordance with the decision of a *beth din* (court), a line of shame is branded upon him by burning" (see Chapter VIII, Section A 2 *b*, above).

---

303. Luria, ibid.; Meir of Lublin, Responsa *Maharam* of Lublin, no. 138.

304. Wettstein, *Ozar Ha'Safrut*, vol. 4, p. 614. For other communal ordinances calling for mutilations, see Halpern, *Takkanot Mehren* (Tel-Aviv, 1948), p. 124, no. 374; see also Section *a*, above.

305. *Nimuke, Maharam* of Merzberg.

306. Judah Ha'Hasid, *Sefer Hasidim* (reprinted Jerusalem, 1973), sec. 631.

307. There is a single exception in Judg. 1:6–7, where amputations were inflicted upon King Adoni Bezek in retaliation for his practice over many years of amputating the limbs of his opponents once he captured them.

308. See "Law in the Ancient Near East," Chapter VIII, Section C 4 *g*, above; Assaf, *Ha'Onshin*, pp. 16, 21.

309. Commentary of Rabbi Jacob, *Baal Ha'Turim* (printed in many editions of the Hebrew Bible), ad loc.

310. See commentary of Moshe ben Nahman (Ramban), ad loc.

311. See Talmud, *Sotah* 10b.

312. Set forth in Finkelstein, *Jewish Self-Government*, p. 363; Assaf, *Ha'Onshin*, p. 9.

3. The ordinances of the Jewish community of Prague in 1612, provided, "Any prostitute that will fornicate from today on, shall have a mark of shame branded upon her through a burning metal, shall be driven from the community by the policemen, and shall never return."[313]

4. In Cracow, Poland, thieves expelled from the city were threatened by the Jewish community with branding if they returned.[314] A similar threat was made with regard to those who would violate Jewish community ordinances.[315] The very fact that such threats were utilized may indicate that branding was not unknown as a sanction during that era.

f. FLOGGING

(1) *In the Talmudic Era*

Flogging in the Middle Ages was predicated upon biblical (Deut. 25:2) and talmudic precedents. The Talmud records more than thirty instances where flogging was actually inflicted during the Talmudic Era, even in cases not authorized by the Bible.[316] Flogging was apparently a common sanction[317] in the Talmudic Era and was the only corporal sanction authorized for the courts other than the death penalty.

Sexual offenses were a prime basis for flogging inflicted by talmudic authorities. The following are representative examples:

(*a*) A man who copulated in public with his wife.[318]

(*b*) A man who fornicated with an Egyptian women.[319]

(*c*) A person who was the subject of rumors of promiscuity.[320]

The Talmud states that floggings not prescribed in the Bible were administered until the recalcitrant agreed to do what he was ordered, or "until his soul departed."[321] Despite this latter phrase, it was generally agreed that, "Biblical floggings are harsher than nonbiblical floggings, because the flogging of the Torah is done on the flesh . . . and, since it is (possible) that the flogged person may die from the blows, a prior estimate must first be made as to how many blows he can withstand."[322] [In any case, no more than thirty-nine lashes could be administered.] With regard to non-

biblical floggings, however, they are not administered in this manner. Instead, a person is flogged in accordance with the discretion of the *beth din* in order to chastise him. Even if he can bear more, he is still only flogged in accordance with the seriousness of his violation.[323] Hai Gaon, however, maintained that only thirteen blows were administered on any part of his body.[324]

(2) IN THE MIDDLE AGES

1. Rav Hai Gaon (Babylonia, *circa* 1050) ordered the flogging of one who violated community mores and stated that this was the common practice.[325]

2. Rabbi Yehudai Gaon (Babylonia, *circa* 800)[326] flogged a deviant.

3. Isaac Alfasi (Morocco, *circa* 1050) authorized flogging.[327]

4. Floggings were administered in France *circa* 1150, even when not authorized or required by biblical law.[328]

5. Moshe ben Maimon (Rambam; Egypt, *circa* twelfth century) ordered the flogging of two men who signed as witnesses to a promissory note but did not know its contents.[329]

6. Rambam also ordered the flogging of a *kohen* (priest) who married a divorcee (contrary to Jewish law) and who then refused to divorce her.[330]

7. Meir of Rothenberg (Germany, *circa* thirteenth century) authorized flogging for one who beat his wife.[331]

---

313. Assaf, ibid., p. 114.
314. Ibid.
315. Ibid.; Wettstein, *Jahrbuch der Judisch-Literarischen Gesellschaft*, vol. 10, p. 313.
316. See, e.g., Talmud, *Shabbat* 40b, *Yebamot* 52a, *Ketubot* 45b, *Nazir* 58b, *Hulin* 141b. For a detailed listing, see Shlomo Duran, Responsa *Rashbash*, no. 510.
317. See footnotes 318–324, below.
318. Talmud, *Yebamot* 90b.
319. Ibid., *Berakhot* 58a.
320. Ibid., *Kiddushin* 81a.
321. Tosefta *Makkot* 3, 10; Jerusalem Talmud, *Nazir* 4, 3.
322. Mishnah, *Makkot* 3:10–11.

323. Isaac ben Sheshet, Responsa *Rivash*, no. 90; see also nos. 87, 91.
324. See Zidkiyahu, the physician, in *Shibale Ha'Leket* (Vilna, 1887), sec. 2; Harkavy, *Tshuvat Ha'Gaonim*, no. 440; Shimon Duran, Responsa *Tashbatz*, vol. 2, no. 51; Ginsberg, *Mishpatim Le'Yisrael*, p. 29; *Avraham*, sec. 496, subsec. 2 (New York, 1946); Assaf, *Ha'Onshin*, p. 51 ff; Z. Leiter, *Tshuvat Ha'Gaonim, Sha'are Tshuva* (New York, 1946), sec. 15; Shlomo ben Aderet, Responsa *Rashba*, vol. 4, no. 264; *Kal Bo*, sec. 136; Hayim ben Yitzhak, *Ohr Zarua, B. K.*, sec. 389. See also Rambam, Laws of the Sanhedrin, 4:5, and Moshe ben Nakhman (Ramban) in his commentary to *Sefer Hamitzvot*, sec. 1; Shlomo Duran, Responsa *Rashbash*, no. 510; Commentary *Ran* to Talmud, *Ketubot*, chap. 4; Commentary of *Tosafot* to Talmud *Sanhedrin* 26b; Levi ben Habib, Responsa *Ralbakh*, the Epistle of Ordination, p. 100a.
325. Responsum cited in Benjamin the Physician, *Shibalei Ha'leket*, sec. 2.
326. See *Ohr Zarua, Baba Kama*, no. 389; B. Halpern, *Toratan Shel Rishonim*, 1, 29; 2, 18.
327. Isaac Alfasi, Responsa *Rif*, no. 302.
328. Benjamin the Physician, *Shibalei Ha'Leket, Shabbat* no. 60, cites a number of instances.
329. Responsa *Rambam* (Blau ed.), sec. 1., no. 71.
330. Responsa *Rambam*, ibid., sec. 2, no. 349; Freiman ed., no. 157. See Rambam, Laws of Murder, 2:5: "The Court may flog and otherwise punish murderers, for whom technically admissible evidence is lacking." See also Rambam, Laws of Theft, 1:10, to the effect that juvenile delinquents may be flogged.
331. Responsa (Prague ed.), nos. 81, 927. See also Rabbi Yerukhem (Germany, *circa* 1250), *Misharim*, sec. 23, subsec. 5.

8. Judah ben Asher (Spain, *circa* 1275) authorized the flogging of a woman who was suspected of fornicating with a non-Jew.[332]

9. He also ordered the flogging of promiscuous couples.[333]

10. Samuel Sardi (*circa* 1550) ruled that one who refused to come to a trial in court could be flogged with rods.[334]

11. Abraham DiBotan (Salonika, *circa* 1550) records a verdict for the flogging of a person who slandered a woman and spread rumors that she was promiscuous.[335]

12. Menahem of Merzberg (Germany, *circa* fourteenth century) cites a number of instances in which the court, apparently in practice, administered flogging to, e.g., one who slandered people and called them names and to one who scoffed at the words of the sages.[336]

13. Jacob Weil (Germany, *circa* 1450) ordered the flogging of one who assaulted another person.[337]

14. Shlomo Duran (Algeria, *circa* 1450) ordered flogging for one who slandered.[338]

15. Moshe Galanti (Israel, *circa* 1550) authorized the flogging of one who persistently embarrassed people in public.[339]

16. Solomon Luria, (Poland, *circa* 1550) authorized the flogging of one who betrothed a woman privately without witnesses (contrary to prescribed norms) and also of others who slandered and told false stories about people.[340]

17. Jacob Emden (Germany, *circa* 1750)[341] ordered the flogging of a thief. He further stated that it was a common occurrence to inflict similar severe sanctions in order to coerce a debtor to pay overdue money owed by him.

(3) *Procedure for Flogging*

The procedure for flogging in Babylonia (based on the talmudic procedure in Mishnah, *Makkot* 3:12–14) is described by Hai Gaon (Babylonia, *circa* eleventh century) as follows:

And with regards to your inquiry as to how one is to be flogged in our time, and whether a strap made of calfskin is required, and whether one is to make the announcements [set forth in Talmud, *Makkot* 22b] or not, and how the rabbis carry all of this out in the Academy:

We have not seen that a strap of calfskin [is utilized] and this is not the custom in the Academies; instead, a strong rope of flax or *kanbas* is brought. (Some fold it over two or three times, in accordance with its thickness and the discretion of the court.) The person to be flogged is brought before the court, with his hands and feet tied: his right hand to his right foot, and his left hand to his left foot. The court hangs his hat around his neck, the court bailiff, who is to flog him, stands by his head, with the rope in his hands, near his shoulder. The court instructs him, and he stands prepared to flog. An announcement is first made to the one to be flogged, concerning the reason for his flogging . . . The bailiff of the court begins to flog him thirteen times on his right side, and the one appointed to count, counts. They then stop and announce to him "If you will not heed [the laws], then the Lord will smite you and your children with distinct blows" (Deut. 28:55–59). He then continues to flog him thirteen more times on his left side, and the counter, counts. They then stop and read before him "And if the guilty person is to be flogged, he shall be flogged forty, but not more" (Deut. 25:2–3). He then continues to flog him thirteen more times on his back, and the counter counts. They then read before him "And you shall keep this covenant" (Deut. 29:8), and they then untie his hands and feet, and he stands on his feet with his hat hanging by his neck and confesses: "I have sinned, I have transgressed, I have rebelled; may my flogging bring forgiveness for my sins." Some stand him up to confess before the flogging. Thereafter, the court prays for mercy for him that he be forgiven. . . ."[342]

While the flogging in Babylonia was done in the courtroom, in other countries it was administered in front of the synagogue,[343] or in the synagogue itself.[344] Where it was felt warranted, the person to be flogged

332. Responsa *Zikhron Yehuda* (Berlin, 1846), no. 80.

333. Ibid., p. 53a.

334. B. G. Palmeza, *Sefer Ha'Terumot*, sec. 3; see Karo, *Beth Yosef, Shulkhan Arukh, Ho. Mis.*, sec. 2.

335. Responsa *Lekhem Rav* (Jerusalem, 1968), no. 7.

336. In his *Nimukim*, printed at the end of standard editions of the Responsa *Mahari Weil*, p. 117b.

337. Responsa *Mahari Weil*, no. 28.

338. Responsa *Rashbash*, no. 511.

339. Responsa, no. 33.

340. Responsa *Maharshal*, nos. 25, 28.

341. Responsa *Ya'Avetz*, (New York, 1964), sec. 1., no. 79. For additional instances, see decisions of Natronai Gaon, in H. Modai, *Shaare Tzedek*, vol. 4, 7:39; Isaac ben Sheshet, Responsa *Rivash*, no. 79 and nos. 238–39; Rambam, Laws of Theft and Lost Articles, 3:11; Binyamin Ze'Ev, Responsa, no. 402; Yitzhak Adarbi, Responsa *Divrei Ribbot*, no. 167; Yair Bakhrakh, Responsa *Khavat Yair*, no. 65, sec. 5; and no. 141; Yosef Ha'Levi, Responsa *Ri Migash*, no. 161; Responsa *Radvaz*, sec. 3, no. 480; Assaf, *Ha'Onshim*, pp. 45, 47.

342. Responsa of the *Gaonim*, Harkavy ed., no. 440; See also the Responsa of Nakhshon in H-Modai, *Sha'Are Tzedek*, vol. 4, sec. 350, no. 34. See also commentary to *Seder Taharot*, attributed to Hai Gaon, *Kelim*, ch. 22; Assaf, *Ha'Onshin*, pp. 23, 55–57.

343. See Solomon Schechter, "The Scroll of Avyatar the Priest" in *Saadyana*, (New York, 1905), p. 90, regarding the practice in Egypt; Wettstein, "The Communal Records of Crakow" in *Ozar Ha'Safrut* (1890), vol. 4, p. 614.

344. Luria, in *Yam Shel Shlomo, Baba Kama*, ch. 8, secs. 48, 49, regarding Poland.

might be required to walk through the entire Jewish neighborhood while being flogged all the way.[345] He might also be flogged on his bare flesh, his shirt first being removed.[346] Often, however, the person to be flogged was permitted to wear clothes to soften the blows.[347]

(4) Extraordinary Flogging

Extraordinary flogging was accorded for crimes that were considered very serious. Where the crime was serious enough, "unmerciful flogging," without any limitations as to the number of blows, was inflicted. This was done, for example, in the case of a man who beat his pregnant wife with a stick until she died.[348] The Great Synod of Valladolid, Spain, in 1432, resolved that one who informed for the first time, or who betrothed a woman against her will, should be flogged one hundred blows.[349] So, too, in one instance, some Jews in Spain who were suspected of heresy were flogged so severely that some of them died.[350] There is one account (based on heresay) by Judah Ha-Hasid (circa twelfth century) that a confessed murderer in Jerusalem, who requested a penance in order to atone for his crime, was taken to the Mount of Olives and the following sanctions were inflicted upon him, with his consent: He was beaten until he bled and his entire body became swollen. Three weeks later, when he recovered somewhat, he was buried in the ground with only a small hole for him to breathe, until he nearly died. This process was repeated three times.[351]

Sometimes one who was to be flogged was permitted to avoid this by paying a fixed fine.[352] This was permitted where the offense, such as embarrassing a person publicly, was not considered serious.[353] One who, however, slandered a woman and impugned her chastity was not permitted to avoid flogging by payment of a fine, since such slander could, in those days, seriously affect her life and that of her entire family.[354] Appar-

ently, however, in Poland, by the seventeenth century, flogging was administered only in a symbolic way that would not be painful.[355]

(5) Flogging of Women

In Babylonia female violators of the law were flogged in the same manner as males.[356] This was also true in Spain.[357] In Europe, however, it appears that women were not flogged. A. S. Bachrach says in his Responsa:[358]

> With regard to flogging, I have not seen fit to arrange flogging for women [who wished to receive penances for various transgressions]. Even though a woman is treated in the same way as a man with regards to all penalties of the Bible, nevertheless, since our flogging is not the biblical flogging, but is only symbolic of biblical flogging, we do not flog women.[359]

It may be that, partly under the influence of the European notions of chivalry, women were treated more leniently in this respect in France and Germany than in Spain or Babylonia.[360]

g. Imprisonment

Imprisonment was one of the most common sanctions employed by Jewish decision-makers in the Middle Ages. In Spain, for example, nearly every Jewish community had its own jail.[361] Imprisonment was a well-established device utilized by Jewish decision-makers for many purposes. These included ensuring that the defendant would appear at trial or for sentencing, and as a means of coercing the performance of an act ordered by the beth din. In the Talmudic Era, imprisonment does not appear to have been very common, in keeping with the practice in ancient Greek and Roman law.[362] In the Middle Ages, however, it was widely utilized as a penalty. Some of the major uses of imprisonment in Jewish law will now be detailed.

345. Spain and North Africa; see Isaac ben Sheshet, Responsa Rivash, no. 351.

346. Isaac ben Sheshet, Rivash, ibid.; Hai Gaon, in Orkhot Khayim (New York, 1946), Laws of the Day Preceding Yom Kippur.

347. Assaf, Ha'Onshin, p. 23.

348. Menahem of Merzberg, Nimuke of Maharam of Merzberg, p. 178.

349. Assaf, Ha'Onshin, p. 23; Finkelstein, Jewish Self-Government, p. 351.

350. Shmuel Ha'Nagid (circa 1055 C.E.), cited in Judah Al-Barceloni, Sefer Ha'Shtarot, p. 277.

351. Y. Ha'Hasid, Sefer Hasidim, sec. 630; see also A. Epstein in Monatsschrift, vol. 47, pp. 340–45; Assaf, Ha'Onshin, p. 23.

352. Luria, in Yam Shel Shlomo, Baba, Kama, ch. 8, sec. 49.

353. Cf. Talmud, Sotah 10b.

354. Assaf, Ha'Onshin, p. 38; Luria, Responsa Maharshal, no. 28, and his Yam Shel Shlomo, to Baba Kama, ch. 8, sec. 49.

355. Luria, Responsa Maharshal, no. 28; Bachrach, Responsa Khut Ha'Shani, no. 47.

356. Decisions of Yehudai Gaon (circa 760), in Y. Halpern, Toratam Shel Rishonim, vol. 1, p. 29, vol. 2, p. 18; Decisions of Nahshon Gaon (circa 880 C.E.), cited in Mordecai ben Hillel, Commentary Mordecai to Baba Kama, ch. 8; Decisions of Tzemah Gaon (circa 890 C.E.), in Ohr Zarua, Baba Kama, sec. 316; Luria, Yam Shel Shlomo, Baba Kama, ch. 8, sec. 27.

357. Judah ben Asher, Responsa Zikhron Yehuda, no. 91.

358. Bachrach, Khut Ha'Shani, no. 47.

359. See Abraham ben David, in his commentary to Rambam, Laws of Marriage, 21:10, that he had never heard of women being flogged. Y. Rosanes (in Magid Mishnah to Rambam) cites Rambam and Rashba to the same effect.

360. See Assaf, Ha'Onshin, p. 78.

361. See Assaf, Ha'Onshin, p. 25.

362. Assaf, Ha'Onshin, p. 25; M. Elon, The Principles of Jewish Law (Jerusalem, 1975), p. 536. See, however, Talmud, Pesakhim 91a.

(1) *As a Penalty*

1. The Bible records, in addition to the imprisonment of Joseph and others in Egypt (Exod. 39:20), a number of other instances of imprisonment[363] imposed as a penalty for crimes.

2. The Bible also relates that one who violated the Sabbath was imprisoned.[364] This may have referred to imprisonment as a penalty.[365]

3. The biblical Book of Ezra (7:26) records an order of the king of Persia that whoever would not obey Ezra could be punished by imprisonment and other penalties. The Talmud[366] relied on this verse as empowering every Jewish court to imprison.[367]

4. The Talmud[368] authorized a penalty of death by imprisonment. The prisoner would be fed exclusively with barley and water, which would cause the intestines to gradually expand until death resulted from extreme intestinal distress. It is not known whether this penalty (borrowed from the Persians and prescribed in the Talmud for recidivists and for murderers, against whom admissible evidence was lacking) was ever carried out in practice.[369] The language of the Talmud seems to indicate that it was an actual practice.

5. The penalty of imprisonment was sometimes made harsher by the practice of confining prisoners in a small cell in which they would be unable to walk, or even to stand up.[370]

In medieval Europe, where imprisonment was extremely common, it was employed as a sanction for many types of offenders. The following are representative samples:

a. Informers in Spain, particularly those who had not yet caused any harm by their informing,[371] were to be imprisoned.

b. Various sexual offenders, including those guilty of intercourse with non-Jewish women,[372] were subject to imprisonment. This sanction was also threatened for householders who would not report such offenses by their servants.[373]

c. Those who were guilty of assault, but had no money with which to pay the fine, were sometimes imprisoned at the rate of one day in prison for each piece of gold unpaid. The intention here was to permit the poor to be penalized "equally" with the rich.[374] It may be questioned, however, whether imprisonment for one day is the equivalent, in terms of punishment, of the payment of one piece of gold.[375]

d. For additional cases, see Isaac Alfasi, Responsa *Rif* no. 146; Yom Tov Ashvili, Responsa *Ritva*, no. 159; Mahari Adrabi, *Divre Rivot*, no. 282; Shimon Duran, Responsa *Tashbatz*, vol. 3, no. 168.

6. The Jews of Mantoba, Italy (*circa* 1725) apparently maintained a prison in which they incarcered both Jews and Christians.[376]

7. In Poland prisons were also a common feature of community life. Some communities, such as Cracow, had two prisons,[377] and Cracow's sanctioning practices are representative of the situation in Poland during the seventeenth and eighteenth centuries.[378] Imprisonment was authorized as a sanction against anybody who violated any of the ordinances of the Jewish community of Cracow, or of the Regional Council of Four Lands, including the following offenses:

a. Any poor person who went from door to door collecting charity, without the authorization of the appropriate community official.

b. A butcher who slaughtered animals during the summer time (because it was believed, based on the then current medical advice, that eating meat at that time was unhealthy).

c. Any parent who did not pay the required tuition for his child.

d. Anyone who removed notices concerning taxation and other serious matters, which had been posted by the lay leaders of the community on the synagogue wall.

e. Women who played with dice or other gambling games. Apparently women were considered to be the chief offenders in this respect. They were liable to one day's imprisonment for this offense but could, instead, pay a fine of three *"edomin"*.

f. There were also provisions for the temporary imprisonment, by appropriate community officials, of

363. Judg. 16:21; 1 Kings 22:27; Jer. 37:15 ff., 38:4 ff.; 2 Chron. 16:10.

364. Num. 16:34.

365. See Ginsberg, *Mishpatim Le'Yisrael*, p. 35.

366. *Mo'ed Katan* 16a.

367. See also Rambam, Laws of the Sanhedrin, 24:91.

368. *Sanhedrin* 81b.

369. *Pesakhim* 8:6, 36a, 91a; *Mo'ed Katan* 3:1; *Sotah* 4:5; *Yoma* 11a.

370. Talmud, *Mo'ed Katan* 16a; see commentaries of Asher ben Yehiel, *Rosh*, and Gerundi, *Ran*, ad. loc.; Rabbi Yerucham, in *Mesharim*, sec. 1, subsec. 2; Talmud, *Sanhedrin* 81b; Rambam, Laws of the Sanhedrin, 18:5; Ginsberg, *Mishpatim Le'Yisrael*, p. 34.

371. Ordinances of the Synod at Valladolid (1432), in Finkelstein, *Jewish Self-Government*, p. 348.

372. Judah ben Asher, Responsa *Zikhron Yehuda*, sec. 91.

373. Ibid.; see also Isaac ben Sheshet, Responsa *Rivash*, no. 351; M. Trani, Responsa *Mabit*, 1:22.

374. Judah ben Asher, Responsa *Zikhron Yehuda*, sec. 36.

375. See the decision of the U.S. Supreme Court on this issue, in *Tate v. Short*, 401 U.S. 395 (1971).

376. Assaf, *Ha'Onshin*, p. 4.

377. Ibid., p. 27.

378. Ibid.

those who were accused of disturbing the peace, raising prices unduly, or using false weights.[379]

8. Another variety of imprisonment, more humiliating than the forms described above, was the *"kona"* (a form of pillory), which was utilized in Poland. This was a device consisting of two bars of iron attached to the wall in the entrance corridor to the synagogue. When it was felt to be appropriate, a prisoner would be chained by his hands to these iron bars for a few hours, while another iron chain would be wrapped around his neck and attached to the wall. He would usually be placed there during the times of prayer services, so that all those who entered and left the synagogue could see him in chains, berate him, and often spit in his face. He might also be tormented by the boys who accompanied their fathers to the synagogue.[380]

(2) *To Ensure Appearance at Trial or for Sentencing*

1. The Bible records,[381] "and he [a blasphemer] was placed in prison until the word of God would be explained to them"[382] [regarding the type of penalty to be imposed]. This is the earliest mention in the Bible of imprisonment by Jewish law.[383]

2. The Talmud[384] records that one who tortiously caused an injury was kept in prison until it could be determined that the victim would not die. This was based upon the talmudic interpretation of a biblical verse.[385] There is, however, no specific mention regarding the extent to which this was carried out in practice.

3. The practice of imprisonment to ensure appearance at trial is referred to by Paltai Gaon (Babylonia, *circa* 858 C.E.)[386] and Sherira Gaon (Babylonia, *circa* 998 C.E.).[387] There is, however, some doubt as to whether Sherira Gaon was the author of this ruling.[388] Nevertheless, it is indicative of the employment of imprisonment for this purpose.

4. Asher ben Yehiel (Spain, *circa* 1250), "Whoever owes taxes to the community, is imprisoned in jail . . .

and does not go out of there, until he posts security or obtains a guarantor, or until he obligates himself in writing to pay."[389]

5. Isaac ben Sheshet (Spain and Algeria, *circa* 1390) ordered the continued imprisonment of one who was accused of being an informer to make sure that he did not flee until the investigation of the case was completed. His order indicates that it was the practice for anyone accused of a crime to be kept in prison until the completion of his trial.[390] The accused could be released, however, upon posting security or providing guarantors, except in capital cases, where it was feared that he might flee and forfeit the security. His guarantors could not, of course, be killed or physically punished in his stead.[391]

6. Shimon Duran (Algeria, *circa* 1425) authorized imprisonment pending investigation of a crime and states that in another case he himself had ordered the imprisonment of a Jew upon receipt of a complaint. (See Section C 2 *f*, above.)

(3) *As a Means of Coercion*

1. The Talmud[392] implies that prison was an established institution during the Second Jewish Commonwealth. While the Talmud does not specifically so state, some commentators[393] have understood this institution to be a means to force a husband to divorce his wife, or to force a debtor to pay debts, when so ordered by the courts.

2. The Talmud[394] records an instance where a suspected thief (who aroused suspicion because he exhibited his disregard for the property of others by wiping his hands on someone else's coat) was tied up until he confessed.

3. Imprisonment was also not unknown in the Middle Ages to coerce a man to marry the woman to whom he had become betrothed.[395]

(4) *For Debt*

Jewish law has always greatly emphasized the perspective requiring dignified treatment of a debtor. The Bible explicitly prohibited entry into a debtor's home in order to seize chattels as security for the repayment

---

379. For all of the above, see the community records of Cracow, from the year 1595 and thereafter in M. Balaban, in *Jahrbuch der Judisch Literarischen Gesellschaft, supra,* vols. 10, 11. See also Wettstein, in *Otzar Ha'Safrut,* vol. 4, pp. 577–641; Assaf, *Ha'Onshin,* pp. 27–28; S. Halpern, *Takkanot Medinat Mehrin,* no. 247; S. Dubnow, *Pinkas Ha'Medinah,* no. 546.

380. Assaf, *Ha'Onshin,* p. 31.
381. Lev. 24:12.
382. Talmud, *Sanhedrin* 78b.
383. See also the imprisonment of Joseph and others in Egypt, Gen. 39:20, 40:3, 42:17, 24.
384. *Sanhedrin* 78b.
385. Exod. 21:19: ". . . and he shall go outside . . ."; see *Mekhilta,* ad loc.
386. Cited in Leiter, *Sha'Are Teshuva,* sec. 182, and Yehodai Gaon, *Halakhot Pesukot* (Jerusalem, 1951), sec. 135.
387. Cited in Yitzhak ben Moshe, *Ohr Zarua,* vol. 1, no. 112; Zidkiyahu the Physician, *Shibbalei Ha'Leket,* no. 60.
388. See Assaf, *Ha'Onshin,* p. 52.

389. Asher ben Yehiel, Responsa *Rosh,* sec. 7, no. 11. See also sec. 13, no. 3, and sec. 68, no. 10.
390. Isaac ben Sheshet, Responsa *Rivash,* no. 236; see also Karo, *Beth Yosef, Ho. Mis.,* sec. 388, subsec. 5.
391. Isaac ben Sheshet, Responsa *Rivash,* ibid.
392. *Pesakhim* 91a.
393. See Shlomo Yitzhaki, *Rashi,* ad loc.
394. *Baba Metzia* 23a. See, below, regarding the practice of coercing confessions; and see the imprisonment of an accused thief, by Shimon Duran, which resulted in a confession in his Responsa *Tashbatz,* vol. 3, no. 165.
395. Yosef Ibn Migash (Spain, *circa* 1050), Responsa *Ri Migash,* no. 122.

of a loan. It further forbids retention of a garment as security if it were needed by a debtor to keep warm at night.[396] Bondage for debt was recognized only in the case of a male thief, who was sold to repay his debt to the victim, and in the case of a person who sold himself as a slave because of his utter poverty, including, presumably inability to pay debts.[397]

In practice, however, debtors were enslaved at various times, at least during the Biblical Era.[398]

The biblical perspective continued in the Talmudic Era too. Talmudic decision-makers ruled that not even a court officer could enter a debtor's home to seize a pledge.[399] While imprisonment for debt was clearly contrary to this perspective, and was not often practiced by Jews in the Talmudic Era, it was not unknown.[400] Nevertheless, a debtor who did possess property, but refused to pay, was to be "flogged until his soul departs"[401] if he persisted in his refusal.

However, the Babylonian *gaonim* (*circa* tenth century), prescribed that a debtor was required to take an oath that he had no property with which to repay his debt. Alfasi (*circa* eleventh century) authorized entry into the home of a debtor who blatantly refused to repay his debts.[402]

In medieval Europe imprisonment for debt became a common method of debt collection by non-Jews,[403] and it became common for loan agreements to provide for imprisonment of debtors in the event of non-payment.[404] This appeared to influence Jewish perspectives, too, and imprisonment of debtors and similar loan agreements began to proliferate in medieval Jewish communities as well.[405] Such provisions have been found in many of the documents of Jews in Spanish communities, particularly Castille, Burgos, Saragossa, and Astudillo, and they have even found their way into privileges of autonomy granted to Jewish communities.[406]

By the twelfth century the change in the treatment of debtors in Jewish law was pronounced. Meir Ha-levi Abulafia (Spain, *circa* twelfth century) ruled that a court officer could enter a borrower's home to search for property if none could be found elsewhere.[407] Rabbi Jacob Tam (France, *circa* twelfth century) and Asher ben Yehiel (Spain, *circa* thirteenth century) ruled that a court officer could enter a borrower's home to seize property in repayment for a loan, and they held the biblical prohibition to be limited to attempted seizure of property *before* a debt was due in order to secure repayment.[408] This was later codified in Jacob ben Asher's Code of Laws,[409] *Turim*.

Although a number of prominent Jewish scholar–decision-makers ruled contractual provisions for imprisonment to be invalid, they began to be upheld frequently by decision-makers during the fourteenth century.[410] One of the most noted scholar–decision-makers of that century said:

> In truth, in this city [Huesca, in the province of Aragon, Spain], the Jewish judges are accustomed to seize a debtor, if the latter had so agreed. This is based on a communal ordinance. There is also an ordinance, that even without such agreement, a debtor may be seized, or must provide security (called, "confirmation of the *beth din*") for a claim against him. I wished to object to this ordinance, since it is not in accordance with the Torah, but was advised that it is an ordinance of the marketplace because of defrauders and in order not to bolt the door against borrowers [to prevent the closing off of the sources of credit], I then acquiesced in this custom.[411]

396. Deut. 24:10–13, 16. See also Exod. 22:24–26. See also Rambam, Laws of Lenders and Borrowers, 2:2.

397. Exod. 22:2; Lev. 25:39.

398. See 2 Kings 4:1; Isa. 50:1; Amos 2:6, 8:4–6; Micah 2:1–2; Neh. 5:1–13. See, in general, Elon, *Freedom of the Individual in the Collection of Debts in Jewish Law* (Heb.; Jerusalem, 1964). Compare the perspective regarding bondage of debtors in the Code of Hammurabi, secs. 113–19, 151–52, and the Roman *Lex Poetelia*, which permitted imprisonment of a debtor, but not his sale into slavery.

399. Rambam, Laws of Lenders and Borrowers, 2:2.

400. See Shlomo Yitzhaki, *Rashi, Pesakhim* 91a, regarding imprisonment for non-payment of debts, apparently taxes; also Rambam, ibid., 2:1; Elon, *Freedom of the Individual*, pp. 13, 112.

401. Talmud, *Ketubot* 86a.

402. See Shmuel Ha'Sardi, *Sefer Ha'Terumot* (Salonika, 1596), sec. 1, pt. 3, 2.

403. See J. Kohler, *Shakespeare vor dem Forum der Jurisprudenz* (Berlin, 1919), p. 16, cited in M. Elon, "The Sources and Nature of Jewish Law," Israel Law Review (1968), vol. 3, p. 108.

404. A. Gulak, "The Foundations of Hebrew Law" (Hebrew; Berlin, 1922; reprinted Tel-Aviv, 1967), 2:124–27; Alfasi, Responsa *Rif*, no. 146.

405. Similar provisions were in widespread use in loan agreements by non-Jews (see O. Gierke, *Schuld und Haftung*

im Alteren Deutschen Recht, pp. 72–74 [Berlin, 1910]; and Kohler, *Shakespeare vor dem Forum*, pp. 136–60). In Babylonia debtors appear to have been excommunicated, not imprisoned (Assaf, *Ha'Onshim*, p. 29).

406. Gulak, "The Foundations of Hebrew Law"; see Baer, *The Jews in Christian Spain*; Elon, *Freedom of the Individual*, pp. 138–40.

407. Cited in Jacob ben Asher, *Tur, Ho. Mis.*, sec. 97, no. 26.

408. Asher ben Yehiel, Commentary *Rosh, Baba Metzia*, p. 46.

409. Jacob ben Asher, *Tur, Ho. Mis.* sec. 97, no. 15 (*circa* fourteenth century).

410. See Alexander Suslin Ha'Cohen, in *Sefer Ha'Agudah, Shabbat*, no. 150; see also Alfasi, Responsa *Rif*, no. 146.

411. Isaac ben Sheshet Perfet, Responsa *Rivash*, no. 484; see also Asher ben Yehiel, Responsa *Rosh*, 18:4 and 65:10; Samuel Di'Medina, Responsa *Maharsham, Ho. Mis.*, no. 390.

Apparently the ordinances providing for imprisonment of debtors were applied even to those who were
clearly unable, rather than unwilling, to pay their
debts.[412] The *Shulkhan Arukh*, the standard Jewish
code of laws, recorded the view of Moses Isserlis (who
reflected the situation in Germany and Poland, *circa*
sixteenth century) that a debtor without means could
not be imprisoned, but one who possessed property, yet
refused to repay his debt, could be imprisoned.[413] This
view was upheld by the majority of Jewish scholar–
edcision-makers.[414]

Although some Jewish communities enacted ordinances that prohibited the incarceration of debtors
without a written order from the proper communal
officials,[415] the practice of imprisonment for debt became widespread in Poland, Lithuania, and Germany
in the seventeenth and eighteenth centuries.[416] Imprisonment was sometimes imposed, almost automatically,
in all cases of non-payment, regardless of whether or
not the debtor had means.[417] The term of imprisonment
varied from eight days to one month, but was later
increased to as much as four months,[418] arousing the
intense opposition of a number of prominent scholar–
decision-makers.[419]

Imprisonment for debt was exemplified by the community ordinances of Cracow, Poland. These provided
that one who persisted, after notice, in not paying his
taxes to the community, would be seized by Shpekil
(the name of one of the two men employed in this
capacity) and placed in prison. The prisoner would
remain in prison until he paid the taxes, and the expenses of his imprisonment, including the fee of three
"*gedolim*" to Shpekil.[420]

Furthermore, any debtor who owed two hundred
Polish gold coins or more, and claimed that he did not
have the wherewithal to pay his debt, was to be imprisoned for alternating periods of thirty days until the
end of two years.[421] The standard practice in most of
Poland, however, was to imprison a debtor who did not
pay his debt for a period of only thirty days.[422]

The reasons for this gradual trend away from the
traditional dignified treatment of debtors in Jewish law
are unclear, despite the occasional voices raised against
this practice by prominent decision-makers.[423] While
some scholars have attributed the development to the
alleged increase of fraudulent practices in commerce
and credit in the thirteenth century,[424] it was clearly
brought about in significant measure by pressure, perhaps unwarranted, from creditors.[425] Nevertheless,
many of the communal ordinances purported to predi-
cate their prescriptions for imprisonment of debtors on
the needs of debtors to continue to have access to
sources of credit and the consequent benefit to debtors
of these prescriptions. It is probable that periodic business contractions resulted in increased creditor pressure
for these measures.

Another important factor spurring imprisonment of
debtors might have been the unconscious assimilation
by Jews of the perspective of their non-Jewish neighbors
that such imprisonment was necessary and proper.[426]
As Lord Hyde, speaking for the English House of Lords
in 1663, put it:

> If a man be taken in execution and he lie in prison
> for debt, neither the plaintiff at whose suit he was
> arrested, nor the sheriff who took him, is bound to
> find meat, drink or clothes; he must live on his own,
> or on the charity of others, and if no man will re-
> lieve him, let him die in the name of God, says the
> Law, and so say I.[427]

It should be noted, however, that Jewish prisons generally had more humane conditions than the non-Jewish
ones.[428] For example, Rabbi Haim Palaggi of Smyrna
(*circa* nineteenth century) ruled that a debtor could
not be imprisoned in a jail that was dark, gloomy, and

412. Elon, "The Sources and Nature of Jewish Law," p. 112.
413. Karo, *Shulkhan Arukh, Ho. Mis.*, sec. 97, nos. 3, 15; see
also Epstein, *Arukh Ha'Shulkhan, H. M.*, sec. 25.
414. Elon, "The Sources and Nature of Jewish Law," p. 114.
415. Ordinances of the Spanish Jewish communities at Valladolid (1492), in Finkelstein, *Jewish Self-Government*, p. 348.
See also Assaf, *Ha'Onshin*; Elon, *Ha'Ma'asar Ba'Mishpat Ha'-
Ivri*, in *Jubilee Volume for Pinkhas Rosen* (Jerusalem, 1962),
p. 171, and *Ha'Mishpat Ha'Ivri*; Waldenberg, *Hilkhot Medina*
(Jerusalem, 1952); Karo, *Beth Yosef, Ho. Mis.*, sec. 96, subsec. 31. Isserlis, *Darkey Moshe*, sec. 97, subsec. 3; Y. T. Lip-
man-Heller, *Pilpulei Kharifta* (printed in standard editions of
the Talmud); Talmud, *Baba Metzia*, secs. 5–38; Samuel Di'-
Medina, Responsa *Maharshdam, Ho. Mis.*, no. 390.
416. Cf. Kolon, who reported that it was not the custom in
his area (Germany, *circa* fifteenth century) to imprison a Jew
who did not pay taxes to his community (Responsa *Mahari
Kolon*, no. 12).
417. Elon, "The Sources and Nature of Jewish Law," p. 116.
418. Ibid.
419. See Eibschutz, *Urim Ve'Tumim, Ho. Mis.* 97:13; Yosef
ben Moshe, *Leket Yosher, Y.D.* (Berlin, 1903), nos. 78, 80.
420. Assaf, *Ha'Onshin*, p. 27. See Ya'Avetz, Responsa, sec.
1, no. 79.

421. Wettstein, *Kadmoniot Mi'Pinkasaot Yeshanim*, p. 24;
Assaf, *Ha'Onshin*, p. 30.
422. Wettstein, *Kadmoniot*, p. 37, and *Divrei Khefetz Mi'-
Pinkasei Ha'Kahal Be'Krakow*, p. 36; Assaf, ibid., p. 30.
423. See, e.g., Eibschutz, *Tumim, Ho. Mis.*, 97:13; Isserlin,
in Yosef ben Moshe, *Leket Yosher, Y.D.*, pp. 79–80.
424. Elon, "The Sources and Nature of Jewish Law," p. 108.
425. See Isaac ben Sheshet Perfet, Responsa *Rivash*.
426. See Section B 6, below; Gierke, *Schuld und Haftung im
Alteren Deutschen Recht* (Berlin, 1910), p. 72; Kohler, *Shakespeare vor der Forum*, p. 16.
427. *Manby vs. Scott*, 86 E.R. 781–786, 1663.
428. Baron, *The Jewish Community*, 2:226.

filthy, but was required to be incarcerated in a prison maintained by the Jewish community in which conditions were much more preferable.[429] The Lithuanian Council (*circa* eighteenth century) also provided, "If anyone causes his debtor to be incarcerated, he is obliged to provide him with food, as the *beth din* sees fit, and the cost thereof may be added to the debt."[430]

h. HOUSE ARREST

Among the spectrum of sanctions employed by the Jewish communities of Europe, house arrest (a milder form of imprisonment) was widely practiced by Spanish and Portuguese communities.[431] The practice was carried over by Portuguese Jewish refugees who settled in Hamburg, Germany.[432]

i. EXCOMMUNICATION

One of the most prevalent and powerful sanctions employed by Jewish communities was excommunication. This could take a variety of forms, but was usually one of two types. In the form generally referred to as "*nidui*," the person at whom it was directed would suffer a relatively "moderate" form of social ostracism: No one was permitted to sit within four "ells" (approximately six to eight feet) of him; he could not be included in a prayer quorum; he was prohibited from taking haircuts; and if he died, a stone would be placed upon his coffin.[433] The excommunicated person would be permitted, however, to speak to other persons, to work for employers and to employ laborers, to study and to teach.

In the more serious form of excommunication known as "*Kherem*" (the "prison without lock, with invisible iron chains"),[434] the excommunicatee was also forbidden to teach others or to study with them, could not be employed or have commercial transactions with others, except for the minimal amount necessary to sustain him.[435]

In Babylonia (in the post-Talmudic Era) excommunication was still more onerous. One responsum from that era alleges that those subject to it could not be married, that their children would not be circumcised, and that they would be expelled from the school. The wife of a man who was banned would be expelled from the synagogue. He was, in effect, regarded as "dead," and when he did physically die, his body would not be buried in the Jewish cemetery.[436] The accuracy of this responsum, however, has been questioned by scholars, who have doubted many of its harsh provisions, which are contrary to other decisions of that era and are not in accord with Jewish traditions. This is particularly true with regard to the expulsion of children from school and of the wife from the synagogue, since they were not responsible for the acts of their father and husband, respectively.[437]

Among the Karaites (a deviant Jewish sect that refused to accept the traditions of the oral law and the Talmud), excommunication was still more onerous. It required physical separation from a spouse, and prohibited all conversation with others.[438]

While most Jewish communities appear to have followed the more moderate forms of excommunication referred to in the Talmud, communities in Poland applied the more severe forms of excommunication.[439]

Excommunication was imposed for a wide variety of offenses that were considered serious: refusal to obey a decision of the court after warning and after the imposition of milder forms of social ostracism;[440] the purchasing of stolen goods; spreading false rumors that a woman had become betrothed; unethical dealings with the estates of Polish noblemen; prohibited types of tax farming;[441] the theft of charity monies from synagogues.[442]

429. Responsa *Khikeke Lev, Ho. Mis.* (Salonika, 1797), vol. 2, no. 5; see also A. Ankavah, *Kerem Hamar* (Berlin, 1834), vol. 2, no. 33, 4a.

430. S. Dubnow, *Pinkas Ha'Medinah*, no. 333.

431. Isaac ben Sheshet, Responsa *Rivash*, secs. 173, 395, 249.

432. See the ordinances of that community for the year 1655–1670, in Balaban, *Jahrbuch der Judisch Literarischen Gesellschaft*, vols. 7–12, notably the ordinance adopted in 1660; see also the examples at Section B 2 *g*, above; Assaf, *Ha'Onshin*, pp. 91, 93.

433. See Rambam, Laws of the Study of the Torah, 7:4; see also Talmud, *Ketubot* 28a, *Tosafot*, ad loc., and Commentary *Rashi* to *Kiddushin* 281, *Mo'ed Katan* 17a.

434. So-called by M. Pines, in *Emek Berakha* (Jerusalem, 1883).

435. Rambam, Laws of the Study of the Torah, 7:4.

436. Responsa of Paltai Gaon (Babylonia, *circa* 850), in Hayim Modai, *Shaare Tzedek*, vol. 4, sec. 4, no. 14.

437. See Luria, *Yam Shel Shlomo, Baba Kama*, ch. 10, sec. 13; see also Assaf, *Ha'Onshin*, pp. 50–51, and Leiter, Responsa of the *Gaonim*, *Shaare Tshuva*, no. 41, which contradicts the aforementioned Responsa of Paltai Gaon, and also no. 42; and Isaac ben Sheshet, Responsa *Rivash*, no. 173; Harkavy, Responsa of the *Gaonim*, no. 182; Y. Miller, Responsa *Gaone Mizrah U'Maariv*, no. 217, Ginsberg, *Sheelot U'Tshuvot Min Ha'Gaonim*, (New York, 1909), p. 154. See, however, the Ordinances of Valladolid, above.

438. See Anan, in his *Sefer Ha'Mitzvot*, Harkavy ed. (Petersburg, 1902), p. 14; L. Nemoy, *Karaite Anthology* (Jerusalem, 1952), p. 13.

439. See the records of the community of Cracow, Poland, in Balaban, *Jahrbuch der Literarischen Gesellschaft, D.X.*, pp. 311–12; Wettstein, *Ozar Ha'Safrut*, vol. 4, p. 585; Assaf, *Ha'-Onshin*, p. 135, citing a letter of the Council of Four Lands to the community of Zabulvadave.

440. Responsa of Paltai Gaon, in H. Modai, *Shaare Tzedek* (Jerusalem, 1966), vol. 4, sec. 14.

441. Balaban, "Records of the Community of Cracow" in *Jahrbuch der Judisch Literarischen Gesellschaft*, vol. 10–11, p. 310; Wettstein, *Ozar Ha'Safrut*.

442. L. Levin, *Jubilee Book in Honor of David Hoffman* (Berlin, 1914).

Until the late eighteenth century, excommunications generally were extremely effective. They could also be reinforced in some communities by having the non-Jewish state government confiscate all of the property of the excommunicatee, if he persisted in his conduct for more than thirty days,[443] or even imprison him. This was true particularly in Poland, Mehren, and Lithuania.[444]

Excommunications were also often used in Central Europe against those who refused to pay large debts pursuant to a court order, and sometimes on the basis of failure to make good on a promissory note.[445] Its frequent use appears to have been influenced by its widespread application by the church.[446]

The "Ban of Excommunication" was normally pronounced in the synagogue in a somber ceremony. Seven scrolls of the Torah were removed from the Holy Ark, candles were extinguished, or black candles were utilized, and a ram's horn was blown.[447] Sometimes the ban would include curses pronounced against the offender. The excommunication would then be announced in all of the synagogues of the city. Sometimes copies of the excommunication would be sent to other communities for public announcement there.[448] In some communities the excommunication was announced in all of the streets and marketplaces.[449]

The severity of the excommunications sometimes brought about sharp reactions. Occasionally attempts were made to influence the non-Jewish authorities to have the ban removed.[450] These efforts were sometimes successful. Holland, for example, prohibited the imposition of bans of excommunication.[451] This also occurred in portions of Germany.[452] Where appropriate, Jewish officials of the communities where excommuni-

cations were prohibited, would sometimes attempt to avoid the prohibition by requesting that excommunications be issued by other communities where they were still permitted.[453]

Some Jewish communities, however, resented excommunications being issued against their citizens by other communities as unwarranted interferences in their own internal affairs. They were also troubled by the ever-increasing numbers of such foreign excommunications. Accordingly, in 1512 and 1628 a number of German communities prescribed that copies of such foreign excommunication decrees directed at local citizens should be publicly burned in the courtyard of the synagogue.[454]

A number of other reactions occurred to limit the arbitrary imposition of excommunications. Among these was the practice in a number of communities not to have an excommunication imposed except with the authorization of both the rabbi and the community.[455] A number of prominent rabbis refused as a matter of principle to issue or participate in any excommunications, except on very rare occasions. Thus, Rabbi Israel Isserlin issued only one ban of excommunication in his entire lifetime,[456] and Rabbi Israel Bruna refused to participate in any bans whatsoever.[457] This form of sanction fell into disuse, although the *Shulkhan Arukh* (the authoritative sixteenth-century Jewish code of laws followed by most traditional Jewish communities all over the world) devotes one of its largest sections to the subject of excommunications, and (based upon precedent in the Talmud[458] and in Rambam's code of laws)[459] lists some twenty-four different cases in which milder forms of excommunication may be imposed. By the twentieth century it was apparently prohibited in most countries of Europe.[460]

j. BANISHMENT

Banishment, a very ancient form of sanction in the Jewish tradition,[461] was one of the more severe forms of penalties employed in the Middle Ages. The modali-

443. J. Kolon, Responsa *Maharik*, no. 166.
444. N. Wolf, "The Ordinances of Mehren" (311 Ordinances) (Jerusalem, 1952), nos. 246–48; Dubnow, The Ordinances of the Lithuanian Council of 1662, sec. 546.
445. Wolf, "Ordinances of Mehren."
446. I. Abrahams, *Jewish Life in the Middle Ages* (New York, 1932), p. 66.
447. Assaf, *Ha'Onshin*, p. 32.
448. Morstein, in *Revue Etudes Juives*, vol. 120, pp. 101–04; Asher ben Yehiel, Responsa *Rosh*, sec. 21, nos. 8–9; See A. Frieman, "David Lida's *Be'er Esete*," in *Jubilee Book in Honor of Sokolov*, regarding the excommunication placed by the Council of Four Lands on the slanderers of David Lida, the Rabbi of Amsterdam; Assaf, *Ha'Onshin*, p. 134.
449. Isaac ben Sheshet, Responsa *Rivash*, nos. 173 and 395.
450. Regne, "Catalogue," sec. 275; see Isserlin, Responsa *Terumat Ha'Deshen*, no. 276; Y. Shoeberg, Responsa *Maharitatz* (Marginata, 1903), no. 255; see the Ordinances of the synod convened by Rabbi Jacob Tam, in Finkelstein, *Jewish Self-Government*, p. 151.
451. See Regne, ibid.; Jacob Sassportas, Responsa *Ohel Yaakov*, (Altona, 1683).
452. Kolon, Responsa *Maharik*, no. 4; H. Graetz, *History of the Jews*, 6:295.

453. Kolon, ibid. See Frieman, "David Lida's *Be'er Esete*," re the ban issued by the Council of Four Lands against those who slandered David Lida.
454. See Shimon of Copenhagen, *Ohr Ha'Yashar* (Amsterdam, 1869).
455. Ordinances of the synod convened by Rabbi Jacob Tam, in Finkelstein, *Jewish Self-Government*; Asher ben Yehiel, Responsa *Rosh*, sec. 43, no. 9.
456. Y. Molin, *Minhage Maharil*.
457. Y. Bruna, Responsa *Mahari Bruna*, no. 188.
458. *Berakhot* 19a.
459. Laws of the Study of the Torah, 7:14.
460. See Epstein, *Arukh Ha'Shulkhan*, sec. 334, and Karo, *Shulkhan Arukh*, sec. 334. See, in general, Moshe ben Nahman, *Mishpat Ha'Kherem*.
461. See the exile of Cain in Gen. 4:12–15; compare Num. 35:9–12.

ties of banishment by Jewish decision-makers in the Middle Ages varied considerably with the severity of the crime. Some offenders were banished forever, some for only a limited period of time. In a number of cases an offender might be permitted to dwell in a nearby area, while in others he would be expelled from the entire country. Occasionally even his family would be expelled with him.[462] Banishment was employed frequently in Poland and Spain and was also utilized, although less often, in other countries.[463]

It should be recalled that the position of many Jewish communities was often extremely precarious during the Middle Ages. All of the members of a community might often be expelled by the ruler on the slightest pretext and be forced to search for another country that might be willing to accept them. Accordingly, undesirables who were thought to endanger the community (especially those who dealt unethically with non-Jews) might be expelled entirely from the Jewish community in order to preserve its existence.

There are records of exile imposed on the following types of offenders:

1. Informers who attempted to incite the non-Jewish authorities against the Jewish communities.[464] In one instance,[465] an informer, together with his wife, children, and son-in-law, was exiled from all of Lithuania and Russia. This was, presumably, because of the great fear that one of them might also attempt to incite the non-Jewish authorities against the Jewish communities.

2. Murderers, especially in the absence of two witnesses to the crime,[466] or in the case of accidental murder. The latter case is reminiscent of the biblical prescription in Numbers 35:9–12.[467] Where the Jewish communities did not have the power to inflict capital punishment, exile might be imposed even for deliberate homicide. Thus, one man who beat his pregnant wife until she died was exiled.[468]

3. Thieves, forgers, and counterfeiters.[469]

4. Prostitutes and fornicators.[470]

5. Those who violated community ordinances regulating dealings with non-Jews; for example, those who borrowed money from non-Jews without the prescribed consent of both the rabbi and one of the community leaders, and who had already used up the money and could not therefore repay it.[471] This issue was particularly sensitive, since the entire Jewish community might be held responsible for such loan and forced to repay it or face mass expulsion.[472]

6. Those who repeatedly engaged in quarrels with non-Jews.[473] The Lithuanian Council also threatened that any community that would fail to expel such persons would not receive any help from the Council if it were required to pay a fine as a result of the incident.[474] In Hamburg the Jewish community was responsible to the Senate of Hamburg for the maintenance of order and was, accordingly, authorized to expel all of those who engaged in unethical or immoral practices. As an interesting sidelight, the Jewish community would occasionally lend money for travel expenses to one who was to be expelled but did not have the funds to travel.[475]

7. Many other offenders, including those who disturbed the peace and failed to obey the community ordinances.[476]

k. EXPULSION FROM THE SYNAGOGUE

A minor form of exile and social ostracism was the "expulsion" of an offender from the synagogue by prohibiting his attendance there for a specified period, commonly three months. This sanction could be very effective, since during the Middle Ages the synagogue was the center of social activity and nearly everyone felt obligated to participate in the prayer services there.

This relatively mild form of sanction was applied in the case of less serious offenses such as gambling,[477]

462. See Assaf, *Ha'Onshin*, p. 35.

463. For Germany, see Menahem of Merzberg (*circa* fourteenth century), *Nimuke* of *Maharam* of Merzberg; for Prague and Bohemia, *circa* 1612, see Assaf, *Ha'Onshin*, p. 114; for Mehren, see Wolf, "Ordinances of Mehren," secs. 261–65.

464. Judah ben Asher, Responsa *Zikhron Yehuda*, no. 63; (Spain, *circa* fourteenth century); for the Ordinances of the Council at Valladolid, Spain (1432), see Finkelstein, *Jewish Self-Government*.

465. Dubnow, Minutes of the Council of Lithuania, sec. 144.

466. Luria, *Yam Shel Shlomo, Baba Kama*, ch. 8, sec. 7 (Poland, *circa* sixteenth century); Judah ben Asher, Responsa *Zikhron Yehuda*, no. 58 (Spain, *circa* fourteenth century).

467. See Isaac ben Sheshet, Responsa *Rivash*, no. 251 (Spain, *circa* fifteenth century).

468. Menahem of Merzberg, *Nimuke* of *Maharam* of Merzberg, (Germany, *circa* fourteenth century).

469. Wolf, *Ordinances of Mehren* (Vienna, 1880), secs. 261 65 (*circa* seventeenth century); Ordinance of 1670, sec. 662, of

the Council of Lithuania; Wettstein, *Ozar Ha'Safrut*, 614, re Cracow, Poland; Levin, in *Jubilee Volume in Honor of David Hoffman*, regarding the expulsion of thieves from Poznan in 1692. In 1695 the community of Opta, Poland, expelled a counterfeiter; see S. Frank, *Lekorot Ha'Khazaka*, in *Ha'Shiloah* (Warsaw, 1898), 2:239–47.

470. Prague, Bohemia, 1612. See Assaf, *Ha'Onshin*, p. 114; and Frank, ibid., concerning the expulsion of a youthful fornicator from Opta, Poland, in 1731.

471. Dubnow, Records of the Lithuanian Council, secs. 163, 637.

472. Balaban, *Jahrbuch*, vol. 3, p. 107, relates such an incident that occurred in Poznan, Poland.

473. Dubnow, Minutes of the Lithuanian Council, sec. 21.

474. Ibid., secs. 201, 241, 242.

475. Balaban, *Jahrbuch*, vol. 3; see also Section B 2 *e*, above.

476. Assaf, *Ha'Onshin*, p. 36.

477. Eliezer ben Nathan (*circa* twelfth century), *Ra'Avan* (New York, 1964), 112a.

assault,[478] serious embarrassment of another,[479] Sabbath violations,[480] and sexual offenses.[481]

A more moderate version of this sanction consisted of prohibiting an offender from occupying his normal place in the synagogue, sometimes assigning a specified, different place for him. This practice was occasionally applied to those who defaulted in the payment of their debts,[482] or to those who were found guilty of slander.[483]

l. HUMILIATION

(1) *By Public Announcement*

As distinct from the humiliation suffered by one who was subjected to such sanctions as flogging, excommunication, or exile, there was the practice of imposing the sanction of humiliation in other forms. The most common form was a public announcement, usually in the synagogue, stating the specific offense committed by the named individual. Where the transgression was considered more serious, the announcement might also be made in all other cities of the district or even the country.[484] Even where more serious forms of sanctions were utilized, such announcement would often also be made.

These humiliating public announcements were made in such cases as informing,[485] sexual promiscuity,[486] or in cases of those who violated one of the many community ordinances (such as drinking wine in a tavern on Saturdays or religious festivals, or drinking in any non-Jewish establishment in Lithuania),[487] or those who violated some of the community restrictions regarding sumptuous dress.[488] Its use was particularly widespread with regard to those who refused to litigate in Jewish

courts or to follow the decision of Jewish courts.[489] It was even utilized against those who refused to accept poor strangers as guests at their home for the Sabbath meals.[490] In some communities the announcement was printed on a black bulletin board that hung in the synagogue.[491]

(2) *By Shaving the Head and Beard*

Another form of humiliation that was occasionally utilized in the Middle Ages was the shaving of the head and beard. This had its roots in antiquity[492] and was considered extremely humiliating; sometimes, allegedly, even more than the amputation of a limb.[493] Occasionally the shorn hair was taken and paraded through the streets.[494] In addition to central Europe, this sanction was also employed in Babylonia.

There are records of the sporadic use of this sanction in a small number of instances including the following:
- *a.* One who assaulted another.[495] In numerous other cases of assault in Babylonia, however, shaving was not used as a sanction. Instead, various degrees of excommunication and the payment of compensation to the victim were required.[496]
- *b.* This was also one of many sanctions imposed upon a man who beat his wife until she died.[497]
- *c.* Adultery and other sexual offenses.[498]
- *d.* One who was convicted of accepting bribes.[499]

While this sanction was commonly employed by non-Jewish courts in the Middle Ages, particularly in Spain,[500] it does not appear to have been employed

478. Ibid.; Responsa *Even Ha'Shosham*, no. 17; Commentaries of *Mordecai* (ben Hillel) and Yitzhak ben Moshe, *Ohr Zarua*, to *Sanhedrin*, ch. 3.

479. Balaban, *Jahrbuch*, vol. 3.

480. Ibid., see also Tzidkiyahu the Physician, *Shibale Ha'-Leket*, sec. 60, regarding the practice in Hungary.

481. Balaban, *Jahrbuch*, vol. 3, regarding the Portuguese community in Hamburg, Germany.

482. See the ordinances of 1726 of the Jewish community in Altona-Hamburg, in Assaf, *Ha'Onshin*, p. 116.

483. Menahem of Merzberg, *Nimuke* of *Maharam* of Merzberg.

484. Assaf, *Ha'Onshin*, p. 39.

485. See the Ordinances of the Spanish Council at Valladolid (1432), published in Finkelstein, *Jewish Self-Government*, p. 348; Assaf, *Ha'Onshin*, p. 89.

486. See the decision of Hai Gaon (Babylonia, *circa* 1032), in R. Ginsberg, *She'Elot U'Tshuvot Ha'Gaonim Min Ha'Gerizay* (New York, 1909), p. 155; Kolon, Responsa *Maharik*, no. 129; Responsa *Khut Ha'Shani*, no. 18; Y. Elesh, Responsa *Beth Yehuda* (Livorno, 1746), p. 113b.

487. See Dubnow, Records of the Lithuanian Council, secs. 134, 1628.

488. M. Levenstein, "History of the Jews in Furth," in *Jahrbuch* (Germany, 1764), vol. 5, p. 190. Similar ordinances existed in Prague and in Poland; see Assaf, *Ha'Onshin*, p. 120.

489. M. Mintz, Responsa *Mahram Mintz*, secs. 38–39; sec. 101; see the records of the community of Zalkava, Poland, in S. Buber, *Kirya Nisgava* (Cracow, 1903), p. 109, citing an ordinance from the year 1691; Yaakov Cohen, in *Magal Ho'-Omer* (Hamburg, 1790), pp. 35–37.

490. Assaf, *Ha'Onshin*, p. 40.

491. See Levenstein, *Jahrbuch*, vol. 8, p. 185, regarding this practice in the city of Furth, Germany, and in the city of Horodna, Poland.

492. See 2 Sam. 10:4–5.

493. Luria, *Yam Shel Shlomo, Baba Kama*, ch. 8, sec. 14; see also Y. Greenwald, *Korot Ha'Torah Ve'Ha'Emuna Be'Hungaria* (Budapest, 1931), p. 9; Cf. Halevi, Responsa *Zekan Aharon*, no. 95.

494. See also Tzemah Duran, Responsa *Yakhin U'Boaz*, no. 149, subsec. 1, and vol. 2, no. 57.

495. Yehudai Gaon (*circa* 760 C.E.), cited in Yitzhak ben Moshe, *Or Zarua, Baba Kama*, sec. 389.

496. Assaf, *Ha'Onshin*, p. 24.

497. Menahem of Merzberg, *Nimuke* of *Maharam* Merzberg, p. 178.

498. Yehudai Gaon (*circa* 760 C.E., in Babylonia), and Natronai Gaon (*circa* 850, in Babylonia); in Miller, *Halakhot Pesukot*, sec. 94; Modai, *Shaare Tzedek*, vol. 3, sec. 6, no. 13; Shimon Duran, Responsa *Tashbatz*, vol. 3, no. 191, Tzemah Duran, Responsa *Yakhin U'Boaz*, vol. 1, no. 143.

499. Asher ben Yehiel, Responsa *Rosh*, 58:4.

500. King Ervig (*circa* 680 C.E.) imposed it as a sanction on those Jews who would not convert to Christianity or would

often by Jewish decision-makers in Babylonia. In Europe it was still more infrequently utilized in the Jewish communities.[501] It also does not even appear to have been commonly practiced in Jewish communities during the Talmudic or Biblical Eras, as evidenced by its scant mention there.[502] Presumably, the effectiveness of this sanction as a humiliation was dependent on the prevailing mores, which determined whether or not it was degrading to appear without a beard or hair on the head.

m. DEPRIVATION OF RIGHTS AND PRIVILEGES

For minor offenses certain rights or privileges might be suspended. One of the most important rights often cancelled, was the right to vote in community affairs and to be selected for community posts. (Often this right was, in any case, reserved for taxpayers—sometimes only major taxpayers—and for those whose scholarly attainments had earned them the title of "Colleague" (*Khaver*) or "Our Teacher" (*morenu*).[503]

There are records of this important right being suspended in the following types of offenses:

a. Failure to pay debts on time.[504]

b. Gambling or drinking in non-Jewish establishments.[505]

c. Threatening to inform.[506]

d. Assaults or threats to assault.[507]

Some of the other privileges that might be suspended were the revocation of the titles of *Khaver* ("Colleague") or *morenu* ("Our Teacher"). Loss of these titles resulted in suspension of the exemption from certain taxes that these groups enjoyed and often the right to vote or to fill community positions,[508] and in disqualification to testify as a witness in court, or to take an oath.

Another mild sanction was refusing to call the offender to the Torah in the synagogue during the prayer services.[509]

n. DENIAL OF THE RIGHT TO ENGAGE IN CERTAIN OCCUPATIONS

Another form of monetary sanction was for offenders to be prohibited from engaging in certain occupations. The length of the prohibitions varied with the seriousness of the offense, and also from community to community. Some of the deviant behavior for which this sanction was levied were:

a. Assaults committed at a wedding.[510]

b. Testifying falsely.[511]

c. Fraudulent commercial practices, such as utilizing inaccurate weights and measures, and diluting food products with water.[512]

d. Tailoring clothes that were prohibited by community regulations restricting luxurious clothing,[512] or behavior by community employees that did not meet the expected standards.[513]

o. THE "DONKEY'S BURIAL"

A form of social ostracism known as the "burial of a donkey" (the term is derived from Jer. 22:19) was also sometimes employed as a sanction. When the one to be subjected to this sanction died, he would not be buried within the cemetery but only at its very edge, alongside the cemetery gate, as though he were an animal, not a person. While this sanction was commonly incorporated as a part of the sweeping ban of excommunication, it was also imposed, by itself, as a sanction against many types of offenders, including informers, forgers of documents, false witnesses, or those who slanderously claimed that a divorce had been executed invalidly.[514] Although this penalty was accepted as legitimate in Poland, some of the Jewish authorities in Spain objected to it.[515]

There is a record of this sanction being imposed in a very extreme form as late as the eighteenth century.

not baptize their children, see Graetz, *History of the Jews*, 3:149.

501. Assaf, *Ha'Onshin*, pp. 24, 25.

502. Isolated instances do, however, appear in Talmud, *Mo'ed Katan* 16a, which refers to the sanction of tearing out hair, and Neh. 13:25, where the use of this penalty was authorized by the Persian authorities. See also *Kalbo*, sec. 136, C. Horowitz, *Toratam Shel Rishonim* (Frankfurt, 1882), vol. 1, p. 20; vol. 2, p. 18, and Ginsberg, *Mishpatim Le'Yisrael*, p. 38.

503. See, in general, Assaf, "Inner Life of the Jews of Poland" (Hebrew), in *Be'Ahale Yaakov* (Jerusalem, 1943).

504. Dubnow, Records of the Lithuanian Council, secs. 331, 332.

505. Ordinances of 1726 of Altona-Hamburg, Germany, secs. 34 and 67; see Assaf, *Ha'Onshin*, p. 116.

506. Decision of Paltai Gaon (Babylonia, *circa* 858 C.E.), in Modai, *Sha'are Tzedek*, vol. 4, sec. 307, no. 42; sec. 1, no. 9; Samuel DiMedina, Responsa *Maharashdam, Ho. Mis.*, no. 355; David Ibn Zimra, Responsa *Radvaz*, vol. 1, no. 345.

507. See Responsa *Maharam* (Prague ed.), no. 383; see also sec. 485.

508. Assaf, *Ha'Onshin*, p. 41.

509. See Levenstein, "History of the Jews in Furth." *Jahrbuch*, vol. 9, p. 330; Assaf, *Ha'Onshin, supra* pp. 92, 119.

510. Records of the Portuguese Community in Hamburg, Germany, in *Jahrbuch*, vol. 6; Assaf, *Ha'Onshin*, p. 43; see Section B 2 *g*, above.

511. Yehiel ben Asher, Responsa *Rosh*, sec. 58, no. 4.

512. Dubnow, Ordinances of the Lithuanian Council, secs. 328, 741; Assaf, *Ha'Onshin*, p. 43.

513. Lithuanian Council, secs. 226, 572, 594; the ordinances of the city of Dubnow, pp. 69, 90.

514. Records of the community of Brody, Poland, in *Jahrbuch*, vol. 12, p. 124; S. B. Nissembaum, *Lekorot Ha'Yehudim Be'Lublin* (2d ed., pp. 142–44, regarding an ordinance of 1694 in Lublin, Poland, which deals with this sanction.

515. Shlomo ben Aderet, Responsa *Rashba*, cited in Karo, *Beth Yosef, Y.D.*, sec. 334.

At the death of a man who had slandered a widely esteemed saint, the members of the Jewish community refused to personally handle his body. Instead, they had non-Jews smear it with mud and throw it into a garbage wagon. They removed one wheel from the wagon and harnessed an old, thin horse to drag it through all of the streets of the community. Gangs of boys, accompanied by many dogs, followed the wagon all the way to the cemetery. The boys threw pieces of cakes and cookies on the wagon, while the dogs jumped up on it to retrieve them. When the wagon finally reached the cemetery, the body was buried near the gate.[516]

As with the other sanctions, this one was sometimes carried to excess. For example, one of the foremost acknowledged Jewish saints and scholars of the nineteenth century, Rabbi Nathan Adler, was buried near the gate in the cemetery at Frankfurt-Am-Main because he refused to heed the orders of the communal rabbi of the city. Rabbi Yom Tov Lipman Heller was also buried near the gate of the cemetery of Cracow, Poland, allegedly at his own request. According to local tradition, he learned that an alleged miser, who had persistently refused to give to charity and had accordingly been given a "donkey's burial," used to, in fact, secretly contribute large sums to support the poor, on condition that no one be told that the monies came from him. Rabbi Heller thereupon requested that when he would die he should be buried alongside the "miser." Subsequently, many other distinguished personages who desired to be buried near Rabbi Heller were also interred near the gate, which became one of the "choice" spots in the cemetery.

p. FINES, LEVIES, AND CONFISCATION OF PROPERTY

Fines of varying amounts, and occasionally confiscation of an offender's entire assets, were commonly levied as sanctions by Jewish decision-makers during the Middle Ages. The amounts of the fines, of course, varied from community to community and with the seriousness of the offense. There are records of this sanction being imposed upon:

1. Those who purchased stolen goods at the commercial fairs.[517] The same ordinance also imposes the penalty of confiscation of all the assets of an offender who "reveals secrets at a fair." The ordinance does not specify the nature of these secrets, but they were presumably trade secrets.

2. Robbers and thieves.[518]

3. One who rented his house to a person who did not have the right to settle in a community.[519] Many communities enacted ordinances restricting the right of immigrants to settle there in order to maintain internal discipline and prevent undue competition.

4. Those who violated community regulations regarding commerce (such as, for example, the ordinance of the Lithuanian Council, which attempted to protect domestic products against foreign competition and prohibited any person from selling merchandise that came on commission from Poland).[520]

5. Those found guilty of assault.[521]

6. Fines were also imposed upon those guilty of disorderly conduct or of gambling.[522]

The fines collected were often turned over to the state or to non-Jewish rulers. This disposition was made either because it had been a condition in granting autonomy to the Jewish community or because of the voluntary action of the Jewish community itself.[523] In a number of cases the monies were not required to be turned over and were, occasionally, retained by the judges who had imposed the fines. This practice was vigorously protested by a number of Jewish leaders.[524] The Lithuanian Council eventually prescribed that no rabbi could keep the monies collected from fines that he had levied, and applied the same rule to judges at the commercial fairs.[525] In many areas, however, the fines were divided among the poor.[526]

6. APPRAISAL OF THE PERSPECTIVES, SOCIAL CONTEXTS, AND OUTCOMES OF EXTRAORDINARY SANCTIONING BY JEWISH DECISION-MAKERS

The following are a number of possible rationales that can be advanced to explain the apparently sharp departure in sanctioning practice from traditional legal principles. The reasons suggested hereafter should be examined both individually and in the aggregate. It should, however, be realized that these ratios are a matter of speculation, without conclusive evidence to support them, and they are put forth as avenues of pos-

516. Assaf, *Reshumot*, vol. 2, p. 453.
517. Ordinances of the Community of Poznan, in *Jahrbuch*, vol. 2, p. 108.
518. The Ordinances of the Community of Cracow, Poland, in Wettstein, pp. 64–65.

519. The Records of the Community of Cracow, Poland, in Balaban, *Jarbuch* vol. 11, p. 90.
520. Dubnow, sec. 172; see also sec. 657 and sec. 664.
521. Responsa *Gaonim Kadmonim*, secs. 125, 135; J. Weil, Responsa *Mahari Weil*, sec. 28.
522. Assaf, *Ha'Onshin*, p. 42.
523. Asher ben Yehiel, Responsa *Rosh*, sec. 21, nos. 8–9; see also sec. 11, no. 9 and sec. 65, no. 27.
524. See the complaint of Luria in his *Yam Shel Shlomo, Baba Kama*, chap. 8, sec. 49.
525. These latter came from many different cities, and the Council had direct jurisdiction over them. See Dubnow, Records of the Lithuanian Council, secs. 688, 529, 188.
526. Yom Tov Lippman Heller, in Responsa *Etan Ha'Ezrahi*, sec. 7; Luria, see also Judah ben Asher, Responsa *Zikhron Yehuda*, sec. 36.

sible approach to be investigated, rather than accepted as proven solutions.

1. It may be that the traditional principles of Jewish Law, which attempted to discourage capital punishment and mutilations, and which provided for substantial mercy in dealing with criminal defendants, were appropriate only for a simple, agricultural-pastoral society, in which there was relatively little violence and crime and in which murder was a rarity. When societal conditions changed (particularly under the pressure of social unrest caused by Hellenist and Roman persecutions, which led to abandonment of traditional cultural and religious perspectives, and perhaps spurred on by rapid urbanization), criminal acts became too rampant to be controlled by traditional legal principles. Consequently, extraordinary sanctioning became necessary to maintain order, and it was gradually imposed.

Would this theory imply that today, too, a "soft" protective approach to criminal defendants is also doomed to failure and that "tough" treatment is necessary to preserve public order? In this connection, it should be noted that most of the instances of extraordinary sanctioning of which we are aware date from the latter part of the Talmudic Era and the Middle Ages. This, however, may be due simply to the existence of more records from these later epochs. Furthermore, some of the instances recorded in the Talmud are from the early Second Commonwealth and Talmudic Eras, such as those involving Simon ben Shetah and the stoning of the Sabbath horseback rider during the time of the Greeks.[527]

2. It is conceivable that many of the protective legal principles thrown about criminal defendants were designed mainly to thwart Roman attempts to have Jewish brigands and other revolutionaries killed. Under this theory, the Romans would have these offenders tried in the autonomous Jewish courts, which they permitted to operate. The judges, accordingly, attempted to frustrate the Romans by developing the defendant-biased legal maxims. When this situation no longer existed, the protective procedures changed too. This thesis, too, is subject to the same objections raised above and below.

3. It has been suggested that the talmudic principles were theoretical only and were not applied in practice.[528] It is difficult to accept this thesis since the Jewish oral tradition, which was so meticulously preserved in the Talmud, records a number of instances that purport to be actual cases of extraordinary sanctioning (e.g., the hanging of the sorceresses by Simon ben Shetah; his inability to have a criminal defendant con-

victed under extremely strong circumstantial evidence; executions by courts only once in seven (or seventy) years; the cessation of murder trials when homicides increased, etc.).[529] It is not persuasive that all of the numerous instances in the Talmud where traditional rules were applied, are all fiction. Furthermore, an enormous amount of discussion is contained in the Talmud regarding these traditional norms. These took place between discussants who are elleged to have either applied these norms themselves, or who lived very shortly after the era in which these norms were alleged to have been applied. Given the intense religious motivations behind the enormous efforts that were expended to transmit the oral law tradition accurately, it is not likely that these discussions relate to a never-never era.

4. Some talmudic authorities[530] have suggested that where the courts were unable to maintain public order by applying traditional norms, the king (or other representative of the community), or even the courts (who also represented the community) applied extraordinary sanctioning to control criminal elements. In effect, then, the court's basic function was simply to apply traditional norms, even if these were unsuccessful in maintaining public order. The main responsibility for effective order was with the king. (In the absence of a king, the court itself, acting as representative of the community, would apply extraordinary sanctioning.) This is perhaps another way of saying that court procedures were intended more as a religious service than as an effective means of ordering society.[531]

According to this thesis, the king and other community officials responsible for public order utilized "extraordinary" sanctions to maintain order during the Second Jewish Commonwealth. Thereafter, with the abolition of Jewish kingship and the destruction of the Jewish state, the Jewish courts became the organs that eventually applied extraordinary sanctioning when this became necessary to maintain order.

5. It is arguable that the loss of power among Jewish communities, and their dispersion as a minority among

527. Talmud, *Makkot* 1:10; *Yebamot* 89b, 90a; *Sanhedrin* 6:4, 37b.

528. See C. Tchernowitz, *Toldot Ha'Halaha* (New York, 1945).

529. Talmud, *Sanhedrin* 6:4, 37b; *Makkot* 1:10; *Shabbat* 15a.

530. N. Gerundi, *Derashot Ha'Ran*, discourse no. 11; Judah Loewe, *Be'Er Ha'Gola*, ch. 2; Horowitz, "Torah She'Biktav, Shoftim" *Shne Lukhot Ha'Brit*.

531. See "An Appraisal of the Function of the Judiciary in Maintaining Public Order and in Imposing Criminal Law Sanctions," in Part Two, Chapter VI, Section E, above. A similar thesis may apply in explaining the reasons for the requirement of witnesses, the exclusion of circumstantial evidence, the disqualification of women as witnesses, and the failure of the court to weigh the credibility and testimony of witnesses, resulting in the rule that the testimony of two witnesses was as weighty as the testimony of one hundred contrary witnesses. See ibid., and Shlomo ben Aderet (Section C 2 b, above) to the effect that elicitation of the true facts was not the purpose of a trial pursuant to talmudic law.

alien, and often hostile, peoples who persecuted them, caused the Jewish communities to take emergency action to preserve their precarious existence. This included extraordinary steps to suppress violent persons who might antagonize non-Jewish peoples and endanger the very existence of the Jewish communities. This applied particularly to informers, who were felt to constitute a grave threat to the Jews.

6. Another thesis is that the changes in criminal law practice were due largely to cultural assimilation. It may be that every epoch is characterized by distinctive modes of thought, which assume certain facts as real and crucial and view certain approaches and methodologies as appropriate to solve societal problems that are considered as urgent and as requiring extreme remedies. The people of any era may not even be consciously aware that they possess these perspectives and modes of thought and that their actions are predicated upon them. The basic notions are part of the epistemological and ontological framework of each era, and they are shaped by many factors, including cultural, political, and economic conditions. This phenomena, which has been explored with regard to the development and progress of the natural sciences,[532] may apply to the approaches utilized by society to resolve the social issues in each era, which are deemed to require solutions.

Since physical mutilations and "extraordinary" sanctioning were common among non-Jews in the Talmudic Era and Middle Ages,[533] and came to be accepted as "natural" sanctions, it is likely that Judaic decision-makers, without being conscious of the gradual change in their thinking, came to view mutilations and extraordinary sanctioning as normal, proper,[534] and even vital to the preservation of the Jewish community, minimum public order, and Jewish religious values.

It is ironic, however, that Jewish decision-makers, who consciously fought so hard and long to preserve religious beliefs and to prevent assimilation, and who were often martyred for this, became themselves unconsciously assimilated culturally with regard to the sanctioning process. Accordingly, it is conceivable that they gradually abandoned[535] a long biblical tradition of humane sanctioning without hardly being aware of it. This phenomena reflects, perhaps, the inevitability of cultural assimilation whenever there is cultural interaction. This was particularly so with the Jews, who were dispersed in exile in alien environments, and it recalls the biblical prophecy, "and you shall serve other Gods there . . ." (Deut. 28:36).

7. Another interesting speculation, which may help to explain Jewish sanctioning developments, is Max Weber's "paradox of consequences" (although Weber himself did not apply this concept to Jewish decision-making). This thesis has been aptly summarized as follows:

[The] result achieved by religious beings is often contrary to their original intention. Every choice has a price; it entails the sacrifice for the sake of estimable values, of others just as estimable. . . .

This paradox of consequences is inherent in every struggle, whatever the sphere in which it occurs. As the struggle develops, it eventually shifts the meaning of the values which it was intended to defend . . . (and) its development sometimes brings men to adopt a course of behavior contrary to their conviction, or to their original intentions. For they very seldom draw the logical conclusions from the causes which they champion, and they try to achieve accommodations, theoretically, in order to safeguard the validity of their convictions, but, in practice, often unconsciously, jettisoning them. . . .[536]

Perhaps one often ends up adopting the methods and values of one's adversaries.

It might then be argued that it was nearly inevitable that Jewish decision-makers should unconsciously abandon the long tradition of humane sanctioning in their prolonged struggle to preserve the physical and religious welfare of Jewish communities. Gradually they adopted the crude values of the Jewish informers, men of violence, and their non-Jewish neighbors.

8. It may also be that the process was aided and became subject to abuse by the lack of clear standards attached to the principles of law that Judaic decision-makers utilized as authority for extraordinary sanctioning, and which permitted Jewish law to be so flexible and resilient in dealing with changed societal conditions. Many prominent Jewish decision-makers themselves criticized the overindulgence in imposing extraordinary sanctioning, particularly with regard to the common practice of imprisoning debtors.[537]

Does this mean that Jewish Law was too *flexible*, contrary to a common misunderstanding that it was too *rigid*?

532. See T. Kuhn, *Structure of Scientific Revolution* (Chicago, 1970).

533. For example, the royal court commonly ordered amputations of tongues; see Baer, *History of the Jews in Christian Spain* (Tel-Aviv, 1959), p. 188.

534. See, e.g., the claim of Avraham Rappaport, Responsa *Etan Ha'Ezrahi*, (circa 1650), that amputations are a potent deterrent, even greater than death.

535. See also Assaf, *Ha'Onshin*, p. 21.

536. J. Freund, *The Sociology of Max Weber* (New York, 1968), p. 215.

537. Y. Sirkis, *Bakh, Tur, Ho. Mis.*, 97:28; Eibschutz, *Urim Ve'Tumim, Ho. Mis.*, 97:13; Elon, *Herot Ha'Prat Be'Darke Ge'Viat Hov* (Heb.; Jerusalem, 1964), p. 172 ff. The thesis that extraordinary sanctioning was carried to excess is stressed by N. Z. Y. Berlin, who also claims that this was the reason why God caused the Second Jewish Commonwealth and the Temple to be destroyed. See his *He'Emek Davar*, Num. 35:34, Deut. 32:5; *Meshiv Davar*, no. 44.

SUGGESTED READINGS

Abrahams, I. *Jewish Life in the Middle Ages.* New York, 1973.

Agus, I. A. *Rabbi Meir of Rothenberg: His Life and Works as Sources for the Religious, Legal and Social History of the Jews of Germany.* New York, 1947.

Baer, Y. *A History of the Jews in Christian Spain.* Philadelphia, 1966.

Baron, S. *The Jewish Community.* Philadelphia, 1942.

Bazak, Y., and S. M. Passamaneck. *Jewish Law and Jewish Life.* New York, 1977.

Ben Sasson, H. H., and S. Ettinger. *Jewish Society through the Ages.* New York, 1971.

Cohn, H. H. *Jewish Law in Ancient and Modern Israel.* New York, 1976.

Dinei Israel: An Annual Journal of Jewish Law. Pub. by the Tel-Aviv University Faculty of Law, Tel Aviv, Israel.

Elon, M., ed. *Principles of Jewish Law.* Jerusalem, 1975.

Epstein, I. *The "Responsa" of Rabbi Solomon Ben Adereth of Barcelona.* London, 1925.

Finkelstein, L. *Jewish Self-Government in the Middle Ages.* New York, 1924.

Freehoff, S. *The Responsa Literature.* Cincinnatti, 1955.

Herzog, I. *Judaism: Law and Ethics.* London, 1976.

The Jewish Law Annual: An Annual Journal of Jerusalem. Leiden, Netherlands.

Katz, J. *Tradition and Crisis.* New York, 1961.

Katz, J. *Exclusiveness and Tolerance.* New York, 1975.

Landman, L. *Jewish Law in the Diaspora: Confrontation and Accomodation.* Philadelphia, 1968.

Roth, C., ed. *World History of the Jewish People,* Vol. XI: *The Dark Ages.* New Brunswick, N.J., 1966.

Shohet, D. M. *The Jewish Court in the Middle Ages.* New York, 1974.

Silberg, M. *Talmudic Law and the Modern State.* New York, 1973.

Twersky, I. *Studies in Jewish Law and Philosophy.* New York, 1978.

Zimmels, H. J. *Ashkenazim and Sephardim.* London, 1958.

Index

Index of Biblical and Talmudic Works

The Pentateuch